Actors, Artists, Authors & Attempted Assassins

THE ALMANAC OF FAMOUS & INFAMOUS PEOPLE

Actors, Artists, Authors & Attempted Assassins

THE ALMANAC OF FAMOUS & INFAMOUS PEOPLE

Susan Stetler

VISIBLE
INK
PRESS

Detroit • Washington D.C. • Chicago • London

Actors, Artists, Authors & Attempted Assassins:
The Almanac of Famous & Infamous People

Published by **Visible Ink Press**
A division of Gale Research Inc.
835 Penobscot Building
Detroit, MI 48226-4094

Visible Ink Press is a trademark of Gale Research Inc.

ISBN 0-8103-9409-X

Art Director: Arthur Chartow
Design Supervisor: Cynthia Baldwin
Cover Design: Jeanne M. Moore
Illustrations: Glenn L. Barr

10 9 8 7 6 5 4 3 2 1

On the front cover: *(clockwise from top) Prince Charles, Josephine Baker, Plato, Andy Warhol, Kitty Kelley, Mark Twain, Genghis Khan, Colin Powell, James Brown, Madonna, Mother Teresa, Mozart, Gloria Steinem, Hugh Hefner, Iggy Pop, Mikhail Gorbachev, Dan Quayle, and Salvador Dali.* **On the back cover:** *Charlton Heston and Frank Sinatra*

CONTENTS

INTRODUCTION

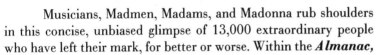

Some 150 years ago on a rainy day with not much to do and lawn work out of the question, Lord Byron *(see Scribes)* presaged Andy Warhol *(Artists),* remarking (that), "I awoke one morning and found myself famous." Many have had a similar experience. Whether famous or infamous for 15 minutes or hundreds of years, their life story is presented within ***Actors, Artists, Authors & Attempted Assassins*** in thirty words or less, enabling you to share with them their modicum of fame and fortune and still have plenty of time for other leisure-time pursuits. Leave the ***Almanac*** next to the television, on the coffee table or in the microwave; we're certain (sort of) that this is one book that even Nancy Reagan *(Potentates)* may keep on her nightstand.

Musicians, Madmen, Madams, and Madonna rub shoulders in this concise, unbiased glimpse of 13,000 extraordinary people who have left their mark, for better or worse. Within the ***Almanac,*** legendary and contemporary figures tangle with the terrestrial transience of fame or infamy, including Mother Teresa and the Singing Nun, Johann Sebastian Bach and the B-52s, Malcolm X and Nelson Mandela, Moammar Khadafy and David Ben-Gurion and of course, Gandhi and Gorbachev. Villains of all sorts share space on these pages: assassins, successful and otherwise (John Wilkes Booth and John Hinkley); big-time criminals of lore such as Clyde Barrow, Al Capone and Jack the Ripper; and Jesse James and the Daltons and the Youngers and other havoc-raising outlaws of the Wild West. In short, after spending a few moments with this book, you'll impress your friends with your new-found ability to identify which Henry (the VIII) had a propensity for marrying and which Henry (Winkler) starred as the Fonz.

The End of Fame and Fortune Overload

A biographical potpourri sure to interest people who watch people, such as detectives and sentries, ***Actors, Artists, Authors & Attempted Assassins*** offers several side benefits as well:
- ◆ You can become fully familiar with the history of the world in less than a day.
- ◆ Who's living, who's not quickly ascertained.
- ◆ Helpful as a primer for achieving trivia pursuit nirvana.

- May serve as a one-stop guide to perhaps all the knowledge you'll ever need in life, other than how to program a VCR or fill out tax forms.
- Handy as a party-planner guest list.
- Instant cure for insomnia, particularly when that nagging question of "Who was she or he?" is keeping you up well into the night, tossing, turning and wondering.
- Instantly improves your chances of becoming a game show host.
- Will lift your SAT scores 300%.
- Prepares you to open any number of conversations with, "Did you know that . . ."

What's Inside the Book

Arranged in seven unlikely chapters for entertaining browsing, *Actors, Artists, Authors & Attempted Assassins* includes (at no extra charge) a handy alphabetic index for those needing a quick fix of fameousitude. Each profile presents the person's name as he or she is most popularly known; pseudonyms, real names or group affiliations in parentheses; nationality (if birth nationality changes, the current nationality or the one at the time of death is cited); occupation, career or best known activity; dates and locations of birth and death (or if not known, the approximate era during which the person flourished); and last but not least, a brief summary of the pertinent biographical facts (just how did these folks earn their stars?).

How Did We Select the Famous Folks Inside?

A good question. Obviously, more than 13,000 people have enjoyed the fleeting fantasy of fame and fortune since human history began. After intense calculation, we believe that number to be 125,857,003. From this vast universe we have selected thousands of names with a claim to fame on the basis of how enduring their contributions are or how well-lodged they have become in the mass culture or because we felt that their now dimming stars deserved a temporary relighting or because their family members plied us with gifts and favors. We have attempted to provide a panoramic encyclopedic survey that rambles merrily through the ages rather than a work which focuses exclusively on a given era. You will perhaps not find names here that you expect; you will likely discover names that you didn't expect as well. The final authority on fame is of course Robin Leach, *and we do have him.*

We invite you to send in information on people you would like to see listed in subsequent editions. If possible, include justification for listing, birth and death dates, occupation, nationality, and a short bio. We'll have Spike II, the office file folder, collect these notes in our Famous Persons' File, where we'll make sure to consult them before undertaking the next edition. Send to:

Assassins Etc.
Visible Ink Press
835 Penobscot Building
Detroit, Michigan 48226

About the author: For ten years, Susan Stetler has been zealously writing very brief notes on 4x6 index cards about the famous and infamous through the ages. Ms. Stetler believes that fame is something shared by a lot of people and that you always wonder where the time goes and that the *Almanac* is the culmination of a life, sometimes lonely and often misunderstood, of work. For their assistance in compiling the *Almanac* she would like to thank Jenny Sweetland and Monty Belfry, Cindy Baldwin and Jeanne Moore, and Neil Walker.

Actors, Artists, Authors & Attempted Assassins

THE ALMANAC OF FAMOUS & INFAMOUS PEOPLE

Stage & Screen: Cher, Chung & Charisse

Actors, Dancers,

Directors,

Television

Entertainers...

Beverly Aadland
American actress–dancer–singer
- In film *Cuban Rebel Girls* with Errol Flynn, 1959; their subsequent romance caused scandal.
- **b.** 1944

Willie Aames
(William Upton)
American actor
- Played Tommy Bradford on TV series "Eight Is Enough," 1977-84.
- **b.** July 15, 1960 in Newport Beach, California

Bud (William A) Abbott
(Abbott and Costello)
American comedian
- Starred in over 35 films with partner, Lou Costello, 1940-65.
- **b.** October 02, 1900 in Asbury Park, New Jersey
- **d.** April 24, 1974 in Woodland Hills, California

George Francis Abbott
American director–dramatist
- Outstanding Broadway figure; won many Tonys including one for *The Pajama Game*, 1955.
- **b.** June 25, 1887 in Forestville, New York

L(enwood) B(allard) Abbott
American filmmaker
- Won four Oscars, numerous Emmys for special effects cinematography.
- **b.** June 13, 1908 in Pasadena, California
- **d.** September 28, 1985 in Los Angeles, California

Abbott and Costello
(Bud Abbott; Lou Costello)
American comedy team
- Starred in over 35 comedy films, 1940-65; known for baseball comedy routine "Who's on First?"

Walter Charles Abel
American actor
- Has appeared in over 80 films including *The Three Musketeers*, 1934; *Man Without a Country*, 1973.
- **b.** June 06, 1898 in Saint Paul, Minnesota
- **d.** March 26, 1987 in Chester, Connecticut

F Murray Abraham
American actor
- Won Oscar for *Amadeus*, 1984.
- **b.** October 24, 1940 in El Paso, Texas

Doris Cole Abrahams
American producer
• Won Tonys for *Equus*, 1975; *Travesties*, 1976.
b. January 29, 1925 in New York, New York

Jim Abrahams
American director
• Co-creator of hit film *Airplane*, 1980.
b. 1944

Harry S Ackerman
American film executive-producer
• Exec. producer, Screen Gems Pictures Corp., 1958-73; developed several TV shows: "Bachelor Father," "Leave It to Beaver," "Gunsmoke," "I Love Lucy."
b. November 17, 1912 in Albany, New York
d. February 03, 1991 in Burbank, California

Robert Allan Ackerman
American director
• Directed on stage *Bent; Extremities; Slab Boys.*
b. 1945

Joss Ackland
English actor
• Character actor typically portraying men of power, especially kings.
b. February 29, 1928 in London, England

Don Adams
(Donald James Yarmy)
American actor-comedian
• Played Maxwell Smart on TV series "Get Smart," 1965-70.
b. April 19, 1926 in New York, New York

Joey Adams
(Joseph Abramowitz)
American comedian-author
• Nightclub, film performer who starred in "Joey Adams" TV show, 1956-58.
b. January 06, 1911 in Brooklyn, New York

Julie Adams
(Betty May Adams)
American actress
• Leading lady in second features; carried off by "Creature from the Black Lagoon," in 1954 film.
b. October 17, 1926 in Waterloo, Iowa

Mason Adams
American actor
• Played Charlie Hume in TV series "Lou Grant," 1977-82; nominated for three Emmys.
b. February 26, 1919 in New York, New York

Maud Adams
(Maud Solveig Christina Wikstrom)
Swedish actress-model
• Starred with Roger Moore in James Bond films *Man with the Golden Gun*, 1974, *Octopussy*, 1983.
b. February 12, 1945 in Lulea, Sweden

Maude Adams
(Maude Kiskadden)
American actress
• Played more than 1,500 performances in title role of *Peter Pan.*
b. November 11, 1872 in Salt Lake City, Utah
d. July 17, 1953 in Tannersville, New York

Nick Adams
(Nicholas Adamschock)
American actor
• Starred in TV series "The Rebel," 1959-61.
b. July 1, 1931 in Nanticoke, Pennsylvania
d. February 05, 1968 in Beverly Hills, California

Tony (Anthony Patrick) Adams
Irish producer
• Films include *10*, 1979; *S.O.B.*, 1981.
b. February 15, 1953 in Dublin, Ireland

Dawn Addams
English actress
• Best known as Charlie Chaplin's leading lady in *A King in New York*, 1957.
b. September 21, 1930 in Felixstowe, England
d. May 07, 1985 in London, England

Sybil Adelman
Canadian writer
• TV shows include "The Mary Tyler Moore Show," 1976-83; "Alice," 1970-77.
b. March 15, 1942 in Winnipeg, Manitoba

Isabelle Adjani
French actress
• Received Oscar nominations for *The Story of Adele H.*, 1975, *Camille Claudel*, 1990.
b. June 27, 1955 in Paris, France

Buddy (Maurice) Adler
American producer
• Won Oscar for *From Here to Eternity*, 1953; succeeded Darryl Zanuck as head of 20th Century Fox.
b. June 22, 1909 in New York, New York
d. July 12, 1960 in Hollywood, California

Aeschylus
("The Father of Tragedy;" "The Founder of the Greek Drama;" Father of Greek Tragedy ")
Greek poet-dramatist
• Wrote *Prometheus Bound;* seven of 90 plays survive.
b. 524?BC in Eleusis, Greece
d. 456?BC in Gela, Sicily

Brian de Lacy Aherne
English actor
• Suave romantic lead, who made 37 films including *Sylvia Scarlett*, 1935; *My Sister Eileen*, 1942.
b. May 02, 1902 in King's Norton, England
d. February 1, 1986 in Venice, Florida

Alvin Ailey
American dancer-choreographer
• Formed Alvin Ailey American Dance Theater, 1958; leading figure in establishment of modern dance as popular art form.
b. January 05, 1931 in Rogers, Texas
d. December 01, 1989 in New York, New York

Anouk Aimee
(Francoise Dreyfus)
French actress
• Nominated for Oscar for role in *A Man and a Woman*, 1966.
b. April 27, 1934 in Paris, France

Jo Anne Akalaitis
American director
• Off-Broadway productions include *Endgame*, 1984; won three Obies.
b. June 29, 1937 in Chicago, Illinois

Claude Akins
American actor
• Played Sonny Pruitt on TV series "Movin' On," 1974-76, title role in "Sheriff Lobo," 1979-81; in film *From Here to Eternity*, 1953.
b. May 25, 1918 in Nelson, Georgia

Zoe Akins
American poet-dramatist
• Wrote 1935 Pulitzer winner *The Old Maid.*
b. October 3, 1886 in Humansville, Missouri
d. October 29, 1958 in Los Angeles, California

Edward Franklin Albee III
American author-dramatist
• Plays critique American society and the loss of contact between individuals: *The Zoo Story*, 1959; won Pulitzers for *A Delicate Balance*, 1967, *Seascape*, 1975; won Tony, 1963, for *Who's Afraid of Virginia Woolf.*
b. March 12, 1928 in Washington, District of Columbia

Eddie Albert
(Edward Albert Heimberger)
American actor
• Played Oliver Douglas on TV comedy "Green Acres," 1965-71; received Oscar nominations for *Roman Holiday*, 1955, *The Heartbreak Kid*, 1972; father of Edward.
b. April 22, 1908 in Rock Island, Illinois

Jack Albertson
American actor
• Won Oscar, 1968, for *The Subject Was Roses;* Emmy, 1976, for "Chico and the Man."
b. June 16, 1910 in Malden, Massachusetts
d. November 25, 1981 in Hollywood, California

Alan Alda
(Alphonso d'Abruzzo)
American actor–director
• Played Hawkeye on "MASH," 1972-83; movie roles in *California Suite*, 1978; *The Four Seasons*, 1981.
b. January 28, 1936 in New York, New York

Robert Alda
(Alphonso Giovanni Giusseppi Roberto d'Abruzzo)
American actor
• Father of Alan Alda; best known for playing George Gershwin in *Rhasody in Blue*, 1945.
b. February 26, 1914 in New York, New York
d. May 03, 1986 in Los Angeles, California

Richard Stoddard Aldrich
American producer–author
• Produced over 30 Broadway plays, including *The Moon Is Blue*, 1951; pioneered growth of summer stock in US.
b. August 17, 1902 in Boston, Massachusetts
d. March 31, 1986 in Williamsburg, Virginia

Robert Aldrich
American director–producer
• Films include *The Dirty Dozen*, 1967; *The Longest Yard*, 1974.
b. August 09, 1918 in Cranston, Rhode Island
d. December 05, 1983 in Los Angeles, California

Ben (Nicholas Benton) Alexander
American actor
• Popular child star in silent films who was Jack Webb's partner on TV series "Dragnet," 1953-59.
b. May 26, 1911 in Garfield, Nevada
d. July 05, 1969 in Hollywood, California

Denise Alexander
American actress
• Played Dr. Leslie Weber on TV soap opera "General Hospital," 1973-84.
b. November 11, 1945 in New York, New York

Jane Alexander
(Jane Quigley)
American actress
• Won Tony for *Great White Hope*, 1969; played Eleanor Roosevelt in TV mini-series.
b. October 28, 1939 in Boston, Massachusetts

Yves Allegret
(Yves Champlain pseud)
French director
• Best known for "film noir" films, 1940s, starring Simone Signoret.
b. October 13, 1907 in Paris, France
d. January 31, 1986 in Paris, France

Byron Allen
American comedian
• Wrote comedy material for Jimmy Walker, Freddie Prinze; co-host, TV series "Real People"; currently a late night talkshow host.
b. April 22, 1961 in Detroit, Michigan

Debbie (Deborah) Allen
(Mrs Norm Nixon)
American actress–dancer
• Starred in TV series "Fame"; won Emmys for choreography, 1982, 1983.
b. January 16, 1950 in Houston, Texas

Gracie Ethel Cecil Rosaline Allen
(Mrs George Burns; Burns and Allen)
American comedienne
• With husband, starred in "Burns and Allen Show," 1922-58.
b. July 26, 1906 in San Francisco, California
d. August 27, 1964 in Hollywood, California

Irwin Allen
American director–producer
• Won Oscar, 1952, for *The Sea Around Us*, based on Rachel Carson's book.
b. June 12, 1916 in New York, New York

Jay Presson Allen
American screenwriter–author
• Noted teleplay, stagewriter who created TV series, "Family," 1976.
b. March 03, 1922 in San Angelo, Texas

Karen Jane Allen
American actress
• Appeared in movies *Animal House*, 1978, *Raiders of the Lost Ark*, 1981.
b. October 05, 1951 in Carrollton, Illinois

Nancy Allen
American actress
• Appeared in movies *Blowout*, 1981, *Dressed to Kill*, 1980.
b. June 24, 1949 in New York, New York

Steve (Stephen Valentine Patrick William) Allen
(William Christopher Stevens pseud)
American TV personality–songwriter
• Versatile entertainer known for ad-libbed witticisms; early host of "Tonight Show," "I've Got a Secret."
b. December 26, 1921 in New York, New York

Woody Allen
(Allen Stewart Konigsberg)
American actor–director
• Won four Oscars, including best picture, director, for *Annie Hall*, 1978.
b. December 01, 1935 in Brooklyn, New York

Kirstie Alley
(Mrs Parker Stevenson)
American actress
• Films include *Star Trek II*, 1982; plays Rebecca Howe on TV series "Cheers," 1987–.
b. January 12, 1955 in Wichita, Kansas

Fran(ces) Allison
American actress
• Best known as the warm-hearted human foil for puppets on the "Kukla, Fran, and Ollie" TV show, 1947-57.
b. November 2, 1924 in La Porte City, Iowa
d. June 13, 1989 in Van Nuys, California

June Allyson
(Ella Geisman)
American actress
• Movie roles project image of cheerful wholesomeness: *The Sailor Takes a Wife*, 1946; *The Three Musketeers*, 1948.
b. October 07, 1917 in Lucerne, New York

Nestor Almendros
Spanish filmmaker
• Award-winning cinematographer whose films include *Sophie's Choice*, 1982; *Places in the Heart*, 1984; won best photography Oscar, 1979, for *Days of Heaven* .
b. October 3, 1930 in Barcelona, Spain

Paul Almond
Canadian producer–screenwriter
• Pres., Quest Films since 1967; films include *Act of the Heart*, 1970; *Journal*, 1972.
b. April 26, 1931 in Montreal, Quebec

Alicia Alonso
(Alicia Ernestina de la Caridad del Cobre Marinez Hoyo)
Cuban dancer
• First Western dancer invited to dance in USSR, 1957; founded Ballet Nacional de Cuba, 1959.
b. December 21, 1921 in Havana, Cuba

Robert B Altman
American director–producer
• Directed *M*A*S*H*, 1970; *A Wedding*, 1978, *Vincent and Theo*, 1990
b. February 2, 1925 in Kansas City, Missouri

Eric Ambler
(Eliot Reed pseud)
English author–screenwriter
• Famed espionage writer who wrote *Mask of Dimitrios*, 1939; filmed, 1944.
b. June 28, 1909 in London, England

Don Ameche
(Dominic Felix Amici)
American actor–radio performer
• Star of over 40 films; won Oscar, 1986, for role in *Cocoon*.
b. May 31, 1908 in Kenosha, Wisconsin

Leon Ames
(Leon Wycoff)
American actor
• Character actor; appeared in over 100 films since 1932.
b. January 2, 1903 in Portland, Indiana

Winthrop Ames
American theater owner–producer
• Built, managed NYC theaters, 1905-15; wrote, produced *Snow White*, 1913, first play especially for children; grandson of Oakes.
b. November 25, 1871 in North Easton, Massachusetts
d. November 03, 1937 in Boston, Massachusetts

John Amos
American actor
• Played Kunte Kinte in TV mini-series "Roots," 1977; James Evans on TV series "Good Times," 1974-76.
b. December 27, 1942 in Newark, New Jersey

Ana-Alicia
(Ana Alicia Ortiz)
American actress
• Plays Melissa Agretti on TV series "Falcon Crest," 1981–.
b. December 12, 1957 in Mexico City, Mexico

Ib Steen Andersen
Danish dancer
• Co-star, with Merrill Ashley, in Balanchine's NYC Ballet, 1980.
b. December 14, 1954 in Copenhagen, Denmark

Daryl Anderson
American actor
• Played Animal in TV series "Lou Grant," 1977-82.
b. July 01, 1951 in Seattle, Washington

Eddie Anderson
American actor
• Played Jack Benny's manservant Rochester on radio, films, TV.
b. September 18, 1905 in Oakland, California
d. February 28, 1977 in Los Angeles, California

Gilbert M Anderson
(Max Aaronson)
American actor
• Starred as first cowboy hero, Broncho Billy, in western serial, 1907-14; awarded special Oscar, 1957.
b. March 21, 1882 in Little Rock, Arkansas
d. January 2, 1971 in South Pasadena, California

Harry Anderson
American actor
• Plays Judge Harry Stone on TV series "Night Court," 1984–.
b. October 14, 1952 in Newport, Rhode Island

Dame Judith Anderson
(Frances Margaret Anderson-Anderson)
Australian actress
• First Australian-born actress invested as Dame Commander, 1960; known for role in film *Rebecca*, 1940.
b. February 1, 1898 in Adelaide, Australia

Loni Anderson
(Mrs Burt Reynolds)
American actress
• Played Jennifer on TV series "WKRP in Cincinnati," 1978-80.
b. August 05, 1945 in Saint Paul, Minnesota

Maxwell Anderson
American dramatist
• Plays include *Winterset*, 1935; *Key Largo*, 1939; Pulitzer-winning *Both Your Houses*, 1933.
b. December 15, 1888 in Atlantic, Pennsylvania
d. February 28, 1959 in Stamford, Connecticut

Melissa Sue Anderson
American actress
• Played Mary Ingalls on TV series, "Little House on the Prairie," 1973-81.
b. September 26, 1962 in Berkeley, California

Michael Anderson
English director
• Films include *Around the World in 80 Days*, 1956; *Logan's Run*, 1976.
b. January 3, 1920 in London, England

Richard Dean Anderson
American actor
• Plays title role in TV action-adventure series "MacGyver," 1985–.
b. January 23, 1950 in Minneapolis, Minnesota

Bibi (Birgitta) Andersson
Swedish actress
• Discovered by Ingmar Bergman, in many of his films: *The Seventh Seal*, 1956; *Brink of Life*, 1958.
b. November 11, 1935 in Stockholm, Sweden

Harriet Andersson
Swedish actress
• Starred in Ingmar Bergman's *Monika*, 1952, written especially for her.
b. January 14, 1932 in Stockholm, Sweden

Ursula Andress
Swiss actress
• First wife of John Derek; movies include *Dr. No*, 1962.
b. March 19, 1936 in Bern, Switzerland

Anthony Andrews
English actor
• Starred in TV movies: "Ivanhoe," 1982; "Sparkling Cyanide," 1983.
b. January 12, 1948 in London, England

Dana (Carver Dana) Andrews
American actor
• Brother of Steve Forrest; starred in *The Ox-Bow Incident*, 1943.
b. January 01, 1909 in Collins, Mississippi

Harry Andrews
English actor
• Character actor; specialized in playing tough, military officers: *The Battle of Britain*, 1969.
b. November 1, 1911 in Tonbridge, England
d. March 06, 1989 in Salchurst, England

Tige Andrews
(Tiger Androwaous)
American actor
• Played Capt. Adam Greer in TV series "The Mod Squad," 1968-73.
b. March 19, 1920 in Brooklyn, New York

Kenneth Anger
American director–author
• Avant-garde filmmaker; films reveal obsessions with occult and fetishism; wrote *Hollywood Babylon*, recounting scandals in film industry, 1959.
b. February 03, 1930 in Santa Monica, California

Edward Anhalt
(Andrew Holt pseud)
American screenwriter
• Original film writer, story adapter; won Oscar, 1964, for *Becket*.
b. March 28, 1914 in New York, New York

Evelyn Ankers
British actress
• Played in Universal B films *Wolf Man*, *Ghost of Frankenstein*, 1940s.
b. August 17, 1918 in Valparaiso, Chile
d. August 29, 1985 in Maui, Hawaii

Ann-Margret
(Ann-Margret Olsson; Mrs Roger Smith)
American dancer–actress
• Oscar nominations for *Carnal Knowledge*, 1971; *Tommy*, 1975.
b. April 28, 1941 in Stockholm, Sweden

Annabella
(Suzanne Georgette Charpentier)
French actress
• Wife of Tyrone Power, 1939-48; films include *Napoleon*, 1926, *Le Million*, 1931.
b. July 14, 1912 in Paris, France

Jean-Jacques Annaud
French director
• Movies include *Quest for Fire*, 1981.
b. January 1, 1943 in Draveil, France

Jean Marie Lucien Pierre Anouilh
French dramatist
• Plays portray human condition with scorn, compassion: *Antigone*, 1944; *Becket*, 1960.
b. June 23, 1910 in Bordeaux, France
d. October 03, 1987 in Lausanne, Switzerland

Susan Anspach
(Mrs Sherwood Ball)
American actress
• In films *Play It Again Sam*, 1972; *Five Easy Pieces*, 1970.
b. November 23, 1945 in New York, New York

Edgar Harold McFarlane Anstey
English director
• Documentary pioneer; won Oscar for *Wild Wings*, 1966.
b. February 16, 1907 in Watford, England
d. September 26, 1987 in London, England

Michelangelo Antonioni
Italian director
• First international hit *L'Avventura*, 1960, described modern man's emotional barrenness.
b. September 29, 1912 in Ferrara, Italy

Fatty (Roscoe Conkling) Arbuckle
(William B Goodrich pseud)
American comedian–director
• Involved in famous Hollywood manslaughter scandal, 1921.
b. March 24, 1887 in Smith Center, Kansas
d. June 29, 1933 in Los Angeles, California

Anne Archer
(Mrs Terry Jastrow)
American actress
• Received Oscar nomination for *Fatal Attraction*, 1987; daughter of Marjorie Lord.
b. August 25, 1947 in Los Angeles, California

Eve Arden
(Eunice Quedens)
American actress
• Starred in "Our Miss Brooks" on radio, TV, 1948-56; nominated for Oscar for *Mildred Pierce*, 1945.
b. April 3, 1912 in Mill Valley, California
d. November 12, 1990 in Los Angeles, California

John Arden
English dramatist
• Controversial, innovative playwright whose modernistic plays include *Mary's Name*, 1977.
b. October 26, 1930 in Barnsley, England

Aristophanes
Greek dramatist
• Greatest comic playwright of ancient world; wrote 55 plays, 11 survive today.
b. 448BC
d. 385BC

Alan Wolf Arkin
(Roger Short)
American actor–director
• Won Tony Award, 1963, for *Enter Laughing*.
b. March 26, 1934 in New York, New York

Samuel Z Arkoff
American producer–film executive
• Has produced films since 1961: *Love at First Bite*, 1979; *Dressed to Kill*, 1980.
b. June 12, 1918 in Fort Dodge, Iowa

Roone Pinckney Arledge
American TV executive
• Pres., ABC News, ABC Sports; changed sports with slow-stop action, split-screens.
b. July 08, 1931 in Forest Hills, New York

Richard Arlen
(Richard Cornelius van Mattimore)
American actor
• Starred in movies *Wings*, 1927; *The Virginian*, 1929.
b. September 01, 1899 in Charlottesville, Virginia
d. March 28, 1976 in North Hollywood, California

Pedro Armendariz
Mexican actor
• Top Mexican film star; appeared in over 75 films: *From Russia With Love*, 1963.
b. May 09, 1912 in Mexico City, Mexico
d. June 18, 1963 in Los Angeles, California

R G Armstrong
American actor
• Gruff character actor whose films include *Ride the Wild Country*, 1962; *Heaven Can Wait*, 1978.
b. April 07, 1917 in Birmingham, Alabama

Robert Armstrong
American actor
• Starred in *King Kong*, 1933, as hunter who brings ape to civilization.
b. November 2, 1896 in Saginaw, Michigan
d. April 2, 1973 in Santa Monica, California

Desi Arnaz
(Desiderio Alberto Arnaz de Acha III)
American actor–singer
• Rumba bandleader; formed Desilu Productions with wife, Lucille Ball, 1950; best known as Ricky Ricardo.
b. March 02, 1917 in Santiago de Cuba, Cuba
d. December 02, 1986 in Del Mar, California

Desi(derio Alberto Arnaz, IV), Jr
American actor
• Son of Desi Arnaz, Lucille Ball; began career as rock singer; film debut, *Red Sky at Morning*, 1972.
b. January 19, 1953 in Los Angeles, California

Lucie Desiree Arnaz
(Mrs Lawrence Luckinbill)
American actress–singer
• Daughter of Desi Arnaz, Lucille Ball; starred in film *The Jazz Singer*, 1980; *They're Playing Our Song* on Broadway.
b. July 17, 1951 in Hollywood, California

James Arness
(James Aurness)
American actor
• Starred as Matt Dillon in TV series "Gunsmoke," 1955-75; brother of Peter Graves.
b. May 26, 1923 in Minneapolis, Minnesota

Danny Arnold
(Arnold Rothman)
American producer
• Pres., Four D Productions, 1958–; produced "Barney Miller," 1973-81.
b. January 23, 1925 in New York, New York

Edward Arnold
(Gunter Edward Arnold Schneider)
American actor
• Starred in *Diamond Jim*, 1935; *Sutter's Gold*, 1936.
b. February 18, 1890 in New York, New York
d. April 26, 1956 in San Fernando, California

Karin von Aroldingen
(Karin Awny Hannelore Reinbold von Aroldingen und Eltzingen)
German dancer
• With NYC Ballet, 1962–.
b. July 09, 1941 in Greiz, Germany

Rosanna Arquette
American actress
• Appeared in films *The Executioner's Song*, 1982; *Desperately Seeking Susan*, 1985; *After Hours*, 1988.
b. August 1, 1959 in New York, New York

Beatrice Arthur
(Bernice Frankel)
American actress
• Starred in TV series "Maude," 1972-78; "The Golden Girls," 1985–; won best actress Emmy, 1988.
b. May 13, 1926 in New York, New York

Jean Arthur
(Gladys Georgianna Greene)
American actress
• Squeaky-voiced leading lady of 1930s-40s films; nominated for Oscar for *The More the Merrier*, 1943.
b. October 17, 1908 in New York, New York

Dorothy Arzner
American director
• First woman director of sound films; credits include *Craig's Wife*, 1935.
b. January 03, 1900 in San Francisco, California
d. October 01, 1979 in La Quinta, California

Hal Ashby
American director
• Directed *Shampoo*, 1975, *Coming Home*, 1978; as film editor, won Oscar for *In the Heat of the Night*, 1967.
b. 1936 in Ogden, Utah
d. December 27, 1988 in Malibu, California

Dame Peggy (Edith Margaret Emily) Ashcroft
English actress
• Best known for role opposite Paul Robeson in *Othello*, 1930; won Oscar for *A Passage to India*, 1984.
b. December 22, 1907 in Croydon, England

Elizabeth Ashley
(Elizabeth Ann Cole)
American actress
• Won Tony, 1962; films include *The Carpet Baggers*, 1963.
b. August 3, 1939 in Ocala, Florida

Sir Frederick William Ashton
English choreographer–dancer
• Created inumerable works for Sadlers Wells, the Royal Ballet director, 1963-70.
b. September 17, 1906 in Guayaquil, Ecuador
d. August 18, 1988 in London, England

Ed(ward) Asner
American actor
• Six-time Emmy winner best known for role of Lou Grant on "Mary Tyler Moore Show," 1970-77.
b. November 15, 1929 in Kansas City, Missouri

Anthony Asquith
English director
• Directed *The Importance of Being Earnest*, 1952.
b. November 09, 1902 in London, England
d. February 2, 1968 in London, England

Adele Astaire
(Adele Austerlitz; Mrs Kingman Douglas)
American dancer–celebrity relative
• Dancing partner, 1916-32, of brother Fred.
b. September 1, 1898 in Omaha, Nebraska
d. January 25, 1981 in Scottsdale, Arizona

Fred Astaire
(Frederick Austerlitz)
American dancer–actor
• Dancing style has influenced all movie musicals; starred in 10 films with best known partner, Ginger Rogers.
b. May 1, 1899 in Omaha, Nebraska
d. June 22, 1987 in Los Angeles, California

Nils Asther
Swedish actor
• Leading man in Swedish and German films; in US film *The Bitter Tea of General Yen*, 1933.
b. January 17, 1901 in Malmo, Sweden
d. October 13, 1981 in Stockholm, Sweden

John Allen Astin
American actor
• Best known as Gomez Addams on "The Addams Family," 1964-66.
b. March 3, 1930 in Baltimore, Maryland

Mary Astor
(Lucille Vasconcellos Langhanke)
American actress
• Made over 100 films in 44-yr. career; best-known role: Brigid O'Shaughnessy in *The Maltese Falcon*, 1941; won Oscar for *The Great Lie*, 1941.
b. May 03, 1906 in Quincy, Illinois
d. September 25, 1987 in Los Angeles, California

William Atherton
(William Atherton Knight II)
American actor
• Starred in films *Sugarland Express*, 1974; *Looking For Mr. Goodbar*, 1977.
b. July 3, 1947 in New Haven, Connecticut

Sir Richard Samuel Attenborough
English actor–producer–director
• Won 1983 best director Oscar for *Gandhi*; film took 20 yrs. to make.
b. August 29, 1923 in Cambridge, England

Lionel Atwill
English actor
• Began career on stage in plays by Shaw, Isben; films include *Son of Frankenstein*, 1939.
b. March 01, 1885 in Croydon, England
d. April 22, 1946 in Hollywood, California

Rene Murat Auberjonois
American actor
• Won Tony for *Coco*, 1969; played Clayton Endicott on TV comedy "Benson," 1980-86.
b. June 01, 1940 in New York, New York

Stephane Audran
(Mrs Claude Chabrol)
French actress
• Sophisticated film beauty who starred in *Les Beches*, 1968; *Violette Noziere*, 1978.
b. 1939 in Versailles, France

Mischa Auer
(Mischa Ounskowski)
Russian actor
• Appeared in over 60 US films; nominated for Oscar, 1936, for *My Man Godfrey*.
b. November 17, 1905 in Saint Petersburg, Russia
d. March 05, 1967 in Rome, Italy

Frank Joseph Augustyn
Canadian dancer
• Star of Canada's National Ballet since 1972.
b. January 27, 1953 in Hamilton, Ontario

George Axelrod
American dramatist
• Wrote plays *The Seven Year Itch*, 1956; *Breakfast at Tiffany's*, 1962.
b. June 09, 1922 in New York, New York

Alan (Roland Allen) Ayckbourn
English dramatist–director
• England's Neil Simon; comedies include *Joking Apart*, 1979.
b. April 12, 1939 in London, England

Dan(iel Edward) Aykroyd
American actor–comedian
• Star of "Saturday Night Live," 1975-79; won Emmy, 1976; in films *The Blues Brothers*, 1980; *Ghostbusters*, 1984.
b. July 01, 1952 in Ottawa, Ontario

Lew Ayres
American actor
• Starred in *All Quiet on the Western Front*, 1930; first actor to register as conscientious objector, WW II.
b. December 28, 1908 in Minneapolis, Minnesota

Emanuel Azenberg
American producer
• Credits include dozens of major Broadway hits; won many Tonys: *Ain't Misbehaving*, 1978.
b. January 22, 1934 in Bronx, New York

Thomas Babe
American dramatist
• Award-winning plays include *Rebel Women*, 1976.
b. March 13, 1941 in Buffalo, New York

Lauren Bacall
(Betty Joan Perske)
American actress
• Won Tonys for *Applause*, 1970; *Woman of the Year*, 1981; once wed to Humphrey Bogart, Jason Robards.
b. September 16, 1924 in New York, New York

Barbara Bach
(Barbara Goldbach; Mrs Ringo Starr)
American actress
• Married Ringo Starr, 1981, after starring together in movie *Caveman*.
b. August 27, 1947 in New York, New York

Jim (James Gilmore) Backus
American actor
• Veteran stage, radio, vaudeville performer; known for voice of Mr. Magoo; role on TV's "Gilligan's Island," 1964-67.
b. February 25, 1913 in Cleveland, Ohio

Frank Bacon
American actor
• Star, co-author of long-running play, *Lightin'*, 1918.
b. January 16, 1864 in Marysville, California
d. November 19, 1922 in Chicago, Illinois

Kevin Bacon
American actor
• Starred in films *Footloose*, 1984; *She's Having a Baby*, 1988; *He Said, She Said*, 1991.
b. July 08, 1958 in Philadelphia, Pennsylvania

Angela (Madeleine Angela Clinton) Baddeley
English actress
• Played Mrs. Bridges, the cook, in PBS TV series "Upstairs Downstairs".
b. July 04, 1900 in London, England
d. February 22, 1976 in Essex, England

Max Baer, Jr
American actor–producer–director
• Played Jethro Bodine on "The Beverly Hillbillies," 1962-71.
b. December 04, 1937 in Oakland, California

Enid Bagnold
(Lady Jones)
English author–dramatist
• Noted for novel *National Velvet*, 1935; prize-winning play *The Chalk Garden*, 1956.
b. October 27, 1889 in Rochester, England
d. March 31, 1981 in London, England

Jack Bailey
American TV personality
• Emceed for several game shows: "Queen for a Day"; "Truth or Consequences"; "Joker's Wild."
b. September 15, 1907 in Hampton, Iowa
d. February 01, 1980 in Santa Monica, California

James Anthony Bailey
(Barnum and Bailey)
American circus owner
• Merged his Cooper and Bailey Circus with P T Barnum's to form "The Greatest Show on Earth," 1881.
b. July 04, 1847 in Detroit, Michigan
d. April 11, 1906 in Mount Vernon, New York

Barbara Bain
American actress
• Played Cinnamon Carter on TV series "Mission Impossible," 1966-69.
b. September 13, 1932 in Chicago, Illinois

Conrad Stafford Bain
Canadian actor
• Starred in TV series "Maude," 1971-78; founded Actors Federal Credit Union, 1962.
b. February 04, 1923 in Lethbridge, Alberta

Scott Vincent Baio
American actor
• Played Chachi on TV series "Happy Days," 1977-82; star of "Charles in Charge," 1984-.
b. September 22, 1961 in Brooklyn, New York

Bil (William Britton) Baird
American puppeteer
• Founded Bil and Cora Baird Puppet Theatre, Greenwich Village, 1966.
b. August 15, 1904 in Grand Island, Nebraska
d. March 18, 1987 in New York, New York

Cora Eisenberg Baird
(Mrs Bil Baird)
American puppeteer
• Puppets appeared in movie *The Sound of Music*, 1965.
b. January 26, 1912 in New York, New York
d. December 07, 1967 in New York, New York

Carroll Baker
American actress
• Nominated for Oscar, 1956, for *Baby Doll*; groomed in 1960s to replace Marilyn Monroe as screen sex goddess.
b. May 28, 1935 in Johnstown, Pennsylvania

Diane Baker
American actress
• Films include *Diary of Anne Frank*, 1959; *Marnie*, 1969.
b. February 25, 1938 in Hollywood, California

Joe Don Baker
American actor
• Best known for role in movie *Walking Tall*, 1973.
b. February 12, 1936 in Groesbeck, Texas

Kenny Baker
English actor
• Played R2-D2 in *Star Wars* films.
b. August 24, 1934 in Birmingham, England

Sir Stanley Baker
Welsh actor
• Films include *The Guns of Navarone*, 1961; *Accident*, 1967.
b. February 28, 1928 in Glamorgan, Wales
d. June 28, 1976 in Malaga, Spain

William Bakewell
American actor
• Films include *All Quiet on the Western Front*, 1930; *Gone With The Wind*, 1939.
b. May 02, 1908 in Hollywood, California

Barney Balaban
American film executive
• Pres., of Paramount Pictures, 1936-64; introduced primitive air-conditioning to movie theaters, 1917.
b. June 08, 1887 in Chicago, Illinois
d. March 07, 1971 in Byram, Connecticut

George Balanchine
(Georges Malitonovitch Balanchivadze; "Mr B")
American dancer–choreographer
• Co-founded Ballet Society, now NYC Ballet, 1946; artistic director, 1948-83.
b. January 09, 1904 in Saint Petersburg, Russia
d. April 3, 1983 in New York, New York

John Lloyd Balderston
American dramatist
• Writings include *Genius of the Marne*, 1919; *Cleopatra and Caesar*, 1952.
b. October 22, 1889 in Philadelphia, Pennsylvania
d. March 08, 1954 in Beverly Hills, California

Alec (Alexander Rae, III) Baldwin
American actor
• Starred in TV series "Knots Landing," 1984-85; films *Working Girl*, 1988, *The Hunt for Red October*, 1990, *Miami Blues*, 1990.
b. April 03, 1958 in Amityville, New York

Lucille Ball
(Mrs Gary Morton)
American actress
• Red-headed actress best known as Lucy Ricardo in TV sitcom "I Love Lucy," 1951-57; show won over 200 awards, including five Emmys.
b. August 06, 1911 in Jamestown, New York
d. April 26, 1989 in Los Angeles, California

William Ball
American director
• Won Obie for *Ivanov*, 1959; received special Tony for contributions to theater, 1979.
b. April 29, 1931 in Chicago, Illinois

Kaye Ballard
(Catherine Gloria Balotta)
American actress
• Stage, TV comedienne, who starred in TV series, "The Mothers-in-Law," 1967-69.
b. November 2, 1926 in Cleveland, Ohio

Martin Henry Balsam
American actor
• Won 1964 Oscar for *A Thousand Clowns*.
b. November 04, 1919 in New York, New York

Anne Bancroft
(Anna Maria Luisa Italiano; Mrs Mel Brooks)
American actress
• Won Oscar, Tony, 1962, for role of Annie Sullivan in *The Miracle Worker*; played Mrs. Robinson in *The Graduate*, 1967.
b. September 17, 1931 in New York, New York

Victor Banerjee
Indian actor
• First Indian actor since Sabu to win world fame in Hollywood movie: *Passage to India*, 1986.
b. October 15, 1946 in Calcutta, India

Leslie Banks
English actor–director
• Played villain in *The Most Dangerous Game*, 1932.
b. June 09, 1890 in Liverpool, England
d. April 21, 1952 in London, England

Monty (Montague) Banks
(Mario Bianchi)
Italian actor–director
• Married to Gracie Fields; appeared in *A Bell for Adano*, 1945.
b. 1897 in Casene, Italy
d. January 07, 1950 in Arona, Italy

Ian Bannen
Scottish actor
• Known for Shakespearean roles including film *Macbeth*, 1959.
b. June 29, 1928 in Airdrie, Scotland

Bob Banner
American producer–director
• Has produced, directed TV series "Solid Gold" since 1980.
b. August 15, 1921 in Ennis, Texas

Adrienne Barbeau
(Mrs John Carpenter)
American actress
• Starred in TV series "Maude," 1972-78; in movie *The Fog*, 1980.
b. June 11, 1945 in Sacramento, California

Brigitte Bardot
(Camille Javal)
French actress
• French sex symbol best known for film *And God Created Woman*, 1956; retired from screen to become conservationist.
b. September 28, 1934 in Paris, France

Lynn Bari
(Marjorie Schuyler Fisher)
American actress
• Husky-voiced siren; played the "other woman" in B films, 1930s-40s.
b. December 18, 1913 in Roanoke, Virginia
d. November 2, 1989 in Goleta, California

Bob (Robert William) Barker
American TV personality
• Hosted TV game shows, "Truth or Consequences"; "The Price is Right."
b. December 12, 1923 in Darrington, Washington

Lex (Alexander Crichlow, Jr) Barker
American actor
• Tenth actor to play Tarzan in five films, 1949-53.
b. May 08, 1919 in Rye, New York
d. April 11, 1973 in New York, New York

Ronnie Barker
English actor–comedian
• Starred in British TV series "The Two Ronnies"; "Porridge"; "Sorry."
b. September 25, 1929 in Bedford, England

Ellen Barkin
American actress
• Supporting film roles include *Down by Law*, 1986; *The Big Easy*, 1987.
b. April 16, 1955 in New York, New York

Binnie (Gertrude Maude) Barnes
English actress
• Starred as Catherine Howard in *The Private Life of Henry VIII*, 1933, with Charles Laughton.
b. March 25, 1905 in London, England

Peter Barnes
English dramatist
• Wrote award-winning play with a "playful nightmare" effect, *The Ruling Class*, 1968.
b. January 1, 1931 in London, England

P(hineas) T(aylor) Barnum
(Barnum and Bailey)
American circus owner
• Opened "The Greatest Show on Earth," 1871, with flashy ads, freak shows; coined expression "There's a sucker born every minute."
b. July 05, 1810 in Bethel, Connecticut
d. April 07, 1891 in Philadelphia, Pennsylvania

Roseanne Barr
(Mrs Tom Arnold)
American comedienne–actress
• Housewife-turned-comedienne; star of TV comedy "Roseanne," 1988–.
b. November 03, 1952 in Salt Lake City, Utah

John L Barrett
American radio performer
• Original voice of the Lone Ranger on radio, early 1930s.
b. 1913
d. May 01, 1984 in Buffalo, New York

Barbara Barrie
(Barbara Ann Berman)
American actress
• Films include *Breaking Away*, 1979; *Private Benjamin*, 1980.
b. May 23, 1931 in Chicago, Illinois

Wendy Barrie
(Marguerite Wendy Jenkins)
English actress
• Radio, TV talk show hostess whose films include *Private Life of Henry VIII*, 1933; *Hound of Baskervilles*, 1939.
b. April 18, 1912 in London, England
d. February 02, 1978 in Englewood, New Jersey

Chuck Barris
American TV personality–producer
• Created, produced "The Dating Game," 1965-73; "The Newlywed Game," 1966-74; created, starred in "The Gong Show."
b. June 02, 1929 in Philadelphia, Pennsylvania

Donald Barry
(Donald Barry de Acosta; "Red")
American actor
• Starred in *Red Ryder* Western film series, 1940s.
b. July 11, 1912 in Houston, Texas
d. July 17, 1980 in North Hollywood, California

Gene Barry
(Eugene Klass)
American actor
• Starred in TV series "Bat Masterson," 1959-61; "Burke's Law," 1963-66; "Name of the Game," 1968-71.
b. June 04, 1922 in New York, New York

Jack Barry
(Jack Barasch)
American TV personality–producer
• Producer of game shows, including "Concentration," 1958-73, longest-running daytime quiz show.
b. March 2, 1918 in Lindenhurst, New York
d. May 02, 1984 in New York, New York

Philip Barry
American dramatist
• Wrote *The Philadelphia Story*; filmed, 1940, starring Katharine Hepburn, Cary Grant.
b. June 18, 1896 in Rochester, New York
d. December 03, 1949 in New York, New York

Diana Barrymore
(Diana Blanche Blythe)
American actress–celebrity relative
• John Barrymore's daughter; starred in 1940s films; wrote autobiography *Too Much, Too Soon*, 1957.
b. March 03, 1921 in New York, New York
d. January 25, 1960 in New York, New York

Drew Barrymore
American actress–celebrity relative
• Granddaughter of John Barrymore; played Gertie in *ET*, 1982.
b. February 22, 1975 in Los Angeles, California

Elaine Jacobs Barrymore
(Elaine Barrie)
American actress
• John Barrymore's wife; wrote autobiography *All My Sins Remembered*, 1977.
b. 1914

Ethel Mae Blythe Barrymore
American actress
• Starred in *Corn Is Green*, 1942, in NYC's Ethel Barrymore Theatre; won Oscar for *None But the Lonely Heart*, 1944; sister of John, Lionel.
b. August 15, 1879 in Philadelphia, Pennsylvania
d. June 18, 1959 in Hollywood, California

Georgiana Emma Drew Barrymore
(Mrs Maurice Barrymore)
American actress
• Starred in *Romeo and Juliet* with husband Maurice, 1883; mother of John, Ethel, Lionel.
b. July 11, 1854 in Philadelphia, Pennsylvania
d. July 02, 1893 in Santa Barbara, California

John Barrymore
(John Sidney Blythe)
American actor
• Box office attraction due to voice, profile; known for roles as lover, grotesque tortured part in *Dr. Jekyll and Mr. Hyde*, 1920.
b. February 15, 1882 in Philadelphia, Pennsylvania
d. May 29, 1942 in Hollywood, California

John Blythe Drew Barrymore, Jr
American actor–celebrity relative
• Appeared in low-budget Italian films; son of John, father of Drew.
b. June 04, 1932 in Beverly Hills, California

Lionel Blythe Barrymore
American actor
• Brother of Ethel, John; first Barrymore to appear in film; won 1931 Oscar for *Free Soul*.
b. April 28, 1878 in Philadelphia, Pennsylvania
d. November 15, 1954 in Van Nuys, California

Maurice Barrymore
(Herbert Blythe)
English actor
• Father of Lionel, Ethel, John; made acting debut, 1872; known for supporting roles on stage.
b. 1847 in Agra, India
d. March 26, 1905 in Amityville, New York

Eva Bartok
(Eva Martha Szoke)
British actress
• Made film debut, 1947; private life love affairs better known; wrote autobiography *Worth Living For*, 1959.
b. June 18, 1926 in Kecskemet, Hungary

Mikhail Baryshnikov
American dancer–director–choreographer
• Artistic director, American Ballet Theatre, 1980-90; films include *The Turning Point*, 1977, *White Knights*, 1985.
b. January 28, 1948 in Riga, U.S.S.R.

Richard Basehart
American actor
• Versatile actor who made film debut, 1947; won 1956 Oscar for *Moby Dick*.
b. August 31, 1914 in Zanesville, Ohio
d. September 17, 1984 in Los Angeles, California

Kim Basinger
American actress–model
• Starred in *Never Say Never Again*, 1983; *The Natural*, 1983; starred in controversial *Nine-and-a-Half Weeks*, 1986; *Batman*, 1990.
b. December 08, 1953 in Athens, Georgia

Alfie (Alfred) Bass
English actor
• Character comedian; works include *Help!*, 1965; *Alfie*, 1966.
b. April 08, 1921 in London, England
d. July 15, 1987 in London, England

Saul Bass
American director–producer
• Revolutionized film credits by animating names; film title designs include *Seven Year Itch*, 1955; *Vertigo*, 1958.
b. May 08, 1920 in New York, New York

Jason Bateman
American actor
• Plays David Hogan on TV comedy "The Hogan Family," 1985; brother of Justine.
b. January 14, 1969 in Westchester, New York

Justine Bateman
American actress
• Played Mallory Keaton on TV series "Family Ties," 1982-89; sister of Jason.
b. February 19, 1966 in Rye, New York

Alan Arthur Bates
English actor
• Starred in films *King of Hearts,* 1967; *An Unmarried Woman,* 1978.
b. February 17, 1934 in Allestree, England

Florence Bates
(Florence Rabe)
American actress
• Made film debut at age 50; starred in *Rebecca,* 1940.
b. April 15, 1888 in San Antonio, Texas
d. January 31, 1954 in Burbank, California

Kathy Bates
(Kathleen Doyle-Bates)
American actress
• Won Best Actress Oscar, 1991, for memorable role in *Misery,* 1991.
b. June 28, 1948 in Memphis, Tennessee

Peg Leg (Clayton) Bates
American dancer
• Amputation of leg forced him to dance with peg leg; in Broadway musical *Blackbirds,* 1925, 1933.
b. November 1, 1907 in Fountain Inn, South Carolina

Frances Bavier
American actress
• Played Aunt Bea in TV series "The Andy Griffith Show," 1960-69.
b. January 14, 1905 in New York, New York
d. December 06, 1989 in Silver City, North Carolina

Anne Baxter
American actress
• Best known for films *The Razor's Edge,* 1946; *All About Eve,* 1950; played Victoria Cabot on TV's "Hotel," 1983-85.
b. May 07, 1923 in Michigan City, Indiana
d. December 12, 1985 in New York, New York

Keith Baxter
(Keith Stanley Baxter Wright)
Welsh actor
• Starred in London and NY stage production of "Sleuth," 1970.
b. April 29, 1935 in Newport, Wales

Warner Baxter
American actor
• Won 1929 Oscar for role of the Cisco Kid in *In Old Arizona.*
b. March 29, 1891 in Columbus, Ohio
d. May 07, 1951 in Beverly Hills, California

Meredith Baxter-Birney
American actress
• Starred in TV series "Bridget Loves Bernie," 1971-72; "Family," 1976-80; "Family Ties," 1982-89.
b. June 21, 1947 in Los Angeles, California

Howard Bay
American designer–director
• Won best set design Tonys for *Toys in the Attic,* 1960; *Man of La Mancha,* 1966.
b. May 03, 1912 in Centralia, Washington
d. November 21, 1986 in New York, New York

Beverly Pearl Bayne
(Mrs Francis X Bushman)
American actress
• Played Juliet in first American film version of *Romeo and Juliet,* 1915.
b. November 22, 1894 in Minneapolis, Minnesota
d. August 18, 1982 in Scottsdale, Arizona

Stephanie Beacham
English actress
• Played Sable Colby on TV series "The Colbys," 1985-87, starring role in TV comedy "Sister Kate," 1989-90.
b. February 28, 1947 in Hertfordshire, England

John Beal
(J Alexander Bliedung)
American actor
• Stage, screen actor since 1930; films include *Madame X,* 1937; *The Sound and the Fury,* 1959.
b. August 13, 1909 in Joplin, Missouri

Jennifer Beals
American actress
• Starred in films *Flashdance,* 1983; *The Bride,* 1985.
b. December 19, 1963 in Chicago, Illinois

Matthew Beard, Jr
(Our Gang; "Stymie")
American actor
• Bald black boy who made 40 "Our Gang" comedies, 1930-35.
b. January 01, 1925 in Los Angeles, California
d. January 08, 1981 in Los Angeles, California

Allyce Beasley
(Allyce Tannenberg)
American actress
• Played Agnes Dipesto on TV series "Moonlighting," 1985-89.
b. July 06, 1954 in New York, New York

Morgan Beatty
American broadcast journalist
• With NBC radio, 1941-67; commentator on "News of the World," 1946-67.
b. September 06, 1902 in Little Rock, Arkansas
d. July 04, 1975 in Putwith, West Indies

Ned Beatty
American actor
• Appeared in films *Deliverance,* 1972; *Superman,* 1978.
b. July 06, 1937 in Louisville, Kentucky

Roger Beatty
American writer–director
• Won five Emmys for writing "The Carol Burnett Show," 1972-78.
b. January 24, 1933 in Los Angeles, California

Warren Beatty
(Henry Warren Beaty)
American actor–director–producer
• Known for off-screen playboy image; award-winning films include *Heaven Can Wait,* 1978; *Reds,* 1981; *Dick Tracy,* 1991; brother of Shirley MacLaine.
b. March 3, 1937 in Richmond, Virginia

Pierre Augustin Caron de Beaumarchais
French author–courtier–dramatist
• Wrote comedies, *Barber of Seville,* 1775; *Marriage of Figaro,* 1784; both later operatized.
b. January 24, 1732 in Paris, France
d. May 18, 1799 in Paris, France

Francis Beaumont
English dramatist
• Collaborated with John Fletcher on about 50 tragicomedies, including *Philaster,* 1610; *A Maid's Tragedy,* 1611.
b. 1584 in Grace-Dieu, England
d. March 06, 1616

Hugh Beaumont
American actor
• Played Ward Cleaver in "Leave It to Beaver" TV series, 1957-63.
b. February 16, 1909 in Lawrence, Kansas
d. May 14, 1982 in Munich, Germany (West)

Louise Beavers
American actress
• One of Hollywood's most frequently employed blacks, usually as maid: *Imitation of Life*, 1934.
b. March 08, 1902 in Cincinnati, Ohio
d. October 26, 1962 in Hollywood, California

John Beck
American actor
• Plays Mark Graison on TV series "Dallas," 1983, 1985–.
b. January 28, 1946 in Chicago, Illinois

Julian Beck
American dramatist–actor
• Founded Living Theater; used improvisation, superrealistic horror to shock audiences.
b. May 31, 1925 in New York, New York
d. September 14, 1985 in New York, New York

Michael Beck
American actor
• Starred in film *Xanadu*, 1980; TV mini-series "Holocaust," "Mayflower."
b. February 04, 1949 in Memphis, Tennessee

Samuel Barclay Beckett
Irish author–dramatist
• Noted for *Waiting for Godot*, 1952; won Obie for *Play*, 1963; won Nobel Prize, 1969.
b. April 13, 1906 in Dublin, Ireland
d. December 22, 1989 in Paris, France

Bonnie Bedelia
(Bonnie Culkin)
American actress–singer–dancer
• Films include *Heart Like a Wheel*, 1983; *They Shoot Horses Don't They?*, 1969.
b. March 25, 1948 in New York, New York

Brace Beemer
American actor
• One of the original radio voices of the Lone Ranger, 1933-54.
b. 1903
d. March 01, 1965 in Oxford, Michigan

Noah Beery
American actor
• Silent screen's most loved villain best known for *Beau Geste*, 1926.
b. January 17, 1884 in Kansas City, Missouri
d. April 01, 1946 in Beverly Hills, California

Noah Beery, Jr
American actor
• Made screen debut with father Noah Beery, 1920; appeared in TV series "The Rockford Files," 1974-80.
b. August 1, 1916 in New York, New York

Wallace Beery
American actor
• Brother of Noah Beery, known for "lovable slob" roles; won Oscar, 1931, for *The Champ*.
b. April 01, 1886 in Kansas City, Missouri
d. April 15, 1949 in Beverly Hills, California

David Begelman
American film executive
• Involved in money scandal that was subject of book *Indecent Exposure*, 1973, by John M MacDonald.
b. August 26, 1921 in New York, New York

Ed(ward James) Begley
American actor
• Began career as radio announcer, 1931; won Oscar, 1964, for *The Unsinkable Molly Brown*.
b. March 25, 1901 in Hartford, Connecticut
d. April 28, 1970 in Hollywood, California

Ed Begley, Jr
American actor
• Played Dr. Victor Ehrlich on TV series "St. Elsewhere," 1982-88.
b. September 16, 1949 in Los Angeles, California

Aphra Behn
English author–dramatist
• First English woman to support herself by writing; most popular play was *The Rover*, 1677.
b. 1640 in Harbledown, England
d. April 16, 1689 in London, England

S(amuel) N(athaniel) Behrman
American author–dramatist–screenwriter
• The American theater's most accomplished specialist in the comedy of manners; plays include *No Time for Comedy*, 1939.
b. June 09, 1893 in Worcester, Massachusetts
d. August 09, 1973 in New York, New York

Albert Bein
Romanian dramatist–author
• Proletarian who wrote social protest drama *Let Freedom Ring*, 1935.
b. May 18, 1902 in Kishinev, Romania

Maurice Bejart
French choreographer
• Avant-garde ballet master of Belgium's nat. dance company since 1959.
b. January 01, 1927 in Marseilles, France

Shari Belafonte-Harper
American actress
• Played Julie Gillette on TV's "Hotel," 1983-88; daughter of Harry.
b. September 22, 1954 in New York, New York

Steve (Stephen Scott) Bell
American broadcast journalist
• Correspondent, ABC News since 1967; one of few journalists in Hanoi for release of American POWs.
b. December 09, 1935 in Oskaloosa, Iowa

Ralph Bellamy
American actor
• Won Tony, 1958, for *Sunrise at Campobello*.
b. June 17, 1904 in Chicago, Illinois

Kathleen Beller
American actress
• Films include *Godfather II*, 1974; TV shows include "Dynasty," 1982-84; "The Bronx Zoo," 1987–.
b. February 1, 1956 in Westchester, New York

Donald P Bellisario
American writer–producer
• Created "Magnum P I" TV series, 1980.
b. August 08, in Charleroi, Pennsylvania

Pamela Bellwood
American actress
• In movie *Airport '77*; played Claudia on TV series "Dynasty."
b. June 26, 1946 in New York, New York

Jean-Paul Belmondo
French actor
• Antihero image established in first feature film *Breathless*, 1960.
b. April 09, 1933 in Neuilly-sur-Seine, France

Jim (James) Belushi
American actor
• Starred on "Saturday Night Live," 1983-85; films include *Trading Places*, 1983; *About Last Night...*, 1986; *Salvador*, 1987.
b. June 15, 1954 in Chicago, Illinois

John Belushi
American actor–comedian
• Starred in films *Animal House*, 1978; *The Blues Brothers*, 1980; died of drug overdose. Fixture on vintage "Saturday Night Live."
b. January 24, 1949 in Chicago, Illinois
d. March 05, 1982 in Hollywood, California

Bea Benaderet
American actress
• Played Kate Bradley on TV series "Petticoat Junction," 1963-68.
b. April 04, 1906 in New York, New York
d. October 13, 1968 in Los Angeles, California

Jacinto Benavente y Martinez
Spanish dramatist
• Wrote over 170 plays, including *Bonds of Interest*, 1907; awarded Nobel Prize, 1922.
b. August 12, 1866 in Madrid, Spain
d. July 14, 1954 in Madrid, Spain

Dirk Benedict
(Dirk Niewoehner)
American actor
• On TV series "Battlestar Galactica," 1978-79; "The A-Team," 1983–.
b. March 01, 1945 in Helena, Montana

Brenda Benet
(Brenda Benet Nelson)
American actress
• Star of TV soap opera "Days of Our Lives"; married to Bill Bixby; committed suicide.
b. August 14, 1945 in Los Angeles, California
d. April 07, 1982 in Los Angeles, California

Richard Benjamin
American actor
• Husband of Paula Prentiss; starred in film *Goodbye Columbus*, 1969; directed *Little Nikita*, 1987.
b. May 22, 1938 in New York, New York

Constance Campbell Bennett
American actress
• Starred in sophisticated comedies: *Topper*, 1937; *Topper Takes a Trip*, 1939; daughter of Richard Bennett.
b. October 22, 1905 in New York, New York
d. July 04, 1965 in Fort Dix, New Jersey

Joan Bennett
(Mrs Walter Wanger)
American actress
• Her 50-year career took her from innocent blonde roles to sultry temptress parts on TV, stage, screen; appeared in 75 films including *Little Women*, 1933; sister of Constance.
b. February 27, 1910 in Palisades, New Jersey
d. December 07, 1990 in White Plains, New York

Michael Bennett
(Michael Bennett DiFiglia)
American choreographer
• Won two Tonys, Pulitzer for conceiving, directing, choreographing *A Chorus Line*, 1975; filmed, 1986.
b. April 08, 1943 in Buffalo, New York
d. July 02, 1987 in Tucson, Arizona

Richard Bennett
American actor
• Leading matinee idol who made stage debut, 1891; father of Joan, Constance.
b. May 21, 1873 in Deacon's Mills, Indiana
d. October 22, 1944 in Los Angeles, California

Jack Benny
(Benjamin Kubelsky)
American comedian
• Known for stinginess and violin playing; starred in "The Jack Benny Program," on TV, 1950-64.
b. February 14, 1894 in Waukegan, Illinois
d. December 26, 1974 in Los Angeles, California

Sir Frank Robert Benson
English actor–manager
• Founded touring Shakespearean Repertory Co., 1880s; only actor to be knighted in a theater, 1916.
b. November 04, 1858 in Alresford, England
d. December 31, 1939 in London, England

Robby Benson
(Robin Segal)
American actor
• Starred in movies *One on One*, 1977; *Ice Castles*, 1979; *The Chosen*, 1982.
b. January 21, 1956 in Dallas, Texas

Nelson (Joseph Nelson, Jr) Benton
American broadcast journalist
• With CBS News, covered 20 yrs. of events including Vietnam War, civil rights movement.
b. September 16, 1924
d. February 14, 1988 in New York, New York

Robert Douglass Benton
American screenwriter–director
• Won Oscars for *Kramer vs. Kramer*, 1979; *Places in the Heart*, 1984.
b. September 29, 1932 in Waxahachie, Texas

John Beradino
American actor–baseball player
• Infielder, 1939-52; plays Dr. Hardy on TV soap opera "General Hospital," 1963–.
b. May 01, 1917 in Los Angeles, California

Tom Berenger
American actor
• Appeared in film *The Big Chill*, 1983; nominated for Oscar for *Platoon*, 1986; *Born on the Fourth of July*, 1989.
b. May 31, 1950 in Chicago, Illinois

Gertrude Berg
American actress
• Starred in "The Goldbergs" on radio, 1929-50, TV, 1949-54.
b. October 03, 1899 in Harlem, New York
d. September 14, 1966 in New York, New York

Candice Bergen
(Mrs Louis Malle)
American actress–photojournalist
• Daughter of Edgar Bergen; plays title role in TV comedy, "Murphy Brown," 1988–; won Emmy, 1989, 1990.
b. May 09, 1946 in Beverly Hills, California

Edgar John Bergen
(Edgar John Bergren)
American ventriloquist–comedian
• Vaudeville, film, TV entertainer for 60 yrs.; with dummy Charlie McCarthy, starred in radio's "Chase & Sanborn Hour," 1937-47; father of Candice.
b. February 16, 1903 in Chicago, Illinois
d. September 3, 1978 in Las Vegas, Nevada

Polly Bergen
(Nellie Paulina Burgin)
American actress
• Radio singer turned actress; won Emmy, 1957, for "The Helen Morgan Story"; played Rhoda Henry on TV miniseries "The Winds of War" and "War and Remembrance."
b. July 14, 1930 in Knoxville, Tennessee

Helmut Berger
(Helmut Steinberger)
Austrian actor
• Known for sinister roles: *The Damned*, 1969; *Dorian Gray*, 1972.
b. May 29, 1944 in Salzburg, Austria

Marilyn Berger
(Mrs Don Hewitt)
American broadcast journalist
• Chief White House correspondent, NBC-TV, 1976-77; with ABC News, 1982–.
b. August 23, 1935 in New York, New York

Senta Berger
Austrian actress
• Star of films *Major Dundee*, 1965; *The Glory Guys*, 1965; *Quiller Memorandum*, 1967.
b. May 13, 1941 in Vienna, Austria

Ingmar Bergman
(Ernest Ingmar Bergman)
Swedish director–producer
• Leading film artist whose works include *The Seventh Seal*, 1957; *Wild Strawberries*, 1957.
b. July 14, 1918 in Uppsala, Sweden

Ingrid Bergman
Swedish actress
• Won Oscars for roles in *Gaslight*, 1944; *Anastasia*, 1956; *Murder on the Orient Express* ,1974.
b. August 29, 1915 in Stockholm, Sweden
d. August 29, 1982 in London, England

Jules Verne Bergman
American broadcast journalist
• Science editor, ABC News, 1961-87; wrote *Anyone Can Fly*, 1965; *Fire*, 1974.
b. March 21, 1929 in New York, New York
d. February 12, 1987 in New York, New York

Elisabeth Bergner
(Elizabeth Ettel)
British actress
• James Barrie wrote his last play *The Boy David*, for her, 1938; Oscar nominee for *Escape Me Never*, 1935.
b. August 22, 1900 in Vienna, Austria
d. May 12, 1986 in London, England

Busby Berkeley
(William Berkeley Enos)
American director–choreographer
• Known for choreography, 1930s movies, using dancing girls to form kaleidoscopic patterns: *42nd Street*, 1933; *No No Nanette*, 1971.
b. November 29, 1895 in Los Angeles, California
d. March 14, 1976 in Palm Springs, California

Bob Berkowitz
American broadcast journalist
• Correspondent, ABC News since 1982.
b. May 15, 1950 in New York, New York

Milton Berle
(Milton Berlinger; "Uncle Miltie" "Mr Television")
American actor–comedian–radio performer–TV personality
• Vaudeville, stage performer; dominated early TV with "The Milton Berle Show," 1948-56; known for collecting colleagues' jokes.
b. July 12, 1908 in New York, New York

Shelley (Sheldon Leonard) Berman
American comedian–actor
• Films include *The Best Man*, 1964; *Divorce American Style*, 1969.
b. February 03, 1926 in Chicago, Illinois

Paul Bern
(Paul Levy)
American director
• MGM exec. who supervised all Garbo's films; committed suicide after marriage to Jean Harlow.
b. December 03, 1889 in Wandsbek, Germany
d. September 04, 1932 in Beverly Hills, California

Sandra Bernhard
American actress–comedienne
• Made film debut in *The King of Comedy*, 1983; had critically acclaimed one-woman Off-Broadway show *Without You I'm Nothing*, 1988.
b. 1955 in Flint, Michigan

Melvin Bernhardt
(Melvin Bernhard)
American director
• Won Tony for *Da*, 1978.
b. February 26, in Buffalo, New York

Sarah Bernhardt
(Rosine Bernard; "The Divine Sarah")
French actress
• Greatest stage tragedienne of her time; noted for emotional acting, dulcet voice.
b. October 23, 1844 in Paris, France
d. March 26, 1923 in Paris, France

Corbin Bernsen
American actor
• Plays Arnie Becker on TV series "LA Law," 1986–; in film *Hello Again*, 1987.
b. September 07, 1955 in North Hollywood, California

Valerie Bertinelli
(Mrs Eddie Van Halen)
American actress
• Played Barbara on TV series "One Day at a Time," 1975-84.
b. April 23, 1960 in Wilmington, Delaware

Bernardo Bertolucci
Italian director
• Directed *Last Tango in Paris*, 1972; won Oscar for *The Last Emperor*, 1988.
b. March 16, 1940 in Parma, Italy

Pierre Berton
Canadian author–TV personality
• Host, weekly TV show "My Country"; wrote 30 books including *Klondike Quest*, 1983; Canada's most popular historian.
b. July 12, 1920 in Whitehorse, Yukon Territory

Ted Bessell
American actor
• Played Donald Hollinger on TV series "That Girl," 1966-71.
b. May 2, 1935 in Flushing, New York

Joe Besser
(The Three Stooges)
American comedian
• One of the members of The Three Stooges, 1956-58, replacing Shemp Howard.
b. 1908
d. March 01, 1988 in Los Angeles, California

Natalya (Igorevna) Bessmertnova
Russian dancer
• Prima ballerina of Bolshoi Ballet; won Lenin Award, 1970, for performance in *Spartacus*.
b. July 19, 1941 in Moscow, U.S.S.R.

Edna Best
American actress
• Made stage debut, 1917; greatest success in "The Constant Nymph," 1926.
b. March 03, 1900 in Hove, England
d. September 18, 1974 in Geneva, Switzerland

Thomas Betterton
English actor
• Opened London Theatre, 1695.
b. August 1635 in London, England
d. April 27, 1710 in London, England

Valerie Bettis
American choreographer
• With Virginia Sampler, first to choreograph a modern dance for ballet co., 1947.
b. December 2, 1919 in Houston, Texas
d. September 26, 1982 in New York, New York

Carl Betz
American actor
• Played husband in "The Donna Reed Show," 1958-66; had own series "Judd for the Defense," 1967-69.
b. March 09, 1920 in Pittsburgh, Pennsylvania
d. January 18, 1978 in Los Angeles, California

Richard (George Richard) Beymer
American actor
• Films include *The Diary of Anne Frank*, 1959; *West Side Story*, 1961.
b. February 21, 1939 in Avoca, Iowa

Charles Ambrose Bickford
American actor
• Three-time Oscar nominee; starred in TV's "The Virginian," 1966-67.
b. January 01, 1889 in Cambridge, Massachusetts
d. November 09, 1967 in Boston, Massachusetts

Theodore Meir Bikel
American actor–singer
• Made film debut in *African Queen*, 1952; Oscar nominee for *The Defiant Ones*, 1958.
b. May 02, 1924 in Vienna, Austria

Tony Bill
American actor–director–producer
• Directed *My Bodyguard*, 1980; won Oscar, 1973, for co-producing *The Sting*.
b. August 23, 1940 in San Diego, California

Barbara Billingsley
American actress
• Played June Cleaver on TV series "Leave It to Beaver," 1957-63.
b. December 22, 1922 in Los Angeles, California

Michael Patrick Bilon
American actor
• Played title role in *ET*, 1982; was 2 feet, 10 inches tall.
b. 1947 in Youngstown, Ohio
d. January 27, 1983 in Youngstown, Ohio

Frank J Biondi, Jr,
American TV executive
• President of Home Box Office (HBO) since 1983.
b. January 09, 1945 in Livingston, New Jersey

David Edwin Birney
American actor
• Star of TV series "Bridget Loves Bernie," 1972, "St. Elsewhere," 1982; married Meredith Baxter, 1974, later divorced.
b. April 23, 1940 in Washington, District of Columbia

Joey Bishop
(Joseph Abraham Gottlieb)
American comedian
• Nightclub entertainer, member of Frank Sinatra's "rat pack," 1950s, who was popular TV personality, 1960s.
b. February 03, 1918 in Bronx, New York

Kelly Bishop
(Carole Bishop)
American actress
• Won Tony for role of Sheila in *A Chorus Line*, 1976.
b. February 28, 1944 in Colorado Springs, Colorado

Patrick (Walter Patrick) Bissell
American dancer
• At time of death from drug overdose, was principal dancer, American Ballet Theater, NY.
b. December 01, 1957 in Corpus Christi, Texas
d. December 29, 1987 in Hoboken, New Jersey

Richard Bissell
American dramatist
• Co-wrote Tony winner *The Pajama Game*, 1954.
b. June 27, 1913 in Dubuque, Iowa
d. May 04, 1977 in Dubuque, Iowa

Jacqueline Fraser Bisset
English actress
• Starred in movies *The Deep*, 1977; *Rich and Famous*, 1981.
b. September 13, 1944 in Weybridge, England

Bill Bixby
American actor
• Starred in TV series "My Favorite Martian"; "The Courtship of Eddie's Father"; "The Incredible Hulk."
b. January 22, 1934 in San Francisco, California

Karen Black
(Karen Blanche Ziegler)
American actress
• Appeared in films *Easy Rider*, 1969; *Five Easy Pieces*, 1970; *The Great Gatsby*, 1975.
b. July 01, 1942 in Park Ridge, Illinois

Shirley Temple Black
(Mrs Charles A Black)
American actress–diplomat
• Child actress who was number one Hollywood attraction, 1938; US ambassador to Ghana, 1974-76.
b. April 23, 1928 in Santa Monica, California

Honor Blackman
English actress
• Played Pussy Galore in Bond film *Goldfinger*, 1964.
b. August 22, 1926 in London, England

Sidney Alderman Blackmer
American actor
• Made Broadway debut, 1917; portrayed Teddy Roosevelt more than a dozen times in films, plays.
b. July 13, 1896 in Salisbury, North Carolina
d. October 05, 1973 in New York, New York

Harry Blackstone
(Henri Bouton)
American magician
• Oldtime vaudeville act, became internationally famous; entertained Pres. Coolidge in White House, troops during WW II.
b. September 27, 1885 in Chicago, Illinois
d. November 16, 1965 in Hollywood, California

James Stuart Blackton
American filmmaker
• Founder, Vitagraph Films, 1896; first to produce film plays.
b. January 05, 1875 in Sheffield, England
d. August 13, 1941 in Los Angeles, California

Taurean Blacque
American actor
• Played Neal Washington on TV series "Hill Street Blues," 1981-87.
b. May 1, 1946 in Newark, New Jersey

Frank Blair
American broadcast journalist
• First newscaster on TV's "Today Show," 1952-75; autobiography *Let's Be Frank About It*, 1979.
b. May 3, 1915 in Yemassee, South Carolina

Janet Blair
(Martha Janet Lafferty)
American actress
• Appeared in *Three Girls about Town*, 1941; *My Sister Eileen*, 1942.
b. April 23, 1921 in Altoona, Pennsylvania

Linda Denise Blair
American actress
• Played the possessed girl whose head spins around in *The Exorcist*, 1973.
b. January 22, 1959 in Saint Louis, Missouri

Amanda Blake
(Beverly Louise Neill)
American actress
• Played Miss Kitty on TV series "Gunsmoke," 1955-75.
b. February 2, 1931 in Buffalo, New York
d. August 16, 1989 in Los Angeles, California

Robert Blake
(Michael Gubitosi; Our Gang)
American actor
• Starred in TV series "Baretta," 1974-78; won Emmy, 1975.
b. September 18, 1934 in Nutley, New Jersey

Colin (George Edward) Blakely
Irish actor
• Played Dr. Watson in film *The Private Life of Sherlock Holmes*, 1970.
b. September 23, 1930 in Bangor, Northern Ireland
d. May 07, 1987 in London, England

Susan Blakely
American actress
• Played in TV miniseries "Rich Man, Poor Man"; movies *The Way We Were*, 1973; *Towering Inferno*, 1974.
b. September 07, 1948 in Frankfurt, Germany (West)

Mel(vin Jerome) Blanc
American actor
• Voice of many cartoon characters: Bugs Bunny, Porky Pig, Daffy Duck.
b. May 3, 1908 in San Francisco, California
d. July 1, 1989 in Los Angeles, California

Holbrook Blinn
American actor–producer
• Silent film star who appeared opposite Marion Davies in *Janice Meredith*, 1924; *Zander the Great*, 1925.
b. 1872 in San Francisco, California
d. June 24, 1928 in Croton-on-Hudson, New York

Bertram Bloch
American dramatist
• Co-wrote play *Dark Victory*, 1934; filmed, 1939.
b. May 05, 1892 in New York, New York
d. June 21, 1987 in New York, New York

Ivan Sol Bloch
American producer–restaurateur
• Co-owner, Sardi's, NYC; Broadway productions include *The Real Thing*; won two Tonys.
b. November 16, 1940 in Detroit, Michigan

Robert Albert Bloch
(Tarleton Fiske; Nathan Hindin; Collier Young pseuds)
American author–screenwriter
• Mystery writer who wrote film version of his novel *Psycho*, 1959, sequel *Psycho II*, 1982.
b. April 05, 1917 in Chicago, Illinois

Dan Blocker
American actor
• Played Hoss Cartwright on TV series "Bonanza," 1959-72.
b. December 1, 1932 in Bowie, Texas
d. May 13, 1972 in Inglewood, California

Joan Blondell
American actress
• Appeared in over 80 films; best known role Aunt Sissy in *A Tree Grows in Brooklyn*, 1945.
b. August 3, 1912 in New York, New York
d. December 25, 1979 in Santa Monica, California

Jean Francois Gravelet Blondin
French entertainer
• Crossed Niagara Falls on a tightrope, 1859, repeating act blindfolded.
b. February 28, 1824 in Saint-Omer, France
d. February 19, 1897 in London, England

Claire Bloom
English actress
• Best known for Chaplin film *Limelight*, 1952; former wife of Rod Steiger.
b. February 15, 1931 in London, England

Kermit Bloomgarden
American producer
• Produced *Diary of Anne Frank*, 1959.
b. December 15, 1904 in Brooklyn, New York
d. September 2, 1976 in New York, New York

Ben Blue
(Benjamin Bernstein)
Canadian comedian–dancer
• Vaudeville star 1916; appeared in film *It's a Mad, Mad, Mad, Mad World*, 1963.
b. September 12, 1901 in Montreal, Quebec
d. March 07, 1975 in Los Angeles, California

Monte Blue
American actor
• Appeared in 200 films, 1915-54; playing romantic leads, 1920s: *Orphans of the Storm*, 1922.
b. January 11, 1890 in Indianapolis, Indiana
d. February 18, 1963 in Milwaukee, Wisconsin

Larry Blyden
(Ivan Lawrence Blieden)
American actor–TV personality
• Made stage debut in *Mr. Roberts*, 1948; in film *On a Clear Day You Can See Forever*, 1969; hosted TV's "What's My Line?"
b. June 23, 1925 in Houston, Texas
d. June 06, 1975 in Agadir, Morocco

Ann Marie Blyth
American actress
• Received Oscar nomination for *Mildred Pierce*, 1945.
b. August 16, 1928 in Mount Kisco, New York

Betty Blythe
(Elizabeth Blythe Slaughter)
American actress
• Popular Vitagraph silent star; title role in *Queen of Sheba*, 1921.
b. September 01, 1893 in Los Angeles, California
d. April 07, 1972 in Woodland Hills, California

Steven Bocho
American writer–producer
• Co-creator of TV show "Hill Street Blues," 1981.
b. December 16, 1943

Hart Bochner
Canadian actor
• Star of film *Breaking Away*, 1979; TV film "East of Eden," 1981.
b. December 03, 1956 in Toronto, Ontario

Lloyd Bochner
Canadian actor
• Played Cecil Colby on TV's "Dynasty," 1981-83.
b. July 29, 1924 in Toronto, Ontario

Dirk Bogarde
(Derek Niven van den Bogaerde)
English actor–author
• Won British Academy Award for *The Servant*, 1963; *Darling*, 1965.
b. March 28, 1921 in London, England

Humphrey de Forest Bogart
American actor
• Starred in *Casablanca*, 1942; won Oscar for *The African Queen*, 1951; a leading cult figure, played quintessential tough guy.
b. December 25, 1899 in New York, New York
d. January 14, 1957 in Los Angeles, California

Neil Bogart
(Neil Bogatz)
American business executive–producer
• Founder, 1974, pres., Casablanca Record and Film Works.
b. February 03, 1943 in Brooklyn, New York
d. May 08, 1982 in Los Angeles, California

Peter Bogdanovich
American director–producer
• Won NY Film Critics Award, best screenplay for *The Last Picture Show*, 1971.
b. July 3, 1939 in Kingston, New York

Eric Bogosian
American actor–dramatist
• Won Obie, Drama Desk awards for one-man show *Drinking in America*, 1986.
b. April 24, 1953 in Boston, Massachusetts

Wojciech Boguslawski
Polish director–dramatist
• Considered father of Polish theater; director, National Theater, 1783-1814; wrote over 80 plays.
b. April 09, 1757 in Glinno, Poland
d. July 23, 1829 in Warsaw, Poland

Heidi Bohay
American actress
• Played Megan Kendal on TV series "Hotel," 1983-88.
b. December 15, 1959 in Bound Brook, New Jersey

Mary Boland
American actress
• Played opposite Charles Ruggles in many 1930s films including *Ruggles of Red Gap*, 1935.
b. January 28, 1880 in Philadelphia, Pennsylvania
d. June 23, 1965 in New York, New York

John Boles
American actor
• Leading man of 30s-40s; films include *Curly Top,* 1935; *The Littlest Rebel,* 1935; *Stella Dallas,* 1937.
b. October 18, 1895 in Greenville, Texas
d. February 27, 1969 in San Angelo, Texas

Ray(mond Wallace) Bolger
American actor–dancer
• Show business veteran best known for playing the Scarecrow in *The Wizard of Oz,* 1939.
b. January 1, 1904 in Dorchester, Massachusetts
d. January 15, 1987 in Los Angeles, California

Joseph Bologna
American actor
• Films include *My Favorite Year,* 1982; *Blame It on Rio,* 1984.
b. 1938 in Brooklyn, New York

Guy Reginald Bolton
English dramatist
• Wrote over 50 musicals including *Lady be Good; Anything Goes.*
b. November 23, 1884 in Brozbourne, England
d. September 05, 1979 in Goring, England

Edward Bond
English dramatist
• Controversial plays include *Saved,* 1965; *Lear,* 1971.
b. July 18, 1934 in London, England

Sudie Bond
American actress
• Played Flo on TV's "Alice," 1980-82.
b. July 13, 1928 in Louisville, Kentucky
d. November 1, 1984 in New York, New York

Tommy Bond
(Our Gang)
American actor
• Played Butch in 1930s "Our Gang" serial.
b. September 16, 1927 in Dallas, Texas

Ward Bond
American actor
• Appeared in over 200 films; starred in TV series "Wagon Train," 1957-61.
b. April 09, 1904 in Denver, Colorado
d. November 05, 1960 in Dallas, Texas

Sergei (Fedorovich) Bondarchuk
Russian director–actor
• Played lead roles in Russian films *Destiny of a Man,* 1961; *War and Peace,* 1966.
b. September 25, 1922 in Byelozerka, U.S.S.R.

Beulah Bondi
American actress
• Oscar nominee for *Gorgeous Hussy; Of Human Hearts;* won 1977 Emmy for "The Waltons."
b. May 03, 1892 in Chicago, Illinois
d. January 12, 1981 in Hollywood, California

Peter Bonerz
American actor–director
• TV actor, director of episodes of "Bob Newhart Show," 1972-78; director *It's Your Move,* 1984.
b. August 06, 1938 in Portsmouth, New Hampshire

Lisa Bonet
American actress
• Played Denise Huxtable on "The Cosby Show," 1984-87, "A Different World," 1987–; *Angel Heart,* 1987.
b. November 16, 1967 in Los Angeles, California

Frank Bonner
(Frank Boers Jr)
American actor
• Played Herb Tarlek on TV series "WKRP in Cincinnati," 1978-82.
b. February 28, 1942 in Little Rock, Arkansas

Sonny (Salvatore Phillip) Bono
(Sonny and Cher)
American actor–politician
• Best known for hits while married to Cher: "The Beat Goes On," 1966; mayor of Palm Springs, CA, 1988–.
b. February 16, 1935 in Detroit, Michigan

Sorrell Booke
American actor
• Best known for role of "Boss" Hogg in TV series "The Dukes of Hazzard," 1979-86.
b. January 04, 1930 in Buffalo, New York

Richard Boone
American actor
• Starred in TV series "Medic," 1954-56, "Have Gun Will Travel," 1957-63.
b. June 18, 1917 in Los Angeles, California
d. January 1, 1981 in St. Augustine, Florida

John Boorman
English director
• Films include *Deliverance,* 1970; *Exorcist II,* 1977.
b. January 18, 1933 in Shepperton, England

Edwin Thomas Booth
American actor
• Brother of John Wilkes Booth; noted Shakespearean actor; founded Players Club, 1888.
b. November 13, 1833 in Bel Air, Maryland
d. June 07, 1893 in New York, New York

Junius Brutus Booth
English actor
• Father of Edwin and John Wilkes; dominated stage for 30 yrs.
b. May 01, 1796 in London, England
d. November 3, 1852

Shirley Booth
(Thelma Booth Ford)
American actress
• Won Oscar for *Come Back, Little Sheba,* 1953; won Emmy for "Hazel," 1963.
b. August 3, 1907 in New York, New York

Powers Boothe
American actor
• Portrayed Rev. Jim Jones in TV movie *Guyana Tragedy: The Story of Jim Jones,* 1980; won Emmy, 1980.
b. June 01, 1949 in Snyder, Texas

Veda Ann Borg
American actress
• Played tough blonde in many 1940s films; face was reconstructed in 10 operations after car crash.
b. January 15, 1915 in Boston, Massachusetts
d. August 16, 1973 in Hollywood, California

Ernest Borgnine
(Ermes Effron Borgnino)
American actor
• Starred in TV series "McHale's Navy," 1962-66; won Oscar for *Marty,* 1955.
b. January 24, 1917 in Hamden, Connecticut

Paolo Bortoluzzi
Italian choreographer–dancer
• Artistic adviser, choreographer for La Scala, Milan.
b. May 17, 1938 in Genoa, Italy

Frank Borzage
American director
• Pioneered use of soft focus for his sentimental love stories; won Oscars for *Seventh Heaven,* 1927; *Bad Girl,* 1931.
b. April 23, 1893 in Salt Lake City, Utah
d. June 19, 1962 in Hollywood, California

Tom Bosley
American actor
• Star of TV series "Happy Days"; won Tony for role in *Fiorello,* 1959.
b. October 01, 1927 in Chicago, Illinois

Barbara Bosson
(Mrs Steven Bochco)
American actress
• Played Fay Furillo on TV drama "Hill Street Blues," 1981-85.
b. November 01, 1939 in Charleroi, Pennsylvania

Barry Bostwick
American actor
• Won 1977 Tony for *The Robber Bridegroom*; also appears on TV, films.
b. February 24, 1945 in San Mateo, California

Stephen Bosustow
Canadian producer
• Co-founded United Productions of America, animation co.; won three Oscars.
b. November 06, 1911 in Victoria, British Columbia
d. 1981

Hobart van Zandt Bosworth
American actor
• Began film career, 1909, in *In the Sultan's Power*, first dramatic film shot on West Coast.
b. August 11, 1867 in Marietta, Ohio
d. December 3, 1943 in Glendale, California

Joseph Bottoms
American actor
• Film debut, 1974, in *The Dove*.
b. April 22, 1954 in Santa Barbara, California

Sam Bottoms
American actor
• Brother of Joseph and Timothy; films include *Apocalyse Now*, 1979; TV film "East of Eden," 1981.
b. October 17, 1955 in Santa Barbara, California

Timothy Bottoms
American actor
• In movie *The Last Picture Show*, 1971.
b. August 3, 1951 in Santa Barbara, California

John Boulting
English director
• Films poked fun at British institutions, featured recurring cast of comic actors including Peter Sellers: *Heavens Above!* 1963.
b. November 21, 1913 in Bray, England
d. June 19, 1985 in Warfield Dale, England

Roy Boulting
English producer
• Founded Charter Films, 1937, with twin brother, John; films include *There's a Girl in My Soup*, 1970.
b. November 21, 1913 in Bray, England

Clara Gordon Bow
(The It Girl)
American actress
• Starred in Roaring 20s silent films; symbol of flapper age.
b. August 25, 1905 in New York, New York
d. September 27, 1965 in Los Angeles, California

Lee (Lucien Lee, Sr) Bowman
American actor
• Played opposite Susan Hayward in film *Smash-Up*, 1947.
b. December 28, 1914 in Cincinnati, Ohio

John Box
English filmmaker
• Art director who won Oscars for *Doctor Zhivago*, 1965; *Oliver*, 1968.
b. January 27, 1920 in Kent, England

Bruce Boxleitner
American actor
• Star of TV series "Scarecrow and Mrs. King," 1983–.
b. May 12, 1951 in Elgin, Illinois

Stephen Boyd
American actor
• Played Messala in *Ben Hur*, 1959.
b. July 04, 1928 in Belfast, Northern Ireland
d. June 02, 1977 in Los Angeles, California

William (Bill) Boyd
American actor
• Best known as Hopalong Cassidy, character he played 66 times, 1935-48.
b. June 05, 1898 in Cambridge, Ohio
d. September 12, 1972 in South Laguna, California

Charles Boyer
French actor
• Romantic lead starred in films *Algiers*, 1938; *Gaslight*, 1944.
b. August 28, 1899 in Figeac, France
d. August 26, 1978 in Phoenix, Arizona

Peter Boyle
American actor
• Films include *Taxi Driver*, 1976; *Joe*, 1970.
b. October 18, 1935 in Philadelphia, Pennsylvania

Anne Bracegirdle
English actress
• Starred in Congreve's comedies, which were written for her, 1690s; favorite of Colley Cibber.
b. 1674
d. September 15, 1748 in London, England

Eddie (Edward Vincent) Bracken
American actor
• Stage, film performer, 1940s-60s; started career in *Our Gang* series, 1920s.
b. February 07, 1920 in New York, New York

Charles Brackett
American producer
• Produced five Oscar-winners; often collaborated with Billy Wilder.
b. November 26, 1892 in Saratoga Springs, New York
d. March 09, 1969

Ed(ward) Bradley
American broadcast journalist
• Co-anchorman, "60 Minutes," replacing Dan Rather, 1981–.
b. June 22, 1941 in Philadelphia, Pennsylvania

Alice Brady
American actress
• Won Oscar for *In Old Chicago*, 1938.
b. November 02, 1893 in New York, New York
d. October 28, 1939 in New York, New York

Pat (Robert Patrick) Brady
(Sons of the Pioneers)
American actor–singer
• Played Roy Rogers sidekick in films, TV.
b. December 31, 1914 in Toledo, Ohio
d. February 27, 1972 in Green Mountain Falls, Colorado

Scott Brady
(Gerard Kenneth Tierney)
American actor
• Played in TV series "Shotgun Slade," 1959-62.
b. September 13, 1924 in Brooklyn, New York
d. April 17, 1985 in Woodland Hills, California

William Aloysius Brady
American actor–producer
• Built Playhouse Theatre, 1910; Forty-eighth Street Theatre, 1912, NYC; produced over 250 plays.
b. June 19, 1863 in San Francisco, California
d. January 06, 1950 in New York, New York

Sonia Braga
Brazilian actress
• Films include *The Milagro Beanfield War*, 1988.
b. 1951

Wilfrid Brambell
Irish actor
• Star of British TV show "Steptoe and Son," which was basis for "Sanford and Son" in US.
b. March 22, 1912 in Dublin, Ireland
d. January 18, 1985 in London, England

Neville Brand
American actor
• Played on TV's "Laredo," 1965-67; films include *The Birdman of Alcatraz*, 1962.
b. August 13, 1921 in Kewanee, Illinois

Klaus Maria Brandauer
Austrian actor
• Stage actor in European theater since 1963; films include *Never Say Never Again*, 1983, *Out of Africa*, 1985.
b. June 22, 1944 in Altausse, Austria

Marlon (Jr) Brando
American actor
• Controversial, acclaimed actor; won Oscars for *On the Waterfront*, 1954; *The Godfather*, 1972.
b. April 03, 1924 in Omaha, Nebraska

Hugh Brannum
American entertainer
• Played Mr. Green Jeans on children's morning TV program, "Captain Kangaroo," for 29 yrs.
b. January 05, 1910 in Sandwich, Illinois
d. April 19, 1987 in East Stroudsburg, Pennsylvania

Rossano Brazzi
Italian actor
• Starred in *The Barefoot Contessa*, 1954; *South Pacific*, 1958.
b. September 18, 1916 in Bologna, Italy

Bertolt Eugene Friedrich Brecht
German poet–dramatist
• Best known for collaboration with Kurt Weill on *Threepenny Opera*, 1928.
b. February 1, 1898 in Augsburg, Germany
d. August 14, 1956 in Berlin, Germany (East)

Edmund Breese
American actor
• Screen character actor, 1915-35; worked with James O'Neill on stage *Count of Monte Cristo*, 1892.
b. June 18, 1871 in Brooklyn, New York
d. April 06, 1936 in New York, New York

Eileen Regina Brennan
American actress
• Nominated for Oscar for role of Capt. Doreen Lewis in *Private Benjamin*, 1980; won Emmy for same role in TV comedy "Private Bejnamin," 1982.
b. September 03, 1935 in Los Angeles, California

Walter Andrew Brennan
American actor
• First actor to win three Oscars, 1936, 1938, 1940; known for character roles, TV series "The Real McCoys," 1957-63.
b. July 25, 1894 in Lynn, Massachusetts
d. September 22, 1974 in Oxnard, California

David Brenner
American comedian
• Nightclub performer; named Las Vegas entertainer of year, 1977; host of syndicated TV show "Nightlife," 1986–.
b. February 04, 1945 in Philadelphia, Pennsylvania

George Brent
(George B Nolan)
American actor
• Played in 11 films with Betty Davis including *Dark Victory*, 1939; *Jezebel*, 1938.
b. March 15, 1904 in Dublin, Ireland
d. May 26, 1979 in Solana Beach, California

Jerry Bresler
American producer
• Won Oscars for *Heavenly Music; Stairway to Light;* known for Our Gang comedies, Gidget series.
b. April 13, 1908 in Denver, Colorado

Robert Bresson
French director
• Stylist who does not use professional actors; films, often character studies, include *Pickpocket*, 1959.
b. September 25, 1907 in Bromont-Lamothe, France

Jeremy Brett
(Jeremy Huggins)
English actor
• Played on PBS "Rebecca"; "The Good Soldier."
b. November 03, 1935 in Berkswell, England

Lee Breuer
American dramatist
• Won Obies for *Shaggy Dog Animation*, 1978; *A Prelude to Death in Venice*, 1980.
b. February 06, 1937 in Philadelphia, Pennsylvania

Donald Brian
American actor–singer
• Starred on Broadway *Chocolate Soldier; Merry Widow; No, No, Nanette.*
b. February 17, 1875 in Saint John's, Newfoundland
d. December 22, 1948 in Great Neck, New York

Beau (Lloyd Vernet III) Bridges
American actor
• Films include *The Other Side of the Mountain*, 1975; *Norma Rae*, 1979; son of actor Lloyd.
b. December 09, 1941 in Los Angeles, California

James Bridges
American director–screenwriter
• Author, director of prize-winning films *China Syndrome*, 1979; *Urban Cowboy*, 1980.
b. February 03, 1936 in Little Rock, Arkansas

Jeff Bridges
American actor
• Nominated for Oscars for roles in *The Last Picture Show*, 1971; *Thunderbolt & Lightfoot*, 1974; *Tron*, 1982; son of Lloyd, brother of Beau.
b. December 04, 1949 in Los Angeles, California

Lloyd (Lloyd Vernet II) Bridges
American actor
• Starred in TV series "Sea Hunt," 1958; films include *High Noon*, 1952; father of actors Jeff, Beau.
b. January 15, 1913 in San Leandro, California

Todd Bridges
American actor
• Played Willis on TV series "Diff'rent Strokes." Has had some problems with the law.
b. May 27, 1965 in San Francisco, California

James Bridie
(Osborne Henry Mavor)
Scottish dramatist
• Witty, fanciful plays include *The Sleeping Clergyman*, 1933; *Storm in a Teacup*, 1936.
b. January 03, 1888 in Glasgow, Scotland
d. January 29, 1951 in Edinburgh, Scotland

John Richard Briley
American screenwriter
• Won 1983 best original screenplay Oscar for *Gandhi*.
b. June 25, 1925 in Kalamazoo, Michigan

Wilford Brimley
American actor
• Star of TV series "Our House," 1986-88; had supporting role in film *The Natural*, 1984; now does oatmeal commercials.
b. September 27, 1934 in Salt Lake City, Utah

David McClure Brinkley
American broadcast journalist
• Co-anchor, with Chet Huntley, 1958-70; host of "This Week," 1981–.
b. July 1, 1920 in Wilmington, North Carolina

May Britt
(Maybritt Wilkens)
Swedish actress
• Starred in *The Blue Angel*, 1959; former wife of Sammy Davis, Jr.
b. March 22, 1933 in Lidingo, Sweden

Morgan Brittany
(Suzanne Cupito; Mrs Jack Gill)
American actress
• Played Katherine Wentworth on TV drama "Dallas," 1981-84.
b. December 05, 1951 in Hollywood, California

Barbara Britton
(Barbara Brantingham)
American actress
• Spokesperson for Revlon cosmetics, 12 yrs.
b. September 26, 1919 in Long Beach, California
d. January 18, 1980 in New York, New York

Kent Broadhurst
American actor
• Films include *The Verdict*, 1982; *Silkwood*, 1983.
b. February 04, 1940 in Saint Louis, Missouri

Helen Broderick
American actress
• Star of first Ziegfeld Follies,1907; mother of actor Broderick Crawford.
b. August 11, 1891 in Philadelphia, Pennsylvania
d. September 25, 1959 in Beverly Hills, California

James Joseph Broderick
American actor
• Played father, Doug Lawrence, in TV series "Family," 1976-81; father of Matthew.
b. March 07, 1927 in Charlestown, New Hampshire
d. November 01, 1982 in New Haven, Connecticut

Matthew Broderick
American actor
• Won 1983 Tony for *Brighton Beach Memoirs*; in films *Ferris Bueller's Day Off*, 1986; *War Games*, 1983; *Glory*, 1990; son of James.
b. March 21, 1962 in New York, New York

Steve Brodie
(John Stevens)
American actor
• Films include *Thirty Seconds Over Tokyo*, 1944; *Winchester '73*, 1950.
b. November 25, 1919 in El Dorado, Kansas

Tom (Thomas John) Brokaw
American broadcast journalist
• Anchor, "NBC Nightly News," 1982–; host, "The Today Show," 1976-82.
b. February 06, 1940 in Webster, South Dakota

James Brolin
American actor
• Won Emmy for "Marcus Welby, MD," 1969; played Peter McDermott in TV series "Hotel," 1983-88.
b. July 18, 1941 in Los Angeles, California

J Edward Bromberg
American actor
• Character actor in films, 1936-50.
b. December 25, 1903 in Temesvar, Hungary
d. 1951

Betty (Elizabeth Ada) Bronson
American actress
• Starred in first film version of *Peter Pan*, 1924.
b. November 17, 1906 in Trenton, New Jersey
d. October 21, 1971 in Pasadena, California

Charles Bronson
(Charles Buchinsky)
American actor
• Known for tough-guy roles: *Death Wish*, 1974; was married to Jill Ireland.
b. November 03, 1922 in Ehrenfeld, Pennsylvania

Clive (Clifford) Brook
English actor
• Played leads, supporting roles for over 40 yrs.; model of British suavity, elegance.
b. June 01, 1887 in London, England
d. November 18, 1974 in London, England

Peter Stephen Paul Brook
English director–producer
• Films include *Lord of the Flies*, 1962; producing started on stage in 1943.
b. March 21, 1925 in London, England

Hillary Brooke
(Beatrice Sofia Mathilda Peterson)
American actress
• Played "bad girl" roles, films, 1940-50.
b. September 08, 1914 in Astoria, New York

Albert Brooks
American comedian–actor–writer
• Roles in *Private Benjamin*, 1980; *Twilight Zone*, 1983; *Broadcast News*, 1988; *Defending your Life*, 1991.
b. July 22, 1947 in Los Angeles, California

Foster Murrell Brooks
American comedian–actor
• Known for "drunk" skits in nightclubs, TV shows.
b. May 11, 1912 in Louisville, Kentucky

James L Brooks
American producer–director–actor–screenwriter
• One of TV's best story minds who co-created "The Mary Tyler Moore Show."
b. May 09, 1940 in Brooklyn, New York

Mel Brooks
(Melvyn Kaminsky)
American producer–director–actor
• Writer, director *Blazing Saddles*, 1974, *Young Frankenstein*, 1975.
b. June 28, 1928 in New York, New York

Richard Brooks
American director–screenwriter
• Won award, screenplay *Elmer Gantry*, 1960; writer-director *Looking for Mr. Goodbar*, 1977.
b. May 18, 1912 in Philadelphia, Pennsylvania

Pierce Brosnan
Irish actor
• Star of TV series "Remington Steele," 1982-86.
b. May 16, 1953 in Limerick, Ireland

Harve Brosten
American writer–director–producer
• Won Emmy for comedy writing for "All in the Family," 1978.
b. May 15, 1943 in Chicago, Illinois

Blair Brown
American actress
• Played Jackie Kennedy in TV miniseries "Kennedy," 1983; in film *Continental Divide*, 1981; star of TV show "The Days and Nights of Molly Dodd," 1987–.
b. 1948 in Washington, District of Columbia

Bryan Brown
Australian actor
• Played Luke O'Neill in TV mini-series "The Thorn Birds," 1983.
b. 1950 in Sydney, Australia

Clarence Brown
American director
• Directed 52 films; received six Oscar nominations; launched Garbo's career, 1927, in *Flesh and the Devil*.
b. May 1, 1890 in Clinton, Massachusetts
d. August 17, 1987 in Santa Monica, California

David Brown
American producer
• Produced films *The Sting*, 1973; *Jaws*, 1975; *Cocoon*, 1985. Husband of Helen Gurley Brown.
b. July 28, 1916

Georgia Brown
English actress
• Stage works include London, Broadway productions of *Threepenny Opera; Oliver* .
b. October 21, 1933 in London, England

Jim (James Nathaniel) Brown
American actor–football player
• Running back, Cleveland, 1957-65; held NFL record for career rushing yds. until broken by Walter Payton, 1984; Hall of Fame. Acted in variety of prison, black exploitation films, including *Riot*.
b. February 17, 1936 in Saint Simons Island, Georgia

Joe E(van) Brown
American comedian–actor
• Known for comical, wide-mouthed expressions in musical comedies of stage, films including *Some Like It Hot*, 1959.
b. July 28, 1892 in Holgate, Ohio
d. July 17, 1973 in Brentwood, California

Johnny Mack Brown
American football player–actor
• Collegiate running back, 1923-25; as actor, known for cowboy roles.
b. September 01, 1904 in Dothan, Alabama
d. November 14, 1974 in Woodland Hills, California

Kelly (Elford Cornelious Kelly Kingman) Brown
American actor–dancer
• Soloist, American Ballet Theater; films include *Daddy Long Legs*, 1955; father of dancer Leslie Browne.
b. September 24, 1928 in Maysville, Kentucky
d. March 13, 1981 in Phoenix, Arizona

Pamela Brown
English actress
• Broadway debut, 1947, opposite John Gielgud in *Importance of Being Earnest;* won 1961 Emmy for "Victoria Regina."
b. July 08, 1917 in London, England
d. September 18, 1975 in London, England

Vanessa Brown
(Smylla Brind)
American actress–author–artist
• Freelance correspondent for "Voice of America"; films include *Late George Apley; Foxes of Harrow; Ghost and Mrs. Muir*.
b. March 24, 1928 in Vienna, Austria

Coral Edith Browne
(Mrs Vincent Price)
Australian actress
• Sophisticated character roles in *Ruling Class; Theater of Blood; Drowning Pool*, 1970s.
b. July 23, 1913 in Melbourne, Australia

Leslie Browne
American dancer–actress
• Soloist, American Ballet Theater, 1976–; starred in *The Turning Point*, 1977.
b. June 29, 1957 in New York, New York

Roscoe Lee Browne
American actor–director
• TV, stage, screen performances include film *The Cowboys*, with John Wayne, 1972.
b. May 02, 1925 in Woodbury, New Jersey

Tod Browning
American director
• Made macabre horror films starring Lon Chaney, Bela Lugosi: *Dracula*, 1931; *Freaks*, 1932.
b. July 12, 1882 in Louisville, Kentucky
d. October 06, 1962 in Santa Monica, California

Lenny Bruce
(Leonard Alfred Schneider)
American author–comedian
• Charged with obscenity for using four-letter words in act; Dustin Hoffman starred in *Lenny*, 1974.
b. October 13, 1925 in Mineola, New York
d. August 03, 1966 in Hollywood, California

Nigel Bruce
American actor
• Played Dr. Watson to Basil Rathbone's Sherlock Holmes in a dozen 1940s films.
b. February 04, 1895 in Ensenada, Mexico
d. October 08, 1953 in Santa Monica, California

Virginia Bruce
(Helen Virginia Briggs)
American actress
• Leading lady in almost 50 films, 1930s-40s: *Great Ziegfield*, 1934.
b. September 29, 1910 in Minneapolis, Minnesota
d. February 24, 1982 in Woodland Hills, California

Erik Belton Evers Bruhn
Danish dancer–producer
• One of greatest classical dancers, 1953-72; appeared with American Ballet Theater.
b. October 03, 1928 in Copenhagen, Denmark
d. April 01, 1986 in Toronto, Ontario

Robert Sanford Brustein
American educator–author
• Award-winning *NY Times, New Republic* drama critic, 1972–; founder, director, American Repertory Theater.
b. April 21, 1927 in New York, New York

Dora Bryan
(Mrs William Lawton Dora Broadbent)
English actress
• Won British Academy Award for *A Taste of Honey*, 1961; appears mostly on stage.
b. February 07, 1924 in Southport, England

Yul Brynner
(Taidje Khan)
American actor
• Won Tony, 1951, Oscar, 1956, for role in *The King and I*.
b. July 11, 1920 in Sakhalin, Russia
d. October 1, 1985 in New York, New York

John Bubbles
(John William Sublett; Buck and Bubbles)
American dancer
• Created rhythm tap dancing; starred in *Porgy and Bess*, 1935; first black to appear on "The Tonight Show."
b. February 19, 1902 in Louisville, Kentucky
d. May 18, 1986 in Baldwin Hills, California

Edgar Buchanan
(J J Jackson)
American actor
• Played Uncle Joe on TV series "Petticoat Junction," 1963-70.
b. March 2, 1903 in Humansville, Missouri
d. April 04, 1979 in Palm Desert, California

Horst Buchholz
German actor
• Films include *Tiger Bay*, 1959; *Fanny*, 1961.
b. December 04, 1933 in Berlin, Germany

Georg Buchner
German dramatist
• Considered one of Germany's greatest playwrights; best known for *Danton's Death*, 1835; unfinished *Woyzeck*, 1836.
b. October 17, 1813 in Goddelan-bei-Darmst, Prussia
d. February 19, 1837 in Zurich, Switzerland

Duke George Villiers Buckingham
English nobleman–dramatist
• Prominent writer of the restoration; satirized Dryden in play *The Rehearsal*, 1671.
b. January 3, 1628 in London, England
d. April 16, 1687 in Yorkshire, England

Betty Lynn Buckley
American actress
• Won Tony for *Cats*, 1983; starred in TV's "Eight Is Enough," 1977-81.
b. July 03, 1947 in Big Spring, Texas

John Baldwin Buckstone
English dramatist–actor
• Wrote over 150 plays, including *Luke the Labourer*, 1826; *Married Life*, 1834.
b. September 14, 1802 in London, England
d. October 31, 1879 in London, England

Genevieve Bujold
Canadian actress
• Golden Globe Award for *Anne of a Thousand Days*, 1972; films include *Coma*, 1978.
b. July 01, 1942 in Montreal, Quebec

Peter Bull
English actor
• Journalist-turned actor, films include *African Queen*, 1952; *Dr. Strangelove*, 1963.
b. March 21, 1912 in London, England
d. May 2, 1984 in London, England

John Bunny
American actor
• First comic film star; joined Vitagraph, 1910; made over 200 shorts in five years.
b. September 21, 1863 in New York, New York
d. April 26, 1915 in Brooklyn, New York

Luis Bunuel
Mexican director
• Started career by working with Salvador Dali on surrealist film *An Andalusian Dog*, 1928.
b. February 22, 1900 in Calanda, Spain
d. July 29, 1983 in Mexico City, Mexico

Victor (Charles Victor) Buono
American actor
• Oscar nominee for first film *Whatever Happened to Baby Jane?*, 1962.
b. February 03, 1938 in San Diego, California
d. January 01, 1982 in Apple Valley, California

James Burbage
English actor
• Built first English playhouse, 1576, called The Theatre.
b. 1530
d. 1597

Richard Burbage
English actor
• Original player of Shakespeare's Hamlet, Lear, Othello; son of James; name synonymous with highest quality acting.
b. 1567
d. 1619

Gary Burghoff
American actor
• Played Radar O'Reilly in film *M*A*S*H*, 1970, and on TV series, 1972-79; only actor to play same character in film, on TV; won Emmy, 1977.
b. May 24, 1943 in Bristol, Connecticut

Billie (Mary William Ethelberg Appleton) Burke
(Mrs Flo Ziegfeld)
American actress
• Played Glinda, the Good Witch, in *The Wizard of Oz*, 1939.
b. August 07, 1886 in Washington, District of Columbia
d. May 14, 1970 in Los Angeles, California

Delta Burke
(Mrs Gerald McRaney)
American actress
• Former beauty queen; plays Suzanne Sugerbaker on TV comedy "Designing Women," 1986–.
b. July 3, 1956 in Orlando, Florida

Carol Burnett
American actress–comedienne
• Best known as host of "The Carol Burnett Show," 1966-77; won many performance awards.
b. April 26, 1936 in San Antonio, Texas

Smiley (Lester Alvin) Burnette
American actor
• Gene Autry's sidekick in 81 films, 1935-42.
b. March 18, 1911 in Summun, Illinois
d. February 16, 1967 in Los Angeles, California

David Burns
American actor
• Won Tony for *The Music Man*.
b. June 22, 1902 in New York, New York
d. March 12, 1971 in Philadelphia, Pennsylvania

George Burns
(Nathan Birnbaum; Burns and Allen)
American comedian–actor
• Veteran comedian whose career spans vaudeville, TV, stage, film, concerts; won Oscar, 1976, for *The Sunshine Boys*.
b. January 2, 1896 in New York, New York

Jack Burns
(Burns and Schrieber)
American comedian
• Played straight man to Avery Schrieber in "Burns and Schrieber Comedy Hour," 1973.

Raymond William Stacey Burr
American actor
• Starred in TV series "Perry Mason," 1957-65; "Ironside," 1967-75.
b. May 21, 1917 in New Westminster, British Columbia

James Burrows
American producer–director
• Has directed "The Mary Tyler Moore Show," other comedies; co-creator, "Cheers," 1982.

Ellen Burstyn
(Edna Rae Gillooly)
American actress
• Won Oscar, 1974, for *Alice Doesn't Live Here Anymore*.
b. December 07, 1932 in Detroit, Michigan

Kate (Katherine) Burton
Actress
• Starred in CBS mini-series "Ellis Island," 1984; daughter of actor Richard.
b. September 1, 1957 in Geneva, Switzerland

LeVar(dis Robert Martyn, Jr) Burton
American actor
• Played Kunta Kinte in TV series "Roots," 1977.
b. February 16, 1957 in Landstuhl, Germany (West)

Richard Burton
(Richard Jenkins)
Welsh actor
• Won Tony, 1961, for *Camelot*; nominated for seven Oscars. Remembered for marriages to Elizabeth Taylor.
b. November 1, 1925 in Pontrhydfen, Wales
d. August 05, 1984 in Geneva, Switzerland

Stephen H Burum
American filmmaker
• Cinematographer whose abstract style of camera work was prominent in *8 Million Ways to Die*, 1986; *Rumble Fish*, 1983.
b. 1940 in California

Gary Busey
(Teddy Jack Eddy pseud)
American actor–musician
• Starred in *The Buddy Holly Story*, 1978; *The Last American Hero*, 1973; *A Star is Born*, 1976.
b. June 29, 1944 in Goose Creek, Texas

Francis X(avier) Bushman
American actor
• Romantic hero of silent films, 1911-28; played Messala in *Ben-Hur*, 1926.
b. January 1, 1883 in Baltimore, Maryland
d. August 23, 1966 in Pacific Palisades, California

Dick (Richard J) Butkus
(Animal; The Enforcer; Maestro of Mayhem; Paddles)
American football player–actor
• Seven-time all-pro linebacker, Chicago, 1965-73; Hall of Fame, 1979.
b. December 09, 1942 in Chicago, Illinois

Daws (Charles Dawson) Butler
American entertainer
• Voice of many cartoon characters including Yogi Bear, Huckleberry Hound, Quick Draw McGraw.
b. November 16, 1916 in Toledo, Ohio
d. May 18, 1988 in Los Angeles, California

John Butler
American choreographer–dancer
• Student of Martha Graham; prolific opera choreographer.
b. September 29, 1920 in Memphis, Tennessee

Robert Butler
American director
• Won Emmy for direction of "Hill Street Blues," 1981.

Red Buttons
(Aaron Chwatt)
American comedian–actor
• Won Oscar, 1957, for *Sayonara*.
b. February 05, 1919 in New York, New York

Pat Buttram
American actor
• Played in TV series "Green Acres," 1965-71.
b. June 19, 1917 in Addison, Alabama

Eddie (Edward) Buzzell
American actor–director
• Star of Broadway musical comedies who became director, 1932.
b. November 13, 1907 in Brooklyn, New York
d. January 11, 1985 in Los Angeles, California

Ruth Ann Buzzi
(Mrs Basil Keko)
American actress–comedienne
• Best known for appearances in TV series "Laugh-In," 1968-73.
b. July 24, 1936 in Westerly, Rhode Island

Spring Byington
American actress
• Star of TV series "December Bride," 1954-59.
b. October 17, 1893 in Colorado Springs, Colorado
d. September 07, 1971 in Hollywood, California

Edd Byrnes
(Edward Breitenberger)
American actor
• Played Kookie on TV series "77 Sunset Strip," 1958-63; his combing hair on show led to fad, song.
b. July 3, 1933 in New York, New York

James Caan
American actor
• Starred in *The Godfather*, 1972; *Misery*, 1991; TV movie "Brian's Song," 1971.
b. March 26, 1939 in New York, New York

Bruce Cabot
(Jacques Etienne de Bujac)
American actor
• Best known as hero who saved Fay Wray in *King Kong*, 1933.
b. April 2, 1904 in Carlsbad, New Mexico
d. May 03, 1972 in Woodland Hills, California

Sebastian Cabot
English actor
• Played Mr. French on TV series "Family Affair," 1966-71.
b. July 06, 1918 in London, England
d. August 23, 1977 in Victoria, British Columbia

Michael Cacoyannis
Greek director
• Films include *Zorba the Greek*, 1964; *The Trojan Women*, 1971.
b. June 11, 1922 in Limassol, Cyprus

Adolph Caesar
American actor
• Nominated for Oscar for *A Soldier's Story*, 1984; appeared in *The Color Purple*, 1985.
b. 1934 in Harlem, New York
d. March 06, 1986 in Los Angeles, California

Sid Caesar
American comedian–actor
• Accomplished mimic, sketch comic; teamed with Imogene Coca in TV's "Caesar's Hour," 1950s; won Emmy, 1956.
b. September 08, 1922 in Yonkers, New York

Nicolas Cage
(Nicholas Coppola)
American actor
• Films include *The Cotton Club*, 1984; *Moonstruck*, 1987; *Peggy Sue Got Married*, 1988; *Wild at Heart*, 1990.
b. January 07, 1964 in Long Beach, California

Conte di Alessandro Cagliostro
(Giuseppe Balsamo)
Italian magician
• Traveled throughout Europe posing as an alchemist; condemned to death in Rome as a heretic.
b. June 02, 1743 in Palermo, Italy
d. August 26, 1795 in Rome, Italy

James (James Francis, Jr) Cagney
American actor
• Best known for tough-guy roles; won Oscar for *Yankee Doodle Dandy*, 1942.
b. July 17, 1899 in New York, New York
d. March 3, 1986 in Stanfordville, New York

Jeanne Cagney
American actress–celebrity relative
• Films include *Town Tamer*, 1965; sister of James Cagney.
b. March 25, 1919 in New York, New York

Michael Caine
(Maurice Joseph Micklewhite)
English actor
• Films include *Educating Rita*, 1983; won 1986 Oscar for *Hannah and Her Sisters*.
b. March 14, 1933 in London, England

Anna Lucia Calder-Marshall
English actress
• TV, stage performer since 1967; starred in numerous Shakesperean roles; won 1970 Emmy.
b. January 11, 1947 in London, England

Zoe Caldwell
Australian actress
• Best known for the title role on stage, TV of "Medea."
b. September 14, 1933 in Melbourne, Australia

Louis Calhern
(Carl Henry Vogt)
American actor
• Stage, screen star, who won many awards for portraying Oliver Wendell Holmes in *Magnificent Yankee*, 1946.
b. February 19, 1895 in New York, New York
d. May 12, 1956 in Nara, Japan

Rory Calhoun
(Francis Timothy Durgin)
American actor
• Western films include *Ticket to Tomahawk; River of No Return; Treasure of Pancho Villa*.
b. August 08, 1923 in Los Angeles, California

Michael Callan
American actor
• Films include *Gidget Goes Hawaiian*, 1961; *Cat Ballou*, 1965.
b. November 22, 1935 in Philadelphia, Pennsylvania

Charlie Callas
American comedian
• Night club performer, 1962–; films include *Pete's Dragon*, 1977.
b. December 2, in Brooklyn, New York

Phyllis Calvert
(Phyllis Bickle)
English actress
• Popular star of 1940s: *Young Mr. Pitt*, 1942; *Fanny by Gaslight*, 1944.
b. February 18, 1915 in London, England

Corinne Calvet
(Corinne Dibos)
French actress
• Film star of 1950s: *What Price Glory?*, 1952; *Flight to Tangiers*, 1953.
b. April 3, 1925 in Paris, France

Marie Anne de Cupis de Camargo
French dancer
• Paris Opera ballerina, 1726-35, 1741-51; introduced shortened ballet skirt, heelless slippers.
b. April 15, 1710 in Brussels, Belgium
d. April 28, 1770 in Paris, France

Godfrey Cambridge
American actor–comedian
• Films include *Purlie Victorious*, 1963; *Cotton Comes to Harlem*, 1970.
b. February 26, 1933 in New York, New York
d. November 29, 1976 in Hollywood, California

James Cameron
Canadian director
• Co-wrote with Sylvester Stallone *Rambo: First Blood, Part II*; directed *Aliens II*, 1986.
b. August 16, 1954 in Kapuskasing, Ontario

Kirk Cameron
American actor
• Plays Mike Seaver in TV show "Growing Pains," 1986–.
b. October 12, 1970 in Panorama City, California

Rod Cameron
(Rod Cox)
American actor
• Played leads in Westerns: *The Bounty Killer*, 1965; *Jessie's Girl*, 1976.
b. December 07, 1912 in Calgary, Alberta
d. December 21, 1983 in Gainesville, Georgia

Joseph Mario Campanella
American actor
• Star of TV series "The Lawyers," 1969-72.
b. November 21, 1927 in New York, New York

Mrs Patrick Campbell
(Beatrice Stella Tanner)
English actress
• G B Shaw wrote Eliza Doolittle role in *Pygmalion* especially for her.
b. February 09, 1865 in London, England
d. April 09, 1940 in Pau, France

Marcel Camus
French director
• Won Oscar, 1958, for *Black Orpheus*.
b. April 21, 1912 in Chappes, France
d. January 13, 1982 in Paris, France

David Canary
American actor
• Played Candy on TV series "Bonanza," 1967-70; 1972-73; won Emmy for role as Adam/Stuart Chandler on "All My Children," 1986.
b. August 25, 1939 in Elwood, Indiana

John (Franklin) Candy
Canadian actor–comedian
• Films include *Splash*, 1984; *Summer Rental*, 1985; *Brewster's Millions*, 1985; *Planes, Trains, and Automobiles*, 1988.
b. October 31, 1950 in Toronto, Ontario

Stephen Joseph Cannell
American producer–writer
• Creator, producer of many TV shows: "Rockford Files"; "A-Team."
b. February 05, 1943 in Los Angeles, California

Dyan Cannon
(Samille Diane Friesen; "Frosty")
American actress
• Former wife of Cary Grant, mother of his only child, Jennifer; films include *Bob & Carol & Ted & Alice*, 1969.
b. January 04, 1938 in Tacoma, Washington

Diana Canova
(Diana Canova Rivero)
American actress
• Star of TV series "Soap."
b. June 02, 1953 in West Palm Beach, Florida

Cantinflas
(Mario Moreno)
Mexican actor–comedian
• Won Oscar, 1957, for *Around the World in 80 Days*.
b. August 12, 1911 in Mexico City, Mexico

Yakima (Enos Edward) Canutt
American stuntman–actor
• Cowboy film star, 1920s, who did own stunts, later doubled for other stars; won special Oscar, 1966, for creating profession of stuntman.
b. November 29, 1895 in Colfax, Washington
d. May 25, 1986 in Los Angeles, California

Virginia Capero
American actress
• Films include *Lady Sings the Blues*, 1972; won Tony for *Raisin*, 1974.
b. September 22, in Sumter, South Carolina

Frank Capra
American director–producer
• Won Oscars for *It Happened One Night*, *Mr. Deeds Goes to Town*; known for folksy, sentimental style.
b. May 18, 1897 in Palermo, Italy

Kate Capshaw
(Mrs. Steven Spielberg)
American actress
• Starred in *Indiana Jones and the Temple of Doom*, 1984.
b. in Fort Worth, Texas

Capucine
(Germaine Lefebvre)
French actress
• Best known among her American films was *What's New, Pussycat?*, 1965; suicide victim.
b. January 06, 1935 in Toulon, France
d. March 17, 1990 in Lausanne, Switzerland

Claudia Cardinale
Italian actress
• Appeared in over 40 films, including *The Pink Panther*, 1963.
b. April 15, 1938 in Tunis, Tunisia

Harry Carey
(Henry Dewitt Carey II)
American actor
• Appeared in 26 westerns for John Ford as "Cheyenne Harry."
b. January 16, 1878 in New York, New York
d. September 21, 1947 in Brentwood, California

Macdonald (Edward Macdonald) Carey
American actor
• Plays Tom Horton in TV soap opera "Days of our Lives," 1965–; had supporting roles in films, 1940s-60s.
b. March 15, 1914 in Sioux City, Iowa

Richard Carle
American actor
• Broadway musical comedian, 1900-20s; character actor in over 80 films, 1928-41.
b. July 07, 1871 in Somerville, Massachusetts
d. June 28, 1941 in North Hollywood, California

George Dennis Carlin
American comedian–actor
• Created characters Biff Burns, sportscaster; Al Sleet, weatherman; broadcast of explicit record led to landmark "Seven Dirty Words" Supreme Court decision.
b. May 12, 1937 in New York, New York

Lewis John Carlino
American dramatist–filmmaker
• Film adaptation of *I Never Promised You a Rose Garden* won Academy Award nomination, 1977.
b. January 01, 1932 in New York, New York

Kitty Carlisle
(Katherine Conn; Mrs Moss Hart)
American actress–singer
• Panelist, TV series "To Tell the Truth," 1956-67.
b. September 03, 1915 in New Orleans, Louisiana

Roger C Carmel
American actor
• Episodic TV actor; voice of Smokey the Bear in commercials.
b. 1932 in Brooklyn, New York
d. November 11, 1986 in Hollywood, California

Judy Carne
(Joyce A Botterill)
English comedienne
• Appeared in TV series "Laugh In," 1968-70; first wife of Burt Reynolds.
b. April 27, 1939 in Northampton, England

Marcel Albert Carne
French director
• Worked with screenwriter Jacques Prevert on *Children of Paradise*, 1945; *Port of Shadows*, 1939.
b. August 18, 1909 in Paris, France

Art (Arthur William Matthew) Carney
American actor
• Won Oscar, 1974, for *Harry and Tonto;* played Ed Norton in TV series "The Honeymooners"; won three Emmys.
b. November 04, 1918 in Mount Vernon, New York

Martine Carol
(Maryse Mourer)
French actress
• French sex symbol of early 1950s; films include *Beauties of the Night*, 1952; *Lola Montes*, 1955.
b. May 16, 1920 in Paris, France
d. February 06, 1967 in Monte Carlo, Monaco

Leslie Clare Margaret Caron
French actress–dancer
• Starred in MGM musicals: *An American in Paris*, 1951; *Gigi*, 1958.
b. July 01, 1931 in Paris, France

John Howard Carpenter
American director
• Known for horror films; directed *Halloween*, 1978, which became the highest grossing independently made movie of all time; married to actress Adrienne Barbeau.
b. January 16, 1948 in Carthage, New York

Allan Carr
(Allan Solomon)
American producer
• Co-produced *Grease* on Broadway, 1977.
b. May 27, 1941 in Chicago, Illinois

David Carradine
(John Arthur Carradine)
American actor
• Son of John Carradine; starred in TV shows "Shane," 1966; "Kung Fu," 1972-75; in films since 1965.
b. October 08, 1940 in Hollywood, California

John Carradine
(Richmond Reed Carradine)
American actor
• Father of David, Keith, Robert; starred in over 500 films.
b. February 05, 1906 in New York, New York
d. November 27, 1988 in Milan, Italy

Keith Ian Carradine
American actor–singer
• Won Oscar for writing, singing "I'm Easy," 1975.
b. August 08, 1950 in San Mateo, California

Robert Reed Carradine
American actor
• Youngest son of John Carradine, half brother of David, who starred in *The Big Red One*, 1979.
b. March 24, 1954 in Los Angeles, California

Barbara Carrera
American actress
• Portrayed Fatima Blush in *Never Say Never Again*, 1983; in TV series "Dallas," 1985–.
b. 1945 in Managua, Nicaragua

Jean-Claude Carriere
French screenwriter
• France's leading scriptwriter, 1960s-70s: *The Discreet Charm of the Bourgeoise*, 1972; *The Tin Drum*, 1978.
b. 1931 in Colombieres, France

Leo Carrillo
American actor
• Played Pancho in *Cisco Kid*, 1951.
b. August 06, 1880 in Los Angeles, California
d. September 1, 1961 in Santa Monica, California

Leo G Carroll
English actor
• Played Cosmo Topper in TV series "Topper," 1953-56; Mr. Waverly in "Man from Uncle," 1964-68.
b. October 18, 1892 in Weedon, England
d. October 16, 1972 in Hollywood, California

Madeleine Carroll
(Marie-Madeline Bernadette O'Carroll)
English actress
• Appeared in over 36 films, including Hitchcock thrillers *The 39 Steps*, 1935; *Secret Agent*, 1936.
b. February 26, 1909 in West Bronwich, England
d. October 02, 1987 in Marbella, Spain

Pat(ricia Ann Angela Bridgit) Carroll
American actress–comedienne
• Won Emmy for "Caesar's Hour," 1956-57; Tony for *Catch a Star*, 1955.
b. May 05, 1927 in Shreveport, Louisiana

Marcia Carsey
American producer
• Senior VP, all prime time series, ABC, 1979-80; executive producer, "The Cosby Show," 1984–.
b. November 21, 1944 in South Weymouth, Massachusetts

Jack Carson
American actor
• Teamed with Dennis Morgan in series of 1940s musicals.
b. October 27, 1910 in Carman, Manitoba
d. January 02, 1963 in Encino, California

Johnny Carson
American comedian–TV personality
• Host of "The Tonight Show," 1962–.
b. October 23, 1925 in Corning, Iowa

Dixie Carter
American actress
• Plays Julia Sugarbaker on TV series "Designing Women," 1986–.
b. May 25, 1939 in McLemoresville, Tennessee

Hodding (William Hodding, III) Carter
American broadcast journalist
• Anchorman, "Inside Story," PBS, 1981–; State Dept. spokesman, 1977-80.
b. April 07, 1935 in New Orleans, Louisiana

Jack Carter
(Jack Chakrin)
American comedian
• Performer in major nightclubs; films include *Viva Las Vegas*, 1964.
b. June 24, 1923 in New York, New York

Lynda Jean Carter
American actress–singer
• Starred in TV series "Wonder Woman," 1977-79; spokeswoman for Max Factor Cosmetics.
b. July 24, 1951 in Phoenix, Arizona

Nell Carter
(Nell Hardy)
American actress–singer
• Appeared on stage in *Ain't Misbehavin'*; played Nell Harper on TV series "Gimme a Break," 1981-86.
b. September 13, 1948 in Birmingham, Alabama

Angela Cartwright
American actress
• In TV series "Lost in Space," 1965-68; "Danny Thomas Show," 1957-64.
b. September 09, 1952 in Cheshire, England

Veronica Cartwright
American actress
• Films include *The Birds*, 1963; *The Right Stuff*, 1983; sister of Angela.
b. 1950 in Bristol, England

Dana Carvey
American comedian–actor
• Plays Church Lady on "Saturday Night Live," 1987–.
b. June 06, 1955 in San Francisco, California

Adriana Caselotti
American entertainer
• Original voice of Snow White in films.
b. 1916

Jim Cash
American educator–screenwriter
• With Jack Epps, wrote screenplays for 1986 films *Top Gun, Legal Eagles*.
b. 1941

Vera Caspary
American author–screenwriter
• Wrote mystery novel *Laura*, 1942; made into film, 1944.
b. November 13, 1904 in Chicago, Illinois
d. June 13, 1987 in New York, New York

Peggy (Mary Margaret) Cass
American actress
• Won Tony for *Auntie Mame*, 1956; regular panelist on TV game show "To Tell the Truth," 1964-67.
b. May 21, 1925 in Boston, Massachusetts

John Cassavetes
American actor–director
• Known for free-wheeling, improvisational directing style in *Faces*, 1968, *A Woman Under the Influence*, 1974; husband of Gena Rowlands.
b. December 09, 1929 in New York, New York
d. February 03, 1989 in Los Angeles, California

Joanna Cassidy
(Joanna Virginia Caskey)
American actress
• Movies include *Blade Runner; Under Fire* ; TV series "Buffalo Bill."
b. August 02, 1944 in Camden, New Jersey

Richard Castellano
American actor
• Appeared in *The Godfather*, 1972; nominated for Oscar, 1970, for *Lovers and Other Strangers*.
b. September 04, 1934 in New York, New York
d. December 1, 1988 in North Bergen, New Jersey

Irene Foote Castle
(Mrs Vernon Castle)
American dancer
• Rogers and Astaire portrayed her and husband in film *Story of Vernon and Irene Castle*, 1939; credited with starting bobbed hair fad.
b. April 07, 1893 in New Rochelle, New York
d. January 25, 1969 in Eureka Springs, Arkansas

Vernon Castle
(Vernon Blythe)
American dancer–aviator
• Dance innovator, 1910s; originated one-step, turkey trot, castle walk; husband of Irene, portrayed by Fred Astaire in 1939 film.
b. May 02, 1887 in Norwich, England
d. February 15, 1918 in Fort Worth, Texas

William Castle
(William Schloss)
American director–producer
• Made over 100 horror films, including *Rosemary's Baby*, 1968.
b. April 24, 1914 in New York, New York
d. May 31, 1977 in Beverly Hills, California

Joseph Cates
Producer–Director
• Won Emmy for "Annie: The Woman in the Life of a Man," 1970; films include *Last Married Couple in America*.
b. 1924

Phoebe Cates
American actress
• In TV movie "Lace," 1984; "Lace II," 1985; in film *Gremlins*, 1984.
b. 1964 in New York, New York

Walter Catlett
American actor
• Comical performer of hundreds of cameo roles.
b. February 04, 1889 in San Francisco, California
d. November 14, 1960 in Woodland Hills, California

Joan Caulfield
American actress
• Ex-model, Broadway, movie star, turned to TV, 1953; starred in "My Favorite Husband."
b. June 01, 1922 in Orange, New Jersey

Maxwell Caulfield
English actor
• Played Miles Colby on TV series "The Colbys," 1985-87; married to Juliet Mills.
b. November 23, 1959 in Derbyshire, England

Dick (Richard Alva) Cavett
American entertainer
• Won Emmy, 1972; host of PBS talk show, 1978–; wrote *Cavett*, 1974.
b. November 19, 1936 in Gibbon, Nebraska

Christopher Cazenove
English actor
• Films include *Heat and Dust*, 1983; plays Ben Carrington on TV's "Dynasty," 1986–.
b. December 17, 1945 in Winchester, England

Claude Chabrol
French director
• Influenced by Hitchcock-style thrillers: *The Champagne Murders*, 1967.
b. June 24, 1930 in Paris, France

Joseph Chaikin
American actor–director
• Founder, director, Open Theater, NYC, 1963-73.
b. September 16, 1935 in Brooklyn, New York

George Chakiris
American dancer–actor
• Won Oscar for role of Bernardo in *West Side Story*, 1961.
b. September 16, 1934 in Norwood, Ohio

Richard (George Richard) Chamberlain
American actor
• Starred in TV series "Dr. Kildare," 1961-65; mini-series "Shogun," 1980; "The Thorn Birds," 1983; "Night of the Hunter," 1991.
b. March 31, 1935 in Beverly Hills, California

Gower Champion
American choreographer–dancer
• Won Tonys for *Bye Bye Birdie*, 1961; *Hello, Dolly*, 1964; *42nd Street*, 1981.
b. June 22, 1921 in Geneva, Illinois
d. August 25, 1980 in New York, New York

Marge Celeste Champion
(Marjorie Celeste Belcher; Mrs Gower Champion)
American dancer–actress
• Teamed with husband, Gower, in film musicals; won Emmy for "Queen of the Stardust Ballroom," 1975.
b. September 02, 1923 in Los Angeles, California

John William Chancellor
American broadcast journalist
• Anchorman, "NBC Nightly News," 1970-81; commentator since 1981.
b. July 14, 1927 in Chicago, Illinois

Lon (Alonso) Chaney
American actor
• Starred in *The Hunchback of Notre Dame*, 1923; *The Phantom of the Opera*, 1925.
b. April 01, 1883 in Colorado Springs, Colorado
d. August 26, 1930 in Los Angeles, California

Lon Chaney, Jr (Creighton)
American actor
• Starred in over 100 films, mostly horror; played Lenny in *Of Mice and Men*, 1940.
b. February 1, 1905 in Oklahoma City, Oklahoma
d. July 12, 1973 in San Clemente, California

Norman Chaney
(Our Gang; "Chubby")
American actor
• Played Joe Cobb, "Our Gang," 1926-34.
b. January 18, 1918 in Baltimore, Maryland
d. May 3, 1936 in Baltimore, Maryland

Carol Channing
(Carol Channing Lowe)
American actress
• Vivacious, husky-voiced blonde best-known for Tony-winning role in *Hello Dolly*, 1964.
b. January 31, 1923 in Seattle, Washington

Stockard Channing
(Susan Stockard)
American actress
• Films include *Grease*, 1978; starred in own TV show, 1979.
b. February 13, 1944 in New York, New York

Charlie Chaplin
(Sir Charles Spencer)
English actor–author–composer
• Known for character created in *The Tramp*, 1915; won special Oscar, 1972; considered greatest comic actor of silents; much imitated style.
b. April 16, 1889 in London, England
d. December 25, 1977 in Vevey, Switzerland

Geraldine Chaplin
American actress
• Daughter of Charlie Chaplin; films include *Doctor Zhivago*, 1965; *Nashville*, 1975.
b. July 31, 1944 in Santa Monica, California

Sydney Dryden Chaplin
English actor–comedian
• Half-brother, manager of Charlie Chaplin, who appeared in comedies, 1920s.
b. March 17, 1885 in Cape Town, South Africa
d. April 16, 1956 in Nice, France

Graham Chapman
(Monty Python's Flying Circus)
English actor–comedian
• Founding member, Monty Python's Flying Circus comedy troupe; TV program broadcast by BBC, 1969-74.
b. January 08, 1941 in Leicester, England
d. October 04, 1989 in Maidstone, England

Cyd Charisse
(Tula Ellice Finklea; Mrs Tony Martin)
American dancer–actress
• Renowned for long, shapely legs; films include *Silk Stockings*, 1957; Fred Astaire's last dancing partner.
b. March 08, 1923 in Amarillo, Texas

Glen Charles
American writer–producer
• Won Emmys, 1979, 1980, 1981, for "Taxi"; 1983, 1984 for "Cheers."
b. in Henderson, New York

Lee Charles
American writer–producer
• Wrote award-winning scripts for several TV shows, including "Taxi"; "Cheers"; "MASH."
b. in Henderson, Nevada

Ian Charleson
Scottish actor
• Starred in Oscar-winning *Chariots of Fire*, 1981; died of AIDS.
b. August 11, 1949 in Edinburgh, Scotland
d. January 06, 1990 in London, England

Tony Charmoli
American choreographer
• Most successful presentation was *Your Hit Parade*, 1950-58.
b. in Mountain Iron, Montana

Robert Chartoff
American producer
• Films include *Rocky III; Right Stuff*; won Oscar for *Rocky*, 1976.
b. August 26, 1933 in New York, New York

Charley Chase
American comedian
• Started acting career in Max Sennett's "Keystone Kop" series; wrote, produced, acted in slapstick-type comedy "shorts."
b. October 2, 1893 in Baltimore, Maryland
d. June 2, 1940 in Hollywood, California

Chevy (Cornelius Crane) Chase
American actor–comedian
• Starred on "Saturday Night Live"; won Emmy, 1976; films include *National Lampoon's Vacation*, 1983; *Fletch*, 1985.
b. October 08, 1943 in New York, New York

David Chase
Writer–Producer
• Winner of four Emmys who produced "Rockford Files"; "Off the Minnesota Strip."
b. August 22, 1945

Lucia Chase
American dancer
• Principal dancer, American Ballet Theatre, 1940-60; co-director, 1945-80.
b. March 27, 1907 in Waterbury, Connecticut
d. January 09, 1986 in New York, New York

Mary Coyle Chase
American dramatist
• Best known for Pulitzer-winning play *Harvey*, 1944.
b. February 25, 1907 in Denver, Colorado
d. October 2, 1981 in Denver, Colorado

Sylvia B Chase
American broadcast journalist
• Correspondent, ABC News "20/20," 1978–; won Emmys, 1978, 1980.
b. February 23, 1938 in Northfield, Minnesota

Ruth Chatterton
American actress
• Wrote several novels in 1950s; Oscar nominee for *Madame X*, 1929; *Sarah and Son*, 1930.
b. December 24, 1893 in New York, New York
d. November 24, 1961 in Norwalk, Connecticut

Paddy (Sidney) Chayefsky
American writer–dramatist
• Best known for screenplays *Marty*, 1953; won Oscar, 1976, for *Network*.
b. January 29, 1923 in New York, New York
d. August 01, 1981 in New York, New York

Cheech and Chong
(Tommy Chong; Cheech Marin)
American comedy team
• First of the rock-culture comedians, 1970s; films include *Up In Smoke*, 1978.

Cher
(Cherylynn LaPiere; Cherilyn Sarkisian; Sonny and Cher)
American singer–actress
• Part of pop duo with ex-husband, Sonny Bono, 1960s-70s; won Oscar, 1988, for *Moonstruck*.
b. May 2, 1946 in El Centro, California

Monzaemon Chikamatsu
(Sugimori Mobumori)
Japanese dramatist
• Prominent author of Joruri, Kabuki plays, based on myths, legends.
b. 1653 in Eichizen Province, Japan
d. January 06, 1725

Julia McWilliams Child
(Mrs Paul Child)
American chef–author–TV personality
• Star of "The French Chef," 1962–; wrote *Mastering the Art of French Cooking*, 1961.
b. August 15, 1912 in Pasadena, California

Alvin Childress
American actor
• Played Amos Jones in TV series "Amos 'n Andy," 1950-53.
b. 1908 in Meridian, Mississippi
d. April 19, 1986 in Inglewood, California

Edward Chodorov
American author–director–producer
• Wrote plays, films, TV series, "The Billy Rose Show"; plays include *Wonder Boy*, 1932; *Kind Lady*, 1935.
b. April 17, 1904 in New York, New York
d. October 09, 1988 in New York, New York

Jerome Chodorov
American dramatist–director
• Collaborated with Joseph Field in plays: *My Sister Eileen*, 1940; *Anniversary Waltz*, 1954.
b. August 1, 1911 in New York, New York

Marvin Chomsky
American director
• TV credits include "Star Trek"; "Roots"; "Gunsmoke."
b. May 23, 1929 in Bronx, New York

Tommy (Thomas) Chong
(Cheech and Chong)
Canadian actor–comedian
• Teamed with Richard Marin in counter-culture records, nightclub acts, film series: *Up in Smoke*, 1978; *Still Smokin'*, 1983.
b. May 24, 1938 in Edmonton, Alberta

Linda Christian
(Blanca Rosa Welter)
American actress
• Married to Tyrone Power, 1949-55.
b. November 13, 1923 in Tampico, Mexico

Christian-Jaque
French director
• Won best director award, Cannes, 1952: *Fanfan la Tulipe*.
b. September 04, 1904 in Paris, France

Julie Christie
English actress
• Won Oscar, 1965, for *Darling*; starred in *Doctor Zhivago*, 1965.
b. April 14, 1940 in Chukua, India

Dennis Christopher
(Dennis Carelli)
American actor
• In films *Breaking Away*, 1979; *Chariots of Fire*, 1981.
b. December 02, 1955 in Philadelphia, Pennsylvania

Sybil Williams Burton Christopher
(Mrs Jordan Christopher; Sybil Williams)
Welsh actress
• First wife of Richard Burton, 1949-63; Burton divorced her to marry Elizabeth Taylor.
b. 1928 in Taylorstown, Wales

William Christopher
American actor
• Played Father Mulchahy on TV series "M*A*S*H," 1972-83.
b. October 2, 1932 in Evanston, Illinois

Grigori Chukrai
Russian director
• Important in Soviet cinema; known for films about war: *Forty-First*, 1956; *Ballad of a Soldier*, 1959.
b. 1921 in Melitopol, U.S.S.R.

Connie (Constance Yu-Hwa) Chung
(Mrs Maury Povich)
American broadcast journalist
• NBC News anchor, 1983-89, CBS News anchor, 1989–; won Emmys, 1978, 1980, 1987.
b. August 2, 1946 in Washington, District of Columbia

Sandra Church
American actress
• Won Tony for performance in *Gypsy*, 1960; stage, film, TV appearances.
b. January 13, 1943 in San Francisco, California

Caryl Churchill
English dramatist
• Explores male-dominated society in Obie-winning plays *Cloud Nine*, 1978; *Top Girls*, 1981.
b. September 03, 1938 in London, England

Diana Josephine Churchill
English actress
• Leading lady on stage, screen; films include *The Winter's Tale*, 1968.
b. August 21, 1913 in Wembley, England

Diane Cilento
Australian actress
• Wife of Sean Connery, 1962-73; Oscar nominee for *Tom Jones*, 1963.
b. October 05, 1933 in Brisbane, Australia

Michael Cimino
American director
• Won Oscar for directing *The Deer Hunter*, 1978. Spent a lot of money on *Heaven's Gate*, 1980.
b. 1943 in New York, New York

Rene Clair
French filmmaker
• Films satirized human behavior; *Sous les Toits de Paris*, 1930.
b. November 11, 1898 in Paris, France
d. March 15, 1981 in Neuilly, France

Ina Claire
(Ina Fagan)
American actress
• Vaudeville performer, later with Ziegfield Follies; portrayed witty, chic sophisticates on stage and screen.
b. October 15, 1895 in Washington, District of Columbia
d. February 21, 1985 in San Francisco, California

Bobby Clark
American comedian
• Known as the "world's funniest clown"; worked in films, vaudeville, circuses, minstrel shows.
b. June 16, 1888 in Springfield, Ohio
d. February 12, 1960 in New York, New York

Dane Clark
(Bernard Zanville)
American actor
• Tough guy leading man in action films, 1940s; on TV, 1950s-60s.
b. February 18, 1913 in New York, New York

Dick (Richard Wagstaff) Clark
American entertainer–business executive–producer
• Host, "American Bandstand," 1952-1990. Known for eternal youthfulness.
b. November 3, 1929 in Mount Vernon, New York

Fred Clark
American actor
• Character parts include Burns and Allen's TV shows, 1950s.
b. March 09, 1914 in Lincoln, California
d. December 05, 1968 in Santa Monica, California

Sir Kenneth MacKenzie Clark
English art historian–TV personality–author
• Preeminent supporter of British arts; created, narrated acclaimed TV series "Civilization," 1969.
b. July 13, 1903 in London, England
d. May 21, 1983 in Hythe, England

Marguerite Clark
American actress
• Rivaled Mary Pickford as silent screen star, 1914-21; best known for *Wildflowers*, 1914; *Uncle Tom's Cabin*, 1919.
b. February 22, 1887 in Avondale, Ohio
d. September 25, 1940 in New York, New York

Susan Nora Goulding Clark
(Mrs Alex Karras)
Canadian actress
• Starred with husband in movies *Babe*; *Jimmy B and Andre*; *Maid in America*.
b. March 08, 1944 in Sarnia, Ontario

Mae Clarke
(Mary Klotz)
American actress
• Starred in *The Public Enemy*, 1931, with James Cagney, when he mashed grapefruit in her face.
b. August 16, 1907 in Philadelphia, Pennsylvania

Shirley Clarke
American director
• Cinema-verite films include *Portrait of Jason*, 1967.
b. October 02, 1927 in New York, New York

Robert Clary
American actor
• Played LaBeau in TV series "Hogan's Heroes," 1965-71.
b. March 01, 1926 in Paris, France

Jill Clayburgh
(Mrs David Rabe)
American actress
• Best known for role in *An Unmarried Woman*, 1978, nominated for Oscar.
b. April 3, 1944 in New York, New York

Jack Clayton
British director
• His first feature film, *Room at the Top*, 1958, started a new trend in British films.
b. March 01, 1921 in Brighton, England

Jan(e Byral) Clayton
American actress
• Played mother in TV series "Lassie," 1954-57.
b. August 26, 1925 in Alamogordo, New Mexico
d. August 28, 1983 in Los Angeles, California

Lou Clayton
(Louis Finkelstein)
American actor
• Starred with Jimmy Durante in vaudeville; featured in *Show Girl*, 1929.
b. 1887 in Brooklyn, New York
d. September 12, 1950 in Santa Monica, California

John Marwood Cleese
(Monty Python's Flying Circus)
English actor–writer
• Created Monty Python, 1969; humor based on conviction of senselessness of life; won 1987 Emmy. Starred in a variety of films, including *Fish Named Wanda*.
b. October 27, 1939 in Weston-super-Mare, England

John Cleland
English author–dramatist
• Wrote erotic classic, *Fanny Hill or Memories of a Woman of Pleasure*, 1749.
b. 1709 in London, England
d. January 23, 1789

Rene Clement
French director
• Won Oscars for best foreign films *Forbidden Games; The Walls of Malapga*, 1952.
b. March 18, 1913 in Bordeaux, France

Montgomery (Edward Montgomery) Clift
American actor
• Known for playing troubled heroes: *From Here to Eternity*, 1953; *The Misfits*, 1961.
b. October 17, 1920 in Omaha, Nebraska
d. July 23, 1966 in New York, New York

Colin Clive
(Clive Greig)
British actor
• Played title role in *Dr. Frankenstein*, 1931; Mr. Rochester in *Jane Eyre*, 1934.
b. January 2, 1900 in Saint-Malo, France
d. June 25, 1937 in Hollywood, California

Glenn Close
American actress
• Received Oscar nominations for *The World According to Garp*, 1982; *The Big Chill*, 1983; *Fatal Attraction*, 1988.
b. March 19, 1947 in Greenwich, Connecticut

Henri-George Clouzot
French director
• Noted for suspense films *The Wage of Fear*, 1953; *The Diaboliques*, 1954.
b. November 2, 1907 in Niort, France
d. January 12, 1977 in Paris, France

Harold Edgar Clurman
American author–director
• Best known for award-winning film *A Member of the Wedding*, 1950.
b. September 18, 1901 in New York, New York
d. September 09, 1980 in New York, New York

Andy Clyde
American actor–comedian
• Played in Mack Sennett two-reel comedies, later as Hopalong Cassidy's sidekick; TV series "No Time for Sergeants," 1960s.
b. March 18, 1892 in Blairgowrie, Scotland
d. May 18, 1967 in Los Angeles, California

Joe Cobb
(Our Gang; "Fat Joe" "Wheezer")
American actor
• First fat boy of Our Gang comedies, 1922.
b. 1917

Lee J (Leo Jacob) Cobb
American actor
• Created role of Willy Loman in *Death of a Salesman* on Broadway, 1949.
b. December 09, 1911 in New York, New York
d. February 11, 1976 in Los Angeles, California

Charles Douville Coburn
American actor–manager
• Won Oscar for *The More the Merrier*, 1943.
b. June 19, 1877 in Savannah, Georgia
d. August 3, 1961 in New York, New York

D(onald) L(ee) Coburn
American dramatist
• Won Pulitzer, 1978, for *The Gin Game*.
b. August 04, 1938 in Baltimore, Maryland

James Coburn
American actor
• Starred in *Our Man Flint*, 1966; *In Like Flint*, 1967.
b. August 31, 1928 in Laurel, Nebraska

Imogene (Fernadez y) Coca
American comedienne–actress
• Appeared with Sid Caesar in "Your Show of Shows," 1950-52; had own show, "Grindl," 1963-64.
b. November 19, 1908 in Philadelphia, Pennsylvania

Steve Cochran
American actor
• Discovered by Mae West; appeared with her in film *Diamond Lil*, 1949.
b. May 25, 1917 in Eureka, California
d. June 15, 1965 in Guatemala

James Emil Coco
American actor
• Oscar nomination for *Only When I Laugh*, 1981.
b. March 21, 1929 in New York, New York
d. February 25, 1987 in New York, New York

Jean Cocteau
French author–director–poet
• Wrote *Les Enfants Terribles*, 1924; *Thomas L'Imposteur*, 1923.
b. July 05, 1889 in Maisons-Lafitte, France
d. October 12, 1963 in Paris, France

Michael Codron
English producer
• Won Tony, 1984, for *The Real Thing*.
b. June 08, 1930 in London, England

Buffalo Bill (William Frederick) Cody
American frontiersman–entertainer
• Buffalo hunter who organized Buffalo Bill's Wild West Show, touring US, Europe, 1883-1901.
b. February 26, 1846 in Scout County, Iowa
d. January 1, 1917 in Denver, Colorado

Iron Eyes Cody
American Indian actor
• Cherokee who wept in TV ecology ads; films include *Grayeagle*, 1977.
b. April 03, 1915 in Oklahoma

Frederick H Coe
American producer–director
• Pioneer TV producer; launched over 500 hour-long teleplays, 1940s-50s; directed Broadway hits *Two for the Seesaw; Miracle Worker*.
b. December 23, 1914 in Alligator, Mississippi
d. April 29, 1979 in Los Angeles, California

George M(ichael) Cohan
American actor–dramatist–producer
• Wrote "Over There," 1917; "Give My Regards to Broadway"; life story filmed: *Yankee Doodle Dandy*, 1942; received special Congressional Medal of Honor, 1940.
b. July 03, 1878 in Providence, Rhode Island
d. November 05, 1942 in New York, New York

Josephine Cohan
American dancer
• Talented sister of George M; performed with him in family acts, 1881-1916.
b. 1876 in Providence, Rhode Island
d. July 12, 1916 in New York, New York

Alexander H Cohen
American producer–actor
• Won two Emmys; producer of Tony Awards, 1967-80; appeared in *The Purple Rose of Cairo*, 1985.
b. July 24, 1920 in New York, New York

Myron Cohen
American comedian
• Known for dialect, government jokes.
b. July 01, 1902 in Grodno, Poland
d. March 1, 1986 in Nyack, New York

Mindy Cohn
American actress
• Played Natalie on TV series "Facts of Life," 1979-88.
b. May 2, 1966 in Los Angeles, California

Nicholas Colasanto
American actor
• Best known as Coach Ernie Pantusso on TV series "Cheers."
b. January 19, 1924 in Providence, Rhode Island
d. February 12, 1985 in Los Angeles, California

Claudette Colbert
(Lily Claudette Chauchoin)
American actress
• Won Oscar for *It Happened One Night*, 1934.
b. September 13, 1905 in Paris, France

Jack Cole
American choreographer
• Introduced jazz style which became US dance trademark; choreographed dance numbers for Rita Hayworth, Marilyn Monroe.
b. April 27, 1914 in New Brunswick, New Jersey
d. February 17, 1974 in Los Angeles, California

Michael Cole
American actor
• Played Pete Cochran in TV series "The Mod Squad," 1968-73.
b. July 03, 1945 in Madison, Wisconsin

Olivia Cole
American actress
• Best known for role of Mathilda in TV miniseries "Roots," 1977, for which she won an Emmy.
b. November 26, 1942 in Memphis, Tennessee

Dabney Coleman
American actor
• Star of TV series "Buffalo Bill," 1983-84; "Slap Maxwell," 1987–; won 1987 Emmy for TV movie "Sworn to Silence."
b. January 03, 1932 in Austin, Texas

Gary Coleman
American actor
• Child actor who played Arnold on TV series "Different Strokes," 1978-86.
b. February 08, 1968 in Zion, Illinois

William Collier, Sr
American actor–director–dramatist
• Appeared as comedian on stage, screen for 60 yrs.
b. November 12, 1866 in New York, New York
d. January 13, 1944 in Beverly Hills, California

Charles Cummings Collingwood
American broadcast journalist
• CBS correspondent who was first American network newsman admitted to N Vietnam, 1968.
b. June 04, 1917 in Three Rivers, Michigan
d. October 03, 1985 in New York, New York

Joan Henrietta Collins
English actress
• Played Alexis Carrington Colby on TV soap opera "Dynasty," 1981-89.
b. May 23, 1933 in London, England

Ray Collins
American actor
• Appeared in TV series "Perry Mason," 1957-64.
b. December 1, 1889 in Sacramento, California
d. July 11, 1965 in Santa Monica, California

Stephen Collins
American actor
• Films include *Star Trek;* starred in TV movie "The Two Mrs. Grenvilles," 1987.
b. October 01, 1947 in Des Moines, Iowa

Bud (Clayton) Collyer
American TV personality
• Hosted TV game show "To Tell the Truth," 1956.
b. June 18, 1908 in New York, New York
d. September 08, 1969 in Greenwich, Connecticut

George Colman
English dramatist
• Wrote comedies: *The Jealous Wife,* 1761; *The Clandestine Marriage,* 1766; managed Covent Garden, Haymarket theaters.
b. April 18, 1732 in Florence, Italy
d. August 14, 1794 in London, England

George Colman
English dramatist
• Wrote comedies, including *John Bull,* 1803.
b. October 21, 1762 in London, England
d. October 17, 1836 in London, England

Ronald Colman
American actor
• Won Oscar for *A Double Life,* 1948; appeared in *A Tale of Two Cities,* 1936.
b. February 09, 1891 in Richmond, England
d. May 19, 1958 in Santa Barbara, California

Coluche
(Michel Colucci)
French entertainer
• Known for vulgar, irreverent humor; most ubiquitous show business star in France.
b. October 28, 1944 in Paris, France
d. June 19, 1986 in Opio, France

Betty Comden
(Mrs Steven Kyle)
American dramatist
• Won Tonys for *Applause,* 1970; *A Doll's Life,* 1982; wrote song "New York, New York," 1945.
b. May 03, 1915 in New York, New York

Ann (Woodruff) Compton
American broadcast journalist
• ABC News White House correspondent, 1979-81, 1984–.
b. January 19, 1947 in Chicago, Illinois

Fay Compton
(Virginia Lilian Emeline Compton)
English actress
• Remembered as the supreme Ophelia of her time; wrote *Rosemary,* 1926.
b. September 18, 1894 in London, England
d. December 12, 1978 in Hove, England

Jeff Conaway
American actor
• Starred on Broadway in *Grease;* played Bobby on TV series "Taxi," 1978-81.
b. October 05, 1950 in New York, New York

Jackie Condon
(Our Gang)
American actress
• Child actor who appeared in *Hallroom Boys, Our Gang* comedies, 1922.
b. March 25, 1918 in Los Angeles, California
d. October 13, 1977 in Inglewood, California

William Congreve
English dramatist
• Wrote *The Way of the World,* a comedy of manners, 1700.
b. January 24, 1670 in Bardsey, England
d. January 19, 1729 in London, England

Chester Conklin
American comedian
• Mustachioed silent screen star in *Keystone Cops* series, 1913-22.
b. January 11, 1888 in Oskaloosa, Iowa
d. October 11, 1971 in Hollywood, California

Christopher Connelly
American actor
• Played Norman Harrington on TV soap opera "Peyton Place," 1964-69.
b. September 08, 1941 in Wichita, Kansas
d. December 07, 1988 in Burbank, California

Marc(us Cook) Connelly
American dramatist
• Won Pulitzer for *The Green Pastures,* 1930.
b. December 13, 1890 in McKeesport, Pennsylvania
d. December 21, 1980 in New York, New York

Sean (Thomas) Connery
Scottish actor
• Originated film role of James Bond in *Dr. No,* 1962; won Oscar for *The Untouchables,* 1988.
b. August 25, 1930 in Edinburgh, Scotland

Walter Connolly
American actor
• Versatile performer best remembered for portrayal in *Nothing Sacred,* 1937.
b. April 08, 1887 in Cincinnati, Ohio
d. May 28, 1940 in Beverly Hills, California

Chuck (Kevin Joseph) Connors
American actor
• Starred in TV show "The Rifleman," 1957-62.
b. April 1, 1921 in New York, New York

Michael Conrad
American actor
• Won Emmy for role of Phil Esterhaus in "Hill Street Blues," 1981, 1982. "Remember, let's be careful out there."
b. October 16, 1927 in New York, New York
d. November 22, 1983 in Los Angeles, California

Robert Conrad
(Conrad Robert Falk)
American actor
• Starred in "Hawaiian Eye," 1959-63; "The Wild, Wild West," 1965-69.
b. March 01, 1935 in Chicago, Illinois

William Conrad
American actor
• Star of "Cannon," 1971-76; "Nero Wolfe," 1981; "Jake and the Fatman," 1987–.
b. September 27, 1920 in Louisville, Kentucky

Hans Conreid
(Frank Foster Conreid)
American actor
• Comedian in over 100 films; played Uncle Tonoose in "Make Room for Daddy," 1957-64.
b. April 01, 1915 in Baltimore, Maryland
d. January 05, 1982 in Burbank, California

Tim Considine
American actor
• Played Mike Douglas on "My Three Sons," 1960-65.
b. December 1, 1941 in Louisville, Kentucky

Michael Constantine
(Constantine Joanides)
American actor
• Won 1970 Emmy for role of Seymour Kaufman on "Room 222," 1969-74.
b. May 22, 1927 in Reading, Pennsylvania

Richard Conte
(Nicholas Peter)
American actor
• Often portrayed loner in stage, screen roles, 1940s-70s; film *Call Northside 777* starred Jimmy Stewart, 1948.
b. March 24, 1914 in Jersey City, New Jersey
d. April 15, 1975 in Los Angeles, California

Tom (Thomas Antonio) Conti
Scottish actor
• Star of BBC TV series "The Glittering Prizes," 1976; won Tony for role in play *Whose Life Is It Anyway?* 1978-79.
b. November 22, 1941 in Paisley, Scotland

Frank Converse
American actor
• Played Johnny Corso on "NYPD," 1967-69.
b. May 22, 1938 in Saint Louis, Missouri

Bert Convy
American TV personality
• Host of game shows "Tattletales"; "People Do the Craziest Things"; "Win, Lose, or Draw."
b. July 23, 1933 in Saint Louis, Missouri

Jack Conway
American actor–director
• Films noted for technical excellence include *A Tale of Two Cities,* 1935.
b. July 17, 1887 in Graceville, Minnesota
d. October 11, 1952 in Pacific Palisades, California

Tim (Thomas Daniel) Conway
American comedian–actor
• Appeared in TV series "McHale's Navy," 1962-66; "The Carol Burnett Show," 1975-78.
b. December 13, 1933 in Willoughby, Ohio

Tom Conway
(Thomas Charles Sanders)
American actor
• Brother of actor George Sanders; played title role in "The Falcon," 1942-46.
b. September 15, 1904 in Saint Petersburg, Russia
d. April 22, 1967 in Culver City, California

Jackie (Jack Leslie) Coogan
American actor
• First child star in movie history, known for role in *The Kid,* 1919; played Uncle Fester on the "Addams Family," 1962-64.
b. October 26, 1914 in Los Angeles, California
d. March 01, 1984 in Santa Monica, California

Michael Cook
Canadian dramatist
• Stage, radio plays include *Deserts of Bohemia,* 1981.
b. February 14, 1933 in London, England

Peter Cook
English actor
• Won Tony for *Beyond the Fridge,* 1963; films include *The Wrong Box,* 1966.
b. November 17, 1937 in Devonshire, England

Joan Ganz Cooney
American producer
• Pres., Children's TV Workshop, 1970–; shows include "Sesame Street"; "Electric Company."
b. November 3, 1929 in Phoenix, Arizona

Gary (Frank James) Cooper
American actor
• Matinee idol, 1930s-50s; won Oscars for *Sergeant York,* 1941; *High Noon,* 1952; special Oscar, 1960.
b. May 07, 1901 in Helena, Montana
d. May 13, 1961 in Hollywood, California

Giles (Stannus) Cooper
British dramatist
• Noted radio dramatist; British award for yr's best radio plays was established in his honor, 1978.
b. August 09, 1918 in Dublin, Ireland
d. December 02, 1966 in Surbiton, England

Dame Gladys Cooper
English actress
• Career on stage, film, TV spanned more than 60 yrs.
b. December 18, 1888 in Lewisham, England
d. November 17, 1971 in Henley-on-Thames, England

Jackie (John, Jr) Cooper
(Our Gang)
American actor–director
• Started acting at age three; starred in *The Champ,* 1931; won Emmys, 1970s for directing.
b. September 15, 1922 in Los Angeles, California

Melville Cooper
American actor
• Character actor for 50 yrs.; films include *The Scarlet Pimpernel,* 1935; *Rebecca,* 1940.
b. October 15, 1896 in Birmingham, England
d. March 29, 1973 in Woodland Hills, California

Robert Coote
English actor
• Played Colonel Pickering, Broadway version of *My Fair Lady,* 1956.
b. February 04, 1909 in London, England
d. November 25, 1982 in New York, New York

Jacques Copeau
French dramatist
• Founder of the Theater Vieux Colombier in Paris, 1913.
b. 1878 in Paris, France
d. October 2, 1949 in Beaune, France

David Copperfield
(David Kotkin)
American magician
• Combines theater, humor with illusions; performed "illusion of century," 1983, making Statue of Liberty disappear.
b. 1957 in Metuchen, New Jersey

Francis Ford Coppola
American director
• Films include *The Godfather I, II,* 1972, 1974; *Apocalypse Now,* 1979. *Godfather III,* 1990.
b. April 07, 1939 in Detroit, Michigan

Benoit Constant Coquelin
(Coquelin Aine)
French actor
• His first part, Cyrano de Bergerac, was always associated with his name; with Comedie-Francaise, 1860-92.
b. January 23, 1841 in Boulogne-sur-Mer, France
d. January 27, 1909 in Pont-aux-Dames, France

Ellen Corby
(Ellen Hansen)
American actress
• Played Grandma on "The Waltons," 1972-79.
b. June 03, 1913 in Racine, Wisconsin

Dan (Howard Dan) Cordtz
American broadcast journalist
• With *Wall Street Journal,* 1955-66; economics editor, ABC News, 1974–.
b. May 01, 1927 in Gary, Indiana

Irwin Corey
American comedian–actor
• Double-talking comedian of stage and screen; films include *Car Wash,* 1976; *The Comeback Trail,* 1982.
b. July 29, 1912 in New York, New York

Jeff Corey
American actor
• Played character roles, 1940s; ran acting school, 1940-59; returned to films later in career: *The Last Tycoon,* 1976.
b. August 1, 1914 in New York, New York

Wendell Corey
American actor
• Former film star; appeared in TV series "The Eleventh Hour," 1962-63; former pres., Academy of Motion Picture Arts and Sciences.
b. March 2, 1914 in Dracut, Massachusetts
d. November 09, 1968 in Woodland Hills, California

Roger William Corman
American producer
• B horror films include Poe's *The Raven*, 1962; *The Bees*, 1980.
b. April 05, 1926 in Detroit, Michigan

Pierre Corneille
French dramatist–poet
• Wrote *Le Cid*, 1637; *Le Menteur*, 1643.
b. June 06, 1606 in Rouen, France
d. October 01, 1684 in Paris, France

Henry Cornelius
British director
• Best known for comedies *Passport to Pimlico*, 1949; *Genevieve*, 1954.
b. August 18, 1913 in South Africa
d. May 03, 1958 in London, England

Lydia Cornell
American actress
• Played Sarah Rush on TV series "Too Close for Comfort," 1980-86.
b. July 23, 1957 in El Paso, Texas

Charles J Correll
(Amos 'n Andy)
American comedian
• Andy of Amos 'n Andy comedy team; on radio, 1928-58.
b. February 02, 1890 in Peoria, Illinois
d. September 26, 1972 in Chicago, Illinois

Adrienne Corri
(Adrienne Riccoboni)
Scottish actress
• Films include *A Clockwork Orange*, 1971.
b. November 13, 1933 in Glasgow, Scotland

Douglas Corrigan
("Wrong Way")
American aviator–actor
• Nicknamed for landing in Ireland after taking off from NY for LA, 1938.
b. 1907

Frank Corsaro
(Francesco Andrea)
American actor–director
• Directed many plays, TV shows, operas; with NYC Opera, 1958–; appeared in *Rachel, Rachel*, 1967.
b. December 22, 1925 in New York, New York

Bud Cort
American actor
• Appeared in *Harold and Maude*, with Ruth Gordon, 1971. Also *M*A*S*H* and *Brewster McCloud*.
b. March 29, 1951 in Rye, New York

Valentina Cortesa
Italian actress
• Appeared in several international films including *Widow's Nest*, 1977.
b. January 01, 1925 in Milan, Italy

Ricardo Cortez
(Jacob Kranz)
American actor
• Matinee idol, 1920s; Garbo's first leading man in *The Torrent*, 1926.
b. September 19, 1899 in Vienna, Austria
d. May 28, 1977 in New York, New York

Norman Corwin
American screenwriter–producer–director
• Screenplay, *Lust for Life* was nominated for Oscar, 1956; won many awards in various fields.
b. May 03, 1910 in Boston, Massachusetts

Bill Cosby
(William Henry Cosby Jr)
American actor–comedian
• Star of hit TV series "The Cosby Show," 1984–; wrote *Fatherhood*, 1986; won Spingarn, 1984.
b. July 12, 1937 in Philadelphia, Pennsylvania

Ernest Cossart
English actor
• Usually cast in portly British butler roles: *Charley's Aunt*, 1941.
b. September 24, 1876 in Cheltenham, England
d. January 21, 1951 in New York, New York

Henri Costa-Gavras
(Kostantinos Gavras)
Greek director
• Won Oscar for *Z*, 1969.
b. 1933 in Athens, Greece

Chris Costello
American actress–author
• Appeared in movie, *Semi-Tough*, 1978; wrote biography of father Lou Costello, *Lou's on First*, 1982.
b. August 15, 1947 in Los Angeles, California

Lou Costello
(Abbott and Costello; Louis Francis Cristillo)
American actor–comedian
• Starred in over 30 films with Bud Abbott; best known for "Who's On First?" routine.
b. March 06, 1908 in Paterson, New Jersey
d. March 03, 1959 in Los Angeles, California

Maurice Costello
American actor
• One of first matinee stage idols; made film triumph in *A Tale of Two Cities*, 1911.
b. 1877 in Pittsburgh, Pennsylvania
d. October 3, 1950 in Hollywood, California

Robert E Costello
American producer
• Won Emmys, 1977, 1979 for soap opera "Ryan's Hope."
b. April 26, 1921 in Chicago, Illinois

Kevin Michael Costner
American actor
• Films include *The Untouchables; No Way Out*, 1987; *Bull Durham*, 1988; *Field of Dreams*, 1989; *Dances with Wolves*, 1990.
b. January 18, 1955 in Lynwood, California

James Costigan
Writer
• Won three Emmys for TV shows including "Eleanor and Franklin," 1976.

Joseph Cotten
American actor
• Starred in *Citizen Kane*, 1941; *Journey into Fear*, 1942.
b. May 15, 1905 in Petersburg, Virginia

George Coulouris
English actor
• Best known for villian roles in films including *For Whom the Bell Tolls*, 1943.
b. October 01, 1903 in Manchester, England
d. April 25, 1989 in London, England

John William Coulter
Canadian dramatist
• Noted for dramas with Irish themes: *Family Portraits*, 1937.
b. February 12, 1888 in Belfast, Northern Ireland
d. December 1980 in Toronto, Ontario

Tom (Thomas Daniel) Courtenay
English actor
• Oscar nominee for *The Dresser*, 1984; *Doctor Zhivago*, 1965; Tony nominee for *Otherwise Engaged*, 1977.
b. February 25, 1937 in Hull, England

Dame Cicely Courtneidge
British actress
• London stage, musical star since 1909; introduced song "The Kings Horses," 1931.
b. April 01, 1893 in Sydney, Australia
d. April 26, 1980 in London, England

Philippe Cousteau
French oceanographer–producer
• Produced TV series "Undersea World of Jacques Cousteau," 1970-75; Emmy nominee, 1971.
b. December 3, 1940 in Toulon, France
d. June 28, 1979 in Alverca, Portugal

Franklin Cover
American actor
• Played Tom Willis on TV series "The Jeffersons," 1975-85.
b. November 2, 1928 in Cleveland, Ohio

Sir Noel Pierce Coward
English dramatist–composer
• Wrote 27 plays, 281 songs; plays include *Private Lives*, 1930; *Blithe Spirit*, 1941.
b. December 16, 1899 in London, England
d. March 26, 1973 in Kingston, Jamaica

Alex Cox
English screenwriter
• Wrote, directed cult films *Repo Man*, 1984; *Sid and Nancy*, 1986.
b. in Liverpool, England

Constance Cox
English dramatist
• Adapted classics for radio, TV; won Screenwriters Guild Award, 1967, for TV series "The Forsyte Saga."
b. October 25, 1915 in Sutton, England

Wally (Wallace Maynard) Cox
American actor–comedian
• Starred in "Mr. Peepers," 1952-55; regular on "Hollywood Squares."
b. December 06, 1924 in Detroit, Michigan
d. February 15, 1973 in Los Angeles, California

Buster (Larry) Crabbe
(Clarence Linden)
American actor–swimmer
• Starred as Flash Gordon, Buck Rogers in 1930s-40s movie serials.
b. February 07, 1908 in Oakland, California
d. April 23, 1983 in Scottsdale, Arizona

Lotta Crabtree
American actress
• Began career entertaining in CA mining camps; appeared in *Old Curiosity Shop*, 1867.
b. November 07, 1847 in New York, New York
d. September 25, 1924 in Boston, Massachusetts

May Craig
Irish actress
• Played in first production of *Playboy of the Western World*, 1907.
b. 1889 in Ireland
d. February 09, 1972 in Dublin, Ireland

May (Elizabeth May) Craig
American broadcast journalist
• Served as war correspondent in 1944; popular panelist on "Meet the Press"; noted for persistent questioning at presidential news conferences.
b. December 24, 1889 in Coosaw, South Carolina
d. July 15, 1975 in Silver Spring, Maryland

Wendy Craig
English actress
• Won BBC TV personality award for "The Nanny," 1970.
b. June 2, 1930 in Sacriston, England

Bob Crane
American actor
• Played Colonel Robert Hogan in "Hogan's Heroes," 1965-71.
b. July 13, 1928 in Waterbury, Connecticut
d. June 29, 1978 in Scottsdale, Arizona

Frank Craven
American actor
• Played stage manager in Broadway, film versions of *Our Town*.
b. 1878 in Boston, Massachusetts
d. September 01, 1945 in Beverly Hills, California

Broderick Crawford
(William Broderick Crawford)
American actor
• Won Oscar, 1949, for *All the King's Men;* known for TV's "Highway Patrol," 1955-59.
b. December 09, 1911 in Philadelphia, Pennsylvania
d. April 26, 1986 in Rancho Mirage, California

Cheryl Crawford
American producer
• Started Actors Studio, 1947, with Robert Lewis, Elia Kazan; produced Broadway hit *Brigadoon.*
b. September 24, 1902 in Akron, Ohio
d. October 07, 1986 in New York, New York

Joan Crawford
(Lucille Fay LeSueur; "Billie")
American actress
• Won Oscar for *Mildred Pierce*, 1945; relationship with daughter subject of novel, film *Mommie Dearest*, 1978, 1981.
b. March 23, 1908 in San Antonio, Texas
d. May 13, 1977 in New York, New York

Michael Patrick Crawford
(Michael Dumble-Smith)
American actor
• Won Tony for musical *Phantom of the Opera*, 1988.
b. January 19, 1942 in Salisbury, England

Richard Crenna
American actor
• Starred in "Our Miss Brooks," 1952-56; "The Real McCoys," 1957-63; films include *The Flamingo Kid*, 1985.
b. November 3, 1927 in Los Angeles, California

Laura Hope Crews
American actress
• Played Aunt Pittypat in *Gone With the Wind*, 1939.
b. December 12, 1879 in San Francisco, California
d. November 13, 1942 in New York, New York

Charles Crichton
English director
• Films include *Hue and Cry*, 1946; *Lavender Hill Mob*, 1951; *A Fish Called Wanda*, 1988.
b. August 06, 1910 in Wallasey, England

(John) Michael Crichton
(Jeffrey Hudson; John Lange pseuds)
American author–director
• Won Edgar for *A Case of Need*, 1968; directed *Coma*, 1977.
b. October 23, 1942 in Chicago, Illinois

Donald Crisp
American actor
• Won Oscar for *How Green Was My Valley*, 1941.
b. April 18, 1880 in Aberfeldy, Scotland
d. May 26, 1974 in Van Nuys, California

Michael Cristofer
(Michael Procaccino)
American dramatist
• Won Pulitzer Prize in drama, 1977, for *The Shadow Box.*
b. January 22, 1945 in Trenton, New Jersey

Michael Croft
English director
• Founder, National Youth Theatre, 1956.
b. March 08, 1922 in Oswestry, England
d. November 15, 1986 in London, England

John Cromwell
American director
• Directed *Of Human Bondage*, 1964.
b. December 23, 1887 in Toledo, Ohio
d. September 26, 1979 in Santa Barbara, California

Walter Leland Cronkite, Jr
American broadcast journalist
• Anchored "CBS Evening News," 1962-81; host "Universe" TV series.
b. November 04, 1916 in Saint Joseph, Missouri

Hume Cronyn
Canadian actor
• Won Tony, 1964, for *Hamlet;* best known for *The Gin Game*, 1978, with wife Jessica Tandy.
b. July 18, 1911 in London, Ontario

Cathy Lee Crosby
American actress
• Co-host of TV show "That's Incredible!," 1980-84.
b. December 02, 1949 in Los Angeles, California

Floyd Delafield Crosby
American filmmaker
• Films include *The Raven*, 1935; won Oscar for *Tabu*, 1930-31.
b. December 12, 1899 in New York, New York
d. September 3, 1985 in Ojai, California

Mary Frances Crosby
American actress–celebrity relative
• Played Kristin Shepherd, who shot JR Ewing, on "Dallas," 1979-81; daughter of Bing Crosby.
b. September 14, 1959 in Los Angeles, California

Norm(an Lawrence) Crosby
American comedian
• Night club, TV routines feature mispronounced malapropisms.
b. September 15, 1927 in Boston, Massachusetts

Ben (Bernard) Cross
English actor
• Played Olympic runner Harold Abrahams in Oscar-winning *Chariots of Fire*, 1981. Now stars in "Dark Shadows" on American television.
b. December 16, 1947 in London, England

Milton John Cross
American radio performer
• Annouced Metropolitan Opera broadcasts, 1931-75.
b. April 16, 1897 in New York, New York
d. January 03, 1975 in New York, New York

Lindsay Ann Crouse
American actress
• Daughter of Russel Crouse; appeared in film *All the President's Men*, 1976.
b. May 12, 1948 in New York, New York

Russel Crouse
American dramatist
• Co-wrote hit Broadway plays *Life with Father*, 1939; *State of the Union*, 1946; wrote book from which *The Sound of Music* was made.
b. February 2, 1893 in Findlay, Ohio
d. April 03, 1966 in New York, New York

Eric John Crozier
English producer
• Co-founded, English Opera Group, 1947; plays include *Noah Gives Thanks*, 1950; translated several classic operas.
b. November 14, 1914 in London, England

Andrew John Cruickshank
Scottish actor
• Star of British theater, film, since 1930s; best known since 1963 for TV series "Dr. Finlay's Casebook."
b. December 25, 1907 in Aberdeen, Scotland
d. April 29, 1988

Tom Cruise
(Thomas Cruise Mapother 4th)
American actor
• Has had roles in six major films, including *Risky Business*, 1983; *Top Gun*, 1986; *Born on the Fourth of July*, 1989.
b. July 03, 1962 in Syracuse, New York

Billy (William) Crystal
American actor–comedian
• Comedic actor known as versatile mimic; starred in "Soap," 1977-81; *When Harry Met Sally*, 1989.
b. March 14, 1947 in Long Island, New York

Lester M Crystal
American TV executive
• Won two Emmys; former exec. vp, NBC News.
b. September 13, 1934 in Duluth, Michigan

George Dewey Cukor
American director
• Won 1964 Oscar for *My Fair Lady;* last film *Rich and Famous*, 1981.
b. July 07, 1899 in New York, New York
d. January 24, 1983 in Los Angeles, California

Bill (William Lawrence) Cullen
American TV personality
• Had 30-year career hosting over 5,000 game show episodes on TV including "The Price Is Right," "The $25,000 Pyramid," "Name That Tune."
b. February 18, 1920 in Pittsburgh, Pennsylvania
d. July 07, 1990 in Los Angeles, California

John Cullum
American actor
• Won Tony awards for *Shenandoah*, 1975; *On the Twentieth Century*, 1978.
b. March 02, 1930 in Knoxville, Tennessee

Robert Culp
American actor
• Starred in "I Spy," 1965-68; "The Greatest American Hero," 1981-83.
b. August 13, 1930 in Berkeley, California

Richard Cumberland
English dramatist
• Wrote over 40 plays, including sentimental comedy *The Brothers*, 1769.
b. February 19, 1732 in Cambridge, England
d. May 07, 1811 in London, England

Bob (Robert Orville) Cummings
American actor
• Starred in early TV sitcoms, including "Love That Bob," 1954-61; most film roles were light comedies, but also co-starred in Hitchcock's *Dial M for Murder*, 1954.
b. June 09, 1910 in Joplin, Missouri
d. December 02, 1990 in Los Angeles, California

Constance Cummings
(Constance Halverstadt)
American actress
• Won Tony award for *Wings*, 1979.
b. May 15, 1910 in Seattle, Washington

Quinn Cummings
American actress
• Nominated for Oscar, 1977, for *The Goodbye Girl*.
b. August 13, 1967 in Hollywood, California

Peggy Cummins
Welsh actress
• Best known for films *English Without Tears*, 1944; *Late George Apley*, 1946.
b. December 18, 1926 in Prestatyn, Wales

Merce Cunningham
American dancer–choreographer
• Martha Graham protege; formed own co., 1952; developed new forms of abstract dance.
b. April 16, 1919 in Centralia, Washington

Finlay Currie
Scottish actor
• Best known for *Great Expectations*, 1946.
b. January 2, 1878 in Edinburgh, Scotland
d. May 09, 1968 in Gerrards Cross, England

Jane Therese Curtin
American actress–comedienne
• Star of NBC TV's "Saturday Night Live," 1975-79; plays Allie on "Kate & Allie," 1984-1989.
b. September 06, 1947 in Cambridge, Massachusetts

Jackie Curtis
American dramatist–screenwriter
• Screenplays include *Women in Revolt*, 1971.
b. February 19, 1947 in Stony Creek, Tennessee

Jamie Lee Curtis
American actress
• Daughter of Tony Curtis, Janet Leigh; star of film *Halloween*, 1981, TV series "Anything But Love," 1989–.
b. November 22, 1958 in Los Angeles, California

Ken Curtis
(Curtis Gates)
American actor
• Best known as Festus Haggen on "Gunsmoke," 1964-75.
b. July 12, 1916 in Lamar, Colorado
d. April 28, 1991 in Fesno, California

Tony Curtis
(Bernard Schwartz)
American actor
• Starred in *The Defiant Ones*, 1958; *Some Like it Hot*, 1959.
b. June 03, 1925 in New York, New York

Michael Curtiz
American director
• Won Oscar for *Casablanca*, 1942; directed over 100 films for Warner Bros.
b. December 24, 1898 in Budapest, Hungary
d. April 11, 1962 in Hollywood, California

Cyril Cusack
Irish actor
• Appeared in TV movies *Catholics; Jesus of Nazareth*.
b. November 26, 1910 in Durban, South Africa

Joan Cusack
American actress
• Received Best Supporting Actress nomination for *Working Girl*, 1988; sister of John.
b. October 11, 1962 in Evanston, Illinois.

John Cusack
American actor
• Starred in numerous films including *A Sure Thing, Say Anything*, and most recently, *Grifters*, 1991.
b. June 28, 1966 in Evanston, Illinois

Peter Cushing
English actor
• Rivals Vincent Price in horror film roles; has played Baron Frankenstein in four movies.
b. May 26, 1913 in Kenley, England

Charlotte Saunders Cushman
American actress
• Acclaimed as foremost actress of her day; noted for Shakespearean tragedies; gave farewell performances from 1857-75.
b. July 23, 1816 in Boston, Massachusetts
d. February 17, 1876 in Boston, Massachusetts

Maryam D'Abo
English actress
• Played Kara Milovy in James Bond film *The Living Daylights*, 1987.
b. 1961 in London, England

Morton DaCosta
(Morton Tecosky)
American producer–director
• Directed Broadway's biggest hits in the 1950s including *Music Man, Auntie Mame, No Time for Sergeants*.
b. March 07, 1914 in Philadelphia, Pennsylvania
d. January 29, 1989 in Danbury, Connecticut

Willem (William) Dafoe
American actor
• Oscar nominee for supporting actor in *Platoon*, 1987; other films include *To Live and Die in L.A.*, 1985; *Wild at Heart*, 1990.
b. July 22, 1955 in Appleton, Wisconsin

Dagmar
(Virginia Ruth Egnor)
American actress
• Played dumb blonde role of TV variety show "Broadway Open House," 1950; own variety show, "Dagmar's Canteen," 1952.
b. November 29, 1926 in Huntington, West Virginia

Lil (Marta Maria Liletta) Dagover
German actress
• International star of 1920s-30s; heroine of classic *The Cabinet of Dr. Caligari*, 1919.
b. September 3, 1897 in Madiven, Indonesia
d. January 3, 1980 in Munich, Germany (West)

Arlene Dahl
American actress
• Glamor star of late 1940s-1950s films; has written column, books on beauty; mother of Lorenzo Lamas.
b. August 11, 1927 in Minneapolis, Minnesota

Roald Dahl
American author–screenwriter
• Wrote macabre children's stories, books for adults, films; *Charlie and the Chocolate Factory*, 1964, adapted for screen as *Willie Wonka and the Chocolate Factory*; wrote screenplay *Chitty Chitty Bang Bang*.
b. September 13, 1916 in Llandaff, Wales
d. November 23, 1990 in Oxford, England

Dan Dailey
American dancer–actor
• Made Broadway debut in *Babes in Arms*, 1939; films include *The Mortal Storm*, 1940.
b. December 14, 1915 in New York, New York
d. October 17, 1978 in Hollywood, California

Grover Dale
(Grover Robert Aitken)
American director–choreographer
• With Michael Bennett, won Tony for *Seesaw*, 1973.
b. July 22, 1935 in Harrisburg, Pennsylvania

Jim Dale
(James Smith)
English actor
• Starred in "Carry On" series of films including *Carry on Again, Doctodr*, 1969.
b. August 15, 1935 in Rothwell, England

Robert H Daley
Producer
• Films include *Play Misty for Me*, 1971; *Prince of the City*, 1981.

John Dall
(John Jenner Thompson)
American actor
• Oscar nominee for *The Corn Is Green*, 1946; star of Hitchcock's *Rope*, 1948.
b. 1918 in New York, New York
d. January 15, 1971 in Beverly Hills, California

Ian (Murray) Dalrymple
British screenwriter
• Won Oscars for *The Citadel; Pygmalion*, 1938.
b. August 26, 1903 in Johannesburg, South Africa

Jean Dalrymple
American producer–director
• Stage productions include *Hope for the Best*, 1944; *King Lear*, 1957.
b. September 02, 1910 in Morristown, New Jersey

Abby Dalton
American actress
• Played Julia Cumson on TV series "Falcon Crest."
b. August 15, 1935 in Las Vegas, Nevada

Timothy Dalton
Welsh actor
• Played James Bond in film *The Living Daylights*, 1987.
b. March 21, 1946 in Colwyn Bay, Wales

Augustin Daly
American dramatist
• Melodramas include *Under the Gaslight*, 1867; established Broadway theater, Daley's, 1879.
b. July 2, 1838 in Plymouth, North Carolina
d. June 07, 1899 in Paris, France

James Daly
American actor
• Played Dr. Paul Lochner on TV series "Medical Center," 1969-76.
b. October 23, 1918 in Wisconsin Rapids, Wisconsin
d. July 03, 1978 in Nyack, New York

John Daly
English producer
• Films include *Return of the Living Dead*, 1983; *Terminator*, 1984; *Falcon and the Snowman*, 1985.
b. 1937 in England

John Charles Daly, Jr
American TV personality
• Best known for hosting "What's My Line," 1950-67. "Voice of America," 1967-.
b. February 2, 1914 in Johannesburg, South Africa
d. February 24, 1991 in Chevy Chase, Maryland

Tyne (Ellen Tyne) Daly
American actress
• Won two Emmys for role of Mary Beth Lacey in TV series "Cagney and Lacey," 1982-88.
b. February 21, 1944 in Madison, Wisconsin

Cathryn Damon
American actress
• Best known for role of Mary Campbell in TV spoof, "Soap," 1977-81; won Emmy, 1980.
b. September 11, 1931 in Seattle, Washington
d. May 06, 1987 in Los Angeles, California

Stuart Damon
(Stuart Michael Zonis)
American actor
• Best known as Dr. Alan Quartermain on TV soap opera "General Hospital."
b. February 05, 1937 in Brooklyn, New York

Bill Dana
American comedian–actor
• Films include *The Busybody*, 1967; *The Harrad Summer*, 1974.
b. October 05, 1924 in Quincy, Massachusetts

Viola Dana
(Violet Flugrath)
American actress
• Silent screen star of over 50 films: *Revelation*, 1924; made Broadway debut, 1913.
b. June 28, 1897 in Brooklyn, New York
d. July 1, 1987 in Woodland Hills, California

John Albert Dancy
American broadcast journalist
• With NBC News since 1973; congressional correspondent, 1982–.
b. August 05, 1936 in Jackson, Tennessee

William Danforth
(William Daniels)
American actor
• Appeared in over 5,000 performances of Gilbert & Sullivan operas; played *The Mikado* 1,000 times.
b. May 13, 1869 in Syracuse, New York
d. April 16, 1941 in Skaneateles, New York

Beverly D'Angelo
American actress–singer
• Former rock singer who appeared in films *Paternity*, 1981; *Coal Miner's Daughter*, 1980.
b. 1952 in Columbus, Ohio

Rodney Dangerfield
(Jacob Cohen real name; Jack Roy pseud)
American comedian
• Films include *Back to School*, 1986; won Grammy for comedy album *No Respect*, 1980.
b. November 22, 1921 in Babylon, New York

Leon Danielian
American dancer–choreographer
• Director, American Ballet Theater Schools, 1967–; performances include *Frankie and Johnny*.
b. October 31, 1920 in New York, New York

Henry Daniell
English actor
• Played Prof. Moriarity in Sherlock Holmes film *The Woman in Green*, 1945.
b. March 05, 1894 in London, England
d. October 31, 1963 in Santa Monica, California

Bebe (Virginia) Daniels
American actress
• Made 200 shorts with Harold Lloyd, 1914-18; wed to Ben Lyon.
b. January 14, 1901 in Dallas, Texas
d. March 16, 1971 in London, England

Frank Daniels
American actor
• Began in Vitagraph films, 1915; played in *Kernel Nutt* series.
b. 1860 in Dayton, Ohio
d. January 12, 1935 in Palm Beach, Florida

Jeff Daniels
American actor
• Films include *Ragtime*, 1982; *Terms of Endearment*, 1984; *Purple Rose of Cairo*, 1985.
b. 1955 in Georgia

Mickey Daniels
(Our Gang)
Actor
• Appeared in first of Our Gang comedies, 1920s.
b. 1914

William Daniels
American actor
• Won Emmy, 1984, 1986, for role of Dr. Mark Craig on TV series "St. Elsewhere," 1982-88.
b. March 31, 1927 in Brooklyn, New York

Alexandra Danilova
American dancer–choreographer
• Best-known ballets include *Le Beau Danube*, *Swan Lake*.
b. January 2, 1904 in Peterhof, Russia

Blythe Katharine Danner
(Mrs Bruce W Paltrow)
American actress
• Won 1971 Tony for *Butterflies Are Free*.
b. February 03, 1943 in Philadelphia, Pennsylvania

Ted (Edward Bridge, III) Danson
American actor
• Plays Sam Malone on TV comedy "Cheers," 1982–; won Emmy, 1990; starred in film *Three Men and a Baby*, 1987.
b. December 29, 1947 in San Diego, California

Nicholas Dante
American dramatist
• Wrote *A Chorus Line*, 1976; won Pulitzer, Tony.
b. November 22, 1941 in New York, New York

Helmut Dantine
American actor
• Known for playing Nazi roles during WW II; films include *Hotel Berlin*, 1945.
b. October 07, 1917 in Vienna, Austria
d. May 03, 1982 in Beverly Hills, California

Ray(mond) Danton
American actor
• Best known for gangster roles *The Rise and Fall of Legs Diamond*, 1960; *Portrait of a Mobster*, 1961.
b. September 19, 1931 in New York, New York

Tony Danza
American actor
• Former middleweight fighter; star of TV series "Taxi," 1982-85; "Who's the Boss?" 1985–.
b. April 21, 1951 in New York, New York

Kim Darby
(Deborah Zerby)
American actress
• Starred with John Wayne in *True Grit*, 1969.
b. July 08, 1948 in Hollywood, California

Denise Darcel
American singer–actress
• Nightclub performer; Hollywood debut, 1947; played sensuous leads in 1950s films.
b. September 08, 1925 in Paris, France

Linda Darnell
American actress
• Famous for role in *Forever Amber*, 1948.
b. October 16, 1921 in Dallas, Texas
d. April 12, 1965 in Chicago, Illinois

James Darren
American actor–singer
• Starred in *Gidget*, 1959; TV series "The Time Tunnel," 1966-67.
b. June 08, 1936 in Philadelphia, Pennsylvania

Danielle Darrieux
French actress
• Epitome of French femininity; films included *Mayerling*, 1936, *La Ronde*, 1950.
b. May 01, 1917 in Bordeaux, France

Frankie Darro
(Frank Johnson)
American actor
• Played tough kids, jockeys in Depression-era films.
b. December 22, 1917 in Chicago, Illinois
d. 1976

Jane Darwell
(Patti Woodward)
American actress
• Won 1940 Oscar as Ma Joad in *Grapes of Wrath*.
b. October 15, 1880 in Palmyra, Missouri
d. August 13, 1967 in Woodland Hills, California

Howard DaSilva
(Harold Silverblatt)
American actor–director–producer
• Career spanned 55 yrs.; best known for playing Benjamin Franklin in Broadway musical *1776*, 1969.
b. May 04, 1909 in Cleveland, Ohio
d. February 16, 1986 in Ossining, New York

Jules Dassin
American director
• Married to Melina Mercouri, who starred in his films *Never on Sunday*, 1960, *Topkapi*, 1964.
b. December 12, 1911 in Middletown, Connecticut

Sir Peter Lauderdale Daubeny
British director
• Plays on London stages include *The Aspern Papers*, 1959; *Chin-Chin*, 1960.
b. April 1921 in Wiesbaden, Germany
d. August 06, 1975 in London, England

Claude Le Grand Maria Eugene Dauphin
French actor
• International film star best known for *April in Paris*, 1952.
b. August 19, 1903 in Corbeil, France
d. November 17, 1978 in Paris, France

Harry George Bryant Davenport
American actor
• Played grandfather roles in films *The Higgins Family* series, 1938-40; *Meet Me in St. Louis*, 1944.
b. January 19, 1886 in New York, New York
d. August 09, 1949 in Los Angeles, California

Nigel Davenport
English actor
• Character actor who appeared in *Look Back in Anger*, 1959; *Chariots of Fire*, 1981.
b. May 23, 1928 in Shelford, England

Marion Davies
(Marion Douras)
American actress
• Mistress of William Randolf Hearst; affair satirized by Orson Welles in *Citizen Kane*, 1941.
b. January 03, 1897 in New York, New York
d. September 22, 1961 in Hollywood, California

Ann Bradford Davis
American actress
• Best known for TV series "The Brady Bunch," 1969-74; "The Bob Cummings Show," 1955-59.
b. May 03, 1926 in Schenectady, New York

Bette (Ruth Elizabeth) Davis
American actress
• Major movie star since 1930s; won Oscars for *Dangerous*, 1935; *Jezebel*, 1938; other films include *The Whales of August*, 1987.
b. April 05, 1908 in Lowell, Massachusetts
d. October 06, 1989 in Paris, France

Brad Davis
American actor
• Appeared in films *Midnight Express*, 1978, *Chariots of Fire*, 1981.
b. November 06, 1949 in Tallahassee, Florida

Elmer Holmes Davis
American journalist–radio performer
• News commentator for CBS, NBC; early opponent of Senator Joseph McCarthy's hearings; books include *Love Among the Ruins*, 1935; *But We Were Born Free*, 1954.
b. January 13, 1890 in Aurora, Indiana
d. May 18, 1958 in Washington, District of Columbia

Geena Davis
American actress
• Won best supporting actress Oscar, 1989, for *The Accidental Tourist*.
b. January 21, 1957 in Wareham, Massachusetts

Jim Davis
American actor
• Played Jock Ewing on TV series "Dallas," 1978-81.
b. August 26, 1916 in Edgerton, Missouri
d. April 26, 1981 in Northridge, California

Joan Davis
American actress–comedienne
• Starred in TV series *I Married Joan*, 1952-55.
b. June 29, 1907 in Saint Paul, Minnesota
d. May 23, 1961 in Palm Springs, California

Judy Davis
Australian actress
• Starred in *My Brilliant Career*, 1981.
b. 1956 in Perth, Australia

Ossie Davis
American actor–dramatist
• Wrote, directed, starred in *Purlie Victorious*, 1961.
b. December 18, 1917 in Cogdell, Georgia

Owen Davis
American dramatist
• Best known for Pulitzer-winning play *Icebound*, 1923.
b. January 29, 1874 in Portland, Maine
d. October 13, 1956 in New York, New York

Peter Frank Davis
American producer–writer
• Won 1975 Oscar for controversial Vietnam documentary, *Hearts and Minds;* won Emmy for "The Selling of the Pentagon," 1971.
b. January 02, 1937 in Los Angeles, California

Sammi Davis
British actress
• Films include *Mona Lisa,* 1986; *Hope and Glory,* 1987.
b. 1964

Bruce Davison
American actor
• Appeared in films *Willard,* 1971; *Mother, Jugs, and Speed,* 1976; in TV shows, made-for-TV films.
b. June 28, 1946 in Philadelphia, Pennsylvania

Pam Dawber
(Mrs Mark Harmon)
American actress
• Played Mindy on TV series "Mork and Mindy," 1978-82; star of "My Sister Sam," 1986–.
b. October 18, 1951 in Farmington, Michigan

Richard Dawson
English TV personality
• Starred in TV series "Hogan's Heroes," 1965-71; host of game show "Family Feud."
b. November 2, 1932 in Gosport, England

Doris Day
(Doris VonKappelhoff)
American actress–singer
• Starred in *The Pajama Game,* 1957; *Pillow Talk,* 1959; star of sit-com, "Doris Day Show," 1968-73.
b. April 03, 1924 in Cincinnati, Ohio

Laraine Day
(Laraine Johnson)
American actress
• Played nurse Mary Lamont in *Dr. Kildare* film series, 1940s.
b. October 13, 1920 in Roosevelt, Utah

Daniel Day-Lewis
Irish actor
• Won best actor Oscar, 1990, for *My Left Foot;* son of England poet laureate, Cecil Day-Lewis.
b. 1957 in London, England

James Dean
(James Byron)
American actor
• Starred in *East of Eden,* 1955; *Rebel Without a Cause,* 1955; *Giant,* 1956; popular teen idol. Died in auto accident.
b. February 08, 1931 in Marion, Indiana
d. September 3, 1955 in Paso Robles, California

Morton (Nissan) Dean
American broadcast journalist
• With CBS News since 1967; part-time anchor of "Newsbreak."
b. August 22, 1935 in Fall River, Massachusetts

Philippe Claude Alex DeBroca
French filmmaker
• Identified with sophisticated, eccentric comedies: *Le Cavaleur,* 1979.
b. March 15, 1933 in Paris, France

Yvonne DeCarlo
(Peggy Yvonne Middleton)
Canadian actress
• Played Lily on TV series "The Munsters," 1964-66.
b. September 01, 1922 in Vancouver, British Columbia

Pedro DeCordoba
American actor
• Character actor in films, 1915-50, including *Winner Take All,* 1939.
b. September 28, 1881 in New York, New York
d. September 17, 1950 in Sunland, California

Frederick Timmins DeCordova
American producer
• With CBS, NBC, 1953–; won Emmys for "The Tonight Show," 1970s.
b. October 27, 1910 in New York, New York

John Dee
English magician
• Practiced magic to entertain; imprisoned for insulting Mary Tudor; released, 1555; wrote on math, astrology.
b. 1527 in London, England
d. December 1608 in Mortlake, England

Ruby Dee
(Mrs Ossie Davis; Ruby Ann Wallace)
American actress
• Starred in stage, movie productions of *Raisin in the Sun,* 1959, 1961.
b. October 27, 1924 in Cleveland, Ohio

Sandra Dee
(Alexandra Zuck)
American actress–singer
• Starred in *Gidget,* 1959; *Tammy Tell Me True,* 1961; was married to Bobby Darrin.
b. April 23, 1942 in Bayonne, New Jersey

Don DeFore
American actor
• Appeared in TV shows "Adventures of Ozzie and Harriet," 1952-58, "Hazel," 1961-65.
b. August 25, 1917 in Cedar Rapids, Iowa

Gloria DeHaven
American actress
• Co-star in 1940s musicals *Broadway Rythm; Three Little Words; Two Girls and a Sailor.*
b. July 23, 1925 in Los Angeles, California

Olivia DeHavilland
American actress
• Played Melanie in *Gone With the Wind,* 1939; won Oscars, 1946, 1949.
b. July 01, 1916 in Tokyo, Japan

John Forkum Dehner
American actor
• Films include *Thirty Seconds over Tokyo,* 1944; *Airplane II: The Sequel,* 1982.
b. November 23, 1915 in New York, New York

Albert Dekker
American actor
• Played mad scientists, other villains, 1937-69: *Dr. Cyclops,* 1940; *The Pretenders,* 1947.
b. December 2, 1905 in New York, New York
d. May 05, 1968 in Hollywood, California

Thomas Dekker
(Thomas Decker)
English dramatist
• Wrote comedy *Old Fortunates,* 1599; pamphlet *The Wonderful Yeare 1603,* described London during plague.
b. 1572 in London, England
d. 1632 in London, England

Dana Delany
American actress
• Plays nurse Colleen McMurphy on TV drama "China Beach," 1987–; won best actress Emmy, 1989.
b. March 13, 1957

Dino DeLaurentiis
Italian producer
• Best known films *Serpico,* 1974; *King Kong,* 1976; *Blue Velvet,* 1986.
b. August 08, 1919 in Torre Annunziata, Italy

Federico DeLaurentiis
Italian producer
• Son of Dino DeLaurentiis; produced film *King of the Gypsies,* 1978.
b. 1955
d. 1981 in Kvichak Bay, Alaska

Ronald Frederick Delderfield
English author–dramatist
• Novels include *Mr. Sermon,* 1963; plays include *And Then There Were None,* 1954.
b. February 12, 1912 in London, England
d. June 24, 1972 in Sidmouth, England

Floyd Dell
American editor–author–dramatist
• Spokesman for "Jazz Age," 1920s; most successful play comedy *Little Accident,* 1928; editor, *The Liberator,* 1918-24.
b. June 28, 1887 in Barry, Illinois
d. July 23, 1969 in Bethesda, Maryland

Gabriel Dell
(Gabriel del Vecchio)
American actor
• Member of group of actors called the Dead End Kids, from Broadway hit, *Dead End,* 1935; also called Bowery Boys, Eastside Kids in films.
b. October 07, 1919 in Barbados, British West Indies
d. July 03, 1988 in North Hollywood, California

Alain Delon
French actor
• Plays romantic gangster leads; films include *Is Paris Burning?,* 1966.
b. November 08, 1935 in Seceaux, France

Dolores DelRio
(Lolita Dolores Martinez Asunsolo Lopez Negrette)
Mexican actress
• Best known for *Journey into Fear,* 1942; *The Fugitive,* 1947.
b. August 03, 1905 in Durango, Mexico
d. April 11, 1983 in Newport Beach, California

Roy DelRuth
American director
• Directed over 100 features in 40 yr. career.
b. October 18, 1895 in Philadelphia, Pennsylvania
d. April 27, 1961 in Sherman Oaks, California

Dom DeLuise
American comedian–actor
• Appeared in films *Blazing Saddles,* 1974; *The End,* 1978.
b. August 01, 1933 in Brooklyn, New York

Jack DeManio
English broadcast journalist
• Host, BBC "Today" show, 1958-71.
b. January 26, 1914 in London, England

William Demarest
American actor
• Appeared in TV series "My Three Sons," 1967-73.
b. February 27, 1892 in Saint Paul, Minnesota
d. December 27, 1983 in Palm Springs, California

Agnes George DeMille
(Mrs Walter Foy Prude)
American dancer–author
• Choreographed musicals *Oklahoma,* 1943; *Carousel,* 1945; *Brigadoon,* 1947; won Tonys, 1947, 1962; niece of Cecil B.
b. September 18, 1905 in New York, New York

Cecil B(lount) DeMille
American director–producer
• With Jesse Lasky, Samuel Goldwyn, formed Jesse Lasky Feature Play Co., 1913; evolved into Paramount Studios; spectacular productions included *The Ten Commandments,* 1956.
b. August 12, 1881 in Ashfield, Massachusetts
d. January 21, 1959 in Hollywood, California

Jonathan Demme
American director
• Directed slices of Americana: *Citizens Band,* 1977; *Swing Shift,* 1984; *Silence of the Lambs,* 1991.
b. 1944 in Baldwin, New York

Rebecca DeMornay
American actress
• In films *Risky Business,* 1983; *The Trip to Bountiful,* 1985.
b. 1962 in Santa Rosa, California

Jacques Demy
French director
• Best known for film *The Umbrellas of Cherbourg,* 1963; only US film was *Model Shop,* 1971.
b. June 05, 1931 in Pont Chateau, France
d. October 27, 1990 in Paris, France

Judith Olivia Dench
English actress
• Stage performances include *Pack of Lies.*
b. December 12, 1934 in York, England

Catherine Deneuve
(Catherine Dorleac)
French actress
• Starred in *Mayerling,* 1968; featured in print, TV ads for Chanel No. 5; image used by French govt. to represent modern "Marianne," 1985.
b. October 22, 1943 in Paris, France

Robert DeNiro
American actor
• Won Oscar, 1981, for *Raging Bull;* other films include *The Deer Hunter,* 1979; *The Mission,* 1986; *Goodfellas* ,1990.
b. August 17, 1943 in New York, New York

Brian Dennehy
American actor
• Films include *Cocoon,* 1985; also known for many TV, stage appearances.
b. July 09, 1938 in Bridgeport, Connecticut

Richard Denning
(Louis Albert Denninger)
American actor
• Films include *Creature from the Black Lagoon,* 1954; *Mary, Queen of Scots,* 1971.
b. March 27, 1914 in Poughkeepsie, New York

Sandy Dennis
American actress
• Won Oscar, 1966, for *Who's Afraid of Virginia Woolf?*
b. April 27, 1937 in Hastings, Nebraska

Reginald Leigh Denny
(Reginald Leigh Daymore)
English actor
• Appeared in 200 films including *Leather Pushers* series, 1922-24.
b. November 2, 1891 in Richmond, England
d. June 16, 1967 in Surrey, England

Sam Denoff
American writer–producer
• Created, produced TV series "That Girl," 1967-71; won Emmys for "The Dick Van Dyke Show," 1964, 1966.
b. July 01, 1928 in Brooklyn, New York

Bob Denver
American actor
• Starred in "The Many Loves of Doby Gillis," 1959-63; "Gilligan's Island," 1964-67.
b. January 09, 1935 in New Rochelle, New York

Brian Russell DePalma
American director
• Inheritor of Alfred Hitchcock's crown "Master of the Macabre"; films include *Dressed to Kill,* 1980; *Body Double,* 1984; *The Untouchables,* 1987; *Bonfire of the Vanities,* 1991.
b. September 11, 1940 in Newark, New Jersey

Gerard Depardieu
French actor
• Leading roles as working-class character: *The Return of Martin Guerre*, 1983; *Danton*, 1983, *Green Card*, 1990.
b. December 27, 1948 in Chateauroux, France

Suzanne De Passe
American screenwriter–producer
• Wrote film *Lady Sings the Blues*, 1972; won Emmy for producing "Forever," 1983.

Bo Derek
(Mary Cathleen Collins; Mrs John Derek)
American actress
• Starred with Dudley Moore in *10*, 1979; fourth wife of John Derek.
b. November 2, 1956 in Long Beach, California

John Derek
(Derek Harris)
American actor
• Starred in *The Ten Commandments*, 1956; former wives Linda Evans, Ursula Andress.
b. August 12, 1926 in Hollywood, California

Maya Deren
American filmmaker
• Producer of avant-garde films; founded Creative Film Foundation, 1955.
b. April 29, 1917 in Kiev, Russia
d. October 13, 1961 in Queens, New York

Joe DeRita
(The Three Stooges; "Curly Joe")
American comedian
• Joined The Three Stooges, 1959.

Bruce MacLeish Dern
American actor
• Films include *Coming Home*, 1978; *That Championship Season*, 1982.
b. June 04, 1936 in Chicago, Illinois

Laura Elizabeth Dern
American actress
• Daughter of Bruce Dern; in 1985 film *Mask*, *Wild at Heart*, 1990.
b. February 1, 1967 in Santa Monica, California

Giuseppe DeSantis
Italian director
• Advocate of neo-realism in film.
b. February 11, 1917 in Fondi, Italy

Vittorio DeSica
Italian actor–director
• Won four Oscars as best director of foreign films.
b. July 07, 1901 in Scra, Italy
d. November 13, 1974 in Paris, France

William Desmond
American actor
• Silent films include *The Extra Girl*, 1923; talking films include *Phantom of the Opera*, 1943.
b. May 21, 1878 in Dublin, Ireland
d. November 03, 1949 in Los Angeles, California

Helen Deutsch
American screenwriter–lyricist
• Her screenplays include *National Velvet*, 1944; *Lili*, 1953.
b. March 21, 1906 in New York, New York

William Devane
American actor
• Star of TV series "Knots Landing," 1983–.
b. September 05, 1937 in Albany, New York

Andy Devine
(Jeremiah Schwartz)
American actor
• Comic sidekick for Roy Rogers; squeaky-voiced character actor of over 300 films.
b. October 07, 1905 in Flagstaff, Arizona
d. February 18, 1977 in Orange, California

Danny (Daniel Michael) DeVito
American actor–director
• Played Louie DePalma on TV comedy "Taxi," 1980-83; won Emmy, 1981; starred in and directed *Throw Momma from the Train*, 1987; *War of the Roses*, 1989.
b. November 17, 1944 in Neptune, New Jersey

Patrick Dewaere
(Patrick Maurin)
French actor
• Films include *Beau Pere*, 1981; *Get Out Your Hankerchiefs*, 1978.
b. January 26, 1947 in Saint-Brieuc, France
d. July 16, 1982 in Paris, France

Colleen Dewhurst
Canadian actress
• Active on stage, screen, TV since mid-1950s; won Tonys for *All the Way Home*, 1962; *Moon for the Misbegotten*, 1974.
b. June 03, 1926 in Montreal, Quebec

Joyce DeWitt
American actress
• Played Janet Wood on TV series "Three's Company."
b. April 23, 1949 in Wheeling, West Virginia

John Dexter
English director
• Stage director, best known for productions of *Equus* and *M. Butterfly*.
b. August 02, 1925 in Derby, England
d. March 23, 1990 in London, England

Susan Hallock Dey
(Susan Smith)
American actress–model
• TV shows include "The Partridge Family," 1970-74; "L.A. Law," 1986–.
b. December 1, 1952 in Pekin, Illinois

Cliff De Young
American actor
• Starred in TV movie *Sunshine*, 1973; theatrical films include *The Hunger*, 1983.
b. February 12, 1945 in Inglewood, California

I(sidore) A L Diamond
American screenwriter
• Films include *Some Like It Hot*, 1959; Oscar-winning *The Apartment*, 1960.
b. June 27, 1920 in Unghani, Romania
d. April 21, 1988 in Beverly Hills, California

Nancy Hanschman Dickerson
American broadcast journalist
• Correspondent, NBC News, 1960-70; news analyst on TV's "Inside Washington" since 1971; heads Television Corp., 1980–.
b. January 19, 1930 in Wauwatosa, Wisconsin

Angie Dickinson
(Angeline Brown)
American actress
• Starred in TV series "Policewoman," 1974-78; film *Dressed to Kill*, 1980.
b. September 3, 1931 in Kulm, North Dakota

Joan Didion
American author–screenwriter
• Writings include *Democracy*, 1984; cowrote film *A Star is Born*, 1976.
b. December 05, 1934 in Sacramento, California

William Dieterle
American director
• Best known for *The Hunchback of Notre Dame*, 1939, *A Portrait of Jennie*, 1948.
b. July 15, 1893 in Ludwigshafen, Germany
d. December 09, 1972 in Ottobrunn, Germany (West)

Marlene Dietrich
(Maria Magdalene von Losch)
American actress–singer
• Had glamorous roles in films *The Blue Angel*, 1930; *Destry Rides Again*, 1939; known for sultry looks, long legs.
b. December 27, 1901 in Berlin, Germany

Dudley Digges
Irish actor
• With Theatre Guild, 1919-30, produced *Pygmalion; Doctor's Dilemma*.
b. June 09, 1880 in Dublin, Ireland
d. October 24, 1947 in New York, New York

Barry Charles Diller
American film executive
• CEO, Twentieth Century Fox Film Corp., 1984–; Fox, Inc., 1985–.
b. February 02, 1942 in San Francisco, California

Phyllis Diller
(Phyllis Driver)
American comedienne
• Known for outrageous appearance, stories about husband, Fang; is also a concert pianist.
b. July 17, 1917 in Lima, Ohio

Bradford Dillman
American actor
• Appeared in *The Way We Were*, 1973.
b. April 13, 1930 in San Francisco, California

Kevin Dillon
American actor
• Films include *Platoon*, 1986; brother of Matt.
b. August 19, 1967 in New Rochelle, New York

Matt Dillon
American actor
• Played bully in *My Bodyguard*, 1980; starred in *Tex*, 1982; *Drugstore Cowboy*, 1989.
b. February 18, 1964 in New Rochelle, New York

Melinda Dillon
American actress
• Best known for *Absence of Malice*, 1981.
b. October 31, 1939 in Hope, Arkansas

Mia Dillon
American actress
• Nominated for Tony for *Crimes of the Heart*, 1982.
b. July 09, 1955 in Colorado Springs, Colorado

Roy E(dward) Disney
American film executive
• VP, Walt Disney Productions, 1970s; pres., Roy E Disney Productions, 1978–; son of Roy Oliver.
b. January 1, 1930 in Los Angeles, California

Roy O(liver) Disney
American film executive
• Pres., chm. of board, Walt Disney Productions; co-founder of entertainment empire with brother Walt, 1923.
b. 1893 in Chicago, Illinois
d. December 2, 1971 in Burbank, California

Richard Dix
(Ernest Carlton Brimmer)
American actor
• Oscar nominee for *Cimarron*, 1931; in DeMille's *The Ten Commandments*, 1928.
b. July 18, 1894 in Saint Paul, Minnesota
d. September 2, 1949 in Los Angeles, California

Ivan Dixon
American actor–director
• Played Cpl. Kinchloe on TV comedy "Hogan's Heroes," 1965-70; has directed many TV shows.
b. April 06, 1931 in New York, New York

Jean Dixon
(Marie Jacques)
American actress
• Broadway, film comedienne for 30 yrs; starred in *Gang's All Here*, 1959.
b. July 14, 1894 in Waterbury, Connecticut
d. February 12, 1981 in New York, New York

Edward Dmytryk
(The Hollywood Ten)
American director
• Spent one yr. in jail for communist affiliations, 1947; directed *The Caine Mutiny*, 1954.
b. September 04, 1908 in Grand Forks, British Columbia

Kevin Dobson
American actor
• Plays Mac Mackenzie on TV series "Knots Landing," 1982–.
b. March 18, 1944 in Jackson Heights, New York

Lloyd Allen Dobyns, Jr
American broadcast journalist
• NBC News correspondent, 1972-86.
b. March 12, 1936 in Newport News, Virginia

Thomas Doggett
Irish actor
• Popular comedian; founded sculling prize, Doggett's Coat and Badge, 1716, to commemorate accession of George I; rowed annually on Thames.
b. 1670 in Dublin, Ireland
d. 1721

Sir Anton Dolin
(Sydney Francis Patrick Chippendall Healey-Kay)
English dancer–choreographer
• Leading authority on classical ballet who was co-founder, principal dancer, London's Festival Ballet, 1950-61.
b. July 27, 1904 in Slinfold, England
d. November 25, 1983 in Paris, France

Elinor Donahue
American actress
• Played Betty Anderson in TV series "Father Knows Best," 1954-62.
b. April 19, 1937 in Tacoma, Washington

Phil(ip John) Donahue
American TV personality
• Host of talk show "Donahue," 1967–; won Emmys, 1977, 1979; wrote *Donahue: My Own Story*, 1980.
b. December 21, 1935 in Cleveland, Ohio

Troy Donahue
(Merle Johnson Jr)
American actor
• Starred in TV series "Hawaiian Eye," 1962-63; "Surfside Six," 1960-62.
b. January 27, 1936 in New York, New York

James Donald
Scottish actor
• Best known for films *Bridge on the River Kwai*, 1957; *The Great Escape*, 1963.
b. May 18, 1917 in Aberdeen, Scotland

Sam(uel Andrew) Donaldson
American broadcast journalist
• ABC News White House correspondent, known as one of TV's most aggressive interviewers.
b. March 11, 1934 in El Paso, Texas

Robert Donat
English actor
• Won Oscar for *Goodbye, Mr. Chips*, 1939.
b. March 18, 1905 in Manchester, England
d. June 09, 1958 in London, England

Stanley Donen
American director
• Best known for *Arabesque*, 1966.
b. April 13, 1924 in Columbia, South Carolina

Brian Donlevy
American actor
• Best known for tough-guy roles in *Beau Geste*, 1939; *The Great McGinty*, 1940.
b. February 09, 1899 in Portadown, Ireland
d. April 05, 1972 in Woodland Hills, California

Jeff (Jean Marie) Donnell
American actress
• Best known for *Gidget Goes Hawaiian,* 1961; *Gidget Goes to Rome,* 1962.
b. July 1, 1921 in South Windham, Maine
d. April 11, 1988 in Hollywood, California

Ruth Donnelly
American actress
• Films include *Mr. Deeds Goes to Town; The Bells of St. Mary's.*
b. May 17, 1896 in Trenton, New Jersey
d. November 17, 1982 in New York, New York

Jack Donohue
American actor–dancer–director
• Best known for *Marriage on the Rocks,* 1965; *Assault on a Queen,* 1966.
b. November 03, 1912 in New York, New York
d. March 27, 1984 in Los Angeles, California

King Donovan
American actor
• Films include *The Enforcer,* 1951; on Broadway in *On the Twentieth Century,* 1986.
b. January 25, 1918 in New York, New York
d. June 3, 1987 in Branford, Connecticut

James Montgomery Doohan
Canadian actor
• Played "Scotty" on "Star Trek," 1966-69; films *Star Trek: The Movie; Star Trek II; Star Trek III.*
b. March 03, 1920 in Vancouver, British Columbia

Rae (Rachel Rice) Dooley
Scottish actress
• Starred with husband Eddie Dowling in Ziegfeld Follies, specialized in bratty kid parts.
b. October 3, 1896 in Glasgow, Scotland
d. January 28, 1984 in East Hampton, New York

Francoise Dorleac
French actress
• Sister of Catherine Deneuve; starred together in *The Young Girls of Rochefort,* 1967.
b. March 21, 1942 in Paris, France
d. June 26, 1967 in Nice, France

Diana Dors
(Diana Fluck)
English actress
• British sex symbol, compared to Marilyn Monroe.
b. October 23, 1931 in Swindon, England
d. May 04, 1984 in New Windsor, England

Fifi D'Orsay
(Yvonne Lussier; "The French Bombshell")
Canadian actress
• Starred in *They Had to See Paris,* 1929; trademark was "Ello beeg boy!"
b. April 16, 1904 in Montreal, Quebec
d. December 02, 1983 in Woodland Hills, California

Bob (Robert Charles) Dotson
American broadcast journalist
• Correspondent, NBC News since 1979.
b. October 03, 1946 in Saint Louis, Missouri

Felia Doubrovska
(Felizata Dluzhnevska; Mrs Pierre Vladimiroff)
Russian dancer
• Known for leading roles in Balanchine ballets; taught at School of American Ballet, NYC, 30 yrs.
b. 1896 in Saint Petersburg, Russia
d. September 18, 1981 in New York, New York

Donna Douglas
(Doris Smith)
American actress
• Played Elly May Clampett in TV series "The Beverly Hillbillies," 1962-71.
b. September 26, 1939 in Baywood, Louisiana

Kirk Douglas
(Issur Danielovich Demsky)
American actor
• Has appeared in over 50 films including *Lust for Life,* 1956; *Spartacus,* 1960; father of actor Michael. Received American Film Institute's Life Achievement Award, 1991.
b. December 09, 1916 in Amsterdam, New York

Melvyn Douglas
(Melvin Hesselberg)
American actor
• 40-yr. film career highlighted by Oscars for *Hud,* 1963; *Being There,* 1979.
b. April 05, 1901 in Macon, Georgia
d. August 04, 1981 in New York, New York

Michael Kirk Douglas
American actor–producer
• Won best producer Oscar for *One Flew over the Cuckoo's Nest,* 1975, best actor Oscar for *Wall Street,* 1988; son of Kirk.
b. September 25, 1944 in New Brunswick, New Jersey

Mike Douglas
(Michael Delaney Dowd Jr)
American TV personality–singer
• Hosted "The Mike Douglas Show," 1960s-70s; has won four Emmys.
b. August 11, 1925 in Chicago, Illinois

Paul Douglas
American actor
• 1,024 performances on Broadway in *Born Yesterday.*
b. November 04, 1907 in Philadelphia, Pennsylvania
d. September 11, 1959 in Hollywood, California

Brad Dourif
American actor
• Received Oscar nomination for *One Flew Over the Cuckoo's Nest,* 1975.
b. March 18, 1950 in Huntington, West Virginia

Suzanne Theodore Vaillande Douvillier
American dancer
• First celebrated American ballerina, 1792; first woman choreographer.
b. September 28, 1778 in Dole, France
d. August 3, 1826 in New Orleans, Louisiana

Alexander Dovzhenko
Ukrainian director
• Best known for silent films: *Zvenigora, Earth,*
b. September 11, 1894 in Sosnytsia, Ukraine
d. November 25, 1956

Tony Dow
American actor
• Played Wally Cleaver on "Leave It to Beaver," 1957-63.
b. April 13, 1945 in Hollywood, California

Anthony James Dowell
English dancer
• With Royal Ballet since 1961; assoc. director, 1985–.
b. February 16, 1943 in London, England

Eddie (Edward) Dowling
(Joseph Nelson Goucher)
American actor–dramatist–producer
• Won four NY Drama Critics awards; won Pulitzer for *Time of Your Life,* 1940.
b. December 11, 1894 in Woonsocket, Rhode Island
d. February 18, 1976 in Smithfield, Rhode Island

Lesley-Anne Down
English actress
• Starred in PBS series "Upstairs, Downstairs"; mini-series "North and South," 1985-86.
b. March 17, 1954 in London, England

Morton Downey, Jr (Sean Morton, Jr)
American TV personality
• Hosted talk show bearing his name, 1987-89; known for confrontational, controversial format.
b. 1932

Robert Downey
American director
• Director of cult-classic *Putney Swope*, 1969; *Greaser's Palace*, 1972; father of Robert.
b. June 1936

Robert Downey, Jr
American actor
• Regular on TV series "Saturday Night Live," 1985-86; starred in film *Chances Are*, 1989; *Air America*, 1990.
b. April 04, 1965 in New York, New York

Hugh (Malcolm) Downs
American TV personality
• Host of ABC newsmagazine show "20/20."
b. February 14, 1921 in Akron, Ohio

Johnny Downs
American actor
• Child actor in *Our Gang* series; juvenile lead in 1930s musicals.
b. October 1, 1913 in New York, New York

David Fitzgerald Doyle
American actor
• Played Bosley in TV series "Charlie's Angels," 1976-81.
b. December 01, 1929 in Omaha, Nebraska

Betsy Drake
American actress
• Married to Cary Grant, 1949-59; films include *Room for One More*, 1952.
b. September 11, 1923 in Paris, France

Tom Drake
(Alfred Alderdice)
American actor
• Appeared in 1940s musicals including *Meet Me in St. Louis*, 1944.
b. August 05, 1918 in New York, New York
d. August 11, 1982 in Torrance, California

Louise Dresser
(Louise Kerlin)
American actress
• Starred with Rudolph Valentino in *The Eagle*, 1925; as Al Jolson's mother in *Mammy*, 1930.
b. October 05, 1882 in Evansville, Indiana
d. April 24, 1965 in Woodland Hills, California

Marie Dressler
(Leila Marie Koerber)
Canadian actress
• Won Oscar for *Min and Bill*, 1930, with Wallace Beery.
b. November 09, 1869 in Cobourg, Ontario
d. July 28, 1934 in Santa Barbara, California

Louisa Lane Drew
(Mrs John Drew)
English actress
• Managed Philadelphia's Arch Street Theatre, 1860-92.
b. January 1, 1820 in London, England
d. August 31, 1897 in Larchmont, New York

Carl Theodore Dreyer
Danish director
• Best known for *Day of Wrath; Passion of Joan of Arc; The Word.*
b. February 03, 1889 in Copenhagen, Denmark
d. March 28, 1968 in Copenhagen, Denmark

Richard Stephan Dreyfuss
American actor
• Starred in films *American Graffiti*, 1973, *Jaws*, 1975, *Moon over Parador*, 1988; won Oscar for *The Goodbye Girl*, 1977.
b. October 29, 1947 in Brooklyn, New York

Bobby Driscoll
American actor
• Won special Oscar as outstanding juvenile actor, 1949; career faltered in teens; allegedly died from drug overdose.
b. March 03, 1937 in Cedar Rapids, Iowa
d. March 3, 1968 in New York, New York

Joanne Dru
(Letitia LaCock)
American actress
• Starred in Westerns *Red River*, 1948; *She Wore a Yellow Ribbon*, 1949; sister of Peter Marshall.
b. January 31, 1923 in Logan, West Virginia

James Drury
American actor
• Title star of TV's "The Virginian," 1962-71.
b. April 18, 1934 in New York, New York

Fred (John Frederick) Dryer
American football player–actor
• Defensive end, NY Giants, 1969-71, LA Rams, 1972-80; plays title role in TV series, "Hunter," 1984–.
b. July 06, 1946 in Hawthorne, California

Jean Francois Ducis
French dramatist–poet
• Adapted Shakespeare for French stage so drastically that only title remained.
b. August 22, 1733 in Versailles, France
d. March 31, 1816 in Versailles, France

Howard Duff
American actor
• Tough-guy actor; starred in TV series "Mr. Adams and Eve," 1957-58; "Felony Squad," 1966-69.
b. November 24, 1917 in Bremerton, Washington
d. July 09, 1990 in Santa Barbara, California

Julia Duffy
American actress
• Played Stephanie Vander Kellan Harris on TV series "Newhart," 1983-90.
b. June 27, 1951 in Saint Paul, Minnesota

Patrick Duffy
American actor
• Plays Bobby Ewing on TV series "Dallas," 1978–.
b. March 17, 1949 in Townsend, Montana

Andrew Duggan
American actor
• Character actor on stage, screen, TV; starred in TV series "Twelve O'Clock High," 1965-67.
b. December 28, 1923 in Franklin, Indiana
d. May 15, 1988 in Los Angeles, California

Olympia Dukakis
American actress
• Won Oscar for *Moonstruck*, 1988; during stage career, won Obie for *A Man's a Man*, 1963; cousin of Michael.
b. June 2, 1931 in Lowell, Massachusetts

Patty Duke
(Mrs John Astin; Anna Marie Patricia Duke)
American actress
• Won Oscar, 1963, Emmy, 1979, for *The Miracle Worker*, playing different roles.
b. December 14, 1946 in New York, New York

Dr (James Henry) Duke Red
American TV personality
• Host of PBS medical show "BodyWatch."
b. 1929

David Dukes
American actor
• Appeared in TV mini-series "The Winds of War," 1983; film *Without a Trace*, 1983.
b. June 06, 1945 in San Francisco, California

Keir Dullea
American actor
• Appeared in *David and Lisa*, 1963; *2001: A Space Odyssey*, 1968.
b. May 3, 1936 in Cleveland, Ohio

Alexandre Dumas
(Dumas Fils)
French dramatist
• Play *La Dame aux Camelias*, 1852, basis for Verdi's opera, *La Traviata*.
b. July 27, 1824 in Paris, France
d. November 27, 1895 in Paris, France

Sir Gerald Hubert DuMaurier
English producer–actor
• Greatest success in *Raffles*, 1906; made hero out of villian; father of Daphne DuMaurier.
b. March 26, 1873 in London, England
d. April 11, 1934 in London, England

Margaret Dumont
(Margaret Baker)
American actress
• Stately matron in seven Marx Brothers films: *Animal Crackers*, 1930; *A Night at the Opera*, 1935.
b. October 2, 1889 in New York, New York
d. March 06, 1965 in Los Angeles, California

Faye (Dorothy Faye) Dunaway
American actress
• Starred in *Bonnie and Clyde*, 1967; *Barfly*, 1987; won Oscar, 1976, for *Network*, 1976.
b. January 14, 1941 in Bascom, Florida

Augustin Duncan
American actor–producer
• Brother of Isadora Duncan; co-founder, NY Theatre Guild.
b. April 12, 1873 in San Francisco, California
d. February 2, 1954 in New York, New York

Isadora Duncan
American dancer
• Revolutionized interpretative dancing; wed to Sergei Yesenin; strangled by scarf in freakish car accident.
b. May 27, 1878 in San Francisco, California
d. September 14, 1927 in Nice, France

Sandy Duncan
American actress
• Starred on Broadway as Peter Pan, 1980; replaced Valerie Harper in TV comedy "The Hogan Family," 1987–.
b. February 2, 1946 in Henderson, Texas

Katherine Dunham
American dancer–choreographer
• First to organize professional black dance troupe; founded own dance school, 1945.
b. June 22, 1910 in Chicago, Illinois

Frank Dunlop
English director
• Founder, director of Young Vic Theatre, 1969.
b. February 15, 1927 in Leeds, England

James Howard Dunn
American actor
• Won Oscar for *A Tree Grows in Brooklyn*, 1945.
b. November 02, 1905 in New York, New York
d. September 03, 1967 in Santa Monica, California

Michael Dunn
(Gary Neil Miller)
American actor
• Dwarf actor whose movie credits include *Ship of Fools*, 1965; appeared in TV series "Wild, Wild West," 1965-70.
b. October 2, 1934 in Shattuck, Oklahoma
d. August 29, 1973 in London, England

Nora Dunn
American comedienne
• Member, "Saturday Night Live" TV series cast, 1984–1990; best known for character, Pat Stevens, and for boycotting Andrew Dice Clay show along with Sinead O'Connor.
b. 1951

Griffin Dunne
American actor–producer
• Produced films *Baby It's You*, 1982; *After Hours*, 1985.
b. June 08, 1955 in New York, New York

Irene Marie Dunne
American actress
• Five-time Oscar nominee; best known for lead in *I Remember Mama*, 1948.
b. December 2, 1904 in Louisville, Kentucky
d. September 04, 1990 in Los Angeles, California

Joseph Dunninger
American astrologer–magician
• Performed telepathic readings on radio, TV.
b. April 28, 1896 in New York, New York
d. March 09, 1975 in Cliffside Park, New Jersey

Mildred Dunnock
American actress
• Oscar nominee for *Death of a Salesman*, 1952, which she also played on Broadway, TV.
b. January 25, 1906 in Baltimore, Maryland

Baron Edward J M Plunkett Dunsany
(Lord Dunsany)
Irish author–dramatist
• Wrote books, plays of fantasy, myth; associated with Abbey Theatre.
b. July 24, 1878 in London, England
d. October 25, 1957 in Dublin, Ireland

Diane Dupuy
Canadian puppeteer
• Founded Famous People Players, puppet troupe largely comprised of mentally handicapped adults.
b. 1948 in Hamilton, Ontario

Jimmy (James Francis) Durante
American entertainer–comedian
• Comedian, singer for over 60 years; nose insured for $100,000 with Lloyd's of London.
b. February 1, 1893 in New York, New York
d. January 29, 1980 in Santa Monica, California

Deanna Durbin
Canadian actress
• Shared special Oscar with Mickey Rooney, 1938; teenage star, 1930s-40s.
b. December 04, 1921 in Winnipeg, Manitoba

Charles Durning
American actor
• Co-starred in *Tootsie*, 1982.
b. February 28, 1923 in Highland Falls, New York

Dan Duryea
American actor
• Character actor, often villain; films include *The Little Foxes*, 1941.
b. January 23, 1907 in White Plains, New York
d. June 07, 1968 in Los Angeles, California

Eleanora Duse
Italian actress
• Famed tragedienne; made NYC debut, 1893; great rival of Bernhardt.
b. 1859 in Vigerano, Italy
d. April 23, 1924 in Pittsburgh, Pennsylvania

Robert Selden Duvall
American actor
• Best known for *Tender Mercies*, 1983; *The Great Santini*, 1980.
b. January 05, 1931 in San Diego, California

Shelley Duvall
American actress
• Appeared in films *Nashville*, 1975; *Popeye*, 1979.
b. July 07, 1949 in Houston, Texas

Julien Duvivier
French director
• Best known for films *Pepe le Moko*; *Maria Chapdelaine*.
b. October 08, 1896 in Lille, France
d. October 29, 1967 in Paris, France

Ann Dvorak
American actress
• Starred in *Scarface*, 1932.
b. August 02, 1912 in New York, New York
d. December 1, 1979 in Honolulu, Hawaii

Allan Dwan
(Joseph Aloysius Dwan)
Canadian director
• Directed estimated 1,850 films, 1909-61.
b. April 03, 1885 in Toronto, Ontario
d. December 21, 1981 in Woodland Hills, California

Richard A(llan) Dysart
American actor
• Plays Leland McKensie on TV series "L.A. Law," 1986–; films include *The Terminal Man,* 1974.
b. March 3, 1929 in Augusta, Maine

Carol Eastman
(Adrien Joyce pseud)
American screenwriter
• Won Oscar for screenplay *Five Easy Pieces,* 1970.

Clint Eastwood
American actor
• Starred in TV series "Rawhide," 1959-66; movie *Dirty Harry,* 1971; mayor of Carmel, CA, 1986-88.
b. May 31, 1930 in San Francisco, California

Mary Eaton
American actress
• In Ziegfeld Follies, 1920-22; starred in *Five O'Clock Girl,* 1927.
b. 1901 in Norfolk, Virginia
d. October 1, 1948 in Hollywood, California

Shirley Eaton
English actress
• Played the girl painted gold in James Bond film *Goldfinger,* 1964.
b. 1936 in London, England

Buddy Ebsen
(Christian Rudolf Ebson Jr)
American actor
• Starred in TV series "The Beverly Hillbillies," 1962-71; "Barnaby Jones," 1973-79.
b. April 02, 1908 in Belleville, Illinois

Jose Echegaray y Eizaguirre
Spanish dramatist
• Shared Nobel Prize for Literature, 1904.
b. April 19, 1831 in Madrid, Spain
d. September 15, 1916 in Madrid, Spain

William Joseph Eckart
American designer–producer
• Designed costumes for films *The Pajama Game,* 1957; *The Night They Raided Minsky's,* 1968.
b. October 21, 1920 in New Iberia, Louisiana

George Eckstein
American writer
• Wrote TV shows "The Untouchables," 1959-63; "Gunsmoke," 1955-75; "Dr. Kildare," 1961-66.
b. May 03, 1928 in Los Angeles, California

Herb Edelman
American actor
• In TV series "The Good Guys," 1968-70; film *The Way We Were,* 1977.
b. November 05, 1933 in Brooklyn, New York

Barbara Eden
(Barbara Jean Huffman)
American actress
• Played title role in TV comedy "I Dream of Jeannie," 1965-70.
b. August 23, 1934 in Tucson, Arizona

David Edgar
English dramatist
• Prolific stage, TV playwright who stresses political, social themes: *Death Story,* 1972.
b. February 26, 1948 in Birmingham, England

Richard Edlund
American special effects technician
• Won Oscars for visual effects in three *Star Wars* films, 1977, 1980, 1983.
b. December 06, 1940 in Fargo, North Dakota

Alan Edwards
American actor
• Films include *The White Sister,* 1933; also appeared in silent films.
b. June 03, 1900 in New York, New York
d. May 08, 1954 in Los Angeles, California

Blake Edwards
(William Blake McEdwards)
American producer–director
• Produced *Pink Panther* film series; husband of Julie Andrews.
b. July 26, 1922 in Tulsa, Oklahoma

Cliff Edwards
American singer–actor
• Played Ukelele Ike in several films; played sidekick, Harmony, in many Westerns; voice of Jiminy Cricket in *Pinocchio,* 1940.
b. July 14, 1895 in Hannibal, Missouri
d. July 17, 1971 in Hollywood, California

Douglas Edwards
American broadcast journalist
• CBS News correspondent, 1942-88; anchored network TVs first nightly news show, 1948; won Peabody, 1955.
b. July 14, 1917 in Ada, Oklahoma
d. October 13, 1990 in Sarasota, Florida

Ralph Livingstone Edwards
American producer–TV personality
• Created, produced, hosted radio, TV series "This Is Your Life," 1940s-70s; exec. producer, "The People's Court," 1980s.
b. June 13, 1913 in Merino, Colorado

Vince Edwards
(Vincent Edward Zoino)
American actor
• Starred in TV series "Ben Casey," 1961-66.
b. July 07, 1928 in Brooklyn, New York

Marshall Efron
American comedian–actor–author
• Best known for comedy TV series "The Great American Dream Machine."
b. 1938

Richard Egan
American actor
• Once considered film successor to Clark Gable, but roles confined to action/Western movies.
b. July 29, 1923 in San Francisco, California
d. July 2, 1987 in Santa Monica, California

Samantha Eggar
English actress
• Won Cannes Film Festival award for *The Collector,* 1965.
b. March 05, 1940 in Hampstead, England

Jill Eikenberry
(Mrs Michael Tucker)
American actress
• Plays Ann Kelsey on TV series "LA Law," 1986–.
b. January 21, 1947 in New Haven, Connecticut

Bob Einstein
American writer–producer
• Won Emmys for writing "The Smothers Brothers Show," 1969; producing "Van Dyke and Company," 1977.
b. November 2, 1940 in Los Angeles, California

Sergei Mikhailovich Eisenstein
Russian director
• Films frequently re-edited to conform to political policy; *October; Battleship Potemkin.*
b. January 23, 1898 in Riga, Russia
d. February 1, 1948 in Moscow, U.S.S.R.

Anita Ekberg
Swedish actress
• Films include *La Dolce Vita; Boccaccio '70.*
b. September 29, 1931 in Malmo, Sweden

Konrad Ekhof
German actor–director
• A founder of the modern German theater; promoted realism.
b. August 12, 1720 in Hamburg, Germany
d. June 16, 1778 in Gotha, Germany

Britt Ekland
Swedish actress
• Married Peter Sellers, 1963-68; starred in James Bond film *Man with the the Golden Gun,* 1974.
b. October 06, 1942 in Stockholm, Sweden

Jack Elam
American actor
• Appeared in over 100 films: *The Way West,* 1967; *Support Your Local Sheriff,* 1969.
b. November 13, 1916 in Phoenix, Arizona

Florence Eldridge
(Mrs Fredric March)
American actress
• Broadway, film star; appeared with husband in films *Studio Murder Mystery,* 1929; *Les Miserables,* 1935.
b. September 05, 1901 in New York, New York
d. August 01, 1988 in Santa Barbara, California

Hector Elizondo
American actor
• In TV shows "Popi," 1976; "Casablanca," 1983; film *American Gigolo,* 1980.
b. December 22, 1936 in New York, New York

Hillard Elkins
American producer
• Films include *A Doll's House,* 1972; stage productions include *Streetcar Named Desire,* 1974.
b. October 18, 1929 in New York, New York

Linda Ellerbee
American broadcast journalist
• With NBC News, 1978-86, ABC News, 1986–.
b. August 15, 1944 in Bryan, Texas

Bob (Robert B) Elliott
(Bob and Ray)
American comedian
• Member of comedy team known for satire, ad-libbing; won Peabody Award, 1952, 1957. Currently stars with son Chris in television's "Get a Life."
b. March 26, 1923 in Boston, Massachusetts

Denholm Mitchell Elliott
English actor
• Supporting actor in *Alfie,* 1966; *Raiders of the Lost Ark,* 1981.
b. May 31, 1922 in London, England

Robin Ellis
English actor
• Lead role in BBC TV series "Poldark," shown on PBS.
b. 1944 in London, England

Fanny Elssler
Austrian dancer
• Introduced folk dancing, especially the tarantella, into theater; made fortune in US tour, 1840s.
b. June 23, 1810 in Vienna, Austria
d. November 27, 1884 in Vienna, Austria

Julian Eltinge
(William Dalton)
American actor
• Female impersonator in plays *The Crinoline Girl; The Fascinating Widow.*
b. May 14, 1883
d. March 07, 1941 in New York, New York

Ron Ely
(Ronald Pierce)
American actor
• Screen's 15th Tarzan who starred in two films, 1970; in TV series, 1968-69.
b. June 21, 1938 in Hereford, Texas

Faye Margaret Emerson
American actress
• Hosted late night talk show "Faye Emerson's Wonderful Town," 1950s; once wed to Elliott Roosevelt, "Skitch" Henderson.
b. July 08, 1917 in Elizabeth, Louisiana
d. March 09, 1983 in Majorca, Spain

Hope Emerson
American actress
• Body measurements (6'2", 200 lbs) exploited in films *Caged; Adam's Rib.*
b. October 29, 1898 in Hawarden, Iowa
d. April 25, 1960 in Hollywood, California

Georgia Bright Engel
American actress
• Played Georgette on TV series "The Mary Tyler Moore Show," 1972-77.
b. July 28, 1948 in Washington, District of Columbia

Robert Englund
American actor
• Plays Freddy Krueger in *Nightmare on Elm Street* films, 1984–.
b. June 06, 1948 in Hollywood, California

Nora Ephron
American author–screenwriter
• Wrote best-seller *Heartburn,* 1983, filmed, 1986; received Oscar nominations for screenplay writing of films *Silkwood,* 1984, *When Harry Met Sally,* 1989. Once married to Carl Bernstein.
b. May 19, 1941

Jack Epps, Jr
American screenwriter
• With Jim Cash, wrote screenplays for 1986 films *Top Gun, Legal Eagles.*
b. 1949 in Detroit, Michigan

Philip G Epstein
American screenwriter–dramatist
• Co-wrote film classics *Casablanca,* 1942; *Arsenic and Old Lace,* 1944.
b. August 22, 1909 in New York, New York
d. February 07, 1952 in Los Angeles, California

Leif Erickson
(William Wycliffe Anderson)
American singer–actor
• Best known for role of Big Jon Cannon on TV series "The High Chaparral."
b. October 27, 1911 in Alameda, California
d. January 3, 1986 in Pensacola, Florida

Paul Karl Friedrich Ernst
German author–critic–dramatist
• Dramas include *Brunhild,* 1909; novels include *Die Selige Insel,* 1909.
b. March 07, 1866 in Elbingerode, Germany
d. May 13, 1933 in Saint Georgen, Germany

Leon Errol
Australian actor
• Comedian, dancer; appeared in 60 films, often as hen-pecked husband.
b. July 03, 1881 in Sydney, Australia
d. October 12, 1951 in Los Angeles, California

Stuart Erwin
American comedian–actor
• Roles in films were usually the hero's friend, Mr. Average: *He Hired the Boss,* 1943.
b. February 14, 1902 in Squaw Valley, California
d. December 21, 1967 in Beverly Hills, California

Jill Esmond
English actress
• Married to Lawrence Olivier, 1930-40; films include *First Lady; Thirteen Women.*
b. January 26, 1908 in London, England
d. July 28, 1990 in Wimbledon, England

Emilio Estevez
American actor
• Son of actor Martin Sheen; films include *The Breakfast Club,* 1985; *St. Elmo's Fire,* 1985.
b. May 12, 1962 in New York, New York

Erik (Henry Enrique) Estrada
American actor
• Played Frank "Ponch" Poncherello on TV series "CHiPS," 1977-83.
b. March 16, 1949 in New York, New York

Till Eulenspiegel
(Tyll Ulenspiegel; Tyll Howleglas; Owlglass)
German clown
• Peasant known for legendary pranks on tradesmen, townspeople throughout Germany; translation of tales first printed in England, 1560.
b. 1290 in Kheitlingen, Germany
d. 1350 in Lubeck, Germany

Euripides
Greek dramatist
• Wrote about 90 tragedies, including *Medea; Electra.*
b. September 23, 480 in Salamis, Greece
d. 406BC in Pella, Greece

Bob (Robert) Evans
American actor–producer
• Films include *The Godfather*, 1972; *Chinatown*, 1974; former husband of Ali McGraw, Phyllis George.
b. June 29, 1930 in New York, New York

Dale Evans
(Mrs Roy Rogers; Frances Smith)
American actress–evangelist
• Starred with husband in TV series "The Roy Rogers Show," 1951-64.
b. October 31, 1912 in Uvalde, Texas

Dame Edith Mary Booth Evans
English actress
• Received Oscar nominations for *Chalk Garden*, 1964; *Tom Jones*, 1963; *The Whispers*, 1966.
b. February 08, 1888 in London, England
d. October 14, 1976 in Kent, England

Linda Evans
(Linda Evenstad)
American actress
• Played Krystle Carrington on TV soap opera "Dynasty," 1981-89; former wife of John Derek.
b. November 18, 1942 in Hartford, Connecticut

Maurice Evans
American actor–manager
• Played Samantha's father on TV's "Bewitched," 1964-72; starred in *Hamlet*, 1940s.
b. June 03, 1901 in Dorchester, England
d. March 12, 1989 in Rottingdean, England

Judith Evelyn
American actress
• Films include *Rear Window*, 1954; *Giant*, 1956; *Brothers Karamazov*, 1958.
b. 1913 in Seneca, South Dakota
d. May 07, 1967 in New York, New York

Chad Everett
(Raymon Lee Cramton)
American actor
• Last performer signed to long-term Hollywood contract when he joined MGM, 1964; played Dr. Joe Gannon on TV series "Medical Center," 1969-76.
b. June 11, 1937 in South Bend, Indiana

Greg(ory Ralph) Evigan
American actor
• Starred in TV series "BJ and the Bear," 1979-81, "My Two Dads," 1987-90.
b. October 14, 1953 in South Amboy, New Jersey

Tom Ewell
(Yewell Tompkins)
American actor
• Films include *Adam's Rib*, 1949; *The Seven Year Itch*, 1955.
b. April 29, 1909 in Owensboro, Kentucky

Tom Eyen
American dramatist–director
• Won Tony, 1982, for play *Dreamgirls.*
b. August 14, 1941 in Cambridge, Ohio

Shelley (Michelle Marie) Fabares
(Mrs Mike Farrell)
American actress–singer
• Played Mary on "The Donna Reed Show," 1958-66; had hit single "Johnny Angel," 1962; appeared with Elvis Presley in *Girl Happy*, 1965, *Clambake*, 1967. Now stars in "Coach."
b. January 19, 1944 in Santa Monica, California

Nanette Fabray
(Ruby Nanette Fabares)
American actress
• Veteran of stage, screen, TV; won Tony for *Love Life*, 1949, Emmy for best comedienne, 1955, 1956; active in handicapped affairs.
b. October 27, 1920 in San Diego, California

Douglas Fairbanks
(Douglas Elton Ulman)
American actor
• Swashbuckler hero in *The Three Musketeers*, 1921; *Robin Hood*, 1922; married Mary Pickford, 1928-36.
b. May 23, 1883 in Denver, Colorado
d. December 12, 1939 in Santa Monica, California

Douglas Fairbanks, Jr
(Douglas Elton Ulman Jr)
American actor–producer
• Appeared in over 75 films; married to Joan Crawford, 1928-33.
b. December 09, 1909 in New York, New York

Morgan Fairchild
(Patsy Ann McClenny)
American actress
• Starred in TV series "Flamingo Road," 1981-82; host of many TV specials.
b. February 03, 1950 in Dallas, Texas

Lola Falana
(Loletha Elaine Falana; "First Lady of Las Vegas")
American entertainer
• Known for fabulous Las Vegas shows, guest spots on TV specials.
b. September 11, 1943 in Philadelphia, Pennsylvania

Louis Falco
American choreographer–dancer
• Staged dances for movie *Fame*, 1980.
b. August 02, 1942 in New York, New York

Peter Falk
American actor
• Starred in TV series "Columbo," 1971-78, 1989-90; won Emmy, 1972, 1990; starred in *Wings of Desire*, 1988.
b. September 16, 1927 in New York, New York

Dennis Farina
American actor
• Star of TV series "Crime Story," 1986-.
b. in Chicago, Illinois

Frances Farmer
American actress
• Stage, film star who spent most of 1940s in mental institution; life was subject of film *Frances*, 1983.
b. September 19, 1914 in Seattle, Washington
d. August 01, 1970 in Indianapolis, Indiana

Richard Farnsworth
American actor
• Spent 40 yrs. as stuntman; appeared in films *Comes a Horseman*, 1979; *The Natural*, 1983.
b. September 01, 1920 in Los Angeles, California

William Farnum
American actor
• Debut film *The Spoilers*, 1914; brother of Dustin Farnum.
b. July 04, 1876 in Boston, Massachusetts
d. June 05, 1953 in Los Angeles, California

George Farquhar
English dramatist
• Comedies include *The Beaux Stratagen*, 1707.
b. 1678 in Londonderry, Northern Ireland
d. April 29, 1707 in London, England

Felicia Farr
(Mrs Jack Lemmon)
American actress
• Movies include *Charley Varrick*, 1973; *The Venetian Affair*, 1967.
b. October 04, 1932 in Westchester, New York

Jamie Farr
(Jameel Joseph Farah)
American actor
• Best known for role as Cpl. Klinger on TV series "M*A*S*H," 1972-83.
b. July 01, 1934 in Toledo, Ohio

Charles Farrell
American actor
• Starred with Janet Gaynor in series of romantic films including 1927 silent classics *Sunrise* and *Seventh Heaven;* former mayor of Palm Springs, CA.
b. August 09, 1901 in Onset Bay, Massachusetts
d. May 06, 1990 in Palm Springs, California

Glenda Farrell
American actress
• Starred as reporter in *Torchy Blane* film series; won Emmy for "Ben Casey," 1963.
b. June 3, 1904 in Enid, Oklahoma
d. May 01, 1971 in New York, New York

Mike Farrell
American actor
• Played B J Hunnicutt on TV series "MASH," 1975-83.
b. February 06, 1939 in Saint Paul, Minnesota

Suzanne Farrell
American dancer
• Principal dancer, NYC Ballet, 1965-69, 1975-.
b. August 16, 1945 in Cincinnati, Ohio

John Villiers Farrow
Australian author-director
• Won Oscar for best screenplay *Around the World in 80 Days*, 1956; father of Mia Farrow.
b. February 1, 1906 in Sydney, Australia
d. January 28, 1963 in Beverly Hills, California

Mia Farrow
(Maria de Lourdes Villiers Farrow)
American actress
• Played Allison MacKenzie on TV drama "Peyton Place," 1964-66; starred in films *Rosemary's Baby*, 1968, *Hannah and Her Sisters*, 1986; former wife of Frank Sinatra, Andre Previn.
b. February 09, 1945 in Los Angeles, California

Rainer Werner Fassbinder
German actor-author-director
• Films included *The Marriage of Maria Brown*, 1978; *Lili Marleen*, 1980; *Lola*, 1981.
b. May 31, 1946 in Bad Worishofen, Germany
d. June 1, 1982 in Munich, Germany (West)

Johann Faust
(Johann Faustus)
German magician
• Was the archtype of character, Dr. Faustus in the writings of Marlowe, Goethe, Mann, also operas by Gounod, Busconi.
b. 1480 in Knittlingen, Germany
d. 1540

William Alfred Faversham
English actor
• Leading man in Charles Frohman's Empire Theatre Co., 1893-1901; in silent films, 1915.
b. February 12, 1868 in London, England
d. April 07, 1940 in Bay Shore, New York

Farrah Leni Fawcett
American actress
• Starred in "Charlie's Angels," 1976-77; TV movies "The Burning Bed," 1983; "Poor Little Rich Girl," 1987.
b. February 02, 1947 in Corpus Christi, Texas

George Fawcett
American actor
• Silent screen star in D W Griffith films: *Intolerance*, 1916; *Once a Gentleman*, 1930.
b. August 25, 1861 in Alexandria, Virginia
d. June 06, 1939 in Nantucket, Massachusetts

Joey Faye
(Joseph Anthony Palladino)
American actor-comedian
• Starred in Minsky's burlesque theatre, 1931-38.
b. July 12, 1910 in New York, New York

Frank Faylen
(Frank Cusik)
American actor
• Best known for film *The Lost Weekend*, 1945; was Dobie's father on "The Many Loves of Dobie Gillis," 1959-63.
b. December 08, 1907 in Saint Louis, Missouri
d. August 02, 1985 in Burbank, California

Louise Fazenda
American actress
• In comedies for Mack Sennett's Keystone studio from 1915.
b. June 17, 1899 in Lafayette, Indiana
d. April 17, 1962 in Beverly Hills, California

Fritz Feld
American actor
• Appeared in 400 major films, 300 TV shows, 500 TV films, since 1920s.
b. October 15, 1900 in Berlin, Germany

Irvin Feld
American businessman-producer
• Pres., producer Ringling Brothers, Barnum & Bailey Circus, 1967-84; founded Clown College, 1968.
b. May 09, 1918 in Hagerstown, Maryland
d. September 06, 1984 in Venice, California

Kenneth Jeffrey Feld
American circus owner
• Owner, president, Ringling Brothers and Barnum & Bailey Combined Shows, Inc., 1984-; son of Irvin.
b. 1948 in Washington, District of Columbia

Marty Feldman
English actor-comedian
• Made American film debut in *Young Frankenstein*, 1974. Remembered for bug-eyed approach to comedy.
b. July 08, 1934 in London, England
d. December 02, 1982 in Mexico City, Mexico

Barbara Feldon
American actress
• Best known for role as Agent 99 on TV series "Get Smart," 1965-70.
b. March 12, 1941 in Pittsburgh, Pennsylvania

Norman Fell
American actor
• Starred on TV's "Three's Company," 1977-79; "The Ropers," 1979-80.
b. March 24, 1925 in Philadelphia, Pennsylvania

Federico Fellini
Italian screenwriter-director
• Won four Oscars for best foreign film, including *La Dolce Vita*, 1960.
b. January 2, 1920 in Rimini, Italy

Edith Fellows
American actress-singer
• 1930s child star in films *Huckleberry Finn; Jane Eyre; Five Little Peppers.*
b. May 2, 1923 in Boston, Massachusetts

George Fenneman
American TV personality
• Announcer for Groucho Marx quiz show, "You Bet Your Life," 1950-61.
b. November 1, 1919 in Peking, China

Elsie Ferguson
American actress
• Silent screen star who played in 16 pictures, 1917-20, including *A Doll's House.*
b. August 19, 1885 in New York
d. November 15, 1961 in New London, Connecticut

John Bailey Fernald
American director
• Known for British stage productions since 1929, including *Dail M for Murder.*
b. November 21, 1905 in California

Fernandel
(Fernand Contandin)
French actor
• Popular in *Don Camillo* series of French comedies in which he portrayed an eccentric priest.
b. May 08, 1903 in Marseilles, France
d. February 26, 1971 in Paris, France

Emilio Fernandez
Mexican director
• Award-winner for films with strong, nationalistic tones: *Maria Candelaria,* 1943.
b. March 26, 1904 in Hondo, Mexico
d. August 06, 1986 in Mexico City, Mexico

Conchata Galen Ferrell
American actress
• Won Obie for *The Sea Horse,* 1974.
b. March 28, 1943 in Charleston, West Virginia

Jose Vicente Ferrer
American actor
• Won 1950 Oscar for *Cyrano de Bergerac.*
b. January 08, 1912 in Santurce, Puerto Rico

Mel(chor Gaston) Ferrer
American actor
• In film *Lili,* 1953; TV series "Falcon Crest," 1983-84; married to Audrey Hepburn, 1954-68.
b. August 25, 1917 in Elberon, New Jersey

Lou Ferrigno
American actor
• Played the Hulk on TV series "The Incredible Hulk," 1977-81; has won many bodybuilding awards, including Mr. Universe, 1973, 1974.
b. November 09, 1952 in Brooklyn, New York

Stepin Fetchit
(Lincoln Theodore Monroe Andrew Perry)
American actor
• Known for portrayal of perpetually bemused Uncle Tom-like character; screen debut, 1927.
b. May 3, 1902 in Key West, Florida
d. November 19, 1985 in Woodland Hills, California

Cy Feuer
American director–producer
• Stage productions include *Guys and Dolls; Can-Can; Silk Stockings.*
b. January 15, 1911 in New York, New York

Louis Feuillade
French director
• Directed over 800 films, 1906-26, wrote almost all of the scripts; best known for his fantasy serials.
b. February 19, 1873 in Lunel, France
d. 1925 in Paris, France

Georges Feydeau
French dramatist
• Comedies of manners include *Lady from Maxims,* 1899; *A Flea in Her Ear,* 1907.
b. December 08, 1862 in Paris, France
d. June 06, 1921 in Rueil-Malmaison, France

Mary Fickett
American actress
• Won 1973 Emmy for role in soap opera "All My Children."
b. May 23, in Bronxville, New York

Betty Field
American actress
• Films include *Of Mice and Men,* 1939; *The Great Gatsby,* 1949; *Peyton Place,* 1957.
b. February 08, 1918 in Boston, Massachusetts
d. September 13, 1973 in Hyannis, Massachusetts

Ron(ald) Field
American choreographer–director
• Best-known musicals: *Cabaret,* 1966; *Applause,* 1970; won two Tonys, two Emmys.
b. 1934 in Queens, New York
d. February 06, 1989 in New York, New York

Sally Margaret Field
(Mrs Alan Greisman)
American actress
• Won Oscars for *Norma Rae,* 1979; *Places in the Heart,* 1985.
b. November 06, 1946 in Pasadena, California

Freddie Fields
American producer
• Films include *Looking for Mr. Goodbar,* 1977; *American Gigolo,* 1980.
b. July 12, 1923 in Ferndale, New York

Gracie Fields
(Grace Stansfield)
English comedienne
• Beloved British night club, music hall entertainer; sang "Biggest Aspidastra in the World."
b. January 09, 1898 in Rochdale, England
d. September 27, 1979 in Capri, Italy

Joseph Fields
American screenwriter–director
• Co-wrote book for musicals *Gentlemen Prefer Blondes,* 1949; *Flower Drum Song,* 1958.
b. February 21, 1895 in New York, New York
d. March 03, 1966 in Beverly Hills, California

Kim Fields
American actress
• Played Tootie on TV series "Facts of Life," 1979-88.
b. May 12, 1969 in Los Angeles, California

Stanley Fields
American actor
• Supporting actor in 90 films, 1930-41, including *Island of Lost Souls,* 1933.
b. 1880 in Allegheny, Pennsylvania
d. April 23, 1941 in Los Angeles, California

Totie Fields
(Sophie Feldman)
American comedienne
• Popular nightclub entertainer known for self-deprecating humor.
b. May 07, 1930 in Hartford, Connecticut
d. August 02, 1978 in Las Vegas, Nevada

W C Fields
(William Claude Dukenfield real name; Charles Bogle Otis J Criblecoblis, Mahatma Kane Jeeves, pseuds.)
American comedian
• Vaudeville, stage, radio performer; noted for hard drinking, dislike of children, pets; starred with Mae West in *My Little Chickadee,* 1940.
b. January 29, 1880 in Philadelphia, Pennsylvania
d. December 25, 1946 in Pasadena, California

Harvey Forbes Fierstein
American dramatist–actor
• Won best play, actor Tonys for *Torch Song Trilogy,* 1983.
b. June 06, 1954 in Brooklyn, New York

Jon Finch
English actor
• Films include *Sunday, Bloody Sunday*, 1971; *Frenzy*, 1972.
b. 1941 in England

Peter Finch
(William Mitchell)
English actor
• Only actor awarded posthumous Oscar for *Network*, 1976.
b. September 28, 1916 in London, England
d. January 14, 1977 in Beverly Hills, California

Larry Fine
(Laurence Fineburg; The Three Stooges)
American comedian–actor
• Member of original Three Stooges; films include *Snow White and the Three Stooges*, 1961.
b. 1911 in Philadelphia, Pennsylvania
d. January 24, 1975 in Woodland Hills, California

Frank Finlay
English actor
• Films include *The Three Musketeers*, 1973.
b. August 06, 1926 in Farnworth, England

Albert Finney
English actor–director
• Starred in *Tom Jones*, 1963; *Murder on the Orient Express*, 1974.
b. May 09, 1936 in Salford, England

Peter Firth
English actor
• Made debut as deranged stable boy in stage, film versions of *Equus*, 1975, 1977.
b. October 27, 1953 in Bradford, England

Carrie Frances Fisher
American actress
• Daughter of Debbie Reynolds, Eddie Fisher; in *Star Wars*, 1977; *The Empire Strikes Back*, 1980. Memoirs, *Postcards from the Edge*, made into movie starring Meryl Streep.
b. October 21, 1956 in Beverly Hills, California

Clara Fisher
American actress
• Noted comic performer; played male, female roles in career that spanned 72 yrs.
b. April 14, 1811 in England
d. November 12, 1898 in Metuchen, New Jersey

Gail Fisher
American actress
• Played Peggy Fair in TV series "Mannix," 1968-74.
b. August 18, 1935 in Orange, New Jersey

Terence Fisher
English director
• Joined Hammer films, 1952, directing horror films *Curse of Frankenstein*, 1957; *Island of Terror*, 1966.
b. 1904 in London, England
d. June 18, 1980 in Twickenham, England

Barry Fitzgerald
(William Joseph Shields)
American actor
• Won 1944 Oscar for *Going My Way*.
b. March 1, 1888 in Dublin, Ireland
d. January 04, 1961 in Dublin, Ireland

Ed(ward) Fitzgerald
American radio performer
• With wife Pegeen broadcast "The Fitzgerald's" radio show for 44 years.
b. 1893 in Troy, New York
d. March 22, 1982 in New York, New York

Geraldine Fitzgerald
American actress
• 1939 Oscar nominee for *Wuthering Heights*.
b. November 24, 1914 in Dublin, Ireland

Pegeen Fitzgerald
American radio performer
• With husband Ed, broadcast "The Fitzgeralds" radio talk show.
b. November 24, 1910 in Norcatur, Kansas
d. January 3, 1989 in New York, New York

Robert Joseph Flaherty
American director
• "Father" of documentary; first was *Nanook of the North*, 1920, on Eskimos.
b. February 16, 1884 in Iron Mountain, Michigan
d. July 23, 1951 in Dummerston, Vermont

Michael Flanders
English actor–author
• Broadcaster with BBC radio, 1948-75.
b. March 01, 1922 in London, England
d. April 14, 1975 in Wales

Susan Flannery
American actress
• Soap opera actress; won Golden Globe for outstanding acting debut in film *The Towering Inferno*, 1974.
b. July 31, 1944 in New York, New York

Ernest O Flatt
Choreographer
• Won Emmys for "Carol Burnett Show," 1971.
b. October 3, 1928

Erin Fleming
Canadian actress
• Groucho Marx's companion, 1970-77.
b. 1941 in New Liskeard, Ontario

Ian Fleming
British actor
• Played Dr. Watson in British film series *Sherlock Holmes*, 1930s.
b. September 1, 1888 in Melbourne, Australia
d. January 01, 1969 in London, England

Rhonda Fleming
(Marilyn Lewis)
American actress
• Played "bad girl" roles, 1945–; films include *Pony Express*, 1953.
b. August 1, 1923 in Los Angeles, California

Victor Fleming
American director
• Won Oscar for *Gone With the Wind*, 1939; films include *Wizard of Oz*, 1939; *Treasure Island*, 1934.
b. February 23, 1883 in Pasadena, California
d. January 06, 1949 in Cottonwood, Arizona

John Fletcher
English author–dramatist
• Collaborated with Francis Beaumont in famed partnership; sold 16 plays.
b. December 2, 1579 in Rye, England
d. August 1625 in London, England

Louise Fletcher
American actress
• Won 1975 Oscar for *One Flew Over the Cuckoo's Nest*.
b. July 1934 in Birmingham, Alabama

Jay C Flippen
American actor
• Character actor in films, 1934-71; in TV series "Ensign O'Toole," 1962-64.
b. March 06, 1900 in Little Rock, Arkansas
d. February 03, 1971 in Hollywood, California

Wayland Parrott Flowers, Jr
American ventriloquist
• Known for cabaret shows, TV series with puppet named "Madame."
b. November 1939 in Dawson, Georgia
d. October 1, 1988 in Hollywood, California

Errol Flynn
American actor
• Swashbuckling star of 1930s-40s adventure films: *Captain Blood*, 1936; *Robin Hood*, 1938; wrote autobiography, *My Wicked, Wicked Ways*.
b. June 2, 1909 in Tasmania, New Zealand
d. October 14, 1959 in Vancouver, British Columbia

Nina Foch
(Nina Consuelo Maud Fock)
American actress
• Oscar nominee for *Executive Suite*, 1954; founder, teacher, Nina Foch Studio, 1973–.
b. April 2, 1924 in Leiden, Netherlands

Michel Fokine
American dancer
• Creator of modern ballet; choreographer of Diaghilev's Ballets Russes in Paris, 1909-14.
b. April 26, 1880 in Saint Petersburg, Russia
d. August 22, 1942 in Yonkers, New York

Bridget Fonda
American actress
• Starred in film *Scandal*, 1989; daughter of Peter and Susan.
b. 1964 in Los Angeles, California

Henry Jaynes Fonda
American actor
• Top film star since 1930s; often cast as upstanding common man; films include *Grapes of Wrath*, 1940; *On Golden Pond* (Oscar), 1981.
b. May 16, 1905 in Grand Island, Nebraska
d. August 12, 1982 in Los Angeles, California

Jane Fonda
American actress–political activist
• Won Oscars for *Klute*, 1971, *Coming Home*, 1978; wrote *Jane Fonda's Workout Book*, 1982; has starred in many fitness videocassettes; daughter of Henry. Romantically linked with Ted Turner.
b. December 21, 1937 in New York, New York

Peter Fonda
American actor
• Wrote, co-produced, and starred in *Easy Rider*, 1969; son of actor Henry, brother of actress Jane.
b. February 23, 1939 in New York, New York

Joan Fontaine
(Joan de Havilland)
American actress
• Won 1941 Oscar for *Suspicion;* sister of Olivia de Haviland.
b. October 22, 1917 in Tokyo, Japan

Tom Fontana
American writer–producer
• Won Emmy for writing "St. Elsewhere," 1984.
b. September 12, 1951

Lynn Fontanne
(Mrs Alfred Lunt)
American actress
• With husband, formed one of great stage duos: *O Mistress Mine*, 1946; *The Visit*, 1960.
b. December 06, 1887 in London, England
d. July 3, 1983 in Genesee, Wisconsin

Dame Margot Fonteyn
(Mrs Roberto de Arias; Margaret Hookham)
English dancer
• Prima ballerina, Britain's Royal Ballet, 1934-75; formed partnership "made in heaven" with Rudolf Nureyev, 1962-79; pres., Royal Academy of Dancing, 1954–.
b. May 18, 1919 in Reigate, England
d. February 21, 1991 in Panama City, Panama

Horton (Albert Horton, Jr) Foote
American author–screenwriter
• Wrote *Trip to Bountiful*, 1953; won Oscars for screenplays of *Tender Mercies*, 1983; *To Kill a Mockingbird*, 1962.
b. March 14, 1916 in Wharton, Texas

Samuel Foote
English dramatist–actor
• One-legged comedian who starred in *Lame Lover*, 1770; mimicked prominent persons; plays include *The Minor*, 1760.
b. January 27, 1720 in Truro, England
d. October 21, 1777 in Dover, England

Dick John Nicholas Foran
American actor
• Made series of Warners films as singing cowboy including *My Little Chickadee*, 1940.
b. June 18, 1910 in Flemington, New Jersey
d. August 1, 1979

Bryan Forbes
English screenwriter–director
• Directed *The Stepford Wives*, 1974; *International Velvet*, 1978.
b. July 22, 1926 in London, England

Sir Johnston Forbes-Robertson
English actor–manager
• Appeared on stage, 1874-1913; said to be greatest Hamlet of his time.
b. 1853 in London, England
d. November 06, 1937 in Saint Margaret's, England

Alexander Ford
Polish director
• Organized Polish army film unit, WW II; director, Film Polski, govt. run film organization.
b. January 24, 1908 in Lodz, Poland

Glenn Ford
(Gwyllyn Samuel Newton Ford)
American actor
• Among his over 100 films are *Gilda*, 1946; *Blackboard Jungle*, 1955; noted for thoughtful leading man roles.
b. May 01, 1916 in Quebec

Harrison Ford
American actor
• Best-known roles as Han Solo in *Star Wars* films, Indiana Jones in *Indiana Jones* films; received Oscar nomination for *Witness*, 1985.
b. July 13, 1942 in Chicago, Illinois

John Ford
English dramatist
• Melancholy plays include *Broken Heart*, 1633.
b. 1586 in Ilsington, England
d. 1640

John Ford
(Sean O'Feeney)
American director
• Best known for western films including *Stagecoach*, 1939; won six Oscars.
b. February 01, 1895 in Cape Elizabeth, Maine
d. August 31, 1973 in Palm Desert, California

Steven Meigs Ford
American actor–celebrity relative
• Son of Gerald and Betty Ford; stars in TV soap opera "The Young and the Restless."
b. May 19, 1956 in Washington, District of Columbia

Wallace Ford
(Samuel Jones Grundy)
English actor
• Character actor, 1903-65; notable film *The Informer*, 1935.
b. February 12, 1899 in Batton, England
d. June 11, 1966 in Woodland Hills, California

Carl Foreman
American director
• Won best director Oscar for *Bridge Over the River Kwai*, 1957.
b. July 23, 1914 in Chicago, Illinois
d. June 26, 1984 in Beverly Hills, California

Richard Foreman
American dramatist–director
• Established avant-garde theatrical company, Ontological-Hysteric Theater, 1968; won Obie Awards for his plays *Rhoda*, 1976; *Film Is Evil; Radio Is Good*, 1987.
b. June 1, 1937 in New York, New York

Milos Forman
Czech director
• Won Oscars for *One Flew Over the Cuckoo's Nest*, 1975; *Amadeus*, 1984.
b. February 18, 1932 in Caslav, Czechoslovakia

Edwin Forrest
American actor
• First actor to encourage US plays; best known for role in *Othello*, 1826.
b. March 09, 1806 in Philadelphia, Pennsylvania
d. December 12, 1872 in Philadelphia, Pennsylvania

Henderson Forsythe
American actor–director
• Won supporting actor Tony for *Best Little Whorehouse in Texas*, 1978; star of TV series "As the World Turns."
b. September 11, 1917 in Macon, Missouri

John Forsythe
(John Lincoln Freund)
American actor
• Played Blake Carrington on TV soap opera "Dynasty," 1981-89.
b. January 29, 1918 in Penns Grove, New Jersey

Bob (Robert Louis) Fosse
American choreographer–director
• Known for bold, innovative direction; won Oscar for *Cabaret*, 1972; other films include autobiographical *All That Jazz*, 1979.
b. June 23, 1927 in Chicago, Illinois
d. September 23, 1987 in Washington, District of Columbia

Jodie (Alicia Christian) Foster
American actress
• Starred in *Taxi Driver*, 1976; *Foxes*, 1980; *Silence of the Lambs*, 1991; Won Oscar for starring role in *The Accused*, 1989.
b. November 19, 1962 in Los Angeles, California

Julia Foster
English actress
• Films include *The Loneliness of the Long Distance Runner*, 1963; *Half a Sixpence*, 1968.
b. 1942 in Lewes, England

Norman Foster
(Norman Hoeffer)
American director
• Leading man, early 1930s; directed numerous hits including *Davy Crockett*, 1955.
b. December 13, 1903 in Richmond, Indiana
d. July 07, 1976

Phil Foster
(Fivel Feldman)
American comedian
• Stand-up comedian best known as Laverne's father on TV series "Laverne and Shirley," 1976-82.
b. March 29, 1914 in Brooklyn, New York
d. July 08, 1985 in Rancho Mirage, California

Preston Foster
American actor
• Two-fisted hero in films, 1930-68, including *The Last Warning*, 1938.
b. August 24, 1900 in Ocean City, New Jersey
d. July 14, 1970 in La Jolla, California

Edward Fox
English actor
• Starred in films *The Day of the Jackal*, 1973; *Gandhi*, 1984.
b. April 13, 1937 in London, England

James Fox
English actor
• In films *The Servant*, 1964; *Isadora*, 1968; became an evangelist, 1973-83.
b. May 19, 1939 in London, England

Michael J Fox
(Michael Andrew Fox)
Canadian actor
• Played Alex Keaton on TV series "Family Ties," 1982-89; starred in *Back to the Future*, 1985; won Emmys, 1986, 1987.
b. June 09, 1961 in Edmonton, Alberta

Robert Foxworth
American actor
• Played Chase Gioberti in TV series "Falcon Crest," 1981-87; films include *The Black Marble*, 1980.
b. November 01, 1941 in Houston, Texas

Redd Foxx
(John Elroy Sanford)
American comedian–actor
• Starred as Fred Sanford in TV series "Sanford and Son," 1972-77, 1980.
b. December 09, 1922 in Saint Louis, Missouri

Eddie Foy
(Edward Fitzgerald)
American actor
• Starred in vaudeville with children as "Eddie and the Seven Little Foys," 1913-27.
b. March 09, 1856 in New York, New York
d. February 16, 1928 in Kansas City, Missouri

Eddie Foy, Jr
American actor–dancer
• Portrayed famed father in films; starred in Broadway's *Pajama Game*, 1954.
b. February 04, 1905 in New Rochelle, New York
d. July 15, 1983 in Woodland Hills, California

Carla Fracci
Italian dancer
• Prima ballerina with La Scala Ballet, 1954-67; American Ballet Theater, 1974–.
b. August 2, 1936 in Milan, Italy

William A Fraker
American filmmaker
• Cinematographer for *The Exorcist*; *Looking for Mr. Goodbar*; *Sharky's Machine*.
b. 1923 in Los Angeles, California

Celia Franca
English dancer–choreographer
• Founded National Ballet of Canada, Toronto, 1951.
b. June 25, 1921 in London, England

Anne Francis
American actress
• Played child roles on radio; was TV detective in "Honey West," 1965-66.
b. September 16, 1930 in Ossining, New York

Arlene Francis
(Mrs Martin Gabel; Arlene Francis Kazanjian)
American actress
• Best known as panelist on TV game show "What's My Line?," 1950-67.
b. October 2, 1908 in Boston, Massachusetts

Freddie Francis
English filmmaker–director
• Won Oscar for cinematography of *Sons and Lovers*, 1960.
b. 1917 in London, England

Genie Francis
American actress
• Played Laura on daytime soap opera "General Hospital," 1977-81.
b. May 26, 1962 in Los Angeles, California

James Grover Franciscus
American actor
• Played in TV series "Mr. Novak," 1963-65; "Longstreet," 1971-72.
b. January 31, 1934 in Clayton, Missouri

Emily Frankel
American dancer–choreographer
• Performances from 1950-73 include "Electra"; "Four Seasons."
b. 1930 in New York, New York

Gene Frankel
American director
• Won Obies for *Volpone*, 1958; *Machinal*, 1960.
b. December 23, 1923 in New York, New York

John Michael Frankenheimer
American director
• Began career in TV; directed over 125 TV plays; films include *Birdman of Alcatraz*, 1961; *The Manchurian Candidate*, 1962.
b. February 19, 1930 in Malba, New York

Bonnie Gail Franklin
American actress–dancer
• Starred on Broadway in *Applause*, 1970-71; TV series "One Day at a Time," 1975-84.
b. January 06, 1944 in Santa Monica, California

Pamela Franklin
English actress
• Films include *The Innocents*, 1961; *David Copperfield*, 1969.
b. February 04, 1950 in Tokyo, Japan

Mary Frann
(Mary Luecke)
American actress
• Played Joanna Louden in TV series "Newhart," 1982-90.
b. February 27, 1943 in Saint Louis, Missouri

Arthur Franz
American actor
• Films include *Jungle Patrol*, 1948; *Member of the Wedding*, 1952.
b. February 29, 1920 in Perth Amboy, New Jersey

Eduard Franz
American actor
• Original member of Provincetown Players; appeared in films *Twilight Zone-The Movie*, 1983; *The Ten Commandments*, 1956.
b. October 31, 1902 in Milwaukee, Wisconsin
d. February 1, 1983 in Los Angeles, California

William Frawley
American actor
• Played Fred Mertz on TV series "I Love Lucy," 1951-60.
b. February 26, 1893 in Burlington, Iowa
d. March 03, 1966 in Los Angeles, California

Pauline Frederick
(Beatrice Pauline Libby)
American actress
• Silent screen star beginning 1915 in *Bella Donna; Madame X.*
b. August 12, 1885 in Boston, Massachusetts
d. August 19, 1938 in Los Angeles, California

Pauline Frederick
American broadcast journalist
• First woman to receive Dupont radio award for news commentating, 1953; career covered TV, radio, political reporting, analysis, 1940's-70's.
b. February 13, 1908 in Gallitzen, Pennsylvania
d. May 09, 1990 in Lake Forest, Illinois

H Gray Frederickson
American producer
• Films include *The Good, the Bad and the Ugly*; won Oscar for *The Godfather, Part II*, 1974.
b. July 21, 1937 in Oklahoma City, Oklahoma

Arthur Freed
American songwriter–producer
• Produced films *Wizard of Oz*, 1939; *Gigi*, 1958; won special Oscar; wrote "Singin' in the Rain," 1929.
b. September 09, 1894 in Charleston, South Carolina
d. April 12, 1973 in Los Angeles, California

Gerald Freedman
American director
• Won Obie award for *Taming of the Shrew*, 1960.
b. June 25, 1927 in Lorain, Ohio

Morgan Freeman
American actor
• Starred in films *Glory*, *Driving Miss Daisy*, 1989; received Oscar nomination, 1990, for *Driving Miss Daisy*.
b. June 01, 1937 in Memphis, Tennessee

Seth Freeman
American writer–producer
• Won Emmy for script of TV show "Lou Grant," 1980.
b. January 06, 1945 in Los Angeles, California

Friz Freleng
American director–producer
• Won Emmys for "Halloween is Grinch Night," 1978; "The Grinch Grinches the Cat-in-The-Hat," 1982.
b. August 21, 1906 in Kansas City, Missouri

Phyllis Frelich
American actress
• Deaf actress who won Tony for *Children of a Lesser God*, 1980.
b. 1944 in Devils Lake, North Dakota

Florida Friebus
American actress
• Played mother on TV's "The Many Loves of Dobie Gillis," 1959-63; patient on "The Bob Newhart Show," 1972-78.
b. October 1, 1909 in Auburndale, Massachusetts
d. May 27, 1988 in Laguna Niguel, California

William Friedkin
American director
• Directed *The Exorcist*, 1973; won best director Oscar, 1971, for *The French Connection*.
b. August 29, 1939 in Chicago, Illinois

Bruce Jay Friedman
American screenwriter
• Wrote films *Doctor Detroit*, 1983; *Splash*, 1984.
b. April 26, 1930 in New York, New York

Ed (Edwin S, Jr) Friendly
American producer
• Co-created TV comedy "Laugh-In," 1973; executive producer, TV series "Little House on the Prairie," 1974-82.
b. April 08, 1922 in New York, New York

Charles W Fries
American producer
• Films include *The Cat People*, 1982; major supplier of made for TV movies.
b. September 3, 1928 in Cincinnati, Ohio

Joe Frisco
American actor
• Vaudevillian; did stuttering comic routine in 1930s films.
b. 1890 in Milan, Illinois
d. February 16, 1958 in Woodland Hills, California

Gerd Frobe
German actor
• Appeared in nearly 100 movies; best known for role of Goldfinger in James Bond film, 1964.
b. February 25, 1912 in Planitz, Germany
d. September 05, 1988 in Munich, Germany (West)

Charles Frohman
American impresario–producer
• Introduced Maude Adams in *Peter Pan*, 1905; helped create "star" system; victim of Lusitania disaster.
b. June 17, 1860 in Sandusky, Ohio
d. May 07, 1915

David Frost
(David Paradine)
English TV personality–author
• Won Emmys, 1970, 1971, for TV interview show; famous for one-on-one interviews with Nixon, Kissinger, others.
b. April 07, 1939 in Tenterden, England

Barbara Frum
Canadian broadcast journalist–author
• Host, interviewer, "As It Happens," CBC radio show; "The Journal," TV show; often compared to Barbara Walters.
b. September 08, 1937 in Niagara Falls, New York

Christopher Fry
English dramatist
• Wrote plays *The Lady's Not for Burning*, 1949; *Venus Observed*, 1950.
b. December 18, 1907 in Bristol, England

Robert Fryer
American producer
• Won Tonys for *Wonderful Town*, 1953; *Redhead*, 1959; *Sweeny Todd*, 1979.
b. December 18, 1920 in Washington, District of Columbia

Robert E Fuisz
American writer–producer
• Won four Emmys for Body Human series including "The Body Human - The Living Code," 1983.
b. October 15, 1934 in Pennsylvania

Charles Fuller
American dramatist
• Won Pulitzer for *A Soldier's Play*, 1982; wrote film *A Soldier's Story*, 1984.
b. March 05, 1939 in Philadelphia, Pennsylvania

Annette Funicello
(Mrs Glen Holt)
American actress–singer
• Disney Mousketeer, 1950s; star of "beach party" films, 1960s.
b. October 22, 1942 in Utica, New York

Allen Funt
American producer
• Creator, host of TV series "Candid Camera."
b. September 16, 1914 in Brooklyn, New York

Sidney J Furie
Canadian director
• Films include *Lady Sings the Blues*; *Gable and Lombard*; *Boys in Company C*.
b. February 28, 1933 in Toronto, Ontario

Roger Furman
Director
• Founder, director, Harlem's Repertory Theater, 1964.
b. 1924
d. November 27, 1983

Martin Gabel
American actor–director
• Won 1961 Tony for *Big Fish, Little Fish*; regular panelist on TV game show "What's My Line?"
b. June 19, 1912 in Philadelphia, Pennsylvania
d. May 22, 1986 in New York, New York

Jean Gabin
(Jean-Alexis Moncorge)
French actor
• World-weary hero in films: *Pepe le Moko*, 1937; *Port of Shadows*, 1938.
b. May 17, 1904 in Paris, France
d. November 15, 1976 in Neuilly, France

Clark (William Clark) Gable
American actor
• Won Oscar, 1934, for *It Happened One Night;* played Rhett Butler in *Gone With the Wind*, 1939.
b. February 01, 1901 in Cadiz, Ohio
d. November 16, 1960 in Hollywood, California

Eva Gabor
Hungarian actress
• Co-starred with Eddie Albert in TV series "Green Acres," 1965-71.
b. February 11, 1921 in Budapest, Hungary

Magda Gabor
Hungarian actress
• Eldest sister of famous trio.
b. July 1, 1917 in Budapest, Hungary

Zsa Zsa (Sari) Gabor
Hungarian actress
• Witty, exotic performer; known for many husbands; films include *Three Ring Circus*, 1954. Recently slapped a police officer.
b. February 06, 1919 in Budapest, Hungary

Max(well Trowbridge, Jr) Gail
American actor
• Played Sergeant Wojciehowicz ("Wojo") on TV series "Barney Miller," 1975-81.
b. April 05, 1943 in Detroit, Michigan

Helen Gallagher
American actress
• Won Emmy for her role in TV soap opera "Ryan's Hope," 1976; won Tonys for *No, No, Nannette*, 1970; *Pal Joey*, 1952.
b. July 19, 1926 in Brooklyn, New York

Don Galloway
American actor
• Played Sergeant Ed Brown in TV series "Ironside," 1967-75.
b. July 27, 1937 in Brooksville, Kentucky

Abel Gance
French director–screenwriter
• Pioneer filmmaker who made 1927 silent epic *Napoleon* (revised 1981); used multiple screens, wide angle lenses.
b. October 25, 1889 in Paris, France
d. November 1, 1981 in Paris, France

Greta Garbo
(Greta Louisa Gustafsson)
Swedish actress
• Starred in film *Anna Karenina*, 1935; won special Oscar, 1954; famous recluse.
b. September 18, 1905 in Stockholm, Sweden
d. April 15, 1990 in New York, New York

Vincent Gardenia
(Vincent Scognamiglio)
American actor
• Won Tony for *Prisoner of Second Avenue*, 1971; Oscar nominee for *Bang the Drum Slowly*, 1973.
b. January 07, 1922 in Naples, Italy

Reginald Gardiner
English actor
• Familiar character actor; has appeared in 100 films since 1936, including *The Great Dictator*, 1940.
b. February 27, 1903 in Wimbledon, England
d. July 07, 1980 in Westwood, California

Ava Gardner
(Lucy Johnson)
American actress
• Screen sex goddess; made over 60 films, 1942-81, including *Mogambo*, 1951, for which she received Oscar nomination; also known for marriages to Mickey Rooney, Artie Shaw, Frank Sinatra.
b. December 24, 1922 in Smithfield, North Carolina
d. January 25, 1990 in London, England

John Garfield
(Julius Garfinkle)
American actor
• Played tough-guy roles in *The Postman Always Rings Twice, Body and Soul;* victim of McCarthy's blacklist.
b. March 04, 1913 in New York, New York
d. May 21, 1952 in New York, New York

Louis Garfinkle
American screenwriter
• Wrote award-winning film *The Deer Hunter*, 1982.
b. February 11, 1928 in Seattle, Washington

William Gargan
American actor
• Played TV's first detective "Martin Kane, Private Eye," 1949.
b. July 17, 1905 in New York, New York
d. February 16, 1979

Beverly Garland
(Beverly Lucy Fessenden)
American actress
• Played in TV shows "My Three Sons," 1969-72; "Scarecrow and Mrs. King," 1983–.
b. October 17, 1926 in Santa Cruz, California

Judy Garland
(Frances Gumm)
American actress–singer
• Played Dorothy in *The Wizard of Oz*, 1939; mother of Liza Minnelli, Lorna Luft.
b. June 1, 1922 in Grand Rapids, Minnesota
d. June 22, 1969 in London, England

James Garner
(James Baumgarner)
American actor
• Starred in "The Rockford Files," 1974-80; appeared in Polaroid commercials with Mariette Hartley; won Emmy, 1977.
b. April 07, 1928 in Norman, Oklahoma

Peggy Ann Garner
American actress
• Won special Oscar, 1945, "Outstanding Child Performer" in *A Tree Grows in Brooklyn*.
b. February 03, 1931 in Canton, Ohio
d. October 17, 1984 in Woodland Hills, California

Teri Garr
American actress
• Starred in *Tootsie*, 1982; *Mr. Mom*, 1983.
b. December 11, 1945 in Hollywood, California

Betty Garrett
American actress
• Played in TV shows "All in the Family," 1973-75; "Laverne and Shirley," 1976-82.
b. May 23, 1919 in Saint Joseph, Missouri

Lila Garrett
American producer–writer–director
• Won Emmys for "Mother of the Bride," 1974; "The Girl Who Couldn't Lose," 1975.
b. November 21, 1925 in New York, New York

David Garrick
English actor
• Greatest actor of 18th-c. English stage; Garrick Club established for actors in his honor, 1831.
b. February 19, 1717 in Hereford, England
d. January 2, 1779 in London, England

Dave (David Cunningham) Garroway
American TV personality
• Original host of "The Today Show," 1952-61.
b. July 13, 1913 in Schenectady, New York
d. July 21, 1982 in Swarthmore, Pennsylvania

Greer Garson
American actress
• Won Oscar, 1942, for *Mrs. Miniver*.
b. September 29, 1908 in County Down, Northern Ireland

Kathy Garver
American actress
• Played Cissy on TV's "Family Affair," 1966-71.
b. December 13, 1947 in Long Beach, California

Vittorio Gassman
Italian actor–director
• Starred in *Bitter Rice*, 1948; *Anna*, 1951; married Shelley Winters, 1952.
b. September 01, 1922 in Genoa, Italy

John Anthony Golenor Gavin
American actor–business executive–diplomat
• Reagan's ambassador to Mexico, 1981-86; films include *Imitation to Life*, 1959.
b. April 08, 1931 in Los Angeles, California

Janet Gaynor
(Laura Gainor)
American actress
• Won first Oscar given, 1928, for films *Sunrise; Seventh Heaven; Street Angel*.
b. October 06, 1906 in Philadelphia, Pennsylvania
d. September 14, 1984 in Palm Springs, California

Anthony Geary
American actor
• Best known for role of Luke Spencer on daytime drama "General Hospital."
b. May 29, 1948 in Coalville, Utah

Barbara Bel Geddes
American actress
• In films, 1947-71; star of TV series "Dallas," 1978-.
b. October 31, 1922 in New York, New York

Will Geer
American actor
• Played grandfather on TV series "The Waltons," 1972-78; won 1975 Emmy.
b. March 09, 1902 in Frankfort, Indiana
d. April 22, 1978 in Los Angeles, California

David Geffen
American producer
• One of most influential people in entertainment industry who produced Tony-winning Broadway musical, *Cats*, 1982.
b. February 21, 1943 in Brooklyn, New York

Larry Gelbart
American producer
• Comedy writer for Bob Hope, Sid Caesar; creator of TV's "M*A*S*H."
b. February 25, 1928 in Chicago, Illinois

Jack Gelber
American author–dramatist
• Avant-garde writer of Off-Broadway plays: *The Connection*, 1959; *The Apple*, 1961.
b. April 12, 1932 in Chicago, Illinois

Bruce Geller
American producer
• Produced action TV series "Rawhide"; "Mannix"; "Mission: Impossible," 1960s-70s.
b. October 13, 1930 in New York, New York
d. May 21, 1976 in Santa Barbara, California

Leo Genn
English actor
• Nominated for Oscar for *Quo Vadis*, 1951.
b. August 09, 1905 in London, England
d. January 26, 1978 in London, England

Peter Gennaro
American choreographer
• Won Tony for *Annie*, 1977; nominee for *Little Me*, 1982.
b. 1924 in Metairie, Louisiana

Chief Dan George
(Geswanouth Slaholt)
Canadian indian chief–actor
• Best known for Oscar-winning role as Cheyenne warrior in *Little Big Man*, 1970.
b. June 24, 1899 in North Vancouver, British Columbia
d. September 23, 1981 in Vancouver, British Columbia

Gladys George
American actress
• Oscar nominee for *Madame X*, 1937; other films include *The Roaring Twenties*, 1939.
b. September 13, 1904 in Hatton, Maine
d. December 08, 1954 in Los Angeles, California

Grace George
American actress
• Married actor, manager William A. Brady; appeared in many of his films including *The First Mrs. Fraser*.
b. December 25, 1879 in New York, New York
d. May 19, 1961 in New York, New York

Susan George
(Mrs Simon McCorkindale)
English actress
• Films include *Dirty Mary, Crazy Larry*, 1974; *Mandingo*, 1975.
b. July 26, 1950 in London, England

Gil Gerard
American actor
- Played on TV show "Buck Rogers in the 25th Century," 1979-81.
b. January 23, 1943 in Little Rock, Arkansas

Steven Geray
(Stefan Gyergyay)
Czech actor
- Character actor in over 100 films from 1941 including *Gentleman Prefer Blondes*, 1953.
b. November 1, 1904 in Uzhored, Czechoslovakia
d. December 26, 1973

Richard Gere
American actor
- Starred in films *American Gigolo*, 1980, *An Officer and a Gentleman*, 1982, *Pretty Woman*, 1990.
b. August 31, 1949 in Philadelphia, Pennsylvania

Pietro Germi
Italian director
- Most films set in Italy, depicted poverty-stricken people; directed *Divorce, Italian Style*, 1961.
b. September 14, 1904 in Genoa, Italy
d. December 05, 1974 in Rome, Italy

Bruno Gerussi
Canadian actor–broadcaster
- Played in TV series "The Beachcombers"; radio show "Gerussi," 1967-71.
b. 1928 in Medicine Hat, Alberta

Estelle Getty
American actress
- Plays Sophia on TV series "The Golden Girls," 1985–; won supporting actress Emmy, 1988.
b. July 25, 1923 in New York, New York

Giancarlo Giannini
Italian actor
- Known for roles in Lina Wertmuller films including *Love and Anarchy*, 1974.
b. August 01, 1942 in Spezia, Italy

Hoot (Edmund Richard) Gibson
American actor
- Western hero whose films include *Outlaw Trail*, 1944; *Ocean's Eleven*, 1960.
b. August 06, 1892 in Tememah, Nebraska
d. August 23, 1962 in Woodland Hills, California

Mel Gibson
American actor
- Films include *The Road Warrior*, 1982; *Lethal Weapon*, 1987; *Hamlet*, 1990.
b. January 03, 1956 in Peekskill, New York

William Gibson
American dramatist
- Best known plays include Tony-winning *The Miracle Worker*, 1960.
b. November 13, 1914 in New York, New York

Sir (Authur) John Gielgud
English actor–director–producer
- Won Oscar for *Arthur*, 1982; distinguished Shakespearean actor with Old Vic, 1920s.
b. April 14, 1904 in London, England

Val Henry Gielgud
British dramatist
- Brother of actor John; books include *In Such a Night*, 1974; *A Fearful Thing*, 1975.
b. April 28, 1900
d. November 3, 1981

Billy Gilbert
American actor
- Trademark was comic sneezing routine used in Disney's *Snow White and the Seven Dwarfs* for the dwarf Sneezy.
b. September 12, 1894 in Louisville, Kentucky
d. September 23, 1971 in Hollywood, California

Bruce Gilbert
American producer
- Films include *Coming Home; China Syndrome; Nine to Five; On Golden Pond*.
b. March 28, 1947 in Beverly Hills, California

John Gilbert
(John Pringle)
American actor
- Starred opposite Greta Garbo in several films; talking pictures destroyed career.
b. July 1, 1897 in Logan, Utah
d. January 09, 1936 in Los Angeles, California

Melissa Gilbert
(Mrs Bo Brinkman)
American actress
- Played Laura Ingalls Wilder on TV series "Little House on the Prairie," 1974-83.
b. May 08, 1964 in Los Angeles, California

Sir William Schwenck Gilbert
(Gilbert and Sullivan)
English dramatist
- Wrote librettos for Gilbert and Sullivan comic operas: *Pirates of Penzance*, 1880; *The Mikado*, 1885.
b. November 18, 1836 in London, England
d. May 29, 1911 in Harrow, England

Jack Gilford
(Jacob Gellman)
American actor
- Versatile comedian; 50-year career began in vaudeville; nominated for Oscar, 1972, for *Save the Tiger*; starred in *Cocoon*, 1985.
b. July 25, 1913 in New York, New York
d. June 04, 1990 in New York, New York

Terry (Vance) Gilliam
(Monty Python's Flying Circus; Jerry Gilian)
American illustrator–writer–director
- Created animated sequences for Monty Python comedy TV series, film *Monty Python and the Holy Grail*, 1975; directed *Brazil*, 1986.
b. November 22, 1940 in Minneapolis, Minnesota

Penelope Ann Douglas Conner Gilliatt
English critic–writer
- Wrote film *Sunday, Bloody Sunday*, 1971; nominated for Oscar; film critic with *New Yorker* mag. since 1968.
b. March 25, 1932 in London, England

Virginia Gilmore
(Sherman Virginia Poole)
American actress
- Broadway star, 1940s, who starred in 40 films; married to Yul Brynner, 1944-60.
b. July 26, 1919 in Del Monte, California
d. March 28, 1986 in Santa Barbara, California

Charles Sidney Gilpin
American actor
- One of first black actors to win wide stage following; played title role in *The Emperor Jones* which ran for three years.
b. November 2, 1878 in Richmond, Virginia
d. May 06, 1930 in Eldridge Park, New Jersey

Suzy Gilstrap
American actress
- Paraplegic star in TV movie "Skyward," 1980; "Skyward Christmas," 1981.
b. January 1966

Hermione Ferdinanda Gingold
English actress
- Films include *Gigi*, 1958; won Grammy for narration of "Peter and the Wolf."
b. December 09, 1897 in London, England
d. May 24, 1987 in New York, New York

Annie Girardot
French actress
• Won the Cesar (French Oscar) for *No Time For Breakfast*, 1975.
b. October 25, 1931 in Paris, France

Dorothy Gish
American actress
• Played in over 100 films, 1912-22, including *Orphans of the Storm*.
b. March 11, 1898 in Dayton, Ohio
d. June 04, 1968 in Rapallo, Italy

Lillian Diana Gish
American actress
• Starred in D W Griffith classics: *Birth of a Nation*, 1915; revivals in *The Wedding*, 1978; *The Whales of August*, 1987.
b. October 14, 1896 in Springfield, Ohio

Robin Givens
American actress
• Plays Darlene on TV series "Head of the Class," 1986–; had tempetuous marriage to Mike Tyson.
b. November 27, 1964 in New York, New York

Paul Michael Glaser
American actor
• Played Starsky on TV series "Starsky and Hutch," 1975-79; AIDS activist.
b. March 25, 1942 in Cambridge, Massachusetts

Susan Keating Glaspell
American author–dramatist
• Awarded Pulitzer for play *Alison's House*, 1930.
b. July 01, 1882 in Davenport, Iowa
d. July 21, 1948

Montague (Marsden) Glass
American lawyer–author–dramatist
• Known for humorous books, plays *Potash and Prelmutter*, 1910-26.
b. July 23, 1877 in Manchester, England
d. February 03, 1934 in Westport, Connecticut

Ron Glass
American actor
• Played Ron Harris on "Barney Miller," 1975-82.
b. July 1, 1945 in Evansville, Indiana

Jackie (Herbert John) Gleason
American actor–comedian
• Best known for role of Ralph Kramden on TV series, "The Honeymooners."
b. February 26, 1916 in Brooklyn, New York
d. June 24, 1987 in Fort Lauderdale, Florida

James Gleason
American actor
• Nominated for 1941 Oscar for *Here Comes Mr. Jordan*.
b. May 23, 1886 in New York, New York
d. April 12, 1959 in Woodland Hills, California

Scott Glenn
American actor
• In films *Urban Cowboy*, 1980; *The Right Stuff*, 1983.
b. January 26, 1942 in Pittsburgh, Pennsylvania

Sharon Gless
American actress
• Played Chris Cagney on TV series "Cagney and Lacey," 1982-88; won two Emmys.
b. May 31, 1943 in Los Angeles, California

Danny Glover
American actor
• Starred in *The Color Purple*, 1985; *Places in the Heart*, 1984; *Lethal Weapon*, 1987.
b. 1947

Julian Glover
English actor
• Films include *Tom Jones*, 1963; *Nicholas and Alexandra*, 1971.
b. March 27, 1935 in London, England

George Leslie Gobel
American comedian
• Won 1954 Emmy for TV show, "The George Gobel Show."
b. May 2, 1919 in Chicago, Illinois
d. February 24, 1991 in Encino, California

Jean Luc Godard
French director
• A founder of French New Wave cinema; controversial films include *Breathless*, 1960; *Hail Mary*, 1985.
b. December 03, 1930 in Paris, France

Paulette Goddard
(Marion Levy)
American actress
• Married Charlie Chaplin, 1936-42, Erich Maria Remarque, 1958-70; appeared in 40 films including *Modern Times*, 1936, with Chaplin.
b. June 03, 1911 in Great Neck, New York
d. April 23, 1990 in Porto Ronco, Switzerland

Arthur Michael Godfrey
American actor–singer
• Hosted TV shows, 1948-59, including "The Arthur Godfrey Show."
b. August 31, 1903 in New York, New York
d. March 16, 1983 in New York, New York

Alexander (Boris Alexander) Godunov
American dancer
• First Bolshoi Ballet member to defect to US, 1979; films include *Witness*, 1985.
b. November 28, 1949 in Sakhalin, U.S.S.R.

Leonard Goldberg
American producer
• With Aaron Spelling, produced TV series "Charlie's Angels," "Hart to Hart."
b. January 24, 1934 in New York, New York

Whoopi Goldberg
(Caryn E Johnson)
American actress–comedienne
• Won Best-Supporting Actress Oscar, 1991, for role in *Ghost* ; starred in film *Color Purple*, 1985; one-women Broadway show, 1984-85.
b. November 13, 1950 in New York, New York

Jeff Goldblum
American actor
• Starred in films *The Big Chill*, 1983; *The Fly*, 1986; memorable cameo in *Annie Hall*.
b. October 22, 1952 in Pittsburgh, Pennsylvania

John Golden
American dramatist–producer
• Produced plays *Let Us Be Gay*, 1928; *Susan and God*, 1937; *Claudia*, 1941; wrote song "Poor Butterfly," 1916.
b. June 27, 1874 in New York, New York
d. June 17, 1955 in New York, New York

Leonard Harry Goldenson
American film executive–TV executive
• Chm., chief exec. of ABC since 1972; played pivotal role in history of commercial network TV.
b. December 07, 1905 in Scottdale, Pennsylvania

Horace Goldin
American magician
• Devised magic trick of "sawing a woman in half."
b. December 17, 1873 in Poland
d. August 22, 1939 in London, England

Bo Goldman
American screenwriter
• Won Oscars for *One Flew Over the Cuckoo's Nest*, 1975; *Melvin and Howard*, 1980.
b. September 1, 1932 in New York, New York

James Goldman
American dramatist–author
• Films include Oscar winners *Butch Cassidy and the Sundance Kid*, 1969; *All the President's Men*, 1976.
b. June 3, 1927 in Chicago, Illinois

William Goldman
American author–screenwriter
• Wrote film scripts *Harper*, 1966; *Marathon Man*, 1976; Oscar-winning *Butch Cassidy and the Sundance Kid*, 1969.
b. August 12, 1931 in Chicago, Illinois

Carlo Goldoni
Italian dramatist
• Creator of modern Italian comedy; plays reflect contemporary Venetian life: *La Locandiera*, 1753.
b. February 25, 1707 in Venice, Italy
d. January 06, 1793 in Versailles, France

Samuel Goldwyn
(Samuel Goldfish)
American producer
• Produced *All Quiet on the Western Front*, 1930; won Oscar for *The Best Years of Our Lives*, 1946; co-founded MGM; noted for malapropisms.
b. August 27, 1882 in Warsaw, Poland
d. January 31, 1974 in Los Angeles, California

Grant Goodeve
American actor
• Played David Bradford on TV series "Eight is Enough," 1977-81.
b. July 06, 1952 in New Haven, Connecticut

Lynda Goodfriend
American actress
• Played Richie's wife, Lori Beth, on TV comedy "Happy Days," 1983.
b. October 31, 1950 in Miami, Florida

John Goodman
American actor
• Plays Dan Conner on TV comedy "Roseanne," 1988–; films include *Sea of Love, Always*, 1989; *King Ralph*, 1991.
b. June 2, 1952 in Affton, Missouri

Frances Goodrich
(Mrs Albert Hacker)
American writer
• With husband, wrote screenplay of *The Diary of Anne Frank*, which won Tony, 1956.
b. 1891 in Belleville, New Jersey
d. January 29, 1984 in New York, New York

Mark Goodson
American producer
• Known as developer of TV game shows; with Bill Todman, created "The Price Is Right"; "Family Feud."
b. January 24, 1915 in Sacramento, California

Leo Gorcey
American actor
• Played Spit, the gang leader, in film series *Dead End Kids; East Side Kids; The Bowery Boys*.
b. June 03, 1915 in New York, New York
d. June 02, 1969 in Oakland, California

C Henry Gordon
(Henry Racke)
American actor
• Suave, cold-hearted villain in films, 1930s-40s.
b. June 17, 1883 in New York, New York
d. December 03, 1940 in Los Angeles, California

Gale Gordon
(Charles T Aldrich Jr)
American actor
• Played Mr. Wilson on "Dennis the Menace," 1962-64; Mr. Mooney on "The Lucy Show," 1968-74.
b. February 02, 1906 in New York, New York

Max Gordon
American producer
• Long-running hits include *Born Yesterday*, 1946; *The Solid Gold Cadillac*, 1953.
b. June 28, 1892 in New York, New York
d. November 02, 1978 in New York, New York

Ruth Gordon
(Ruth Jones; Mrs Garson Kanin)
American actress
• With husband co-wrote *Adam's Rib*, 1952; won Oscar for *Rosemary's Baby*, 1968.
b. October 3, 1896 in Wollaston, Massachusetts
d. August 28, 1985 in Martha's Vineyard, Massachusetts

Steve Gordon
American author–director
• Author, director of comedy *Arthur*, 1981.
b. 1940 in Toledo, Ohio
d. November 27, 1982 in New York, New York

Charles Edward Gordone
American dramatist
• Won 1970 Pulitzer for drama *No Place to Be Somebody*.
b. October 12, 1925 in Cleveland, Ohio

Marius Goring
English actor
• Films include *Lilli Marlene*, 1944; *The Red Shoes*, 1948; *Exodus*, 1960.
b. May 23, 1912 in Newport, England

Maxim Gorky, pseud
(Maxim Gorki; Alexie M Peshov; Aleksey Maximovich Pyeshkov)
Russian author–dramatist
• Wrote *The Lower Depths*, 1902; *Mother*, 1907; considered father of Soviet literature.
b. March 14, 1868 in Nizhni-Novgorod, Russia
d. June 18, 1936 in Moscow, U.S.S.R.

Cliff Gorman
American actor
• Won Tony for *Lenny*, 1971; TV appearances include "Class of '63," 1973.
b. October 13, 1936 in New York, New York

Frank John Gorshin
American actor–comedian
• Played the Riddler on "Batman," 1966-68.
b. April 05, 1934 in Pittsburgh, Pennsylvania

Marjoe (Hugh Ross) Gortner
American evangelist–actor
• Ordained minister, 1948; name is amalgam of Mary and Joseph; won Oscar, 1972, for autobiographical documentary, *Marjoe*.
b. January 14, 1945 in Long Beach, California

Freeman Fisher Gosden
(Amos 'n Andy)
American comedian
• Amos of "Amos 'n Andy" radio show, 1926-58; show denounced by NAACP.
b. May 05, 1899 in Richmond, Virginia
d. December 1, 1982 in Los Angeles, California

Lou(is, Jr) Gossett
American actor
• Won best supporting actor Oscar for *An Officer and a Gentleman*, 1983.
b. May 27, 1936 in Brooklyn, New York

Morton Edgar Gottlieb
American producer
• Won Tony for *Sleuth*, 1970; produced film version, 1972.
b. May 02, 1921 in Brooklyn, New York

Elliott Gould
(Elliott Goldstein)
American actor
• Starred in films *Bob and Carol and Ted and Alice*, 1969, *M*A*S*H*, 1970; former husband of Barbra Streisand.
b. August 29, 1938 in Brooklyn, New York

Edmund Goulding
American director
• Films include *Grand Hotel*, 1932; *Nightmare Alley*, 1949.
b. March 2, 1891 in London, England
d. December 24, 1959 in Hollywood, California

Ray(mond Walter) Goulding
("Bob and Ray")
American comedian
• Member of comedy team, Bob and
Ray, known for satire, ad-libbing; won
Peabody Award, 1952, 1957.
b. March 20, 1922 in Lowell, Massachusetts
d. March 24, 1990 in Manhasset, New York

Betty Grable
(Elizabeth Grasle)
American actress
• WW II pin-up girl; married Jackie
Coogan, 1937-40, Harry James, 1943-
65.
b. December 18, 1916 in Saint Louis, Missouri
d. July 03, 1973 in Beverly Hills, California

Don Grady
(Don L Agrati)
American actor
• Played Robbie Douglas on TV comedy
"My Three Sons," 1960-72; was a Mouseketeer on "The Mickey Mouse Club,"
1957.
b. June 08, 1944 in San Diego, California

Martha Graham
American dancer–choreographer
• Doyenne of modern dance; founder, director, Martha Graham Dance Co.,
1926–; choreographed over 150 works.
b. May 11, 1893 in Pittsburgh, Pennsylvania
d. April

Virginia Graham
(Virginia Komiss)
American TV personality–actress
• Active in TV, 1950s-60s; honored by
many groups for her charitable work;
wrote *If I Made It So Can You*, 1979;
films include *Slapstick of Another Kind*,
1984.
b. July 04, 1912 in Chicago, Illinois

Gloria Grahame
(Gloria Grahame Hallward)
American actress
• Won 1952 Oscar for *The Bad and the
Beautiful*.
b. November 28, 1925 in Los Angeles, California
d. October 05, 1981 in New York, New York

Fred(erick Lawrence) Grandy
American politician–actor
• Parlayed fame from role on TV series
"Love Boat," 1977-86 to win election as
Rep. congressman from IA, 1986.
b. June 29, 1948 in Sioux City, Iowa

Farley Granger
American actor
• Played in Hitchcock films *Rope*, 1948;
Strangers on a Train, 1951.
b. July 01, 1925 in San Jose, California

Stewart Granger
(James Lablache Stewart)
American actor–author
• Wrote autobiography *Sparks Fly Up-
ward*; films include *Caesar and Cleopatra*,
1945.
b. May 06, 1913 in London, England

Cary Grant
(Archibald Alexander Leach; "Archie")
American actor
• One of Hollywood's most enduring
leading men; starred in *The Philadelphia
Story*, 1940; *North by Northwest*, 1959.
b. January 18, 1904 in Bristol, England
d. November 29, 1986 in Davenport, Iowa

Lee Grant
(Mrs Joseph Feury; Lyova Haskell Ro-
senthal)
American actress
• Won Emmy for "Peyton Place," 1965;
Oscar for *Shampoo*, 1975.
b. October 31, 1931 in New York, New York

Bonita Granville
American actress
• Played Nancy Drew in 1930s film series.
b. February 02, 1923 in New York, New
York
d. October 11, 1988 in Santa Monica, California

Charley (Charles) Grapewin
American actor
• Character actor in over 100 films including *The Grapes of Wrath*, 1940; *Tobacco Road*, 1941.
b. December 2, 1875 in Xenia, Ohio
d. February 02, 1956 in Corona, California

Karen Gene Grassle
American actress
• Played Caroline Ingalls on "Little
House on the Prairie," 1973-81.
b. February 25, 1944 in Berkeley, California

Ben(jamin Franklin) Grauer
American broadcast journalist
• NBC commentator, announcer; covered
wide variety of events, 1930-73.
b. June 02, 1908 in New York, New York
d. May 31, 1977 in New York, New York

Peter Graves
English actor
• Character actor mainly in British films
since 1941.
b. October 21, 1911 in London, England

Peter Graves
(Peter Aurness)
American actor
• Played Jim Phelps in "Mission: Impos-
sible," 1967-73; brother of James
Arness.
b. March 18, 1926 in Minneapolis, Minnesota

Dolores Gray
American actress
• Appeared on Broadway in *Annie Get
Your Gun*, 1947-50; won Tony for *Car-
nival in Flanders*, 1954.
b. June 07, 1924 in Chicago, Illinois

Dulcie Gray
(Dulcie Bailey)
British actress–author
• Noted for London stage career; writings
include mystery/horror books: *Murder in
Mind*, 1963.
b. November 2, 1919 in Kuala Lampur, Ma-
laysia

Linda Gray
American actress
• Appeared in over 400 TV commercials; plays Sue Ellen Ewing on "Dallas," 1978–.
b. September 12, 1941 in Santa Monica, California

Simon James Holliday Gray
English dramatist
• Wrote *Wise Child*, 1968; *Butley*,
1971; *Otherwise Engaged*, 1975.
b. October 21, 1936 in Hayling Island, England

Kathryn Grayson
(Zelma Hedrick)
American actress
• Starred in *Show Boat*, 1951; *Kiss Me
Kate*, 1953; *The Vagabond King*, 1956.
b. February 09, 1923 in Winston-Salem,
North Carolina

Jose Greco
American dancer–choreographer
• Debut in *Carmen*, 1937; appeared in
Ship of Fools, 1965.
b. December 23, 1918 in Montorio, Italy

Abel Green
American screenwriter–actor
• Wrote film *Mr. Broadway*, 1947; appeared in *Copacabana*, 1947.
b. June 03, 1900 in New York, New York
d. May 1, 1973 in New York, New York

Gerald Green
American writer
• Documentary TV films include Emmy-
winner "Holocaust," 1978.
b. April 08, 1922 in Brooklyn, New York

Guy Green
English director
• Won 1947 Oscar for *Great Expectations.*
b. 1913 in Frome, England

Mitzi Green
American actress
• Child star who played Annie in *Little Orphan Annie;* Becky Thatcher in *Tom Sawyer, Huckleberry Finn;* retired age 14.
b. October 22, 1920 in New York, New York
d. May 24, 1969 in Huntington, California

Paul Eliot Green
American dramatist–screenwriter
• Writings portray NC, black themes; wrote 1927 Pulitzer play *In Abraham's Bosom.*
b. March 17, 1894 in Lillington, North Carolina
d. May 04, 1981 in Chapel Hill, North Carolina

Lorne Greene
American actor
• Best known for role of Ben Cartwright on TV western "Bonanza," 1959-73.
b. February 12, 1915 in Ottawa, Ontario
d. September 11, 1987 in Santa Monica, California

Richard Greene
English actor
• Played the original Robin Hood in British TV series "Robin Hood," 1950s.
b. August 25, 1918 in Plymouth, England
d. June 01, 1985 in Norfolk, England

Robert Greene
English dramatist
• His dramatic works *Friar Bacon* and *Friar Bungay,* 1594, were models for Shakespeare's comedies.
b. July 11, 1558 in Norwich, England
d. September 03, 1592 in London, England

Shecky Greene
(Fred Sheldon Greenfield)
American actor–comedian
• Las Vegas comedian since 1953; in film *Tony Rome,* 1967.
b. April 08, 1926 in Chicago, Illinois

Bud Greenspan
American producer–director
• Known for sports documentaries for TV, albums.
b. September 18, 1927 in New York, New York

Sydney Hughes Greenstreet
English actor
• Best known roles in *The Maltese Falcon,* 1941; *Casablanca,* 1942.
b. December 27, 1879 in Sandwich, England
d. January 19, 1954 in Los Angeles, California

Charlotte Greenwood
American actress
• Comedienne best known for her high kicking dance routines.
b. June 25, 1893 in Philadelphia, Pennsylvania
d. January 18, 1978 in Los Angeles, California

Joan Greenwood
English actress
• Films include *The Man in the White Suit,* 1951.
b. March 04, 1921 in London, England
d. March 02, 1987 in London, England

Bettina Louise Gregory
American broadcast journalist
• Corrsepondent, ABC News, 1974–; White House correspondent, 1979–.
b. June 04, 1946 in New York, New York

Cynthia Kathleen Gregory
American dancer
• Principal dancer with American Ballet Theatre, 1967–.
b. July 08, 1946 in Los Angeles, California

Dick (Richard Claxton) Gregory
American comedian–author–political activist
• Noted for social consciousness expressed through fasting, lifestyle; first black comedian to perform for white audiences.
b. October 12, 1932 in Saint Louis, Missouri

Lady Isabella Augusta Persse Gregory
Irish dramatist
• A founder, Irish National Theater; directed Abbey Theater, 1904; her plays depict Irish peasants.
b. March 15, 1852 in Roxborough, Scotland
d. May 22, 1932 in County Galway, Ireland

James Gregory
American actor
• Starred on Broadway in *Death of a Salesman;* in films *PT-109; The In-Laws.*
b. December 23, 1911 in New York, New York

John Gregson
English actor
• Played in British TV police series "Gideon's Way."
b. March 15, 1919 in Liverpool, England
d. January 08, 1975 in Porlock Weir, England

Joyce Irene Grenfell
English actress
• Presented her own monologues in one-woman shows, 1939; few films as character actress *Yellow Rolls Royce.*
b. February 1, 1910 in London, England
d. November 3, 1979 in London, England

Jennifer Grey
American actress
• Films include *Ferris Bueller's Day Off,* 1986; *Dirty Dancing,* 1987; daughter of Joel.
b. March 26, 1960 in New York, New York

Joel Grey
(Joel Katz)
American singer–actor–dancer
• Won Tony for *Cabaret,* 1967; Oscar for film, 1972.
b. April 11, 1932 in Cleveland, Ohio

Virginia Grey
American actress
• Began career as Little Eva in *Uncle Tom's Cabin,* 1927.
b. March 22, 1917 in Los Angeles, California

Harry Wagstaff Graham Gribble
English dramatist–director
• Wrote Broadway hit *Elizabeth and Essex,* 1930; dircted *Johnny Belinda,* 1940.
b. March 27, 1896 in Sevenoaks, England
d. January 28, 1981 in New York, New York

Pamela Suzette Grier
American actress
• Films include *On The Edge,* 1985; *Something Wicked This Way Comes,* 1983; TV show "Roots II."
b. May 26, 1949 in Winston-Salem, North Carolina

Merv(yn Edward) Griffin
American TV personality
• Hosted "The Merv Griffin Show," 1960s-80s; produces TV game show "Wheel of Fortune."
b. July 06, 1925 in San Mateo, California

Andy (Andrew) Griffith
American actor
• Made stage and film debut in *No Time for Sergeants,* 1955; played Andy Taylor on TV comedy "The Andy Griffith Show," 1960-69, title role on TV series "Matlock," 1988–.
b. June 01, 1926 in Mount Airy, North Carolina

D(avid Lewelyn) W(ark) Griffith
American director–actor
• Introduced techniques that changed movies into art form; films include *Birth of a Nation,* 1915.
b. January 22, 1875 in La Grange, Kentucky
d. July 23, 1948 in Los Angeles, California

Hugh Emrys Griffith
Welsh actor
• Won Oscar for *Ben Hur,* 1959.
b. May 3, 1912 in Anglesey, Wales
d. May 14, 1980 in London, England

Melanie Griffith
(Mrs Don Johnson)
American actress
• Received Oscar nomination for role in *Working Girl*, 1988; daughter of Tippi Hedren.
b. August 09, 1957 in New York, New York

Yuri Nikolaevich Grigorovich
Russian dancer
• Chief Ballet Master, Bolshoi Theater, 1970–.
b. January 01, 1927

John Grillo
English dramatist–actor
• Bizarre plays include *Hello Goodbye Sebastian*, 1965.
b. November 29, 1942 in Watford, England

Franz Grillparzer
Austrian dramatist
• Best-known works include *The Golden Fleece*, 1821; *Hero and Leander*, 1831.
b. January 15, 1791 in Vienna, Austria
d. January 21, 1872 in Vienna, Austria

Joseph Grimaldi
English clown
• Popular attraction in Covent Gardens, 1806-23; created archetypal clown "Joey."
b. December 18, 1779
d. May 31, 1837

J William Grimes
American TV executive
• Chm., CEO, cable sports network, ESPN, 1982–.
b. March 07, 1941 in Wheeling, West Virginia

Tammy Lee Grimes
American actress
• Won Tonys for *Unsinkable Molly Brown*, 1961; *Private Lives*, 1970; married Christopher Plummer, 1956-60.
b. January 3, 1936 in Lynn, Massachusetts

George Grizzard
American actor
• Broadway appearances include *The Happiest Millionaire*, 1958; *The Country Girl*, 1972; *The Royal Family*, 1975.
b. April 01, 1928 in Roanoke Rapids, North Carolina

Charles Grodin
American actor–director–writer
• Films include *Heartbreak Kid*, 1972; *The Woman in Red*, 1984; *Movers and Shakers*, 1985.
b. April 21, 1935 in Pittsburgh, Pennsylvania

David Lawrence Groh
American actor
• Played Joe Girard on TV comedy "Rhoda," 1974-77; starred in Broadway production of *Chapter Two*, 1978.
b. May 21, 1939 in New York, New York

Michael Gross
American actor
• Played Steven Keaton on TV series "Family Ties," 1982-89.
b. June 21, 1947 in Chicago, Illinois

Harry Guardino
American actor
• Played on Broadway in *Woman of the Year*; films include *Dirty Harry*, 1971; *Any Which Way You Can*, 1980.
b. December 23, 1925 in New York, New York

John Guare
American dramatist
• Won 1971 Tony for best musical: *Two Gentlemen of Verona*.
b. February 05, 1938 in New York, New York

Peter (Howard Peter) Guber
American producer
• Produced *Missing*, 1982; *Flashdance*, 1983.
b. March 01, 1942 in Boston, Massachusetts

Burnett Guffey
American filmmaker
• Won Oscars for *From Here to Eternity*, 1953; *Bonnie and Clyde*, 1967.
b. May 26, 1905 in Del Rio, Tennessee
d. May 3, 1983 in Goleta Valley, California

Robert Guillaume
(Robert Peter Williams)
American actor
• Played Benson DuBois on TV comedys "Soap," 1977-79, "Benson," 1979-86; won Emmys, 1979, 1985.
b. November 3, 1937 in Saint Louis, Missouri

Sylvie Guillem
French dancer
• Featured ballerina with Paris Opera Ballet Co., 1984–; ballets include *Cinderella*.
b. 1965 in LeBlanc-Mesnil, France

Texas (Mary Louise Cecilia) Guinan
American actress
• Nightclub owner known for saying "Hello, Sucker!"; Betty Hutton portrayed her in movie *Incendiary Blonde*, 1945.
b. 1889 in Waco, Texas
d. November 05, 1933 in Vancouver, British Columbia

Sir Alec Guinness
English actor
• Versatile stage screen performer; played eight roles in *Kind Hearts and Coronets*, 1949; won Oscar for *The Bridge on the River Kwai*, 1958.
b. April 02, 1914 in London, England

Sacha Guitry
French filmmaker
• French films where he was actor, writer, director include *Pearls of the Crown*, 1938.
b. February 21, 1885 in Saint Petersburg, Russia
d. July 24, 1957 in Paris, France

Clu Gulager
American actor
• Films include *The Last Picture Show*, 1971.
b. November 16, 1928 in Holdenville, Oklahoma

Bryant Charles Gumbel
American broadcast journalist
• Hosted "NBC Sports," 1975-82; won Emmys 1976, 1977; host, "Today Show," 1982–.
b. September 29, 1948 in New Orleans, Louisiana

Moses Gunn
American actor–director
• Broadway plays include *First Breeze of Summer*, 1975; *I Have a Dream*, 1977; joined Negro Ensemble Co., 1967-68.
b. October 02, 1929 in Saint Louis, Missouri

A(lbert) R(amsdell) Gurney, Jr
(Pete Gurney psued)
American dramatist
• Plays describe WASP society: *Scenes from American Life*, 1971.
b. November 01, 1930 in Buffalo, New York

Steve Guttenberg
American actor
• Starred in films *Cocoon*, 1985, *Three Men and a Baby*, 1987.
b. August 24, 1958 in Brooklyn, New York

Alice Guy-Blanche
French director
• World's first woman director; first film *La Fee aux Choux*, 1896; made US films, 1910-20.
b. July 01, 1873 in Paris, France
d. 1968 in Mahwah, New Jersey

Edmund Gwenn
Welsh actor
• Won Oscar for role of Santa Claus in *Miracle on 34th Street*, 1947.
b. September 26, 1875 in Glamorgan, Wales
d. September 06, 1959 in Woodland Hills, California

Fred (Frederick Hubbard) Gwynne
American actor–children's author
• Played Herman Munster in TV comedy "The Munsters," 1964-68; starred in films *On the Waterfront*, 1954, *Cotton Club*, 1984. Also writes and illustrates children's books.
b. July 1, 1926 in New York, New York

Shelley Hack
American model–actress
• Revlon's "Charlie Girl" in TV commercials; starred in TV series "Charlie's Angels," 1979.
b. July 06, 1952 in Greenwich, Connecticut

Buddy Hackett
(Leonard Hacker)
American comedian
• Starred in *God's Little Acre*, 1958; *The Love Bug*, 1969; known for popular stand-up acts on TV, in nightclubs.
b. August 31, 1924 in New York, New York

Joan Hackett
American actress
• Starred in *The Group*, 1966; nominated for Oscar, 1982, for *Only When I Laugh*.
b. March 01, 1934 in New York, New York
d. October 08, 1983 in Encino, California

Taylor Hackford
American director–producer
• Films include *An Officer and A Gentleman*, 1983; *Against All Odds*, 1984.
b. December 31, 1944 in Santa Barbara, California

Gene (Eugene Alden) Hackman
American actor
• Won Oscar for *The French Connection*, 1972.
b. January 3, 1931 in San Bernardino, California

Reed Hadley
(Reed Herring)
American actor
• Starred in TV series "Racket Squad," 1951-53; "Public Defender," 1954.
b. 1911 in Petralia, Texas
d. December 11, 1974 in Los Angeles, California

Jean Hagen
(Jean Shirley VerHagen)
American actress
• Starred in TV series "Make Room for Daddy," 1953-57; films *Singin' in the Rain*, 1952; *Adam's Rib*, 1949.
b. August 03, 1923 in Chicago, Illinois
d. August 29, 1977 in Woodland Hills, California

Uta Thyra Hagen
American actress
• Won Tonys for *The Country Girl*, 1951; *Who's Afraid of Virginia Woolf?* 1963.
b. June 12, 1919 in Gottingen, Germany

Dan Haggerty
American actor
• Starred in TV series "Life and Times of Grizzly Adams," 1977-78.
b. November 19, 1941 in Hollywood, California

Larry Hagman
American actor
• Played Tony Nelson on TV comedy "I Dream of Jeannie," 1965-70; plays J R Ewing on TV series "Dallas," 1978–; son of Mary Martin.
b. September 21, 1931 in Fort Worth, Texas

Charles Haid
American actor
• Played Andy Renko on TV series "Hill Street Blues," 1981-87.
b. June 02, 1944 in San Francisco, California

Robert Terrel Haines
American actor
• Starred in vaudeville, radio, film, and on stage in career spanning four decades.
b. February 03, 1870 in Muncie, Indiana
d. May 06, 1943 in New York, New York

William Haines
American actor
• Appeared in silent films and early talkies; retired to become interior decorator.
b. January 01, 1900 in Staunton, Virginia
d. November 26, 1973 in Santa Monica, California

Alan Hale
(Rufus Alan McKahan)
American actor
• Character actor best known as Errol Flynn's sidekick in films such as *The Adventures of Robin Hood*, 1938.
b. February 1, 1892 in Washington, District of Columbia
d. January 22, 1950 in Hollywood, California

Alan Hale, Jr
American actor
• Played the Skipper on TV series "Gilligan's Island," 1964-67; son of Alan.
b. March 08, 1918 in Los Angeles, California
d. January 02, 1990 in Los Angeles, California

Barbara Hale
American actress
• Played Della Street on TV series "Perry Mason," 1957-66; mother of actor William Katt.
b. April 18, 1922 in De Kalb, Illinois

Ludovic Halevy
French dramatist–author
• With Henri Meilhac, wrote libretti for Bizet's *Carmen*, Offenbach's light operas; best known novel: *L'Abbe Constantin*.
b. July 01, 1834 in Paris, France
d. May 08, 1908 in Paris, France

Jack Haley
American actor
• Best known for role of the Tin Man in film *Wizard of Oz*, 1939.
b. August 1, 1900 in Boston, Massachusetts
d. June 06, 1979 in Los Angeles, California

Jack Haley, Jr (John J)
American director–producer
• Has produced many TV specials and awards shows; directed film *That's Entertainment*, 1974; son of Jack Haley; former husband of Liza Minnelli.
b. October 25, 1933 in Los Angeles, California

Adrian Hall
American director
• Award-winning stage work includes *Buried Child*, 1979; won special Tony, 1981.
b. December 03, 1927 in Van, Texas

Anthony Michael Hall
American actor
• Films include *The Breakfast Club*, 1985; *Out of Bounds*, 1986; *Edward Scissorhands*, 1991.
b. April 14, 1968 in Boston, Massachusetts

Arsenio Hall
American comedian–actor
• Stand-up comic; host, "The Arsenio Hall Show," 1988–; starred with Eddie Murphy in *Coming to America*, 1987.
b. February 12, 1955 in Cleveland, Ohio

Huntz (Henry) Hall
American actor
• Played Dippy in *The Dead End Kids*; Satch in *The Bowery Boys* film series, 1930s-40s.
b. 1920 in New York, New York

Monty Hall
(Monty Halparin)
Canadian TV personality
• Host of "Let's Make a Deal," 1963-77.
b. August 25, 1924 in Winnipeg, Manitoba

Sir Peter Reginald Frederick Hall
English director
• National Theatre Co., director since 1973.
b. November 22, 1930 in Bury St. Edmunds, England

Richard Halliday
American producer
• Producer, stage production of *Sound of Music*, stage, film productions of *Peter Pan*; married Mary Martin, 1940.
b. April 03, 1905 in Denver, Colorado
d. March 03, 1973 in Brasilia, Brazil

Florence Halop
American actress
• Played bailiff on TV series "Night Court," 1985-86.
b. January 23, 1923 in New York, New York
d. July 15, 1986 in Los Angeles, California

Veronica Hamel
American model–actress
• Played Joyce Davenport on TV series "Hill Street Blues," 1981-87.
b. November 2, 1945 in Philadelphia, Pennsylvania

Robert Hamer
English director
• Best known for *Kind Hearts and Coronets,* 1949.
b. March 31, 1911 in Kidderminster, England
d. December 04, 1963 in London, England

Rusty (Russell Craig) Hamer
American actor
• Played Rusty in TV series "Make Room for Daddy," 1953-64, "Make Room for Granddaddy," 1970-71; suicide victim.
b. February 15, 1947 in Tenafly, New Jersey
d. January 18, 1990 in De Ridder, Louisiana

Mark Hamill
American actor
• Played Luke Skywalker in *Star Wars,* 1977; *The Empire Strikes Back,* 1980.
b. September 25, 1952 in Oakland, California

Carrie Hamilton
American actress
• Daughter of Carol Burnett; in film *Tokyo Pop,* 1987, with mother in TV movie "Hostage," 1988.
b. December 05, 1963 in New York, New York

George Hamilton
American actor
• Star, producer of *Love at First Bite,* 1979; *Zorro, the Gay Blade,* 1981.
b. August 12, 1939 in Memphis, Tennessee

Guy Hamilton
British director
• Best known for James Bond films *Goldfinger,* 1964; *Diamonds Are Forever,* 1971.
b. 1922 in Paris, France

Linda Hamilton
American actress
• Played Catherine Chandler on TV series "Beauty and the Beast," 1987-89.
b. September 26, in Salisbury, Maryland

Margaret Brainard Hamilton
American actress
• Best known for role of Miss Gulch/Wicked Witch of the West in film *The Wizard of Oz,* 1939.
b. September 12, 1902 in Cleveland, Ohio
d. May 16, 1985 in Salisbury, Connecticut

Harry Robinson Hamlin
American actor
• Plays Michael Kuzack on TV series "LA Law," 1986–.
b. October 3, 1951 in Pasadena, California

Earl Henry Hamner, Jr
American writer
• Creator of TV series "The Waltons," "Falcon Crest."
b. July 1, 1923 in Schuyler, Virginia

Walter Hampden
(Walter Hampden Dougherty)
American actor
• Starred in *Hamlet, Cyrano de Bergerac*; fourth pres., Players' Club, 1927-54.
b. June 3, 1879 in New York, New York
d. June 11, 1955 in Los Angeles, California

Susan Hampshire
English actress
• Won Emmys, 1970, 71, 73; appeared in series "The Forsythe Saga," "The First Churchills."
b. May 12, 1942 in London, England

Christopher James Hampton
British dramatist
• Wrote 1971 Tony Award winner *The Philanthropist.*
b. January 26, 1946 in Fayal, Azores

Hope Hampton
American socialite–actress
• Silent film star, NYC socialite; noted for lavish dress.
b. 1901 in Houston, Texas
d. January 02, 1982 in New York, New York

James Hampton
American actor
• In films *Condorman,* 1981; *The China Syndrome,* 1979.
b. July 09, 1936 in Oklahoma City, Oklahoma

Terry (Terence David) Hands
English director
• London stage productions include *Cyrano de Bergerac,* 1985.
b. January 09, 1941 in Aldershot, England

Carol Haney
American choreographer–dancer
• In Broadway musical *Pajama Game,* 1954; choreographed *Funny Girl,* 1964.
b. December 24, 1924 in Bedford, Massachusetts
d. May 1, 1964 in Saddle River, New Jersey

Tom Hanks
American actor
• Funnyman noted for comedy films: *Splash,* 1984; *Big,* 1988; some TV guest spots; costarred in TV's "Bosom Buddies."
b. July 09, 1956 in Oakland, California

William Hanley
American dramatist
• Films include *The Gypsy Moths;* plays include *No Answer.*
b. October 22, 1931 in Lorain, Ohio

Daryl Hannah
American actress
• Films include *Splash,* 1984; *Legal Eagles,* 1986; *Steel Magnolias,* 1990.
b. 1961 in Chicago, Illinois

Lorraine Hansberry
American author–dramatist
• Wrote *A Raisin in the Sun,* 1959; first play by black woman produced on Broadway.
b. May 19, 1930 in Chicago, Illinois
d. January 02, 1965 in New York, New York

Ann Harding
(Dorothy Walton Gatley)
American actress
• 1930s film star; received Oscar nomination for *Holiday,* 1930.
b. August 17, 1904 in San Antonio, Texas
d. September 01, 1981 in Sherman Oaks, California

Sir Cedric Webster Hardwicke
English actor
• Character actor in authoritative, villain roles: *The Hunchback of Notre Dame,* 1939; *Suspicion,* 1941.
b. February 19, 1893 in Lye, England
d. August 06, 1964 in New York, New York

Oliver Hardy
(Laurel and Hardy; Norvell Hardy)
American comedian
• First film with Laurel: *Putting Pants on Philip,* 1926.
b. January 18, 1892 in Atlanta, Georgia
d. August 07, 1957 in Hollywood, California

David Hare
English dramatist
• Award-winning playwright: *Knuckle,* 1974; *Plenty,* 1978.
b. June 05, 1947 in Saint Leonards, England

Sir John Hare
English actor–manager
• Noted character actor; managed Garrick Theatre, 1889-1905, built for him by W S Gilbert.
b. May 16, 1844 in Yorkshire, England
d. December 28, 1921 in London, England

Dorian Harewood
American actor
• Appeared in TV mini-series "Roots–The Next Generations," 1979-81; film, *Against All Odds*, 1984.
b. August 06, 1951 in Dayton, Ohio

Jean Harlow
(Harlean Carpenter; "Blonde Bombshell")
American actress
• Platinum blonde star of *Hell's Angels*, 1930; *Dinner at Eight*, 1933; sex queen of 1930s.
b. March 03, 1911 in Kansas City, Missouri
d. June 07, 1937 in Los Angeles, California

Mark Harmon
American actor
• Son of Tom Harmon and Elyse Knox; starred in "St. Elsewhere," 1984-86; movies include *Summer School*, 1987; married Pam Dawber, 1987.
b. September 02, 1951 in Burbank, California

Ken Harper
American producer
• Best-known Broadway musical, *The Wiz*, opened, 1975; won seven Tonys.
b. 1940
d. January 2, 1988 in New York, New York

Tess Harper
(Tessie Jean Washam)
American actress
• In movies *Silkwood, Tender Mercies*. 1983.
b. 1950 in Mammoth Spring, Arkansas

Valerie Harper
American actress
• Won four Emmys for role of Rhoda in "The Mary Tyler Moore Show," 1970-74; "Rhoda," 1974-78; star of TV show "Valerie," 1986-87.
b. August 22, 1941 in Suffern, New York

Woody Harrelson
American actor
• Plays Woody Boyd on TV comedy "Cheers," 1985–.
b. July 23, 1961

Pat Harrington
(Daniel Patrick Harrington Jr)
American actor
• Played Schneider on TV series "One Day at a Time," 1975-84.
b. August 13, 1929 in New York, New York

Barbara Harris
American actress
• Films include *Plaza Suite*, 1971; *Nashville*, 1975; won Tony for *The Apple Tree*, 1966.
b. July 25, 1935 in Evanston, Illinois

Jed Harris
(Jacob Horowitz)
American producer–director
• Had four Broadway hits in 1928: *Broadway; Coquette; The Front Page; The Royal Family;* considered theater genius.
b. February 25, 1900 in Vienna, Austria
d. November 14, 1979 in New York, New York

Jonathan Harris
American actor
• Starred in TV series "Lost in Space," 1965-68.
b. 1919 in New York, New York

Julie Harris
American actress
• Starred in films *Member of the Wedding*, 1952; *East of Eden*, 1955; won Tony for *The Last of Mrs. Lincoln*, 1973.
b. December 02, 1925 in Grosse Pointe Park, Michigan

Neil Patrick Harris
American actor
• Plays title role in TV series "Doogie Howser, MD," 1989–.
b. June 15, 1973

Sir Richard Harris
Irish actor
• Won Golden Globe for *Camelot*, 1968; appeared in *A Man Called Horse*, 1970; Oscar-nominated for best actor for *The Field*, 1990.
b. October 01, 1930 in Limerick, Ireland

Sam Henry Harris
American producer
• Credited with 28 Broadway plays, 1920s-30s, including three Pulitzer winners.
b. February 03, 1872 in New York, New York
d. July 03, 1941 in New York, New York

Gregory Harrison
American actor
• Played Gonzo Gates in "Trapper John, MD," 1979-86.
b. May 31, 1950 in Avalon, California

Rex (Reginald Carey) Harrison
English actor
• Won 1957 Tony, 1964 Oscar for role of Henry Higgins in *My Fair Lady*; considered a master of light comedy.
b. March 05, 1908 in Huyton, England
d. June 02, 1990 in New York, New York

Ray Harryhausen
American special effects technician
• Trick film specialist: *Clash of the Titans*, 1981.
b. June 29, 1920 in Los Angeles, California

Mary Hart
American TV personality
• Co-host of syndicated TV series "Entertainment Tonight," 1982–.
b. November 08, 1951 in Madison, South Dakota

Moss Hart
(Robert Arnold Conrad)
American director–dramatist–author
• Won Tony for directing *My Fair Lady*, 1959.
b. October 24, 1904 in New York, New York
d. December 2, 1961 in Palm Springs, California

William Surrey Hart
American actor–author
• Stone-faced Western star, 1914-25; wrote Western novels, autobiography, *My Life: East and West*, 1929.
b. December 06, 1872 in Newburgh, New York
d. June 23, 1946 in Newhall, California

Mariette Hartley
(Mrs Patrick Boyriven)
American actress
• Best known for Polaroid commercials with James Garner; won Emmy for "The Incredible Hulk," 1979.
b. June 21, 1940 in New York, New York

Elizabeth Hartman
American actress
• Oscar nominee for first film: *A Patch of Blue*, 1965; committed suicide.
b. December 23, 1941 in Boardman, Ohio
d. June 11, 1987 in Pittsburgh, Pennsylvania

David Downs Hartman
American TV personality
• Hosted ABC's "Good Morning America," 1975-87.
b. May 19, 1935 in Pawtucket, Rhode Island

Grace Hartman
American dancer–comedienne
• Wife of Paul, formed comedy dance team.
b. 1907 in San Francisco, California
d. August 08, 1955 in Van Nuys, California

Paul Hartman
American actor
• Comic dance team with wife Grace on Broadway; won Tony, 1948, for *Angel in the Wings*.
b. March 01, 1904 in San Francisco, California
d. October 02, 1973 in Los Angeles, California

Anthony (Kesteven) Harvey
English director
• Best known for *Lion in Winter*, 1968; *They Might Be Giants*, 1972.
b. June 03, 1931 in London, England

Frank Laird Harvey
English screenwriter
• Wrote screenplay for *Poltergeist*, 1946.
b. August 11, 1912 in Manchester, England

Laurence Harvey
(Larushke Mischa Skikne)
British actor
• Oscar nominee for *Room at the Top*, 1958.
b. October 01, 1928 in Janiskis, Lithuania
d. November 25, 1973 in London, England

Paul Harvey
(Paul Harvey Aurandt; "Voice of US Heartland")
American broadcast journalist
• Opinionated, colorful ABC News commentator, 1957–; syndicated columnist, *LA Times* since 1954.
b. September 04, 1918 in Tulsa, Oklahoma

Ernie Harwell
American broadcaster–author
• Baseball broadcaster, songwriter; wrote *Tuned to Baseball*, 1985; Hall of Fame, 1981.
b. January 25, 1918 in Atlanta, Georgia

Vanessa Clare Harwood
Canadian dancer
• Star, National Ballet of Canada, 1970–.
b. 1947 in Cheltenham, England

Signe Eleonora Cecilia Hasso
Swedish actress
• Sweden's leading lady; first Hollywood starring role: *Assignment in Brittany*, 1943.
b. August 15, 1915 in Stockholm, Sweden

Hurd Hatfield
American actor
• Starred in film *The Picture of Dorian Gray*, 1945.
b. December 07, 1918 in New York, New York

Henry Hathaway
(Henri Leopold de Fiennes)
American director
• Best known for directing *True Grit*, 1969.
b. March 13, 1898 in Sacramento, California
d. February 11, 1985 in Los Angeles, California

Rutger Hauer
Dutch actor
• Films include *Blade Runner*, 1982; *A Breed Apart*, 1984.
b. January 23, 1944 in Breukelen, Netherlands

June Haver
(June Stovenour; Mrs Fred MacMurray)
American actress
• Personified *The Girl Next Door*, title of movie she starred in, 1953.
b. June 1, 1926 in Rock Island, Illinois

June Havoc
(Ellen Evangeline Hovick; "Baby June")
American actress
• Sister of Gypsy Rose Lee; author of two autobiographies, numerous plays.
b. November 08, 1916 in Seattle, Washington

Jack Hawkins
English actor
• Lost voice, 1966, due to cancer, but continued to act, with speaking parts dubbed by others.
b. September 14, 1910 in London, England
d. July 18, 1973 in London, England

Howard Winchester Hawks
American director–producer
• Best known for films *Bringing Up Baby*, 1938; *The Big Sleep*, 1946.
b. May 3, 1896 in Goshen, Indiana
d. December 26, 1977 in Palm Springs, California

Goldie (Jean) Hawn
American actress
• Won Oscar for *Cactus Flower*, 1969; other films include *Protocol*, 1984.
b. November 21, 1945 in Washington, District of Columbia

Sessue (Kintaro) Hayakawa
Japanese actor
• Oscar nominee for *Bridge on the River Kwai*, 1957.
b. June 1, 1886 in Chiba, Japan
d. November 23, 1974 in Tokyo, Japan

Russell Hayden
(Pate Lucid; "Lucky")
American actor
• Played Lucky Jenkins in *Hopalong Cassidy* western films.
b. June 12, 1912 in Chico, California
d. June 09, 1981 in Palm Springs, California

Sterling Relyea Walter Hayden
(John Hamilton; Stirling Hayden)
American actor–author
• Rugged character actor; best known for roles in *The Asphalt Jungle*, 1950; *Dr. Strangelove*, 1964; wrote of wanderlust, love of sea in popular novel *Voyage*, 1976.
b. March 26, 1916 in Montclair, New Jersey
d. May 23, 1986 in Sausalito, California

Richard Haydn
English actor–director
• Starred in *Please Don't Eat the Daisies*, 1960; *The Sound of Music*, 1965.
b. 1905 in London, England
d. April 25, 1985 in Pacific Palisades, California

Gabby (George Francis) Hayes
American actor
• Comic sidekick in over 200 westerns.
b. May 07, 1885 in Wellsville, New York
d. February 09, 1969 in Burbank, California

Helen Hayes
(Mrs Charles MacArthur; Helen H Brown; "First Lady of the American Theater")
American actress
• Won Oscars for *The Sin of Madelon Claudet*, 1931; *Airport*, 1970; adoptive mother of James MacArthur.
b. October 1, 1900 in Washington, District of Columbia

John Michael Hayes
American screenwriter
• Won awards for scripts for *Rear Window*, 1954; *To Catch a Thief*, 1955.
b. May 11, 1919 in Worcester, Massachusetts

Lloyd (Samuel Lloyd) Haynes
American actor
• Best known portrayal of history teacher Pete Dixon on TV series "Room 222," 1969-74.
b. October 19, 1935 in South Bend, Indiana
d. December 31, 1986 in Coronado, California

Robert Hays
American actor
• Starred in *Airplane!*, 1980; *Airplane II*, 1982.
b. July 24, 1947 in Bethesda, Maryland

Leland Hayward
American producer
• Top Hollywood agent, 1940s; produced Broadway hits *South Pacific*, 1949; *Sound of Music*, 1959.
b. September 13, 1902 in Nebraska City, Nebraska
d. March 18, 1971 in Yorktown Heights, New York

Louis Hayward
(Seafield Grant)
American actor
• Played swashbucklers in 1940s adventure films; last film was *Terror in the Wax Museum*, 1973.
b. March 19, 1909 in Johannesburg, South Africa
d. February 21, 1985 in Palm Springs, California

Susan Hayward
(Edythe Marrener)
American actress
• Won Oscar for *I Want to Live*, 1958.
b. June 3, 1919 in New York, New York
d. March 14, 1975 in Beverly Hills, California

Rita Hayworth
(Margarita Carmen Cansino; "The Love Goddess")
American actress
• Made 60 films in 37 yrs.; known for WW II pinup photo in *Life* mag., 1941.
b. October 17, 1918 in New York, New York
d. May 14, 1987 in New York, New York

Katherine Healy
American dancer–actress
• Won gold medal, Varna International Ballet Competition; in film *Six Weeks*, 1982.
b. 1969 in New York, New York

Mary Healy
(Mrs Peter Lind Hayes)
American entertainer
• Teamed with husband, Peter Lind Hayes, for radio, TV shows, 1950s; wrote *Only Twenty-Five Minutes from Broadway*, 1961.
b. April 14, 1918 in New Orleans, Louisiana

Ted Healy
American actor
• Films include *Reckless*, 1935; *Hollywood Hotel*, 1937.
b. October 01, 1896 in Houston, Texas
d. December 21, 1937 in Los Angeles, California

John Heard
American actor
• Films include *Cat People*, 1982; *CHUD*, 1984; won Obie for *Othello and Split*, 1980.
b. March 07, 1945 in Washington, District of Columbia

Gabriel Heatter
American radio performer–journalist
• Opening words for his news broadcasts, "Ah-there's good news tonight," became nat. catch phrase.
b. September 17, 1890 in New York, New York
d. March 3, 1972 in Miami Beach, Florida

Ben Hecht
American author–dramatist
• Wrote novels of city life; co-wrote many Hollywood, Broadway hits, including *Front Page*, 1928.
b. February 28, 1893 in New York, New York
d. April 18, 1964 in New York, New York

Harold Hecht
American producer
• Won best picture Oscar, 1955, for *Marty*.
b. June 01, 1907 in New York, New York
d. May 25, 1985 in Beverly Hills, California

Eileen (Anna Eileen) Heckart
American actress
• Won 1972 Oscar for *Butterflies Are Free*.
b. March 29, 1919 in Columbus, Ohio

Amy Heckerling
American director
• Films include *Fast Times at Ridgemont High*, 1982; *National Lampoon's European Vacation*, 1985.
b. May 07, 1954 in New York, New York

Tippi (Natalie Kay) Hedren
American actress
• Cool blonde star of Hitchcock films: *The Birds*, 1963; *Marnie*, 1964; mother of Melanie Griffith.
b. January 19, 1935 in New Ulm, Minnesota

Van Emmett Evan Heflin
American actor
• Won Oscar for *Johnny Eager*, 1942; also in film *Shane*, 1953.
b. December 13, 1910 in Walters, Oklahoma
d. July 23, 1971 in Hollywood, California

O P Heggie
Australian actor
• Films include *Anne of Green Gables*, 1934; *Bride of Frankenstein*, 1935.
b. November 17, 1879 in Angaston, Australia
d. February 07, 1936 in Los Angeles, California

Robert Hegyes
American actor
• Played Epstein on TV series "Welcome Back, Kotter," 1975-79.
b. May 07, 1951 in New Jersey

Theresa Helburn
American producer
• With Theatre Guild, 1918-53; produced *Oklahoma*, 1943.
b. January 12, 1887 in New York, New York
d. August 18, 1959 in Weston, Connecticut

Anna Held
American actress
• Broadway star; first wife of Flo Ziegfeld; starred in *Anna Held*, 1902; known for expressive eyes, milk baths.
b. March 08, 1873 in Paris, France
d. August 12, 1918 in New York, New York

Lillian Hellman
American dramatist–author
• Wrote *The Little Foxes*, 1939; movie *Julia*, based on *Pentimento*, 1973.
b. June 2, 1905 in New Orleans, Louisiana
d. June 3, 1984 in Martha's Vineyard, Massachusetts

Katherine Helmond
American actress
• Starred as Jessica Tate on TV's "Soap," 1977-80. Also, "Who's the Boss."
b. June 05, 1933 in Galveston, Texas

Tom Helmore
English actor
• Films include *Designing Woman*, 1957; *Vertigo*, 1958.
b. January 04, 1912 in London, England

Sir Robert Murray Helpmann
Australian dancer–actor
• Flamboyant star of British ballet, 1934-50; known for theatricality; films include *The Mango Tree*, 1981.
b. April 09, 1909 in Mount Gambier, Australia
d. September 28, 1986 in Sydney, Australia

Margaux Hemingway
American model–actress
• Granddaughter of Ernest Hemingway; starred in *Lipstick*, 1976.
b. February 19, 1955 in Portland, Oregon

Mariel Hemingway
(Mrs Steve Douglas Crisinan)
American actress
• Granddaughter of Ernest Hemingway; starred in *Lipstick*, 1976; *Manhattan*, 1979.
b. November 21, 1961 in Mill Valley, Idaho

David Leslie Edward Hemmings
(Leslie Edward)
English actor
• Starred in films *Blow-Up*, 1966, *Camelot*, 1967.
b. November 18, 1941 in Guildford, England

Sherman Hemsley
American actor
• Played George Jefferson on "The Jeffersons," 1975-85; star of "Amen," 1986–.
b. February 01, 1938 in Philadelphia, Pennsylvania

Florence Henderson
American actress–singer
• Starred in TV series "The Brady Bunch," 1969-75.
b. February 14, 1934 in Dale, Indiana

Ian Hendry
English actor
• Best known for *Theatre of Blood*, 1973.
b. 1931 in Ipswich, England

Beth (Elizabeth Becker) Henley
American dramatist
• Won Pulitzer, 1981, for *Crimes of the Heart*, filmed 1986.
b. May 08, 1952 in Jackson, Mississippi

Doug(las James) Henning
Canadian magician
• Created, starred in musical *The Magic Show*; host of TV specials.
b. May 03, 1947 in Fort Gary, Manitoba

Linda Kaye Henning
American actress
• Played Betty Jo Bradley on TV series "Petticoat Junction," 1963-70.
b. September 16, 1944 in Toulca Lake, California

Paul Henreid
(Paul G Julius VonHernreid)
Italian actor–director
• Discovered by Otto Preminger, 1933; starred in *Casablanca*, 1943.
b. January 1, 1908 in Trieste, Italy

Buck Henry
(Buck Zuckerman)
American screenwriter–actor
• Wrote, appeared in film: *The Graduate*, 1967; wrote *Protocol*, 1984.
b. December 09, 1930 in New York, New York

Charlotte Henry
American actress
• Had title role in *Alice in Wonderland*, 1933.
b. March 03, 1913 in Charlotte, New York
d. April 1980 in San Diego, California

Jim (James Maury) Henson
American puppeteer
• Created the Muppets who first appeared on "Sesame Street," 1969; produced "The Muppet Show," 1976-81, which won three Emmys; and three feature films starring the Muppets.
b. September 24, 1936 in Greenville, Mississippi
d. May 16, 1990 in New York, New York

Audrey Hepburn
(Mrs Andrea Dotti; Edda Hepburn)
American actress
• Won Oscar for *Roman Holiday*, 1953; starred in *My Fair Lady*, 1964.
b. May 04, 1929 in Brussels, Belgium

Katharine Houghton Hepburn
American actress
• Has received more Oscar nominations–12–and won more Oscars–four–than any other actor; among her films: *The Philadelphia Story*, 1940, several with lover Spencer Tracy.
b. November 08, 1907 in Hartford, Connecticut

Hugh Herbert
American actor
• Comedian whose signature was fluttery hands and expression "Woo-Woo!"
b. August 1, 1887 in Binghamton, New York
d. March 13, 1951 in Hollywood, California

Eileen Herlie
(Eileen Herlihy)
Scottish actress
• Played Queen Gertrude in *Hamlet*, opposite Laurence Olivier, 1948, Richard Burton, 1964.
b. March 08, 1920 in Glasgow, Scotland

George Edward Herman
American broadcast journalist
• Moderator on TV show "Face the Nation," 1969-84; Washington, DC correspondent, 1954–.
b. January 14, 1920 in New York, New York

Pee-Wee Herman
(Paul Reubens)
American comedian
• His child-like character became basis for hit film *Pee-wee's Big Adventure*, 1985; children's TV show "Pee-wee's Playhouse," 1986–.
b. August 27, 1952 in Peekskill, New York

Edward Herrmann
American actor
• Won Tony, 1976, for *Mrs. Warren's Profession*; played FDR on TV's "Eleanor and Franklin."
b. July 21, 1943 in Washington, District of Columbia

Barbara Hershey
(Barbara Herzstein; Barbara Seagull)
American actress
• In TV series "The Monroes," 1966-67; films *The Natural*, 1984; *A World Apart*, 1988; *Hannah and Her Sisters*, 1986.
b. February 05, 1948 in Hollywood, California

Jean Hersholt
Danish actor
• Special Oscar, Jean Hersholt Humanitarian Award, given in his honor since 1956; star of radio show "Dr. Christian," 1937-54.
b. July 12, 1886 in Copenhagen, Delaware
d. June 02, 1956 in Beverly Hills, California

Werner Herzog
(Werner H Stipetic)
German director
• Films include *Aguirre, the Wrath of God*, 1973, *Fitzcarraldo*, 1982.
b. 1942 in Munich, Germany

Howard Hesseman
American actor
• Played Dr. Johnny Fever on TV comedy "WKRP in Cincinnati," 1978-82; star of TV comedy "Head of the Class," 1986-90.
b. February 27, 1940 in Lebanon, Ohio

Charlton Heston
American actor
• Won Oscar for *Ben Hur*, 1959; president of Screen Actors Guild, 1966-71.
b. October 04, 1922 in Evanston, Illinois

Alan Hewitt
American actor
• Film work included *That Touch of Mink*, 1962; *Sweet Charity*, 1969; recorded over 200 books for the blind.
b. January 21, 1915 in New York, New York
d. November 07, 1986 in New York, New York

Jon-Erik Hexum
American actor
• In TV series "Cover-Up," 1984; accidentally killed himself playing Russian Roulette.
b. November 05, 1958 in Englewood, New Jersey
d. October 18, 1984 in Los Angeles, California

Thomas Heywood
English dramatist
• Said to have written 220 plays including *The Captives*, 1634.
b. 1574 in Lincoln, England
d. August 1641 in London, England

Dwayne B Hickman
American actor
• Starred in "The Many Loves of Dobie Gillis," 1959-63; exec. producer of comedies, CBS, 1979–.
b. May 18, 1934 in Los Angeles, California

Wild Bill (James Butler) Hickok
American frontiersman–entertainer
• Toured with Buffalo Bill as legendary gunfighter, 1872-73; killed while playing poker.
b. May 27, 1837 in Troy Grove, Illinois
d. August 02, 1876 in Deadwood, South Dakota

Colin Higgins
French writer
• Films include *Harold and Maude*, 1971; *Nine to Five*, 1980; TV movies include *Out on a Limb*, 1987.
b. July 28, 1941 in Noumea, New Caledonia

Arthur Hill
Canadian actor
• Won 1962 Tony for *Who's Afraid of Virginia Woolf?*, starred in TV show "Owen Marshall, Counselor at Law," 1971-74.
b. August 01, 1922 in Melfort, Saskatchewan

Benny (Benjamin) Hill
(Alfred Hawthorn Hill)
English comedian
• Star of internationally syndicated TV series, "The Benny Hill Show."
b. January 21, 1925 in Southampton, England

George Roy Hill
American director
• Directed *Butch Cassidy and the Sundance Kid*, 1969; *The Sting*, 1973; won Oscar for *The Sting*.
b. December 2, 1922 in Minneapolis, Minnesota

Virginia Hill
American actress–criminal
• Appeared in 1930s musicals; mistress of gangsters Joe Adonis, Bugsy Siegel; key witness, 1951 Kefauver Crime Investigation.
b. August 26, 1916 in Lipscomb, Alabama
d. March 25, 1966 in Salzburg, Austria

Arthur Hiller
American director
• Best known for *Love Story*, 1970.
b. November 22, 1923 in Edmonton, Alberta

Wendy Hiller
English actress
• Won 1958 Oscar for *Separate Tables*.
b. August 15, 1912 in Bramhall, England

John Benedict Hillerman
American actor
• Played Jonathan Higgins on "Magnum PI," 1980-88; won Emmy, 1987.
b. December 2, 1932 in Denison, Texas

Daisy Hilton
(The Hilton Sisters)
English entertainer–siamese twins
• Siamese twin in films *Freaks*, 1932; *Chained for Life*, 1950.
b. February 05, 1908 in Brighton, England
d. January 04, 1969 in Charlotte, North Carolina

Violet Hilton
(The Hilton Sisters)
English entertainer–siamese twins
• One of Siamese twin in vaudeville act; made film *Chained for Life*, 1950.
b. February 05, 1908 in Brighton, England
d. January 04, 1969 in Charlotte, North Carolina

Gregory Oliver Hines
American dancer–actor
• Tap dancer, known for jazz numbers in musical *Eubie*, 1978; film *The Cotton Club*, 1984.
b. February 14, 1946 in New York, New York

Pat (Martin Patterson) Hingle
American actor
• Films include *Splendor in the Grass*, 1961; *Norma Rae*, 1979.
b. July 19, 1924 in Denver, Colorado

Judd Hirsch
American actor
• Played Alex on TV series "Taxi," 1978-85; won 1986 Tony for *I'm Not Rappaport*. Currently starring in "Dear John."
b. March 15, 1935 in New York, New York

Sir Alfred Joseph Hitchcock
English director
• Famous thrillers include *North by Northwest*, 1959; *Psycho*, 1960; won 1940 Oscar for *Rebecca*.
b. August 13, 1899 in London, England
d. April 29, 1980 in Beverly Hills, California

Raymond Hitchcock
American actor
• Vaudeville, film comedian who did three films for Mack Sennett, 1915.
b. 1865 in Auburn, New York
d. December 24, 1929 in Beverly Hills, California

Valerie Babette Hobson
British actress
• Leading lady in British films, 1936-54; retired, married to John Profumo since 1954.
b. April 14, 1917 in Larne, Northern Ireland

Rolf Hochhuth
German author–dramatist
• Due to subject matter (guilt, moral responsibility), his play *The Deputy* brought him int'l. fame, 1963.
b. April 01, 1931 in Germany

John Hodiak
American actor
• Best known for film *Lifeboat*, 1944.
b. April 16, 1914 in Pittsburgh, Pennsylvania
d. October 19, 1955 in Tarzana, California

Dustin Hoffman
American actor
• Starred in *The Graduate*, 1967; *Kramer vs. Kramer*, 1979; *Tootsie*, 1982; won Emmy for TV movie *Death of a Salesman*, 1986. Won Oscar for Best Actor in *Rain Man*, 1988.
b. August 08, 1937 in Los Angeles, California

Jack Bernard Hofsiss
American director
• Won Tony for *Elephant Man*, 1979.
b. September 28, 1950 in Brooklyn, New York

Paul Hogan
Australian actor
• Wrote, directed, starred in *Crocodile Dundee*, 1986; *Crocodile Dundee II*, 1988; married co-star Linda Kozlowski, 1990.
b. October 08, 1939 in Lightning Ridge, Australia

Hal (Harold Rowe, Jr) Holbrook
American actor
• Won Tony, NY Drama Critics citation for *Mark Twain Tonight*, 1966.
b. February 17, 1925 in Cleveland, Ohio

Fay Holden
(Fay Hammerton)
English actress
• Portrayed Mickey Rooney's mother in Andy Hardy film series.
b. September 26, 1895 in Birmingham, England
d. June 23, 1973 in Los Angeles, California

William Holden
(William Franklin Beedle Jr)
American actor
• Starred in over 50 films; won Oscar for *Stalag 17*, 1953.
b. April 17, 1918 in O'Fallon, Illinois
d. November 12, 1981 in Santa Monica, California

Geoffrey Holder
Actor
• Won Tony Awards as director, costume designer of *The Wiz*, 1975.
b. August 01, 1930 in Trinidad

Judd Clifton Holdren
American actor
• Starred in 1950s film series *Captain Video; Zombies of the Stratosphere; Last Planet.*
b. October 16, 1915 in Iowa
d. March 11, 1974 in Los Angeles, California

Polly Dean Holliday
American actress
• Starred in TV series "Alice," 1976-80; in own series "Flo," 1981.
b. July 02, 1937 in Jasper, Alabama

Earl Holliman
(Anthony Numkena)
American actor
• Starred, with Angie Dickinson, in TV series "Police Woman," 1974-78.
b. September 11, 1928 in Delhi, Louisiana

Stanley Holloway
English actor
• Played Eliza Doolittle's father in *My Fair Lady,* 1964.
b. October 01, 1890 in London, England
d. January 3, 1982 in Littlehampton, England

Sterling Price Holloway
American actor
• Voice of many Disney animals, including Winnie the Pooh; supporting actor in over 100 films.
b. January 04, 1905 in Cedartown, Georgia

Hollywood Ten
(Alvah Bessie; Herbert Biberman; Lester Cole; Edward Dmytryk; Ring Lardner, Jr.; John Howard Lawson; Albert Maltz; Samuel Ornitz; Adrian Sc)
American filmmakers
• Blacklisted group who refused to testify before House Un-American Activities Committee about alleged membership in Communist Party; sentenced to jail, 1948.

Celeste Holm
American actress
• Won 1947 Oscar for *Gentleman's Agreement.*
b. April 29, 1919 in New York, New York

Ian Holm
(Ian Holm Cuthbert)
English actor
• Received Oscar nomination for *Chariots of Fire,* 1981.
b. September 12, 1931 in Goodmayes, England

John Cecil Holm
American dramatist–actor
• Co-wrote Broadway comedy *Three Men in a House.*
b. November 04, 1904 in Philadelphia, Pennsylvania
d. October 24, 1981 in Rhode Island

Anna Marie Holmes
Canadian dancer
• Performances with husband, David, include *Romeo and Juliet, Taras Bulba.*
b. April 17, 1943 in Mission City, British Columbia

Burton Holmes
American producer
• Presented travelogues, 1890-1958; known for tag line: "Sun sinks slowly in the West."
b. January 08, 1870 in Chicago, Illinois
d. July 22, 1958 in Hollywood, California

Taylor Holmes
American actor
• Had title role in *Ruggles of Red Gap,* 1918.
b. 1878 in Newark, New Jersey
d. September 3, 1959 in Hollywood, California

Fritz (George William III) Holt
American producer
• Best known for co-producing Broadway hit *La Cage Aux Folles,* 1983; revival of *Gypsy,* 1974.
b. 1941 in San Francisco, California
d. July 14, 1987 in Montclair, New Jersey

Jack (Charles John) Holt
American actor
• Father of Tim Holt; hero in many silent Westerns.
b. May 31, 1888 in Winchester, Virginia
d. January 18, 1951 in Los Angeles, California

Tim Holt
(Charles John Holt Jr)
American actor
• Best known for *Treasure of the Sierra Madre,* 1948.
b. February 05, 1918 in Beverly Hills, California
d. February 15, 1973 in Shawnee, Oklahoma

Oscar Homolka
Austrian actor
• Oscar nominee for *I Remember Mama,* 1948.
b. August 12, 1903 in Vienna, Austria
d. January 27, 1978 in Sussex, England

Darla Jean Hood
(Our Gang)
American actress
• Curly-headed sweetheart of *Our Gang* comedies, 1935-42.
b. November 04, 1931 in Leedey, Oklahoma
d. June 13, 1979 in Canoga Park, California

Kevin Hooks
American actor
• Best known for role of Morris Thorpe on TV series "The White Shadow," 1978-81.
b. September 19, 1958 in Philadelphia, Pennsylvania

Robert Hooks
American actor
• Founder, Negro Ensemble Co.; appeared in TV series "NYPD," 1967-69.
b. April 18, 1937 in Washington, District of Columbia

Bob (Leslie Townes) Hope
American comedian–actor
• Made annual trips to entertain American troops, 1940-72; won four special Oscars; theme song: "Thanks for the Memory."
b. May 29, 1903 in Eltham, England

Anthony Hopkins
Welsh actor
• Won Emmy, 1976, for "The Lindbergh Kidnapping Case"; films include *Magic,* 1978; *The Elephant Man,* 1980; *Silence of the Lambs,* 1991.
b. December 31, 1937 in Port Talbot, Wales

Arthur Hopkins
American director–producer
• Best known for plays *Poor Little Rich Girl; Glory Road.*
b. October 04, 1878 in Cleveland, Ohio
d. March 22, 1950 in New York, New York

Bo Hopkins
American actor
• Known for "tough guy" roles: *The Wild Bunch,* 1969; *American Graffiti,* 1973.
b. February 02, 1942 in Greenwood, South Carolina

Miriam Hopkins
American actress
• Sophisticated blonde in films: *Design for Living,* 1933; *Becky Sharp,* 1935.
b. October 18, 1902 in Bainbridge, Georgia
d. October 09, 1972 in New York, New York

Dennis Hopper
American actor–director
• Cult figure who directed, starred in *Easy Rider,* 1969; also starred in *Blue Velvet,* 1986.
b. May 17, 1936 in Dodge City, Kansas

De Wolfe (William De Wolfe) Hopper
American actor
• Noted for recitations of "Casey at the Bat."
b. March 3, 1858 in New York, New York
d. September 23, 1935 in Kansas City, Missouri

Hedda Hopper
(Elda Furry)
American journalist–actress
• Began 28-year career as Hollywood gossip columnist, 1938; famous for her hats.
b. June 02, 1890 in Hollidaysburg, Pennsylvania
d. February 01, 1966 in Hollywood, California

William Hopper
American actor
• Starred as Paul Drake on TV's "Perry Mason," 1957-65; son of Hedda Hopper.
b. January 26, 1915 in New York, New York
d. March 06, 1970 in Palm Springs, California

Israel Arthur Horovitz
American dramatist
• Plays include *The Bottom; The Widow's Blind Date.*
b. March 31, 1939 in Wakefield, Massachusetts

Louis Horst
American dancer
• Musical director, Martha Graham Dance Company, 1926-48.
b. January 12, 1884 in Kansas City, Missouri
d. January 23, 1964 in New York, New York

Edward Everett Horton
American actor
• Known for tag line in comic roles: "Oh dear, oh dear"; often Fred Astaire's sidekick.
b. March 18, 1886 in New York, New York
d. September 29, 1970 in Encino, California

Allen Clayton Hoskins
(Our Gang; "Farina")
American actor
• Played pigtailed Farina in over 100 *Our Gang* episodes.
b. August 09, 1920 in Chelsea, Massachusetts
d. July 26, 1980 in Oakland, California

Bob Hoskins
English actor
• Cockney actor; won Cannes best actor honors for *Mona Lisa,* 1986.
b. October 26, 1942 in Bury St. Edmunds, England

Jean Eugene Robert Houdin
French magician
• First magician to use electricity; debunked "fakes"; Harry Houdini named himself after him.
b. 1805 in Blois, France
d. 1871

Harry Houdini
(Ehrich Weiss; Erik Weisz)
American magician
• America's most celebrated magician; known for escapes from bonds, many of which have not been duplicated; worked to improve quality, ethics of industry.
b. March 24, 1874 in Budapest, Hungary
d. October 31, 1926 in Detroit, Michigan

Katharine Houghton
American actress–celebrity relative
• Niece of Katherine Hepburn; starred with her in *Guess Who's Coming to Dinner?* 1967.
b. March 1, 1945 in Hartford, Connecticut

John Hough
English director
• Directed movie *Eyewitness,* 1981; TV series "The Avengers," "The Saint," 1960s.
b. November 21, 1941 in London, England

John Houseman
(Jacques Haussmann)
American actor–director–producer
• Won Oscar, 1973, for *The Paper Chase;* recreated role in TV series.
b. September 22, 1902 in Bucharest, Romania
d. October 31, 1988 in Malibu, California

Bronson Crocker Howard
American dramatist
• First professional American playwright; 21 plays include *Shenandoah,* 1888.
b. October 07, 1842 in Detroit, Michigan
d. August 04, 1908 in Avon, New Jersey

Clint Howard
American actor
• Starred in TV's "Gentle Ben," 1967-69; brother of Ron Howard.
b. April 2, 1959 in Burbank, California

Curly (Jerry) Howard
(The Three Stooges)
American comedian
• Member of popular 1940s comedy team.
b. 1906 in Brooklyn, New York
d. January 19, 1952 in San Gabriel, California

Leslie Howard
(Leslie Stainer)
English actor
• Played Ashley Wilkes in *Gone with the Wind,* 1939.
b. April 03, 1893 in London, England
d. June 02, 1943 in Bay of Biscay

Moe Howard
(The Three Stooges)
American comedian
• Last survivor of 1940s comedy team.
b. June 19, 1897 in Brooklyn, New York
d. May 24, 1975 in Hollywood, California

Ron Howard
American actor–director
• Played Opie on "The Andy Griffith Show," 1960-68, Richie Cunningham on "Happy Days," 1974-80; directed *Splash; Cocoon.*
b. March 01, 1954 in Duncan, Oklahoma

Shemp (Samuel) Howard
(The Three Stooges)
American comedian
• Member of 1940s comedy team.
b. March 17, 1900 in New York, New York
d. November 22, 1955 in Hollywood, California

Sidney Coe Howard
American dramatist–journalist
• Won Oscar for screenplay of *Gone With the Wind,* 1939; won Pulitzer for *They Knew What They Wanted,* 1924.
b. June 26, 1891 in Oakland, California
d. August 23, 1939 in Tyringham, Massachusetts

Susan Howard
(Jeri Lynn Mooney)
American actress
• Played Donna Culver Krebs on TV series "Dallas," 1978-87.
b. January 28, 1943 in Marshall, Texas

Tom Howard
British actor
• Starred in two-reel comedies, 1930-36.
b. 1886 in Ireland
d. February 27, 1955 in Long Branch, New Jersey

Trevor Wallace Howard
English actor
• Starred in over 70 films spanning five decades; known for portrayal of military officers, including Captain Bligh in *Mutiny on the Bounty,* 1962.
b. September 29, 1916 in Cliftonville-Margate, England
d. January 07, 1988 in London, England

Willie Howard
American comedian
• Starred on Broadway with brother Eugene from 1912; on radio, 1930s.
b. April 13, 1886 in Germany
d. January 14, 1949 in New York, New York

James Wong Howe
American filmmaker
• Cameraman who helped establish distinctive look of Warner Brothers pictures, 1940.
b. August 28, 1899 in Kwangtung, China
d. July 12, 1976 in Hollywood, California

Sally Ann Howes
English actress–singer
• Child star of 1940 British films, later in *Chitty Chitty Bang Bang*, 1968.
b. July 2, 1934 in London, England

Beth Howland
American actress
• Played Vera on TV series "Alice," 1976-85.
b. May 28, 1941 in Boston, Massachusetts

Rock Hudson
(Roy Harold Scherer Jr; Roy Fitzgerald)
American actor
• Known for light romantic comedy: *Pillow Talk*, 1959; nominated for Oscar for *Giant*, 1956; died of AIDS.
b. November 17, 1925 in Winnetka, Illinois
d. October 02, 1985 in Beverly Hills, California

Barnard Hughes
American actor
• TV series include "Doc," 1975-76, "Mr. Merlin," 1981; won 1978 Emmy.
b. July 16, 1915 in Bedford Hills, New York

Victor Marie Hugo
French dramatist–author
• Best known for *Les Miserables*, 1862.
b. February 26, 1802 in Besancon, France
d. May 22, 1885 in Paris, France

Thomas Hulce
American actor
• Made debut in *Those Lips, Those Eyes*, 1980; nominated for Oscar, 1984, for title role in *Amadeus*.
b. December 06, 1953 in White Water, Wisconsin

Henry Hull
American actor
• Created role of Jeeter Lester in *Tobacco Road*, Broadway, 1934; title in film *The Werewolf of London*, 1935.
b. October 03, 1890 in Louisville, Kentucky
d. March 08, 1977 in Cornwall, England

Doris Humphrey
American dancer–choreographer
• Artistic director for Jose Limon, 1946; founded Julliard Dance Theater, 1955.
b. October 17, 1895 in Oak Park, Illinois
d. December 29, 1958 in New York, New York

Arthur Hunnicutt
American actor
• Received Oscar nomination for *The Big Sky*, 1952.
b. February 17, 1911 in Gravelly, Arkansas
d. September 27, 1979 in Woodland Hills, California

Gayle Hunnicutt
American actress
• Starred in TV movies "The Golden Bowl"; "A Man Called Intrepid."
b. February 06, 1943 in Fort Worth, Texas

Linda Hunt
American actress
• Won Oscar, 1983, for role of man in *The Year of Living Dangerously*.
b. April 02, 1945 in Morristown, New Jersey

Martita Hunt
English actress
• Played Miss Havisham in 1947 film *Great Expectations*.
b. January 3, 1900 in Argentina
d. June 13, 1969 in London, England

Evan Hunter
(Ed McBain pseud)
American author–screenwriter
• Books include *Eight Black Horses*, 1985; films include *The Birds*, 1962.
b. October 15, 1926 in New York, New York

Holly Hunter
American actress
• Star of many major motion pictures including *Raising Arizona*, 1987, and *Always*, 1989.
b. March 20, 1958 in Atlanta, Georgia.

Ian Hunter
South African actor
• Played nice guys in Hollywood films: *Adventures of Robin Hood*, 1938.
b. June 13, 1900 in Cape Town, South Africa
d. September 24, 1975 in England

Kim Hunter
(Janet Cole)
American actress
• Won 1951 Oscar for *Streetcar Named Desire*, for role of Stella.
b. November 12, 1922 in Detroit, Michigan

Ross Hunter
(Martin Fuss; "Last of the Dream Merchants")
American producer
• Films include *Flower Drum Song*, 1961; *Airport*, 1970; famous for great scale of stories, sumptuous sets.
b. May 06, 1924 in Cleveland, Ohio

Tab Hunter
(Arthur Gelien)
American actor
• Teen idol, 1950s; in films *Damn Yankees*, 1958; *Ride the Wild Surf*, 1964.
b. July 11, 1931 in New York, New York

Charlayne Hunter-Gault
American broadcast journalist
• Won 1983 Emmy for reporting in Grenada after the US invasion.
b. February 27, 1942 in Due West, South Carolina

Chet (Chester Robert) Huntley
American broadcast journalist
• Teamed with David Brinkley for nightly newscasts, 1956-70; author *The Generous Years*, 1968.
b. December 1, 1911 in Cardwell, Montana
d. March 2, 1974 in Bozeman, Montana

Isabelle Huppert
French actress
• Won 1978 best actress award, Cannes Festival, for *Violette Noziere*.
b. March 16, 1955 in Paris, France

John Hurt
English actor
• Starred in *The Elephant Man*, 1980; *Champions*, 1984.
b. January 22, 1940 in Chesterfield, England

Mary Beth Supinger Hurt
American actress
• In films *The World According to Garp*, 1982; *A Change of Seasons*, 1980; Tony nominee for *Crimes of the Heart*, 1981.
b. September 26, 1948 in Marshalltown, Iowa

William Hurt
American actor
• Won Oscar for *Kiss of the Spider Woman*, 1985; other films include *Broadcast News*, 1987, *Big Chill*.
b. March 2, 1950 in Washington, District of Columbia

Anjelica Huston
American actress
• Won best supporting actress Oscar for *Prizzi's Honor*, 1985; daughter of John; best actress Oscar nomination for *Grifters*, 1991.
b. July 08, 1951 in Los Angeles, California

John Huston
Irish actor–director
• Won Oscar for *Treasure of the Sierra Madre*, 1948; also directed *The African Queen*, 1952; *Prizzi's Honor*, 1985; *The Dead*, 1987.
b. August 05, 1906 in Nevada, Missouri
d. August 28, 1987 in Middletown, Rhode Island

Walter Huston
(Walter Houghston)
American actor
• Won 1948 Oscar for *The Treasure of the Sierra Madre*, which his son John directed.
b. April 06, 1884 in Toronto, Ontario
d. April 07, 1950 in Beverly Hills, California

William Ian Dewitt Hutt
Canadian director–producer
• Member, Stratford, ON Shakespeare Festival Co., as actor, director, since 1953.
b. May 02, 1920 in Toronto, Ontario

Betty Hutton
(Betty Thornburg)
American actress–singer
• Blonde bombshell of 1940s films; noted for *Annie Get Your Gun*, 1950.
b. February 26, 1921 in Battle Creek, Michigan

Jim Hutton
American actor
• Starred in films *Where the Boys Are*, 1960; *The Trouble with Angels*, 1966; father of Timothy Hutton.
b. May 31, 1938 in Binghamton, New York
d. June 02, 1979 in Los Angeles, California

Lauren (Mary Laurence) Hutton
American model–actress
• Film career since 1968; films include *The Gambler; American Gigolo*.
b. November 17, 1944 in Charleston, South Carolina

Timothy James Hutton
American actor
• Won Oscar for *Ordinary People*, 1980; star of *The Falcon and the Snowman*, 1985; married Debra Winger.
b. August 16, 1960 in Malibu, California

David (Henry) Hwang
American dramatist
• His drama, *M. Butterfly*, won best play Tony, 1988; won Obie for *The Dance and the Railroad*, 1981.
b. August 11, 1957 in Los Angeles, California

Wilfrid Hyde-White
English actor
• Played Colonel Pickering in film version of *My Fair Lady*, 1964. Starred in the 1979 TV series *The Associates*.
b. May 12, 1903 in Gloucester, England
d. May 06, 1991 in Los Angeles, California

Martha Hyer
American actress
• Received 1959 Oscar nomination for *Some Came Running*.
b. August 1, 1924 in Fort Worth, Texas

Henrik Ibsen
Norwegian dramatist–author
• Depicted 19th c. women in *A Doll's House*, 1879; *Hedda Gabler*, 1890.
b. March 2, 1828 in Skien, Norway
d. May 23, 1906 in Christiania, Norway

Eric Idle
(Monty Python's Flying Circus)
British actor–author
• Co-winner, 1983 Cannes Film Festival for *Monty Python's Meaning of Life*.
b. March 29, 1943 in Durham, England

Frieda Inescort
(Frieda Wightman)
Scottish actress
• Character actress in films *Mary of Scotland*, 1936; *Pride and Prejudice*, 1940.
b. June 29, 1901 in Edinburgh, Scotland

William Inge
American dramatist
• Wrote *Come Back, Little Sheba*, 1950; *Bus Stop*, 1955.
b. May 03, 1913 in Independence, Kansas
d. June 1, 1973 in Hollywood Hills, California

Rex Ingram
American actor
• Best known as slave Jim in film *Adventures of Huckleberry Finn*, 1939.
b. October 2, 1895 in Cairo, Illinois
d. September 19, 1969 in Los Angeles, California

Albert Innaurato
American dramatist
• Won Obie for *Gemini*, 1977.
b. June 02, 1948 in Philadelphia, Pennsylvania

Eugene Ionesco
French author–dramatist
• Theater of the absurd: *The Bald Prima Donna*, 1950; *The Rhinoceros*, 1959.
b. November 26, 1912 in Slatina, Romania

Jill Ireland
(Mrs Charles Bronson)
American actress
• Starred with Charles Bronson in several films: *Breakheart Pass*, 1976; autobiography *Life Wish*, 1987, deals with her fight with cancer; died of cancer.
b. April 24, 1936 in London, England
d. May 18, 1990 in Malibu, California

John Ireland
Canadian actor
• Oscar nominee for *All the King's Men*, 1949.
b. January 3, 1915 in Victoria, British Columbia

Jeremy John Irons
English actor
• Won best actor Tony for *The Real Thing*, 1984; TV appearances include series "Brideshead Revisited," 1980-81. Won Oscar for best actor for *Reversal of Fortune*, 1990.
b. September 19, 1948 in Cowes, England

Amy Irving
American actress
• Films include *Yentl*, 1983; *Micki & Maude*, 1984. Married to Steven Spielberg, divorced 1988.
b. September 1, 1953 in Palo Alto, California

George Steven Irving
(George Irving Shelasky)
American actor
• Won Tony for *Irene*, 1973; began Broadway career with *Oklahoma*, 1943.
b. November 01, 1922 in Springfield, Massachusetts

Sir Henry Irving
(John Henry Brodribb)
English actor
• Noted for Shakespearian roles; first actor to be knighted, 1895.
b. February 06, 1838 in Glastonbury, England
d. October 13, 1905 in Bradford, England

Bill (William) Irwin
American actor–choreographer
• Performing artist; best-known act, *The Regard of Flight*, 1982, was highest grossing show at American Palace Theatre, NYC.
b. April 11, 1950 in Santa Monica, California

May Irwin
(May Campbell)
Canadian actress
• Made screen history in Thomas Edison's *The Kiss*, 1896; denounced as immoral; noted farce comedienne with Tony Pasteur, 1877-83.
b. June 27, 1862 in Whitby, Ontario
d. October 22, 1938 in New York, New York

Christopher William Isherwood
American author–dramatist
• Play *Cabaret,* 1966 was based on his stories *Goodbye to Berlin,* 1935.
b. August 26, 1904 in Cheshire, England
d. January 04, 1986 in Santa Monica, California

Judith Ivey
American actress
• Won Tony Awards for *Steaming,* 1982; *Hurlyburly,* 1984.
b. September 04, 1951 in El Paso, Texas

James Ivory
American director–producer
• With Ismail Merchant, formed longest producer-director team in film history; films include *A Room With a View,* 1986.
b. June 07, 1928 in Berkeley, California

Jackee
(Jackee Harry)
American actress
• Played Sandra Clark on TV comedy "227," 1985-89; won Emmy, 1987.
b. August 14, 1957 in Winston-Salem, North Carolina

Anne Jackson
(Mrs Eli Wallach)
American actress
• Appeared on stage with husband Eli Wallach in *The Typists and the Tiger,* 1963; *The Waltz of the Toreadores,* 1973.
b. September 03, 1926 in Allegheny, Pennsylvania

Glenda Jackson
English actress
• Won Oscars for *Women in Love,* 1970; *A Touch of Class,* 1973.
b. May 09, 1937 in Birkenhead, England

Gordon Cameron Jackson
Scottish actor
• Won Emmy for role of Hudson the butler in PBS series "Upstairs, Downstairs," 1970s.
b. December 19, 1923 in Glasgow, Scotland
d. January 14, 1990 in London, England

Kate Jackson
American actress
• TV series include "The Rookies," 1972-76; "Charlie's Angels," 1976-79; "Scarecrow and Mrs. King," 1983-.
b. October 29, 1948 in Birmingham, Alabama

Derek George Jacobi
English actor
• Had title role in PBS series "I, Claudius"; nominated for Tony, 1980, for *The Suicide;* highly regarded for skills in British stage, TV roles.
b. October 22, 1938 in London, England

Richard Hanley Jaeckel
American actor
• Oscar nominee for *Sometimes a Great Notion,* 1971; character actor usually in role of the heavy.
b. October 26, 1926 in Long Beach, California

Sam Jaffe
American actor
• Played Dr. Zorba on TV's "Ben Casey," 1961-66.
b. March 08, 1893 in New York, New York
d. March 24, 1984 in Beverly Hills, California

Sam(uel Anderson) Jaffe
American broadcast journalist
• ABC News correspondent, 1961-69; covered Vietnam War.
b. 1924 in San Francisco, California
d. February 08, 1985 in Bethesda, Maryland

Bianca Teresa Jagger
(Bianca Perez Morena de Macias)
English socialite–actress
• Married to Mick Jagger, 1971-79; youngest member, best-dressed Hall of Fame.
b. May 02, 1945 in Managua, Nicaragua

Dean Jagger
American actor
• Oscar winner for *Twelve O'Clock High,* 1950.
b. November 07, 1903 in Columbus Grove, Ohio
d. February 05, 1991 in Santa Monica, California

Marine Jahan
French dancer
• Did dance scenes in *Flashdance,* 1983, for Jennifer Beals, but didn't get credit in film.

Dennis James
American TV personality
• Game shows include "Chance of a Lifetime," 1952-56; daytime "Name That Tune," 1980s.
b. August 24, 1917 in Jersey City, New Jersey

John James
American actor
• Played Jeff Colby on TV dramas "Dynasty," 1981-85, 1987-89, "The Colbys," 1985-87.
b. April 18, 1956 in Minneapolis, Minnesota

House Jameson
American actor
• Played father in radio, TV series "The Aldrich Family," 1949-53.
b. 1902
d. April 23, 1971 in Danbury, Connecticut

Bob (Robert John) Jamieson
American broadcast journalist
• NBC News correspondent; won 1981 Emmy for coverage of Iranian hostage crisis.
b. February 01, 1943 in Streator, Illinois

Judith Jamison
American dancer
• Lead dancer, Alvin Ailey's Dance Theater, 1967-80; starred in Broadway show "Sophisticated Ladies," 1980; formed own company, the Jamison Project, 1988; director, Alvin Ailey American Dance Theater, 1989-.
b. May 1, 1934 in Philadelphia, Pennsylvania

Elsie Janis
(Elsie Bierbower)
American actress
• First American to entertain troops in WW I.
b. March 16, 1889 in Columbus, Ohio
d. February 26, 1956 in Beverly Hills, California

Russell Dixon Janney
American author–producer
• Co-wrote, produced hit Broadway musical *The Vagabond King,* 1925.
b. April 14, 1885 in Wilmington, Ohio
d. July 14, 1963 in New York, New York

Emil Jannings
(Theodor Friedrich Emil Janenz)
American actor
• Won Oscar for *The Last Command; The Way of All Flesh,* 1928.
b. July 26, 1886 in Rorschach, Switzerland
d. January 03, 1950 in Lake Wolfgang, Austria

David Janssen
(David Harold Meyer)
American actor
• Starred in TV series "The Fugitive," 1963-67; "Harry-O," 1974-76.
b. March 27, 1931 in Naponee, Nebraska
d. February 13, 1980 in Malibu Beach, California

Claude Jarman, Jr
American actor
• Won special Oscar for debut in *The Yearling,* 1946.
b. September 27, 1934 in Nashville, Tennessee

Tom (Thomas Edwin) Jarriel
American broadcast journalist
• Correspondent, ABC News since 1965; contributor to "20/20."
b. December 29, 1934 in La Grange, Georgia

Alfred Jarry
French poet–dramatist
• Wrote first theatrical work of the absurd: *Ubu Roi*, 1896.
b. October 08, 1873 in Laval, France
d. November 01, 1907 in Paris, France

Joseph Jefferson
American actor
• Identified with title role in play *Rip Van Winkle;* had 72-yr. stage career.
b. February 2, 1829 in Philadelphia, Pennsylvania
d. April 23, 1905 in Palm Beach, Florida

Thomas Jefferson
American actor
• Son of Joseph Jefferson, 5th generation of theatrical family; entered films with D W Griffith, 1909.
b. 1859
d. April 02, 1923 in Hollywood, California

Lionel Charles Jeffries
English actor
• Character actor, 1950–; directed films including *The Railway Children*, 1971; *Water Babies*, 1979.
b. 1926 in London, England

Allen Jenkins
(Al McConegal)
American actor
• Played character roles in 175 films from 1931.
b. April 09, 1900 in New York, New York
d. July 2, 1974 in Santa Monica, California

Peter Charles Jennings
Canadian broadcast journalist
• Anchorman, "ABC World News Tonight," 1983–; won 1982 Emmy.
b. July 29, 1938 in Toronto, Ontario

Talbot Jennings
American dramatist–screenwriter
• Co-authored screenplays *The Good Earth*, 1937; *Mutiny on the Bounty*, 1935.
b. 1895 in Shoshone, Ohio
d. May 3, 1985 in East Glacier Park, Montana

Salome Jens
American actress
• Films include *Angel Baby*, 1961; *Harry's War*, 1981.
b. May 08, 1935 in Milwaukee, Wisconsin

Mike (Michael C) Jensen
American broadcast journalist
• NBC News correspondent who specializes in business, economics.
b. November 01, 1934 in Chicago, Illinois

Adele Jergens
American actress
• Played brassy blonde in 50 B-films, including *The Day the World Ended*, 1956.
b. 1922 in New York, New York

Henry Jewett
American actor
• Built Repertory Theatre of Boston, 1924; first in US.
b. June 04, 1862 in Warrnambool, Australia
d. June 24, 1930 in West Newton, Massachusetts

Norman Jewison
American director
• Best known for *Fiddler on the Roof*, 1971, *Moonstruck*.
b. July 21, 1926 in Toronto, Ontario

Ruth Prawer Jhabvala
British author
• Won Oscar for screenplay adaptation for *A Room with a View*, 1986.
b. May 07, 1927 in Cologne, Germany

Ann Jillian
(Ann Jura Nauseda; Mrs Andrew Murcia)
American actress
• Starred on Broadway in *Sugar Babies*, 1979-80; starred in own life story, 1987, which focused on her double mastectomy, 1985.
b. January 29, 1951 in Cambridge, Massachusetts

Jimmy the Greek
(James Snyder; Demetrius George Synodinos)
American journalist–sportscaster
• Former pro gambler; analyst for CBS Sports, fired, 1988, for controversial racial statements.
b. September 09, 1919 in Steubenville, Ohio

Robert Joffrey
(Abdullah Jaffa Bey Khan)
American choreographer
• Founder, artistic director, Joffrey Ballet Co., 1956, renowned for wide-ranging repertory.
b. December 24, 1930 in Seattle, Washington
d. March 25, 1988 in New York, New York

Glynis Johns
English actress
• Noted for role of mother in film *Mary Poppins*, 1964; won Tony for *A Little Night Music*, 1973.
b. October 05, 1923 in Pretoria, South Africa

Arte Johnson
American actor–comedian
• Best known for character acting in TV's "Laugh-In," 1968-71; popularized expression "Velly interesting"; won Emmy, 1969.
b. January 2, 1934 in Benton Harbor, Michigan

Ben Johnson
American actor
• Won Oscar for *The Last Picture Show*, 1971.
b. June 13, 1918 in Pawhuska, Oklahoma

Dame Celia Johnson
English actress
• Starred in films *Brief Encounter*, 1945, *In Which We Serve*, 1942.
b. December 18, 1908 in Richmond, England
d. April 25, 1982 in Nettlebed, England

Chic (Harold Ogden) Johnson
(Olsen and Johnson)
American actor–comedian
• Vaudeville star with Ole Olsen, 1914; *Hellzapoppin* became great Broadway, film success, 1941.
b. March 05, 1891 in Chicago, Illinois
d. February 1962 in Las Vegas, Nevada

Don Johnson
(Donald Wayne)
American actor
• Played Sonny Crockett on TV series "Miami Vice," 1984-89; married to Melanie Griffith.
b. December 15, 1950 in Galena, Missouri

Nunnally Johnson
American director–screenwriter–producer
• Best-known films *The Grapes of Wrath*, 1940; *The Three Faces of Eve*, 1957.
b. December 05, 1897 in Columbus, Georgia
d. March 25, 1977 in Los Angeles, California

Richard Johnson
English actor
• Films include *Take All of Me*, 1978; *The Comeback*, 1982.
b. July 3, 1927 in Upminster, England

Anissa Jones
American actress
• Played Buffy in "Family Affair," 1966-71; died of drug overdose.
b. 1958 in West Lafayette, Indiana
d. 1976

Barry Jones
English actor
• Best known for film *Brigadoon*, 1954.
b. March 06, 1893 in Guernsey, Channel Islands

Buck Jones
(Charles Frederick Gebhart)
American actor
• Western hero in "Rough Rider" serials with horse "Silver."
b. December 04, 1891 in Vincennes, Indiana
d. November 3, 1942 in Boston, Massachusetts

Carolyn Jones
American actress
• Played Morticia on TV series "The Addams Family," 1964-66.
b. April 28, 1933 in Amarillo, Texas
d. August 03, 1983 in Los Angeles, California

Christopher Jones
American actor
• Best known for films *The Looking Glass War,* 1969; *Ryan's Daughter,* 1971.
b. August 18, 1941 in Jackson, Tennessee

Dean Carroll Jones
American actor
• Starred in 1960s Disney films such as *That Darn Cat,* 1965; *The Love Bug,* 1968.
b. January 25, 1936 in Morgan County, Alabama

Henry Jones
American actor
• Won Tony for *Sunrise at Campobello,* 1958.
b. August 01, 1912 in Philadelphia, Pennsylvania

James Earl Jones
American actor
• Won Tonys for *The Great White Hope,* 1969; *Fences,* 1987.
b. January 17, 1931 in Arkabutla, Mississippi

Jennifer Jones
(Phyllis Isley)
American actress
• Won Oscar, 1943, for *The Song of Bernadette.*
b. March 02, 1919 in Tulsa, Oklahoma

Leroi Jones
(Imamu Amiri Baraka)
American poet–dramatist
• Wrote *Black Magic,* 1969; *It's Nation Time,* 1971.
b. October 07, 1934 in Newark, New Jersey

Preston St Vrain Jones
American actor–dramatist
• Wrote *A Texas Trilogy,* 1974.
b. April 07, 1936 in Albuquerque, New Mexico
d. September 19, 1979 in Dallas, Texas

Robert C Jones
American writer
• Won Oscar for screenplay *Coming Home,* 1978.
b. March 3, 1930 in Los Angeles, California

Shirley Jones
(Mrs Marty Ingels)
American actress
• Won Oscar, 1960, for *Elmer Gantry;* also starred in *Oklahoma,* 1954; *Music Man,* 1962; TV includes "The Partridge Family," 1970-74.
b. March 31, 1934 in Smithtown, Pennsylvania

Terry Jones
(Monty Python's Flying Circus)
Welsh actor–director–writer
• Directed film *Monty Python's Life of Brian;* wrote *Fairy Tales,* 1981; *Erik the Viking,* 1983.
b. February 01, 1942 in Colwyn Bay, Wales

Tommy Lee Jones
American actor
• Films include *Coal Miner's Daughter,* 1981; *River Rat,* 1984; won Emmy, 1983.
b. September 15, 1946 in San Saba, Texas

Ben(jamin) Jonson
English dramatist–poet
• Master of dramatic satire; wrote *Volpone,* 1606.
b. June 11, 1572 in Westminster, England
d. April 06, 1637 in Westminster, England

Kurt Jooss
German choreographer
• Combined classical ballet with modern dance; known for antiwar play *The Green Table,* 1932.
b. January 12, 1901 in Wasseralfingen, Germany
d. May 22, 1979 in Heilbronn, Germany (West)

Bobby Jordan
American actor
• Best known for role of Bobby in Bowery Boy films.
b. 1923
d. September 1, 1965 in Los Angeles, California

Jim (James Edward) Jordan
American radio performer
• Played Fibber McGee in classic radio show "Fibber McGee and Molly," 1935-60.
b. November 16, 1896 in Peoria, Illinois
d. April 01, 1988 in Los Angeles, California

Marian Driscoll Jordan
(Mrs Jim Jordan; "Molly McGee")
American radio performer
• With husband, formed one of radio's most famous comedy teams: "Fibber McGee and Molly," 1935-60.
b. April 15, 1897 in Peoria, Illinois
d. April 07, 1961 in Encino, California

Richard Jordan
American actor
• Starred in TV mini-series "The Captains and the Kings," 1976.
b. July 19, 1938 in New York, New York

Victor Jory
American actor
• Often cast as villain in 40-year career; among films *Gone With the Wind,* 1939.
b. November 23, 1902 in Dawson City, Alaska
d. February 12, 1982 in Santa Monica, California

Allyn Morgan Joslyn
American actor
• Performed on 3,000 radio programs; Broadway work included: *Boy Meets Girl; Arsenic and Old Lace.*
b. July 21, 1905 in Milford, Pennsylvania
d. January 21, 1981 in Woodland Hills, California

Louis Jourdan
(Louis Gendre)
French actor
• Best known for film *Gigi,* 1958.
b. June 19, 1920 in Marseilles, France

Leatrice Joy
(Leatrice Joy Zeidler)
American actress
• Star of Cecil B DeMille silent films; credited with popularizing bobbed hair.
b. November 07, 1893 in New Orleans, Louisiana
d. May 13, 1985 in Riverdale, New York

Alice Joyce
American actress
• Voted most popular actress in America, 1913-17.
b. October 01, 1890 in Kansas City, Missouri
d. October 09, 1955 in Hollywood, California

Peggy Hopkins Joyce
(Margaret Upton; "A Circle of the Cinema")
American actress
• In Ziegfeld Follies; six marriages given wide publicity.
b. 1893 in Norfolk, Virginia
d. June 12, 1957 in New York, New York

Raul Julia
(Raul Rafael Carlos Julia y Arcelay)
American actor
• Films include *Tempest; One From the Heart*, 1982.
b. March 09, 1940 in San Juan, Puerto Rico

Katy Jurado
(Maria Christina Jurado Garcia)
Mexican actress
• Oscar nominee for role of Senora Devereaux in *Broken Lance*, 1954.
b. January 16, 1927 in Guadalajara, Mexico

Curt Jurgens
German actor
• Appeared in over 150 films, including *The Enemy Below*, 1957; *The Spy Who Loved Me*, 1977.
b. December 12, 1915 in Munich, Germany
d. June 18, 1982 in Vienna, Austria

James Robertson Justice
British actor
• Best known for film *Doctor in the House*, 1954, and sequels.
b. June 15, 1905 in Wigtown, Scotland
d. July 02, 1975 in Winchester, England

Madeline Gail Kahn
American actress
• Oscar nominee for *Paper Moon, Blazing Saddles*; star of TV series "Oh Madeline," 1983.
b. September 29, 1942 in Boston, Massachusetts

Karen Alexandria Kain
Canadian dancer
• Principal dancer, National Ballet of Canada, 1971–.
b. March 28, 1951 in Hamilton, Ontario

Georg Kaiser
German dramatist
• A leader of German Expressionism; plays banned by Nazis, after 1933; wrote *Gas I*, 1918.
b. November 25, 1878 in Magdeburg, Germany
d. June 05, 1945 in Ascona, Switzerland

Mikhail Kalatozov
(Mikhail Kalatozishvili)
Russian director
• Early films banned for negativism; won Cannes Award for *Cranes Are Flying*, 1958.
b. December 23, 1903 in Tiflis, Russia
d. March 28, 1973 in Moscow, U.S.S.R.

Marvin Leonard Kalb
American broadcast journalist
• Chief diplomatic correspondent, NBC News since 1980; permanent panel member of "Meet the Press."
b. June 09, 1930 in New York, New York

H(ans) V(on) Kaltenborn
American editor–broadcast journalist
• Best known for series of nonstop broadcasts during Munich crisis, 1938; wrote autobiography *Fifty Fabulous Years*, 1956.
b. July 09, 1878 in Milwaukee, Wisconsin
d. June 14, 1965 in Brooklyn, New York

Ida Kaminska
Russian actress
• Oscar nominee for *The Shop on Main Street*, 1965; founded two theaters in Warsaw, Poland.
b. September 04, 1899 in Odessa, Russia
d. May 21, 1980 in New York, New York

Carol Kane
American actress
• Played Simka Gravas on TV comedy "Taxi," 1981-83; won Emmys, 1982, 1983.
b. June 18, 1952 in Cleveland, Ohio

Fay Kanin
(Fay Mitchell)
American writer–producer
• Oscar nominee for original screenplay of *Teacher's Pet*, 1959; won Peabody for TV film *Heartsounds*, 1984.
b. in New York, New York

Garson Kanin
American author–director
• Wrote *Tracy and Hepburn: An Intimate Memoir*, 1971; directed *Funny Girl*, 1964.
b. November 24, 1912 in Rochester, New York

Hal Kanter
(Henry Irving)
American screenwriter–director–producer
• Co-wrote film *Pocketful of Miracles*, 1961; won 1954 Emmy for TV show "George Gobel Show," 1954-60.
b. December 18, 1918 in Savannah, Georgia

Gabe (Gabriel) Kaplan
American actor–comedian
• Starred in TV series "Welcome Back, Kotter," 1975-79.
b. March 31, 1945 in Brooklyn, New York

Valerie Kaprisky
French actress
• Starred in film *Breathless* with Richard Gere, 1983.
b. 1963 in Paris, France

Boris Karloff
(William Henry Pratt)
English actor
• In horror films *Frankenstein*, 1931; *The Mummy*, 1933.
b. November 23, 1887 in London, England
d. February 02, 1969 in Middleton, England

Roscoe Karns
American comedian
• Known for cynical, fast-talking roles as journalists, press agents; best-known film *20th Century*, 1934.
b. September 07, 1893 in San Bernardino, California
d. February 06, 1970 in Los Angeles, California

Tamara (Platonova) Karsavina
(Tamara Karsavin; "La Tamara")
Russian dancer
• Ballerina known for highly expressive, intelligent interpretations of Mariinsky, Dyagilev.
b. 1885 in Saint Petersburg, Russia
d. May 26, 1978 in London, England

Lawrence Edward Kasdan
American screenwriter
• Co-wrote *Empire Strikes Back*, 1980; *The Big Chill*, 1983; won Clios for TV commercials.
b. January 14, 1949 in Miami Beach, Florida

Kurt Kasznar
(Kurt Serwischer)
Austrian actor
• Appeared in 1,000 Broadway performances of *The Sound of Music*; also appeared in *Barefoot in the Park*, 1964.
b. August 13, 1913 in Vienna, Austria
d. August 06, 1979 in Santa Monica, California

William Katt
American actor
• Starred in TV series "The Greatest American Hero," 1981-83.
b. February 16, 1955 in Los Angeles, California

Andy Kaufman
American actor–comedian
• Best known for appearances on "Saturday Night Live," 1975-78; played Latka Gravas on TV comedy "Taxi," 1978-83.
b. January 17, 1949 in New York, New York
d. May 16, 1984 in Los Angeles, California

Boris Kaufman
Polish filmmaker
• Noted Hollywood cameraman; won 1954 Oscar for best black-and-white cinematography for *On the Waterfront*.
b. August 24, 1906 in Bialystok, Poland
d. June 24, 1980 in New York, New York

George S(imon) Kaufman
(Kaufman and Hart; "The Great Collaborator")
American dramatist–journalist
• With Moss Hart, wrote some of Broadway's most popular plays: *You Can't Take It With You*, 1936 Pulitzer winner; *The Man Who Came to Dinner*, 1939.
b. November 16, 1889 in Pittsburgh, Pennsylvania
d. June 02, 1961 in New York, New York

Murray Kaufman
American radio performer
• Promoted The Beatles' first tour, 1964.
b. February 14, 1922 in New York, New York
d. February 21, 1982 in Los Angeles, California

Helmut Kautner
German screenwriter–director
• Led revival of German cinema: *Romanze in Moll*, 1942.
b. March 25, 1908 in Dusseldorf, Germany
d. April 2, 1980 in Castellina, Italy

Julie Deborah Kavner
American actress
• Played Brenda Morgenstern on TV series "Rhoda," 1974-78; won Emmy, 1978; regular on "Tracey Ullman Show," 1987-1990.
b. September 07, 1951 in Los Angeles, California

Dianne Kay
American actress
• Played Nancy Bradford on TV series "Eight Is Enough," 1977-81.
b. 1956

Danny Kaye
(David Daniel Kominsky)
American actor–comedian
• Films include *The Secret Life of Walter Mitty*, 1947; *Hans Christian Andersen*, 1952; UNICEF ambassador-at-large, noted for comic patter-songs.
b. January 18, 1913 in New York, New York
d. March 03, 1987 in Los Angeles, California

Nora Kaye
(Nora Koreff)
American dancer–actress
• With NYC Ballet, 1951-54; retired from dancing, 1961; films include *The Turning Point*, 1977; *Pennies From Heaven*, 1981.
b. 1920 in New York, New York
d. February 28, 1987 in Santa Monica, California

Stubby Kaye
American actor–comedian
• Best known for role of Nicely-Nicely Johnson in Broadway, film *Guys and Dolls*.
b. November 11, 1918 in New York, New York

Elia Kazan
(Elia Kazanjoglou)
American director
• Won 1954 Oscar for *On the Waterfront*; co-founded Actor's Studio, 1947.
b. September 07, 1909 in Constantinople, Turkey

Stacy Keach, Sr
American actor–director
• Active in Hollywood since early 1940s; plays Clarence Bird's Eye in TV commercials; father of Stacy Jr.
b. May 29, 1914 in Chicago, Illinois

John Brendon Keane
Irish dramatist–poet
• First, most popular play in Ireland at time: *Sive*, 1959; other works include *Values*, 1973; *The Crazy Wall*, 1974.
b. July 21, 1928 in Listowel, Ireland

Buster (Joseph Francis) Keaton
American actor–comedian
• Perfected deadpan stare in *The Navigator*, 1924; *The General*, 1927.
b. October 04, 1896 in Piqua, Kansas
d. February 01, 1966 in Hollywood, California

Diane Keaton
(Diane Hall)
American actress
• Won 1977 Oscar for *Annie Hall*; wrote *Reservations*, 1980.
b. January 05, 1946 in Los Angeles, California

Michael Keaton
(Michael Douglas)
American actor–comedian
• Starred in *Night Shift*, 1982; *Mr. Mom*, 1983, *Batman*, 1989.
b. September 09, 1951 in Pittsburgh, Pennsylvania

Barrie Colin Keefe
English dramatist
• Wrote award-winning play *My Girl*, 1975.
b. October 31, 1945 in London, England

Howard Keel
(Harold Clifford Leek)
American actor–singer
• Plays Clayton Farlow on TV series, "Dallas"; singing star in *Showboat*, 1951; *Kiss Me Kate*, 1953.
b. April 13, 1919 in Gillespie, Illinois

Ruby Keeler
(Ethel Hilda Keeler)
American dancer–actress
• Star of lavish musicals, 1930s: *42nd Street*, 1933; once wed to Al Jolson.
b. August 25, 1909 in Halifax, Nova Scotia

Laura Keene
English actress
• First woman theatrical producer in US, 1855-1863; at Ford's Theater starred in *Our American Cousin* the night Lincoln was assassinated.
b. July 2, 1820 in London, England
d. November 04, 1873 in Montclair, New Jersey

Bob (Robert James) Keeshan
American TV personality–author
• Star of "Captain Kangaroo," 1955-81, longest-running children's program in network history.
b. June 27, 1927 in Lynbrook, New York

Garrison (Gary Edward) Keillor
American author–producer
• Created radio program "A Prairie Home Companion" about fictional Lake Wobegon, MN, 1974-87; wrote *Lake Wobegon Days*, 1985.
b. August 07, 1942 in Anoka, Minnesota

Harvey Keitel
American actor
• Best-known films include *Mean Streets*, 1973; *Alice Doesn't Live Here Anymore*, 1975; *Taxi Driver*, 1976.
b. 1941 in Brooklyn, New York

Benjamin F Keith
American entertainer
• Established Vaudeville, 1800s, catering to respectable, family entertainment.
b. 1846 in Hillsboro, New Hampshire
d. March 26, 1914

Brian Michael Keith
(Robert Keith Jr)
American actor
• Played Bill Davis on TV comedy "Family Affair," 1966-71, Milton Hardcastle on "Hardcastle and McCormick," 1983-86.
b. November 14, 1921 in Bayonne, New Jersey

David Lemuel Keith
American actor
• In films *An Officer and a Gentleman*, 1982; *The Lords of Discipline*, 1983.
b. May 08, 1954 in Knoxville, Tennessee

Ian Keith
(Keith Ross)
American actor
• Broadway matinee idol; supporting actor, 1924-56, in films *Abraham Lincoln*, 1930; *The Ten Commandments*, 1956; *Cleopatra*, 1963.
b. February 27, 1899 in Boston, Massachusetts
d. March 26, 1960 in New York, New York

Cecil Kellaway
American actor
• Oscar nominee: *The Luck of the Irish*, 1948; *Guess Who's Coming to Dinner*, 1967.
b. August 22, 1893 in Cape Town, South Africa
d. February 28, 1973 in Los Angeles, California

Marthe Keller
Swiss actress
• Films include *Marathon Man; Bobby Deerfield; Fedora*.
b. 1945 in Basel, Switzerland

Sally Claire Kellerman
American actress
• Oscar nominee for role of Hot Lips Houlihan in film *M*A*S*H*, 1970.
b. June 02, 1937 in Long Beach, California

DeForrest Kelley
American actor
• Played Dr. McCoy in TV series, film *Star Trek*, 1967-69.
b. January 2, 1920 in Atlanta, Georgia

Mike Kellin
(Myron Kellin)
American actor
• Won 1976 Obie for *American Buffalo*.
b. April 26, 1922 in Hartford, Connecticut
d. August 26, 1983 in Nyack, New York

Emmett Kelly
American clown
• Created character of "Weary Willie," 1931.
b. December 09, 1898 in Sedan, Kansas
d. March 28, 1979 in Sarasota, Florida

Gene Kelly
(Eugene Curran)
American dancer–actor
• Starred in *An American in Paris*, 1951; *Singing in the Rain*, 1952; known for energetic, innovative style; also directed, choreographed many films.
b. August 23, 1912 in Pittsburgh, Pennsylvania

Grace Patricia Kelly
(Princess Grace Grimaldi; Princess Grace of Monaco)
American actress–princess
• Won 1954 Oscar for *The Country Girl*; married Prince Rainier, 1956.
b. November 12, 1929 in Philadelphia, Pennsylvania
d. September 14, 1982 in Monte Carlo, Monaco

Jack Kelly
American actor
• Played in TV series "Maverick," 1957-62.
b. September 16, 1927 in Astoria, New York

Nancy Kelly
American actress
• Won Tony for *The Bad Seed*, 1955; also played the same role in film, 1956.
b. March 25, 1921 in Lowell, Massachusetts

Patsy (Sarah Veronica Rose) Kelly
American comedienne
• In films, 1930s-40s; won Tony for Broadway revival: *No, No, Nanette*, 1971.
b. January 12, 1910 in Brooklyn, New York
d. September 24, 1981 in Hollywood, California

Paul Kelly
American actor
• Child star, supporting actor, 1908-56, who served two years in prison for manslaughter, 1920s.
b. August 09, 1899 in New York, New York
d. November 06, 1956 in Los Angeles, California

Linda Kelsey
American actress
• Played Billie on TV series "Lou Grant," 1977-82.
b. July 28

Charles Kemble
English actor
• Acted with daughter, Fanny, 1829-34; manager, Covent Garden, 1822-40; first to use historical sets, authentic costumes; noted for comic roles.
b. November 25, 1775 in Brecknock, Wales
d. November 12, 1854 in London, England

John Philip Kemble
English actor
• Brother of Charles; manager, Covent Gardens, 1803-17; introduced live animals to stage; Shakespearian actor.
b. February 01, 1757 in Prescott, England
d. February 26, 1823 in Lausanne, Switzerland

Rachel Kempson
(Mrs Michael Redgrave)
English actress
• Films include *Jane Eyre*, 1971; mother of Vanessa, Lynn Redgrave.
b. May 28, 1910 in Dartmouth, England

Dame Madge Kendal
English actress
• Twenty-second child of an actor; played Shakespeare, Old English comedies with husband, William.
b. March 15, 1848 in Cleethorpes, England
d. September 14, 1935 in Chorley Wood, England

Kay Kendall
(Justine McCarthy)
English actress
• Married, Rex Harrison, 1957-59; starred in *Genevieve*, 1953.
b. 1926 in Hull, England
d. September 06, 1959 in London, England

Arthur (John Arthur) Kennedy
American actor
• Won Tony award for *Death of a Salesman*, 1949; films include *The Desperate Hours*, 1955, *The Glass Menagerie*, 1950.
b. February 17, 1914 in Worcester, Massachusetts
d. January 05, 1990 in Branford, Connecticut

Edgar Kennedy
American actor
• Comedian in films since 1914, including *The Edgar Kennedy*, series, 1931-48.
b. April 26, 1890 in Monterey, California
d. November 09, 1948 in Woodland Hills, California

George Kennedy
American actor
• Won 1967 Oscar for *Cool Hand Luke*; often in strong supporting roles: *Airport*, 1970, *Charade*, 1963.
b. February 18, 1925 in New York, New York

Jayne Harrison Kennedy
American actress
• Co-hosted CBS's "NFL Today"; first black woman with network sports.
b. October 27, 1951 in Washington, District of Columbia

Madge Kennedy
American actress
• Silent film star, 1917-26; considered last of Sam Goldwyn's original glamorous leading ladies; starred on Broadway with WC Fields in *Poppy*, 1923.
b. 1892 in Chicago, Illinois
d. June 1, 1987 in Woodland Hills, California

Douglas C Kenney
American editor–screenwriter
• Co-founded, edited *National Lampoon*, 1969-75; wrote film *Animal House*, 1978.
b. December 1, 1947 in Cleveland, Ohio
d. August 27, 1980 in Kauai Island, Hawaii

Ken Kercheval
American actor
• Plays Cliff Barnes on TV series "Dallas," 1978–.
b. July 15, 1935 in Wolcottville, Tennessee

Joanna Kerns
(Joanna DeVarona)
American actress
• Plays Maggie Seaver on TV comedy "Growing Pains," 1985–; sister of Donna DeVarona.
b. February 12, 1953 in San Francisco, California

Deborah Kerr
(Deborah Jane Kerr-Trimmer)
American actress
• Starred in *From Here to Eternity*, 1953; *Tea and Sympathy*, 1956.
b. September 3, 1921 in Helensburgh, Scotland

Graham Kerr
English chef–TV personality
• Star of TV series "Galloping Gourmet," 1969-73; "Take Kerr," 1976–.
b. January 22, 1934 in London, England

Jean Kerr
(Bridget Jean Collins)
American author–dramatist
• Wrote humorous autobiographical work *Please Don't Eat the Daisies*, 1957; adapted to film, 1960; wife of Walter Francis.
b. July 1, 1923 in Scranton, Pennsylvania

Joseph Otto Kesselring
American dramatist
• Wrote suspense comedy *Arsenic and Old Lace*, 1941; screenplay, 1944.
b. June 21, 1902 in New York, New York
d. November 05, 1967

Evelyn Louise Keyes
American actress
• Artie Shaw's eighth wife; wrote autobiography *Scarlet O'Hara's Younger Sister*, 1977.
b. November 2, 1919 in Port Arthur, Texas

Yevgeni Kharitonov
Russian poet–dramatist
• Attempted to form experimental literary workshop which was suppressed by Soviets, 1980; wrote *Under House Arrest*.
b. 1941
d. June 29, 1981 in Moscow, U.S.S.R.

Guy Kibbee
American actor
• Character actor, 1931-49; played title role in *Scattergood Baines* series, 1941-42.
b. March 06, 1882 in El Paso, Texas
d. May 24, 1956 in East Islip, New York

Michael Kidd
(Milton Greenwald)
American choreographer
• Won five Tonys, 1940s-50s, including one for *Guys and Dolls*, 1957.
b. August 12, 1919 in Brooklyn, New York

Margot Kidder
American actress
• Played Lois Lane in movies *Superman*, 1978; *Superman II*, 1981.
b. October 17, 1948 in Yellowknife, Northwest Territories

Richard Kiel
American actor
• Stands seven feet, two inches; played part of Jaws in James Bond films *The Spy Who Loved Me, Moonraker*.
b. September 13, 1939 in Redford, Michigan

John Francis Kieran
American editor–TV personality
• Radio, TV panelist of "Information Please" from 1938; edited *Information Please Almanac*.
b. August 02, 1892 in New York, New York
d. December 1, 1981 in Rockport, Massachusetts

Douglas Kiker
American broadcast journalist–author
• Correspondent, NBC News since 1966; author of several books.
b. January 07, 1930 in Griffin, Georgia

Percy Kilbride
American actor
• Played Pa Kettle in film series, 1947-55.
b. July 16, 1888 in San Francisco, California
d. December 11, 1964 in Los Angeles, California

Richard Paul Kiley
American actor–singer
• Won 1966 Tony Award as Don Quixote in *Man of La Mancha*.
b. March 31, 1922 in Chicago, Illinois

Dorothy Kilgallen
(Mrs Richard Kollmar)
American journalist–TV personality
• Reporter, gossip columnist, NY *Journal-American*, beginning 1930s.
b. July 03, 1913 in Chicago, Illinois
d. November 08, 1965 in New York, New York

Joseph Kilgour
Actor
• Silents, 1915-26, include *Let's Get Married*, 1926; *Try and Get It*, 1924.
b. 1863 in Ayr, Ontario
d. April 21, 1933 in Bay Shore, New York

Victor Kilian
American actor
• Played the "Fernwood Flasher" on TV series "Mary Hartman, Mary Hartman."
b. March 06, 1898 in Jersey City, New Jersey
d. March 11, 1979 in Hollywood, California

Thomas Killigrew
English dramatist
• Most popular play comedy *The Parson's Wedding*, 1637; established Drury Lane Theatre, 1663.
b. February 07, 1612 in London, England
d. May 19, 1683 in London, England

Alan King
(Irwin Kniberg)
American comedian–actor
• Films include *Author! Author!*, 1982; *Lovesick*, 1983.
b. December 26, 1927 in New York, New York

Cammie King
American actress
• Played Bonnie Blue Butler in *Gone with the Wind*, 1939.
b. August 05, 1934 in Los Angeles, California

Charles King
American actor
• Song, dance man in film musical *Broadway Melody*, 1929.
b. October 31, 1894 in New York, New York
d. January 11, 1944 in London, England

Dennis King
(Dennis Pratt)
American actor
• Co-starred with Jeanette MacDonald in *The Vagabond King*, 1930.
b. November 02, 1897 in Coventry, England
d. May 21, 1971 in New York, New York

Henry King
American director
• Co-founder, Academy of Motion Picure Arts & Sciences; organizer of Oscars; films include *Carousel*, 1956.
b. January 24, 1896 in Christianburg, Virginia
d. June 29, 1982 in Toluca Lake, California

Larry King
(Larry Zeiger)
American radio performer–TV personality
• Hosts nat'l. cable TV talk show, "Larry King Live!"
b. November 19, 1933 in Brooklyn, New York

Morganna King
American actress
• Played mother of Corleone family in *The Godfather I, II*.
b. June 04, 1930

Perry King
American actor
• Played in films *Lords of Flatbush; Mandingo;* TV movies *Captains and Kings; Riptide*.
b. April 3, 1948 in Alliance, Ohio

Yolanda Denise King
American actress
• Daughter of Martin Luther King, Jr.; formed theatre troupe, Nucleus, with Attallah Shabazz, daughter of Malcolm X.
b. 1955

Ben Kingsley
(Krishna Bhanji)
English actor
• Won 1983 Best Actor Oscar for *Gandhi*.
b. December 31, 1943 in Snaiton, England

Sidney Kingsley
(Sidney Kieschner)
American dramatist
• Won Pulitzer for play *Men in White*, 1934.
b. October 18, 1906 in New York, New York

Klaus Kinski
(Nikolaus Gunther Nakszynski)
American actor
• Star of German, American films known for intense portrayals: *Fitzcarraldo*, 1982; father of Nastassja.
b. October 18, 1926 in Sopot, Poland

Nastassja Kinski
(Nastassja Nakszynski; Mrs Ibrahim Moussa; "Nasti")
German actress
• Starred in films *Tess*, 1978; *Unfaithfully Yours*, 1984.
b. January 24, 1960 in Berlin, Germany (West)

Robert Edmonds Kintner
American radio executive–TV executive
• Pres., ABC, 1950-56; NBC, 1958-65; televised McCarthy hearings, 1950s; criticized for violence-oriented programs.
b. September 12, 1909 in Stroudsburg, Pennsylvania
d. December 2, 1980 in Washington, District of Columbia

Teinousuke Kinugasa
Japanese director
• Won Oscar for best foreign film *Gate of Hell*, 1954.
b. 1898 in Mie, Japan
d. February 26, 1982

Claude Kipnis
French entertainer–pantomimist
• Mime; trained with Marcel Marceau; traveled internationally; wrote *The Mime Book*, 1974.
b. April 22, 1938 in Paris, France
d. February 08, 1981 in New York, New York

Durward Kirby
American actor
• Co-host of TV show "Candid Camera," 1961-66.
b. August 24, 1912 in Covington, Kentucky

George Kirby
American comedian
• First black stand-up comic, known for repertoire of over 100 impersonations; starred in own TV comedy-variety show, 1972-73.
b. June 08, 1923 in Chicago, Illinois

Phyllis Kirk
(Phyllis Kirkegaard)
American actress
• Nora Charles on TV series "The Thin Man," 1957-59.
b. September 18, 1930 in Plainfield, New Jersey

Gelsey Kirkland
American dancer
• With American Ballet Theatre, 1974-81.
b. December 29, 1952 in Bethlehem, Pennsylvania

James Kirkwood
American writer
• Won Pulitzer, Tony, for musical play, *Chorus Line*, 1976.
b. August 22, 1930 in Los Angeles, California
d. April 21, 1989 in New York, New York

Karoly Kisfaludy
Hungarian dramatist
• Founder of Hungarian drama; wrote historical play, *The Tatars in Hungary*, 1819.
b. February 06, 1788 in Tete, Hungary
d. November 21, 1830 in Pest, Hungary

Darci Anna Kistler
American dancer
• Youthful star of NYC Ballet since 1980; principal dancer, 1982–.
b. June 04, 1964 in Riverside, California

Iva Kitchell
American dancer
• Dance comedienne who impersonated great dancers, satirized classical ballet; featured dancer at Radio City Music Hall, NYC.
b. March 31, 1908 in Junction City, Kansas
d. November 19, 1983 in Ormond Beach, Florida

Robert Klein
American comedian–actor
• Won Tony, 1979, for *They're Playing Our Song;* known for records, TV appearances.
b. February 08, 1942 in New York, New York

Werner Klemperer
German actor
• Won Emmys for role of Colonel Klink on TV series "Hogan's Heroes," 1968, 1969; son of Otto.
b. March 22, 1920 in Cologne, Germany

Ivan Klima
Czech dramatist
• Began as novelist; antirealist plays are rich in symbols, myths: *The Castle*, 1964.
b. September 14, 1931 in Prague, Czechoslovakia

Kevin Delaney Kline
American actor
• Won Tonys for *On the Twentieth Century*, 1978; *The Pirates of Penzance*, 1981; in film *Sophie's Choice*, 1982.
b. October 24, 1947 in Saint Louis, Missouri

Jack Klugman
American actor
• Played Oscar Madison on TV comedy "The Odd Couple," 1970-75, title role in TV drama "Quincy," 1976-83; won three Emmys.
b. April 27, 1922 in Philadelphia, Pennsylvania

Shirley Knight
American actress
• Oscar nominee for *The Dark at the Top of the Stairs*, 1959; *Sweet Bird of Youth*, 1962; won Tony for *Kennedy's Children*, 1975.
b. July 05, 1937 in Goessel, Kansas

Ted Knight
(Tadeus Wladyslaw Konopka)
American actor
• Starred in TV series "The Mary Tyler Moore Show," 1970-77; "Too Close for Comfort," 1980-86; won three Emmys.
b. December 07, 1923 in Terryville, Connecticut
d. August 26, 1986 in Pacific Palisades, California

Don Knotts
American comedian–actor
• Won five Emmys for role of Barney Fife on TV comedy "The Andy Griffith Show," 1960-68.
b. July 21, 1924 in Morgantown, West Virginia

James Sheridan Knowles
British dramatist
• Plays include tragedy, *William Tell,*
1825; comedy, *The Hunchback,* 1832.
b. May 12, 1784 in Cork, Ireland
d. November 3, 1862 in Torquay, England

Patric Knowles
(Reginald Lawrence Knowles)
English actor
• Films include *Adventures of Robin
Hood,* 1938; *How Green Was My Valley,*
1941.
b. November 11, 1911 in Horsforth, England

Alexander Knox
Canadian actor
• Oscar nominee for *Wilson,* 1944; other
films include *Gorky Park,* 1983.
b. January 16, 1907 in Strathroy, Ontario

Walter Koenig
American actor
• Played Pavel Chekov in TV's "Star
Trek," 1967-69; same role in film se-
ries, 1979-86.
b. September 14, 1936 in Chicago, Illinois

Sir Fred Kohler
American actor
• Played villain in films *The Iron Horse,*
1924; *The Plainsman,* 1937; *Way of All
Flesh,* 1927.
b. April 2, 1889 in Kansas City, Missouri
d. October 28, 1938 in Los Angeles, California

Susan Kohner
American actress
• Oscar nominee for role of bi-racial
Sarah Jane in *Imitation of Life,* 1959.
b. November 11, 1936 in Los Angeles, Cali-
fornia

Richard Kollmar
American producer–actor
• Played radio detective Boston Blackie;
with wife, Dorothy Kilgallen, broadcast
"Dick and Dorothy," 1954-63.
b. December 31, 1910 in Ridgewood, New
Jersey
d. January 07, 1971 in New York, New York

Bernie (Bernard Morton) Kopell
American actor
• Played Dr. Adam Bricker on TV series
"The Love Boat," 1976-86.
b. June 21, 1933 in Brooklyn, New York

Arthur Lee Kopit
American dramatist
• Wrote play *Oh Dad, Poor Dad,
Mama's Hung You in the Closet and I'm
Feelin' So Sad,* 1960; became film,
1967.
b. May 1, 1937 in New York, New York

Ted (Edward James) Koppel
American broadcast journalist
• Anchor, ABC News "Nightline,"
1980–; program started in order to cover hostages in Iran.
b. February 08, 1940 in Lancashire, England

Sir Alexander Korda
(Sandor Kellner; Sandor Korda)
English producer
• Developed British film industry with
London Films Co.; made 112 films, in-
cluding *The Third Man,* 1950.
b. September 16, 1893 in Turkeve, Hungary
d. January 23, 1956 in London, England

Harvey Herschel Korman
American comedian
• Regular on "The Carol Burnett Show,"
1967-77; won four Emmys; films include
Blazing Saddles, 1974.
b. February 15, 1927 in Chicago, Illinois

Mary Kornman
(Our Gang)
American actress
• "Our Gang" first leading lady, 1923.
b. 1917 in Idaho Falls, Idaho
d. June 01, 1973 in Glendale, California

Yaphet Frederick Kotto
American actor
• Starred as Idi Amin in *Raid on En-
tebbe,* 1976; other films include *Alien,*
1979; *Brubaker,* 1980.
b. November 15, 1937 in New York, New
York

**August Friedrich Ferdinand von
Kotzebue**
German dramatist
• Wrote 200 plays including *The Stranger,* 1798; killed by U. student.
b. May 03, 1761 in Weimar, Germany
d. March 23, 1819 in Mannheim, Germany

Ernie Kovacs
American actor
• Played Ernie in TV show "Kovacs-
land," 1951; "Tonight," 1956-57; married Edie Adams.
b. January 23, 1919 in Trenton, New Jersey
d. January 13, 1962 in Hollywood, California

Stanley E Kramer
American director–producer
• Among his 15 Oscar-winning movies
are *High Noon,* 1952, *Judgment at Nur-
emberg,* 1961, *Guess Who's Coming to
Dinner?* 1967.
b. September 29, 1913 in New York, New
York

Joseph Kramm
American dramatist–actor–director
• Actor-turned-director; won 1952 Pulitzer for ninth play he wrote, first play
produced, *The Shrike.*
b. September 3, 1907 in Philadelphia, Pennsylvania

Norman Krasna
American dramatist–critic
• Won Oscar for screenplay: *Princess
O'Rourke,* 1943.
b. November 07, 1909 in New York, New
York
d. November 01, 1984 in Los Angeles, Cali-
fornia

Werner Krauss
German actor
• Played insane doctor in silent horror
classic *Cabinet of Dr. Caligari,* 1919.
b. 1884 in Gestungshausen, Germany
d. October 2, 1959 in Vienna, Austria

Kreskin
(George Joseph Kresge Jr; "The Amazing
Kreskin")
American psychic–entertainer
• Uses telepathy, traditional magic; wrote
Use Your Head to Get Ahead, 1977.
b. January 12, 1935 in Montclair, New Jersey

Kurt Kreuger
American actor
• Supporting actor in 1943 films *Enemy
Below; The Moon Is Down.*
b. July 23, 1917 in Saint Moritz, Switzerland

Alfred Kreymborg
American dramatist–poet
• Experimental poet; first collection,
Mushrooms, 1916; wrote autobiography,
Troubadour, 1925.
b. December 1, 1883 in New York, New
York
d. August 14, 1966 in Milford, Connecticut

Alice Krige
South African actress
• In TV mini-series "Ellis Island,"
1984; "Dream West," 1986; in film
Chariots of Fire, 1983.
b. 1955 in South Africa

Sylvia Kristel
Dutch actress
• Star of erotic French film *Emmanuelle,*
1974.
b. September 28, 1952 in Utrecht, Netherlands

Marty Krofft
American puppeteer–producer
• With brother, Sid, created various pup-
pet, cartoon TV shows including "H R
Pufnstuf," 1970s.
b. in Montreal, Quebec

Sid Krofft
American puppeteer–producer
• With brother, Marty, created various puppet, cartoon TV shows.
b. in Athens, Greece

Hardy (Eberhard) Kruger
German actor
• Films include *The One That Got Away; Wild Geese*, 1943.
b. April 12, 1928 in Berlin, Germany

Otto Kruger
American actor
• Broadway matinee idol, 1920s; film lead in *Dr. Ehrlich's Magic Bullet*, 1940.
b. September 06, 1885 in Toledo, Ohio
d. September 06, 1974 in Woodland Hills, California

Stanley Kubrick
American director
• Films include *2001: A Space Odyssey*, 1968; *A Clockwork Orange*, 1971.
b. July 26, 1928 in New York, New York

Nancy Jane Kulp
American actress
• Played Jane Hathaway on "The Beverly Hillbillies," 1962-71.
b. August 28, 1921 in Harrisburg, Pennsylvania
d. February 03, 1991 in Palm Desert, California

Irv Kupcinet
American journalist–TV personality
• Columnist, *Chicago Sun Times*, 1943–; hosted "Kup's Show," 1959-86.
b. July 31, 1912 in Chicago, Illinois

Charles Bishop Kuralt
American broadcast journalist
• Correspondent with CBS News, 1959–; known for "On the Road" segments; won three Peabodys, three Emmys.
b. September 1, 1934 in Wilmington, North Carolina

Harry Kurnitz
(Marco Page pseud)
American dramatist–screenwriter–author
• Wrote screenplay of his novel *Fast Company*, 1938; other films include *Once More with Feeling*, 1960; *Goodbye Charlie*, 1964.
b. January 05, 1909 in New York, New York
d. March 18, 1968 in Los Angeles, California

Akira Kurosawa
Japanese director
• Best known for action films; directed epic *Ran*, 1985.
b. March 23, 1910 in Tokyo, Japan

Bill (William Horton) Kurtis
American broadcast journalist
• Correspondent, co-anchor, CBS Morning News, 1982-86.
b. September 21, 1940 in Pensacola, Florida

Swoosie Kurtz
American actress
• Won Tony, 1980, for *Fifth of July*.
b. September 06, 1944 in Omaha, Nebraska

Nancy Kashen Kwan
Chinese actress
• Starred in *The World of Suzie Wong*, 1960; *Flower Drum Song*, 1961.
b. May 19, 1939 in Hong Kong

Jiri Kylian
Czech dancer
• Director, choreographer for Netherlands Dance Theater, 1978–.
b. March 21, 1945 in Prague, Czechoslovakia

Rudolf von Laban
Czech choreographer
• Founded dance-drama; originated method of recording dance instructions similar to music scores.
b. December 15, 1879 in Bratislava, Czechoslovakia
d. July 01, 1958 in London, England

Kenneth Lackey
American actor
• Best known as original member of Three Stooges, 1923-25.
b. 1902 in Indiana
d. April 16, 1976 in Columbus, North Carolina

Alan Ladd
American actor
• Appeared in 150 films, including *Shane*, 1954.
b. September 03, 1913 in Hot Springs, Arkansas
d. January 29, 1964 in Palm Springs, California

Alan Walbridge Ladd, Jr
American producer
• Pres., 20th Century-Fox, 1976-79; pres., Ladd Co., 1979–.
b. October 22, 1937 in Los Angeles, California

Cheryl Ladd
(Cheryl Stoppelmoor; Mrs Brian Russell)
American actress
• Played Kris on "Charlie's Angels," 1977-81.
b. July 02, 1952 in Huron, South Dakota

Diane Ladd
(Rose Diane Ladner)
American actress
• Oscar nominee for *Alice Doesn't Live Here Anymore*, 1975.
b. November 29, 1932 in Meridian, Mississippi

Carl Laemmle, Sr
American film executive
• Formed IMP Co., 1909, which was first to publicize its stars including Mary Pickford; became Universal Studio, 1912; sold, 1935.
b. January 17, 1867 in Laupheim, Germany
d. September 24, 1939 in Hollywood, California

Bert Lahr
(Irving Lahrheim)
American actor–comedian
• Starred as Cowardly Lion in *The Wizard of Oz*, 1939.
b. August 13, 1895 in New York, New York
d. December 04, 1967 in New York, New York

Christine Lahti
American actress
• Oscar nominee for *Swing Shift*, 1984; other films include *Just Between Friends*, 1986.
b. April 04, 1950 in Detroit, Michigan

Hugh Laing
(Hugh Skinner)
English dancer
• Best-known ballets written for him by Anthony Tudor, 1930s-50s; with NYC Ballet, 1950-52.
b. June 06, 1911 in Barbados
d. May 1, 1988 in New York, New York

Arthur Lake
(Arthur Silverlake)
American actor
• Played comic strip character Dagwood Bumstead in over two dozen *Blondie* films, 1939-50.
b. April 17, 1905 in Corbin, Kentucky
d. January 09, 1987 in Indian Wells, California

Veronica Lake
(Constance Frances Marie Ockleman)
American actress
• Popular in 1940s films; known for style-setting long, straight hair.
b. November 15, 1919 in Brooklyn, New York
d. July 07, 1973 in Burlington, Vermont

Barbara LaMarr
(Rheatha Watson)
American actress
• Played in 22 silent movies; best known for her exotic beauty; private life was scandal plagued; died from drug overdose.
b. July 28, 1896 in Richard, Virginia
d. January 3, 1926 in Altadena, California

Hedy Lamarr
(Hedwig Eva Marie Kiesler; Hedy Kieslerova)
American actress
• Gained notoriety for her 10-minute nude sequence in film *Ecstasy*, 1933; billed as world's most beautiful woman.
b. September 11, 1913 in Vienna, Austria

Fernando Lamas
American actor–director
• Typecast as a "Latin lover" in 1950s films; TV series include "Falcon Crest"; married Esther Williams, Arlene Dahl.
b. January 09, 1925 in Buenos Aires, Argentina
d. October 08, 1982 in Los Angeles, California

Lorenzo Lamas
American actor
• Son of Fernando Lamas, Arlene Dahl; played Lance Cumson on TV series "Falcon Crest," 1981-90.
b. January 2, 1958 in Santa Monica, California

Gil Lamb
American actor
• Film comedian, 1941–; films include *The Fleet's In*, 1949; *The Love Bug*, 1968.
b. June 14, 1906 in Minneapolis, Minnesota

Christopher Lambert
American actor
• 17th actor to play Tarzan; in 1984 film *Greystoke: The Legend of Tarzan, Lord of the Apes.*
b. 1957 in New York, New York

Dorothy Lamour
(Dorothy Kaumeyer)
American actress–singer
• Best known for 1940s "road" films with Bing Crosby, Bob Hope.
b. December 1, 1914 in New Orleans, Louisiana

Zohra Lampert
American actress
• Starred in film *Let's Scare Jessica to Death*, 1971; TV series "The Girl with Something Extra," 1973-74.
b. May 13, 1936 in New York, New York

Burt(on Stephen) Lancaster
American actor
• Won Oscar, 1960, for *Elmer Gantry*; in major films since 1946.
b. November 02, 1913 in New York, New York

Elsa Lanchester
(Elizabeth Sullivan; Mrs Charles Laughton)
English comedienne–actress
• Known for eccentric, comic roles: *The Bride of Frankenstein*, 1935.
b. October 28, 1902 in Lewisham, England
d. December 26, 1986 in Woodland Hills, California

Ely A Landau
American producer
• Noted for telefilms of hit plays; founded American Film Theater, 1972.
b. January 2, 1920 in New York, New York

Martin Landau
American actor
• Starred in "Mission Impossible," 1966-69; "Space 1999," 1974-77. Oscar-nominated for *Crimes and Misdemeanors*, 1989.
b. June 3, 1933 in New York, New York

Toni Lander
(Toni Pihl Peterson)
Danish dancer
• Known for unparalleled style, especially in *Etudes*, 1950.
b. June 19, 1931 in Copenhagen, Denmark
d. May 19, 1985 in Salt Lake City, Utah

Audrey Landers
American actress
• Played Afton Cooper in recurring role on TV series "Dallas."
b. July 18, 1959 in Philadelphia, Pennsylvania

Harry Landers
American actor
• Character actor in films *The Ten Commandments*, 1956; *Rear Window*, 1954.
b. 1921 in New York, New York

Judy Landers
American actress
• Starred in TV series "BJ and the Bear" and "Vegas"; sister of Audrey.
b. October 07, 1961 in Philadelphia, Pennsylvania

Steve Landesberg
American actor–comedian
• Played Arthur Dietrich on TV series "Barney Miller," 1976-82.
b. November 23, in Bronx, New York

Elissa Landi
(Elizabeth Marie Zanardi-Landi)
Italian actress
• Best known for role in *The Sign of the Cross*, 1932.
b. December 06, 1904 in Venice, Italy
d. October 31, 1948 in Kingston, New York

Carole Landis
(Frances Lillian Mary Ridste)
American actress
• One of favorite WW II pinups who starred in film *Four Jills in a Jeep*, 1944, based on her adventures entertaining troops.
b. January 01, 1919 in Fairchild, Wisconsin
d. July 05, 1948 in Brentwood Heights, California

Jessie Royce Landis
(Jessie Royse Medbury)
American actress
• Character actress in mother roles in films *North by Northwest*, 1959; *To Catch a Thief*, 1955.
b. November 25, 1904 in Chicago, Illinois
d. February 02, 1972 in Danbury, Connecticut

John David Landis
American director
• First success: *National Lampoon's Animal House*, 1978; acquitted, 1987 of involuntary manslaughter of Vic Morrow, others during filming *Twilight Zone–The Movie*, 1983.
b. August 03, 1950 in Chicago, Illinois

Michael Landon
(Eugene Michael Orowitz)
American actor–director–writer
• TV series include "Bonanza"; "Little House on the Prairie"; "Highway to Heaven."
b. October 31, 1937 in Forest Hills, New York

Diane Lane
American actress
• Films include *Rumble Fish*, 1983; *Cotton Club*, 1984.
b. January 1963 in New York, New York

Lola Lane
(Dorothy Mullican)
American actress–singer
• Co-starred with sisters Priscilla, Rosemary in sentimental films of late 1930s-40s.
b. May 21, 1906 in Macy, Indiana
d. June 22, 1981 in Santa Barbara, California

Priscilla Lane
(Priscilla Mullican)
American actress–singer
• Starred in *Brother Rat*, 1938; *Arsenic and Old Lace*, 1944.
b. June 12, 1917 in Indianola, Iowa

Rosemary Lane
(Rosemary Mullican)
American singer–actress
• Co-starred in films with sisters Priscilla, Lola, late 1930s-40s.
b. April 04, 1914 in Indianola, Iowa
d. November 25, 1974 in Woodland Hills, California

Stewart F Lane
American producer
• Theatrical producer; won Tony, 1984, for *La Cage Aux Folles*.
b. May 03, 1951 in New York, New York

Fritz Lang
Austrian director
• Films include *The Big Heat*, 1953.
b. December 05, 1890 in Vienna, Austria
d. August 02, 1976 in Los Angeles, California

Harry Langdon
American actor
• Joined Mack Sennett comedies, 1923; screen character was a baby-faced simpleton.
b. June 15, 1884 in Council Bluffs, Iowa
d. December 22, 1944 in Los Angeles, California

Jessica Lange
American actress
• Won best supporting actress Oscar for *Tootsie*, 1983; starred in *King Kong*, 1976.
b. April 2, 1949 in Cloquet, Minnesota

Lawrence Langer
American producer–dramatist
• Founded Washington Square Players, 1914; Theatre Guild, 1919.
b. May 3, 1890 in Swansea, South Wales
d. December 26, 1962 in New York, New York

Noel Langley
American screenwriter
• Wrote MGM classic screenplay *Wizard of Oz*, 1939.
b. December 25, 1911 in Durban, South Africa
d. November 04, 1980 in Desert Hot Springs, California

Lillie Langtry
(Emilie Charlotte LeBreton; "The Jersey Lily")
American actress
• Famed for her beauty; mistress of Edward VII; wrote autobiography *The Days I Knew*, 1925.
b. October 13, 1853 in Isle of Jersey
d. February 12, 1929 in Monte Carlo, Monaco

Angela Brigid Lansbury
(Mrs Peter Shaw)
American actress–singer
• Won four Tonys; star of TV's "Murder, She Wrote," 1984–.
b. October 16, 1925 in London, England

Sherry Lee Lansing
American film executive
• First woman in charge of production at major film studio: 20th Century Fox, 1980-82.
b. July 31, 1944 in Chicago, Illinois

Jane Lapotaire
English actress
• Won 1981 Tony for title role in *Piaf*.
b. December 26, 1944 in Ipswich, England

Ring(gold Wilmer) Lardner, Jr
(The Hollywood Ten)
American screenwriter
• Won Oscars for *M*A*S*H*, 1970; *Woman of the Year*, 1942.
b. August 19, 1915 in Chicago, Illinois

Rod LaRocque
(Roderick la Rocque de la Rour)
American actor
• Matinee idol of silent films including *Ten Commandments*; *Notoriety*.
b. November 29, 1898 in Chicago, Illinois
d. October 15, 1969 in Beverly Hills, California

Rose LaRose
(Rosina Dapelle)
American entertainer
• Burlesque performer, 1940s-50s, who earned $2,500 a week.
b. 1913 in Brooklyn, New York
d. July 27, 1972 in Toledo, Ohio

John Larroquette
American actor
• Plays Dan Fielding on TV show "Night Court," 1983–; won Emmy, 1985, 1986, 1987.
b. November 25, 1947 in New Orleans, Louisiana

Jack LaRue
(Gaspere Biondolillo)
American actor
• Made a career as a sneering bad guy in 200 films.
b. May 03, 1902 in New York, New York
d. January 11, 1984 in Santa Monica, California

Jesse L(ouis) Lasky
American film executive
• With brother-in-law, Samuel Goldwyn, formed film studio, 1913, that became Paramount Studios, 1916.
b. September 13, 1880 in San Jose, California
d. January 13, 1958 in Beverly Hills, California

Jesse Louis Lasky, Jr
(Frances Smeed pseud)
American writer
• Screenplays include *Samson and Delilah*, 1950; *Ten Commandments*, 1956; also wrote novels, plays; son of Hollywood film pioneer.
b. September 19, 1910 in New York, New York
d. April 11, 1988 in London, England

Louise Lasser
American actress
• Starred in "Mary Hartman, Mary Hartman"; was married to Woody Allen.
b. April 11, 1939 in New York, New York

Charles Laughton
American actor
• Won Oscar, 1933, for *The Private Lives of Henry VIII*; noted for *Mutiny on the Bounty*, 1935.
b. July 01, 1899 in Scarborough, England
d. December 15, 1962 in Los Angeles, California

Stan Laurel
(Arthur Stanley Jefferson; Laurel and Hardy)
American comedian–actor
• Joined with Oliver Hardy, 1926; made over 200 films.
b. June 16, 1890 in Ulverston, England
d. February 23, 1965 in Santa Monica, California

Arthur Laurents
American dramatist–author
• Wrote musical *West Side Story*, 1958; wrote novels, screenplays *The Way We Were*, 1972; *The Turning Point*, 1977.
b. July 14, 1918 in New York, New York

Piper Laurie
(Rosetta Jacobs)
American actress
• Oscar nominee for her role as mother in *Carrie*, 1976; won 1987 Emmy for "Promise."
b. January 22, 1932 in Detroit, Michigan

Linda Lavin
(Mrs Kip Niven)
American actress–singer
• Starred in TV series "Alice," 1976-85; won Tony for *Broadway Bound*, 1987.
b. October 15, 1939 in Portland, Maine

John Philip Law
American actor
• Films include *The Russians Are Coming, the Russians Are Coming*; *Barbella*.
b. September 07, 1937 in Hollywood, California

Peter Lawford
English actor
• Played Nick Charles in TV series "The Thin Man," 1957-59.
b. September 07, 1923 in London, England
d. December 24, 1984 in Los Angeles, California

Florence Lawrence
American actress
• First film star, 1908-24, to be known by name, previously, silent stars had been anonymous.
b. January 02, 1886 in Hamilton, Ontario
d. December 27, 1938 in Beverly Hills, California

Jerome Lawrence
(Jerome Lawrence Schwartz)
American dramatist–author
• Wrote prize-winning plays *Inherit the Wind*, 1955; *Auntie Mame*, 1956.
b. July 14, 1915 in Cleveland, Ohio

John Howard Lawson
(The Hollywood Ten)
American dramatist
• Co-founder, first pres., Screen Writers Guild, 1933; films include *Marching Song*, 1939.
b. September 25, 1895 in New York, New York
d. August 12, 1977 in San Francisco, California

Leigh Lawson
English actor
• Films include *Tess*, 1981; TV show "Lace," 1984.
b. July 21, 1945 in Atherston, England

Joe Layton
(Joseph Lichtman)
American choreographer
• Won Tonys for *No Strings*, 1962; *George M!*, 1969; Emmy for "My Name Is Barbra," 1965.
b. May 03, 1931 in Brooklyn, New York

Robin Leach
English TV personality
• Hosts "Lifestyles of Rich and Famous," 1983–; one of most popular syndicated TV shows in Amercia.
b. August 29, 1941 in Perivale, England

Will (Wilford Carson) Leach
American director
• Director, NY Shakespeare Festival, 1978–; won Tony, 1981, Obie, 1972, 1981.
b. August 26, 1934 in Petersburg, Virginia
d. June 2, 1988 in Rocky Point, New York

Cloris Leachman
American actress
• Won Oscar, 1971, for *The Last Picture Show*; won Emmy, 1975, for "The Mary Tyler Moore Show."
b. April 3, 1925 in Des Moines, Iowa

Sir David Lean
English director
• Won Oscars for *Bridge on the River Kwai*, 1957; *Lawrence of Arabia*, 1962.
b. March 25, 1908 in Croydon, England
d. April 16, 1991

Norman Milton Lear
American producer
• TV comedy empire reshaped the sitcom; created "All in the Family"; "The Jeffersons"; "Maude."
b. July 27, 1922 in New Haven, Connecticut

Michael Learned
American actress
• Played Olivia on "The Waltons," 1972-79; won three Emmys.
b. April 09, 1929 in Washington, District of Columbia

Jean-Pierre Leaud
French actor
• Played same character in five Truffaut films, 1959-79, including *Stolen Kisses*.
b. May 05, 1944 in Paris, France

Francis Lederer
(Frantisek or Franz Lederer)
Czech actor
• Films include German *Pandora's Box*, 1929; *Gay Deception*, 1936.
b. November 06, 1906 in Prague, Czechoslovakia

Bernard Lee
English actor
• Played M in James Bond films, 1962-79.
b. January 1, 1908 in London, England
d. January 16, 1981 in London, England

Bruce Lee
(Lee Siu Loong; Lee Yuen Kam; "The Little Dragon")
American actor
• Best known for martial arts films: *Enter the Dragon*, 1973.
b. November 27, 1940 in San Francisco, California
d. July 3, 1973 in Hong Kong

Christopher Lee
(Christopher Frank Carandini Lee)
English actor
• Vincent Price's rival for horror film portrayals; films include *Corridor of Mirrors*, 1947; *Dracula*, 1958; *An Eye for an Eye*, 1981.
b. May 27, 1922 in London, England

Gypsy Rose Lee
(Rose Louise Hovick)
American entertainer
• Burlesque queen; autobiography *Gyspy*, 1957 basis for Broadway musical,1959, movie, 1962.
b. February 09, 1914 in Seattle, Washington
d. April 26, 1970 in Los Angeles, California

Michele Lee
(Michele Lee Dusiak)
American actress–dancer
• Plays Karen Fairgate MacKenzie on TV series "Knots Landing"; Tony nomination for musical *Seesaw*.
b. June 24, 1942 in Los Angeles, California

Spike (Shelton Jackson) Lee
American actor–director
• Produced, directed, starred in 1989 smash film *Do the Right Thing*; work often compared with Woody Allen.
b. 1956 in Atlanta, Georgia

Will Lee
American actor
• Played Mr. Hooper, the storekeeper, on "Sesame Street," 1969-82.
b. August 06, 1908 in Brooklyn, New York
d. December 07, 1982 in New York, New York

Eva LeGallienne
American actress–author
• Founded Civic Repertory Theatre, 1926-32; won special Tony, 1964; Emmy for "The Royal Family," 1978.
b. January 11, 1899 in London, England

Jim (James Charles) Lehrer
American broadcast journalist
• Associate editor, co-anchor "The MacNeil-Lehrer Report," 1975–.
b. May 19, 1934 in Wichita, Kansas

Ron Leibman
American actor
• Starred in film *Norma Rae*, 1979; played Martin Kazinski on TV series "Kaz," 1978-79; won Emmy, 1979; former husband of Linda Lavin; currently married to Jessica Walter.
b. October 11, 1937 in New York, New York

Janet Leigh
(Jeanette Helen Morrison)
American actress
• Starred in *Psycho*, 1960; mother of actress Jamie Lee Curtis.
b. July 06, 1927 in Merced, California

Vivien Leigh
(Vivian Mary Hartley)
English actress
• Played Scarlett O'Hara in *Gone With the Wind*, 1939.
b. November 05, 1913 in Darjeeling, India
d. July 07, 1967 in London, England

Margaret Leighton
English actress
• Won Tonys for *Separate Tables; Night of the Iguana.*
b. February 26, 1922 in Barnt Green, England
d. January 13, 1976 in Chichester, England

Lillian Leitzel
(Mrs Alfredo Codona; Leopoldina Alitza Pelikan)
German circus performer–gymnast
• One of Ringling Brothers' top attractions, 1915-31; queen of circus aerialists; died after 29-ft. plunge.
b. 1892 in Breslau, Germany
d. February 15, 1931 in Copenhagen, Denmark

Claude LeLouch
French director
• Won Best Foreign Film Oscar for *A Man and a Woman*, 1966.
b. October 3, 1937 in Paris, France

Harvey Lembeck
American actor
• Comedian in 250 TV performances; with Phil Silvers in "You'll Never Get Rich," 1955-59.
b. April 15, 1923 in New York, New York
d. January 05, 1982 in Los Angeles, California

Jack (John Uhler, III) Lemmon
American actor
• Won Oscars for *Mister Roberts*, 1955; *Save the Tiger*, 1971; received Life Achievement Award, 1988.
b. February 08, 1925 in Boston, Massachusetts

W(illiam) J Lemoyne
American actor
• Played in first 100 productions of "Uncle Tom's Cabin"; noted Dickens performer.
b. April 29, 1831 in Boston, Massachusetts
d. November 06, 1905 in New York, New York

Jay (James Douglas Muir) Leno
American comedian
• Noted for "attitude comedy"; performances include TV talk shows, sold-out concert at NYC's Carnegie Hall, 1986.
b. April 28, 1950 in New Rochelle, New York

Rula Lenska
(Roza-Maria Lubienska; "The Fair One")
English actress
• Rita Hayworth look-alike; noted for early 1980s TV commercials, "Who the hell is Rula Lenska?" fad.
b. September 3, 1947 in St. Neots, England

Eddie Leonard
(Lemuel Gordon Toney)
American actor
• Worked in vaudeville minstrel shows for 45 yrs.; composed "Ida, Sweet as Apple Cider."
b. October 18, 1875 in Richmond, Virginia
d. July 29, 1941 in New York, New York

Hugh Leonard, pseud
(John Keyes Byrne)
Irish dramatist
• Won 1978 Tony for *Da.*
b. November 09, 1926 in Dublin, Ireland

Jack E Leonard
(Leonard Lebitsky; "Fat Jack")
American comedian
• Nightclub comedian whose trademark was one-line insults.
b. April 24, 1911 in Chicago, Illinois
d. May 09, 1973 in New York, New York

Sheldon Leonard
(Sheldon Leonard Bershad)
American actor–producer
• Produced TV shows "The Dick Van Dyke Show"; "I Spy."
b. February 22, 1907 in New York, New York

Sergio Leone
Italian director–screenwriter
• Noted for Westerns: *A Fistful of Dollars*, 1964; *For a Few Dollars More*, 1967.
b. January 03, 1929 in Rome, Italy
d. April 3, 1989 in Rome, Italy

Eugenie Leontovich
American actress–director
• On stage since 1922; won Tony for *Anastasia*, 1959; founded Actors Workshops, 1953, 1973.
b. March 21, 1900 in Moscow, Russia

Jules Leotard
French circus performer
• Trapeze artist; original "daring young man on the flying trapeze"; first to call costume leotard.
b. 1830 in Toulouse, France
d. 1870

Mervyn Leroy
American director–producer
• Films include *The Wizard of Oz*, 1939; won Oscar for *Random Harvest*, 1942; won two special Oscars.
b. October 15, 1900 in San Francisco, California
d. September 13, 1987 in Beverly Hills, California

Jack Lescoulie
American TV personality
• Founding personality on NBC's "Today" show, 1960s; spoke first words on show's first broadcast; played second banana to Dave Garroway, was resident jester, 1952-67.
b. May 17, 1917 in Sacramento, California
d. July 22, 1987 in Memphis, Tennessee

Mark Lester
English actor
• Played title role in film *Oliver*, 1968.
b. July 11, 1958 in Richmond, England

Richard Lester
American director
• Films include *Superman II*, 1980; *Four Musketeers*, 1975.
b. January 19, 1932 in Philadelphia, Pennsylvania

David Letterman
American TV personality
• Hosts "Late Night with David Letterman," 1982–; known for offbeat, droll humor; won two Emmys, 1981, 1984.
b. April 12, 1947 in Indianapolis, Indiana

Sam Levene
(Samuel Levine)
American actor
• On Broaday since 1927; hits include *Sunshine Boys*, 1972-75.
b. August 28, 1905 in New York, New York
d. December 29, 1980 in New York, New York

Irving R(askin) Levine
American broadcast journalist
• Award-winning foreign correspondent with NBC since 1950; wrote *Main Street, Italy*, 1963.
b. August 26, 1922 in Pawtucket, Rhode Island

Joseph Edward Levine
American producer
• Pioneer independent producer called one of last movie moguls; films include *The Graduate*, 1967; *Carnal Knowledge*, 1971.
b. September 09, 1905 in Boston, Massachusetts
d. July 31, 1987 in Greenwich, Connecticut

Barry Levinson
American director
• Won best director Oscar, 1989, for *Rain Man*.
b. June 02, 1932 in Baltimore, Maryland

Jerry Lewis
(Joseph Levitch)
American comedian
• Zany film, TV star whose telethons for muscular dystrophy have raised over $300 million.
b. March 16, 1926 in Newark, New Jersey

Joe E Lewis
American actor–comedian
• Nightclub comedian whose problems with gangsters were depicted in film *The Joker Is Wild*, 1957, starring Frank Sinatra.
b. January 12, 1902 in New York, New York
d. June 04, 1971 in New York, New York

Shari Lewis
(Shari Hurwitz; Mrs Jeremy Tarcher)
American ventriloquist–author
• Starred on TV with puppet Lamb Chop; won five Emmys.
b. January 17, 1934 in New York, New York

David Lichine
Russian choreographer–ballet dancer
• With Ballet Russe de Monte Carlo; ballets include "Graduation Ball," 1940.
b. October 25, 1910 in Rostov-on-Don, Russia
d. June 26, 1972 in Los Angeles, California

Max Liebman
American director–producer–writer
• Produced TV's Emmy-winning "Your Show of Shows," 1949-54; discovered Danny Kaye, other stars.
b. August 05, 1902 in Vienna, Austria
d. July 21, 1981 in New York, New York

Serge Lifar
Russian dancer–choreographer
• Director, Paris Opera Ballet, 1929-58; ballets include *The Prodigal Son; Apollo*.
b. April 02, 1905 in Kiev, Russia
d. December 15, 1986 in Lausanne, Switzerland

Judith Ellen Light
American actress
• Played Karen Wolek on soap opera "One Life to Live," won two Emmys for role; plays Angela Bower on TV's "Who's the Boss," 1985–.
b. February 09, 1950 in Trenton, New Jersey

Beatrice Gladys Lillie
English comedienne
• Had 50-year entertainment career, beginning 1914; known for signature song, "Mad Dogs and Englishmen."
b. May 29, 1898 in Toronto, Ontario
d. January 2, 1989 in Henley-on-Thames, England

Elmo Lincoln
(Otto Elmo Linkenhelter)
American actor
• First screen Tarzan in *Tarzan of the Apes*, 1918.
b. 1899 in Rochester, New York
d. June 27, 1952 in Hollywood, California

Hal Linden
(Harold Lipschitz)
American actor
• Starred in TV series "Barney Miller," 1975-82; won Tony for musical *The Rothchilds*, 1971.
b. March 2, 1931 in Bronx, New York

Audra Lindley
American actress
• Played Mrs. Roper in TV series "Three's Company," 1977-79; "The Ropers," 1979-80.
b. September 24, 1918 in Los Angeles, California

Howard Lindsay
American dramatist–producer–actor
• Co-wrote, with Russel Crouse, *Life With Father*, 1939; *Sound of Music*, 1959; starred in *Life With Father*, 1939-46, a record run on Broadway.
b. March 29, 1889 in Waterford, New York
d. February 11, 1968 in New York, New York

Margaret Lindsay
(Margaret Kies)
American actress
• Veteran character player of over 80 films; starred in numerous *Ellery Queen* mysteries.
b. September 19, 1910 in Dubuque, Iowa
d. May 08, 1981 in Los Angeles, California

Leopold Lindtberg
Swiss director
• Prominent stage, film director,1926-84; *Last Chance*, 1945, won special Cannes Peace Prize.
b. June 01, 1902 in Vienna, Austria

Art(hur Gordon) Linkletter
American TV personality
• Star of radio, TV shows "People Are Funny"; "House Party."
b. July 17, 1912 in Moose Jaw, Saskatchewan

Bambi Linn
American dancer
• Noted for TV variety dance numbers with Rod Alexander, 1950s.
b. April 26, 1926 in Brooklyn, New York

Larry Lavon Linville
American actor
• Played Frank Burns on TV series "M*A*S*H," 1972-77.
b. September 29, 1939 in Ojai, California

Clara Lipman
American actress
• Writer, star of stage comedy *Julie Bon Bon: It Depends on a Woman*.
b. December 06, 1889 in Chicago, Illinois
d. 1952 in New York, New York

Peggy Lipton
American actress
• Starred in TV series "The Mod Squad," 1968-73; married to Quincy Jones, 1974-87; now in "Twin Peaks."
b. August 3, 1947 in New York, New York

Virna Lisi
(Virna Pieralisi)
Italian actress
• Leading lady in *Duel of the Titans*, 1963; *How to Murder Your Wife*, 1965.
b. September 08, 1937 in Ancona, Italy

John Arthur Lithgow
American actor
• Character actor who appeared in *The World According to Garp*, 1982; *Terms of Endearment*, 1983.
b. October 19, 1945 in Rochester, New York

Rich(ard Caruthers) Little
Canadian entertainer
• Impressionist who can do 160 different personalities.
b. November 26, 1938 in Ottawa, Ontario

Little Tich
(Harry Relph)
English comedian
• Popular British, Parisian music-hall comic, noted for impersonations, pantomimes; friend of Lautrec.
b. 1868 in England
d. February 1, 1928 in London, England

Joan Littlewood
English director
• Founded, directed London's experimental Theatre Workshop, 1945-61; produced *O What a Lovely War*, 1963.
b. 1916 in London, England

Anatole Litvak
(Michael Anatol Litwak)
French director
• Films include *Snake Pit; Sorry Wrong Number*, 1948.
b. May 21, 1902 in Kiev, Russia
d. December 15, 1974 in Neuilly, France

Roger Livesey
Welsh actor
• Starred in film *The Life and Death of Colonel Blimp*, 1943.
b. June 25, 1906 in Barry, Wales
d. February 05, 1976

Barry Livingston
American actor
• Played Ernie Douglas on TV's "My Three Sons," 1963-72.
b. December 17, 1953 in Los Angeles, California

Stanley Livingston
American actor
• Played Chip on TV series, "My Three Sons," 1960-72.
b. November 24, 1950 in Los Angeles, California

Mary Livingstone
(Sadye Marks; Mrs Jack Benny)
American comedienne
• Played with husband, Jack Benny on radio, TV, 1930s-65.
b. June 22, 1908 in Seattle, Washington
d. June 3, 1983 in Holmby Hills, California

Christopher Lloyd
American actor
• Played Jim on TV series "Taxi"; starred in *Back to the Future*, 1985.
b. October 22, 1938 in Stamford, Connecticut

Frank Lloyd
American director
• Directed over 100 films; won Oscars for *Divine Lady; Cavalcade*.
b. February 02, 1888 in Glasgow, Scotland
d. August 1, 1960 in Santa Monica, California

Harold Lloyd
American comedian–actor
• Highest paid film star of 1920s; noted for thrill-comedy scenes; won special Oscar, 1952.
b. April 2, 1893 in Burchard, Nebraska
d. March 08, 1971 in Hollywood, California

Marie Lloyd
(Matilda Alice Wood)
English entertainer
• Legendary British music-hall idol, noted for Cockney impersonations; toured worldwide.
b. February 12, 1870 in London, England
d. October 07, 1922 in London, England

Gene (Eugene) Lockhart
American actor
• Father of June Lockhart; character actor in over 100 films.
b. July 18, 1891 in London, Ontario
d. March 31, 1957 in Santa Monica, California

June Lockhart
American actress
• Starred in TV series "Lassie," 1958-64; "Lost in Space," 1965-68.
b. June 25, 1925 in New York, New York

Heather Locklear
(Mrs Tommy Lee)
American actress
• TV series include "Dynasty"; "T J Hooker."
b. September 25, 1961 in Los Angeles, California

Margaret Mary Lockwood
(Margaret Day)
American actress
• Most popular actress in Britain, 1940s; films include *The Wicked Lady*, 1946; *The Man in Grey*, 1943.
b. September 15, 1916 in Karachi, India
d. July 15, 1990 in London, England

John Loder
(John Lowe)
English actor
• Films include *Lorna Doone*, 1935; *King Solomon's Mines*, 1937.
b. January 03, 1898 in London, England

Cissie Loftus
(Marie Cecilia McCarthy)
Scottish actress
• Best known for her impersonations of stage, film stars.
b. October 26, 1876 in Glasgow, Scotland
d. July 12, 1943 in New York, New York

Josh(ua Lockwood) Logan
American director–dramatist
• Directed some of Broadway's biggest hits: *South Pacific, Annie Get Your Gun, Mister Roberts*.
b. October 05, 1908 in Texarkana, Texas
d. July 12, 1988 in New York, New York

Gina Lollobrigida
Italian actress
• Italy's first post-war sex-symbol; films include *Trapeze*, 1956; *Solomon and Sheba*, 1959.
b. July 04, 1928 in Subiaco, Italy

Herbert Lom
(Herbert C Angelo Kuchacevich)
Czech actor
• Films include *The Return of the Pink Panther*, 1974.
b. January 09, 1917 in Prague, Czechoslovakia

Carole Lombard
(Jane Alice Peters)
American actress
• Zany blonde comic who was married to Clark Gable at time of death in plane crash; films include *My Man Godfrey*, 1936.
b. October 06, 1909 in Fort Wayne, Indiana
d. January 16, 1942 in Las Vegas, Nevada

John Luther Long
American author–dramatist
• His short story "Madame Butterfly," 1898, served as libretto for Puccini's opera, 1906.
b. January 01, 1861 in Pennsylvania
d. October 31, 1927

Shelley Long
(Mrs Bruce Tyson)
American actress
• Played Diane Chambers on TV series "Cheers," 1982-87; won Emmy, 1983; films include *Outrageous Fortune*, 1986.
b. August 23, 1950 in Fort Wayne, Indiana

Richard Loo
American actor
• Played villainous Japanese soldiers in WW II movies: *God Is My Co-Pilot; Tokyo Rose*.
b. 1903 in Maui, Hawaii
d. November 2, 1983 in Burbank, California

Anita Loos
American author–dramatist
• Wrote *Gentlemen Prefer Blondes*, 1925.
b. April 26, 1893 in Sisson, California
d. August 18, 1981 in New York, New York

Lope de Vega
(Lope Felix de Vega Carpio)
Spanish dramatist–poet
• Tragic personal life; wrote 1500 plays including *The King the Greatest Mayor*, 1620-23.
b. November 25, 1562 in Madrid, Spain
d. August 27, 1635 in Madrid, Spain

Lydia Vasilievna Lopokova
(Mrs John Maynard Keynes)
Russian dancer–actress
• Starred with Ballet Russe, 1920s; London ballets, 1930s.
b. October 21, 1892 in Saint Petersburg, Russia
d. June 08, 1981 in Seaford, England

Jack Lord
(John Joseph Ryan)
American actor–producer–artist
• Produced, starred in TV series "Hawaii Five-O," 1968-80.
b. December 3, 1930 in New York, New York

Marjorie Lord
American actress
• Played in TV show "Make Room for Daddy," 1957-64; mother of actress Anne Archer.
b. July 26, 1922 in San Francisco, California

Pauline Lord
American actress
• Stage performances include Anna Christie, 1921-25; Ethan Frome, 1936.
b. 1890 in Hanford, California
d. October 11, 1950 in Alamogordo, New Mexico

Sophia Loren
(Sophia Lazarro; Sofia Scicolone; Mrs Carlo Ponti)
Italian actress
• Won Oscar, 1961, for Two Women; wrote autobiography Sophia: Living and Loving, 1979; awarded special Oscar, 1991.
b. September 2, 1934 in Rome, Italy

Eugene Loring
(LeRoy Kerpestein)
American dancer–choreographer
• Wrote ballet Billy the Kid, 1938.
b. 1914 in Milwaukee, Wisconsin
d. August 3, 1982 in Kingston, New York

Gloria Jean Loring
American singer–actress
• Star of TV soap opera "Days of Our Lives," 1980-.
b. December 1, 1946 in New York, New York

Peter Lorre
(Laszlo Loewenstein)
American actor
• Played sinister villain in many 1930s-40s films including The Maltese Falcon, 1941.
b. June 26, 1904 in Rosenberg, Hungary
d. March 24, 1964 in Hollywood, California

Richard Lortz
American author–dramatist–editor
• Wrote novel: The Bethrothed, 1975;drama: The Juniper Tree, 1972; many 1950s TV plays.
b. January 13, 1930 in New York, New York
d. November 05, 1980 in New York, New York

Joseph Losey
(Victor Hanbury pseud)
American director
• Blacklisted for refusing to testify before House Un-American Activities Committee, 1951; films include Don Giovanni, 1979; The Steaming, 1984.
b. January 14, 1909 in La Crosse, Wisconsin
d. July 22, 1984 in London, England

Dorothy Loudon
American actress
• Won Tony, 1977, for role of Miss Hannigan in Broadway musical Annie.
b. September 17, 1933 in Boston, Massachusetts

Anita Louise
(Louise Fremault)
American actress
• Played in TV show "My Friend Flicka," 1956-58; films from 1929-52 include Madame DuBarry; Midsummer Night's Dream.
b. January 09, 1917 in New York, New York
d. April 25, 1970 in West Los Angeles, California

Tina Louise
(Tina Blacker)
American actress
• Played Ginger Grant on TV comedy "Gilligan's Island," 1964-67.
b. February 11, 1938 in New York, New York

Bessie Love
(Juanita Horton)
English actress
• Career stretched from silent films to 1980 TV; nominated for Oscar, 1929, for Broadway Melody.
b. September 1, 1898 in Midland, Texas
d. April 26, 1986 in London, England

Frank Lovejoy
American actor
• Supporting roles in films, 1948-58, include Home of the Brave, 1949; House of Wax, 1953.
b. March 28, 1914 in New York, New York
d. October 02, 1962 in New York, New York

Linda Lovelace
(Linda Boreman Marciano)
American actress–author
• Starred in pornographic film Deep Throat, 1972; wrote autobiography Ordeal, 1984.

Rob(ert Hepler) Lowe
American actor
• Part of "Brat Pack"; films include Masquerade, 1988; St. Elmo's Fire, 1984.
b. March 17, 1964 in Charlottesville, Virginia

Myrna Loy
(Myrna Williams)
American actress
• Played Nora Charles in The Thin Man film series, 1930s-40s.
b. August 02, 1905 in Helena, Montana

Ernst Lubitsch
American director
• Noted for sophisticated comedies of manners, inventive camera work; won special Oscar, 1937.
b. January 28, 1892 in Berlin, Germany
d. November 3, 1947 in Los Angeles, California

Lar Lubovitch
American dancer–choreographer
• Modernist; known for groupings in abstract shapes; creates dances for own co. since 1963.
b. in Chicago, Illinois

George Lucas
American director
• Films include Star Wars, 1977; The Empire Strikes Back, 1980; Return of the Jedi, 1983.
b. May 14, 1944 in Modesto, California

Nick Lucas
American entertainer
• Starred in vaudeville; hit song "Tiptoe Through the Tulips with Me," 1929.
b. August 22, 1897 in Newark, New Jersey
d. July 28, 1982 in Colorado Springs, Colorado

Susan Lucci
American actress
• Plays Erica Kane on daytime soap opera "All My Children," 1970-.
b. December 23, 1948 in Scarsdale, New York

Allen Ellsworth Ludden
American TV personality–producer
• Hosted game show "Password," 1961-67; married to Betty White.
b. October 05, 1918 in Mineral Point, Wisconsin
d. June 09, 1981 in Los Angeles, California

Charles Ludlam
American dramatist–actor–producer
• Known for offbeat, classically comic theater co., begun, 1960; played title role in his version of *Camille*, 1973; won many Obies.
b. April 12, 1943 in Floral Park, New York
d. May 28, 1987 in New York, New York

Kurt (Mamre) Luedtke
American screenwriter
• Wrote screenplays *Absence of Malice*, 1981; *Out of Africa*, 1985, won Oscar.
b. September 28, 1939 in Grand Rapids, Michigan

Bela Lugosi
(Bela Ferenc Blasko)
American actor
• Master of horror films, 1930s-40s; noted for *Dracula*, 1930.
b. October 2, 1882 in Lugos, Hungary
d. September 16, 1956 in Hollywood, California

Paul Lukas
American actor
• Won Oscar for *Watch on the Rhine*, 1943.
b. May 26, 1894 in Budapest, Hungary
d. August 15, 1971 in Tangiers, Morocco

Keye Luke
American actor
• Appeared in 150 movies, 13 as Charlie Chan's "Number One Son."
b. June 18, 1904 in Canton, China
d. January 12, 1991 in Whittier, California

Sidney Lumet
American director
• Films include *Network*, 1976, *The Verdict*, 1982.
b. June 25, 1924 in Philadelphia, Pennsylvania

Joan Lunden
American broadcast journalist
• Reporter, interviewer, "Good Morning, America," since 1980.
b. September 19, 1951 in Sacramento, California

Alfred Lunt
(Lunt and Fontaine)
American actor
• Co-starred with wife Lynn Fontaine in over 24 plays beginning in 1922 including *The Visit*.
b. August 18, 1892 in Milwaukee, Wisconsin
d. August 02, 1977 in Chicago, Illinois

Ida Lupino
American actress–director
• Often portrayed tough, lower-class characters; films include *High Sierra*, 1941.
b. February 04, 1918 in London, England

Stanley Lupino
English actor–dramatist–producer
• British revue, film comedian; father of Ida Lupino.
b. June 17, 1896 in London, England
d. June 1, 1942 in London, England

Patti Ann LuPone
American actress
• Won Tony, 1980, for *Evita*.
b. April 21, 1949 in Northport, New York

Peter Lupus
American actor
• Played Willie Armitage in TV series "Mission Impossible," 1966-73.
b. June 17, 1937 in California

David K Lynch
American director–screenwriter
• Films include *The Elephant Man*, 1980, *Blue Velvet*, 1986; directs innovative TV series "Twin Peaks," 1990–.
b. January 2, 1946 in Missoula, Montana

Paul Edward Lynde
American comedian–actor
• Known for one-liners as panelist on game show "Hollywood Squares."
b. June 13, 1926 in Mount Vernon, Ohio
d. January 09, 1982 in Beverly Hills, California

Carol Lynley
(Carol Ann Jones)
American actress
• Films include *Return to Peyton Place*, 1961; *The Poseidon Adventure*, 1972.
b. February 13, 1942 in New York, New York

Sir Henry Alfred Lytton
English actor
• Appeared on stage, 1884-1934; operas include *Pirates of Penzance*.
b. January 03, 1867 in London, England
d. August 15, 1936 in London, England

Charles MacArthur
American dramatist
• Wrote *The Front Page*, 1928; *Twentieth Century*, 1932, with Ben Hecht; husband of Helen Hayes.
b. November 05, 1895 in Scranton, Pennsylvania
d. April 21, 1956 in New York, New York

James MacArthur
American actor
• Adopted son of Helen Hayes; starred in TV series "Hawaii Five-O," 1968-80.
b. December 08, 1937 in Los Angeles, California

Ralph George Macchio, Jr
American actor
• In films *The Karate Kid*, 1984; *The Karate Kid II*, 1986.
b. November 04, 1962 in Long Island, New York

Leueen (Emily) MacGrath
English actress
• Stage star in several plays including *No Exit*, 1936; collaborated with then-husband, George S Kaufman, on various works.
b. July 03, 1914 in London, England

Ali MacGraw
American actress
• Starred in *Love Story*, 1971; TV mini-series "Winds of War," 1983; appeared on "Dynasty," 1985. Was wed to Steve McQueen.
b. April 01, 1938 in Westchester, New York

Ted Mack
(William E Maguiness)
American TV personality–musician
• Hosted amateur show on radio, TV, 1945-70; helped discover Frank Sinatra.
b. February 12, 1904 in Greeley, Colorado
d. July 12, 1976 in Tarrytown, New York

Alexander Mackendrick
American director
• Noted for *Sweet Smell of Success*, 1957; *The Ladykillers*, 1956.
b. 1912 in Boston, Massachusetts

Catherine Patricia Mackin
American broadcast journalist
• First woman to anchor nighttime network newscast.
b. August 28, 1939 in Baltimore, Maryland
d. November 2, 1982 in Towson, Maryland

Shirley MacLaine
(Shirley Beaty; Mrs Steve Parker)
American actress–author
• Oscar nominee in films since 1954; best-selling books include *Out on a Limb*, 1983.
b. April 23, 1934 in Richmond, Virginia

Barton MacLane
American actor
• Appeared in over 200 films; co-starred with Glenda Farrell in *Torchy Blane* films; TV series "The Outlaws," 1960-61.
b. December 25, 1900 in Columbia, South Carolina
d. January 01, 1969 in Santa Monica, California

Don Maclaughlin
American actor
• Member, original cast of "As the World Turns," 1956, first US daily drama.
b. 1907
d. May 28, 1986 in Goshen, Indiana

Gavin MacLeod
American actor
• Starred in "The Mary Tyler Moore Show," 1970-77, "The Love Boat," 1977-86.
b. February 28, 1930 in Mount Kisco, New York

Michael MacLiammoir
Irish actor–designer–director
• Co-founder of Dublin Gate Theatre, 1928; acted in and designed over 300 productions.
b. October 25, 1899 in Cork, Ireland
d. March 06, 1978 in Dublin, Ireland

Fred(erick Martin) MacMurray
American actor
• Starred in TV series "My Three Sons," 1960-72; film *Double Indemnity*, 1944.
b. August 3, 1908 in Kankakee, Illinois

Patrick MacNee
English actor
• Played John Steed on TV's "The Avengers," 1966-69; "The New Avengers,"1978.
b. February 06, 1922 in England

Robert Breckenridge Ware MacNeil
American broadcast journalist
• Co-anchor, PBS's "MacNeil/Lehrer Report," 1975–; won Emmy, 1974.
b. January 19, 1931 in Montreal, Quebec

Meredith MacRae
(Mrs Greg Mullavey)
American actress
• Daughter of Sheila and Gordon MacRae; starred in TV series "Petticoat Junction," 1966-70.
b. May 3, 1944 in Houston, Texas

George Macready
American actor
• Screen villain, 1942-71; played in *Gilda*, 1946; *Paths of Glory*, 1957.
b. August 29, 1909 in Providence, Rhode Island
d. July 02, 1973 in Los Angeles, California

Bill Macy
(William Macy Garber)
American actor
• Played Walter Findlay in TV series "Maude," 1972-78.
b. May 18, 1922 in Revere, Massachusetts

Donald Madden
American actor
• Classical actor on Broadway in *Hamlet; Julius Caesar.*
b. November 05, 1933 in New York, New York
d. January 22, 1983 in Central Islip, New York

Guy Madison
(Robert Moseley)
American actor
• Hero of action films and spaghetti westerns; starred in TV series "Wild Bill Hickok," 1951-58.
b. January 19, 1922 in Bakersfield, California

Patrick Magee
Irish actor
• Won Tony, 1965, for *Marat/Sade.*
b. 1924 in Armagh, Northern Ireland
d. August 14, 1982 in London, England

Anna Magnani
Italian actress
• Won 1955 Oscar for *The Red Tattoo.*
b. March 07, 1909 in Alexandria, Egypt
d. September 26, 1973 in Rome, Italy

John Lee Mahin
American screenwriter
• Wrote script for *Dr. Jekyll and Mr. Hyde,* 1941; *Quo Vadis,* 1951.
b. 1902 in Evanston, Illinois
d. April 18, 1984 in Santa Monica, California

Marjorie Main
(Mary Tomlinson Krebs)
American actress
• Played Ma Kettle in nine films, 1949-57, with Percy Kilbride.
b. February 24, 1890 in Acton, Illinois
d. April 1, 1975 in Los Angeles, California

Lee Majors
(Harvey Lee Yeary)
American actor–producer
• Star of three hit TV series: "The Big Valley," 1965-69; "The Six Million Dollar Man," 1974-78; "The Fall Guy," 1981-86.
b. April 23, 1940 in Wyandotte, Michigan

Karl Malden
(Mladen Sekulovich)
American actor
• Won Oscar for *A Streetcar Named Desire,* 1951; star of TV series "Streets of San Francisco," 1972-77.
b. March 22, 1913 in Gary, Indiana

John Malkovich
American actor
• Won Obie for performance in *True West,* 1982; films include *Places in the Heart,* 1984; *Making Mr. Right,* 1987; *Dangerous Liasons,* 1989.
b. December 09, 1953 in Christopher, Illinois

Louis Malle
French director
• First US-made film *Pretty Baby,* 1978; others include *Goodbye, Children,* 1988; *Au revoir les enfants,* 1989.
b. October 3, 1932 in Thumeries, France

Dorothy Malone
(Dorothy Maloney)
American actress
• Won 1956 Oscar for *Written on the Wind;* played in TV series "Peyton Place," 1964-69.
b. January 3, 1925 in Chicago, Illinois

Richard Eldridge Maltby, Jr
American director
• Won 1978 Tony for *Ain't Misbehavin';* 1984 nominee for *Baby.*
b. October 06, 1937 in Ripon, Wisconsin

Albert Maltz
(Hollywood Ten)
American author–screenwriter
• Wrote screenplays for several films: *Destination Tokyo,* 1944; *The Naked City,* 1948; jailed, 1950, blacklisted.
b. October 08, 1908 in Brooklyn, New York
d. April 26, 1985 in Los Angeles, California

David Alan Mamet
American dramatist
• Won Obies for *American Buffalo,* 1976; *Edmond,* 1983; Pulitzer for *Glengarry Glen Ross,* 1984.
b. November 3, 1947 in Chicago, Illinois

Rouben (Zachary) Mamoulian
American director
• Films include Hollywood's first Technicolor feature *Becky Sharp,* 1935; *Silk Stockings,* 1957.
b. October 08, 1897 in Tiflis, Russia
d. December 04, 1987 in Los Angeles, California

Robert Mandan
American actor
• Played Chester Tate on TV series "Soap," 1977-80.
b. February 02, in Clever, Missouri

Howie Mandel
Canadian comedian
• Played Dr. Wayne Fiscus on "St. Elsewhere," 1982-88.
b. November 29, 1955 in Toronto, Ontario

Larry Manetti
American actor
• Played Rick on "Magnum, P I,"
1980-88.
b. in Chicago, Illinois

Silvana Mangano
Italian actress
• Films include *Death in Venice*, 1971;
Bitter Rice, 1950.
b. April 21, 1930 in Rome, Italy
d. December 16, 1989 in Madrid, Spain

Joseph Leo Mankiewicz
American director–producer
• Won Oscars for best director, best
screenplay: *A Letter to Three Wives*,
1949; *All About Eve*, 1950.
b. February 11, 1909 in Wilkes-Barre, Pennsylvania

Abby Mann
(Abraham Goodman)
American screenwriter
• Oscar nominee for *Judgment at Nuremberg*, 1961; *Ship of Fools*, 1965.
b. December 01, 1927 in Philadelphia, Pennsylvania

Michael Mann
American writer–producer
• TV shows include Emmy-winning "The
Jericho Mile," 1979; "Miami Vice,"
1984–.
b. 1943 in Chicago, Illinois

Theodore Mann
American producer
• Co-founded Circle in the Square Theatre, 1951; won Tony, Pulitzer, for co-
producing *Long Day's Journey Into Night*,
1956.
b. May 13, 1924 in New York, New York

Irene Manning
(Inez Harvout)
American actress–singer–author
• Wrote column "Girl About Town";
films include *Desert Song*, 1943; *Yankee
Doodle Dandy*, 1942.
b. July 17, 1918 in Cincinnati, Ohio

Jayne Mansfield
(Mrs Mickey Hargitay; Vera Jayne Palmer)
American actress
• Known for breathless, dizzy blonde
roles in films, 1950s-60s, similar to
Marilyn Monroe: *Will Success Spoil Rock
Hunter?* 1957; killed in auto accident.
b. April 19, 1932 in Bryn Mawr, Pennsylvania
d. June 29, 1967 in New Orleans, Louisiana

Richard Mansfield
English actor
• Stage roles in *Dr. Jekyll and Mr.
Hyde*, 1887; *Beau Brummell*, 1890.
b. May 24, 1854 in Berlin, Germany
d. August 3, 1907 in New London, Connecticut

Martin Manulis
American producer–director
• Won five Emmys for "Playhouse 90."
b. May 3, 1915 in New York, New York

Jean Marais
(Jean Alfred Villain-Marais)
French actor
• France's most popular leading man,
1940s-50s; many of his films directed
by Jean Cocteau.
b. December 11, 1913 in Cherbourg, France

Marcel Marceau
French actor–pantomimist
• World's most famous mime; created
character "Bip," 1947.
b. March 22, 1923 in Strasbourg, France

Fredric March
(Frederick McIntyre Bickel)
American actor
• Won Oscars, 1932, 1946, for *Dr. Jekyll and Mr. Hyde*; *The Best Years of
Our Lives*.
b. August 31, 1897 in Racine, Wisconsin
d. April 14, 1975 in Los Angeles, California

Hal March
American actor
• Emcee of TV's "$64,000 Question,"
1955-58.
b. April 22, 1920 in San Francisco, California
d. January 11, 1970 in Los Angeles, California

Nancy Marchand
American actress
• Played Mrs. Pynchon on "Lou Grant,"
1977-81; won two Emmys.
b. June 19, 1928 in Buffalo, New York

Frank Marcus
English dramatist
• Won Cleo Award for *The Killing of
Sister George*, 1965.
b. June 3, 1928 in Breslau, Germany

Margo
(Maria Marguerita Boldao y Castillo; Mrs
Eddie Albert)
American actress
• Introduced the Rumba with her uncle
Xavier Cugat's band; films include *From
Hell to Texas*, 1958.
b. May 1, 1918 in Mexico City, Mexico
d. July 17, 1985 in Pacific Palisades, California

Janet Margolin
American actress
• Starred in *David and Lisa*, 1962; *Annie Hall*, 1977.
b. July 25, 1943 in New York, New York

Richard Marin
(Cheech and Chong; "Cheech")
American actor–comedian
• Teamed with Tommy Chong in counterculture records, nightclub acts, and
film series: *Up in Smoke*, 1978; *Still
Smokin'*, 1983.
b. July 13, 1946 in Los Angeles, California

Ed(ward Francis) Marinaro
American actor–football player
• All-American running back, set 17
NCAA records; in NFL, 1972-77, mostly
with Minnesota; played Joe Coffey on
TV's "Hill Street Blues," 1980-86.
b. March 03, 1950 in New York, New York

Frances Marion
American screenwriter
• Won Oscars for film scripts *The Big
House*, 1930; *The Champ*, 1931; used
statues for doorstops.
b. November 18, 1888 in San Francisco, California
d. May 12, 1973 in Los Angeles, California

Pierre Carlet de Marivaux
French author–dramatist
• Among his 30 comedies still being
staged in France: *The Surprise of Love*,
1722; *The Game of Love and Chance*,
1737.
b. February 04, 1688 in Paris, France
d. February 12, 1763 in Paris, France

Russell Markert
American choreographer
• Formed what was to become the Radio
City Music Hall Rockettes, 1925; staged
their dance routines for 39 years.
b. 1899
d. December 01, 1990 in Waterbury, Connecticut

Enid Markey
American actress
• Played Jane in *Tarzan of the Apes*,
1918.
b. February 22, 1886 in Dillon, Colorado
d. November 15, 1981 in Bay Shore, New York

Pigmeat (Dewey M) Markham
American comedian
• Known for "Here come de judge" skit;
appeared on "Laugh-In" TV show.
b. April 18, 1904 in Durham, North Carolina
d. December 13, 1981 in Bronx, New York

Dame Alicia Markova
(Lillian Alicia Marks)
English dancer
• First prima ballerina with the Royal Ballet, 1933-35; formed own ballet co., 1935; guest dancer in major ballets.
b. December 01, 1910 in London, England

Charles Marks
(Smith and Dale)
American actor–comedian
• Teamed with Joe Smith, 1898-1960s; play *Sunshine Boys* loosely based on their lives.
b. September 06, 1882 in New York, New York
d. 1971

John Marley
American actor
• Character actor nominated for Oscar for role of Phil Cavilleri in *Love Story*, 1971.
b. October 17, 1916 in New York, New York
d. April 22, 1984 in Los Angeles, California

Hugh Marlowe
(Hugh Hipple)
American actor
• Played Jim Matthews on TV soap "Another World," 1969-82.
b. January 3, 1914 in Philadelphia, Pennsylvania
d. May 02, 1982 in New York, New York

Julia Marlowe
(Sarah Frances Frost)
American actress
• Known for Shakespearean roles: *Romeo and Juliet; Twelfth Night; Hamlet.*
b. August 17, 1866 in Cumberland, England
d. November 12, 1950 in New York, New York

Richard Marquand
English director
• Best known for films *Return of the Jedi*, 1983; *Jagged Edge*, 1985; won Emmy, 1972, for "Search for the Nile."
b. 1938 in Cardiff, Wales
d. September 04, 1987 in London, England

Jean Marsh
(Jean Lyndsey Torren Marsh)
English actress
• Starred in British series "Upstairs, Downstairs"; won Emmy, 1975.
b. July 01, 1934 in London, England

Mae Marsh
American actress
• Starred in silent film classic *Birth of a Nation*, 1915.
b. November 19, 1895 in Madrid, New Mexico
d. February 13, 1968 in Hermosa Beach, California

Dame Ngaio Marsh
New Zealander author–producer
• Created character of Roderick Alleyn in over 30 mysteries, 1934-82.
b. April 23, 1899 in Christchurch, New Zealand
d. February 18, 1982 in Christchurch, New Zealand

Alan Marshal
Australian actor
• Supporting actor, 1936-59; in film *The Hunchback of Notre Dame*, 1939.
b. January 29, 1909 in Sydney, Australia
d. July 09, 1961 in Chicago, Illinois

Alan Peter Marshall
English producer
• Films include *Midnight Express*, 1978; *Fame*, 1980; *Angel Heart*, 1986; won four Oscars.
b. August 12, 1938 in London, England

Brenda Marshall
(Ardis Anderson Gaines)
American actress
• Married William Holden, 1941-71; starred opposite Errol Flynn in *The Sea Hawk*, 1940.
b. September 29, 1915 in Philadelphia, Pennsylvania

E G (Edda Gunnar) Marshall
American actor
• Versatile film, Broadway, TV actor since late 1930s; won two Emmys for "The Defenders," 1962, 1963.
b. June 18, 1910 in Owatonna, Minnesota

Garry Kent Marshall
American producer
• Created, produced comedy shows "Happy Days," 1974-84; "Mork and Mindy," 1978-82.
b. November 13, 1934 in New York, New York

Herbert Marshall
American actor
• Leading man: *A Bill of Divorcement, 1940; The Letter, 1940.*
b. May 23, 1890 in London, England
d. January 22, 1966 in Beverly Hills, California

Penny Marshall
American actress–director
• Played Laverne in TV series "Laverne and Shirley," 1976-83. Directed popular movie *Big*, 1988; *Awakenings*, 1991.
b. October 15, 1945 in New York, New York

Peter Marshall
(Pierre LaCock)
American TV personality
• Best known for hosting over 5,000 shows of "The Hollywood Squares."
b. March 3, 1930 in Huntington, West Virginia

Tully Marshall
(William Phillips)
American actor
• Character actor in over 100 films, 1914-43.
b. April 13, 1864 in Nevada City, California
d. March 1, 1943 in Encino, California

William Marshall
American actor
• Screen debut in *Lydia Bailey*, 1952; starred as black vampire in *Blacula*, 1972; *Scream Blacula Scream*, 1973.
b. August 19, 1924 in Gary, Indiana

John Marston
English author–dramatist
• Plays include *What You Will*, 1601; *Sophonisba*, 1605.
b. 1575 in Wardington, England
d. June 25, 1634 in London, England

Dean Paul (Dino, Jr) Martin
(Dino Desi and Billy)
American actor
• Son of Dean Martin; formed successful rock group with Desi Arnaz, Jr. as teen; in film *Players*, 1979; killed piloting Air Force jet.
b. November 17, 1951 in California
d. March 21, 1987 in California

Dick Martin
(Rowan and Martin)
American comedian
• Co-host of "Laugh-In," 1967-73.
b. January 3, 1923 in Battle Creek, Michigan

George Martin
English producer
• With The Beatles, 1962-70.
b. January 03, 1926 in London, England

Jared Martin
American actor
• Played Dusty Farlow on "Dallas," 1979-81, 1985-86.
b. December 11, 1949 in New York, New York

Kiel Martin
American actor
• Played JD LaRue on TV series "Hill Street Blues," 1981-87.
b. July 26, 1945 in Pittsburgh, Pennsylvania
d. December 28, 1990 in Rancho Mirage, California

Mary Martin

American actress–singer
• Starred in long-running Broadway plays *South Pacific*, *The Sound of Music*, and *Peter Pan*, with favorite role that of Peter Pan; won Tonys for all three; mother of Larry Hagman.
b. December 01, 1914 in Weatherford, Texas
d. November 03, 1990 in Rancho Mirage, California

Millicent Martin

English singer–actress
• Broadway performances include *King of Hearts*, 1978.
b. June 08, 1934 in Romford, England

Pamela Sue Martin

American actress
• Played Fallon Carrington Colby on TV series "Dynasty," 1981-84.
b. January 05, 1954 in Westport, Connecticut

Quinn Martin

(Martin Cohen Jr)
American producer
• One of TV's most successful producers; QM Productions produced 16 network shows, including "The Fugitive"; "Streets of San Francisco"; "Cannon."
b. May 22, 1927 in Los Angeles, California
d. September 05, 1987 in Santa Fe, California

Ross Martin

(Martin Rosenblatt)
American actor
• Played Artemus Gordon on "The Wild, Wild West," 1965-69.
b. March 22, 1920 in Gradek, Poland
d. July 03, 1981 in Ramona, California

Steve Martin

American comedian–actor
• Won two Grammys for comedy albums, 1977, 1978; films include *Roxanne*, 1987; *Planes, Trains, and Automobiles*, 1988.
b. August 14, 1945 in Waco, Texas

Strother Martin

American actor
• Character actor, 1950-80; films include *Harper*, 1966; *Cool Hand Luke*, 1967; *True Grit*, 1969.
b. March 26, 1919 in Kokomo, Indiana
d. August 01, 1980 in Thousand Oaks, California

Roger Martin du Gard

French author–dramatist
• Wrote long novel *Les Thibault*, 1922-40; won Nobel Prize, 1937.
b. March 22, 1881 in Neuilly-sur-Seine, France
d. August 22, 1958 in Belleme, France

Wink (Winston Conrad) Martindale

American TV personality
• Host of numerous game shows including "Tic Tac Dough."
b. December 04, 1934 in Bells, Tennessee

Elsa Martinelli

Italian actress
• Discovered by Kirk Douglas; starred with him in *The Indian Fighter*, 1954; became fashion designer, 1975.
b. August 03, 1933 in Rome, Italy

Lee Marvin

American actor
• Tough-guy actor in 45 films; won Oscar, 1965, for *Cat Balou*; part of first "palimony" lawsuit, 1979.
b. February 19, 1924 in New York, New York
d. August 29, 1987 in Tucson, Arizona

Chico (Leonard) Marx

(The Marx Brothers)
American comedian
• Known for outrageous puns, exaggerated accent.
b. March 22, 1891 in New York, New York
d. October 11, 1961 in Hollywood, California

Groucho (Julius Henry) Marx

(The Marx Brothers)
American comedian
• Famous for ad-lib insults, radio-TV series "You Bet Your Life"; wrote autobiography *Groucho and Me*, 1959.
b. October 02, 1890 in New York, New York
d. August 19, 1977 in Los Angeles, California

Gummo (Milton) Marx

(The Marx Brothers)
American talent agent–comedian
• Left Marx Brothers early to become business manager for act.
b. 1894 in New York, New York
d. April 21, 1977 in Palm Springs, California

Harpo (Arthur) Marx

(The Marx Brothers)
American comedian
• Harp-playing, non-speaking member; autobiography *Harpo Speaks*, 1961.
b. November 23, 1893 in New York, New York
d. September 28, 1964 in Hollywood, California

Zeppo (Herbert) Marx

(The Marx Brothers)
American comedian
• Romantic straight man of act; later a successful agent.
b. February 25, 1901 in New York, New York
d. November 3, 1979 in Palm Springs, California

The Marx Brothers

(Chico (Leonard) Marx; Groucho (Julius) Marx; Gummo (Milton) Marx; "Harpo" (Arthur) Marx; "Zeppo" (Herbert) Marx)
American comedy team
• Starred in *Duck Soup*, 1933; *A Night at the Opera*, 1935.

Giuletta Masina

Italian actress
• Married Federico Fellini, 1943; films include *La Strada*, 1956; *Nights of Cabiria*, 1957.
b. March 22, 1921 in Bologna, Italy

John Nevil Maskelyne

English magician
• Noted for exposing the Davenport Brothers as imposter spirtualists, 1865.
b. 1839
d. 1917

Jackie Mason

(Yacov Moshe Maza)
American comedian
• Rabbi comedian, star of successful Broadway show, *The World According to Me*, 1986.
b. June 09, 1934 in Sheboygan, Wisconsin

James Neville Mason

English actor
• Starred in *A Star is Born*, 1955; wrote *Before I Forget*, 1981.
b. May 15, 1909 in Huddersfield, England
d. July 27, 1984 in Lausanne, Switzerland

Marsha Mason

American actress
• Starred in films *Cinderella Liberty*, 1973, *The Goodbye Girl*, 1977 *Chapter Two*, 1979; has received four Oscar nominations; former wife of Neil Simon.
b. April 03, 1942 in Saint Louis, Missouri

Pamela Helen Mason

English actress
• Married James Mason, 1941-64; host of TV, radio talk shows.
b. March 1, 1922 in London, England

Anna Massey

English actress
• Daughter of Raymond Massey; TV shows include "Mayor of Casterbridge"; "Rebecca"; films include *Frenzy*, 1972.
b. August 11, 1937 in Thakeham, England

Daniel Raymond Massey

English actor
• Son of Raymond Massey; Oscar nominee for *Star*, 1968.
b. October 1, 1933 in London, England

Raymond Hart Massey
American actor–producer
• Noted for stage, film portrayals of Abraham Lincoln; starred as Dr. Gillespie on TV's "Dr. Kildare," 1961-66.
b. August 3, 1896 in Toronto, Ontario
d. July 29, 1983 in Los Angeles, California

Leonide Fedorovich Massine
American choreographer–dancer
• Legendary name in ballet history; with Ballet Russe, Ballet Russe de Monte Carlo, American Ballet Theater, from 1920s.
b. August 09, 1896 in Moscow, Russia
d. March 16, 1979 in Cologne, Germany (West)

Philip Massinger
English dramatist
• Plays include *New Way to Pay Old Debts*, 1633; frequently colloborated with Fletcher.
b. 1583 in Salisbury, England
d. March 1640 in London, England

Marcello Mastroianni
Italian actor
• 1947 films include *La Dolce Vita*; *Marriage Italian Style* .
b. September 28, 1924 in Fontana Liri, Italy

Jerry Mathers
American actor–businessman
• Played the Beaver on TV series "Leave It to Beaver," 1957-63.
b. June 02, 1948 in Sioux City, Iowa

Murray Matheson
Australian actor
• Films include *Twilight Zone: The Movie*, 1983; TV series "Banacek," 1972-74.
b. July 01, 1912 in Casterton, Australia
d. April 25, 1985 in Woodland Hills, California

Richard Burton Matheson
American screenwriter
• Films include *Twilight Zone–The Movie*; *Jaws 3-D*, 1983.
b. February 2, 1926 in Allendale, New Jersey

Tim Matheson
American actor
• Played in TV series "Bonanza," 1972-73; film part in *Animal House*, 1978.
b. December 31, 1948 in Los Angeles, California

Melissa Mathison
(Mrs Harrison Ford)
American screenwriter
• Received Oscar nomination, 1983, for screenplay of *ET*.
b. 1949

Marlee Matlin
American actress
• Deaf actress; won Oscar, 1987, for very first film role in *Children of a Lesser God*, 1986.
b. 1965 in Chicago, Illinois

Walter Matthau
American actor
• Best known for role of Oscar Madison in play, film *The Odd Couple*, 1965, 1968; won Oscar for *The Fortune Cookie*, 1972.
b. October 01, 1920 in New York, New York

Jessie Matthews
American actress
• Popular London musical comedy star, 1920s-30s; plays include *This Year of Grace*, 1928.
b. March 11, 1907 in London, England
d. August 19, 1981 in Pinner, England

Victor Mature
American actor
• Leading man in films *Samson and Delilah*, 1949; *The Robe*, 1953.
b. January 29, 1916 in Louisville, Kentucky

Francois Mauriac
French author–dramatist
• Won Nobel Prize in literature, 1952; psychological novels include *Le Noeud de Viperes*, 1932; *Asmodee*, 1938.
b. October 11, 1885 in Bordeaux, France
d. September 01, 1970 in Paris, France

Elaine May
(Elaine Berlin)
American actress–director
• Appeared in revue with Mike Nichols, 1960-61; directed, acted in film *A New Leaf*, 1971.
b. April 21, 1932 in Philadelphia, Pennsylvania

Eddie Mayehoff
American actor
• TV shows include "The Adventures of Fenimore J. Mayehoff," 1946; "That's My Boy," 1954.
b. July 07, 1914 in Baltimore, Maryland

Arthur Loeb Mayer
American film executive
• Paramount Studios publicist, exhibitor; nickname from policy of distributing low-budget horror films.
b. May 28, 1886 in Demopolis, Alabama
d. April 14, 1981 in New York, New York

L(ouis) B(urt) Mayer
American producer–film executive
• Co-founded MGM Studios, 1924; founder, 1927, pres., 1931-36, Academy of Motion Picture Arts and Sciences.
b. July 04, 1885 in Minsk, Russia
d. October 29, 1957 in Santa Monica, California

Ken Maynard
American actor
• Popular cowboy star, known for riding stunts on horse, Tarzan.
b. July 21, 1895 in Ve Vay, Indiana
d. March 23, 1973 in Woodland Hills, California

Virginia Mayo
(Virginia Jones)
American actress
• Glamorous star of 1940s-50s; films include *Secret Life of Walter Mitty*, 1947.
b. November 3, 1920 in Saint Louis, Missouri

Mike Mazurki
(Mikhail Mazurwski)
American actor
• Appeared in adventure films, crime melodramas: *Farewell My Lovely*, 1944, *Donovan's Reef*, 1963.
b. December 25, 1909 in Tarnopal, Austria
d. December 09, 1990 in Glendale, California

Paul Mazursky
American director
• Films include *Tempest; Unmarried Woman; Bob & Carol & Ted & Alice* .
b. April 25, 1930 in Brooklyn, New York

May McAvoy
American actress
• Played Al Jolson's leading lady in first feature length talking picture, *The Jazz Singer*, 1927.
b. September 18, 1901 in New York, New York
d. April 26, 1984 in Los Angeles, California

Mary Margaret McBride
(Martha Deane)
American radio performer
• Columnist, travel writer who conducted popular daytime radio show, 1934-56.
b. November 16, 1899 in Paris, Missouri
d. April 07, 1976 in West Shokun, New York

Patricia McBride
American dancer
• NYC Ballet star, 1959–; made numerous TV appearances; won *Dance* mag. award, 1980.
b. August 23, 1942 in Teaneck, New Jersey

Lon McCallister
(Herbert Alonzo McCallister Jr)
American actor
• Juvenile actor, 1936-53; films include *Adventures of Tom Sawyer*, 1938; *Yankee Doodle Dandy*, 1942.
b. April 17, 1923 in Los Angeles, California

David McCallum
Scottish actor
• Played Illya Kuryakin on TV series "The Man from UNCLE," 1964-67.
b. September 19, 1933 in Glasgow, Scotland

Mercedes (Charlotte Mercedes) McCambridge
American actress
• Won 1949 Oscar for *All the King's Men*.
b. March 17, 1918 in Joliet, Illinois

Elizabeth Ireland (Liz) McCann
American producer
• Won Tonys for *The Elephant Man*, 1978; *Amadeus*, 1980.
b. 1932 in New York, New York

Leo McCarey
American director
• Won Oscars for *The Awful Truth*, 1937; *Going My Way*, 1944.
b. October 03, 1898 in Los Angeles, California
d. July 05, 1969 in Santa Monica, California

Frank McCarthy
American producer
• Films include *Patton*, 1970; *MacArthur*, 1977.
b. July 08, 1912 in Richmond, Virginia
d. December 01, 1986 in Los Angeles, California

J(oseph) P(riestley) McCarthy
American radio performer
• One of most respected interviewers in US; considered king of Detroit radio.
b. March 22, 1934 in New York, New York

Kevin McCarthy
American actor
• Film debut in *Death of a Salesman*, 1951; TV shows include "Flamingo Road."
b. February 15, 1914 in Seattle, Washington

Constance Broman McCashin
American actress
• Plays Laura Avery on TV series "Knots Landing."
b. June 18, 1947 in Chicago, Illinois

Rue (Eddi-Rue) McClanahan
American actress
• Starred in TV shows "Maude," 1972-78; "Golden Girls," 1986–; won 1987 Emmy.
b. February 21, 1936 in Healdton, Oklahoma

Guthrie McClintic
American producer
• Produced, directed over 90 stage plays, many of which starred wife, Katherine Cornell.
b. August 06, 1893 in Seattle, Washington
d. October 29, 1961 in Sneden's Landing, New York

Doug McClure
American actor
• Played Trampas in TV series "The Virginian," 1962-71.
b. May 11, 1938 in Glendale, California

Kent McCord
American actor
• Starred in TV series "Adam-12," 1968-75.
b. September 26, 1942 in Los Angeles, California

Myron McCormick
American actor
• Stage: *South Pacific*, 1949-54; *No Time for Sergeants*, 1955-57; film: *No Time For Sergeants*, 1958; *The Hustler*, 1961.
b. February 08, 1908 in Albany, Indiana
d. July 3, 1962 in New York, New York

Alec (Alexander Duncan) McCowen
English actor
• Originated stage role of Equus, 1973; films include *Frenzy, Never Say Never Again*.
b. May 26, 1926 in Tunbridge Wells, England

Joel McCrea
American actor
• Appeared in nearly 90 films, best known for Westerns: *Sullivan's Travels*, 1941, *Buffalo Bill*, 1944.
b. November 05, 1905 in South Pasadena, California
d. October 2, 1990 in Woodland Hills, California

Hattie McDaniel
American actress
• Won 1939 Oscar for *Gone With The Wind*.
b. June 1, 1895 in Wichita, Kansas
d. October 26, 1952 in Hollywood, California

Roddy (Roderick Andrew) McDowall
English actor
• Starred in *My Friend Flicka*, 1943; *Planet of the Apes*, film, TV series.
b. September 17, 1928 in London, England

Malcolm McDowell
English actor
• Films include *Clockwork Orange*, 1971; *Cat People*, 1982.
b. June 13, 1943 in Leeds, England

Spanky (George Emmett) McFarland
(Our Gang)
American actor
• Fat boy in "Our Gang" series, 1931-45.
b. October 02, 1928 in Fort Worth, Texas

Darren McGavin
American actor
• Starred in TV series "The Night Stalker," 1974-75.
b. May 07, 1922 in Spokane, Washington

Patrick (Joseph) McGoohan
American actor
• Played in TV series, Disney films; won Emmy for "Columbo," 1975.
b. March 19, 1928 in New York, New York

Elizabeth McGovern
American actress
• Played in films *Ordinary People*, 1980 Oscar winner; *Ragtime*, 1981.
b. July 18, 1961 in Evanston, Illinois

Dorothy Hackett McGuire
American actress
• Star of stage, film *Claudia*, 1941; won Drama Critics Circle Award, 1941; TV show "Rich Man, Poor Man."
b. June 14, 1918 in Omaha, Nebraska

Frank (Francis Curray) McHugh
American actor
• Character actor with Warner Bros., 1930-42, generally as the hero's best-friend in over 150 films.
b. May 23, 1898 in Homestead, Pennsylvania
d. September 11, 1981 in Greenwich, Connecticut

John McIntire
American actor
• Played wagon master on long-running TV series "Wagon Train," 1961-64; often appeared with wife Jeannette Nolan.
b. June 27, 1907 in Spokane, Washington
d. January 3, 1991 in Laguna Beach, California

James McIntyre
American actor
• With partner Thomas Heath appeared in minstrel shows as blackface comedian for over 50 years, beginning 1874.
b. August 08, 1857 in Kenosha, Wisconsin
d. August 18, 1937 in Southampton, New York

Michael McKean
American actor
• Played Lenny on TV series "Laverne & Shirley," 1976-83.
b. October 17, 1947 in New York, New York

Donna McKechnie
American dancer–actress
• Won Tony, 1975, for A Chorus Line.
b. November 16, 1942 in Pontiac, Michigan

Ian Murray McKellen
English actor–director
• Won 1981 Tony for his role, Salieri, in Amadeus.
b. May 25, 1939 in Burnley, England

Siobhan McKenna
Irish actress
• Stage debut, 1940; films include Doctor Zhivago, 1965.
b. May 24, 1922 in Belfast, Northern Ireland
d. November 16, 1986 in Dublin, Ireland

Nancy McKeon
American actress
• Played Jo on TV series "Facts of Life," 1980-88.
b. April 04, 1966 in Westbury, New York

Leo McKern
(Reginald McKern)
English actor
• Films include A Man for All Seasons, 1952.
b. March 16, 1920 in Sydney, Australia

Amanda McKerrow
American dancer
• Won gold prize, Moscow International Ballet Competition, 1981, highest honor ever given to American.
b. November 07, 1964 in New Mexico

Victor McLaglen
American actor
• Former boxer promoted as "great white hope" against black boxer Jack Johnson to whom he lost; Oscar winner for The Informer, 1935.
b. December 11, 1886 in Tunbridge Wells, England
d. November 07, 1959 in Newport Beach, California

Norman McLaren
Canadian filmmaker
• Innovator in animation who won Academy Award for short Neighbors, 1952.
b. April 11, 1914 in Stirling, Scotland
d. January 26, 1987 in Montreal, Quebec

Ed(ward Lee) McMahon
American entertainer
• Best known as Johnny Carson's right-hand man on "The Tonight Show," 1962–; host of syndicated "Star Search," late 1980s–.
b. March 06, 1923 in Detroit, Michigan

Horace McMahon
American actor
• Character actor in over 125 films, 1937-68; played in TV series "Naked City," 1959-63.
b. May 17, 1907 in Norwalk, Connecticut
d. August 17, 1971 in Norwalk, Connecticut

Don(ald Thomas) McNeill
American radio performer
• Hosted "Breakfast Club," longest-running morning show on radio, 1933-68.
b. December 03, 1907 in Galena, Illinois

Kristy McNichol
American actress
• Played Buddy Lawrence on TV series "Family," 1976-80; won Emmys, 1977, 1979; plays Barbara Weston on TV comedy "Empty Nest," 1988–.
b. September 09, 1962 in Los Angeles, California

Butterfly (Thelma) McQueen
American actress
• Played Prissy in Gone With the Wind, 1939; other films include Mildred Pierce, 1945; The Mosquito Coast, 1986.
b. January 07, 1911 in Tampa, Florida

Steve (Terence Stephen) McQueen
American actor
• Starred in Bullitt, 1968; The Getaway, 1973.
b. March 24, 1930 in Indianapolis, Indiana
d. November 07, 1980 in Juarez, Mexico

Gerald McRaney
American actor
• Played Rick Simon on TV series "Simon and Simon," 1981-88, Mac MacGillis on "Major Dad," 1989–; married to Delta Burke.
b. August 19, 1948 in Collins, Mississippi

Vaughn Meader
American actor
• Did impersonations of JFK; album The First Family, 1962, sold 2 1/2 million copies; career ended when Kennedy died.
b. 1936 in Boston, Massachusetts

Audrey Meadows
American actress
• Played Alice Kramden on TV series "The Honeymooners."
b. 1924 in Wu Chang, China

Jayne Cotter Meadows
(Mrs Steve Allen)
American actress
• Married Steve Allen, 1954–; TV shows include "I've Got a Secret," 1952-58; "Medical Center," 1969-72.
b. September 27, 1926 in Wu Chang, China

Anne Meara
(Mrs Jerry Stiller; Stiller and Meara)
American actress–comedienne
• Played Veronica Rooney on TV series "Archie Bunker's Place," 1979-82.
b. September 2, 1924 in New York, New York

Patricia Medina
American actress
• Married Joseph Cotten, 1960–; heroine of swashbucklers The Three Musketeers, 1948; Fortunes of Captain Blood, 1950; Black Knight, 1954.
b. July 19, 1920 in London, England

Mark Howard Medoff
American dramatist
• Wrote award-winning play Children of a Lesser God, 1981.
b. March 18, 1940 in Mount Carmel, Illinois

Thomas Edward Meehan
American writer
• Wrote Annie; basis for Braodway smash hit; won Tony, 1977.
b. August 14, 1932 in Ossining, New York

Donald Meek
Scottish actor
• Character actor 1929-46; Stagecoach, 1939; My Little Chickadee, 1940; Top Hat, 1935.
b. July 14, 1880 in Glasgow, Scotland
d. November 18, 1946 in Los Angeles, California

Ralph Meeker
(Ralph Rathgeber)
American actor
• Known for roles in action, adventure films; played Mike Hammer in Kiss Me Deadly, 1955.
b. November 21, 1920 in Minneapolis, Minnesota
d. August 05, 1988 in Los Angeles, California

Thomas Meighan
American actor
• Star of Paramount, 1915-32, in over 80 films including Miracle Man, 1932.
b. April 09, 1879 in Pittsburgh, Pennsylvania
d. July 08, 1936 in Great Neck, New York

Austin (Alfred Austin) Melford
English actor–director–producer
• London stage performer since 1904.
b. August 24, 1884 in Alverstoke, England
d. August 19, 1971

Georges Melies
French director–producer
• Originator of fiction and fantasy film; best known film *A Trip to the Moon*, 1902.
b. December 08, 1861 in Paris, France
d. January 21, 1938 in Paris, France

Daniel Melnick
American film executive–producer
• Films include *All That Jazz*, 1979; *Altered States*, 1980; won Emmys for"Death of a Salesman," 1951; "Ages of Man."
b. April 21, 1932 in New York, New York

Jean-Pierre Melville
(Jean-Pierre Grumbach)
French director
• Pseud. is from favorite novelist, Herman Melville; films include *Les Enfants Terribles*, 1949.
b. October 2, 1917 in Paris, France
d. August 02, 1973 in Paris, France

Adolphe Jean Menjou
American actor
• Starred in Chaplin's *A Woman of Paris*, 1923; Oscar nominee for *The Front Page*, 1931.
b. February 08, 1890 in Pittsburgh, Pennsylvania
d. October 29, 1963 in Beverly Hills, California

Helen Menken
American actress–producer
• First wife of Humphrey Bogart; produced *Stage Door Canteen*, 1942-46; *Second Husband*, 1937-46.
b. December 12, 1901 in New York, New York
d. March 27, 1966 in New York, New York

Jiri Menzel
Czech director
• Won Oscar for best foreign language film *Closely Watched Trains*, 1966.
b. 1938

Ismail Merchant
American producer
• With director James Ivory, formed the longest producer-director team in film history (25 years); films include *A Room With a View*, 1986.
b. December 25, 1936 in Bombay, India

Vivien Merchant
(Ada Thomson)
English actress
• Starred in *The Homecoming*, 1967; written by ex-husband Harold Pinter.
b. July 22, 1929 in Manchester, England
d. October 03, 1982 in London, England

Melina (Maria Amalia) Mercouri
(Mrs Jules Dassin)
Greek actress–politician
• Starred in *Never on Sunday*; minister, Greek culture, sciences, 1981–.
b. October 18, 1925 in Athens, Greece

Burgess Meredith
American actor
• Best known for role in *Rocky* films, 1977-81; played on Broadway in *The Playboy of the Western World*, 1946.
b. November 16, 1909 in Cleveland, Ohio

Lee Meriwether
American actress–beauty contest winner
• Miss America, 1955; co-star, "Barnaby Jones," 1973-80.
b. May 27, 1935 in Los Angeles, California

Una Merkel
American actress
• Career began in silent films with W C Fields; won Tony for *The Ponder Heart*, 1956.
b. December 1, 1903 in Covington, Kentucky
d. January 04, 1986 in Los Angeles, California

David Merrick
(David Margulois)
American producer
• Plays include *Fanny*, 1954; *Gypsy*, 1958; *Promises, Promises*, 1969.
b. November 27, 1912 in Saint Louis, Missouri

Gary Franklin Merrill
American actor
• Acting career spanned 50 years; best known for marriage to Bette Davis, 1950-60; starred with her in *All About Eve*, 1950.
b. August 02, 1915 in Hartford, Connecticut
d. March 06, 1990 in Falmouth, Maine

Nicholas Meyer
American screenwriter–director
• Wrote *Seven-Per-Cent Solution*, 1974; directed *Star Trek II*, 1982.
b. December 24, 1945 in New York, New York

Russ Meyer
American director
• Noted for sexploitation films: *Vixen*, 1969; *Fanny Hill*.
b. 1922 in Oakland, California

Ari(adne) Meyers
American actress
• Plays Emma McArdle on TV series "Kate & Allie."
b. 1970 in New York, New York

Lorne Michaels
Canadian producer–writer
• Producer of "Saturday Night Live" TV show; won four Emmys for various other shows.
b. November 17, in Toronto, Ontario

Ray Middleton
American actor
• Played on stage in *Annie Get Your Gun*; *South Pacific*.
b. February 08, 1907 in Chicago, Illinois
d. April 1, 1984 in Panorama City, California

Thomas Middleton
English dramatist
• Satirical comedies include *Chaste Main in Cheapside*, 1630; often collaborated with Dekker, Rowley.
b. April 18, 1570 in London, England
d. July 04, 1627 in Newington Butts, England

Bette Midler
(Mrs Harry Kipper; "The Divine Miss M" "The Last of the Tacky Ladies")
American singer–actress
• Concert, recording, film star; Oscar nominee for *The Rose*, 1979; other films include *Outrageous Fortune*, 1987; *Beaches*, 1989.
b. December 01, 1945 in Honolulu, Hawaii

Sarah Miles
(Mrs Robert Bolt)
English actress
• Oscar nominee for *Ryan's Daughter*, 1970; other films include *Hope and Glory*, 1987.
b. December 31, 1943 in Igatestone, England

Sylvia Miles
American actress–comedienne
• Oscar nominee for *Midnight Cowboy*; *Farewell My Lovely*.
b. September 09, 1932 in New York, New York

Vera Miles
American actress
• Films include *The Searchers*, 1956; *Psycho*, 1960; *Psycho II*, 1983.
b. August 23, 1930 in Boise City, Oklahoma

Lewis Milestone
American director
• Won Oscars for *Two Arabian Knights*; *All Quiet on the Western Front*.
b. September 3, 1895 in Chisinau, Russia
d. September 25, 1980 in Los Angeles, California

Ray(mond Alton) Milland
(Reginald Alfred John Truscott-Jones)
American actor–director
• Debonair leading man who made more than 120 movies; won Oscar, 1945, for *The Lost Weekend.*
b. January 03, 1908 in Neath, Wales
d. March 1, 1986 in Torrance, California

Ann Miller
(Lucille Ann Collier)
American dancer–actress–singer
• Star of *Sugar Babies,* 1979-86; known for MGM musicals: *On the Town,* 1949.
b. April 12, 1923 in Cherino, Texas

Arthur Miller
American dramatist
• Wrote *Death of a Salesman,* 1949; *The Crucible,* 1953; married Marilyn Monroe, 1956-61; won Pulitzer, 1949; Tonys, 1947, 1949, 1953; Emmys, 1976, 1981.
b. October 17, 1915 in New York, New York

Barry Miller
American actor
• Won Tony, 1985, for *Biloxi Blues;* in movie *Fame.*
b. February 08, 1958

Jason Miller
American dramatist–actor
• Won Tony, Pulitzer, for writing *That Championship Season,* 1973.
b. April 22, 1939 in Scranton, Pennsylvania

Spike (Terence Alan) Milligan
British director–author
• Best known for "The Goon Show" with Peter Sellers, Harry Secombe on BBC, 1950s.
b. April 16, 1918 in Ahmaddnagar, India

Donna Mills
(Donna Jean Miller)
American actress
• Plays Abby Ewing on TV series "Knots Landing," 1980-.
b. December 11, 1943 in Chicago, Illinois

Florence Mills
American entertainer
• Starred in black musical revues on Broadway, 1920s: *Blackbirds of 1926.*
b. January 25, 1895 in Washington, District of Columbia
d. November 01, 1927 in New York, New York

Hayley Mills
(Hayley Catherine Rose Vivian Mills)
English actress
• Known for child, adolescent roles in Walt Disney films; won Oscar for *Polyanna,* 1960.
b. April 18, 1946 in London, England

Sir John Mills
(Lewis Ernest Watts Mills)
English actor
• Won Oscar for *Ryan's Daughter,* 1970; father of Hayley, Juliet Mills
b. February 22, 1908 in Felixstowe, England

Juliet Mills
(Mrs Maxwell Caulfield)
English actress
• Starred in "Nanny and the Professor," 1970-71; daughter of John Mills.
b. November 21, 1941 in London, England

Martin Sam Milner
American actor
• Played Pete Malloy in "Adam-12," 1968-75.
b. December 28, 1931 in Detroit, Michigan

Yvette Carmen M Mimieux
American actress
• Films include *The Black Hole,* 1979; appeared in many TV movies.
b. January 08, 1939 in Los Angeles, California

Sal(vatore) Mineo
American actor–singer
• Oscar nominations for *Rebel Without a Cause,* 1955; *Exodus,* 1960.
b. January 1, 1939 in New York, New York
d. February 12, 1976 in Los Angeles, California

Worthington C Miner
American producer
• Created "The Ed Sullivan Show," 1948-71.
b. November 13, 1900 in Buffalo, New York
d. December 11, 1982 in New York, New York

Vincente Minnelli
American director
• Won Oscar for *Gigi,* 1958; married Judy Garland, 1945-50; father of Liza Minnelli.
b. February 28, 1913 in Chicago, Illinois
d. July 25, 1986 in Beverly Hills, California

Abraham Bennett Minsky
(The Minsky Brothers)
American producer
• With brothers, owned chain of burlesque houses; helped sponsor Bert Lahr, Abbott and Costello.
b. March 01, 1881 in New York, New York
d. September 05, 1949 in New York, New York

Harold Minsky
(The Minsky Brothers)
American producer
• Diehard supporter of old-time striptease burlesque; ran show around US; son of Abraham.
b. 1915
d. December 28, 1977 in Las Vegas, Nevada

Carmen Miranda
Brazilian singer–dancer–actress
• Flamboyant musical comedy star, 1940s; noted for fast-tempo songs, elaborate hats; films include *Down Argentine Way,* 1940.
b. February 09, 1909 in Marco Canavezes, Portugal
d. August 05, 1955 in Beverly Hills, California

Walter Mortimer Mirisch
American director–producer
• Films include *In the Heat of the Night,* 1967; *Same Time, Next Year,* 1978.
b. November 08, 1921 in New York, New York

Helen Mirren
English actress
• Films include *O Lucky Man,* 1973; *Excalibur,* 1981.
b. 1946

Arthur Adam Mitchell
American dancer–choreographer
• First black man to achieve prominence in classical dance; with NYC Ballet, 1952-69; founded Dance Theater of Harlem Inc.
b. March 27, 1934 in New York, New York

Cameron Mitchell
(Cameron Mizell)
American actor
• On stage, in film *Death of a Salesman;* in TV show "High Chaparral," 1967-71.
b. November 04, 1918 in Dallastown, Pennsylvania

Grant Mitchell
American actor
• Starred in over 80 films including *Mr. Smith Goes to Washington.*
b. June 17, 1875 in Columbus, Ohio
d. May 01, 1957 in Los Angeles, California

Thomas Mitchell
American actor
• Won Oscar for *Stagecoach,* 1939; played Scarlett O'Hara's father in *Gone With the Wind.*
b. July 11, 1892 in Elizabeth, New Jersey
d. December 17, 1962 in Beverly Hills, California

Robert (Robert Charles Duran) Mitchum
American actor
• One of the first anti-hero actors; over 45 films include *The Story of G I Joe*, 1945; *Crossfire*, 1947.
b. August 06, 1917 in Bridgeport, Connecticut

Tom Mix
American actor
• Starred in over 400 westerns, usually with his horse, Tony.
b. January 06, 1880 in Mix Run, Pennsylvania
d. October 12, 1940 in Florence, Arizona

Kenji Mizoguchi
Japanese director
• Films created realistic, unified universe; *The Life of Oharu*, 1952, considered masterpiece.
b. May 16, 1898 in Tokyo, Japan
d. August 24, 1956 in Kyoto, Japan

Helena Modjeska
(Helena Opid)
Polish actress
• Introduced Ibsen to American theater in *A Doll's House*.
b. October 12, 1840 in Krakow, Poland
d. 1909

Donald Moffat
English actor
• Films include *Rachel, Rachel; Eleanor and Franklin; Popeye*.
b. December 26, 1930 in Plymouth, England

Al Molinaro
American actor
• Played Murray the Cop on "The Odd Couple," Al on "Happy Days."
b. June 24, 1919 in Kenosha, Wisconsin

Ferenc Molnar
Hungarian dramatist–author–journalist
• Noted for light sophisticated plays including *Liliom*, 1909; source for Broadway's *Carousel*, 1945.
b. 1878 in Budapest, Hungary
d. April 01, 1952 in New York, New York

Paul Monash
American producer–writer
• Produced TV show, "Peyton Place," 1964-69.
b. in New York, New York

Mario Monicelli
Italian director
• Directed *The Big Deal on Madonna Street*, 1960; wrote *Crackers*, 1984.
b. May 15, 1915 in Rome, Italy

Meredith Jane Monk
American choreographer
• "Next Wave" choreographer known for Obie-winning *Vessel*, 1971; *Quarry*, 1975.
b. November 2, 1942 in Lima, Peru

Bill (William Blanc, Jr) Monroe
American broadcast journalist
• Moderator, exec. producer, NBC's "Meet the Press" since 1975.
b. July 17, 1920 in New Orleans, Louisiana

Marilyn Monroe
(Norma Jean (Mortenson) Baker)
American actress
• Ultimate pin-up girl, cult figure; starred in *Some Like It Hot*, 1959; *Bus Stop*, 1956; died of drug overdose.
b. June 01, 1926 in Los Angeles, California
d. August 05, 1962 in Hollywood, California

Ricardo Montalban
Mexican actor
• Played Mr. Rourke on TV series "Fantasy Island," 1978-83.
b. November 25, 1920 in Mexico City, Mexico

Yves Montand
(Ivo Livi)
French singer–actor
• Vocalist, international film star whose films include *Let's Make Love*, 1960; husband of Simone Signoret.
b. October 13, 1921 in Monsummano, Italy

Elizabeth Montgomery
American actress
• Played Samantha on "Bewitched," 1964-72; daughter of Robert Montgomery.
b. April 15, 1933 in Hollywood, California

Robert Henry Montgomery
(Henry Montgomery Jr)
American actor–director
• Starred in *Here Comes Mr. Jordan*, 1941; TV adviser to Eisenhower; father of Elizabeth Montgomery.
b. May 21, 1904 in Beacon, New York
d. September 27, 1981 in New York, New York

Gloria Monty
(Gloria Montemuro)
American producer
• Known for turning daytime drama "General Hospital" into top-rated show; won Emmys 1981, 1984.
b. August 12, 1921 in Union Hill, New Jersey

Monty Python's Flying Circus
(Graham Chapman; John Cleese; Terry Gilliam; Eric Idle; Terry Jones; Michael Palin)
British comedy team
• Zany comedy group, starring in TV series, movies, 1969–; at one time, highest-rated comedy show in Britain, US.

Clayton Moore
American actor
• Starred in "The Lone Ranger," 1949-56.
b. September 14, 1914 in Chicago, Illinois

Colleen Moore
(Kathleen Morrison)
American actress
• Bobbed-haired flapper star of numerous 1920s films; wrote *Silent Star*, an autobiography.
b. August 19, 1902 in Port Huron, Michigan
d. January 25, 1988 in Paso Robles, California

Demi Moore
(Demi Guynes; Mrs Bruce Willis)
American actress
• In films *Blame It on Rio*, 1984, *St. Elmo's Fire*, 1985, *Ghost*, 1990.
b. November 11, 1962 in Roswell, New Mexico

Dick(ie) Moore
(John Richard Moore Jr; Our Gang)
American actor
• Child actor who appeared in many "Our Gang" episodes; gave Shirley Temple first screen kiss in *Miss Andy Rooney*, 1942.
b. September 12, 1925 in Los Angeles, California

Dudley Stuart John Moore
English actor–musician
• Starred in *10*, 1979; *Arthur*, 1981; won Grammy, 1974; special Tonys, 1969, 1974.
b. April 19, 1935 in London, England

Garry Moore
(Thomas Garrison Morfit)
American TV personality
• Writer, "Jimmy Durante-Garry Moore Show," 1943-48; star, "Garry Moore Show," 1950-54, 1966-67; moderator, "To Tell The Truth," 1969-77.
b. January 31, 1915 in Baltimore, Maryland

Mary Tyler Moore
American actress
• Star of "Mary Tyler Moore Show," 1970-77; 1981 Oscar nominee for *Ordinary People*.
b. December 29, 1936 in Brooklyn, New York

Roger George Moore
English actor
• Starred in "The Saint," 1967-69; movie role as James Bond, Agent 007.
b. October 14, 1928 in London, England

Terry Moore
(Helen Koford)
American actress
• After seven-year legal battle was recognized as widow of Howard Hughes and inherited part of his estate; married, 1949.
b. January 01, 1932 in Los Angeles, California

Victor Moore
American actor
• Vaudeville comedian in films, 1915-55.
b. February 24, 1876 in Hammonton, New Jersey
d. July 23, 1962 in Long Island, New York

Erin Moran
American actress
• Played Joanie on "Happy Days," 1974-83.
b. October 18, 1961 in Burbank, California

George Moran
American actor
• Moran & Mack comedy team in vaudeville appeared in films with W C Fields: *My Little Chickadee*, 1940.
b. 1882 in Elwood, Kansas
d. August 01, 1949 in Oakland, California

Polly Moran
American comedienne–actress
• Teamed with Marie Dressler in movies: *The Passionate Plumber*, 1932.
b. June 28, 1883 in Chicago, Illinois
d. January 25, 1952 in Los Angeles, California

Kenneth Gilbert More
English actor
• Played title role in "Father Brown" series, 1974; wrote autobiographies *Happy Go Lucky*, 1959; *More of Less*, 1978.
b. September 2, 1914 in Gerrards Cross, England
d. July 12, 1982 in London, England

Jeanne Moreau
French actress
• Films include *Frantic; Lovers.*
b. January 23, 1928 in Paris, France

Ward Morehouse
American drama critic–dramatist
• Wrote syndicated column "Broadway After Dark," 1926-66.
b. November 24, 1899 in Savannah, Georgia
d. December 07, 1966 in New York, New York

Rita Moreno
(Mrs Leonard Gordon; Rosita Dolores Alverio)
American actress–singer
• Only woman to win show business' four top awards: Oscar, Grammy, Tony, Emmy; starred in *West Side Story*, 1961.
b. December 11, 1931 in Humacao, Puerto Rico

Dennis Morgan
(Stanley Morner)
American actor–singer
• Musicals, comedies include *Desert Song*, 1943; *Christmas in Connecticut*, 1945; *My Wild Irish Rose*, 1947.
b. December 1, 1920 in Prentice, Wisconsin

Frank Morgan
(Francis Phillip Wupperman)
American actor
• Played title role in *The Wizard of Oz*, 1939.
b. July 01, 1890 in New York, New York
d. September 18, 1949 in Beverly Hills, California

Harry Morgan
(Harry Bratsburg)
American actor
• Starred in TV series "Dragnet," 1967-70; "M*A*S*H," 1975-83.
b. April 1, 1915 in Detroit, Michigan

Henry Morgan
American TV personality
• Appeared on TV quiz show, "I've Got a Secret," 1952-76.
b. March 31, 1915 in New York, New York

Michele Morgan
(Simone Roussel)
French actress
• Won best actress award at Cannes festival for *Symphonie Pastorale*, 1946.
b. February 29, 1920 in Neuilly, France

Ralph Morgan
(Raphael Kuhner Wupperman)
American actor
• Brother of Frank Morgan; character actor in over 100 films, 1923-53, including *Gang Busters; Power and the Glory.*
b. July 06, 1883 in New York, New York
d. June 11, 1956 in New York, New York

Terence Morgan
English actor
• Leading man in British films *Captain Horatio Hornblower*, 1951; *It Started in Paradise*, 1952.
b. December 08, 1921 in London, England

Cathy Moriarty
American actress
• Starred in *Raging Bull*, 1981; *Neighbors*, 1982.
b. November 29, 1960 in Bronx, New York

Michael Moriarty
American actor
• Won Tony for *Find Your Way Home*, 1974; Emmy for *The Glass Menagerie*, 1974.
b. April 05, 1942 in Detroit, Michigan

Pat (Noriyuki) Morita
American actor–comedian
• TV shows include "Happy Days," 1975-76, 1982-83; "Ohara," 1987–; films include *The Karate Kid* series, 1984, 1986.
b. 1932 in Isleton, California

Chester Morris
American actor
• Oscar nominee for *Alibi*, 1929; played Boston Blackie in 13 films, 1941-49.
b. February 16, 1901 in New York, New York
d. September 11, 1970 in New Hope, Pennsylvania

Greg Morris
American actor
• Starred in TV series "Mission Impossible," 1966-73.
b. September 26, 1934 in Cleveland, Ohio

Howard Morris
American actor–director
• Directed comedies *Who's Minding the Mint?*, 1967; *With Six You Get Eggroll*, 1968.
b. September 04, 1919 in New York, New York

Vic Morrow
American actor
• Starred in "Combat," 1962-67; died in helicopter crash making movie.
b. February 14, 1932 in New York, New York
d. July 23, 1982 in Castaic, California

Robert Alan Morse
American actor
• Won 1961 Tony for *How to Succeed in Business without Really Trying*; starred in film version, 1967.
b. May 18, 1931 in Newton, Massachusetts

Bruce Alexander Morton
American journalist
• CBS News Washington anchorman since 1975.
b. October 28, 1930 in Norwalk, Connecticut

Tad Mosel
American dramatist
• Won Pulitzer for play *All the Way Home*, 1961; wrote screenplay for *Up the Down Staircase*, 1967.
b. May 01, 1922 in Steubenville, Ohio

Gilbert Moses, III,
American director
• Won Obies for *Slaveship*, 1973; *The Taking of Miss Janie*, 1977.
b. August 2, 1942 in Cleveland, Ohio

Arnold Moss
American actor–director
• Acclaimed classical actor; known for Shakespearean roles on stage, villains in films.
b. January 28, 1911 in Brooklyn, New York
d. December 15, 1989 in New York, New York

Donny Most
American actor
• Played Ralph Malph on TV series "Happy Days," 1974-80.
b. August 08, 1953 in New York, New York

Zero (Samuel Joel) Mostel
American actor
• Played Tevye in *Fiddler on the Roof*; won three Tonys.
b. February 28, 1915 in Brooklyn, New York
d. September 08, 1977 in Philadelphia, Pennsylvania

Alan Mowbray
English actor
• Character actor in 200 films, 1931-62, including *My Man Godfrey*.
b. August 18, 1897 in London, England
d. March 25, 1969 in Hollywood, California

Bill (William Don) Moyers
American broadcast journalist
• Correspondent, CBS News since 1981; author of *Listening to America*; won several Emmys.
b. June 05, 1934 in Hugo, Oklahoma

Roger Harrison Mudd
American broadcast journalist
• Newscaster, CBS, 1961-80; NBC, 1980-86; PBS, 1987–; won several Emmys.
b. February 09, 1928 in Washington, District of Columbia

Jean Muir
American actress
• Hired to play in TV series "The Aldrich Family," 1950 blacklisted as a communist sympathizer, career virtually destroyed.
b. February 13, 1911 in New York, New York

Martin Mull
American actor–comedian
• Played on TV shows "Mary Hartman, Mary Hartman"; "Fernwood 2-Night."
b. August 18, 1943 in Chicago, Illinois

Richard Mulligan
American actor
• Played Burt Campbell on TV comedy "Soap," 1977-81, Harry Weston on "Empty Nest," 1988–; won Emmys, 1980, 1989.
b. November 13, 1932 in Bronx, New York

Paul Muni
(Muni Weisenfreund)
American actor
• Won Oscar for *The Story of Louis Pasteur*, 1936.
b. September 22, 1895 in Lemberg, Austria
d. August 25, 1967 in Montecito, California

Jules Munshin
American actor
• Broadway star of *Call Me Mister*, 1946.
b. 1915 in New York, New York
d. February 19, 1970 in New York, New York

Ona Munson
American actress
• Played Belle Watling in *Gone With the Wind*, 1939.
b. June 16, 1906 in Portland, Oregon
d. February 11, 1955 in New York, New York

Friedrich W Murnau
(Friedrich Wilhelm Plumpe)
German director
• Made German, American films, 1920s; used novel camera techniques.
b. December 28, 1899 in Bielefeld, Germany
d. March 11, 1931 in California

Audie Murphy
American actor
• Received 24 decorations to become WW II's most decorated soldier; most film roles in low-budget Westerns.
b. June 2, 1924 in Kingston, Texas
d. June 01, 1971 in Roanoke, Virginia

Eddie Murphy
American comedian
• Former regular of "Saturday Night Live"; starred in *Beverly Hills Cop*, 1984.
b. April 03, 1961 in Roosevelt, New York

George Lloyd Murphy
American actor–politician
• Tap-dancing star of numerous 1930-40s musicals; won special Oscar, 19 50; senator from CA, 1965-71.
b. July 04, 1902 in New Haven, Connecticut

Rosemary Murphy
American actress
• Won Emmy for "Eleanor and Franklin," 1976; three-time Tony nominee.
b. January 13, 1927 in Munich, Germany

Arthur Murray
(Arthur Murray Teichman)
American dancer
• Began Arthur Murray School of Dancing; over 450 schools throughout US.
b. April 04, 1895 in New York, New York
d. March 03, 1991 in Honolulu, Hawaii

Bill Murray
American actor–comedian
• Cast member on "Saturday Night Live," 1977-80; films include *Ghostbusters*, 1984.
b. September 21, 1950 in Wilmette, Illinois

Don(ald Patrick) Murray
American actor
• Oscar nominee for *Bus Stop*, 1956; played on TV's "Knot's Landing."
b. July 31, 1929 in Hollywood, California

Kathryn Hazel Murray
(Mrs Arthur Murray)
American dancer
• Was mistress of ceremonies for TV's "Arthur Murray Party," 1950-60.
b. September 15, 1906 in Jersey City, New Jersey

Mae Murray
(Marie Koenig)
American dancer–actress
• Appeared in dozens of films, 1916-31: *The Merry Widow*, 1925; subject of biography, *The Self-Enchanted*, 1965.
b. April 1, 1889 in Portsmouth, Virginia
d. March 23, 1965 in Woodland Hills, California

Edward R(oscoe) Murrow
American broadcast journalist
• TV moderator, "See It Now," 1951-58; director, US Information Agency, 1961-64.
b. April 25, 1908 in Greensboro, North Carolina
d. April 27, 1965 in Pawling, New York

Jim (James Thurston) Nabors
American actor–singer
• Played Gomer Pyle on TV comedies "The Andy Griffith Show," 1963-64, "Gomer Pyle, USMC," 1964-69; has several gold albums as singer.
b. June 12, 1932 in Sylacauga, Alabama

George Nader
American actor
• Leading man in action pictures, 1950s; did series of thrillers in Germany playing an FBI agent.
b. October 09, 1921 in Pasadena, California

Michael Nader
American actor
• Played Dex Dexter on TV soap opera "Dynasty," 1983-89.
b. February 18, 1945

Conrad Nagel
American actor
• Matinee idol, 1920-35; received special Oscar for work on Motion Picture Relief Fund, 1947.
b. March 16, 1897 in Keokuk, Iowa
d. February 21, 1970 in New York, New York

J(oseph) Carrol Naish
American actor
• Character actor in over 200 films; Oscar nominee for *Sahara; A Medal for Benny.*
b. January 21, 1900 in New York, New York
d. January 24, 1973 in La Jolla, California

Mikio Naruse
Japanese filmmaker
• Directed film *Late Chrysanthemums,* 1954; at first considered culturally alien to W audiences.
b. August 2, 1905 in Tokyo, Japan
d. 1969 in Tokyo, Japan

Clarence Nash
American entertainer
• Voice of Donald Duck since cartoon character's inception, 1934.
b. 1905 in Independence, Missouri
d. February 2, 1985 in Burbank, California

George Frederick Nash
American actor
• Films include *Oliver Twist,* 1933; silent films: *The Great Gatsby,* 1926.
b. 1873 in Philadelphia, Pennsylvania
d. December 31, 1944 in Amityville, New York

Thomas Nash
(Pasquil pseud)
English author–dramatist
• Only surviving play is satirical masterpiece *Summer's Last Will and Testament,* 1593.
b. 1567 in Lowestoft, England
d. 1601 in Yarmouth, England

Mildred Natwick
American actress
• Oscar nominee for *Barefoot in the Park,* 1967.
b. June 19, 1908 in Baltimore, Maryland

Alla Nazimova
Russian actress
• Known for her expressive pantomime in silent films, 1916-25; also bold acting style in *Camille; A Doll's House.*
b. June 04, 1879 in Yalta, Russia
d. July 13, 1945 in Hollywood, California

Dame Anna Neagle
(Florence Marjorie Robertson)
English actress–producer
• First lady of British screen, 1930s-40s; set West End record with 2,062 performances in *Charlie Girl,* 1965-71.
b. October 2, 1904 in London, England
d. June 03, 1986 in London, England

Larry (Lawrence P) Neal
American poet–dramatist
• Major influence in black arts movement; editor, *Liberator* art mag., 1960s; co-founded, Black Arts Theater, NYC, 1965.
b. September 05, 1937 in Atlanta, Georgia
d. January 06, 1981 in Hamilton, New York

Patricia Neal
(Patsy Lou Neal)
American actress
• Won Tony for *Another Part of the Forest,* 1947; Oscar for *Hud,* 1963.
b. January 2, 1926 in Packard, Kentucky

James Morton Nederlander
American producer–theater owner
• Owns theatres nationwide; has produced *Annie; Hello Dolly; Woman of the Year.*
b. March 21, 1922 in Detroit, Michigan

Hal Needham
American director–stuntman
• Directed five films starring Bert Reynolds: *Smokey and the Bandit,* 1977; *Cannonball Run,* 1981.
b. March 06, 1931 in Memphis, Tennessee

Pola Negri
(Barbara Appolonia Chalupiec)
American actress
• Star of silent German films, 1917-22; known for Hollywood vamp role, off-screen affair with Rudolph Valentino.
b. December 31, 1894 in Janowa, Poland
d. August 01, 1987 in San Antonio, Texas

Jean Negulesco
American director
• Films include *Daddy Long Legs,* 1955; *Johnny Belinda,* 1948.
b. February 29, 1900 in Craiova, Romania

Barry Nelson
(Robert Haakon Nielson)
American actor
• Star of Broadway's *Rat Race; Cactus Flower;* appeared on TV show "The Hunter."
b. April 16, 1920 in San Francisco, California

David Nelson
American actor
• Son of Ozzie and Harriet; appeared on their TV show, 1952-65.
b. October 24, 1936 in New York, New York

Gene Nelson
(Eugene Leander Berg)
American actor–dancer
• Films include *Tea For Two,* 1950; *Three Sailors and a Girl,* 1953.
b. March 24, 1920 in Seattle, Washington

Harriet Nelson
(Harriet Hilliard; Mrs Ozzie Nelson)
American actress–singer
• Began career as singer in Ozzie Nelson's orchestra; starred on TV, 1952-65.
b. July 18, 1912 in Des Moines, Iowa

Judd Nelson
American actor
• Films include *The Breakfast Club,* 1985; member of young actors known as "brat pack."
b. in Portland, Maine

Ozzie (Oswald George) Nelson
American actor–bandleader
• Starred in TV series "The Adventures of Ozzie and Harriet," 1952-65.
b. March 2, 1906 in Jersey City, New Jersey
d. June 03, 1975 in Hollywood, California

Ralph Nelson
American director
• Films include *Requiem for a Heavyweight,* 1962; *Lillies of the Field,* 1963; also directed TV shows.
b. August 12, 1916 in New York, New York
d. December 21, 1987 in Santa Monica, California

Tracy Nelson
(Mrs William Moses)
American actress–celebrity relative
• Daughter of Rick, Kris Nelson, niece of Mark Harmon; appeared on TV show "Square Pegs," 1982-83; stars in TV series "Father Dowling's Mysteries".

Jan Nemec
Czech director
• Films include *Diamonds of the Night.*
b. July 02, 1936 in Prague, Czechoslovakia

Vladimir I Nemirovich-Danchenko
Russian author–dramatist–producer
• Co-founder, Moscow Art Theatre; author, *My Life in the Russian Theatre*, 1937.
b. December 23, 1858 in Tiflis, Russia
d. April 25, 1943 in Moscow, U.S.S.R.

Franco Nero
Italian actor
• Played the role of Lancelot in 1967 film *Camelot*.
b. 1941

Evelyn Nesbit
(Evelyn Nesbit Thaw; "The Girl on the Red Velvet Swing")
American actress
• Showgirl, whose husband, Harry Thaw, killed Stanford White in jealousy over her, 1906.
b. 1885 in Tarentum, Pennsylvania
d. January 18, 1967 in Santa Monica, California

Cathleen Mary Nesbitt
English actress
• Originated stage role of Mrs. Higgins in *My Fair Lady*, 1956.
b. November 24, 1889 in Liskeard, England
d. August 02, 1982 in London, England

Olga Nethersole
English actress
• Arrested in NY for alleged indecency in play *Sapho*, 1900; acquitted; symbol to younger generation of revolt against prudery.
b. January 18, 1870 in London, England
d. January 09, 1951 in Bournemouth, England

John Neville
English actor–director
• English matinee idol, 1950s; artistic director, Canada's Stratford Festival, 1986–.
b. May 02, 1925 in London, England

Bob (George Robert) Newhart
American comedian
• Known for low-key, dry humor; starred in TV comedies "The Bob Newhart Show," 1972-78, "Newhart," 1982-90.
b. September 05, 1929 in Chicago, Illinois

David Newman
American screenwriter
• Films include *Bonnie and Clyde*, 1967; *Superman*, 1978.
b. February 04, 1937 in New York, New York

Paul Newman
American actor–director–producer–sportsman
• Starred in *The Sting*, 1973; *The Verdict*, 1982; races Formula One cars.
b. January 26, 1925 in Cleveland, Ohio

Julie Newmar
(Julia Charlene Newmeyer)
American dancer–actress
• Played Catwoman on TV series "Batman"; won Tony, 1959, for *Marriage Go 'Round*.
b. August 16, 1935 in Los Angeles, California

Robert Newton
English actor
• Character actor in British films of the 1930s-40s; films include *Treasure Island*, 1950.
b. June 01, 1905 in Shaftesbury, England
d. March 25, 1956 in Beverly Hills, California

Fred Niblo
(Federico Nobile)
American director
• Directed Valentino in films *Mark of Zorro; Three Musketeers; Blood and Sand*.
b. January 06, 1874 in York, Nebraska
d. November 11, 1948 in New Orleans, Louisiana

Denise Nicholas
American actress
• Played in TV series "Room 222," 1969-74; also had roles in feature films.
b. July 12, 1944 in Detroit, Michigan

Mike Nichols
(Michael Igor Peschkowsky)
American director
• Noted for works on Broadway, film; won many Tonys, including one for *The Odd Couple*, 1965; won Oscar for *The Graduate*, 1967.
b. November 06, 1931 in Berlin, Germany

Peter Nichols
English dramatist
• Published play *A Day in the Death of Joe Egg*, 1967; wrote screenplay for *Georgy Girl*, 1966.
b. July 31, 1927 in Bristol, England

Jack Nicholson
American actor
• Won Oscars for *One Flew Over the Cuckoo's Nest*, 1975; *Terms of Endearment*, 1983.
b. April 22, 1937 in Neptune, New Jersey

Leslie Nielsen
Canadian actor
• Starred in *The Poseidon Adventure*, 1972; *Airplane*, 1980.
b. February 11, 1926 in Regina, Saskatchewan

Vaslav Nijinsky
(Waslaw Nijinsky)
Russian dancer
• One of world's greatest dancers, 1909-19, known for performances of *The Rite of Spring*.
b. February 28, 1890 in Kiev, Russia
d. April 08, 1950 in London, England

Anna Q(uerentia) Nilsson
Swedish actress
• Silent screen star, 1911-28; fall ended her leading roles but she was able to appear as character actress.
b. March 3, 1888 in Ystad, Sweden
d. February 11, 1974 in Hemet, California

Leonard Nimoy
American actor–producer–director
• Played Mr. Spock on TV series "Star Trek," 1966-69; also in film series; has directed and produced several major movies.
b. March 26, 1931 in Boston, Massachusetts

David (James David Graham) Niven
Scottish actor–author
• Won 1958 Oscar for *Separate Tables*; book *The Moon's A Balloon*, 1972, sold over four million copies.
b. March 01, 1910 in Kirriemuir, Scotland
d. July 29, 1983 in Chateau D'Oex, Switzerland

Lloyd Nolan
American actor
• Character actor known for gangster and cop roles; co-starred in "Julia," 1968-71.
b. August 11, 1902 in San Francisco, California
d. September 27, 1985 in Brentwood, California

Nick Nolte
American actor
• Star of TV mini-series "Rich Man, Poor Man," 1976; films include *48 Hours*, 1982; *Down and Out in Beverly Hills*, 1986.
b. February 08, 1942 in Omaha, Nebraska

Marsha Williams Norman
American dramatist
• Won Pulitzer, 1983 for play *'Night Mother*; work characterized by honesty, natural dialogue, broken dramas; filmed, 1986.
b. September 21, 1947 in Louisville, Kentucky

Mabel Normand
American actress
• Silent screen comedienne; co-star with Chaplin in *Tillie's Punctured Romance*, 1914; credited with throwing first custard pie, ca. 1913.
b. November 1, 1894 in Boston, Massachusetts
d. February 23, 1930 in Monrovia, California

Christopher Norris
American actress
• Played Nurse Gloria Brancusi in TV series "Trapper John, MD," 1979-86.
b. October 07, 1953 in New York, New York

Chuck (Carlos Ray) Norris
American actor
• Karate champion; known for tough guy roles in action-adventure films: *Delta Force*, 1986, *Firewalker*, 1986, *Delta Force 2*, 1990; wrote autobiography *The Secret of Inner Strength: My Story*, 1988.
b. March 1, 1940 in Ryan, Oklahoma

Jay North
American actor
• Played Dennis the Menace in TV series, 1959-63.
b. August 03, 1952 in North Hollywood, California

Sheree North
(Dawn Bethel)
American actress
• Groomed by Fox Studios as sexpot substitute for Monroe but film career was limited; had lots of TV appearances.
b. January 17, 1933 in Los Angeles, California

Jack Norton
American actor
• Character actor whose speciality was the amiable drunk, 1934-48.
b. 1889 in New York, New York
d. October 15, 1958 in Saranac Lake, New York

Judy Norton-Taylor
American actress
• Played Mary Ellen on "The Waltons," 1972-81.
b. January 29, 1958 in Santa Monica, California

Deborah Norville
American broadcast journalist
• Replaced Jane Pauley as co-anchor of the "Today Show," 1990–. Replaced in 1991.
b. August 08, 1958 in Dalton, Georgia

Viscountess Diana (Manners) Cooper Norwich
(Diana Olivia Winifred Maud Manners)
British actress–socialite
• Eccentric beauty who inspired poetry, comedy; immortalized by Hilaire Belloc, Evelyn Waugh; played the Madonna in *The Miracle*, for 12 yrs.
b. August 29, 1892 in London, England
d. June 16, 1986 in London, England

Jack Norworth
American actor
• Composed "Shine On, Harvest Moon"; appeared in vaudeville as blackface comedian.
b. January 05, 1879 in Philadelphia, Pennsylvania
d. September 01, 1959 in Beverly Hills, California

Kim Novak
(Marilyn Pauline Novak)
American actress
• Starred in *Vertigo*, 1959; played Kit Marlowe on TV series "Falcon Crest," 1986-87.
b. February 18, 1933 in Chicago, Illinois

Ramon Novarro
(Ramon Samaniegos)
Mexican actor
• Silent screen leading man best known for title role in *Ben Hur*, 1926.
b. February 06, 1899 in Durango, Mexico
d. October 31, 1968 in Hollywood, California

Don Novello
American comedian
• Best known as Father Guido Sarducci on TV's "Saturday Night Live," 1978-80.
b. January 01, 1943 in Ashtabula, Ohio

Elliott Nugent
American dramatist–director–producer
• Co-authored *Male Animal* with James Thurber, 1940; co-produced *The Seven Year Itch* on Broadway.
b. September 2, 1899 in Dover, Ohio
d. August 09, 1980 in New York, New York

Nelle Nugent
American producer
• Partner, Elizabeth McCann; stage productions include *The Dresser; Mass Appeal*; won five Tonys.
b. March 24, 1939 in Jersey City, New Jersey

Trevor Robert Nunn
English director
• Master of London stage, Broadway; noted for running four hits at one time; won three Tonys.
b. January 14, 1940 in Ipswich, England

Rudolf Hametovich Nureyev
Russian dancer
• Defected from Soviet Union, 1961; partnered with Margot Fonteyn, 1962-79.
b. March 17, 1938 in Irkutsk, U.S.S.R.

France Nuyen
(France Nguyen Vannga)
American actress
• Starred on stage in *The World of Suzie Wong*, 1958; films include *South Pacific*, 1958; starred on TV's "St. Elsewhere," 1985-88.
b. July 31, 1939 in Marseilles, France

Sven Vilhem Nykvist
Swedish filmmaker
• Best known as Ingmar Bergman's cameraman, 1960s; won Oscars for *Cries and Whispers*, 1973; *Fanny and Alexander*, 1983.
b. December 03, 1922 in Moheda, Sweden

Jack Oakie
American actor
• Known for comic roles in over 100 films, 1930s-40s; Oscar nominee for *The Great Dictator*, 1940.
b. November 12, 1903 in Sedalia, Missouri
d. February 23, 1978 in Los Angeles, California

Warren Oates
American actor
• Starred in *In the Heat of the Night*, 1967; *Stripes*, 1981.
b. July 05, 1928 in Depoy, Kentucky
d. April 03, 1982 in Hollywood Hills, California

Merle Oberon
(Estelle Merle O'Brien Thompson)
American actress
• Films include *Divorce of Lady X; Wuthering Heights*, 1930s-40s.
b. February 19, 1911 in Bombay, India
d. November 23, 1979 in Los Angeles, California

Edmond O'Brien
American actor
• Won Oscar for *The Barefoot Contessa*, 1954.
b. September 1, 1915 in New York, New York
d. May 08, 1985 in Inglewood, California

George O'Brien
American actor
• Starred in *The Iron Horse*, 1924; Western hero in 1930s films.
b. April 19, 1900 in San Francisco, California
d. September 04, 1985 in Broken Arrow, Oklahoma

Pat (William Joseph Patrick) O'Brien
American actor
● Starred in *Knute Rockne-All American,* 1940; won two Emmys for "The Other Woman," 1974; often portrayed priests, Irish cops.
b. November 11, 1899 in Milwaukee, Wisconsin
d. October 15, 1983 in Santa Monica, California

Arthur O'Connell
American actor
● Oscar nominee for *Picnic; Anatomy of a Murder.*
b. March 29, 1908 in New York, New York
d. May 19, 1981 in Los Angeles, California

Carroll O'Connor
American actor
● Played Archie Bunker in "All in the Family"; earned more awards than any actor for a single characterization.
b. August 02, 1924 in New York, New York

Una O'Connor
(Agnes Teresa McGlade)
Irish actress
● Horror films include *The Bride of Frankenstein; The Invisible Man.*
b. October 23, 1881 in Belfast, Northern Ireland
d. February 04, 1959 in New York, New York

Clifford Odets
American dramatist
● Wrote *The Country Girl,* 1950; best known for plays of social protest.
b. July 18, 1906 in Philadelphia, Pennsylvania
d. August 14, 1963 in Los Angeles, California

Ian Ogilvy
English actor
● Played in PBS TV series "Upstairs, Downstairs"; "Return of the Saint."
b. September 3, 1943 in Woking, England

Maureen O'Hara
(Maureen Fitzsimmons)
American actress
● Star of films, 1939-71: *How Green Was My Valley,* 1941; *Miracle on 34th Street,* 1947.
b. August 17, 1921 in Milltown, Ireland

Dan (Daniel Peter) O'Herlihy
Irish actor
● Oscar nominee for *The Adventures of Robinson Crusoe,* 1952; *The Dead,* 1987.
b. May 01, 1919 in Wexford, Ireland

Tom O'Horgan
American director
● Won Obie Award for *Futz,* 1967; Tony nominee for *Hair,* 1968.
b. May 03, 1926 in Chicago, Illinois

Walter O'Keefe
American author-actor
● Host of 1940s radio quiz show "Double or Nothing"; popularized song "The Man on the Flying Trapeze," 1930s.
b. August 18, 1900 in Hartford, Connecticut
d. June 26, 1983 in Torrance, California

John O'Keeffe
Irish dramatist
● Comedies, farces include *Wild Oats,* 1791.
b. June 24, 1747 in Dublin, Ireland
d. February 04, 1833 in Southampton, England

Warner Oland
Swedish actor
● Played Charlie Chan in films, 1931-38.
b. October 03, 1880 in Umea, Sweden
d. August 05, 1938 in Stockholm, Sweden

Ken Olin
American actor
● Plays Michael Steadman on TV series "Thirtysomething," 1987–.
b. July 3, 1954 in Chicago, Illinois

Edna May Oliver
(Edna May Cox Nutter)
American actress
● Films include *Little Women,* 1933; *David Copperfield,* 1935.
b. November 09, 1883 in Malden, Massachusetts
d. November 09, 1942 in Hollywood, California

Sir Laurence Kerr Olivier Olivier
(Baron Olivier of Brighton; "Sir Larry")
English actor-producer-director
● The English-speaking world's most revered actor; won Oscar for *Hamlet,* 1948; once wed to Vivien Leigh.
b. May 22, 1907 in Dorking, England
d. July 11, 1989 in Amhurst, England

Ole Olsen
(Olsen and Johnson)
American comedian
● Starred in over 1,400 performances of *Hellzapoppin,* 1938-41.
b. November 06, 1892 in Peru, Indiana
d. January 26, 1963 in Albuquerque, New Mexico

Johnny Olson
American TV personality
● TV announcer whose cry "Come on down!" was trademark of game show "The Price Is Right."
b. 1910
d. October 12, 1985 in Santa Monica, California

Patrick O'Neal
American actor
● TV shows include "Emerald Point," 1983; films include *The Way We Were,* 1973.
b. September 26, 1927 in Ocala, Florida

Ryan (Patrick Ryan) O'Neal
American actor
● Starred in film *Love Story,* 1970; TV series "Peyton Place," 1960s.
b. April 2, 1941 in Los Angeles, California

Tatum O'Neal
(Mrs John McEnroe)
American actress
● Youngest Oscar winner in history for *Paper Moon,* 1973; daughter of Ryan.
b. November 05, 1963 in Los Angeles, California

Eugene Gladstone O'Neill
American dramatist
● Considered America's finest playwright; won Pulitzer's for many works, including *The Iceman Cometh,* 1946; awarded 1936 Nobel Prize.
b. October 16, 1888 in New York, New York
d. November 27, 1953 in Boston, Massachusetts

James O'Neill
American actor
● Best known for 1913 film *The Count of Monte Cristo;* made int'l. tour in stage version; father of playwright Eugene.
b. October 14, 1847 in County Kilkenny, Ireland
d. August 1, 1920 in New London, Connecticut

Jennifer O'Neill
(Mrs James Lederer)
American actress-model
● Starred in *The Summer of '42,* 1971.
b. February 2, 1949 in Rio de Janeiro, Brazil

Marcel Ophuls
American director
● Son of Max Ophuls; made controversial documentary *The Sorrow and the Pity* about France under German occupation.
b. November 01, 1927 in Frankfurt, Germany

Max Ophuls
(Max Oppenheimer)
French director
● Known for fluid motion camera technique: *Caught; Reckless Movement.*
b. May 06, 1902 in Saarbrucken, Germany
d. March 26, 1957 in Hamburg, Germany (West)

Jerry Orbach
American actor
• Leading man in films since 1961, including *Prince of the City*, 1981; won Tony for *Promises, Promises*, 1969.
b. October 2, 1935 in New York, New York

Santos Ortega
American actor
• Played in TV soap opera "As the World Turns," 1956-76.
b. 1899 in New York, New York
d. April 1, 1976 in Fort Lauderdale, Florida

Joe (John Kingsley) Orton
English dramatist
• Writings include *Mr. Sloane*, 1964; *What the Butler Saw*, 1969.
b. 1933 in Leicester, England
d. August 09, 1967 in London, England

Paul Osborn
American dramatist–screenwriter
• Won Tony for *Morning's at Seven*, 1980; films include *The Yearling*, 1947; *South Pacific*, 1958.
b. September 04, 1901 in Evansville, Indiana
d. May 12, 1988 in New York, New York

John James Osborne
English dramatist–author
• Won 1963 Tony for *Luther*; Oscar for *Tom Jones*, 1978.
b. December 12, 1929 in London, England

Michael O'Shea
American actor
• TV shows include "It's a Great Life," 1954-56; films include *Jack London*, 1943; *Last of the Redmen*, 1947.
b. March 17, 1906 in Hartford, Connecticut
d. December 1973 in Dallas, Texas

Milo O'Shea
Irish actor
• Nominated for Tony, 1982, for *Mass Appeal*.
b. June 02, 1926 in Dublin, Ireland

Tessie O'Shea
English comedienne–singer
• Character actress since 1950s; films include *Bedknobs and Broomsticks*, 1971.
b. March 13, 1918 in Cardiff, Wales

Ken Osmond
American actor
• Played Eddie Haskell on "Leave It to Beaver," 1957-63.
b. June 07, 1943 in Los Angeles, California

Maureen O'Sullivan
American actress
• Played Jane in Johnny Weissmuller's Tarzan films; appeared in *Hannah and Her Sisters*, 1986; mother of Mia Farrow.
b. May 17, 1911 in Boyle, Ireland

Peter Seamus O'Toole
Irish actor
• Won international fame for portrayal of T E Lawrence in award-winning film *Lawrence of Arabia*, 1962.
b. August 02, 1932 in County Galway, Ireland

Our Gang
("The Little Rascals"); Matthew Beard (Stymie); Tommy Bond (Butch"); Norman Chaney ("Chubby"); Joe Cobb ("Fat Joe")
Americans child actors
• Highly popular children's film comedy group, 1930s-40s; syndicated TV reruns continue today.

Maria Ouspenskaya
Russian actress
• Oscar nominee for *Dodsworth*, 1936; *Love Affair*, 1939.
b. July 29, 1876 in Tula, Russia
d. December 03, 1949 in Los Angeles, California

(John) Reginald Owen
English actor
• Only actor to play both Dr. Watson in *Sherlock Holmes*, 1932, Sherlock Holmes in *A Study in Scarlet*, 1933.
b. August 05, 1887 in Wheathampstead, England
d. November 05, 1972 in Boise, Idaho

Gary Owens
American actor
• Featured in TV series "Laugh-In," 1968-73.
b. May 1, 1935 in Mitchell, South Dakota

Rochelle Owens
(Rochelle Bass)
American dramatist–poet
• Writings include *The String Game*, 1965; *He Wants Shih*, 1972; won Obie for *Futz*, 1968.
b. April 02, 1936 in Brooklyn, New York

Frank Oz
(Frank Richard Oznowicz)
American puppeteer
• Performs voices of many of Muppet, Sesame Street characters; won three Emmys.
b. May 24, 1944 in Hereford, England

Paulina Porizkova
(Mrs Ric Ocasek)
Czech actress–model
• Cover model known for swimsuit issues of *Sports Illustrated* magazine; starred with Tom Selleck in film *Her Alibi*, 1989.
b. April 09, 1965 in Czechoslovakia

Jack Paar
American entertainer
• Pioneer talk show host; star of "Tonight Show," 1957-62; "Jack Paar Show," 1962-65, 1973.
b. May 01, 1918 in Canton, Ohio

Georg Wilhelm Pabst
Austrian director
• Used pessimistic realism in his films *Pandora's Box; Diary of a Lost Girl.*
b. August 27, 1885 in Raudnitz, Bohemia
d. May 29, 1967 in Vienna, Austria

Al(fredo James) Pacino
American actor
• Starred in *The Godfather*, 1972; *Serpico*, 1974; *Cruising*, 1980; won two Tonys.
b. April 25, 1940 in East Harlem, New York

Geraldine Page
American actress
• Stage actress best known for playing Tennessee Williams' heroines; won Oscar, 1986, for *A Trip to Bountiful*.
b. November 22, 1924 in Kirksville, Missouri
d. June 13, 1987 in New York, New York

Nicola Pagett
(Nicola Scott)
English actress
• Played in TV shows "Upstairs, Downstairs"; "Ana Karenina."
b. June 15, 1945 in Cairo, Egypt

Marcel Paul Pagnol
French dramatist–producer
• Wrote Marseilles trilogy: *Marius*, 1929; *Fanny*, 1931; *Cesar*, 1936.
b. April 18, 1895 in Aubagne, France
d. April 18, 1974 in Paris, France

Janis Paige
(Donna Mae Jaden)
American singer–actress
• Stage, film musical comedy star, 1940s-60s; trained as opera singer.
b. September 16, 1923 in Tacoma, Washington

Alan Jay Pakula
American director
• Films include *Klute*, 1971; *All the President's Men*, 1976; *Sophie's Choice*, 1982.
b. April 07, 1928 in New York, New York

George Pal
American producer–director
• Won Oscars for special effects for *When Worlds Collide*, 1951; *War of the Worlds*, 1952; *The Time Machine*, 1960.
b. February 01, 1908 in Cegled, Hungary
d. May 02, 1980 in Beverly Hills, California

Jack Palance
(Walter Jack Palahnuik)
American actor
• Oscar nominee for *Sudden Fear*, 1952; *Shane*, 1953; hosts TV show "Ripley's Believe It Or Not," 1983–.
b. February 18, 1920 in Lattimore Mines, Pennsylvania

William Samuel Paley
American radio executive–TV executive
• Bought United Independent Broadcasting Co., 1928, which later became CBS.
b. September 28, 1901 in Chicago, Illinois
d. October 26, 1990 in Manhattan, New York

Ron Palillo
American actor
• Played a Sweathog on "Welcome Back, Kotter," 1975-79.
b. April 02, 1954 in New Haven, Connecticut

Eugene Pallette
American actor
• Popular, 1913-46; films include *Topper*, 1937; *My Man Godfrey*, 1936.
b. July 08, 1889 in Winfield, Kansas
d. September 03, 1943 in Los Angeles, California

Michael Palin
(Monty Python's Flying Circus)
British actor–author
• Zany films include *The Missionary*, 1982; *The Meaning of Life*, 1983.
b. May 05, 1943 in Sheffield, England

Betsy Palmer
(Patricia Hrunek)
American actress
• Panelist on "I've Got a Secret," 1957-67.
b. November 01, 1926 in East Chicago, Indiana

Lilli Palmer
(Mrs Carlos Thompson; Lilli Marie Peiser)
German actress–author
• Married to Rex Harrison, 1943-57; films include *Body and Soul*, 1948; *The Boys from Brazil*, 1978.
b. May 24, 1914 in Posen, Germany
d. January 27, 1986 in Los Angeles, California

Peter Palmer
American actor–singer
• Played title role in film *Lil' Abner*, 1959.
b. September 2, 1931 in Milwaukee, Wisconsin

Bruce Paltrow
American director–producer
• Exec. producer-director of TV series "St. Elsewhere," 1982-88.
b. November 26, 1943 in New York, New York

Norman Panama
American screenwriter
• Films include *My Favorite Blonde*, 1942; *White Christmas*, 1954.
b. April 21, 1914 in Chicago, Illinois

Franklin Pangborn
American actor
• Known for roles in over 150 films as prissy hotel manager, bank clerk, including *A Star Is Born*, 1937.
b. January 23, 1893 in Newark, New Jersey
d. July 2, 1958 in Santa Monica, California

Valery Panov
Israeli dancer
• Principal dancer, Maly Theatre of Opera and Ballet, 1957-63; wrote *To Dance*, 1978.
b. March 12, 1938 in Vilno, U.S.S.R.

Irene Papas
Greek actress
• Films include *Zorba the Greek*, 1964; *The Trojan Women*, 1971.
b. September 03, 1926 in Chiliomondion, Greece

Joseph Papp
(Joseph Papirofsky)
American director–producer
• Founded NY Shakespeare Festival; won six Tonys, six Obies.
b. June 22, 1921 in Brooklyn, New York

Jerry Paris
American actor–director
• Directed, played the neighbor in "The Dick Van Dyke Show," 1961-66.
b. July 25, 1925 in San Francisco, California
d. April 02, 1986 in Los Angeles, California

Alan William Parker
English director
• Films include *Midnight Express*, 1978; *Fame*, 1980.
b. February 14, 1944 in London, England

Eleanor Parker
American actress
• Films include *Return to Peyton Place*, 1961; *The Sound of Music*, 1965.
b. June 26, 1922 in Cedarville, Ohio

Fess Parker
American actor
• Played Davy Crockett and Daniel Boone in movies, on TV.
b. August 16, 1927 in Fort Worth, Texas

Jameson Parker
American actor
• Plays A J Simon on TV series "Simon & Simon," 1982–.
b. November 18, 1950 in Baltimore, Maryland

Jean Parker
(Mae Green; Luise Stephanie Zelinska)
American actress
• Played hard-boiled characters in 1940s films including *Little Women*, 1949.
b. August 11, 1912 in Butte, Montana

Barbara Parkins
Canadian actress
• Starred in *Valley of the Dolls*, 1961; TV series "Peyton Place," 1963-67.
b. May 22, 1942 in Vancouver, British Columbia

Bert Parks
(Bert Jacobson)
American actor
• Hosted Miss America Pageant, 1954-79.
b. December 3, 1914 in Atlanta, Georgia

Gordon Alexander Buchanan Parks
American director
• Photographer for *Life* mag., 1948-72; directed film *Shaft*, 1972; won Spingarn, 1972.
b. October 3, 1912 in Fort Scott, Kansas

Larry Parks
(Samuel Klausman)
American actor
• Played Al Jolson in *The Jolson Story*, 1946; *Jolson Sings Again*, 1949; victim of 1950s Communist witch-hunts.
b. December 03, 1914 in Olathe, Kansas
d. April 13, 1975 in Studio City, California

Gabriel Pascal
Hungarian producer
• Persuaded GB Shaw to sell film rights to his plays; productions include *Pygmalion*, 1938; *Major Barbara*, 1941; *Caesar and Cleopatra*, 1945.
b. June 04, 1894 in Hungary
d. July 06, 1954 in New York, New York

Pier Paolo Pasolini
Italian director
• Clashed frequently with authorities over contents of films because of sex, violence including *Canterbury Tale*, 1944.
b. March 05, 1922 in Bologna, Italy
d. November 02, 1975 in Ostia, Italy

Joe (Joseph Vincent) Pasternak
American producer
• Saved Universal from bankruptcy by producing successful Deanna Durbin musicals.
b. September 19, 1901 in Silagy, Romania

Tony (Antonio) Pastor
American actor–manager
• Pioneer developer of vaudeville; managed Fourteenth Street Theatre, 1881-1908.
b. May 28, 1837 in New York, New York
d. August 26, 1908 in Elmhurst, New York

Charles Pathe
French filmmaker
• Introduced the newsreel, 1909 in France, 1910 in US.
b. December 25, 1863 in Chevry Cossigny, France
d. December 25, 1957 in Monte Carlo, Monaco

Mandy (Mandel) Patinkin
American actor
• Won Tony for *Evita*, 1980; films include *Ragtime*, 1981; *Yentl*, 1983.
b. November 3, 1952 in Chicago, Illinois

Gail Patrick
(Margaret Fitzpatrick)
American producer–actress
• Exec. producer of "Perry Mason" TV series, 1957-66.
b. June 2, 1911 in Birmingham, Alabama
d. July 06, 1980 in Hollywood, California

John Patrick, pseud
(John Patrick Goggan)
American dramatist
• Plays include *The Hasty Heart*, 1945; Pulitzer-winner *Teahouse of the August Moon*, 1954.
b. May 17, 1905 in Louisville, Kentucky

Lorna Patterson
American actress
• Star of TV series "Private Benjamin"; films include *Airplane!* 1980.
b. July 01, 1957 in Whittier, California

Tom (Harry Thomas) Patterson
Canadian producer
• Founded Stratford Shakespearean Festival, Stratford, ON, 1952.
b. June 11, 1920 in Stratford, Ontario

Jane (Margaret Jane) Pauley
(Mrs Garry Trudeau)
American broadcast journalist
• Succeeded Barbara Walters on "The Today Show," 1976-90; resigned to pursue other TV endeavors; replaced on "Today" by Deborah Norville.
b. October 31, 1950 in Indianapolis, Indiana

Pat Paulsen
American comedian
• Regular on "The Smothers Brothers Show," 1966-68; ran for pres., 1968.
b. July 06, 1927 in South Bend, Washington

Marisa Pavan
(Marisa Pierangeli)
Italian actress
• Oscar nominee for her role in *Rose Tattoo*, 1955.
b. June 19, 1932 in Cagliari, Sardinia

Anna Pavlova
Russian dancer
• Most celebrated dancer of her time who performed in Paris, New York.
b. January 31, 1885 in Saint Petersburg, Russia
d. January 23, 1931 in Netherlands

Katina Paxinou
Greek actress
• Won Oscar for her role in *For Whom the Bell Tolls*, 1943.
b. December 17, 1900 in Piraeus, Greece
d. February 22, 1973 in Athens, Greece

John Payne
American actor
• Leading man in 1940s-50s films; portrayed Kris Kringle's lawyer in Christmas classic *Miracle on 34th Street*, 1947.
b. May 23, 1912 in Roanoke, Virginia
d. December 05, 1989 in Malibu, California

John Howard Payne
American actor–dramatist
• Wrote, adapted at least 60 plays; wrote lyrics for "Home Sweet Home," 1823.
b. June 09, 1791 in New York, New York
d. April 09, 1852 in Tunis, Tunisia

Pamela Payton-Wright
American actress
• Won Obies for *Effect of Gamma Rays on Man-in-the-Moon Marigolds*; *Jessie and the Bandit Queen*, 1976.
b. November 01, 1941 in Pittsburgh, Pennsylvania

Josephine Preston Peabody
American poet–dramatist
• Wrote plays *The Piper*, 1910; *Marlowe*, 1901.
b. May 3, 1874 in Brooklyn, New York
d. December 04, 1922

Jack Pearl
American radio performer
• Popularized expression "Vas you dere, Sharlie?" on radio program, 1932-47.
b. October 29, 1895 in New York, New York
d. December 25, 1982 in New York, New York

Minnie Pearl
(Sarah Ophelia Colley Cannon)
American comedienne
• Trademark is straw hat with price tag hanging on it; appeared on TV's "Hee Haw"; Country Hall of Fame, 1975.
b. October 25, 1912 in Centerville, Tennessee

Harold Peary
American actor
• Played the Great Gildersleeve in movies, radio for 16 years.
b. 1908
d. March 3, 1985 in Torrance, California

Gregory Peck
(Eldred Gregory Peck)
American actor
• Won Oscar, 1962, for *To Kill a Mockingbird*; other films include *The Omen*, 1976; *Gentleman's Agreement*, 1947.
b. April 05, 1916 in La Jolla, California

Sam (David Samuel) Peckinpah
American director
• Best known for glorifying anti-hero in violent Westerns: *The Wild Bunch*, 1969.
b. February 21, 1925 in Fresno, California
d. December 28, 1984 in Inglewood, California

Elizabeth Pena
American actress
• Films include *La Bamba*, 1986; star of "I Married Dora," 1987.
b. September 23, in Elizabeth, New Jersey

Austin Pendleton
American actor–director
• Won Obie, Drama Desk Award for *The Last Sweet Days of Isaac*, 1970.
b. March 27, 1940 in Warren, Ohio

Arthur Hiller Penn
American director
• Films include *The Miracle Worker*, 1962; *Bonnie and Clyde*, 1967.
b. September 27, 1922 in Philadelphia, Pennsylvania

Sean Penn
American actor
• In movies *Fast Times at Ridgemont High*, 1982; *Shanghai Surprise*, 1986; known for temper, trouble with media.
b. August 17, 1960 in Santa Monica, California

Joe Penner
(Joseph Pinter)
American comedian
• Famous for phrase "Wanna buy a duck?"; in films, 1934-40.
b. November 11, 1904 in Budapest, Hungary
d. January 1, 1941 in Philadelphia, Pennsylvania

George Peppard
American actor
• Star of TV shows "Banacek," 1972-74; "The A-Team," 1983–; films include *Breakfast at Tiffany's*, 1961.
b. October 01, 1928 in Detroit, Michigan

Anthony Perkins
American actor
• Best known for role of Norman Bates in *Psycho* films, 1960, 1983, 1986; son of Osgood.
b. April 14, 1932 in New York, New York

Marlin (Richard Marlin) Perkins
American TV personality–adventurer
• Pioneer in filming wild animals in natural surroundings; host, "Wild Kingdom," 1963-85.
b. March 28, 1902 in Carthage, Missouri
d. June 14, 1986 in Saint Louis, Missouri

Millie Perkins
American actress
• Films include title role in *Diary of Anne Frank*, 1959.
b. May 12, 1940 in Passaic, New Jersey

Osgood (James Ridley Osgood) Perkins
American actor
• Films include *Scarface*, 1932; *The Front Page*, 1931; father of Anthony.
b. May 16, 1892 in West Newton, Massachusetts
d. September 23, 1937 in Washington, District of Columbia

Rhea Perlman
(Mrs Danny DeVito)
American actress
• Plays Carla Tortelli on TV comedy "Cheers," 1982–; won Emmys, 1984, 1985, 1986.
b. March 31, 1948 in Brooklyn, New York

Ron Perlman
American actor
• Played Vincent on TV series "Beauty and the Beast," 1987-89.
b. April 13, 1950 in New York, New York

Gene Perret
American writer
• TV scriptwriter; won Emmys for "Carol Burnett Show," 1974, 1975, 1978.
b. April 03, 1937 in Philadelphia, Pennsylvania

Valerie Perrine
American actress
• Films include *Lenny*, 1974; *Superman II*, 1981.
b. September 03, 1943 in Galveston, Texas

Antoinette Perry
American actress–director
• Tony Award is named for her; prominent in American Theater Wing, other welfare groups.
b. June 27, 1888 in Denver, Colorado
d. June 28, 1946 in New York, New York

Eleanor Bayer Perry
(Oliver Weld Bayer pseud)
American screenwriter–author
• Oscar nominee for *David and Lisa*, 1962; other films include *The Man Who Loved Cat Dancing*, 1973.
b. 1915 in Cleveland, Ohio
d. March 14, 1981 in New York, New York

Jill Perryman
Australian actress
• Award-winning stage performances include *No, No, Nanette*, 1972; *Palace of Dreams*, 1980.
b. May 3, 1933 in Melbourne, Australia

Nehemiah Persoff
American actor
• Films include *On the Waterfront*, 1954; *Some Like It Hot*, 1959; *Yentyl*, 1983.
b. August 14, 1920 in Jerusalem, Palestine

Donna Pescow
American actress
• Star of TV series "Angie"; in film *Saturday Night Fever*, 1977.
b. March 24, 1954 in New York, New York

Bernadette Peters
(Bernadette Lazzara)
American actress–singer
• Won Tony for *Song and Dance*, 1986; films include *The Jerk*, 1979; *Pennies from Heaven*, 1981.
b. February 28, 1948 in Queens, New York

Brandon Peters
American actor
• Stage actor, 1924-56; appearances include *Life With Father; Love on the Dole*.
b. 1893 in Troy, New York
d. February 27, 1956 in New York, New York

Brock Peters
(Brock Fisher)
American actor–singer
• Award-winning star of stage, screen; films include *To Kill a Mockingbird*, 1962.
b. July 27, 1927 in New York, New York

Jean Peters
American actress
• Screen debut, 1947, with Tyrone Power in *Captain from Castile*; married to Howard Hughes, 1957-71.
b. October 15, 1926 in Canton, Ohio

Jon Peters
American producer–business executive
• Produced films *A Star Is Born*, 1976; *The Color Purple*, 1985; turned his hair-styling business into major production co.
b. 1945 in Van Nuys, California

Susan Peters
(Suzanne Carnahan)
American actress
• Oscar nominee for *Random Harvest*, 1942; paralyzed in accident, 1944.
b. July 03, 1921 in Spokane, Washington
d. October 23, 1952 in Visalia, California

Wolfgang Petersen
German director
• Nominated for best director Oscar for *Das Boot* (The Boat), 1983.
b. March 14, 1941 in Emden, Germany

Paul Peterson
American actor–singer
• Played Jeff on TV series "The Donna Reed Show," 1958-66; brief recording career included song "My Dad," 1962.
b. September 23, 1945 in Glendale, California

Marius Petipa
French dancer–choreographer
• Developed classical ballet in Russia; founded Bolshoi and Kirov ballets.
b. March 11, 1822 in Marseilles, France
d. June 02, 1910 in Gurzuf, Russia

Roland Petit
French dancer–choreographer
• Founded Les Ballets de Paris, 1948; noted for *An American in Paris*, 1944.
b. January 13, 1924 in Villemomble, France

William Thomas Pettit
American journalist
• Reporter with NBC News since 1968; chief national affairs correspondent, 1985–; has won three Emmys.
b. April 23, 1931 in Cincinnati, Ohio

Michelle Pfeiffer
American actress
• Sultry actress; starred in films *The Fabulous Baker Boys*, 1989, *Dangerous Liaisons*, 1989, *Married to the Mob*, 1988.
b. 1957 in Santa Ana, California

Gerard Philipe
French actor–director
• France's leading romantic star of postwar years; starred in *Devil in the Flesh*, 1947.
b. December 04, 1922 in Cannes, France
d. November 27, 1959 in Paris, France

Irna Phillips
American writer
• Scriptwriter for TV's longest-running soap opera, "Guiding Light," 1938-73.
b. July 01, 1901 in Germany
d. December 22, 1973 in Chicago, Illinois

Lou Diamond Phillips
(Lou Upchurch)
American actor
• Starred in films *La Bamba*, 1987, *Young Guns*, 1988.
b. February 17, 1962 in Philippines

MacKenzie (Laura MacKenzie) Phillips
American actress
• Daughter of John Phillips; starred in TV series "One Day at a Time," 1975-80, 1981-83.
b. November 1, 1959 in Alexandria, Virginia

River Phoenix
American actor
• Appeared in films *Stand By Me*, 1986, *I Love You to Death*, 1990; received Oscar nomination, 1988, for *Running on Empty*.
b. August 23, 1970 in Madras, Oregon

Slim Pickens
(Louis Bert Lindley Jr)
American actor
• Best known for role in *Dr. Strangelove*, 1964; Cowboy Hall of Fame, 1984.
b. June 29, 1919 in Kingsberg, California
d. December 08, 1983 in Modesto, California

Jack Pickford
(Jack Smith)
Canadian actor
• Child star, romantic lead, 1910-28; Mary Pickford's brother.
b. August 18, 1896 in Toronto, Ontario
d. January 03, 1933 in Paris, France

Mary Pickford
(Gladys Mary Smith; "America's Sweetheart")
Canadian actress
• Won Oscar, 1929, for *Coquette*; married to Douglas Fairbanks, Sr. and Buddy Rogers.
b. April 08, 1894 in Toronto, Ontario
d. May 29, 1979 in Santa Monica, California

Molly Picon
American actress
• Starred in Yiddish theater, 1923; films include *Fiddler on the Roof*, 1971; *Come Blow Your Horn*, 1963.
b. February 28, 1898 in New York, New York

Walter Pidgeon
American actor
• Films from, 1925-77 include *Mrs. Miniver; Madame Curie*.
b. September 23, 1898 in Saint John, New Brunswick
d. September 25, 1984 in Santa Monica, California

Frank R(omer) Pierson
American screenwriter
• Won Oscar for *Dog Day Afternoon*, 1975.
b. May 12, 1925 in Chappaqua, New York

Bronson Alcott Pinchot
American actor
• Films include *Beverly Hills Cop*, 1984; star of TV comedy "Perfect Strangers," 1985–.
b. May 2, 1959 in New York, New York

Miguel Pinero
Puerto Rican dramatist–actor
• While in prison for armed robbery, wrote award-winning play *Short Eyes*, 1974.
b. December 19, 1946 in Gurabo, Puerto Rico
d. June 16, 1988 in New York, New York

Gordon Edward Pinsent
Canadian actor–writer
• Wrote, starred in film *The Rowdyman*, 1969.
b. July 12, 1930 in Grand Falls, Newfoundland

Harold Pinter
English dramatist
• Wrote *The Dumb Waiter*, 1957; screenplay *The French Lieutenant's Woman*, 1981.
b. October 1, 1930 in London, England

Luigi Pirandello
Italian author–dramatist
• Awarded Nobel Prize in literature, 1934; created "theater within the theater."
b. June 28, 1867 in Agriegento, Sicily
d. December 1, 1936 in Rome, Italy

Joe (Joseph Charles) Piscopo
American comedian
• Repertory player, "Saturday Night Live," 1980-84; in film *Johnny Dangerously*, 1984.
b. June 17, 1951 in Passaic, New Jersey

Marie-France Pisier
French actress
• Films include *Other Side of Midnight*, 1977; *Cousin Cousine*, 1976.
b. May 1946 in Da Lat, Vietnam

Noam Pitlik
American director
• Won Emmy, 1979, for directing "Barney Miller."
b. November 04, 1932 in Philadelphia, Pennsylvania

Robert W(arren) Pittman
American TV executive
• Responsible for planning, developing MTV, cable music network.
b. December 28, 1953 in Jackson, Mississippi

Zasu (Eliza Susan) Pitts
American actress
• Comedienne in over 100 films, 1917-63, including *Life With Father*, 1947.
b. January 03, 1900 in Parsons, Kansas
d. June 07, 1963 in Hollywood, California

Mary Kay Place
American actress
• Starred in *The Big Chill*, 1983; won Emmy for "Mary Hartman, Mary Hartman," 1977.
b. September 23, 1947 in Tulsa, Oklahoma

Donald Pleasence
English actor
• Made stage debut, 1939; appeared in *Oh God*, 1977; *Halloween*, 1978.
b. October 05, 1919 in Worksop, England

John Pleshette
American actor
• Played Richard Avery in TV series "Knots Landing," 1979-83.

Suzanne Pleshette
(Mrs Thomas Gallagher III)
American actress
• Played Emily Hartley on TV series "The Bob Newhart Show," 1972-78.
b. January 31, 1937 in New York, New York

Maya Mikhailovna Plisetskaya
Russian dancer
• Prima ballerina with Bolshoi Ballet, 1960s; leading roles include *Swan Lake*, *Sleeping Beauty*, *Don Quixote*.
b. November 2, 1925 in Moscow, U.S.S.R.

Roy Plomley
English dramatist–radio performer
• Creator, host of world's longest-running radio show "Desert Island Discs," 1942-85.
b. January 2, 1914 in Kingston-upon-Thames, England
d. May 29, 1985 in London, England

Joan Anne Plowright
(Mrs Laurence Olivier)
English actress
• Won NY Drama Critics Award for *A Taste of Honey*, 1961.
b. October 28, 1929 in Scunthorpe, England

Amanda Plummer
American actress
• Daughter of Tammy Grimes and Christopher Plummer; won Tony, 1982, for *Agnes of God*.
b. March 23, 1957 in New York

Christopher (Arthur Christopher) Plummer
Canadian actor
• Played Baron von Trapp in *The Sound of Music*, 1965; noted Shakespearian actor; won Tony, 1974.
b. December 13, 1929 in Toronto, Ontario

Rossana Podesta
Italian actress
• Films include *Helen of Troy*, 1956.
b. June 2, 1934 in Tripoli, Libya

James Poe
American screenwriter
• Won Oscar for *Around the World in Eighty Days*, 1957.
b. October 04, 1921 in Dobbs Ferry, New York
d. January 24, 1980 in Malibu, California

Sidney Poitier
American actor–director
• First black man to win Oscar for best actor: *Lilies of the Field*, 1963; other films include *Shoot to Kill*, 1988.
b. February 2, 1924 in Miami, Florida

Roman Polanski
Polish director
• Received critical acclaim for *Rosemary's Baby*, 1968; *Chinatown*, 1974.
b. August 18, 1933 in Paris, France

Sydney Pollack
American director
• Films include *They Shoot Horses, Don't They?*, 1969; *Absence of Malice*, 1981; won Emmy for "The Game," 1966; won Best Director Oscar for *Out of Africa*, 1985.
b. July 01, 1934 in South Bend, Indiana

Michael J Pollard
American actor
• Oscar nominee for *Bonnie and Clyde*, 1967; other films include *Melvin and Howard*, 1980.
b. May 3, 1939 in Passaic, New Jersey

Channing Pollock
American author–dramatist
• Wrote over 30 plays including *Harvest of My Years*, 1943; wrote song made famous by Frannie Brice, "My Man," 1920.
b. March 04, 1880 in Washington, District of Columbia
d. August 17, 1946 in New York, New York

Carlo Ponti
Italian producer
• Credited with discovering Sophia Loren, whom he later married; won Oscar for *La Strada*, 1956.
b. December 11, 1913 in Milan, Italy

Oleg Konstantinovich Popov
Russian clown
• Russia's "Chaplin"; much-loved entertainer with Moscow's State Circus, 1955–.
b. August 03, 1930 in Moscow, U.S.S.R.

Edwin Porter
American director
• Films include *Great Train Robbery; Uncle Tom's Cabin*, 1903.
b. April 21, 1870 in Connellsville, Pennsylvania
d. April 3, 1941 in New York, New York

Eric Portman
English actor
• Character actor, 1934-69; films include *Mark of Cain; Prince and the Pauper*.
b. July 13, 1903 in Halifax, England
d. December 07, 1969 in Saint Veep, England

Vladimir Posner
Russian TV personality
• Popular TV host in Soviet Union; co-hosted with Phil Donahue, 1985.
b. April 01, 1934 in Paris, France

Tom Poston
American comedian–actor
• Broadway, stage actor; played George Utley on TV comedy "Newhart," 1982-90.
b. October 17, 1927 in Columbus, Ohio

Maury Povich
American TV personality
• Hosted TVs "A Current Affair," 1986-90; married to Connie Chung.
b. 1939 in Washington, District of Columbia

Dick Powell
American actor
• Starred in 1930s musicals, 1940s thrillers; 1950's,60's TV series.
b. November 24, 1904 in Mountain View, Arkansas
d. January 02, 1963 in Hollywood, California

Eleanor Powell
American dancer–actress
• Billed as "world's greatest tap dancer" while with MGM.
b. November 21, 1912 in Springfield, Massachusetts
d. February 11, 1982 in Beverly Hills, California

Jane Powell
(Suzanne Burce)
American singer–actress
• In MGM musicals, 1940s-50s, including *Seven Brides for Seven Brothers*, 1954.
b. April 01, 1928 in Portland, Oregon

Michael Latham Powell
English director–producer
• Innovative filmmaker; films include *Life and Death of Colonel Blimp*, 1943, *The Red Shoes*, 1948, and 30 others.
b. September 3, 1905 in Canterbury, England
d. February 19, 1990 in Avening, England

Robert Powell
English actor
• Starred in TV epic "Jesus of Nazareth."
b. June 01, 1944 in Salford, England

William Powell
American actor
• Starred with Myrna Loy in six *Thin Man* films, 1934-47.
b. July 29, 1892 in Pittsburgh, Pennsylvania
d. March 05, 1984 in Palm Springs, California

Jules Power
American producer
• TV productions include ABC's "AM America," PBS's "Over Easy"; winner of Emmy, Peabody awards.
b. October 19, 1921 in Hammond, Indiana

Tyrone Power, Jr
American actor
• Handsome leading man better known for his looks than his talent.
b. May 05, 1914 in Cincinnati, Ohio
d. November 15, 1958 in Madrid, Spain

Tyrone (Frederick Tyrone Edmond) Power
American actor
• Broadway matinee idol; films, 1914-30; father of Tyrone, Jr.
b. 1869 in London, England
d. December 3, 1931 in Hollywood, California

Stefanie Powers
(Stefania Zofia Ferderkievicz)
American actress
• Played Jennifer Hart on TV series "Hart to Hart," 1979-84.
b. November 12, 1942 in Hollywood, California

Otto Ludwig Preminger
American director–producer
• Films include *Laura*, 1944; *Anatomy of a Murder*, 1959; *Exodus*, 1960.
b. December 05, 1906 in Vienna, Austria
d. April 23, 1986 in New York, New York

Paula Prentiss
(Mrs Richard Benjamin; Paula Ragusa)
American actress
• Starred in *What's New, Pussycat?*, 1965; TV series with husband, "He and She," 1967-68.
b. March 04, 1939 in San Antonio, Texas

Micheline Presle
(Micheline Chassagne)
French actress
• In films since 1938, including *Devil in the Flesh*, 1947.
b. August 22, 1922 in Paris, France

Priscilla Ann Beaulieu Presley
American celebrity relative–actress
• Married to Elvis Presley, 1967-73; played Jenna Wade on TV series "Dallas," 1983-88; wrote autobiography *Elvis and Me*, 1985, made into TV movie, 1988.
b. May 24, 1946 in Brooklyn, New York

Harve Presnell
American actor–opera singer
• Films include *Unsinkable Molly Brown*, 1964; *Paint Your Wagon*, 1969.
b. September 14, 1933 in Modesto, California

David Pressman
American actor
• Appeared on TV soap opera "One Life to Live" since 1970; won four Emmys.
b. October 1, 1913 in Tiflis, Russia

Robert Preston
(Robert Preston Meservey)
American actor
• Best known for role of Professor Harold Hill in Broadway (1,375 performances), film (1962) versions of *The Music Man*.
b. June 08, 1918 in Newton Highlands, Massachusetts
d. March 21, 1987 in Santa Barbara, California

Dennis Price
(Dennistoun Frankly John Rose-Price)
English actor
• Leading man in British films including *Kind Hearts and Coronets; Theatre of Blood*.
b. June 23, 1915 in Twyford, England
d. October 07, 1973 in Guernsey, Channel Islands

Nancy (Lillian Nancy Bache) Price
British actress–producer
• Founded People's National Theatre, 1939.
b. February 03, 1880 in Kinver, England
d. March 31, 1970 in England

Vincent Price
American actor
• Starred in horror films *House of Wax*, 1953; *Theatre of Blood*, 1973.
b. May 27, 1911 in Saint Louis, Missouri

Hal (Harold Smith) Prince
American producer–director
• Plays include *Damn Yankees, West Side Story, Fiddler on the Roof, Phantom of the Opera;* has produced more Tony Award winners than any other Broadway producer.
b. January 3, 1928 in New York, New York

William Prince
American actor
• Character actor since 1943; films include *Destination: Tokyo*, 1944; *The Soldier*, 1982.
b. January 26, 1913 in Nichols, New York

Victoria Principal
(Mrs Harry Glassman)
American actress
• Played Pamela Ewing on TV series "Dallas," 1978-87.
b. January 03, 1944 in Fukuoka, Japan

Aileen Pringle
American actress
• Silent movie leading lady known for exotic siren roles in *Three Weeks, Souls for Sale.*
b. July 23, 1895 in San Francisco, California
d. December 16, 1989 in Manhattan, New York

Freddie Prinze
American actor–comedian
• Starred in TV series *Chico and the Man*, 1974-77; suicide ruled accidental, 1983.
b. June 22, 1954 in New York, New York
d. January 28, 1977 in Los Angeles, California

Robert Joseph Prosky
American actor
• Played Sgt. Jablonski on "Hill Street Blues," 1984-87.
b. December 13, 1930 in Philadelphia, Pennsylvania

Juliet Prowse
American dancer–actress
• Had film debut in *Can-Can*, 1960; TV series "Mona McClusky," 1966.
b. September 25, 1936 in Bombay, India

Richard Franklin Lennox Thomas Pryor
American actor–comedian
• Stand-up comic; films include *Stir Crazy*, 1980; semi-autobiographical *Jo Jo Dancer*, 1986; won five Grammys for comic albums.
b. December 01, 1940 in Peoria, Illinois

Vsevolod Pudovkin
Russian director
• Pioneer of Soviet cinema; films include *Mother*, 1926; *End of St. Petersburg*, 1927.
b. February 06, 1893 in Penza, Russia
d. June 3, 1953 in Riga, U.S.S.R.

Keshia Knight Pulliam
American actress
• Plays Rudy Huxtable on TV comedy "The Cosby Show," 1984–.
b. April 09, 1979 in Newark, New Jersey

B S Pully
Comedian–Actor
• Films include *Nob Hill*, 1945; *The Bellboy*, 1960.
b. 1910
d. January 06, 1972 in Philadelphia, Pennsylvania

Sarah Purcell
(Sarah Pentecost)
American TV personality
• Co-host of TV series "Real People," 1979-84.
b. October 08, 1948 in Richmond, Indiana

Linda Purl
American actress
• Appears in TV movies, shows, including "Happy Days," 1982-83.
b. September 02, 1955 in Greenwich, Connecticut

Edna Purviance
American actress
• Starred in Chaplin films, 1915-23, including *The Tramp*, 1915; made one talking film, 1947.
b. 1894 in Reno, Nevada
d. January 13, 1958 in Woodland Hills, California

William Henry Putch
American director
• Producer, director, Totem Pole Playhouse, Fayetteville, PA, 1954-83; married to Jean Stapleton.
b. April 22, 1924 in Pittsburgh, Pennsylvania
d. November 23, 1983 in Syracuse, New York

David Terence Puttnam
British producer
• Films include Oscar-winner *Chariots of Fire*, 1981; chm. of Columbia Pictures, Aug-Nov 1987.
b. February 25, 1941 in London, England

Denver Pyle
American actor
• TV shows include "Dukes of Hazard," 1979-85.
b. May 11, 1920 in Bethune, Colorado

Joe Pyne
Entertainer
• Talk show interviewer known for aggressive style.
b. 1925 in Chester, Pennsylvania
d. March 23, 1970 in Hollywood, California

Dennis William Quaid
American actor
• Starred in film *The Right Stuff*, 1983; *Great Balls of Fire*, 1989; married to actress Meg Ryan.
b. April 09, 1954 in Houston, Texas

Randy Quaid
American actor
• Oscar nominee for *The Last Detail*, 1973; other films include *National Lampoon's Vacation*, 1983; brother of Dennis.
b. May 11, 1950 in Houston, Texas

John Mandt Qualen
Canadian actor
• Films include *Anatomy of a Murder*, 1959; *A Patch of Blue*, 1966.
b. December 08, 1899 in Vancouver, British Columbia
d. September 12, 1987 in Torrance, California

Anna Quayle
English actress
• Won Tony for *Stop the World I Want to Get Off*, 1962.
b. October 06, 1936 in Birmingham, England

Anthony (John Anthony) Quayle, Sir
English actor–director
• Versatile actor; built Stratford-upon-Avon into a center of British theater; received Oscar nomination for *Anne of a Thousand Days*, 1969.
b. September 07, 1913 in Ainsdale, England
d. October 2, 1989 in London, England

Eddie Quillan
American actor
• Appeared in over 150 films in 60-year career including *Grapes of Wrath*, 1940, *Brigadoon*, 1954.
b. March 31, 1907 in Philadelphia, Pennsylvania
d. July 19, 1990 in Burbank, California

Richard Quine
American actor–director
• Child performer in vaudeville; directed *Sex and the Single Girl*, 1964, *How to Murder Your Wife*, 1965; suicide victim.
b. November 12, 1920 in Detroit, Michigan
d. June 1, 1989 in Los Angeles, California

Kathleen Quinlan
American actress
• Films include *I Never Promised You a Rose Garden*, 1977; *The Promise*, 1979.
b. November 19, 1954 in Pasadena, California

Anthony Rudolph Oaxaca Quinn
American actor
• Won Oscars for *Viva Zapata*, 1952; *Lust for Life*, 1956.
b. April 21, 1916 in Chihuahua, Mexico

Martha Quinn
American TV personality
• Video Jockey for MTV, 1981–.
b. May 11, 1959 in Albany, New York

Jose Benjamin Quintero
Panamanian director
• Won Tony, 1973, for *A Moon for the Misbegotten*.
b. October 15, 1924 in Panama City, Panama

Jean Baptiste Racine
French dramatist
• Plays include tragedy *Andromaque*, 1667; comedy *Les Plaideurs*, 1668.
b. December 1639 in Laferte-Milon, France
d. April 26, 1699 in Paris, France

Gilda Radner
(Mrs Gene Wilder)
American actress–comedienne
• Original cast member of TV series "Saturday Night Live," 1975-80; won Emmy, 1978; autobiography *It's Always Something*, 1989, details her fight against cancer.
b. June 28, 1946 in Detroit, Michigan
d. May 2, 1989 in Los Angeles, California

Charlotte Rae
(Charlotte Rae Lubotsky)
American actress
• Starred on TV shows "Diff'rent Strokes," 1978-79; "Facts of Life," 1980-86.
b. April 22, 1926 in Milwaukee, Wisconsin

Chips Rafferty
(John Goffage)
Australian actor
• Best-known Australian films include *The Rat of Tobruk; The Overlanders; Outback*.
b. March 26, 1909 in Australia
d. May 27, 1971 in Sydney, Australia

Deborah Raffin
American actress
• Films include *Once is Not Enough*, 1975; *Touched by Love*, 1980.
b. March 13, 1953 in Los Angeles, California

George Raft
(George Ranft)
American actor
• Played gangsters in *Scarface*, 1932; *Each Dawn I Die*, 1939.
b. September 26, 1895 in New York, New York
d. November 24, 1980 in Hollywood, California

Raimu
(Jules Muraire)
French actor
• Character star of French stage, films including *Fanny*.
b. December 17, 1883 in Toulon, France
d. September 2, 1946 in Paris, France

Luise Rainer
Austrian actress
• Won Oscars for *The Great Ziegfeld*, 1936; *The Good Earth*, 1937.
b. January 12, 1912 in Vienna, Austria

Claude Rains
American actor
• Starred in *The Invisible Man*, 1933; *Casablanca*, 1942; *Notorious*, 1946.
b. November 09, 1889 in London, England
d. May 3, 1967 in Sandwich, New Hampshire

Esther Ralston
American actress
• Played heroine roles in over 150 films, 1918-40.
b. September 17, 1902 in Bar Harbor, Maine

Marjorie Rambeau
American actress
• Broadway, film star; Oscar nominee for *Promise Path*, 1940.
b. July 15, 1889 in San Francisco, California
d. July 07, 1970 in Palm Springs, California

Dame Marie Rambert
(Cyvia Rambam; Myriam Rambam)
English dancer–director
• Key figure in development of ballet in Britain; founded Ballet Rambert, 1926.
b. February 2, 1888 in Warsaw, Poland
d. June 12, 1982 in London, England

Dack Rambo
(Norman J Rambo)
American actor
• Plays Jack Ewing on TV series "Dallas."
b. November 13, 1941 in Delano, California

Charlotte Rampling
(Mrs Jean-Michel Jarre)
English actress
• Best known for role in *Georgy Girl*, 1966; other films include *DOA*, 1988; *The Verdict*, 1982.
b. February 05, 1946 in Sturmer, England

Anne Ramsey
American actress
• Had 37-year show business career, but best known for one of last roles–as mother in *Throw Momma From the Train*, 1987, for which she received Oscar nomination.
b. 1929
d. August 11, 1988 in Los Angeles, California

Sally Rand
(Helen Beck)
American dancer
• Exotic fan dance was sensation of 1933 Chicago World's Fair.
b. January 02, 1904 in Elkton, Missouri
d. August 31, 1979 in Glendora, California

Tony Randall
(Leonard Rosenberg)
American actor
• Played Felix Unger in TV comedy "The Odd Couple," 1970-75; won Emmy, 1975.
b. February 26, 1924 in Tulsa, Oklahoma

J(oseph) Arthur Rank
English film executive
• Monopolized British film industry, 1930-40s; owned over half of the studios, 1,000 theaters.
b. December 23, 1888 in Hull, England
d. March 29, 1972 in Sutton Scotney, England

Martin Ransohoff
American producer
• Films include *Cincinnati Kid*, 1965; *Catch 22*, 1970; *Class*, 1983.
b. 1927 in New Orleans, Louisiana

Frederic Michael Raphael
English screenwriter
• Won Oscar for *Darling*, 1965.
b. August 14, 1931 in Chicago, Illinois

Samson Raphaelson
American author–screenwriter
• Wrote play *The Jazz Singer*, 1925.
b. March 3, 1896 in New York, New York
d. July 16, 1983 in New York, New York

Joseph Raposo
American composer–puppeteer
• Co-creator of TVs "Sesame Street" with Jim Henson; wrote song "It's Not Easy Being Green"; nominated for Oscar for music for *The Great Muppet Caper*.
b. February 08, 1937 in Fall River, Massachusetts
d. February 05, 1989 in Bronxville, New York

Phylicia Rashad
(Mrs Ahmad Rashad; Phylicia Ayers-Allen)
American actress
• Plays Claire Huxtable on "The Cosby Show," 1984–.
b. June 19, 1948 in Houston, Texas

Basil Rathbone
English actor
• Played Sherlock Holmes in series of 1930-40s films.
b. June 13, 1892 in Johannesburg, South Africa
d. July 21, 1967 in New York, New York

Dan(iel Irvin) Rather
American broadcast journalist
• Anchor, "The CBS Evening News," 1977–; co-editor, "60 Minutes," 1975-81; won five Emmys.
b. October 31, 1931 in Wharton, Texas

Gregory Ratoff
American actor–director
• Directed *Intermezzo*, 1939; starred in *Seventh Heaven*, 1937; *All About Eve*, 1950.
b. April 2, 1893 in Petrograd, Russia
d. December 14, 1960 in Solothurn, Switzerland

Sir Terence Mervyn Rattigan
English dramatist
• Wrote *The Windslow Boy*, 1946; *Separate Tables*, 1956.
b. June 1, 1911 in Cornwall Gardens, England
d. November 3, 1977 in Hamilton, Bermuda

John Dezso Ratzenberger
American actor
• Plays Clifford Claven in TV series "Cheers," 1982–.
b. April 06, 1947 in Bridgeport, Connecticut

Herbert Rawlinson
English actor
• Screen career, 1911-51; films include *Count of Monte Cristo; Swiss Family Robinson.*
b. 1883 in Brighton, England
d. July 12, 1953 in Woodland Hills, California

Aldo Ray
(Aldo DaRe)
American actor
• Played tough guy roles since 1951 in films *Green Berets; The Naked and the Dead.*
b. September 25, 1926 in Pen Argyl, Pennsylvania
d. March 27, 1991 in Martinez, California

Charles Ray
American actor
• Star of 118 silent, talking films, including *Nobody's Widow*, 1927.
b. March 15, 1891 in Jacksonville, Illinois
d. November 23, 1943 in Los Angeles, California

Nicholas Ray
(Raymond N Kienzle)
American director
• Films include *They Live By Night*, 1948; *Rebel Without a Cause*, 1955.
b. August 07, 1911 in La Crosse, Wisconsin
d. June 16, 1979 in New York, New York

Satyajit Ray
Indian director
• India's best-known filmmaker; works include trilogy about Bengali village life, *World of Apu*, 1960.
b. May 02, 1921 in Calcutta, India

Martha Raye
(Margaret Theresa Yvonne Reed)
American comedienne–singer
• Known for wide-mouthed zaniness; in films since 1936; won special Oscar, 1968.
b. August 27, 1916 in Butte, Montana

Gene Raymond
American actor
• Married Jeanette MacDonald, 1937-65; leading man in B-pictures, 1940s-50s.
b. August 13, 1908 in New York, New York

Harry Reasoner
American broadcast journalist
• Original co-editor, with Mike Wallace, of "60 Minutes," 1968-70, 1978–.
b. April 17, 1923 in Dakota City, Iowa

Robert Redford
(Charles Robert Redford Jr)
American actor–director–author
• Box office draw since film *Barefoot in the Park*, 1967; won Oscar for directing *Ordinary People*, 1980.
b. August 18, 1937 in Santa Monica, California

Corin Redgrave
English actor
• Son of Sir Michael; brother of Vanessa, Lynn; films include *A Man for all Seasons*, 1966.
b. July 16, 1939 in London, England

Lynn Redgrave
English actress
• Starred in *Georgy Girl*, 1967; TV series "House Calls," 1979-81; TV spokeswoman for Weight Watchers.
b. March 08, 1943 in London, England

Sir Michael Scudamore Redgrave
English actor
• Starred in *The Quiet American*, 1958; *The Go-Between*, 1970.
b. March 2, 1908 in Bristol, England
d. March 21, 1985 in Denham, England

Vanessa Redgrave
English actress
• Won 1977 Oscar for *Julia;* starred in *Blow-up; Camelot; Playing for Time.*
b. January 3, 1937 in London, England

Alan Reed
(Teddy Bergman)
American actor
• Cartoon voice of Fred Flintstone; played Falstaff Openshaw on radio show "Allen's Alley."
b. August 2, 1907 in New York, New York
d. June 14, 1977 in Los Angeles, California

Sir Carol Reed
English director
• Won Oscar for *Oliver*, 1968; films include *Third Man; Fallen Idol.*
b. December 3, 1906 in London, England
d. April 25, 1976 in London, England

Donna Reed
(Donna Belle Mullenger)
American actress
• Won Oscar for *From Here To Eternity*, 1953, but gained greatest success on TVs "Donna Reed Show," 1958-66.
b. January 27, 1921 in Denison, Iowa
d. January 14, 1986 in Beverly Hills, California

Oliver (Robert Oliver) Reed
English actor
• Leading man, 1960–; films include *Oliver!*, 1968; *The Three Musketeers*, 1974.
b. February 13, 1938 in London, England

Robert Reed
(John Robert Rietz)
American actor
• Played the father on TV series "The Brady Bunch," 1969-74.
b. October 19, 1932 in Chicago, Illinois

Harry Reems
(Herbert Streicher)
American actor
• Pornography star in films: *Deep Throat; Devil and Miss Jones.*
b. August 27, 1947 in New York, New York

Roger Rees
Welsh actor
• Star of *Nicholas Nickleby* in London, on Broadway, TV; won Tony, 1982.
b. May 05, 1944 in Aberystwyth, Wales

Christopher Reeve
American actor
• Best known for title role in *Superman* film series, 1978, 1980, 1983, 1987.
b. September 25, 1952 in New York, New York

George Reeves
(George Basselo)
American actor
• Typecast in TV series "The Adventures of Superman."
b. April 06, 1914 in Ashland, Kentucky
d. June 16, 1959 in Beverly Hills, California

Steve Reeves
American actor
• Former "Mr. World," "Mr. Universe," who gained fame in Italian costume epics *Hercules*, 1957; *Goliath and the Barbarians*, 1959.
b. January 21, 1926 in Glasgow, Montana

Ada Rehan
American actress
• Leading lady of Daly's Theater in NY, 1879-99; best known for her rolee of Katherine in *Taming of the Shrew.*
b. April 22, 1860 in Limerick, Ireland
d. January 08, 1916 in New York, New York

Beryl Reid
English actress
• Won 1967 Tony for *The Killing of Sister George.*
b. June 17, 1920 in Hereford, England

Elliott Reid
American actor
• Supporting actor since 1940 in films *Gentlemen Prefer Blondes*, 1953; *Absent-Minded Professor*, 1961.
b. January 16, 1920 in New York, New York

Kate (Daphne Kate) Reid
Canadian actress
• Won critical acclaim, 1984, playing Linda Loman in revival of *Death of a Salesman* on Broadway.
b. November 04, 1930 in London, England

Tim Reid
American actor
• Played Venus Flytrap in TV series "WKRP in Cincinnati," 1978-82; plays Frank Parrish in "Frank's Place," 1987–.
b. December 19, 1944 in Norfolk, Virginia

Wallace Eugene Reid
American actor
• Silent screen star in over 100 films, 1910-22; died from morphine drug addiction.
b. April 15, 1891 in Saint Louis, Missouri
d. January 18, 1923 in Los Angeles, California

Charles Nelson Reilly
American comedian
• Won Tony for *How to Succeed in Business without Really Trying*, 1961; TV includes game shows, situation comedies, varieties.
b. January 13, 1931 in New York, New York

Carl Reiner
American actor–author
• Creative force behind TV's "The Dick Van Dyke Show," 1961-66; won several Emmys; appeared on Broadway, TV, film.
b. March 2, 1922 in New York, New York

Rob(ert) Reiner
American actor–director
• Played Michael Stivic on "All in the Family," 1971-78; directed *When Harry Met Sally*, 1990; won two emmys; son of Carl Reiner
b. March 06, 1947 in New York, New York

Max Reinhardt
(Maximilian Goldman)
American director–producer
• Expressionism in German films was directly influenced by his way of handling lights, sets, crowds.
b. September 09, 1873 in Baden, Austria
d. October 31, 1943 in New York, New York

Judge (Edward Ernest) Reinhold
American actor
• Films include *Ruthless People*, 1986; *Beverly Hills Cop*, 1984.
b. 1958 in Wilmington, Delaware

Ann H Reinking
American actress–dancer
• Two-time Tony nominee whose plays include *Pippin*, 1972; films include *Annie*, 1982.
b. November 1, 1949 in Seattle, Washington

Paul Reiser
American actor–comedian
• Stand-up comic; starred in TV comedy "My Two Dads," 1987-90.
b. in New York, New York

Karel Reisz
British director
• Films include *Morgan; Isadora; Saturday Night & Sunday Morning.*
b. July 21, 1926 in Ostrava, Czechoslovakia

John Charles Walsham Reith
(First Baron Reith; "Father of BBC")
English government official–broadcast executive
• First director of the BBC, 1920s.
b. July 2, 1889 in Stonehaven, Scotland
d. June 16, 1971 in Edinburgh, Scotland

Ivan Reitman
Canadian director–producer
• Films include box office hits: *Stripes*, 1981; *Ghostbusters*, 1984.
b. October 26, 1946 in Komarno, Czechoslovakia

Lee Remick
(Mrs William Kip Gowans)
American actress
• Made Broadway debut, 1953; noted for role of mother in film *The Omen*, 1976; frequently in TV mini series.
b. December 14, 1935 in Boston, Massachusetts

Duncan Renaldo
American actor–producer
• Best known as star of Western series, playing the Cisco Kid.
b. April 23, 1904 in Camden, New Jersey
d. September 03, 1980 in Santa Barbara, California

Jules Renard
French dramatist–author
• Wrote autobiography, *Poil de Carotte*, 1894, which was basis for his best-known play, 1900.
b. February 22, 1864 in Chalons-sur-Mayenne, France
d. May 22, 1910 in Paris, France

Jean Renoir
French director–screenwriter
• Best known for film *The Rules of the Game*, 1939; son of artist, Auguste Renoir.
b. September 15, 1894 in Paris, France
d. February 12, 1979 in Beverly Hills, California

Alain Resnais
French director
• Films include *Hiroshima Mon Amour*; *Last Year at Marienbad*.
b. June 03, 1922 in Vannes, France

Anne Revere
American actress
• Best known for playing wise mothers in films, 1940s-50s; won supporting actress Oscar for role as Elizabeth Taylor's mother in *National Velvet*, 1945; career cut short for refusing to testify about alleged communism.
b. June 25, 1903 in New York, New York
d. December 18, 1990 in Locust Valley, New York

Clive Selsby Revill
New Zealander actor
• Character actor, 1959–; films include *The Empire Strikes Back*, 1980; *Zorro, the Gay Blade*, 1981.
b. April 18, 1930 in Wellington, New Zealand

Fernando Rey
(Fernando Casado Arambillet)
Spanish actor
• Character actor, 1945–; played criminal mastermind in *The French Connection*, 1971.
b. September 2, 1917 in La Coruna, Spain

Burt Reynolds
American actor
• First *Cosmopolitan* centerfold; films include *Best Friends*, 1983; *Sharky's Machine*, 1984; *Stick*, 1985; stars in TV series "Evening Shade".
b. February 11, 1936 in Lansing, Michigan

Debbie (Marie Frances) Reynolds
American actress–singer
• Starred in *The Unsinkable Molly Brown*, 1964; *Singing in the Rain*, 1952.
b. April 01, 1932 in El Paso, Texas

Frank Reynolds
American broadcast journalist
• Chief anchorman, ABC World News Tonight, 1978-83.
b. November 29, 1923 in East Chicago, Indiana
d. July 2, 1983 in Washington, District of Columbia

Marjorie Reynolds
(Marjorie Goodspeed)
American actress
• Played wife of William Bendix on TV's "Life of Riley," 1953-58.
b. August 12, 1921 in Buhl, Idaho

William Reynolds
American actor
• Played special agent Tom Colby on TV show "The FBI," 1967-73.
b. December 09, 1931 in Los Angeles, California

Hari Rhodes
American actor–author
• Played in TV series "Daktari," 1966-68; "Bold Ones," 1969-71.
b. April 1, 1932 in Cincinnati, Ohio

Elmer Rice
(Elmer Leopold Reizenstein)
American dramatist
• Wrote Pulitzer-winner *Street Scene*, 1929; *We, The People*, 1933.
b. September 28, 1892 in New York, New York
d. May 08, 1967 in Southampton, England

Thomas Dartmouth Rice
American actor
• Known for song-and-dance act, "Jim Crow," that perpetuated the popular minstrel shows of 19th c.
b. May 2, 1808 in New York, New York
d. September 19, 1860 in New York, New York

Mandy Rice-Davies
English call girl–restaurateur–actress
• Involved in 1963 British political-sex scandal known as Profumo affair.
b. 1944

Adam Rich
American actor
• Played Nicholas Bradford on TV series "Eight Is Enough" 1977-81.
b. October 12, 1968 in Brooklyn, New York

Irene Rich
(Irene Luther)
American actress
• Radio star of "Dear John"; featured in films, 1918-50; radio sponsor for Welch's Grape Juice, 1930s.
b. October 13, 1897 in Buffalo, New York
d. April 23, 1988 in Santa Barbara, California

John Rich
American director–producer
• Won Emmys for "The Dick Van Dyke Show," 1963; "All in the Family," 1972.
b. July 06, 1925 in Rockaway Beach, New York

Lee Rich
American TV executive
• Pres., Lorimar Productions; co. produces TV shows "Dallas," "Knots Landing."
b. in Cleveland, Ohio

Lloyd George Richards
American director–actor
• First black director of Broadway play, *A Raisin in the Sun*, 1959; dean of drama school, Yale U., 1979–.
b. 1922 in Toronto, Ontario

Stanley Richards
American dramatist–author
• Wrote dozens of plays, many produced around the world: *Journey to Bahia*, 1964.
b. April 23, 1918 in Brooklyn, New York
d. July 26, 1980 in New York, New York

Jack Richardson
American dramatist
• Won Obie for *The Prodigal*, 1960.
b. February 18, 1935 in New York, New York

Lee Richardson
(Lee David Richard)
American actor
• Played in TV soap operas "Search for Tomorrow," "Guiding Light."
b. September 11, 1926 in Chicago, Illinois

Sir Ralph David Richardson
English actor
• One of most acclaimed figures in English-speaking theater; starred in over 200 plays, 100 films.
b. December 19, 1902 in Cheltenham, England
d. October 1, 1983 in London, England

Susan Richardson
American actress
• Played Susan Bradford on TV series "Eight Is Enough," 1977-81.
b. March 11, 1952

Tony Richardson
English producer–director
• Produced, directed films *A Taste of Honey*, 1962; *Tom Jones*, 1963.
b. June 05, 1929 in Shipley, England

Charles Richman
American actor
• Film star, 1915-42; films include *Life of Emile Zola*, 1937; *Dark Victory*, 1939.
b. January 12, 1870 in Chicago, Illinois
d. December 01, 1940 in Bronx, New York

Hans Richter
German filmmaker
• Made first abstract film *Rhythm 21*, 1921; known for *Dada: Art and Anti-art*, 1964.
b. 1888 in Berlin, Germany
d. February 01, 1976 in Locarno, Switzerland

Don Rickles
American comedian
• Well known for comedy style based on insults.
b. May 08, 1926 in New York, New York

Leni (Helene Bertha Amalie) Riefenstahl
German director
• Friend of Hitler, who filmed propaganda documentary, *Triumph of the Will*, 1934; imprisoned by French following WW II.
b. August 22, 1902 in Berlin, Germany

Harry Rigby
American producer
• Co-produced long-running Broadway hit musicals *Sugar Babies; Irene*.
b. February 21, 1925 in Pittsburgh, Pennsylvania
d. January 17, 1985 in New York, New York

Diana Rigg
English actress
• Played Emma Peel on TV series "The Avengers," 1965-68.
b. July 2, 1938 in Doncaster, England

Lynn Riggs
American dramatist
• Noted for romantic comedy, *Green Grow the Lilacs*, 1931.
b. August 31, 1899 in Claremore, Oklahoma
d. June 3, 1954 in New York, New York

Charles Ringling
(Ringling Brothers)
American circus owner
• With four brothers, started small circus, 1880s; merged with Forepaugh-Sells, Barnum & Bailey, 1907; established Sarasota as winter resort.
b. December 02, 1863 in McGregor, Iowa
d. December 03, 1926 in Sarasota, Florida

Ringling Brothers
(Alfred C Alfred T Charles John and Otto Ringling)
American circus owners
• Brothers who started small circus in Baraboo, WI, 1880s; merged with Forepaugh-Sells, Barnum & Bailey, 1907.

Molly Ringwald
American actress
• Star of five feature films, including *The Breakfast Club*, 1985; *Pretty in Pink*, 1986.
b. February 18, 1968 in Roseville, California

Rodney Allen Rippy
American actor
• 1970s child commercial star for Jack-in-the Box hamburger chain.
b. 1968

Elizabeth Risdon
American actress
• Played in over 60 films beginning in 1913; films include *Huckleberry Finn; Random Harvest*.
b. April 26, 1888 in London, England
d. December 2, 1956 in Santa Monica, California

Cyril Ritchard
Australian actor–director
• Best known for portrayal of Captain Hook in Broadway's *Peter Pan*, won Tony, 1954.
b. December 01, 1897 in Sydney, Australia
d. December 18, 1977 in Chicago, Illinois

Martin Ritt
American director
• Maverick director of *Norma Rae*, 1979, *Hud*, 1963, *The Long Hot Summer*, 1958; once blacklisted in Hollywood.
b. March 02, 1920 in New York, New York
d. December 08, 1990 in Santa Monica, California

John(athan Southworth) Ritter
American actor
• Won Emmy for role in "Three's Company," 1977-83; plays Harry Hooperman in "Hooperman," 1987-; son of Tex Ritter.
b. September 17, 1948 in Burbank, California

Tex (Woodward Maurice) Ritter
American singer–actor
• Singing cowboy in over 60 films; won Oscar, 1952, for *High Noon*; first country music Hall of Famer, 1964.
b. January 12, 1907 in Murval, Texas
d. January 02, 1974 in Nashville, Tennessee

Thelma Ritter
American actress
• Films include *All About Eve*, 1950; *Pillow Talk*, 1959; *Bird Man of Alcatraz*, 1961; six-time Oscar nominee.
b. February 14, 1905 in New York, New York
d. February 05, 1969 in New York, New York

Ritz Brothers
(Al Ritz; Harry Ritz; Jimmy Ritz)
American comedy team
• Slapstick routines featured in 1930s-40s films; highlights include *The Three Musketeers*, 1939.

Al Ritz
American comedian
• Eldest member of comedy team; appeared in 21 films with brothers.
b. August 27, 1901 in Newark, New Jersey
d. December 22, 1965 in New Orleans, Louisiana

Harry Ritz
(Herschel Joachim)
American comedian
• The youngest, last surviving brother of famous comedy team, the Ritz Brothers.
b. May 22, 1906 in Newark, New Jersey
d. March 29, 1986 in San Diego, California

Jimmy Ritz
(James Joachim)
American comedian
• Member of comedy team with brothers; appeared in film *The Three Musketeers*, 1939.
b. October 05, 1905 in Brooklyn, New York
d. November 17, 1985 in Los Angeles, California

Chita Rivera
(Concita del Rivero)
American singer–actress
• Created role of Anita in *West Side Story* on Broadway, 1957; won Tony for role of Anna in *The Rink*, 1984.
b. January 23, 1933 in Washington, District of Columbia

Geraldo Rivera
American journalist
• Investigative reporter; TV shows include "20/20," 1978-85; "Geraldo," 1987–; won Emmys, 1980, 1981.
b. July 04, 1943 in New York, New York

Joan Rivers
(Joan Alexandra Molinsky; Mrs Edgar Rosenberg)
American comedienne
• Known for daring wit; had own talk show "The Late Show," 1986-87; won Emmy for guest hosting "The Tonight Show," 1983.
b. June 08, 1933 in New York, New York

Hal Roach
American director–producer
• Developed comedy serials, "Laurel & Hardy"; "Our Gang"; later produced feature films only; won Oscars for *The Music Box*, 1932; *Bored of Education*, 1936.
b. January 14, 1892 in Elmira, New York

Jason Robards
American actor
• Stage actor who became leading screen star in over 100 films, 1921-61.
b. December 31, 1892 in Hillsdale, Michigan
d. April 04, 1963 in Sherman Oaks, California

Jason Robards, Jr
American actor
• Won Oscars for *All the President's Men*, 1976, *Julia*, 1977; won Tony for *The Disenchanted*, 1959; once wed to Lauren Bacall.
b. July 22, 1922 in Chicago, Illinois

Jerome Robbins
(Jerome Rabinowitz)
American choreographer
• With NY City Ballet, 1949–; won Tony, Oscar for *West Side Story*.
b. October 11, 1918 in New York, New York

Doris Roberts
American actress
• Won Emmy, 1983, for "St. Elsewhere"; nominated for "Remington Steele," 1985; plays include *Cheaters*, 1978.
b. November 04, 1930 in Saint Louis, Missouri

Eric Roberts
American actor
• Films include *Star 80*, 1983, *The Pope of Greenwich Village*, 1984; brother of Julia.
b. April 18, 1956 in Biloxi, Mississippi

Julia Roberts
American actress
• Starred in films *Pretty Woman*, 1990, *Flatliners*, 1990; received Oscar nomination for *Steel Magnolias*, 1989.
b. October 25, 1967 in Smyrna, Georgia

Pernell Roberts
American actor
• TV series roles in "Bonanza," 1959-65; "Trapper John, MD," 1979-86.
b. May 18, 1930 in Waycross, Georgia

Rachel Roberts
Welsh actress
• Starred in *Saturday Night and Sunday Morning; This Sporting Life; O Lucky Man*.
b. September 2, 1927 in Llanelly, Wales
d. November 26, 1980 in Los Angeles, California

Tony (David Anthony) Roberts
American actor
• Stage performances received two Tony nominations; *How Now, Dow Jones*, 1967; *Play It Again, Sam*, 1969; appeared in films, TV.
b. October 22, 1939 in New York, New York

Cliff Robertson
American actor
• Won Oscar, 1969, for *Charley*; starred in *PT 109*, 1962.
b. September 09, 1925 in La Jolla, California

Dale Robertson
American actor
• Appeared in TV series "Death Valley Days," 1968-72; "Tales of Wells Fargo," 1957-62.
b. July 14, 1923 in Oklahoma City, Oklahoma

Pat (Marion Gordon) Robertson
American evangelist–TV personality
• Founder, pres., Christian Broadcasting Network, 1977–; host of "700 Club," 1968–; ran for pres., 1988.
b. March 22, 1930 in Lexington, Virginia

Paul Leroy Robeson
American singer–actor
• Jerome Kern wrote "Ol' Man River" for him, which he sang in play, movie *Showboat*, 1928, 1936.
b. April 09, 1898 in Princeton, New Jersey
d. January 23, 1976 in Philadelphia, Pennsylvania

Sir George Robey
English comedian–actor
• Films include *Birds of a Feather*, 1935; *The Pickwick Papers*, 1952.
b. September 2, 1869 in London, England
d. November 29, 1954 in Saltdean, England

Bill Robinson
American actor–dancer
• Tap dancer known for stairway dance, appearances in Shirley Temple films.
b. May 25, 1878 in Richmond, Virginia
d. November 25, 1949 in New York, New York

Jay Robinson
American actor
• Played in films, 1953-58, until drug conviction led to long career decline; came back in 1970s in *The Robe; Wild Party*.
b. April 14, 1930 in New York, New York

Max C Robinson
American broadcast journalist
• First black to anchor network TV news, 1978 on ABC; won several Emmys; died of AIDS.
b. May 01, 1939 in Richmond, Virginia
d. December 2, 1988 in Washington, District of Columbia

Dame Flora McKenzie Robson
English actress
• Actress since age five; played in over 100 plays, more than 60 films.
b. March 28, 1902 in South Shields, England
d. July 07, 1984 in Brighton, England

May Robson
(Mary Jeanette Robison)
American actress
• Oscar nominee for Apple Annie in *Lady for a Day*, 1933.
b. April 19, 1858 in Melbourne, Australia
d. October 2, 1942 in Beverly Hills, California

Gene (Eugene Wesley) Roddenberry
American writer–producer
• Creator of TV series "Star Trek," 1966-69; wrote screenplays for *Star Trek* films; won Hugo, 1967.
b. August 19, 1921 in El Paso, Texas

Albert S Rogell
American director–producer
• Made Hollywood's first coop. film, 1921; worked on over 2,000 films including *The Black Cat*, 1941.
b. August 21, 1901 in Oklahoma City, Oklahoma

Buddy (Charles) Rogers
American actor
• Starred in *Wings*, 1927, first picture to win Oscar; husband of Mary Pickford.
b. August 13, 1904 in Olathe, Kansas

Fred McFeely Rogers
American educator–TV personality
• Producer, host, "Mister Rogers Neighborhood," 1965-75; "Old Friends, New Friends," 1978–; ordained Presbyterian minister.
b. March 2, 1928 in Latrobe, Pennsylvania

Ginger Rogers
(Virginia Katherine McNath)
American dancer
• Won Oscar, 1940, for *Kitty Foyle;* frequent dance partner of Fred Astaire.
b. July 16, 1911 in Independence, Missouri

Roy Rogers
(Leonard Slye; "King of the Cowboys")
American actor–singer
• With *Sons of the Pioneers*, 1932-38; in TV series "The Roy Rogers Show," 1951-64.
b. November 05, 1912 in Cincinnati, Ohio

Wayne Rogers
American actor
• Played Trapper John in TV series "M*A*S*H," 1972-75.
b. April 07, 1933 in Birmingham, Alabama

Will(iam Penn Adair) Rogers
American actor–lecturer
• "Comedy roper" in Ziegfield Follies from 1914; columnist, 1926-35; killed with Wiley Post in plane crash.
b. September 05, 1879 in Oologah, Oklahoma
d. August 15, 1935 in Point Barrow, Alaska

Will Rogers, Jr
American actor–lecturer
• Portrayed father in film *The Story of Will Rogers*, 1950.
b. October 12, 1912 in New York, New York

Eric Rohmer
(Jean-Marie Maurice Scherer)
French director
• Films include *My Night at Maud's*, 1970; *Full Moon in Paris*, 1984.
b. December 01, 1920 in Nancy, France

Roxie Roker
American actress
• Played Helen Willis on "The Jeffersons," 1975-85.
b. August 28, 1929 in Miami, Florida

Gilbert Roland
American actor
• Latin lover in films including *Camille*, 1936.
b. December 11, 1905 in Juarez, Mexico

Esther Rolle
American actress
• Played Florida Evans in two TV series "Maude," 1972-74; "Good Times," 1974-78.
b. November 08, 1933 in Pompano Beach, Florida

Howard Ellsworth Rollins, Jr
American actor
• In feature films *Ragtime*, 1981; *A Soldier's Story*, 1984.
b. October 17, 1950 in Baltimore, Maryland

Cesar Romero
American actor
• Latin lover in films, 1933–; played The Joker in "Batman" TV series.
b. February 15, 1907 in New York, New York

George A Romero
American filmmaker–screenwriter
• Wrote, directed cult classic *Night of the Living Dead*, 1968.
b. 1940 in New York, New York

Andy (Andrew Aitken) Rooney
American author–producer
• Feature commentator on "60 Minutes" since 1978; author of five books.
b. January 14, 1919 in Albany, New York

Mickey Rooney
(Joe Yule Jr)
American actor
• Played Andy Hardy in film series, 1937-46; on Broadway in *Sugar Babies*.
b. September 23, 1920 in Brooklyn, New York

Pat Rooney
American actor
• Vaudeville star in *Show Business*, 1924; silent films, 1915-33.
b. July 04, 1880 in New York, New York
d. September 09, 1962 in New York, New York

Lynn Root
American dramatist
• Wrote Broadway play with all-black cast: *Cabin In the Sky*, 1940; filmed, 1942.
b. April 11, 1905 in Morgan, Minnesota

Hayden Rorke
American actor
• Best known as Dr. Alfred Bellows on TV's "I Dream of Jeannie," 1965-70; appeared in over 50 films, 70 plays.
b. October 23, 1910 in Brooklyn, New York
d. August 19, 1987 in Toluca Lake, California

Francoise Rosay
(Francoise Brandy de Naleche)
French actress
• Star in over 100 films, 1913-74.
b. April 19, 1891 in Paris, France
d. March 28, 1974 in Paris, France

George Walter Rose
English actor
• Won Tonys for *The Mystery of Edwin Drood*, 1986; *My Fair Lady*, 1976.
b. February 19, 1920 in Bicester, England
d. May 05, 1988 in Puerto Plata, Dominican Republic

Rose-Marie
(Rose-Marie Mazzatta)
American comedienne
• Played Sally Rogers on "The Dick Van Dyke Show," 1961-66.
b. August 15, in New York, New York

Maxie Rosenbloom
American boxer–actor–TV personality
• Colorful light-heavyweight champion, 1930-34; Hall of Fame, 1973.
b. September 06, 1906 in New York, New York
d. March 06, 1976 in South Pasadena, California

David Ross
American director–producer
• Won Obies for *Uncle Vanya*, 1956; *Hedda Gabler*, 1960.
b. 1891 in New York, New York
d. November 12, 1975 in New York, New York

Herbert David Ross
American director
• Films include *The Turning Point*, 1977; *Footloose*, 1984.
b. May 13, 1927 in Brooklyn, New York

Joe E Ross
American comedian
• Films since 1960s include *The Love Bug*, 1969; *The Boatniks*, 1970.
b. 1905
d. August 13, 1982 in Los Angeles, California

Katharine Ross
American actress
• Starred in *The Graduate*, 1967; *Butch Cassidy and the Sundance Kid*, 1969; *The Stepford Wives*, 1975.
b. January 29, 1943 in Hollywood, California

Marion Ross
American actress
• Best known for her role as Marion Cunningham on "Happy Days," 1974-83.
b. October 25, 1928 in Albert Lea, Minnesota

Isabella Rossellini
Italian actress–model
• Daughter of Ingrid Bergman and Roberto Rossellini; films since 1976 include *A Matter of Time*, 1976; *Blue Velvet*, 1987.
b. June 18, 1952 in Italy

Roberto Rossellini
Italian director
• Directed *Open City*, 1946; *Stromboli*, 1950; husband of Ingrid Bergman.
b. May 08, 1906 in Rome, Italy
d. June 03, 1977 in Rome, Italy

Robert Rossen
American director–producer
• Won Oscar for *All the King's Men*, 1949; other films include *Body and Soul*, 1947; *Hustler*, 1961.
b. March 16, 1908 in New York, New York
d. February 18, 1966 in New York, New York

Edmond Alexis Rostand
French dramatist
• Wrote *Cyrano de Bergerac*, 1897.
b. April 01, 1868 in Marseilles, France
d. December 02, 1918 in Paris, France

Richard Roundtree
American actor
• Best-known film, *Shaft*, 1971; others include *City Heat*, 1984.
b. September 07, 1942 in New Rochelle, New York

Robert Field Rounseville
American actor–opera singer
• Films include *Tales of Hoffman*, 1951; *Carousel*, 1955.
b. March 25, 1914 in Attleboro, Massachusetts
d. August 06, 1974 in New York, New York

Mickey Rourke
(Philip Andre Rourke Jr)
American actor
• Films include *9 1/2 Weeks*, 1986; *Bar Fly*, 1987; known for playing difficult characters.
b. 1956 in Schenectady, New York

Dan Rowan
(Rowan and Martin)
American comedian
• Co-star of TV comedy series "Laugh-In," 1968-73; straight man to Dick Martin for over 20 yrs.; won two Emmys.
b. July 02, 1922 in Beggs, Oklahoma
d. September 22, 1987 in Englewood, Florida

Gena (Catherine) Rowlands
(Mrs John Cassavetes)
American actress
• Oscar nominee, 1980, for *Gloria*; won 1987 Emmy for *The Betty Ford Story*.
b. June 19, 1936 in Cambria, Wisconsin

Alma Rubens
American actress
• Silent film star, 1916-29; heroin addiction cut career short.
b. 1897 in San Francisco, California
d. January 23, 1931 in Los Angeles, California

Benny Rubin
American comedian
• Vaudeville comedian, tap dancer; worked with Jack Benny, Eddie Cantor, 1920s; helped launch careers of Milton Berle, George Burns.
b. 1899 in New York, New York
d. July 16, 1986 in Los Angeles, California

John Arthur Rubinstein
American actor
• Won Tony for *Children of a Lesser God*, 1980; son of Arthur Rubinstein.
b. December 08, 1946 in Beverly Hills, California

Hughes Day Rudd
American broadcast journalist
• Correspondent, ABC News, 1979–; won Emmy, Peabody.
b. September 14, 1921 in Wichita, Kansas

Paul Ryan Rudd
American actor
• TV shows include "Beacon Hill," 1975; "Beaulah Land," 1980; "Knots Landing," 1980.
b. May 05, 1940 in Boston, Massachusetts

Al(bert Stotland) Ruddy
Canadian producer
• Films include *The Godfather*, 1972; *Cannonball Run II*, 1984.
b. March 28, 1934 in Montreal, Quebec

Louis Richard Rukeyser
American broadcast journalist–author
• Host, PBS series "Wall Street Week," 1970–; author *How To Make Money in Wall Street*.
b. January 3, 1933 in New York, New York

Janice Rule
(Mrs Ben Gazzara)
American actress
• Former nightclub dancer, leading lady; became psychoanalyst, mid-1970s.
b. August 15, 1931 in Norwood, Ohio

Sig(fried) Rumann
German actor
• Character actor, 1929-66; made over 100 films: *A Night at the Opera*.
b. 1884 in Hamburg, Germany
d. February 14, 1967 in Julian, California

Gail Russell
American actress
• Films include *The Unlimited; The Unseen*; career ended by alcoholism, emotional problems.
b. September 23, 1924 in Chicago, Illinois
d. August 26, 1961 in Los Angeles, California

Jane Russell
American actress
• Better known for buxom pinup poster accompanying 1943's *The Outlaw* than for film itself.
b. June 21, 1921 in Bemidji, Minnesota

Ken (Henry Kenneth Alfred) Russell
English director
• BBC feature film director; films include *Altered States*, 1980.
b. July 03, 1927 in Southampton, England

Kurt (Von Vogel) Russell
American actor
• Films include *Silkwood*, 1983; *Big Trouble in Little China*, 1986; Elvis Presley look alike.
b. March 17, 1951 in Springfield, Massachusetts

Mark Russell
(Mark Ruslander)
American comedian
• Political humorist who rose to popularity after the Watergate scandal.
b. August 23, 1932 in Buffalo, New York

Nipsey Russell
American comedian–actor
• Co-hosted "The Les Crane Show" on TV; first black regularly employed as MC on national TV.
b. October 13, 1924 in Atlanta, Georgia

Rosalind Russell
American actress
• Films include *His Girl Friday; My Sister Eileen; Auntie Mame*.
b. June 04, 1911 in Waterbury, Connecticut
d. November 28, 1976 in Beverly Hills, California

Ann Rutherford
Canadian actress
• Played Polly Benedict in Andy Hardy series, 1940s; films include *Secret Life of Walter Mitty*, 1947; retired, 1950.
b. November 02, 1917 in Toronto, Ontario

Margaret Rutherford
(Dame Margot Rutherford)
English actress
• Won 1963 Oscar for *The VIP's*; played Miss Marple in four Agatha Christie films.
b. May 11, 1892 in Balham, England
d. May 22, 1972 in Chalfont, England

Irene Noblette Ryan
American actress
• Played Granny Clampett on TV series "Beverly Hillbillies," 1962-71.
b. October 17, 1903 in El Paso, Texas
d. April 26, 1973 in Santa Monica, California

Peggy (Margaret O'Rene) Ryan
American actress
• Played Jenny on TV show "Hawaii Five-O," 1969-76.
b. August 28, 1924 in Long Beach, California

Robert (Bushnell) Ryan
American actor
• Leading man, 1940-73, whose films include Crossfire, 1947; The Dirty Dozen, 1967.
b. November 11, 1913 in Chicago, Illinois
d. July 11, 1973 in New York, New York

Winona Ryder
(Winona Laura Horowitz)
American actress
• Played Myra Gale Lewis in film Great Balls of Fire! 1989; Beetle Juice, 1988; Edward Scissorhands, 1991.
b. October 29, 1971 in Rochester, Minnesota

Morrie Ryskind
American journalist–dramatist
• Won Pulitzer for play Of Thee I Sing, 1932; wrote film My Man Godfrey, 1936; co-authored several Marx Brothers films.
b. October 2, 1895 in New York, New York
d. August 24, 1985 in Crystal City, Virginia

Sabu
(Sabu Dastagir)
Indian actor
• Best known for title role in Elephant Boy, 1937.
b. March 15, 1924 in Mysore, India
d. December 02, 1963 in Chatsworth, California

Howard Oliver Sackler
American dramatist
• Won Pulitzer, 1969, for The Great White Hope.
b. December 19, 1929 in New York, New York
d. October 14, 1982 in Ibiza, Spain

Donald Saddler
American choreographer
• Won Tonys for Wonderful Town, 1953; No, No, Nanette, 1971.
b. January 24, 1920 in Van Nuys, California

Morley Safer
Canadian broadcast journalist
• Vietnam correspondent, 1964-71, who has been a cohost of "60 Minutes" since 1970.
b. November 08, 1931 in Toronto, Ontario

Bob (Robert) Saget
American actor–comedian
• Plays Danny Tanner on TV comedy "Full House," 1987; hosts TV show "America's Funniest Home Videos," 1990–.
b. May 17, 1956 in Philadelphia, Pennsylvania

Mort (Lyon) Sahl
American comedian
• Offbeat nightclub, TV political satirist; known for ironic views of passing scene; wrote autobiography, Heartland, 1976.
b. May 11, 1927 in Montreal, Quebec

Eva Marie Saint
American actress
• Won Oscar, 1955, for On the Waterfront, her first film; other films include North by Northwest, 1959; Grand Prix, 1966.
b. July 04, 1924 in Newark, New Jersey

Lillian Saint Cyr
(Marie VanShaak)
American entertainer
• Burlesque queen who made as much as $7,500 per week at height of career.
b. June 03, 1917 in Minneapolis, Minnesota

Susan Saint James
(Susan Miller)
American actress
• Appeared in TV series "The Name of the Game"; "McMillan and Wife"; "Kate and Allie."
b. August 14, 1946 in Long Beach, California

Betta Saint John
(Betty Streidler)
American actress
• Ingenue in original Broadway cast of South Pacific, 1949; films include The Law vs. Billy the Kid, 1954.
b. November 26, 1929 in Hawthorne, California

Jill Saint John
(Jill Oppenheim; Mrs Robert Wagner)
American actress
• Began acting at age 6; has appeared on radio, TV, film; appeared in film Tony Rome, 1967.
b. August 09, 1940 in Los Angeles, California

Arnold Saint-Subber
American producer
• Productions include The Little Foxes, 1967; Gigi, 1973.
b. February 18, 1918 in Washington, District of Columbia

Pat Sajak
American TV personality
• Host of game show "Wheel of Fortune," 1981–, most successful show ever syndicated.
b. October 26, 1946 in Chicago, Illinois

S Z Sakall
(Eugene Gero Szakall; "Cuddles")
Hungarian actor
• Films include Casablanca, 1942; Tea for Two, 1950.
b. February 02, 1884 in Budapest, Hungary
d. February 12, 1955 in Los Angeles, California

Gene Saks
American director
• Won Tony for musical, I Love My Wife, 1977.
b. November 08, 1921 in New York, New York

Soupy Sales
(Milton Hines; Morton Supman)
American TV personality
• Starred in "Soupy Sales Show," 1953-66; known for pie-throwing act.
b. January 08, 1930 in Wake Forest, North Carolina

Pierre Emil George Salinger
American broadcast journalist–politician
• Press secretary to JFK; chief foreign correspondent for ABC News, 1983–.
b. June 14, 1925 in San Francisco, California

Albert Salmi
American actor
• TV western actor; films include Caddy Shack, 1980.
b. 1928 in New York, New York
d. April 22, 1990 in Spokane, Washington

Jennifer Salt
American actress
• Leading lady, 1960s-70s: Midnight Cowboy, 1969; Play It Again Sam, 1972.
b. September 04, 1944 in Los Angeles, California

Waldo Salt
American screenwriter
• Won Oscars, 1969, 1978 for screenplays: Midnight Cowboy; Coming Home.
b. October 18, 1914 in Chicago, Illinois
d. March 09, 1987 in Los Angeles, California

Emma Samms
(Emma Samuelson)
English actress
• Succeeded Pamela Sue Martin in role of Fallon Carrington Colby in TV series "Dynasty," "The Colbys."
b. August 28, 1960 in London, England

Junior (Alvin) Samples
American comedian
• Bib-overalled, 300 lb. star of TV's "Hee-Haw," 1969-83.
b. 1927
d. November 13, 1983 in Cumming, Georgia

George Sanders
American actor
• Won Oscar, 1950, for *All About Eve*; married to Zsa Zsa and Magda Gabor.
b. July 03, 1906 in Saint Petersburg, Russia
d. April 25, 1972 in Castelldefels, Spain

Marlene Sanders
American broadcast journalist
• Correspondent, producer of CBS News documentaries since 1978.
b. January 1, 1931 in Cleveland, Ohio

Richard Kinard Sanders
American actor
• Played Les Nessman on TV series "WKRP in Cincinnati," 1978-82.
b. August 23, 1940 in Harrisburg, Pennsylvania

Eugene Sandow
(Karl Frederick Mueller; "The Mighty Monarch of Muscle")
German entertainer
• Physical cultist; performed in London's music halls, 1800s.
b. April 1, 1867 in Konigsberg, Germany
d. October 14, 1925 in London, England

Jay H Sandrich
American director
• Has directed TV sitcoms, including "Mary Tyler Moore Show," 1970-77; "Soap," 1977-79.
b. February 24, 1932 in Los Angeles, California

Dorothy Sands
American actress–director
• One of top performers in Grand Street Follies, 1920s.
b. March 05, 1893 in Cambridge, Massachusetts
d. September 11, 1980 in Croton-on-Hudson, New York

Gary Sandy
American actor
• Played Andy Travis on TV series "WKRP in Cincinnati," 1978-82.
b. December 25, 1946 in Dayton, Ohio

Isabel Gwendolyn Sanford
American actress
• Best known for role of Louise Jefferson on TV series "The Jeffersons," 1974-85.
b. August 29, 1933 in New York, New York

Chris Sarandon
American actor
• Starred in *Dog Day Afternoon*, 1975; *Protocol*, 1984.
b. July 24, 1942 in Beckley, West Virginia

Susan Abigail Sarandon
(Susan Abigail Tomalin)
American actress
• Played Janet in cult film classic, *Rocky Horror Picture Show*, 1975; has starred in many major films including, *Atlantic City*, 1981; *Bull Durham*, 1988; *White Palace*, 1991.
b. October 04, 1946 in New York, New York

Victorien Sardou
French dramatist
• Wrote over 70 popular plays including historical melodramas starring Sarah Bernhardt.
b. September 07, 1831 in Paris, France
d. November 08, 1908 in Paris, France

Tony (Anthony Frederick) Sarg
American puppeteer–children's author
• Created his famed marionettes, 1915; wrote, illustrated *Tony Sarg's Wonder Zoo*, 1927.
b. April 24, 1882 in Guatemala
d. March 07, 1942 in Nantucket, Massachusetts

Alvin Sargent
American screenwriter
• Wrote Oscar-winning screenplays for *Julia*, 1977; *Ordinary People*, 1980.

Dick Sargent
American actor
• Replaced Dick York as Darrin on TV series "Bewitched," 1969-72.
b. April 19, 1933 in Carmel, California

Herb Sargent
Writer
• Won Emmys for "Lily," 1974; "Saturday Night Live," 1976, 1977.

David Sarnoff
American radio executive–TV executive
• Chairman, RCA; one of first to see that TV would replace radio in popularity.
b. February 27, 1891 in Minsk, Russia
d. December 12, 1971 in New York, New York

Michael Sarrazin
(Jacques Michel Andre Sarrazin)
Canadian actor
• Starred in *The Reincarnation of Peter Proud*, 1975.
b. May 22, 1940 in Quebec City, Quebec

Robert Saudek
American TV executive
• Known for producing cultural programming, including "Omnibus"; past president, NY's Museum of Broadcasting.
b. April 11, 1911 in Pittsburgh, Pennsylvania

Lori Saunders
American actress
• Played Bobbi Jo on TV series "Petticoat Junction," 1965-70.
b. October 04, 1941 in Kansas City, Missouri

Carlos Saura (Atares)
Spanish director–screenwriter
• Leading figure in Spanish cinema; films include *Cria*, 1976; *Carmen*, 1983.
b. January 04, 1932 in Huesca, Spain

Fred Savage
American actor
• Plays Kevin Arnold on TV comedy "The Wonder Years," 1988–.
b. July 09, 1976 in Highland Park, Illinois

John Savage
(John Youngs)
American actor
• Films include *Salvador*, 1986; *The Onion Field*, 1979.
b. 1950 in Old Bethpage, New York

Telly (Aristoteles) Savalas
American actor
• Played Kojak on TV police drama of same name, 1973-78; first shaved head for role of Pontius Pilate in *The Greatest Story Ever Told*, 1965.
b. January 21, 1923 in Garden City, New York

Jessica Beth Savitch
American broadcast journalist
• With NBC News, 1977-83; wrote autobiography, *Anchorwoman*, 1982. Killed in auto accident.
b. February 02, 1948 in Kennett Square, Pennsylvania
d. October 23, 1983 in New Hope, Pennsylvania

Diane K Sawyer
(Mrs Mike Nichols)
American broadcast journalist
• Former staff assistant to Nixon; first female co-anchor on TVs "60 Minutes," 1984-88; co-anchor, ABC's "Prime Time Live," 1989–.
b. December 22, 1945 in Glasgow, Kentucky

John Saxon
(Carmen Orrico)
American actor
• Starred in TV series "The Bold Ones," 1969-72; film *The Cardinal*, 1963.
b. August 05, 1935 in Brooklyn, New York

Gia Scala
(Giovanna Sgoglio)
American actress
• Leading lady, 1950s-60s: *The Guns of Navarone*, 1961; died of accidental drug, alcohol overdose.
b. March 03, 1934 in Liverpool, England
d. April 3, 1972 in Hollywood Hills, California

John Alfred Scali
American journalist–diplomat
• Senior correspondent, ABC News, 1975–; US ambassador to UN, 1973-75.
b. April 27, 1918 in Canton, Ohio

Natalie Schafer
American actress
• Veteran stage comedienne since 1944; starred in TV series "Gilligan's Island," 1964-67.
b. November 05, 1912 in Rumson, New Jersey

Franklin James Schaffner
American director
• Won best director Oscar, 1970, for *Patton*.
b. May 03, 1920 in Tokyo, Japan
d. July 02, 1989 in Santa Monica, California

Jerry Ned Schaltzberg
American director
• Films include *Panic in Needle Park*, 1972; *Honeysuckle Rose*, 1980.
b. June 26, 1927 in Bronx, New York

Roy Richard Scheider
American actor
• Starred in *Jaws I, II*, 1975, 1978; Oscar nominee: *All That Jazz*, 1979.
b. November 1, 1935 in Orange, New Jersey

Maximilian Schell
Austrian actor
• Won Oscar, 1961, for *Judgment at Nuremberg*; brother of Maria Schell.
b. December 08, 1930 in Vienna, Austria

Joseph M Schenck
American film executive–producer
• Chm., 20th Century-Fox, 1935-41; produced all of Buster Keaton's Silent films.
b. December 25, 1878 in Rybinsk, Russia
d. October 22, 1961 in Beverly Hills, California

Bob Schieffer
American broadcast journalist
• Anchor, correspondent, CBS News, since 1969.
b. February 25, 1937 in Austin, Texas

Joseph Schildkraut
American actor
• Won Oscar, 1937, for *The Life of Emile Zola*; son of Rudolph.
b. March 22, 1896 in Vienna, Austria
d. January 21, 1964 in New York, New York

Friedrich von (Johann Christoph Friedrich von) Schiller
German author–dramatist
• Leading German playwright; wrote historical drama *Wilhelm Tell*, 1804.
b. November 1, 1759 in Marbach, Germany
d. May 09, 1805 in Weimar, Germany

Murray Joseph Schisgal
American dramatist
• Avant-garde playwright with comic-sad heroes: *Luv*, 1963, ran on Broadway for 900 performances; sreenplays include *Tootsie*, 1982.
b. November 25, 1926 in Brooklyn, New York

John Richard Schlesinger
English director
• Won Oscar, 1969, for *Midnight Cowboy*.
b. February 16, 1926 in London, England

Volker Schlondorff
German director–screenwriter
• Directed, wrote screen adaptation of *The Tin Drum*, 1980; won best foreign film Oscar.
b. March 31, 1939 in Wiesbaden, Germany

Alan Schneider
(Abram Leopoldovich)
American director
• Won Tony, 1962, for *Who's Afraid of Virginia Woolf*.
b. December 12, 1917 in Kharkov, U.S.S.R.
d. May 03, 1984 in London, England

John Schneider
American actor–singer
• Played Bo Duke on TV series "The Dukes of Hazard."
b. April 08, 1954 in Mount Kisco, New York

Maria Schneider
French actress
• Starred with Marlon Brando in controversial film *Last Tango in Paris*, 1972.
b. March 27, 1952 in Paris, France

Romy Schneider
(Rosemarie Albach-Retty)
Austrian actress
• Starred in *The Cardinal*, 1963.
b. September 23, 1938 in Vienna, Austria
d. May 29, 1982 in Paris, France

Daniel Louis Schorr
American broadcast journalist
• Controversial CBS News correspondent, 1943-76; won three Emmys for Watergate coverage; suspended for disclosing confidential govt. information to *Village Voice* newspaper, 1976.
b. August 31, 1916 in New York, New York

Paul Joseph Schrader
American director–writer
• Directed, wrote films *American Gigolo*, 1980; *Blue Collar*, 1978; *Hardcore*, 1979.
b. July 22, 1946 in Grand Rapids, Michigan

Avery Schreiber
(Burns and Schreiber)
American actor–comedian
• Starred with Jack Burns in "Burns and Schreiber Comedy Hour," 1973.
b. April 09, 1935 in Chicago, Illinois

Ricky Schroder
American actor
• Appeared in remake of *The Champ*, 1979; won Golden Globe award.
b. April 13, 1970 in Staten Island, New York

Stuart Schulberg
American producer
• Exec. producer of news documentaries for NBC; producer, "Today" show, 1968-76.
b. November 17, 1922 in Los Angeles, California
d. June 28, 1979 in New York, New York

Maurice Schwartz
American actor–director–producer
• Films include *Bird of Paradise*, 1951; *Slaves of Babylon*, 1953.
b. June 18, 1890 in Sedikov, Russia
d. May 1, 1960 in Tel Aviv, Israel

Ronald L Schwary
American producer
• Films include *A Soldier's Story*, 1984; won Oscar for *Ordinary People*, 1980.
b. May 23, 1944 in Oregon

Arnold Alois Schwarzenegger
American actor
• Five times Mr. Universe, six times Mr. Olympia; films include *Twins*, 1988, *Total Recall*, 1990; heads President Bush's Council on Physical Fitness; married to Maria Shriver.
b. July 3, 1947 in Graz, Austria

Paul (David Paul) Scofield
English actor
• Won Oscar, 1966, for *A Man for All Seasons*.
b. January 21, 1922 in Hurstpierpoint, England

Martin Scorsese
American director–screenwriter
• Known for films *The Color of Money*, 1986; *Taxi Driver*, 1976; *Goodfellows*, 1991.
b. November 17, 1942 in Flushing, New York

Adrian Scott
(The Hollywood Ten)
American producer–screenwriter
• Blacklisted as Communist by film industry; sentenced to one yr. in prison.
b. February 06, 1912 in Arlington, New Jersey
d. 1973

George C(ampbell) Scott
American actor
• First performer to refuse Oscar, 1970, for *Patton*.
b. October 18, 1927 in Wise, Virginia

Gordon Scott
(Gordon M Werschkul)
American actor
• Was the 11th Tarzan in films, 1955-60.
b. August 03, 1927 in Portland, Oregon

Martha Ellen Scott
American actress
• Broadway, film character actress nominated for Oscar for *Our Town*, 1940.
b. September 22, 1914 in Jamesport, Missouri

Randolph Scott
American actor
• Made name as a Western hero who was fast on the draw but short on words: *Ride the High Country*, 1962.
b. January 23, 1903 in Orange County, Virginia
d. March 02, 1987 in Los Angeles, California

Ridley Scott
English director
• Films include *Alien*, 1979; *Blade Runner*, 1982; *Legend*, 1985.
b. 1939 in South Shields, England

Willard Herman Scott, Jr
American TV personality
• Weathercaster for the "Today Show" since 1980.
b. March 07, 1934 in Alexandria, Virginia

Zachary Scott
American actor
• Films include *Bandido*, 1956; *It's Only Money*, 1962.
b. February 24, 1914 in Austin, Texas
d. October 03, 1965 in Austin, Texas

Elizabeth Seal
Italian actress
• Won Tony for *Irma La Douce*, 1961.
b. August 28, 1933 in Genoa, Italy

George Seaton
American screenwriter
• Won Oscars for *Miracle on 34th Street*, 1947; *The Country Girl*, 1954.
b. April 17, 1911 in South Bend, Indiana
d. July 28, 1979 in Beverly Hills, California

Jean Seberg
American actress
• Discovered by Otto Preminger; films include *Saint Joan*, 1957; *Lilith*, 1964.
b. November 13, 1938 in Marshalltown, Iowa
d. August 31, 1979 in Paris, France

Joe (John Josef) Sedelmaier
American director–filmmaker
• Advertising director who created "Where's the Beef" commercial for Wendy's, 1984.
b. May 31, 1933 in Orrville, Ohio

Blossom Seeley
(Mrs Benny Fields)
American actress
• Vaudville performer with husband; their life filmed as *Somebody Loves Me*.
b. 1892 in San Pablo, California
d. April 17, 1974 in New York, New York

Erich Wolf Segal
American author–dramatist
• Wrote *Love Story*, 1970; translated into 23 languages, filmed, 1970; *Oliver's Story*, 1977, filmed, 1978.
b. June 16, 1937 in Brooklyn, New York

George Segal
American actor
• Starred in *A Touch of Class*, 1973; *Carbon Copy*, 1981.
b. February 13, 1934 in New York, New York

Vivienne Segal
American actress
• Broadway star of operettas, musicals: *Desert Song*, 1926; *Pal Joey*, 1940.
b. April 19, 1897 in Philadelphia, Pennsylvania

Susan Seidelman
American director–producer
• Directed film *Desperately Seeking Susan*, 1984.
b. December 11, 1952 in Philadelphia, Pennsylvania

David Selby
American actor
• Starred in TV soap opera "Dark Shadows," 1966-71; played Richard Channing on TV drama "Falcon Crest," 1982-90.
b. in Morganstown, West Virginia

Connie Sellecca
American actress
• Played Christine Francis on TV series "Hotel," 1983-88.
b. May 25, 1955 in Bronx, New York

Tom (Thomas William) Selleck
American actor
• Played Thomas Magnum on TV series "Magnum PI," 1980-88; won Emmy, 1984; star of film *Three Men and a Baby*, 1987.
b. January 29, 1945 in Detroit, Michigan

Peter Sellers
(Richard Henry Peter Sellers)
English actor
• Played Inspector Jacques Clouseau in *The Pink Panther* films, 1963-76.
b. September 08, 1925 in Portsmouth, England
d. July 24, 1980 in London, England

David O(liver) Selznick
American producer
• Won Oscar, 1939, for producing *Gone With the Wind*.
b. May 1, 1902 in Pittsburgh, Pennsylvania
d. June 22, 1965 in Hollywood, California

Marina Semyonova
Russian dancer
• Russia's first prima ballerina; best known for role of Nikya in *La Bayadere*.
b. June 12, 1908 in Saint Petersburg, Russia

Lucius Annaeus Seneca, the Younger
Roman philosopher–statesman–dramatist
• Famed stoic; wrote eight tragedies; committed suicide at Nero's command.
b. 4 in Cordoba, Spain
d. 65

Mack Sennett
(Michael Sinnott; "King of Comedy")
American director–producer
• Created Keystone Kops; directed Charlie Chaplin, Harold Lloyd.
b. January 17, 1884 in Richmond, Quebec
d. November 05, 1960 in Woodland Hills, California

Rod Serling
American author–producer
• Created, hosted TV series "Twilight Zone," 1959-65; "Night Gallery," 1970-73.
b. December 25, 1924 in Syracuse, New York
d. June 28, 1975 in Rochester, New York

Michel Serrault
French actor
• Played the transvestite Zara in *La Cage aux Folles*, 1978.
b. 1928

(Arnold) Eric Sevareid
American broadcast journalist
• Joined CBS as member of original news team assembled, 1939.
b. November 26, 1912 in Velva, North Dakota

Jane Seymour
(Joyce Penelope Wilhelmina Frankenberg)
English actress
• Starred in TV mini-series, "East of Eden," 1980; *Somewhere in Time*, 1980.
b. February 15, 1951 in Hillingdon, England

Lynn Seymour
Canadian dancer
• Popular dramatic ballerina with Royal Ballet, 1957-77; director, prima ballerina, Bayerische Staatsoper, Munich, 1978-79.
b. March 08, 1939 in Wainwright, Alberta

Attallah Shabazz
American celebrity relative–actress
• Daughter of Malcolm X; formed theater troupe, Nucleus, with Yolanda King, daughter of Martin Luther King, Jr.
b. 1959 in Mount Vernon, New York

Ted Shackelford
American actor
• Plays Gary Ewing on TV series "Knots Landing," 1980–.
b. June 23, 1946 in Oklahoma City, Oklahoma

Peter Levin Shaffer
English dramatist
• Wrote plays *Five Finger Exercise*, 1958; Tony-winner *Equus*, 1975; *Amadeus*, 1981.
b. May 15, 1926 in Liverpool, England

Steve (Stephen H) Shagan
American screenwriter
• Oscar nominee for best screenplay: *Save the Tiger*, 1973; *Voyage of the Damned*, 1976.
b. October 25, 1927 in New York, New York

William Shakespeare
(Bard of Avon)
English dramatist–poet
• Considered greatest dramatist ever; wrote 154 sonnets, 37 plays.
b. April 23, 1564 in Stratford-on-Avon, England
d. April 23, 1616 in Stratford-on-Avon, England

Gene Shalit
American critic–journalist
• With NBC since 1969; regular commentator, 1973–.
b. 1932 in New York, New York

Garry Shandling
American comedian
• Star of cable TV sitcom "It's Garry Shandling's Show."
b. 1950 in Tucson, Arizona

Ntozake Shange
(Paulette L Williams)
American dramatist–poet
• Wrote play *For Colored Girls Who Have Considered Suicide/When the Rainbow is Enuf*, 1977, won Obie.
b. October 18, 1948 in Trenton, New Jersey

Arnold Shapiro
American producer
• Won Oscar for documentary *Scared Straight*, 1978.
b. February 01, 1941 in Los Angeles, California

Stanley Shapiro
American screenwriter–producer
• Co-wrote screenplay for Oscar-winning film *Pillow Talk*, 1959.
b. July 16, 1925 in New York, New York
d. July 21, 1990 in Los Angeles, California

Omar Sharif
(Michael Shalhoub)
Egyptian actor
• Starred in *Dr. Zhivago*, 1965, *Funny Girl*, 1968; bridge expert–daily bridge lessons published in syndicated newspapers.
b. October 1, 1932 in Alexandria, Egypt

William Shatner
American actor
• Best known as James T Kirk on TV series "Star Trek," 1966-69, films based on series, 1979-87.
b. March 22, 1931 in Montreal, Quebec

George Bernard Shaw
English dramatist–critic
• Greatest British dramatist since Shakespeare; wrote *Pygmalion*, 1913; won Nobel Prize, 1925.
b. July 26, 1856 in Dublin, Ireland
d. November 02, 1950 in Ayot St. Lawrence, England

Mary Shaw
American actress
• One of first actresses to introduce American audiences to Ibsen, Shaw.
b. January 25, 1854 in Boston, Massachusetts
d. May 18, 1929 in New York, New York

Robert Shaw
English actor–dramatist–author
• Starred in *Jaws*, 1975; *The Deep*, 1977.
b. August 09, 1927 in Westhoughton, England
d. August 28, 1978 in Tourmakeady, Ireland

Dick Shawn
(Richard Schulefand)
American actor–comedian
• Appeared in films *It's a Mad Mad Mad Mad World*, 1963; *The Producers*, 1968.
b. December 01, 1929 in Buffalo, New York
d. April 17, 1987 in La Jolla, California

Wallace Shawn
American actor–dramatist
• Known for collaboration, starring role in film *My Dinner with Andre*, 1981.
b. November 12, 1943 in New York, New York

John (Victor III) Shea
American actor
• Films include *Missing*, 1982; *Windy City*, 1984.
b. April 14, 1949 in North Conway, New Hampshire

Al Shean
(Alfred Schoenberg)
American actor
• Films include *52nd Street*, 1937; *People Are Funny*, 1946.
b. May 12, 1868 in Dornum, Germany
d. August 12, 1949 in New York, New York

Norma Shearer
American actress
• Won 1930 Oscar for *The Divorcee*; married to Irving Thalberg, 1927.
b. August 1, 1904 in Montreal, Quebec
d. June 12, 1983 in Woodland Hills, California

Ally Sheedy
American actress
• Films include *The Breakfast Club*; *St. Elmos Fire*, 1985.
b. June 12, 1962 in New York, New York

Charlie Sheen
(Carlos Irwin Estevez)
American actor
• Son of Martin Sheen; brother of Emilio Estevez; in films *Ferris Bueller's Day Off*, *Platoon*, 1986, *Major League*, 1988.
b. September 03, 1965 in New York, New York

Martin Sheen
(Ramon Estevez)
American actor
• Films include *Apocalypse Now*, 1979; *Gandhi*, 1982; father of Charlie, Emilio Estevez.
b. August 03, 1940 in Dayton, Ohio

Carole Augusta Shelley
English actress
• Won Tony, 1979, for *The Elephant Man*; Obie, 1982, for *Twelve Dreams*.
b. August 16, 1939 in London, England

Sam Shepard
(Samuel Shepard Rogers)
American dramatist–actor
• Won Pulitzer for *Buried Child*, 1979; won several Obies; wrote film *The Right Stuff*, 1983; appeared in some films.
b. November 05, 1943 in Fort Sheridan, Illinois

Cybill Lynne Shepherd
American model–actress
• Played Maddie Hayes on TV series "Moonlighting," 1985-89.
b. February 18, 1950 in Memphis, Tennessee

Jean Parker Shepherd
American actor–author
• Writings include *The America of George Ade*, 1961; *The Ferrari in the Bedroom*, 1973.
b. July 26, 1929 in Chicago, Illinois

Ann Sheridan
(Clara Lou Sheridan; "Oomph Girl")
American actress
• Pin-up favorite, 1940s; films include *The Man Who Came to Dinner*, 1942.
b. February 21, 1915 in Denton, Texas
d. January 21, 1967 in Hollywood, California

Nicollette Sheridan
American actress
• Plays Paige Mathison on TV series "Knots Landing," 1988-.
b. November 21, 1963 in Sussex, England

Richard Brinsley Sheridan
Irish dramatist–politician
• Noted for three great comedies: *The Rivals*, 1775; *School for Scandal*, 1777; farce *The Critic*, 1779.
b. October 3, 1751 in Dublin, Ireland
d. July 07, 1816 in London, England

Allan Sherman
American comedian
• Known for satiric song, "Hello Muddah, Hello Faddah," 1963.
b. November 3, 1924 in Chicago, Illinois
d. November 2, 1973 in Los Angeles, California

Harry R Sherman
American producer
• TV productions include "Eleanor and Franklin," 1976; "The Gathering," 1978; won three Emmys.
b. September 21, 1927 in Los Angeles, California

Lowell Sherman
American actor–director
• Films include *Morning Glory*, 1933; *Born to Be Bad*, 1934.
b. October 11, 1885 in San Francisco, California
d. December 28, 1934 in Hollywood, California

Vincent Sherman
(Abram Orovitz)
American director
• TV shows include "The Waltons," 1972-81; "Baretta," 1975-78.
b. July 16, 1906 in Vienna, Georgia

Robert Emmet Sherwood
American dramatist–author
• Won Pulitzer for *Idiot's Delight*, 1936; *Abe Lincoln in Illinois*, 1938.
b. April 04, 1896 in New Rochelle, New York
d. November 14, 1955 in New York, New York

Brooke Shields
(Christa Brooke Camille Shields; "Brookie")
American model–actress
• Appeared on over 30 magazine covers, 1981.
b. May 31, 1965 in New York, New York

Shields and Yarnell
(Robert Shields; Lorene Yarnell)
American entertainers
• Mime duo; won first place Ted Mack amateur contest; on numerous TV specials.

Talia Rose Coppola Shire
(Mrs Jack Schwartzman)
American actress
• Played Adrian in *Rocky* films; sister of director Francis Ford Coppola.
b. April 25, 1946 in Jamaica, New York

Anne Shirley
(Dawn O'Day; Dawn Evelyeen Paris)
American actress
• Child star under name Dawn O'Day, 1922-34; received Oscar nomination for *Stella Dallas*, 1937.
b. April 17, 1918 in New York, New York

James Shirley
English dramatist
• Wrote 40 plays, including tragedy *The Traitor*, 1631; comedy of manners, *Lady of Pleasure*, 1635.
b. 1596 in London, England
d. October 29, 1666 in London, England

Martin Short
Canadian actor–comedian
• Regular cast member, "Saturday Night Live," 1984-85; created characters Ed Grimley, Nathan Thurm.
b. March 26, 1950 in Hamilton, Ontario

Herb Shriner
American TV personality
• Pioneer TV humorist, emcee; known for his Hoosier stories, 1950s.
b. May 29, 1918 in Toledo, Ohio
d. April 23, 1970 in Delray Beach, Florida

Maria Owings Shriver
(Mrs Arnold Schwarzenegger)
American broadcast journalist–celebrity relative
• Daughter of Sargent Shriver, Eunice Kennedy; co-anchor, "CBS Morning News," 1985-86.
b. November 06, 1955 in Chicago, Illinois

Jacob J Shubert
American manager–producer
• One of three brothers who built powerful Broadway theatrical empire; principal backer of Flo Ziegfield.
b. August 15, 1880 in Shirvanta, Russia
d. December 26, 1963 in New York, New York

Lee Shubert
American theater owner–producer
• With brothers, major owner of legitimate theater empire, 1920-53; produced countless Broadway hits.
b. March 15, 1875 in Shirvanta, Russia
d. December 25, 1953 in New York, New York

Max Shulman
American author–dramatist
• Humorous works include *Barefoot Boy with Cheek*, 1943; adapted to musical comedy, 1947; cowrote play *The Tender Trap*, 1954; creator, writer, TV series "The Many Loves of Dobie Gillis," 1959-63.
b. March 14, 1919 in Saint Paul, Minnesota
d. August 28, 1988 in Los Angeles, California

Frank Shuster
(Wayne and Shuster)
Canadian comedian
• Had documentary-style TV show with partner Johnny Wayne, "Wayne and Schuster Take an Affectionate Look at...," 1966.
b. 1916

Rosie Shuster
American writer
• Multiple Emmy winner for NBC's "Saturday Night Live," 1970s.
b. June 19, 1950 in Toronto, Ontario

Charles Shyer
American screenwriter
• Films include *Smokey and the Bandit*, 1977; *Private Benjamin*, 1980.
b. October 11, 1941 in Los Angeles, California

Andy Sidaris
American producer–director
• Won Emmys for "1968 Summer Olympics," 1969; "XII Winter Olympics," 1976.
b. February 2, 1932 in Chicago, Illinois

Sarah Kemble Siddons
English actress
• Best known for tragic roles, especially Lady MacBeth, 1785-1812.
b. July 05, 1755 in Brecon, Wales
d. June 08, 1831 in London, England

George Sidney
American director–producer
• Won Oscars for shorts *Quicker'n A Wink*, 1940; *Of Pups and Puzzles*, 1941.
b. October 04, 1916 in New York, New York

Sylvia Sidney
(Sophia Kosow)
American actress
• Oscar nominee, 1973, for *Summer Wishes, Winter Dreams*.
b. August 08, 1910 in New York, New York

Larry Siegel
American writer
• Won Emmys for "The Carol Burnett Show," 1971, 1973, 1978.
b. October 29, 1925 in New York, New York

Simone Henrietta Charlotte Signoret
(Simone Kaminker; Mrs Yves Montand)
German actress
• Won Oscar for *Room at the Top*, 1958.
b. March 25, 1921 in Wiesbaden, Germany
d. September 3, 1985 in Normandy, France

James B Sikking
American actor
• Played Lt. Howard Hunter on TV series "Hill Street Blues," 1981-87.
b. March 05, in Los Angeles, California

Stirling Dale Silliphant
American screenwriter–producer
• Won Oscar, Edgar for writing *In the Heat of the Night*, 1968.
b. January 16, 1918 in Detroit, Michigan

Leonard Sillman
American producer–actor–author
• Wrote film *New Faces*, 1954; produced *An Angel Comes to Brooklyn*, 1945.
b. May 09, 1908 in Detroit, Michigan
d. January 23, 1982 in New York, New York

Milton Sills
American actor
• Leading man in over 75 films, 1914-30.
b. January 1, 1882 in Chicago, Illinois
d. September 15, 1930 in Santa Barbara, California

Franelle Silver
Canadian writer
• Won Emmy for "The Carol Burnett Show," 1978.
b. September 12, 1952 in Toronto, Ontario

Ron Silver
American actor
• Won best actor Tony for *Speed-the-Plow*, 1988; films include *Silkwood*, 1983.
b. July 02, 1946 in New York, New York

Frank Silvera
American actor
• Character actor, 1952-70; appeared in TV series "High Chaparral," 1967-70.
b. July 24, 1914 in Kingston, Jamaica
d. June 11, 1970 in Pasadena, California

Jay Silverheels
American actor
• Played Tonto in *Lone Ranger* movies and TV series, 1948-61.
b. May 26, 1922 in Ontario
d. March 05, 1980 in Woodland Hills, California

Fred Silverman
American TV executive
• Only man to run all three TV networks' entertainment divisions; CBS, 1963-75; ABC, 1975-78; NBC, 1978-81.
b. September 13, 1937 in New York, New York

Phil Silvers
(Philip Silversmith)
American comedian
• Won three Emmys for playing Sergeant Bilko in TV series "The Phil Silvers Show," 1955-59; films include *A Funny Thing Happened on the Way to the Forum*, 1966.
b. May 11, 1911 in Brooklyn, New York
d. November 01, 1985 in Los Angeles, California

Elliot Silverstein
American director
• Films include *Cat Ballou*, 1965; *A Man Called Horse*, 1970.
b. 1927 in Boston, Massachusetts

Alastair Sim
English producer–director
• Films include *The Lavender Hill Mob*, 1951; starred in *A Christmas Carol*, 1951.
b. October 09, 1900 in Edinburgh, Scotland
d. August 19, 1976 in London, England

Jean Simmons
English actress
• Appeared in British, US films including *Big Country*, 1958; TV movies include "Thornbirds," 1983.
b. January 31, 1929 in London, England

Richard Simmons
("Pied Piper of Pounds")
American TV personality–author
• Host of syndicated exercise TV show; wrote *Never Say Diet*, 1980.
b. July 12, 1948 in New Orleans, Louisiana

Hilda Simms
American actress
• Made Broadway debut in first play in US with all-black cast, *Anna Lucasta*, 1944.
b. April 15, 1920 in Minneapolis, Minnesota

Neil (Marvin Neil) Simon
American dramatist
• Has produced more Broadway hits than any other American playwright; most of his plays have been adapted to film, including *The Goodbye Girl*, 1977.
b. July 04, 1927 in New York, New York

Simone Simon
French actress
• Movie idol in France, 1930s; US films include *Seventh Heaven*, 1937; *The Cat People*, 1942.
b. April 23, 1913 in Marseilles, France

Donald C Simpson
American producer
• Films include *Flash Dance*, 1983; *Beverly Hills Cop*, 1984; *Top Gun*, 1986.
b. October 29, 1945 in Anchorage, Alaska

Madge Sinclair
(Madge Walters)
American actress
• Three-time Emmy nominee for role on TV's "Trapper John, MD," 1980-86.
b. April 28, in Kingston, Jamaica

Donald (Alfred) Sinden
English actor
• British films include *The Cruel Sea*, 1953; *That Lucky Touch*, 1975.
b. October 09, 1923 in Plymouth, England

Penny Singleton
(Dorothy McNulty)
American actress
• Starred as "Blondie" in film series, 1938-50.
b. September 15, 1908 in Philadelphia, Pennsylvania

Douglas Sirk
(Dietlef Sierck)
Danish director
• Films include *Magnificent Obsession*, 1954; *Imitation of Life*, 1959.
b. April 26, 1900 in Skagen, Denmark
d. January 14, 1987 in Lugano, Switzerland

Victor Sjostrom
Swedish director
• Pioneer of Swedish film industry.
b. September 2, 1879 in Silbodal, Sweden
d. January 03, 1960 in Stockholm, Sweden

Red (Richard) Skelton
American comedian–actor
• Master of pantomime and slapstick comedy; hosted comedy-variety TV show, 1951-71.
b. July 18, 1913 in Vincennes, Indiana

Tom (Thomas Roy) Skerritt
American actor
• Films include *The Dead Zone*, 1983; *Alien*, 1979.
b. August 25, 1933 in Detroit, Michigan

Otis Skinner
American actor
• One of American theater's greatest character actors; known for role in *Kismet*, 1911-14.
b. June 28, 1858 in Cambridge, Massachusetts
d. January 04, 1942 in New York, New York

Spyros Panagiotes Skouras
American producer
• Pres., 20th Century Fox, 1942-62; launched cinemascope.
b. March 28, 1893 in Skourokhori, Greece
d. August 16, 1971 in Mamaroneck, New York

Menasha Skulnik
Polish actor
• Stage comedian, 1920-50, in Yiddish theater.
b. May 15, 1898 in Warsaw, Poland
d. June 04, 1970 in New York, New York

Bernard Slade, pseud
(Bernard Slade Newbound)
Canadian dramatist
• Stage plays include *Same Time Next Year*, 1975; *Fatal Attraction*, 1984; also wrote screenplays, TV scripts.
b. May 02, 1930 in Saint Catherines, Ontario

Mia Slavenska
(Mia Corak)
Yugoslav dancer
• Ballerina best known for role of "Blanche" in *Streetcar Named Desire*, 1952.
b. February 2, 1914 in Slavonski-Brod, Yugoslavia

Henry Slesar
American writer
• With soap opera "The Edge of Night," since 1968; won Emmy, 1974.
b. June 12, 1927 in Brooklyn, New York

Erika Slezak
American actress
• Won Emmys, 1984, 1986, for role of Victoria Lord Buchanan in soap opera "One Life to Live."
b. August 05, 1946 in Los Angeles, California

Walter Slezak
American actor
• Won 1955 Tony for *Fanny*, best known film role in *Lifeboat*, 1944.
b. May 03, 1902 in Vienna, Austria
d. April 21, 1983 in Flower Hill, New York

Michael Sloan
American writer
• Wrote for TV detective shows "Columbo," 1971-77; "Harry-O," 1974-76; "Switch," 1975-78.
b. October 14, 1946 in New York, New York

Everett Sloane
American actor
• Films include *The Patsy*, 1964; *Brushfire*, 1962.
b. October 01, 1909 in New York, New York
d. August 06, 1965 in Brentwood, California

Jack Scott Smart
American actor
• Films include *Some Like It Hot*, 1939; *The Fat Man*, 1951.
b. 1903
d. January 15, 1960 in Springfield, Illinois

Yakov Smirnoff
(Yakov Pokhis)
American comedian
• Known for TV beer commercial; comedy about native land.
b. January 24, 1951 in Odessa, U.S.S.R.

Alexis Smith
(Mrs Craig Stevens)
American actress
• Won 1971 Tony award for *Follies*.
b. June 08, 1921 in Penticton, British Columbia

Allison Smith
American actress
• Plays Jennie Lowell on TV series "Kate & Allie," 1984-1989.
b. 1970 in Bergen County, New Jersey

Bob Smith
American entertainer
• Creator, star of children's TV show "Howdy Doody," 1947-60.
b. November 27, 1917 in Buffalo, New York

C Aubrey Smith
English actor
• Noted character actor in over 80 films, 1920s-40s.
b. July 21, 1863 in London, England
d. December 2, 1948 in Beverly Hills, California

Dodie (Dorothy Gladys) Smith
(C L Anthony pseud)
English dramatist–author
• Wrote *The One Hundred and One Dalmations*, 1956; filmed by Walt Disney, 1960.
b. May 03, 1896 in Whitefield, England

Howard K(ingsbury) Smith
American broadcast journalist
• Correspondent, CBS News, 1941-61; reporter, commentator, ABC News, 1961-79.
b. May 12, 1914 in Ferriday, Louisiana

Jaclyn Smith
(Mrs Tony Richmond)
American actress
• Starred in "Charlie's Angels," 1976-80; TV movie *Rage of Angels*, 1983.
b. October 26, 1948 in Houston, Texas

Joe Smith
(Joseph Seltzer; Smith and Dale)
American comedian
• Part of vaudeville team, Smith and Dale, for 73 yrs.
b. February 17, 1884 in New York, New York
d. February 22, 1981 in Englewood, New Jersey

Kent Smith
American actor
• Films include *Games*, 1967; *Taking Tiger Mountain*, 1983.
b. March 19, 1907 in New York, New York
d. April 23, 1985 in Los Angeles, California

Maggie Natalie Smith
English actress
• Won Oscars for *The Prime of Miss Jean Brodie*, 1969; *California Suite*, 1978.
b. December 28, 1934 in Ilford, England

Oliver Smith
American producer–designer
• Winner of eight Tonys for designs including *The Sound of Music*, 1960.
b. February 13, 1918 in Waupun, Wisconsin

Pete Smith
(Peter Schmidt)
American producer
• Produced, narrated shorts for MGM, 1936-55; over 20 nominated for Oscars.
b. September 04, 1892 in New York, New York
d. 1979 in Los Angeles, California

Robert Lee Smith
American inventor–TV personality
• Founder, Equal Relationships Institute, 1981–; host, TV series "You and Your Big Ideas," 1959-64.
b. September 18, 1928 in Saint Louis, Missouri

Roger Smith
American actor
• Films include *The First Time*, 1969; husband, manager of Ann-Margret.
b. December 18, 1932 in South Gate, California

Samantha Smith
American student–actress
• Wrote letter to Soviet leader Andropov, 1982, visited USSR as his guest, 1983; died in plane crash.
b. June 29, 1972 in Manchester, Maine
d. August 25, 1985 in Auburn, Maine

Jan Smithers
American actress
• Played Bailey on TV series "WKRP in Cincinnati," 1978-82.
b. July 03, 1949 in North Hollywood, California

Jimmy Smits
American actor
• Plays Victor Sifuentes on TV drama "LA Law," 1986–; won supporting actor Emmy, 1990.
b. July 09, 1958 in New York, New York

Dick (Richard) Smothers
(The Smothers Brothers)
American comedian–singer
• Starred with brother Tommy in 1960s TV series, in Broadway play *I Love My Wife*, 1978-79.
b. November 2, 1938 in New York, New York

Michael Smuin
American choreographer
• Won Tony for musical revival *Anything Goes*, 1988.
b. October 13, 1938 in Missoula, Montana

Carrie Snodgress
American actress
• 1970 Oscar nominee for *Diary of a Mad Housewife*.
b. October 27, 1946 in Chicago, Illinois

Tom Snyder
American broadcast journalist–TV personality
• Best known as host of NBC latenight interview show "Tomorrow," 1973-81.
b. May 12, 1936 in Milwaukee, Wisconsin

Carol Sobieski
American writer
• TV shows include "Peyton Place," 1964-69; films include *The Toy, Annie,* 1982.
b. March 16, 1939 in Chicago, Illinois

Steven Soderbergh
American filmmaker
• Wrote, edited, directed *Sex, Lies, and Videotape*, winner of several awards, 1989 Cannes Film Festival.
b. 1963 in Georgia

Suzanne Somers
(Mrs Alan Hamel; Suzanne Mahoney)
American actress
• Star of TV's "Three's Company," 1977-81.
b. October 16, 1946 in San Bruno, California

Michael Somes
English dancer
• Leading male dancer with Royal Ballet, 1951-68.
b. September 28, 1917 in Horsley, England

Elke Sommer
(Elke Schletze)
American actress
• Sexy blonde in films since 1959.
b. November 05, 1940 in Berlin, Germany

Gale (Edith Holm) Sondergaard
(Mrs Herbert Biberman)
American actress
• Known for playing villainous women; won first supporting actress Oscar for *Anthony Adverse*, 1937; blacklisted with husband, late 1940s-50s.
b. February 15, 1899 in Litchfield, Minnesota
d. August 14, 1985 in Woodland Hills, California

Jack Soo
(Goro Suzuki)
American actor
• Played Yemana on TV series "Barney Miller," 1975-79.
b. October 28, 1915 in Oakland, California
d. January 11, 1979 in Los Angeles, California

Ann Sothern
(Harriet Lake)
American actress
• Lighthearted heroine of *Maisie* film series, 1939-47; starred on TV in comedies "Private Secretary," 1954-57; "The Ann Sothern Show," 1958-61.
b. January 22, 1909 in Valley City, North Dakota

Edward Askew Sothern
English entertainer
• Noted for role in *Our American Cousin*, from 1858; appeared night of Lincoln assassination.
b. April 01, 1826 in Liverpool, England
d. January 2, 1881 in London, England

Edward Hugh Sothern
American entertainer
• Founded Shakespearian Repertory Co. with wife, Julia Marlowe, 1900-16; son of Edward Askew.
b. December 06, 1859 in New Orleans, Louisiana
d. 1933 in New York, New York

David Soul
American actor
• Starred in TV shows "Here Come the Brides," "Starsky and Hutch."
b. August 28, 1946 in Chicago, Illinois

Olan Soule
American actor
• Films include *The Apple Dumpling Gang*, 1975; *St. Ives*, 1976.
b. February 28, 1909 in La Harpe, Illinois

Sissy (Mary Elizabeth) Spacek
(Mrs Jack Fiske)
American actress
• Won Oscar, 1980, for *Coal Miner's Daughter*.
b. December 25, 1949 in Quitman, Texas

James Spader
American actor
• Achieved stardom for role in the award-winning film, *Sex, Lies & Videotape*, 1989.
b. February 7, 1960

Joe Spano
American actor
• Played Henry Goldblum on TV series "Hill Street Blues," 1981-87.
b. July 07, 1946 in San Francisco, California

Phil(lip Harvey) Spector
American producer
• Devised "wall of sound" technique of sound arrangement, 1962; highlights lead vocals.
b. December 25, 1940 in New York, New York

Johnny Speight
English writer
• Created BBC series "Till Death Do Us Part," 1966-75; adapted in US as "All in the Family," 1971.
b. June 02, 1921 in London, England

Aaron Spelling
American producer
• Most successful TV producer; shows include "Charlie's Angels," "Dynasty," "Hotel."
b. April 22, 1925 in Dallas, Texas

Bella Cohen Spewack
(Mrs Samuel Spewack)
American dramatist–journalist
• With husband, wrote Broadway hits *Boy Meets Girl*, 1935, *Kiss Me Kate*, 1949.
b. March 25, 1899 in Bucharest, Romania
d. April 27, 1990 in New York, New York

Samuel Spewack
Russian dramatist
• With wife Bella, wrote Broadway hits *Boy Meets Girl*, 1935, *Kiss Me Kate*, 1949.
b. September 16, 1899 in Bachmut, Russia
d. October 14, 1971 in New York, New York

Sam Spiegel
(S P Eagle)
American producer
• Won Oscars for *On the Waterfront*, 1954; *The Bridge on the River Kwai*, 1957; *Lawrence of Arabia*, 1962.
b. November 11, 1904 in Jaroslau, Austria
d. December 31, 1985 in St. Martin Island, West Indies

Steven Spielberg
American director
• Films include *Jaws*, 1975; *ET*, 1982; *The Color Purple*, 1986.
b. December 18, 1947 in Cincinnati, Ohio

Leonard Spigelgass
American dramatist
• Oscar nominee for best original story: *Mystery Street*, 1950.
b. November 26, 1908 in New York, New York
d. February 14, 1985 in Los Angeles, California

Lawrence Spivak
American TV personality–producer
• Co-founder, producer, panel member, *Meet the Press*, on radio, TV, 1945–.
b. June 11, 1900 in Brooklyn, New York

Robert Langford Stack
American actor
• Starred in TV series "The Untouchables," 1959-63.
b. January 13, 1919 in Los Angeles, California

James Stacy
(Maurice W Elias)
American actor
• Lost arm, leg in motorcycle accident; starred in TV movie *Just a Little Inconvenience*, 1977; once married to Connie Stevens.
b. December 23, 1936 in Los Angeles, California

Lesley Rene Stahl
American broadcast journalist
• Correspondent, CBS News, 1974–; coined expression "The Peggy Principle."
b. December 16, 1941 in Lynn, Massachusetts

Sylvester (Michael Sylvester) Stallone
American actor–director
• Best known for *Rocky* film series, 1976-85; *Rambo* films, 1984, 1985.
b. July 06, 1946 in New York, New York

John Stamos
American actor
• Plays Jesse on TV series "Full House," 1987–.
b. August 19, 1963

Terence Stamp
English actor
• Films include *Superman II*, 1980; *Monster Island*, 1981.
b. July 22, 1940 in London, England

Lionel (Jay) Stander
American actor
• Played Max on TV series "Hart to Hart," 1979-84.
b. January 11, 1909 in New York, New York

Sir Guy Standing
Actor
• Prominent on British, American stage; appeared in Hollywood films, 1930s: *Death Takes a Holiday*, 1934.
b. September 01, 1873 in London, England
d. February 24, 1937 in Los Angeles, California

Arnold Stang
American comedian–actor
• Performer on radio beginning 1935; known for film performance in *The Man With the Golden Arm*, 1955.
b. September 28, 1925 in Chelsea, Massachusetts

Konstantin Sergeyevich Stanislavsky
(Konstantin Sergeyevich Alexeyev)
Russian actor–director
• Co-founder, Moscow Art Theatre; developed theory of actor identifying with role, called Stanislavsky System.
b. January 17, 1863 in Moscow, Russia
d. August 07, 1938 in Moscow, U.S.S.R.

Kim Stanley
(Patricia Kimberly Reid)
American actress
• Method actress; nominated for Oscar, 1964, for *Seance on a Wet Afternoon*, 1964.
b. February 11, 1925 in Tularosa, New Mexico

Frank Stanton
American TV executive
• Pres. of CBS, 1946-71; TV Academy Hall of Fame, 1986.
b. March 2, 1908 in Muskegon, Michigan

Barbara Stanwyck
(Ruby Stevens)
American actress
• Starred in over 80 films; received Oscar nominations for *Stella Dallas*, 1937, *The Lady Eve*, 1941, *Double Indemnity*, 1944, *Sorry, Wrong Number*, 1948; won Emmys for "The Big Valley" and "The Thorn Birds."
b. July 16, 1907 in Brooklyn, New York
d. January 2, 1990 in Santa Monica, California

Jean Stapleton
(Jeanne Murray; Mrs William Putch)
American actress
• Played Edith Bunker on TV series "All in the Family," 1971-79.
b. January 19, 1923 in New York, New York

Maureen (Lois Maureen) Stapleton
American actress
• Won Tony for *The Gingerbread Lady*, 1970; won Oscar for *Reds*, 1982.
b. June 21, 1925 in Troy, New York

Dawn Steel
American producer–film executive
• Films include *Fatal Attraction*, 1987; chairman of Columbia Pictures, 1987-1990.
b. August 19, 1946 in New York, New York

Bob Steele
(Robert North Bradbury Jr)
American actor
• Cowboy star in over 150 films, 1927-71; appeared in TV comedy "F-Troop." 1965-67.
b. January 23, 1906 in Pendleton, Oregon
d. December 21, 1988 in Burbank, California

Tommy Steele
English actor
• Films include *The Happiest Millionaire*, 1967; *Finian's Rainbow*, 1968.
b. December 17, 1936 in London, England

Mary Steenburgen
(Mrs Malcolm McDowell)
American actress
• Won Oscar, 1981, for *Melvin and Howard.*
b. 1953 in Little Rock, Arkansas

Rod Steiger
American actor
• Won Oscar, 1967, for *In the Heat of the Night.*
b. April 14, 1925 in Westhampton, New York

James R Stein
American writer
• Won Emmys for "Lily," 1974; "The Carol Burnett Show," 1978.
b. January 09, 1950 in Chicago, Illinois

David Steinberg
Canadian actor–comedian
• Off-beat comic; hosted David Frost, Dick Cavett shows on TV; directed film *Paternity,* 1981.
b. August 09, 1942 in Winnipeg, Manitoba

Robert Stephens
English actor
• Films include *Cleopatra,* 1963; *The Shout,* 1978.
b. July 14, 1931 in Bristol, England

Henry Stephenson
British actor
• Character actor in over 100 films, 1917-49.
b. April 16, 1871 in West Indies
d. April 24, 1956 in San Francisco, California

Skip (Charles Frederick) Stephenson
American TV personality–comedian
• Co-host of TV series "Real People."
b. 1948 in Omaha, Nebraska

Jan Sterling
(Jan Sterling Andriance; Mrs Paul Douglas)
American actress
• Made Broadway debut, 1938; nominated for Oscar for *The High and the Mighty,* 1954.
b. April 03, 1923 in New York, New York

Robert Sterling
(William Sterling Hart)
American actor
• Played George Kerby in TV's "Topper," 1953-56; appeared in some films.
b. November 13, 1917 in New Castle, Pennsylvania

Leonard B Stern
Writer–Producer
• Won Emmys for scripts of "The Bilko Show," 1956; "Get Smart," 1967.
b. December 23, 1923

Sandor Stern
Canadian writer–director
• Wrote screenplays *Fast Break; The Amityville Horror.*
b. July 13, 1936 in Timmins, Ontario

Stewart Stern
American screenwriter
• Films include *Rebel Without a Cause,* 1955; Oscar-winning *Rachel, Rachel,* 1966.
b. March 22, 1922 in New York, New York

Andrew Stevens
American actor
• Films include *The Fury,* 1978; played Casey Denault on TV series "Dallas," 1987-88; son of Stella.
b. June 1, 1955 in Memphis, Tennessee

Connie Stevens
(Concetta Ingolia)
American actress–singer
• Starred in TV series "Hawaiian Eye," 1959-63; "Wendy and Me," 1964-65, with George Burns.
b. August 08, 1938 in Brooklyn, New York

Emily A Stevens
American actress
• Known for alluring woman roles: *The Unchastened Woman,* 1915; died of drug overdose; cousin of Minnie Fiske.
b. 1882 in New York
d. January 02, 1928 in New York, New York

George (Cooper) Stevens
American director
• Won Oscars for *A Place in the Sun,* 1951; *Giant,* 1956.
b. December 18, 1904 in Oakland, California
d. March 08, 1975 in Lancaster, California

Inger Stevens
(Inger Stensland)
American actress
• Starred in "The Farmer's Daughter," 1963-66.
b. October 18, 1934 in Stockholm, Sweden
d. April 3, 1970 in Hollywood, California

Leslie Stevens
American screenwriter
• Co-wrote science fiction film *Buck Rogers in the 25th Century,* 1979.
b. February 13, 1924 in Washington, District of Columbia

Onslow Stevens
(Onslow Ford Stevenson)
American actor
• Appeared in films *This Side of Heaven,* 1934; *The Couch,* 1962.
b. March 29, 1906 in Los Angeles, California
d. January 05, 1977 in Van Nuys, California

Roger L(acey) Stevens
American producer
• Won Tonys for Broadway productions of *A Man For All Seasons,* 1962; *Death of a Salesman,* 1984; chm. of board, Kennedy Center, Washington, DC, 1961-88.
b. March 12, 1910 in Detroit, Michigan

Stella Stevens
(Estelle Eggleston)
American actress
• Best known for role of Appassionata von Climax in film *Lil' Abner,* 1959.
b. October 01, 1938 in Hot Coffee, Mississippi

McLean Stevenson
American actor
• Played Henry Blake on "M*A*S*H," 1972-75.
b. November 14, 1929 in Bloomington, Illinois

Parker Stevenson
American actor
• Starred in TV series "Hardy Boys Mysteries," 1978-79.
b. June 04, 1951 in Philadelphia, Pennsylvania

Robert Stevenson
American director
• Films include Disney classics *Mary Poppins,* 1964; *The Love Bug,* 1968.
b. 1905 in London, England
d. April 3, 1986 in Santa Barbara, California

Ellen Stewart
American producer
• Opened boutique, La Mama, NYC, 1962; produced, directed plays by int'l., avant-garde playwrights.
b. October 07, 1931 in New Orleans, Louisiana

Jimmy (James Maitland) Stewart
American actor
• Hollywood great; best known for *Mr. Smith Goes to Washington,* 1939, *It's a Wonderful Life,* 1946.
b. May 2, 1908 in Indiana, Pennsylvania

Michael Stewart
(Michael Rubin)
American dramatist
• Won Tonys for *Bye, Bye Birdie,* 1961; *Hello Dolly!* 1964.
b. August 01, 1929 in New York, New York
d. September 2, 1987 in New York, New York

Paul Stewart
American actor
• Made acting debut in Orson Welles' *Citizen Kane,* 1941; typically cast in gangster roles.
b. March 13, 1908 in New York, New York
d. February 17, 1986 in Los Angeles, California

Dorothy Stickney
American actress
• Co-starred in Broadway's *Life With Father* with husband Howard Lindsay, 1939-43.
b. June 21, 1900 in Dickinson, North Dakota

David Ogden Stiers
American actor
• Played Major Winchester on "M*A*S*H," 1977-83.
b. October 31, 1942 in Peoria, Illinois

Robert Colin Stigwood
Australian producer
• Won Tony for *Evita,* 1980.
b. April 16, 1934 in Adelaide, Australia

Jerry Stiller
(Stiller and Meara)
American comedian–actor
• Formed successful comedy team with wife Anne Meara; in film *Those Lips, Those Eyes,* 1980.
b. June 08, 1926 in New York, New York

Mauritz Stiller
Swedish director
• Pioneer of Swedish cinema; discovered Greta Garbo.
b. July 17, 1883 in Helsinki, Finland
d. November 08, 1928 in Stockholm, Sweden

Dean Stockwell
American actor
• Child star of 1940s; in screen musical *Anchors Aweigh,* 1945; brother of Guy.
b. March 05, 1936 in Hollywood, California

Guy Stockwell
American actor
• Films include *Please Don't Eat the Daisies,* 1960; *Airport 1975,* 1974.
b. November 16, 1938 in North Hollywood, California

Dorothy Stone
American actress–dancer
• Daughter of Fred Stone; dance partner with husband, Charles Collins, in *The Gay Divorcee,* 1933, 1941; *The Red Mill,* 1945.
b. June 03, 1905 in Brooklyn, New York
d. September 24, 1974 in Montecito, California

Ezra (Chaim) Stone
American director–producer
• Best known as Henry Aldrich on radio show "The Aldrich Family"; director of numerous movies, plays, TV shows.
b. December 02, 1917 in New Bedford, Massachusetts

Fred Stone
American actor
• Scarecrow in original Broadway version of *The Wizard of Oz,* 1903.
b. August 19, 1873 in Denver, Colorado
d. March 06, 1959 in North Hollywood, California

Lewis Stone
American actor
• Was Judge Hardy in Andy Hardy film series.
b. November 15, 1879 in Worcester, Massachusetts
d. September 11, 1953 in Los Angeles, California

Milburn Stone
American actor
• Played Doc Adams on "Gunsmoke," 1955-75; won Emmy, 1968.
b. July 05, 1904 in Burton, Kansas
d. June 12, 1980 in La Jolla, California

Oliver Stone
American screenwriter–director
• Won best picture, best director Oscars for *Platoon,* 1986; best director Oscar for *Born on the Fourth of July,* 1990.
b. September 15, 1946 in New York, New York

Paula Stone
American producer
• Starred with family as *The Stepping Stones* in vaudeville.
b. January 2, 1916 in New York, New York

Peter H Stone
American screenwriter
• Won Oscar for *Father Goose,* 1964; won Tonys for *1776,* 1969; *Woman of the Year,* 1980.
b. February 27, 1930 in Los Angeles, California

Sidney Stone
American TV personality
• Commercial announcer for Milton Berle's TV series, 1948-51; coined phrase, "Tell ya what I'm gonna do!"
b. 1903
d. February 12, 1986 in New York, New York

Tom Stoppard
(Thomas Straussler)
British author–dramatist
• Award-winning dramatist: *Rosencrantz and Guildenstern Are Dead,* 1967; *The Real Thing,* 1984.
b. July 03, 1937 in Zlin, Czechoslovakia

Gale Storm
(Josephine Cottle)
American actress
• Starred in "My Little Margie," 1952-55; "The Gale Storm Show," 1956-62.
b. April 05, 1922 in Bloomington, Texas

Beatrice Whitney Straight
American actress
• Won Tony, 1953, for performance in *The Crucible;* Oscar, 1976, for *Network.*
b. August 02, 1918 in Long Island, New York

Paul Strand
American photographer–filmmaker
• First to use "candid camera" trick; produced film documentaries.
b. October 16, 1890 in New York, New York
d. March 31, 1976 in Yvelines, France

Lee Strasberg
(Israel Strassberg)
American actor–acting teacher
• Directed Actor's Studio, 1950-82; taught Stanislavsky acting method.
b. November 17, 1901 in Budzanow, Austria
d. February 17, 1982 in New York, New York

Susan Elizabeth Strasberg
American actress–author
• Created lead role on stage in *Diary of Anne Frank,* 1955.
b. May 22, 1938 in New York, New York

Dorothy Stratten
(Dorothy Hoogstratten; Mrs Paul Snider)
Canadian actress–model
• Former Playboy centerfold shot to death by estranged husband; life story subject of film *Star 80,* 1983.
b. February 28, 1960 in Vancouver, British Columbia
d. August 14, 1980 in Los Angeles, California

Peter Strauss
American actor
• Won Emmy, 1979, for *The Jericho Mile;* starred in *Rich Man, Poor Man,* 1976.
b. February 2, 1947 in Croton-on-Hudson, New York

Robert Strauss
American actor
• In films, 1942-61; appeared in *Stalag 17*, 1953; *The Seven Year Itch*, 1955.
b. November 08, 1913 in New York, New York
d. February 2, 1974 in New York, New York

Meryl (Mary Louise) Streep
American actress
• Won Oscar for *Sophie's Choice*, 1983; Emmy, 1978, for *Holocaust*.
b. June 22, 1949 in Summit, New Jersey

August (Johan August) Strindberg
Swedish dramatist–author
• Developed realism, symbolism in work: *Miss Julie; The Ghost Sonata*.
b. January 22, 1849 in Stockholm, Sweden
d. May 14, 1912 in Stockholm, Sweden

Woody Strode
American actor
• In films since 1941: *The Cotton Club*, 1984.
b. July 25, 1914 in Los Angeles, California

Hunt Stromberg
American producer
• Produced Nelson Eddy-Jeanette MacDonald films, *The Thin Man* series for MGM, 1930s.
b. July 12, 1894 in Louisville, Kentucky
d. August 23, 1968 in Los Angeles, California

Shepperd Strudwick
American actor
• Career began in 1928; over 200 roles in plays, movies, TV.
b. September 22, 1907 in Hillsboro, North Carolina
d. January 15, 1983 in New York, New York

Karl Struss
American filmmaker
• Won first Oscar given for cinematography, 1927.
b. November 3, 1886 in New York, New York
d. December 16, 1981 in Santa Monica, California

Sally Anne Struthers
American actress
• Played Gloria on "All in the Family," 1971-78; won two Emmys.
b. July 28, 1948 in Portland, Oregon

Mel Stuart
American director
• Won Emmys for "The Roots of Madness," 1967; "Making of the President," 1970.
b. September 02, 1928 in New York, New York

Preston Sturges
(Edmond P Biden)
American director–screenwriter
• Wrote, directed Oscar-winning *The Great McGinty*, 1940.
b. August 29, 1898 in Chicago, Illinois
d. August 06, 1959 in New York, New York

Hermann Sudermann
German dramatist
• Works concerned ideas of honor, reputation: *Honor*, 1893; *St. John's Fire*, 1900.
b. September 3, 1857 in Matziken, Prussia (East)
d. November 21, 1928 in Berlin, Germany

Margaret Sullavan
American actress
• First wife of Henry Fonda; won Drama Critics award for *The Voice of the Turtle*, 1943.
b. May 16, 1896 in Norfolk, Virginia
d. January 01, 1960 in New Haven, Connecticut

Barry Sullivan
(Patrick Barry)
American actor
• Leading man in films since 1940s: *Another Time, Another Place*, 1958; *Harlow*, 1965.
b. August 12, 1912 in New York, New York

Ed(ward Vincent) Sullivan
American TV personality
• "Toast of the Town" variety show evolved into "The Ed Sullivan Show," 1948-71.
b. September 28, 1902 in New York, New York
d. October 13, 1974 in New York, New York

Francis Loftus Sullivan
English actor
• Character actor, often in villainous roles: *Oliver Twist*, 1948; *The Prodigal*, 1955.
b. January 06, 1903 in London, England
d. November 19, 1956 in New York, New York

Kathleen Sullivan
American broadcast journalist
• Anchored "ABC World News This Morning."
b. 1954 in Pasadena, California

Susan Sullivan
American actress
• Played Maggie Gioberti Channing on TV series "Falcon Crest," 1981-89.
b. November 18, 1944 in New York, New York

Slim (George J) Summerville
American comedian
• One of original Keystone Cops, known for "hick" roles; films include *All Quiet on the Western Front*, 1930.
b. July 1, 1896 in Albuquerque, New Mexico
d. January 06, 1946 in Laguna Beach, California

David Howard Susskind
American producer
• Well-known TV talk show host; producer of films, plays, TV shows; won Emmys, 1970s.
b. December 19, 1920 in Brookline, Massachusetts
d. February 22, 1987 in New York, New York

Donald Sutherland
Canadian actor
• Played Hawkeye in film version of *MASH*, 1970; other films include *Ordinary People*, 1980.
b. July 17, 1934 in Saint John, New Brunswick

Keifer Sutherland
Canadian actor
• Films include *Stand By Me*, 1986, *Bright Lights, Big City*, 1988, *Flatliners*, 1990; son of Donald.
b. December 21, 1966 in London, England

John Sutton
British actor
• In films since 1937, usually playing hero's rival: *Of Human Bondage*, 1964.
b. October 22, 1908 in Rawalpindi, India
d. 1963

Janet Suzman
South African actress
• Active in British theater since 1962; Oscar nominee for *Nicholas and Alexandra*, 1971.
b. February 09, 1939 in Johannesburg, South Africa

Gloria May Josephine Swanson
(Josephine Swenson)
American actress
• Starred in *Sunset Boulevard*, 1950.
b. March 27, 1899 in Chicago, Illinois
d. April 04, 1983 in New York, New York

Patrick Swayze
American actor
• Played Orry Main in TV mini-series "North and South," 1985-86; in films *Dirty Dancing*, 1987, *Ghost*, 1990.
b. August 18, 1955 in Houston, Texas

Blanche (Sarah Blanche) Sweet
American actress
• Starred in first feature length film made in US: *Judith of Bethulia*, 1913.
b. June 18, 1896 in Chicago, Illinois
d. September 06, 1986 in New York, New York

Inga Swenson
American actress
• Played Gretchen Kraus on TV series "Benson," 1979-85.
b. December 29, 1932 in Omaha, Nebraska

Jo Swerling
American screenwriter–dramatist
• Co-author of play *Guys and Dolls*, 1951; won Tony.
b. May 18, 1897 in Russia

Loretta Swit
(Mrs Dennis Holahan)
American actress
• Played Margaret Houlihan in TV series "MASH," 1972-83.
b. November 04, 1937 in Passaic, New Jersey

Carl Switzer
(Our Gang; "Alfalfa")
American actor
• In *Our Gang* film series, 1935-42; specialty was off-key singing; shot in brawl.
b. August 08, 1926 in Paris, Illinois
d. January 21, 1959 in Sepulveda, California

Paul Sylbert
Designer–Director
• Won Oscar, 1978, for *Heaven Can Wait.*
b. 1928

Sylvia Syms
English actress
• Leading lady in films: *The World of Suzie Wong*, 1960; *The Victim*, 1961.
b. 1934 in London, England

John Millington Synge
Irish author–dramatist
• Wrote about peasants of W Ireland; *The Playboy of the Western World*, 1907.
b. April 16, 1871 in Dublin, Ireland
d. March 24, 1909 in Dublin, Ireland

Mr T
(Lawrence Tero Lawrence Tureaud)
American actor
• Former celebrity bodyguard; star of TV's "A-Team."
b. May 21, 1952 in Chicago, Illinois

William Tabbert
American actor–singer
• Broadway shows include *South Pacific; Seven Lively Arts; Fanny.*
b. October 05, 1921 in Chicago, Illinois
d. October 2, 1974 in Dallas, Texas

Martin Tahse
American producer
• Exec. producer of ABC's "Afternoon Specials"; won Emmys, 1980, 1981.
b. April 24, 1930 in Cincinnati, Ohio

George Takei
American actor
• Played Sulu on TV's "Star Trek," 1966-69, also in film series.
b. April 2, in Los Angeles, California

Lyle Talbot
(Lysle Henderson)
American actor
• Character actor in over 100 films since 1932; in TV series "The Bob Cummings Show," 1955-59.
b. February 08, 1902 in Pittsburgh, Pennsylvania

Nita Talbot
American comedienne–actress
• Appeared in film *The Day of the Locust*, 1975.
b. August 08, 1930 in New York, New York

Maria Tallchief
American dancer
• Prima ballerina who appeared in film *Million Dollar Mermaid*, 1952.
b. January 24, 1925 in Fairfax, Oklahoma

Constance Talmadge
American actress–comedienne
• Silent film star, 1914-29; retired when talking pictures began.
b. April 19, 1900 in Brooklyn, New York
d. November 23, 1973 in Los Angeles, California

William Talman
American actor
• Played D.A. Burger on TV show "Perry Mason," 1957-66.
b. February 04, 1915 in Detroit, Michigan
d. August 3, 1968 in Encino, California

Russ Tamblyn
American actor
• Oscar nominee for *Peyton Place*, 1957; dancing star of *Seven Brides for Seven Brothers*, 1954; *West Side Story*, 1961.
b. December 3, 1935 in Los Angeles, California

Helen Tamiris
American choreographer–dancer
• Choreographed Broadway musical *Annie Get Your Gun*, 1948.
b. April 24, 1902 in New York, New York
d. August 25, 1966 in New York, New York

Akim Tamiroff
American actor
• Character actor who played villain roles, 1933-70; Oscar nominee for *For Whom the Bell Tolls.*
b. October 29, 1901 in Baku, Russia
d. September 17, 1972 in Palm Springs, California

Jessica Tandy
(Mrs Hume Cronyn)
English actress
• Three-time Tony winner; performances include *A Streetcar Named Desire*, 1948; oldest to win Oscar, 1990, for *Driving Miss Daisy.*
b. June 07, 1909 in London, England

Ned Stone Tanen
Producer
• Films include *The Breakfast Club*, 1985; *St. Elmo's Fire*, 1985.
b. 1931 in Los Angeles, California

Fran(cis Asbury) Tarkenton
American football player–TV personality
• Scrambling quarterback, 1961-79; mostly with Minnesota; Hall of Fame, 1986; co-host TV series, "That's Incredible," 1980-84.
b. February 03, 1940 in Richmond, Virginia

Booth Tarkington
American author–dramatist
• Won Pulitzers for *The Magnificent Ambersons*, 1919; *Alice Adams*, 1922.
b. July 29, 1869 in Indianapolis, Indiana
d. May 16, 1946 in Indianapolis, Indiana

Richard Tarlton
English comedian
• Queen Elizabeth I's favorite clown; probably model for Yorick in Shakespeare's *Hamlet.*

Brandon Tartikoff
American TV executive
• Pres., NBC Entertainment, since 1980, credited with successes "The Cosby Show," "Cheers."
b. January 13, 1949 in Long Island, New York

Lilyan Tashman
American actress
• Elegant leading lady of silents and early talkies, 1921-34, in *No, No Nanette.*
b. October 23, 1899 in Brooklyn, New York
d. March 21, 1934 in New York, New York

Sharon Tate
(Mrs Roman Polanski)
American actress
• Murdered by Charles Manson family.
b. 1943 in Dallas, Texas
d. August 09, 1969 in Bel Air, California

Jacques Tati
(Jacques Tatischeff)
French comedian–director
• Won Oscar, 1958, for *Mon Oncle;* inspired by Charlie Chaplin and Buster Keaton.
b. October 09, 1908 in Le Pecq, France
d. November 05, 1982 in Paris, France

Norman Taurog
American director
• Won Oscar for *Skippy,* 1931.
b. February 23, 1899 in Chicago, Illinois
d. April 07, 1981 in Rancho Mirage, California

Bertrand Tavernier
French director
• Films center around basic human experiences: *'Round Midnight,* 1986; *Let Joy Reign Supreme,* 1975.
b. April 25, 1941 in Lyon, France

Vic Tayback
(Victor Tabback)
American actor
• Played Mel on TV series "Alice," 1976-85.
b. January 06, 1929 in Brooklyn, New York
d. May 25, 1990 in Glendale, California

Elizabeth Rosemond Taylor
English actress
• Won Oscars for *Butterfield 8,* 1960; *Who's Afraid of Virginia Woolf?* 1966.
b. February 27, 1932 in London, England

Estelle Taylor
(Estelle Boylan)
American actress
• Married Jack Dempsey, 1925-31; films include *The Ten Commandments,* 1956.
b. May 2, 1899 in Wilmington, Delaware
d. April 15, 1958 in Hollywood, California

Kent Taylor
(Louis Weiss)
American actor
• Hero in B-pictures: *Tangier, Tombstone;* began film career, 1931; played Blackie in TV series "Boston Blackie," 1951-53.
b. May 11, 1907 in Nashua, Iowa
d. April 13, 1987 in Los Angeles, California

Laurette Taylor
(Laurette Cooney)
American actress
• Star of plays *Peg o' My Heart,* 1912; *Glass Menagerie,* 1945.
b. April 01, 1887 in New York, New York
d. December 07, 1946 in New York, New York

Paul Taylor
American choreographer
• Award-winning productions include *Musette,* 1983; formed own co., NYC, 1952–.
b. July 29, 1930 in Allegheny, New York

Robert Taylor
(Arlington Spangler Brugh; "The Man with the Perfect Profile")
American actor
• Romantic star with MGM for 25 years.
b. August 05, 1911 in Filley, Nebraska
d. June 08, 1969 in Santa Monica, California

Rod(ney) Taylor
Australian actor
• Best known as resourceful hero in Hitchcock's *The Birds,* 1963.
b. January 11, 1930 in Sydney, Australia

Ronnie Taylor
English filmmaker
• Won Oscar for cinematography of *Gandhi,* 1982.

Samuel (Albert) Taylor
American dramatist
• Plays include *Sabrina Fair,* 1953; *No Strings,* 1962.
b. June 13, 1912 in Chicago, Illinois

William Desmond Taylor
(William Cunningham Dean Tanner)
American director
• Pres., Screen Actors Guild; homocide victim whose death was a scandal when affairs with popular leading ladies discovered.
b. April 26, 1877 in Ireland
d. February 02, 1922 in Hollywood, California

Marianna Alexsavena Tcherkassky
American dancer
• Principal dancer, American Ballet Theatre since 1976, known for purity of style.
b. October 28, 1952 in Glen Cove, New York

John Michael Tebelak
American dramatist–director
• Wrote, directed rock musical *Godspell.*
b. 1949
d. April 02, 1985 in New York, New York

Howard Miles Teichmann
American dramatist–biographer
• Best-known play: *The Solid Gold Cadillac,* 1953; biographies include those of Henry Fonda, Alexander Woollcott.
b. January 22, 1916 in Chicago, Illinois
d. July 07, 1987 in New York, New York

Marie Tempest
English actress
• Appeared in stage comedies, 1899-1942, including *Marriage of Kitty.*
b. July 15, 1864 in London, England
d. October 15, 1942 in London, England

Veronica Tennant
Canadian dancer
• Principal dancer with National Ballet Canada, 1965–.
b. January 15, 1946 in London, England

Terence
(Publius Terentius Afer)
Roman dramatist–poet
• Comedies modeled on Greek originals; more subtle, refined than Plautus'.
b. 185?BC
d. 159BC

Dame Ellen Alicia Terry
English actress
• Acting partner with Henry Irving, 1878-1902; carried on famed correspondence with George Bernard Shaw.
b. February 27, 1848 in Coventry, England
d. July 21, 1928 in Kent, England

Megan Terry
(Megan Duffy)
American dramatist
• Plays include Obie winner, *The Tommy Allen Show,* 1970.
b. July 22, 1932 in Seattle, Washington

Terry-Thomas
(Thomas Terry Hoar-Stevens)
English actor–comedian
• Character actor known for gap-toothed smile; films include *I'm All Right, Jack,* 1960, *Those Magnificent Men in Their Flying Machines,* 1965.
b. July 14, 1911 in London, England
d. January 08, 1990 in Godalming, England

Hiroshi Teshigahara
Japanese director
• Films include *The Pitfall; Woman in the Dunes.*
b. 1927 in Tokyo, Japan

Steve Tesich
(Stoyan Tesich)
American screenwriter
• Best known for *Breaking Away,* 1979; *The World According to Garp,* 1982.
b. September 29, 1942 in Titovo Utice, Yugoslavia

Tex and Jinx
(Jinx Falkenburg; Tex McCrary)
American radio performers
• Husband and wife team; produced own radio, TV shows, 1940s-50s.

Twyla Tharp
American choreographer–dancer
• Organized modern dance troupe, 1965–.
b. July 01, 1941 in Portland, Indiana

Phyllis Thaxter
American actress
• Mother of Skye Aubrey; films include *Sea of Grass*, 1947.
b. November 2, 1920 in Portland, Maine

Tiffany Ellsworth Thayer
American screenwriter–actor
• Appeared in films, 1920-25; wrote *Devil on Horseback*, 1936; *Chicago Deadline*, 1949.
b. March 01, 1902 in Freeport, Illinois
d. August 23, 1959 in Nantucket, Massachusetts

Thespis
Greek actor–dramatist–poet
• Invented tragedy in Greek tradition; originated actor's role; actors called thespians in his honor.
b. 6thBC in Attica, Greece

Alan Thicke
Canadian actor
• Star of TV series "Growing Pains," 1985–.
b. March 01, 1947 in Kirkland Lake, Ontario

Betty Thomas
(Betty Thomas Nienhauser)
American actress
• Played Lucy Bates on TV series "Hill Street Blues," 1981-87.
b. July 27, 1948 in Saint Louis, Missouri

Billy Thomas
(Our Gang; "Buckwheat")
American actor
• Played Buckwheat in "Our Gang" comedies, 1934-44.
b. March 12, 1931 in Los Angeles, California
d. October 1, 1980 in Los Angeles, California

Danny Thomas
(Amos Jacobs)
American actor–comedian–producer
• Starred in "Make Room for Daddy," 1953-64, later called "Danny Thomas Show"; father of Marlo.
b. January 06, 1914 in Deerfield, Michigan
d. February 06, 1991 in Los Angeles, California

Dave Thomas
(McKenzie Brothers; Doug McKenzie)
Canadian comedian–screenwriter
• As Doug McKenzie, had hit album with Rick Moranis *Great White North*, 1981.
b. 1949 in Saint Catherines, Ontario

Gerald Thomas
English producer–director
• Noted for *Carry On* comedy film series, 1957-70s.
b. 1920 in Hull, England

Henry Thomas
American actor
• Played Elliott, ET's "friend," in film *ET*, 1981.
b. September 08, 1972

Lowell Jackson Thomas
American author–radio performer
• Wrote *With Lawrence in Arabia*, 1924; hosted "High-Adventure," 1957-59.
b. April 06, 1892 in Woodington, Ohio
d. August 29, 1981 in Pawling, New York

Marlo Thomas
(Mrs Phil Donahue; Margaret Thomas)
American actress
• Starred in "That Girl," 1966-71; won Emmys for "Free to Be...You and Me,"1977; "Nobody's Child," 1986.
b. November 21, 1938 in Detroit, Michigan

Philip Michael Thomas
American actor
• Played Ricardo Tubbs on TV series "Miami Vice," 1984-89.
b. May 26, 1949 in Los Angeles, California

Richard Earl Thomas
American actor
• Played John Boy in "The Waltons," 1972-77; published two books of poetry.
b. June 13, 1951 in New York, New York

Anthony Denis Thomopoulos
American TV executive
• Pres., ABC Broadcast Group, 1983–; pres., ABC, 1978-83.
b. February 07, 1938 in Mount Vernon, New York

Sada Carolyn Thompson
American actress
• Played Kate Lawrence in "Family," 1976-79; won Tony for *Twigs*, 1971.
b. September 27, 1929 in Des Moines, Iowa

Gordon Thomson
Canadian actor
• Played Adam Carrington on TV drama "Dynasty," 1982-89.
b. March 02, 1951 in Ottawa, Ontario

Dame Sybil Thorndike
English actress
• Best known for her lead role in *Saint Joan*, 1923.
b. October 24, 1882 in Gainsborough, England
d. June 06, 1976 in Chelsea, England

The Three Stooges
(Joe DeRita; Larry Fine; Curly Howard; Moe Howard; Shemp Howard;Joe Besser)
American comedy team
• Performed in vaudeville, 1923; made 200 short films, 1934-58.

Ingrid Thulin
Swedish actress
• Films include *Wild Strawberries; The Damned; Cries and Whispers*.
b. January 27, 1929 in Solleftea, Sweden

Howard Thurston
American magician
• Practiced magic since childhood; toured US, 1907-08.
b. July 2, 1869 in Columbus, Ohio
d. April 13, 1936

Ernest Tidyman
American author–screenwriter
• Wrote novel, screenplay *Shaft*, won best screenplay Oscar for *The French Connection*, 1971.
b. January 01, 1928 in Cleveland, Ohio
d. July 14, 1984 in London, England

Gene Tierney
American actress
• Played title role in *Laura*, 1944; wrote *Self-Portrait*, 1979.
b. November 11, 1920 in Brooklyn, New York

Pamela Kimberley Tiffin
American model–actress
• Films include *The Pleasure Seekers*, 1964; *Harper*, 1966.
b. October 13, 1942 in Oklahoma City, Oklahoma

Burr Tillstrom
American puppeteer
• Creator, puppeteer, "Kukla, Fran, & Ollie" puppet show, on TV, 1947-57.
b. October 13, 1917 in Chicago, Illinois
d. December 06, 1985 in Palm Springs, California

Charlene Tilton
American actress
• Plays Lucy Ewing Cooper on TV drama "Dallas," 1978-85, 1988–.
b. December 01, 1958 in San Diego, California

Grant Almerin Tinker
American TV executive–producer
• Pres., MTM Enterprises, 1970-81; chairman, CEO, NBC, 1981-86; former husband of Mary Tyler Moore.
b. January 11, 1926 in Stamford, Connecticut

Tiny Tim
(Herbert Buckingham Khaury)
American entertainer
• Falsetto singer, best known for song "Tiptoe through the Tulips."
b. April 12, 1922 in New York, New York

George Tobias
American actor
• Character actor as the hero's sidekick, 1939-70; films include *Ninotchka; Silk Stockings.*
b. 1905 in New York, New York
d. February 27, 1980 in Hollywood, California

Ann Todd
English actress
• Films include *The Paradine Case,* 1947; *The Seventh Veil,* 1946.
b. January 24, 1909 in Hartford, England

Mike (Michael) Todd
(Avron Hirsch Goldbogen)
American producer
• Produced 1956 Oscar-winning *Around the World in 80 Days;* wed to Elizabeth Taylor; killed in plane crash.
b. June 02, 1907 in Minneapolis, Minnesota
d. March 22, 1958 in Grants, Minnesota

Richard Todd
(Richard Andrew Palethorpe-Todd)
Irish actor
• Oscar nominee for *The Hasty Heart,* 1949.
b. June 11, 1919 in Dublin, Ireland

Thelma Todd
American actress
• Made over 60 films, 1926-36.
b. July 29, 1905 in Lawrence, Massachusetts
d. December 18, 1935 in Santa Monica, California

Bill (William Selden) Todman
American producer
• With Mark Goodson, created TV game shows "What's My Line"; "Match Game."
b. July 31, 1916 in New York, New York
d. July 29, 1979 in New York, New York

General Tom Thumb
(Charles Sherwood Stratton)
American circus performer
• Midget, whose height never exceeded 33 inches; hired by PT Barnum, 1842.
b. January 04, 1838 in Bridgeport, Connecticut
d. July 15, 1883 in Middleboro, Massachusetts

Helgi Tomasson
Icelandic dancer
• "Premier danseur" with NY City Ballet, 1970-85; artistic director, San Francisco ballet, 1985-.
b. October 08, 1942 in Reykjavik, Iceland

Lily (Mary Jean) Tomlin
American actress–comedienne
• Starred in *Nine to Five,* 1980; won Tony for *The Search for Signs of Intelligent Life in the Universe,* 1986.
b. September 01, 1939 in Detroit, Michigan

Franchot Tone
(Stanislas Pascal Franchot Tone)
American actor
• Typecast in playboy roles at MGM, 1930s; Oscar nominee for *Mutiny on the Bounty,* 1935.
b. February 27, 1905 in Niagara Falls, New York
d. September 18, 1968 in New York, New York

Regis Toomey
American actor
• Character actor in over 150 films, 1929–, TV shows "Burke's Law," 1963-65.
b. August 13, 1902 in Pittsburgh, Pennsylvania

Chaim Topol
Israeli actor
• Oscar nominee for Tevye in *Fiddler on the Roof,* 1971.
b. September 09, 1935 in Tel Aviv, Palestine

Rip Torn
(Elmore Torn Jr)
American actor
• Films from 1956 include *Sweet Bird of Youth; Heartland;* married Geraldine Page, 1961.
b. February 06, 1931 in Temple, Texas

Leopoldo Torre-Nilsson
Argentine director
• Art cinema director; *The House of the Angel,* 1957, brought world attention to him, Argentinian films.
b. May 05, 1924 in Buenos Aires, Argentina
d. September 08, 1978 in Buenos Aires, Argentina

Ridgely (Frederic Ridgely) Torrence
American poet–dramatist
• His *Plays for a Negro Theater,* 1917, sparked interest in blacks as a source of literary material; won many awards for poetry, admired by A E Houseman, other poets.
b. February 27, 1875 in Xenia, Ohio
d. December 25, 1950 in New York, New York

Ivan Tors
Hungarian producer–director
• Produced TV shows "Sea Hunt," 1957-61; "Flipper," 1964-68.
b. June 12, 1916 in Budapest, Hungary
d. June 04, 1983 in Mato Grosso, Brazil

Tamara Toumanova
Russian dancer
• Prima ballerina since age 12; starred in film *Days of Glory,* 1944.
b. 1917

Cyril Tourneur
English dramatist
• *The Revenger's Tragedy,* 1607; *The Atheist's Tragedy,* 1611, are considered most important of his dramas.
b. 1575
d. February 28, 1626 in Kinsdale, Ireland

Robert (Burton) Towne
American screenwriter
• Won Oscar for *Chinatown,* 1974.
b. 1936 in San Pedro, California

Spencer Bonaventure Tracy
American actor
• Leading man considered one of world's greatest actors; won Oscars for *Captains Courageous,* 1937; *Boy's Town,* 1938; co-starred with Katharine Hepburn in nine films.
b. April 05, 1900 in Milwaukee, Wisconsin
d. June 1, 1967 in Beverly Hills, California

Shepard Traube
American producer–director
• Founder, Society of Stage Directors and Choreographers; directed *Angel Street,* 1940s.
b. February 27, 1907 in Malden, Massachusetts
d. July 23, 1983 in New York, New York

Daniel J(ohn) Travanti
American actor
• Won two Emmys for role of Frank Furillo on TV series "Hill Street Blues," 1981-87.
b. March 07, 1940 in Kenosha, Wisconsin

Bill Travers
English actor–producer–director
• Films include *Born Free,* 1966; *Ring of Bright Water,* 1969.
b. January 03, 1922 in Newcastle-upon-Tyne, England

John Travolta
American actor–singer
• Starred in TV's "Welcome Back Kotter," 1975-79; films: *Saturday Night Fever,* 1977, *Grease,* 1978, *Look Who's Talking,* 1989.
b. February 18, 1954 in Englewood, New Jersey

Arthur Treacher
(Arthur Veary)
American actor
• Played butler in films, 1930s-40s; sidekick on Merv Griffin's TV show.
b. July 02, 1894 in Brighton, England
d. December 14, 1975 in Manhasset, New York

Terri Treas
American actress
• Films include *All That Jazz*, 1979; *The Best Little Whorehouse in Texas*, 1982.
b. July 19, 1959 in Kansas City, Kansas

Alex Trebek
Canadian TV personality
• Host of syndicated TV game show "Jeopardy!," 1984-.
b. July 22, 1940 in Sudbury, Ontario

Les Tremayne
American actor
• Long-time radio actor in "The First Nighter," 1933-43; "The Thin Man," 1945-50; had character roles in US films from 1951: *The Fortune Cookie*, 1966.
b. April 16, 1913 in London, England

George Washington Trendle
American producer
• Creator of "The Lone Ranger," "The Green Hornet," "Sergeant Preston of the Yukon" radio series, 1930s-40s.
b. July 04, 1884 in Norwalk, Ohio
d. May 11, 1972 in Grosse Pointe, Michigan

Claire Trevor
American actress
• Won Oscar for *Key Largo*, 1948.
b. March 08, 1909 in New York, New York

Jean-Louis Xavier Trintignant
French actor
• Films include *And God Created Woman*, 1957; *A Man and a Woman*, 1966.
b. December 11, 1930 in Polenc, France

Paul Tripp
American children's author-actor-producer
• Created, produced TV shows for children; wrote script, lyrics for film *The Christmas That Almost Wasn't*, 1966; also starred in film.
b. February 2, 1916 in New York, New York

Jiri Trnka
Czech filmmaker-illustrator
• Award-winning puppet film producer: *The Animals and the Brigands*, 1946; *Favorite Tales from Grimm and Andersen*, 1959.
b. February 24, 1912 in Pilsen, Czechoslovakia
d. December 3, 1969 in Prague, Czechoslovakia

Jan Troell
Swedish director
• Films include *The Emigrants*, 1971; *The New Land*, 1973; *Flight of the Eagle*, 1978; often edits, photographs works.
b. July 23, 1931 in Limhamn, Sweden

Ernest Truex
American actor
• Films include *It's a Wonderful World*, 1939; *Fluffy*, 1965.
b. September 19, 1890 in Kansas City, Missouri
d. June 27, 1973 in Fallbrook, California

Francois Truffaut
French director
• New Wave director who was admired for depictions of children, obsessed men, and women driven by strong passions; won Oscar, 1973.
b. February 06, 1932 in Paris, France
d. October 21, 1984 in Neuilly-sur-Seine, France

Dalton Trumbo
(The Hollywood Ten)
American screenwriter-author
• Wrote novel *Johnny Got His Gun*, 1939; screenplays *Thirty Seconds Over Tokyo*, 1945; *Exodus*, 1960.
b. December 09, 1905 in Montrose, Colorado
d. September 1, 1976 in Los Angeles, California

Thomas Tryon
American author-actor
• Writes supernatural fiction: *The Other*, 1971; *Harvest Home*, 1973.
b. January 14, 1926 in Hartford, Connecticut

Forrest Meredith Tucker
American actor
• Crusty character actor best known as Sgt. O'Rourke on TV series "F Troop," 1965-67.
b. February 12, 1919 in Plainfield, Indiana
d. October 25, 1986 in Woodland Hills, California

Lorenzo Tucker
American actor
• One of the first major black screen actors; starred in many all-black movies, 1920s-40s.
b. June 27, 1907 in Philadelphia, Pennsylvania
d. August 19, 1986 in Los Angeles, California

Antony Tudor
(William Cook)
English choreographer
• Best known for revolutionary use of psychological themes in ballet.
b. April 04, 1908 in London, England
d. April 2, 1987 in New York, New York

Sonny Tufts
(Bowen Charles Tufts III)
American actor
• Began film career, 1943; appeared in *No Escape*, 1953.
b. July 16, 1911 in Boston, Massachusetts
d. June 05, 1970 in Santa Monica, California

Tom Tully
American actor
• Oscar nominee for *The Caine Mutiny*, 1954.
b. August 21, 1902 in Durango, California
d. April 27, 1982 in Newport Beach, California

Tommy (Thomas James) Tune
American director-choreographer
• Won Tonys for *A Day in Hollywood/A Night in the Ukraine*, 1980; *Nine*, 1982.
b. February 28, 1939 in Wichita Falls, Texas

Kathleen Turner
American actress
• Star of feature films *Romancing the Stone*, 1984; *Jewel of the Nile*, 1985.
b. June 19, 1954 in Springfield, Missouri

Lana (Julia Jean Mildred Frances) Turner
American actress
• Allegedly discovered while drinking a soda at Schwab's Drugstore; films include *Imitation of Life*, 1959.
b. February 08, 1920 in Wallace, Idaho

Rita Tushingham
English actress
• Had award-winning performance in *A Taste of Honey*, 1961.
b. March 14, 1942 in Liverpool, England

Lurene Tuttle
American actress
• TV shows include "Life With Father," 1953-55; "Julia," 1968-71.
b. August 2, 1906 in Pleasant Lake, Indiana
d. May 28, 1986 in Encino, California

George Tyne
American actor–director
• Directed TV shows: "Sanford and Son," 1972-77; "The Ghost and Mrs. Muir," 1968-70.
b. August 06, 1917 in Philadelphia, Pennsylvania

Susan Tyrrell
American actress
• Oscar nominee for *Fat City*, 1972.
b. 1946 in San Francisco, California

Cicely Tyson
(Mrs Miles Davis)
American actress
• Won Emmy, 1973, for "The Autobiography of Miss Jane Pitman"; star of film, *Sounder*, 1972.
b. December 19, 1939 in New York, New York

Margaret Maud Tyzack
British actress
• Noted for work on London stage; plays include *Mornings as Seven*, 1984; also on TV, films.
b. September 09, 1931

Nicholas Udall
English dramatist
• Wrote *Ralph Roister Doister*, first complete English comedy, c. 1553.
b. 1505 in Hampshire, England
d. December 1556 in London, England

Bob (Robert George) Uecker
American baseball player–actor
• Mediocre catcher, 1962-67, known for beer commercials, starring role in TV series "Mr. Belvedere," 1984–.
b. January 26, 1935 in Milwaukee, Wisconsin

Alfred Uhry
American dramatist
• Won 1988 Pulitzer for first play, *Driving Miss Daisy*.
b. 1937

Tracey Ullman
English singer–actress
• First American hit "They Don't Know," 1984; star of TV show "The Tracey Ullman Show," 1986–.
b. December 3, 1959 in Cliveden, England

Liv Johanne Ullmann
(Mrs Donald Saunders)
Norwegian actress
• Star of Ingmar Bergman films; goodwill ambassador, UNICEF, 1980–.
b. December 16, 1939 in Tokyo, Japan

Lenore Ulric
American actress
• Played in *Tiger Rose; Camille; Intrigue.*
b. July 21, 1894 in New Ulm, Minnesota
d. December 3, 1970 in Orangeburg, New York

Miyoshi Umeki
Japanese singer–actress
• Films include *Flower Drum Song*, 1961; won Oscar for *Sayonara*, 1957.
b. April 03, 1929 in Holdaido, Japan

Mary Ure
Scottish actress
• Married John Osborne, Robert Shaw; films include *Sons and Lovers*, 1960.
b. February 18, 1933 in Glasgow, Scotland
d. April 03, 1975 in London, England

Robert Urich
American actor
• Starred in TV series "Vega$," 1978-80; "Spencer for Hire," 1985–.
b. December 19, 1947 in Toronto, Ohio

Peter Alexander Ustinov
English actor
• All-around entertainer in films, stage, TV; Oscar nominee for *Quo Vadis*, 1951.
b. April 16, 1921 in London, England

(Clifton) Garrick Utley
American broadcast journalist
• Foreign correspondent for NBC, 1963-64; British correspondent, 1973–.
b. November 19, 1939 in Chicago, Illinois

Brenda Vaccaro
American actress
• Husky-voiced entertainer on TV, film, stage; nominated for three Tonys, won Emmy for "The Shape of Things," 1974.
b. November 18, 1939 in Brooklyn, New York

Roger Vadim
(Roger Vadim Piemiannikov)
French director
• Wrote book about former wives: *Bardot, Deneuve, Fonda*, 1983.
b. January 26, 1928 in Paris, France

Luis Valdez
American director–writer
• Founder, El Teatro Campesino, 1965–, most influential Chicano theater in US; won Obie, 1968; Emmy, 1973.
b. June 26, 1940 in Delano, California

Karen Valentine
American actress
• TV shows include "Room 222," 1969-74; "Karen," 1975.
b. May 25, 1947 in Santa Rosa, California

Scott Valentine
American actor
• Played Nick in TV series "Family Ties," 1985-87.
b. June 03, 1958 in Saratoga Springs, New York

Rudolph Valentino
(Rodolfo d'Antonguella)
American actor
• Starred in *The Sheik*, 1921; *Blood and Sand*, 1922.
b. May 06, 1895 in Castellaneta, Italy
d. August 23, 1926 in New York, New York

Alida Valli
(Alida Maria Altenburger)
Italian actress
• Films include *Third Man; Paradine Case*.
b. May 31, 1921 in Pola, Italy

Raf(faele) Vallone
Italian actor
• Leading man in Italian films, 1948–; films include *Obsession*, 1976.
b. February 17, 1918 in Tropea, Italy

Joan Van Ark
American actress
• Plays Val Ewing on TV series "Knots Landing," 1979–.
b. June 16, 1946 in New York, New York

Vivian Vance
American actress
• Best known as Ethel Mertz in "I Love Lucy," 1951-59; also starred in "The Lucy Show," 1962-65.
b. July 26, 1912 in Cherryvale, Kansas
d. August 17, 1979 in Belvedere, California

Lee Van Cleef
American actor
• Western/action films include *High Noon*, 1952; *The Good, the Bad, and the Ugly*, 1967.
b. January 09, 1925 in Somerville, New Jersey
d. December 16, 1989 in Oxnard, California

Trish Van Devere
(Patricia Dressel; Mrs George C Scott)
American actress
• Co-starred with husband in several films: *Where's Poppa?*, 1970, *Day of the Dolphin*, 1973.
b. March 09, 1945 in Englewood Cliffs, New Jersey

Mamie Van Doren
(Joan Lucille Olander)
American actress
• Films include *Untamed Youth; Ain't Misbehavin'.*
b. February 06, 1933 in Rowena, South Dakota

John William Van Druten
English dramatist
• Plays include *I Remember Mama*, 1944, from Kathryn Forbes' book; *Anatomy of Murder*, 1957, from Robert Traver's book.
b. June 01, 1901 in London, England
d. December 19, 1957 in Indio, California

Dick Van Dyke
American actor–comedian
• Won three Emmys for TV series "The Dick Van Dyke Show," 1961-66.
b. December 13, 1925 in West Plains, Missouri

Jerry Van Dyke
American actor
• Brother of Dick Van Dyke; starred in TV series "My Mother the Car," 1965-66.
b. July 27, 1931 in Danville, Illinois

W(oodbridge) S(trong) Van Dyke
American director–producer
• Nickname earned from reputation as casual director; resulted in spontaneous performances from actors.
b. March 21, 1887 in San Diego, California
d. February 05, 1943 in Brentwood, California

Jo Van Fleet
(Mrs William Bales)
American actress
• Won Oscar for her first film *East of Eden*, 1955; Tony for *Trip to Bountiful*, 1954.
b. December 3, 1919 in Oakland, California

Martine Van Hamel
Canadian dancer
• Principal dancer, American Ballet Theatre, 1973–; won dance awards.
b. November 16, 1945 in Brussels, Belgium

Jean-Claude Van Itallie
American dramatist
• Won Obie for *The Serpent*, 1969; other plays include *The Traveler*, 1986.
b. May 23, 1936 in Brussels, Belgium

Sander Vanocur
American broadcast journalist
• With ABC News since 1977; chief diplomatic correspondent since 1981.
b. January 08, 1928 in Cleveland, Ohio

Dick Vincent Van Patten
American actor
• Appeared in "I Remember Mama," 1949-57; played Tom Bradford on "Eight Is Enough," 1977-81.
b. December 09, 1928 in Kew Gardens, New York

Joyce Van Patten
American actress
• Began career as child actress in radio, stage; TV shows include "Danny Kaye Show."
b. March 09, 1934 in New York, New York

Vince(nt) Van Patten
American actor–tennis player
• Supporting actor, 1970s; films include *Wild Horses*; son of Dick Van Patten.
b. October 17, 1957 in Brooklyn, New York

Melvin Van Peebles
American actor–dramatist–composer
• Wrote, directed play *Ain't Supposed to Die a Natural Death*, 1971.
b. August 21, 1932 in Chicago, Illinois

Monique Van Vooren
American actress–author
• Appeared in movie *Damn Yankees*, 1958; wrote novel *Night Sanctuary*, 1981.
b. March 17, 1933 in Brussels, Belgium

Agnes Varda
French screenwriter–director
• Directed *Elsa*, 1966; *Lions Love*, 1969.
b. May 3, 1928 in Brussels, Belgium

Jim Varney
American actor
• Plays TV commercial character Ernest P Worrell; star of film *Ernest Goes to Camp*, 1987.
b. June 15, 1949 in Lexington, Kentucky

Diane Varsi
American actress
• Won Oscar for her first film *Peyton Place*, 1957.
b. February 23, 1938 in San Francisco, California

Robert Vaughn
American actor
• Played Napoleon Solo in TV series "The Man from UNCLE," 1964-67.
b. November 22, 1932 in New York, New York

Eddie (Edwin) Velez
American actor
• Best known for episodic TV; films include *Extremities*, 1986.
b. June 04, 1958 in New York, New York

Lupe Velez
(Maria Guadalupe Velez de Villalobos)
Mexican actress
• Starred in *Mexican Spitfire* film series, 1940s; married Johnny Weissmuller, 1933-38.
b. July 18, 1908 in San Luis Potosi, Mexico
d. December 14, 1944

Benay Venuta
(Venuta Rose Crooke)
American actress–singer
• Played on stage since 1928 in *Anything Goes; Annie Get Your Gun*.
b. January 27, 1911 in San Francisco, California

Vera-Ellen
(Vera-Ellen Rohe)
American dancer–actress
• Films include *White Christmas*, 1954; *Web of Violence*, 1959.
b. February 16, 1926 in Cincinnati, Ohio
d. August 3, 1981 in Los Angeles, California

Gwen (Gwyneth Evelyn) Verdon
American dancer–actress
• Won Tonys for *Can Can*, 1953; *Damn Yankees*, 1956; *New Girl in Town*, 1958; *Red Head*, 1959.
b. January 13, 1925 in Culver City, California

Elena Verdugo
American actress
• Played Millie Bronson in "Meet Millie," 1952-56; Nurse Consuelo Lopez in "Marcus Welby, MD," 1969-76.
b. April 2, 1926 in Hollywood, California

Ben(jamin Augustus) Vereen
American entertainer
• Won Tony for *Pippin'*, 1972; played Chicken George in TV miniseries "Roots," 1977.
b. October 1, 1946 in Miami, Florida

Jackie Vernon
American comedian
• Known for off-beat, satirical humor; played nightclubs, TV, films; trademark saying, "You had to be there."
b. 1928 in New York, New York
d. November 1, 1987 in Los Angeles, California

John Vernon
(Adolphus Vernon Agopsowicz)
Canadian actor
• Films include *Dirty Harry; Topaz; National Lampoon's Animal House.*
b. February 24, 1932 in Regina, Saskatchewan

Martha Vickers
(Martha MacVicar)
American actress
• Married Mickey Rooney, 1949-51; films include *The Big Sleep*, 1946.
b. May 28, 1925 in Ann Arbor, Michigan
d. November 02, 1971 in Van Nuys, California

Florence Vidor
(Florence Cobb)
American actress
• Successful on silent films; career ended with talkies.
b. July 23, 1895 in Houston, Texas
d. November 03, 1977 in Pacific Palisades, California

King Wallis Vidor
American director
• Directed *Hallelujah*, 1929; first Hollywood movie with all black cast.
b. February 08, 1894 in Galveston, Texas
d. November 01, 1982 in Paso Robles, California

Jean Vigo
French director
• Experimental films banned as "anti-French" because they attacted the establishment.
b. April 26, 1905 in Paris, France
d. October 05, 1934 in Paris, France

Abe Vigoda
American actor
• Played Detective Fish on "Barney Miller," 1975-77.
b. February 24, 1921 in New York, New York

Herve Jean Pierre Villechaize
French actor
• Played Tattoo on TV series "Fantasy Island," 1978-83.
b. April 23, 1943 in Paris, France

Jan-Michael Vincent
American actor
• Films include *Buster and Billie; White Line Fever.*
b. July 15, 1944 in Ventura, California

Luchino Visconti
Italian director
• Films recurrent theme was moral disintegration of a family including *The Damned*, 1961.
b. November 02, 1906 in Milan, Italy
d. March 17, 1976 in Rome, Italy

Milly Vitale
Italian actress
• Films since 1950s include *The Juggler*, 1953; *War and Peace*, 1956.
b. July 16, 1938 in Rome, Italy

Monica Vitti
(Maria Louisa Ceciarelli)
Italian actress
• Appeared mostly on stage in classical roles; first leading role in film: *L'Avventura.*
b. November 03, 1931 in Rome, Italy

Jon Voight
American actor
• Won Oscar, 1979, for *Coming Home.*
b. December 29, 1938 in Yonkers, New York

Lula Vollmer
American dramatist
• Plays include *The Shame Woman*, 1923; *Sentinels*, 1931.
b. 1898 in Keyser, North Carolina
d. May 02, 1955

Betsy VonFurstenberg
(Elizabeth Caroline Maria Agatha Felicitas Therese von Furstenberg-Hedringen)
German actress
• Stage performances include *Wonderful Town*, 1959, 1967.
b. August 16, 1932 in Westphalia, Germany

Josef VonSternberg
Austrian director
• Films include *The Blue Angel*, 1931, which starred Marlene Dietrich, whom he discovered.
b. May 29, 1894 in Vienna, Austria
d. December 22, 1969 in Hollywood, California

Erich VonStroheim
(Erich Oswald Stroheim)
German actor-director
• As actor, called "the man you love to hate"; directed many silent films including *Greed*, 1928.
b. September 22, 1885 in Vienna, Austria
d. May 12, 1957 in Paris, France

Max Carl Adolf VonSydow
Swedish actor
• Sensitive, versatile, powerful screen actor: *Hannah and Her Sisters*, 1985, *Pelle the Conqueror*, 1988.
b. April 1, 1929 in Lund, Sweden

Harry Von Zell
American actor
• Known for mellow voice; featured on "George Burns and Gracie Allen Show," 1956-58; appeared in 30 movies.
b. July 11, 1906 in Indianapolis, Indiana
d. November 21, 1981 in Woodland Hills, California

George Voskovec
Czech actor-director-dramatist
• On Broadway *Cabaret*, 1969; in film *Twelve Angry Men*, 1957.
b. June 19, 1905 in Sazova, Czechoslovakia
d. July 01, 1981 in Pearblossom, California

Lyle Waggoner
American actor
• TV shows include "Wonder Woman," 1977-79; "Carol Burnett Show," 1967-74.
b. April 13, 1935 in Kansas City, Kansas

Jack Peter Wagner
American actor-singer
• Plays Frisco Jones on daytime drama "General Hospital"; hit single "All I Need," 1984.
b. October 03, 1959 in Washington, Missouri

Jane Wagner
American writer-director
• Won three Emmys for Lily Tomlin specials; wrote film *The Incredible Shrinking Woman*, 1980.
b. February 02, 1935 in Morristown, Tennessee

Lindsay J Wagner
American actress
• Emmy-winning star of TV series "Bionic Woman," 1976-78; TV films include *This Child Is Mine*, 1985.
b. June 22, 1949 in Los Angeles, California

Robert John Wagner, Jr
American actor
• Star of TV series, 1960s-80s: "It Takes a Thief"; "Switch"; "Hart to Hart"; in films since 1951: *Prince Valiant*, 1954; widower of Natalie Wood.
b. February 1, 1930 in Detroit, Michigan

Wieland Adolf Gottfried Wagner
German director-producer
• Scenic director of Bayreuth Festival from 1951; grandson of Richard Wagner, son of Siegfried.
b. January 05, 1917 in Bayreuth, Germany
d. October 16, 1966 in Munich, Germany (West)

Wolfgang Wagner
German producer
• Director of Bayreuth Festival since 1966; grandson of Richard Wagner, son of Siegfried.
b. August 3, 1919 in Bayreuth, Germany

Ken Wahl
American actor
• Played undercover cop Vinnie Terranova on TV series, "Wiseguy," 1987-90.
b. 1957 in Chicago, Illinois

Kenneth Waissman
American producer
• Won Tony for *Torch Song Trilogy*, 1983.
b. January 24, 1940 in Baltimore, Maryland

Ralph Waite
American actor
• Played John Walton in TV series "The Waltons," 1972-80.
b. June 22, 1928 in White Plains, New York

Andrzej Wajda
Polish director
• Films include *Man of Marble*, 1977; *Man of Iron*, 1981, about Solidarity labor movement.
b. March 06, 1926 in Suwalki, Poland

Anton Walbrook
(Adolf Anton Wilhelm Wohlbruck)
British actor
• Films include *The Red Shoes*, 1948; *Gaslight*, 1940.
b. November 19, 1900 in Vienna, Austria
d. August 09, 1967 in Munich, Germany (West)

Raymond Walburn
American actor
• Character actor in over 80 films, 1929-55, including *Broadway Bill*, 1934.
b. September 09, 1887 in Plymouth, Indiana
d. July 26, 1969 in New York, New York

Jerry (Jerome Irving) Wald
American producer
• Films include *Flamingo Road*, 1949; *Mildred Pierce*, 1945; *Peyton Place*, 1957.
b. September 16, 1911 in New York, New York
d. July 13, 1962 in Beverly Hills, California

Robert Walden
American actor
• Played Joe Rossi on TV series "Lou Grant."
b. September 25, 1943 in New York, New York

Charles D Waldron
American actor
• Specialized in playing stern fathers; films include *The Nurse's Secret*, 1941; *The Gay Sisters*, 1942.
b. December 23, 1875 in Waterford, New York
d. March 04, 1946 in Hollywood, California

Christopher Walken
American actor
• Won Oscar, 1978, for *The Deer Hunter*.
b. March 31, 1943 in Astoria, New York

Clint Walker
American actor
• Star of TV series "Cheyenne," 1955-63.
b. May 3, 1927 in Hartford, Illinois

Jimmie (James Carter) Walker
American actor–comedian
• Played J J on TV series "Good Times," 1974-78; known for phrase "Dy-no-mite."
b. June 25, 1948 in New York, New York

Nancy Walker
(Anna Myrtle Swoyer)
American actress
• TV shows include "McMillan and Wife," 1971-76, "Rhoda," 1974-76.
b. May 1, 1921 in Philadelphia, Pennsylvania

Robert Walker
American actor
• Starred in Hitchcock's *Strangers on a Train*, 1951.
b. October 13, 1914 in Salt Lake City, Utah
d. August 28, 1951 in Santa Monica, California

Zena Walker
English actress
• Won Tony for *A Day in the Death of Joe Egg*, 1968.
b. March 07, 1934 in Birmingham, England

Chris Wallace
American broadcast journalist
• White House correspondent, NBC News, 1982–; son of Mike Wallace.
b. October 12, 1947 in Chicago, Illinois

Mike (Myron Leon) Wallace
American broadcast journalist
• CBS correspondent, 1963-76;; co-editor, "60 Minutes," 1968–.
b. May 09, 1918 in Brookline, Massachusetts

Eli Wallach
American actor
• Films include *Baby Doll*, 1956; *The Misfits*, 1961.
b. December 07, 1915 in New York, New York

Karl Wallenda
American circus performer
• Patriarch of famed high-wire troupe; killed in 100-foot fall.
b. 1905
d. March 22, 1978 in San Juan, Puerto Rico

Deborah Walley
American actress
• Played in TV show "Mothers-in-law," 1967-69; starred in film *Gidget Goes Hawaiian*, 1961.
b. August 13, in Bridgeport, Connecticut

Jimmy (James S) Wallington
American actor
• Radio announcer on "The Eddie Cantor Show," "The Burns and Allen Show."
b. September 15, 1907 in Rochester, New York
d. December 22, 1972 in Fairfax, Virginia

Sir Barnes Neville Wallis
American producer
• Produced over 400 films, including *Casablanca*, 1942; *The Maltese Falcon*, 1941; 32 of his films won Oscars.
b. September 14, 1899 in Chicago, Illinois
d. October 05, 1986 in Rancho Mirage, California

Shani Wallis
English actress
• Films include *Terror in the Wax Museum*, 1973.
b. April 16, 1933 in London, England

Jon Walmsley
American actor
• Played Jason Walton on TV series "The Waltons," 1972-79.
b. 1956

Raoul Walsh
American actor–director
• Directed Hollywood's first outdoor talking movie, *In Old Arizona*, 1929.
b. March 11, 1887 in New York, New York
d. December 31, 1980 in Los Angeles, California

Ray Walston
American actor–director
• Won Tony for *Damn Yankees*, 1955; starred in TV series "My Favorite Martian," 1963-66.
b. November 22, 1918 in New Orleans, Louisiana

Jessica Walter
(Mrs Ron Leibman)
American actress
• Won Emmy for "Amy Prentiss," 1974-75; films include *Play Misty For Me*, 1971.
b. January 31, 1944 in Brooklyn, New York

Barbara Walters
(Mrs Merv Adelson)
American broadcast journalist
• First woman to co-anchor "The Today Show," 1963-76; with ABC News since 1976; known for one-on-one interviews.
b. September 25, 1931 in Boston, Massachusetts

Charles Walters
American director
• Directed musicals *Easter Parade*, 1948; *Unsinkable Molly Brown*, 1964.
b. November 17, 1903 in Pasadena, California
d. August 13, 1982 in Malibu, California

Julie Walters
English actress
• Received Oscar nomination for role of Rita in film *Educating Rita*, 1984.
b. 1950 in Birmingham, England

Henry B Walthall
American actor
• First actor to wear motion picture makeup, 1914; starred in film *Birth of a Nation*, 1915.
b. March 16, 1878 in Shelby City, Alabama
d. June 17, 1936 in Monrovia, California

Sam Wanamaker
American actor–director
• On Hollywood black list, 1950s, for leftist political associations.
b. June 14, 1919 in Chicago, Illinois

Walter Wanger
(Walter Feuchtwanger)
American producer
• Regarded his films as foremost medium of communication, instrument to promote int'l. understanding: *Stagecoach*, 1939.
b. July 11, 1894 in San Francisco, California
d. November 18, 1968 in New York, New York

Joseph A Wapner
American TV personality
• Arbitrates cases as presiding judge on syndicated TV series "The People's Court," 1981–; California Superior Court judge, 1961-79.
b. November 15, 1919 in Los Angeles, California

Burt Ward
(Bert John Gervais Jr)
American actor
• Played Robin on TV series "Batman," 1966-68.
b. July 06, 1946 in Los Angeles, California

David S Ward
American screenwriter
• Wrote films *The Sting*, 1973; *The Sting II*, 1983; won Oscar, 1973.
b. October 24, 1945

Douglas Turner Ward
American director–dramatist–actor
• Artistic director, co-founder, Negro Ensemble Co., 1967; won Obie for distinguished performance in *River Niger*, 1973.
b. May 05, 1930 in Burnside, Louisiana

Fannie Ward
American actress
• Films include *The Cheat*, 1915; *Betty to the Rescue*, 1917.
b. November 23, 1872 in Saint Louis, Missouri
d. January 27, 1952 in New York, New York

Rachel Ward
(Mrs Bryan Brown)
English actress–model
• Starred in TV mini-series "The Thorn Birds," 1983; film *Against All Odds*, 1984.
b. 1957 in London, England

Simon Ward
English actor
• Portrayed Winston Churchill in film *Young Winston*, 1971.
b. October 19, 1941 in London, England

Jack Warden
American actor
• Oscar nominee for *Shampoo*, 1975; *Heaven Can Wait*, 1978; starred in mid-1980s TV show "Crazy Like a Fox."
b. September 18, 1920 in Newark, New Jersey

David Warfield
American actor
• Starred in Belasco plays including *Return of Peter Grimm*, 1911.
b. November 28, 1866 in San Francisco, California
d. June 27, 1951 in New York, New York

Marsha Warfield
American actress–comedienne
• Plays bailiff Roz Russell on TV series "Night Court," 1986–.
b. 1955

Albert Warner
(Warner Brothers)
American film executive
• Co-founded Warner Brothers Pictures, Inc., 1923.
b. July 23, 1884 in Poland
d. November 26, 1967 in Miami Beach, Florida

David Warner
English actor
• Starred in *Morgan*, 1965; *Time After Time*, 1979; *Time Bandits*, 1980.
b. July 29, 1941 in Manchester, England

Harry Morris Warner
(Warner Brothers)
American film executive
• Co-founder, pres., Warner Brothers Pictures, Inc., 1923-56.
b. December 12, 1881 in Kraznashiltz, Poland
d. July 25, 1958 in Hollywood, California

Jack Warner, Jr
American film executive
• Organized Jack M Warner Productions, Inc., 1949.
b. March 27, 1916 in San Francisco, California

Jack Leonard Warner
(Warner Brothers; Jack Eichelbaum)
American film executive
• With brothers, introduced first successful sound film, *The Jazz Singer*, 1927; produced award-winning *My Fair Lady*, 1964.
b. August 02, 1892 in London, Ontario
d. September 09, 1978 in Los Angeles, California

Malcolm-Jamal Warner
American actor
• Plays Theo Huxtable on "The Cosby Show," 1984–.
b. August 18, 1970 in Jersey City, New Jersey

Sam(uel Louis) Warner
(Warner Brothers)
American film executive
• Opened studios in CA with brothers, 1918.
b. August 1, 1887 in Baltimore, Maryland
d. October 05, 1927 in Los Angeles, California

Lesley Ann Warren
American actress–dancer
• Made TV debut in musical "Cinderella," 1964.
b. August 16, 1946 in New York, New York

Michael Warren
American actor
• Played Bobby Hill on TV series "Hill Street Blues," 1981-87; former All-American basketball player.
b. March 05, 1946 in South Bend, Indiana

Ruth Warrick
American actress
• In film *Citizen Kane*, 1941; long-time role on TV daytime drama "All My Children."
b. June 29, 1915 in Saint Louis, Missouri

Robert Warwick
(Robert Taylor Bien)
American actor
• Matinee idol of Broadway, films, 1914-59; in film *Adventures of Robin Hood*, 1938.
b. October 09, 1876 in Sacramento, California
d. June 04, 1964 in Los Angeles, California

Wisner McCamey Washam
American writer
• Head writer for soap opera "All My Children," 1971–.
b. September 08, 1931 in Mooresville, North Carolina

Denzel Washington, Jr
American actor
• Played Dr. Phillip Chandler on TV series "St. Elsewhere," 1982-88; won best supporting actor Oscar, 1990, for *Glory*.
b. December 28, in Mount Vernon, New York

Dale Wasserman
American dramatist
• Won best musical Tony for *Man of La Mancha*, 1965.
b. November 02, 1917 in Rhinelander, Wisconsin

Lew(is Robert) Wasserman
American film executive
• Chief exec., MCA, Inc.; won special Oscar, 1973.
b. March 15, 1913 in Cleveland, Ohio

Ethel Waters
American singer–actress
• Starred in plays *Cabin in the Sky*, 1940; *The Member of the Wedding*, 1950; Oscar nominee for *Pinky*, 1949; active in Billy Graham's crusades from 1950s.
b. October 31, 1900 in Chester, Pennsylvania
d. September 01, 1977 in Chatsworth, California

Sam(uel Atkinson) Waterston
American actor
• Film, TV, stage performer since 1963; Oscar nominee for *The Killing Fields*, 1984.
b. November 15, 1940 in Cambridge, Massachusetts

Al Waxman
Actor
• Played Lt. Samuels in TV series "Cagney and Lacey," 1982-88.
b. 1934 in Toronto, Ontario

David Wayne
(Wayne James McMeekan)
American actor
• Films include *Three Faces of Eve*, 1957; *Front Page*, 1931.
b. January 3, 1914 in Traverse City, Michigan

John Wayne
(Marion Michael Morrison; "Duke")
American actor–director
• Biggest box office attraction in Hollywood history; starred in over 200 westerns; won Oscar, 1968, for *True Grit*.
b. May 26, 1907 in Winterset, Iowa
d. June 11, 1979 in Los Angeles, California

Johnny Wayne
(Wayne and Shuster)
Canadian comedian
• Had documentary-style TV show with Frank Shuster, "Wayne and Shuster Take an Affectionate Look at...," 1966; got first break in US on Ed Sullivan's show, 1950s.
b. 1918
d. July 18, 1990 in Toronto, Ontario

Patrick Wayne
American actor
• Son of John Wayne, appeared with father in several films: *McClintock!*, 1963; leading man in own right, 1970s.
b. July 15, 1939 in Los Angeles, California

Paula Wayne
American actress
• Career in theater, TV, films; dubbed voices for over 50 foreign films.
b. November 03, 1937 in Hobart, Oklahoma

Wayne and Shuster
(Frank Shuster; Johnny Wayne)
Canadian comedy team
• Ed Sullivan first gave them US exposure, 1950s; popular on Canadian radio, TV, 1940s-60s.

Dennis Weaver
American actor
• Starred in TV series "Gunsmoke," 1955-64; "McCloud," 1970-77; "Buck James," 1987–.
b. June 04, 1925 in Joplin, Missouri

Doodles (Winstead Sheffield Glendening Dixon) Weaver
American actor
• Played hayseed comedic roles in over 60 films, 1930s-40s; appeared with Spike Jones band as Professor Feedelbaum, 1948-51.
b. May 11, 1914 in Los Angeles, California
d. January 15, 1983 in Burbank, California

Fritz William Weaver
American actor
• Won Tony for *Child's Play*, 1970.
b. January 19, 1926 in Pittsburgh, Pennsylvania

Sigourney Weaver
(Susan Weaver)
American actress
• Starred in *Alien*, 1979; *Eyewitness*, 1981; *The Year of Living Dangerously*, 1983.
b. 1949 in New York, New York

Clifton Webb
(Webb Parmelee Hollenbeck)
American actor
• Oscar nominee for *Laura*, 1944; *Razor's Edge*, 1946.
b. November 19, 1891 in Indianapolis, Indiana
d. October 13, 1966 in Beverly Hills, California

Jack Randolph Webb
(John Farr; Tex Grady pseuds)
American director–author
• Played Sgt. Joe Friday on Emmy-winning TV series "Dragnet," 1952-59, 1967-70; also produced "Adam 12," 1968-75.
b. April 02, 1920 in Santa Monica, California
d. December 23, 1982 in Los Angeles, California

Carl Weber
Director
• Has directed for stage, TV, all over the world; won Obie Award, 1973, for *Kaspar*.
b. August 07, 1925 in Dortmund, Germany

Lois Weber
American actress–director–screenwriter
• First woman film director, early 1900s.
b. June 13, 1881 in Allegheny, California
d. November 13, 1939 in Los Angeles, California

Ben(jamin) Webster
English actor
• Movies include *Mrs. Miniver*, 1942; *Lassie Come Home*, 1943; father of Margaret Webster.
b. June 02, 1864 in London, England
d. February 26, 1947 in Hollywood, California

John Webster
English dramatist
• Wrote *The White Devil*, 1612; *The Duchess of Malfi*, 1613.
b. 1580 in London, England
d. 1634

Margaret Webster
American actress–director
• Revived Shakespeare on Broadway stage, 1930s-40s; daughter of May Whitty.
b. March 15, 1905 in New York, New York
d. November 13, 1972 in London, England

Frank Wedekind
German dramatist
• Expressionist, social critic; plays on sexual issues include *Pandora's Box*, 1918; play's character, Lulu, subject of Alban Berg's opera, *Lulu*, 1934.
b. July 24, 1864 in Hannover, Germany
d. March 09, 1918 in Munich, Germany

Charles Weidman
American dancer
• Best known for enhancing the participation of men in dance.
b. July 22, 1901 in Lincoln, Nebraska
d. July 15, 1975 in New York, New York

Claudia Weill
American director
• Films include *It's My Turn*, 1980; *Girlfriends*, 1977.
b. 1947 in New York, New York

Edwin B Weinberger
Writer
• Won Emmys for "Mary Tyler Moore Show"; "Taxi."

Jerry Weintraub
American producer–talent agent
• Produced *The Karate Kid*, 1984; agent for Frank Sinatra, Neil Diamond, John Denver.
b. September 26, 1937 in Brooklyn, New York

Peter Weir
Australian director
• Compared with Alfred Hitchcock for ability to combine everyday life with unspeakable terror: *The Year of Living Dangerously*, 1983.
b. August 08, 1944 in Sydney, Australia

Bob Weiskopf
American writer–producer
• Won Emmys for "Red Skelton Show," 1971; "All in the Family," 1978.

Peter Weiss
Swedish dramatist
• Wrote *Marat/Sade*; won Tony, 1966.
b. November 08, 1916 in Nowawes, Germany
d. May 1, 1982 in Stockholm, Sweden

Johnny Weissmuller
American actor–swimmer
• Played Tarzan in 19 movies, 1934-48; won five gold medals in 1924, 1928 Olympics.
b. June 02, 1904 in Chicago, Illinois
d. January 2, 1984 in Acapulco, Mexico

Bruce Peter Weitz
American actor
• Played Mick Belker on TV series "Hill Street Blues," 1981-87; won Emmy award, 1984.
b. May 27, 1943 in Norwalk, Connecticut

Raquel Welch
(Raquel Tejada; Mrs Andre Weinfeld)
American actress–model
• Film star known for figure, sexiness: *One Million Years, BC*, 1967; starred on Broadway in *Woman of the Year*, 1982.
b. September 05, 1942 in Chicago, Illinois

Tuesday (Susan Kerr) Weld
American actress
• Starred in *Return to Peyton Place*, 1961; *Looking for Mr. Goodbar*, 1977.
b. August 27, 1943 in New York, New York

Joan Weldon
American actress
• Films include *So This Is Love*, 1953; *Home Before Dark*, 1958.
b. August 05, 1933 in San Francisco, California

John Weldon
(Brinsley MacNamara pseud)
Irish actor–dramatist
• Plays include *Margaret Gillan*, 1935.
b. September 06, 1890 in Hiskenstown, Ireland
d. February 04, 1963 in Dublin, Ireland

Colin Welland
English screenwriter
• Wrote Oscar-winning film *Chariots of Fire*, 1981.
b. July 04, 1934 in England

Michael Weller
American dramatist–screenwriter
• Wrote films *Hair*, 1979; *Ragtime*, 1981.
b. September 27, 1942 in New York, New York

Orson (George Orson) Welles
American actor–director–producer–writer
• Considered major film genius; gained reputation with 1938 radio adaptation of *War of the Worlds*; starred in *Citizen Kane*, 1940.
b. May 06, 1915 in Kenosha, Wisconsin
d. October 1, 1985 in Los Angeles, California

William Augustus Wellman
American director
• Films known for "documentary realism" include *Wings*, 1927; *The High and the Mighty*, 1954.
b. February 29, 1896 in Brookline, Massachusetts
d. December 09, 1975 in Los Angeles, California

George Wells
Screenwriter
• Won Oscar for *Designing Woman*, 1957.
b. 1909

George Wendt
American actor
• Plays Norm Peterson on TV series "Cheers," 1982–.
b. October 17, 1948 in Chicago, Illinois

Oskar Werner
(Oskar Josef Bschliessmayer)
Austrian actor
• Starred in *Jules et Jim*, 1961; *Ship of Fools*, 1965; *Fahrenheit 451*, 1966.
b. November 13, 1922 in Vienna, Austria
d. October 23, 1984 in Marburg, Germany (West)

Lina von Eigg Wertmuller
(Arcangela Felice Assunta Wertmuller von Elgg)
Italian director
• In popular films: *Seven Beauties*, 1976; *Seduction of Mimi*, 1974.
b. August 14, 1928 in Rome, Italy

Arnold Wesker
English dramatist
• Plays include *Their Very Own Golden City*, 1966; *The Merchant*, 1977.
b. May 24, 1932 in London, England

Adam West
(William West Anderson)
American actor
• Played Bruce Wayne/Batman on TV series "Batman," 1966-68.
b. September 19, 1938 in Walla Walla, Washington

Mae West
American actress
• Known for sex appeal, frankness, films with W C Fields, including *My Little Chickadee*, 1940.
b. August 17, 1892 in Brooklyn, New York
d. November 22, 1980 in Hollywood, California

Helen Westley
(Henrietta Meserole Manney)
American actress
• Helped found the Theater Guild, 1918-36.
b. March 28, 1879 in Brooklyn, New York
d. December 12, 1942 in Franklin County, New Jersey

Jack Weston
(Morris Weinstein)
American actor
• Supporting actor in films *The Four Seasons*, 1981; *High Road to China*, 1983.
b. August 21, 1915 in Cleveland, Ohio

Haskell Wexler
American director–filmmaker
• Won Oscars for cinematography for *Who's Afraid of Virginia Woolf?* 1966; *Bound for Glory* 1976.
b. 1926 in Chicago, Illinois

Norman Wexler
American screenwriter
• Films include *Joe*, 1970; *Saturday Night Fever*, 1977.
b. August 16, 1926 in New Bedford, Massachusetts

John Wexley
American dramatist
• Wrote film *Hangmen Also Die*, 1943; blacklisted by studio.
b. 1907 in New York, New York
d. February 04, 1985 in Doylestown, Pennsylvania

James Whale
English director
• Films include *Frankenstein*, 1931; *Invisible Man*, 1933.
b. July 22, 1896 in Dudley, England
d. May 29, 1957 in Hollywood, California

Michael Whalen
(Joseph Kenneth Shovlin)
American actor
• Leading man of B-films, 1936-60, including *Sing, Baby, Sing*; *Poor Little Rich Girl*.
b. June 3, 1902 in Wilkes-Barre, Pennsylvania
d. April 14, 1974 in Woodland Hills, California

Bert (Albert Jerome) Wheeler
(Wheeler and Woolsey)
American comedian
• Teamed with Robert Woolsey in over 30 films, including *On Again, Off Again*, 1937.
b. April 07, 1895 in Paterson, New Jersey
d. January 18, 1968 in New York, New York

Lisa Whelchel
American actress
• Played Blair on TV series "Facts of Life," 1979-88.
b. May 29, 1963 in Fort Worth, Texas

Johnny Whitaker
American actor
• Played Jody on TV series "Family Affair," 1966-71.
b. December 13, 1959 in Van Nuys, California

Betty White
(Mrs Allen Ludden)
American actress
• Played Sue Ann Nevins on "The Mary Tyler Moore Show," 1970-77; Rose on "Golden Girls," 1985-.
b. January 17, 1917 in Oak Park, Illinois

George White
(George Weitz)
American actor–director–producer
• Produced rival of *Ziegfeld Follies*, *George White's Scandals*, 1919-31.
b. 1890 in Toronto, Ontario
d. October 11, 1968 in Los Angeles, California

Jesse White
(Jesse Marc Weidenfeld)
American actor–comedian
• TV spokesman for Maytag Co., 1967–; coined slogan "the loneliest man in the world."
b. January 03, 1919 in Buffalo, New York

Michael Simon White
Scottish producer
• Won Tony for *Sleuth*, 1971; films include *The Rocky Horror Picture Show*, 1975.
b. January 16, 1936 in Scotland

Slappy White
American comedian
• Popular on screen, 1970s; films include *Amazing Grace*, 1974.

Vanna Marie White
American model–TV personality
• Hostess of TV game show "Wheel of Fortune," 1982–; wrote autobiography: *Vanna Speaks*, 1987.
b. February 18, 1957 in Conway, South Carolina

Robert Whitehead
Canadian producer
• Plays include *Member of the Wedding*, 1950; won Tony for *A Man for All Seasons*, 1962.
b. March 03, 1916 in Montreal, Quebec

Billie Whitelaw
English actress
• Films include *Charlie Bubbles*, 1968; *The Omen*, 1976.
b. June 06, 1932 in Coventry, England

Leonard Whiting
British actor
• Film debut as Romeo in *Romeo and Juliet*, 1968.
b. 1950

Albert Whitlock
English special effects technician
• Won Oscars for *Earthquake*, 1974; *The Hindenburg*, 1975.
b. 1915 in London, England

Stuart Whitman
American actor
• Oscar nominee for *The Mark*, 1961.
b. February 01, 1926 in San Francisco, California

James Allen Whitmore
American actor
• Famous for one-man shows *Will Rogers, USA*, and *Give 'Em Hell, Harry*.
b. October 01, 1921 in White Plains, New York

C(ornelius) V(anderbilt) Whitney
American businessman–producer
• Founder, board director, Pan Am Airways, 1927-41; co-produced *Gone With the Wind*, 1939.
b. February 2, 1899 in New York, New York

Dame May Whitty
English actress
• Oscar nominee for *Night Must Fall*, 1937.
b. June 19, 1865 in Liverpool, England
d. May 29, 1948 in Beverly Hills, California

Richard Whorf
American actor–director
• Films include *Love from a Stranger*, 1947; *The Burning Hills*, 1956.
b. June 04, 1906 in Winthrop, Massachusetts
d. December 14, 1966 in Santa Monica, California

Ireene Seaton Wicker
(Lady ")
American TV personality
• Children's storyteller on TV, radio, 1931-75; won over 30 awards.
b. November 24, 1905 in Quincy, Illinois
d. November 17, 1987 in West Palm Beach, Florida

James Widdoes
American actor
• Best known for film debut in *Animal House*, 1977.
b. November 15, 1953 in Pittsburgh, Pennsylvania

Kathleen Effie Widdoes
American actress
• TV performances include "Much Ado about Nothing"; "Edith Wharton: Looking Back."
b. March 21, 1939 in Wilmington, Delaware

Bo Widerberg
Swedish director
• Films include *Adalen 31*, 1969; *Joe Hill*, 1971.
b. June 08, 1930 in Malmo, Sweden

Richard Widmark
American actor
• Starred in *Judgment at Nuremberg*, 1961; *Murder on the Orient Express*, 1974.
b. December 26, 1914 in Sunrise City, Minnesota

Dianne Wiest
American actress
• Won 1986 Oscar for *Hannah and Her Sisters*.
b. March 28, 1948 in Kansas City, Missouri

Herbert Wilcox
British producer
• Films include *No, No, Nanette*, 1940; *Heart of a Man*, 1959.
b. April 19, 1891 in Cork, Ireland
d. May 15, 1977 in London, England

Larry Dee Wilcox
American actor
• Played Officer Jon Baker on TV series "CHiPs," 1977-82.
b. August 08, 1947 in San Diego, California

Henry Wilcoxon
(Harry Wilcoxon)
British actor-producer
• Starred in Cecil B. DeMille films, *Cleopatra*, 1934; *The Crusades*, 1935.
b. September 08, 1905 in Dominica, British West Indies

Jack Wild
English actor
• Oscar nominee for debut in movie *Oliver*, 1968, as the Artful Dodger.
b. September 3, 1952 in Manchester, England

Cornel Wilde
American actor-producer-director
• Oscar nominee for role of Chopin in *A Song to Remember*, 1945.
b. October 13, 1915 in New York, New York
d. October 16, 1989 in Los Angeles, California

Oscar Fingal O'Flahertie Wills Wilde
Irish poet-dramatist-author
• Flamboyant wit; wrote *The Importance of Being Earnest*, 1895; imprisoned for sodomy, 1890s.
b. October 16, 1856 in Dublin, Ireland
d. November 3, 1900 in Paris, France

Billy (Samuel) Wilder
American director-producer
• Has over 50 films, six Oscars to credit; films include *Double Indemnity*, 1944; *Some Like It Hot*, 1959; won Lifetime Achievement Award, 1986; Thalberg Award, 1988.
b. June 22, 1906 in Vienna, Austria

Gene Wilder
(Jerome Silberman)
American actor
• Starred in *Blazing Saddles*, 1974; *Young Frankenstein*, 1974; *Stir Crazy*, 1980.
b. June 11, 1934 in Milwaukee, Wisconsin

Thornton Niven Wilder
American author-dramatist
• Won Pulitzers for novel, *The Bridge of San Luis Rey*, 1928; plays, *Our Town*, 1938; *Skin of Our Teeth*, 1942.
b. April 17, 1897 in Madison, Wisconsin
d. December 07, 1975 in Hamden, Connecticut

Michael Wilding
English actor
• Married to Elizabeth Taylor, 1952-57; debonair leading man of British films, 1933-73.
b. July 28, 1912 in Westcliff-on-Sea, England
d. July 09, 1979 in Chichester, England

George F Will
American journalist-TV personality
• Conservative political syndicated columnist; won Pulitzer, 1977; commentator, ABC News.
b. May 04, 1941 in Champaign, Illinois

Jess Willard
American boxer-actor
• World heavyweight champ, 1915-16, lost to Jack Dempsey; starred in film *The Heart Punch*, 1919.
b. December 29, 1881 in Kansas
d. December 15, 1968 in Los Angeles, California

Anson Williams
(Anson William Heimlick)
American actor-singer
• Played Potsie on TV series "Happy Days," 1974-83.
b. September 25, 1949 in Los Angeles, California

Barry Williams
American actor
• Played Greg on TV series "The Brady Bunch," 1969-74.
b. September 3, 1954 in Santa Monica, California

Bert (Egbert Austin) Williams
American actor-comedian
• Best known as star comedian of Ziegfeld Follies, 1909-19, where his most famous song was "Nobody."
b. 1876 in New Providence Island, Bahamas
d. March 04, 1922 in New York, New York

Billy Williams
English filmmaker
• Won Oscar for cinematography of *Gandhi*, 1982.
b. 1929 in England

Billy Dee Williams
American actor
• Best known for playing Gale Sayers in TV movie "Brian's Song," 1971, Louis McKay in film *Lady Sings the Blues*, 1972.
b. April 06, 1937 in New York, New York

Cindy Williams
(Mrs Bill Hudson)
American actress
• Starred in TV series "Laverne and Shirley," 1976-82.
b. August 22, 1948 in Van Nuys, California

Clarence Williams, III
American actor
• Starred in TV series "The Mod Squad," 1968-73.
b. August 21, 1939 in New York, New York

Darnell Williams
American actor
• Won Emmy for role as Jesse Hubbard on soap opera "All My Children," 1983.
b. March 03, in London, England

Emlyn (George Emlyn) Williams
Welsh dramatist-actor
• Wrote, starred in *The Corn Is Green*, 1930s; best known for one-man show on Charles Dickens.
b. November 26, 1905 in Mostyn, Wales
d. September 25, 1987 in London, England

Esther Williams
(Mrs Fernando Lamas)
American actress-swimmer
• Starred in MGM aquatic musicals *Neptune's Daughter*, 1949; *Dangerous When Wet*, 1953.
b. August 08, 1923 in Los Angeles, California

Gus Williams
American actor
• Comedian at Tony Pastor's theatre, 1868-79, starred in *Our German Senator*.
b. July 19, 1847 in New York, New York
d. January 16, 1915 in Yonkers, New York

JoBeth (Margaret JoBeth) Williams
American actress
• Films include *The Big Chill*, 1983; *Murder Ordained*, 1987.
b. 1953 in Houston, Texas

Robin Williams
American comedian-actor
• Starred in TV's "Mork and Mindy," 1978-81; won Grammy, 1979, for album, *Reality, What a Concept*; films include *Good Morning, Vietnam*, 1987.
b. July 21, 1952 in Chicago, Illinois

Samm-Art Williams
American actor–dramatist
• Plays include *Home*, 1979; *The Sixteenth Round*, 1980.
b. 1946 in Burgaw, North Carolina

Simon Williams
English actor
• Played James Bellamy in PBS series "Upstairs, Downstairs."
b. June 16, 1946 in Windsor, England

Tennessee (Thomas Lanier) Williams
American dramatist–author
• Won Pulitzers for classic plays *A Streetcar Named Desire*, 1947; *Cat on a Hot Tin Roof*, 1955.
b. March 26, 1911 in Columbus, Mississippi
d. February 25, 1983 in New York, New York

Treat (Richard Treat) Williams
American actor
• Starred in films *Hair*, 1979, *Prince of the City*, 1981, *Dead Heat*, 1988.
b. December 01, 1951 in Stamford, Connecticut

Wendy O(rlean) Williams
(The Plasmatics)
American entertainer
• Lead singer known for outrageous appearance and stage antics.
b. 1946 in Rochester, New York

David Williamson
Australian screenwriter
• Films include *The Year of Living Dangerously*, 1983.
b. February 24, 1942 in Melbourne, Australia

Nicol Williamson
Scottish actor
• Films include *The Seven-Percent Solution*, 1976; *Excaliber*, 1980.
b. September 14, 1938 in Hamilton, Scotland

George Willig
American actor–stuntman
• Became instant celebrity when he climbed World Trade Center, NYC, 1977; wrote *Going It Alone*, 1979.
b. June 11, 1949 in New York, New York

Bruce Walter Willis
American actor
• Played David Addison on TV series "Moonlighting," 1985-89; won 1987 Emmy; starred in film *Die Hard*, 1988, *Die Harder*, 1990; married to Demi Moore.
b. March 19, 1955 in Germany (West)

Gordon Willis
American filmmaker
• Cinematographer whose major films include *Klute*, 1971; *Annie Hall*, 1983.

Chill Wills
American actor
• Voice of Francis the Talking Mule in film series, 1940s-50s.
b. July 18, 1903 in Seagoville, Texas
d. December 15, 1978 in Encino, California

August Wilson
American dramatist
• Won 1987 Pulitzer, Tony for drama: *Fences*, about a 1950s black American family.
b. 1945 in Pittsburgh, Pennsylvania

Demond Wilson
American actor
• Starred in "Sanford and Son," 1972-77; "The New Odd Couple," 1982-83.
b. October 13, 1946 in Valdosta, Georgia

Don(ald Harlow) Wilson
American radio performer–TV personality
• Jack Benny's announcer, foil on TV, radio shows over 40 yrs.
b. September 01, 1900 in Lincoln, Nebraska
d. April 25, 1982 in Palm Springs, California

Dooley (Arthur) Wilson
American actor–musician
• Played Sam, the piano player, in *Casablanca*, 1943.
b. April 03, 1894 in Tyler, Texas
d. May 3, 1953 in Los Angeles, California

Flip (Clerow) Wilson
American actor–comedian
• Star of TV series "The Flip Wilson Show," 1970-74; best known character, Geraldine.
b. December 08, 1933 in Jersey City, New Jersey

Lanford Wilson
American dramatist
• Won Pulitzer Prize, 1980, for *Talley's Folley*.
b. April 13, 1937 in Lebanon, Missouri

Marie (Katherine Elizabeth) Wilson
American actress
• Starred on film, radio, TV, as "My Friend Irma."
b. August 19, 1916 in Anaheim, California
d. November 23, 1972 in Hollywood Hills, California

Robert M Wilson
American dramatist–producer
• Won special Obie for *The Life and Times of Joseph Stalin*, 1974; has won many awards for contributions to theater.
b. October 04, 1944 in Waco, Texas

Paul Winchell
American ventriloquist–actor
• Had TV show with dummy, "The Paul Winchell-Jerry Mahoney Show," 1950-54; voice of "Smurfs" cartoon show.
b. December 21, 1922 in New York, New York

William Windom
American actor
• Starred in "The Farmer's Daughter," 1962-65; "My World and Welcome to It," 1969-70.
b. September 28, 1923 in New York, New York

Claire Windsor
(Claire Viola Cronk)
American actress
• Starred in 45 silent films, 1920-29.
b. April 14, 1897 in Coffee City, Kansas
d. October 24, 1972 in Los Angeles, California

Marie Windsor
(Emily Marie Bertelson)
American actress
• Known for supporting roles in films: *Outpost in Morocco*, 1949; *Support Your Local Gunfighter*, 1971.
b. December 11, 1924 in Marysvale, Utah

Paul Edward Winfield
American actor
• Oscar nominee for *Sounder*, 1973; Emmy nominee for *King*, 1978; *Roots II*, 1980.
b. May 22, 1941 in Los Angeles, California

Oprah Gail Winfrey
American TV personality–actress
• Received Oscar nomination for role of Sophia in *The Color Purple*, 1985; hosts nationally syndicated talk show.
b. January 29, 1954 in Kosciusko, Mississippi

Debra (Mary Debra) Winger
(Mrs Timothy Hutton)
American actress
• Oscar nominee for *Terms of Endearment*, 1983; also starred in *Urban Cowboy*, 1980; *An Officer and a Gentleman*, 1982.
b. May 17, 1955 in Cleveland, Ohio

Henry Franklin Winkler
American actor
• Played Fonzie on TV series "Happy Days," 1974-84.
b. October 3, 1945 in New York, New York

Irwin Winkler
American producer
• Films include *They Shoot Horses Don't They?*, 1969; *Raging Bull*, 1980; *The Right Stuff*, 1983.
b. May 28, 1931 in New York, New York

Charles Winninger
American actor
• Played Cap'n Andy in original Broadway production of *Show Boat*, 1927-30.
b. May 26, 1884 in Athens, Wisconsin
d. January 1969 in Palm Springs, California

Jonathan (Harshman, III) Winters
American comedian–actor
• Known for characterizations, improvizations; films since 1963 include *The Loved One*, 1965.
b. November 11, 1925 in Dayton, Ohio

Shelley Winters
(Shirley Schrift)
American actress
• Won Oscars for *The Diary of Anne Frank*, 1959; *A Patch of Blue*, 1966.
b. August 18, 1922 in Saint Louis, Missouri

Estelle Winwood
(Estelle Goodwin; "Cow Eyes")
English actress
• Character actress whose career spanned 90 years; played the fairy godmother in *The Glass Slipper*, 1955.
b. January 24, 1883 in Leeds, England
d. June 2, 1984 in Los Angeles, California

Norman Wisdom
English actor–comedian
• Starred in plays *Where's Charley*, 1960; *Walking Happy*, 1970.
b. February 04, 1925 in London, England

Robert Wise
American director–producer
• Won Oscars for direction of *West Side Story*, 1961; *Sound of Music*, 1965.
b. September 1, 1914 in Winchester, Indiana

Joseph Wiseman
Canadian actor
• Played villainous title role in first James Bond film *Dr. No*, 1962.
b. May 15, 1918 in Montreal, Quebec

Walt Witcover
(Walter Witcover Scheinman)
American director–actor
• Won best actor Obies for *Maedchen in Uniform*, 1955; *Exiles*, 1957.
b. August 24, 1924 in New York, New York

Googie Withers
(Georgina McCallum)
British actress
• British films include *Miranda; Lady Vanishes*.
b. March 12, 1917 in Karachi, Pakistan

Jane Withers
American actress
• Child star of 1930s films; TV commercials as Josephine the Plumber.
b. April 12, 1926 in Atlanta, Georgia

Paul Junger Witt
American producer–director
• TV shows include "The Rookies," 1972-76; won Emmy for "Brian's Song," 1972.
b. March 2, 1943 in New York, New York

Margaret Woffington
Irish actress
• Best role as male in *Constant Couple*.
b. October 18, 1714 in Dublin, Ireland
d. March 28, 1760 in London, England

Digby Wolfe
English writer
• Emmy winner for writing TV specials, shows including "Laugh-In," 1968.
b. June 04, 1932 in England

Sir John Frederick Wolfenden
English museum director
• Director, British Museum, 1969-73; led com. which recommended liberalizing nation's homosexuality laws, 1967.
b. June 26, 1906 in Swindon, England
d. January 18, 1985 in London, England

Iggie Wolfington
American actor
• Tony nominee for *The Music Man*, 1958.
b. October 14, 1920 in Philadelphia, Pennsylvania

Wolfman Jack
(Robert Smith)
American radio performer
• Best known for wild, jive-talking radio program, 1970s; in film *American Graffiti*, 1973.
b. January 21, 1938 in Brooklyn, New York

Louis Wolheim
American actor
• Character actor, 1917-31, in films *Dr. Jekyll and Mr. Hyde; America*.
b. March 23, 1880 in New York, New York
d. February 18, 1931 in Los Angeles, California

David Lloyd Wolper
American producer–business executive
• Produces documentaries, TV shows, including "Roots," 1976; won 11 Emmys, one special Oscar.
b. January 11, 1928 in New York, New York

Anna May (Lu Tsong) Wong
American actress
• Star in 1920s-30s as mysterious Oriental in *Shanghai Express; Thief of Bagdad*.
b. January 03, 1907 in Los Angeles, California
d. February 03, 1961 in Santa Monica, California

John Wood
English actor
• Won 1976 Tony for *Travesties*.
b. 1930 in Derbyshire, England

Natalie Wood
(Natasha Gurdin; Mrs Robert Wagner)
American actress
• Starred in *Miracle on 34th Street*, 1946; *Rebel Without a Cause*, 1955; *West Side Story*, 1961.
b. July 2, 1939 in San Francisco, California
d. November 29, 1981 in Catalina Island, California

Peggy Wood
American actress–author
• Played in TV show "Mama," 1949-57; Oscar nominee for *Sound of Music*, 1965.
b. February 09, 1892 in New York, New York
d. March 18, 1978 in Stamford, Connecticut

Robert Dennis Wood
American TV executive
• Pres., CBS, 1969-76; introduced comedies "The Mary Tyler Moore Show"; "All in the Family"; "MASH."
b. April 17, 1925 in Boise, Idaho
d. May 2, 1986 in Santa Monica, California

Samuel Grosvenor Wood
American director
• Directed Marx Brothers film *A Night at the Opera*, 1935.
b. July 1, 1884 in Philadelphia, Pennsylvania
d. September 22, 1949 in Hollywood, California

Mary Woodall
British museum director
• First female director of major British provincial museum, Birmingham Museum and Art Gallery, 1956-64.
b. March 06, 1901
d. March 01, 1988

Alfre Woodard
American actress
• Award-winning TV roles include "St. Elsewhere," "L.A. Law," "Hill Street Blues"; cable TV film *Mandela*, 1987.
b. 1953 in Tulsa, Oklahoma

Barbara Blackburn Woodhouse
British TV personality
• Hosted popular dog training show on BBC, 1980; wrote *Dog Training My Way*, 1981; *No Bad Dogs: The Woodhouse Way*, 1982.
b. May 09, 1910 in Rathfarnham, Ireland
d. July 09, 1988 in Buckinghamshire, England

Donald Woods
(Ralph L Zink)
American actor–real estate executive
• Appeared in over 40 films, including
True Grit, 1969.
b. December 02, 1904 in Brandon, Manitoba

James Woods
American actor
• Films include *Against All Odds*, 1984;
Salvador, 1986; won Emmy, 1987.
b. April 18, 1947 in Vernal, Utah

Edward Woodward
English actor
• Starred in Shakespearian roles, British
TV, films; star of TV series "The Equalizer," 1986–.
b. June 01, 1930 in Croydon, England

Joanne Gignilliat Woodward
(Mrs Paul Newman)
American actress
• Won Oscar, 1957, for *The Three
Faces of Eve*.
b. February 27, 1930 in Thomasville, Georgia

Sheb Wooley
American singer–musician–actor
• Films include *Giant*, 1956; *High Noon*,
1952.
b. April 1, 1921 in Erick, Oklahoma

Monty (Edgar Montillion) Woolley
American actor
• Best known for stage, screen title role
in *The Man Who Came to Dinner*.
b. August 17, 1888 in New York, New York
d. May 06, 1962 in Albany, New York

Robert Woolsey
(Wheeler and Woolsey)
American actor–comedian
• Teamed with Bert Wheeler in Broadway musical, film *Rio Rita*, 1929; vaudeville and comedy film stars, 1927-38.
b. August 14, 1889 in Oakland, California
d. October 1938 in Malibu Beach, California

Tom Wopat
American actor
• Co-star of TV series "The Dukes of
Hazzard," 1979-85.
b. September 09, 1951 in Lodi, Wisconsin

Jo Anne Worley
American comedian–actress–singer
• Starred on TV series "Laugh-In,"
1968-73.
b. September 06, 1937 in Lowell, Indiana

Irene Worth
American actress
• Won Tony for *Sweet Bird of Youth*,
1976.
b. June 23, 1916 in Nebraska

Herman Wouk
American author–dramatist
• Wrote *The Caine Mutiny; The Winds
of War*, 1971; *War and Remembrance*,
1978; won Pulitzer for *The Caine Mutiny*.
b. May 27, 1915 in New York, New York

Fay Wray
Canadian actress
• Starred in *King Kong*, 1933.
b. September 1, 1907 in Alberta

Martha Wright
American singer–actress
• Replaced Mary Martin in *South Pacific*,
1951; played Nellie Forbush role 1,080
times.
b. March 23, 1926 in Seattle, Washington

Steven Wright
American comedian
• Stand-up comic since 1979; films include *Desperately Seeking Susan*, 1985.
b. December 06, 1955 in New York, New York

Teresa Wright
American actress
• Won 1941 Oscar for *Mrs. Miniver*;
nominated in same year for *Pride of the
Yankees*.
b. October 27, 1918 in New York, New York

Jane Wyatt
American actress
• Starred in TV series "Father Knows
Best," 1954-62.
b. August 13, 1912 in Campgaw, New York

Margaret Wycherley
American actress
• 1941 Oscar nominee for *Sergeant
York*.
b. 1881 in London, England
d. June 06, 1966 in New York, New York

Gretchen Wyler
(Gretchen Wienecke)
American actress
• Stage performances include *Silk Stockings*, 1955; *Damn Yankees*, 1956.
b. February 16, 1932 in Oklahoma City,
Oklahoma

William Wyler
American director–producer
• Won Oscars for *Mrs. Miniver*, 1942;
The Best Years of Our Lives, 1946; *Ben
Hur*, 1959.
b. July 01, 1902 in Muhlhausen, Germany
d. July 28, 1981 in Beverly Hills, California

Jane Wyman
(Sarah Jane Fulks)
American actress
• Won Oscar, 1948, for *Johnny Belinda*;
starred in TV series "Falcon Crest,"
1981-90; first wife of Ronald Reagan.
b. January 04, 1914 in Saint Joseph, Missouri

Thomas Hunt Wyman
American TV executive
• President, CEO of CBS, 1983–.
b. November 3, 1929 in Saint Louis, Missouri

Ed Wynn
(Isiah Edwin Leopold)
American comedian
• Ziegfeld Follies star; won Emmy for
"Requiem for a Heavyweight," 1956;
films include *Mary Poppins*, 1964.
b. November 09, 1886 in Philadelphia, Pennsylvania
d. June 19, 1966 in Beverly Hills, California

Keenan Wynn
(Francis Xavier Aloysius Wynn)
American actor
• Mustachioed character actor best remembered for film roles in *Dr. Straangelove*, 1964; *Kiss Me Kate*, 1953; son of
comedian Ed.
b. July 27, 1916 in New York, New York
d. October 14, 1986 in Brentwood, California

Tracy Keenan Wynn
American writer
• Won Emmys for "Tribes," 1971; "The
Autobiography of Miss Jane Pittman,"
1974.
b. February 28, 1945 in Los Angeles, California

Dana Wynter
(Dagmar Spencer-Marcus)
English actress
• Appeared in many TV shows including
"Gunsmoke," 1969; films include *Airport*, 1970.
b. June 08, 1932 in London, England

Diana Wynyard
(Dorothy Isobel Cox)
English actress
• Oscar nominee for *Cavalcade*, 1933.
b. January 16, 1906 in London, England
d. May 13, 1964 in London, England

Frank Yablans
American producer
• Films include *The Other Side of Midnight*, 1977; *Mommie Dearest*, 1982.
b. August 27, 1935 in New York, New York

Bruce Yarnell

American actor
• Appeared on stage with Ethel Merman in revival of *Annie Get Your Gun*.
b. December 28, 1938 in Los Angeles, California
d. November 3, 1973 in California

Peter Yates

English director
• Oscar nominee for *Breaking Away*, 1979; other films include *The Deep*, 1977.
b. July 24, 1929 in Aldershot, England

Philip Yordan

American screenwriter
• Won Oscar for *Broken Lance*, 1954; films include *God's Little Acre*, 1958.
b. 1913 in Chicago, Illinois

Dick (Richard Allen) York

American actor
• Played the first Darrin in TV series "Bewitched," 1964-69.
b. September 04, 1928 in Fort Wayne, Indiana

Michael York

(Michael York-Johnson)
English actor
• Starred in *The Island of Dr. Moreau*, 1977; on tour in *Cyrano de Bergerac*, 1981.
b. March 27, 1942 in Fulmer, England

Susannah York

(Susannah Yolande Fletcher)
English actress
• 1969 Oscar nominee for *They Shoot Horses, Don't They?*
b. January 09, 1941 in London, England

Tina Yothers

American actress
• Played Jennifer Keaton on TV comedy "Family Ties," 1982-89.
b. May 05, 1973 in Whittier, California

Alan (Angus) Young

American comedian-actor
• Starred in TV series "Mister Ed," 1961-65.
b. November 19, 1919 in North Shields, England

Burt Young

American actor-screenwriter
• Oscar nominee for *Rocky*, 1976.
b. April 3, 1940 in New York, New York

Gig Young

(Bryon Barr)
American actor
• Won Oscar for *They Shoot Horses, Don't They?*, 1969.
b. November 04, 1913 in Saint Cloud, Minnesota
d. October 19, 1978 in New York, New York

Loretta Gretchen Young

American actress
• Won Oscar for *The Farmer's Daughter*, 1947; star of TV series "The Loretta Young Show," 1953-61.
b. January 06, 1913 in Salt Lake City, Utah

Marian Young

(Martha Deane)
American radio performer
• Noted for hosting daily radio program, 1941-73; editor of daily newspapers.
b. November 21, 1908 in Star Lake, New York
d. December 09, 1973 in New York

Robert George Young

American actor
• Starred in TV series "Father Knows Best," 1954-62; "Marcus Welby, MD," 1969-76.
b. February 22, 1907 in Chicago, Illinois

Roland Young

English actor
• Oscar nominee for *Topper*, 1937.
b. November 11, 1887 in London, England
d. June 05, 1953 in New York, New York

Terence Young

American director
• Noted for James Bond films *Dr. No*, 1963; *From Russia With Love*, 1965; *Thunderball*, 1967.
b. June 2, 1915 in Shanghai, China

Henny (Henry) Youngman

American comedian
• Best known for line "Take my wife, please!"
b. January 12, 1906 in Liverpool, England

Igor Youskevitch

Russian dancer
• Debuted in US at NY Met., 1938; starred in film *Invitation to the Dance*, 1956.
b. March 13, 1912 in Kiev, Russia

Victor Sen Yung

American actor
• Played Hop Sing on TV series "Bonanza," 1959-73.
b. 1915 in San Francisco, California
d. November 09, 1980 in North Hollywood, California

Blanche Yurka

American actress
• Numerous classical roles included 130 performances of *Hamlet* with John Barrymore, 1922.
b. June 19, 1887 in Saint Paul, Minnesota
d. June 06, 1974 in New York, New York

Saul Zaentz

American producer
• Won Oscars for *Amadeus*, 1984; *One Flew Over the Cuckoo's Nest*, 1975.
b. in Passaic, New Jersey

Roxana Zal

American actress
• Won Emmy for title role in *Something About Amelia*, 1984.
b. November 08, 1969 in Los Angeles, California

Luigi Zampa

Italian director
• Films include *A Yank in Rome*, 1945; *Difficult Years*, 1948; *Anyone Can Play*, 1967.
b. January 02, 1905 in Rome, Italy

Darryl Francis Zanuck

American film executive-producer
• Produced first sound film, 1927; co-founded 20th Century Pictures, 1933; won three special Oscars.
b. September 05, 1902 in Wahoo, Nebraska
d. December 22, 1979 in Palm Springs, California

Richard Darryl Zanuck

American film executive-producer
• Produced two of the biggest box office draws in film history: *The Sting*, 1973, *Jaws*, 1975; won Oscar for *Driving Miss Daisy*, 1990; son of Darryl.
b. December 13, 1934 in Los Angeles, California

Franco Zeffirelli

Italian director
• Films include *Taming of the Shrew*, 1967; *Romeo and Juliet*, 1968; TV work includes mini-series *Jesus of Nazareth*, 1977.
b. February 12, 1923 in Florence, Italy

Anthony Zerbe

American actor
• Won Emmy, 1976, for "Harry-O."
b. in Long Beach, California

Howard Zieff

American director
• Films include *Private Benjamin*, 1980; *Unfaithfully Yours*, 1984.
b. 1943 in Los Angeles, California

Flo(renz) Ziegfeld
American producer
• Produced lavish, musical revues, "Ziegfeld Follies," 1907-30.
b. March 21, 1867 in Chicago, Illinois
d. July 22, 1932 in Hollywood, California

Efrem Zimbalist, Jr
American actor–composer
• Played Lewis Erskine on TV series "The FBI," 1965-74.
b. November 3, 1923 in New York, New York

Stephanie Zimbalist
American actress
• Daughter of Efrem Zimbalist, Jr.; starred in TV series "Remington Steele," 1982-87.
b. October 08, 1956 in Encino, California

Paul Zindel
American author–dramatist
• Won 1971 Pulitzer for *The Effects of Gamma Rays on Man-in-the-Moon Marigolds.*
b. May 15, 1936 in New York, New York

Fred Zinnemann
American director
• Won Oscars for *From Here to Eternity,* 1953; *A Man for All Seasons,* 1966.
b. April 25, 1907 in Vienna, Austria

Adrian Zmed
American actor
• Made Broadway debut as Danny Zuko in *Grease,* 1977; played Johnny Nogerilli in film *Grease 2,* 1982, Vince Romano on TV series "T J Hooker," 1982-85.
b. March 14, 1954 in Chicago, Illinois

Vera Zorina
(Eva Brigitta Hartwig)
German dancer–actress
• Appeared on Broadway in *On Your Toes,* 1954; films include *The Goldwyn Follies,* 1938.
b. January 02, 1917 in Berlin, Germany

Vilmos Zsigmond
Hungarian filmmaker
• Won Oscar for cinematography for *Close Encounters of the Third Kind,* 1977.
b. June 16, 1930 in Czeged, Hungary

George Zucco
English actor
• Had villainous supporting roles in over 100 films, 1931-51.
b. January 11, 1886 in Manchester, England
d. May 28, 1960 in Hollywood, California

Carl Zuckmayer
German dramatist
• Best known for satire *The Captain of Kopenick;* wrote film *The Blue Angel,* 1930.
b. December 27, 1896 in Nackenheim, Germany
d. January 18, 1977 in Visp, Switzerland

Adolph Zukor
American film executive–producer
• Founded Famous Players Lasky Corp., 1916; Paramount Pictures, 1927.
b. January 07, 1873 in Riese, Hungary
d. June 1, 1976 in Los Angeles, California

Arnold Zweig
German author–dramatist
• Best known for novel *Case of Sergeant Grischa,* 1927.
b. November 1, 1887 in Prussia
d. November 26, 1968 in Berlin, Germany (East)

MADAMS, MODELS, MYTHS & BLOOD LINES

Call Girls,

Celebrity Relatives,

Courtesans,

Fashion Mavens,

Legendary

Figures...

Scott Abbott
Canadian journalist–inventor
• With Chris and John Haney, invented board game Trivial Pursuit, 1979.

Polly Adler
(Pearl Adler)
American madam
• Began career, 1920; wrote *A House Is Not a Home*, 1953.
b. April 16, 1900 in Yanow, Poland
d. June 09, 1962 in Hollywood, California

Philip Agee
American government official–author
• Former CIA agent who wrote expose *Inside the Company: CIA Diary*, 1975.
b. July 19, 1935 in Tacoma Park, Florida

Prince Albert
(Albert Francis Charles Augustus Emmanuel of Saxe-Coburg-Gotha)
German consort
• Married Queen Victoria, Feb 1840; used influence to avert war with US in Trent Affair, 1861.
b. August 26, 1819 in Rosenau, Germany
d. December 13, 1861 in London, England

Alexandra Caroline Mary Charlotte
English consort
• Queen of Edward VII, remembered for beauty, goodness.
b. December 01, 1844 in Copenhagen, Denmark
d. November 2, 1925 in Sandringham, England

Alexandra Feodorovna
(Alix Victoria Helene Luise Beatrix)
Russian consort
• Married Nicholas II, last czar of Russia, 1894; slain with family by Bolsheviks.
b. 1872 in Hesse-Darmstadt, Germany
d. July 16, 1918 in Ekaterinburg, U.S.S.R.

Kim Alexis
American model
• Has appeared on covers of over 400 magazines in US and abroad; fashion editor of TV program "Good Morning America," since 1987.
b. July 15, 1960 in Lockport, New York

Alice (Mary Victoria Augusta Pauline)
(Countess of Athlone)
English princess
• Last surviving grandchild of Queen Victoria; great aunt of Queen Elizabeth II; wrote memoirs: *For My Grandchildren: Some Reminiscences.*
b. February 25, 1883 in Windsor, England
d. January 03, 1981 in London, England

Theodosia Burr Alston
(Mrs Joseph Alston)
American celebrity relative
• Daughter of Aaron Burr; stood loyally by father through all disasters; lost at sea.
b. June 21, 1783 in Albany, New York
d. January 01, 1813

Carol Alt
(Mrs Ron Greschner)
American model
• Has appeared on over 500 magazine covers; made three films in Italy, 1987.
b. December 01, 1960 in Queens, New York

Anne
(Anne Elizabeth Alice Louise)
English princess
• Only daughter of Queen Elizabeth II and Prince Philip, currently eighth in line to British throne; accomplished horsewoman, has represented England in Olympics; children are Peter and Zara Phillips.
b. August 15, 1950 in London, England

Anne of Bohemia
English consort
• First queen of Richard II, 1382-94.
b. March 11, 1366 in Prague, Bohemia
d. June 07, 1394 in Sheen, Bohemia

Anne of Cleves
German consort
• Protestant princess; fourth wife of Henry VIII, Jan-Jul 1540; marriage annulled.
b. September 22, 1515 in Cleves, Germany
d. July 16, 1557 in London, England

Army (Armand) Archerd
American journalist–actor
• Announcer, "pre-Oscar" show, 1958–; columnist, *Daily Variety*, since 1953.
b. January 13, 1919 in New York, New York

Giorgio Armani
Italian fashion designer
• Founded Giorgio Armani Co., 1975; developed unconstructed blazer.
b. 1936 in Piacenza, Italy

King Arthur
British legendary figure
• Celtic chieftain whose medieval legends began with Monmouth book *History of the Kings of Britain*, 12th c.

Ellen Lewis Herndon Arthur
(Mrs Chester A Arthur)
American celebrity relative
• Soprano soloist; died suddenly year before husband became president.
b. August 3, 1837 in Frederick, Virginia
d. January 12, 1880 in New York, New York

Susan Denise Atkins
American cultist–murderer
• Convicted, with Charles Manson, of Tate-LaBianca murders, 1969.
b. 1948

Charles Atlas
(Angelo Siciliano)
American physical fitness expert–bodybuilder
• Developed dynamic tension method of bodybuilding.
b. October 3, 1894 in Acri, Italy
d. December 23, 1972 in Long Beach, New York

Hugh D Auchincloss
American celebrity relative
• Stepfather of Jacqueline Onassis.
b. 1897
d. November 2, 1976 in Washington, District of Columbia

Ayesha
Arabian celebrity relative
• Daughter of Abu-Bakr; second wife of Mohammad.
b. 614 in Medina, Arabia
d. 678

Babur
(Zahir un-Din Muhammad; "Tiger")
Turkish military leader
• Descendant of Genghis Khan who was founder, first ruler of Mogul empire.
b. February 14, 1483 in Farghana, Turkey
d. December 26, 1530 in Agra, India

Tammy Faye Bakker
(Mrs Jim Bakker)
American evangelist–celebrity relative
• Wife of TV evangelist forced out, along with husband, during PTL ministry scandal, 1987; noted for heavy makeup.
b. 1942

Amelia Batchler
American model
• Posed for Columbia Pictures logo–the woman with torch, 1936.
b. 1916

Geoffrey Beene
American fashion designer
• Pres., designer, Geoffrey Beene, Inc. since 1962.
b. August 30, 1927 in Haynesville, LA

Alva Erskine Smith Vanderbilt Belmont
American socialite–suffragette
• Militant feminist, once wife of William K Vanderbilt.
b. January 17, 1853 in Mobile, Alabama
d. January 26, 1933

Prince Bernhard
(Bernhard Leopold Friedrich Eberhard Julius Kurt Karl Gottfried Peter)
German consort
• Married Queen Juliana of the Netherlands, Jan 7, 1937.
b. June 29, 1911 in Jena, Germany

Mr. (Richard) Blackwell
American fashion critic
• Famous for yearly list of "worst dressed" women in world
b. in Brooklyn, New York

Countess Marguerite Power Blessington
English socialite
• Renowned beauty; headed intellectual circle; wrote memoir of Byron, 1834.
b. September 01, 1789 in Knockbrit, Ireland
d. June 04, 1849 in Paris, France

Arndt von Bohlem
German celebrity relative
• Last heir to Krupp industrial fortune.
b. 1938
d. May 13, 1986 in Essen, Germany (West)

Anne Boleyn
English consort
• Second wife of Henry VIII, whose marriage was voided by church, May 17, 1536; mother of Elizabeth I.
b. 1507
d. May 19, 1536 in London, England

Elizabeth Patterson Bonaparte
American celebrity relative–socialite
• Marriage to Napoleon's youngest brother, Jerome, 1803; annulled, 1805.
b. February 06, 1785 in Baltimore, Maryland
d. April 04, 1879

Louis Lucien Bonaparte
French scholar–celebrity relative
• Philologist who was made prince by Napoleon III, 1863.
b. 1813 in Mangrove, England
d. 1891

Lucien Bonaparte
French statesman–celebrity relative
• Exiled for opposing brother, Napoleon's polices, 1810.
b. 1775
d. 1840 in Italy

Maria Letizis Bonaparte
French celebrity relative
• Mother of Napoleon I.
b. 1750
d. 1836

Chastity Bono
American celebrity relative
• Daughter of Sonny and Cher.
b. March 04, 1969 in Los Angeles, California

Rebecca B Boone
American celebrity relative
• Wife of Daniel Boone.
b. 1739
d. 1813

Maria Paolina Borghese
French celebrity relative
• Sister of Napoleon I.
b. 1780
d. 1825

Belle (Isabellle) Boyd
American spy–actress
• Confederate spy, 1861-62.
b. May 08, 1843 in Martinsburg, Virginia
d. June 11, 1900 in Kilbourne, Wisconsin

Eva Braun
(Mrs Adolf Hilter)
German celebrity relative
• Married Hitler a few days before their suicides.
b. February 06, 1912
d. April 3, 1945 in Berlin, Germany

Christie Brinkley
(Mrs Billy Joel)
American model
• Super model credited with several cover pgs, commercials.
b. February 02, 1953 in Monroe, Michigan

Helen Gurley Brown
American author–fashion editor
• *Cosmopolitan* magazine editor, 1965–; wrote best-selling novel *Sex & the Single Girl*, 1962. Wife of producer David Brown.
b. February 18, 1922 in Green Forest, Arkansas

Louise Joy Brown
English test tube baby
• First test tube baby; procedure developed by Drs. Patrick Steptoe, Robert Edwards.
b. July 25, 1978 in Oldham, England

Tina Brown
English fashion editor–journalist
• Editor-in-chief, *Vanity Fair*, 1984–.
b. November 21, 1953 in Maidenhead, England

Beau (George Bryan) Brummell
English dandy–gambler
• Set fashion standards for English society: trousers instead of breeches.
b. June 07, 1778 in London, England
d. March 31, 1840 in Caen, France

Calpurnia
Roman celebrity relative
• Third wife of Julius Caesar; had prophetic dream of Caesar's assassination.
b. 59BC

Teresa Capone
Italian celebrity relative
• Mother of Al Capone.
b. 1867 in Italy
d. November 29, 1952 in Chicago, Illinois

Pierre Cardin
French fashion designer
• Founded fashion house, 1949; purchased Paris restaurant, Maxim's, 1981.
b. July 7, 1922 in Venice, Italy

Princess Caroline
(Caroline Louise Marguerite Grimaldi)
Monacan princess
• Daughter of Princess Grace and Prince Rainier of Monaco; has taken on many of mother's official duties.
b. January 23, 1957 in Monte Carlo, Monaco

Elizabeth Jordan Carr
American test tube baby
• First test tube baby born in US.
b. December 28, 1981 in Norfolk, Virginia

Amy Lynn Carter
American celebrity relative
• Only daughter of Jimmy, Rosalynn Carter; involved in various forms of political activism in college.
b. October 19, 1967 in Plains, Georgia

Billy Carter
American celebrity relative
• Brother of Jimmy Carter.
b. March 29, 1937 in Plains, Georgia
d. September 25, 1988 in Plains, Georgia

Chip (James Earl, III) Carter
American celebrity relative
• Second son of Jimmy and Rosalynn Carter.
b. April 12, 1950 in Honolulu, Hawaii

Jack (John William) Carter
American celebrity relative
• First child of Jimmy and Rosalynn Carter.
b. July 03, 1947 in Portsmouth, Virginia

Jeff (Donnel Jeffrey) Carter
American celebrity relative
• Third son of Jimmy and Rosalynn Carter.
b. August 18, 1952 in New London, Connecticut

Lillian (Bessie Lillian Gordy) Carter
American celebrity relative–nurse
• Mother of Jimmy Carter; joined Peace Corps serving in India at age 68.
b. August 15, 1898 in Richmond, Georgia
d. October 3, 1983 in Americus, Georgia

Stefano Casiraghi
Italian celebrity relative
• Second husband of Princess Caroline of Monaco, married Dec 29, 1983; killed in power boating accident.
b. September 08, 1960 in Italy
d. October 03, 1990 in Monte Carlo, Monaco

Oleg Lolewski Cassini
French fashion designer
• Official White House designer for Jacqueline Kennedy, 1961-63.
b. April 11, 1913 in Paris, France

Raul Castro
Cuban political leader–celebrity relative
• First vice premier; younger brother of Fidel Castro.
b. June 03, 1931 in Biran, Cuba

Catherine de Medici
Italian consort
• Daughter of Lorenzo de Medici who married Henry II, 1533, adviser to son Charles IX, 1560-74.
b. April 13, 1519 in Florence, Italy
d. January 05, 1589 in Blois, France

Catherine of Aragon
English consort
• Mother of Mary I; marriage voided, 1533, so Henry could marry Anne Boleyn.
b. December 16, 1485 in Alcala, Spain
d. January 07, 1536 in Kimbolton, England

Catherine of Valois
French consort
• Lived in obscurity after death of husband, Henry V, due to unpopular remarriage to poor commoner.
b. October 27, 1401 in Paris, France
d. January 03, 1437 in Bermondsey Abbey, England

"Coco" (Gabrielle) Chanel
French fashion designer
• Created Chanel No. 5 perfume, 1924; subject of Broadway play, *Coco*.
b. August 19, 1882 in Saumur, France
d. January 10, 1971 in Paris, France

Chang and Eng
(Chang and Eng Bunker)
American siamese twins
• Toured carnivals in US, Europe, 1829-54; Chang died first, Eng died of fright two hrs. later.
b. May 11, 1811 in Meklong, Thailand
d. January 17, 1874 in Mount Airy, North Carolina

Sydney Chaplin
American celebrity relative
• Broadway musicals include *Funny Girl*; son of Charlie Chaplin, Lita Grey.
b. March 3, 1926 in Los Angeles, California

Charles
(Charles Philip Arthur George; Prince of Wales)
English Prince
• First child of Queen Elizabeth II and Prince Philip; currently heir to British throne.
b. November 14, 1948 in London, England

Suzette Charles
(Suzette DeGaetano)
American beauty contest winner
• First runner-up in Miss America pageant, 1983; succeed Vanessa Williams, Jul 1983 when she was forced to give up crown.
b. 1963 in Philadelphia, Pennsylvania

Charlotte Sophia
English consort
• Queen of George III.
b. 1744
d. November 17, 1818 in Kew, England

Baroness Clementine Ogilvy (Hozier) Spencer Churchill
English celebrity relative
• Wife of Winston Churchill.
b. April 01, 1885 in London, England
d. December 12, 1977 in London, England

Jennie Jerome Churchill
American celebrity relative
• Vivacious society leader, mother of Winston Churchill.
b. 1850 in New York, New York
d. June 29, 1921

Randolph Churchill
English celebrity relative
• Son of Winston Churchill.
b. May 28, 1911 in London, England
d. June 06, 1968 in London, England

Liz (Elisabeth) Claiborne
(Mrs. Arthur Ortenberg)
American fashion designer
• Specialist in moderate-priced sportswear; founded Liz Claiborne, Inc. 1976.
b. March 31, 1929 in Brussels, Belgium

Claire (Clara Mary Jane) Clairmont
English celebrity relative
• Stepdaughter of William Godwin; friend of Percy, Mary Shelley; mother of Lord Byron's daughter, Allegra.
b. April 27, 1798
d. 1879 in Florence, Italy

Hope Cooke
(Hope Namgyal Maharani of Sikkim)
American consort
• Married Prince Palden Thondup Namgyal, 1963; first native-born American to become queen.
b. June 21, 1940 in San Francisco, California

Wilhelmina Behmenburg Cooper
American model–business executive
• Founded Wilhelmina Models, Inc. in 1967; appeared on record 28 *Vogue* covers, 1960s.
b. 1940
d. March 01, 1980 in Greenwich, Connecticut

Edward Finch Cox
American lawyer–celebrity relative
• Married Tricia Nixon, Jun 1971.
b. October 02, 1946 in Southampton, New York

Cheryl Crane
American celebrity relative
• Daughter of Lana Turner; killed mother's lover, gangster Johnny Stompanato, 1958; wrote autobiography *Detour: A Hollywood Story*, 1988.
b. 1944

Kathryn Crosby
(Mrs Bing Crosby; Kathryn Grandstaff; Kathryn Grant)
American celebrity relative
• Married Bing, 1957, appeared with family in TV Christmas specials.
b. November 25, 1933 in Houston, Texas

Nathaniel Crosby
American golfer–celebrity relative
• Youngest son of Bing; won US Amateur Golf Championship, 1981.
b. 1961 in Los Angeles, California

Pauline Cushman
(Harriet Wood; "Spy of the Cumberland")
American actress–spy
• Spy for the Union; captured, found guilty by Confederates, but rescued by Union advance.
b. June 1, 1833 in New Orleans, Louisiana
d. December 02, 1893 in San Francisco, California

Gala Dali
(Mrs Salvador Dali; Elena Diaranoff)
Model–Celebrity Relative
• For over 50 years was inspiration for husband, surrealist painter Salvador Dali.
b. 1893 in Kazan, Russia
d. June 1, 1982 in Gerona, Spain

Damocles
Courtier
• Attended to Dionysius; story told by Cicero.
b. 370?BC in Syracuse, Sicily

Lord Henry Stuart Darnley
English celebrity relative
• Second husband of Mary Queen of Scots; victim of murder plot.
b. 1545
d. February 09, 1567

Barbara Davis
American celebrity relative
• Wrote memoir *My Mother's Keeper*, 1985; daughter of Bette Davis.

Loyal Davis
American surgeon–celebrity relative
• Stepfather of Nancy Reagan, known for practice, teaching of brain surgery.
b. January 17, 1896 in Galesburg, Illinois
d. August 19, 1982 in Scottsdale, Arizona

Oscar De La Renta
American fashion designer
• Known for lavish evening clothes; won Cody awards, 1967, 1968.
b. July 22, 1932 in Santo Domingo, Dominican Republic

Ferdinand Waldo Demara, Jr
American imposter
• Master identity thief; subject of biography, film *The Great Imposter*, 1961.
b. December 12, 1921 in Lawrence, Massachusetts
d. June 07, 1982 in Anaheim, California

Robert Devereaux
(Earl of Essex)
English courtier
• Liked by Queen Elizabeth until his secret marriage caused disfavor; prosecuted for treason, executed; enjoyed literature, writing sonnets.
b. November 19, 1566
d. February 25, 1601

Princess Diana of Whales
(Lady Diana Frances Spencer; "Lady Di")
English princess
• Married Prince Charles, 1981; mother of Princes William, Henry.
b. July 01, 1961 in Sandringham, England

Emilie Dionne
(Dionne Sisters)
Canadian quintuplet
• One of world's first recorded surviving quintuplets; films *Reunion*, 1936; *Five of a Kind*, 1938, were biographical.
b. May 28, 1934 in Callander, Ontario
d. August 06, 1954 in Saint Agathe, Quebec

Marie Dionne
(Dionne Sisters)
Canadian quintuplet
• One of world's first recorded surviving quintuplets; films *The Country Doctor*, 1936; *Five of a Kind*, 1938, were biographical.
b. May 28, 1934 in Callander, Ontario
d. February 27, 1970 in Montreal, Quebec

Dionne Sisters
(Annette Dionne; Cecile Dionne; Emilie Dionne; Marie Dionne; Yvonne Dionne)
Canadian quintuplets
• World's first recorded surviving quintuplets; appeared in two films as toddlers.
b. May 28, 1934 in Callander, Ontario

Christian Dior
French fashion designer
• Introduced long hemlines, full skirts; controversial before accepted, called "new look."
b. January 21, 1905 in Granville, France
d. October 24, 1957 in Montecatini, Italy

Count Alfred Guillaume D'Orsay
French socialite–dandy
• Famed Paris, London dandy, wit; arbiter of fashion.
b. September 04, 1801 in Paris, France
d. August 04, 1852 in Paris, France

Comtesse Marie Jeanne Gomard de Vaubernier Du Barry
(Madame Du Barry)
French mistress
• Royal mistress to Louis XV, 1769-74; nursed him until his death; appeared before Revolutionary Tribunal, guillotined.
b. August 19, 1746 in Paris, France
d. December 07, 1793 in France

Kitty (Katharine Dickson) Dukakis
(Mrs Michael Dukakis)
American celebrity relative
• Married Michael Dukakis, 1963; autobiography *Now You Know*, 1990, details alcohol, drug addiction.
b. 1937

Doris Duke
American socialite–philanthropist
• Only child of tobacco magnate James Buchanan Duke; heiress to fortune.
b. November 22, 1912 in New York, New York

Marie Duplessis
(Alphonsine Plessis)
French courtesan–model
• Well-known in Paris, 1840s; first *Dame aux Camelias*.
b. 1824 in Normandy, France
d. 1847 in Paris, France

David Eisenhower
American celebrity relative
• Grandson of Dwight Eisenhower, husband of Julie Nixon; presidential retreat "Camp David" named for him.
b. April 01, 1947 in West Point, New York

Julie Nixon Eisenhower
(Mrs David Eisenhower)
American celebrity relative–author
• Younger daughter of Richard Nixon; wrote *Special People*, 1977, biography of mother *Pat Nixon: The Untold Story*, 1986.
b. July 05, 1948 in Washington, District of Columbia

Ruth Elder
American aviatrix–actress
• Made unsuccessful attempts to become first woman to fly across Atlantic, 1927; starred in several vaudeville films.
b. September 08, 1905 in Anniston, Alabama
d. October 09, 1977 in San Francisco, California

Eleanor of Aquitaine
(Eleanor of Guienne)
French consort
• Marriage to Louis VII annulled; married Henry II, 1154; mother of Richard the Lion-Hearted; story told in Oscar-winning *The Lion in Winter*, 1968.
b. 1122 in Aquitaine, France
d. April 01, 1204 in Maine-et-Loire, France

The Queen Mother Elizabeth
(Elizabeth Angela Marguerite)
English consort
• Wife of King George VI; mother of Queen Elizabeth II, Princess Margaret.
b. August 04, 1900 in Hertfordshire, England

Perry Edwin Ellis
American fashion designer
• Created the "American Look," easy to wear, youthful garments in natural fibers, colors, 1976.
b. March 3, 1940 in Churchland, Virginia
d. May 30, 1986 in New York, New York

Ada Everleigh
American madam
• Known in Chicago for expensive, high-class bordello, 1900s.
b. 1876 in Kentucky
d. January 03, 1960 in Roanoke, Virginia

Minna Everleigh
American madam
• Known in Chicago for expensive bordello that was virtually a city landmark.
b. 1878 in Kentucky
d. September 16, 1948 in New York, New York

Judith Campbell Exner
(Judith Eileen Katherine Immoor)
American celebrity friend
• Alleged mistress of JFK; mobster Sam Giancana; wrote *My Story*, 1977.
b. 1934 in Pacific Palisades, California

Fabiola, Queen of Belgium
Belgian celebrity relative
• Wife of King Baudouin of Belgium.
b. June 11, 1928

Sally (Sarah Cary) Fairfax
(Mrs Will Fairfax)
American celebrity friend
• Wife of George Washington's best friend; object of Washington's lifelong (probably unconsummated) obsession; played by Jaclyn Smith in TV miniseries, 1984.
b. 1730
d. 1811

Jinx (Eugenia Lincoln) Falkenburg
(Jinx McCrary)
American model
• Highest paid model, 1941; had radio show "Tex and Jinx Show."
b. January 21, 1919 in Barcelona, Spain

Fatima
Arabian celebrity relative
• Daughter of Mohammed, wife of Ali.
b. 606 in Mecca, Arabia
d. 632 in Medina, Arabia

Sarah Margaret Ferguson
(Duchess of York; "Fergie")
English consort
• Commoner who married Prince Andrew Jul 23, 1986.
b. October 15, 1959 in London, England

Christina Ferrare
(Mrs Anthony Thomopolos)
American model
• Former wife of John DeLorean; appeared on mag. covers, some films, weight-loss ads.
b. 1951

Caroline Carmichael McIntosh Fillmore
American celebrity relative
• Second wife of US Pres. Millard Fillmore.
b. October 21, 1813 in Morristown, New Jersey
d. August 11, 1881

Althea Sue Flynt

(Althea Leasure; Mrs Larry Flynt)
American publisher
• Co-publisher, *Hustler* magazine, 1974-87; editorial director, *Chic* magazine, 1976-87.
b. November 06, 1953 in Marietta, Ohio
d. June 27, 1987 in Los Angeles, California

Larry Claxton Flynt

American publisher
• Publishes *Hustler* magazine, 1974–; paralyzed in assassination attempt.
b. November 01, 1942 in Magoffin County, Kentucky

Anne McDonnell Ford

(Mrs Deane Johnson)
American celebrity relative
• First wife of Henry Ford II, 1940-64; mother of Charlotte, Ann, Edsel II.

Charlotte Ford

(Mrs Edward Downe Jr)
American socialite–designer–celebrity relative
• Daughter of Henry Ford II; etiquette columnist who wrote *Charlotte Ford's Book of Modern Manners*.
b. April 03, 1941

Christina Ford

(Maria Christina Vettore Austin Ford)
Italian celebrity relative
• Second wife of Henry Ford II.
b. 1927

Eleanor Clay Ford

American celebrity relative
• Wife of Edsel B Ford, mother of Henry Ford II.
b. 1896
d. October 19, 1976 in Detroit, Michigan

Jack (John Gardner) Ford

American celebrity relative
• Second son of Gerald and Betty Ford.
b. March 16, 1952 in Washington, District of Columbia

Kathleen DuRoss Ford

(Mrs Henry Ford II)
American celebrity relative
• Third wife of Henry Ford II.
b. February 11, 1940 in Belding, Michigan

Michael Gerald Ford

American celebrity relative
• Oldest son of Gerald, Betty Ford.
b. March 14, 1950 in Washington, District of Columbia

Susan Elizabeth Ford

American celebrity relative
• Only daughter of Gerald and Betty Ford.
b. July 06, 1957 in Washington, District of Columbia

Brenda Diana Dudd Frazier

(Mrs Robert F Chatfield-Taylor)
American socialite
• Made headlines, 1930s-40s, for glamorous life with friends such as Bette Davis, Duke of Windsor.
b. 1921
d. May 03, 1982 in Boston, Massachusetts

Frederika Louise

Greek consort
• Queen of Greece, 1947-64; in self-imposed exile after monarchy overthrow, 1973.
b. April 18, 1917 in Blankenburg, Germany
d. February 06, 1981 in Madrid, Spain

Lynette Alice Fromme

American attempted assassin–cultist
• Charles Manson follower, convicted of attempting to assassinate Gerald Ford, 1975.
b. 1949

Diane Halfin von Furstenberg

Fashion Designer
• Began designing, 1971; first effort was jersey wrapdress.
b. December 31, 1946 in Brussels, Belgium

Egon von Furstenberg

Fashion Designer
• Developed ready to wear line of fashion.
b. June 29, 1946 in Lausanne, Switzerland

John Clark Gable

American celebrity relative
• Son of Clark Gable.
b. March 2, 1961

Jolie Gabor

(Jancsi Tilleman)
Hungarian celebrity relative
• Mother of glamorous Gabor sisters.
b. September 29, 1896 in Hungary

Sanjay Gandhi

Indian celebrity relative
• Son of Indira Gandhi.
b. December 14, 1946 in New Delhi, India
d. June 23, 1980 in New Delhi, India

Phyllis George

(Mrs John Y Brown Jr)
American sportscaster–beauty contest winner
• Miss America, 1971; sportscaster, CBS NFL Today Show, 1970s-80s.
b. June 25, 1949 in Denton, Texas

Rudi Gernreich

American fashion designer
• Introduced topless bathing suits, 1974.
b. August 8, 1922 in Vienna, Austria
d. April 21, 1985 in Los Angeles, California

Hubert James Marcel Taffin de Givenchy

French fashion designer
• Opened couture house, 1952, known for elegant day, evening wear.
b. February 21, 1927 in Beauvais, France

Raisa Maksimovna Titorenko Gorbachev

(Mrs Mikhail Gorbachev)
Russian celebrity relative
• Stylish wife of general secretary of USSR since 1956; known for charm, considered most visibile wife of any Soviet leader.
b. 1934 in Rubtsovsk, U.S.S.R.

Sheilah Graham

(Lily Shiel)
American journalist–celebrity friend
• Syndicated Hollywood columnist for 33 yrs.; known for affair with F Scott Fitzgerald described in autobiographies *Beloved Infidel*, 1958 and *The Rest of the Story*, 1964.
b. September 1908 in London, England
d. November 17, 1988 in West Palm Beach, Florida

Rodolfo Gucci

Italian fashion designer
• With brothers, made Gucci name synonymous with quality, elegance in fashion.
b. 1902
d. May 15, 1983 in Milan, Italy

Bob (Robert Charles Joseph Edward Sabatini) Guccione

American publisher
• Founder, publisher, adult mags. *Penthouse*, 1965; *Omni*, 1978; *Spin*, 1985.
b. December 17, 1930 in Brooklyn, New York

Peggy Marguerite Guggenheim

American art collector–socialite
• Collected 20th c. art; patron to Jackson Pollock, Robert Motherwell.
b. August 26, 1898 in New York, New York
d. December 23, 1979 in Venice, Italy

Baron Nicolas de Gunzberg

American fashion editor
• Elegant senior fashion editor, *Vogue* mag., from 1940s.
b. 1904 in Paris, France
d. February 2, 1981 in New York, New York

Jerry Hall

(Mrs Mick Jagger; "Tall Hall")
American model
• Top fashion model; longtime companion of Mick Jagger and mother of two of his children; married him, Nov 1990.
b. July 02, 1956 in Mesquite, Texas

Halston
(Roy Halston Frowick)
American fashion designer
• Top American fashion designer; won fame for "pillbox" hat worn by Jackie Onassis; died of AIDS complications.
b. April 23, 1932 in Des Moines, Iowa
d. March 26, 1990 in San Francisco, California

Emma Hamilton
(Emma Lyon)
English mistress
• Mistress of Horatio Nelson; known for her beauty, 1798-1805.
b. 1761
d. 1815

Chris Haney
Canadian photojournalist–inventor
• With Scott Abbott, John Haney, invented board game Trivial Pursuit, 1979.
b. 1949

Nancy Hanks
(Mrs Thomas Lincoln)
American celebrity relative
• Mother of Abraham Lincoln; died when son was nine.
b. 1784
d. 1818 in Spencer County, Indiana

Bill (William Fisk) Harrah
American gambler–businessman
• Founded Harrah's Casino, 1937; Harrah's Tahoe Casino, 1955.
b. September 02, 1911 in Pasadena, California
d. June 3, 1978 in Rochester, Minnesota

Mary Scott Lord Dimmick Harrison
(Mrs Benjamin Harrison)
American celebrity relative
• Second wife of Benjamin Harrison, married 1896.
b. April 3, 1858 in Honesdale, Pennsylvania
d. January 05, 1948 in New York, New York

Anne Hathaway
(Mrs William Shakespeare)
English celebrity relative
• Married Shakespeare, 1582; home is open for tours in Stratford-upon-Avon.
b. 1557 in Temple Grafton, England
d. 1623

Elisabeth Hawes
American fashion designer–feminist–author
• Wrote best-seller Fashion Is Spinach, 1938.
b. December 16, 1903 in Ridgewood, New Jersey
d. September 06, 1971 in New York, New York

Christie (Christine Ann) Hefner
American celebrity relative–business executive
• Daughter of Hugh Hefner; pres., Playboy Enterprises, 1982–.
b. November 08, 1952 in Chicago, Illinois

Hugh Marston Hefner
American publisher
• Founded adult mags. Playboy, 1953; VIP, 1963-75; Oui, 1972-81.
b. April 09, 1926 in Chicago, Illinois

Helen of Troy
Greek legendary figure
• Daughter of Zeus and Leda; was abducted by Paris and taken to Troy; husband's attempts to reclaim her led to Trojan War.

Heloise
(Heloise Bowles Reese)
American journalist–author
• Wrote syndicated column Hints from Heloise, 1961-77.
b. May 04, 1919 in Fort Worth, Texas
d. December 28, 1977 in San Antonio, Texas

Sally Hemings
American slave–celebrity friend
• Believed by some to have been mistress of Thomas Jefferson; subject of book by Barbara Chase-Riboud, 1979.
b. 1773
d. 1835

Hiawatha
American Indian legendary figure
• Subject of Henry Wadsworth Longfellow's Song of Hiawatha, 1855.
b. 1530

Duncan Hines
American author–publisher
• His books, Adventures in Good Eating, 1936-59, influenced the culinary and sanitary practices of American restaurants.
b. March 26, 1880 in Bowling Green, Kentucky
d. March 15, 1959 in Bowling Green, Kentucky

Xaviera Hollander
Dutch author–call girl
• Former call girl who wrote of her experiences in The Happy Hooker, 1972.
b. 1943

Doc (John Henry) Holliday
American dentist–gambler–criminal
• Frontier gambler who was friend of Wyatt Earp and with him at OK Corral gunfight, 1882.
b. 1851 in Griffin, Georgia
d. November 08, 1887 in Glenwood Springs, Colorado

Catherine Howard
English consort
• Fifth wife of Henry VIII, 1540; beheaded for adultery.
b. 1520
d. 1542

Adele Hugo
French celebrity relative
• Daughter of Victor Hugo whose life was filmed as Story of Adele H., 1975.
b. 1830
d. 1915

Muriel Fay Buck Humphrey
(Mrs Hubert Humphrey)
American celebrity relative–politician
• Completed husband's final senate term, 1978-79.
b. February 2, 1912 in Huron, South Dakota

Barbara Woolworth Hutton
American socialite
• Granddaughter of FW Woolworth, heir to family fortune; married seven times; life story subject of TV mini series, 1987.
b. November 14, 1912 in New York, New York
d. May 11, 1979 in Los Angeles, California

William Henry Ireland
English imposter
• Wrote two "pseudo-Shakespearian" plays, Vortigern and Rowena; Henry II.
b. 1777
d. 1835

Irene
Dutch princess
• Daughter of Queen Julianna and Prince Bernhard; sister of Christina.
b. August 05, 1939 in Soestdijk, Netherlands

Jade Jagger
British celebrity relative
• Daughter of Mick and Bianca Jagger.
b. October 21, 1971

Mary Jefferson
(Mrs John Wayles Eppes; "Marie" "Polly")
American celebrity relative
• Daughter of Thomas Jefferson in constant competition with older sister, Martha; died in childbirth during father's second term as pres.
b. August 01, 1778 in Albemarle County, Virginia
d. April 17, 1804 in Albemarle County, Virginia

Martha Jefferson
(Mrs Thomas Mann Randolph)
American celebrity relative
• Eldest daughter of Thomas Jefferson; headed father's household after mother's death.
b. September 27, 1772 in Albemarle County, Virginia
d. October 1, 1836 in Washington, District of Columbia

Martha Wayles Skelton Jefferson
(Mrs Thomas Jefferson)
American celebrity relative
• Married Thomas Jefferson, Jan 1, 1772; died before he became pres., 1801.
b. October 19, 1748 in Charles City, Virginia
d. September 06, 1782 in Albemarle County, Virginia

Betsey Lee Johnson
American fashion designer
• Designer of children's, maternity, women's clothes; owner, NYC's Betsey Johnson store, 1979-.
b. August 10, 1942

Beverly Johnson
American model
• First black woman on cover of *Vogue*, 1975; won outstanding US model award, 1975.
b. October 13, 1951 in Buffalo, New York

Luci Baines Johnson
American celebrity relative
• Younger daughter of Lyndon Johnson.
b. July 02, 1947 in Washington, District of Columbia

Lynda Bird Johnson
(Mrs Charles Robb)
American celebrity relative
• Elder daughter of Lyndon Johnson.
b. March 19, 1944 in Washington, District of Columbia

Candy Jones
(Mrs John Nebel)
American model–business executive
• Cover girl, 1940s; founded Candy Jones Career Girls School, 1947; author of many books of advice on beauty, fashion, modeling.
b. December 31, 1925 in Wilkes-Barre, Pennsylvania
d. January 18, 1990 in New York, New York

Count of Barcelona Juan Carlos
(Don Juan de Borbon y Battenberg; "The King Who Never Reigned")
Spanish prince–celebrity relative
• Father of King Juan Carlos I; helped ease nation's transition to democracy; was denied throne, backed son.
b. June 2, 1913 in Madrid, Spain

Eliza Jumel
(Betsey Bowen; Eliza Brown)
American celebrity relative
• Eccentric, social climber who married Stephen Jumel, coffee planter; Aaron Burr, former US vp.
b. 1769
d. July 16, 1865 in New York, New York

Philippe Junot
French banker–celebrity relative
• Married Princess Caroline of Monaco, 1978-1980.
b. 1942

Norma Kamali
American fashion designer
• Fashion line, Norma Kamali Inc., is known for sexy ensembles, coats.
b. June 27, 1945 in New York, New York

Donna Faske Karan
American fashion designer
• Owner, chief designer, Donna Karan Co., NYC, 1984-; designer with Anne Klein & Co., 1974-84; Coty Hall of Fame, 1984.
b. October 2, 1948

Irene Chamie Kassorla
American psychologist–author
• Psychologist to Hollywood stars; wrote best-selling sex manual *Nice Girls Do*, 1981.
b. August 18, 1931 in Los Angeles, California

Christine Keeler
English call girl
• Involved in 1963 British political-sex scandal known as Profumo affair.
b. 1942

Annette Kellerman
("Mermaid")
Australian swimmer–actress
• Introduced the one-piece bathing suit; Esther Williams portrayed her in *Million Dollar Mermaid*, 1952.
b. July 06, 1888 in Sydney, Australia
d. October 3, 1975 in Southport, Australia

John Brenden Kelly
American sportsman–celebrity relative
• Father of Princess Grace; won gold medals in sculling, 1920, 1924 Olympics.
b. October 04, 1890 in Philadelphia, Pennsylvania
d. June 2, 1960 in Philadelphia, Pennsylvania

John Brenden Kelly, Jr
American olympic official–celebrity relative
• Brother of Princess Grace; sculling champion, pres., US Olympic Committee, 1984-85.
b. May 24, 1927 in Philadelphia, Pennsylvania
d. March 02, 1985 in Philadelphia, Pennsylvania

Patrick Kelly
American fashion designer
• Black fashion designer popular for button-studded dresses. First American to be inducted into the 44-member French designer organization called Chambre Syndicale.
b. September 24, 1950 in Vicksburg, Mississippi
d. January 1, 1990 in Paris, France

Caroline Bouvier Kennedy
(Mrs Edwin Arthur Schlossberg)
American celebrity relative
• Daughter of John F Kennedy and Jacqueline Onassis.
b. November 27, 1957 in New York, New York

David Anthony Kennedy
American celebrity relative
• Son of Robert and Ethel Kennedy; died of drug overdose.
b. 1955
d. April 26, 1984 in Palm Beach, Florida

Ethel Skakel Kennedy
(Mrs Robert F Kennedy)
American celebrity relative
• Married Robert Kennedy, June 17, 1950; mother of his 11 children.
b. April 11, 1928 in Greenwich, Connecticut

Joan Bennett Kennedy
American celebrity relative–pianist
• Wife of Edward Kennedy, 1958-81; active in Joseph Kennedy Jr. Foundation for Mental Retardation.
b. September 05, 1936 in New York, New York

John Fitzgerald Kennedy, Jr
American celebrity relative
• Son of John and Jacqueline Kennedy; as three-year-old, remembered for saluting father's casket at funeral, 1963.
b. November 25, 1960 in Washington, District of Columbia

Joseph Patrick Kennedy, Jr
American celebrity relative
• Eldest Kennedy brother; TV movie based on his life: "Young Joe, the Forgotten Kennedy, 1977; killed in WW II plane crash.
b. 1915
d. August 12, 1944

Joseph Patrick Kennedy, II
American politician–celebrity relative
• Eldest son of Robert and Ethel Kennedy; Democratic congressman from MA, 1987–.
b. September 24, 1952 in Boston, Massachusetts

Patrick Bouvier Kennedy
American celebrity relative
• Third child of John F Kennedy, first born to president while in office in 68 yrs.; buried next to father in Arlington National Cemetery.
b. August 07, 1963 in Falmouth, Massachusetts
d. August 09, 1963 in Boston, Massachusetts

Danny (Daniel) Keough
American celebrity relative
• Married Lisa Marie Presley, Elvis's only daughter and sole heir, Oct 3, 1988.
b. November 06, 1964 in Chicago, Illinois

Princess Yasmin Aga Khan
American celebrity relative
• Daughter of Rita Hayworth and Prince Aly Khan; established fund-raiser in mother's name for Alzheimer's Disease research.
b. 1950

Nina Petrovna Khrushchev
Russian celebrity relative
• Wife of Nikita Khrushchev, 1924-71; worked as teacher.
b. 1900
d. August 08, 1984 in Moscow, U.S.S.R.

Alberta Christine Williams King
American celebrity relative
• Mother of Martin Luther King, Jr.; shot to death.
b. 1904
d. June 3, 1974 in Atlanta, Georgia

Nancy Maginnes Kissinger
American celebrity relative
• Wife of Henry Kissinger.
b. 1934 in White Plains, New York

Anne Klein
American fashion designer
• Known for sophisticated sportswear.
b. August 3, 1923 in Brooklyn, New York
d. March 19, 1974 in New York, New York

Calvin (Richard) Klein
American fashion designer
• Designer of elegant, modern classics since 1969.
b. November 19, 1942 in New York, New York

Evel (Robert Craig) Knievel
American stuntman
• Known for outrageous motorcycle stunts involving jumping over trucks, people, canyons.
b. October 17, 1938 in Butte, Montana

Patricia Krenwinkel
American cultist–murderer
• Member, Charles Manson's "family"; convicted of killing Sharon Tate, six others, 1969.
b. 1947

Bertha Krupp von Bohlen und Halbach
German celebrity relative
• Cannon produced by Krupp Manufacturing during WW II named for her; daughter of Friedrich Krupp.
b. 1886 in Essen, Germany
d. September 21, 1957 in Essen, Germany

Christian Lacroix
French fashion designer
• Known for using old styles to create a "regeneration" effect on clothes.
b. May 17, 1950 in Arles, France

Karl Lagerfeld
German fashion designer
• Designer for House of Chloe.
b. September 10, 1938 in Hamburg, Germany

Jack LaLanne
American physical fitness expert–bodybuilder
• Hosted syndicated physical fitness TV series, late 1950s-70s.
b. September 26, 1914 in San Francisco, California

Lady Caroline Ponsonby Lamb
English author–celebrity friend
• Noted for affair with Lord Byron, 1812; husband prime minister Melbourne later left her, 1825.
b. November 13, 1785 in Roehampton, England
d. January 24, 1828 in London, England

Ralph Lauren
(Ralph Lifshitz)
American fashion designer
• Known for elegant, classic menswear and women's wear. Head of Polo Fashions, Inc., 1969-.
b. October 14, 1939 in New York, New York

Pat(ricia Kennedy) Lawford
American celebrity relative
• Sister of John F Kennedy; was married to Peter Lawford.

Frieda Lawrence
(Frieda von Richthofen)
German celebrity relative
• Wife of D H Lawrence, 1912-30; wrote memoir Not I, But the Wind, 1934; Baron Richthofen's sister.
b. 1879
d. 1956

Larry (Lawrence John) Layton
American cultist
• Member, Peoples Temple; accused of killing Congressman Leo Ryan, four others in Jonestown, Guyana, 1978.
b. January 1946

Ninon de Lenclos
(Anne DeLenclos)
French courtesan
• Her beauty, wit attracted famous men of the day; wrote La Coquette vengee, 1659.
b. 1620 in Paris, France
d. 1705 in Paris, France

L'Esperance Quintuplets
(Alexandria; Danielle; Erica; Raymond and Veronica L'Esperance)
American quintuplets
• First US test-tube fertilization to result in five babies; parents are Raymond and Michelle.
b. January 11, 1988 in Royal Oak, Michigan

Ada Leverson
(Elaine pseud; "Wittiest Woman in the World")
English author–celebrity friend–socialite
• Close friend of Oscar Wilde; wrote novel Love at Second Sight, 1916.
b. 1865 in London, England
d. 1936 in London, England

Robert Todd Lincoln
American lawyer–celebrity relative
• First child of Abraham Lincoln; secretary of war, 1889-93; minister to Great Britain, 1889-93.
b. August 01, 1843 in Springfield, Illinois
d. July 26, 1926 in Manchester, Vermont

Charles Augustus Lindbergh
American celebrity relative
• Son of Charles A, Anne Morrow; kidnapped, murdered by Bruno Hauptmann, who was electrocuted for crime.
b. 1931
d. 1932

Pia Lindstrom
American journalist–celebrity relative
• Daughter of Ingrid Bergman, who is film, theater critic in NYC.
b. September 2, 1938 in Stockholm, Sweden

Alice Roosevelt Longworth
American author–socialite–celebrity relative
• Daughter of Theodore Roosevelt; noted for caustic remarks.
b. February 12, 1884 in Long Island, New York
d. February 2, 1980 in Washington, District of Columbia

Magda (Elena) Lupescu
Romanian mistress
• King Carol of Romania's paramour for 22 yrs.; married him in exile, 1947.
b. 1896
d. June 29, 1977 in Estoril, Portugal

Bob (Robert Gordon) Mackie
American fashion designer
• Designed clothes for "Carol Burnett Show," 1967-77; won Emmys, 1969, 1976. Known for designing evening wear for Cher and other stars.
b. March 24, 1940 in Monterey Park, California

Francoise d'Aubigne Maintenon, Marquise
French consort
• Second wife of King Louis XIV, 1684; author of essays, letters on education.
b. 1635
d. 1719

Manco Capac
Legendary Figure
• Supposedly the founder of Inca Dynasty in Peru.

Charles Manson
(No Name Maddox)
American murderer–cultist
• In prison for 1969 murders of actress Sharon Tate, eight others.
b. November 11, 1934 in Cincinnati, Ohio

Imelda Romualdez Marcos
(Mrs Ferdinand Marcos; "Iron Butterfly")
Philippine celebrity relative
• Wife of former pres. who fled country with him, 1986; known for extravagant life style.
b. 1931 in Tacloban, Philippines

Margaret of Anjou
French consort
• Married Henry VI, 1445; brought on War of Roses, 1453.
b. March 23, 1430 in Lorraine, France
d. April 25, 1482 in London, England

Mariamne the Hasmonaean
Celebrity Relative
• Ordered executed by Herod in fit of jealousy.
b. 60?BC
d. 29?BC

Marie Antoinette
(Josephe-Jeanne-Marie-Antoinette)
Austrian consort
• Guillotined for encouraging civil war, betraying her country; known for flippant saying, "Let them eat cake."
b. November 02, 1755 in Vienna, Austria
d. October 16, 1793 in Paris, France

Marie de Medicis
Italian consort
• Queen of Henry IV of France; mother of Louis XIII; banished from France, 1631.
b. 1573 in Florence, Italy
d. 1642

Marie Louise
French celebrity relative
• Second wife of Napoleon I, 1810; mother of Napoleon II.
b. 1791
d. 1847

Marina
(Duchess of Kent)
English consort
• Married Prince George, fourth son of King George V; pres., All England Tennis Club.
b. December 13, 1906 in Athens, Greece
d. August 27, 1968 in London, England

Judith Martin
American author–journalist
• Author, syndicated newspaper column, "Miss Manners," since 1978; *Miss Manners' Guide to Excruciatingly Correct Behavior*, 1982.
b. September 13, 1938 in Washington, District of Columbia

Michelle Triola Marvin
American celebrity friend
• Live-in lover of Lee Marvin, responsible for first palimony case involving unmarried couples and property rights, 1979.
b. 1932

Mary
(Victoria Mary Augusta Louise Olga)
English consort
• Married George V, 1893; mother of Edward VIII, George VI; grandmother of Queen Elizabeth II.
b. 1867
d. March 24, 1953 in London, England

Mata Hari
(Margaretha Geertruida Macleod)
Dutch dancer–spy
• Executed by the French for being double agent for Germans.
b. August 07, 1876 in Leeuwarden, Netherlands
d. October 15, 1917 in Vincennes, France

Mary Josephine McFadden
American fashion designer
• Clothes have distinctive dramatic look, include vibrant colors, fine pleating.
b. October 1, 1938 in New York, New York

Evalyn Walsh McLean
American socialite
• Owned famed Hope diamond; gave lavish Washington parties.
b. August 01, 1886 in Denver, Colorado
d. April 26, 1947 in Washington, District of Columbia

Frederick Mellinger
American fashion designer
• The "Frederick" in Frederick's of Hollywood. Introduced French bikini underwear to the U.S., along with the push-up bra, front-hook bra, and the derriere enhancer. The 160 Frederick's stores nationwide made more than $80 million in 1989.
b. 1914 in New York, New York
d. June 2, 1990 in Los Angeles, California

Martha Elizabeth Beall Mitchell
(Mrs John Mitchell)
American celebrity relative
• Known for calling reporters in middle of night with Washington gossip.
b. September 02, 1918 in Pine Bluff, Arkansas
d. May 31, 1976 in New York, New York

John T Molloy
American author–journalist–critic–businessman
• "Wardrobe engineer"; author of *Dress for Success*, 1975; syndicated column.
b. 1937

Joan Adams Mondale
(Mrs Walter Mondale; "Joan of Art")
American celebrity relative–author
• VP's wife, who wrote *Politics in Art*, 1972.
b. August 08, 1930 in Eugene, Oregon

Duke James Scott Monmouth
(James Crofts; James Fitzroy)
English imposter
• Led unsuccessful uprising against James II; beheaded.
b. April 09, 1649 in Rotterdam, Netherlands
d. July 25, 1685 in London, England

Michel Eyquem de Montaigne
French essayist–courtier
• Introduced the essay as a literary form, often using quotations from classical writers.
b. February 28, 1533 in Bordeaux, France
d. September 13, 1592 in Bordeaux, France

Vicki Morgan
American mistress
• Mistress of Alfred Bloomingdale; unsuccessfully sued estate for $10 million.
b. 1952
d. July 07, 1983 in North Hollywood, California

Edwina Mountbatten
(Countess Mountbatten of Burma)
English celebrity relative
• Colorful, charming wife of Louis Mountbatten, last viceroy of India.
b. November 28, 1901 in London, England
d. February 21, 1960 in Jesselton, North Borneo

Rachele Guidi Mussolini
Italian celebrity relative
• Widow of Benito Mussolini; wrote autobiography *My Life with Mussolini*.
b. 1890 in Forli, Italy
d. October 3, 1979 in Forli, Italy

Bess Myerson
American government official–beauty contest winner
• First Jewish Miss America, 1945; commissioner of cultural affairs, NYC, 1983–.
b. July 16, 1924 in New York, New York

Empress Nagako
Japanese consort
• Princess who married Emperor Hirohito of Japan, Jan 26, 1924.
b. 1903

Nick the Greek
(Nicholas Andrea Dandolos)
American gambler
• Gained fame as fastest crap shooter in US; estimated he won, lost $500 million.
b. 1896 in Rethymon, Crete
d. December 25, 1966 in Los Angeles, California

Albert Nipon
American fashion designer
• Head of Albert Nipon, Inc., 1971-78; arrested for tax fraud, 1978. Sentenced to three years in prison in 1985.
b. September 11, 1927 in Philadelphia, Pennsylvania

Tricia (Patricia) Nixon
(Mrs Edward Cox)
American celebrity relative
• Elder daughter of Richard Nixon.
b. February 21, 1946 in San Francisco, California

Queen Noor
(Lisa Najeeb Halaby)
American consort
• Wife of King Hussein of Jordan; has played major role in education, social welfare, arts in Jordan.
b. August 23, 1951 in Washington, District of Columbia

Serge Obolensky
Russian businessman–socialite
• Distant relative of Czar Nicholas II; with Hilton Hotels, 1940s; later had own consulting firm.
b. October 03, 1890 in Tsarskoe Selo, Russia
d. September 29, 1978 in Grosse Pointe, Michigan

Octavia
Roman celebrity relative
• Roman empress divorced by Mark Anthony so he could marry Cleopatra.
b. 69BC
d. 11BC

Kenneth P O'Donnell
American government official–celebrity friend
• Best friend of John F Kennedy; wrote *Johnny We Hardly Knew Ye*.
b. March 04, 1924 in Worchester, Massachusetts
d. September 09, 1977 in Boston, Massachusetts

Olga
(Olga Erteszek)
American fashion designer
• Designs intimate apparel for women; Olga Co. employs more than 1,200 people.
b. in Krakow, Poland

Arthur Orton
English imposter
• Claimed to be heir to Lady Tichborne, 1868; imprisoned, 1870-84.
b. 1834 in London, England
d. April 01, 1898 in London, England

Marina Nikolaevna Oswald
(Marina Nikolaevna Pruskova; Mrs Ken Porter)
Russian celebrity relative
• Wife of Lee Harvey Oswald at time he allegedly killed John Kennedy.
b. 1941

Riza Cyrus Pahlevi
Iranian celebrity relative
• Son of Shah of Iran who proclaimed himself Shah following father's death, 1980.
b. October 31, 1960

Barbara Cushing Paley
(Mrs William S Paley; "Babe")
American socialite
• Described as one of world's great beauties, who was perennially on best-dressed lists.
b. July 05, 1915 in Boston, Massachusetts
d. July 06, 1978 in New York, New York

Suzy Parker
(Cecelia Parker)
American model
• Highest-paid fashion model, cover girl in US, 1950s; unsuccessful movie career.
b. October 28, 1933 in San Antonio, Texas

Catherine Parr
English consort
• Sixth wife of Henry VIII, 1543; survived him.
b. 1512
d. 1548

Clara Petacci
Italian mistress
• Benito Mussolini's mistress.
b. 1912
d. April 29, 1945 in Milan, Italy

Lorraine Collett Peterson
American model
• Was model for Sun-Maid raisin logo, 1915; still used today.
b. 1893 in Kansas City, Missouri
d. March 3, 1983 in Fresno, California

Prince Philip
(Duke of Edinburgh)
English consort
• Married Elizabeth II, 1947; became British citizen, renouncing Greek, Danish ties same year.
b. June 1, 1921 in Corfu, Greece

Mark Anthony Peter Phillips
English celebrity relative
• Married Princess Anne, Nov 14, 1973; children Peter and Zara are highest ranking commoners.
b. September 22, 1948 in England

Phryne
(Mnesarete)
Greek courtesan
• Model for Apelle's *Aphrodite Emerging*; Praxitele's *Aphrodite*.
b. 300BC in Athens, Greece

Paloma Picasso
French celebrity relative–designer
• Daughter of Pablo Picasso; designs jewelry for Tiffany and Co.
b. April 19, 1949 in Paris, France

Jeanne Antoinette Poisson Pompadour
French mistress
• Influential mistress of Louis XV from 1745; patronized authors, artists; hair style named for her.
b. December 29, 1721 in Paris, France
d. April 15, 1764 in Versailles, France

Paulina Porizkova
American model
• Modeling career began in 1980; became star in US with 1983 *Sports Illustrated* swimsuit issue.
b. April 9, 1965 in Czechoslovakia

Lisa Marie Presley
(Mrs Danny Keough)
American celebrity relative
• Only child of Elvis, Priscilla Presley.
b. February 01, 1968 in Memphis, Tennessee

George Psalmanazar
French imposter
• Posed as Formosan Christian; sent to Oxford to teach fictitious language, 1704.
b. 1679 in Languedoc, France
d. May 03, 1763 in London, England

Yemelyan I Pugachev
Russian imposter
• Cossack soldier, posed as Peter III; led army, peasants rebellion against Catherine II; defeated, captured, executed.
b. 1741
d. 1775

Roxanne Pulitzer
American celebrity relative
• Ex-wife of Peter Pulitzer; granted headline-making divorce, 1982.
b. 1952

Mary Quant
English fashion designer
• Credited with starting Mod Look in London; also hot pants, body stockings.
b. February 11, 1934 in London, England

Marilyn Tucker Quayle
(Mrs Dan Quayle)
American celebrity relative
• Lawyer; married Dan Quayle, 1972.
b. July 29, 1949 in Indianapolis, Indiana

Lee (Caroline Lee Bouvier) Radziwill
American celebrity relative
• Wrote childhood memoir, *One Special Summer*, with sister, Jacqueline Onassis.
b. March 03, 1933 in New York, New York

Maureen Elizabeth Reagan
(Mrs Dennis Revell)
American celebrity relative–politician
• Daughter of Ronald Reagan, Jane Wyman; active in CA politics.
b. January 04, 1941 in Los Angeles, California

Michael Edward Reagan
American businessman–celebrity relative
• Adopted son of Ronald Reagan, Jane Wyman; wrote family expose, 1988.
b. March 18, 1946 in Los Angeles, California

Ronald Prescott Reagan
American celebrity relative
• Son of Ronald, Nancy Reagan; former ballet dancer.
b. May 2, 1958 in Los Angeles, California

Madame (Jeanne Francoise) Julie(tte) Adelaide Recamier
French socialite
• Queen of Parisian society, 1815-49; friend of Chateaubriand; portrait by Jacques Louis David in Louvre.
b. 1777 in Lyons, France
d. 1849 in Paris, France

Lance Reventlow
American celebrity relative–auto racer
• Son of millionairess Barbara Hutton; developed *Scarab* racing car to compete with Europeans, late 1950s; died in plane crash.
b. February 24, 1936 in London, England
d. July 25, 1972 in Colorado

Robin Hood
English legendary figure–hero
• Legendary 12th c. hero who robbed from rich to give to poor.

Happy (Margaretta Large) Rockefeller
(Mrs Nelson Rockefeller)
American celebrity relative
• Second wife, widow of former vp, NY governor.
b. June 09, 1926

Sharon Percy Rockefeller
American celebrity relative
• Wife of John D, IV; daughter of Charles H Percy; twin sister, Valerie, murdered in bizarre unsolved mystery, 1960s.
b. December 1, 1944 in Oakland, California

Anastasia Romanov
Russian celebrity relative
• Daughter of Czar Nicholas II; long thought to have escaped family's execution, but never proven.
b. June 1901
d. July 16, 1918 in Ekaterinburg, U.S.S.R.

Romulus
Roman legendary figure
• Twin brother of Remus whose father was god Mars; founder, 753 BC, first king of Rome, 753-716 BC.

Alice Lee Roosevelt
(Mrs Theodore Roosevelt)
American celebrity relative
• First wife of Theodore Roosevelt; mother of Alice Longworth.
b. July 29, 1861 in Chestnut Hill, Massachusetts
d. February 14, 1884 in New York, New York

Anna Eleanor Roosevelt
(Mrs James A Halsted)
American celebrity relative
• Only daughter of Franklin and Eleanor Roosevelt; author of children's books.
b. May 03, 1906 in Hyde Park, New York
d. December 01, 1975 in New York, New York

Elliott Roosevelt
American celebrity relative–military leader–author
• Son of Franklin and Eleanor Roosevelt; as WW II Air Corps general played key role in D-Day Invasion of Normandy, 1944; mayor of Miami Beach, 1065-69; author of trilogy on family.
b. September 23, 1910 in New York, New York
d. October 27, 1990 in Scottsdale, Arizona

James Roosevelt
American celebrity relative–politician
• First son of Franklin and Eleanor Roosevelt; Democratic congressman from CA, 1955-66; author of several books on family.
b. December 23, 1907 in Hyde Park, New York

John Aspinal Roosevelt
American celebrity relative
• Youngest child of Franklin and Eleanor Roosevelt; supported Republican candidates in later years.
b. March 13, 1916 in Hyde Park, New York
d. April 27, 1981 in New York, New York

Kermit Roosevelt
American celebrity relative
• Son of Theodore Roosevelt; traveled with father to Africa, S America; wrote *War in the Garden of Eden*, 1919; died in military service.
b. October 1, 1889 in Oyster Bay, New York
d. June 04, 1943 in Alaska

Quentin Roosevelt
American celebrity relative
• Son of Theodore Roosevelt; shot down, killed in action, WW I.
b. November 19, 1897 in Washington, District of Columbia
d. July 14, 1918 in France

Sara Delano Roosevelt
American celebrity relative
• Mother of President Franklin D Roosevelt.
b. September 21, 1855
d. September 07, 1941 in Hyde Park, New York

Theodore Roosevelt, Jr
American celebrity relative–military leader
• Eldest son of Theodore Roosevelt; only general to land with first wave of troops in D-Day Invasion of Normandy, June 6, 1944.
b. September 13, 1887 in Oyster Bay, New York
d. July 12, 1944 in Cherbourg, France

Arnold Rothstein
American gambler
• Accused of masterminding "Black Sox" baseball scandal, 1919; murdered in hotel room while playing cards.
b. 1882 in New York, New York
d. 1928

Roxana
Celebrity Relative
• Married Alexander the Great, 327 BC; murdered along with son, Alexander IV.

Lucy Page Mercer Rutherfurd
American secretary–celebrity friend
• Social secretary to Eleanor Roosevelt, who allegedly had affair with FDR; with him at his death.
b. 1891
d. 1948

Jehan Raouf Sadat
Egyptian celebrity relative–educator
• Widow of Anwar Sadat; lecturer in Arabic literature at Cairo U; outspoken advocate of women's rights; wrote autobiography *A Woman of Egypt*, 1987.
b. August 1934 in Cairo, Egypt

Yves Mathieu Saint Laurent
French fashion designer
• Responsible for "chic beatnik" and "little boy look" of 1960s; current line emphasizes classic look, textures.
b. August 1, 1936 in Oran, Algeria

Jane Seymour
English consort
• Married Henry VIII, 1536; mother of Edward VI; died 12 days after son's birth.
b. 1509
d. October 24, 1537

Jean Rosemary Shrimpton
English model
• Popular model at same time as Twiggy, 1960s.
b. November 06, 1942 in High Wycombe, England

Eunice Mary Kennedy Shriver
(Mrs Robert Sargent Shriver)
American celebrity relative
• Sister of John F Kennedy; vp, Joseph P Kennedy Foundation, 1950–.
b. July 1, 1920 in Brookline, Massachusetts

Silvia
Swedish consort
• Commoner who married King Carl Gustaf of Sweden, 1976.
b. December 23, 1943 in Heidelberg, Germany

Simonetta
Italian author–fashion designer
• Rome's leading designer, 1950s; established first "haute boutique," 1965.
b. 1922 in Rome, Italy

Wallis (Bessie Wallis Warfield) Simpson
(Duchess of Windsor)
American celebrity relative
• Two-time divorcee for whom Edward VIII abdicated his throne to marry, 1936.
b. June 19, 1896 in Blue Ridge Summit, Pennsylvania
d. April 24, 1986 in Paris, France

Barbara Marx Spencer Sinatra
(Mrs Frank Sinatra)
American celebrity relative
• Fourth, current wife of Frank Sinatra.
b. 1926

Christina Sinatra
American celebrity relative
• Youngest daughter of Frank Sinatra.
b. June 2, 1948

Frances Scott Fitzgerald Lanahan Smith
American celebrity relative–writer
• Only child of F Scott, Zelda Fitzgerald; wrote for *Washington Post; New Yorker*.
b. 1922
d. June 18, 1986 in Montgomery, Georgia

Willi Donnell Smith
American fashion designer
• Considered one of America's most innovative and successful clothing designers, taking the country by storm in late 1970s with WilliWear. Won Coty Award in 1983.
b. February 29, 1948 in Philadelphia, Pennsylvania
d. April 17, 1987 in New York, New York

Carmel White Snow
American fashion editor
• Edited *Harper's Bazaar*, 1932-57; promoted Parisian designers.
b. August 21, 1887 in Dublin, Ireland
d. May 07, 1961 in New York, New York

Svetlana Alliluyeva Stalina
(Svetlana Peters)
Russian author–celebrity relative
• Daughter of Joseph Stalin who defected to West, 1967; wrote memoirs *Twenty Letters to a Friend*, 1967.
b. February 28, 1926 in Moscow, U.S.S.R.

Sally Stanford
(Marcia Busby; Sally Gump)
American politician–madam
• Ran San Francisco's most celebrated brothel, 1930s-40s; mayor of Sausalito, CA, 1976-78.
b. May 05, 1903 in Baker City, Oregon
d. February 02, 1982 in Greenbrae, California

Ruth Carter Stapleton
American celebrity relative
• Baptist evangelist, spiritual healer; sister of Jimmy Carter.
b. August 07, 1929 in Archery, Georgia
d. September 26, 1983 in Fayetteville, North Carolina

Koo (Kathleen) Stark
American actress
• Involved in publicized romance with Britain's Prince Andrew, 1982.
b. 1957 in New York, New York

Hendrijke Stoffels
Dutch mistress–model
• Housekeeper, mistress of Rembrandt, 1645-63.
b. 1622
d. 1663

Charles Edward Louis Philip Stuart
English celebrity relative
• Grandson of James II who unsuccessfully tried to seize Hanoverian throne, 1745.
b. December 31, 1720 in Rome, Italy
d. January 31, 1788 in Rome, Italy

Marion Tanner
American philanthropist–socialite
• Real life model for Auntie Mame, immortalized in novel by nephew Patrick Dennis.
b. March 06, 1891 in Buffalo, New York
d. October 3, 1985 in New York, New York

William (Wilhelm) Tell
Swiss legendary figure
• In legend, shot an apple from son's head with arrow.
b. f. 1282

Theodora
Roman consort
• Married Justinian I, 523; became joint ruler of Byzantine empire, 527.
b. 508
d. 548

Cheryl Tiegs
American actress–model
• Highest paid model of 1970s; wrote *The Way to Natural Beauty*, 1980.
b. September 25, 1947 in Minnesota

Margaret Joan Sinclair Trudeau
(Mrs Pierre Trudeau)
Canadian author–socialite
• Separated from husband, 1977; wrote *Beyond Reason*, 1979.
b. September 1, 1948 in Vancouver, British Columbia

Mary Bradham Tucker
American model
• The first Pepsi girl, seen on calendars, early 1900s.
b. 1903
d. May 26, 1984 in Edenton, North Carolina

Madame (Marie Gresholtz) Tussaud
Swiss wax modeler
• Created Madame Tussaud museum of waxwork figures in London.
b. December 07, 1760 in Bern, Switzerland
d. April 15, 1850 in London, England

Twiggy
(Leslie Hornby; Mrs Michael Whitney)
English model
• Ultra-thin model, 1966-76; starred in *The Boy Friend*, 1971.
b. September 19, 1949 in London, England

Sir James Tyrrell
English courtier
• Sir Thomas More claimed he was responsible for murders of Edward V, brother Richard.

Emanuel Matteotti Ungaro
French fashion designer
• Avant-garde designs are noted for print patterns, flowers, abstracts.
b. February 13, 1933 in Aix-en-Provence, France

Hannah Hoes Van Buren
(Mrs Martin Van Buren)
American celebrity relative
• Died 18 yrs. before husband became president.
b. March 08, 1783 in Kinderhook, New York
d. February 05, 1819 in Albany, New York

Amy Vanderbilt
American journalist–author
• Etiquette expert who wrote syndicated newspaper column, regularly revised *Complete Book of Etiquette*, 1952.
b. July 22, 1908 in Staten Island, New York
d. December 27, 1974 in New York, New York

Gianni Versace
Italian fashion designer
• Among a handful of designers credited with making Milan an international fashion center. Best known for metal-mesh dresses and wide-shoulder suits, favoring loose, comfortable clothes described as having the feel of casual luxury.
b. December 2, 1946 in Reggion Calabria, Italy

Veruschka
(Countess Vera VonLehndorff)
German model–actress
• Films include *Blow Up*, 1966.
b. 1943

Luz Corral de Villa
(Mrs Francisco Pancho Villa; "Dona Lucha")
Mexican celebrity relative
• Known for her successful efforts to gain official recognition of her husband's revolutionary contributions to Mexico.
b. 1892 in Chihuahua, Mexico
d. July 06, 1981 in Chihuahua, Mexico

Sunny (Martha Sharp Crawford) Von Bulow
(Mrs Claus Von Bulow)
American socialite–victim
• Husband convicted, 1982, of trying to murder her with insulin injection. Claus was subsequently freed upon appeal; situation was subject of movie, *Reversal of Fortune*, 1990.
b. 1932

Diana Dalziel Vreeland
American fashion editor
• Fashion editor, *Harper's Bazaar*, 1937-62, editor-in-chief, *Vogue*, 1962-71; created spectacular fashion exhibits at Metropolitan Museum of Art.
b. 1903 in Paris, France
d. August 22, 1989 in New York, New York

Cosima Liszt Wagner
(Mrs Richard Wagner)
Hungarian celebrity relative
• Daughter of Franz Liszt; married Wagner, 1870; created Bayreuth Festival.
b. December 25, 1837 in Bellagio, Italy
d. April 01, 1930 in Bayreuth, Germany

Cornelia Folsom Wallace
American celebrity relative
• Second wife of AL governor, George Wallace, 1971-78.
b. 1939

Marie Therese Walter
French model
• Mistress of Pablo Picasso.
b. 1909
d. 1977 in Antibes, France

Lawrence Washington
American celebrity relative
• Half-brother of George Washington; George inherited Mount Vernon from him.
b. 1718
d. July 1752

Charles Watson
American cultist
• Member of Manson cult.
b. 1945

Anna Matilda McNeill Whistler
American celebrity relative
• Best known as subject of son James' painting.
b. 1804
d. 1881

Vanessa Williams
American beauty contest winner
• First black crowned Miss America, 1983; first to give up title for violating pageant's moral code.
b. March 18, 1963 in New York, New York

Sarah Wilson
(Marchioness de Waldegrave)
English imposter
• Escaped US indentured servitude to pose as sister of Queen Charlotte of England.
b. 1750 in Staffordshire, England

Zita of Bourbon-Parma
Italian consort
- Wife of Karl I; last empress of Austria and queen of Hungary; crowned on death of Franz Josef, 1916, reigned two years.
  b. 1892 in Viareggio, Italy
  d. March 14, 1989 in Zizers, Switzerland

ARTISTS: DaVinci, Degas & Dali

Cartoonists,

Illustrators,

Painters,

Photographers,

Sculptors...

Berenice Abbott
American photographer
• Best known for black and white architectural, documentary images of NYC, 1930s.
b. July 17, 1898 in Springfield, Ohio

Ken Adam
English art director–designer
• Won Oscar for *Barry Lyndon*, 1975; other films include several of James Bond series.
b. February 05, 1921 in Berlin, Germany

Ansel Easton Adams
American photographer
• Best known photographer in US, noted for landscape images of western US; helped establish photography as art form.
b. February 2, 1902 in San Francisco, California
d. April 22, 1984 in Monterey, California

Charles Samuel Addams
American cartoonist
• Known for ghoulish humor appearing in *New Yorker*, 1935-80s; cartoons basis for "Addams Family" TV series, 1960s.
b. January 07, 1912 in Westfield, New Jersey
d. September 29, 1988 in New York, New York

Peter Agostini
American sculptor
• Known for humorous "frozen life" plaster castings.
b. February 13, 1913 in New York, New York

Agostino di Duccio
Italian sculptor
• Examples of his reliefs are at Rimini, Perugia, Bologna, Florence, Italy, museums.
b. 1418 in Florence, Italy
d. 1481 in Florence, Italy

Robert Aitken
American sculptor
• Works include Hann Memorial, Arlington Cemetery; Pioneer Lumberman Monument, Huron National Forest, MI.
b. May 08, 1878 in San Francisco, California
d. January 03, 1949 in New York, New York

Constantin Alajalov
American artist–illustrator
• Muralist, portrait painter best known for watercolor covers of *New Yorker* magazine.
b. November 18, 1900 in Rostov-on-Don, Russia
d. October 24, 1987 in Amenia, New York

Josef Albers
American artist
• Known as teacher, color theorist, paint-er of *Homage to the Square*, series of several hundred works of squares of col-or.
b. March 19, 1888 in Bottrop, Germany
d. March 25, 1976 in New Haven, Connecti-cut

Ivan Le Lorraine Albright
American artist
• "Magic realism" painter who empha-sized details, emotions.
b. February 2, 1897 in Chicago, Illinois
d. November 18, 1983 in Woodstock, Ver-mont

Alcamenes
Greek sculptor
• Noted for antiquity masterpieces *Aphro-dite of the Gardens, Hermes Propylaeus.*
b. 5thBC

Washington Allston
American artist–poet
• Preeminent Romantic painter known for dramatic subjects; published poetry, a novel, *Monaldi.*
b. November 05, 1779 in Georgetown County, South Carolina
d. July 09, 1843 in Cambridgeport, Massachu-setts

Irving Amen
American artist
• Designed Peace Medal for end of Viet-nam War.
b. July 25, 1918 in New York, New York

Carl Thomas Anderson
American cartoonist
• Created cartoon, "Henry," 1932, which currently runs in 196 daily newspapers.
b. February 14, 1865 in Madison, Wisconsin
d. November 04, 1948 in Madison, Wisconsin

Carl Andre
American sculptor
• Influential minimalist whose work is simple, serenely ordered, quiet.
b. September 16, 1935 in Quincy, Massachu-setts

Fra Angelico
(Guido di Pietro; Giovanni da Fiesole)
Italian artist
• Painter who used strong, pure colors, simple subjects, reflecting new ideas of time.
b. 1387 in Vicchio, Italy
d. March 18, 1455 in Rome, Italy

Pietro Annigoni
Italian artist
• Portrait painter of the famous: Eliza-beth II, 1955, 1970; John F Kennedy, 1961; Shah of Iran, 1968.
b. June 07, 1910 in Milan, Italy

Horst Antes
German artist
• Post-war painter; later works include strange, massive, "gnome" people.
b. October 28, 1936 in Heppenheim, Germa-ny

Antonello da Messina
Italian artist
• First Italian to master technique of painting with oils.
b. 1430 in Messina, Sicily
d. February 15, 1479 in Messina, Sicily

Richard Joseph Anuszkiewicz
American artist
• Master of dizzying, optical art.
b. May 23, 1930 in Erie, Pennsylvania

Apelles
Greek artist
• Best known work *Aphrodite Anadyo-mene*, painted for temple of Aesculapius at Cos.
b. 4thBC in Ionia, Asia Minor

Karel Christian Appel
Dutch artist
• Self-taught abstract expressionist; uses rich, swirling colors.
b. April 25, 1921 in Amsterdam, Netherlands

Diane Arbus
American photographer
• Best known for photographs of "freaks"–midgets, giants, etc.
b. March 14, 1923 in New York, New York
d. July 26, 1971 in New York, New York

Joe (Joseph Stopford) Archibald
American cartoonist–author
• Wrote *The Fifth Base*, 1973; created first story comic strip "Saga of Steve West," 1928-29.
b. September 02, 1898 in Newington, New Hampshire
d. March 01, 1986 in Barrington, New Hamp-shire

Edward Jeffrey Irving Ardizzone
English author–illustrator
• Illustrated over 120 books; official war artist, 1940-45.
b. October 16, 1900 in Haiphong, Vietnam
d. November 08, 1979 in London, England

Antony Charles Robert Armstrong-Jones
(Earl of Snowden)
English photographer–socialite
• Ex-husband of Britain's Princess Mar-garet; known for celebrity portraits, TV documentaries.
b. March 07, 1930 in London, England

Peter Arno
(Curtis Arnoux Peters Jr)
American cartoonist
• With *New Yorker* as cartoonist, 1925-68; established tone of magazine.
b. January 08, 1904 in New York, New York
d. February 22, 1968 in Port Chester, New York

Hans Arp
(Jean Arp)
French author–sculptor
• Founded Dadaist movement; wrote *Dreams and Projects*, 1952.
b. September 16, 1887 in Strasbourg, France
d. June 07, 1966 in Basel, Switzerland

Boris Mikhailovich Artzybasheff
American author–illustrator
• Designed over 200 *Time* magazine cov-ers; illustrated book jackets, children's books.
b. May 25, 1899 in Kharkov, Russia
d. July 16, 1965 in Old Lyme, Connecticut

Eugene (Jean-Eugene-Auguste) Atget
French photographer
• Documentary photographer, known for photos of Paris.
b. 1855 in Libourne, France
d. August 1927 in Paris, France

George Christian Ault
American artist
• Precisionist who drew nocturnes, citys-capes.
b. October 11, 1891 in Cleveland, Ohio
d. December 3, 1948 in Woodside, New York

Richard Avedon
American photographer
• One of world's greatest photographers credited with making fashion photography art form.
b. May 15, 1923 in New York, New York

Milton Clark Avery
American artist
• Works influenced by Matisse; known as pioneer in American abstractionism.
b. March 07, 1893 in Altmar, New York
d. January 03, 1965 in New York, New York

Tex (Frederick Bean) Avery
American cartoonist
• Developed Daffy Duck, Bugs Bunny; made animated TV commercials.
b. February 26, 1908 in Taylor, Texas
d. August 27, 1980 in Burbank, California

Francis Bacon
English artist
• Self-taught modern artist whose permanent exhibits are in NYC, other cities.
b. October 28, 1910 in Dublin, Ireland

Peggy Bacon
American artist
• Wrote, illustrated *The Good American Witch*, 1957; did caricatures of notables, NYC alley cats.
b. May 02, 1895 in Ridgefield, Connecticut
d. January 04, 1987 in Kennebunk, Maine

Bruce Bairnsfather
English cartoonist
• Official cartoonist, WW II; war cartoons, *Fragments from France*, published in six volumes.
b. July 09, 1888 in Murree, India
d. September 29, 1959 in Norton, England

Rick Baker
American artist–designer
• Make-up artist specializing in horror, science fiction films: *King Kong*, 1976; *Star Wars*, 1977.
b. 1950 in New York

Ralph Bakshi
American cartoonist
• Produced, directed animated version of Tolkien's *Lord of the Rings*, 1978.
b. October 26, 1938 in Haifa, Palestine

Kenneth Bald
(K Bruce pseud)
American cartoonist
• Created "Captain Marvel"; "Doc Savage"; "Captain Battle," 1941-43.
b. 1920 in New York, New York

Alesso Baldovinetti
Italian artist
• Mosaicist, decorator at Bapistry in Florence, 1456; painting *Madonna* hangs in Louve.
b. 1425
d. August 29, 1499

Hans Baldung(-Grien)
(Hans Gruen)
German artist–printmaker
• Did portraits, woodcuts, demonic allegories; altar of Freiburg Cathedral, 1512.
b. 1484 in Strassburg, Germany
d. 1545 in Strassburg, Germany

Thomas Ball
American sculptor
• Greatest work equestrian statue of Washington, built in Boston Public Garden, 1869.
b. June 03, 1819 in Charlestown, Massachusetts
d. December 11, 1911 in Montclair, New Jersey

Giacomo Balla
Italian artist
• Member, Italian Futurist Group, 1916-30; art emphasized movement, machines, warfare.
b. July 18, 1871 in Turin, Italy
d. March 01, 1958 in Rome, Italy

Balthus
(Comte Balthazar Klossowski de Rola)
French artist
• Self-taught painter, noted for doll-like portraits of Miro, Derain, 1936.
b. February 29, 1908 in Paris, France

Constance Gibbs Bannister
American photographer
• Gained worldwide recognition, 1940s-50s, as specialist in photographing babies.
b. February 11, 1919 in Ashland, Tennessee

Edward Mitchell Bannister
American artist
• First black artist to win first place at Philadelphia Centennial Exhibition, 1876.
b. 1833 in Saint Andrew's, New Brunswick
d. 1901 in Providence, Rhode Island

Joseph Roland Barbera
(Hanna and Barbera)
American cartoonist
• With Bill Hanna, created cartoons "Huckleberry Hound"; "The Smurfs"; "The Flintstones."
b. March 24, 1911 in New York, New York

McClelland Barclay
American artist–illustrator
• Illustrated stories for *Ladies Home Journal*; *Saturday Evening Post*; designed recruiting posters for both world wars; created "Fisher Body Girl."
b. May 09, 1893 in Saint Louis, Missouri
d. July 18, 1943 in South Pacific

Carl Barks
American cartoonist
• Illustrated Donald Duck, Uncle Scrooge McDuck comic strips.
b. March 27, 1901 in Merrill, Oregon

George Grey Barnard
American sculptor
• One of his most important works: 31 statues in Pennsylvania Capitol Building.
b. May 24, 1863 in Bellefonte, Pennsylvania
d. April 24, 1938 in New York, New York

Will Barnet
American artist–educator
• Painter, printmaker who calls style Abstract Reality; professor, Cooper Union Art School, 1945-78.
b. May 25, 1911 in Beverly, Massachusetts

Daniel Barry
American cartoonist
• Drew "Flash Gordon," "Doc Savage," "Commando York" for comic books.
b. July 11, 1923 in Long Branch, New Jersey

Richmond Barthe
American sculptor
• Known for realistic busts of black historical figures, celebrities.
b. January 28, 1901 in Bay St. Louis, Mississippi
d. March 06, 1989 in Pasadena, California

Auguste (Frederic Auguste) Bartholdi
French sculptor
• Designed Statue of Liberty, France's gift to America, 1886.
b. April 02, 1834 in Colmar, France
d. October 04, 1904 in Paris, France

Paul Wayland Bartlett
American sculptor
• Known for portrait statues; Columbus, Michelangelo at Library of Congress, Lafayette at Louvre.
b. January 24, 1865 in New Haven, Connecticut
d. September 2, 1925 in Paris, France

Fra Bartolommeo
(Bartolommeo di Pagolo del Fatorino; Baccio della Porta)
Italian artist
• Paintings reflect composition balance, color harmony of High Renaissance; known for "St. Mark," 1517, now in Louvre.
b. March 28, 1475 in Florence, Italy
d. October 31, 1517 in Florence, Italy

Leonard Baskin
American artist–illustrator
• Sculptor, later print maker; founded Gehanna Press, producer of limited editions, 1952.
b. August 15, 1922 in New Brunswick, New Jersey

Jacopo Bassano
(Giacomo da Ponte)
Italian artist
• One of earliest genre painters; noted for *The Good Samaritan*.
b. 1510 in Bassano, Italy
d. February 13, 1592 in Bassano, Italy

Clarence Daniel Batchelor
American cartoonist
• Work appeared in *NY Daily News*, 1931-69; won Pulitzer, 1937.
b. April 01, 1888 in Osage City, Kansas
d. September 05, 1977 in Deep River, Connecticut

Henry Mayo Bateman
Welsh cartoonist
• Most highly paid British cartoonist of his time.
b. February 15, 1887 in New South Wales, Australia
d. February 11, 1970 in Gozo, Malta

Willi Baumeister
German artist
• Abstractionist, who used ideograms, biomorphic shapes; condemned by Nazis, 1937.
b. January 22, 1889 in Stuttgart, Germany
d. August 31, 1955 in Stuttgart, Germany (West)

William Baziotes
American artist
• Abstract Expressionist; co-founded art school which became meeting place for *avant-garde* artists, "The Club."
b. June 11, 1912 in Pittsburgh, Pennsylvania
d. June 05, 1963 in New York, New York

Dan(iel Carter) Beard
American artist
• Founded Boy Scouts of America, 1910; only recipient of Golden Eagle Medal.
b. June 21, 1850 in Cincinnati, Ohio
d. June 11, 1941 in Suffern, New York

Peter Hill Beard
American photographer
• Known for color photography of dead, decaying animals of Africa.
b. January 22, 1938 in New York, New York

Romare Howard Bearden
American artist
• America's foremost collagist, portraying images common to all cultures; brought recognition to the black American artist.
b. September 02, 1914 in Charlotte, North Carolina
d. March 11, 1988 in New York, New York

Sir Cecil Walter Hardy Beaton
English photographer–designer
• Major 1930s fashion photographer; won Oscars for costume design for *Gigi*, 1959; *My Fair Lady*, 1965.
b. January 14, 1904 in London, England
d. January 18, 1980 in Salisbury, England

C(harles) C(larence) Beck
American cartoonist
• Created Captain Marvel, the super hero who came to life at the word "shazam," using actor Fred MacMurray as model, 1939.
b. June 08, 1910 in Zumbrota, Minnesota
d. November 22, 1989 in Gainesville, Florida

Max Beckmann
German artist
• Leading German expressionist; works depict social commentaries, grotesque scenes.
b. February 12, 1884 in Leipzig, Germany
d. December 12, 1950 in New York, New York

Vanessa Bell
(Mrs Clive Bell)
English artist
• Sister of Virginia Woolf; member of Bloomsburg group of painters.
b. May 3, 1879 in London, England
d. April 07, 1961 in East Sussex, England

Gentile Bellini
Italian artist
• Prominent portraitist, also noted for processions, panoramic views.
b. 1429 in Venice, Italy
d. February 23, 1507 in Venice, Italy

Giovanni Bellini
Italian artist–architect
• Teacher of Giorgione and Titian; founded Venetian school.
b. 1430 in Venice, Italy
d. November 29, 1516 in Venice, Italy

Jacopo Bellini
Italian artist
• Venetian religious painter; father of Gentile, Giovanni Bellini.
b. 1400
d. 1470

Bernardo Bellotto
Italian artist
• Court painter for king of Poland, known for paintings of Warsaw.
b. January 3, 1720 in Venice, Italy
d. October 17, 1780 in Warsaw, Poland

George Wesley Bellows
American artist
• Associated with "The Eight"; painted boxing scenes, landscapes: "Stag at Sharkey's," 1907.
b. August 12, 1882 in Columbus, Ohio
d. January 08, 1925 in New York, New York

Jeanne Bendick
American author–illustrator
• Prolific writer, illustrator of children's science books: *Living Things*, 1969.
b. February 25, 1919 in New York, New York

Thomas Hart Benton
American artist
• Regionalist whose paintings depict life in Midwest, South.
b. April 15, 1889 in Neosho, Missouri
d. January 19, 1975 in Kansas City, Missouri

Eugene Berman
American artist–designer
• Neo-romantic painter, also known for theater sets, interiors.
b. November 04, 1899 in Saint Petersburg, Russia
d. December 14, 1972 in Rome, Italy

Bruno Bernard
American photographer
• Known for shots of film stars including famed photo of Marilyn Monroe in windblown skirt.
b. 1912
d. June 04, 1987 in Los Angeles, California

Walter Berndt
American cartoonist
• Best known for syndicated comic strip "Smitty," 1922-73.
b. November 22, 1899 in Brooklyn, New York
d. August 13, 1979 in Port Jefferson, New York

Giovanni Lorenzo Bernini
Italian sculptor–architect
• Created Baroque style in sculpture; noted as famed architect of St. Peter's, from 1629.
b. December 07, 1598 in Naples, Italy
d. November 28, 1680 in Rome, Italy

Jim Berry
American cartoonist
• Editorial cartoonist who draws "Berry's World," 1963–.
b. January 16, 1932 in Chicago, Illinois

Clifford Kennedy Berryman
American cartoonist
• Editorial cartoonist, Washington *Star*, 1907-49; created "Teddy Bear" after Theodore Roosevelt's bear-hunting trip, 1902.
b. April 02, 1869 in Versailles, Kentucky
d. December 11, 1949 in Washington, District of Columbia

Harry Bertoia
American artist–designer
• Noted for abstract, metal sculptures; prize-winning wire shell chairs.
b. March 1, 1915 in San Lorenzo, Italy
d. November 06, 1978 in Barto, Pennsylvania

Joseph Beuys
German artist
• Sculptor, political activist who saw art as means of reshaping society.
b. May 12, 1921 in Krefeld, Germany
d. January 23, 1986 in Dusseldorf, Germany (West)

George Biddle
American artist–author
• Leader of Federal Arts Project during Depression; known for portraits, murals.
b. January 24, 1885 in Philadelphia, Pennsylvania
d. November 06, 1973 in Croton-on-Hudson, New York

George Caleb Bingham
American artist
• Portrait, genre painter of old-time Missouri life: *Jolly Flatboatman*, 1846.
b. March 2, 1811 in Augusta County, Virginia
d. July 07, 1879 in Kansas City, Missouri

Sir Oswald Hornby Joseph Birley
English artist
• Commissioned by Royal Naval College to paint portraits of George VI, his admirals, Winston Churchill, WW II.
b. March 31, 1880 in Auckland, New Zealand
d. May 06, 1952 in London, England

Isabel Bishop
American artist
• Known for representational paintings, drawings of women in everyday settings.
b. March 03, 1902 in Cincinnati, Ohio
d. February 19, 1988 in New York, New York

George William Bitzer
American filmmaker–photographer
• Pioneer cameraman; filmed D W Griffith's *Birth of a Nation*, 1914.
b. April 21, 1872 in Boston, Massachusetts
d. April 29, 1944 in Los Angeles, California

William Blake
English poet–artist
• Wrote *Songs of Innocence*, 1789; engraved, published own poetry.
b. November 28, 1757 in London, England
d. August 12, 1827 in London, England

Ralph Albert Blakelock
American artist
• Original self-taught landscapist who did moody scenes, often with Indians.
b. October 15, 1847 in New York, New York
d. August 09, 1919 in Elizabethtown, New York

Peter Blume
American artist
• Surrealist painter with meticulous style: "The Eternal City," 1937.
b. October 27, 1906 in Smorgon, Russia

Umberto Boccioni
Italian artist
• Futurist painter, sculptor; helped draft "Futurist Manifests," 1910.
b. 1882
d. 1916

Vaughn Bode
American cartoonist
• Underground comic artist; strips show worlds of beauty, cruelty; best known for lizards.
b. July 22, 1941 in Syracuse, New York

Aaron Bohrod
American artist
• Realistic painter, commissioned by *Life* to record WW II; does outstanding examples of *trompe-l'-o eil*.
b. November 21, 1907 in Chicago, Illinois

Hannes Vajn Bok
(Dolbokov joint pseud)
American artist–author
• Famed fantasy illustrator who drew woodcut-like scenes for *Weird Tales*.
b. July 02, 1914 in Minnesota
d. April 11, 1964 in New York

Ilya Bolotowsky
American artist–sculptor
• Painter, known for diamond-shaped canvases; co-founder, American Abstract Artists, 1936.
b. July 01, 1907 in Saint Petersburg, Russia
d. November 21, 1981 in New York, New York

Dave (David) Bomberg
English artist
• Original member of the "London Group," 1914; landscape paintings have a documentary character.
b. December 05, 1890 in Birmingham, England
d. August 19, 1951 in London, England

Pierre Bonnard
French artist
• Subjects for paintings include still lifes, women bathing, self-portraits.
b. October 3, 1867 in Fontenay, France
d. January 23, 1947 in LeCannet, France

Paul-Emile Borduas
Canadian artist
• Leader of Montreal "Automatistes," exponents of objective painting.
b. November 01, 1905 in Saint Hilaire, Quebec
d. February 22, 1960 in Paris, France

Gutzon Borglum
American sculptor
• Best known as sculptor of US presidents on Mt. Rushmore, 1927-41.
b. March 25, 1867 in Bear Lake, Idaho
d. March 06, 1941 in Chicago, Illinois

James Lincoln Delamothe Borglum
American sculptor
• Completed statues on Mt. Rushmore after death of father, Gutzon, 1941.
b. April 09, 1912 in Stamford, Connecticut
d. January 27, 1986 in Corpus Christi, Texas

Hieronymus Bosch
(Hieronymus VanAeken)
Dutch artist
• Allegorical painter who depicted evil with fantastic images: "Seven Deadly Sins"; influenced Pieter the Elder, considered forerunner of surrealism.
b. 1450 in Hertogenbosch, Netherlands
d. 1516

Blackbear Bosin
American Indian artist–designer
• Award-winning painter, who draws birds, animals, Indian lore in flat, two-dimensional style.
b. June 05, 1921 in Anadarko, Oklahoma

Fernando Botero (Angulo)
Colombian artist
• Figurative painter; exhibits in Europe, North, South America.
b. April 19, 1932 in Medellin, Colombia

Sandro Botticelli
(Alessandrodi Mariano dei Filipipi)
Italian artist
• Favorite artist, protege of Medici family; best known work "The Birth of Venus."
b. 1444 in Florence, Italy
d. May 17, 1510 in Florence, Italy

Eugene Louis Boudin
French artist
• His seascapes strongly influenced the impressionist painters.
b. July 12, 1824 in Honfleur, France
d. August 08, 1898 in Deauville, France

Dierick C Bouts
Dutch artist
• Painted austere religious works: "The Last Supper," 1464; "Last Judgment," 1468.
b. 1420 in Haarlem, Netherlands
d. 1475 in Louvain, Belgium

Mathew B Brady
American photographer
• Accompanied Union army, 1861-65; photographed all aspects of Civil War.
b. 1823 in Warren County, New York
d. January 15, 1896 in New York, New York

Constantin Brancusi
Romanian sculptor
• Leader in growth of modern sculpture famous for simple, abstract style: "Bird in Space," 1919.
b. February 21, 1876 in Pestisanigorj, Romania
d. March 16, 1957 in Paris, France

Brumsic Brandon, Jr
American artist–author
• Best known for syndicated comic strip "Luther," 1970–; first major strip to highlight a black character.
b. April 1, 1927 in Washington, District of Columbia

Bill (William) Brandt
English photographer
• Landscape, portrait photographer known for series of distorted female nudes: *Perspectives of Nudes*, 1961.
b. 1904 in London, England
d. December 2, 1983 in London, England

Sir Frank Brangwyn
English artist
• Official war artist during WW I; best known for marine paintings; murals hang in RCA Building, NYC, British House of Lords.
b. May 13, 1867 in Bruges, Belgium
d. June 11, 1956 in Ditchling, England

Georges Braque
French artist
• Founded Cubism with Picasso, 1907; developed the collage, 1911.
b. May 13, 1882 in Argenteuil, France
d. August 31, 1963 in Paris, France

Brassai
(Gyula Halasz)
French photographer
• Best known for pictures of the night people of Paris, 1930s; reproduced in *The Secret Paris of the 30s*, 1976.
b. September 09, 1899 in Brasso, Hungary
d. July 08, 1984 in Nice, France

Berke Breathed
American cartoonist
• Pulitzer-winning creator of comic strip, "Bloom County," 1980–; has written books based on strip.
b. June 21, 1957 in Encino, California

Dave Breger
American cartoonist–illustrator
• Originated term "G I Joe" with WW II cartoon series.
b. 1908 in Chicago, Illinois
d. January 16, 1970 in South Nyack, New York

Jules Adolphe Breton
French artist–author
• Harmonizes landscapes, human nature in paintings: "A Gleaner," 1877; "The Weed-Gathers," 1861.
b. 1827 in Calais, France
d. 1906

Morrie Brickman
American cartoonist
• Wrote *This Little Pigeon Went to Market*, 1965; syndicated cartoonist, 1954–.
b. July 24, 1917 in Chicago, Illinois

Austin Eugene Briggs
American artist–illustrator
• Illustrated Henry Ford's *Dearborn Independent*, 1925-27; cofounder, member, Famous Artists School, 1950-73.
b. September 08, 1908 in Humboldt, Minnesota
d. October 13, 1973 in Paris, France

Alexey Brodovitch
American photographer–designer
• Award-winning works exhibited throughout US; art director, *Harper's Bazaar* mag., 1934-58.
b. 1898 in Russia
d. April 15, 1971 in Lethor, France

Bronzino Il
(Agnoli di Cosimo Allori)
Italian artist
• Florentine portraitist whose best-known work was *Eleanora of Toledo with Her Son*, c. 1545.
b. November 17, 1503 in Montecelli, Italy
d. November 23, 1572

Alexander Brook
American artist
• Portraitist, landscape painter called the "unstruggling artist"; best known for 1940 portrait of Katherine Hepburn.
b. July 14, 1898 in Brooklyn, New York
d. February 26, 1980 in Sag Harbor, New York

Adriaen C Brouwer
Flemish artist
• Pupil of Frans Hals, genre painter whose landscapes were among greatest of his age.
b. 1606 in Oudenaarde, Belgium
d. January 1638 in Antwerp, Belgium

Dik Browne
American cartoonist
• Created "Hi and Lois," 1954; "Hagar the Horrible," 1973.
b. August 11, 1917 in New York, New York
d. June 03, 1989 in Sarasota, Florida

Phiz (Hablot Knight) Browne
English artist–illustrator
• Remembered as Dickens' chief illustrator; depicted *Pickwick Papers*, 1837; *David Copperfield*, 1850.
b. June 15, 1815 in Kensington, England
d. July 08, 1882 in West Brighton, England

Jennie Augusta Brownscombe
American artist
• Painted genre, American historical scenes.
b. December 1, 1850 in Honesdale, Pennsylvania
d. August 05, 1936 in New York, New York

Pieter Bruegel, (The Elder)
(Pieter Breughel or Brueghel; "Peasant Breughel" "The Droll")
Flemish artist
• Regarded as finest Flemish painter of 16th c.; known for landscapes, peasant scenes: "The Peasant Dance."
b. 1525
d. September 05, 1569 in Brussels, Belgium

Jan Brughel
(Jan Breughel or Brueghel; "Velvet Brueghel" "Flower Brueghel")
Flemish artist
• Noted for painting landscapes, flowers; did backgrounds for figure painters, especially Rubens; son of Pieter.
b. 1568 in Brussels, Belgium
d. 1625

Filippo Brunelleschi
Italian architect–sculptor
• Considered greatest architect, engineer of time; designed dome for Florence cathedral.
b. 1377 in Florence, Italy
d. April 16, 1446 in Florence, Italy

Laurent de Brunhoff
French author–illustrator
• Continues "Barbar" children's books his father originated.
b. August 3, 1925 in Paris, France

George Brush
American artist
• Prize-winning portraitist of Indians, family groups.
b. September 28, 1855
d. April 24, 1941

Bernard Buffet
French artist
• One of the leading artists of the 20th c.; paintings in genre of post-war France.
b. July 1, 1928 in Paris, France

Charles Ephraim Burchfield
American artist
• Watercolorist, painted urban scenes, landscapes; won 1960 Gold medal for painting.
b. April 09, 1893 in Ashtabula, Ohio
d. January 1, 1967 in Gardenville, New York

Jacob Burck
American cartoonist
• Created daily editorial cartoon in *Chicago Sun Times*; won Pulitzer, 1941.
b. January 1, 1904 in Poland
d. May 11, 1982 in Chicago, Illinois

Carl Victor Burger
American author–illustrator
• Illustrated nature, children's books; wrote and illustrated popular "All About" series.
b. June 18, 1888 in Maryville, Tennessee
d. December 3, 1967 in Mount Kisco, New York

Edward Coley Burne-Jones, Sir
English artist–designer
• Late Pre-Raphaelite painter; joined with William Morris in Arts & Crafts movement to design furniture, books, tapestries.
b. August 23, 1833 in Birmingham, England
d. June 17, 1898 in London, England

Wilhelm Busch
German poet–illustrator
• Illustrated, wrote book of verses *Max and Moritz*, 1865.
b. April 15, 1832 in Hannover, Germany
d. January 09, 1908 in Mechtshausen, Germany

Ernie (Ernest Paul) Bushmiller
American cartoonist
• Created comic strip "Nancy."
b. August 23, 1905 in New York, New York
d. August 15, 1982 in Stamford, Connecticut

Paul Cadmus
American artist
• Best known during WW II for his tempera portraits of realism.
b. December 17, 1904 in New York, New York

Jacques Caffieri
French artist
• Bronze founder; member of respected family of artists; executed rococo decorations for Versailles.
b. 1678
d. 1755

Randolph Caldecott
English artist
• Caldecott Medal given annually to outstanding children's book illustrator established, 1938.
b. March 22, 1846 in Chester, England
d. February 12, 1886 in Saint Augustine, Florida

Alexander Calder
American artist
• Best known for abstract sculptures of metal, bent wire called "mobiles."
b. July 22, 1898 in Philadelphia, Pennsylvania
d. November 11, 1976 in New York, New York

Dick Calkins
American cartoonist
• Drew science-fiction comic strip "Buck Rogers," 1929-47; wrote stories for Red Ryder comic books, 1950s.
b. 1895 in Grand Rapids, Michigan
d. May 13, 1962 in Tucson, Arizona

Jacques Callot
French artist
• First to make engraving an independent art; produced over 1,600 caricatures, engravings.
b. 1592 in Nancy, France
d. March 24, 1635 in Nancy, France

E Simms Campbell
American cartoonist
• First black artist to work for nat. publications; cartoonist for *Esquire*, other leading periodicals, 1933-71.
b. January 02, 1906 in Saint Louis, Missouri
d. January 27, 1971 in White Plains, New York

Robert Campin
(")
Flemish artist
• Considered founder, with Van Eyck, of Netherlandish school; did Merode Altarpiece, c. 1428.
b. 1375
d. 1444

Antonio Canaletto
(Giovanni Canal)
Italian artist
• Widely imitated painter of atmospheric Venetian scenes.
b. October 18, 1697 in Venice, Italy
d. April 2, 1768 in Venice, Italy

Milt(on Arthur) Caniff
American cartoonist
• Created comic strips "Terry and the Pirates," "Steve Canyon," 1934.
b. February 28, 1907 in Hillsboro, Ohio
d. April 03, 1988 in New York, New York

Antonio Canova
Italian artist
• Neo-classic sculptor: "Cupid and Psycje," 1793; "Tomb of Maria Christina," 1798.
b. November 01, 1757 in Passagno, Italy
d. October 13, 1822 in Venice, Italy

Cornell Capa
American journalist–photographer
• Gives a visual history of our century with his documentary scenes.
b. April 19, 1918 in Budapest, Hungary

Robert Capa
(Andrei Friedmann)
American photographer
• First war photographer to get dramatic close-ups of action; photographs in *Images of War*, 1964.
b. 1913 in Budapest, Hungary
d. May 25, 1954 in Hanoi, Vietnam

Al Capp
(Alfred Gerald Caplin)
American cartoonist
• Created "Li'l Abner," 1934-77; syndicated in over 900 newspapers.
b. September 28, 1909 in New Haven, Connecticut
d. November 05, 1979 in Cambridge, Massachusetts

Michelangelo da Caravaggio
(Michelangelo Merisi)
Italian artist
• Interpreted religious figures, scenes as contemporary events, people; early exponent of "chiaroscuro."
b. September 08, 1573 in Caravaggio, Italy
d. July 18, 1610

Eric Carle
American artist–illustrator
• On *New York Times* 10 Best list for his self-illustrated *The Very Hungry Caterpillar*, 1969.
b. June 25, 1929 in Syracuse, New York

Wally (Wallace A) Carlson
American cartoonist
• Drew comic strip "The Nebbs," 1923-46.
b. March 28, 1894 in St. Louis, Missouri
d. 1969

Franklin Carmichael
(Group of Seven)
Canadian artist
• Oil landscape painter; original Group of Seven member, 1919.
b. 1890 in Orillia, Ontario
d. October 24, 1945 in Toronto, Ontario

Anthony Caro
English sculptor
• Known for abstract, complex steel, aluminum sculptures; often painted in primary colors.
b. March 08, 1924 in London, England

Vittore Carpaccio
Italian artist
• Painted colorful, detailed narrative scenes; noted for St. Ursula series.
b. 1455 in Venice, Italy
d. 1525 in Venice, Italy

Emily Carr
Canadian artist–author
• Painted, wrote about British Columbia Indians: *Heart of a Peacock*, 1953.
b. December 12, 1871 in Victoria, British Columbia
d. March 02, 1945 in Victoria, British Columbia

Carlo Carra
Italian artist
• Founded Italian metaphysical school, futurist movement, 1910; paintings include *Lot's Daughters*.
b. 1881
d. April 13, 1966 in Milan, Italy

Annibale Carracci
Italian artist
• Did first of great baroque ceilings, frescoes of Farness Palace, 1597-1604; a work, once bought for $22, brought $1.52 million, 1987.
b. November 03, 1560 in Bologna, Italy
d. July 15, 1609 in Rome, Italy

Lodovico Carracci
Italian artist
• Founded, with cousins Agostino and Annibale, famed art academy, Accademia degli Incamminati, 1582.
b. April 21, 1555 in Bologna, Italy
d. November 13, 1619 in Bologna, Italy

Albert Ernest Carrier-Belleuse
French sculptor
• Works include *Bacchante*; taught Rodin, 1864-70.
b. 1824
d. 1887

Rosalba Carriera
Italian artist
• Miniature painter, specialist in pastel portraits.
b. 1675 in Venice, Italy
d. 1757 in Venice, Italy

Henri Cartier-Bresson
French photographer
• Black and white photographer known for brilliant clarity; published *The Decisive Moment*, 1952.
b. August 22, 1908 in Chanteloup, France

Jean Carzou
French artist
• Landscape, still-life painter, who uses linear style, rich colors.
b. January 01, 1907 in Alep, Syria

Mary Stevenson Cassatt
American artist
• Impressionist noted for paintings of mother and child; friend of Degas.
b. May 22, 1844 in Allegheny, Pennsylvania
d. June 14, 1926 in Paris, France

George Catlin
American explorer–artist
• Best known for paintings of Indians, tribal life, 1829-38.
b. July 26, 1796 in Wilkes-Barre, Pennsylvania
d. December 23, 1872 in Jersey City, New Jersey

Pietro Cavallini
Italian artist
• Mosaicist, frescoist; an innovator of naturalism who broke with Byzantine style.
b. 1250 in Rome, Italy
d. 1330

Benvenuto Cellini
Italian sculptor
• Goldsmith; designed intricate metalwork; noted for *Autobiography*, first printed, 1728.
b. November 01, 1500 in Florence, Italy
d. February 14, 1571 in Florence, Italy

Paul Cezanne
French artist
• Post-impressionist painter; his geometric forms influenced cubism.
b. January 19, 1839 in Aix-en-Provence, France
d. October 22, 1906 in Aix-en-Provence, France

Marc Chagall
Russian artist
• Influenced by cubism; paintings depict Russian village life.
b. July 07, 1887 in Vitebsk, Russia
d. March 28, 1985 in Saint-Paul-de-Vence, France

Samuel Chamberlain
American author–photographer
• Produced etchings, photographs of European, American landscapes; co-wrote popular books on foreign cuisine.
b. October 28, 1895 in Cresco, Iowa
d. January 1, 1975 in Marblehead, Massachusetts

Sir Francis Legatt Chantrey
English artist
• Famous sculptures include equestrians of Wellington, George IV, London.
b. April 07, 1781 in Jordanthorpe, England
d. November 25, 1841 in London, England

Jean Baptiste Simeon Chardin
French artist
• Wholesome still lifes include "Le Benedicte," 1740.
b. November 02, 1699 in Paris, France
d. December 06, 1779 in Paris, France

Chares
Greek sculptor
• Carved Colossus of Rhodes, one of the seven wonders of the ancient world.
b. 320BC

Siegfried Charoux
British sculptor
• Best known for works in London: *The Judge; The Cellist; The Motor Cyclist*.
b. 1896
d. April 26, 1967 in London, England

Sandro Chia
Italian artist
• Among most successful of neoexpressionists: *The Idleness of Sisyphus;* painter, printmaker, sculptor with exhibits in US, Europe.
b. April 1946 in Florence, Italy

Judy Chicago
(Judy Cohen)
American artist–feminist
• Most well-known work is "The Dinner Party," a monumental work conveying the social history of women.
b. July 2, 1939 in Chicago, Illinois

Eduard Chillida
Spanish artist
• Abstract sculptor whose works are on display in Germany, Switzerland, US.
b. January 1, 1924 in San Sebastian, Spain

Giorgio de Chirico
Italian artist
• Founded Italian school of metaphysical painting.
b. July 1, 1888 in Volos, Greece
d. November 2, 1978 in Rome, Italy

Albert Christ-Janer
American artist–author–educator
• Watercolorist, graphic designer, who wrote numerous biographies of artists.
b. June 13, 1910 in Appleton, Wisconsin
d. December 12, 1973 in Como, Italy

Christo
(Christo Javacheff)
Bulgarian artist
• Created 24-mile long fabric fence in Sonoma, Marin Counties, CA, 1972-76.
b. June 13, 1935 in Gabrovo, Bulgaria

Howard Chandler Christy
American artist
• Created the "Christy Girl"; paintings include "Signing the Constitution," 1940, in the Capitol building, Washington, DC.
b. January 1, 1873 in Morgan County, Ohio
d. March 04, 1952 in New York, New York

Giovanni Cimabue
(Cenni de Pepo; "Father of Italian Painting")
Italian artist
• Considered first modern painter; developed space, figure modelling; noted for Assisi church frescoes.
b. 1240 in Florence, Italy
d. 1302 in Florence, Italy

Bob (Robert) Clampett
American cartoonist–filmmaker
• Animator; worked at Warner Brothers, 1930s-40s; created "Looney Tune," "Merry Melodie" cartoons.
b. May 08, 1913 in San Diego, California
d. May 02, 1984 in Detroit, Michigan

Joos van Cleve
Flemish artist
• Royalty portraitist, religious painter; works include *Lamentation*, c. 1530.
b. 1485
d. 1540 in Antwerp, Belgium

Shobal Vail Clevenger
American sculptor
• His bust of Daniel Webster was selected by Post Office for 15 cent stamp.
b. October 22, 1812 in Middletown, Ohio
d. September 23, 1843

Francois Clouet
French artist
• Chief painter to Francis I, 1523; portraitist of royalty; son of Jean.
b. 1510 in Tours, France
d. 1572 in Paris, France

Jean Clouet
French artist
• Painter to four French kings; did portraits, genre scenes.
b. 1485 in Netherlands
d. 1540 in Paris, France

Thomas Cole
American artist
• One of the founders of the Hudson River School, first American movement in painting.
b. February 01, 1801 in Bolton, England
d. February 11, 1848 in Catskill, New York

Samuel Colman
American artist
• A founder, first president, American Watercolor Society, 1866.
b. March 04, 1832 in Portland, Maine
d. March 27, 1920 in New York, New York

Alex (David Alexander) Colville
Canadian artist
• Realist painter who captured people, places, animals of Maritime Provinces.
b. August 24, 1920 in Toronto, Ontario

Paul Francis Conrad
American cartoonist–author
• LA *Times* syndicated editorial cartoonist, 1973–; won three Pulitzers.
b. June 27, 1924 in Cedar Rapids, Iowa

John Constable
English artist
• Romantic landscape painter; influenced Barbizon, impressionist schools.
b. June 11, 1776 in East Bergholt, England
d. March 3, 1837 in London, England

Samuel Cooper
English artist
• Miniaturist painter; among the subjects for his portraits were Mrs. Pepys, Cromwell, Milton.
b. 1609
d. 1672

John Singleton Copley
American artist
• Considered greatest American old master; known for perceptive portraits of Paul Revere, Samuel Adams, others.
b. July 03, 1733 in Boston, Massachusetts
d. September 09, 1815 in London, England

Richard Vance Corben
American artist
• Horror illustrator who invented fantasy strip "Rowlf."
b. October 01, 1940 in Anderson, Missouri

Lovis Corinth
German artist
• Proponent of Sezession modernistic movement who strongly influenced German expressionism.
b. 1858
d. 1925

Corneille
(Cornelis Guillaume van Beverloo)
Dutch artist
• Abstract colorist, illustrator; co-founded Cobra group, 1947.
b. 1922 in Liege, Belgium

Jean Baptiste Camille Corot
French artist
• Barbizon school landscape painter whose works include *Ponte de Mantes*, 1870.
b. July 16, 1796 in Paris, France
d. February 22, 1875 in Paris, France

Antonio Allegri da Correggio
Italian artist
• Most famous work *The Assumption of the Virgin* in dome of Parma cathedral.
b. August 3, 1494 in Italy
d. March 05, 1534

Piero di Cosimo
Italian artist–architect
• Painter of religious, mythological works, often in bizarre style *Death of Procris*, c. 1500.
b. 1462
d. 1521

Gustave Courbet
French artist
• Realist painter whose works include *Burial at Ornans* in the Louvre.
b. June 1, 1819 in Ornans, France
d. December 31, 1877 in Vevey, Switzerland

Fleur Fenton Cowles
American author–illustrator
• Wrote *The Case of Salvador Dali*, 1960; illustrated *Tiger Flower*, 1968.
b. February 13, 1910 in New York, New York

Allyn Cox
American artist
• Known for completing mural in rotunda of US capitol, 1954, begun 100 yrs. earlier by Constantino Brumidi.
b. June 05, 1896 in New York, New York
d. September 26, 1982 in Washington, District of Columbia

Gardner Cox
American artist
• Portrait painter whose subjects include Robert Frost, Dean Acheson, Robert Kennedy.
b. January 22, 1906 in Holyoke, Massachusetts

John Rogers Cox
American artist
• Landscape painter known for color design *Gray and Gold*, 1942.
b. March 24, 1915 in Terre Haute, Indiana

Lucas Cranach

(Lucas Kranach; Lucas Muller; "The Elder")
German artist–designer
• Originated Protestant religious painting; known for altarpieces, portraits of Martin Luther, other reformer friends; court painter to electors of Saxony, 1552-53.
b. October 04, 1472 in Kronach, Germany
d. October 16, 1553 in Weimar, Germany

Roy(ston Campbell) Crane

American cartoonist
• Wrote "Buz Sawyer" cartoon, 1943-77.
b. November 22, 1901 in Abilene, Texas
d. July 07, 1977 in Orlando, Florida

Thomas Crawford

American sculptor
• Works include equestrian *George Washington*, 1857; *Armed Liberty*, on Capitol dome, 1860.
b. March 22, 1813 in New York, New York
d. October 1, 1857 in London, England

William Hulfish Crawford

American cartoonist
• Political cartoonist Newark, *News*, 1938-77; work appeared in over 700 newspapers.
b. March 18, 1913 in Hammond, Indiana
d. January 06, 1982 in Washington, District of Columbia

John Crome

English artist
• Founded Norwich school of painting; known for romanticized scenes of rural life.
b. December 22, 1768 in Norwich, England
d. April 22, 1821 in Norwich, England

Percy L Crosby

American cartoonist
• Drew syndicated comic strip Skippy, 1920s-43; became film starring Jackie Cooper, 1931.
b. December 08, 1891 in Brooklyn, New York
d. December 08, 1964 in New York, New York

George Cruikshank

English artist–illustrator
• Noted for humorous satirical sketches in *Oliver Twist*, 1838;Grimm's *Popular Stories*, 1826.
b. September 27, 1792 in London, England
d. February 01, 1878 in London, England

Robert Crumb

American cartoonist
• Known for 1970s underground comics with biting satire; started *Zap Comix* series, 1967.
b. August 3, 1943 in Philadelphia, Pennsylvania

Peyo (Pierre) Culliford

Belgian author–cartoonist
• Created the Smurfs, 1957; top children's TV show in US, early 1980s.
b. June 25, 1928 in Brussels, Belgium

Terence Tenison Cuneo

English artist
• Portrait and figure painter; best known for works with royal subjects.
b. November 01, 1907

Imogen Cunningham

American photographer
• Experimental, portrait photographer whose career spanned 75 yrs.
b. April 12, 1883 in Portland, Oregon
d. June 24, 1976 in San Francisco, California

John Steuart Curry

American artist
• Murals, oil paintings deal with rural America.
b. November 14, 1897 in Dunavant, Kansas
d. August 29, 1946 in Madison, Wisconsin

Edward Sheriff Curtis

American photographer
• Interest in Indians resulted in 20-volume series *The North American Indian*, 1907-30.
b. February 19, 1868 in Madison, Wisconsin
d. October 19, 1952 in Los Angeles, California

Louise Dahl-Wolfe

American photographer
• The doyenne of fashion, portrait photography; with *Harper's Bazaar*, 1936-58.
b. 1895 in San Francisco, California

Salvador Dali

Spanish artist
• Leader of Surrealist Movement; best-known work *Persistence of Memory*, 1931.
b. May 11, 1904 in Figueras, Spain
d. January 23, 1989 in Figueras, Spain

Cyrus Edwin Dallin

American sculptor
• Best known for statues of Paul Revere, Sir Isaac Newton.
b. November 22, 1861 in Springville, Vermont
d. November 14, 1944 in Boston, Massachusetts

Tom (Thomas) Darcy

American cartoonist
• Known for bold lines, facial expressions; won Pulitzer for editorial cartooning, 1970.
b. June 07, 1916 in Saint Louis, Missouri

Jay Norwood Darling

(J N Ding pseud)
American cartoonist
• On staff, *Des Moines Register;* won two Pulitzers.
b. October 21, 1876 in Norwood, Michigan
d. February 12, 1962 in Des Moines, Iowa

Whitney Darrow, Jr

American cartoonist
• With *New Yorker* mag. since 1934; cartoon books include *You're Sitting on My Eyelashes*, 1943.
b. August 22, 1909 in Princeton, New Jersey

Charles Francois Daubigny

French artist
• Landscape painter who influenced Impressionists: *Lever de Lune*, 1877.
b. February 15, 1817 in Paris, France
d. February 19, 1878 in Auvers, France

Honore Daumier

French artist
• Noted for over 7,500 lithographs, illustrations satirizing French politics, society.
b. February 26, 1808 in Marseilles, France
d. February 11, 1879 in Valmondois, France

Homer Calvin Davenport

American cartoonist
• Political cartoonist whose most famous cartoon is Uncle Sam's endorsement of T Roosevelt: "He's Good Enough for Me."
b. March 08, 1867 in Silverton, Oregon
d. May 02, 1912 in New York, New York

Gerard David

Dutch artist
• Paintings include *Madonna with Angels and Saints*, 1509; known for skill in using color.
b. 1460 in Oudewater, Netherlands
d. August 13, 1523 in Bruges, Netherlands

Jacques Louis David

French artist
• Foremost French classicist; named court painter to Napoleon; best known for *Death of Marat*, 1793.
b. August 3, 1748 in Paris, France
d. December 29, 1825 in Brussels, Belgium

d'Angers David

(Pierre Jean David)
French sculptor
• Did national figures–nudes, statues, busts, medallions; executed pediment of Pantheon, Paris.
b. March 12, 1788 in Angers, France
d. January 04, 1856 in Paris, France

Jo Davidson

American sculptor
• Most famous busts include those of Walt Whitman, Will Rogers.
b. March 3, 1883 in New York, New York
d. January 02, 1952 in Bercheron, France

Alan Davie
Scottish artist
• Colorful painting style influenced by Picasso, post-war Americans; one-man int'l. showings since 1949.
b. 1920 in Grangemouth, Scotland

Jim (James Robert) Davis
American cartoonist
• Created comic strip character Garfield; syndicated in 500 newspapers.
b. July 28, 1945 in Marion, Indiana

Stuart Davis
American artist
• Exhibited at 1913 Armory show; precursor of 1960s pop-art; did abstract works of urban life.
b. December 07, 1894 in Philadelphia, Pennsylvania
d. June 24, 1964 in New York, New York

Chon (Chauncey Addison) Day
American cartoonist–author
• Known for well-designed gag cartoons; books include *Brother Sebastian at Large*, 1961; cartoon Hall of Famer.
b. April 06, 1907 in Chatham, New Jersey

Jose DeCreeft
American sculptor
• Works of bronze include Alice in Wonderland 16 foot group, NY, 1957; works exhibited in museums.
b. November 27, 1884 in Guadalajara, Spain
d. 1982

John De Cuir
American art director
• Won Oscars for *Cleopatra*, 1963; *Hello, Dolly*, 1969; other films include *Ghostbusters*, 1984.
b. 1918 in San Francisco, California

(Hilaire Germain) Edgar Degas
French artist
• Impressionist painter whose favorite subjects were ballet dancers, cafe life.
b. July 19, 1834 in Paris, France
d. September 27, 1917 in Paris, France

Adolf Arthur Dehn
American artist
• Prolific lithographer, watercolor landscapist.
b. November 22, 1895 in Waterville, Minnesota
d. May 19, 1968 in New York, New York

Kim Deitch
American cartoonist
• Known for underground comic strips since 1967: "Sunshine Girl"; "Uncle Ed."
b. May 21, 1944

Elaine Marie Catherine Fried DeKooning
(Mrs Willem DeKooning)
American artist–critic
• Paintings and portraits combine abstract expressionism and representational style; favorite subjects bullfighters, athletes in action, landscapes.
b. March 12, 1920 in New York, New York
d. February 01, 1989 in Southampton, New York

Willem DeKooning
American artist
• Abstract Expressionism leader, 1940s; known for distorted portraits of women.
b. April 24, 1904 in Rotterdam, Netherlands

(Ferdinand Victor) Eugene Delacroix
French artist
• Leading Romantic painter; noted for historical, colorful Moroccan scenes: *Liberty Leading the People*, 1831.
b. April 26, 1798 in Charenton, France
d. August 13, 1863 in Paris, France

Hippolyte Delaroche
(Paul Delaroche)
French artist
• Large historical paintings include *Joas Saved By Josabeth*, 1822.
b. 1797
d. 1856

Robert Delaunay
French artist
• Known for linking color with movement; works include *Ville de Paris*.
b. April 12, 1885 in Paris, France
d. October 25, 1941 in Montpellier, France

Sonia Delaunay-Terk
French artist–designer
• Noted for exuberant use of vibrant color, geometric designs.
b. November 14, 1885 in Gradizhsk, Russia
d. December 05, 1979 in Paris, France

Luca DellaRobbia
Italian sculptor
• Developed enameling technique of terra-cotta figures, c. 1440; started famed family workshop.
b. 1400 in Florence, Italy
d. February 23, 1482 in Florence, Italy

Philip James DeLoutherbourg
English artist–designer
• Oil painter, dramatic stage designer; introduced act-drops, invented moving peep-show.
b. October 31, 1740 in Strasbourg, Germany
d. March 11, 1812 in Chiswick, England

William Frend De Morgan
English artist–author
• Potter who made colored lusterware; popular novelist later in life: *Joseph Vance*, 1906; son of Augustus.
b. November 16, 1839 in London, England
d. January 15, 1917 in London, England

Charles Demuth
American artist
• Leader of the Precisionist school; known for watercolors, series of flowers, circuses.
b. November 08, 1883 in Lancaster, Pennsylvania
d. October 23, 1935 in Lancaster, Pennsylvania

Andre Derain
French artist
• Known for Fauvist paintings: *The Bathers*, 1907; refused to paint cubism.
b. June 1, 1880 in Chatou, France
d. September 1, 1954 in Chambourcy, France

Jose Ruiz DeRivera
American artist–sculptor
• Began exhibiting work, 1930, in museums, galleries.
b. September 18, 1904 in West Baton Rouge, Louisiana
d. March 21, 1985 in New York, New York

Narciso Virgilio Diaz de la Pena
French artist
• Landscape painter; best known for his scenes from forest of Fontainbleau.
b. 1807 in Bordeaux, France
d. 1876

Edwin W Dickinson
American artist
• Painted in Romantic style; never finished *The Fossil Hunters*, 1926-28.
b. October 11, 1891 in Seneca Falls, New York
d. December 02, 1978 in Cape Cod, Massachusetts

Richard Clifford Diebenkorn, Jr
American artist
• Exhibits held in museums, galleries; writings include *The Search for Meaning in Modern Art*, 1964.
b. April 22, 1922 in Portland, Oregon

Diane Claire Sorber Dillon
(Mrs Leo Dillon)
American author–illustrator
• Won Caldecott medal with husband, Leo, for illustrating children's tales *Ashanti to Zulu*, 1976.
b. March 13, 1933 in Glendale, California

Leo Dillon
American author–illustrator
• Co-illustrator with wife, Diane, of children's and science fiction books: *Why Mosquitoes Buzz in People's Ears*, 1975.
b. March 02, 1933 in Brooklyn, New York

Jim Dine
American artist
• Nonconformist works are in museums, one-man shows; wrote *Welcome Home Lovebirds*, 1969.
b. June 16, 1935 in Cincinnati, Ohio

Rudolph Dirks
American cartoonist
• One of founding fathers of American comics, created "Katzenjammer Kids," 1897.
b. February 26, 1877
d. April 2, 1968 in New York, New York

Walt(er Elias) Disney
(Retlaw Yensid pseud)
American cartoonist–producer
• Introduced Mickey Mouse in "Steamboat Willie," 1928; won 29 Oscars; opened Disneyland, 1955, creating family entertainment empire.
b. December 05, 1901 in Chicago, Illinois
d. December 15, 1966 in Los Angeles, California

Mark DiSuvero
American sculptor
• Abstract expressionist whose massive works of steel, wood beams include LA Tower of Peace, 1966, protesting Vietnam War.
b. September 18, 1933 in Shanghai, China

Otto Dix
German artist
• Realistic work depicted working class life, social criticism; banned by Nazis, WW II.
b. December 02, 1891 in Gera, Germany
d. June 25, 1969

Ed(ward) Benton Dodd
American cartoonist
• Cartoon strips include "Back Home Again," 1930-45; "Mark Trail," 1946–.
b. November 07, 1902 in Lafayette, Georgia

Mrs John Bruce (Sonora Louise Smart) Dodd
American author–artist
• Founder of Father's Day, first observed, 1910.
b. 1882 in Jenny Lind, Arkansas
d. March 22, 1978 in Spokane, Washington

Theo van Doesburg
(Christian Emil Marie Kupper)
Dutch artist
• With others founded group, de Stijl; published art review *De Stijl*, 1917.
b. 1883
d. 1931

Il Domenichino
(Domenico Zampieri)
Italian artist
• Major figure in the Baroque eclectic school; chief architect for Vatican, 1621-23; Naples, 1630-38.
b. October 21, 1581 in Bologna, Italy
d. April 06, 1641 in Naples, Italy

Veneziano Domenico
(Domenico di Bartolomeo da Venezia)
Italian artist
• A founder of Florentine school of painting; known for *St. Lucy Altarpiece*, Florence.
b. 1438 in Venice, Italy
d. 1461

Donatello
(Donatodi Niccolo di Betto Bardi)
Italian artist
• Considered finest sculptor of his century; masterpieces include *David; John the Evangelist*; mentor of Michelangelo.
b. 1386 in Florence, Italy
d. December 13, 1466 in Florence, Italy

Kees van Dongen
(Cornelius Theodorus Dongen)
French artist–illustrator
• Fauvist painter who did landscapes of Holland, Paris; noted for riotous use of color.
b. January 26, 1877 in Delfshaven, Netherlands
d. May 28, 1968 in Monte Carlo, Monaco

Thomas Aloysius Dorgan
American cartoonist–journalist
• Cartoons, sports columns in *San Francisco Bulletin*, 1892-1902; *NY Journal*, 1902-29; coined term "yes-man," 1913.
b. April 29, 1877 in San Francisco, California
d. 1929 in Great Neck, New York

Aaron Douglas
American artist
• Major figure in American Black art; numerous NYC murals depict black heritage.
b. 1899 in Topeka, Kansas
d. February 02, 1979 in Nashville, Tennessee

Sir Henry Doulton
English artist
• Joined father's pottery firm, 1835; introduced stoneware drainpipes, appliances, which made Doulton famous.
b. 1820 in England
d. 1897

Arthur Garfield Dove
American artist
• Paintings are of large masses of muted colors; worked in collage, nonobjective approach.
b. August 02, 1880 in Canandaigua, New York
d. November 23, 1946 in Huntington, New York

Dan(iel Blair) Dowling
American cartoonist
• Exaggerated, humorous political cartoons appeared in newspapers, 1940-73.
b. November 16, 1906 in O'Neill, Nebraska

Richard Doyle
English artist
• Regular contributor to *Punch* mag., 1843-50; drew endearing elfish figures in *In Fairyland;* uncle of Arthur Conan.
b. September 1824 in London, England
d. December 11, 1883 in London, England

Stanley Albert Drake
American cartoonist
• Created comic strip "The Heart of Juliet Jones," 1953–; illustrator for *Golf Digest* mag., 1969–.
b. November 09, 1921 in Brooklyn, New York

William Bryan DuBay
American artist–editor
• Editor, *Warren Comics*, 1972-76; created characters Creepy, Errie, Rook.
b. 1948 in San Francisco, California

Jean Dubuffet
French artist
• Post-WW II artist, known for primitive-style paintings, large-scale representational sculptures.
b. July 31, 1901 in Le Havre, France
d. May 12, 1985 in Paris, France

Duccio di Buoninsegna
Italian artist
• Founded Sienese School; noted for Maesta altarpiece, Siena church, 1308-11.
b. 1278 in Siena, Italy
d. 1319 in Siena, Italy

Marcel Duchamp
French artist
• Dadaist painter; *Nude Descending a Staircase*, 1912, among his most controversial works.
b. July 28, 1887 in Blainville, France
d. October 01, 1968 in Neuilly, France

Edmund Duffy
American cartoonist
• Won three Pulitzers, 1931, 1934, 1940, for political cartoons.
b. March 01, 1899 in Jersey City, New Jersey
d. September 13, 1962 in New York, New York

Charles Dufresne
French artist
• Prolific painter of exotic, Fauvist-cubist landscapes.
b. 1876 in Millemont, France
d. 1938 in Seyne-sur-Mer, France

Raoul (Ernest Joseph) Dufy
French artist
• Modernist painter, fabric designer; known for huge panel *History of Electricity*, at 1937 Paris Exhibition.
b. June 03, 1877 in Le Havre, France
d. March 23, 1953 in Forcalquier, France

Edmund Dulac
English artist
• Created fantastic, intricate scenes for fairy tales: *The Arabian Nights*; designed cornation stamps, 1937, 1953.
b. October 22, 1882 in Toulouse, France
d. May 25, 1953 in England

George Louis P B DuMaurier
English author–artist
• Satirized upper classes in *Punch* cartoons, 1864-96; wrote *Trilby*, 1894.
b. March 06, 1834 in Paris, France
d. October 08, 1896 in London, England

David Douglas Duncan
American photojournalist
• Covered most major events of past 35 yrs., including Japan's surrender to US aboard *USS Missouri*, 1945.
b. January 23, 1916 in Kansas City, Missouri

William Dunlap
American dramatist–artist
• Did portrait of George Washington; Wrote 65 plays: *History of American Theater*, 1832.
b. February 11, 1766 in Perth Amboy, New Jersey
d. September 28, 1839 in New York, New York

Alan Dunn
American cartoonist–artist
• With *New Yorker* mag. for over 40 yrs.
b. August 11, 1900 in Belmar, New Jersey
d. May 2, 1974 in New York, New York

Andre Dunoyer de Segonzac
French artist
• Leader in naturalistic tradition; painting subjects include boxers, dancers.
b. July 06, 1884 in France
d. September 17, 1974

Asher Brown Durand
American artist
• Co-founded Hudson River school of landscape painting with Thomas Cole.
b. August 21, 1796 in Jefferson, New Jersey
d. September 17, 1886 in Jefferson, New Jersey

Albrecht Durer
German artist
• Leading German Renaissance artist; excelled in engraving as well as painting; noted for religious themes.
b. May 21, 1471 in Nuremberg, Germany
d. April 06, 1528 in Nuremberg, Germany

Frank Duveneck
American artist–educator
• Noted for brushwork; defined planes of the face on canvas.
b. October 09, 1848 in Covington, Kentucky
d. January 03, 1919 in Cincinnati, Ohio

William Dyce
Scottish artist
• Historical, portrait painter of House of Parliament frescoes, 1848.
b. September 19, 1806 in Aberdeen, Scotland
d. February 14, 1864 in Streatham, England

Anthony van Dyck
Flemish artist
• Religious, portrait painter who was Ruben's pupil, court painter to England's Charles I, 1632.
b. 1599 in Antwerp, Belgium
d. 1641 in London, England

Thomas Eakins
American artist
• Realist painter known for sporting scenes, surgical operations, portraits.
b. July 25, 1844 in Philadelphia, Pennsylvania
d. June 25, 1916 in Philadelphia, Pennsylvania

Ralph Earle
(Ralph Earl)
American artist
• Itinerant, primitive painter known for Concord butterflies, stern portraits.
b. May 11, 1751 in Shrewsbury, Massachusetts
d. November 24, 1801 in Pendleton, South Carolina

Gus Edson
American cartoonist
• Cartoon characters include *Streaky*, 1933-35; *The Gumps*, 1935-66; *Dondi*, 1955-66.
b. September 2, 1901 in Stamford, Connecticut
d. September 26, 1966 in Stamford, Connecticut

Gerbrand van den Eeckhout
Dutch artist
• Genre, religious painter; pupil of Rembrandt: *Family of Darius*.
b. August 19, 1621 in Amsterdam, Netherlands
d. September 29, 1674 in Amsterdam, Netherlands

The Eight
(Arthur B Davies; William J Glackens; Robert Henri; Ernest Lawson; George Luks; Maurice Pendergast; Everett Shinn; John Sloan)
American artists
• Established "Ashcan School" of painting, circa 1907.

Alfred Eisenstaedt
American photojournalist
• Father of photojournalism whose photographs included more than 90 *Life* mag. covers.
b. December 06, 1898 in Dirschau, Prussia

Eliot Elisofon
American photographer–artist–filmmaker
• Master of color, black and white photography, renowned watercolor artist.
b. April 17, 1911 in Manhattan, New York
d. April 07, 1973 in New York, New York

Charles Loring Elliott
American artist
• Over 700 portraits include those of James E Freeman, Governor Hunt.
b. October 12, 1812 in Scipio, New York
d. August 25, 1868 in Albany, New York

Adam Elsheimer
(Adam Tedesco)
German artist
• Founder of modern landscape painting; works, chiefly done on copper, are usually religious, mythological.
b. March 18, 1578 in Frankfurt, Germany
d. December 1610 in Rome, Italy

Peter Henry Emerson
English photographer
• Pioneer in field; wrote classic, *Naturalistic Photography*, 1889.
b. 1856
d. 1936

Elizabeth Enright
American artist–author–illustrator
• Books for children include Newbery-winner *Thimble Summer*, 1939; adults include *The Moment Before the Rain*, 1959.
b. September 17, 1909 in Oak Park, Illinois
d. June 08, 1968

James Sydney Ensor, Baron
Belgian artist
• Considered most original artist of his time; forerunner of expressionism, surrealism; works include *The Entry of Christ into Brussels*, 1888.
b. April 13, 1860 in Ostend, Belgium
d. November 19, 1949 in Ostend, Belgium

Sir Jacob Epstein
English sculptor
• Known for peculiar rough-hewn style in bronze busts, Oscar Wilde's tomb in Paris.
b. August 09, 1880 in London, England
d. August 09, 1959 in London, England

Jimmy Ernst
American author–artist
• Son of Max Ernst; one of leading abstractionists in US.
b. June 24, 1920 in Cologne, Germany
d. February 06, 1984 in New York, New York

Kenneth Ernst
American cartoonist
• Known for clean, tasteful craftmanship; drew "Mary Worth"; "Clyde Beatty."
b. 1918 in Illinois

Max Ernst
German artist
• Co-founded Dadaist group, 1919; helped found Surrealist group, 1931; worked chiefly in sculpture.
b. April 02, 1891 in Cologne, Germany
d. April 01, 1976 in Paris, France

Erte
(Romain de Tirtoff)
Russian fashion designer–artist
• Prolific designer thought to epitomize the elegance of art deco; designed every *Harper's Bazaar* cover, 1915-36.
b. November 23, 1892 in Saint Petersburg, Russia
d. April 21, 1990 in Paris, France

Maurits Cornelis Escher
Dutch artist
• Surrealist; paintings mixed reality with symbolism; used math concepts in later works.
b. 1898
d. 1972 in Hilversum, Netherlands

Walker Evans
American photographer–journalist
• Writer, photographer, *Fortune* mag., 1945-65, known for pictures of Depression Era.
b. November 03, 1903 in Saint Louis, Missouri
d. April 1, 1975 in New Haven, Connecticut

Philip (Howard Francis Dixon) Evergood
American artist
• Produced realistic murals of Depression Era; noted for satiric pictures dealing with social causes.
b. October 26, 1901 in New York, New York
d. March 11, 1973 in Bridgewater, Connecticut

Moses Jacob Ezekiel
American sculptor
• Largely idealized busts include those of Eve, Homer, Christ in the Tomb; also did Arlington National Cemetery's Confederate Monument.
b. October 28, 1844 in Richmond, Virginia
d. March 27, 1917

Horst Faas
German photographer
• Photographer in Vietnam; won Pulitzer for spot news photography, 1972.
b. April 28, 1933 in Berlin, Germany

Carel Fabritius
Dutch artist
• Student of Rembrandt, influenced by Vermeer; paintings include *A View of Delft*, 1652; *The Goldfinch*, 1654.
b. 1622 in Netherlands
d. October 12, 1654 in Delft, Netherlands

Lee Harrison Falk
American cartoonist–author
• Created comic strips "Mandrake the Magician," 1934; "The Phantom," 1936.
b. 1915 in Saint Louis, Missouri

Jules Ralph Feiffer
American cartoonist–screenwriter
• Philosophizing satirist for *Village Voice*, 1956–; wrote screenplay *Carnal Knowledge*, 1971; won Obie, 1969; Pulitzer, 1986.
b. January 26, 1929 in New York, New York

Andreas Bernhard Lyonel Feininger
American photographer
• With *Life* mag., 1943-62; known for work in telephoto, close-up photography; noted for poetic views of cities.
b. December 27, 1906 in Paris, France

Lyonel Feininger
(Charles Adrian Feininger)
American artist–cartoonist
• Pioneer of modern American art whose unique style of dividing forms, space by segmented planes of color was influenced by cubism.
b. July 17, 1871 in New York, New York
d. January 13, 1956

Arthur Fellig
American photographer
• Black-and-white news photographer known for pictures of NYC violence, 1940s-50s.
b. July 12, 1899 in Zloczew, Austria
d. December 26, 1968 in New York, New York

Jose Antonio Fernandez-Muro
Argentine artist
• Abstract painter, member of Group of Concrete Artists, 1952; awarded Guggenheim, 1960.
b. March 01, 1920 in Madrid, Spain

Domenico Feti
Italian artist
• Religious artist influenced by Caravaggio, Ruben: *Six Sainted Martyrs*, 1613.
b. 1589 in Rome, Italy
d. 1623 in Venice, Italy

Anselm Feuerbach
German artist
• Romantic classicist painter famous for "Judgment of Paris," 1870.
b. September 12, 1829
d. January 04, 1880

Leonor Fini
Italian artist
• Noted theatrical designer, book illustrator; does sensual, surrealistic paintings of women.
b. August 3, 1918 in Buenos Aires, Argentina

John Fischetti
American editor–cartoonist
• Syndicated political cartoonist; won Pulitzer, 1969; wrote autobiography, *Zinga Za*, 1973.
b. September 27, 1916 in Brooklyn, New York
d. 1978 in New Haven, Connecticut

Eric Fischl
American artist
• Known for paintings that resemble giant movie stills; major exhibition, 1986, NYC's Whitney Museum.
b. March 09, 1948 in New York, New York

Bud (Harry Conway) Fisher
American cartoonist
• Created "Mutt and Jeff" comic strip, 1907.
b. April 03, 1885 in Chicago, Illinois
d. September 07, 1954 in New York, New York

Ham(mond Edward) Fisher
American cartoonist
• Created Joe Palooka comic strip.
b. September 24, 1900 in Wilkes-Barre, Pennsylvania
d. December 27, 1955 in New York, New York

Daniel R Fitzpatrick
American cartoonist
• His outspoken political drawings, syndicated from 1912-57, won Pulitzer, 1926, 1955.
b. March 05, 1891 in Superior, Wisconsin
d. May 18, 1969 in Saint Louis, Missouri

James Montgomery Flagg
American artist–author
• His WW I recruiting poster with Uncle Sam, modeled on himself, pointing finger, with caption "I Want You!" brought him fame.
b. June 18, 1877 in Pelham Manor, New York
d. May 27, 1960 in New York, New York

John Bernard Flannagan
American sculptor
• Renowned for animal sculptures: "Triumph of the Egg," 1941.
b. April 07, 1895 in Fargo, North Dakota
d. January 06, 1942 in New York, New York

John Flaxman
English artist
• Neoclassic Wedgwood pottery designer, 1775-87; known for line drawings of Homer's *Iliad*, *Odyssey*. 1793.
b. July 06, 1755 in York, England
d. December 07, 1826 in London, England

Max Fleischer
American cartoonist
• Created cartoon characters Betty Boop. Popeye.
b. July 19, 1883 in Vienna, Austria
d. September 11, 1972 in Los Angeles, California

Govert Flinck
Dutch artist
• Pupil of Rembrandt, noted for portraits, religious narratives: *Blessing of Jacob*.
b. January 25, 1615 in Cleves, Germany
d. February 02, 1660 in Amsterdam, Netherlands

James Royer Flora
American author–illustrator
• Self-illustrated children's books include *Grandpa's Ghost Stories*, 1978; *Wanda and the Bumbly Wizard*, 1980.
b. January 25, 1914 in Bellefontaine, Ohio

Sean Flynn
American photographer–actor–celebrity relative
• Son of Errol Flynn; disappeared in Vietnam covering war, 1970.
b. 1941
d. 1970

Jean-Michel Folon
Belgian artist–illustrator
• Designer of magazine covers, bold posters; did book of watercolors *The Eyewitness*, 1980.
b. March 01, 1934 in Uccle, Belgium

Hal (Harold Rudolf) Foster
American cartoonist
• Created "Prince Valiant" comic strip.
b. August 16, 1892 in Halifax, Nova Scotia
d. July 25, 1982 in Spring Hill, Florida

Jean Fouquet
French artist
• Works include portrait of Charles VII, illuminations for Chevalier's *Book of Hours*, 1450-60.
b. 1420 in Tours, France
d. 1480 in Tours, France

Fontaine Talbot Fox, Jr
American illustrator–cartoonist
• Created syndicated comic strip "Toonerville Folks," 1915-30s.
b. March 03, 1884 in Louisville, Kentucky
d. August 1, 1964 in Greenwich, Connecticut

Dana Fradon
American cartoonist
• Contributor to *New Yorker*, 1950–; known for cartoons satirizing local politics.
b. April 14, 1922 in Chicago, Illinois

Jean-Honore Fragonard
French artist–engraver
• Painted landscapes, elegant outdoor social affairs in Rococo style: *The Swing*, c. 1766.
b. April 05, 1732 in Grasse, France
d. August 22, 1806 in Grasse, France

Marcantonio Franceschini
Italian artist
• Last leader of Bolognese school; painted large frescoes, ceiling decorations.
b. April 05, 1648 in Bologna, Italy
d. December 14, 1729

Sam Francis
American artist
• Abstract expressionist painter, internationally exhibited.
b. July 25, 1923 in San Mateo, California

Helen Frankenthaler
(Mrs Robert Motherwell)
American artist
• Abstract expressionist; had numerous one-woman shows since 1950s.
b. December 12, 1928 in New York, New York

Antonio Frasconi
American artist–author
• Woodcut artist, illustrations in children's books: *See and Say*, 1955; designed commemorative stamps, 1963, 1968.
b. April 28, 1919 in Montevideo, Uruguay

James Earle Fraser
American sculptor
• Noted for Old West motifs; best-known sculpture: "The End of the Trail," 1898; designed buffalo nickel, many medals.
b. November 04, 1876 in Winona, Minnesota
d. October 11, 1953 in Westport, Connecticut

Frank Frazetta
American artist–cartoonist
• Drew Buck Rogers, Flash Gordon; known for Tarzan, Conan comic book covers.
b. February 09, 1928 in Brooklyn, New York

Daniel Chester French
American sculptor
• Among most famous pieces are "The Minute Man," Concord, MA, 1873; "Lincoln," Lincoln Memorial, Washington, DC, 1922.
b. April 2, 1850 in Exeter, New Hampshire
d. October 07, 1931 in Stockbridge, Massachusetts

Lucian Freud
English artist
• Prominent modern oil painter of nudes, still life, interiors.
b. December 08, 1922 in Berlin, Germany

William Freyse
American cartoonist
• Continued syndicated comic strip by Gene Ahern, "Our Boarding House," 1936-69.
b. 1899 in Detroit, Michigan
d. March 03, 1969 in Tucson, Arizona

Caspar David Friedrich
German artist
• Romantic landscape paintings had mystical tone, limited impact on art: *Man and Woman Gazing at the Moon.*
b. September 05, 1774 in Greifswald, Germany
d. May 07, 1840 in Dresden, Germany

William Edward Friese-Greene
(William Edward Green)
British inventor–photographer
• Built first practical movie camera, 1889; subject of film *The Magic Box,* 1951.
b. September 07, 1855 in Bristol, England
d. 1921 in London, England

Othon Friesz
French artist
• Designed Gobelin tapestry, *Peace.*
b. 1879 in Le Havre, France
d. January 11, 1949 in Paris, France

Toni Frissell
American photographer
• First to photograph formally dressed models outdoors; worked for top fashion magazines from 1931.
b. March 1, 1907 in New York, New York
d. April 17, 1988 in Saint James, New York

Roger Eliot Fry
English artist–critic
• Introduced modern French painters to English public; coined phrase, Post-Impressionists, 1910.
b. December 14, 1866 in London, England
d. September 09, 1934 in London, England

Louis Agassiz Fuertes
American ornithologist–artist
• Finely detailed paintings illustrate handbooks of birds in eastern, western US.
b. February 07, 1874 in Ithaca, New York
d. August 22, 1927

Harry Furniss
English cartoonist–illustrator
• Noted for political lampoons in *Punch,* 1880s-90s; illustrated works of Charles Dickens.
b. March 26, 1854 in Wexford, England
d. January 14, 1925 in Hastings, England

Henry Fuseli
Swiss artist–author
• Romantic painter of eerie imaginery including *The Nightmare,* 1781; active in Britain.
b. February 07, 1741 in Zurich, Switzerland
d. April 16, 1825 in London, England

Naum Pevsner Gabo
American sculptor
• Founded contemporary art movement, Constructivism; wrote *Realist Manifesto,* 1920.
b. August 05, 1890 in Briansk, Russia
d. August 23, 1977 in Waterbury, Connecticut

Thomas Gainsborough
English artist
• Painted elegant portraits, country children, pastoral subjects; well known for "Blue Boy," 1770.
b. May 14, 1727 in Sudbury, England
d. 1788 in London, England

Ron Galella
American photographer
• Famous for his pursuit to photograph Jacqueline Onassis.
b. January 1, 1931 in Bronx, New York

Frank Gallo
American artist
• Pop artist, sculptor; specializes in life-size figures of epoxy-type materials.
b. January 13, 1933 in Toledo, Ohio

Paul (Eugene Henri Paul) Gauguin
French artist
• Post-impressionist painter whose work is noted for massive simplified forms, impassive figures, exotic backgrounds.
b. June 07, 1848 in Paris, France
d. June 06, 1903 in Marquesas Islands

Giovanni Battista Gaulli
(Il Baciccio)
Italian artist
• Painted altarpieces, portraits: *Assumption of St. Francis Xavier,* in the Gesu, Rome.
b. 1639
d. 1709

Arnold Genthe
American journalist–photographer
• Known for pictures of San Francisco earthquake, presidents; wrote *As I Remember,* 1936.
b. January 08, 1869 in Berlin, Germany
d. August 08, 1942

Gentile da Fabriano
Italian artist
• Gothic-style painter; best-known works: *St. John the Baptist; Adoration of the Magi,* 1422.
b. 1370 in Fabriano, Italy
d. 1427 in Rome, Italy

Artemisia Gentileschi
Italian artist
• Painted portraits, colorful Biblical scenes including *Judith and Holofernes,* 1618; daughter of Orazia.
b. 1597 in Italy
d. 1651

Orazio Gentileschi
Italian artist
• Adopted Caravaggio's chiaroscuro style; court painter to England's Charles I, 1626; known for *The Annunciation,* 1623.
b. 1562
d. 1647

Dave Gerard
American cartoonist
• Drew syndicated comic strip, "Will-Yum," 1953-67.
b. June 18, 1909 in Crawfordsville, Indiana

Francois Gerard
French artist
• Court painter to Napoleon, Louis XVII; works include *Empress Josephine,* 1802.
b. May 04, 1770 in Rome, Italy
d. January 11, 1837 in Paris, France

Jean Louis Andre Theodore Gericault
French artist
• Painted bold romantic historical scenes; drew famous *Raft of the Medusa,* 1819.
b. September 26, 1791 in Rouen, France
d. January 26, 1824 in Paris, France

Lorenzo Ghiberti
Italian artist
• Sculpted north, east doors of the baptistry of Florence; portals called *Gates of Paradise.*
b. 1378 in Florence, Italy
d. December 01, 1455 in Florence, Italy

Domenico Ghirlandaio
(Domenico di Tommaso Bigordi)
Italian artist
• Among his noted works are wall frescoes in the Sistene Chapel, with Botticelli.
b. 1449 in Florence, Italy
d. January 11, 1494 in Florence, Italy

Alberto Giacometti
Swiss sculptor
• Known for sculptures of wiry, torment-ed figures: "Man Pointing," 1947.
b. October 1, 1901 in Stampa, Switzerland
d. January 11, 1966 in Chur, Switzerland

Kahlil George Gibran
American sculptor
• Exhibited paintings, 1949-52, life-sized steel sculpture, 1953–.
b. November 29, 1922 in Boston, Massachu-setts

Sir John Gilbert
English artist–illustrator
• Painted historical scenes; illustrated works of Shakespeare, Scott.
b. July 21, 1817 in Blackheath, England
d. October 05, 1897 in London, England

Eric Gill
English author–sculptor–engraver
• Did wood engravings for prestigious Golden Cockerel Press, from 1924; de-signed numerous typefaces.
b. February 22, 1882 in Brighton, England
d. November 18, 1940

James Gillray
English cartoonist
• Political cartoonist whose work covered Napoleonic War, c.1802; credited with introducing English style, format of car-toon to Europe.
b. 1757 in London, England
d. June 01, 1815 in London, England

Francoise Gilot
French author–artist
• Mistress of Pablo Picasso, 1946-53; had two children with him; wrote *Life with Picasso*, 1964.
b. November 26, 1921 in Neuilly-sur-Seine, France

Laura Gilpin
American photographer–author
• Known for photographic studies of Na-vaho Indians.
b. April 22, 1891 in Colorado Springs, Colo-rado
d. November 3, 1979 in Santa Fe, New Mexi-co

Luca Giordano
Italian artist
• Student of Ribera; lively, airy composi-tions combined Neapolitan, Venetian styles; painted ceiling of Escorial, Ma-drid, 1692.
b. 1632 in Naples, Italy
d. 1705

Francesco di Giorgio
Italian architect–artist–sculptor
• Paintings include *The Rape of Europa, The Chess Players.*
b. 1439 in Siena, Italy
d. 1502

Il Giorgione
(Giorgio Barbarelli; Giorgione da Castel-franco)
Italian artist
• Renaissance painter, chief master of Venetian school of his time; influenced contemporaries such as Titian: *The Tem-pest,* c. 1505.
b. 1477 in Venice, Italy
d. 1511

Giotto di Bondone
Italian artist–architect
• His paintings among the greatest in Italian, European art; designed campanile, "Giotti's Tower," at cathedral in Flor-ence.
b. 1266 in Vespignamo, Italy
d. January 08, 1337 in Florence, Italy

Giovanni di Paulo
Italian artist
• Major painter of Sienese school.
b. 1403
d. 1483

Francois Girardon
French sculptor
• Louis XIV's designer who produced decorative Apollo series for Versailles, 1670s; also designed Richelieu's tomb.
b. March 17, 1628 in Troyes, France
d. September 01, 1715 in Paris, France

Thomas Girtin
English artist
• Landscape watercolorist; introduced new techniques in shading, tinting: *The White House at Chelsea,* 1800.
b. February 18, 1775 in Southwark, England
d. November 09, 1802 in London, England

William James Glackens
American artist
• Impressionist, one of Eight-later Ash-can school: *Central Park-Winter, Prome-nade.*
b. March 13, 1870 in Philadelphia, Pennsyl-vania
d. May 22, 1938 in Westport, Connecticut

Albert L Gleizes
French artist
• Prominent cubist; founding member, Section d'Or group, 1912; works include *Harvest Threshing,* 1912.
b. 1881 in Creteil, France
d. June 23, 1953 in France

Hugo van der Goes
Flemish artist
• Best-known work: Portinari altarpiece, Uffizi, Florence, 1476.
b. 1440
d. 1482

Rube (Reuben Lucius) Goldberg
American cartoonist
• Created comic strips "Mike & Ike," "Lucifer Butts"; known for drawings of absurd mechanical contraptions.
b. July 04, 1883 in San Francisco, California
d. December 07, 1970 in New York, New York

William Golden
American artist
• Designed the CBS eye as TV trade-mark, 1951.
b. March 31, 1911 in New York, New York
d. October 23, 1959 in Stony Pointe, New York

Leon Albert Golub
American artist
• Figurative painter whose works have strong political overtones, 1976–.
b. January 23, 1922 in Chicago, Illinois

John Strickland Goodall
English artist–illustrator
• Children's books include *Adventures of Paddy Pork,* 1968; *The Story of Main Street,* 1987.
b. June 07, 1908 in Heacham, England

Robert Gordy
American artist
• Painted flat, whimsical works with re-peated patterns and abstracts of human heads.
b. October 14, 1933 in Jefferson Island, Lou-isiana
d. September 24, 1986 in New Orleans, Loui-siana

Edward St John Gorey
American author–illustrator
• Won Tony for costumes, set designs for *Dracula,* 1976; known for macabre illustrated children's books.
b. February 22, 1925 in Chicago, Illinois

Arshile Gorky
(Vosdanik Adoian)
American artist
• Abstract expressionist; works include "Dark Green Painting."
b. October 25, 1904 in Armenia
d. July 03, 1948 in New York, New York

Rene Goscinny
French cartoonist
• Co-founded French comic weekly, *Pi-lote,* 1959.
b. August 14, 1926 in Paris, France
d. November 05, 1977 in Paris, France

Adolph Gottlieb
American artist
• Founding member of The Ten, 1935, a group of abstract expressionists; works include *Voyager's Return*, 1946; *Expanding*, 1962.
b. March 14, 1903 in New York, New York
d. March 04, 1974 in New York, New York

Chester Gould
American cartoonist
• Cartoon comic strip pioneer who created "Dick Tracy," 1931.
b. November 2, 1900 in Pawnee, Oklahoma
d. May 11, 1985 in Woodstock, Illinois

Francisco Jose de Goya y Lucientes
Spanish artist
• Executed portraits, etchings, genre scenes; most noted for depictions of war: *Disasters of War* series, 1810-13.
b. March 3, 1746 in Aragon, Spain
d. April 18, 1828 in Bordeaux, France

Jan Josephszoon van Goyen
Dutch artist
• Created naturalistic landscapes; influenced later Dutch artists.
b. 1596 in Leiden, Netherlands
d. 1656 in The Hague, Netherlands

Benozzo Gozzoli
(Benozzo di Lese di Sandro)
Italian artist
• Frescoes include *The Journey of the Magi*, 1459-60.
b. 1420 in Florence, Italy
d. October 04, 1497 in Pistoria, Italy

Gordon Grant
American illustrator–artist
• Marine painter whose *Old Ironsides* hangs in Oval Office; best known for illustrations for Tarkington's *Penrod* stories.
b. June 07, 1875 in San Francisco, California
d. May 06, 1962 in New York, New York

Morris Cole Graves
American artist
• Noted for somber, expressionist bird paintings: *Blind Bird*, 1940.
b. August 28, 1910 in Fox Valley, Oregon

Nancy Stevenson Graves
American artist
• Known for sculptures of camels, camouflage paintings, lunar landscapes; work called imaginative, technically exact.
b. December 23, 1940 in Pittsfield, Massachusetts

Harold Lincoln Gray
American cartoonist
• Created comic strip "Little Orphan Annie," 1924, syndicated until 1968.
b. January 2, 1894 in Kankakee, Illinois
d. May 09, 1968 in La Jolla, California

El Greco
(Kyriakas Theotokopoulos)
Spanish artist
• Works include *Assumption of the Virgin*, 1577; *Burial of the Count of Orgaz*, 1586; noted for elongated figures, mystical mannerism style.
b. 1541 in Candia, Crete
d. April 06, 1614 in Toledo, Spain

Juan Gris
(Jose Victoriano Gonzales)
Spanish artist
• Major contributor to synthetic Cubism; works are of geometric form; spent most of life in France.
b. March 13, 1887 in Boulogne-sur-Seine, Spain
d. May 11, 1927 in Paris, France

Matt Groening
American cartoonist
• Created TV's first animated prime-time series, "The Simpsons," 1990.
b. February 15, 1954 in Portland, Oregon

Red (Charles Roger) Grooms
American artist
• Produces animated, experimental films; mixed-media constructions.
b. June 02, 1937 in Nashville, Tennessee

William Gropper
American artist
• Liberal cartoonist for *NY Herald Tribune*, 1919-35; executed murals for public buildings, illustrated his own children's books.
b. December 03, 1897 in New York, New York
d. January 06, 1977 in Manhasset, New York

Antoine Jean Gros
French artist
• Romantic painter of Napoleon's war campaigns: *Napoleon at Eylau*, 1808.
b. March 16, 1771 in Paris, France
d. June 26, 1835 in Meudon, France

George Ehrenfried Grosz
American artist
• Violent drawings were social critiques; series included *Ecce Homo*, 1922; *The Stickman*, 1947.
b. July 26, 1893 in Berlin, Germany
d. July 06, 1959 in Berlin, Germany (West)

John August Groth
American artist–journalist
• Illustrated, wrote introductions for books: *Grapes of Wrath*, 1947; *War and Peace*, 1961; *Exodus*, 1962.
b. February 26, 1908 in Chicago, Illinois
d. June 27, 1988 in New York, New York

Group of Seven
(Frank Carmichael; Lauren Harris; A(lexander) Y(oung) Jackson; Frank Johnston; Arthur Lismer; J(ames) E(dward) H(ervey) MacDonald; F(rederi) Canadian artists
• Canadian art movement inspired by northern Ontario landscapes; offically formed, exhibited, 1920.

Johnny (John Barton) Gruelle
American cartoonist–author
• Created series *Raggedy Ann*, 1918, *Raggedy Andy*, 1920.
b. December 24, 1880 in Arcola, Illinois
d. January 09, 1938 in Miami Beach, Florida

Matthias Grunewald
(Mathis Gothart Nithart)
German artist
• Considered finest painter of German Gothic school; masterpiece, *Isenheim Altarpiece*, 1515, is now in Colmar.
b. 1470 in Wurzburg, Germany
d. 1528 in Halle, Germany

Francesco Guardi
Italian artist
• Noted for imaginary landscapes, views of Venice.
b. October 05, 1712 in Venice, Italy
d. January 01, 1793 in Venice, Italy

Guercino
(Giovanni Francesco Barbieri; "The Squinting One")
Italian artist
• Religious, Baroque artist, painted illusionistic ceiling at Villa Ludovisi, Rome, 1621.
b. 1591 in Cento, Italy
d. 1666 in Bologna, Italy

Jules Guerin
American artist
• Painted murals in Lincoln Memorial, Washington, DC; LA state capitol.
b. 1866 in Saint Louis, Missouri
d. June 13, 1946 in Neptune, New Jersey

Guido of Sienna
(Guido da Siena)
Italian artist
• Considered innovator of Italian art; broke away from Byzantyne style; authenticity, date of painting *Madonna Hodetria* disputed.
b. 13thAD

Cathy Lee Guisewite
American cartoonist
• Created syndicated "Cathy" comic strip, 1976; wrote *The Cathy Chronicles*, 1978.
b. September 05, 1950 in Dayton, Ohio

Philip Guston
American artist
• Muralist for WPA projects, 1936-40, developed into abstract expressionist; works include *Altar*, 1953.
b. June 27, 1913 in Montreal, Quebec
d. June 07, 1980 in Woodstock, New York

Hans Christoph Haacke
German artist–sculptor
• Controversial graphic artist known for visual attacks on society; had first one-man show in US, 1986.
b. August 12, 1936 in Cologne, Germany

Harry William Haenigsen
American cartoonist
• Created comic strips "Our Bell," 1939-66; "Penny," 1943-70.
b. July 14, 1902 in New York, New York

Frans Hals
Dutch artist
• Famed portraitist known for characterization: *Laughing Cavalier*.
b. 1580 in Antwerp, Belgium
d. August 26, 1666

Philippe Halsman
American photographer
• Noted for honest realism in portraits; has over 100 *Life* covers to credit.
b. May 02, 1906 in Riga, Russia
d. June 25, 1979 in New York, New York

William Hamilton
American cartoonist–author
• *New Yorker* cartoonist, 1965–; wrote syndicated "Now Society" column since 1973.
b. June 02, 1939 in Palo Alto, California

Frank Hampson
English cartoonist–author
• Created science fiction cartoon character Dan Dare, 1950.
b. December 21, 1918 in Manchester, England
d. July 08, 1985 in Surrey, England

William Denby Hanna
(Hanna and Barbera)
American cartoonist
• With Joseph Barbera, created cartoons "Yogi Bear," "The Flintstones."
b. July 14, 1910 in Melrose, New Mexico

Chester Harding
American artist
• Portraitist; popular in London, Boston; sitters included John Marshall, 1828.
b. September 01, 1792 in Conway, Massachusetts
d. April 01, 1866 in Boston, Massachusetts

Keith Haring
American artist
• Graffiti artist known for drawings in NYC subways; died of AIDS.
b. May 04, 1958 in Kutztown, Pennsylvania
d. February 16, 1990 in New York, New York

Fred Harman
American cartoonist
• Created syndicated "Red Ryder" comic strips for 25 yrs.
b. February 09, 1902 in Saint Joseph, Missouri
d. January 02, 1982 in Phoenix, Arizona

Hugh Harman
American cartoonist
• Created *Looney Tunes* and *Merry Melodies* cartoon series.
b. 1903 in Pagosa Springs, Colorado
d. November 26, 1982 in Chatsworth, California

William Michael Harnett
American artist
• Master of Trompe L'oeil (Fool the Eye); still life works include *After the Hunt*.
b. August 1, 1848 in County Cork, Ireland
d. October 29, 1892 in New York, New York

Henri Harpignies
French artist
• Landscape painter of Barbizon School; in first Impressionist exhibition, 1874.
b. 1819 in Valenciennes, France
d. 1916 in Saint-Prive, France

Lauren Harris
(Group of Seven)
Canadian artist
• Painted simplified Canadian landscapes.
b. October 23, 1885 in Brantford, Ontario
d. January 29, 1970 in Vancouver, British Columbia

John(ny Lewis) Hart
American cartoonist
• Draws "BC," 1958–; "The Wizard of Id," 1964–.
b. February 18, 1931 in Endicott, New York

Marsden Hartley
American artist
• Painted still-lifes, harsh landscapes of Maine, US Southwest; used flat, somber forms.
b. January 04, 1877 in Lewiston, Maine
d. September 02, 1943 in Ellsworth, Maine

Hans Hartung
French artist
• Early abstract expressionist; black splashes reminiscent of Japanese calligraphy.
b. September 21, 1904 in Leipzig, Germany
d. December 07, 1989 in Antibes, France

Suzuki Harunobu
Japanese artist
• Master of woodblock printing; perfected brocade painting; admired by Degas in 19th c.
b. 1718 in Edo, Japan
d. 1770 in Edo, Japan

Childe Hassam
American artist
• Major American Impressionist; known for NYC, New England scenes.
b. October 17, 1859 in Dorchester, Massachusetts
d. August 27, 1935 in East Hampton, New York

Jimmy Hatlo
American cartoonist
• Created comic character Little Iodine.
b. September 01, 1898 in Providence, Rhode Island
d. November 3, 1963 in Carmel, California

Hugh Haynie
American cartoonist
• Liberal political cartoonist, *Louisville Courier-Journal;* syndicated with Los Angeles Times, 1958–.
b. February 06, 1927 in Reedville, Virginia

Stanley William Hayter
English artist
• Pioneer of graphic art; influenced Picasso, Miro; founded print shop, 1927.
b. December 27, 1901 in London, England
d. May 04, 1988 in Paris, France

Erich Heckel
German artist
• Expressionist; a founder of Die Bruecke school of painting, 1905; art denounced by Nazis.
b. July 31, 1883 in Dobeln, Germany
d. January 27, 1970 in Radolfzell, Germany (West)

Jan Davidsz de Heem
Dutch artist
• Known for realistic still lifes, portraits: *Still Life with Books*, 1628.
b. 1606 in Utrecht, Netherlands
d. 1684 in Antwerp, Belgium

Peter (Clarence Peter) Helck
American artist–illustrator
• Automobiles serve as painting subjects; entered illustrators Hall of Fame, 1968.
b. June 17, 1893 in New York, New York

Al Held
American artist
• Paintings developed from abstract expressionism to massive black and white geometrics: *Albany Mural*, 1971.
b. October 12, 1928 in New York, New York

John Held, Jr
American cartoonist–illustrator
• His line drawings captured spirit of "flaming youth" and "flappers" during 1920s.
b. January 1, 1889 in Salt Lake City, Utah
d. March 02, 1958 in Belmar, New Jersey

Jean Helion
French artist
• Pioneer in abstract school of painting, 1929-39; later works tended toward reality.
b. April 21, 1904 in Coyterne, France
d. October 27, 1987 in Paris, France

Jean Jacques Henner
French artist
• Drew historical subjects, female portraits, sensuous nudes in Italian settings: "Sleeping Bather," 1863.
b. 1829 in Bernweiler, Alsace
d. 1905 in Paris, France

Robert Henri
American artist
• A major influence on group of now-famous artists known as the Ashcan School.
b. June 25, 1865 in Cincinnati, Ohio
d. July 12, 1929 in New York, New York

Barbara Hepworth, Dame
English sculptor
• Designed large geometric shapes from wood, stone; introduced the "hole," painted hollows to abstract sculpture.
b. January 1, 1903 in Wakefield, England
d. May 2, 1975 in Saint Ives, England

Herblock
(Herbert Lawrence Block)
American cartoonist
• Political cartoonist, Washington *Post*, 1946-; won Pulitzers, 1942, 1954, 1979; coined term McCarthyism, 1950.
b. October 13, 1909 in Chicago, Illinois

George Herriman
American cartoonist
• Created cartoon character Krazy Kat.
b. August 22, 1880 in New Orleans, Louisiana
d. April 25, 1944 in Hollywood, California

Harry Hershfield
American cartoonist
• Created comic strip Abie the Agent.
b. October 13, 1885 in Cedar Rapids, Iowa
d. December 15, 1974 in New York, New York

Sol Hess
American cartoonist
• Founded cartoon strip "The Nebbs," 1923.
b. October 14, 1872 in Northville, Illinois
d. December 31, 1941 in Chicago, Illinois

Eva Hesse
German artist–sculptor
• Major conceptualist sculptor; created disquieting hanging modular forms.
b. January 11, 1936 in Hamburg, Germany
d. May 29, 1970 in New York, New York

Edward Hicks
American artist
• Quaker folk painter remembered for beloved *The Peaceable Kingdom*.
b. April 04, 1780 in Attleboro, Pennsylvania
d. August 23, 1849 in Newtown, Pennsylvania

Nicholas Hilliard
English artist
• Best known for miniature portraits of Queen Elizabeth I set in jeweled lockets.
b. 1537 in Exeter, England
d. 1619

Lewis Wickes Hine
American photographer
• Noted for photographs of Ellis Island immigrants, 1905.
b. September 26, 1874 in Oshkosh, Wisconsin
d. November 03, 1940 in Hastings-on-Hudson, New York

Ando Hiroshige
Japanese artist
• Member, Ukiyo-e school; master of colored woodcut; noted for landscapes which influenced European impressionists.
b. 1797
d. 1858

Al(bert) Hirschfeld
American cartoonist–artist–author
• Well-known theatrical caricaturist with *NY Times*, 1925-.
b. June 21, 1903 in Saint Louis, Missouri

Russell Hoban
American artist–author
• Writes children's books: *The Atomic Submarine; Bedtime for Frances*, 1960; adult fiction includes *Riddley Walker*, 1986.
b. February 04, 1925 in Lansdale, Pennsylvania

Meindert Hobbema
Dutch artist
• Last of 17th-c. Dutch landscapists; most famous work: *The Avenue at Middleharnia*, 1689.
b. October 31, 1638 in Netherlands
d. December 07, 1709 in Netherlands

David Hockney
English artist
• Graphic, pop artist whose early success came with a set of satirical etchings: *The Rake's Progress*, 1963; books include *Paper Pools*, 1980.
b. July 09, 1937 in Bradford, England

Ferdinand Hodler
Swiss artist
• Post-Impressionist; used parallelism compositions; awarded Gold Medal, 1900 Paris World's Fair.
b. March 14, 1853 in Bern, Switzerland
d. May 19, 1918 in Geneva, Switzerland

Bill (William) Hoest
American cartoonist
• Created syndicated cartoons "The Lockhorns," 1968; "Agatha Crumm," 1977.
b. February 07, 1926 in Newark, New Jersey
d. November 07, 1988 in New York, New York

Karl Hofer
German artist
• Expressionist, known for emaciated mannequin figures.
b. 1878 in Karlsruhe, Germany
d. April 03, 1955 in Berlin, Germany (West)

Sydney Hoff
American illustrator–author
• Cartoonist for syndicated comic strip, "Laugh It Off," 1957-71; children's book illustrator: *Danny and the Dinosaur*, 1958.
b. September 04, 1912 in New York, New York

Malvina Hoffman
American sculptor
• Her greatest achievement: group of 101 life-size bronze statues, *Races of Mankind*, for the Field Museum, Chicago, 1930-35.
b. June 15, 1887 in New York, New York
d. July 1, 1966 in New York, New York

Hans Hofmann
German artist
• His paintings inspired Abstract Expressionism movement.
b. March 21, 1880 in Weissenburg, Germany
d. February 17, 1966 in New York, New York

Burne Hogarth
American cartoonist
• Created, drew "Tarzan," 1937-50; pres., Pendragon Press, 1975-79.
b. November 25, 1911 in Chicago, Illinois

William Hogarth
English artist–engraver
• Engraved series of morality scenes: *Rake's Progress*, 1735; *Marriage a la Mode*, 1745.
b. November 1, 1697 in London, England
d. October 26, 1764 in London, England

Hans Holbein, the Younger
German artist
• Called one of world's greatest portraitists; subjects included Erasmus, Henry VIII, Sir Thomas More; son of Hans the Elder.
b. 1497 in Augsburg, Germany
d. 1543 in London, England

Bill Holman
American cartoonist
• Created, drew comic strip "Smokey Stover," 1935-75.
b. 1903 in Crawfordsville, Indiana
d. February 27, 1987 in New York, New York

Winslow Homer
American artist
• Excelled in watercolors of seascapes, including *Breaking Storm, Maine Coast.*
b. February 24, 1836 in Boston, Massachusetts
d. September 29, 1910 in Prouts Neck, Maine

Edward Hopper
American artist
• Known for starkly realistic scenes of city streets, theater interiors, lunch counters, etc.: "Early Sunday Morning," 1930.
b. July 22, 1882 in Nyack, New York
d. May 15, 1967 in New York, New York

John Hoppner
English artist
• Portrait painter to Prince of Wales, 1789; said to be illegitimate son of George III.
b. April 04, 1758 in London, England
d. January 23, 1810

Horst P(aul) Horst
American photographer
• Fashion photographer for *Vogue* mag., 1932–.
b. August 14, 1906 in Weissenfels, Germany

Eric J Hosking
English ornithologist–photographer
• One of his many self-illustrated bird books: *British Birds*, 1961-76.
b. October 02, 1909 in London, England

Harriet Goodhue Hosmer
American sculptor
• Her most popular statue: *Puck*, of which she made 30 copies.
b. October 09, 1830 in Watertown, Massachusetts
d. February 21, 1908 in Watertown, Massachusetts

Jean Antoine Houdon
French sculptor
• Neoclassicist; did busts of Voltaire, Thomas Jefferson, George Washington, Napoleon I.
b. March 2, 1741 in Versailles, France
d. July 15, 1828 in Paris, France

Arthur Hughes
English artist–illustrator
• Pre-Raphaelite whose paintings are characterized by detail, bright palette: *Home from the Sea*, 1856; *The Long Engagement*, 1859.
b. January 27, 1832 in London, England
d. December 22, 1915 in Kew Green, England

Berta Hummel
(Sister Maria Innocentia)
German artist
• Hummel figurines inspired by her drawings; international industry by 1935.
b. 1909 in Massing, Bavaria
d. 1946

Friedensreich Hundertwasser
(Friedrich Stowasser real name)
Austrian artist
• Abstract painter who developed grammar of vision theory: *Regenstag* series.
b. December 15, 1928 in Vienna, Austria

Holman (William Holman) Hunt
English artist
• A founder of pre-Raphaelite Brotherhood, 1848; painted *Light of the World*, 1854.
b. April 02, 1827 in London, England
d. September 07, 1910 in London, England

William Morris Hunt
American artist
• Portraitist; introduced Millet, French Barbizon school to US; brother of Richard Morris.
b. March 31, 1824 in Brattleboro, Vermont
d. September 08, 1879 in Isles of Shoals, Vermont

Clementine Hunter
American artist
• One of the South's most important folk artists; known for primitive visions of rural life.
b. January 19, 1887 in Natchitoches, Louisiana
d. January 01, 1988 in Natchitoches, Louisiana

Daniel Huntington
American artist
• Works include *Mercy's Dream, The Sibyl;* portraits of presidents Lincoln, Van Buren.
b. October 14, 1816 in New York, New York
d. 1906 in New York, New York

George Hurrell
American photographer
• Noted for classic black and white shots of legendary Hollywood Stars, 1920s-50s.
b. 1904 in Cincinnati, Ohio

Leslie Gilbert Illingworth
Welsh cartoonist
• Cartoonist for *Daily Mail*, 1939-68.
b. September 02, 1902 in Barry, South Wales
d. 1979

Robert Indiana
(Robert Clarke)
American artist
• Creates art out of words; called designer of trivia.
b. September 13, 1928 in New Castle, Indiana

Jean Auguste Dominique Ingres
French artist
• Famed Draughtsman; did portraits, sensual nudes in neoclassic linear style: *Madame Riviere*, 1806.
b. August 29, 1780 in Montauban, France
d. January 13, 1867 in Paris, France

James Merritt Ives
(Currier and Ives)
American artist
• Partner, from 1857, with Nathaniel Currier, Currier and Ives Lithograph Publishers.
b. March 05, 1824 in New York, New York
d. January 03, 1895 in Rye, New York

Ub(be) Iwerks
American cartoonist
• Developed character of Mickey Mouse for Walt Disney, 1927; won Oscars, 1959, 1965.
b. March 24, 1901 in Kansas City, Missouri
d. July 08, 1971

A(lexander) Y(oung) Jackson
(Group of Seven)
Canadian artist
• Co-founder, Group of Seven, 1920; drew rural Quebec arctic scenes.
b. October 03, 1882 in Montreal, Quebec
d. April 06, 1974 in Kleinburg, Ontario

John Adams Jackson
American sculptor
• Best known for busts including Musidora, 1873; Hylas, 1875.
b. November 05, 1825 in Bath, Maine
d. August 3, 1879 in Pracchia, Italy

William Henry Jackson
American artist–photographer
• Best known for photographic record of development of West.
b. April 04, 1843 in Keeseville, New York
d. June 3, 1942 in New York, New York

Albert Jaegers
American sculptor
• Known for busts of marble, bronze; commissioned to do statue of Baron von Steuben by US government.
b. March 28, 1868 in Elberfeld, Germany
d. July 22, 1925

Allan Jaffee
American cartoonist–author
• Illustrator for *Mad* magazine; created their "Fold-In."
b. March 13, 1921 in Savannah, Georgia

Philip Duane Jamison, Jr
American artist
• Realistic watercolorist, known for flowers, interiors, ME landscapes.
b. July 03, 1925 in Philadelphia, Pennsylvania

John Wesley Jarvis
American artist
• Noted for full-length portraits of military heroes; nephew of John Wesley.
b. 1781 in South Shields, England
d. January 14, 1839

Paul Jenkins
American artist
• Noted for "pouring" pigments on floor canvasses; wrote *Painters Country*, 1958.
b. July 12, 1923 in Kansas City, Missouri

Alfred Julio Jensen
Artist
• Did bright, checkerboard works inspired by architecture, mathematical themes.
b. December 11, 1903 in Guatemala City, Guatemala
d. April 04, 1981 in Livingston, New Jersey

Augustus Edwin John
British artist
• Noted for portraits of celebrities including Shaw, Yeats; remembered as nonconformist.
b. January 04, 1878 in Tenby, Wales
d. October 31, 1961 in Fordingbridge, England

Gwendolyn Mary John
Welsh artist
• Painted interiors, austere female portraits; Whistler's pupil.
b. 1876 in Haverfordwest, Wales
d. 1939 in Dieppe, France

Jasper Johns, Jr
American artist
• Pop artist known for using flags, letters, numbers in work.
b. May 15, 1930 in Augusta, Georgia

Crockett Johnson
(David Johnson Leisk)
American cartoonist–author
• Created comic strip "Barnaby," 1941-62; author, illustrator of several children's books.
b. October 2, 1906 in New York, New York
d. July 11, 1975 in Norwalk, Connecticut

Eastman Johnson
American artist
• Painted genre pictures of black life in the South, portraits of presidents, authors.
b. July 29, 1824 in Lovell, Maine
d. April 05, 1906 in New York, New York

Joshua Johnson
American artist
• Former slave; self-taught portrait painter.
b. 1796
d. 1824

Frances Benjamin Johnston
American photographer
• Pioneer in photojournalism; took photos of White House interior, 1893.
b. January 15, 1864 in Grafton, West Virginia
d. May 16, 1952 in New Orleans, Louisiana

Frank H Johnston
(Group of Seven)
Canadian artist
• Landscape painter, illustrator; apathetic member, Group of Seven, 1916-22.
b. June 19, 1888 in Toronto, Ontario
d. July 1, 1949

Chuck Jones
American cartoonist
• Animation director, Warner Brothers; created characters Road Runner, Pepe Le Pew, Wiley Coyote.
b. September 21, 1912 in Spokane, Washington

Joseph John (Joe) Jones
American artist
• Self-taught landscape painter, lithographer, muralist; did mural for ocean liner *Independence*.
b. April 07, 1909 in Saint Louis, Missouri
d. April 09, 1963 in Morristown, New Jersey

Thomas Hudson Jones
American sculptor
• Best-known works include "Tomb of the Unknown Soldier," Arlington National Cemetery.
b. July 24, 1892 in Buffalo, New York
d. November 04, 1969 in Hyannis, Massachusetts

Johan Barthold Jongkind
Dutch artist
• Juxtaposed strokes of unmixed colors to illustrate effects of light; helped develop Impressionism.
b. June 03, 1819 in Lattrop, Netherlands
d. February 09, 1891 in Cote-Saint-Andre, Netherlands

Jacob Jordaens
Flemish artist
• Known for baroque religious, historical paintings: *Jesus Among the Doctors*, 1663.
b. May 19, 1593 in Antwerp, Belgium
d. October 18, 1678 in Antwerp, Belgium

Roy Braxton Justus
American editor–cartoonist
• Syndicated, political cartoonist, Washington, DC, since 1927.
b. May 16, 1901 in Avon, South Dakota
d. 1984

Charles William Kahles
American cartoonist
• Innovative comic strips include first suspense serial; first superhero, Hairbreadth Harry, 1906.
b. January 12, 1878 in Lengfurt, Germany
d. January 21, 1931

Frida Kahlo
(Mrs Diego Rivera)
Mexican artist
• Majority of paintings are self-portraits; biography *Frida* written by Hayden Herrera.
b. 1919 in Coyoacan, Mexico
d. 1954 in Coyoacan, Mexico

Jacob Kainen
American artist
• Works span four decades, range from etchings, lithographs to oils and geometric abstractions.
b. December 07, 1909 in Waterbury, Connecticut

Willem Kalf
Dutch artist
• Genre, still-life painter influenced by Vermeer: *Peasant Interior*.
b. 1619 in Rotterdam, Netherlands
d. 1693 in Amsterdam, Netherlands

Max Kalish
Polish sculptor
• Commissioned, 1944, to create bronze statues of WW II personalities.
b. March 01, 1891 in Valojen, Poland
d. March 18, 1945 in New York, New York

Wassily Kandinsky
Russian artist
• A founder of modern abstract art; started Blue Rider group, 1911-14; Bauhaus teacher, 1921-33; noted for bright colors, geometric abstractions.
b. December 04, 1866 in Moscow, Russia
d. December 17, 1944 in Paris, France

Motonobu Kano
Japanese artist
• Founder, Motonobu school which subordinated color to design; celebrated for exquisite landscapes, screens, murals.
b. 1476
d. 1559

Allan Kaprow
American artist
• Pioneer in performance art; known for expansionistic works called "Happenings"; "Activities."
b. August 23, 1927 in Atlantic City, New Jersey

Bernard Karfiol
American artist
• Post-impressionist painter of children, interiors, nudes.
b. May 06, 1886 in Budapest, Hungary
d. August 16, 1952 in New York, New York

Yousuf Karsh
Canadian photographer–journalist
• Best known for photos of Winston Churchill, other famous people; wrote *Faces of Our Time*, 1971.
b. December 23, 1908 in Mardin, Armenia

Bil Keane
American cartoonist
• Creator of the "Family Circus," 1960–.
b. October 05, 1922 in Philadelphia, Pennsylvania

Charles Samuel Keene
English artist
• Illustrator for *Punch*, 1851-91; satirized middle-classes.
b. August 1, 1823 in Hornsey, England
d. January 04, 1891 in London, England

William Keith
American artist
• Prolific painter of colorful CA landscapes; 2,000 works destroyed in 1906 fire.
b. 1839 in Aberdeen, Scotland
d. 1911 in Berkeley, California

Ellsworth Kelly
American artist
• Painter, sculptor known for irregular geometric forms in bright colors on huge canvases.
b. May 31, 1923 in Newburgh, New York

Walt Kelly
American cartoonist
• Created comic strip "Pogo," 1943, nationally syndicated, 1949.
b. August 25, 1913 in Philadelphia, Pennsylvania
d. October 18, 1973 in Hollywood, California

Edward W(indsor) Kemble
American cartoonist–illustrator
• Political cartoonist, book illustrator; noted for sensitive Negro cartoons.
b. January 18, 1861 in Sacramento, California
d. September 19, 1933 in Ridgefield, Connecticut

David Hume Kennerly
American photographer
• Personal photographer to Gerald Ford, 1974-77; won Pulitzer, 1972, for feature photography of Vietnam war.
b. March 09, 1947 in Roseburg, Oregon

Corita Kent
(Frances Kent)
American artist
• Best known for designing "Love" postage stamp.
b. November 2, 1918 in Fort Dodge, Iowa
d. September 18, 1986 in Boston, Massachusetts

Rockwell Kent
(William Hogarth Jr; "RK")
American artist
• Noted for his stark dramatic lithographs, exotic landscapes.
b. June 21, 1882 in Tarrytown, New York
d. March 13, 1971 in Plattsburg, New York

Andre Kertesz
American photographer
• Pioneered use of 35-mm camera in photojournalism.
b. July 02, 1894 in Budapest, Hungary
d. September 27, 1985 in New York, New York

Hank (Henry King) Ketcham
American cartoonist
• Created comic strip "Dennis the Menace," 1952.
b. March 14, 1920 in Seattle, Washington

Ted (Theodore) Key
American cartoonist
• Created "Hazel," appeared in *Saturday Evening Post*, 1943-69; syndicated, 1969–.
b. August 25, 1912 in Fresno, California

Thomas De Keyser
Dutch artist
• Outstanding Dutch portrait painter prior to Rembrandt: *Burgomasters of Amsterdam*.
b. 1596 in Amsterdam, Netherlands
d. 1667 in Amsterdam, Netherlands

Anselm Karl Albert Kiefer
German artist
• Noted for multimedia works of varied, complex subjects, including Nazism.
b. March 08, 1945 in Donaueschingen, Germany

Al Kilgore
American cartoonist
• Drew "Bullwinkle" comic strip; co-author *Laurel and Hardy*.
b. December 19, 1983 in Newark, New Jersey
d. August 15, 1983 in New York, New York

Frank King
American cartoonist
• Creator of comic strip "Gasoline Alley."
b. April 09, 1883 in Cashon, Wisconsin
d. June 24, 1969 in Winter Park, Florida

Warren Thomas King
American cartoonist
• Editorial cartoonist, *NY Daily News*, 1955-77.
b. January 03, 1916 in Queens, New York
d. February 09, 1978

Dong Moy Shu Kingman
(Tsang King-Man)
American artist
• Watercolorist; illustrator of children's books; has contributed artwork to several films including *Lost Horizon*, 1973.
b. March 31, 1911 in Oakland, California

Jack Kirby
American cartoonist
• Created numerous comic book heroes: *Captain America*, 1951; *Fantastic Four*, 1961.
b. August 28, 1917 in New York, New York

Rollin Kirby
American cartoonist
• Pulitzer-winning political cartoons highlighted by attacks on establishment.
b. September 04, 1876 in Galva, Illinois
d. May 08, 1952 in New York, New York

Ernst Ludwig Kirchner
(L de Marsalle pseud)
German artist
• German expressionist; did street scenes, landscapes of vibrant color, distorted forms: "Street, Berlin," 1907.
b. May 06, 1880 in Aschaffenburg, Germany
d. June 15, 1938 in Davos, Switzerland

Paul Klee
Swiss artist
• Abstract painter noted for fantastic shapes, exotic colors.
b. December 18, 1879 in Bern, Switzerland
d. June 29, 1940 in Muralto, Switzerland

Gustav Klimt
Austrian artist
• Founded Vienna Secession school of painting, 1897.
b. July 04, 1862 in Vienna, Austria
d. February 06, 1918 in Vienna, Austria

Franz Joseph Kline
American artist
• Abstract painter, noted for huge scale black and white compositions; introduced color into later works.
b. May 23, 1919 in Wilkes-Barre, Pennsylvania
d. May 13, 1962 in New York, New York

Max Klinger
German artist
• Produced imaginative etchings, grandiose scale paintings, polychromatic statues.
b. February 18, 1857 in Leipzig, Germany
d. July 05, 1920 in Grossjena, Germany

Karl (Otto Karl) Knaths
American artist
• Abstractionist with unique cubist style; known for still-lifes, Cape Cod landscapes.
b. October 21, 1891 in Eau Claire, Wisconsin
d. March 09, 1971 in Hyannis, Massachusetts

Sir Godfrey Kneller
(Gottfried Kniller)
British artist
• Became leading portraitist in England, after 1675; founded first English academy of painting, 1711; painted 10 reigning monarchs.
b. August 08, 1646 in Lubeck, Germany
d. November 07, 1723 in London, England

H(arold) H Knerr
American cartoonist
• Drew syndicated comic strip, "Katzenjammer Kids," 1914-49.
b. 1883 in Bryn Mawr, Pennsylvania
d. July 08, 1949 in New York, New York

John Koch
American artist
• Prize-winning, self-taught painter of elegant Manhattan interiors, celebrities.
b. August 16, 1909 in Toledo, Ohio
d. April 19, 1978 in New York, New York

Oskar Kokoschka
Austrian artist–author
• Expressionist painter; work typified by use of symbolism, distortion; helped found German expressionist drama through melodramatic plays.
b. March 01, 1886 in Austria
d. February 22, 1980 in Montreux, Switzerland

Kathe Schmidt Kollwitz
German artist
• Prints conveyed social justice themes: *The Peasant War*.
b. July 08, 1867 in Konigsberg, Germany
d. April 22, 1945 in Dresden, Germany

Edward Benjamin Koren
American cartoonist–educator
• Known for woolly characters in *New Yorker* cartoons, 1962–; illustrator of numerous books.
b. December 13, 1935 in New York, New York

Ogata Korin
Japanese artist
• Finest painter of decorative style started by Koetsu, Sotatso: *God of the Wind*.
b. 1658 in Japan
d. 1716

Lee Krasner
(Mrs Jackson Pollock)
American artist
• Abstract expressionist whose paintings were characterized by bold, outlined images.
b. October 27, 1908 in Brooklyn, New York
d. June 19, 1984 in New York, New York

Fritz Kredel
American artist–illustrator
• Prestigious illustrator of children's classics, limited editions, club vols.
b. February 08, 1900
d. June 1, 1973 in New York, New York

Leon Kroll
American artist
• Landscape, portrait painter, known for his nudes; created mosaic dome at US Military Cemetery, Omaha Beach, France.
b. December 06, 1884 in New York, New York
d. October 25, 1974 in Gloucester, Massachusetts

Edward Daniel Kuekes
American artist–cartoonist
• Won Pulitzer for cartoon of irony of soldiers too young to vote fighting in Korea, 1953.
b. February 02, 1901 in Pittsburgh, Pennsylvania
d. January 13, 1987 in Oklahoma City, Oklahoma

Yasuo Kuniyoshi
American artist
• Noted for paintings of women, figure studies, still lifes, carnival scenes.
b. September 01, 1893 in Okayama, Japan
d. May 14, 1953

Frank (Frantisek) Kupka
Czech artist
• Pioneer in abstract movement called Orphism; known for satirical drawings, caricatures appearing in French periodicals.
b. September 03, 1871 in Opocno, Czechoslovakia
d. January 21, 1957 in Puteaux, France

Gaston Lachaise
American sculptor
• Noted for voluptuous female nudes, portrait busts of literary figures.
b. March 19, 1882 in Paris, France
d. October 18, 1935 in New York, New York

Sir Osbert Lancaster
English cartoonist
• Created character Maudie Littlehampton for *London Daily Express*, 1939-81.
b. August 04, 1908 in London, England
d. July 27, 1986 in London, England

Nicolas Lancret
French artist
• Rococco painter; did genre, theatrical scenes including *The Music Lesson*, 1743.
b. January 22, 1690 in Paris, France
d. September 14, 1743 in Paris, France

Dorothea Nutzhorn Lange
American photographer
• Called greatest documentary photographer in US; best known for pictures of migrant workers.
b. 1895 in Hoboken, New Jersey
d. October 11, 1965 in San Francisco, California

Walter Lantz
American cartoonist
• Created Woody Woodpecker, 1941; won Honorary Oscar, 1978.
b. April 27, 1900 in New Rochelle, New York

Gary Larson
American cartoonist
• Created "The Far Side," comic feature syndicated in hundreds of newspapers since 1979.
b. August 14, 1950 in Tacoma, Washington

Jacques-Henri Lartique
French photographer–artist
• Known for photographs of everyday objects, sense of movement captured: *Diary of a Century*, 1970.
b. June 13, 1894 in Paris, France
d. September 12, 1986 in Nice, France

Fred Lasswell
American cartoonist
• Noted for "Barney Google" comic strip since 1930s.
b. 1916 in Kennett, Missouri

Alicia Bay Laurel
American author–illustrator
• Children's books include *The Goodnight Hug; The Talking Whale*.
b. May 14, 1949 in Los Angeles, California

Marie Laurencin
French artist
• Drew portraits of females in soft pastels; friend of Picasso, Matisse.
b. 1885 in Paris, France
d. 1956 in Paris, France

Sir John Lavery
Irish artist
• Painted interiors, landscapes, portaits of notables.
b. March 1856 in Belfast, Northern Ireland
d. January 1, 1941 in Kilmoganny, Ireland

Jacob Armstead Lawrence
American artist
• Noted for gouache or egg tempura series on War, Harlem life, John Brown; awarded Spingarn medal, 1970.
b. September 07, 1917 in Atlantic City, New Jersey

Sir Thomas Lawrence
English artist
• Romantic portraits of English society; succeeded Reynolds as court painter, 1792.
b. May 04, 1769 in Bristol, England
d. January 07, 1830 in London, England

Lee Lawrie
American artist
• Architectural sculptor known for bronze Atlas in Rockefeller Center, NYC.
b. October 16, 1877 in Rixdorf, Germany
d. January 23, 1961 in Easton, Maryland

Mell Lazarus
(Mell pseud)
American cartoonist
• Draws, writes comics "Miss Peach," 1957–, "Momma," 1970–.
b. May 03, 1927 in Brooklyn, New York

Charles Le Brun
French artist
• Painter to Louis XIV, 1662; head of Gobelins, 1663; designed royal furnishings; decorated Versailles, especially the Galerie de Glaces.
b. February 24, 1619 in Paris, France
d. February 22, 1690 in Paris, France

Munro (Wilbur Munro) Leaf
(John Calvert; Mun pseuds)
American author–illustrator
• Created children's classic *The Story of Ferdinand*, 1936.
b. December 04, 1905 in Hamilton, Maryland
d. December 21, 1976 in Garrett Park, Maryland

Rico (Frederico) Lebrun
American artist
• Painted grim good-evil theme murals; did crucifixion, concentration camp series.
b. December 1, 1900 in Naples, Italy
d. May 1, 1964 in Malibu, California

Doris Emrick Lee
American artist
• Noted for primitivistic folksy scenes: "Thanksgiving Day," 1936.
b. February 01, 1905 in Aledo, Illinois

Stan Lee
(Stanley Lieber)
American cartoonist
• Editor, publisher, Marvel Comics empire, 1961–; created superhero, Spider-Man.
b. December 28, 1922 in New York, New York

John Leech
English cartoonist–illustrator
• Political cartoonist for *Punch*, 1841-64; illustrated works of Dickens.
b. August 29, 1817 in London, England
d. October 29, 1864 in London, England

Fernand Leger
French artist
• Cubist; drew mechanical subjects, monumental figures; made experimental films.
b. February 04, 1881 in Argentan, France
d. August 17, 1955 in Gif-sur-Yvette, France

Clare Veronica Hope Leighton
English illustrator–author
• Her unique wood-engravings enhance classics, modern, children's books including *Four Hedges*, 1935.
b. April 12, 1900 in London, England
d. January 1990 in Waterbury, Connecticut

Sir Peter Lely
Dutch artist
• Painted English aristocracy, ladies of Charles II's court, the "Windsor Beauties" series, 1660s.
b. September 14, 1618 in Soest, Netherlands
d. December 07, 1680 in London, England

Leonardo da Vinci
Italian artist
• Greatest paintings: *The Last Supper*, 1498; *Mona Lisa*, 1503.
b. April 15, 1452 in Vinci, Italy
d. May 02, 1519 in Amboise, France

Emanuel Leutze
American artist
• Works include *Washington Crossing the Delaware; Columbus Before the Queen*.
b. May 24, 1816 in Gumund, Germany
d. July 18, 1868 in Washington, District of Columbia

David Levine
American artist–illustrator–author
• Illustrated award-winning juvenile books: *Fables of Aesop; The Heart of Stone*, 1964; known for caricatures of composers, performers.
b. December 2, 1926 in Brooklyn, New York

Jack Levine
American artist
• Expressionist noted for satirical portraits, social commentaries: *Pawnshop*.
b. January 03, 1915 in Boston, Massachusetts

Edmonia Lewis
American artist
• First afro-american woman sculptor; *Death of Cleopatra* shown at Centennial Exposition, PA, 1876.
b. July 04, 1845 in Albany, New York
d. 1911 in Rome, Italy

Wyndham Lewis
English author–artist
• Leader, Vorticist movement, edited *Blast*, 1914; wrote satire trilogy, *The Human Age*, 1928.
b. November 18, 1884 in Maine
d. March 07, 1957 in London, England

Sol LeWitt
American artist
• Conceptual/minimal sculptor, using square, cube, line as basic components.
b. September 09, 1928 in Hartford, Connecticut

Joseph Christian Leyendecker
American artist
• Produced over 300 covers for *Saturday Evening Post*, 1910-30s.
b. March 23, 1874 in Montabour, Germany
d. July 25, 1951 in New Rochelle, New York

Leon Augustin L'Hermitte
French artist
• Drew realistic scenes of peasant life: *The Harvest*, 1874.
b. 1844 in Mont-Saint-Pere, France
d. 1925 in Paris, France

Alexander Semeonovitch Liberman
American editor–artist–photographer
• Editorial director of Conde Nast, 1962–; minimal painter who does geometrics, circle drawings.
b. September 04, 1912 in Kiev, Russia

Patrick (Earl Thomas Patrick John Anson) Lichfield
(Viscount Anson; Baron Soberton)
English photographer–celebrity relative
• Cousin of Queen Elizabeth II; took official photos of Prince Charles' wedding, 1981.
b. April 25, 1939

Roy Lichtenstein
American artist
• Pioneered 1960s Pop Art movement, noted for comic strip-inspired paintings.
b. October 27, 1923 in New York, New York

George Lichty
(George Maurice Lichtenstein)
American cartoonist
• Creator of "Grin and Bear It," 1932-74.
b. May 16, 1905 in Chicago, Illinois
d. July 18, 1983 in Santa Rosa, California

Max Liebermann
German artist
• Postimpressionist; known for genre scenes of humble people: *Women Plucking Geese*, 1872; forbidden by Nazis to paint.
b. July 2, 1847 in Berlin, Germany
d. February 08, 1935 in Berlin, Germany

Richard Lindner
German artist–illustrator
• Unique figurative painter; flat, geometric shapes combine cubism, symbolism, pop art.
b. November 11, 1901 in Hamburg, Germany
d. April 16, 1978 in New York, New York

Jacques Lipchitz
French sculptor
• A founder, cubist school of sculptor, 1916; noted for heavy stone abstractions, monumental figures, "aerial transparencies."
b. August 22, 1891 in Lithuania
d. May 26, 1973 in New York, New York

Filippino Lippi
Italian artist–religious figure
• Son of Filippo; masterpieces include *Madonna and Child Enthroned*.
b. 1459
d. 1504

Fra Filippo (Lippo) Lippi
Italian artist
• Florentine monk, painted religious frescoes, canvases: *Adoration of the Magi*.
b. 1406 in Florence, Italy
d. October 09, 1469 in Florence, Italy

Richard Lippold
American sculptor
• Noted for large stainless steel wood or wire sculptural constructions.
b. May 03, 1915 in Milwaukee, Wisconsin

Arthur Lismer
(Group of Seven)
Canadian artist
• Founding member, Group of Seven, 1919; paintings depict Northern Canada.
b. June 27, 1885 in Sheffield, England
d. March 23, 1969 in Montreal, Quebec

Scott Long
American editor–cartoonist
• Editorial cartoonist, Minneapolis *Tribune* since 1940s.
b. February 24, 1917 in Evanston, Illinois

Ambrogio Lorenzetti
Italian artist
• A leading early Sienese painter, noted for frescoes: *Good and Bad Government*, 1330s.
b. 1265
d. 1348

Bernard Joseph Pierre Lorjou
French artist
• A leader, Social Realist group, 1940s-50s; later developed strong expressionist style.
b. September 09, 1908 in Blois, France
d. January 26, 1986 in Blois, France

Claude Lorrain
(Claude Gellee; Claude Gelee; "Le Lorrain")
French artist
• Painted idyllic seascapes, landscapes which are noted for light, atmosphere including *Expulsion of Hagar*, 1668.
b. 1600 in Lorraine, France
d. November 21, 1682 in Rome, Italy

Morris Louis
(Morris Louis Bernstein)
American artist
• Abstract Expressionist; often poured paint on unsized canvas; did colored stripes in vertical patterns; *Veils* series, 1954-58.
b. November 28, 1912 in Baltimore, Maryland
d. September 07, 1962 in Washington, District of Columbia

Sir David Low
English cartoonist
• Created comic character, "Colonel Blimp" satirizing the pompous British ultraconservative, 1940s.
b. April 07, 1891 in Dunedin, New Zealand
d. September 11, 1963 in London, England

Lawrence Stephen Lowry
English artist
• Painter, lithographer, best known for industrial scenes.
b. November 01, 1887 in Manchester, England
d. February 23, 1976 in Glossop, England

Lucas Van Leyden
(Lucas Hugensz)
Dutch artist
• Noted for copperplate engravings; considered founder of Dutch genre painting.
b. 1494 in Leiden, Netherlands
d. 1533 in Leiden, Netherlands

Henry A Lukeman
American sculptor
• Did memorials, equestrian statues; noted for large relief of Robert E Lee on Atlanta's Stone Mountain.
b. January 28, 1871 in Richmond, Virginia
d. April 03, 1935 in Norway

George Benjamin Luks
American artist–cartoonist
• Member, Ashcan school of realistic painting; created comic strip "Hogan's Alley" featuring the Yellow Kid.
b. August 13, 1867 in Williamsport, Pennsylvania
d. October 29, 1933 in New York, New York

Jean Marie Lurcat
French artist
• Responsible for revivial of French tapestry after WW II.
b. July 01, 1892 in Bruyeres, France
d. January 06, 1966 in Saint-Paul-de-Vence, France

Lysippus
Greek sculptor
• Introduced new system of bodily proportions; reported to have made over 1,500 bronzes, none extant.
b. 4thBC

Hermon Atkins MacNeil
American sculptor–designer
• Designed US quarter; works depict Indians, Western life.
b. February 27, 1866 in Chelsea, Massachusetts
d. October 02, 1947 in New York, New York

Jan de Mabuse
(Jan Gossart; Jan Gossaert)
Flemish artist
• Did portraits, religious works; introduced Italian High Renaissance to the Netherlands.
b. 1478 in Maubeuge, France
d. 1533 in Antwerp, Belgium

J(ames) E(dward) H(ervey) MacDonald
(Group of Seven)
Canadian artist
• Original member, Group of Seven, 1920; known for landscapes, Rocky Mountain scenes.
b. May 12, 1873 in Durham, England
d. November 26, 1932 in Toronto, Ontario

Stanton MacDonald-Wright
American artist
• Co-found, Synchromism, 1913, a style where color generates form; later turned to Oriental art.
b. July 08, 1890 in Charlottesville, Virginia
d. August 22, 1973 in Pacific Palisades, California

Loren MacIver
American artist
• Career as painter has spanned six decades; work doesn't fall into definite art movement or style, but sometimes called symbolic or romantic: *Winter Dunes*, 1932.
b. February 22, 1909 in New York, New York

Daniel Maclise
Irish artist–illustrator
• Portrait painter who illustrated some of Dickens' Christmas books.
b. 1806
d. 1870

Jeff(rey Kenneth) MacNelly
American cartoonist
• Draws comic strip "Shoe"; won Pulitzers, 1972, 1978.
b. September 17, 1947 in New York, New York

Alessandro Lissandrino Magnasco
Italian artist
• Painted mystical, gloomy religious genre scenes including *Baptism of Christ*.
b. 1667 in Genoa, Italy
d. March 12, 1749 in Genoa, Italy

Rene Magritte
Belgian artist
• Noted Surrealist painter; used iconographic images as lions, men in bowler hats.
b. November 21, 1898
d. August 08, 1967 in Brussels, Belgium

Aristide Maillol
French artist
• Neoclassical sculptor known for massive but graceful female nudes.
b. December 08, 1861 in Banyuls sur Mer, France
d. October 05, 1944 in Banyuls sur Mer, France

Kasimir Severinovich Malevich
Russian artist
• Founded suprematist school of abstract art, 1913.
b. February 26, 1878 in Kiev, Russia
d. May 15, 1935 in Leningrad, U.S.S.R.

Alfred Manessier
French artist
• Abstractionist whose *The Crown of Thorns* was the first non-figurative painting to win Carnegie Award, 1955.
b. December 05, 1911 in Saint-Ouen, France

Edouard Manet
French artist
• Main forerunner of Impressionism; noted for *Olympia*, 1863; *Bar at the Folles Bergere*, 1882.
b. January 23, 1832 in Paris, France
d. April 3, 1883 in Paris, France

Paul Manship
American sculptor
• Works include large Prometheus figure at NYC's Rockefeller Plaza.
b. December 25, 1885 in Saint Paul, Minnesota
d. January 31, 1966 in Massachusetts

Andrea Mantegna
Italian artist
• Historical, religious painter whose frescoes include *Triumph of Caesar*.
b. 1431 in Isola Carturo, Italy
d. September 13, 1506 in Mantua, Italy

Robert Mapplethorpe
American photographer
• His homoerotic photographs brought shock waves to art world; were subject of controversy, lawsuits; died of AIDS.
b. November 04, 1946 in Floral Park, New York
d. March 09, 1989 in Boston, Massachusetts

Franz Marc
German artist
• Expressionist whose paintings include *Blue Horses*.
b. 1880
d. March 04, 1916 in Verdun, France

Conrad Marca-Relli
American artist
• Abstract expressionist painter who developed the "collage" technique, 1950s.
b. June 05, 1913 in Boston, Massachusetts

John Marin
American artist
• Expressionist whose seascapes include *Maine Island*.
b. December 23, 1872 in Rutherford, New Jersey
d. October 01, 1953 in Addison, Maine

Marino Marini
Italian sculptor
• Best known for equestrian figures.
b. February 27, 1901 in Pistoria, Italy
d. August 06, 1980 in Viareggio, Italy

Marisol (Escobar)
Venezuelan sculptor
• Pop artist noted for large wooden sculptures.
b. May 22, 1930 in Paris, France

Albert Marquet
French artist
• Noted for French cityscapes.
b. 1875 in Bordeaux, France
d. 1947 in Paris, France

Fletcher Martin
American artist
• Subject matter ranged from rodeo, baseball, racing; painted N African warfront scenes for *Life* magazine.
b. April 29, 1904 in Palisade, Colorado
d. May 3, 1979 in Guanajuato, Mexico

Homer Dodge Martin
American artist
• Landscapes featuring aspects of Impressionism include *Normandy Farm*.
b. November 28, 1836 in Albany, New York
d. February 12, 1897 in Saint Paul, Minnesota

Simone Martini
Italian artist
• Influential Sienese painter noted for color, decorative lines; works include *Annunciation Triptych*, 1333.
b. 1284 in Siena, Italy
d. 1344 in Avignon, Italy

Masaccio
(Tommaso di Giovanni di Simone Cassai)
Italian artist
• Major figure of Florentine Renaissance; only four works survive; first to use linear perspective in frescoes.
b. December 21, 1401 in San Giovanni Valdarno, Italy
d. 1428 in Rome, Italy

Quentin Massys
Flemish artist
• Painted portraits, religious, genre subjects including *Money Changer and His Wife*, 1514.
b. 1466 in Louvain, Belgium
d. 1530 in Antwerp, Belgium

Andre (Aime Rene) Masson
French artist
• Pioneer of surrealism; known for wild brush strokes, body movement, "action" technique.
b. January 04, 1896 in Balagny-sur-Therain, France
d. October 28, 1987 in Paris, France

Henri Matisse
French artist–author
• Pioneer of modern art known for vivid female nudes, still lifes, interiors.
b. December 31, 1869 in Le Cateau, France
d. November 03, 1954 in Nice, France

Roberto Sebastian Antonio Echaurren Matta
Chilean artist
• Abstract surrealist painter: *Untitled*, 1961.
b. November 11, 1911 in Santiago, Chile

Tompkins Harrison Matteson
American artist
• Pictures of American history include *The Spirit of '76*.
b. May 09, 1813 in Peterboro, New York
d. February 02, 1884 in Sherburne, Nevada

Bill (William Henry) Mauldin
American cartoonist
• Prominent during WW II; GI characters Willie, Joe were most realistic of period.
b. October 29, 1921 in Mountain Park, New Mexico

Peter Max
American artist–designer
• Best known for colorful, psychedelic posters, murals, 1960s.
b. October 19, 1937 in Berlin, Germany

Winsor McCay
American cartoonist
• Best known for "Little Nemo" cartoons.
b. September 26, 1869 in Spring Lake, Michigan
d. July 26, 1934

Donald McCullin
English photographer
• Free-lance photographer known for war photography in Cyprus, 1964.
b. October 09, 1935 in London, England

John Tinney McCutcheon
American cartoonist
• *Chicago Tribune* political cartoonist, 1903-45; won Pulitzer, 1932.
b. May 06, 1870 in South Raub, Indiana
d. June 1, 1949 in Lake Forest, Illinois

Walt(er) McDougall
American cartoonist
• Introduced cartooning, news illustration to daily newspaper, 1884.
b. February 1, 1858 in Newark, New Jersey
d. 1938

Henry Lee McFee
American artist
• Painted landscapes, still-lifes; influenced by Cezanne, cubism.
b. April 14, 1886 in Saint Louis, Missouri
d. March 19, 1953 in Claremont, California

Alden McWilliams
American cartoonist
• Known for comic strips "Twin Earths," 1953-63; "Dateline: Danger!," 1968-74.
b. 1916 in Greenwich, Connecticut

Jean Louis Ernest Meissonier
French artist
• Noted for genre scenes, military subjects.
b. February 21, 1815 in Lyons, France
d. January 31, 1891 in Paris, France

Gari (Julius Gari) Melchers
American artist
• Did portraits, landscapes, sacred scenes, murals for Library of Congress.
b. August 11, 1860 in Detroit, Michigan
d. November 3, 1932 in Fredericksburg, Virginia

Hans Memling
Flemish artist
• Portraitist, religious painter; noted for color, detail; works include *Last Judgement Altarpiece*.
b. 1430 in Seligenstadt, Belgium
d. August 11, 1494 in Bruges, Belgium

Anton Raphael Mengs
German artist
• Historical, portrait painter; neoclassicist; wrote treatise on taste in painting, 1762.
b. 1728 in Aussig, Bohemia
d. 1779 in Rome, Italy

Carlos Merida
Mexican artist
• Leading abstract expressionist of Mexico; his murals, bas-reliefs, mosaics adorn many important buildings in Mexico City.
b. December 02, 1891 in Guatemala City, Guatemala

Dale Messick
American cartoonist
• Created popular comic strip "Brenda Starr, Reporter," 1940.
b. 1906 in South Bend, Indiana

Otto Messmer
American cartoonist
• Created "Felix the Cat," 1919; featured in over 300 shorts, 1920s-30s.
b. 1892 in Union City, New Jersey
d. October 28, 1983 in Teaneck, New Jersey

Ivan Mestrovic
American sculptor
• First living artist to have one-man show at NYC's Met. Museum, 1947.
b. August 15, 1883 in Vrpolje, Croatia
d. January 16, 1962

Duane Steven Michals
American photographer
• Member sharp focus school of photography, with fanatical devotion to realism, technical perfection.
b. February 18, 1932 in McKeesport, Pennsylvania

Henri Michaux
French artist
• Paintings focused on subconscious mind, effects of drugs; wrote several critically acclaimed poems.
b. May 24, 1899 in Namur, Belgium
d. October 17, 1984 in Paris, France

Michelangelo
(Michelangelo di Lodovico Buonarroti Simoni)
Italian artist–poet
• Leader of High Renaissance; works include marble sculpture *David*, 1504; paintings of Sistine Chapel, 1508-12.
b. March 06, 1475 in Caprese, Italy
d. February 18, 1564 in Rome, Italy

Henning Dahl Mikkelsen
(Mik pseud)
American cartoonist
• Created comic trip "Ferd'nand," 1937-82.
b. January 09, 1915 in Skive, Denmark
d. June 01, 1982

Gjon Mili
American photographer
• Worked for *Life* magazine 45 yrs.; pioneered use of high-speed flash, multi-exposure prints.
b. November 28, 1904 in Kerce, Albania
d. February 14, 1984 in Stamford, Connecticut

Sir John Everett Millais
English artist
• A founder, pre-Raphaelite Brotherhood, 1848; works included controversial *Christ in House of His Parents*, 1850.
b. June 08, 1829 in Southampton, England
d. August 13, 1896 in London, England

Jeff(rey) Lynn Millar
American journalist–critic–cartoonist
• Created syndicated comic strip "Tank McNamera," 1974–.
b. July 1, 1942 in Pasadena, Texas

Alfred Jacob Miller
American artist
• Sketched American Indians; works long forgotten; rediscovered, 1930s.
b. January 02, 1810 in Baltimore, Maryland
d. June 26, 1874 in Baltimore, Maryland

Carl Wilhelm Emil Milles
American sculptor
• Famous for huge sculptures, fountains at Chicago Exhibition, NY World's Fair, 1930s.
b. June 23, 1875 in Lagga, Sweden
d. September 19, 1955 in Stockholm, Sweden

Jean Francois Millet
French artist
• Paintings on pleasant subjects include *The Gleaners*, 1857; *Man With the Hoe*, 1863.
b. October 04, 1814 in Gruchy, France
d. January 2, 1875 in Barbizon, France

David Brown Milne
Canadian artist
• Painter of rural Ontario landscapes; pioneered post-impressionism in Canada.
b. January 1882 in Paisley, Ontario
d. December 26, 1953 in Toronto, Ontario

Joan Miro
Spanish artist
• Member, French school of surrealist painters, 1930s; works express nightmare, horror.
b. April 2, 1893 in Barcelona, Spain
d. December 25, 1983 in Palma de Majorca, Spain

Joan Mitchell
American artist
• One of finest painters of second generation of abstract expressionists; large, colorful works called "metaphors of natural world."
b. February 12, 1926 in Chicago, Illinois

Amedeo Modigliani
Italian artist
• Noted for elongated portraits, nudes.
b. July 12, 1884 in Leghorn, Italy
d. January 25, 1920 in Paris, France

Laszlo Moholy-Nagy
American artist–photographer–designer
• Noted constructivist; developed "photogram" technique; organized Chicago's New Bauhaus, 1937.
b. July 2, 1895 in Bacsbarsod, Hungary
d. November 24, 1946 in Chicago, Illinois

Piet(er Cornelis) Mondrian
Dutch artist
• Abstract painter influenced by cubism; developed geometric style called neoplasticism.
b. March 07, 1872 in Amersfoort, Netherlands
d. February 01, 1944 in New York, New York

Claude-Oscar Monet
French artist
• Leader of impressionists whose painting *Impression: Sunrise* gave group its name.
b. November 14, 1840 in Paris, France
d. December 05, 1926 in Giverny, France

Jean-Baptiste Monnoyer
French artist
• Noted floral painter; decorated Versailles.
b. 1636 in Lille, France
d. 1699 in London, England

Phil Monroe
American cartoonist
• Created cartoon characters the Road Runner, Tony the Tiger, Charley Tuna, and others.
b. 1917
d. July 14, 1988 in Los Angeles, California

Bob Montana
American cartoonist
• Created syndicated comic strip "Archie," 1942.
b. October 23, 1920 in Stockton, California
d. January 04, 1975 in Meredith, New Hampshire

Don W Moore
American cartoonist
• Drew "Flash Gordon" comic strip, 1934-54; wrote TV show "Captain Video," 1949.
b. 1901
d. April 07, 1986 in Venice, Florida

Henry Spencer Moore
English sculptor
• Sculptures fused abstract, distorted figures with traditional concepts; known for *Reclining Figure*, 1929.
b. July 3, 1898 in Castleford, England
d. August 31, 1986 in London, England

Dick (Richard Arnold) Moores
American cartoonist
• Drew syndicated comic strip "Gasoline Alley," after death of creator Frank King.
b. December 12, 1909 in Lincoln, Nebraska
d. April 22, 1986 in Asheville, North Carolina

Gustave Moreau
French artist
• Symbolist who left paintings, including *Dance of Salome*, to form Moreau Museum; noted for violent scenes.
b. April 06, 1826 in Paris, France
d. April 18, 1898 in Paris, France

Berthe Morisot
French artist
• Impressionist, noted for soft-colored landscapes, portraits; often modeled for brother-in-law, Edouard Manet.
b. January 14, 1841 in Bourges, France
d. March 02, 1895 in Paris, France

James Wilson Morrice
Canadian artist
• Landscape painter who greatly influenced young Canadian artists; works include *The Ferry*.
b. August 1, 1865 in Montreal, Quebec
d. January 23, 1924 in Tunis, Tunisia

Robert Morris
American sculptor
• Minimalist; works in gray painted plywood and plastic cubes, pyramids, and polyhedreon forms.
b. February 09, 1931 in Kansas City, Missouri

Grandma (Anna Mary Robertson) Moses
American artist
• Started painting in her late 70's; subjects are rural life, including *Black Horses*, 1941.
b. August 07, 1860 in Greenwich, New York
d. December 13, 1961 in Hoosick Falls, New York

Zack Terrell Mosley
American cartoonist
• Created nationally syndicated cartoon, "Smilin' Jack," 1933-73.
b. December 12, 1906 in Hickory, Oklahoma

Geoffrey Moss
American cartoonist–illustrator
• Syndicated political cartoonist with *Washington Post*, 1974–; first to be featured without captions.
b. June 3, 1938 in Brooklyn, New York

Robert Burns Motherwell
American artist
• One of founders of Abstract Expressionism, 1940s.
b. January 24, 1915 in Aberdeen, Washington

William Sidney Mount
American artist
• Portrait, genre painter, known for scenes of black life.
b. November 26, 1807 in Setauket, New York
d. November 19, 1868 in Setauket, New York

Alphonse Marie Mucha
Czech artist
• Specialized in designing posters in art nouveau style.
b. 1860 in Ivancice, Bohemia
d. 1938 in Prague, Czechoslovakia

Willard Mullin
American cartoonist
• Noted sports cartoonist; created the Brooklyn Dodger Bum; drawings appeared in hundreds of mags.
b. 1902 in Ohio
d. December 21, 1978 in Corpus Christi, Texas

Edvard Munch
Norwegian artist
• Early expressionist noted for lithographs, woodcuts, macabre paintings including *Vampire*, 1894.
b. December 12, 1863 in Loyten, Norway
d. January 23, 1944 in Oslo, Norway

Sir Alfred James Munnings
English artist
• Finest painter of animals of his time.
b. October 08, 1878 in Suffolk, England
d. July 17, 1959 in Dedham, England

Bartolome Esteban Murillo
Spanish artist
• Painter of sentimental Baroque religious scenes: *Vision of St. Anthony*.
b. January 01, 1618 in Seville, Spain
d. April 03, 1682 in Cadiz, Spain

Jimmy (James Edward) Murphy
American cartoonist
• Created "Toots and Casper" syndicated comic strip.
b. November 2, 1891 in Chicago, Illinois
d. March 09, 1965 in Beverly Hills, California

Eadweard Muybridge
(Edward James Muggeridge)
English photographer
• Took first pictures of objects in rapid motion; proved that horse is completely off ground during part of stride, circa 1877.
b. April 09, 1830 in Kingston, England
d. May 08, 1904 in Kingston, England

Carl M Mydans
American photographer
• On staff of *Life*, 1936-72; author, *China: A Visual Adventure*, 1979.
b. May 2, 1907 in Boston, Massachusetts

Jerome Myers
American artist
• Depicted NYC street scenes; an initiator of 1913 Armory Show.
b. March 2, 1867 in Petersburg, Virginia
d. June 19, 1940

Russell Myers
American cartoonist
• Created comic strip "Broom Hilda," 1970–.
b. October 09, 1938 in Pittsburg, Kansas

Myron
Greek sculptor
• Considered one of the greatest Attic sculptors of time; works include *Discus Thrower*.
b. 480BC
d. 440BC

Nadar
(Gaspard-Felix Tournachon)
French balloonist–photographer
• Known for mapmaking by surveying from a ballon; invented the photo-essay.
b. 1820
d. 1910

Paul Nash
English artist–designer
• Official artist during both world wars; noted for finding unusual scenes to paint.
b. May 11, 1889 in London, England
d. July 11, 1946 in London, England

Thomas Nast
American cartoonist–illustrator
• Political cartoonist; originated elephant, donkey as symbols of Rep., Dem. parties; biting style popularized term "nasty."
b. September 27, 1840 in Landau, Germany
d. December 07, 1902 in Guayaquil, Ecuador

Jean Marc Nattier
French artist
• Often painted royalty, nobility in guise of mythological characters: *Portrait of a Lady as Diana*, 1756.
b. 1685 in Paris, France
d. 1766 in Paris, France

Fred Neher
American cartoonist
• Draws cartoon "Life's Like That," 1934–.
b. September 29, 1903 in Nappanee, Indiana

LeRoy Neiman
American artist
• Known for paintings of athletes; collected in *Leroy Neiman Posters*, 1980.
b. June 08, 1926 in Saint Paul, Minnesota

Louise Berliawsky Nevelson
American artist
• Pioneer creator of large wall, environmental sculpture: *Sky Gate, New York*, 1978.
b. September 23, 1899 in Kiev, Russia
d. April 17, 1988 in New York, New York

Arnold Abner Newman
American photographer
• Best known for environmental symbolic portraiture, especially portraits of famous artists.
b. March 03, 1918 in New York, New York

Barnett Newman
American artist
• Abstract expressionist best known for *Stations of the Cross* series, 1958-66.
b. January 29, 1905 in New York, New York
d. July 03, 1970 in New York, New York

Ben Nicholson
English artist
• Abstract painter who won Guggenheim International Award, 1956.
b. April 1, 1894 in Uxbridge, England
d. February 06, 1982 in London, England

Isamu Noguchi
American sculptor–designer
• Works contributed to modern abstract art movement.
b. November 17, 1904 in Los Angeles, California
d. December 3, 1988 in New York, New York

Kenneth Clifton Noland
American artist
• Paintings emphasized pure color, made color the subject; experimented with bull's eye, chevron motifs.
b. April 1, 1924 in Asheville, North Carolina

Emil Nolde
(Emil Hansen)
German artist
• Expressionist, influenced by primative art; forbidden to paint by Nazis, but continued to do landscapes, seascapes.
b. August 07, 1867 in Nolde, Germany
d. April 15, 1956 in Seebull, Sweden

Phil Nowlan
(Frank Phillips pseud)
American cartoonist
• Best known for creating comic strip character, Buck Rogers, 1929.
b. 1888 in Philadelphia, Pennsylvania
d. February 01, 1940 in Philadelphia, Pennsylvania

Willis Harold O'Brien
American special effects technician–cartoonist
• Best known for special effects in *King Kong*, 1933; won Oscar for *Mighty Joe Young*, 1949.
b. 1886 in Oakland, California
d. November 08, 1962 in Hollywood, California

Georgia O'Keeffe
(Mrs Alfred Stieglitz)
American artist
• One of founders of Modernism known for brilliant paintings of flowers, bleached skulls, Western terrain.
b. November 15, 1887 in Sun Prairie, Wisconsin
d. March 06, 1986 in Santa Fe, New Mexico

Claes Thure Oldenburg
American artist–sculptor
• Known for "soft" sculptures of ice cream cones, hamburgers, etc.
b. January 28, 1929 in Stockholm, Sweden

Patrick Bruce Oliphant
American cartoonist
• Syndicated cartoonist for *Washington Star*, 1975–; won Pulitzer for editorial cartooning, 1967.
b. July 24, 1935 in Adelaide, Australia

Jules Olitski
American artist
• Noted for misty color-fields, spraying paint directly on canvas; first living American to have one-man show at NYC's Met. Museum, 1969.
b. March 27, 1922 in Snovsk, U.S.S.R.

Rose Cecil O'Neill
American illustrator–author
• Created Kewpie doll, 1909; wrote several Kewpie books.
b. June 25, 1874 in Wilkes-Barre, Pennsylvania
d. April 06, 1944 in Springfield, Missouri

Yoko Ono
(Mrs John Lennon)
Japanese artist–musician
• Married John Lennon, 1969; recorded, with husband, *Double Fantasy*, 1980.
b. February 18, 1933 in Tokyo, Japan

Ruth Orkin
American photographer
• Her black and white photographs of American street life are in permanent museum collections.
b. September 03, 1921 in Boston, Massachusetts
d. January 16, 1985 in New York, New York

Jose Clemente Orozco
Mexican artist
• A leader of the Mexican muralist movement; frescoes include *Quetzalcoatl*, 1930s.
b. November 23, 1883 in Zapotlan, Mexico
d. September 07, 1949 in Mexico City, Mexico

Adriaen van Ostade
Dutch artist
• Genre painter of peasant life; among 1000 oils: *Cottage Dooryard*, 1640s.
b. December 1, 1610 in Haarlem, Netherlands
d. May 02, 1685 in Haarlem, Netherlands

Richard Felton Outcault
American cartoonist
• Best known for characters "Yellow Kid"; "Buster Brown."
b. January 14, 1863 in Lancaster, Ohio
d. September 25, 1928 in Flushing, New York

Erastus Dow Palmer
American sculptor
• His most famous work in marble, *The White Captive*, 1858, in Metropolitan Museum, NYC.
b. April 02, 1817 in Pompey, New York
d. 1904 in Albany, New York

Frances Flora Bond Palmer
American artist
• Produced over 200 lithographs for Currier and Ives, 1849-59.
b. June 26, 1812 in Leicester, England
d. August 2, 1876 in Brooklyn, New York

Giovanni Paolo Pannini
(Giovanni Paolo Panini)
Italian artist
• Drew cityscapes, ancient Roman landmarks: *View of Roman Forum*, 1735.
b. 1691 in Piacenza, Italy
d. 1765 in Rome, Italy

Brant (Julian) Parker
American cartoonist
• Created nat. syndicated comic strips, "Wizard of Id," 1964; "Crock," 1975; "Goosemeyer," 1980.
b. August 26, 1920 in Los Angeles, California

Norman Parkinson
(Ronald Smith)
English photographer
• Known for fashion, celebrity portraits; has photographed British royalty since 1931.
b. April 21, 1913 in Roehampton, England
d. February 15, 1990 in Singapore

Parmigiano
(Francesco Mazzola)
Italian artist
• Mannerist painter noted for *Mystic Marriage of St. Catherine*, c. 1521; influenced by Correggio.
b. January 11, 1503 in Parma, Italy
d. August 24, 1540 in Casalmaggiore, Italy

Parrhasius
Greek artist
• Representative of the Ionic School; the master of outline drawing.
b. 4th?BC in Ephesus, Greece

Maxfield Parrish
American artist
• Student of Howard Pyle; known for original posters, book illustrations.
b. July 25, 1870 in Philadelphia, Pennsylvania
d. March 3, 1966 in Plainfield, New Hampshire

Virgil Franklin Partch, II
(Vip pseud)
American cartoonist
• Created comic strip "Big George."
b. October 17, 1916 in Saint Paul Island, Alaska
d. August 1, 1984 in Newhall, California

Mervyn Laurence Peake
English illustrator–author
• Wrote *Titus* trilogy novels, 1946-59; illustrated books by Lewis Carroll, R L Stevenson.
b. July 09, 1911 in Kuling, China
d. November 17, 1968 in Burcot, England

Charles Willson Peale
American artist–naturalist
• Best known for painting portraits of Revolutionary War figures; founded Peale Museum, 1786.
b. April 15, 1741 in Queen Annes County, Maryland
d. February 22, 1827 in Philadelphia, Pennsylvania

Raphael Peale
American artist
• Miniaturist; established portrait gallery of distinguished persons with brother, Rembrandt; son of Charles Wilson.
b. February 17, 1774 in Annapolis, Maryland
d. March 04, 1825

Rembrandt Peale
American artist
• Historical painter noted for portraits of Washington, Jefferson; son of Charles Wilson.
b. February 22, 1778 in Richboro, Pennsylvania
d. October 03, 1860

Waldo Peirce
American illustrator–artist
• Works include *Maine Swimming Hole*, 1944; illustrated juvenile poetry book *The Children's Hour*, 1944.
b. December 17, 1884 in Bangor, Maine
d. March 08, 1970 in Searsport, Maine

Irving Penn
American photographer
• Known for fashion photographs in *Vogue*, often compared to paintings.
b. June 16, 1917 in Plainfield, Pennsylvania

Perugino
Italian artist
• Painted Sistine Chapel fresco "Christ Delivering Keys to St. Peter," 1500; Raphael's teacher.
b. 1445 in Perugia, Italy
d. 1523 in Perugia, Italy

Antoine Pevsner
French artist–sculptor
• Founded Constructivist school, which applies cubism principles to sculpture.
b. January 18, 1886 in Orel, Russia
d. April 12, 1962 in Paris, France

Marjorie Acker Phillips
American artist–art patron
• Established first major modern art museum in US, 1921.
b. October 25, 1894 in Bourbon, Indiana
d. June 19, 1985 in Washington, District of Columbia

Francis Picabia
French artist
• Early cubist, surrealist; introduced DaDa movement to Paris, NYC, 1918; known for machinist works, human figure paintings.
b. January 22, 1879 in Paris, France
d. November 3, 1953 in Paris, France

Pablo Ruiz y Picasso
Spanish artist
• Profoundly influenced 20th c. art; masterpiece, *Guernica*, 1937, denounced war.
b. October 25, 1881 in Malaga, Spain
d. April 09, 1973 in Mougins, France

Piero della Francesca
(Pietro di Benedetto dei Franceschi)
Italian artist
• Major Renaissance painter who developed perspective; court portraits, altarpieces include *Resurrection*, c. 1463.
b. 1420 in Borgo San Sepolcro, Italy
d. October 12, 1492 in Borgo San Sepolcro, Italy

Pinturicchio
(Betto di Biago)
Italian artist
• Umbrian school historical painter; did Sistine Chapel frescoes with Perugino.
b. 1454 in Perugia, Italy
d. December 11, 1513 in Siena, Italy

Horace Pippin
American artist
• Self-taught primative painter, one of America's leading black artists; did *The End of the War: Starting Home*, 1931.
b. February 22, 1888 in West Chester, Pennsylvania
d. July 06, 1946 in West Chester, Pennsylvania

Andrea Pisano
(Andrea da Pontedera)
Italian architect–sculptor
• Noted for famed bronze doors on baptistery, Florence Cathedral, 1330-36.
b. 1290 in Pisa, Italy
d. 1348

Antonio Pisano
(Pisanello)
Italian artist
• Int'l. Gothic-style painter, medalist; with da Fabriano executed frescoes of Venice's Doge's Palace.
b. 1395 in Pisa, Italy
d. 1455 in Rome, Italy

Nicola Pisano
Italian sculptor
• Earliest great Italian sculptor; executed hexagonal marble pulpit, Pisa Baptistery.
b. 1220
d. 1283

Filippo Tibertelli de Pisis
Italian artist
• Painted architecture, landscapes, still lifes; influenced by French impressionism.
b. 1896 in Ferrara, Italy
d. April 02, 1956 in Milan, Italy

Lucien Pissaro
English artist
• One of most original book designers of all time; painted modified form of *pointillisme*.
b. February 2, 1863 in Paris, France
d. July 1, 1944 in Chard, England

Camille Jacob Pissarro
French artist
• Impressionist painter known for Parisian street scenes, views of Normandy countryside, sunlit village road scenes.
b. July 1, 1831 in Saint Thomas, West Indies
d. November 13, 1903 in Paris, France

Leo Politi
American author–illustrator
• Won 1950 Caldecott for *Song of the Swallows*.
b. 1908 in Fresno, California

Jackson Pollock
American artist–author
• Founded "action painting" and Abstract Expressionism movement.
b. January 28, 1912 in Cody, Wyoming
d. August 11, 1956 in East Hampton, New York

Polycletus the Elder
Greek sculptor
• Greatest Greek sculptor of his time; greatest achievement was figure of Hera in temple near Argos.
b. 5th?BC in Argos, Greece

Polygnotus
Greek artist
• Greatest Greek painter of his time, taking subject matter from epic poetry; first to draw open mouth with teeth showing, facial expressions.
b. 490?BC in Thaos, Greece
d. 425?BC in Athens, Greece

Lawrence (Larry) Poons
American artist
• Op art painter; prominent member of Colour Field school of art.
b. October 01, 1937 in Tokyo, Japan

Fairfield Porter
American artist
• Representative painter; had several one-man shows, 1950s-70s.
b. June 1, 1907 in Winnetka, Illinois
d. September 18, 1975 in Southhampton, New York

Beatrix (Helen Beatrix) Potter
English illustrator–author
• Wrote *The Tale of Peter Rabbit*, 1902.
b. July 06, 1866 in London, England
d. December 22, 1943 in Sawrey, England

Hiram Powers
American sculptor
• Noted for famed neoclassic marble: *The Greek Slave*, 1843.
b. July 29, 1805 in Woodstock, Vermont
d. June 27, 1873 in Florence, Italy

Frank Powolny
American photographer
• Best known for pinup of Betty Grable that GI's carried to battle, WW II.
b. 1902
d. January 09, 1986 in Valencia, California

Dith Pran
American photographer
• Film *The Killing Fields*, 1984, depicted his ordeal in Cambodia under Khmer Rouge.
b. 1943 in Cambodia

Bela Lyon Pratt
American sculptor
• Best-known work *Peace Restraining War*.
b. December 11, 1867 in Norwich, Connecticut
d. May 18, 1917 in Jamacia Plains, Massachusetts

Praxiteles
Greek sculptor
• Second only in reputation to Phidias; lone surviving work: *Hermes with the Infant Dionysus*.
b. 370?BC in Athens, Greece
d. 330?BC

Maurice Brazil Prendergast
(The Eight)
American artist
• Post-impressionist watercolorist; paintings include *Umbrellas in the Rain*.
b. October 1861 in Boston, Massachusetts
d. February 01, 1924 in New York, New York

Gregorio Prestopino
American artist
• Expressionist; used oils, watercolors to paint Manhattan, Harlem subjects; later turned to impressionist rural scenes.
b. June 21, 1907 in New York, New York
d. December 16, 1984 in Princeton, New Jersey

George Price
American cartoonist
• Regular contributor, *New Yorker*, 1926–; collections appear in *People's Zoo*, 1971.
b. June 09, 1901 in Coytesville, New Jersey

Pierre-Paul Prudhon
French artist
• Romanticist whose paintings include *Crime Pursued by Vengeance and Justice*, 1808.
b. April 04, 1758 in Cluny, France
d. February 16, 1823 in Paris, France

Susan Gold Purdy
American author–illustrator
• Self-illustrated children's books include *Costumes for You to Make*, 1971; *Books for Your to Make*, 1973.
b. May 17, 1939 in New York, New York

Howard Pyle
American author–illustrator
• Known for juvenile tales: *Story of King Arthur and His Knights*, 1903.
b. March 05, 1853 in Wilmington, Delaware
d. November 09, 1911 in Florence, Italy

Ellen Gertrude Emmet Rand
American artist
• Celebrity portrait painter, noted for craftmanship, coloring; after 1929 crash, sold paintings for up to $5,000 each.
b. March 04, 1875 in San Francisco, California
d. December 18, 1941 in New York, New York

Raphael
(Raffaello Sanzio d'Urbino)
Italian artist–architect
• Master of the High Renaissance; responsible for many paintings inside Vatican: *The School of Athens*.
b. March 28, 1483 in Urbino, Italy
d. April 06, 1520 in Rome, Italy

Abraham Rattner
American artist
• Paintings known for intense, vivid colors depicting religious or moral themes.
b. July 08, 1895 in Poughkeepsie, New York
d. February 14, 1978 in New York, New York

Robert Rauschenberg
(Milton Rauschenberg)
American artist
• Collages, called "combines," include *Gloria*, 1956; *Summer Rental*, 1960.
b. October 22, 1925 in Port Arthur, Texas

Man Ray
American artist–photographer
• Co-founded Dadaism, 1917; developed rayograph photographical technique.
b. August 27, 1890 in Philadelphia, Pennsylvania
d. November 18, 1976 in Paris, France

Alex(ander Gillespie) Raymond
American cartoonist
• Best known for characters: Flash Gordon, Jungle Jim.
b. October 02, 1909 in New Rochelle, New York
d. September 06, 1956 in Westport, Connecticut

James C Raymond
American cartoonist
• Worked on "Blondie" for over 40 yrs.
b. February 25, 1917 in Riverside, Connecticut
d. October 14, 1981 in Boynton Beach, Florida

Odilon Redon
French artist
• Noted for delicate floral studies, fantastic imagery.
b. April 22, 1840 in Bordeaux, France
d. July 06, 1916 in Paris, France

Sir William Reid Dick
English sculptor
• Did stone carvings of royalty, large bronzes.
b. January 13, 1878 in Glasgow, Scotland
d. October 01, 1961 in London, England

Ad(olph Frederick) Reinhardt
American artist
• Precursor of minimal art; known for monochromatic, black works.
b. December 24, 1913 in Buffalo, New York
d. August 3, 1967

Charles S Reinhart
American artist
• Revolutionized art of magazine, book illustration; most noted works in oil and watercolor: *September Morning*, 1879; *Fishermen of Villerville*, 1886.
b. May 16, 1844 in Pittsburgh, Pennsylvania
d. August 3, 1896 in New York, New York

Rembrandt (Harmenszoon van Rijn)
Dutch artist
• Master of light, shadow; notable works include *Nightwatch*, 1642; *Flight into Egypt*, 1627.
b. July 15, 1607 in Leiden, Netherlands
d. October 04, 1669 in Netherlands

Frederic Remington
American artist–sculptor
• Paintings, bronze sculptures depict the Old West.
b. October 04, 1861 in Canton, New York
d. December 26, 1909 in Ridgefield, Connecticut

Guido Reni
Italian artist
• Painted mythological, religius scenes; noted for *Crucifixion of St. Peter*.
b. November 04, 1575 in Bologna, Italy
d. August 18, 1642 in Bologna, Italy

(Pierre) Auguste Renoir
French artist
• Impressionist painter; subjects: nudes, flowers, social scenes, represent optimistic view of life.
b. February 25, 1841 in Limoges, France
d. December 17, 1919 in Cagnes-sur-Mer, France

Ilya Yefimovich Repin
Russian artist
• Leading Russian painter, 1800s; many portraits of Tolstoy have often been reproduced.
b. 1844
d. 1930

Joshua Reynolds, Sir
English artist
• Painted over 2000 portraits, historical scenes; first pres., Royal Academy, 1768; intimate of Johnson, Garrick.
b. July 16, 1723 in Plympton, England
d. February 23, 1792 in London, England

William Trost Richards
American artist
• Painted landscapes, sea pictures; some work in NY Metropolitan Museum's permanent collection.
b. November 14, 1838 in Philadelphia, Pennsylvania
d. 1905 in Newport, Rhode Island

George Warren Rickey
American sculptor
• Major figure in kinetic sculpture; works in Museum of Modern Art, NYC; edited *Contemporary Art, 1942-72*, 1973.
b. June 06, 1907 in South Bend, Indiana

Don(ato) Rico
American illustrator–writer
• Edited Marvel Comics: *Captain America; Daredevil*, 1939-57, 1977-85.
b. September 26, 1917 in Rochester, New York
d. March 27, 1985 in Los Angeles, California

Bridget Riley
English artist
• Op-artist; early work is in black & white geometric shapes, lines; won many awards.
b. April 24, 1931 in London, England

Jean-Paul Riopelle
Canadian artist
• Leading exponent of nonfigurative and "action" painting.
b. 1923 in Montreal, Quebec

Robert Leroy Ripley
American cartoonist
• First published *Believe It or Not* cartoons, 1918.
b. December 25, 1893 in Santa Rosa, California
d. May 27, 1949 in New York, New York

Diego Rivera
Mexican artist
• Painted murals depitcing peasants, workers; revived fresco technique.
b. December 08, 1886 in Guanajuato, Mexico
d. November 25, 1957 in Mexico City, Mexico

Larry Rivers
American artist
• Pioneered in pop art movement: *Double Portrait of Birdie*, 1954.
b. August 17, 1923 in New York, New York

Frank Robbins
American cartoonist
• Drew comic strip "Johnny Hazard," 1944-84; comic books include *Batman*.
b. September 09, 1917 in Boston, Massachusetts

Ercole Roberti
Italian artist
• One of greatest Ferrara painters; did portraits, altarpieces.
b. 1450 in Ferrara, Italy
d. 1496

Boardman Robinson
American artist–illustrator
• Widely reprinted, influential political cartoonist, *NY Tribune*, 1910-14; illustrated books include *Moby Dick*, 1942.
b. September 06, 1876 in Somerset, Nova Scotia
d. September 05, 1952 in Stamford, Connecticut

Auguste (Francois Auguste Rene) Rodin
French sculptor
• Works include *The Thinker; The Kiss; The Burghers of Calais*.
b. November 12, 1840 in Paris, France
d. November 17, 1917 in Meudon, France

Randolph Rogers
American sculptor
• Neo-classicist; did Columbus doors for US capital.
b. July 06, 1825 in Waterloo, New York
d. January 15, 1892 in Rome, Italy

Feodor Stepanovich Rojankovsky
Russian artist
• Won 1956 Caldecott for *Frog Went A-Courtin'*.
b. December 24, 1891 in Mitava, Russia
d. October 21, 1970

Umberto Romano
American artist–educator
• Noted for portraits of Martin Luther King, Jr., John F Kennedy.
b. February 26, 1906 in Bracigliano, Italy
d. September 27, 1982 in New York, New York

George Romney
English artist
• Famed London portraitist; painted Emma Hart (Lady Hamilton) over 50 times.
b. December 15, 1734 in Lancashire, England
d. November 15, 1802 in Kendal, England

Salvator Rosa
Italian artist–poet
• Member, Neapolitan school; painted battle scenes, marines, romantic landscapes.
b. July 1615 in Naples, Italy
d. March 15, 1673 in Rome, Italy

Evelyn Edelson Rosenberg
American artist
• Sculptor, printmaker; innovative works produced by using plastic explosives.
b. 1942 in Washington, District of Columbia

James Albert Rosenquist
American artist
• Pop artist; known for controversial *F-1-11*, 1965 on canvas that was 11 ft. longer than original US bomber.
b. November 29, 1933 in Grand Forks, North Dakota

Joe (Joseph J) Rosenthal
American photojournalist
• Won Pulitzer for picture of Marines raising US flag on Iwo Jima, during WW II.
b. October 09, 1911 in Washington, District of Columbia

Dante Gabriel Rossetti
English poet–artist
• Pre-Raphaelite paintings include *Dante's Dream*, 1871; wrote famed sonnet "The Blessed Damozel," 1850; son of Gabriele.
b. May 12, 1828 in London, England
d. April 09, 1882 in Birchington, England

Susan Rothenberg
American artist
• Painter who used horse as major motif, 1970s, human images, 1980s.
b. January 2, 1945 in Buffalo, New York

Sir William Rothenstein
English artist
• Portraits, lithographs now in Tate, National Portrait Galleries.
b. January 29, 1872 in Bradford, England
d. February 14, 1945 in Oxford, England

Mark Rothko
(Marcus Rothkovich)
American artist
• Pioneer abstract expressionist; known for huge canvases containing simple rectangles of glowing, shifting color.
b. September 25, 1903 in Daugavpils, Russia
d. February 25, 1970 in New York, New York

Georges Rouault
French artist
• Expressionistic paintings include "The Old King."
b. May 27, 1871 in Paris, France
d. February 13, 1958 in Paris, France

Henri Rousseau
(LeDouanier)
French artist
• Primitive painter whose works possess dreamlike quality: *The Sleeping Gypsy,* 1897.
b. May 21, 1844 in Laval, France
d. September 02, 1910 in Paris, France

(Pierre Etienne) Theodore Rousseau
French artist
• Landscapes include *Under the Birches;* led Barbizon School, painted dirctly from nature.
b. April 15, 1812 in Paris, France
d. December 22, 1867 in Barbizon, France

Sir Peter Paul Rubens
Flemish artist
• Baroque style painter, known for brilliant coloring; sacred, historical subjects include *Rape of the Sabines.*
b. June 29, 1577 in Siegen, Prussia
d. May 3, 1640 in Antwerp, Belgium

Reuven Rubin
Israeli artist
• Romantic impressionist, noted for landscapes of Holy Land; first minister to Romania from Israel, 1948-49.
b. November 13, 1893 in Galati, Romania
d. October 13, 1974 in Tel Aviv, Israel

Charles Marion Russell
American artist
• Great painter of American West; museum in Great Falls, MT.
b. March 19, 1864 in Saint Louis, Missouri
d. October 24, 1926

Jacob van Ruysdael
(Jacob van Ruisdael)
Dutch artist
• Landscape painter, etcher known for forest, shore, mountain scenes.
b. 1628 in Haarlem, Netherlands
d. March 14, 1682 in Amsterdam, Netherlands

Tom Kreusch Ryan
American cartoonist
• Draws syndicated cartoon, "Tumbleweeds," 1965–; published 18 paperback compilations, 1970-80.
b. June 06, 1926 in Anderson, Indiana

Albert Pinkham Ryder
American artist
• Legendary hermit-crank of American art; early landscapes may be tiniest ever exhibited as finished work: *The Golden Hour,* 1870s, measures 7 1/2 by 12 1/2.
b. March 19, 1847 in New Bedford, Massachusetts
d. March 28, 1917 in Elmhurst, New York

Augustus Saint Gaudens
American sculptor
• Leading sculptor of late 19th c. known for equestrian statue of General Sherman in Central Park, NYC.
b. March 01, 1848 in Dublin, Ireland
d. August 03, 1907 in Cornish, New Hampshire

Yoshishige Saito
Japanese artist
• Rose to prominence with his surrealistic series of Japanese demons, 1956; later works moved to non-expressive mode.
b. May 04, 1904 in Tokyo, Japan

Lucas Samaras
American artist
• Experimental artist, noted for his "assemblages," three dimensional still lifes: *The Room,* 1964.
b. September 14, 1936 in Kastoria, Greece

Paul Starrett Sample
American artist
• Paintings of genre subjects in a simplified manner include *Janitor's Holiday.*
b. September 14, 1896 in Louisville, Kentucky
d. February 26, 1974 in Norwich, Vermont

Andrea Sansovino
(Andrea Andrea)
Italian artist
• Renaissance sculptures include *Baptism of Christ.*
b. 1460 in Monte Sansavino, Italy
d. 1529

Jacopo Sansovino
(Jacopo Tatti)
Italian artist
• Renaissance sculptures include *St. John the Baptist.*
b. 1486 in Florence, Italy
d. 1570

Ben Sargent
American cartoonist–author
• Won 1982 Pulitzer for editorial cartooning.
b. November 26, 1948 in Amarillo, Texas

John Singer Sargent
American artist
• Portrait painter who had many famous subjects; *Madame X* is in Metropolitan Museum of Art, NYC.
b. January 12, 1856 in Florence, Italy
d. April 15, 1925 in London, England

Andrea del Sarto
(Andrea Domenico d'Agnolodi Francisco; "Andrew the Faultless")
Italian artist
• Noted for superbly colored religious frescoes, easel painting: *Madonna of the Harpies,* 1517.
b. July 16, 1486 in Florence, Italy
d. September 29, 1531 in Florence, Italy

Sassetta
(Stefano di Giovanni)
Italian artist
• Noted painter of international Gothic style; drew panels on life of St. Francis, 1437-44.
b. 1395 in Siena, Italy
d. 1450 in Siena, Italy

Augusta Christine Savage
American sculptor
• First black member National Assn. of Women Painters and Sculptors, 1934; noted for portrait sculpture.
b. February 29, 1892 in Green Cove Springs, Florida
d. March 26, 1962 in Bronx, New York

Charles David Saxon
American cartoonist
• Best known for humorous, satiric commentary on suburban upper class liftstyle in cartoons appearing on covers of *New Yorker* magazine since 1956.
b. November 13, 1920 in New York, New York
d. December 06, 1988 in Stamford, Connecticut

Francesco Scavullo
American photographer
• Freelance photographer known for pictures of models, celebrities appearing in popular magazines.
b. January 16, 1929 in Staten Island, New York

(Johann) Gottfried Schadow
German sculptor
• Member of Neo-classic school; best known for monuments of Fredrick the Great, Blucher, Luther.
b. 1764
d. 1850

Karl Schmidt-Rottluf
German artist
• Helped form German Expressionist group, Die Brucke, 1905; drew vividly colored landscapes, nudes.
b. December 01, 1884 in Rottluff, Germany
d. August 09, 1976 in Wiesbaden, Germany (West)

Julian Schnabel
American artist
• Neo-expressionist whose paintings are encrusted with crockery, plaster; had one-man show, NYC, 1981.
b. October 26, 1951 in Brooklyn, New York

Martin Schongauer
German artist–engraver
• First painter to practice engraving; historical, religious subjects include *Madonna of the Rose Bower*, 1473.
b. 1450 in Colmar, Germany
d. February 02, 1491 in Breisach, Germany

Charles Monroe Schulz
American cartoonist
• Created "Peanuts" comic strip, 1950; won Emmy, 1966.
b. November 26, 1922 in Minneapolis, Minnesota

Scopas
Greek sculptor
• First to depict violent emotions on marble faces; known for architectural works, statues.
b. 6thBC in Paros, Greece

Arthur (Holland Arthur) Secunda
American artist
• Abstract paintings reflect California environment through use of vibrant colors.
b. November 12, 1927 in Jersey City, New Jersey

George Segal
American sculptor
• Known for life-size sculpture done in plaster.
b. November 26, 1924 in New York, New York

Giovanni Segantini
Italian artist
• Portrayed allegorical scenes, peasants, alpine landscapes: *At The Watering Place*.
b. 1858 in Italy
d. 1899

Elzie Crisler Segar
American cartoonist
• Created comic strip "Popeye," 1929.
b. December 08, 1894 in Chester, Illinois
d. October 13, 1938 in Santa Monica, California

Maurice Bernard Sendak
American author–illustrator
• Won Caldecott for *Where the Wild Things Are*, 1963; first American to win H C Anderson's illustrator's award, 1970.
b. June 1, 1928 in Brooklyn, New York

Richard Anthony Serra
American artist
• Most innovative of minimalist sculptors.
b. November 02, 1939 in San Francisco, California

Toyo Sesshu
Japanese artist
• Zen priest, master of ink paintings; noted for landscape scrolls: *Four Seasons Landscape*, ca. 1470-90.
b. 1420
d. 1506

Georges Pierre Seurat
French artist
• Devised pointillist style of painting, tiny dots of color.
b. December 02, 1859 in Paris, France
d. March 29, 1891 in Paris, France

Gino Severini
Italian artist
• Futurist, cubist whose paintings include *Dynamic Hieroglyph of the Bal Tabarin*.
b. 1883 in Italy
d. February 29, 1966 in Paris, France

Ben(jamin) Shahn
American artist
• Noted for posters; used social, political themes in paintings: *Handball*.
b. September 12, 1898 in Kaunas, Lithuania
d. March 14, 1969 in New York, New York

Charles Sheeler
American artist–photographer
• Abstractionist whose paintings include *Upper Deck*; depicted factories, machines.
b. July 16, 1883 in Philadelphia, Pennsylvania
d. May 07, 1965 in Dobbs Ferry, New York

Ernest Howard Shepard
English artist–illustrator
• Gained fame as illustrator of Milne's *Pooh* books.
b. December 1, 1879 in London, England
d. March 24, 1976 in Midhurst, England

Everett Shinn
American artist
• One of "the eight" versatile creator of mag., children's book illustrations; pastel scenes of Paris, NYC.
b. November 07, 1876 in Woodstown, New Jersey
d. May 01, 1953 in New York, New York

Vaughn Richard Shoemaker
American cartoonist
• Political cartoons found in *Chicago Daily News* won Pulitzers, 1938, 1947.
b. August 11, 1902 in Chicago, Illinois

Joe Shuster
American cartoonist
• Best known for "Superman" cartoons.
b. July 1, 1914 in Toronto, Ontario

Jerry Siegel
American cartoonist
• Created comic book's most lucrative character, Superman, 1933; mistakenly sold rights for only $130 in 1938.
b. October 17, 1914 in Cleveland, Ohio

Paul Signac
French artist
• Leading spokesman for the neo-impressionist movement; painted European coastal scenes.
b. November 11, 1863 in Paris, France
d. August 15, 1935 in Paris, France

Luca Signorelli
Italian artist
• Member of Umbrian school; best-known frescoe: *Heaven and Hell*, 1499-1504.
b. 1441 in Cortona, Italy
d. October 16, 1523 in Cortona, Italy

George Silk
American photographer–journalist
• Staff photographer, *Life* magazine, 1943-72; best known for sports, war pictures.
b. November 17, 1916 in Levin, New Zealand

Franklin Simmons
American sculptor
• Marble, bronze portraits, monuments include General Grant in the capital rotunda, 1900.
b. January 11, 1839 in Webster, Maine
d. December 08, 1913 in Rome, Italy

David A Siqueiros
Mexican artist
• Last of Mexican Renaissance giants; did boldly colored murals promoting proletarian revolution.
b. December 29, 1896 in Chihuahua, Mexico
d. January 06, 1974 in Cuernavaca, Mexico

Mario Sironi
Italian artist
• Founding member of the Novecento group: *House and Trees*, 1948.
b. May 12, 1885 in Tempio Pausania, Sardinia
d. August 13, 1961 in Milan, Italy

Alfred Sisley
French artist
• Impressionist painter; *The Flood at Port Marly; Snow at Louveciennes*, both at Louvre.
b. October 3, 1839 in Paris, France
d. January 29, 1899 in Moret, France

John F Sloan
American artist
• Member "The Eight" or "Ashcan" school; drew somber genre scenes of NY working people: *McSorley's Bar*, 1912.
b. August 02, 1871 in Lock Haven, Pennsylvania
d. September 08, 1951 in Hanover, New Hampshire

Louis Slobodkin
American sculptor–author–illustrator
• Won Caldecott Medal for illustrating James Thurber's *Many Moons*, 1943; did sculptures for govt. buildings, wrote *Sculpture: Principles and Practice*, 1949.
b. February 19, 1903 in Albany, New York
d. May 08, 1975 in Miami Beach, Florida

Claus Sluter
Dutch sculptor
• Master of early Burgundian school, noted for works at Dijon.
b. 1350
d. 1406 in Dijon, France

David Smith
American sculptor
• Welded metal sculptures include *Zig*.
b. March 09, 1906 in Decatur, Indiana
d. May 23, 1965 in Albany, New York

(Robert) Sidney Smith
American cartoonist
• Started Andy Gump comic strip, 1917; considered first to introduce continuity to strips by continuing stories day after day.
b. February 13, 1877 in Bloomington, Illinois
d. October 2, 1935 in Harvard, Illinois

Tony (Anthony Peter) Smith
American sculptor
• Created huge minimalist sculptures: *Cigarette*, 1961; *Throwback*, 1978.
b. 1912 in Orange, New Jersey
d. December 26, 1980 in New York, New York

Reginald Smythe
English cartoonist
• Created "Andy Capp," daily comic strip for London's *Daily Mirror*, 1956–.
b. 1917 in Hartlepool, England

Frederick Sommer
American photographer–artist
• Known for 1940s "assemblage" pictures: *Coyotes*, 1945; works have also included landscapes, geometric forms.
b. September 07, 1905 in Angri, Italy

Chaim Soutine
French artist
• Expressionist, used heavy impasto; often painted distorted portraits, slaughterhouse scenes.
b. 1894 in Smilovich, Russia
d. August 09, 1943 in Paris, France

Isaac Soyer
American artist
• With brothers, Moses, Raphael, leading exponent of realism; paintings of Depression Era working class: *Employment Agency*, 1941.
b. April 2, 1907 in Tambov, Russia
d. July 08, 1981 in New York, New York

Moses Soyer
American artist
• Twin brother of Raphael; social realism genre painter; major works include *Girl at Sewing Machine*, 1940.
b. December 25, 1899 in Tambov, Russia
d. September 02, 1974 in New York, New York

Raphael Soyer
American artist
• Social realist; known for paintings showing men, women during the Depression.
b. December 25, 1899 in Tambov, Russia
d. November 04, 1987 in New York, New York

Sir Stanley Spencer
British artist
• Drew surrealistic religious paintings including *Resurrection* series, 1945-50.
b. 1891
d. December 14, 1959 in Cliveden, England

Peter Edward Spier
American artist–author
• Self-illustrated children's books include *Gobble, Growl, Grunt*, 1971.
b. June 06, 1927 in Amsterdam, Netherlands

Spy pseud
(Leslie Ward)
English cartoonist
• Contributed to *Vanity Fair* for 36 yrs; recollections in *Forty Years of Spy*, 1915.
b. November 21, 1851 in London, England
d. May 15, 1922 in London, England

Jannis Spyropoulos
Greek artist
• Painting style ranged from naturalistic to abstract to non-objective abstract; later paintings concentrate on surface, texture.
b. March 12, 1912 in Pylos, Greece

Nicolas de Stael
French artist
• Painted mainly in watercolor; known for *Footballers* series, 1952; suicide victim.
b. 1914 in Saint Petersburg, Russia
d. March 22, 1955 in Antibes, France

Ben(jamin Albert) Stahl
American artist–illustrator
• Best known for illustrations in the *Saturday Evening Post*, 1933-63; won many awards.
b. September 07, 1910 in Chicago, Illinois
d. October 19, 1987 in Sarasota, Florida

Richard Peter Stankiewicz
American artist
• Pioneer in junk art; created sculptures from scrap metal *The Bride*.
b. October 18, 1922 in Philadelphia, Pennsylvania
d. March 27, 1983 in Worthington, Massachusetts

Jan Steen
Dutch artist
• Prolific painter of genre scenes depicting taverns, middle-class life.
b. 1626 in Leiden, Netherlands
d. February 03, 1679 in Leiden, Netherlands

Saul Steinberg
American artist–cartoonist
• Known for cartoons, cover-art for *New Yorker*; works combine many styles including cubism, pointalism.
b. June 15, 1914 in Romanic-Sarat, Romania

Frank Philip Stella
American artist
• Leader of "Minimal Art" movement; paintings emphasize shape and color.
b. May 12, 1936 in Malden, Massachusetts

Joseph Stella
American artist
• Realist-turned-semiabstractionist painter: *Battle of Lights, Coney Island*, 1913; *Brooklyn Bridge*, 1919.
b. June 13, 1880 in Munra Lucano, Italy
d. November 05, 1946 in New York, New York

Bert Stern
American photographer
• Commercial photographer who ascribed to motto "less is more"; known for Smirnoff ads of martini glass in front of pyramids, 1955, portfolio of Marilyn Monroe silkscreen prints, 1967.
b. October 03, 1929 in New York, New York

Maurice Sterne
American artist
• Modern classicist, painted 20 murals for Dept. of Justice Bldg.; works done on Bali made island famous.
b. July 13, 1878 in Libau, Russia
d. July 23, 1957

Alfred Stieglitz
American photographer–editor
• Work characterized by technical innovations taking pictures at night or in rain; influenced by artists Matisse, Picasso; husband of Georgia O'Keefe.
b. January 01, 1864 in Hoboken, New Jersey
d. July 13, 1946 in New York, New York

Clyfford Still
American artist
• Pioneer in use of mural sized canvas.
b. October 3, 1904 in Grandin, North Dakota
d. June 23, 1980 in Baltimore, Maryland

Veit Stoss
German sculptor
• Master wood carver, active in Krakow, Nuremberg.
b. 1445 in Nuremberg, Germany
d. 1533 in Nuremberg, Germany

Gilbert Charles Stuart
American artist
• Noted for three portraits of George Washington, 1795-96.
b. December 03, 1755 in North Kingstown, Rhode Island
d. July 09, 1828 in Boston, Massachusetts

James Stuart
English architect–artist
• Published *The Antiquities of Athens*, 1762, which had first illustrations of Greek architecture; work spurred the classic revival period.
b. 1713
d. 1788

George Stubbs
English artist
• Animal painter, noted for drawings of horses.
b. 1724 in Liverpool, England
d. 1806

Thomas Sully
American artist
• Painted over 2,000 portraits, 500 historical scenes.
b. June 08, 1783 in Horncastle, England
d. November 05, 1872 in Philadelphia, Pennsylvania

Graham Vivian Sutherland
English artist
• Commissioned to paint a portrait of Winston Churchill, 1954; so disliked, Churchill's family destroyed it.
b. August 24, 1903 in London, England
d. February 17, 1980 in Hampstead, England

Richard Sylbert
American art director
• Films include *Breathless; The Cotton Club;* won Oscar for *Who's Afraid of Virginia Woolf*, 1966.
b. April 16, 1928 in New York, New York

Arthur Szyk
Polish artist
• Miniaturist, manuscript illuminator; noted for fine book illustration.
b. June 03, 1894 in Lodz, Poland
d. September 13, 1951 in New Canaan, Connecticut

Sophie Taeuber-Arp
Swiss artist
• Sculptor; active in Dada movement; wed to Jean Arp; best work done, 1935-38.
b. January 19, 1889 in Davos, Switzerland
d. January 13, 1943 in Zurich, Switzerland

Arthur Fitzwilliam Tait
English artist
• Self-taught painter for Currier & Ives; specialized in animal subjects: *The Life of a Hunter*, 1928.
b. August 05, 1819 in Liverpool, England
d. 1905 in Yonkers, New York

William Henry Fox Talbot
English photographer–inventor
• Developed several photographic processes, including method for taking instant pictures, 1851.
b. February 11, 1800 in Lacock Abbey, England
d. September 17, 1877 in Lacock Abbey, England

Rufino Tamayo
Mexican artist
• Fused ancient Mexican with modern French art; painted nationalistic murals in Mexico City, 1950s.
b. August 26, 1899

Yves Tanguy
American artist
• Surrealist painter whose permanent collections are in museums throughout US, Paris.
b. January 05, 1900 in Paris, France
d. January 15, 1955

Henry Ossawa Tanner
American artist
• Most renowned of all black artists; member National Academy of Art and Design.
b. June 21, 1859 in Pittsburgh, Pennsylvania
d. May 25, 1937 in Etaples, France

Tao-chi
(Shih-Tao)
Chinese artist
• One of first Individualist painters well known in China, the West; landscapes have often been forged.
b. 1630 in Wu-Chou, China
d. 1717

David Teniers, the Younger
Flemish artist
• Paintings express tone, atmosphere: *The Dance in Front of the Castle*, 1645.
b. December 14, 1610 in Antwerp, Belgium
d. April 25, 1690 in Brussels, Belgium

Sir John Tenniel
English illustrator–artist
• Best known for illustrations in *Alice's Adventures in Wonderland*.
b. February 28, 1820 in London, England
d. February 25, 1914 in London, England

Gerard Ter Borch
Dutch artist
• Noted for small portraits, genre painting, including *Guitar Lesson*.
b. 1617 in Zwolle, Netherlands
d. December 08, 1681 in Deventer, Netherlands

Hendrick Terbrugghen
Dutch artist
• Genre works, influenced by Caravaggio, include *The Flute Player*, 1621.
b. 1588
d. 1629

Paul H Terry
American cartoonist–producer
• Best known for animation of Mighty Mouse.
b. February 19, 1887 in San Mateo, California
d. October 25, 1971 in New York, New York

(Morton) Wayne Thiebaud
American artist
• Realist painter best known for use of light, structure.
b. November 15, 1920 in Mesa, Arizona

Hans Thoma
German artist
• Influenced by Courbet; early landscapes depict native Black Forest.
b. 1839 in Bernau, Germany
d. 1924 in Karlsruhe, Germany

Tom Thomson
Canadian artist
- Short painting career ended when found mysteriously drowned; his Canadian landscapes directly influenced the Group of Seven.
- **b.** 1877 in Claremont, Ontario
- **d.** July 08, 1917 in Canoe Lake, Ontario

Jack Randolph Thornell
American photographer
- With AP, 1964–; won Pulitzer, 1967.
- **b.** August 29, 1939 in Vicksburg, Mississippi

Giambattista (Giovanni Battista) Tiepolo
Italian artist
- Works include frescos, portraits, palace facades.
- **b.** March 05, 1696 in Venice, Italy
- **d.** March 27, 1770

Louis Comfort Tiffany
American artist–designer
- VP, director, Tiffany and Co. who discovered formula for making decorative glass, "Tiffany Favrile glass"; known for Tiffany lamps.
- **b.** February 18, 1848 in New York, New York
- **d.** January 17, 1933 in New York, New York

Jean Tinguely
Swiss sculptor
- Began using motion in sculpture, 1940s; advanced to complex machine art: *Homage to NY*, 1960.
- **b.** 1925

Tintoretto
(Jacopo Robusti)
Italian artist
- Paintings known for unusual body movement, light, spacing.
- **b.** 1518 in Venice, Italy
- **d.** May 31, 1594 in Venice, Italy

Titian
(Tiziano Vecellio)
Italian artist
- Works include *Assumption of the Virgin*, 1518; *La Bella*, 1537; master colorist.
- **b.** 1477 in Preve di Cadore, Italy
- **d.** August 27, 1576 in Venice, Italy

Feliks Topolski
British artist
- Official war artist, 1940-45; mural in Buckingham Palace: *The Coronation of Elizabeth II*.
- **b.** August 14, 1907 in Warsaw, Poland
- **d.** August 24, 1989 in London, England

(Henri Marie Raymond de) Toulouse-Lautrec (Monfa)
French artist
- Postimpressionist painter known for physical deformity; drawings of Paris cabarets.
- **b.** November 24, 1864 in Albi, France
- **d.** September 09, 1901 in Malrome, France

Constant Troyon
French artist
- Member, Barbizon School; noted for landscapes and animal scenes, particularly cows.
- **b.** August 18, 1810 in Sevres, France
- **d.** February 21, 1865 in Paris, France

Garry (Garretson Beckman) Trudeau
American cartoonist
- Created comic strip "Doonesbury"; won Pulitzer, 1975.
- **b.** 1948 in New York, New York

Cosme Tura
(Cosimo Tura)
Italian artist
- Founder, master of Ferrarese school of painting; works include allegorical frescoes, Pieta, 1472.
- **b.** 1430 in Ferrara, Italy
- **d.** 1495 in Ferrara, Italy

Joseph Mallord William Turner
English artist
- Foremost English Romantic painter; noted for impressionistic oils, watercolors of seascapes.
- **b.** April 23, 1775 in London, England
- **d.** December 19, 1851 in London, England

Morrie Turner
American cartoonist–author
- Broke cartoon strip color barrier with syndicated comic *Wee Pals*, 1970s; books include *All God's Chillun Got Soul*, 1980.
- **b.** December 11, 1923 in Oakland, California

John Henry Twachtman
American artist
- Impressionist landscape painter; known for scenes of Yellowstone, Niagara: "Snowbound," 1902.
- **b.** 1853 in Cincinnati, Ohio
- **d.** 1902

Paolo Uccello
(Paolo di Dono)
Italian artist
- Developed foreshortening, linear perspective: *Rout of San Romano*, 1450s.
- **b.** 1396 in Florence, Italy
- **d.** December 1, 1475 in Florence, Italy

Huynh Cong Ut
Vietnamese photojournalist
- Won 1973 Pulitzer for photograph of children running, crying from their napalmed village near Saigon.
- **b.** March 29, 1951 in Saigon, Vietnam

Kitagawa Utamaro
Japanese artist
- Best known Japanese master of color print; paintings center around beautiful women's occupations, amusements.
- **b.** 1753
- **d.** 1806

Maurice Utrillo
French artist
- Style based on modified form of Cubism; known for Parisian street scenes, houses.
- **b.** December 25, 1883 in Paris, France
- **d.** November 05, 1955 in Dax, France

Suzanne Valadon
French artist
- Mother of Utrillo; influenced in painting by Gauguin, Degas; figures usually from working class.
- **b.** 1869 in Bessines, France
- **d.** 1938 in Paris, France

Edmund Siegfried Valtman
American cartoonist
- Won 1962 Pulitzer for political, anti-Castro cartoon.
- **b.** May 31, 1914 in Tallinn, Russia

John Vanderlyn
American artist
- First nude exhibited in US caused scandal, 1815; portraits of famous people include Andrew Jackson, James Monroe.
- **b.** October 15, 1775 in Kingston, New York
- **d.** September 23, 1852 in Kingston, New York

James Van Der Zee
American photographer
- Known for photographs of Harlem, begun in 1915.
- **b.** June 29, 1886 in Lenox, Massachusetts
- **d.** May 15, 1983 in Washington, District of Columbia

Sir Anthony Van Dyck
Flemish artist
- Court painter to Charles I of England; set style for English portraiture which lasted a century.
- **b.** March 22, 1599 in Antwerp, Belgium
- **d.** December 09, 1641

Hubert Van Eyck
Flemish artist
• Co-founder, with brother Jan, of Flemish School; only extant piece, Lamb altarpiece, Ghent.
b. 1370
d. 1426

Jan Van Eyck
Flemish artist
• Noted for descriptive realism, intensive color; perfected, but did not discover oil technique.
b. 1371 in Maeseyck, Netherlands
d. 1440

Vincent Willem Van Gogh
Dutch artist
• Works in brilliant colors, swirling brush strokes became popular 50 years after death, include *Sunflowers*.
b. March 3, 1853 in Groot Zundert, Netherlands
d. July 29, 1890 in Auvers, France

Alberto Vargas
(Joaquin Alberto Vargas y Chavez)
American artist
• Created pinups for *Esquire*; *Playboy* magazines.
b. February 09, 1895 in Arequipa, Peru
d. December 3, 1983 in Los Angeles, California

F(rederick) H(orseman) Varley
(Group of Seven)
Canadian artist
• Landscape, portrait painter; original member of group influential in Canadian painting, 1920s; famous for *Stormy Weather, Georgian Bay*, 1920.
b. January 02, 1881 in Sheffield, England
d. September 08, 1969 in Toronto, Ontario

Victor Vasarely
French artist
• Considered originator of post-war Op Art; geometric works include *Orion MC*, 1963.
b. April 09, 1908 in Pecs, Hungary

Elihu Vedder
American artist
• Painted five decorative panels, mosaic Minerva in the Congressional Library in Washington, DC.
b. February 26, 1836 in New York
d. January 29, 1923

Diego Rodriguez de Silva Velazquez
Spanish artist
• Greatest Spanish Baroque painter; superb colorist, noted for portraits, genre scenes.
b. June 06, 1599 in Seville, Spain
d. August 06, 1660 in Madrid, Spain

Willem van de Velde
Dutch artist
• Known for paintings of naval battles; member of family of famous 17th century painters, draftsmen.
b. 1633 in Leiden, Netherlands
d. 1707 in London, England

Jan Vermeer
(Jan van der Meer; Jan van Delft)
Dutch artist
• Painted Dutch interiors, genre subjects; interested in light, color: *The Lacemaker*.
b. October 3, 1632 in Delft, Netherlands
d. December 15, 1675 in Delft, Netherlands

Paolo Veronese
(Paolo Caliari; "Painter of Pageants")
Italian artist
• Noted for decorative, many-figured frescos, altarpieces: *Marriage of Cana*.
b. 1528 in Verona, Italy
d. April 19, 1588

Andrea del Verrocchio
(Andrea di Michele di Francesco Cioni)
Italian artist
• Sculptures include bronze of David; paintings include *Baptism of Christ*.
b. 1435 in Florence, Italy
d. October 07, 1488 in Venice, Italy

Marcel Vertes
Hungarian artist
• Designed scenery, costumes for ballets: *Bluebeard; Helen of Troy*; exhibits in museums around the world.
b. August 1, 1895 in Ujpest, Hungary
d. October 31, 1961 in Paris, France

Robert (Remsen) Vickrey
American artist
• Paintings are of detailed, eerie tempera: *The Labyrinth*, 1951.
b. August 2, 1926 in New York, New York

Marie-Louise-Elisabeth Vigee-Lebrun
French artist
• Best known for her portraits, including over 25 of Marie-Antoinette.
b. 1755
d. 1842

Roman Vishniac
American photographer
• Best known for photographs documenting doomed Jews in Nazi Germany.
b. August 19, 1897 in Saint Petersburg, Russia
d. January 22, 1990 in New York, New York

Maurice de Vlaminck
French artist
• Painted in broad strokes, straight from paint tube to canvas; began with Fauvism ended with sinister realism.
b. April 04, 1876 in Paris, France
d. October 11, 1958 in Paris, France

Alfredo Volpi
Brazilian artist
• Abstract paintings marked by intricate geometric forms in bright colors.
b. 1895 in Lucca, Italy
d. May 3, 1988 in Sao Paolo, Brazil

Robert William Vonnoh
American artist
• Paintings exhibited at Metropolitan Museum, NYC, include *President Wilson's Family, La Mere Adele*.
b. September 17, 1858 in Hartford, Connecticut
d. December 28, 1933 in Lyme, Connecticut

Chris Von Wangenheim
German photographer
• Fashion photographer whose admirable love of women produced "daring, provacative, brilliantly inventive" photos.
b. 1942 in Breslau, Germany
d. March 09, 1981 in St. Martin Island

Simon Vouet
French artist
• Best-known paintings: *The Presentation*, 1641; *Allegory of Peace*, 1648.
b. January 09, 1590
d. June 3, 1649

(Jean) Edouard Vuillard
French artist
• Painted commonplace subjects, domestic interiors: *Woman Sweeping*, 1892.
b. November 11, 1868 in Cuiseaux, France
d. June 21, 1940 in La Baule, France

Mary Morris Vaux Walcott
American artist–naturalist
• Illustrated five-volume *North American Wild Flowers*, 1925.
b. July 31, 1860 in Philadelphia, Pennsylvania
d. August 22, 1940 in Saint Andrew's, New Brunswick

Max Waldman
American photographer
• Known for black and white theater and classical dance subjects, 1947-81.
b. 1920 in New York, New York
d. March 01, 1981 in New York, New York

Henry Oliver Walker
American artist
• Figural, mural painter; did congressional library scenes.
b. May 14, 1843 in Boston, Massachusetts
d. January 14, 1929 in Belmont, Massachusetts

Mort Walker
(Mortimer Walker Addison)
American cartoonist
• Created *Beetle Bailey*, 1950; *Hi and Lois*, 1954.
b. September 03, 1923 in El Dorado, Kansas

Jay Ward
American cartoonist
• Created cartoon characters Rocky the Flying Squirrel and Bullwinkle Moose with partner Bill Scott, 1959.
b. September 21, 1920 in San Francisco, California
d. October 12, 1989 in Los Angeles, California

Lynd Ward
American artist
• Noted for woodcutt illustrations; won 1952 Caldecott for *The Biggest Bear*.
b. June 26, 1905 in Chicago, Illinois
d. June 28, 1985 in Reston, Virginia

Andy Warhol
(Andrew Warhola)
American artist–author
• Leader of pop artists since early 1960s; known for paintings of soup cans, celebrities; published *Interview* mag., made several films.
b. August 06, 1927 in McKeesport, Pennsylvania
d. February 22, 1987 in New York, New York

Jean Antoine Watteau
French artist
• Rococo painter; noted for pastel coloring, courtly fantasies: *Embarkation of Cythera*, 1717.
b. October 1, 1684 in Valenciennes, France
d. July 18, 1721 in Nogent sur Marne, France

Bill (William B, II) Watterson
American cartoonist
• Created syndicated comic strip "Calvin and Hobbes," 1985.
b. 1958

George Frederic Watts
English artist–sculptor
• Best known for 19th-c. British portraiture, busts.
b. 1817 in London, England
d. 1904 in London, England

Frederick Judd Waugh
American artist
• Principally painted marine scenes; designed church of St. Mary's of the Harbor, Provincetown, MA.
b. September 13, 1861 in Bordentown, New Jersey
d. September 11, 1940

Max Weber
American artist–author
• Social themes depicted in *Chinese Restaurant* .
b. April 18, 1881 in Bialystok, Russia
d. October 04, 1961 in Great Neck, New York

Robert Maxwell Weber
American cartoonist
• With *New Yorker* mag. since 1962; contributor of cartoons to US newspapers.
b. April 22, 1924 in Los Angeles, California

H(arold) T(ucker) Webster
American cartoonist
• Newspaper cartoonist known for "The Timid Soul," its character Caspar Milquetoast.
b. September 21, 1885 in Parkersburg, West Virginia
d. September 22, 1952 in Stamford, Connecticut

Josiah Wedgwood
English artist
• Founded firm, 1759; invented translucent, unglazed semiporcelain called jasper ware.
b. July 12, 1730 in Burslem, England
d. January 03, 1795 in Etruria, England

Adolph A Weinman
American sculptor
• Designed 1916 dime, half dollar.
b. December 11, 1870 in Karlsruhe, Germany
d. August 08, 1952

John F(erguson) Weir
American artist
• Industrial scenes include *Forging the Shaft;* son of Robert.
b. August 28, 1841 in West Point, New York
d. April 08, 1926 in Providence, Rhode Island

Julian Alden Weir
American artist
• Semi-Impressionist works include *The Green Bodice;* son of Robert.
b. August 3, 1852 in West Point, New York
d. December 08, 1919

Tom Wesselmann
American artist
• Best known for series of *The Great American Nude* paintings in different setups, media.
b. February 23, 1931 in Cincinnati, Ohio

Benjamin West
American artist
• Realistic, historic paintings include *Death of General Wolfe*.
b. October 1, 1738 in Springfield, Pennsylvania
d. March 11, 1820 in London, England

H(orace) C(lifford) Westermann
American sculptor
• Works of metal, wood take on a comic strip flare; known for surrealist displacement.
b. December 11, 1922 in Los Angeles, California
d. November 03, 1981 in Danbury, Connecticut

Edward Weston
American photographer
• One of most influential photographers of 20th c.; was subject of film *The Photographer*, 1948.
b. March 24, 1886 in Highland Park, Illinois
d. January 01, 1958 in Carmel, California

Rogier van der Weyden
(Roger de la Pasture)
Flemish artist
• Religious, portrait painter; noted for color, emotion, *Descent From the Cross*, 1435.
b. 1399 in Tournai, Belgium
d. June 16, 1464 in Brussels, Belgium

James Abbott McNeill Whistler
American artist–author
• Famous for *Arrangement in Gray and Black No.1: The Artist's Mother*, 1872 or, "Whistler's Mother."
b. July 1, 1834 in Lowell, Massachusetts
d. July 17, 1903 in London, England

Gertrude Vanderbilt Whitney
(Mrs William Collins Whitney)
American sculptor–art patron
• Founded Whitney Museum of American Art, NYC; opened, 1931.
b. 1877 in New York, New York
d. April 18, 1942 in New York, New York

Thomas Worthington Whittredge
American artist
• Painted Western scenes, romantic landscapes; posed as Washington in Leutze's *Washington Crossing the Delaware*.
b. May 22, 1820 in Springfield, Ohio
d. February 25, 1910 in New Jersey

Olaf Wieghorst
Danish artist
• Drew horses, Navajo portraits; a painting sold for $1 million, highest price ever paid to living American artist at the time.
b. 1899 in Jutland, Denmark
d. April 27, 1988 in La Mesa, California

Sir David Wilkie
Scottish artist
• Influenced by Spanish art, Flemish realists; pioneered English school of anecdotal or "subject" painting.
b. November 18, 1785 in Cults, Scotland
d. June 01, 1841

Archibald MacNeal Willard
American artist
- Painted *The Spirit of '76.*
b. August 22, 1836 in Bedford, Ohio
d. October 11, 1918 in Cleveland, Ohio

Frank Henry Willard
American cartoonist
- Created "Moon Mullins," "Kitty Higgins" cartoons.
b. September 21, 1893 in Chicago, Illinois
d. January 12, 1958 in Los Angeles, California

Gluyas Williams
American cartoonist
- Satirized middle-class America in *The New Yorker,* 1928-53.
b. July 23, 1888 in San Francisco, California
d. February 13, 1982 in Boston, Massachusetts

Edward Arthur Wilson
American artist–illustrator
- Noted woodcut illustrator of sea adventures: *The Pirate's Treasure,* 1926.
b. March 04, 1886 in Glasgow, Scotland
d. October 02, 1970 in Dobbs Ferry, New York

Tom Wilson
American cartoonist
- Created "Ziggy" comic strip; syndicated since 1971.
b. August 01, 1931 in Grant Town, West Virginia

Konrad Witz
Swiss artist
- Among first to use realistic landscapes in religious scenes: *Christ Walking on the Waters.*
b. 1400 in Rottweil, Germany
d. 1447 in Basel, Switzerland

Grant Wood
American artist
- Depicted rural life in Midwest: *American Gothic,* 1930.
b. February 13, 1892 in Anamosa, Iowa
d. February 12, 1942 in Iowa City, Iowa

George S Wunder
American cartoonist
- Succeeded Caniff as artist for comic strip "Terry and the Pirates," 1947-73.
b. April 24, 1912 in New York, New York
d. December 13, 1987 in New Milford, Connecticut

Andrew Wyeth
American artist
- Son of Newell Convers Wyeth; subjects are people, place of northeastern states; best-known painting: *Christina's World.*
b. July 12, 1917 in Chadds Ford, Pennsylvania

Henriette (Zirngiebel) Wyeth
(Mrs Peter Hurd)
American artist
- Specialized in portraits, murals; sister of Andrew.
b. October 22, 1907 in Wilmington, Delaware

Jamie (James Browning) Wyeth
American artist
- Called most commercially successful artist of his generation; member, Nat. Endowment for Arts, 1972–; son of Andrew.
b. July 06, 1946 in Wilmington, Delaware

N(ewell) C(onvers) Wyeth
American illustrator–artist
- Illustrated popular children's novels; father of Andrew, grandfather of Jamie.
b. October 22, 1882 in Needham, Massachusetts
d. October 19, 1945 in Chadds Ford, Pennsylvania

Bill Yates
(Floyd Buford Yates)
American cartoonist
- Drew comic strip "Professor Phumble," 1960-78; comics feature editor of King Features Syndicate, 1978–.
b. July 05, 1921 in Samson, Alabama

Art(hur Henry) Young
American cartoonist–author
- Contributed cartoons to *Life; Puck; Colliers* magazines.
b. January 14, 1866 in Orangeville, Illinois
d. December 29, 1943 in Bethel, Connecticut

Chic (Murat Bernard) Young
American cartoonist
- Created comic strip "Blondie," 1930.
b. January 09, 1901
d. March 14, 1973 in Saint Petersburg, Florida

Mahonri Mackintosh Young
American sculptor
- Executed Mormon statues, Indian groups; first prize for sculpture, 1932 Olympic Games.
b. August 09, 1877 in Salt Lake City, Utah
d. November 02, 1957 in New York, New York

Jack Youngerman
American artist
- Abstract paintings include "Dive," 1980; "Ohio," 1977.
b. March 25, 1926 in Webster Grove, Missouri

Ossip Zadkine
Russian artist
- Sculptures include *The Destroyed City; Musicians.*
b. July 14, 1890
d. November 25, 1967 in Paris, France

Zao-Wou-Ki
French artist
- Known for imaginative landscapes, animals; brushstrokes resemble a type of calligraphy.
b. 1921 in Peking, China

Korczak Ziolkowski
American sculptor
- Spent 35 years blasting Thunderhead Mt. creating monument to Crazy Horse.
b. September 06, 1908 in Boston, Massachusetts
d. October 2, 1982 in Sturgis, South Dakota

William Zorach
American artist–sculptor
- Sculptures include post office in Washington, DC; facade for Mayo Clinic Building.
b. February 28, 1887 in Eurburg, Lithuania
d. November 15, 1967 in Bath, Maine

Anders Leonhard Zorn
Swedish artist
- Paintings are usually Swedish subjects, nudes, portraits including *Portrait of the Artist and his Wife.*
b. 1860 in Mora, Sweden
d. 1920

Francisco Zurbaran
Spanish artist
- Baroque painter known for religious, monastic work: *Immaculate Conception,* 1616.
b. November 07, 1598 in Fuentes de Cantos, Spain
d. August 27, 1664 in Madrid, Spain

SAINTS, SINNERS & SUFFRAGETTES

Anarchists, Assassins, Civil Rights Leaders, Feminists, Hunger Strikers...

Aaron
Religious Leader–Biblical Character
• Brother of Moses; founded Hebrew priesthood.

Grace Abbott
American social reformer
• Influential in having child-labor laws declared unconstitutional, 1918.
b. November 17, 1878 in Grand Island, Nebraska
d. June 19, 1939 in Chicago, Illinois

Saint Thomas A'Becket
(Thomas Becket; Thomas of Canterbury; Thomas of London)
English religious leader
• Archbishop of Canterbury, 1162-70; conflict with Henry II, martyrdom were subject of T S Eliot's *Murder in the Cathedral*, 1935.
b. December 21, 1118 in London, England
d. December 29, 1170 in Canterbury, England

Ralph David Abernathy
American clergyman–civil rights leader
• Close friend of Martin Luther King, Jr.; succeeded King as pres. of SCLC, 1968-77; wrote controversial autobiography *And the Walls Came Tumbling Down*, 1989.
b. March 11, 1926 in Linden, Alabama
d. April 17, 1990 in Atlanta, Georgia

Morris Berthold Abram
American civil rights leader–lawyer
• First head of Peace Corps legal department, 1961.
b. June 19, 1918 in Fitzgerald, Georgia

Abu Bakr
Arabian religious leader
• Father-in-law, first convert, successor of Mohammed; helped make Islam a world religion.
b. 573 in Mecca, Arabia
d. August 634

Abu Daoud
(Muhamman Daoud Audeh; Tarik Shakir Mahdi)
Palestinian terrorist
• Most wanted, feared int'l. criminal of 1980s; thought responsible for many terrorist attacks.
b. 1937

Jane (Laura Jane) Addams
American social worker–suffragette
• Organized Hull House, Chicago, 1889; first American woman to receive Nobel Peace Prize, 1931.
b. September 06, 1860 in Cedarville, Illinois
d. May 21, 1935 in Chicago, Illinois

Felix Adler
American reformer
• Founder, Ethical Culture Society, 1876, which aided NY poor.
b. August 13, 1851 in Alzey, Germany
d. April 24, 1933 in New York, New York

Joe Adonis
(Joe Doro; "Joey A")
Italian criminal
• Headed Broadway mob that controlled bootleg liquor in Manhattan; deported, 1956.
b. November 22, 1902 in Montemarano, Italy
d. November 26, 1971 in Aucona, Italy

Adrian II
(Hadrian II)
Italian religious leader
• Last pope to be married; approved Slavic liturgy.
b. 792 in Rome, Italy
d. 872

Aga Khan IV
(Prince Karim Khan)
Religious Leader
• Descendant of Mohammed; grandson of Aga Khan III, who succeeded him as Imam, spiritual leader of Ismaili Moslems, 1957–.
b. December 13, 1936 in Geneva, Switzerland

Mehmet Ali Agca
(Faruk Ozgun)
Turkish terrorist–attempted assassin
• Convicted of attempting to assassinate Pope John Paul II, May 1981.
b. 1958 in Malatya, Turkey

Saint Agnes
Roman religious figure
• Well-born virgin martyr; patron saint of young girls.
b. 291 in Rome
d. 304 in Rome

Salvador Agron
American murderer
• Youngest person, at age 16, to receive death sentence in NY state, 1959; sentence commuted, 1962; paroled, 1979.
b. 1944 in New York
d. April 22, 1986 in New York, New York

Thomas Leo Ahern, Jr
(The Hostages)
American hostage in Iran
• One of 52 held by terrorists, Nov 1979 - Jan 1981.
b. 1932 in Falls Church, Virginia

Saint Albertus Magnus
(Albert Count of Bollstadt; Albrecht von Koln; "Doctor Universalis" "The Great" "LePetit Albert")
German philosopher–religious figure
• Paraphrased Aristotle's works; canonized, 1932.
b. 1193 in Lauingen, Germany
d. November 15, 1280 in Cologne, Germany

Alexander VI
(Rodrigo de Borja y Doms; Rodrigo Borgia; "The Worst Pope")
Spanish religious leader
• Pope, 1492-1503, elected by corrupt conclave; father of Cesare and Lucrezia Borgia.
b. January 01, 1431 in Xativa, Spain
d. August 18, 1503

Ali
Arabian religious leader
• Fourth caliph of Arab, Islamic Empire; cousin of Muhammed; division of Islam into Sunni, Shiites began during reign.
b. 600
d. 661 in Al Kufa, Iraq

Richard Allen
American religious leader
• First black ordained in Methodist Episcopal Church, 1799; founded African Methodist Church, 1816.
b. February 14, 1760 in Philadelphia, Pennsylvania
d. March 26, 1831 in Philadelphia, Pennsylvania

Clay Allison
American outlaw
• "Fast gun," who killed at least 15 other gunmen in NM area, 1870s.
b. 1840 in Tennessee
d. 1877

Rulon Clark Allred
American religious leader
• Founded Apostolic United Brethren, a Fundamentalist Mormon, polygamy-practicing group.
b. March 29, 1906 in Chihuahua, Mexico
d. May 1, 1977 in Murray, Utah

Saint Ambrose
Italian religious leader
• Bishop of Milan who was first to use hymns extensively as divine praise.
b. 340 in Trier, Germany
d. April 04, 397 in Milan, Italy

Jessie Daniel Ames
American reformer
• Founded Assn. of Southern Women for Prevention of Lynching, 1930.
b. November 02, 1883 in Palestine, Texas
d. February 21, 1972 in Austin, Texas

Amos
Prophet–Biblical Character
• Visions recorded in Old Testament book of Amos.
b. 750BC

Albert Anastasia
American criminal–murderer
• Joined Louis Buchalter and Murder Inc., 1931; extorted "sweetheart contracts" from unions.
b. September 26, 1902 in Tropea, Italy
d. October 29, 1957 in New York, New York

Terry A Anderson
American journalist
• Chief Middle East correspondent for AP; hostage in Lebanon since 1985. Longest-held hostage.
b. October 27, 1947

William Anderson
American murderer
• Confederate officer; raided MO-KS border towns during Civil War; killed unarmed men, boys.

Saint Angela Merici
(Angela of Brescia)
Italian religious figure
• Founded company of St. Ursula, 1534, first teaching order of women devoted to educating women.
b. 1474 in Desenzano, Italy
d. 1540

Saint Anselm
Italian religious leader
• Archbishop of Canterbury, 1093-1109, called founder of scholasticism; writings characterized by rational argument.
b. 1033 in Aosta, Italy
d. April 21, 1109 in Canterbury, England

Saint Anthony
(Saint Anthony the Abbot)
Egyptian religious leader
• Founded Christian monasticism, c. 305.
b. 251 in Memphis, Egypt
d. 350 in Mount Kolzim, Egypt

Saint Anthony of Padua
French religious figure
• Biblical scholar with reputation as miracle worker; patron saint of lost articles.
b. August 15, 1195 in Lisbon, Portugal
d. June 13, 1231 in Padua, Italy

Earl Anthony
American author–civil rights leader
• Joined Black Panthers, 1967, wrote *Picking Up the Gun: A Report on the Black Panthers*, 1970.
b. 1941 in Roanoke, Virginia

Susan B(rownell) Anthony
American reformer–suffragette
• Early advocate of women's equality; led women's suffrage movement.
b. February 15, 1820 in Adams, Massachusetts
d. March 13, 1906 in Rochester, New York

Apache Kid
American criminal
• Indian, cavalry scout, convicted of murder, then pardoned by Pres. Cleveland.
b. 1868
d. 1894 in Tucson, Arizona

Gaius Sollius Apollinaris Sidonius
(Saint Sidonius)
French religious figure
• Letters describe life during breakup of Roman Empire; feast day Aug 21.
b. 430 in Lyons, France
d. 487 in Clermont, France

Thomas Aquinas, Saint
(Tommaso d'Aquino; "Angelic Doctor" "Doctor of the School")
Italian theologian–philosopher
• Synthesis of theology, philosophy known as Thomism; wrote *Summa Theologica*.
b. 1225 in Roccasecca, Italy
d. March 07, 1274 in Fossannova, Italy

Herbert W Armstrong
American evangelist
• Founded Worldwide Church of God, 1947; used media to spread fundamentalist beliefs: radio show "The World Tomorrow"; father of Garner Ted.
b. July 31, 1892 in Des Moines, Iowa
d. January 16, 1986 in Pasadena, California

Benedict Arnold
American army officer–traitor
• Revolutionary patriot; betrayed American cause by offering military information to British, 1779-80.
b. January 14, 1741 in Norwich, Connecticut
d. June 14, 1801 in London, England

Andrija Artukovic
German Nazi leader
• WW II Nazi police minister convicted, 1986, of ordering massacre of villagers, 450 people at Kerestinec camp near Zagreb, 1942.
b. November 29, 1899 in Croatia, Austria-Hungary
d. January 16, 1988 in Zagreb, Yugoslavia

Saint Athanasius
(odoxy ")
Greek religious leader
• Patriarch of Eastern church; constantly opposed Arianism; wrote *Four Orations Against the Arians*, 362.
b. 293
d. 373

Athenagoras I
Greek religious leader
• Led Eastern Orthodox Christians, 1948-72; advocated reunion with Roman Catholic Church.
b. March 25, 1886 in Vassilikon, Greece
d. July 06, 1972 in Istanbul, Turkey

Ti-Grace Atkinson
American feminist
• Active in women's lib movements; known for helping to pass NY State abortion law, 1970.
b. 1939 in Baton Rouge, Louisiana

Saint Augustine
(Aurelius Augustinus; Saint Augustine of Hippo)
Roman religious figure–philosopher
• Early bishop regarded as founder of Christian theology; defended orthodoxy in extensive writings: *City of God*, 413-426.
b. November 13, 354 in Agaste, Numidia
d. 430 in Hippo, Numidia

Saint Augustine of Canterbury
Roman religious leader
• First archbishop of Canterbury, 601; feast day May 26.

Axis Sally
(Mildred Elizabeth Gillars)
American traitor
• Broadcast Nazi propoganda during WW II; imprisoned by Allies for 12 years.
b. November 1900 in Portland, Maine
d. June 25, 1988 in Columbus, Ohio

Andreas (Bernd Andreas) Baader
German terrorist–revolutionary
• Co-leader, with Ulrike Meinhof, of the Baader-Meinhof Gang, 1968-72; trail lasted two years; convicted, 1977; committed suicide.
b. May 06, 1943 in Munich, Germany
d. October 18, 1977 in Stuttgart, Germany

Israel Ba'al Shem Tov
(Israel ben Eliezer)
Polish religious leader
• Founded modern Hasidism, a mystical interpretaion of Judaism.
b. 1700 in Akopy, Poland
d. 1760 in Mezshbozsh, Poland

Lady Olave St Claire Baden-Powell
English social reformer
• Founded International Girl Scout Movement, 1909; wrote *Training Girls As Guides*, 1917.
b. February 22, 1889 in Chesterfield, England
d. June 26, 1977 in Guildford, England

Baha'u'llah
(Mirza Husayn Ali Nuri)
Persian religious leader
• Founded Baha'i faith; writings revealed in over 100 volumes, 1853-92.
b. November 12, 1817 in Teheran, Persia
d. May 29, 1892 in Akko, Palestine

Bill Baird
(William Ritchie Baird Jr; "Father of the Abortion Movement")
American reformer
• Abortion rights advocate; opened first birth control, abortion clinic in US, 1963.
b. June 2, 1932 in New York, New York

Sara Josephine Baker
American physician–feminist
• Child health pioneer; first director, Bureau of Child Hygiene, 1909.
b. November 15, 1873 in Poughkeepsie, New York
d. February 22, 1945 in New York, New York

Jim (James Orsen) Bakker
American evangelist–TV personality
• Spiritual leader, PTL TV ministry; resigned over sex scandal involving Jessica Hahn; sentenced to 45-year jail term, 1989, for defrauding his followers.
b. January 02, 1939 in Muskegon, Michigan

Mikhail Aleksandrovich Bakunin
(Jules Elizard pseud)
Russian anarchist
• A founder of Nihilism, who wrote *God and the State*, 1872-74.
b. May 18, 1814 in Tver, Russia
d. July 13, 1876 in Bern, Switzerland

Roger Nash Baldwin
American social reformer
• Founded ACLU, 1920, with Norman Thomas, Felix Frankfurter; director until 1950.
b. January 21, 1884 in Wellesley, Massachusetts
d. August 26, 1981 in Ridgewood, New Jersey

Gertrude Wright Baniszewski
American murderer
• Known for torture murder of female
boarder, 16 yr. old Sylvia Likens, 1965.
b. 1929 in Indiana

Dennis J Banks
American reformer
• Champion of Native American rights;
co-founded American Indian Movement,
1968.
b. 1930 in Minnesota

Klaus Barbie
(Klaus Altmann alias; "The Butcher of
Lyon")
German Nazi leader
• Captain of Gestapo, Lyon, France,
1942-44; accused of crimes against hu-
manity; extradited to France, 1983.
b. 1914 in Germany

Velma Barfield
American criminal
• First woman executed in US since
1962.
b. 1932
d. November 02, 1984 in Raleigh, North Carolina

Bernard L Barker
American Watergate participant
• Recruited by E Howard Hunt as one
of Watergate burglars, Jan 17, 1972.
b. 1917 in Havana, Cuba

Doc (Arthur) Barker
American criminal
• Robber, murderer, kidnapper, captured
by Melvin Purvis, 1935, killed in escape
attempt, 1939.
b. 1899 in Aurora, Missouri
d. June 13, 1939 in Alcatraz, California

Fred Barker
American criminal
• Added Alvin Karpis to Barker gang;
killed with mother in battle with FBI.
b. 1902 in Aurora, Missouri
d. January 16, 1935 in Oklawaha, Florida

Herman Barker
American criminal
• Member, Kimes-Terrill Gang, early
1920s, robbing banks; committed suicide.
b. 1894 in Aurora, Missouri
d. September 19, 1927 in Newton, Kansas

Lloyd Barker
American criminal
• Only Barker brother who did not join
a gang; jailed for robbing post office,
1922-47.
b. 1896 in Aurora, Missouri
d. 1949 in Colorado

Ma (Arizona Donnie Clark) Barker
American criminal
• Planned bank robberies with sons; ran
hideout in OK for escaped convicts.
b. 1872 in Springfield, Missouri
d. January 16, 1935 in Oklawaha, Florida

Thomas John Barnardo
Irish social reformer
• Pioneer in care of destitute children;
opened Dr. Barnardo's Homes for Boys,
1870.
b. July 04, 1845 in Dublin, Ireland
d. September 19, 1905 in Surbiton, Ireland

Clair Cortland Barnes
(The Hostages)
American hostage in Iran
• One of 52 held by terrorists, Nov
1979 - Jan 1981.

Clyde Barrow
(Bonnie and Clyde; "Public Enemy 1 of
the Southwest")
American outlaw
• With Bonnie Parker, accused of 12
murders during two-year crime spree in
Southwest.
b. March 24, 1909 in Telice, Texas
d. May 23, 1934 in Gibsland, Louisiana

Clara Harlowe Barton
American social reformer
• Founded American Red Cross, 1881-
82; pres. until 1904.
b. December 25, 1821 in Oxford, Massachusetts
d. April 12, 1912 in Glen Echo, Maryland

Saint Basil (the Great)
Greek religious leader
• Father of Eastern communal monasticism; feast day Jun 14.
b. 330 in Caesarea, Cappadocia
d. January 01, 379 in Caesarea, Cappadocia

Sam Bass
American outlaw
• Train robber, ambushed by Texas
Rangers, who was hero of Western ballads.
b. July 21, 1851 in Mitchell, Indiana
d. July 21, 1878 in Round Rock, Texas

Mary Bateman
English murderer
• Pathological criminal who dispensed
magical charms to defraud, kill; died on
gallows.
b. 1768 in Aisenby, England
d. March 2, 1809

Mary Elizabeth Bates
American surgeon-reformer
• First female intern at Cook County
Hospital, Chicago, 1882; worked to reform child abuse laws, 1905.
b. February 25, 1861 in Manitowoc, Wisconsin
d. 1954

Elizabeth Bathory
(Countess Nadasdy; "The Blood Countess")
Hungarian murderer
• Killed 610 servant girls; believed human blood baths essential to retaining
youth.
b. 1560
d. 1614

William Beadle
American murderer
• Slaughtered his family, then killed him-
self.

Henry Ward Beecher
American clergyman-social reformer
• Forceful orator who spoke out on social, political issues, including slavery,
Civil War, Reconstruction.
b. June 24, 1813 in Litchfield, Connecticut
d. March 08, 1887 in Brooklyn, New York

Clifford Whittingham Beers
American reformer
• Founded National Committee for Mental
Hygiene, 1909, to prevent mental disor-
ders, care for mentally ill.
b. March 3, 1876 in New Haven, Connecticut
d. July 09, 1943 in Providence, Rhode Island

William E Belk
(The Hostages)
American hostage in Iran
• One of 52 held by terrorists, Nov
1979 - Jan 1981.
b. 1938 in Winnsboro, South Carolina

Eleanor Robson Belmont
(Mrs August Belmont)
American actress-philanthropist
• Associated with Red Cross for over 25
yrs.; Shaw wrote play *Major Barbara*
based on her life.
b. December 13, 1879 in Wigan, England
d. October 24, 1979 in New York, New York

Saint Benedict
(Benedict of Nursia)
Italian religious figure
• Patriarch of Western monks who
founded Benedictine monasticism.
b. 480 in Norcia, Italy
d. March 21, 547 in Monte Cassino, Italy

Pope Benedict XV
(Giacomo della Chiesa; "The Pope of the Missions")
Italian religious leader
• In 1914-22 pontificate, maintained neutrality, urged peace; spurred missionary activity.
b. November 21, 1854 in Genoa, Italy
d. January 22, 1922 in Rome, Italy

Benedictos I
(Vassilios Papadopoulos)
Turkish religious leader
• Greek Orthodox leader, 1957-80; had historical meeting with Pope Paul VI, 1964.
b. 1892 in Brusa, Asia Minor
d. December 1, 1980 in Jerusalem, Israel

Ezra Taft Benson
American government official–religious leader
• Secretary of Agriculture, 1953-61; succeeded Spencer Kimball as leader of Mormon Church, 1985–.
b. September 03, 1899 in Whitney, Idaho

David Berger
Israeli olympic athlete–victim
• One of 11 members of Israeli Olympic team kidnapped and killed by Arab terrorists during Summer Olympic Games.
b. 1944
d. September 05, 1972 in Munich, Germany (West)

Henry Bergh
American reformer
• Shipbuilder, founder, first pres., ASPCA, 1866; co-founder, ASPCC, 1875.
b. August 29, 1811 in New York, New York
d. March 12, 1888 in New York, New York

Alexander Berkman
Russian anarchist
• Believed ideal society based on voluntary anarchist collectivism; wrote *Prison Memoirs of an Anarchist*, 1912.
b. November 21, 1870 in Vilna, Russia
d. June 28, 1936 in Nice, France

David Berkowitz
(Son of Sam)
American murderer
• Killed six people in NYC, Jul, 1976-Aug, 1977.
b. June 01, 1953

Bernadette of Lourdes
(Marie Bernarde Soubirous; Soubiroux; Saint Bernadette)
French religious figure
• Nun who saw 18 visions of Virgin Mary in grotto in Lourdes, 1858; canonized, 1933; subject of 1943 Oscar-winning *Song of Bernadette*.
b. January 07, 1844 in Lourdes, France
d. April 16, 1879 in Nevers, France

Saint Bernard of Clairvaux
French religious leader
• Monk who preached in Second Crusade, 1146; canonized 1174.
b. 1090 in Fontaines-les-Dijon, France
d. August 2, 1153 in Clairvaux, France

Bernard of Cluny
French religious figure
• Wrote poem *De Contempu Mundi*; hymn "Jerusalem the Golden" is based on it.
b. 1100
d. 1156

Saint Bernardine of Siena
Italian religious figure
• Preacher who was leader in Franciscan order; promoted Holy Name of Jesus; feast day May 20.
b. 1380 in Massa di Carrera, Italy
d. 1444 in Aquila, Italy

Mary McLeod Bethune
American educator–reformer
• Founder, pres., National Council of Negro Women, 1935-49; adviser to FDR, Truman.
b. July 1, 1875 in Mayesville, South Carolina
d. May 18, 1955 in Daytona Beach, Florida

Ronald Arthur Biggs
British criminal
• With 14 others, stole $7.3 million from mail train, 1963; escaped prison, 1965.
b. 1929

John Billington
American murderer
• One of pilgrims who arrived on the Mayflower; first murderer in US.

Billy the Kid
(William H Bonney)
American outlaw
• Had career of killing and cattle rustling; fatally shot by Sheriff Pat Garrett.
b. November 23, 1859 in New York, New York
d. July 15, 1881 in Fort Sumner, New Mexico

Blackbeard
(Edward Teach)
English pirate
• Privateer during War of Spanish Succession, 1701-14; became pirate at end of war.
b. 1680 in Bristol, England
d. November 22, 1718 in Ocracoke Island, North Carolina

Antoinette Louisa Brown Blackwell
American abolitionist–feminist–clergyman
• First woman ordained minister in US, 1853; wrote *The Making of the Universe*, 1914.
b. 1825 in Henrietta, New York
d. 1921

Saint Blaise
Religious Figure
• Patron of throat ailments; bishop of Sebastea, Armenia; commemorated, Feb 2.

Harriot Eaton Stanton Blatch
American feminist–lecturer
• Daughter of Elizabeth Cody Stanton; founded Women's Political Union, 1908; leader in women's suffrage movement.
b. January 2, 1856 in Seneca Falls, New York
d. November 2, 1940 in Greenwich, Connecticut

Amelia Jenks Bloomer
American social reformer
• Advocate of women's rights, dress reform; led to costume called "bloomers."
b. May 27, 1818 in Homer, New York
d. December 3, 1894 in Council Bluffs, Iowa

Mother Ella Reeve Bloor
American feminist
• Leading US female communist, 1930s-40s; helped organize Communist Labor Party, 1919.
b. July 08, 1862 in Staten Island, New York
d. August 1, 1951 in Richlandtown, Pennsylvania

Robert Olof Blucker
(The Hostages)
American hostage in Iran
• One of 52 held by terrorists, Nov 1979-Jan 1981.
b. October 21, 1927 in North Little Rock, Arkansas

Isadore Blumenfeld
American criminal
• Bootlegger acquitted in kidnapping, murder, fraud charges; finally convicted, jailed for jury tampering, 1961-67.
b. 1901 in Minneapolis, Minnesota
d. 1981 in New York, New York

Jakob Boehme
German mystic–religious leader
• Claimed divine revelation; wrote *Mysterium Magnum*, 1623.
b. 1575 in Gorlitz, Prussia
d. 1624

Allan Aubrey Boesak
South African clergyman–social reformer
• President, World Alliance of Reformed Churches, 1982–.
b. February 23, 1945 in Kakamas, South Africa

Joseph Bonanno
American criminal
• Sought to increase power against other Mafia families in Banana crime war, 1964-69.
b. 1904

Saint Bonaventure
(Bonaventura; Giovanni DeFidenza; "Seraphic Doctor")
Italian religious figure
• Developed scholasticism in medievil thought.
b. 1221 in Bagnoregio, Italy
d. July 15, 1274 in Lyons, France

Julian Bond
American politician–civil rights leader
• First black to be nominated for vp, 1968; member, GA senate, 1975–.
b. January 14, 1940 in Nashville, Tennessee

Saint Boniface
English missionary–religious figure
• Advanced Christianity; founded monasteries in Germany; martyred.
b. 680
d. 755

Yelena Bonner
(Mrs Andrei Sakharov)
Russian reformer
• Accepted husband's Nobel Peace Prize, 1975; formed group of dissidents, 1976; internally exiled, 1984-86.
b. February 15, 1923 in Moscow, U.S.S.R.

Anne Bonny
(Anne Bonney)
Irish pirate
• With a series of husbands operated in vicinity of West Indies; captured, 1720; released, then disappeared.
b. 1700
d. 1720

Ella Alexander Boole
American reformer
• Pres., of World WCTU, 1931-47; wrote *Give Prohibition Its Chance*, 1929.
b. July 26, 1858 in Van Wert, Ohio
d. March 13, 1952 in Brooklyn, New York

Ballington Booth
American social reformer
• Son of William, Catherine Booth; withdrew from Salvation Army to found Volunteers of America, 1896.
b. July 28, 1859 in Brighouse, England
d. October 05, 1940 in Blue Point, New York

Catherine Mumford Booth
(Mrs William Booth)
English social reformer
• Played leading role in founding, developing Salvation Army.
b. 1829 in Derbyshire, England
d. 1890

Charles Brandon Booth
American social reformer
• Head of Volunteers of America, 1949-58; grandson of Salvation Army founder William Booth.
b. December 26, 1887 in Brooklyn, New York
d. April 14, 1975 in La Mesa, California

Evangeline Cory Booth
American social reformer
• Daughter of William, Catherine Booth; with Salvation Army, beginning 1895, general, 1934-39.
b. December 25, 1865 in London, England
d. July 17, 1950 in Hartsdale, New York

John Wilkes Booth
American assassin
• Shakespearean actor; shot, killed Lincoln at Ford's Theatre, Apr 14, 1865.
b. August 26, 1838 in Hartford City, Maryland
d. April 26, 1865 in Virginia

William Booth
English religious leader–social reformer
• Started Christian Mission in E London, 1865, became Salvation Army, 1878.
b. April 1, 1829 in Nottinghamshire, England
d. August 2, 1912 in London, England

Lizzie Andrew Borden
American murderer
• Arrested for murdering father, stepmother, Aug 4, 1892; acquitted, 1893.
b. July 19, 1860 in Fall River, Massachusetts
d. June 01, 1927 in Fall River, Massachusetts

Martin Ludwig Bormann
German Nazi leader
• Pronounced dead, 1973, when skeleton was found near Hitler's bunker.
b. 1900
d. 1945

Charles Borromeo, Saint
Italian religious leader
• Archbishop of Milan, 1560s; noted for ecclesiastical reforms; canonized, 1610.
b. October 02, 1538 in Rocca d'Arona, Italy
d. November 03, 1584 in Milan, Italy

Malcolm Boyd
American author–clergyman
• Episcopalian priest whose books deal with spirituality, human rights: *Are You Running with Me, Jesus?*, 1965.
b. June 08, 1923 in Buffalo, New York

Charles Loring Brace
American reformer
• Cofounded Children's Aid Society, 1853; concerned himself with immigration problems, stressed self-reliance.
b. June 19, 1826 in Litchfield, Connecticut
d. August 11, 1890 in Campfer, Switzerland

Sophonisba Preston Breckinridge
American social reformer
• First woman admitted to Bar in KY, 1897.
b. April 01, 1866 in Lexington, Kentucky
d. July 3, 1948

Arthur Herman Bremer
American attempted assassin
• Shot George Wallace, May 5, 1972 in Lowell, MD.
b. August 21, 1950 in Milwaukee, Wisconsin

Saint Brendan of Clonfert
Irish religious figure
• Subject of 10th c. tale *Brendan's Voyage*, recounting adventures; feast day May 16.
b. 484 in Tralee, Ireland
d. 577 in Annaghdown, Ireland

Margaret Brent
American feminist
• First woman landowner in MD.
b. 1600 in Gloucester, England
d. 1671

Brigid of Kildare
Irish religious figure
• Founded first religious community for women in Ireland; revered only less that St. Patrick.
b. 453 in Faughart, Ireland
d. 523 in Kildare, Ireland

Samuel Bronfman
Canadian kidnap victim
• Heir to Seagram's fortune; kidnapped, 1975.
b. 1954

Charlie Brooks, Jr
American murderer
• First US felon executed by injection.
b. 1942
d. December 07, 1982 in Huntsville, Texas

David Owen Brooks
American murderer
• Killed 27 young boys, TX, 1973.
b. 1955

Phillips Brooks
American religious leader
• Episcopal minister who said sermon over Abraham Lincoln's body, 1865; wrote "O Little Town of Bethlehem."
b. December 13, 1835 in Boston, Massachusetts
d. January 23, 1893 in Boston, Massachusetts

H(ubert) Rap Brown
(Jamiel Abdul Al-Amin)
American civil rights leader
• Chairman, SNCC, 1967; converted to Islam while serving prison term.
b. October 04, 1943 in Baton Rouge, Louisiana

Judie Brown
American reformer
• Founder, pres., American Life League, American Life Lobby, 1979–; goal to amend Constitution to prohibit abortion.
b. March 04, 1944 in Los Angeles, California

Lepke (Louis) Buchalter
American criminal
• Number one labor racketeer; led professional "hit" squad, 1930s.
b. 1897 in Manhattan, New York
d. March 04, 1944 in Ossining, New York

Frank Nathan Daniel Buchman
American religious leader
• Founded religious sect, Oxford Group, 1921; Moral Re-Armament, 1938, to prevent war.
b. June 04, 1878 in Pennsburg, Pennsylvania
d. August 07, 1961

Buddha
(Siddhartha Gautama; "Bhagavat" "Sugata" "Tathagata")
Indian religious leader–philosopher
• Renounced world at age 29 to search for solution to human suffering; founded Buddhism, ca. 528 BC.
b. 563BC in Kapilavastu, India
d. 483BC in Kusinagara, India

Ted (Theodore Robert) Bundy
American murderer
• Serial killer; convicted of three murders, confessed to killing over 20 women, 1970s, before death by electrocution.
b. November 24, 1946 in Burlington, Vermont
d. January 24, 1989 in Starke, Florida

William Burke
(Burke and Hare)
Irish murderer
• With William Hare, killed 15 people, sold bodies to surgeons for dissection; hanged.
b. 1792 in Orrery, Ireland
d. January 28, 1829 in Edinburgh, Scotland

Horace Bushnell
(Father of American Religious Liberalism)
American religious leader
• Wrote Forgiveness and Law, 1874.
b. April 14, 1802 in Bantam, Connecticut
d. February 17, 1876 in Hartford, Connecticut

J(oseph) Fred Buzhardt, Jr
American Watergate participant–lawyer
• Special counsel to Richard Nixon on Watergate matters, 1973-74.
b. February 21, 1924 in Greenwood, South Carolina
d. December 16, 1978 in Hilton Head Island, South Carolina

Saint Frances Xavier Cabrini
(Mother Cabrini)
American religious figure
• First American saint; founded convents, orphanages, hospitals in Europe, US; canonized, 1946.
b. July 15, 1850 in Saint' Angelo, Italy
d. December 22, 1917 in Chicago, Illinois

Saint Caedmon
Anglo-Saxon poet
• Monk; wrote scripture history.
b. 650 in England
d. 680 in England

Helen Broinowski Caldicott
Australian reformer
• Leader, Physicians for Social Responsibility, an antinuclear coalition, 1978–.
b. August 07, 1938 in Melbourne, Australia

Pope Callistus II
(Calixtus II; Guido di Borgogne)
French religious leader
• Signed Concordat of Worms, 1122; called first Lateran Council, 1123.
b. 1050
d. December 14, 1124

John Calvin
(Jean Chauvin)
French theologian–reformer
• Established Calvinism; recognized Bible as only source of knowledge.
b. July 1, 1509 in Noyon, France
d. May 27, 1564 in Geneva, Switzerland

Al(phonse) Capone
American criminal
• Dominated Chicago crime scene, gang warfare, 1920s; implicated in St. Valentine's Day massacre, 1929.
b. January 17, 1899 in Brooklyn, New York
d. January 25, 1947 in Miami Beach, Florida

Carlos
(Ilitch Ramirez Sanchez; "The Jackel")
Venezuelan terrorist–murderer
• Most-wanted man in world, 1981; linked to Red Brigade, Khadafi, etc.
b. 1947 in Venezuela

Stokely Carmichael
(Kwame Toure)
American civil rights leader
• Responsible for Black Power concept, 1960s.
b. June 29, 1941 in Port of Spain, British West Indies

Giovanni de Piano Carpini
Italian religious figure–traveler
• Wrote first account of court of Great Khan in Mongolia, 1246.
b. 1180 in Pian di Carpine, Italy
d. 1252

John Carroll
American religious leader
• First Roman Catholic bishop in US; founded Georgetown, 1789.
b. January 08, 1735 in Upper Marlboro, Maryland
d. December 03, 1815 in Baltimore, Maryland

Louis Dominique Cartouche
(Louis Dominique Bourguignon)
French criminal
• Legendary figure; leader of bank robbers.
b. 1693
d. November 28, 1721

Saint Casimir
Polish celebrity relative–religious figure
• Imprisoned at age 15 for refusing to obey orders of his father, King Casimir IV.
b. 1458
d. 1484

Butch Cassidy
(Robert Leroy Parker)
American outlaw
• Train robber whose life was subject of hit film Butch Cassidy and the Sundance Kid, 1969; fled to S America with partner, fate uncertain.
b. April 06, 1867 in Circleville, Utah
d. 1912

Saint Catherine of Alexandria
Religious Figure
• Condemned to torture on a spiked wheel, later named "Catherine wheel"; later beheaded.

Saint Catherine of Genoa
(Caterina Fieschi)
Italian religious figure
• Converted from pleasure-loving Genoese society to spiritual life, 1473; doctrine contained in Vita e dottrinea, 1551.
b. 1447 in Genoa, Italy
d. September 14, 1510 in Genoa, Italy

Catherine of Siena
(Caterina Benincasa)
Italian religious leader
• Influenced Pope Gregory XI to return papacy to Rome from Avignon, 1376.
b. 1347 in Siena, Italy
d. April 29, 1380 in Rome, Italy

Carrie Chapman Catt
American feminist
• Organized League of Women Voters, 1920; helped win women's suffrage.
b. January 09, 1859 in Ripon, Wisconsin
d. March 09, 1947 in New Rochelle, New York

Saint Cecelia
Religious Figure
• Martyr, regarded as patroness of musicians; feast day Nov 22.

Saint Celestine V
(Pietro da Morrone)
Italian religious leader
• Only pope to voluntarily resign, 1294; five-month pontificate marked by chaos.
b. 1210 in Isernia, Italy
d. May 19, 1296 in Rome, Italy

Cassie L Chadwick
(Elizabeth Bigley; "Queen of Ohio")
Canadian criminal–imposter
• Notorious swindler; masqueraded as Andrew Carnegie's illegitimate daughter.
b. 1859 in Strathroy, Ontario
d. 1907

Dwight Lee Chapin
American Watergate participant
• Organized "dirty tricks" unit to harass Democrats; convicted of perjury, 1974.
b. December 02, 1940 in Wichita, Kansas

Mark David Chapman
American murderer
• Shot, killed John Lennon, Dec 8, 1980.
b. May 1, 1955 in Fort Worth, Texas

Ben(jamin Franklin) Chavis
(Wilmington 10)
American civil rights leader
• Central figure of Wilmington 10; imprisoned, 1972, released, 1980; director of a civil rights commission, 1980s–.
b. 1948

Caryl Whittier Chessman
American criminal–author
• Lived on Death Row 12 years; Alan Alda starred in movie of his life, 1977.
b. May 27, 1921 in Saint Joseph, Michigan
d. May 02, 1960 in San Quentin, California

John Reginald Halliday Christie
English murderer
• Strangled at least six women, including wife, 1943-53; hanged.
b. 1899 in England
d. July 15, 1953 in England

Saint Christopher
Religious Figure
• Martyr, patron saint of travelers, until dropped from liturgical calendar, 1969.

Saint John Chrysostom
Syrian religious leader
• Doctor of the church; beloved for his preaching, charity; archbishop of Constantinople, 398-404, banished due to controversy over sermons.
b. 345 in Antioch, Syria
d. September 14, 407 in Comana, Pontus

May (Beatrice Desmond) Churchill
(May Lambert; "Chicago May" "Queen of the Badgers")
Criminal
• Red-headed beauty who blackmailed lovers; planned robbery, Parisian American Express, 1901.
b. 1876 in Sligo, Ireland
d. 1929 in Philadelphia, Pennsylvania

Tennessee Celeste Claflin
American social reformer
• With sister, Victoria Woodhull, founded *Woodhull and Claflin's Weekly*, 1870, which advocated equal rights for women.
b. October 26, 1846 in Homer, Ohio
d. January 18, 1923 in London, England

Saint Clare
Italian religious figure
• Influenced by St. Francis to become nun; founded Poor Clares order; feast day Aug 12.
b. 1194 in Assisi, Italy
d. 1253 in Assisi, Italy

Joan B Claybrook
American government official–reformer
• Headed National Highway Traffic Safety Administration, 1977-81; pres. of consumer group, Public Citizen, 1982–.
b. June 12, 1937 in Baltimore, Maryland

Saint Clement I
(Clemens Romanus)
Religious Leader
• Fourth pope; known for *First Epistle of Clement*, c. 96, which asserted authority of Roman church; feast day Nov 23.

Clement VII
(Giulio DeMedici)
Florentine religious leader
• Pope, 1523-34; Henry VIII attempted to divorce Catherine of Aragon during his reign.
b. 1475 in Florence, Italy
d. September 25, 1534 in Rome, Italy

Clement VIII
(Gil Sanchez Munoz)
Spanish religious leader
• Last of the antipopes, 1423-29; voluntarily renounced rank, was reconciled with church.
b. 1360 in Teruel, Spain
d. December 28, 1446

Pope Clement XIV
(Giovanni Vincenzo Antonio Ganganelli)
Italian religious leader
• Pope, 1769-74; his suppression of Jesuits, 1773, weakened church for years.
b. October 31, 1705 in Sant'Arcangelo, Italy
d. September 22, 1774 in Rome, Italy

George Harold Clements
American clergyman–civil rights leader
• Black priest known for adopting son, 1981; heads largest black Catholic school in US, emphasizing discipline, rigorous academics.
b. January 26, 1932 in Chicago, Illinois

William Montague Cobb
American civil rights leader–educator
• President, NAACP, 1976-82; editor, *Journal of National Medical Assn.*, 1949-77.
b. October 12, 1904 in Washington, District of Columbia
d. November 2, 1990 in Washington, District of Columbia

Mickey (Meyer) Cohen
American criminal
• Leader of CA gambling rackets, 1940s-50s.
b. 1913 in Brooklyn, New York
d. July 29, 1976 in Los Angeles, California

Gaspard de Chatillon Coligny
French religious leader
• Leader of Huguenots, 1560s; killed in St. Bartholomew's Massacre.
b. February 16, 1519 in Chatillon-sur-Loing, France
d. August 24, 1572 in Paris, France

Oscar Collazo
Puerto Rican attempted assassin
• With Griselio Torresola, tried to assassinate Harry Truman, Nov 1, 1950.
b. 1914

Frank Collin
(Frank Cohn)
American Nazi leader
• Son of Jewish refugee who is active in Chicago Nazi Party.
b. November 03, 1944 in Chicago, Illinois

Marva Deloise Nettles Collins
American teacher–reformer
• Started Chicago's one-room school, Westside Preparatory, 1975.
b. August 31, 1936 in Monroeville, Alabama

Joseph Anthony Colombo
American criminal
• Headed one of Mafia's biggest crime families; organized Italian-American Civil Rights League, 1970, to fight gangster stereotype.
b. June 16, 1923 in Brooklyn, New York
d. May 23, 1978 in Newburgh, New York

Chuck (Charles Wendell) Colson
American Watergate participant
• Special counsel to Nixon; became born-again Christian during Watergate trial; wrote *Born Again*, 1976.
b. October 16, 1931 in Boston, Massachusetts

Saint Columban
Irish religious figure
• Missionary to Europe whose practices alienated religious, political powers; founded abbey at Luxeil, 590.
b. 543 in Lenister, Ireland
d. 615 in Bobbia, Italy

Confucius
(Kung Fu-Tzu)
Chinese philosopher
• Developed religious system for management of society; emphasized good family relationships for social stability.
b. August 27, 551 in Lu, China
d. 479BC

Donald Cooke
(The Hostages)
American hostage in Iran
• One of 52 held by terrorists, Nov 1979-Jan 1981.
b. 1955 in Long Island, New York

D B Cooper
American criminal
• Skyjacker; disappeared after parachuting with ransom money, 1971.

(Marie Anne) Charlotte Corday d'Armount
French revolutionary–assassin
• Murdered Jean Paul Marat in his bath, Jul 13, 1793; guillotined.
b. July 27, 1768 in Saint-Saturnin, France
d. July 17, 1793 in Paris, France

Juan Corona
American murderer
• Convicted of murdering 25 migrant workers, 1970-71.
b. 1934 in Mexico

Mairead Corrigan
Irish reformer
• With Betty Williams, won Nobel Peace Prize for forming N Ireland Peace Movement, 1976.
b. January 27, 1944 in Belfast, Northern Ireland

John Cotton
(The Patriarch of New England)
American religious leader
• Headed Congregationalists in America; preached adherence to authority, resistance to democratic institutions.
b. December 04, 1584 in Derby, England
d. December 23, 1652 in Boston, Massachusetts

Father (Charles Edward) Coughlin
American clergyman–radio performer
• Controversial "radio priest" of Depression Era; published *Social Justice*, 1934-42; took violent anti-Roosevelt, anti-Semetic stand.
b. October 25, 1891 in Hamilton, Ontario
d. October 27, 1979 in Bloomfield Hills, Michigan

Ernest Kent Coulter
American social reformer
• Children's court clerk who founded first Big Brother agency, NYC, 1904.
b. November 14, 1871 in Columbus, Ohio
d. May 01, 1952 in Santa Barbara, California

Harvey Gallagher Cox, Jr
American theologian–social reformer
• Wrote *Secular City*, 1965; believes in socially relevant church.
b. May 19, 1929 in Chester County, Pennsylvania

Jacob Sechler Coxey
American reformer
• Leader of 1894 march of unemployed on Washington, DC.
b. April 16, 1854 in Selinsgrove, Pennsylvania
d. May 18, 1951 in Massillon, Ohio

Thomas Cranmer
English religious leader
• Archbishop of Canterbury, 1533; burned at stake for promoting English Reformation, 1556.
b. July 02, 1489 in Aslacton, England
d. March 21, 1556 in Oxford, England

Sir William Randal Cremer
English reformer
• Secretary, Workmen's Peace Assn., 1871-1908; won Nobel Peace Prize, 1903.
b. March 18, 1838 in Fareham, England
d. July 22, 1908 in London, England

Hawley Harvey Crippen
English murderer
• Capture aided by one of earliest uses of shipboard radio telephone, 1910.
b. 1862 in Michigan
d. November 23, 1910 in Pentonville, England

Samuel Adjai Crowther
Nigerian religious leader
• Explored Niger River, 1841; first African Anglican bishop in Nigeria.
b. 1808 in Ochuga, Nigeria
d. December 31, 1891

George David Cummins
American religious leader
• Founder, first bishop, Reformed Episcopal Church, 1873.
b. December 11, 1822 in Smyrna, Delaware
d. June 25, 1876 in Lutherville, Maryland

Richard James Cushing, Cardinal
American religious leader
• Archbishop of Boston, 1944-70.
b. August 24, 1895 in Boston, Massachusetts
d. November 02, 1970 in Boston, Massachusetts

Moll Cutpurse
(Mary Frith; "Queen of Misrule")
English criminal
• First professional female criminal; dressed as man; pickpocket, highway robber.
b. 1589 in London, England
d. 1662 in London, England

Saint Cyril of Alexandria
Greek religious figure
• Patriarch of Alexandria, 412-44, whose writings dealt with problems of the Trinity; feast day, Feb 9.
b. 376 in Alexandria, Egypt
d. June 27, 444 in Alexandria, Egypt

Leon F Czolgosz
American assassin
• Shot William McKinley at Pan-American Exposition, Buffalo, NY, Sep 6, 1901; sent to electric chair.
b. 1873 in Detroit, Michigan
d. October 29, 1901 in New York

Dalai Lama

(Gejong Tenzin Gyatsho; "The 14th Incarnate")
Tibetan ruler–religious leader
• Exiled religious and political leader of Tibet now living in India; won Nobel Peace Prize, 1989, in recognition of his nonviolent campaign to end China's domination of Tibet.
b. July 06, 1935 in Chhija Nangso, Tibet

Emmett Dalton

(Dalton Brothers)
American outlaw
• Realtor, screenwriter after prison term; wrote saga *When the Daltons Rode*, 1931.
b. 1871 in Cass County, Missouri
d. July 13, 1937 in Los Angeles, California

Gratton Dalton

(Dalton Brothers)
American outlaw
• Cousin of Younger Brothers; killed by armed citizens after trying to rob two banks at once.
b. 1862 in Cass County, Missouri
d. October 05, 1892 in Coffeyville, Kansas

Robert Dalton

(Dalton Brothers)
American outlaw
• Was marshal before becoming bankrobber, trainrobber; killed with brother Gratton trying to rob two banks at once.
b. 1867 in Cass County, Missouri
d. October 05, 1892 in Coffeyville, Kansas

William Dalton

(Dalton Brothers)
American outlaw
• Robbed banks and trains with brothers and Doolin gang; killed by lawmen on front porch.
b. 1873 in Cass County, Missouri
d. 1893

Saint Damian

Religious Figure
• Martyr; became doctor but accepted no payment; feast day, Sept 27.

Samuel Dash

American Watergate participant–lawyer
• Chief counsel US Senate Watergate committee, 1973-74; wrote *The Eavesdroppers*, 1959.
b. February 27, 1925 in Camden, New Jersey

William J Daugherty

(The Hostages)
American hostage in Iran
• One of 52 held by terrorists, Nov 1979 - Jan 1981.
b. 1948

Saint David

(Dewi)
Religious Figure
• Patron saint of Wales said to have founded 12 monasteries; feast day Mar 1.
b. 495 in Henfynw, Wales
d. 589 in Mynyw, Wales

David

Hebrew ruler–biblical character
• Prominent Old Testament figure; second king of Israel, Judah; considered author of many Psalms.
b. 1000BC
d. 960BC

Rennie Davis

(The Chicago 7)
American reformer
• Coordinated Pentagon march against Vietnam War, 1967; codefendant, Chicago Seven case.
b. May 23, 1941 in Lansing, Michigan

Emily Wilding Davison

English feminist–hunger striker
• Imprisoned eight times for militant campaigning; force fed during 49 hunger strikes; threw herself under King's horse.

John Wesley Dean

American lawyer–Watergate participant
• Counsel to Richard Nixon, 1971-73; key prosecution witness in Watergate hearings; wrote *Blind Ambition*, 1976.
b. October 14, 1938 in Akron, Ohio

Cardinal John Francis Dearden

American religious leader
• Archbishop of Detroit, 1959-80; as pres. of National Conference of Catholic Bishops, was key figure in transformation of US church after Vatican II.
b. October 15, 1907 in Valley Falls, Rhode Island
d. August 01, 1988 in Southfield, Michigan

Sigurd Friedrich Debus

German terrorist–hunger striker
• Red Army extremist who starved to death striking for better prison conditions, 1981.
b. 1943
d. April 16, 1981 in Hamburg, Germany (West)

Charles Edwin Dederich

American social reformer
• Founder, chief exec., Synanon Foundation, Inc., 1958-.
b. March 22, 1913 in Toledo, Ohio

Ronald Defeo

American murderer
• Killing of parents, siblings known as "Amityville Horror"; Long Island, NY house supposedly haunted; subject of films.
b. 1951

John Demjanjuk

American Nazi leader
• Convicted, sentenced to death by hanging, for operating gas chamber, 1942-43, at Treblinka concentration camp.
b. 1921 in Ukraine

Albert DeSalvo

(Boston Strangler)
American criminal
• Never tried for slayings of 13 women, confessed to psychiatrist; stabbed to death in jail cell.
b. 1931
d. December 27, 1973 in Walpole, Massachusetts

Catherine Deshayes

French criminal
• Sorceress who gave poison to aristocracy; killed over 2,000 infants in Black Mass services.

Michael Devine

Irish hunger striker–revolutionary
• IRA member; one of 10 hunger strikers to die in prison, demanding political prisoner rather than criminal status.
b. 1954 in Londonderry, Northern Ireland
d. August 2, 1981 in Belfast, Northern Ireland

Anagarika Dharmapala

(David Hewivitarne)
Ceylonese religious leader
• One of founders of Buddhism in US, Europe.
b. September 27, 1864 in Columbo, Ceylon
d. April 29, 1933 in Sarnath, India

Legs (Jack) Diamond

(John Thomas Diamond)
American criminal
• 1920s gangster, bootlegger, killer, whose ability to elude police earned him nickname; murdered by other gangsters.
b. 1896 in Philadelphia, Pennsylvania
d. December 18, 1931 in Albany, New York

John Herbert Dillinger

American criminal–murderer
• "Public Enemy Number One," 1930s; known for daring bank robberies, jail escapes.
b. June 28, 1902 in Indianapolis, Indiana
d. July 22, 1934 in Chicago, Illinois

Johnny Dio
(John DioGuardi)
American criminal
• Labor racketeer; worked with Jimmy Hoffa; sentenced to prison for stock fraud, for 15 yrs.
b. 1915
d. 1979 in Pennsylvania

Jenny Diver
(Mary Jones)
British criminal
• England's greatest pickpocket or "diver"; immortalized in *Beggar's Opera*.
b. 1700
d. March 18, 1740 in London, England

Father Major Jealous Divine
(George Baker)
American religious leader
• Founded International Peace Movement, 1919.
b. 1874
d. September 1, 1965 in Philadelphia, Pennsylvania

Dorothea Lynde Dix
American reformer
• Instrumental in building state hospitals for the insane.
b. April 04, 1802 in Hampden, Maine
d. July 17, 1887 in Trenton, New Jersey

Kieran Doherty
Irish hunger striker–revolutionary
• IRA member; one of 10 hunger strikers to die in prison, demanding political prisoner rather than criminal status.
b. 1956
d. August 02, 1981 in Belfast, Northern Ireland

Saint Dominic
(Domingo DeGuzman)
Spanish religious figure
• Founded Dominican religious order, 1216.
b. 1170
d. 1221

Emmitt Douglas
American civil rights leader
• LA NAACP head, 1968-81; initiated lawsuit that desegregated local schools, 1956.
b. 1926
d. March 25, 1981 in New Roads, Louisiana

Helen Mary Gahagan Douglas
American singer–politician
• Dem. con. from CA, 1944-50; bid for US Senate stopped by opponent Richard Nixon, who insinuated she favored communism; wife of actor Melvyn Douglas.
b. November 25, 1900 in Boonton, New Jersey
d. June 28, 1980 in New York, New York

Frederick Douglass
(Frederick Augustus W Bailey)
American lecturer–author
• Escaped slavery, 1838; took active part in antislavery cause, edited antislavery journal.
b. February 14, 1817 in Tuckahoe, Maryland
d. February 2, 1895 in Anacosta Heights, Maryland

John Alexander Dowie
Scottish evangelist
• Founded Christian Catholic Apostolic Church; came to US, settled sect near Chicago, 1903-05.
b. May 25, 1847 in Scotland
d. March 09, 1907

Mary Katherine Drexel
American religious leader
• Founder, Catholic Order for Indians and Blacks, 1891.
b. November 26, 1858
d. March 03, 1955

Charles Dumurcq
(Alain Gauthier; Charles Gurmukh Sobhraj)
French murderer
• Subject of Thomas Thompson's book *Serpentine*, 1979.
b. 1944 in Saigon, Vietnam

Sheena Duncan
South African social reformer
• Member, former pres. of South African women's group, Black Sash; attempts to help blacks with race laws, change whites' views of apartheid through peaceful protest.
b. 1932 in Johannesburg, South Africa

Abigail Jane Scott Duniway
American feminist–suffragette
• First registered woman voter in Oregon.
b. October 22, 1834 in Groveland, Illinois
d. October 11, 1915

Johannes Eckhart
German philosopher–mystic
• Had conflicts with Church for heresy, 1326; thoughts were influential for Quakers after his death.
b. 1260 in Hochheim, Germany
d. 1327 in Avignon, France

Mary Baker Morse Eddy
American religious leader
• Founded Christian Science Religious Movement; organized first church, 1879.
b. July 16, 1821 in Bow, New Hampshire
d. December 03, 1910 in Chestnut Hill, Massachusetts

John Daniel Ehrlichman
American Watergate participant
• Served 18 months in prison for involvement in Watergate, 1976-78.
b. March 2, 1925 in Tacoma, Washington

Adolf (Otto Adolf) Eichmann
Austrian Nazi leader
• In charge of Hitler's death camps; escaped to Argentina, 1946; captured by Israelis, 1960; hung, 1962.
b. March 19, 1906 in Solingen, Germany
d. May 31, 1962 in Jerusalem, Israel

Amy Eilberg
American religious leader
• First woman rabbi in Judaism's Conservative branch, 1985.
b. 1955

David Einhorn
German religious leader
• Leader of the Reform movement in Judaism, US; supported liberal views on practice of Judaism.
b. November 1, 1809 in Dispeck, Bavaria
d. November 02, 1879 in New York, New York

Saint Elizabeth of Hungary
Hungarian religious figure
• Daughter of Andrew II, king of Hungary; devoted to religion, charity; canonized, 1235.
b. 1207
d. 1231

Ruth Ellis
Welsh murderer
• Last woman hanged in England; murdered her lover.
b. 1927 in Rhyl, Wales
d. July 13, 1955 in London, England

Robert A Englemann
(The Hostages)
American hostage in Iran
• One of 52 held by terrorists, Nov 1979 - Jan 1981.
b. 1947 in Pasadena, California

Joseph Esposito
American criminal
• Labor organizer accused of murder, operating illegal stills during Prohibition.
b. April 28, 1872 in Acerra, Italy
d. March 21, 1928 in Chicago, Illinois

Billie Sol Estes
American financier–criminal
• Called "world's best salesman" for con-man deals made in TX; served several prison terms.
b. 1925

James Charles Evers
American civil rights leader
• First black mayor of Fayette, MS, 1969; ran unsuccessfully for governor, 1971; brother of Medgar.
b. September 11, 1923 in Decatur, Mississippi

Medgar Wiley Evers
American civil rights leader
• Brother of Charles; shot to death in front of home; became martyr for civil rights cause; awarded 1963 Spingarn Medal.
b. July 02, 1926 in Decatur, Mississippi
d. June 12, 1963 in Jackson, Mississippi

Ezekiel
Prophet
• Major Hebrew prophet; foretold coming of a messiah, restoration of Jewish kingdom, c.586 BC.

James Farmer
American civil rights leader
• Founded CORE, 1942, national director, 1961-66; pres., Council on Minority Planning and Strategy, 1973-76.
b. January 12, 1920 in Marshall, Texas

Dame Millicent Garrett Fawcett
(Mrs Henry Fawcett)
English feminist
• Leader of women's suffrage movement, 1867.
b. 1847 in Adleburgh, England
d. August 05, 1929 in London, England

Fyodor Fedorenko
Nazi leader
• First accused Nazi war criminal deported by US, 1984; execution date kept secret.
b. 1908
d. 1987 in U.S.S.R.

David Dudley Field
American lawyer–reformer
• Noted for legal reform; adopted Code of Civil Procedure, 1848, which was later used throughout US, Britain.
b. February 13, 1805 in Haddam, Connecticut
d. April 13, 1894 in New York, New York

Albert Fish
(Robert Hayden; Frank Howard; John W Pell; Thomas A Sprague alaises; "The Moon Maniac")
American murderer
• Molested 400 children, killed at least six; practiced cannibalism.
b. 1870 in Washington, District of Columbia
d. January 16, 1936 in Ossining, New York

John Fisher
English clergyman–author
• Beheaded for refusing to acknowledge Henry VIII as head of church; canonized, 1935.
b. 1469 in Beverley, England
d. June 22, 1535 in London, England

Arthur Allen Fletcher
American government official
• First black football player for Baltimore Colts, 1950; as asst. secretary for Wage and Labor Standards, Dept. of Labor, 1969-71, was highest ranking black in Nixon administration.
b. December 22, 1924 in Phoenix, Arizona

Andre Hercule de Fleury
French religious leader–statesman
• Cardinal; chief advisor to Louis XV, 1726-43.
b. 1653
d. 1743

Pretty Boy (Charles Arthur) Floyd
American criminal
• "Public enemy No. 1," 1933; killed in gun battle with FBI's Melvin Purvis.
b. 1904 in Akins, Oklahoma
d. October 22, 1934 in East Liverpool, Ohio

Ginny Foat
(Virginia Galluzzo)
American feminist
• Pres., CA NOW, arrested on 18-yr.-old murder charge, 1983; acquitted.
b. June 21, 1941 in New York, New York

Steve (Stephen, Jr) Fonyo
Canadian track athlete–victim
• After losing leg to cancer, ran 4,924 miles across Canada to raise money for cancer research, 1984-85.
b. June 29, 1965 in Montreal, Quebec

Andrew Hull Foote
American reformer
• Temperance activist who abolished rum ration in US Navy, 1862; worked to suppress slave trade; wrote *Africa & the American Flag*, 1854.
b. September 12, 1806 in New Haven, Connecticut
d. June 26, 1863 in New Haven, Connecticut

Bob (Robert Newton) Ford
American murderer
• Fellow gang member who shot Jesse James in back, 1882.
b. 1860
d. June 24, 1892 in Creede, Colorado

James Forten
American reformer
• Influential spokesman for the abolition movement.
b. September 02, 1766 in Philadelphia, Pennsylvania
d. March 04, 1842 in Philadelphia, Pennsylvania

George Fox
English religious leader
• Founded Society of Friends, the Quakers, 1671; frequently persecuted.
b. July 1624 in Leicester, England
d. January 13, 1691 in Sussex, England

Terry (Terrance Stanley) Fox
Canadian track athlete–victim
• After losing leg to cancer began marathon run across Canada to raise money for research; never completed, but raised $24 million.
b. July 28, 1958 in Winnipeg, Manitoba
d. June 28, 1981 in New Westminster, British Columbia

Abraham H Foxman
American civil rights leader
• National director of the Anti-Defamation League of B'nai B'rith, 1987–.
b. 1940 in Baranovichi, Poland

Saint Francis of Assisi
(Giovanni di Bernardone)
Italian religious leader
• Called greatest of all Christian saints; founded Franciscans, 1209; often depicted preaching to birds.
b. 1182 in Assisi, Italy
d. October 03, 1226 in Porzivncola, Italy

Hans Frank
German Nazi leader
• Hitler's head of programming, 1939 to war's end; hung for war crimes.
b. May 23, 1900
d. October 16, 1946 in Nuremberg, Germany

Joseph Paul Franklin
(James Clayton Vaughan Jr)
American murderer
• Arrested for killing eight blacks, wounding National Urban League pres. Vernon Jordan, 1980.
b. 1950

Wilhelm Frick
German Nazi leader
• Hitler's minister of interior, 1933-43; hanged at Nuremburg trails.
b. March 03, 1877 in Alsenz, Germany
d. October 16, 1946 in Nuremberg, Germany

Betty Naomi Goldstein Friedan
American feminist–author
• Founded NOW, 1966, pres. until 1970; wrote *The Feminine Mystique*, 1963.
b. February 04, 1921 in Peoria, Illinois

Ze'ev Friedman
Israeli olympic athlete–victim
• One of 11 members of Israeli Olympic team kidnapped and killed by Arab terrorists during Summer Olympic Games.
b. 1944
d. September 05, 1972 in Munich, Germany (West)

Joseph Richard Frings
German religious leader
• Cardinal who denounced Nazis in sermons during WW II.
b. February 06, 1887 in Neuss, Germany
d. December 17, 1978 in Cologne, Germany (West)

Hans Fritzsche
German Nazi leader
• Radio, news propaganda chief under Goebbels; pardoned at Nuremburg trials.
b. April 21, 1900 in Bochum, Germany
d. September 27, 1953 in Cologne, Germany (West)

Elizabeth Gurney Fry
English reformer–philanthropist
• Dedicated life to improving condition of the poor, women in prison.
b. May 21, 1780 in Ramsgate, England
d. 1845 in Earlham, England

Caril Ann Fugate
American murderer
• Friend of Charles Starkweather allegedly involved in NE murders; spent 18 years in prison.
b. 1943

Ida Fuller
American social reformer
• Received first US Social Security check, 1940; invested $22 in program, received over $20,000.
b. September 06, 1875 in Ludlow, Vermont
d. January 27, 1975 in Brattleboro, Vermont

Margaret Fuller
(Sarah Margaret Fuller Ossoli)
American critic–social reformer
• Women's rights leader; first US foreign correspondent, 1848; edited *The Dial*, 1840-42; drowned with family off NY coast.
b. May 23, 1810 in Cambridge, Massachusetts
d. July 19, 1850 in Fire Island, New York

Walther Funk
German Nazi leader–banker
• Reichsbank pres., 1939-45; responsible for Nazi finances; jailed as war criminal until 1957.
b. August 18, 1890 in Trakehnen, Prussia (East)
d. May 31, 1960 in Dusseldorf, Germany (West)

John Wayne Gacy, Jr
American murderer
• Convicted, 1980, of murders of 33 boys in Chicago area, 1972-78.
b. 1942

Milton Arthur Galamison
American clergyman–civil rights leader
• Pastor, Siloam Presbyterian Church, Brooklyn, 1949–; active in civil rights movement, especially in desegregation of NYC schools, 1960s.
b. January 25, 1923 in Philadelphia, Pennsylvania

William Gallegos
(The Hostages)
American hostage in Iran
• One of 52 held by terrorists, Nov 1979 - Jan 1981.
b. 1959

Gamaliel the Elder
Palestinian religious leader–scholar
• Made innovations in Jewish ritual.

Don Carlo Gambino
American criminal
• Leader of NY Mafia family, 1960s-70s.
b. 1902 in Sicily, Italy
d. October 15, 1976 in Massapequa, New York

Ed Gein
American murderer
• Farmer who was reportedly model for slayer in film *Psycho*.
b. 1906 in Plainfield, Wisconsin
d. July 26, 1984 in Madison, Wisconsin

Saint Genevieve
French religious figure
• Patron saint of Paris said to have averted Attila the Hun's attack on city with fasting, prayer.
b. 422 in Nanterre, France
d. 512 in Paris, France

Kitty Genovese
American victim
• Stabbed, as 38 neighbors watched, but did nothing to help.
b. 1935
d. March 13, 1964 in New York, New York

Vito Genovese
Italian criminal
• Gangster who rose to power in underworld through narcotics, murder of Albert Anastasia.
b. November 27, 1879 in Rosiglino, Italy
d. February 14, 1969 in Springfield, Missouri

Saint George
English religious figure
• Patron saint of England portrayed in legend as slayer of the dragon.

Paul(us) Gerhardt
German poet–theologian
• Wrote over 120 Protestant hymns.
b. March 12, 1607 in Saxony, Germany
d. May 27, 1676 in Lubbenau, Germany

Bruce W German
(The Hostages)
American hostage in Iran
• One of 52 held by terrorists, Nov 1979-Jan 1981.
b. March 31, 1936

Elbridge Thomas Gerry
American lawyer–social reformer
• Grandson of Elbridge Gerry; co-founded ASPCC, 1875; pres., 1879-1901.
b. December 25, 1837 in New York, New York
d. February 18, 1927

Saint Gertrude the Great
German religious figure
• Mystic, known for supernatural visions.
b. 1256
d. 1311

Anthony Giacalone
American criminal
• Mafia leader; allegedly connected with disappearance of Jimmy Hoffa when blood was found in his car.
b. 1919

Salvatore (Sam) Giancana
American criminal
• Chicago gang boss who was invloved in CIA plot to kill Castro, 1961.
b. 1894
d. June 19, 1974 in Oak Park, Illinois

Duane Gillette
(The Hostages)
American hostage in Iran
• One of 52 held by terrorists, Nov 1979 - Jan 1981.
b. 1957

Gary Mark Gilmore
American murderer
• First execution, by firing squad, following reinstatement of death penalty. Story followed in "Executioner's Song" by Norman Mailer.
b. 1941
d. January 18, 1977 in Point of Mountain, Utah

Ira Glasser
American social reformer
• Exec. director, ACLU, 1978–.
b. April 18, 1938 in New York, New York

Jozef Glemp, Cardinal
Polish religious leader
• Elevated to cardinal Feb 2, 1983, by Pope John Paul II; head of Polish Catholic church, 1981–.
b. December 18, 1929 in Inowroclaw, Poland

Hermann Gmeiner
Austrian social reformer
• Founded SOS-Children's Village movement for orphans, 1949; twice nominated for Nobel Prize.
b. June 23, 1919 in Alberschwende, Austria
d. April 26, 1986 in Innsbruck, Austria

Lady Godiva
(Godgifu)
English social reformer–legendary figure
• Made legendary ride naked through Coventry to win tax relief for townspeople.
b. 1010
d. 1067

Joseph (Paul Joseph) Goebbels
German Nazi leader
• Minister of propaganda under Hitler; committed suicide as Berlin fell to Russians.
b. October 29, 1897 in Rheydt, Germany
d. May 03, 1945 in Berlin, Germany

Hermann Wilhelm Goering
German Nazi leader
• Hitler's minister of aviation; founder of Gestapo.
b. January 12, 1893 in Rosenheim, Germany
d. October 15, 1946 in Nuremberg, Germany

Alan Bruce Golacinski
(The Hostages)
American hostage in Iran
• One of 52 held by terrorists, Nov 1979 - Jan 1981.
b. June 04, 1950 in Austria

Emma Goldman
American anarchist
• Important figure in American radicalism who published *Anarchism and Other Essays,* 1910.
b. June 27, 1869 in Kaunas, Lithuania
d. May 14, 1940 in Toronto, Ontario

Judith Ann Becker Goldsmith
American feminist
• Pres. of NOW, 1982-85.
b. November 26, 1938 in Manitowoc, Wisconsin

Israel Goldstein
American religious leader
• Co-founded National Conference of Christians and Jews, 1928; Brandeis U, 1946.
b. June 18, 1896 in Philadelphia, Pennsylvania
d. April 11, 1986 in Tel Aviv, Israel

Robert O Goodman, Jr
American naval officer–hostage
• Shot down, held by Syrians in Lebanon; released after intercession by Jesse Jackson, 1984.
b. 1956 in San Juan, Puerto Rico

Samuel Gorton
American religious leader
• His followers, Gortonites, flourished in 1600s, founded Shawomet (later Warwick), RI, 1643.
b. 1592 in Gorton, England
d. 1677 in Warwick, Rhode Island

Barbara Graham
American murderer
• Life and execution portrayed by Susan Hayward in film *I Want to Live,* 1958.
b. 1923
d. June 03, 1955 in San Quentin, California

Billy (William Franklin) Graham
American evangelist
• Wrote *The Seven Deadly Sins,* 1955; *Challenge,* 1969; has conducted evangelistic tours throughout the world.
b. November 07, 1918 in Charlotte, North Carolina

Sylvester W Graham
American reformer
• Health evangelist who spoke on diet, wholesome living; invented the graham cracker.
b. July 05, 1794 in West Suffield, Connecticut
d. September 11, 1851 in Northampton, Massachusetts

Lester Granger
American government official–civil rights leader
• Executive director, National Urban League, 1941-61; worked to develop economic opportunities for blacks.
b. September 16, 1896 in Newport News, Virginia
d. January 09, 1976 in Alexandria, Louisiana

John Earl Graves
(The Hostages)
American hostage in Iran
• One of 52 held by terrorists, Nov 1979-Jan 1981.
b. May 16, 1927 in Detroit, Michigan

Dana McLean Greeley
American religious leader
• First pres., Unitarian Universalist Assn., 1961-69; co-founded World Conference on Religion and Peace.
b. July 05, 1908 in Lexington, Massachusetts
d. June 13, 1986 in Concord, Massachusetts

Pope Gregory XIII
(Ugo Boncompagni)
Italian religious leader
• Catholic reformer who created Gregorian calendar, 1582, replacing Julian calendar.
b. January 01, 1502 in Bologna, Italy
d. April 1, 1585

Pope Gregory XV
(Alessandro Ludovisi)
Italian religious leader
• Reformed papal elections; founded Congregation for Propagation of Faith, 1622, to coordinate missionary activities.
b. January 09, 1554 in Bologna, Italy
d. 1623

Saint Gregory the Great
(Gregory I Pope)
Italian religious leader
• Doctor of the Church who extended its temporal power; supposedly responsible for Gregorian chant.
b. 540 in Rome, Italy
d. 604

Irma Grese
("Blood Angel of Hell")
German Nazi leader
• Camp guard in charge of 18,000 female prisioners at Auschwitz; known for brutality; sentenced to death.
b. 1923
d. December 13, 1945 in Hamelin, Germany

Gerhard Groote
(Geerte Groete)
Dutch mystic–reformer
• Founded religious order, Brothers of the Common Life.
b. 1340 in Deventer, Netherlands
d. August 2, 1384 in Deventer, Netherlands

Romano Guardini
Italian religious leader–philosopher
• Leading Catholic theologian who founded German Catholic Youth Movement after WW II.
b. February 17, 1885 in Verona, Italy
d. October 01, 1968 in Munich, Germany (West)

Charles Julius Guiteau
American assassin
• Shot, killed James Garfield, Washington, DC, Jul 2, 1881; hanged.
b. 1844 in Illinois
d. June 3, 1882 in Washington, District of Columbia

Thomas J Gumbleton
American religious leader
• Bishop of Detroit, 1968–; visited hostages in Iran; critic of US foreign policy, urges disarmament.
b. January 26, 1930 in Detroit, Michigan

Yosef Gutfreund
Israeli olympic athlete–victim
• One of 11 members of Israeli Olympic team kidnapped and killed by Arab terrorists during Summer Olympic games.
b. 1931 in Romania
d. September 05, 1972 in Munich, Germany (West)

David Leigh Guyer
American social reformer
• President of Save the Children Federation, 1977–.
b. September 24, 1925 in Pasadena, California

H(arry) R(obert) Haldeman
American Watergate participant
• Convicted for involvement in Watergate, 1975; jailed, 1977-78.
b. October 27, 1926 in Los Angeles, California

Clara McBride Hale
American social reformer
• Organized Hale House, 1969, in Harlem to care for babies born to drug-addicted mothers.
b. April 01, 1905 in Philadelphia, Pennsylvania

Edward Everett Hale
American clergyman–author
• Active in founding Unitarian Church of America; wrote novel *Man Without a Country*, made into opera, produced by Met. Opera Co., 1937.
b. April 03, 1822 in Boston, Massachusetts
d. June 1, 1909 in Roxbury, Massachusetts

Eliezer Halfin
Israeli olympic athlete–victim
• One of 11 members of Israeli Olympic team kidnapped and killed by Arab terrorists during Summer Olympic games.
b. 1948 in U.S.S.R.
d. September 05, 1972 in Munich, Germany (West)

Joseph M Hall
(The Hostages)
American hostage in Iran
• One of 52 held by terrorists, Nov 1979 - Jan 1981.
b. 1950 in Oklahoma

Fannie Lou Townsend Hamer
American civil rights leader
• Founder of MS Freedom Dem. Party, 1972.
b. 1917 in Mississippi
d. March 1977 in Mound Bayou, Mississippi

Alice Hamilton
American physician–reformer
• Pioneer in industrial toxicology.
b. February 27, 1869 in New York, New York
d. September 22, 1970 in Hadlyne, Connecticut

Floyd (Garland) Hamilton
American criminal
• Public enemy number one, 1930s; pardoned for work with ex-convicts.
b. 1908
d. June 26, 1984 in Grand Prairie, Texas

William Hare
(Burke and Hare)
Irish murderer
• With William Burke murdered 15 people, sold bodies to school of anatomy.
b. 1792 in Derry, Northern Ireland
d. 1870

Jean Witt Struven Harris
American murderer
• Convicted of murder of former lover, Dr. Herman Tarnower, 1980; wrote autobiography *Stranger in Two Worlds*, 1986.
b. 1924

LaDonna Crawford Harris
American social reformer–feminist
• Feminist, Comanche Indian; ran for VP on Citizens Party ticket, 1980.
b. 1931

Pearl Hart
American outlaw
• Last bandit to rob stagecoach in US, 1899.
b. 1878
d. 1925

Bruno Richard Hauptmann
German criminal–murderer
• Kidnapped son of Charles Lindbergh, Mar 1, 1932; convicted, executed for murder.
b. November 26, 1900 in Kamenz, Germany
d. April 03, 1936 in Trenton, New Jersey

Karl Haushofer
German Nazi leader
• Geographer who used geopolitical theories to justify Germany's expansion; influenced, advised Hitler on foreign affairs.
b. August 27, 1869 in Munich, Germany
d. March 13, 1946 in Paehl bei Weilheim, Germany

Patty (Patricia Campbell) Hearst
(Mrs Bernard Shaw; "Tanya")
American victim–author
• Kidnapped by SLA, Feb 5, 1974; wrote *Every Secret Thing*, 1981.
b. February 2, 1954 in San Francisco, California

Reginald Heber
English religious leader
• Anglican bishop of Calcutta, 1822-26; wrote beloved hymns including "Holy, Holy, Holy."
b. April 21, 1783 in Malpas, England
d. April 03, 1826 in Trichinopoly, India

Barbara Ruckle Heck
Irish religious leader
• Helped establish first Methodist chapel in America, 1768.
b. 1734 in County Limerick, Ireland
d. August 17, 1804 in Augusta, Ontario

Heloise
(Heloise and Abelard)
French religious figure
• Best known for love affair with Pierre Abelard; immortalized in their letters.
b. 1101
d. 1164

Kevin Jay Hermening
(The Hostages)
American hostage in Iran
• One of 52 held by terrorists, Nov 1979 - Jan 1981.
b. 1960 in Milwaukee, Wisconsin

Abraham Joshua Heschel
Polish religious leader
• First Jewish scholar on staff of Union Theological Seminary.
b. 1907 in Warsaw, Poland
d. December 23, 1972 in New York, New York

Rudolf (Walter Richard Rudolf) Hess
German Nazi leader
• Hitler's deputy; coined phrase "Heil Hitler!"; imprisoned suicide victim.
b. April 26, 1894 in Alexandria, Egypt
d. August 17, 1987 in Berlin, Germany (West)

Reinhard Tristan Eugen Heydrich
German Nazi leader
• Aide to Himmler in Gestapo; early director of death camps; assassinated.
b. March 09, 1904 in Halle, Germany
d. June 04, 1942 in Lidice, Czechoslovakia

James Aloysius Hickey, Cardinal
American religious leader
• Archbishop of Washington, DC, 1980–; made cardinal, 1988.
b. October 11, 1920 in Midland, Michigan

Richard Eugene Hickock
American murderer
• Subject of Truman Capote's *In Cold Blood*, who murdered family with partner Perry Smith, 1959.
b. 1931
d. April 14, 1965

Elias Hicks
American religious leader
• Led liberal faction of Quakers; followers called Hicksites.
b. March 19, 1748 in Hempstead Township, New York
d. February 27, 1830 in Jericho, New York

Saint Hildegard of Bingen
German religious figure
• Benedictine nun; noted for prophecies recorded in *Scivias*.
b. 1098
d. September 17, 1179

Morton A(nthony) Hill
American social reformer–clergyman
• Founder, pres., Morality in Media, Inc., 1962-85; co-authored Hill-Link Report on obscenity, 1970.
b. July 13, 1917 in Brooklyn, New York
d. November 04, 1985 in New York, New York

Heinrich Himmler
German Nazi leader
• Head of SS, 1929, which merged with Gestapo, 1934; minister of interior, 1943-45; captured by British; committed suicide.
b. November 07, 1900 in Munich, Germany
d. May 23, 1945 in Luneburg, Germany

John Warnock Hinckley, Jr
American attempted assassin
• Acquitted, 1982, by reason of insanity for shooting Ronald Reagan, Mar 30, 1981.
b. May 29, 1955 in Ardmore, Oklahoma

Saint Hippolytus
Religious Leader
• First antipope, leader of first schism in Catholic church; eventually was reconciled.
b. 170
d. 235

Adolf Hitler
(Adolf Schickelgruber; "Der Fuhrer")
German Nazi leader
• Founded National Socialism; invasion of Poland, 1939, started WW II; engineered Holocaust, in which over six million Jews and their supporters were murdered.
b. April 2, 1889 in Braunau, Austria
d. April 3, 1945 in Berlin, Germany

Abbie (Abbott) Hoffman
(Spiro Igloo; The Chicago 7)
American author–political activist
• Flamboyant revolutionary, antiwar activist; co-founded Yippies; tried as one of Chicago 7 for conspiring to disrupt Democratic National Convention, 1968; wrote *Revolution for the Hell of It*, 1968; suicide victim.
b. November 3, 1936 in Worcester, Massachusetts
d. April 12, 1989 in New Hope, Pennsylvania

Cardinal Joseph Hoffner
German religious leader
• Archbishop of Cologne, 1969-87; opposed liberalization of Roman Catholic Church.
b. December 24, 1906 in Trier, Germany
d. October 16, 1987 in Cologne, Germany (West)

Donald Hohman
(The Hostages)
American hostage in Iran
• One of 52 held by terrorists, Nov 1979 - Jan 1981.
b. 1943 in Yuma City, California

Leland James Holland
(The Hostages)
American hostage in Iran
• One of 52 held by terrorists, Nov 1979 - Jan 1981.
b. 1928 in Shullsburg, Wisconsin
d. October 02, 1990 in Washington, District of Columbia

John Haynes Holmes
American clergyman–reformer
• Modernist Unitarian who combined religious, political beliefs; wrote *I Speak for Myself*, 1959.
b. November 09, 1879 in Philadelphia, Pennsylvania
d. April 03, 1964 in New York, New York

Benjamin Lawson Hooks
American civil rights leader–clergyman
• Director, NAACP, 1977–, succeeding Roy Wilkins; won Spingarn, 1985.
b. January 31, 1925 in Memphis, Tennessee

John Henry Hopkins
American religious leader–author
• First Episcopal bishop of VT, 1832; wrote *The American Citizen*, 1857.
b. January 3, 1792 in Dublin, Ireland
d. January 09, 1868 in Rock Pointe, Vermont

Tom Horn
American lawman–murderer
• Hired by WY Cattleman's Assn. to eliminate small ranchers, rustlers; hanged for murder.
b. 1860 in Memphis, Missouri
d. November 2, 1903 in Cheyenne, Wyoming

Hosea
Prophet
• Call for Israel to repent sins recorded in Old Testament book of Hosea.

Charles Hamilton Houston
American lawyer–civil rights leader
• Member of NAACP's legal committee, 1940s; awarded Spingarn Medal, 1950.
b. September 03, 1895 in Washington, District of Columbia
d. April 22, 1950 in Washington, District of Columbia

Samuel Gridley Howe
American educator–social reformer
• First to educate a blind deaf-mute child, Laura Dewey Bridgman, 1837; pioneer in education of mentally retarded children.
b. November 1, 1802 in Boston, Massachusetts
d. January 09, 1876 in Boston, Massachusetts

Michael Howland
(The Hostages)
American hostage in Iran
• One of 52 held by terrorists, Nov 1979-Jan 1981.
b. 1947

L(afayette) Ron(ald) Hubbard
American religious leader
• Founded Church of Scientology, 1954, based on his book *Dianetics: The Modern Science of Mental Health.*
b. March 13, 1911 in Tilden, Nebraska
d. January 24, 1986 in San Luis Obispo, California

Saint Hubert
Religious Figure
• Patron saint of hunters and trappers.
b. 655
d. 727

Francis Hughes
Irish hunger striker–revolutionary
• IRA member; one of 10 hunger strikers to die in prison, demanding political prisoner rather than criminal status.
b. 1955 in Bellaghy, Northern Ireland
d. May 12, 1981 in Belfast, Northern Ireland

Rex Humbard
American evangelist
• TV, radio evangelist since 1930; reaches 20 million people on 360 stations.
b. August 13, 1919 in Little Rock, Arkansas

Raymond Gerhardt Hunthausen
American religious leader
• Archbishop of Seattle, 1975–; highest-ranking US Roman Catholic prelate to urge unilateral nuclear disarmament; subject of controversial Vatican investigation, 1983-86.
b. August 21, 1921 in Anaconda, Montana

Henry S Huntington, Jr
American reformer
• Pioneer in organized nudism; founded early nudist camp, 1933; wrote *Defense of Nudism*, 1958.
b. 1882 in Gorham, Maine
d. February 16, 1981 in Philadelphia, Pennsylvania

Martin Hurson
Irish hunger striker–revolutionary
• IRA member; one of 10 hunger strikers to die in prison, demanding political prisoner rather than criminal status.
b. September 13, 1954 in Cappagh, Northern Ireland
d. July 13, 1981 in Belfast, Northern Ireland

Jan Hus
(John Huss)
Czech religious leader
• Burned at stake for urging reform; his loyalists started political party, fought civil war, as Hussites.
b. 1369 in Husinec, Czechoslovakia
d. July 06, 1415 in Constance, Germany

Anne Hutchinson
(Anne Marbury)
English religious leader
• Belief in covenant of grace opposed Puritan covenant of works; banished from MA Bay, 1637.
b. 1591 in Alford, England
d. August 1643 in Long Island, New York

Archbishop Demetrios A Coucouzis Iakovos
Greek religious leader
• Greek Orthodox archbishop of North, South America, Holy Synod of Ecumenical Patriarchate, 1959–.
b. July 29, 1911 in Imvros, Turkey

Fusae Ichikawa
Japanese feminist–politician
• Founded Woman's Suffrage League of Japan; elected to Parliament, 1953-71; 1974-81.
b. 1893 in Aichi Prefecture, Japan
d. February 11, 1981 in Tokyo, Japan

Saint Ignatius of Loyola
(Inigo do Onez y Loyola)
Spanish religious leader
• Founded Society of Jesus or Jesuits, 1540; concerned with education, missionary work; canonized 1622.
b. 1491 in Loyola, Spain
d. July 31, 1556 in Rome, Italy

Reverend Ike
(Frederick Joseph Eikerenkoetter II)
American evangelist–educator
• Founder, pres., United Christian Evangelist Assn., 1962–; Reverend Ike Foundation, 1973–.
b. June 01, 1935 in Ridgeland, South Carolina

Roy Emile Alfredo Innis
American civil rights leader
• Nat. director, CORE, 1968-81; nat. chm., 1981–.
b. June 06, 1934 in St. Croix, Virgin Islands

Pope Innocent XI
(Benedetto Odescalchi)
Italian religious leader
• During 1676-89 pontificate, stressed moral reform, clashed frequently with Louis XIV; considered finest pontiff of 17th c.
b. May 19, 1611 in Como, Italy
d. August 12, 1689 in Rome, Italy

Irish Hunger Strikers
(Michael Devine; Kieran Doherty; Francis Hughes; Martin Hurson; Kevin Lynch; Raymond McCreesh; Joe McDonnell; Thomas McIlwee; Patrick O'Hara; Bobby Sands)
Irish revolutionaries
• IRA members who starved themselves to death in Belfast's Maze Prison, 1981, demanding they be known as political prisoners rather than criminals.

Edward Irving
Scottish mystic–religious leader
• Influential in founding of Catholic Apostolic Church; deposed from Scottish church.
b. August 04, 1792 in Annan, Scotland
d. December 07, 1834 in Glasgow, Scotland

Isaiah
(Isaias)
Hebrew prophet
• His prophesies are collected in book of Old Testament; the first, longest book of the Major Prophets.
b. 740?BC

Vladimir Evgenevich Jabotinsky
Russian religious leader
• Founder, pres., World Union of Zionist-Revisionists, 1922; New Zionist Organization, 1935.
b. October 18, 1880 in Odessa, Russia
d. August 03, 1940

Jack the Ripper
English murderer
• Nickname from ferocity of crimes; five London women killed, 1888; never caught.

George Jackson
American criminal
• Robber who wrote *Soledad Brother*, 1970.
b. September 23, 1941 in Chicago, Illinois
d. August 21, 1971 in San Quentin, California

Jesse Louis Jackson
American civil rights leader–religious leader
• Founded Operation PUSH, 1971; chm., National Rainbow Coalition; Dem. presidential candidate, 1984, 1988.
b. October 08, 1941 in Greenville, South Carolina

John Edward Jacob
American social reformer
• Pres., National Urban League, 1982–.
b. December 16, 1934 in Trout, Louisiana

Michael Faraday Jacobson
American reformer
• Co-founded Center for Science in the Public Interest, 1971–; books include *The Fast Food Guide*, 1986; *The Booze Merchants*, 1983.
b. July 29, 1943 in Chicago, Illinois

Immanuel Jakobovits
German religious leader
• Chief Rabbi of Great Britain and the Commonwealth, 1967–.
b. February 08, 1921 in Koenigsberg, Germany

Frank James
(Alexander Franklin James)
American outlaw
• Only brother of Jesse James; after brother's death he surrendered to governor's office.
b. January 1, 1843 in Clay County, Missouri
d. February 18, 1915 in Clay County, Missouri

Jesse Woodson James
American outlaw
• Leader of outlaw gang known for spectacular bank, train robberies; killed by Robert Ford for reward.
b. September 05, 1847 in Centerville, Missouri
d. April 03, 1882 in Saint Joseph, Missouri

Anna Jarvis
American reformer
• Founded Mother's Day to commemorate anniversary of mother's death.
b. May 01, 1864
d. November 24, 1948 in West Chester, Pennsylvania

Howard Arnold Jarvis
American social reformer
• Force behind CA's Proposition 13, which reduced property taxes 57%, 1978.
b. September 22, 1902 in Magna, Utah
d. August 11, 1986 in Los Angeles, California

Jeremiah
Prophet
• One of major Old Testament prophets who foretold destruction of temple in Jerusalem.
b. 650

Saint Jerome
Religious Figure
• Translated Bible into Latin; feast day: Sep 30.
b. 345 in Strido, Dalmatia
d. 420 in Bethlehem, Judea

Jesus Christ
(Son of Man; Messiah; Anointed One; King of the Jews; Son of God)
Roman religious leader
• Founded Christianity through teaching, healing; became one of world's largest, most influential religions.
b. 4?BC in Bethlehem, Judea
d. 29?AD in Jerusalem, Judea

Pope John XXIII
(Angelo Guiseppe Roncalli)
Italian religious leader
• Pope, 1958-63; convened Vatican II, 1962, to effect reforms within church; promoted unity of Christians.
b. November 25, 1881 in Sotto il Monte, Italy
d. June 03, 1963 in Rome, Italy

Saint John of the Cross
(San Juan de la Cruz; Juan de Yepes y Alvarez; "Ecstatic Doctor")
Spanish poet
• Poems are a mix of religion, poetic imagery; canonized, 1726.
b. June 24, 1542 in Avila, Spain
d. December 14, 1591 in Penuela, Spain

Pope John Paul I
(Albino Luciani)
Italian religious leader
• Pope for 34 days, 1978, before dying of heart attack.
b. October 17, 1912 in Belluno, Italy
d. September 28, 1978 in Vatican City, Italy

Pope John Paul II
(Karol Jozef Wojtyla)
Polish religious leader
• First non-Italian pope since Renaissance, 1978–; most traveled, known for conservatism in doctrine, expanding college of cardinals.
b. May 18, 1920 in Wadowice, Poland

Sonia Johnson
American feminist
• ERA support led to excommunication by Mormon Church, 1979; wrote *From Housewife to Heretic*, 1981.
b. February 27, 1936 in Malad, Idaho

Bob Jones
American religious leader
• Evangelist whose message was heard in every US state, 30 foreign countries; founded Bob Jones U. in SC.
b. October 3, 1883 in Dale County, Alabama
d. January 16, 1968

Charles A Jones, Jr
(The Hostages)
American hostage in Iran
• One of 52 held by terrorists, Nov 1979-Jan 1981.
b. July 01, 1940 in Memphis, Tennessee

Reverend Jim (James) Jones
American religious leader
• Founded People's Temple; led mass suicide of nearly 1,000 followers in Guyana, 1978.
b. May 31, 1931 in Lynn, Indiana
d. November 18, 1978 in Jonestown, Guyana

Fred Jordan
American religious leader
• Founder of int'l. missions since 1949; noted for TV program, "Church in the Home," 1951-88.
b. 1910
d. April 24, 1988 in Glendora, California

Vernon Eulion Jordan, Jr
American civil rights leader
• Pres., National Urban League, 1972-81.
b. August 15, 1935 in Atlanta, Georgia

William Joyce
German social reformer
• Made English language propaganda broadcasts for Nazis; hung for treason.
b. 1906
d. January 05, 1946 in Wandsworth, England

Winnie Ruth McKinnell Judd
American murderer
• Committed to insane asylum for killing, dismembering two people, 1931; escaped seven times.
b. 1905

Steven Judy
American murderer
• Executed by electrocution.
b. 1957 in Indianapolis, Indiana
d. March 09, 1981 in Michigan City, Indiana

Pope Julius II
(Giuliano della Rovere)
Italian religious leader
• Pope, 1503-13; noted patron of the arts; laid cornerstone of St. Peters.
b. 1443 in Albisola, Italy
d. 1513

Pope Julius III
(Giammaria Ciocchi del Monte)
Italian religious leader
• Pope, 1550-55; promoted Jesuits, began reforms, founded Collegium Germanicum, 1552.
b. 1487
d. 1555

Meir David Kahane
American religious leader
• Founded Jewish Defense League, 1968; tactics inspired by Black Panthers.
b. August 01, 1932 in Brooklyn, New York
d. November 05, 1990 in New York, New York

Herbert Warren Kalmbach
American lawyer–Watergate participant
• Personal counsel to Nixon, 1968-73; finance chm. for Nixon's presidential campaigns; linked to Watergate trail for handling secret Rep. fund.
b. October 19, 1921 in Port Huron, Michigan

Malcolm Kalp
(The Hostages)
American hostage in Iran
• One of 52 held by terrorists, Nov 1979-Jan 1981.
b. 1939

Mordecai Kaplan
American religious leader–author
• Founded Jewish Reconstruction movement; outlined philosophy of Judaism.
b. June 11, 1881 in Swenziany, Lithuania
d. November 08, 1983 in New York, New York

Alvin Karpis
(Alvin Karpowicz; "Old Creepy")
Canadian criminal
• Public Enemy number one, 1930s; member Ma Barker's gang; paroled after 32 yrs. in prison, 1969.
b. 1908 in Montreal, Quebec
d. August 12, 1979 in Torremolinos, Spain

Wilhelm Keitel
German Nazi leader
• Chief of the high command of Nazi Armed Forces, WW II; tried, condemned by Int'l. Military Tribunal for war crimes.
b. September 22, 1882
d. October 16, 1946 in Nuremberg, Germany

Machine Gun (George R) Kelly
(E W Moore; J C Tichenor)
American criminal
• Public Enemy Number One, 1930s; died serving life term for 1933 kidnapping of Charles F. Urschel.
b. 1897 in Tennessee
d. July 18, 1954 in Leavenworth, Kansas

Ned (Edward) Kelly
Australian outlaw
• Folk-hero, bankrobber, killer; hanged at 26.
b. 1854 in Beveridge, Australia
d. November 11, 1880 in Melbourne, Australia

Florynce Kennedy
American lawyer–feminist
• Founded Feminist Party, 1971.
b. February 11, 1916 in Kansas City, Missouri

Moorehead Cowell Kennedy, Jr
(The Hostages)
American hostage in Iran
• One of 52 held by terrorists, Nov 1979-Jan 1981.
b. November 05, 1930 in New York

William Francis Keough, Jr
(The Hostages)
American hostage in Iran
• One of 52 held by terrorists, Nov 1979 - Jan 1981.
b. 1931 in Waltham, Massachusetts
d. November 29, 1985 in Washington, District of Columbia

Ayatollah Ruhollah Khomeini
Iranian religious leader
• Leader of Shite Moslems in Iran; supported taking American hostages, 1979.
b. May 17, 1900 in Khomein, Persia
d. June 03, 1989 in Tehran, Iran

William (Captain) Kidd
Scottish pirate
• Poe's story *The Gold Bug*, Stevenson's novel *Treasure Island* based on his exploits.
b. 1645 in Greenock, Scotland
d. May 23, 1701 in London, England

Spencer Woolley Kimball
American religious leader
• Pres., Mormon Church, 1973-85; called America's richest, largest, fastest growing church.
b. March 28, 1895 in Salt Lake City, Utah
d. November 05, 1985 in Salt Lake City, Utah

Coretta Scott King
American celebrity relative–lecturer–author–civil rights leader
• Widow of Martin Luther King, Jr.; pres., MLK Center for Nonviolent Social Change, Atlanta.
b. April 27, 1927 in Marion, Alabama

Martin Luther King, Jr
(Michael Luther King Jr; "The Prince of Peace")
American clergyman–civil rights leader
• Led Civil Rights movement, 1950-68; won Nobel Prize, 1964; birthday is federal holiday. Assassinated.
b. January 15, 1929 in Atlanta, Georgia
d. April 04, 1968 in Memphis, Tennessee

Steven William Kirtley
(The Hostages)
American hostage in Iran
• One of 52 held by terrorists, Nov 1979-Jan 1981.
b. 1958

Beate Klarsfeld
German reformer
• Crusader to track down and bring to trial former Nazi war criminals.
b. February 13, 1931 in Berlin, Germany

Nathan Homer Knorr
American religious leader
• Pres., Jehovah's Witnesses, 1942-77, representing over one million members.
b. April 23, 1905 in Bethlehem, Pennsylvania
d. June 15, 1977 in Wallkill, New York

John Knox
("Apostle of the Scottish Reformers"; "The Reformer of a Kingdom"; "Apostle of Presbytery")
Scottish religious leader–reformer
• Chief leader of the Protestant Reformation in Scotland.
b. 1505 in Haddington, Scotland
d. November 24, 1572 in Edinburgh, Scotland

Ilse Koch
German Nazi leader
• Imprisoned for life for sadistic murders, atrocities at Nazi prison camp; had lampshades made from human skin.
b. 1907 in Dresden, Germany
d. 1967

Maximilian Kolbe, Saint
(Maksymilian Kolbe)
Polish religious figure
• Catholic priest who chose death in place of condemned prisoner; canonized, 1982.
b. 1894 in Poland
d. August 14, 1941 in Auschwitz, Poland

Kathryn L Koob
(The Hostages)
American hostage in Iran
• One of 52 held by terrorists, Nov 1979 - Jan 1981.
b. 1939

Reggie (Reginald) Kray
English criminal–murderer
• With brother ran crime "firm" in London's East End, 1960s; both convicted, sentenced to life in jail, 1969.
b. October 24, 1933 in London, England

Ronnie (Ronald) Kray
English criminal–murderer
• With brother ran crime "firm" in London's East End, 1960s; both convicted, sentenced to life in jail, 1969.
b. October 24, 1933 in London, England

Egil Krogh, Jr
American Watergate participant
• Asst. to John Erhichman, 1969-74; tried, convicted of burglary of Daniel Ellsberg's psychiatrist, 1971, receiving five-yr. sentence for conspiracy.
b. 1939 in Chicago, Illinois

John Krol, Cardinal
American religious leader
• Archbishop of Philadelphia, 1961-88; influential in the election of Pope John Paul II.
b. October 26, 1910 in Cleveland, Ohio

Kathryn Kuhlman
American evangelist
• Faith healer said to produce spontaneous cures; wrote inspirational boook *I Believe in Miracles*, 1962.
b. 1910 in Concordia, Missouri
d. February 2, 1976 in Tulsa, Oklahoma

Maggie (Margaret E) Kuhn
American social reformer
• Founded Gray Panthers, 1971.
b. August 03, 1905 in Buffalo, New York

Hans Kung
(Hans Kueng)
Swiss religious leader–theologian
• Roman Catholic priest; named official theologian of Second Vatican Council, 1962; wrote *The Council, Reform, and Reunion*, 1962.
b. March 19, 1928 in Sursee, Switzerland

Frederick Lee Kupke
(The Hostages)
American hostage in Iran
• One of 52 held by terrorists, Nov 1979-Jan 1981.
b. 1948 in Oklahoma

Walter Kutschmann
(Pedro Olmo)
German Nazi leader
• Nazi lieutenant, accused of killing over 1,500 Jews in Poland during WW II; escaped to Argentina, never prosecuted.
b. 1914
d. August 3, 1986 in Buenos Aires, Argentina

William Ladd
American social reformer
• Founded American Peace Society, 1828.
b. May 1, 1778 in Exeter, Netherlands
d. April 09, 1841 in Portsmouth, Netherlands

Marie Lafarge
(Marie Fortunee Capelle)
French murderer
• Defendant in sensational poisoning trial, 1840; first time forensic medicine decided verdict.
b. 1816 in Picardy, France
d. 1852 in Ussat, France

Jean Laffite
French pirate
• Colorful New Orleans smuggler, privateer; fought heroically for US, War of 1812; disappeared.
b. August 29, 1780 in Bayonne, France
d. 1825

(Lowell) Bruce Laingen
(The Hostages)
American diplomat–hostage in Iran
• One of 52 held by terrorists, Nov 1979 - Jan 1981.
b. August 06, 1922 in Odin Township, Minnesota

Jean Baptist Lamy
American religious leader
• Archbishop of Santa Fe, 1875-85; *Death Comes for the Archbishop* , by Willa Cather, 1927, based on his career.
b. October 14, 1814 in Lempdes, France
d. February 13, 1888 in Santa Fe, New Mexico

Diego de Landa
Spanish religious leader
• First bishop of Yucatan; helped decipher Mayan hieroglyphs.
b. 1524 in Spain
d. 1579

Henri Desire Landru
French murderer
• French "Bluebeard" who murdered 10 women; guillotined.
b. 1869
d. February 25, 1922

Stephen Langton
English religious leader
• Archbishop of Canterbury, 1207; signed Magna Carta as leader of barons against King John.
b. 1155
d. July 29, 1228

Meyer Lansky
(Maier Suchowljansky; "Meyer the Bug")
American criminal
• Jailed only once for two-month period on gambling conviction; called financial genius of underworld.
b. July 04, 1902 in Grodno, Russia
d. January 15, 1983 in Miami Beach, Florida

Lao-Tzu
(Lao-Tse; Li Erh)
Chinese philosopher
• Founder of Taoism whose philosophy of quietism urged renunciation of desire.
b. 570BC
d. 490BC

Frederick Chaney Larue
American Watergate participant
• Shredded Watergate documents; spent six months in prison for obstructing justice, 1973.
b. 1928 in Mississippi

Hugh Latimer
English religious leader
• Protestant bishop known for defending Henry VIII's divorce from Katherine of Aragon; burned at stake for heresy by Mary I.
b. 1485 in Thurcaston, England
d. October 16, 1555 in Oxford, England

William Laud
("Parva Laus"; "The Urchin")
English religious leader
• Archbishop of Canterbury, 1633-40; impeached for high treason, beheaded.
b. October 07, 1573 in Reading, England
d. January 1, 1645 in London, England

Steven Lauterbach
(The Hostages)
American hostage in Iran
• One of 52 held by terrorists, Nov 1979-Jan 1981.
b. 1952

Bernard Francis Law, Cardinal
American religious leader
• Archbishop of Boston, 1984–; became cardinal, 1985.
b. November 04, 1931 in Torreon, Mexico

Ann Lee
American religious leader
• Founded first Shaker settlement in America, Watervliet, NY, 1776.
b. February 29, 1736 in Manchester, England
d. September 08, 1784 in Watervliet, New York

Gary Earl Lee
(The Hostages)
American hostage in Iran
• One of 52 held by terrorists, Nov 1979-Jan 1981.
b. February 04, 1943 in New York, New York

Marcel Francois Lefebvre
French religious leader
• Arch-conservative Catholic archbishop opposed to Vatican II changes; excommunicated for consecrating bishops against pope's wishes, 1988.
b. November 29, 1905 in Tourcoing, France

Pope Leo XIII
(Gioacchino Vincenzo Raffaele Luigi Pecci)
Italian religious leader
• Known for many encyclicals: *Rerum Novarum*, 1891; his 1878-1903 pontificate perhaps century's most productive.
b. March 02, 1810 in Carpineto, Italy
d. July 2, 1903 in Rome, Italy

Nathan Freudenthal Leopold
(Morton D Ballard; George Johnson alaises; William F Lanne; Richard A Lawrence, pseuds.; Leopold and Loeb; "Babe")
American criminal–murderer
• Millionaire's son who committed murder, with Richard Loeb, to attempt the "perfect" crime.
b. November 19, 1904 in Kenwood, Illinois
d. August 28, 1971 in San Juan, Puerto Rico

James W Lewis
(Robert Richardson alias)
American criminal
• Accused of extorting from Johnson & Johnson during Chicago's Tylenol poisonings, 1982.
b. 1946

John Robert Lewis
American civil rights leader
• A founder, long-term chairman of Student Nonviolent Coordinating Committee, 1960.
b. February 21, 1940 in Troy, Alabama

Paul Edward Lewis
(The Hostages)
American hostage in Iran
• One of 52 held by terrorists, Nov 1979-Jan 1981.
b. 1957

Robert Ley
German Nazi leader
• Anti-semitic head of Germany's Labor Front, 1933-45; committed suicide while awaiting trial.
b. February 15, 1890 in Niederbreitenbach, Germany
d. October 25, 1945 in Nuremberg, Germany

Peter Joseph Licavoli, Sr
American criminal
• Founder, leader of organized crime gang, Detroit's Purple Gang.
b. 1902
d. January 11, 1984 in Tucson, Arizona

Thomas Licavoli
American criminal
• Controlled much of Prohibition era crime in Detroit; sentenced to prison for murder, 1934; released, 1971.
b. 1904
d. September 16, 1973 in Columbus, Ohio

G(eorge) Gordon Liddy
American Watergate participant
• An original break-in defendant; 20-yr. sentence commuted by Jimmy Carter; released, 1977.
b. November 3, 1930 in New York, New York

Joshua Loth Liebman
American broadcaster–religious leader
• Rabbi, preached popular radio sermons, 1939; wrote best-seller *Peace of Mind*, 1946.
b. April 07, 1907 in Hamilton, Ohio
d. June 09, 1948

Candy Lightner
American reformer
• Founded Mothers Against Drunk Driving (MADD), 1980.
b. May 3, 1946 in Pasadena, California

John William Limbert, Jr
(The Hostages)
American hostage in Iran
• One of 52 held by terrorists, Nov 1979-Jan 1981.
b. March 1, 1943 in Washington, District of Columbia

Benjamin Barr Lindsey
American judge–reformer
• Founded American juvenile court system, advocating treatment, not punishment, 1899.
b. November 25, 1869 in Jackson, Tennessee
d. March 26, 1943 in Los Angeles, California

Saint Linus
Italian religious leader
• Regarded as successor to St. Peter; pope for nearly 12 years.

Joan Little
American victim
• Jailed for shoplifting, 1974; while in prison gained national attention for killing white jailer who sexually abused her.
b. May 08, 1954 in Washington, North Carolina

Viola Liuzzo
American civil rights leader
• Assassinated while driving marchers from Montgomery to Selma, AL.
b. 1925 in California, Pennsylvania
d. March 25, 1965 in Selma, Alabama

Mary Ashton Rice Livermore
American journalist–reformer–lecturer
• Edited *The Agitator*, 1869; *Woman's Journal*, 1870-72; lectured for 25 yrs. for temperance, suffrage.
b. December 19, 1820 in Boston, Massachusetts
d. May 23, 1905 in Melrose, Massachusetts

Belva Ann Bennett Lockwood
American social reformer–lawyer
• First woman to practice before US Supreme Court, 1879; effective women's right advocate.
b. October 24, 1830 in Royalton, New York
d. May 19, 1917 in Washington, District of Columbia

Richard A Loeb
(Leopold and Loeb)
American criminal–murderer
• With Nathan Leopold, committed "crime of century"; defended by Clarence Darrow.
b. 1907 in Chicago, Illinois
d. January 1936 in Stateville, Illinois

Ann Trow Lohman
American criminal
• Quack physician; notorious NYC abortionist from 1840; slit her throat.
b. 1812 in Painswick, England
d. April 01, 1878 in New York, New York

Bernard J F Lonergan
Canadian religious leader
• Wrote *Insight: A Study of Human Understanding*.
b. December 17, 1904 in Buckingham, Quebec
d. November 26, 1984 in Pickering, Ontario

James Michael (Jimmy) Lopez
(The Hostages)
American hostage in Iran
• One of 52 held by terrorists, Nov 1979-Jan 1981.
b. 1959

Clarence Earle Lovejoy
American author–editor
• Originator, *Lovejoy's College Guide*, 1973.
b. June 26, 1894 in Waterville, Maine
d. January 16, 1974 in Red Bank, New Jersey

Juliette Gordon Low
American social reformer
• Founded Girl Guides in US, 1912; name changed to Girl Scouts, 1913.
b. October 31, 1860 in Savannah, Georgia
d. January 18, 1927 in Savannah, Georgia

Joseph E Lowery
American civil rights leader–clergyman
• Co-founded SCLC; pres., 1977-.
b. October 06, 1924 in Huntsville, Alabama

Myroslav Ivan Lubachivsky, Cardinal
American religious leader
• Archbishop of Lwow, UK, since 1985; head of Ukrainian Roman Catholic Church.
b. 1914 in Dolina, Ukraine

Thomas Lucchese
American criminal
• Worked for "Lucky" Luciano as hired killer; headed Mafia family; never arrested after 1923.
b. 1903
d. 1967

Lucky (Charles) Luciano
(Salvatore Luciana)
American criminal
• Established national crime syndicate, 1930s; deported, 1946.
b. November 24, 1897 in Palermo, Sicily
d. January 26, 1962 in Naples, Italy

Martin Luther
German religious leader
• Led Protestant Reformation, 1517; Lutheran religion named for him.
b. November 1, 1483 in Eisleben, Germany
d. February 18, 1546 in Eisleben, Germany

Albert John Luthuli
South African political leader–reformer
• Won 1960 Nobel Peace Prize for leading peaceful resistance to apartheid; pres., African National Congress (ANC).
b. 1898 in Rhodesia
d. July 21, 1967 in Groutville, South Africa

Kevin Lynch
Irish hunger striker–revolutionary
• IRA member; one of 10 hunger strikers to die in prison, demanding political prisoner rather than criminal status.
b. 1956 in Dungiven, Northern Ireland
d. August 01, 1981 in Belfast, Northern Ireland

Sophie Levy Lyons
American criminal
• Internationally famous swindler, bank robber who later became America's first society columnist, 1897.
b. December 24, 1848 in New York, New York
d. May 08, 1924 in Detroit, Michigan

Francis MacNutt, Father
American religious leader
• Urged prayer for healing; founding editor *Preaching*, 1950-70.
b. April 22, 1925 in Saint Louis, Missouri

Terence MacSwiney
Irish hunger striker–revolutionary
• Nationalist hero; died on 74th day of hunger fast; wrote *Principles of Freedom*, 1921.
b. 1879 in Cork, Ireland
d. October 24, 1920 in Brixton Prison, England

Owen Victor Madden
American criminal
• Gang leader involved with Dutch Schultz, "Legs" Diamond; employed by Lindbergh to help find kidnapped son.
b. June 1892 in Liverpool, England
d. April 24, 1965 in Hot Springs, Arkansas

Jeb Stuart Magruder
American Watergate participant
• Deputy director of Nixon's re-election committee, CREEP; confessed illegal involvement during Watergate trail; served about one yr. in federal prison.
b. November 05, 1934 in Staten Island, New York

Guru Maharaj Ji
(Prem Pal Singh Rawat)
Indian religious leader
• Controversial messenger of God who led Divine Light Mission, 1960s-70s; followers, including some Americans, are called premies.
b. December 1, 1957 in Hardwar, India

Mahavira
Indian religious leader
• Last of Jain Tirthankaras, who founded Jainism, offshoot of Hinduism.
b. 599BC in Vaardhamana, India
d. 527BC in Ksatriyakundagrama, India

Mohammed Ahmed Mahdi
Sudanese religious leader
• Declared himself Mahdi, 1881, united Sudan in religiopolitical movement that began modern history of country.
b. 1844 in Dongola, Sudan
d. June 22, 1885 in Omdurman, Sudan

Maharishi Mahesh Yogi
Indian religious leader
• Founded Spiritual Regeneration Movement, 1959; proponent of TM whose early converts included The Beatles, The Rolling Stones.
b. 1911

James P Mahoney
Canadian religious leader
• Bishop of Saskatoon, 1967–.
b. December 07, 1927 in Saskatoon, Saskatchewan

Roger Michael Mahony
American religious leader
• Roman Catholic priest, 1962–; archbishop of CA, 1985–.
b. February 27, 1936 in Hollywood, California

Moses Maimonides
Spanish philosopher–religious leader
• Major intellectual of medieval judaism; wrote *Guide of the Perplexed*, 1190.
b. March 3, 1135 in Cordova, Spain
d. December 13, 1204 in Cairo, Egypt

Malcolm X
(Malcolm Little)
American political activist–civil rights leader
• Radical civil rights leader; formed Organization for Afro-American Unity, 1964.
b. May 19, 1925 in Omaha, Nebraska
d. February 21, 1965 in New York, New York

Fredericka Mandelbaum
American criminal
• Most successful fence in NY, 1862-84; handled over 12 million dollars in goods.
b. 1818 in New York
d. 1889

Mani
(Manes; Manichaeus)
Persian religious leader
• Founded Manichaeism, 242; concerned with conflict between Light (goodness) and Dark (evil).
b. April 24, 216 in Persia
d. 276 in Persia

Henry Edward Manning
English religious leader
• Archbishop of Westminister, 1865; cardinal, 1875; promoted English Catholicism.
b. July 15, 1808 in Totteridge, England
d. January 14, 1892 in London, England

Maria Manning
(Maria de Roux)
Swiss murderer
• Murdered her lover with the help of her husband, 1849; Dickens profiled her in *Bleak House*.
b. 1825
d. November 13, 1849 in London, England

Timothy Manning, Cardinal
American religious leader
• Archbishop of Los Angeles, 1970-85; made cardinal, 1973.
b. November 15, 1909 in Cork, Ireland

Pope Marcellus II
(Marcello Cervini)
Italian religious leader
• First reform pope; 22-day pontificate marked by neutrality.
b. May 06, 1501 in Montepulciano, Italy
d. May 01, 1555 in Rome, Italy

Paul Casimir Marcinkus
American religious leader
• Pres., Vatican Bank, 1971–; involved in monetary scandal, mid-1980s.
b. January 15, 1922 in Cicero, Illinois

Robert Charles Mardian
American Watergate participant–lawyer
• At Nixon's request, he leaked confidential information on Daniel Ellsberg, Thomas Eagleton during Watergate hearings, 1973.
b. October 23, 1923 in Pasadena, California

Eugene Antonio Marino
American religious leader
• As archbishop of Atlanta, 1988, was highest-ranking black Catholic in US; resigned office, 1990, for violating priestly celibacy.
b. May 29, 1934 in Biloxi, Mississippi

Peter Marshall
American religious leader
• Senate chaplain, 1947-48; subject of *A Man Called Peter*, written by wife Catherine, 1951.
b. May 27, 1902 in Coatbridge, Scotland
d. January 25, 1949 in Washington, District of Columbia

Eugenio R Martinez
Cuban Watergate participant
• Miami-based Cuban hired to break into Democratic headquarters in Watergate, 1972.
b. 1922

The Virgin Mother Mary
("Immaculate Mary")
Roman religious figure
• Mother of Jesus Christ; with him at Crucifixion, with apostles at Pentecost; venerated by Christians, especially Roman Catholics.
b. 1stBC in Judea
d. 1stAD

Cotton Mather
American clergyman–author
• Writings contributed to hysteria of Salem witchcraft trials, 1692; helped found Yale U, 1703.
b. February 12, 1663 in Boston, Massachusetts
d. February 13, 1728 in Boston, Massachusetts

S(helton) Burnita Matthews
American judge–feminist
• First woman to serve as federal district judge, 1949-83; noted women's rights pioneer.
b. December 28, 1894 in Burnell, Mississippi
d. April 25, 1988 in Washington, District of Columbia

Jules Mazarin, Cardinal
(Giulio Mazarini)
French religious leader–statesman
• Succeeded Richelieu, 1643-61; laid foundations for monarchy of Louis XIV.
b. July 14, 1602 in Pescina, Italy
d. March 09, 1661 in Vincennes, France

James Walter McCord
American Watergate participant
• CIA officer; with six others, found guilty of Watergate break-in, 1973; served time in prison, 1975.
b. 1918

Raymond McCreesh
Irish hunger striker–revolutionary
• IRA member; one of 10 hunger strikers to die in prison, demanding political prisoner rather than criminal status.
b. 1957 in Camlough, Northern Ireland
d. May 21, 1981 in Belfast, Northern Ireland

Joe (Joseph) McDonnell
Irish hunger striker–revolutionary
• IRA member; one of 10 hunger strikers to die in prison, demanding political prisoner rather than criminal status.
b. 1951 in Belfast, Northern Ireland
d. July 08, 1981 in Belfast, Northern Ireland

Thomas McIlwee
Irish hunger striker–revolutionary
• IRA member; one of 10 hunger strikers to die in prison, demanding political prisoner rather than criminal status.
b. 1957 in Bellaghy, Northern Ireland
d. August 08, 1981 in Belfast, Northern Ireland

Carl McIntire
American evangelist
• Founder, Bible Presbyterian Church, 1936, Int'l. Council of Christian Churches, 1948; daily radio program, "20th C. Reformation Hour," combines fundamentalist Christianity, hawkish patriotism.
b. May 17, 1906 in Ypsilanti, Michigan

David O McKay
American religious leader
• Led Church of Jesus Christ of Latter-Day Saints, since 1951.
b. September 08, 1873 in Huntsville, Utah
d. January 18, 1970 in Salt Lake City, Utah

Johnny (John D, Jr) McKeel
(The Hostages)
American hostage in Iran
• One of 52 held by terrorists, Nov 1979 - Jan 1981.
b. 1954

Floyd Bixler McKissick
American civil rights leader
• Nat. director, CORE, 1963-68, succeeded by Roy Innis; as lawyer, involved in civil rights cases. In 1951, successfully sued to gain admission to the University of North Carolina at Chapel Hill Law School.
b. March 09, 1922 in Asheville, North Carolina
d. April 28, 1991 in Durham, North Carolina

Aimee Semple McPherson
American evangelist
• Founded International Church of Foursquare Gospel, 1918; ministry characterized by spectacle, optimistic Fundamentalism.
b. October 09, 1890 in Ingersoll, Ontario
d. September 27, 1944 in Oakland, California

Russell Charles Means
American civil rights leader
• Co-founded AIM, 1960s; retired from group, 1988; led 71-day takeover of Wounded Knee, SD, 1973.
b. November 1, 1940 in Pine Ridge, South Dakota

Humberto Medeiros, Cardinal
American religious leader
• Spiritual leader of Boston's Roman Catholics, 1970-83.
b. October 15, 1915 in Portuguese Azores
d. September 17, 1983 in Boston, Massachusetts

Ulrike Marie Meinhof
German terrorist–revolutionary
• Co-leader of Baader-Meinhof Gang, W German terrorists in 1970s; committed suicide in prison.
b. 1934 in Oldenburg, Germany
d. May 09, 1976 in Stuttgart, Germany

Philip Schwarzerd Melanchthon
German religious leader–reformer
• Wrote guidelines for churches, schools which led to first modern public school system in Saxony; tried to unit Catholics, Protestants.
b. February 16, 1497
d. April 19, 1560

Josef Mengele
German Nazi leader
• Doctor at Auschwitz concentration camp; known for medical experimentation; subject of intense manhunt for alleged war crimes.
b. March 16, 1911 in Gunzburg, Bavaria
d. February 07, 1979 in Bertioga, Brazil

Ramon Mercader
(Frank Jacson)
Cuban assassin
• Assassinated Russian leader Leon Trotsky, 1940.
b. 1914
d. October 18, 1978 in Havana, Cuba

James Howard Meredith
American civil rights leader
• Involved in peaceful desegregation of public schools, registering blacks to vote; wrote *Three Years in Mississippi*, 1966.
b. June 25, 1933 in Kosciusko, Mississippi

Michael John Metrinko
(The Hostages)
American hostage in Iran
• One of 52 held by terrorists, Nov 1979-Jan 1981.
b. November 11, 1946 in Pennsylvania

Moina Belle Michael
American social reformer
• Originated Poppy Day, 1918, to raise money for war veterans.
b. August 15, 1869 in Good Hope, Georgia
d. May 1, 1944 in Athens, Georgia

Jerry J Miele
(The Hostages)
American hostage in Iran
• One of 52 held by terrorists, Nov 1979-Jan 1981.
b. 1939

Elizabeth Smith Miller
American reformer–suffragette
• Originated "Bloomer costume," 1851, made popular by Amelia Bloomer.
b. September 2, 1822 in Hampton, New York
d. May 22, 1911 in Geneva, New York

William Miller
American religious leader
• Prophesied second coming of Christ, 1843, 1844; followers called Millerites, then Adventists; Seventh-Day Adventists founded, based on his teachings, 1860s.
b. February 15, 1982 in Pittsfield, Massachusetts
d. December 2, 1849 in Hampton, New York

Kate Millett
(Katherine Murray Millett)
American feminist
• Supports many women's issues groups; member of CORE, 1965–; books include *Sexual Politics*, 1970.
b. September 14, 1934 in Saint Paul, Minnesota

Cardinal Jozsef Mindszenty
Hungarian religious leader
• Regarded in West as symbol of resistance to totalitarian regimes; imprisoned by Nazis, Communists.
b. March 29, 1892 in Hungary
d. May 06, 1975 in Vienna, Austria

Ernesto Miranda
American criminal
• US Supreme Court ruling, 1966, that an individual must be advised of rights at time of arrest was the result of his case.
b. 1940
d. January 31, 1976 in Phoenix, Arizona

Clarence M Mitchell
American diplomat–civil rights leader
• Chief Washington lobbyist for NAACP; played prominent role in passage of Fair Housing Act of 1968.
b. March 08, 1911 in Baltimore, Maryland
d. March 18, 1984 in Baltimore, Maryland

John Newton Mitchell
American government official–Watergate participant
• Attorney General, 1969-72; convicted in Watergate scandal, Jan 1, 1975.
b. September 15, 1913 in Detroit, Michigan
d. November 09, 1988 in Washington, District of Columbia

Michael E Moeller
(The Hostages)
American hostage in Iran
• One of 52 held by terrorists, Nov 1979-Jan 1981.
b. 1950 in Loup City, Nebraska

Mohammed
(Muhammad; Mahomet; "Prophet of Allah")
Arabian religious leader
• Prophet who founded Islam, 622; wrote *The Koran;* considered by most Muslims to have been sinless.
b. 570 in Mecca, Arabia
d. June 08, 632

graf von Helmuth James Moltke
German social reformer
• Opposed Nazi regime; organized group to plan post-Hitler order; executed in prison.
b. March 11, 1907 in Kreisau, Silesia
d. January 23, 1945

Maria Montessori
Italian educator–reformer
• Opened first Montessori school for children, Rome, 1907; wrote *The Montessori Method*, 1912.
b. August 31, 1870 in Chiaravalle, Italy
d. May 06, 1952 in Noordwijk, Netherlands

Dwight Lyman Moody
American evangelist
• With Ira Sankey, promoted Evangelism in US, Britain; published *Gospel Hymns*, 1875.
b. February 05, 1837 in East Northfield, Massachusetts
d. December 22, 1899 in Northfield, Massachusetts

Sung Myung Moon
(Yong Myung Moon)
Korean religious leader
• Head of Unification Church, reported to have 3,000,000 members worldwide; converts called "Moonies."
b. January 06, 1920 in Kwangju Sangsa Ri, Korea

Bert C Moore
(The Hostages)
American hostage in Iran
• One of 52 held by terrorists, Nov 1979 - Jan 1981.
b. March 03, 1935 in Kentucky

Sara Jane Moore
American attempted assassin
• Tried to kill Gerald Ford, Sep 22, 1975; sentenced to life in prison.
b. February 15, 1930 in Charleston, West Virginia

Bugs (George C) Moran
American criminal
• Gangster who rivaled Al Capone for control of Chicago crime, 1920s; target of St. Valentine's Day Massacre, 1929.
b. 1893 in Minnesota
d. February 25, 1957 in Leavenworth, Kansas

Richard H Morefield
(The Hostages)
American hostage in Iran
• One of 52 held by terrorists, Nov 1979-Jan 1981.
b. 1930

Sir Henry Morgan
Welsh pirate–statesman
• Led buccaneers, 1660s; captured Panama City, 1671, becoming English hero; governor of JA, 1674.
b. 1635
d. 1688

Marabel Morgan
American anti-feminist–author
• Developed concept of "Total Woman," which advises women to improve their marriages through submission to husbands.
b. June 25, 1937 in Crestline, Ohio

John R Mott
American evangelist
• Won Nobel Peace Prize, 1946, as leader in founding World Council of Churches.
b. May 25, 1965 in Livingston Manor, New York
d. January 31, 1955 in Orlando, Florida

Lucretia Coffin Mott
American social reformer
• Co-founded women's right movement in US, 1848.
b. January 03, 1793 in Nantucket, Massachusetts
d. November 11, 1880 in Philadelphia, Pennsylvania

Herman Webster Mudgett
(Dr Harry Holmes alias)
American murderer
• Owned home known as "Murder Castle" in Chicago where he killed more than 200 women.
b. in Gilmanton, New Hampshire
d. May 07, 1896

Reuben Herbert Mueller
American religious leader
• Methodist bishop who founded National Council of Churches, 1950; pres., 1963-66.
b. June 02, 1897 in Saint Paul, Minnesota
d. July 05, 1982 in Franklin, Indiana

Elijah Muhammad
American religious leader
• Follower of Wali Farad; leader of Black Muslims, 1934.
b. October 1, 1897 in Sandersville, Georgia
d. February 25, 1975 in Chicago, Illinois

Wallace D Muhammad
American religious leader
• Leader, American Muslim Mission, 1975–; won numerous humanitarian awards; wrote *Religion on the Line,* 1983.
b. October 3, 1933 in Detroit, Michigan

Heinrich Melchior Muhlenberg
American religious leader
• Organized the Lutheran Church in America.
b. September 06, 1711 in Einbeck, Germany
d. October 07, 1786 in New Providence, Pennsylvania

Jack R Murphy
American criminal
• Convicted murderer, jewel thief; stole Star of India sapphire from American Institute of Natural History, NYC, 1964; paroled, 1986.
b. May 26, 1937 in Los Angeles, California

John Murray
American religious leader
• Regarded as father of American Universalism; established first Universalist church in US, 1779.
b. December 1, 1741 in Alton, England
d. September 03, 1815 in Boston, Massachusetts

Nanak
Indian religious figure
• First Sikh Guru; poems are in Sikh bible *Adi Granth.*
b. 1469
d. 1538

Carry A(melia Moore) Nation
American social reformer
• Proponent of temperance; known for using hatchet to smash saloons.
b. November 25, 1846 in Garrard County, Kentucky
d. June 09, 1911 in Leavenworth, Kansas

Paul M Needham, Jr
(The Hostages)
American hostage in Iran
• One of 52 held by terrorists, Nov 1979-Jan 1981.
b. 1951

Baby Face (George) Nelson
(Lester N Gillis)
American criminal
• Member of John Dillinger's outlaw gang, 1930s.
b. December 06, 1908 in Chicago, Illinois
d. November 27, 1934 in Fox River Grove, Illinois

Eliot Ness
(The Untouchables)
American government official
• FBI special agent who headed investigation of Al Capone's gangsterism in Chicago, 1929-32; exploits popularized in books, films, TV series.
b. April 19, 1903 in Chicago, Illinois
d. May 07, 1957 in Cleveland, Ohio

Nestorius
Syrian religious leader
• Patriarch of Constantinople, 428-431, who believed in both divine, human nature of Christ.
b. 389 in Germanicia, Syria
d. 451 in Oasis, Egypt

Constantin Freiherr von Neurath
(Konstantin von Neurath)
German Nazi leader
• Appointed "protector" of Czechs, 1939; considered too lenient, later replaced; tried, sentenced in Nuremberg trail for war crimes, 1946.
b. February 02, 1873 in Klein Glattbach, Germany
d. August 14, 1956 in Enzweihingen, Germany (West)

Cardinal John Henry Newman
English theologian–author
• Catholic convert, cofounded Oxford Movement; *Apologia Pro Vita Sua,* 1864, considered masterpiece; helped define liberal arts education.
b. February 21, 1801 in London, England
d. August 11, 1890 in Birmingham, England

Huey P(ercy) Newton
American political activist–civil rights leader
• Founded Black Panther Party with Bobby Seale, 1966; shot to death outside "crack" cocaine house.
b. February 17, 1942 in New Orleans, Louisiana
d. August 22, 1989 in Oakland, California

Prince Michel de la Moskova Ney
French military leader
• Known for defense in retreat from Moscow, 1812; commanded Napoleon's Waterloo campaign, 1815.
b. January 1, 1769 in Saarlouis, France
d. December 07, 1815 in Paris, France

Nicholas of Cusa
German religious leader–scientist
• Cardinal, 1448-64; believed earth revolved on axis around sun before Newton, Copernicus.
b. 1401 in Cusa, Germany
d. August 11, 1446 in Todi, Italy

Saint Nicholas
(Nicholas of Myra)
Roman religious leader
• Bishop who is patron saint of children; "Santa Claus" derived from Dutch form of name "Sinte Klaas."
b. 3rdAD in Lycia, Asia Minor
d. December 06, 345

Donald Lee Nickles
American politician
• Rep. senator from OK, 1980–.
b. December 06, 1948 in Ponca City, Oklahoma

Jean Nicot
French diplomat
• Ambassador to Portugal; best known for tobacco, Nicotiana, named in his honor; used as a cure all.
b. 1530 in Nimes, France
d. May 05, 1600 in Paris, France

Abu Nidal
(Sabri Khalil al-Banna)
Palestinian terrorist
• Founder, leader, Fatah-Revolutionary Council, 1973–.
b. May 1937 in Jaffa, Palestine

Reinhold Niebuhr
American clergyman–author
• Pioneered philosophy of "Christian realism"; wrote *Nature and Destiny of Man*, 1943; received Presidential Medal of Freedom, 1964.
b. June 21, 1892 in Wright City, Missouri
d. June 01, 1971 in Stockbridge, Massachusetts

Florence Nightingale
English nurse–reformer
• Introduced improved nursing practices in Crimean War; made nursing respected medical profession.
b. May 15, 1820 in Florence, Italy
d. August 13, 1910 in London, England

E(dgar) D(aniel) Nixon
American civil rights leader
• Organized Brotherhood of Sleeping Car Porters, the first successful black union.
b. 1899
d. February 25, 1987 in Montgomery, Alabama

John Humphrey Noyes
American social reformer
• Perfectionist; established utopistic Oneida Community, 1848; noted for starting leading flatware co.
b. September 03, 1811 in Brattleboro, Vermont
d. April 13, 1886 in Niagara Falls, Ontario

Violette Noziere
French murderer
• Murdered her father and attempted to murder her mother with poison in order to obtain their savings; sentenced to life imprisonment.
b. 1915

Miguel Obando (y Bravo)
Nicaraguan religious leader
• Cardinal since 1985; played leading role in ousting Somoza, 1979; vocal critic of Sandinistas.
b. February 02, 1926 in La Libertad, Nicaragua

Patrick Aloysius O'Boyle, Cardinal
American religious leader
• First Roman Catholic archbishop of Washington, DC, 1948-73; championed civil rights, defended church orthodoxy.
b. July 18, 1896 in Scranton, Pennsylvania
d. August 1, 1987 in Washington, District of Columbia

John Joseph O'Connor, Cardinal
American religious leader
• Succeeded Terence Cardinal Cooke as archbishop of NY, 1984.
b. January 15, 1920 in Philadelphia, Pennsylvania

Robert C Ode
(The Hostages)
American hostage in Iran
• One of 52 held by terrorists, Nov 1979 - Jan 1981.
b. December 1, 1915 in Illinois

Patrick O'Hara
Irish hunger striker–revolutionary
• IRA member; one of 10 hunger strikers to die in prison, demanding political prisoner rather than criminal status.
b. 1957 in Londonderry, Northern Ireland
d. May 21, 1981 in Belfast, Northern Ireland

Omar I
(Omar ibn al-Khattab)
Arabian religious leader
• Succeeded Abu Bakr as second caliph; made Islam an imperial power; founded Cairo, c. 642.
b. 581
d. 644 in Medina, Arabia

Origen Adamantius
Egyptian religious figure–philosopher
• Most influential theologian before St. Augustine; tried to prove Christian view of universe compatible with Greek thought.
b. 185 in Alexandria, Egypt
d. 254

Lee Harvey Oswald
American assassin
• Allegedly shot John Kennedy, Nov 22, 1963; killed two days later by Jack Ruby.
b. October 18, 1939 in New Orleans, Louisiana
d. November 24, 1963 in Dallas, Texas

Cardinal Alfredo Ottaviani
Italian religious leader
• Spokesman for ultra-orthodox wing of church during Vatican II Council, 1962-65.
b. October 29, 1890 in Rome, Italy
d. August 03, 1979 in Vatican City, Italy

Mary White Ovington
American reformer
• White social worker, a founder of NAACP, 1908; board chm., 1919-32.
b. April 11, 1865 in Brooklyn, New York
d. July 15, 1951 in Newton Highlands, Massachusetts

G(arfield) Bromley Oxnam
American religious leader
• Pres. of De Pauw U, IN, 1928-36; wrote *A Testament of Faith*, 1958.
b. August 14, 1891 in Sonora, California
d. March 12, 1963 in White Plains, New York

Elizabeth Parsons Ware Packard
American reformer–author
• Crusaded for married women's rights, legislation for insane.
b. December 28, 1816 in Ware, Massachusetts
d. July 25, 1897 in Chicago, Illinois

Alfred G Packer
American murderer
• Murdered and ate five prospectors, 1873.
b. 1842 in Colorado
d. April 24, 1907 in Denver, Colorado

William Palmer
English murderer–physician
• Hanged for poisoning three, suspected of killing 13; case led to "Palmer Act" which allowed change of venue to London for sensational trials.
b. 1824
d. 1856 in London, England

Dame Christabel Harriette Pankhurst
English suffragette
• Daughter of woman-suffrage advocate, Emmeline; published mother's biography, 1935.
b. 1880 in Manchester, England
d. February 14, 1958 in Santa Monica, California

Emmeline Goulden Pankhurst
English suffragette–hunger striker
• Militant reformer known for hunger strikes, bombings; wrote first British woman-suffrage bill, 1860s.
b. July 14, 1858 in Manchester, England
d. June 14, 1928

(Estelle) Sylvia Pankhurst
English suffragette
• With daughters, launched British feminist movement; forerunner of the US version; won women's voting rights, 1918.
b. May 05, 1882 in Manchester, England
d. September 27, 1960 in Addis Ababa, Ethiopia

Franz von Papen
German diplomat–Nazi leader
• Hitler's foreign ambassador to Austria, Turkey; acquitted at Nuremberg.
b. October 29, 1879 in Werl, Germany
d. May 02, 1969

Maud May Wood Park
American suffragette
• First pres., League of Women Voters, 1919.
b. January 25, 1871 in Boston, Massachusetts
d. May 08, 1955 in Reading, Massachusetts

Bonnie Parker
(Bonnie and Clyde)
American criminal
• Two-year crime spree in southwest included 12 murders, numerous robberies.
b. October 01, 1910 in Rowena, Texas
d. May 23, 1934 in Gibsland, Louisiana

Theodore Parker
American religious leader–reformer
• Liberal Unitarian minister; transcendentalist, friend of Emerson; antislavery leader.
b. August 24, 1810 in Lexington, Massachusetts
d. May 1, 1860 in Florence, Italy

Rosa Lee McCauley Parks
American civil rights leader
• Initiated bus boycott, Montgomery, AL, 1955, that led to civil rights movement in the south; won 1978 Spingarn.
b. February 04, 1913 in Tuskegee, Alabama

Saint Patrick
Irish religious figure
• Patron saint of Ireland; called one of most successful missionaries in history; brought organized church to Ireland.
b. 385 in Bannavem Taberniae, England
d. 461 in Saul, Ireland

Ted Patrick
American reformer
• Crusader against religious cults who has deprogrammed nearly 2,000 members since 1972.
b. 1930

Pope Paul III
(Alessandro Farnese)
Italian religious leader
• His pontificate, 1534-49, marked first stages of Counter-Reformation; convened Council of Trent, 1545; gave approval to Jesuits, 1540.
b. February 29, 1468 in Canino, Italy
d. November 1, 1549 in Rome, Italy

Pope Paul VI
(Giovanni Battista Montini)
Italian religious leader
• Carried through Vatican II reforms in 1963-78 pontificate; issued controversial encyclical, *Humanae Vitae*, which condemned birth control.
b. September 26, 1897 in Concesio, Italy
d. August 06, 1978 in Castel Gandolfo, Italy

Nathan Perlmutter
American civil rights leader
• Director, Anti-Defamation League of B'nai B'rith, 1979-87; awarded Presidential Medal of Freedom, 1987.
b. March 02, 1923 in New York, New York
d. July 12, 1987 in New York, New York

Gregory A Persinger
(The Hostages)
American hostage in Iran
• One of 52 held by terrorists, Nov 1979-Jan 1981.
b. December 25, 1957

Kim (Harold Adrian Russell) Philby
English traitor
• Agent for Soviets, 1933-63; defected to Moscow, 1963.
b. 1912 in Ambala, India
d. May 11, 1988 in Moscow, U.S.S.R.

Lena Madesin Phillips
American feminist–lawyer
• Founded National Federation of Business and Professional Women's Clubs, 1919.
b. September 15, 1881 in Nicholasville, Kentucky
d. May 21, 1955 in Marseilles, France

Jeannette Ridlon Piccard
(Mrs Jean Piccard)
American balloonist–religious leader
• Piloted balloon to record 57,559 ft., 1934; consultant to NASA, 1963; ordained Episcopal priest, 1973.
b. January 05, 1895 in Chicago, Illinois
d. May 17, 1981 in Minneapolis, Minnesota

Philippe Pinel
French physician–reformer
• Pioneered humane treatment of insane; established psychiatry as medical field.
b. April 2, 1745 in Saint-Andre, France
d. October 26, 1826 in Paris, France

Father (Francesco Forgione) Pio da Pietrelcina
(Padre Pio)
Italian religious figure
• Capuchin monk believed to have been marked by *stigmata*, or stains of crucified Christ, 1918.
b. May 25, 1887 in Pietrelcina, Italy
d. September 23, 1968 in San Giovanni Rotondo, Italy

Pope Pius IX
(Giovanni Maria Mastai-Ferretti; "Pio Nono")
Italian religious leader
• In longest pontificate (1846-78), convened First Vatican Council, defined dogma of Immaculate Conception, centralized authority in Vatican.
b. May 13, 1792 in Senigallia, Italy
d. February 07, 1878 in Rome, Italy

Saint Pius X
(Giuseppe Melchiorre Sarto)
Italian religious leader
• Widely venerated pope, 1903-14; known for staunch opposition to Modernism, pioneering liturgical changes.
b. June 02, 1835 in Riese, Italy
d. August 2, 1914 in Rome, Italy

Pope Pius XI
(Ambrogio Damiano Achille Ratti)
Italian religious leader
• Pope, 1922-39; best known for negotiating Lateran Treaty, 1929, which established Vatican's independence from Italy; also condemned communism, Nazism, promoted missions.
b. May 31, 1857 in Desio, Italy
d. February 1, 1939

Pope Pius XII
(Eugenio Maria Giuseppi Giovanni Pacelli)
Italian religious leader
• During 1939-58 pontificate, opposed communism, defined dogma of Assumption; maintained neutrality in WW II.
b. March 02, 1876 in Rome, Italy
d. October 09, 1958 in Rome, Italy

Samuel Plimsoll
English politician–social reformer
• The "Plimsoll Line," the load line amidship on cargo ships, is result of his campaigning for safe shipping, 1876.
b. February 1, 1824 in England
d. 1898

Jerry Plotkin
(The Hostages)
American hostage in Iran
• One of 52 held by terrorists, Nov 1979-Jan 1981.
b. 1935 in New York, New York

Daniel A Poling
American evangelist
• Leading temperance leader; editor,
Christian Herald, 1926-66.
b. November 3, 1884 in Portland, Oregon
d. February 07, 1968 in Philadelphia, Pennsylvania

Saint Pontian
Roman religious leader
• Pope, 230-235; first to abdicate.

David de Sola Pool
American religious leader
• Founded several Jewish organizations
including Synagogue Council of America,
1938; wrote *Why I Am a Jew*, 1957.
b. May 16, 1885 in London, England
d. December 01, 1970 in New York, New
York

Henry Codman Potter
American religious leader–social reformer
• Episcopal bishop of NYC, 1887-1908;
initiated building of still-unfinished Cathedral of St. John the Divine, 1892; outspoken critic of civic corruption.
b. June 25, 1834 in Schenectady, New York
d. July 21, 1908 in Cooperstown, New York

Sally Jane Priesand
American religious leader
• First ordained female rabbi, 1972;
wrote *Judaism and the New Woman*,
1975.
b. June 27, 1946 in Cleveland, Ohio

Gavrilo Princip
Serbian assassin
• Assassinated Archduke Ferdinand and
wife, 1914; sparked WW I.
b. 1895 in Bosnia, Austria-Hungary
d. April 3, 1918 in Prague, Czechoslovakia

Joe (Joseph) Profaci
Criminal
• One of the original five Mafia families
in NY.
b. 1898
d. June 06, 1962 in Bay Shore, New York

Pierre Joseph Proudhon
French anarchist–journalist
• Regarded as father of anarchism, wrote
What Is Property?, 1840; influenced European revolutionists.
b. January 15, 1809 in Besancon, France
d. January 16, 1865 in Paris, France

Melvin Purvis
American government official
• FBI agent credited with capturing or
killing John Dillinger, Pretty Boy Floyd,
1930s.
b. 1903
d. February 29, 1960 in Florence, South Carolina

William Clarke Quantrill
(Charley Hart)
American soldier–outlaw
• Confederate sympathizer who killed
180 citizens in Lawrence, KS, 1863;
called "bloodiest man in American history."
b. July 31, 1837 in Canal Dover, Ohio
d. June 06, 1865 in Louisville, Kentucky

Richard Queen I
(The Hostages)
American hostage in Iran
• Held with 52 other Americans by terrorists; the only hostage released early
(mid-1980) due to illness.
b. 1952

Karen Ann Quinlan
American victim
• Comatose since 1975; parents won
landmark court decision to remove life-support systems.
b. March 29, 1954
d. June 11, 1985 in Morris Plains, New Jersey

Vidkun Abraham Quisling
Norwegian government official–traitor
• Minister of Defense, 1931-33; founded
political party similar to Nazis, 1931;
helped Hitler invade Norway, 1940; executed for treason; name became synonymous with "traitor."
b. July 18, 1887 in Fryesdal, Norway
d. October 24, 1945 in Oslo, Norway

Erich Raeder
German Nazi leader
• Commander-in-chief, German Navy;
tried at Nuremberg, sentenced to Spandau.
b. April 24, 1876
d. November 06, 1960 in Kiel, Germany
(West)

Regis Ragan
(The Hostages)
American hostage in Iran
• One of 52 held by terrorists, Nov
1979-Jan 1981.
b. 1942

Bhagwan Shree Rajneesh
(Osho Rajneesh)
Indian religious leader
• Cult leader known for preaching blend
of Eastern religion, pop psychology, free
love; deported from US, 1985, for immigration violations.
b. December 11, 1931 in Kuthwara, India
d. January 19, 1990 in Pune, India

Sri Ramakrishna
Indian religious leader
• Considered sainted wise man by Hindus; followers founded Ramakrishna Mission, 1897.
b. 1834
d. 1886

Arthur Michael Ramsey, Lord
English religious leader
• Archbishop of Canterbury, 1961-74;
pres., World Council of Churches, 1961-68.
b. November 14, 1904 in Cambridge, England
d. April 23, 1988 in Oxford, England

George Rapp
German religious leader
• Founded religious communistic societies
in PA, IN; followers called Rappites.
b. November 01, 1757 in Iptingen, Germany
d. August 07, 1847 in Economy, Pennsylvania

Grigori Efimovich Rasputin
Russian religious figure
• Known for strong influence in court of
Czar Nicholas II; assassinated.
b. 1871 in Tobolsk, Russia
d. December 31, 1916 in Russia

Joseph Alois Ratzinger, Cardinal
German religious leader
• Heads Sacred Congregation for the Defense of Faith, a Vatican agency.
b. April 16, 1927 in Marktyl am Inn, Germany

Lady Dhanvanthi Rama Rau
(Dhanvanthi Handoo)
Indian feminist
• Pres. of International Planned Parenthood Federation, 1963-71; mother of
Santha Rama Rau.
b. May 1, 1893 in Hubli, India
d. July 19, 1987 in Bombay, India

Francois Ravaillac
French assassin
• Assassinated Henry IV of France May
14, 1610; executed for crime.
b. 1578 in Angouleme, France
d. May 27, 1610

James Earl Ray
American assassin
• Killed Martin Luther King, Jr., April
4, 1968; sentenced to 99 years in prison.
b. March 1, 1928 in Alton, Illinois

Joachim von Ribbentrop
German Nazi leader
• German foreign affairs minister, 1938-45; hanged as war criminal.
b. April 3, 1893 in Wesel, Germany
d. October 16, 1946 in Nuremberg, Germany

John(ny) Ringo
American outlaw
• Idealized figure of "gentleman bandit"; member of Clanton gang, enemy of the Earps.
b. 1844
d. July 14, 1882

George Ripley
American clergyman–social reformer
• Transcendentalist, founded the *Dial*, 1840.
b. October 03, 1802 in Greenfield, Massachusetts
d. July 04, 1880 in New York, New York

Oral Roberts
American evangelist
• Founder, pres., Oral Roberts U, Tulsa, OK, 1963–.
b. January 24, 1918 in Ada, Oklahoma

David Roeder
(The Hostages)
American hostage in Iran
• One of 52 held by terrorists, Nov 1979-Jan 1981.
b. 1940

Adrian Pierce Rogers
American religious leader
• Pres., Southern Baptist Convention, largest Protestant denomination in US, 1979-80, 1986–.
b. September 12, 1931 in West Palm Beach, Florida

John Rogers
American religious leader
• Founded the Rogerenes, liberal religious sect advocating pacifism, separation of church and state.
b. December 12, 1648 in Milford, Connecticut
d. October 28, 1721 in New London, Connecticut

Mary Cecilia Rogers
American victim
• Murder was inspiration for Edgar Allan Poe's story *Mystery of Marie Roget*.
b. 1820
d. July 25, 1841 in Weehawken, New Jersey

Ernst Rohm
German Nazi leader
• Leader of Storm Troops (SS, SA), 1930-34; executed.
b. 1887 in Munich, Germany
d. 1934 in Munich, Germany

Joseph Romano
Israeli olympic athlete–victim
• One of 11 members of Israeli Olympic team kidnapped and killed by Arab terrorists during Summer Olympic Games.
b. 1940 in Libya
d. September 05, 1972 in Munich, Germany (West)

Oscar Arnulfo Romero y Galdamez
Salvadoran religious leader
• Archbishop of San Salvador who advocated human rights; assassinated.
b. August 15, 1917 in Ciudad Barrios, El Salvador
d. March 24, 1980 in San Salvador, El Salvador

Eleanor (Anna Eleanor) Roosevelt
(Mrs Franklin Delano Roosevelt; "The First Lady of the World")
American first lady–social reformer
• Married Franklin D Roosevelt, 1905; US representative to UN, 1945, 1947-52, 1961; often chosen in polls as "world's most influential woman."
b. October 11, 1884 in New York, New York
d. November 07, 1962 in New York, New York

Barry Rosen
(The Hostages)
American hostage in Iran
• One of 52 held by terrorists, Nov 1979-Jan 1981.
b. 1944

Moishe Martin Rosen
American religious leader
• Founded Jews for Jesus, 1970.
b. April 12, 1932 in Kansas City, Missouri

Alfred Rosenberg
German Nazi leader–author
• Nazi ideologist; molded Hitler's policies; hanged by war tribunal.
b. January 12, 1893 in Reval, Russia
d. October 16, 1946 in Nuremberg, Germany

Ethel Greenglass Rosenberg
American traitor
• US communist convicted of giving secrets to USSR; first civilian executed for espionage.
b. September 28, 1915 in New York, New York
d. June 19, 1953 in Ossining, New York

Julius Rosenberg
American traitor
• With wife Ethel convicted of espionage; executed.
b. May 12, 1918 in New York, New York
d. June 19, 1953 in Ossining, New York

Roy G Ross
American religious leader
• Co-founder, National Council of Churches, 1950, serving as general secretary, 1952-63.
b. June 25, 1898 in Forrest, Illinois
d. January 08, 1978 in Pompano Beach, Florida

William Blackburn Royer, Jr
(The Hostages)
American hostage in Iran
• One of 52 held by terrorists, Nov 1979-Jan 1981.
b. October 21, 1931 in Pennsylvania

Jack Ruby
(Jacob Rubenstein)
American murderer
• Killed Lee Harvey Oswald on TV, 1963.
b. 1911
d. January 03, 1967 in Dallas, Texas

Morris Rudensky
(Max Motel Friedman; "Red")
American criminal
• Safecracker with Al Capone, Bugsy Moran; spent 35 yrs. in prison; released, 1944, became law-abiding citizen.
b. 1908 in New Yrok, New York
d. April 21, 1988 in Saint Paul, Minnesota

Robert Alexander Kennedy Runcie
English religious leader
• Archbishop of Canterbury, 1980–.
b. October 21, 1921 in Liverpool, England

Charles Taze Russell
American religious leader
• Founded Russellites, 1878, which became Jehovah's Witnesses, 1931.
b. February 16, 1852 in Pittsburgh, Pennsylvania
d. October 31, 1916 in Pampa, Texas

Edward Frederick Langley Russell, Baron of Liverpool
English judge–author
• Prosecuted war criminals after WW II; wrote *Scourge of the Swastika*.
b. April 1, 1895 in Liverpool, England
d. April 08, 1981 in Hastings, England

John Brown Russwurm
American journalist–abolitionist
• Co-founded first black newspaper: *Freedom's Journal*, 1827.
b. October 01, 1799 in Port Antonio, Jamaica
d. June 17, 1851 in Liberia

Bayard Rustin
American civil rights leader
• Adviser to Rev. M L King, Jr.; organized first Freedom Ride, "Journey of Reconciliation," 1947; march on Washington, 1963.
b. March 17, 1910 in West Chester, Pennsylvania
d. August 24, 1987 in New York, New York

Joseph Franklin Rutherford
American religious leader
• Legal adviser for "Russellites," 1907; leader, 1917; founder, president Jehovah's Witnesses, 1925.
b. November 1869 in Versailles, Missouri
d. January 09, 1942 in San Diego, California

Ernest Edwin Ryden
American religious leader
• Wrote, translated over 40 hymns; helped form Lutheran Church in America, 1962.
b. September 12, 1886 in Kansas City, Missouri
d. January 01, 1981 in Providence, Rhode Island

Bobby (Robert Gerard) Sands
Irish hunger striker–revolutionary
• IRA member, elected to Parliament while in prison; first of 10 hunger strikers to die demanding political prisoner rather than criminal status.
b. March 09, 1954 in Belfast, Northern Ireland
d. May 05, 1981 in Belfast, Northern Ireland

Margaret Sanger
(Margaret Higgins)
American nurse–social reformer
• Founded National Birth Control League, 1914; wrote *Women, Morality, and Birth Control*, 1931.
b. September 14, 1883 in Corning, New York
d. September 06, 1966 in Tucson, Arizona

Margaret Elizabeth Sangster
(Margaret Elizabeth Murson)
American reformer
• Founded American Birth Control League, 1917; opened first clinic, 1921.
b. February 22, 1838 in New Rochelle, New York
d. June 04, 1912 in Glen Ridge, New Jersey

Girolamo Savonarola
Italian religious leader
• Preached against corruptions in secular life; burned at stake for heresy, 1498.
b. September 21, 1452 in Ferrara, Italy
d. May 23, 1498 in Florence, Italy

Thomas E Schaefer
(The Hostages)
American hostage in Iran
• One of 52 held by terrorists, Nov 1979-Jan 1981.
b. 1931

Alexander Moshe Schindler
American religious leader
• Leader in nat. Jewish, Zionist organizations since early 1960s; pres., Union of American Hebrew Congregations, 1973–.
b. October 04, 1925 in Munich, Germany

Phyllis Stewart Schlafly
American anti-feminist–author–politician
• Outspoken ultra-conservative opponent of ERA; wrote many books championing conservatism, warning against communism: *A Choice, Not an Echo*, 1964.
b. August 15, 1924 in Saint Louis, Missouri

Dutch Schultz
(Arthur Flegenheimer; "The Dutchman")
American criminal
• Major NYC bootlegger, racketeer of Prohibition era; known for ruthlessness; ordered rival "Legs" Diamond killed, 1931.
b. August 06, 1900 in Bronx, New York
d. October 24, 1935 in Newark, New Jersey

Charles Wesly Scott
(The Hostages)
American hostage in Iran
• One of 52 held by terrorists, Nov 1979-Jan 1981.
b. 1933

Scottsboro Nine
(Olen Montgomery; Clarence Norris; Haywood Patterson; Ozie Powell; Willie Roberson; Charlie Weems; Eugene Williams; Andy Wright; Roy Wright)
American victim
• Young defendants charged with rape; case dragged on for 20 years even though one of rape charges was recanted.

Samuel Seabury
(A Westchester Farmer pseud)
American theologian–pamphleteer–religious leader
• Loyalist during Revolution who was first American-born Episcopalian bishop.
b. November 3, 1729 in Groton, Connecticut
d. February 25, 1796 in New London, Connecticut

Bobby G Seale
American political activist–author–civil rights leader
• Co-founder, chairman, Black Panthers, 1966.
b. October 2, 1936 in Dallas, Texas

Donald H Segretti
American lawyer–Watergate participant
• His "dirty trick" activities were the first uncovered by Woodward & Bernstein, 1972; convicted of political espionage.
b. September 17, 1941 in San Marino, California

Hannah Senesh
Hungarian reformer
• Anti-Nazi activist; shot by Nazi firing squad.
b. 1921 in Budapest, Hungary
d. November 07, 1944

Franjo Seper
Yugoslav religious leader
• Cardinal, Prefect, Sacred Congregation Doctrine of Faith, 1968-81.
b. October 02, 1905 in Osijek, Yugoslavia
d. December 31, 1981 in Rome, Italy

Saint Elizabeth Ann Bayley Seton
(Mother Seton)
American religious leader
• Laid foundation of US parochial school system; founded Sisters of Charity, 1809; first American canonized, 1975.
b. August 28, 1774 in New York, New York
d. January 04, 1821 in Emmitsburg, Maryland

Artur von Seyss-Inquart
Austrian Nazi leader
• German High Commissioner of The Netherlands, 1940-46; condemned, hanged by Int'l. Military Tribunal for "ruthless terrorism."
b. July 02, 1892 in Stannern, Czechoslovakia
d. October 16, 1946 in Nuremberg, Germany

Amitzur Shapira
Israeli olympic athlete–victim
• One of 11 members of Israeli Olympic team kidnapped, killed by Arab terrorists during Summer Olympic Games.
b. 1932
d. September 05, 1972 in Munich, Germany (West)

Donald A Sharer
(The Hostages)
American hostage in Iran
• One of 52 held by terrorists, Nov 1979-Jan 1981.
b. 1941

Ayatollah Seyed Sharietmadari
Iranian religious leader
• Islamic scholar who opposed Shah of Iran, led nation's conservative forces with Khomeini in exile.
b. 1902

Bishop Fulton John Sheen
American religious leader–author
• Well-known spokesman for Catholic perspective, 1930s-70s; reached millions through radio, TV series, books: *Peace of Soul*, 1949.
b. May 08, 1895 in El Paso, Illinois
d. December 1, 1979 in New York, New York

Bernard James Sheil, Archbishop
American religious leader
• Auxilary bishop of Chicago, 1928-69; founder, director, Catholic Youth Organization, 1930-54.
b. February 18, 1888 in Chicago, Illinois
d. September 13, 1969 in Tucson, Arizona

Jack (John) Sheppard
English criminal
• Thief, known for many escapes from prison; hanged; career is theme of several books, plays.
b. 1702 in Stepney, England
d. November 16, 1724 in London, England

Mark Shinburn
(Baron Shindell Jimmy Valentine aliases)
American criminal
• Fenced stolen goods through Fredericka Mandelbaum, eventually retired to Monaco under alias.
b. 1842
d. 1916

Kehat Shorr
Israeli olympic athlete–victim
• One of 11 members of Israeli Olympic team kidnapped, killed by Arab terrorists during Summer Olympic games.
b. 1919 in Romania
d. September 05, 1972 in Munich, Germany (West)

Fred Lee Shuttlesworth
American clergyman–civil rights leader
• Aid to Martin Luther King, Jr.; founder, pres., AL Christian Movement for Human Rights, 1956-69.
b. March 18, 1922 in Mugler, Alabama

Daniel Edgar Sickles
American government official–soldier
• Acquitted for shooting Philip Key, son of Francis Scott; first time plea of temporary insanity used, 1859; credited with obtaining Central Park for NYC.
b. October 2, 1825 in New York, New York
d. May 03, 1914 in New York, New York

Rodney Virgil Sickmann
(The Hostages; "Rocky")
American hostage in Iran
• One of 52 held by terrorists, Nov 1979-Jan 1981.
b. 1958

Stephanos Sidarouss, Cardinal
Egyptian religious leader
• Patriarch of Coptic Catholic Church, 1958-85; became cardinal, 1965.
b. February 22, 1904 in Cairo, Egypt
d. August 23, 1987 in Cairo, Egypt

Bugsy (Benjamin) Siegel
American criminal
• Helped organize Murder, Inc; began syndicate-controlled gambling in Las Vegas.
b. February 28, 1906 in Brooklyn, New York
d. June 2, 1947 in Beverly Hills, California

Etienne de Silhouette
French reformer
• Controller of finance, 1759, scorned by nobility for savings reforms; name used for anything plain or cheap; "silhouette" applied to profile outlines, the poor man's miniature.
b. July 05, 1709
d. 1767

Abba Hillel Silver
American religious leader
• Zionist leader, early advocate of the state of Israel.
b. January 28, 1893 in Lithuania
d. November 28, 1963 in Cleveland, Ohio

Saint Simeon Stylites
(Simeon the Elder)
Syrian religious leader
• First most famed stylite "Pillar Dweller"; spent 35 yrs. on top of 50-ft. high pillar.
b. 390
d. 459

Sirhan Bishara Sirhan
Jordanian assassin
• Shot Robert Kennedy, Jun 5, 1968; serving life sentence in San Quentin Prison.
b. March 19, 1944 in Jerusalem, Palestine

Mark Slavin
Israeli olympic athlete–victim
• One of 11 members of Israeli Olympic team kidnapped and killed by Arab terrorists during Summer Olympic Games.
b. 1954 in U.S.S.R.
d. September 05, 1972 in Munich, Germany (West)

Curtis Sliwa
American social reformer
• Founder, pres., Guardian Angels, 1979, civilian patrol group launched to help combat crime in NYC.
b. March 26, 1954 in Brooklyn, New York

Eleanor Marie Cutri Smeal
American feminist
• Pres. of NOW, 1977-82, 1985-87.
b. July 3, 1939 in Ashtabula, Ohio

Cathy Evelyn Smith
Canadian singer
• Convicted, sentenced to three yrs. in prison, for injecting fatal drug dose to John Belushi, 1986; paroled, 1988.
b. 1947

Joseph Smith
American religious leader
• Founded Mormons, 1830; murdered by non-believers.
b. December 23, 1805 in Sharon, Vermont
d. June 27, 1844 in Carthage, Illinois

Joseph Fielding Smith
American religious leader
• 10th pres., Mormon Church, pres., Council of Apostles.
b. July 19, 1876 in Salt Lake City, Utah
d. July 02, 1972 in Salt Lake City, Utah

Madeline Hamilton Smith
Scottish murderer
• Allegedly poisoned lover, who had blackmailed her with letters she'd written him, 1857.
b. 1835
d. April 12, 1928

Perry Edward Smith
American murderer
• Subject of Truman Capote's book, In Cold Blood; killed family of four with partner Richard Hickock, 1959; hanged after many appeals.
b. 1928
d. April 14, 1965

Robert Holbrook Smith
American social reformer
• Founded Alcoholics Anonymous, 1935.
b. August 08, 1879 in Saint Johnsbury, Vermont
d. November 06, 1950 in Akron, Ohio

Paul Snider
Canadian murderer
• Husband of Dorothy Stratten; killed wife, himself in lover's quarrel.
b. 1951
d. August 14, 1980 in Los Angeles, California

Ralph W Sockman
American religious leader
• Popular NYC pastor, 1916-61; broadcast weekly sermons for 35 yrs.
b. October 01, 1889 in Mount Vernon, Ohio
d. August 29, 1970 in New York, New York

Hannah Greenebaum Solomon
American reformer
• Founded National Council of Jewish Women, 1890.
b. January 14, 1858 in Chicago, Illinois
d. December 07, 1942 in Chicago, Illinois

Richard Franklin Speck
American murderer
• Killed eight student nurses in Chicago, July 13-14, 1966.
b. December 06, 1941 in Kirkwood, Illinois

Albert Speer
German architect–Nazi leader
• Germany's official architect under Hitler; helped plan war economy with Goering.
b. March 19, 1905 in Mannheim, Germany
d. September 01, 1981 in London, England

Francis Joseph Spellman
American religious leader
• Appointed Archbishop of NY, 1939, cardinal, 1946 by Pope Pius XII.
b. May 04, 1889 in Whitman, Massachusetts
d. December 02, 1967 in New York, New York

John Arthur Spenkelink
American murderer
• First person involuntarily executed in US since 1967.
b. 1949 in Buena Park, California
d. May 25, 1979 in Starke, Florida

Arthur Barnett Spingarn
American lawyer–civil rights leader
• Pres., NAACP, 1940-65; honorary pres., 1966-71.
b. March 28, 1878 in New York, New York
d. December 01, 1971 in New York, New York

Andre Spitzer
Israeli olympic athlete–victim
• One of 11 members of Israeli Olympic team kidnapped and killed by Arab terrorists during Summer Olympic Games.
b. 1945 in Romania
d. September 05, 1972 in Munich, Germany (West)

Stephen Gill Spottswood
American religious leader
• African Methodist Episcopal Zion bishop, who was chm., NAACP, 1961-74.
b. July 18, 1897 in Boston, Massachusetts
d. December 01, 1974 in Washington, District of Columbia

Ya'acov Springer
Israeli olympic athlete–victim
• One of 11 members of Israeli Olympic team kidnapped and killed by Arab terrorists during Summer Olympic Games.
b. 1920
d. September 05, 1972 in Munich, Germany (West)

Franz Paul Stangl
Austrian Nazi leader
• Commanded Nazi concentration camps in Poland, 1942-43, where 400,000 Jews were killed under his supervision.
b. 1908 in Austria
d. June 28, 1971 in Dusseldorf, Germany (West)

Elizabeth Cady Stanton
(Mrs Henry Brewster Stanton)
American feminist–social reformer
• Co-founded women's rights movement with Lucretia Mott; first pres., National Woman Suffrage Assn., 1869-90.
b. November 12, 1815 in Johnstown, New York
d. October 26, 1902 in New York, New York

Henry Brewster Stanton
American reformer
• Active in anti-slavery activities, beginning 1834; married Elizabeth Cady, 1840.
b. June 27, 1805 in Griswold, Connecticut
d. January 07, 1887 in New York, New York

Charles Starkweather
American murderer
• Killed 11 people, 1958; executed, 1959.
b. 1940 in Lincoln, Nebraska
d. June 24, 1959 in Nebraska

Belle Starr
(Myra Belle Shirley)
American pioneer–outlaw
• Cattle rustler; harbored Jesse James, 1881.
b. February 05, 1848 in Carthage, Missouri
d. February 03, 1889 in Briartown, Oklahoma

Serge Alexandre Stavisky
French criminal
• Swindler; sold worthless bonds to French working people.
b. 1886 in Russia
d. 1934

Gloria Steinem
American feminist–journalist
• Well-known activist for women's rights; co-founded Ms. mag., 1971; founded groups Coalition of Labor Union Women, Women USA.
b. March 25, 1934 in Toledo, Ohio

Alojzije Stepinac
Yugoslav religious leader
• Roman Catholic archbishop of Zagreb, 1937-53; cardinal, 1953-60; imprisoned by Communists, 1946-51.
b. May 08, 1898 in Krasic, Croatia
d. February 1, 1960 in Krasic, Yugoslavia

Johnny Stompanato
American criminal
• Killed by Lana Turner's daughter after argument; death judged justifiable homocide.
b. 1926
d. April 04, 1958 in Hollywood, California

Lucy Stone
American feminist–suffragette–editor
• Founded Woman's Journal, 1870; voice of Woman's Suffrage Assn. for 50 yrs.
b. August 13, 1818 in West Brookfield, Massachusetts
d. October 18, 1893 in Dorchester, Massachusetts

Julius Streicher
German Nazi leader
• Edited anti-Semitic The Stormer, 1923-45; executed after Nuremberg trial.
b. February 12, 1885
d. October 16, 1946 in Nuremberg, Germany

Robert Franklin Stroud
American ornithologist–criminal
• 60 yrs. in prison for murder portrayed in film starring Burt Lancaster, Birdman of Alcatraz, 1961.
b. 1890 in Seattle, Washington
d. November 21, 1963 in Springfield, Missouri

Joseph Subic, Jr
(The Hostages)
American hostage in Iran
• One of 52 held by terrorists, Nov 1979-Jan 1981.
b. 1957

Daniel P Sullivan
American government official
• FBI agent who helped track down John Dillinger and Barker-Karpis gang.
b. 1912 in Washington, District of Columbia
d. July 04, 1982 in Miami, Florida

Charles Sumner
American politician–orator
• Senator from MA, 1851-74; abolitionist; injured by Southern colleague for ardent attacks against slavery, 1856.
b. January 06, 1811 in Boston, Massachusetts
d. March 11, 1874 in Washington, District of Columbia

The Sundance Kid
(Harry Longabaugh)
American outlaw
• Celebrated bankrobber, trainrobber, 1901-09; portrayed by Robert Redford in popular 1969 film.

Billy (William Ashley) Sunday

American baseball player–evangelist
• Outfielder, 1883-90, known for fielding, base stealing; as popular evangelist, fought against Sunday baseball.
b. November 18, 1862 in Ames, Iowa
d. November 06, 1935 in Chicago, Illinois

John Harrison Surratt

American criminal
• Friend of John Wilkes Booth, tried as conspirator in assassination of A Lincoln.
b. 1844 in Prince George's County, Maryland
d. April 21, 1916

Mary Eugenia Jenkins Surratt

American criminal
• Boardinghouse operator; hanged as conspirator in Lincoln's assassination.
b. May 1820 in Waterloo, Maryland
d. July 07, 1865 in Washington, District of Columbia

Willie (William Francis) Sutton

("The Actor")
American criminal
• Stole $2 million in 35 years of bank robbing; disguises earned him nickname.
b. 1901
d. November 02, 1980 in Spring Hill, Florida

Daisetz Teitaro Suzuki

Japanese author–educator–philosopher
• Introduced Zen Buddhism to Western world.
b. October 18, 1870 in Kanazawa, Japan
d. July 12, 1966 in Tokyo, Japan

Jimmy Lee Swaggart

American evangelist
• TV preacher who claims to have 200 million followers; strong right-wing views; involved in sex scandal, banned from pulpit, 1988.
b. March 15, 1935 in Ferriday, Louisiana

Elizabeth Ann Swift

(The Hostages)
American hostage in Iran
• One of 52 held by terrorists, Nov 1979-Jan 1981.
b. December 03, 1940 in Washington, District of Columbia

Cardinal Edmund Casimir Szoka

American religious leader
• Archbishop of Detroit, 1981-90; chief financial officer at the Vatican, 1990–.
b. September 14, 1927 in Grand Rapids, Michigan

Henrietta Szold

American social reformer
• Founder, pres., Hadassah, US women's Zionist group, 1912-26; practiced nursing in Holy Land.
b. December 21, 1860 in Baltimore, Maryland
d. February 13, 1945 in Jerusalem, Palestine

Lucy Hobbs Taylor

American dentist–reformer
• First woman to receive degree in dentistry, 1866.
b. March 14, 1833 in New York
d. October 03, 1910 in Lawrence, Kansas

Saint Kateri Tekakwitha

(Catherine Tegakovita; "Lily of the Mohawks")
American Indian religious figure
• First American Indian to be made a saint.
b. 1656 in New York
d. April 17, 1680 in Caughnawaga, Quebec

Mother Teresa

(Agnes Gonxha Bojaxhiu; "Saint of the Gutters")
Albanian nun–missionary
• Catholic nun widely respected for int'l. humanitarian efforts for poor; founded Missionaries of Charity, 1950; awarded 1979 Nobel Peace Prize.
b. August 27, 1910 in Skopje, Yugoslavia

Mary Church Terrell

American social reformer
• Worked to improve women's rights, equality for black people; first pres., Nat. Association of Colored Women, 1896-1901.
b. September 23, 1863 in Memphis, Tennessee
d. July 24, 1954 in Annapolis, Maryland

Quintus Septimus Florens Tertullian

Roman writer
• Known as one of fathers of church; writings attack official attitude toward Christianity.
b. 160
d. 230

Harry Kendall Thaw

American murderer
• Killed architect Stanford White in Madison Square Garden, 1906; ruled insane.
b. February 01, 1871 in Pittsburgh, Pennsylvania
d. February 22, 1947 in Miami Beach, Florida

Saint Theresa

Spanish religious figure–author
• Noted for mystic visions; reformed Carmelite order.
b. 1515 in Avila, Spain
d. 1582

Saint Therese of Lisieux

(Marie Francoise-Therese Martin)
French religious figure
• Carmelite nun called the "greatest saint of modern times"; patron of aviators, foreign ministers.
b. 1873 in Alencon, France
d. September 3, 1897 in Lisieux, France

Thomas a Kempis

(Thomas Hamerken)
German theologian–author
• Wrote influential The Imitation of Christ, c. 1427.
b. 1380 in Kempen, Germany
d. July 25, 1471 in Agnietenberg, Netherlands

Martha Carey Thomas

American educator–feminist
• Pres., Bryn Mawr College, 1894-1922.
b. January 02, 1857 in Baltimore, Maryland
d. December 02, 1935 in Philadelphia, Pennsylvania

Frank Tieri

Italian criminal
• First man ever convicted of heading an organized-crime family, 1980; died before serving 10 yr. sentence.
b. 1904 in Castel Gandolfo, Italy
d. March 29, 1981 in New York, New York

Channing Heggie Tobias

American reformer
• Minister active in NAACP, 1940s-50s.
b. February 01, 1882 in Augusta, Georgia
d. November 05, 1961 in New York, New York

Sweeney Todd

English murderer
• Life was subject of Broadway musical Sweeney Todd; supposedly slashed his victims throats, used bodies in meat pies.

Tokyo Rose

(Iva Toguri d'Aquino)
American traitor
• WW II propaganda commentator for Radio Tokyo; imprisoned, then received presidential pardon, 1977.
b. July 04, 1916 in Los Angeles, California

Victor Lloyd Tomseth

(The Hostages)
American hostage in Iran
• One of 52 held by terrorists, Nov 1979-Jan 1981.
b. April 14, 1941 in Oregon

Tomas de Torquemada
Spanish religious figure
• Monk, Inquisitor-General, who organized the Spanish Inquisition, 1483; in charge of removing Jews, Muslims from Spain.
b. 1420 in Spain
d. 1498

Griselio Torresola
Puerto Rican attempted assassin
• Tried to shoot way into Blair House to kill Harry Truman; killed in attempt.

Roger Touchy
American criminal
• Chicago bootlegger, who was convicted for kidnapping, 1934; released, 1959; murdered.
b. 1898 in Chicago, Illinois
d. December 17, 1959 in Chicago, Illinois

Santo Trafficante, Jr
American criminal
• Mafia don; testified before Congress that he was part of a 1960 assassination plot against Fidel Castro.
b. 1915
d. March 17, 1987 in Houston, Texas

Valerian Trifa
American religious leader
• Orthodox archbishop ordered out of U.S. for hiding pro-Nazi activities while a student leader in pre-WW II Romania.
b. June 28, 1914 in Campeni, Romania
d. January 28, 1987 in Cascais, Portugal

Sojourner Truth
(Isabella VanWagener)
American abolitionist–feminist
• Freed slave who advocated emancipation, women's rights; noted orator.
b. 1797 in Ulster County, New York
d. November 26, 1883 in Battle Creek, Michigan

Sterling Tucker
American civil rights leader
• Executive director, Washington, DC Urban League, 1956-78; books include *Black Reflections on White Power*, 1969; *For Blacks Only*, 1970.
b. December 21, 1923 in Akron, Ohio

Henry McNeal Turner
American religious leader
• Commissioned chaplain by Lincoln, first black commissioned, 1863; forced out, 1865.
b. February 01, 1834 in Abbeville, South Carolina
d. May 08, 1915

Thomas Wyatt Turner
American civil rights leader–educator
• Charter member, NAACP; founded Federation of Colored Catholics, 1915; active in black voter registration, 1920s.
b. April 16, 1877 in Hughesville, Maryland
d. April 21, 1978 in Washington, District of Columbia

Dick (Richard) Turpin
English criminal
• Horse thief hanged at York; subject of W H Ainsworth's novel, *Rockwood*, 1834.
b. 1706 in Essex, England
d. April 1, 1739 in York, England

Desmond Mpilo Tutu
South African religious leader
• First black Anglican bishop of Johannesburg, S Africa; won Nobel Peace Prize, 1984.
b. October 07, 1931 in Klerksdrop, South Africa

Howard B Unruh
American murderer
• Killed 13 people in 12 minutes in Camden, NJ, Jun 9, 1949.
b. 1921 in Camden, New Jersey

Pope Urban II
(Odo of Lagery)
French religious leader
• French pope, 1088-99; launched First Crusade, 1095.
b. 1035 in Chatillon-sur-Marne, France
d. October 29, 1099

James Ussher
Irish religious leader
• Archbishop of Armagh, 1625; upheld doctrine of divine right of kings.
b. January 04, 1581 in Dublin, Ireland
d. March 21, 1656 in Reigate, England

Joe (Joseph M) Valachi
American criminal
• Hit man, turned informer to Justice Dept., 1963.
b. September 22, 1904 in New York, New York
d. April 03, 1971 in El Paso, Texas

Saint Veronica Giuliani
Italian religious figure
• Legandary woman who wiped Jesus' brow as he bore the cross.

Helen Francis Garrison Villard
American social reformer
• Worked to further the women's movement, advancement of black people.
b. 1844 in Boston, Massachusetts
d. 1928 in Dobbs Ferry, New York

Saint Vincent de Paul
French religious leader
• Founded charities, Vincentians, Sisters of Charity, circa 1625; helped revive French Catholicism.
b. April 24, 1581 in Pouy, France
d. September 27, 1660 in Paris, France

Willem Adolf Visser T Hooft
Dutch religious leader
• Founding general-secretary, World Council of Churches, 1948-66.
b. September 2, 1900 in Haarlem, Netherlands
d. July 04, 1985 in Geneva, Switzerland

Terry (Terence Hardy) Waite
English clergyman–diplomat–hostage
• Special Anglican Church envoy to Mideast who helped negotiate release of hostages in Lebanon, 1986-87; kidnapped, held hostage himself, 1987–.
b. May 31, 1939 in Styal, England

James Edward Walsh
American religious leader
• Roman Catholic bishop who spent more than 40 yrs. as missionary to China, 12 yrs. in Shanghai prison.
b. April 3, 1891 in Cumberland, Maryland
d. July 29, 1981 in Ossining, New York

Phillip R Ward
(The Hostages)
American hostage in Iran
• One of 52 held by terrorists, Nov 1979 - Jan 1981.
b. March 22, 1940

William Warham
English religious leader
• Archbishop of Canterbury, 1504-15; signed Henry VIII's petition to pope for divorce from Katherine of Aragon, 1527.
b. 1450 in England
d. August 22, 1532 in England

Booker T(aliafero) Washington
American educator–author
• Leading black of his time; founded Tuskegee Institute, 1881, turned it into foremost college for blacks; wrote autobiographical *Up From Slavery*, 1901.
b. April 05, 1856 in Franklin County, Virginia
d. November 14, 1915 in Tuskegee, Alabama

Annie Dodge Wauneka
American Indian reformer
• Won Medal of Freedom, 1963, for efforts to improve health services among Navajos.
b. 1912

Joseph R Weil
American criminal
• Made over $8 million as a con man; known for innovative swindles.
b. 1875 in Chicago, Illinois
d. February 26, 1976

Moshe Weinberg
Israeli olympic athlete–victim
• One of 11 members of Israeli Olympic team kidnapped and killed by Arab terrorists during Summer Olympic Games.
b. 1940
d. September 05, 1972 in Munich, Germany (West)

Ida Bell Wells
American reformer
• Launched anti-lynching crusade; founder, first pres., Negro Fellowship League, 1910.
b. July 16, 1862 in Holly Springs, Mississippi
d. March 25, 1931 in Chicago, Illinois

John Wesley
English religious leader
• Founded Methodism at Oxford U, 1729; name derived from methodical devotion to study, religion.
b. June 28, 1703 in Lincoln, England
d. March 03, 1791 in London, England

Ellen Gould Harmon White
American religious leader
• Co-founder, Seventh-Day Adventists, 1860; claimed 2000 visions.
b. November 26, 1827 in Gorham, Maine
d. July 16, 1915 in Saint Helena, California

Ryan White
American victim
• Hemophiliac; contracted AIDS from tainted blood transfusion, 1985; waged five-year battle against the disease and prejudiced public opinion.
b. December 06, 1971 in Kokomo, Indiana
d. April 08, 1990 in Indianapolis, Indiana

Walter Francis White
American author–civil rights leader
• Active in NAACP, other civil liberties organizations; consultant to UN, 1945, 1948.
b. July 01, 1893 in Atlanta, Georgia
d. March 21, 1955 in New York, New York

George Whitefield
English religious leader
• Joined Methodists, 1732; adapted Calvinist views to Methodism, 1741.
b. December 27, 1714 in Gloucester, England
d. September 3, 1770 in Newburyport, Massachusetts

Charles Joseph Whitman
American murderer
• Shooting spree on Texas U campus left 18 dead, 30 wounded.
b. 1941
d. August 1966 in Austin, Texas

Victor Paul Wierwille
American religious leader–clergyman
• Founder, director of religious group The Way, 1942-82.
b. December 31, 1916 in New Knoxville, Ohio
d. May 2, 1985

Donald Ellis Wildmon
American religious leader–reformer
• Conservative minister, founder of Nat. Federation of Decency; launched crusade to rid media of sexually explicit material.
b. January 18, 1938 in Dumas, Mississippi

George A Wiley
American educator–civil rights leader
• Founded National Welfare Rights Organization, 1966; nat. coordinator, Movement for Economic Justice.
b. February 26, 1931 in Bayonne, New Jersey
d. August 08, 1973 in Maryland

Harvey Washington Wiley
American chemist–reformer
• Wrote books on chemistry including *Foods and Their Adulteration*, 1917.
b. October 18, 1844 in Kent, Indiana
d. June 3, 1930 in Washington, District of Columbia

John Wilkes
English reformer
• Radical critic of govt. policies who became MP, lord mayor of London; helped secure many political rights.
b. October 17, 1727 in London, England
d. March 02, 1797 in London, England

Roy Wilkins
American social reformer–civil rights leader
• Moderate exec. secretary of NAACP, 1955-77.
b. August 3, 1901 in Saint Louis, Missouri
d. September 08, 1981 in New York, New York

Frances Elizabeth Caroline Willard
American social reformer
• President, Women's Christian Temperance Union, 1879-98; toured US, speaking on temperance, women's suffrage.
b. September 28, 1839 in Churchville, New York
d. February 18, 1898 in New York, New York

William of Waynflete
(William Patyn)
English religious leader
• Bishop of Winchester, 1447-86; founded Magdalen College, Oxford, 1448.
b. 1395
d. August 11, 1486

Elizabeth Betty Smyth Williams
(Mrs J T Perkins)
Irish civil rights leader
• Shared 1976 Nobel Peace Prize with Mairead Corrigan; co-founded Peace People to end fighting in N Ireland.
b. May 22, 1943 in Belfast, Northern Ireland

Wayne Bertram Williams
American murderer
• Freelance photographer convicted of Atlanta's child killings, 1982.
b. May 27, 1958

Willmar 8
(Glennis Andresen; Doris Boshart; Sylvia Erickson; Jane Harguth; Teren Novotny; Shirley Solyntjes; Sandi Treml; Irene Wallin)
American social reformers
• Women employees of Citizens National Bank, Willmar, MN; staged strike, 1976, over sexual discrimination.

Isaac Mayer Wise
American religious leader
• Founded Reform Judaism in US; pres., Hebrew Union College, Cincinnati,ati, 1875-1900.
b. March 29, 1819 in Steingrub, Bohemia
d. March 26, 1900 in Cincinnati, Ohio

Stephen Samuel Wise
American religious leader
• Zionist spokesman; founded Federation of American Zionists, 1898, Jewish Institute of Religion, 1922; worked to establish Palestine as national home for Jews.
b. March 17, 1874 in Budapest, Hungary
d. April 19, 1949 in New York, New York

Nicholas Patrick Stephen Wiseman
British religious leader
• First archbishop of Westminister, 1850.
b. August 02, 1802 in Seville, Spain
d. February 15, 1865 in London, England

John Witherspoon
American educator–religious leader–continental congressman
• Only clergyman in first Continental Congress; signed Declaration of Independence; president, Princeton College; coined term "Americanism."
b. February 05, 1723 in Gifford, Scotland
d. November 15, 1794 in Princeton, New Jersey

Annie Turner Wittenmyer
American social reformer
• First president, Woman's Christian
Temperance Union; known for church,
charity work.
b. August 26, 1827 in Sandy Springs, Ohio
d. February 02, 1900

Thomas Wolsey, Cardinal
English religious figure
• Cardinal and lord chancellor with papal
ambitions; Henry VIII's ally in attempt to
secure divorce from Catherine of Aragon.
b. 1475 in Ipswich, England
d. November 29, 1530 in Leicester, England

Louise Aletha Wood
American reformer
• Nat. exec. director, Girl Scouts of the
USA, 1961-72; recreational supervisor,
Federal Works Agency, 1934-42; won
Medal of Freedom, 1947.
b. February 19, 1910 in Mankato, Minnesota
d. May 16, 1988 in Aurora, California

Victoria Claflin Woodhull
American social reformer
• With sister, Tennessee Claflin, founded
Woodhull and Claflin's Weekly, 1870,
which advocated equal rights for women;
Equal Rights Party presidential candidate,
1872.
b. September 23, 1838 in Homer, Ohio
d. June 1, 1927 in Norton Park, England

John Woolman
American religious leader
• Quaker preacher, 1743-72; best known
for his journal, first published in 1774.
b. October 19, 1720 in Ancochs, New Jersey
d. October 07, 1772 in New York, New York

Wovoka
(Jack Wilson)
American Indian religious leader–mystic
• Originator of "Ghost Dance," 1890-91
regarded as messiah by followers.
b. 1856 in Esmeralda County, Nevada
d. October 1932 in Schurz, Nevada

Frances (Fanny) Wright
American reformer–author
• Scandalized America by lecturing on
birth control, woman's rights; co-founded
colony for freed slaves, 1827.
b. September 06, 1795 in Dundee, Scotland
d. December 13, 1852 in Cincinnati, Ohio

John Joseph Wright
American religious leader
• Cardinal who was highest ranking
American in Vatican, 1967-79; author,
The Christian and the Law, 1962.
b. July 18, 1909 in Boston, Massachusetts
d. August 1, 1979 in Cambridge, Massachu-
setts

John Wycliffe
English reformer–theologian
• Involved in rejection of formalism; major force behind Protestant Reformation;
compiled English translation of Bible.
b. December 31, 1320 in Richmond, England
d. 1384

Stefan Wyszynski
Polish religious leader
• Responsible for peaceful co-existence of
Roman Catholic church and socialist state
in Poland.
b. August 03, 1901 in Zuzela, Russia
d. May 28, 1981 in Warsaw, Poland

Molly (Mary Alexander) Yard
American political activist–feminist
• President of NOW, 1987–.
b. 1910 in Shanghai, China

Brigham Young
American religious leader
• Baptized into Mormon faith, 1832; emigrated church to Utah, 1848, governor,
1850-58; had 27 wives, 47 children.
b. June 01, 1801 in Whitingham, Vermont
d. August 29, 1877 in Salt Lake City, Utah

Whitney Moore Young, Jr
American civil rights leader
• Director, National Urban League,
1961-71; wrote *Beyond Racism*, 1969.
b. July 31, 1921 in Lincoln Ridge, Kentucky
d. March 11, 1971 in Lagos, Nigeria

Bob (Robert) Younger
(Younger Brothers)
American outlaw
• Started life of crime with brothers at
age 12; died in jail.
b. 1853 in Lee's Summitt, Missouri
d. 1889 in Minnesota

Cole (Thomas Coleman) Younger
(Younger Brothers)
American outlaw
• Known for famous Northfield, MN,
bank raid, 1876; wrote *The Story of
Cole Younger*, 1903.
b. January 15, 1844 in Jackson County, Missouri
d. March 21, 1916 in Jackson County, Missouri

Jim (James) Younger
(Younger Brothers)
American outlaw
• Famous for raids with brothers; committed suicide after release from jail.
b. 1850 in Lee's Summitt, Missouri
d. 1902 in Minnesota

The Younger Brothers
(Bob Younger; Cole Younger; Jim Youn-
ger)
American criminals
• Famous gang of robbers, murderers;
rode with James brothers.

Joseph (Guiseppe) Zangara
American assassin
• Shot mayor of Chicago, in attempt to
kill FDR, Feb 15, 1933.
b. 1900 in Italy
d. March 21, 1933

Zodiac Killer
American murderer
• Killed at least six in CA beginning
1966; letters, cryptograms sent to papers; nothing heard since mid-1970s;
never caught.

Zoroaster
(Zarathustra)
Persian religious leader–prophet
• Founded Zoroastrianism, circa 575 BC,
which replaced Persian polytheism.
b. 628BC in Persia
d. 551BC

Elmo Russell Zumwalt III
American author–soldier–victim
• Believed to have contracted cancer
from exposure to chemical Agent Orange,
ordered used in Vietnam by father; with
father, wrote *My Father, My Son*, 1986.
b. 1946 in Tulare, California
d. August 13, 1988 in Fayetteville, North Carolina

Huldreich Zwingli
Swiss reformer
• Sermons criticizing the Mass started
Reformation in Switzerland.
b. January 01, 1484 in Wildhause, Germany
d. October 1, 1531 in Kappel, Switzerland

MUSIC MAKERS: MOZART, MONK & MADONNA

Bandleaders,

Composers,

Conductors, Rock

Stars, Singers...

ABBA
(Benny Andersson; Annifrid Lyngstad-Fredriksson; Agetha Ulvaeus; Bjorn Ulvaeus)
Swedish music group
• Formed 1973; hit singles "Dancing Queen," 1977; "Take a Chance on Me," 1978.

Claudio Abbado
Italian conductor
• Music director, Milan's La Scala, 1968–; led Vienna Philharmonic, 1971; guest conductor, Chicago Symphony, 1982–.
b. June 26, 1933 in Milan, Italy

Gregory Abbott
American singer
• Had number one solo debut album *Shake You Down*, 1986.
b. in Harlem, New York

ABC
(Martin Fry; David Palmer; Stephen Singleton; Mark White)
English music group
• Hit albums include *Lexicon of Love*, 1983; *How to be a Zillionaire*, 1985.

Paula Abdul
American singer–dancer
• Choreographer; first album *Forever Your Girl*, 1989, sold four million copies, had three no. 1 singles.
b. June 19, 1962 in North Hollywood, California

Karl Friedrich Abel
German musician–composer
• Considered last great viola da gamba virtuoso.
b. December 22, 1723 in Cothen, Germany
d. June 2, 1787 in London, England

AC-DC
(Mark Evans; Brian Johnson; Phil Rudd; Bon Scott; Cliff Williams;Angus Young; Malcolm Young)
Australian music group
• Heavy-metal band formed 1973; had number one album in US *For Those About to Rock*, 1981.

Ace
(Fran Byrne; Parul Carrack; Tex Comer; Phil Harris; Alan King)
English music group
• London pop-rock band formed 1973-76; hit single, "How Long," 1973.

Johnny Ace
(Johnny Marshall Alexander Jr)
American singer
• "Pledging My Love," 1955, became hit after his accidental death from Russian Roulette.
b. June 09, 1929 in Memphis, Tennessee
d. December 25, 1954 in Houston, Texas

Will (G William) Ackerman
American musician–music executive
• Soft rock, soft jazz guitarist; founded Windham Hill Records, 1975.
b. November 1949 in Eslingen, Germany (West)

Roy Acuff
American singer
• Country singer who has sold over 30 million records including "Wabash Cannoball."
b. September 15, 1903 in Maynardville, Tennessee

Adam de la Halle
French musician–dramatist
• Famed troubadour; wrote Le Jeu de la Feuillee, 1262, called earliest French comedy.
b. 1240 in Arras, France
d. 1287 in Naples, Italy

Adam and the Ants
(Adam Ant; Matthew Ashman; David Barbe; Chris Hughes; Terry Lee Miall; Kevin Mooney; Marco Pirroni; Gary Tibbs; Andrew Warren)
English music group
• Fantasy-oriented, new Romantic group, 1977-82; had number one album Kings of the Wild Frontier, 1981.

Bryan Adams
Canadian singer–musician
• Debut album produced first hit "Lonely Nights," 1982; hit single "Heaven," 1985.
b. November 05, 1959 in Vancouver, British Columbia

Edie Adams
(Elizabeth Edith Enke)
American singer–actress
• Wife of Ernie Kovacs; appeared in It's a Mad, Mad, Mad, Mad World, 1963.
b. April 16, 1929 in Kingston, Pennsylvania

Frank Ramsay Adams
American author–songwriter
• Wrote lyrics for over 200 songs; scripts for 25 films.
b. July 07, 1883 in Morrison, Illinois
d. October 08, 1963 in White Lake, Michigan

Cannonball (Julian Edwin) Adderley
American musician
• Alto-saxophonist who played with Miles Davis in 1950s; had 1960s hit "Mercy, Mercy, Mercy."
b. September 09, 1928 in Tampa, Florida
d. August 08, 1975 in Gary, Indiana

Richard Addinsell
English composer
• Compositions for films include Blithe Spirit, 1945; Under Capricorn, 1949; Macbeth, 1960.
b. January 13, 1904 in Oxford, England
d. November 15, 1977 in London, England

John Addison
English composer
• Known for film scores including Oscar-winning Tom Jones, 1963.
b. March 16, 1920 in West Cobham, England

Larry (Lawrence Cecil) Adler
American musician
• Considered world's best harmonica player; performed since 1928.
b. February 1, 1914 in Baltimore, Maryland

Richard Adler
American composer
• Musical film scores include Damn Yankees, 1958; Pajama Game, 1957; won Tonys for Broadway versions, 1954. 1955.
b. August 03, 1921 in New York, New York

Aerosmith
(Tom Hamilton; Joey Kramer; Joe Perry; Steve Tyler; Brad Whitford)
American music group
• Heavy metal band formed 1970; known for blues-based, hard-rock style; hit single "Dream On," 1975.

Milton Ager
American composer
• Popular balladist; wrote "Ain't She Sweet?," 1927; "Happy Days Are Here Again," 1929.
b. October 06, 1893 in Chicago, Illinois
d. May 06, 1979 in Los Angeles, California

Air Supply
(Russell Hitchcock; Graham Russell)
Australian music group
• Light pop-rock group, formed 1976; hits include "The One That You Love," 1981.

Hugh Aitken
American composer
• Works include chamber music, oratorios, opera, Felipe, 1981.
b. September 07, 1924 in New York, New York

Alabama
(Jeff Cook; Teddy Gentry; Mark Herndon; Randy Owen)
American music group
• Country-rock group, formed 1969; album Forty Hour Week, was number 1 on country charts, 1985; album sales exceed 10 million.

Licia Albanese
Italian opera singer
• Soprano; with NY Met., 1940s-70s; broadcast with Toscanini.
b. July 22, 1913 in Bari, Italy

Anna Maria Alberghetti
American singer–actress
• Operatic soprano who starred in films, Broadway musicals; won Tony for Carnival, 1962.
b. May 15, 1936 in Pasaro, Italy

Stephen Joel Albert
American composer
• Won Pulitzer, 1985, for music for his Symphony River Run.
b. February 06, 1941 in Brooklyn, New York

Tommaso Albinoni
Italian composer–violinist
• Wrote 53 operas, instrumental music.
b. 1671 in Venice, Italy
d. 1750 in Venice, Italy

Gregorio Allegri
Italian composer
• His "Miserere" is sung annually in Sistine Chapel on Good Friday.
b. 1582 in Rome, Italy
d. February 17, 1652 in Rome, Italy

Deborah Allen
American singer–songwriter
• Country singer who wrote, sang hit single "Baby I Lied," 1983.
b. September 3, 1953 in Memphis, Tennessee

Duane David Allen
(The Oak Ridge Boys)
American singer–musician
• Guitarist, lead singer with country-pop group; hit single "Bobby Sue," 1982; has won several Grammys since 1970.
b. April 29, 1943 in Taylortown, Texas

Elizabeth Allen
(Elizabeth Ellen Gillease)
American actress–singer
• Nominated for Tony, 1962, for The Gay Life.
b. January 25, 1934 in Jersey City, New Jersey

Peter Woolnough Allen
Australian songwriter–singer
• Discovered in Hong Kong by Judy Garland, 1964; wrote songs "I Honestly Love You," recorded by Olivia Newton-John, 1974, "Don't Cry Out Loud," sung by Melissa Manchester, 1978; former husband of Liza Minnelli.
b. February 1, 1944 in Tenterfield, Australia

Red (Henry James, Jr) Allen
American jazz musician–bandleader
• Dixieland trumpeter; with Louis Armstrong, 1937-40; led sextet, 1950s.
b. January 07, 1908 in New Orleans, Louisiana
d. April 17, 1967 in New York, New York

Rex E Allen, Sr
American actor–singer–songwriter
• Star of cowboy films, 1950s; wrote 300 songs including "Crying in the Chapel," 1953.
b. December 31, 1924 in Wilcox, Arizona

Rick Allen
(Def Leppard)
English musician
• Drummer with British heavy-metal, new wave group; lost arm in car crash, 1984.
b. November 01, 1963 in Sheffield, England

Duane (Howard Duane) Allman
(Allman Brothers Band; "Skydog")
American singer
• Formed band with brother, Gregg, 1968; debut album, *The Alman Brothers Band*, 1969; died in motorcycle accident.
b. November 2, 1946 in Nashville, Tennessee
d. October 29, 1971 in Macon, Georgia

Gregg (Gregory Lenoir) Allman
(Allman Brothers Band)
American singer–musician
• Formed band with brother, Duane, 1968; recorded solo album *Laid Back*, 1974.
b. December 07, 1947 in Nashville, Tennessee

Allman Brothers Band
(Duane Allman; Gregg Allman; Dicky Betts; Jaimoe (Jai Johnny) Johanson; Chuck Leavell; (Raymond) Berry Oakley; "Butch" (Claude Huds)
American music group
• Formed in Macon, GA, 1968; *Brothers and Sisters* album contained biggest hit, "Ramblin' Man," 1973.

Laurindo Almeida
Spanish musician–composer
• Jazz guitarist featured in Modern Jazz Quartet tours; has won five Grammys.
b. September 02, 1917 in Sao Paulo, Brazil

Herb Alpert
(Tijuana Brass)
American musician–bandleader
• Trumpeter; led Tijuana Brass, 1960s-70s; responsible for new era in instrumental music; hits include "The Lonely Bull," 1962, "Rise," 1979.
b. March 31, 1935 in Los Angeles, California

Lorenzo Alvary
American opera singer
• Bass; with NY Met., 1942-79; host, weekly radio opera program, 1964–.
b. February 2, 1909 in Hungary

Max Alvary
(Max Achenbach)
German opera singer
• Tenor; with NY Met., 1884-98; first to sing Wagner without a beard.
b. May 03, 1856 in Dusseldorf, Germany
d. November 07, 1898 in Gross-Tabarz, Germany

The Amboy Dukes
(Greg Arama; Cliff Davies; Rusty Day; Steve Farmer; Rob Grange; Vic Mastrianni; Ted Nugent; Dave Palmer; Derek St. Holmes; Andy Solomon)
American music group
• Formed by Ted Nugent, 1965; had hit "Journey to the Center of Your Mind," 1968.

Elly Ameling
Dutch opera singer
• Soprano with NY Met., 1950; made numerous recordings.
b. February 08, 1938 in Rotterdam, Netherlands

America
(Gerry Beckley; Dewey Bunnell; Daniel Peek)
American music group
• First million selling record was "A Horse with No Name," 1972; other hits include "You Can Do Magic," 1982.

Ed(mund Dantes) Ames
(The Ames Brothers; Ed Urick)
American singer–actor
• Solo recording artist, 1963–; played Mingo in TV series "Daniel Boone," 1963-68.
b. July 09, 1927 in Boston, Massachusetts

The Ames Brothers
(Ed Gene Joe and Vic Ames; given name Urick)
American music group
• Sang together, 1949-59; had 1953 hit single "You, You, You."

David Werner Amram, III
American composer–conductor
• Scored films, Broadway plays; won 1959 Obie for works for NY Shakespeare Festival.
b. November 17, 1930 in Philadelphia, Pennsylvania

Bill Anderson
("Whispering Bill")
American singer–songwriter
• Top country music star of 1960s; wrote "Walk Out Backward," 1962; "Strangers," 1965.
b. November 01, 1937 in Columbia, South Carolina

Cat (William Alonzo) Anderson
American composer–musician
• Jazz trumpeter, who recorded "Take the A Train" with Duke Ellington Orchestra, 1940s.
b. September 12, 1916 in Greenville, South Carolina
d. April 3, 1981 in Norwalk, California

Ian Anderson
(Jethro Tull)
Scottish musician–singer
• Flute-playing lead vocalist since 1968, known for outlandish stage costumes, antics.
b. August 1, 1947 in Dunfermline, Scotland

Ivie Anderson
American singer
• Jazz vocalist with Duke Ellington Band, 1931-42; hits include "I Got It Bad."
b. 1904 in Gilroy, California
d. December 28, 1949 in Los Angeles, California

John Anderson
American singer–musician
• Country hits include "Swingin'," 1983.
b. December 13, 1954 in Apopka, Florida

Jon Anderson
(Yes)
English singer–musician
• Drummer, vocalist who formed Yes, 1968; wrote most of group's lyrics; had three solo albums.
b. October 25, 1944 in Lancashire, England

Leroy Anderson
American composer–conductor
• Compositions include "The Typewriter"; "Blue Tango"; "Forgotten Dreams."
b. June 29, 1908 in Cambridge, Massachusetts
d. May 18, 1975 in Woodbury, Connecticut

Lynn Anderson
American singer
• Country hit "Rose Garden," rose to top of country, pop charts, 1970; won Grammy, 1970.
b. September 26, 1947 in Grand Forks, North Dakota

Marian Anderson
American singer
• Contralto; first black soloist with NY Met., 1955; received Presidential Medal of Freedom, 1963.
b. February 17, 1902 in Philadelphia, Pennsylvania

Benny Andersson
(ABBA)
Swedish singer–musician
• Part of most successful Swedish singing group, formed 1973; hits include "Fernando," 1976.
b. December 16, 1946 in Stockholm, Sweden

Julie Andrews
(Mrs Blake Edwards; Julia Elizabeth Wells)
English singer–actress
• Won Oscar, 1964, for *Mary Poppins*; Oscar nominee, 1965, for *The Sound of Music*.
b. October 01, 1935 in Walton-on-Thames, England

LaVerne Andrews
(Andrews Sisters)
American singer
• With sisters, popular on radio, in WW II musical movies, 1940s: *Buck Privates*, 1941.
b. July 06, 1915 in Minneapolis, Minnesota
d. May 08, 1967 in Brentwood, California

Maxine Andrews
(Andrews Sisters)
American singer
• With sisters, popular on radio, in WW II musical movies, 1940s: *Private Buckaroo*, 1942.
b. January 03, 1918 in Minneapolis, Minnesota

Patti (Patricia) Andrews
(Andrews Sisters)
American singer
• With sisters, popular on radio, in WW II musical movies: *Follow the Boys*, 1944.
b. February 16, 1920 in Minneapolis, Minnesota

Andrews Sisters
(LaVerne Andrews; Maxine Andrews; Patti Andrews)
American music group
• Harmony trio of sisters known for 1940s hits: "Boogie Woogie Bugle Boy from Company B."

Victoria de los Angeles
Spanish opera singer
• Soprano, who performed famous title roles in *Madame Butterfly*; *Carmen*, 1950s.
b. November 01, 1923 in Barcelona, Spain

The Animals
(Eric Burdon; Bryan Chandler; Barry Jenkins; Alan Price; Dave Rowberry; John Steel; Hilton Valentine)
English music group
• Part of "British Invasion" of early 60s; hit singles: "House of the Rising Sun," 1964; "Don't Let Me Be Misunderstood," 1965.

Giovanni Animuccia
Italian composer
• Developed oratorio musical form with "Laudi Spirtuali," 1563, 1570.
b. 1500 in Florence, Italy
d. 1571 in Rome, Italy

Paul Anka
Canadian singer–songwriter
• Wrote songs "Diana," 1957; "My Way," 1967; has 15 gold records.
b. July 3, 1941 in Ottawa, Ontario

Annabella
(Myant Myant Aye; Bow Wow Wow; Annabella Lwin)
Burmese singer
• Lead singer with Bow Wow Wow, 1980-83.
b. October 31, 1965 in Rangoon, Burma

Ernest Alexandre Ansermet
Swiss conductor
• Founded, conducted Orchestre de la Suisse Romande, Geneva, 1918-67.
b. November 11, 1883 in Vevey, Switzerland
d. February 2, 1969 in Geneva, Switzerland

Adam Ant
(Stewart Goddard; Adam and the Ants)
English singer
• Vocalist, guitarist, pianist; had top solo single "Goody Two Shoes," 1982.
b. November 03, 1954 in London, England

George Antheil
American composer
• Wrote concert music, opera, movie scores; films include *Once in a Blue Moon*, 1935.
b. July 08, 1900 in Trenton, New Jersey
d. February 12, 1959 in New York, New York

Michael Anthony
(Van Halen)
American musician
• Bassist with group since 1974.
b. June 2, 1955 in Chicago, Illinois

Ray Anthony
(Raymond Antonini)
American bandleader–songwriter
• Trumpeter; led popular dance band, 1950s; cowrote "The Bunny Hop," 1952.
b. January 2, 1922 in Bentleyville, Pennsylvania

Susan Anton
American actress–singer
• Nightclub performer; starred in film *Golden Girl*, 1979.
b. October 12, 1950 in Yucaipa, California

Carmine Appice
(Vanilla Fudge)
American musician
• Session drummer; often backs Rod Stewart.
b. December 15, 1946 in Staten Island, New York

April Wine
(Myles Goodwin; Brian Greenway; Steve Lang; Jerry Mercer; Gary Moffet)
Canadian music group
• Earned 10 gold albums in Canada; had platinum album *World's Goin' Crazy*, 1976.

Argent
(Rod Argent; Russ Ballard; John Grimaldi; Robert Henrit; Jim Rodford; John Verity)
English music group
• Group formed, 1969-76; hits include "Hold Your Head Up," 1972.

Rod(ney Terence) Argent
(Argent; Zombies)
English musician–singer
• Keyboardist, vocalist with Zombies, Argent, 1960s-70s.
b. June 14, 1945 in Saint Albans, England

Harold Arlen
(Hyman Arluck; Chaim Arluk)
American songwriter
• Wrote over 500 hits including Oscar winner "Over the Rainbow," 1939; "Stormy Weather," 1933; "Old Black Magic," 1942.
b. February 15, 1905 in Buffalo, New York
d. April 23, 1986 in New York, New York

Joan Armatrading
British singer–songwriter
• Acoustic-based album, *Joan Armatrading*, best-seller in England, 1976; other albums include *Secret Secrets*, 1985.
b. December 09, 1950 in Saint Kitts, West Indies

Lil(lian Hardin) Armstrong
American jazz musician
• Ex-wife of Louis Armstrong; pianist, arranger, vocalist, composer, 1920s-60s.
b. February 03, 1902 in Memphis, Tennessee
d. August 27, 1971 in Chicago, Illinois

Louis Daniel Armstrong
American musician–bandleader
• Called world's greatest trumpeter; introduced "scat" singing.
b. July 04, 1900 in New Orleans, Louisiana
d. July 06, 1971 in New York, New York

Thomas Augustine Arne
English composer
• His patriotic song "Rule Britannia" is from masque *Alfred*, 1740.
b. March 12, 1710 in London, England
d. March 05, 1778 in London, England

Eddy Arnold
American singer–musician
• Country singer, guitarist, who made debut, 1936; country Music Hall of Fame, 1966.
b. May 15, 1918 in Henderson, Tennessee

Sir Malcolm Arnold
English composer
• Film compositions include *Island in the Sun*, 1957; *Trapeze*, 1984.
b. October 21, 1921 in Northampton, England

Claudio Arrau
Chilean pianist
• International concertist; performed publicly since age 5; recorded complete sonatas, Mozart's works.
b. February 06, 1903 in Chillan, Chile

Martina Arroyo
American opera singer
• Leading soprano with NY Met., 1970-74; noted for Verdi, Rossini roles.
b. February 02, 1937 in New York, New York

Peter Asher
(Peter and Gordon)
English singer–producer
• Part of Peter and Gordon duo, 1961-68; has produced albums for James Taylor, Linda Ronstadt.
b. June 22, 1944 in London, England

Nickolas Ashford
(Ashford and Simpson)
American singer–songwriter
• Wrote song "Ain't No Mountain High Enough," 1967, recorded by the Supremes.
b. May 04, 1942 in Fairfield, South Carolina

Ashford and Simpson
(Nickolas Ashford; Valerie Simpson)
American music group
• Husband-wife writers, performers; responsible for some of Motown's biggest hits.

Vladimir Davidovich Ashkenazy
Russian musician
• Considered among best of Russian pianists; co-winner of Tchaikovsky piano award, 1962.
b. July 06, 1937 in Gorki, U.S.S.R.

The Association
(Gary Alexander; Ted Bluechel; Brian Cole; Russ Giguere; Terry Kirkman; Jim Yester)
American music group
• Pop-rock band, 1960s; won gold records for "Cherish," 1966; "Never My Love," 1967.

Rick (Richard Paul) Astley
English singer
• Top dance sales artist, 1988; had hit singles "Never Gonna Give You Up," "She Wants to Dance With Me."
b. June 02, 1966 in Newton-le-Willows, England

Chet (Chester B) Atkins
American musician
• Virtuoso guitarist, associated with Grand Ole Opry since 1950.
b. June 2, 1924 in Luttrell, Tennessee

Atlanta Rhythm Section
(Barry Bailey; J R Cobb; Dean Daugherty; Paul Goddard; Ronnie Hammond; Robert Nix)
American music group
• Had platinum album *Champagne Jam*, 1978; hit singles "So into You," 1977; "Imaginary Lover," 1978.

Daniel Francois Esprit Auber
French composer
• Father of French grand opera; greatest work *La Muette de Portici*, 1828.
b. January 19, 1782 in Caen, France
d. May 12, 1871 in Paris, France

Leopold Auer
American violinist–teacher
• Soloist for the Czar; taught Zimbalist, Heifetz; wrote manuals on violin playing.
b. June 07, 1845 in Vesprem, Hungary
d. July 15, 1930 in Loschwitz, Germany

Brian Auger
English musician–songwriter
• Keyboardist who formed Brian Auger's Trinity, 1964; fused jazz-rock hybrids.
b. July 18, 1939 in London, England

Georges Auric
(Les Six)
French composer
• Scored over 100 films, including *Roman Holiday*, 1953; *Beauty and the Beast*, 1946.
b. February 15, 1899 in Lodeve, France
d. July 23, 1983 in Paris, France

Gene Austin
American actor–songwriter
• Songs include "How Come You Do Me Like You Do?" 1924; "Lonesome Road," 1928.
b. June 24, 1900 in Gainesville, Texas
d. January 24, 1972 in Palm Springs, California

Patti Austin
American singer
• With James Ingram, had hit single "Baby Come to Me," 1982, love theme for soap opera "General Hospital."
b. August 1, 1948 in New York, New York

Gene (Orvon Gene) Autry
American actor–singer–baseball executive
• Starred in 82 movie Westerns, 1934-54; wrote over 250 songs, including "Here Comes Santa Claus"; owner, CA Angels baseball team.
b. September 29, 1907 in Tioga, Texas

Frankie Avalon
(Francis Thomas Avalone)
American actor–singer–entertainer
• Teen idol, 1960s; starred with Annette Funicello in *Beach* movies; had hit song, "Venus," 1959.
b. September 18, 1940 in Philadelphia, Pennsylvania

The Average White Band
(Roger Ball; Malcolm Duncan; Steven Ferrone; Alan Gorrie; Onnie McIntire; Robbie McIntosh; Michael Rosen; Hamish Stuart)
English music group
• Formed 1972; best-selling albums *Cut the Cake,* 1975; *Cupid's in Fashion,* 1982.

Hoyt Wayne Axton
American singer–songwriter
• Country music singer; has sold over 25 million records in 20-year career.
b. March 25, 1938 in Duncan, Oklahoma

Mitchell Ayres
American bandleader
• Led band that backed singer Perry Como on radio, TV, 1940s-60s.
b. December 24, 1910 in Milwaukee, Wisconsin
d. September 05, 1969 in Las Vegas, Nevada

Charles Aznavour
(Shahnour Varenagh Aznavourian)
French singer–actor
• Diminutive, foggy-voiced singer who gained fame, 1950s; most memorable film *Shoot the Piano Player,* 1950.
b. May 22, 1924 in Paris, France

B-52's
(Kate Pierson; Fred Schneider; Keith Strickland; Cindy Wilson; Ricky Wilson)
American music group
• Formed 1976; known for party music with 50s, 60s vocals, lyrics; debut album *Wild Planet,* 1980.

Milton Byron Babbitt
American composer
• First composer to work on RCA's Mark II synthesizer; wrote *Compositionn for Synthesizer,* 1961.
b. May 1, 1916 in Philadelphia, Pennsylvania

Victor Babin
(Vronsky and Babin)
American pianist
• Formed two-piano team with wife Vitya Vronsky, 1933.
b. December 12, 1908 in Moscow, Russia
d. March 01, 1972 in Cleveland, Ohio

The Babys
(Tony Brock; Jonathan Cain; Mike Corby; Ricky Phillips; Wally Stocker; John Waite)
English music group
• Power pop group, 1976-81; hits include "Isn't It Time"; "Head First."

Carl Philipp Emanuel Bach
German composer
• Pioneered sonata-allegro musical form; wrote influential study on clavier playing, 1753; son of Johann Sebastian.
b. March 08, 1714 in Weimar, Germany
d. December 15, 1788 in Hamburg, Germany

Johann Christian Bach
German composer
• Wrote operas, taught music to Britain's royalty, 1762-82; eleventh son of Johann Sebastian.
b. September 03, 1735 in Leipzig, Germany
d. January 01, 1782 in London, England

Johann Sebastian Bach
German composer–organist
• Master of church music; father of church dynasty; masterpieces include *Brandenburg Concerti,* 1721; *Well-Tempererd Clavier,* 1722-44.
b. March 21, 1685 in Eisenach, Germany
d. July 28, 1750 in Leipzig, Germany

Wilhelm Friedemann Bach
German composer–organist
• Wrote concertos, organ works; eldest son of Johann Sebastian.
b. November 22, 1710 in Weimar, Germany
d. July 01, 1784 in Berlin, Germany

Burt Bacharach
American composer–musician–conductor
• Best known for collaborations with Hal David; won Oscar for "Raindrops Keep Falling on My Head," 1970.
b. May 12, 1929 in Kansas City, Missouri

Gina Bachauer
Greek pianist
• Made US debut, 1950, NYC; repertoire ranged from Mozart to Stravinsky.
b. May 21, 1913 in Athens, Greece
d. August 22, 1976 in Athens, Greece

Randy Bachman
(Bachman-Turner Overdrive; Guess Who)
Canadian singer–musician
• Guitarist; co-founded Guess Who, 1963, Bachman-Turner Overdrive, 1972.
b. September 27, 1943 in Winnipeg, Manitoba

Bachman-Turner Overdrive
(Chad Allen; Randy Bachman; Robin Bachman; Timothy Bachman; Jim Clench; Blair Thornton; C F Turner)
Canadian music group
• Heavy-metal group with blue-collar image, 1972-79; hits include "You Ain't Seen Nothin' Yet," 1974.

Wilhelm Backhaus
German pianist
• Concert pianist who toured Europe, US, Australia, Japan, S America, 1905-69.
b. March 26, 1884 in Leipzig, Germany
d. July 05, 1969 in Villach, Austria

Bad Company
(Boz Burrell; Simon Kirke; Michael Ralphs; Paul Rodgers)
English music group
• Debut album *Bad Company,* 1974 was number one worldwide; hit singles include "Rock and Roll Fantasy," 1979.

Badfinger
(Tom Evans; Mike Gibbons; Ronald Griffiths; Peter Ham; Joey Molland)
English music group
• Liverpool quintet formed mid-60s-1975, promoted by Beatles; hit album *Maybe Tomorrow,* 1969.

Paul Badura-Skoda
Austrian pianist
• Made concert debut in Vienna, 1948; wrote books on interpreting Mozart.
b. January 15, 1927 in Munich, Germany

Joan Baez
American singer–political activist
• Folk singer, proponent of human rights, 1960s; founded Humanitas/International Human Rights Committee, 1979.
b. January 09, 1941 in New York, New York

Pearl Mae Bailey
American singer–actress
• Vaudeville, cabaret performer, best known for starring role in Broadway musical *Hello Dolly,* 1967-69.
b. March 28, 1918 in Newport News, Virginia
d. August 17, 1990 in Philadelphia, Pennsylvania

Philip Bailey
(Earth Wind and Fire)
American singer–musician
• With Phil Collins, sang "Easy Lover," 1984.
b. May 08, 1951 in Denver, Colorado

Anita Baker
American singer
• Album *Rapture,* 1986, sold over two million copies; won two Grammys, 1987, including best rhythm and blues song for "Sweet Love."
b. January 26, 1958 in Toledo, Ohio

Bonnie Baker
American singer
• Had number one record: "Oh Johnny, Oh Johnny," 1940.
b. April 01, 1917 in Orange, Texas

Ginger (Peter) Baker
(Blind Faith; Cream)
English musician–singer
• Leading British drummer, percussionist, 1960s-70s; formed group Cream, with Eric Clapton, 1967-69,
b. August 19, 1940 in Lewisham, England

Dame Janet Abbott Baker
English opera singer
• Mezzo-soprano, English Opera Group, 1961-76; Britten wrote a part for her.
b. August 21, 1933 in York, England

Josephine Baker
French singer
• Folies-Bergere's "Dark Star," 1920s; noted for banana dance, introduced hot jazz to Paris; active in Resistance, WWII.
b. June 03, 1906 in Saint Louis, Missouri
d. April 12, 1975 in Paris, France

Julius Baker
American musician
• Principal flutist, NY Philharmonic, 1965-83; soloist in concerts throughout US, Europe, Japan.
b. September 23, 1915 in Cleveland, Ohio

Kenny (Kenneth Lawrence) Baker
American actor–singer
• Nightclub singer who was regular vocalist on Jack Benny's radio show, 1930s.
b. September 3, 1912 in Monrovia, California
d. August 1, 1985 in Solvang, California

Phil Baker
American comedian–composer
• Films include *The Goldwyn Follies*, 1938; *The Gang's All Here*, 1943.
b. August 24, 1896 in Philadelphia, Pennsylvania
d. November 3, 1963 in Copenhagen, Denmark

Shorty (Harold) Baker
American jazz musician
• Trumpeter, 1930-65; played with Duke Ellington, Bud Freeman.
b. May 26, 1914 in Saint Louis, Missouri
d. November 08, 1966 in New York, New York

Marty Balin
(Martyn Jerel Buchwald; Jefferson Airplane)
American singer–songwriter
• Founder, Jefferson Airplane/Starship, 1965-71, 75-85; wrote hits "It's No Secret", "Fantastic Lover."
b. January 3, 1943 in Cincinnati, Ohio

Ernest Ball
American composer
• Compositions include "A Little Bit of Heaven"; "When Irish Eyes Are Smiling."
b. July 22, 1878 in Cleveland, Ohio
d. May 03, 1927 in Santa Ana, California

Florence Ballard
(The Supremes)
American singer
• Member of original Supremes; grew up with Diana Ross.
b. June 3, 1943 in Detroit, Michigan
d. February 22, 1976 in Detroit, Michigan

Hank Ballard
(John Kendricks; The Midnighters)
American singer
• Had 1960 hit "The Twist," before Chubbie Checker.
b. November 18, 1936 in Detroit, Michigan

Russ(ell) Ballard
(Argent)
English singer–musician
• Singer, guitarist with Argent, 1969-74.
b. October 31, 1947 in Waltham Cross, England

Artur Balsam
Polish pianist
• Accompanist to celebrated artists; has recorded all works of Mozart, Haydn.
b. February 08, 1906 in Warsaw, Poland

Bananarama
(Sarah Dallin; Siobhan Fahey; Keren Woodward)
British music group
• British invasion pop/rock group; had hit songs "Venus," 1986, "Cruel Summer," 1984.

The Band
(Rick Danko; Levon Helm; Garth Hudson; Richard Manuel; Robbie Robertson)
American music group
• Frequently worked with Bob Dylan; last concert filmed by Martin Scorsese as *The Last Waltz*, 1976.

The Bangles
(Susanna Hoffs; Debbi Peterson Vicki Peterson; Michael Steele)
English music group
• Pop group; had number one hit single "Walk Like an Egyptian," top 10 hit "Manic Monday," from album *Different Light*, 1986.

Tony Banks
(Genesis)
English musician
• Keyboardist, original member of Genesis.
b. March 27, 1950 in England

David Jacob Bar-Ilian
Israeli musician
• Concert pianist, worldwide recitalist, 1960–.
b. February 07, 1930 in Haifa, Palestine

Samuel Barber
American composer
• First composer to win Pulitzer twice; best known for "Adagio on Strings," 1936.
b. March 09, 1910 in West Chester, Pennsylvania
d. January 23, 1981 in New York, New York

Jules Barbier
French librettist
• Co-wrote, with Carre, texts for famous operas including Gounod's *Faust*.
b. March 08, 1825 in Paris, France
d. January 16, 1901 in Paris, France

Sir John Barbirolli
English conductor
• Succeeded Toscanini as permanent conductor, NY Philharmonic, 1937-43.
b. December 02, 1899 in London, England
d. July 28, 1970 in London, England

Daniel Barenboim
Israeli pianist–conductor
• Piano debut, age seven; led international orchestras since 1962; over 100 recordings as pianist, conductor.
b. November 15, 1942 in Buenos Aires, Argentina

Howard Barlow
American conductor
• Noted conductor on several radio shows; led CBS Symphony, 1927-43; Voice of Firestone, 1943-59.
b. May 01, 1892 in Plain City, Ohio
d. January 31, 1972 in Portland, Oregon

Billy (William Christopher) Barnes
American lyricist–composer
• Wrote songs "Too Long at the Fair," "Make a Little Magic."
b. January 27, 1927 in Los Angeles, California

Charlie (Charles Daly) Barnet
American bandleader–jazz musician
• Saxist, vocalist; led big-name band, 1930s-40s.
b. October 26, 1913 in New York, New York

Samuel Baron
American musician
• Noted flutist; led Bach Aria Group, 1980–.
b. April 27, 1925 in Brooklyn, New York

Syd (Roger Keith) Barrett
(Pink Floyd)
English singer–songwriter
• Founded, named Pink Floyd, 1964; released two solo albums, early 1970s.
b. January 1946 in Cambridge, England

Blue Barron
American bandleader
• Led popular, stylized dance band, 1930s-60s.
b. March 22, 1911 in Cleveland, Ohio

Keith E Barrow
American singer–songwriter
• Popular gospel composer; formed the Soul Shakers.
b. September 27, 1954 in Chicago, Illinois
d. October 22, 1983 in Chicago, Illinois

John Barry
English composer
• Wrote music for several James Bond films; won Oscars for scores of *Lion in Winter*, 1968; *Out of Africa*, 1985.
b. November 03, 1933 in York, England

Lionel Bart
(Lionel Begleiter)
English composer–lyricist–dramatist
• Stage musicals include *La Strada*, 1969; Tony award-winning *Oliver*, 1963.
b. August 01, 1930 in London, England

Bela Bartok
Hungarian composer–pianist
• Works include opera *Bluebeard's Castle*, 1927; *Concerto for Orchestra*, 1943; published over 6,000 folk tunes.
b. May 25, 1881 in Nagyszentmiklos, Hungary
d. September 29, 1945 in New York, New York

Count (William James, Jr) Basie
American jazz musician–bandleader
• Pianist; revolutionized jazz; one of most influential Big Band leaders, 1930s-50s; hits include "One O'Clock Jump," 1941.
b. August 21, 1904 in Red Bank, New Jersey
d. April 26, 1984 in Hollywood, Florida

Shirley Bassey
Welsh singer
• Sang title song from James Bond film *Goldfinger*, 1964.
b. January 08, 1937 in Cardiff, Wales

Mattia Battistini
Italian opera singer
• Was greatest living Italian baritone; had 50-yr. career; never sang in U.S.
b. February 27, 1856 in Rome, Italy
d. November 07, 1928 in Collebaccaro, Italy

Harold Bauer
English pianist–violinist
• Celebrated pianist with U.S. orchestras, from 1900; founded NYC's Beethoven Association, 1918.
b. April 28, 1873 in London, England
d. March 12, 1951 in Miami, Florida

Sir Arnold Edward Trevor Bax
(Dermont O'Byrne pseud)
English composer–author
• Master of Music for Elizabeth II, George VI; composed march played at coronation of Queen Elizabeth II.
b. November 08, 1883 in Streatham, England
d. October 03, 1953 in Cork, Ireland

Les Baxter
American bandleader
• Played keyboards for Neil Norman's Cosmic Orchestra, 1975-80.
b. March 14, 1922 in Mexia, Texas

The Bay City Rollers
(Eric Faulkner; Alan Longmuir; Derek Longmuir; Leslie McKeown; Stuart "Woody" Wood)
Scottish music group
• Group named when manager stuck pin in map hitting Bay City, MI; hit single "Saturday Night," 1976.

Nora Bayes
(Dora Goldberg)
American singer–actress
• Vaudeville, musical comedy star; co-wrote "Shine On, Harvest Moon," with husband Jack Norwood, 1908.
b. January 1, 1880 in Los Angeles, California
d. March 19, 1928 in New York, New York

Mrs H H A Beach
(Amy Marcy Cheney)
American composer
• "Gaelic" Symphony, 1896, first symphonic work composed by American woman.
b. September 05, 1867 in Henniker, New Hampshire
d. December 27, 1944 in New York, New York

The Beach Boys
(Al Jardine; Bruce Johnson; Mike Love; Brian Wilson; Carl Wilson;Dennis Wilson)
American music group
• Personified CA life-style with mellow songs about surfing, cars, young love: "Surfin' USA," 1963; Hall of Fame, 1988.

The Beatles
(George Harrison; John Lennon; Paul McCartney; Ringo Starr)
English music group
• Most influential music group of all time; hits include "I Want to Hold Your Hand," 1963; Hall of Fame, 1988.

Gilbert (Francois Silly) Becaud
French singer–songwriter
• Wrote, sang many French ballads: "What Now, My Love?"; wrote for films, 1950s-70s.
b. October 24, 1927 in Toulon, France

Sidney Bechet
American jazz musician–bandleader
• Clarinetist, early jazz soprano sax innovator; led own bands, 1920s-40s.
b. May 14, 1897 in New Orleans, Louisiana
d. May 14, 1959 in Paris, France

Jeff Beck
(Honeydrippers; Yardbirds)
English musician
• Established reputation as guitarist with Yardbirds, 1965; founded Jeff Beck Group, 1967.
b. June 24, 1944 in Surrey, England

Molly Bee
(Molly Beachboard)
American singer
• Country singer; successful singles 1950s-60s include "I Saw Mommy Kissing Santa Claus."
b. August 18, 1939 in Oklahoma City, Oklahoma

The Bee Gees
(Barry Gibb; Maurice Gibb; Robin Gibb)
English music group
• Soundtrack album *Saturday Night Fever*, 1977, sold over 15 million copies; was first ever triple platinum album.

Sir Thomas Beecham
English conductor
• Founded British National Opera Co., 1932; London Philharmonic, 1932; Royal Philharmonic, 1946.
b. April 29, 1879 in Saint Helens, England
d. March 08, 1961 in London, England

Ludwig van Beethoven
German composer
• Master of classical music; composed *Ninth Symphony*, 1817-23, when totally deaf.
b. December 16, 1770 in Bonn, Germany
d. March 26, 1827 in Vienna, Austria

Bix (Leon Bismark) Beiderbecke
American jazz musician
• Legendary coronetist, pianist; wrote "In a Mist"; recognized posthumously as one of jazz greats.
b. March 1, 1903 in Davenport, Iowa
d. August 07, 1931 in New York, New York

Eduard van Beinum
Dutch conductor
• Led Amsterdam's famed Concertgebouw Orchestra, 1945-59.
b. September 03, 1900 in Arnheim, Netherlands
d. April 13, 1959

Harry (Harold George, Jr) Belafonte
American singer–actor
• Helped popularize calypso music; won Tony, 1953, for *John Murray Anderson's Almanac.*
b. March 01, 1927 in New York, New York

Kool (Robert) Bell
(Kool and the Gang)
American singer–musician
• Leader of rhythm and blues-pop group; number one hit "Celebration," 1980.
b. October 08, 1950 in Youngstown, Ohio

Ronald Bell
(Kool and the Gang)
American musician
• Plays tenor sax with Kool and the Gang.
b. November 01, 1951 in Youngstown, Ohio

The Bellamy Brothers
(David Bellamy; Howard Bellamy)
American music group
• Pop-country duo from FL who had gold record for 1976 hit "Let Your Love Flow."

Vincenzo Bellini
Italian composer
• Noted bel canto composer who wrote operas *Il Pirata*, 1827; *Norma*, 1831.
b. November 03, 1801 in Catania, Sicily
d. September 23, 1835 in Puteaux, France

Pat Benatar
(Patricia Andrzejewski; Mrs Neil Geraldo)
American singer
• Has two platinum albums: *In the Heat of the Night; Precious Time;* single hit "Love Is a Battlefield," 1985.
b. January 1, 1952 in Brooklyn, New York

Ariel Bender
(Luther James Grosvenor; Mott the Hoople)
English musician
• Guitarist with hard rock group, 1973-74.
b. December 23, 1949 in Evesham, England

Tex (Gordon) Beneke
American singer–bandleader
• Popular saxophonist, vocalist with Glenn Miller; led orchestra after Miller's death, 1946-50.
b. February 12, 1914 in Fort Worth, Texas

Robert Russell Bennett
American composer
• Orchestrated over 300 Broadway musicals including *Show Boat; South Pacific;* won Oscar for *Oklahoma*, 1955.
b. June 15, 1894 in Kansas City, Missouri
d. August 18, 1981 in New York, New York

Tony Bennett
(Joe Bari; Anthony Dominick Benedetto; "The Singer's Singer")
American singer
• Biggest hit "I Left My Heart in San Francisco," 1963.
b. August 03, 1926 in New York, New York

George Benson
American singer–musician
• Jazz guitarist; won three Grammys, including record of the year for "This Masquerade," 1977; album *Breezin'* is largest selling jazz album of all time.
b. March 22, 1943 in Pittsburgh, Pennsylvania

Brook Benton
(Benjamin Franklin Peay)
American singer
• One of few black singers of his era to write own material; best known hit "Boll Weevil Song," 1961.
b. September 19, 1931 in Camden, South Carolina
d. April 09, 1988 in New York, New York

Cathy Berberian
(Mrs Luciano Berio)
American opera singer–comedienne
• Known for singing avant-garde works: John Cage's "Fontana Mix"; Luciana Berio's "Circles."
b. July 04, 1928 in Attleboro, Massachusetts
d. March 06, 1983 in Rome, Italy

Alban Berg
Austrian composer
• Wrote opera *Wozzeck*, 1921, in which atonality blends with elements of Viennese tradition.
b. February 09, 1885 in Vienna, Austria
d. December 24, 1935 in Vienna, Austria

Al Berger
(Southside Johnny and the Asbury Jukes)
American singer–musician
• Bassist, vocalist with group since 1974.
b. November 08, 1949

Alan Bergman
American lyricist
• With wife Marilyn, wrote numerous award-winning songs for stage, screen: *The Way We Were*, 1974.
b. September 11, 1925 in Brooklyn, New York

Marilyn Keith Bergman
(Mrs Alan Bergman)
American lyricist
• Won Oscars for *Yentl*, 1983; *The Way We Were*, 1974.
b. November 1, 1929 in Brooklyn, New York

Carl Bergmann
German conductor
• NY Philharmonic conductor, 1855-76, who introduced Wagner, Liszt to American audiences.
b. April 11, 1821 in Ebersbach, Germany
d. August 16, 1876 in New York, New York

Bunny (Rowland Bernart) Berigan
American jazz musician–bandleader
• Trumpeter, known for theme song "Can't Get Started with You."
b. November 02, 1909 in Hilbert, Wisconsin
d. June 02, 1942 in New York, New York

Irving Berlin
(Israel Baline)
American composer
• America's best-loved composer; wrote "God Bless America," 1939, "Easter Parade," 1933, "White Christmas," which won Oscar, 1942.
b. May 11, 1888 in Temun, Russia
d. September 22, 1989 in Manhattan, New York

Lazar Berman
Russian pianist
• Concert virtuoso, 1957–; made Carnegie Hall debut, 1976.
b. February 26, 1930 in Leningrad, U.S.S.R.

Ben Bernie
(The Old Maestro)
American comedian–bandleader
• Vaudeville, radio entertainer; led band, 1920s; used phrase "Yowsah, Yowsah."
b. May 3, 1891 in New York, New York
d. October 2, 1943 in Beverly Hills, California

Leonard Bernstein
American composer–conductor–musician–author
• First American-born conductor of NY Philharmonic, 1957; best known work was *West Side Story*, 1957; also composed theater and chamber music, symphonies, ballets.
b. August 25, 1918 in Lawrence, Massachusetts
d. October 14, 1990 in New York, New York

Michel Beroff
French pianist
• Toured as concert pianist, from age 16, often performing modernistic French composers.
b. 1950 in Epinal, France

Chuck (Charles Edward Anderson) Berry
American singer–songwriter
• Influential figure in development of rock music, 1950s-60s; wrote songs "Roll Over Beethoven," 1956; "Johnny B Goode," 1958.
b. January 15, 1926 in San Jose, California

Jan Berry
(Jan and Dean)
American singer
• Co-wrote duo's hit single "Surf City," 1963; suffered brain damage in car crash, 1966.
b. April 03, 1941 in Los Angeles, California

Walter Berry
Austrian opera singer
• Bass-baritone; NY Met. debut, 1966; known for Wagnerian roles; often sang with wife, Christa Ludwig.
b. April 08, 1929 in Vienna, Austria

Peter Best
English musician
• Replaced by Ringo Starr as drummer for The Beatles, 1962.
b. 1941 in Liverpool, England

Thomas Greene Bethune
American musician
• Retarded black who toured US, 1850s demonstrating uncanny musical memory.
b. 1849 in Georgia
d. 1908 in New York

The Big Bopper
(J P Richardson)
American radio performer–singer
• Disc jockey/pop star; had rockabilly hit, "Chantilly Lace," 1958; killed with Buddy Holly, Richie Valens in plane crash.
b. October 24, 1930 in Sabine Pass, Texas
d. February 03, 1959 in Clear Lake, Iowa

Big Brother and the Holding Company
(Peter Albin; Sam Andrew; David Getz; James Gurley; Janis Joplin)
American music group
• Blues band featuring vocals by Janis Joplin; album Cheap Thrills had hit single "Piece of My Heart," 1968.

Big Country
(Stuart Adamson; Mark Brzezick; Tony Butler; Bruce Watson)
Scottish music group
• Scottish band; debut album, The Crossing, had hit single "In a Big Country," 1983.

Albany Barney Leon Bigard
American jazz musician
• Jazz clarinetist; played with King Oliver, Louis Armstrong, Duke Ellington; co-wrote "Mood Indigo," 1931.
b. March 03, 1906 in New Orleans, Louisiana
d. June 27, 1980 in Culver City, California

Elvin Bishop
American musician
• Hit single "Fooled Around and Fell in Love," 1976, from eighth solo album Struttin' My Stuff.
b. October 21, 1942 in Tulsa, Oklahoma

Stephen Bishop
American singer–songwriter
• Hit songs include "Save It for a Rainy Day," 1976; theme from Tootsie, "It Might Be You," 1983.
b. November 14, 1951 in San Diego, California

Roy Bittan
(E Street Band; "Professor")
American musician
• Keyboardist, accordion player with Bruce Springsteen, 1974–.
b. July 02, 1949 in Rockaway Beach, New York

Georges (Alexandre Cesar Leopold) Bizet
French composer
• Wrote great opera comique Carmen, 1873; published, 1875.
b. October 25, 1838 in Paris, France
d. June 03, 1875 in Bougival, France

Jussi Bjoerling
(Stora Tuna Dalarna)
Swedish opera singer
• Tenor; made NY Met. debut, 1938; starred in over 50 operas, noted for French, Italian roles.
b. February 02, 1911 in Stora Tuna, Sweden
d. September 09, 1960 in Siar Oe, Sweden

David Black, Jay
(Jay and the Americans)
American singer
• Lead singer, group's second "Jay," 1962-70.
b. November 02, 1941

Frank J Black
American composer–musician
• Organized music dept., NBC, 1928; general music director, NBC, 1932-48.
b. November 28, 1896 in Philadelphia, Pennsylvania
d. January 29, 1968 in Atlanta, Georgia

Black Oak Arkansas
(Pat Daugherty; Wayne Evans; Jimmy Henderson; Stan Goober Knight; Jim "Dandy" Mangrum; Ricky Reynolds)
American music group
• Southern band named after group's hometown, 1969; number one hit "Jim Dandy to the Rescue," 1973.

Black Sabbath
(Terry Geezer Butler; Ronnie Dio; Jan Gillan; Anthony Iommi; (John) "Ozzie" Osbourne; William Ward)
English music group
• Heavy-metal band formed, 1969, under name Earth; changed name when material became mystical; hit album Paranoid, 1970.

Ritchie Blackmore
(Deep Purple; Ritchie Blackmore's Rainbow)
English musician
• Co-founded Deep Purple, 1968; had hit "Stone Cold."
b. April 14, 1945 in Weston-Super-Mare, England

Ruben Blades
Panamanian singer–songwriter
• Revolutionized salsa music, universalized appeal; first salsa singer to write own songs.
b. July 16, 1948 in Panama City, Panama

Eubie (James Hubert) Blake
American pianist–composer
• Ragtime pioneer, whose best known songs include "I'm Just Wild About Harry," 1921; "Memories of You," 1930.
b. February 07, 1883 in Baltimore, Maryland
d. February 12, 1983 in Brooklyn, New York

Ronee Blakeley
American actress–singer
• Screen debut in Nashville, 1975; received Oscar nomination.
b. 1946 in Stanley, Idaho

Art Blakey
American jazz musician
• Drummer, major innovator of modern jazz; best known for leading Jazz Messengers, 1954-90, and turning group into jazz training ground; created "hard bop" school that added blues, gospel rhythms to music.
b. October 11, 1919 in Pittsburgh, Pennsylvania
d. October 16, 1990 in New York, New York

Bobby Blue (Robert Calvin) Bland
American singer
• Blues albums include *Blues in the Night,* 1985.
b. January 27, 1930 in Rosemark, Tennessee

Jules Bledsoe
American actor–singer
• Sang "Ol' Man River" in *Show Boat,* 1927 stage, 1929 film.
b. December 29, 1898
d. July 14, 1943 in Hollywood, California

Archie Bleyer
American musician
• Head of Cadence records, 1952; had hit single "Mr. Sandman," 1954.
b. June 12, 1909 in Corona, New York

Blind Faith
(Ginger Baker; Eric Clapton; Rick Grech; Stevie Winwood)
English music group
• Only album *Blind Faith,* 1969, with hits "Can't Find My Way Home"; "Presence of the Lord."

Sir Arthur Bliss
English composer
• Master of the Queen's Music, 1953-75; wrote ballet *Lady of Shallott,* 1958.
b. August 02, 1891 in London, England
d. March 27, 1975 in London, England

Marc Blitzstein
American composer–author
• Wrote *The Cradle Will Rock,* libretto for American version of *Three Penny Opera,* 1952.
b. March 02, 1905 in Philadelphia, Pennsylvania
d. January 22, 1964 in Martinique

Ernest Bloch
American composer
• Noted for tone poem, "Israel Symphony"; "America," 1926; Bloch Society founded in London, 1937.
b. July 24, 1880 in Geneva, Switzerland
d. July 15, 1959 in Portland, Oregon

Blondie
(Clem Burke; Jimmy Destri; Nigel Harrison; Deborah Harry; Frank Infante; Chris Stein)
American music group
• Forerunner of original punk rock, formed 1976-82; had four number-one hits including "Rapture," 1981.

Sweat and Tears Blood
(Dave Bargeron; David Clayton-Thomas; Bobby Colomby; Steve Fieldeer; Jerry Fisher; Dick Halligan; Jeff Hyman; Steve Katz; Al Kooper)
American music group
• Group formed 1968; hit singles "Spinning Wheel"; "And When I Die."

Eric Bloom
(Blue Oyster Cult)
American singer–musician
• Guitarist, vocalist with hard rock group since 1969.
b. December 01, 1944 in Long Island, New York

Mickey (Milton) Bloom
American musician–composer
• Trumpeter with Hal Kemp, 1935-39.
b. August 26, 1906 in Brooklyn, New York

Mike (Michael) Bloomfield
American musician–singer
• Blues guitarist; formed supergroup Electric Flag, 1967-68; album *My Labors,* 1971.
b. July 28, 1944 in Chicago, Illinois
d. February 15, 1981 in San Francisco, California

John Blow
English composer
• Wrote over 100 anthems; his *Venus and Adonis,* 1685, considered first true English opera.
b. February 1649 in Newark-on-Trent, England
d. October 01, 1708 in London, England

Blue Oyster Cult
(Eric Bloom; Albert Bouchard; Joe Bouchard; Rick Downey; Allen Lanier; Donald "Buck Dharma" Roeser)
American music group
• Major heavy metal band; hit single "Don't Fear the Reaper," 1976.

Colin Blunstone
(The Zombies)
English musician
• Rock singer; founded the Zombies, 1962; solo album *Journey,* 1974.
b. June 24, 1945 in Hatfield, England

Carey Blyton
English author–composer
• Composer for documentary films, TV commercials and plays; author of children's nonsense poems and books.
b. March 14, 1932 in Beckenham, England

Luigi Boccherini
Italian composer–violinist
• Prolific composer of chamber music; created the string quintet.
b. February 19, 1743 in Lucca, Italy
d. May 28, 1805 in Madrid, Spain

Jerry (Jerrold Lewis) Bock
American composer
• Broadway scores include Pulitzer-winning *Fiorello,* 1959.
b. November 23, 1928 in New Haven, Connecticut

Angela Bofill
American singer–songwriter
• Album *Something About You* was in top five on jazz charts.
b. 1955 in New York, New York

Tim Bogert
(Vanilla Fudge)
American singer–musician
• Bassist, vocalist with group formed 1966.
b. August 27, 1944 in New York, New York

Karl Bohm
(Karl Boehm)
Austrian conductor
• Noted for interpretations of Mozart, Wagner, Strauss; usually associated with Vienna Philharmonic, Salzburg Festival.
b. August 28, 1894 in Graz, Austria
d. August 14, 1981 in Salzburg, Austria

Francois Adrien Boieldieu
French composer
• Wrote piano music, scores of comic operas including *Jean de Paris,* 1812.
b. December 16, 1775 in Rouen, France
d. October 08, 1834 in Jarcy, France

Marc Bolan
(Mark Feld; T Rex)
English musician
• Co-founder, lead vocalist, T. Rex; died in car crash; recorded 16 albums including *Slider,* 1972.
b. May 08, 1948 in London, England
d. September 16, 1977 in London, England

William Elden Bolcom
American composer–pianist
• Recorded, performed ragtime piano music; wrote concertos, keyboard pieces.
b. May 26, 1938 in Seattle, Washington

Buddy (Charles) Bolden
American jazz musician
• Cornettist who is credited with originating jazz, 1890s.
b. 1868 in New Orleans, Louisiana
d. November 04, 1931 in New Orleans, Louisiana

Jorge Bolet
Cuban pianist
• Romantic concert pianist; recorded piano soundtrack for *Song Without End*, 1960, film about life of Franz Liszt.
b. November 15, 1914 in Havana, Cuba
d. October 16, 1990 in Mountain View, California

Alessandro Bonci
Italian opera singer
• Tenor who is often ranked second to Caruso.
b. February 1, 1870 in Cesena, Italy
d. August 08, 1940 in Vitterba, Italy

Victoria Bond
American conductor
• First woman to co-conduct major US symphony; assisted Previn in leading Pittsburgh Orchestra, 1978-80.
b. May 06, 1950 in Los Angeles, California

Gary U S Bonds
(Gary Anderson)
American singer–songwriter
• Had hit single "Quarter to Three," 1961 teamed with Bruce Springsteen on *Dedication* album, 1981.
b. June 06, 1939 in Jacksonville, Florida

John Henry Bonham
(Led Zeppelin; "Bonzo")
English musician
• Led Zeppelin drummer; group disbanned after his death.
b. May 31, 1949 in Redditch, England
d. September 25, 1980 in Windsor, England

Bon Jovi
(Jon Bon Jovi; Dave Bryan; Alec Johnsuch; Richie Sambora; Tico Torres)
American music group
• Rock band formed, 1980s; had number one album *Slippery When Wet*, 1987.

Jon Bon Jovi
(Jon Bongiovi)
American singer–bandleader
• Founder, lead singer of rock group Bon Jovi, 1984–; had number-one hit album, *Slippery When Wet*, 1987.
b. March 02, 1962 in Sayreville, New Jersey

Karla Bonoff
(Mrs Robby Benson)
American singer–songwriter
• Writer of Linda Ronstadt's "Someone to Lay Down Beside Me," 1976; solo albums include *Wild Heart of the Young*, 1981.
b. December 27, 1952 in Los Angeles, California

Giovanni Battista Bononcini
Italian composer
• Operas include *Astarto*, 1715; *Griselda*, 1722.
b. July 18, 1670 in Modena, Italy
d. July 09, 1747 in Vienna, Austria

Joe Bonsall
(The Oak Ridge Boys)
American singer
• Tenor with country-pop group; hit single "So Fine," 1982.
b. May 18, 1948 in Philadelphia, Pennsylvania

Richard Bonynge
Australian conductor
• Musical director, Australian Opera, 1975–.
b. September 29, 1930 in Sydney, Australia

Booker T and the MG's
(Steve Cropper; Donald Dunn; Al Jackson Jr; Booker T Jones; Bobby Manuel; Carson Whitsett)
American music group
• First hit single "Green Onions," 1962; group disbanded, 1972.

Boomtown Rats
(Pete Briquette; Gerry Cott; Johnny Fingers; Bob Geldof; Simon Grove; Garry Roberts)
Irish music group
• Punk band, formed late 1970s; albums include *Boomtown Rats*, 1978.

Debby (Deborah Ann) Boone
(Mrs Gabriel Ferrer)
American singer
• Daughter of Pat Boone; best known for "You Light Up My Life," 1977.
b. September 22, 1956 in Hackensack, New Jersey

Pat (Charles Eugene) Boone
American singer
• Noted for clean cut image, white buck shoes; starred in *April Love*, 1957.
b. June 01, 1934 in Jacksonville, Florida

Victor Borge
(Borge Rosenbaum)
American pianist–comedian
• Combines music with humor to create musical satire.
b. January 03, 1909 in Copenhagen, Denmark

Boston
(Brad Delp; Barry Goudreau; Sib Hashian; Tom Scholz; Fran Sheehan)
American music group
• Debut album *Boston*, 1976, sold 6.5 million copies.

Connee Boswell
(Boswell Sisters)
American singer–actress
• Enjoyed long career after trio disbanded in 1935; performed in wheelchair.
b. December 03, 1912 in New Orleans, Louisiana
d. October 11, 1976 in New York, New York

Martha Boswell
(Boswell Sisters)
American singer
• Member of singing group trio with sisters.
b. 1905 in New Orleans, Louisiana
d. July 02, 1958 in Peekskill, New York

Vet (Helvetia) Boswell
(Boswell Sisters)
American singer
• In films with sisters *Big Broadcast*, 1932; *Moulin Rouge*, 1934.
b. 1911 in New Orleans, Louisiana
d. November 12, 1988 in Peekskill, New York

Boswell Sisters
(Connee Boswell; Martha Boswell; Vet Boswell)
American music group
• Three Southern girls who blended voices in a way never heard before; made three movies, 1930s.

Nadia Juliette Boulanger
French composer–conductor–teacher
• Influential teacher; first female instructor at the Paris Conservatory; first woman to conduct the Boston Symphony.
b. September 16, 1887 in Paris, France
d. October 22, 1979 in Paris, France

Pierre Boulez
French composer–conductor
• Influential figure in avant-garde French music; music director, New York Philharmonic, 1971-77.
b. March 26, 1925 in Montbrison, France

Bow Wow Wow
(Annabella; Matthew Ashman; Dave Barbarossa; Leroy Gorman)
British music group
• New Wave band, 1980-83; combined African rhythms, chants, surf instrumentals, pop melodies.

Billy Bowen
(Ink Spots)
American singer
• One of first black groups to break color barrier over airwaves.
b. 1909 in Birmingham, Alabama
d. September 27, 1982 in New York, New York

David Bowie
(David Robert Hayward-Jones)
English singer–songwriter–actor
• Pop-rock singer, 1970s-80s; starred in film *The Man Who Fell to Earth*, 1976; songs include "Let's Dance," 1983, "Loving the Alien," 1985.
b. January 08, 1947 in Brixton, England

Roger Bowling
American songwriter
• Wrote songs "Lucille" and "Coward of the County."
b. 1944
d. December 25, 1982 in Clayton, Georgia

The Box Tops
(Rick Allen; Thomas Boggs; Alex Chilton; Harold Cloud; William Cunningham; John Evans; Swain Scharfer; Daniel Smythe; Gary Talley)
American music group
• Memphis-based "blue-eyed soul" band, 1965-70; hit single "The Letter," 1967.

Boy George
(George Alan O'Dowd; Culture Club)
English singer
• Flamboyant lead singer, known for avant-garde dress, make-up; had number-one hit, "Karma Chameleon," 1983.
b. June 14, 1961 in Bexley Heath, England

Bill Boyd
(Cowboy Rambler)
American singer
• Popular Dallas dj for over 35 years; songs include "Under the Double Eagle"; "Ridin' on a Humpback Mule."
b. 1911 in Fannin County, Texas

Liona Maria Boyd
(First Lady of Classical Guitar)
Canadian musician
• Won Canadian instrumentalist awards, 1982, 1985.
b. 1949 in London, Ontario

Will Bradley
(Wilbur Schwichtenberg)
American jazz musician–bandleader
• Trombonist; led swing band that featured boogie woogie, 1940s.
b. July 12, 1912 in Newton, New Jersey
d. July 15, 1989 in Flemington, New Jersey

Ruby Braff
American jazz musician
• Trumpeter of Dixieland, mainstream jazz, 1940s-50s.
b. March 16, 1927 in Boston, Massachusetts

Johannes Brahms
German composer–pianist
• Combined romanticism, classicism in works; best known "Brahms' Lullaby" officially called "Opus 49, no. 4."
b. May 07, 1833 in Hamburg, Germany
d. April 03, 1897 in Vienna, Austria

Alexander Brailowsky
American pianist
• Performed complete cycle of Chopin's works, 1930s.
b. February 16, 1896 in Kiev, Russia
d. April 25, 1976 in New York, New York

Oscar Brand
Canadian singer–composer
• Prolific country performer; won many awards.
b. February 07, 1920 in Winnipeg, Manitoba

Laura Branigan
American singer
• Hit singles include "Gloria," 1982; "Solitaire," 1983; "Self Control," 1984.
b. July 03, 1957 in Brewster, New York

Richard Branson
English airline executive–music executive
• Founder, president, Virgin Records, Virgin Atlantic Airways.
b. July 1951 in Surrey, England

Georges Brassens
French singer–poet
• Wrote over 140 songs describing lives of everyday people; best known was anti-war song "The Two Uncles."
b. October 22, 1921 in Sete, France
d. October 3, 1981 in Sete, France

Bread
(Mike Botts; David Gates; James Gordon; James Grifin; Larry Knechtel; Robb Royer)
American music group
• Soft-rock hit songs include "Lost Without Your Love," 1976; "Make It with You," 1970.

Julian Bream
English musician
• Guitarist, lutenist; known for Elizabethan lute music.
b. July 15, 1933 in London, England

Jacques Brel
Belgian songwriter
• Known for popular revue containing 25 songs: *Jacques Brel Is Alive and Well and Living in Paris.*
b. April 08, 1929 in Brussels, Belgium
d. October 09, 1978 in Bobigny, France

Alfred Brendel
Austrian pianist
• Gives recitals, appears with major orchestras world wide; interpreter of Vienna classics.
b. January 05, 1931 in Wisenberg, Austria

Teresa (Theresa) Brewer
American singer–actress
• 1950s pop hits had upbeat tone: "Music! Music! Music!," 1950; started singing at age two, still performing in clubs.
b. May 07, 1931 in Toledo, Ohio

Brewer and Shipley
(Michael Brewer; Thomas Shipley)
American music group
• Folk-rock duo formed, 1968; hit "One Toke Over the Line," 1971.

Fanny Brice
(Fanny Borach; "Baby Snooks")
American actress–singer
• Ziegfeld Follies star, noted for torch song "My Man"; created radio character, "Baby Snooks"); life portrayed in *Funny Girl*, 1968.
b. October 29, 1891 in New York, New York
d. May 29, 1951 in Beverly Hills, California

Bricktop
(Ada Beatrice Queen Victoria Louise Virginia Smith)
American singer–restaurateur
• Had famous pre-WW II nightclub in Paris; Cole Porter wrote "Miss Otis Regrets" for her.
b. August 14, 1894 in Iderson, West Virginia
d. January 31, 1984 in New York, New York

Antonia Brico
American conductor
• First woman to conduct LA Philharmonic Orchestra, several other major symphony orchestras; subject of film documentary *Portrait of Antonia*, 1975.
b. June 26, 1902 in Rotterdam, Netherlands
d. August 03, 1989 in Denver, Colorado

Leslie Bricusse
English lyricist–composer
• Won Grammy for "What Kind of Fool Am I?," 1962; Oscar for "Talk to the Animals," 1967.
b. January 29, 1931 in London, England

Frank Bridge
English composer
• Composed chamber music; one of his pupils was Benjamin Britten.
b. February 26, 1879 in Brighton, England
d. January 11, 1941 in London, England

Dee Dee Bridgewater
American singer–actress
• Won Tony for *The Wiz*, 1975.
b. May 27, 1950 in Memphis, Tennessee

Eddie Brigati
(The Rascals)
American singer
• Vocalist with blue-eyed soul group, 1965-71; composed most of groups songs with Frank Cavaliere.
b. October 22, 1946 in New York, New York

(Edward) Benjamin Britten
English composer
• Best known for modern operas, including *Gloriana*, 1953, written for coronation of Elizabeth II.
b. November 22, 1913 in Lowestoft, England
d. December 04, 1976 in Aldeburgh, England

Alice May Brock
American author–restaurateur
• Owner, Alice's Restaurant; Arlo Guthrie's song of same name was written about her.
b. February 28, 1941 in Brooklyn, New York

Big Bill Broonzy
American singer–musician
• One of the greatest country blues singers of all time.
b. June 26, 1893 in Scott, Mississippi
d. August 14, 1958 in Chicago, Illinois

The Brothers Johnson
(George Johnson; Louis Johnson)
American music group
• Hit singles include "Strawberry Letter 23," 1977; "I'll Be Good to You," 1976.

James Brown
(Godfather of Soul)
American singer
• Has 38 gold records in 20 years; won Grammy, 1965; songs include "Living in America," 1986. Recently released from prison.
b. May 03, 1934 in Augusta, Georgia

Jim Ed (James Edward) Brown
American singer
• Country music singer popular in 1950s, 60s.
b. April 01, 1934 in Sparkman, Arkansas

Les(ter Raymond) Brown
American bandleader
• Often played with Bob Hope; wrote "Sentimental Journey."
b. March 12, 1912 in Reinerton, Pennsylvania

Lew Brown
American songwriter
• Songs include "Button Up Your Overcoat"; "Beer Barrel Polka."
b. December 1, 1893 in Odessa, Russia
d. February 05, 1958 in New York, New York

Nacio Herb Brown
American songwriter
• Composed scores, songs, for MGM: "You Were Meant for Me"; "Singin' in the Rain."
b. February 22, 1896 in Deming, New Mexico
d. September 28, 1964 in San Francisco, California

Oscar Brown, Jr
American actor–composer
• Wrote "Brown Baby", 1960, sung by Mahalia Jackson.
b. October 1, 1926 in Chicago, Illinois

Peter Brown
English singer–songwriter
• Best known for songwriting with Jack Bruce; songs for group Cream include "Sunshine of Your Love," 1968.
b. 1940 in London, England

Jackson Browne
American singer–songwriter
• Hit single "Doctor My Eyes," 1971; gold album *The Pretender*, 1976. Known for anti-war, pro-Central America stance.
b. October 09, 1950 in Heidelberg, Germany (West)

John Browning
American pianist
• Child prodigy, international concertizer; had Carnegie Hall debut, 1956.
b. May 23, 1933 in Denver, Colorado

Dave (David Warren) Brubeck
American jazz musician
• Avant-garde pianist, noted for modernistic chords; led popular jazz quartet, 1951-67.
b. December 06, 1920 in Concord, California

Jack Bruce
(John Bruce; Cream)
Scottish musician
• Vocalist/bassist with Cream, 1966-69; solo albums include *I've Always Wanted To Do This*, 1980.
b. May 14, 1943 in Glasgow, Scotland

Max Bruch
German conductor–composer
• Wrote concertos, operas, including *Hermione*, 1872.
b. January 06, 1838 in Cologne, Germany
d. October 02, 1920 in Friedenau, Germany

Anton Bruckner
Austrian composer–organist
• Virtuoso organist influenced by Wagner; music includes nine symphonies, three masses.
b. September 04, 1824 in Ausfelden, Austria
d. October 11, 1896 in Vienna, Austria

George Brunis
American jazz musician
• Member, New Orleans Rhythm Kings, founded in Chicago, 1921, an early northern Dixieland.
b. February 06, 1902 in New Orleans, Louisiana
d. November 19, 1974 in Chicago, Illinois

Anita Jane Bryant
American singer
• Lost contract promoting orange juice due to views on homosexuals.
b. March 25, 1940 in Barnsdall, Oklahoma

Boudleaux Bryant
American songwriter
• With wife Felice, wrote over 1,500 songs including early rock hit "Bye Bye Love," 27 for Everly Brothers: "Wake Up Little Susie," "All I Have to Do Is Dream."
b. February 13, 1920 in Shellman, Georgia
d. June 26, 1987 in Knoxville, Tennessee

Felice Bryant
American songwriter
• Songs include "Wake Up Little Susie"; "Bye, Bye Love"; "Raining in My Heart."
b. August 07, 1925 in Milwaukee, Wisconsin

Hugh Bryant
(Delta Rhythm Boys)
American singer
• Member, Delta Rhythm Boys, 1962; died singing at Lee Gaines' funeral.
b. 1929
d. July 23, 1987 in Helsinki, Finland

Jack Brymer
English musician
• Clarinetist with Royal Philharmonic Orchestra; autobiography, *From Where I Sit*, 1979.
b. January 27, 1915 in South Shields, England

Peabo (Robert Peabo) Bryson
American singer
• Rhythm, blues balladeer; had hit single with Roberta Flack: "Lookin' Like Love," 1984.
b. April 13, 1951 in Greenville, South Carolina

Gene Buck
American songwriter
• Co-founder ASCAP, 1914, pres., 1924-41; composed Ziegfeld Follies hits.
b. August 08, 1886 in Detroit, Michigan
d. February 24, 1957 in Manhasset, New York

Lindsey Buckingham
(Fleetwood Mac)
American musician
• Joined Fleetwood Mac, 1975; solo LP *Law and Order*, 1981. No longer performing with band.
b. October 03, 1947 in Palo Alto, California

The Buckinghams
(Nick Fortune; Carl Giamarese; Marty Grebb; Jon Paulos; Denny Tufano)
American music group
• Chicago area band popular 1966-68; had number one hit "Kind of a Drag," 1966.

Tim Buckley
American singer–songwriter
• Pop singer-guitarist, 1960s; albums include *Goodbye and Hello*, 1967.
b. February 17, 1947 in Washington, District of Columbia
d. June 29, 1975 in Santa Monica, California

Buffalo Springfield
(Richie Furay; Dewey Martin; Jim Messina; Bruce Palmer; Stephen Stills; Neil Young)
American music group
• W coast folk rockers, 1966-68; who had hit single, "For What It's Worth," 1966.

Jimmy Buffet
(Jimmy Buffett)
American singer–songwriter
• Had hit single "Margaritaville," 1977.
b. December 25, 1946 in Pascagoula, Mississippi

John Bull
English organist–composer
• Supposedly wrote early form of melody "God Save the King," 1619.
b. 1563 in Somerset, England
d. March 12, 1622 in Antwerp, Belgium

Ole Bornemann Bull
Norwegian musician–composer
• Internationally known violinist who attempted to found Norwegian settlement in PA, 1852.
b. February 05, 1810 in Bergen, Norway
d. August 17, 1880 in Lysoe, Norway

Hans Guido von Bulow
German conductor–pianist
• Directed Wagner premieres, Munich Opera, 1860s; wed Liszt's daughter, Cosima, who later married Wagner.
b. January 08, 1830 in Dresden, Germany
d. February 12, 1894 in Cairo, Egypt

Grace Ann Jaeckel Bumbry
American opera singer
• Noted mezzo-soprano; first black to star in role of goddess, 1961; NY Met. debut, 1965; 1979 Grammy winner.
b. January 04, 1937 in Saint Louis, Missouri

Eric Burdon
(The Animals)
English singer
• Vocalist for the Animals, War; solo albums include hit singles, "Sky Pilot"; "San Franciscan Nights."
b. April 05, 1941 in Walker-on-Tyne, England

Johnny Burke
American songwriter
• Lyricist for many Bing Crosby films, 1930s-50s; songs include "Pennies from Heaven."
b. October 03, 1908 in Antioch, California
d. February 25, 1964 in New York, New York

Harry Thacker Burleigh
American singer–songwriter
• Collected, arranged black spirituals including "Swing Low, Sweet Chariot"; "Go Down Moses."
b. December 02, 1866 in Erie, Pennsylvania
d. September 12, 1949 in Stamford, Connecticut

Johnny Burnette
American singer–composer
• Guitarist; hits include "You're Sixteen," 1961.
b. March 25, 1934 in Memphis, Tennessee
d. August 14, 1964 in Clear Lake, California

Bob Burns
American musician–actor
• Nicknamed "Bazooka" after wind instrument he invented and played.
b. August 02, 1893 in Van Buren, Alaska
d. February 02, 1956 in San Fernando, California

Henry Burr
(Harry H McClaskey; "Dean of Ballad Singers")
American singer
• Known through radio, concerts, recordings; song "Goodnight Little Girl, Goodnight" sold over 3,000,000 copies.
b. January 15, 1885
d. April 06, 1941 in Chicago, Illinois

James Burton
American musician
• Guitarist; played with Rick Nelson, Everly Brothers.
b. August 21, 1939 in Shreveport, Louisiana

Kate Bush
English singer–songwriter
• Hit singles include "Wuthering Heights," 1978; "Running Up That Hill," 1985.
b. July 3, 1958 in Kent, England

Joe (Joseph) Bushkin
American jazz musician–bandleader
• Pianist, trumpeter; led own quartet, 1950s-60s; accompanied Bing Crosby, late 1970s.
b. November 06, 1916 in New York, New York

Ferruccio Benvenuto Busoni
Italian pianist–composer
• Acclaimed concert pianist; his opera *Dokter Faust*, produced 1925, seldom performed today.
b. April 01, 1866 in Empoli, Italy
d. July 27, 1924 in Berlin, Germany

Henry Busse
American jazz musician–bandleader
• Trumpeter for Paul Whiteman, 1918-28; noted for exaggerated vibrato; led own bands, 1930s-40s.
b. May 19, 1894 in Magdeburg, Germany
d. April 23, 1955 in Memphis, Tennessee

Tony Butala
(The Letterman)
American singer
• Member of trio who rejuvenated group, expanded touring, 1970s-80s.
b. November 2, 1940 in Sharon, Pennsylvania

Billy Butterfield
American jazz musician
• Bib Band trumpeter, recorder; with World's Greatest Jazzband, 1968-73; introduced song "What's New?," 1930s.
b. January 14, 1917 in Middletown, Ohio
d. March 18, 1988 in North Palm Beach, Florida

Paul Butterfield
American singer
• Albums include *An Offer You Can't Refuse*, 1982.
b. December 17, 1942 in Chicago, Illinois

Dietrich Buxtehude
Danish organist–composer
• Organ virtuoso; Bach walked 200 miles to hear his famed music series.
b. 1637 in Elsinore, Denmark
d. May 09, 1707 in Lubeck, Germany

Charlie (Charles Lee) Byrd
American jazz musician
• Guitarist who promoted bossa nova craze, 1960s; headed own trio.
b. September 16, 1925 in Chuckatuck, Virginia

Donald Byrd
American jazz musician
• Trumpet, fluegelhorn player; albums include *Ethiopian Knights*, 1972; *Black Byrd*, 1975.
b. December 09, 1932 in Detroit, Michigan

Henry Byrd
American composer–musician
• New Orleans rock-n-roll pianist, songwriter, who wrote "Go to the Mardi Gras," "Big Chief."
b. December 19, 1918 in Bogalusa, Louisiana
d. January 3, 1980 in New Orleans, Louisiana

William Byrd
English organist–composer–songwriter
• Wrote anthems, Roman Masses, first English madrigals, during reign of Elizabeth I.
b. 1542 in London, England
d. July 04, 1623 in London, England

The Byrds
(Skip Battin; Michael Clark; Gene Clarke; David Crosby; Chris Hillman; Kevin Kelly; Roger McGuinn; Gram Parsons)
American music group
• Pioneer folk-rock band, 1964-73; hits include "Mr. Tambourine Man," "Turn! Turn! Turn!," 1965.

David Byrne
(The Talking Heads)
Scottish musician
• Leader of Talking Heads often compared to Bob Dylan; composed music for Broadway's *The Catherine Wheel*, 1981.
b. May 14, 1952 in Scotland

Montserrat Folch Caballe
Spanish opera singer
• Soprano; sang, recorded over 120 roles; noted for Mozart, bel canto parts.
b. April 12, 1933 in Barcelona, Spain

Giulio Caccini
Italian composer–musician
• His *Euridice*, 1601, was first published opera.
b. 1546 in Rome, Italy
d. December 1, 1618 in Florence, Italy

Charles Wakefield Cadman
American composer
• Used American Indian melodies; wrote opera *The Sunset Trail*, 1925; song, "From the Land of Sky-Blue Water," 1908.
b. December 04, 1881 in Johnstown, Pennsylvania
d. December 3, 1946 in Los Angeles, California

Irving Caesar
American songwriter
• Popular during 1920s-30s; wrote "Tea for Two," 1925.
b. July 04, 1895 in New York, New York

John Milton Cage, Jr
American composer–author
• Composed scores for choreography by Merce Cunningham; writes essays, books on music, dance; noted for "prepared piano" procedure.
b. September 05, 1912 in Los Angeles, California

Sammy Cahn
American lyricist
• Won Oscars for title songs "Three Coins in the Fountain," 1954; "All the Way," 1957.
b. June 18, 1913 in New York, New York

Sarah Caldwell
American conductor–director
• Founded Opera Co. of Boston, 1957; first woman to conduct at NY Met., 1976.
b. March 06, 1924 in Maryville, Missouri

J J Cale
American singer–songwriter
• Guitarist, composer, who wrote Eric Clapton's hit single, "After Midnight," 1970.
b. December 05, 1938 in Oklahoma City, Oklahoma

John Cale
English singer–musician
• Formerly with Velvet Underground; solo hits include "Black Rose," 1985.
b. 1942 in Garnant, England

Maria Callas
(Maria Kalogeropoulou; Maria Meneghini)
American opera singer
• Soprano, 1938-60; romantically involved with Aristotle Onassis, 1960s.
b. December 03, 1923 in New York, New York
d. September 16, 1977 in Paris, France

Cab(ell) Calloway
American bandleader–singer
• Acclaimed "scat" singer; noted for song "Minnie the Moocher"; role in *Porgy and Bess*, 1953.
b. December 25, 1907 in Rochester, New York

Robert Cambert
French composer
• Wrote first French operas, including *Pomone*, 1671; co-founded first French opera company, 1669.
b. 1628 in Paris, France
d. 1677 in London, England

Glen Travis Campbell
American singer–musician
• Country-pop singer with 12 gold, seven platinum albums; number one singles "Rhinestone Cowboy," 1975; "Southern Nights," 1977.
b. April 22, 1938 in Delight, Arkansas

Thomas Campion
English poet–composer
• Wrote graceful songs for the lute and lyric poems set to music for court presentations.
b. February 12, 1567 in London, England
d. March 01, 1620 in London, England

Canned Heat
(Ronnie Baron; Bob Hite; Richard Hite; Chris Morgan; Adolfo Fito "de la Palma; Mark Skyer)
American music group
• Blues-styled group, 1966-70; songs include "Let's Work Together," 1970.

Judy Canova
American singer–actress–comedienne
• Popular hillbilly-type entertainer; radio program "Judy Canova Show," 1930s-40s; mother of Diana.
b. November 2, 1916 in Jacksonville, Florida
d. August 05, 1983 in Hollywood, California

Eddie Cantor
(Edward Israel Itskowitz; "Izzie")
American comedian–singer
• Starred on Broadway in *The Ziegfeld Follies*; won special Oscar, 1956.
b. January 31, 1892 in New York, New York
d. October 1, 1964 in Beverly Hills, California

Lana Cantrell
Australian singer–actress
• Popular recording star; won Grammy Award, 1967.
b. August 07, 1943 in Sydney, Australia

Jim Capaldi
(Traffic)
English singer–musician
• Drummer for Traffic, 1967-71; had solo hit single "Living on the Edge," 1983.
b. August 24, 1944 in Evesham, England

The Captain and Tennille
(Daryl Dragon; Toni Tennille)
American music group
• Pop-rock husband and wife team; won 1975 Grammy for "Love Will Keep Us Together."

Captain Beefheart
(Captain Beefheart and the Magic Band; Don Van Vliet)
American singer–musician
• Music combines blues, jazz, classic, rock; is more influential than popular; album *Ice Cream for Crow*, 1982.
b. January 15, 1941 in Glendale, California

Irene (Escalera) Cara
American actress–singer
• Starred in movie *Fame*, 1980; sang Oscar-winning song, theme from *Flashdance*, 1983; won Obie for *The Me Nobody Knows*, 1970.
b. March 18, 1959 in Bronx, New York

Henry Carey
English composer–poet
• Alleged author of "God Save the King"; most remembered song, "Sally in Our Alley."
b. 1687 in Yorkshire, England
d. October 05, 1743 in London, England

Belinda Carlisle
(The Go-Go's)
American singer
• Lead singer for Go-Go's, 1978-85; solo hits include "Mad About You," 1986; "Heaven on Earth," 1987; "Circle in the Sand," 1988.
b. August 17, 1958 in Hollywood, California

Larry (Lawrence Eugene) Carlton
(The Crusaders)
American musician
• Guitarist with Crusaders 1973-76; solo albums include *Sleepwalk*, 1982; *Friends*, 1983.
b. 1948 in Torrance, California

Eric Carmen
(The Raspberries)
American singer–musician
• Had hit singles "All By Myself," 1975, "Make Me Lose Control," 1988.
b. August 11, 1949 in Cleveland, Ohio

Hoagy (Hoagland Howard) Carmichael
American songwriter
• Music characterized by slow, dreamy melodies; wrote "Stardust," 1927, "Georgia On My Mind," 1930.
b. November 22, 1899 in Bloomington, Indiana
d. December 27, 1981 in Rancho Mirage, California

Al(vin Allison Jr) Carmines
American composer
• Prolific songwriter in non-Broadway musical theater; wrote music, lyrics, book for "A Look at the Fifties," 1972.
b. July 25, 1937 in Hampton, Virginia

Kim Carnes
American singer–songwriter
• Known for deep, raw voice; won Grammy for "Bette Davis Eyes," 1981.
b. July 2, 1946 in Hollywood, California

Harry Howell Carney
American jazz musician
• Baritone saxophonist with Duke Ellington since 1927.
b. April 01, 1910 in Boston, Massachusetts
d. October 08, 1974 in New York, New York

John Alden Carpenter
American composer
• Used jazz motifs in ballets, orchestral suites: *Adventures in a Perambulator*, 1915.
b. February 28, 1876 in Park Ridge, Illinois
d. April 26, 1951 in Chicago, Illinois

Karen Ann Carpenter
(The Carpenters)
American singer
• With brother, Richard, sold over 80 million records; first hit "Close to You," 1970. Died of complications from anorexia.
b. March 02, 1950 in New Haven, Connecticut
d. February 04, 1983 in Downey, California

Richard Lynn Carpenter
(The Carpenters)
American singer–musician–songwriter
• With sister, Karen, had several hits including "We've Only Just Begun," 1970.
b. October 15, 1946 in New Haven, Connecticut

The Carpenters
(Karen Carpenter; Richard Carpenter)
American music group
• Pop brother-sister team with many hits, 1970s: "For All We Know," 1971; "Top of the World," 1973.

Vikki Carr
(Florencia Bisenta de Casillas)
American singer
• Multilingual pop songstess; records include *It Must Be Him*.
b. July 19, 1941 in El Paso, Texas

Paul Carrack
(Ace; Squezze)
English singer–musician
• Original member of Ace, who joined Squezze, 1981-82.
b. April 1951 in Sheffield, England

Jose Carreras
Spanish opera singer
• Lyric tenor; NY Met. debut, 1974; TV, film roles.
b. December 05, 1946 in Barcelona, Spain

Diahann Carroll
(Carol Diahann Johnson; Mrs Vic Damone)
American actress–singer
• Won Tony, 1962, for performance in Broadway musical *No Strings*, which Richard Rodgers wrote for her; starred in TV comedy, "Julia," 1968-71, becoming first black performer to star on TV in non-stereotypical role.
b. July 17, 1935 in New York, New York

Earl Carroll
American producer
• Lyricist of over 400 songs; produced "Earl Carroll Vanities," 1923-36.
b. September 16, 1893 in Pittsburgh, Pennsylvania
d. June 17, 1948

Jim Carroll
American poet–singer
• Rock composer who depicts NYC brutality; wrote Pulitzer nominee book of verse *Living at the Movies*, 1973.
b. August 01, 1951 in New York, New York

The Cars
(Elliot Easton; Greg Hawkes; Ric Ocasek; Ben Orr; David Robinson)
American music group
• Pop music quintet, formed, 1976; platinum albums *The Cars*, 1978; *Panarama*, 1980.

Mindy Carson
American actress–singer
• Popular radio vocalist, late 1940s; hosted own TV show, 1950s; sang "Wake the Town and Tell the People," 1954.
b. July 16, 1926 in New York, New York

Richard d'Oyly Carte
English opera singer
• Responsible for bringing composer Arthur Sullivan, librettist William Gilbert together, 1871.
b. May 03, 1844 in London, England
d. April 03, 1901 in London, England

Benny (Bennett Lester) Carter
American jazz musician
• Helped shape jazz music; known for alto sax playing; wrote "Melancholy Lullaby," 1939.
b. August 08, 1907 in New York, New York

Betty Carter
(Lillie Mae Jones)
American singer
• Jazz vocalist little known until appearence in show *Don't Call Me Man,* 1975.
b. May 16, 1930 in Flint, Michigan

Carlene Carter
(Mrs Nick Lowe)
American singer–songwriter
• Daughter of June Carter; stepdaughter of Johnny Cash.
b. 1957 in Madisonville, Tennessee

Elliott Cook Carter, Jr
American composer
• Won Pulitzer in music, 1960, 1973; works include "Concerto for Orchestra," 1969.
b. December 11, 1908 in New York, New York

June Carter
(The Carter Family; Mrs Johnny Cash)
American singer
• Country singer; songs include "He Don't Love Me Anymore"; married Johnny Cash, 1968.
b. June 23, 1929 in Maces Spring, Virginia

Mother Maybelle Carter
(The Carter Family)
American singer–songwriter
• Grand Ole Opry star 1950-67; formed Carter Family, 1927; mother of June.
b. May 1, 1909 in Nickelsville, Virginia
d. October 23, 1978 in Nashville, Tennessee

Wilf Carter
Canadian singer–songwriter
• Pioneer western singer; known for plaintive ballads, yodels; wrote over 500 songs.
b. December 12, 1904 in Port Hilford, Nova Scotia

The Carter Family
(A P Carter; Anita Carter; Helen Carter; June Carter; Maybelle Carter)
American music group
• Recorded over 250 hits, 1927-43; first group honored in Country Music Hall of Fame, 1970.

Enrico Caruso
Italian opera singer
• Legendary tenor, chief attraction of NY Met., 1903-20.
b. February 25, 1873 in Naples, Italy
d. August 02, 1921 in Naples, Italy

Gaby Lhote Casadesus
French musician
• Wife of Robert, performed with him in his two piano concertos.
b. August 09, 1901 in Marseilles, France

Jean Casadesus
French musician
• Pianist son of Robert, performed with him and his mother in three piano concertos.
b. July 07, 1927 in Paris, France
d. January 2, 1972 in Renfrew, Ontario

Robert Casadesus
French musician–composer
• Noted interpreter of Mozart; wrote neo-classic style symphonies.
b. April 07, 1899 in Paris, France
d. September 19, 1972 in Paris, France

Jack Casady
(Jefferson Airplane)
American musician–singer
• One of original members of group, 1965-70; with Hot Tuna, 1970-77.
b. April 13, 1944 in Washington, District of Columbia

Pablo (Pau Carlos Salvador) Casals
Spanish musician
• Modernized playing techniques of cello, elevating status to serious solo orchestral instrument.
b. December 29, 1876 in Vendrell, Spain
d. October 22, 1973 in Rio Piedras, Puerto Rico

H(arry) W(ayne) Casey
(K C and the Sunshine Band)
American singer–musician
• Lead singer, keyboardist who co-founded band, 1973; hit single "Shake Your Booty," 1975.
b. January 31, 1951 in Hialeah, Florida

Johnny Cash
(Tennessee Three; "The Man in Black")
American singer–songwriter
• Country-western hit songs include "I Walk the Line," 1964, "A Boy Named Sue," 1969.
b. February 26, 1932 in Kingsland, Arkansas

Roseanne Cash
(Mrs Rodney Crowell)
American singer–celebrity relative
• Country-rock singer, who is daughter of Johnny Cash; albums include *Seven-Year Ache,* 1981; *Interiors,* 1990.
b. May 24, 1955 in Memphis, Tennessee

David Bruce Cassidy
American singer–actor
• Played Keith Partridge on TV series "The Partridge Family," 1970-74; son of Jack Cassidy.
b. April 12, 1950 in New York, New York

Jack Cassidy
American actor–singer–dancer
• Won Tony for *She Loves Me,* 1964; Shirley Jones was second wife.
b. March 05, 1927 in New York, New York
d. December 12, 1976 in West Hollywood, California

Shaun Paul Cassidy
American singer–actor
• Starred in TV series "Hardy Boys Mysteries," 1977-79.
b. September 27, 1958 in Los Angeles, California

Mario Castelnuovo-Tedesco
American composer
• Wrote piano music, film scores, overtures to 12 Shakespearean plays; composed opera *La Mandragola,* 1923.
b. April 03, 1895 in Florence, Italy
d. March 15, 1968 in Hollywood, California

Alfredo Catalani
Italian composer
• Operas included *La Wally,* 1852; work admired by Toscanini.
b. June 19, 1854 in Lucca, Italy
d. August 07, 1893 in Milan, Italy

Big Sid (Sidney) Catlett
American jazz musician
• A leading Big Band drummer, 1930s-40s.
b. January 17, 1910 in Evansville, Idaho
d. March 25, 1951 in Chicago, Illinois

Felix Cavaliere
(The Rascals)
American singer–musician
• Keyboardist, vocalist with blue-eyed soul group; has recorded several solo albums.
b. November 29, 1944 in Pelham, New York

Lina (Natalina) Cavalieri
Italian opera singer
• Dramatic soprano noted for her beauty; Gina Lollobrigida starred in film of her life, 1957.
b. December 25, 1874 in Viterbo, Italy
d. February 08, 1944 in Florence, Italy

Carmen Cavallaro
American bandleader–composer
• Big Band pianist, noted for chording technique; played soundtrack *Eddy Duchin Story*, 1956.
b. May 06, 1913 in New York, New York

Francesco Cavalli
Italian composer
• Developed modern opera; wrote over 40 operas, some revived in 1970s.
b. February 14, 1602 in Crema, Italy
d. January 14, 1676 in Venice, Italy

Corey Cerovsek
Canadian violinist
• Prodigy compared to Yehudi Menuhin, Mozart in talent; has performed with over 12 Canadian, American orchestras.
b. 1972 in Vancouver, British Columbia

Peter Cetera
(Chicago)
American singer–musician
• Lead singer with Chicago; had solo hit "Glory of Love," 1986.
b. September 13, 1944 in Chicago, Illinois

Emmanuel (Alexis Emmanuel) Chabrier
French composer
• Wrote operas, vocal works; best known for piano pieces, "Espana," 1883, and "Habanera," 1885.
b. January 18, 1841 in Ambert, France
d. September 13, 1894 in Paris, France

Chad and Jeremy
(Jeremy Clyde; Chad Stuart)
English music group
• Soft-rock group, 1964-66; hits include "Yesterday's Gone," "A Summer Song," "Distant Shores."

George Whitefield Chadwick
American composer
• Wrote symphonies, choral pieces; orchestral works include *Rip Van Winkle*, 1879.
b. November 13, 1854 in Lowell, Massachusetts
d. April 07, 1931 in Boston, Massachusetts

Feodor Ivanovitch Chaliapin
(Feodor Ivanovich Shaliapin; Fyodor Shalyapin)
Russian opera singer
• Bass, unrivalled as singing actor; known for role in *Boris Gudunov*, 1890-1930s.
b. February 13, 1873 in Kazan, Russia
d. April 12, 1938 in Paris, France

Cecile Chaminade
(Louise Stephanie Chaminade)
French composer–pianist
• Wrote over 500 enormously popular piano pieces.
b. August 08, 1861 in Paris, France
d. April 18, 1944 in Monte Carlo, Monaco

Harry Foster Chapin
American singer–songwriter
• Popular 1960s ballader, known for story songs like "Taxi," 1972 and humanistic efforts.
b. December 07, 1942 in New York, New York
d. July 16, 1981 in Jericho, New York

Saul Chaplin
American songwriter–producer
• Often collaborated with Sammy Cahn; scored films *Kiss Me Kate*, 1953; *West Side Story*, 1961; wrote "Anniversary Song."
b. February 19, 1912 in New York, New York

Tracy Chapman
American singer–songwriter
• Folksinger; won several Grammys, 1989, for hit single "Fast Car."
b. 1964 in Cleveland, Ohio

Ray Charles
(Charles Raymond Offenberg)
American composer
• Won Emmys for "The First Nine Months Are the Hardest," 1971; "The Funny Side of Marriage," 1972.
b. September 13, 1918 in Chicago, Illinois

Ray Charles
(Ray Charles Robinson; "The Genius of Soul")
American singer–songwriter–musician
• Blind 10-time Grammy winner; signature song is his 1960 version of "Georgia on My Mind."
b. September 23, 1930 in Albany, Georgia

The Charlie Daniels Band
(Tom Bigfoot Crain; Charlie Daniels; Joe Taz DiGregorio; FredEdwards; Charlie Hatward; Don Murray)
American music group
• Country-rock band, formed 1973; biggest hit, "The Devil Went Down to Georgia," 1979, popularized in film *Urban Cowboy*.

Charo
(Maria Rosario Pilar Martinez)
Spanish actress–singer
• Recorded several albums; appeared on TV shows including "Love Boat."
b. January 15, 1951 in Murcia, Spain

Marc-Antoine Charpentier
French composer
• Seventeen operas include *Medee*, 1693.
b. 1634 in Paris, France
d. February 24, 1704 in Paris, France

Abram Chasins
American pianist–composer
• His over 100 compositions include piano work "Three Chinese Pieces"; directed classical music broadcasts, 1941-65.
b. August 17, 1903 in New York, New York
d. June 21, 1987 in New York, New York

Cheap Trick
(Bun E Carlos; Rick Nielsen; Tom Petesson; Robin Zander)
American music group
• IL-based foursome started 1972, known for weird antics.

Chubby Checker
(Ernest Evans)
American singer
• Had hit "The Twist," 1960; created dance sensation of early 1960s.
b. October 03, 1941 in South Philadelphia, Pennsylvania

Luigi Carlo Zenobio Salvadore Maria Cherubini
Italian composer
• A founder of Romantic opera; master of counterpoint; wrote opera *Medee*, 1797.
b. September 14, 1760 in Florence, Italy
d. March 15, 1842 in Paris, France

Maurice Auguste Chevalier
French actor–singer
• Most popular French entertainer of century; starred in film *Gigi*, 1958; won special Oscar, 1958.
b. September 12, 1888 in Paris, France
d. January 01, 1972 in Paris, France

Chic
(Claire Beth; Bernard Edwards; Norma
Jean; Kenny Lehman; Nile Rodgers;
Andy Schwartz; Tony Thompson)
American music group
• Disco group, formed 1977; hits include
"Dance Dance Dance," 1977; "Good
Times," 1979.

Chicago
(Peter Cetera; Donnie Dacus; Laudir
DeOliveira; Terry Kath; Robert Lamm;
Lee Loughnane; James Pankow Walter
Parazaider; Walt Perry; Daniel)
American music group
• Jazz-oriented rock band, formed 1967;
first called Chicago Transit Authority; hits
include "Saturday in the Park," 1972.

Alex Chilton
(The Box Tops)
American singer
• Lead singer with Memphis-based blue-
eyed soul group, late 1960s. Immortalized by Replacements.
b. December 28, 1950 in Memphis, Tennessee

Frederic Francois Chopin
(Fryderyk Franciszek Chopin)
Polish pianist–composer
• Legendary virtuoso; piano compositions
include concertos, etudes; good friend of
George Sand.
b. February 22, 1810 in Zelazowa Wola, Poland
d. October 17, 1849 in Paris, France

Daniel Walter Chorzempa
American musician–composer
• Has given int'l. piano, organ recitals,
1968–; won Leipzig Bach prize, 1968.
b. December 07, 1944 in Minneapolis, Minnesota

Charlie (Charles) Christian
American jazz musician
• Guitarist who pioneered use of electri-
cal amplification; with Benny Goodman
sextet, 1940s.
b. 1919 in Dallas, Texas
d. March 02, 1942 in New York, New York

Sarah Churchill
(Lady Audley; "Mule")
English singer–actress–celebrity relative
• Second daughter of Winston Churchill;
wrote A Thread in the Tapestry, memoir
of father.
b. October 07, 1914 in London, England
d. September 24, 1982 in London, England

Domenico Cimarosa
Italian composer
• Wrote opera Il Matrimonio Segreto,
1792; noted for opera buffa.
b. December 17, 1749 in Aversa, Italy
d. January 11, 1801 in Venice, Italy

Eric Clapton
(Blind Faith; Eric Clap; Eric Patrick
Clapp; Cream; Yardbirds)
English musician
• Top guitarist in British rock, 1960s.
Now has successful solo career.
b. March 3, 1945 in Ripley, England

Dave Clark
(Dave Clark Five)
English musician–singer
• Formed Dave Clark Five, 1964-73.
b. December 15, 1942 in London, England

Petula Clark
English singer
• Won Grammys for "Downtown," 1964;
"I Know a Place," 1965.
b. November 15, 1932 in Epsom, England

Roy Linwood Clark
American singer–songwriter
• Named Entertainer of the Year by
CMA, 1973; banjo-playing host of TV's
"Hee Haw," 1969–.
b. April 15, 1933 in Meherrin, Virginia

Steve (Stephen Maynard) Clark
(Def Leppard; "Steamin'")
English musician
• Guitarist with heavy-metal band since
1978.
b. April 23, 1960 in Sheffield, England
d. January 08, 1991 in London, England

Allan Clarke
(The Hollies)
English singer
• Formed Hollies with childhood friend
Graham Nash, 1962.
b. April 15, 1942 in Salford, England

Jeremiah Clarke
English composer
• Organist, St. Paul's Cathedral, 1695,
who composed church harpsichord pieces.
b. 1673 in London, England
d. December 01, 1701 in London, England

Stanley Marvin Clarke
American musician–composer
• Known for jazz-funk style; hit albums
include Find Out, 1985; often teamed
with George Duke.
b. June 3, 1951 in Philadelphia, Pennsylvania

The Clash
(Topper Headon; Mick Jones; Paul Simo-
non; Joe Strummer)
English music group
• London-based band started, 1976; hit
album Combat Rock, 1982. Band's in
Splitsville with members pursuing various
solo careers.

Richard Clayderman
(The Prince of Romance)
French musician
• Popular pianist who has sold over 40
million records, including 177 gold, 42
platinum.
b. December 28, 1953 in France

Buck Clayton
American jazz musician
• Trumpeter; with Count Basie, 1936-43;
led own sextet, bands, 1950s.
b. November 12, 1911 in Parsons, Kansas

Muzio Clementi
Italian pianist–composer
• Leader in modern piano technique;
noted London music publisher, 1799.
b. 1752 in Rome, Italy
d. March 1, 1832 in Evesham, England

Clarence Clemons
(E Street Band; "The Big Man" "King
of the World" "Master of the Universe")
American musician–singer
• Tenor saxophonist with Bruce Springsteen; solo album Rescue, 1983.
b. January 11, 1942 in Norfolk, Virginia

James Cleveland
American clergyman–singer
• Founded Gospel Music Workshop of
America, 1968; hits include "Peace Be
Still," 1963. Instructed Aretha Franklin.
b. December 05, 1931 in Chicago, Illinois
d. February 09, 1991 in Los Angeles, Califor-
nia

Van (Harvey Lavan, Jr) Cliburn
American pianist
• Classical concert pianist; won Interna-
tional Tchaikovsky Piano Competition,
Moscow, 1958.
b. July 12, 1934 in Shreveport, Louisiana

Jimmy Cliff
(James Chambers)
Jamaican singer–songwriter
• Helped popularize reggae outside Jamaica; albums include The Power and
the Glory, 1983.
b. 1948 in Saint Catherine, Jamaica

The Climax Blues Band
(Colin Cooper; John Cuffley; Peter Haycock; Derek Holt; Richard Jones; George Newsome; Arthur Wood)
English music group
• Founded 1969; first US hit single "Couldn't Get It Right," 1977.

Maggie Cline
American singer
• Vaudeville performer, first woman Irish comedy singer.
b. January 01, 1857 in Haverhill, Massachusetts
d. June 11, 1934 in Fair Haven, New Jersey

Patsy Cline
(Virginia Patterson Hensley)
American singer
• Country singer; had hits "Crazy," "I Fall to Pieces," 1961; killed in plane crash; Jessica Lange played her in film *Sweet Dreams*, 1985.
b. September 08, 1932 in Winchester, Virginia
d. March 05, 1963 in Camden, Tennessee

George Clinton
American composer–producer–singer
• Best known for producing groups Parliament, Funkadelic; hits include "One Nation Under a Groove," 1978.
b. July 22, 1940 in Blainfield, Ohio

Larry Clinton
American bandleader
• Composer, arranger during big band era; tune "The Dipsy Doodle" was one of top hits, late 1930s.
b. August 17, 1909 in Brooklyn, New York
d. May 02, 1985 in Tucson, Arizona

Rosemary Clooney
American actress–singer
• Had million-selling single "Come On-a My House," 1951; autobiography *This for Remembrance*, 1979.
b. May 23, 1928 in Maysville, Kentucky

Club Nouveau
(Denzil Foster; Jay King; Thomas McElroy; Samuelle Prater; Valerie Watson)
American music group
• Dance band, formed 1980s; their hit "Lean on Me," 1987, sold over six million copies.

The Coasters
(Carl Gardner; Cornelius Gunter; Billy Guy; Adolph Jacobs)
American music group
• Rock 'n' roll band known for humorous, off-beat songs: "Yakety-Yak," 1958; "Charlie Brown," 1959; "Love Potion No. 9," 1971.

Edith Coates
English singer
• Founding member of Covent Garden Opera Co., 1937.
b. May 31, 1908 in Lincoln, England
d. January 07, 1983 in Worthing, England

Arnett Cleophus Cobb
American jazz musician–composer
• Noted tenor sax star of 1940s-50s; with Lionel Hampton, 1943-47.
b. August 1, 1918 in Houston, Texas
d. March 24, 1989 in Houston, Texas

Will D Cobb
American songwriter
• Often collaborated with Gus Edwards; hits include "School Days"; "Sunbonnet Sue."
b. July 06, 1876 in Philadelphia, Pennsylvania
d. January 2, 1930 in New York, New York

Billy Cobham
American jazz musician–composer
• Albums include *Flight Time*, 1981.
b. May 16, 1944 in Panama

Eddie Cochran
American singer–songwriter
• Had British hit single "Three Steps to Heaven," 1960; albums include *Words and Music*, 1982.
b. October 03, 1938 in Oklahoma City, Oklahoma
d. April 17, 1960 in London, England

Joe (Robert John) Cocker
English musician–singer
• Recorded "Up Where We Belong" from *An Officer and a Gentleman*, with Jennifer Warnes, 1983. Recognized for spastic stage movements.
b. May 2, 1944 in Sheffield, England

Leonard Cohen
Canadian singer–songwriter
• Wrote song "Beautiful Losers," 1966.
b. September 21, 1934 in Montreal, Quebec

Al Cohn
American jazz musician–composer
• Tenor saxophonist with Big Bands, 1940s; wrote scores for Broadway shows, TV specials.
b. November 24, 1925 in Brooklyn, New York
d. February 14, 1988 in Stroudsburg, Pennsylvania

Isabella Colbran
Spanish opera singer
• Dramatic coloratura soprano; married Rossini, starred in his operas.
b. February 02, 1785 in Madrid, Spain
d. October 07, 1845 in Bologna, Italy

Cozy (William Randolph) Cole
American musician
• Big band drummer; recorded "Topsy," 1958, only drum solo ever to sell over one million copies.
b. October 17, 1909 in East Orange, New Jersey
d. January 29, 1981 in Columbus, Ohio

Maria Cole
American singer–celebrity relative
• With Duke Ellington Band, 1945-46; widow of Nat King Cole.
b. August 01, 1920 in Boston, Massachusetts

Nat King (Nathaniel Adams) Cole
American singer–bandleader
• Known for easy-listening songs including "Mona Lisa," 1950; "Ramblin' Rose," 1962; first black to host TV series, 1950s.
b. March 17, 1919 in Montgomery, Alabama
d. February 15, 1965 in Santa Monica, California

Natalie (Stephanie Natalie Maria) Cole
American singer
• Won Grammy, 1976, for debut album *Inseparable*; daughter of Nat "King" Cole.
b. February 06, 1949 in Los Angeles, California

Cy Coleman
(Seymour Kaufman)
American songwriter
• Wrote song "If My Friends Could See Me Now."
b. June 14, 1929 in New York, New York

Ornette Coleman
American jazz musician
• Alto, tenor saxophonist; wrote over 100 jazz compositions; albums include *Song X*, 1986.
b. March 19, 1930 in Fort Worth, Texas

Samuel Coleridge-Taylor
English composer
• Wrote *24 Negro Melodies*, 1905; Hiawatha trilogy, 1898-1900.
b. August 15, 1875 in London, England
d. September 01, 1912 in Thornton, England

Dorothy Collins
(Marjorie Chandler)
Canadian singer
• Pop singer; star of "Hit Parade," 1950s.
b. November 18, 1926 in Windsor, Ontario

Judy (Judith Marjorie) Collins
American singer
• Hits include "Both Sides Now," 1968; "Send in the Clowns," 1975.
b. May 01, 1939 in Seattle, Washington

Lee Collins
American jazz musician
• Trumpeter, vocalist; led own ragtime band, Chicago, 1930s-50s.
b. October 17, 1901 in New Orleans, Louisiana
d. July 07, 1960 in Chicago, Illinois

Phil Collins
(Genesis)
English singer–musician
• Drummer, lead singer for Genesis; has successful solo career, including singles "Against All Odds," 1984; "One More Night," 1985.
b. January 3, 1951 in Chiswick, England

Jerry (Gerald) Colonna
American comedian–musician
• Accompanied Bob Hope on overseas troop tours; movies with Hope include *Road to Singapore,* 1940.
b. September 17, 1905 in Boston, Massachusetts
d. November 21, 1986 in Woodland Hills, California

John William Coltrane
("Trane")
American jazz musician
• Tenor sax virtuoso; played with Dizzy Gillespie, Miles Davis; helped create "new black music."
b. September 26, 1926 in Hamlet, North Carolina
d. July 17, 1967 in Huntington, New York

Russ Columbo
(Ruggerio de Rudolpho Columbo)
American bandleader–singer
• Baritone; formed band, 1931; died in tragic shooting incident.
b. January 04, 1908 in Philadelphia, Pennsylvania
d. September 02, 1934 in Hollywood, California

The Commodores
(William King; Ronald LaPread; Thomas McClary; Walter Clyde Orange; Lionel Richie, Jr.; Milan Williams)
American music group
• Formed, 1968; number one hits include "Three Times a Lady," 1978; "Sail On," 1979.

Perry (Pierino Roland) Como
American singer
• Popular, easy-going crooner for over 40 years; TV show, 1948-63; hits include "Prisoner of Love," 1956.
b. May 18, 1912 in Canonsburg, Pennsylvania

Richard P Condie
American conductor
• Director, Mormon Tabernacle Choir, 1957-74; brought it to world prominence.
b. July 05, 1898 in Springville, Utah
d. December 22, 1985 in Salt Lake City, Utah

Eddie Condon
American bandleader–jazz musician
• Jazz guitarist noted for "Chicago style" jazz, 1920s; opened NYC nightclub, 1946.
b. November 16, 1905 in Goodland, Indiana
d. August 03, 1973 in New York, New York

Zez (Edward E) Confrey
American composer
• Pianist, bandleader, 1920s; piano works include "Kitten on the Keys."
b. April 03, 1895 in Peru, Illinois
d. November 22, 1971 in Lakewood, New Jersey

Nadine Conner
American opera singer
• Lyric soprano; NY Met. debut, 1942.
b. February 2, 1913 in Compton, California

Harry Connick, Jr
American musician–songwriter
• Jazz pianist and singer of torch ballads, reviving the music of the past.
b. 1967 in New Orleans, Louisiana

Ray Conniff
American bandleader
• "Ray Conniff" sound launched with album *S'Wonderful,* 1956; combined strong beat with "swing" effect, strong choruses.
b. November 06, 1916 in Attleboro, Massachusetts

Con Conrad
(Conrad K Dober)
American songwriter–publisher
• Stage, film composer, 1920s-30s; wrote "Margie," 1920.
b. June 18, 1891 in New York, New York
d. September 28, 1938 in Van Nuys, California

Bill Conti
American composer
• Won Oscar for score of *The Right Stuff,* 1983; TV theme songs include "Dynasty"; "Falcon Crest"; "Cagney and Lacey."
b. April 13, 1942 in Providence, Rhode Island

Dick Contino
American musician
• Popular nightclub, film accordion player.
b. 1930 in Fresno, California

Frederick Shepherd Converse
American composer
• Wrote *Pipe of Desire,* first American opera produced by NY Met., 1910.
b. January 05, 1871 in Newton, Massachusetts
d. June 08, 1940 in Boston, Massachusetts

Ry(land Peter) Cooder
American musician
• Session guitarist, whose movie scores include *The Long Riders,* 1980.
b. March 15, 1947 in Los Angeles, California

Barbara Cook
American actress–singer
• Performed on Broadway musical stage, concerts; TV shows include "The Ed Sullivan Show"; "Chevy Show," 1960s.
b. October 25, 1927 in Atlanta, Georgia

Will Marion Cook
American composer–musician
• Created music for black musicals, 1900s; wrote song "Mandy Lou."
b. January 27, 1869 in Washington, District of Columbia
d. July 19, 1944 in New York, New York

Sam Cooke
American singer–musician
• Hits include "You Send Me," 1957; "Another Saturday Night," 1963.
b. January 22, 1935 in Chicago, Illinois
d. December 11, 1964 in Los Angeles, California

Rita Coolidge
American singer
• Ex-wife of Kris Kristofferson; platinum album *Anytime...Anywhere,* 1977.
b. May 01, 1945 in Nashville, Tennessee

Alice Cooper
(Vincent Damon Furnier)
American singer–songwriter
• One of original "shock-rock" groups, 1970s; hit albums include *Welcome to My Nightmare,* 1975.
b. February 04, 1948 in Detroit, Michigan

J Fred Coots
American songwriter
• Wrote "Santa Claus Is Comin' To Town," 1934; "You Go To My Head," 1938.
b. May 02, 1897 in Brooklyn, New York
d. April 08, 1985 in New York, New York

Stewart Copeland
(Police)
American songwriter
• Wrote hits for rock/pop group, Police: "King of Pain," 1984; film scores include *Bachelor Party,* 1983.
b. July 16, 1952 in Maclean, Virginia

Aaron Copland
American composer
• America's best-known composer; works include *Billy the Kid*, 1938, *Rodeo*, 1942; won Pulitzer for *Appalachian Spring*, 1944.
b. November 14, 1900 in Brooklyn, New York
d. December 02, 1990 in North Tarrytown, New York

Carmine Coppola
American composer–conductor
• Father of Francis Ford Coppola; won Oscar for co-writing music for *Godfather II*, 1974.
b. June 11, 1910 in New York, New York
d. April 26, 1991 in Los Angeles, California

Chick (Armando) Corea
American jazz musician
• Pianist; founded group, Return to Forever, 1971; won four Grammys.
b. June 12, 1941 in Chelsea, Massachusetts

Arcangelo Corelli
Italian violinist
• Virtuoso; regarded as founder of modern violin technique.
b. February 17, 1653 in Fusignano, Italy
d. January 08, 1713 in Rome, Italy

Franco Corelli
Italian opera singer
• Heroic tenor; NY Met. debut, 1961.
b. April 08, 1923 in Ancona, Italy

Peter Cornelius
German composer
• Wrote operas *Barbier von Bagdad*, 1858; *Der Cid*, 1865; friend of Liszt, Wagner.
b. December 24, 1824 in Mainz, Germany
d. October 26, 1874 in Mainz, Germany

Don Cornell
(Louis F Varlaro)
American singer
• High baritone vocalist; starred with Sammy Kaye's band, 1950s.
b. April 21, 1919 in New York, New York

Gene Cornish
(The Rascals)
Canadian musician
• Guitarist with blue-eyed soul group, 1965-71.
b. May 14, 1945 in Ottawa, Ontario

Larry Coryell
American musician–composer
• Jazz guitarist; work mixes jazz rock/hard rock: *The Firebird & Petrushka*, 1984.
b. April 02, 1943 in Galveston, Texas

Sam Coslow
American songwriter
• Songs include "Sing You Sinners," 1930; "Cocktails for Two," 1934.
b. December 27, 1905 in New York, New York
d. April 02, 1982 in Bronxville, New York

Don Costa
American conductor
• Arranger of over 200 hit recordings by Frank Sinatra, Perry Como, others.
b. June 1, 1925 in Boston, Massachusetts
d. January 19, 1983 in New York, New York

Elvis Costello
(Declan Patrick McManus)
English singer–songwriter
• Best-known albums: *Armed Forces*, 1979; *Good Year For The Roses*, 1981.
b. August 25, 1955 in London, England

Ileana Cotrubas
Romanian opera singer
• Soprano; NY Met. debut, 1977; noted for lyrico-dramatic roles.
b. June 09, 1939 in Galati, Romania

Country Joe and the Fish
(Bruce Barthol; David Cohen; Chicken Hirsch; Joseph McDonald; Barry Melton)
American music group
• Appeared at Monterey, Woodstock festivals; albums include *Here We Are Again*, 1969.

Couperin
(Armand-Louis Couperin; Charles Couperin; Francois Couperin; Francois-Gervais Couperin; Louis Couperin; Marguerite-Antoinette Couperin; Mar)
French musicians
• Family best known as organists at St. Gervais, Paris, 1650-1826.

Francois Couperin
(LeGrand Couperin)
French musician–composer
• Harpsichordist; organist; influenced keyboard technique of Bach; leading French composer of his day.
b. November 1, 1668 in Paris, France
d. September 12, 1733 in Paris, France

Warren Covington
American musician–bandleader–singer
• Trombonist, 1940s-50s; led Tommy Dorsey's orchestra after Dorsey's death, late 1950s.
b. August 07, 1921 in Philadelphia, Pennsylvania

Henry Dixon Cowell
American composer–pianist
• Introduced innovations: "tone clusters," playing directly on piano strings; invented instrument called Rhythmicon, 1930s.
b. March 11, 1897 in Menlo Park, California
d. December 1, 1965 in Shady, New York

The Cowsills
(Barbara Cowsill; Barry Cowsill; John Cowsill; Paul Cowsill; Richard Cowsill; Robert Cowsill; Susan Cowsill; William Cowsill)
American music group
• Family group which inspired TV's "Partridge Family"; hit single theme from *Hair*, 1960s.

Jean Cox
American opera singer
• Outstanding Heldentenor; Bayreuth debut, 1956; acclaimed as Siegfried.
b. January 16, 1932 in Gadsden, Alabama

Crash (Billy) Craddock
(Mr Country Rock)
American singer
• Rock and roll performer; member, Dream Lovers since 1974; had hit song "Knock Three Times," 1971.
b. June 16, 1940 in Greensboro, North Carolina

Robert Craft
American conductor
• Musical asst., adviser to Igor Stravinsky for 23 yrs.
b. October 2, 1923 in Kingston, New York

Floyd Cramer
(Mister Keyboards)
American singer–pianist
• Member, Grand Ole Opry, 1950s-60s; wrote hit instrumental "Last Date," 1960; established the "Cramer Style."
b. October 27, 1933 in Shreveport, Louisiana

Johann Baptist Cramer
German pianist–composer
• Wrote sonatas, famed pianoforte studies; founded English firm for publishing, piano-making.
b. 1771 in Mannheim, Germany
d. 1858

Robert Cray
American singer–songwriter
• Guitarist; won Grammys for blues albums *Showdown*, 1987; *Strong Persuader*, 1988.
b. August 01, 1953 in Columbus, Georgia

Crazy Horse
(Tim Drummond; Ben Keith; Joe Lala; Ralph Molina; Bruce Palmer; Frank Sampedro; Billy Talbot; Danny Whitten) American music group
• Country-rock group, late 1960s-70s; albums include *Crazy Horse*, 1971.Frequently backs Neil Young. Known for larger-than-a-garage sound.

Papa (John) Creach
American musician
• Rock fiddler; probably was oldest rock-and-roll performer.
b. May 17, 1917 in Beaver Falls, Pennsylvania

Cream
(Ginger Baker; Jack Bruce; Eric Clapton) English music group
• First 1960s "supergroup"; hits include "Sunshine of Your Love," 1968.

Linda Creed
American songwriter
• With Thom Bell wrote hits "You Make Me Feel Brand New," 1974, "Could It Be I'm Falling in Love?," 1973.
b. 1949
d. April 1, 1986 in Ambler, Pennsylvania

Creedence Clearwater Revival
(Douglas Ray Clifford; Stuart Cook; John Fogerty; Thomas Fogerty) American music group
• Rock band of late 1960-70s; hits include "Proud Mary," 1969; "Who'll Stop the Rain," 1970.

Paul Creston
American composer
• Wrote over 100 major compositions including six symphonies, choral works, piano pieces.
b. October 1, 1906 in New York, New York
d. August 24, 1985 in Poway, California

Jim Croce
American singer-songwriter
• Hits include "Operator," 1972; "Bad Bad Leroy Brown," 1973. Went down with his plane when it crashed.
b. January 1, 1943 in Philadelphia, Pennsylvania
d. September 2, 1973 in Natchitoches, Louisiana

Dash Crofts
(Seals and Crofts) American singer-songwriter
• Member of soft rock duo with Jim Seals; greatest hits: "Summer Breeze," 1973; "Takin' It Easy," 1978.
b. 1940 in Cisco, Texas

Bing (Harry Lillis) Crosby
American actor-singer
• Won Oscar for *Going My Way*, 1944; biggest hit "White Christmas," 1942; crooner known for "road" movies with Bob Hope, Dorothy Lamour.
b. May 02, 1904 in Tacoma, Washington
d. October 14, 1977 in Madrid, Spain

Fanny (Frances Jane) Crosby
American composer
• Wrote over 600 hymns, including "Safe in the Arms of Jesus"; blinded when a baby.
b. March 24, 1820 in Southeast, New York
d. February 12, 1915 in Bridgeport, Connecticut

Bob (George Robert) Crosby
American bandleader-celebrity relative
• Led Dixieland-style big band, 1935-50s; brother of Bing.
b. August 23, 1913 in Spokane, Washington

David Crosby
(The Byrds; Crosby Stills Nash and Young) American musician-songwriter
• Rhythm quitarist, The Byrds, 1960s; Stills, Nash and Young, 1970s-80s; hit songs include "Deja Vu."
b. August 14, 1941 in Los Angeles, California

Stills Crosby, Nash, Young
(David Crosby; Graham Nash; Stephen Stills; Neil Young) American music group
• Hits include "Woodstock; Teach Your Children," 1970.

Christopher Cross
(Christopher Geppert) American singer-songwriter
• Known for number one singles "Sailing," 1980; Oscar-winner "Arthur's Theme," 1981.
b. May 03, 1951 in San Antonio, Texas

Scatman (Benjamin Sherman) Crothers
American actor-singer
• Known for TV role in "Chico and the Man," 1974-78; film roles in *The Shining*, 1980; *Twilight Zone: The Movie*, 1983.
b. May 23, 1910 in Terre Haute, Indiana
d. November 22, 1986 in Los Angeles, California

Rodney Crowell
American musician-songwriter
• Many of his songs recorded by Emmylou Harris; has produced wife Roseanne Cash's albums.
b. August 07, 1950 in Houston, Texas

The Crusaders
(Larry Eugene Carlton; Witon Felder; Wayne Henderson; Stix Hooper; Joe Sample) American music group
• Best known for hit single "Uptight (Everything's Alright)," 1966.

The Crystals
(Barbara Alston; Lala Brooks; Dee Dee Kenniebrew; Mary Thomas; Pat Wright) American music group
• Brooklyn schoolgirls; 1960s hits include "He's a Rebel," 1962; "Da Doo Ron Ron," 1963.

Xavier Cugat
Spanish bandleader
• Introduced Americans to tropical rhythms of the rumba, 1930s; with band, the Gigolos, featured in films that made name a household word, 1940s-50s.
b. January 01, 1900 in Barcelona, Spain
d. October 27, 1990 in Barcelona, Spain

Culture Club
(Boy George; Micheal Craig; Roy Hay; Jon Moss; Helen Terry) English music group
• Most commercially successful of British rock-theater bands, 1980s; first hit "Do You Really Want to Hurt Me?" 1982.

Burton Cummings
(Guess Who) Canadian singer-musician
• Founding member of Guess Who, 1960s; solo hits include "Stand Tall," 1976.
b. December 31, 1947 in Winnipeg, Manitoba

Phyllis Smith Curtin
American singer
• Classical soprano who championed modern American opera; identified with title role, Susannah, 1955.
b. December 03, 1927 in Clarksburg, West Virginia

Clifford Michael Curzon, Sir
English pianist
• Noted for interpretations of Schubert, Brahms; knighted, 1977.
b. May 18, 1907 in London, England
d. September 01, 1982 in London, England

Eugene D'Albert
German pianist-composer
• 20 operas include *Tiefland*, 1903; pupil of Liszt.
b. April 1, 1864 in Glasgow, Scotland
d. March 03, 1932 in Riga, U.S.S.R.

Alan Dale

American musician–singer
• Leading pop singer, 1940s-50s; recorded "Oh, Marie."
b. July 09, 1926 in Brooklyn, New York

Clamma Churita Dale

American singer
• Dramatic soprano of Houston, NYC Opera cos.; won awards for *Porgy and Bess*, 1976.
b. July 04, 1948 in Chester, Pennsylvania

Gilda Dalla Rizza

Italian opera singer
• Soprano; sang over 50 roles at La Scala, 1915-39; admired by Puccini, Toscanini.
b. October 12, 1892 in Verona, Italy
d. July 05, 1975

Luigi Dallapiccola

Italian musician–composer
• First Italian to write atonal music: opera *The Prisoner*, 1948.
b. February 03, 1904 in Pisino, Yugoslavia
d. February 19, 1975 in Florence, Italy

Jorge Dalto

Argentine pianist
• Jazz-fusion hits include 1976 Grammy winner "This Masquerade."
b. July 07, 1948 in Jorge Perez, Argentina
d. October 27, 1987 in New York, New York

Lacy J Dalton

American singer
• Country-western albums include *Hard Times*; *Lacy J Dalton*, 1980.
b. October 13, 1946

Roger Daltrey

(The Who)
English singer–actor
• Appeared in *Tommy*, 1974; *The Kids Are Alright*, 1979.
b. March 01, 1945 in Hammersmith, England

The Damned

(Bryn; Roman Jugg; Rat Scabies; Dave Vanian)
British music group
• Hard rock group formed 1976; albums include *Glad It's All Over*, 1984.

Vic Damone

(Vito Farinola)
American singer
• Starred in own radio show, late 1940s; own TV series, 1956-57, 1967.
b. June 12, 1928 in Brooklyn, New York

Walter Johannes Damrosch

German conductor–composer
• Directed NY Symphony, 1903-26; formed Damrosch Opera Co., 1895; pioneered in weekly music appreciation broadcasts, 1928.
b. January 3, 1862 in Breslau, Prussia
d. December 22, 1950 in New York, New York

Dorothy Dandridge

American singer–actress
• Starred in Otto Preminger's film *Carmen Jones*, 1954.
b. November 09, 1922 in Cleveland, Ohio
d. September 08, 1965 in West Hollywood, California

Dino Danelli

(The Rascals)
American musician
• Drummer with blue-eyed soul group; hit single "How Can I Be Sure," 1967.
b. July 23, 1945 in New York, New York

Billy Daniels

American singer
• Popular vocalist, showman; noted for rendition of "That Old Black Magic."
b. September 12, 1915 in Jacksonville, Florida
d. October 07, 1988 in Los Angeles, California

Charlie Daniels

(The Charlie Daniels Band)
American musician–songwriter
• Nashville session guitarist, who formed Charlie Daniels Band, 1973; wrote Grammy-winning song "Devil Went Down to Georgia," 1979.
b. October 28, 1936 in Wilmington, North Carolina

John Philip William Dankworth

English composer–conductor
• Jazz saxophonist, orchestra leader, 1950s; scored many British films; wed to singer Cleo Laine.
b. September 2, 1927 in London, England

Danny and the Juniors

(Frank Maffei; Danny Rapp; Joe Terranova; Dave White)
American music group
• PA group, formed 1957; recorded classics "At the Hop," 1957; "Rock and Roll Is Here to Stay," 1958.

Bobby Darin

(Walden Robert Cassotto)
American singer–actor
• Best-known song "Mack the Knife," won two Grammys, 1960.
b. May 14, 1936 in New York, New York
d. December 2, 1973 in Hollywood, California

Joseph Darion

American lyricist
• Won 1965 Tony for lyrics of *Man of La Mancha*.
b. January 3, 1917 in New York, New York

Erik Darling

(The Weavers; The Rooftop Singers)
American singer–musician
• Replaced Pete Seeger in the Weavers group, 1958; formed Rooftop Singers, 1962, had gold record with "Walk Right In," 1963.
b. September 25, 1933 in Baltimore, Maryland

The Dave Clark Five

(Dave Clark; Lenny Davidson; Rick Huxley; Denis Payton; Michael Smith)
English music group
• "British invasion" group formed, 1963; hit singles include "Red Balloon," 1968; "Everybody Get Together," 1970.

Hal David

American lyricist
• Former partner of Burt Bacharach; won Oscar, 1969, for "Raindrops Keep Fallin' on My Head."
b. May 25, 1921 in New York, New York

Mack David

American composer
• Film scores include *To Kill a Mockingbird*, 1963; *It's a Mad, Mad, Mad, Mad, World*, 1963.
b. July 05, 1912 in New York, New York

John Davidson

American singer–actor
• Starred in *The Happiest Millionaire*, 1967; TV series, "That's Incredible," 1980-85.
b. December 13, 1941 in Pittsburgh, Pennsylvania

Dave (David) Davies

(Kinks)
English singer–musician
• Rhythm guitarist of hard rock-turned pop group; hit single "You Really Got Me," 1964.
b. February 03, 1947 in Muswell Hill, England

Peter Maxwell Davies

English composer
• Founded Orkney Island's annual St. Magnus Festival, 1977; wrote *Eight Songs for a Mad King*, 1969.
b. September 08, 1934 in Manchester, England

Ray(mond Douglas) Davies
(The Kinks)
English singer–musician
• Lead guitarist for band formed with
brother Dave, 1963.
b. June 21, 1944 in Muswell Hill, England

Billy Davis, Jr
(Fifth Dimension)
American singer
• Vocalist with pop-soul group; had num-
ber-one hit "Wedding Bell Blues," 1969.
b. June 26, 1940 in Saint Louis, Missouri

Clifton Davis
American actor–singer–composer
• Wrote gold-record song "Never Can
Say Goodbye," 1970; stars in TV series
"Amen," 1986–.
b. October 04, 1945 in Chicago, Illinois

Clive Jay Davis
American music executive–lawyer
• Pres., Columbia Records, 1966-73;
pres., co-owner, Arista Records, 1974–.
b. April 04, 1932 in Brooklyn, New York

Colin Davis
English conductor
• Director, London's Covent Garden Royal Opera since 1971; noted for Mozart,
Berlioz interpretations.
b. September 25, 1927 in Weybridge, England

Janette Davis
American singer
• Husky-voiced entertainer; with Arthur
Godfrey's radio, TV shows, 1940s-50s.
b. in Memphis, Tennessee

Mac Davis
American singer–actor–songwriter
• Hit song "I Believe in Music," 1972;
starred in *North Dallas Forty*, 1979.
b. January 21, 1942 in Lubbock, Texas

Meyer Davis
American bandleader–agent
• Often played at White House; could
provide dance bands in 24-hour notice,
1920s-70s.
b. January 1, 1895 in Ellicott City, Maryland
d. April 05, 1976 in New York, New York

Miles Dewey Davis
American jazz musician–composer
• Often considered top jazz trumpeter,
1950s–; formed Miles Davis Quintet,
1955; with Charlie Parker, 1940s.
b. May 25, 1926 in Alton, Illinois

Sammy Davis, Jr
American actor–singer–dancer
• Versatile entertainer; 60-year career
spanned vaudeville, stage, movies, recording, nightclubs, TV; last movie role in
Tap, 1989.
b. December 08, 1925 in New York, New
York
d. May 16, 1990 in Los Angeles, California

Skeeter Davis
American singer
• Country-western star; hit song "The
End of the World," 1963.
b. December 3, 1931 in Dry Ridge, Kentucky

Spencer Davis
(The Spencer Davis Group)
English singer–musician
• Formed rock band featuring Stevie
Winwood, 1963-69; known for hit "I'm
a Man," 1968.
b. July 17, 1942 in England

Wild Bill (William) Davison
American jazz musician
• Dixieland style cornetist; 50-yr. career
as soloist, bandleader.
b. January 05, 1906 in Defiance, Ohio
d. November 14, 1989 in Santa Barbara, California

Hazel Dawn
American actress–singer
• Starred in Broadway musicals, 1911-
20s; silent films, 1914-17.
b. March 23, 1898 in Ogden, Utah
d. August 28, 1988 in New York, New York

Dennis Day
(Eugene Denis McNulty)
American actor–singer
• Golden-voiced Irish tenor best known
as comic target for Jack Benny on radio,
TV, film.
b. May 21, 1917 in New York, New York
d. June 22, 1988 in Los Angeles, California

Dazz Band
(Bobby Harris; Keith Harrison; Sennie
Skip Martin III; Kenny Pettus; Isaac Wi-
ley, Jr.; Michael Wiley)
American music group
• Danceable jazz band; won Grammy,
1982, for "Let It Whip."

Jimmy Dean
(Seth Ward)
American singer–business executive
• Country star, best known for song
"Big Bad John," 1961. Also owns sau-
sage company.
b. August 1, 1928 in Plainview, Texas

Laura Dean
American choreographer–composer
• Founded controversial Dean Dancers
and Musicians, 1976; composed score
for *Enochian*, 1983.
b. December 03, 1945 in Staten Island, New
York

DeBarge
(Bunny DeBarge; Eldra DeBarge; James
DeBarge; Mark DeBarge; RandyDeBarge)
American music group
• Family singing group from Grand Rap-
ids, MI; had hit single "Rhythm of the
Night," 1985.

Michel H Debost
French musician
• First flutist of Paris Orchestra since
1967; winner of numerous international
awards.
b. 1934 in Paris, France

Claude Achille Debussy
French composer
• Creator of musical impressionism; wrote
opera *Pelleas et Melisande,* 1902; piano
piece "Clair de Lune," 1905.
b. August 22, 1862 in Saint-Germain-en-Laye,
France
d. March 25, 1918 in Paris, France

Jeanine Deckers
Belgian nun–singer
• Had hit single "Dominique," 1963;
movie *The Singing Nun*, 1966, based on
her life. Committed suicide in pact with
friend.
b. 1933
d. March 31, 1985 in Wavre, Belgium

Kiki Dee
(Pauline Matthews)
English singer
• Rock vocalist; formed own band,
1970s; was teamed with Elton John.
b. March 06, 1947 in Bradford, England

Deep Purple
(Ritchie Blackmore; Thomas Bolin; David
Coverdale; Rod Evans; IanGillan; Roger
Glover; Glenn Hughs; Jon Lord; Ian
Paige; Nicholas Simper)
American music group
• Heavy rock band, formed 1968; hits
include "Black Night," 1970.

Def Leppard
(Rick Allen; Steve Clark; Phil Collen; Joe
Elliott; Rick Savage;Pete Willis)
British music group
• Heavy metal, new wave group formed
1977; popularity attributed to MTV in
US.

Buddy DeFranco
American jazz musician–bandleader
• Outstanding modern-style clarinetist with name bands, 1940s-50s; led Glenn Miller band, 1966-74.
b. 1933

Jan De Gaetani
American singer
• Versatile mezzo-soprano, leading interpreter of new vocal music known for chamber, orchestral performances.
b. July 1, 1933 in Massillon, Ohio
d. September 17, 1989 in Rochester, New York

(Henry Louis) Reginald DeKoven
American composer–critic
• Founded, conducted, Washington Philharmonic, 1902-05; wrote operettas *Robin Hood*, 1890, *Student King*, 1906.
b. April 03, 1861 in Middletown, Connecticut
d. January 16, 1920 in Chicago, Illinois

Delaney and Bonnie
(Delaney Bramlett; Bonnie Lynn)
American music group
• Southern husband-wife team combining soul, boogie, country; hit album *Down Home*, 1969.

Norman Joseph Dello Joio
American composer
• Won 1957 Pulitzer for *Meditations on Ecclesiastes*; noted exponent of neo-classical manner.
b. January 24, 1913 in New York, New York

Mario DelMonaco
Italian opera singer
• Tenor, most noted for rendition of Verdi's *Otello*, performed 427 times.
b. July 27, 1915 in Florence, Italy
d. October 16, 1982 in Mestre, Italy

Giuseppe DeLuca
Italian opera singer
• Baritone, famed bel canto singer; made over 700 appearances in 80 different operas.
b. December 29, 1876 in Rome, Italy
d. August 27, 1950 in New York, New York

Joreg Demus
Austrian pianist
• Award-winning Viennese concert performer, made over 200 recordings.
b. December 02, 1928 in Saint Poelten, Austria

John Densmore
(The Doors)
American singer–musician
• Drummer, keyboardist with The Doors, mid-60s-1973.
b. December 01, 1945 in Los Angeles, California

John Denver
(Henry John Deutschendorf)
American singer–songwriter–actor
• Hits include "Take Me Home Country Road," 1971; "Rocky Mountain High," 1972; appeared in *Oh, God!*, 1977.
b. December 31, 1943 in Roswell, New Mexico

Deodato
(Eumir DeAlmeida)
Brazilian musician–composer
• Keyboard player best known for background music; albums include *Motion*, 1984.
b. June 22, 1942 in Rio de Janeiro, Brazil

Wilbur DeParis
American jazz musician
• Trombonist, drummer with Duke Ellington, 1940s; led own bands, NYC, from 1950s.
b. September 2, 1900 in Crawfordsville, Indiana
d. January 1973 in New York, New York

Gene Vincent DePaul
American composer
• Noted for Oscar-winning score, *Seven Brides for Seven Brothers*, 1954; Songwriter's Hall of Fame, 1985.
b. June 17, 1919 in New York, New York
d. February 27, 1988 in Los Angeles, California

Derek and the Dominoes
(Eric Clapton; Jim Gordon; Carl Radle; Bobby Whitlock)
American music group
• Encouraged by fame of Cream, formed 1970; albums include *In Concert*, 1973.

Edouard DeReszke
Polish opera singer
• One of opera's greatest basses, 1870-1903; noted for Mephistopheles in *Faust*.
b. December 22, 1853 in Warsaw, Poland
d. May 25, 1917 in Garnek, Poland

Jean DeReszke
(Jan Mieczyslaw)
Polish opera singer
• Tenor with NY Met., 1891-1901; often sang with brother Edouard.
b. January 14, 1850 in Warsaw, Poland
d. April 03, 1925 in Nice, France

Peter DeRose
American songwriter–pianist
• Hit songs include "Deep Purple," 1939; in radio series "Sweethearts of the Air," 1923-39.
b. March 1, 1900 in New York, New York
d. April 23, 1953 in New York, New York

Rick Derringer
(Rick Zehringer)
American singer–musician
• Singer-guitarist with 1960s McCoys; wrote hit "Hang on, Sloopy," 1965; formed own band, 1976.
b. 1947 in Union City, Illinois

Jackie DeShannon
American singer–songwriter
• Concert, TV, folk, pop star, 1960s-70s; wrote over 500 songs.
b. August 21, 1944 in Hazel, Kentucky

Johnny Desmond
(Giovanni Alfredo DeSimone; "GI Sinatra")
American singer–actor
• Popular radio, TV baritone, 1940s-50s; long stint on Breakfast Club Show, 1950s.
b. November 14, 1919 in Detroit, Michigan
d. September 06, 1985 in Los Angeles, California

Paul Breitenfeld Desmond
American jazz musician
• Renowned cool jazz saxist; with Dave Brubeck, 1950s.
b. November 25, 1924 in San Francisco, California
d. May 3, 1977 in New York, New York

Josquin DesPres
(Josse Depres)
Flemish composer
• Considered greatest Renaissance composer; wrote over 20 masses, 100 motets; developed antiphonal techniques.
b. 1445 in Conde sur l'Escaut, France
d. August 27, 1521 in Conde, France

Buddy (George Gard) DeSylva
American songwriter–producer
• Produced five Shirley Temple films; wrote librettos for numerous George White Scandals, 500 songs including "Sonny Boy," 1928.
b. January 27, 1896 in New York, New York
d. July 11, 1950 in Oak Park, Illinois

Robert Nathaniel Dett
American composer
• Choral pieces evolved from black spirituals: "Chariot Jubilee."
b. October 11, 1882 in Drummondsville, Ontario
d. October 02, 1943 in Battle Creek, Michigan

Adolph Deutsch
American composer
• MGM musical director whose scores include Oscar-winning *Oklahoma!*, 1955; *Annie Get Your Gun*, 1950.
b. October 2, 1897 in London, England
d. January 01, 1980 in Palm Desert, California

Tommy DeVito
(The Four Seasons)
American singer–musician
• One of group's original members, 1962.
b. June 19, 1936 in Belleville, New Jersey

Devo
(Bob Casale; Jerry Casale; Bob Mothersbaugh; Mark Mothersbaugh; Alan Myers)
American music group
• Weirdly garbed Akron, OH quintet known for synthesizer-oriented rhythm; hit single "Whip It," 1980.

Barry De Vorzon
American composer
• Wrote "Bless the Beasts and the Children," 1971; Grammy-winning "Nadia's Theme," 1977.
b. July 31, 1934 in New York, New York

Al Dexter
(Clarence Albert Poindexter)
American singer–songwriter
• Biggest hit, "Pistol Packin' Mama," 1943, sold over 10 million copies.
b. May 04, 1902 in Jacksonville, Texas
d. January 28, 1984 in Lake Lewisville, Texas

Dennis DeYoung
(Styx)
American singer
• As solo performer had hit single "Desert Moon," 1984.
b. February 18, 1947 in Chicago, Illinois

David Diamond
American composer
• Noted for prize-winning symphonies, string quartets; his 50th birthday honored by concerts throughout US.
b. July 09, 1915 in Rochester, New York

Neil Diamond
American singer–songwriter–actor
• Pop singer with over 20 gold, platinum records; number one single "Song Sung Blue," 1972.
b. January 24, 1941 in Brooklyn, New York

Charles Dibdin
English dramatist–songwriter
• Wrote 30 popular plays, one-man "table entertainments"; his 1,400 songs include "Tom Bowling."
b. March 04, 1745 in Southampton, England
d. April 25, 1814 in London, England

Thomas Pitt Dibdin
English dramatist–songwriter
• Thought to have written 2,000 songs, 200 operas, plays.
b. March 21, 1771 in London, England
d. September 16, 1841 in London, England

Mischa Dichter
American musician
• Int'l. concert pianist since 1966.
b. September 27, 1945 in Shanghai, China

Little Jimmy Dickens
American singer–songwriter
• Grand Ole Opry guitarist who wrote pop-country novelties: "Hillbilly Fever," 1950.
b. December 19, 1925 in Bolt, West Virginia

Bo Diddley
(Ellas McDaniels; The Originator)
American musician–songwriter
• Best known for "I'm Sorry," 1959.
b. December 3, 1928 in McComb, Mississippi

Emma Lou Diemer
American composer–organist
• Wrote over 100 choral, instrumental works including "Suite for Orchestra," 1981.
b. November 24, 1927 in Kansas City, Missouri

Howard M Dietz
American songwriter
• With Arthur Schwartz, wrote over 500 songs, including "Dancing in the Dark"; "That's Entertainment."
b. September 08, 1896 in New York, New York
d. July 3, 1983 in New York, New York

Chris Difford
(Squeeze)
English singer–musician
• Guitarist, vocalist; collaborated with Glenn Tilbrook on over 600 songs.
b. April 11, 1954 in London, England

Al DiMeola
American musician–songwriter
• Jazz guitarist; albums include *Soaring Through a Dream*, 1985; won Grammy, 1975.
b. July 22, 1954 in Jersey City, New Jersey

Mark Dinning
American singer
• Known for hit song, "Teen Angel," 1959; banned in Britain because it was so sad.
b. 1935
d. March 22, 1986 in Jefferson City, Missouri

Dion
(Dion and the Belmonts; Dion DiMucci)
American singer–songwriter
• As solo performer, had major hits "Runaround Sue," 1961, "Abraham, Martin, and John," 1968.
b. July 18, 1939 in Bronx, New York

Dion and the Belmonts
(Angelo D'Angelo; Dion DiMucci; Carlo Mastangelo; Fred Milano)
American music group
• Bronx-born group formed, 1958-60; biggest hits "A Teenager in Love," 1959, "Where or When," 1960.

Dire Straits
(John Illsley; Dave Knopfler; Mark Knopfler; Pick Withers)
English music group
• Guitar-oriented band, formed 1977; hit single "Walk of Life," 1985.

Giuseppe DiStefano
Italian opera singer
• Tenor; made NY Met. debut, 1948; noted for Verdi, Puccini roles.
b. July 24, 1921 in Catania, Sicily

Karl Ditters
(Karl Ditters von Dittersdorf)
Austrian musician–composer
• 44 operas include *Doktor und Apotheker*, 1786; developed German Singspiel.
b. November 02, 1739 in Vienna, Austria
d. December 24, 1799 in Neuhof, Bohemia

Dean Dixon
American conductor
• First black to lead major orchestra, NY Philharmonic, 1944.
b. January 1, 1915 in New York, New York
d. November 03, 1976

Mort Dixon
American lyricist
• Wrote "That Old Gang of Mine," 1923; often collaborated with Billy Rose, Harry Warner.
b. March 2, 1892 in New York, New York
d. March 23, 1956 in Bronxville, New York

Dr Hook
(Rik Elswit; William Francis; Jance Garfat; Dennis Locorriere; Rod Smarr; John Wolters)
American music group
• Parody rock group formed 1968; hits include "When You're in Love with a Beautiful Woman," 1979.

Dr John
(Malcolm John Mac Rebennack)
American pianist–singer
• Rock/blues albums include *I Been Hoodood*, 1984; noted for voodoo stage costumes.
b. 1941 in New Orleans, Louisiana

Baby (Warren) Dodds
American jazz musician
• New Orleans-style drummer, 1920s-50s; with brother, Johnny's band, 1930s.
b. December 24, 1898 in New Orleans, Louisiana
d. February 14, 1959 in Chicago, Illinois

Johnny Dodds
American jazz musician–bandleader
• Clarinetist; led own band, 1930s.
b. April 12, 1892 in New Orleans, Louisiana
d. August 08, 1940 in Chicago, Illinois

Bill Doggett
American singer–musician–songwriter
• Popularised use of Hammond organ in R&B; had hit single "Honky Tonk," 1956.
b. February 06, 1916 in Philadelphia, Pennsylvania

Christoph von Dohnanyi
German conductor
• Led Hamburg State Opera, 1977-84; became music director of Cleveland Orchestra, 1984.
b. September 08, 1929 in Berlin, Germany

Erno von Dohnanyi
(Ernst von Dohnanyi)
Hungarian composer–musician–conductor
• Keyboard virtuoso; wrote piano works; grandfather of Christoph.
b. July 27, 1877 in Presburg, Hungary
d. 1960 in New York, New York

Paul Karl Doktor
American musician
• Violinist-violist who founded many string ensembles.
b. 1919 in Vienna, Austria

Thomas Dolby
(Thomas Morgan Dolby Robertson)
British singer–musician
• Keyboardist, who had hit single "She Blinded Me with Science," 1983.
b. October 14, 1958 in Cairo, Egypt

Mickey (George Michael) Dolenz
(The Monkees)
American singer
• Vocalist, drummer with The Monkees on popular TV series, 1966-68; part of group's late-1980s revival.
b. March 08, 1945 in Los Angeles, California

Placido Domingo
Spanish opera singer
• Tenor; recorded hit single "Perhaps Love" with John Denver, 1981; played 50 operatic roles.
b. January 21, 1941 in Madrid, Spain

Fats (Antoine) Domino
American singer
• Mixed blues with rock; best known for hit song "Blueberry Hill," 1956.
b. February 26, 1928 in New Orleans, Louisiana

Sam Koontz Donahue
American musician
• Led Big Band, 1940s; directed Dorsey band after Dorsey's death, 1960s.
b. March 08, 1918 in Detroit, Michigan

Walter Donaldson
American songwriter
• Hits songs include "My Buddy," 1922; "My Blue Heaven," 1927.
b. February 15, 1893 in Brooklyn, New York
d. July 15, 1947 in Santa Monica, California

Lonnie Donegan
Scottish singer–musician
• Hits include "Lorelei," 1960; "The Party's Over," 1962.
b. April 29, 1931 in Glasgow, Scotland

Gaetano Donizetti
Italian composer
• A master of musical theater, forerunner of Verdi; wrote *Lucia di Lammermoor*, 1835; *Don Pasquale*, 1843.
b. November 29, 1797 in Bergamo, Italy
d. April 08, 1848 in Bergamo, Italy

Donovan
(Donovan P Leitch)
Scottish singer–songwriter
• Hits include "Sunshine Superman," 1966; "Mellow Yellow," 1966.
b. May 1, 1943 in Glasgow, Scotland

The Doobie Brothers
(Jeff Baxter; Little John Hartman; Mike Hossack; Tom Johnston;Keith Knudson; Michael McDonald; Tiran Porter; Dave Shogren; Pat Simmons)
American music group
• Hit albums include *Minute by Minute*, 1978; *One Step Closer*, 1980.

The Doors
(John Densmore; Bobby Krieger; Ray Manzarek; Jim Morrison)
American music group
• Had number-one song, "Light My Fire," 1967; late 1960s band, controversial for lyrics, lifestyles.

Antal Dorati
American conductor–composer
• Led London's Royal Philharmonic, 1974-81; Detroit Symphony, 1977-81; Stockholm Symphony, 1981-88.
b. April 09, 1906 in Budapest, Hungary
d. November 13, 1988 in Gerzensee, Switzerland

Jimmy (James) Dorsey
American bandleader
• Played clarinet, saxophone in his sweet-swing band, 1930s-40s; joined brother Tommy's band, 1953.
b. February 29, 1904 in Shenandoah, Pennsylvania
d. June 12, 1957 in New York, New York

Thomas Andrew Dorsey
American clergyman–composer
• Coined term gospel music, wrote over 400 songs including, "Precious Lord, Take My Hand."
b. July 01, 1900 in Villa Rica, Georgia

Tommy (Thomas Francis) Dorsey
American bandleader
• Trombonist who led swing dance bands, 1930s-40s; with brother Jimmy starred in film *The Fabulous Dorseys*, 1947.
b. November 19, 1905 in Mahonoy Plains, Pennsylvania
d. November 26, 1956 in Greenwich, Connecticut

John Dowland
English composer–musician
• Greatest lutenist of his age; wrote popular tunes *Songs of Ayres*, 1597-1603.
b. January 1563 in Dublin, Ireland
d. April 07, 1626 in London, England

Morton Downey
American singer
• Irish tenor popular, 1930s-40s; made over 1,500 recordings.
b. November 14, 1902 in Wallingford, Connecticut
d. October 25, 1985 in Palm Beach, Florida

Daryl Dragon
(The Captain and Tennille)
American musician–songwriter
• 1970s hits include "Love Will Keep Us Together."
b. August 27, 1942 in Studio City, California

Jessica Dragonette
Indian opera singer
• Light classical soprano; elected Queen of Radio, 1935; starred eight years on Cities Service Concerts, 1930s.
b. February 14, 1910 in Calcutta, India
d. March 18, 1980 in New York, New York

Alfred Drake
(Alfred Capurro)
American singer–actor–director
• Hit Broadway musicals include *Kiss Me Kate*, 1948; won Tony for *Kismet*, 1954.
b. October 07, 1914 in New York, New York

The Drifters
(Clyde McPhatter; Billy Pickney; Andrew Thrasher; Gerhart Thrasher)
American music group
• Hits included "Save the Last Dance for Me," 1960; "Under the Boardwalk," 1964; Hall of Fame, 1988.

Jacob Raphael Druckman
American composer
• Electronic composer known for ballet scores; won Pulitzer for orchestral work *Windows*, 1972.
b. June 26, 1928 in Philadelphia, Pennsylvania

Spencer Dryden
(Jefferson Airplane)
American singer–musician
• Drummer with Jefferson Airplane, 1965-71.
b. April 07, 1943 in New York, New York

Al Dubin
Swiss lyricist
• Often collaborated with Harry Warren; wrote "42nd Street," "Tiptoe Through the Tulips," 1929.
b. June 1, 1891 in Zurich, Switzerland
d. February 11, 1945 in New York, New York

Eddy Duchin
(Edwin Frank Duchin; "Magic Fingers of Radio")
American bandleader–pianist
• Sophisticated musician known for elegant, intricate style; wrote several books on piano technique.
b. April 01, 1909 in Cambridge, Massachusetts
d. February 09, 1951 in New York, New York

Peter Oelrichs Duchin
American bandleader–pianist
• Son of Eddy Duchin; follows father's style in numerous hotel performances.
b. July 28, 1937 in New York, New York

Vernon Duke
(Vladimir Dukelsky)
American composer
• Film scores include *Cabin in the Sky*, 1940; wrote song "April in Paris."
b. October 1, 1903 in Pskov, Russia
d. January 17, 1969 in Santa Monica, California

Todd (Robert Todd) Duncan
American singer
• Broadway star; performed in over 1,500 concerts, 1944-65; sang at Lyndon Johnson's inaugural concert.
b. February 12, 1903 in Danville, Kentucky

Sonny (Elmer Lewis) Dunham
American musician
• Trumpeter, bandleader, 1930s-40s; soloist with Glen Gray, 1932-40.
b. 1914 in Brockton, Massachusetts

Jacqueline DuPre
English musician
• Cellist, Britain's greatest string player; career cut short when stricken with Multiple Sclerosis, 1972.
b. January 26, 1945 in Oxford, England
d. October 19, 1987 in London, England

Marcel DuPre
French composer–organist
• International concertist; made NYC debut, 1921; wrote organ works.
b. May 03, 1886 in Rouen, France
d. May 3, 1971 in Meudon, France

Duran Duran
(Simon LeBon; Nick Rhodes; Andy Taylor; John Taylor; Roger Taylor)
English music group
• New Romantic band formed, 1978; hit single "Hungry Like a Wolf," 1982.

Ian Dury
English singer–composer
• Blends soul, disco; albums include *Laughter*, 1980.
b. 1942 in Billericay, England

Charles Dutoit
Swiss conductor
• Music director, Montreal Symphony Orchestra, 1977–.
b. October 07, 1936 in Lausanne, Switzerland

Anton Dvorak
Czech composer
• Best known for symphony in E minor, *From the New World*, 1892-95.
b. September 08, 1841 in Nalahozeves, Bohemia
d. May 01, 1904 in Prague, Bohemia

John Bacchus Dykes
English composer–clergyman
• Hymns include "Nearer, My God to Thee," "Lead, Kindly Light."
b. March 1, 1823 in Kingston-upon-Hull, England
d. January 2, 1876 in Ticehurst, England

Bob Dylan
(Robert Zimmerman)
American singer–songwriter
• Songs include "Blowin' in the Wind," 1962; "The Times They Are a'Changin'," 1964; Rock Hall of Fame, 1988.
b. May 24, 1941 in Hibbing, Minnesota

E-Street Band
(Roy Bittan, Clarence Clemons, Daniel Federici, Nils Lofgren, Patty Scialfa, Garry Wayne Tallent, Max M. Weinberg)
American music group
• Back-up band for Bruce Springsteen. Often called world's greatest.

The Eagles
(Don Felder; Glenn Frey; Don Henley; Bernie Leadon; Randy Meiser;Tim Schmidt; Joe Walsh)
American music group
• Sold over 40 million albums; *The Long Run*, 1979, was double platinum.

Emma Hayden Eames
American opera singer
• Soprano; with NY Met., 1891-1909; extremely popular in both Britain, US.
b. August 13, 1865 in Shanghai, China
d. June 13, 1952 in New York, New York

Wind Earth, and Fire
(Philip Bailey; Roland Bautista; Jessica Cleaves; Larry Dunn; Johnny Graham; Ralph Johnson; Al McKay; Fred White; Maurice White; Verdine Wh)
American music group
• Changed sound of black pop music, 1970s; sold over 19 million albums; won six Grammys for *Touch the World*, 1987.

Sheena Easton
(Sheena Shirley Orr)
Scottish singer
• Pop singer who had hit song "Morning Train," 1981; appeared as Sonny's wife on "Miami Vice," 1987.
b. April 27, 1959 in Bellshill, Scotland

Fred Ebb
American lyricist
• With John Kander, wrote song "New York, New York"; won Tonys for *Cabaret*, 1967, *Woman of the Year*, 1980; Songwriter's Hall of Fame, 1983.
b. April 08, 1933 in New York, New York

Ray Eberle
(The Eberle Brothers)
American singer
• Star vocalist for Glen Miller, 1940s; brother of Bob.
b. January 19, 1919 in Hoosick Falls, New York

Bob Eberle
(Robert Eberle; The Eberle Brothers)
American singer–bandleader
• Singer with Dorsey Brothers band; who popularized 1940s hits "Tangerine," 1942; "Green Eyes," 1931.
b. July 24, 1916 in Mechanicville, New York
d. November 17, 1981 in Glen Burnie, Maryland

Billy Eckstine
American singer
• Hits include "Cottage for Sale," 1945; "Prisoner of Love," 1945.
b. July 08, 1914 in Pittsburgh, Pennsylvania

Duane Eddy
American musician
• Guitarist whose instrumental hits include "Rebel Rouser," 1958; "Peter Gunn," 1960.
b. April 26, 1938 in Corning, New York

Nelson Eddy
American singer–actor
• Starred with Jeanette MacDonald 1930's musicals; had voice range of three octaves.
b. June 29, 1901 in Providence, Rhode Island
d. March 06, 1967 in Miami, Florida

Dave Edmunds
(Rockpile)
Welsh musician–producer
• Guitarist who formed Rockpile with Nick Lowe, 1978; hits include "Cruel to be Kind."
b. April 15, 1944 in Cardiff, Wales

Dennis Edwards
(The Temptations)
American singer
• Original member of Temptations; solo single "Don't Look Any Further," 1984.
b. February 03, 1943 in Birmingham, Alabama

Gus Edwards
American songwriter
• Vaudeville star of int'l. fame; portrayed by Bing Crosby in *The Star Maker*, 1939.
b. August 18, 1879 in Hohensaliza, Germany
d. November 07, 1945 in Los Angeles, California

Joan Edwards
American singer–songwriter
• Co-starred with Frank Sinatra in radio show "Your Hit Parade," 1941-46.
b. February 13, 1919 in New York, New York
d. August 27, 1981 in New York, New York

Sherman Edwards
American composer–lyricist
• Wrote music, lyrics for *1776*, 1969; composed scores for Elvis Presley films, 1960s.
b. April 03, 1919 in New York, New York
d. March 3, 1981 in New York, New York

Raymond B Egan
Canadian songwriter
• Popular lyricist, 1920s-30s; hits include "Sleepy Time Gal," 1925.
b. November 14, 1890 in Windsor, Ontario
d. November 13, 1952 in Westport, Connecticut

Walter Lindsay Egan
American singer–songwriter
• Country-rock lyricist, guitarist who had hit album *Hi Fi*, 1979.
b. July 12, 1948 in Jamaica, New York

Marta Eggerth
Hungarian actress–singer
• Starred with husband Jan Kiepura in many filmed operettas in Germany, Austria, 1930s.
b. April 17, 1916 in Budapest, Hungary

Werner Egk
(Werner Mayer)
German composer
• Operas include *Peer Gynt*, 1938; *The Magic Violin*, 1935.
b. May 17, 1901 in Auchsensheim, Germany
d. July 1, 1983 in Inning, Germany (West)

Youri Egorov
Russian pianist
• Concertist; made NYC debut, 1978; noted for virtuoso technique, romantic style.
b. May 28, 1954 in Kazan, Russia
d. April 15, 1988 in Amsterdam, Netherlands

Sixten Ehrling
Swedish conductor
• Head of conducting dept. of Juilliard School, NYC, 1973–; led Detroit Symphony, 1963-73.
b. April 03, 1918 in Malmo, Sweden

Roy (David Roy) Eldridge
American jazz musician
• Trumpeter, drummer; bandleader since 1927; with Goodman, 1950s; became popular as a soloist with Fletcher Henderson band, 1936.
b. January 29, 1911 in Pittsburgh, Pennsylvania
d. February 26, 1989 in Valley Stream, New York

Electric Light Orchestra
(Michael Alberquerque; Bev Bevan; Michael Edwards; Melvyn Gale; Wilf Gibson; Kelly Groucutt; Mik Kaminski; Jeff Lynne; Hugh MacDowell)
English music group
• Orchestral rock group formed, 1971; hits include "Roll Over Beethoven," 1973; "Evil Woman," 1976.

Edward William Elgar, Sir
English composer–conductor–musician
• Best known for oratorios, pomp and circumstance marches, symphonic works in romantic style.
b. June 02, 1857 in Broadheath, England
d. February 23, 1934 in London, England

Les Elgart
American bandleader
• Led popular swing bands, 1950s-60s.
b. August 03, 1918 in New Haven, Connecticut

Yvonne Elliman
(Mrs William Oakes)
American singer
• Sang "I Don't Know How to Love Him," in *Jesus Christ Superstar*.
b. December 29, 1953 in Hawaii

Duke (Edward Kennedy) Ellington
American bandleader–songwriter
• Wrote over 5,000 original works, including "Take the A Train," "Moon Indigo"; outstanding jazz personality; won 1959 Spingarn.
b. April 29, 1899 in Washington, District of Columbia
d. May 24, 1974 in New York, New York

Mercer Ellington
American musician–bandleader
• Son of Duke Ellington; took over orchestra, 1974.
b. March 11, 1919 in Washington, District of Columbia

Cass Elliot
(Ellen Naomi Cohen; Mamas and the Papas)
American singer
• Solo career, 1967-74; hit song "Dream a Little Dream of Me," 1968.
b. February 19, 1943 in Arlington, Virginia
d. July 29, 1974 in London, England

Joe Elliott
(Def Leppard)
English singer
• Lead singer; group named for poster he designed.
b. August 01, 1959 in Sheffield, England

Mischa Elman
American violinist
• Among greatest virtuosos of his time; made NY debut, 1908; noted for romantic interpretations: "Elman Tone."
b. January 21, 1891 in Talnoye, Russia
d. April 05, 1967 in New York, New York

Ziggy Elman
(Harry Finkelman)
American musician
• Trumpet star, 1930s-40s; with Benny Goodman, 1936-40; wrote, recorded hit song "And the Angels Sing," 1939.
b. May 26, 1914 in Philadelphia, Pennsylvania
d. June 26, 1968 in Los Angeles, California

Joe Ely
American musician–singer
• Country-rock singer who had hit album *Notta Gotta Lotta*, 1981.
b. 1947 in Lubbock, Texas

Keith Emerson
(Emerson Lake and Palmer; The Nice)
English musician
• Known for flamboyant performance at keyboards.
b. November 01, 1944 in Todmorden, England

Lake Emerson, and Palmer
(Keith Emerson; Gregory Lake; Carl Palmer)
English music group
• 1960s-70s classical rock band known for hit albums: *Trilogy* ; their biggest song: "Lucky Man," 1971.

Daniel Decatur Emmett
American songwriter
• Early minstral credited with writing "Dixie," 1859.
b. October 29, 1815 in Clinton, Ohio
d. June 28, 1904 in Mount Vernon, Ohio

Georges Enesco
(Georges Enescu)
Romanian violinist–composer
• Wrote opera *Oedipe,* 1936; led NY Philharmonic, 1930s; taught Yehudi Menuhin.
b. August 07, 1881 in Cordaremi, Romania
d. May 04, 1955 in Paris, France

England Dan and John Ford Coley
(John Edward Coley; Danny Seals)
American music group
• Formed during early 1970s; had hit song "I'd Really Love to See You Tonight," 1976.

English Beat
(Dave Blockhead; Andy Cox; Wesley Magoogan; Everett Morton; Ranking Roger; Dave Steele; Dave Wakeling)
English music group
• Revivalist group founded 1979-83; hit album *Special Beat Forces,* 1983.

Skinnay Ennis
American singer–bandleader
• Drummer, noted vocalist with Hal Kemp, 1925-38; band often on Bob Hope's radio shows, 1940s.
b. August 13, 1908 in Salisbury, North Carolina
d. June 05, 1963 in Beverly Hills, California

Brian Eno
(Roxy Music)
English musician–producer
• Co-founder Roxy Music, 1971; solo act since 1973; produced three Talking Heads albums.
b. May 15, 1948 in Woodbridge, England

Phillippe Entremont
French pianist–conductor
• Principal conductor with New Orleans Philharmonic Symphony Orchestra, 1981–; nominated for Grammy, 1972.
b. June 07, 1934 in Reims, France

John Alec Entwistle
(The Who)
English musician–singer
• Joined group, 1964; had solo hit "Too Late the Hero," 1981.
b. September 1, 1944 in London, England

Pee Wee (George) Erwin
American jazz musician–composer
• Swing-era trumpeter who played with Benny Goodman, Tommy Dorsey bands, 1930s; led own band, 1940s-50s.
b. May 3, 1913 in Falls City, Nebraska
d. June 2, 1981 in Teaneck, New Jersey

David Essex
(David Cook)
English singer–actor
• Drummer whose records include "Rock On," 1973; appeared in films *That'll Be the Day,* 1973; *Stardust,* 1975.
b. July 23, 1947 in Plaistow, England

Gloria Estefan
(Gloria Estefan and the Miami Sound Machine)
American singer
• Leading force, principal singer behind Latin-influenced pop band, Miami Sound Machine; first million-selling album *Primitive Love,* 1986.
b. September 01, 1957 in Havana, Cuba

Ruth Etting
American singer
• Popular Ziegfeld, radio star, 1920s-30s; revived "Shine On Harvest Moon"; Doris Day portrayed her in *Love Me Or Leave Me,* 1955.
b. November 23, 1897 in David City, Nebraska
d. September 24, 1978 in Colorado Springs, Colorado

Eurythmics
(Annie Lennox; David Stewart)
British music group
• Synthesizer-based duo who had number-one hit "Sweet Dreams," 1983; "Missionary Man," 1986.

Bill (William John) Evans
American pianist–composer
• Jazz virtuoso who formed trio, 1956, won five Grammys.
b. August 16, 1929 in Plainfield, New Jersey
d. September 01, 1980 in New York, New York

Ray Evans
American composer
• Won Oscars for songs "Buttons and Bows," 1948; "Mona Lisa," 1950; "Que Sera Sera," 1956.
b. February 04, 1915 in Salamanca, New York

Don Everly
(Everly Brothers)
American singer–musician
• With brother Phil, had international country hit, "Bye Bye Love," 1957.
b. February 01, 1937 in Brownie, Kentucky

Phil Everly
(Everly Brothers)
American singer–musician
• With brother Don, had two million-selling single, "Cathy's Clown," 1962.
b. January 19, 1939 in Chicago, Illinois

Everly Brothers
(Don Everly; Phil Everly)
American music group
• Number-one hits include "Let It Be Me," 1960; "All I Have to Do Is Dream," 1958; disbanded, 1973, reunited, 1980s.

Exile
(Buzz Cornelison; Steven Goetzman; Mark Gray; Marlon Hargis; Sonny Lemaire; J P Pennington; Jimmy Stokley; Les Taylor)
American music group
• Country group from KY; had number one hit "Kiss You All Over," 1978.

Fabian
(Fabian Forte)
American singer–actor
• Teen idol of 1950-60s; 1959 hits include "Turn Me Loose"; "Hound Dog Man."
b. February 06, 1943 in Philadelphia, Pennsylvania

The Faces
(Kenney Jones; Ronnie Lane; Ian MacLagan; Rod Stewart; Ron Wood)
British music group
• High energy rock band, formed 1968; hit singles include "Stay With Me," 1971. Known for sloppy, inspired playing.

Donald Fagen
(Steely Dan)
American singer–songwriter
• Wrote songs for Steely Dan; solo single "New Frontier," 1983.
b. January 1, 1948 in Passaic, New Jersey

Sammy Fain
American singer–pianist
• Prolific songwriter, 1920s-60s; had 10 Oscar nominations; hits include "I'll Be Seeing You," 1938; "That Old Feeling," 1937.
b. June 17, 1902 in New York, New York
d. December 05, 1989 in Los Angeles, California

Fairport Convention
(Simon Nichol; Dave Pegg; Bruce Rowland; Dave Swarbrick)
British music group
• Music mixes rock, blues, celtic, cajun; albums include *Farewell Farewell*, 1979.

Adam Faith
(Terence Nelhams)
English singer–actor
• Hit songs include "We Are in Love," 1963; in film *Stardust*, 1974.
b. June 23, 1940 in London, England

Percy Faith
Canadian conductor
• Nominated for Oscar for film score *Love Me or Leave Me*, 1955; wrote "My Heart Cries for You," 1950; noted for full, mellow sound in albums since 1940s.
b. April 07, 1908 in Toronto, Ontario
d. February 09, 1976 in Los Angeles, California

Marianne Faithfull
English singer–actress
• Had hit with Jagger/Richard song "As Tears Go By," 1964.
b. December 29, 1946 in London, England

Abdul Fakir
(Four Tops)
American singer
• With Motown group formed 1954; achieved success, 1964, with top single "Baby I Need Your Loving."
b. 1938 in Detroit, Michigan

Falco
(Johann Holzel)
Austrian musician
• Int'l. rock performer known for Mozart character in videos; recorded top-10 hit "Rock Me, Amadeus," 1985.
b. February 19, 1957 in Vienna, Austria

Agnetha Faltskog
(ABBA)
Swedish singer
• Known for high vocal range; solo single "Can't Shake Loose," 1983.
b. April 05, 1950 in Stockholm, Sweden

Georgie Fame
(Clive Powell)
English singer–musician–composer
• Songs include "Sunny," 1966; "Ballad of Bonnie and Clyde," 1967.
b. June 26, 1943 in Leigh, England

Donna Fargo
(Yvonne Vaughan)
American singer–songwriter
• Country singer; hits include "Happiest Girl in the USA"; "Funny Face."
b. November 1, 1949 in Mount Airy, North Carolina

Richard Farina
American author–singer
• Part of folk music scene, 1960s; wrote *Been Down So Long It Looks Like Up To Me*, 1966.
b. 1936 in Brooklyn, New York
d. April 3, 1966 in Carmel, California

Farinelli
(Carlo Broschi; "Il Ragazzo")
Italian opera singer
• Most famed male soprano of 18th century; women fainted in Venice, London while listening.
b. January 24, 1705 in Andria, Italy
d. July 15, 1782 in Bologna, Italy

Arthur Stewart Farmer
American jazz musician
• Trumpeter, fluegelhornist; led own combo, 1960s.
b. August 21, 1928 in Council Bluffs, Arkansas

Geraldine Farrar
American opera singer
• Celebrated soprano; sang 500 times in 29 roles, NY Met., 1906-22; often starred with Caruso.
b. February 28, 1882 in Melrose, Massachusetts
d. March 11, 1967 in Ridgefield, Connecticut

Eileen Farrell
American opera singer
• Popular soprano; starred in own radio show, 1940s; made NY Met., debut, 1960; noted Wagnerian singer; Grammy winner.
b. February 13, 1920 in Willimantic, Connecticut

Johann Friedrich Fasch
German composer
• Wrote operas, church cantatas, 12 Masses, 69 overtures.
b. April 15, 1688 in Buttelstedt, Germany
d. December 05, 1758 in Zerbst, Germany

Gabriel Urbain Faure
French composer–musician
• Wrote piano works, chamber music; known for grace, delicacy, finesse; wrote *Requiem*, 1888; song "Clair de Lune."
b. May 12, 1845 in Pamiers, France
d. November 04, 1924 in Paris, France

Charles Simon Favart
French composer
• Originated modern light opera; director, Opera Comique, Paris, 1758-69; wrote 150 comedies, operettas.
b. November 13, 1710 in Paris, France
d. March 12, 1792 in Belleville, France

Alice Faye
(Ann Leppert)
American actress–singer
• Beautiful blonde musical star, 1930s-40s; wife of Phil Harris; in *Alexander's Ragtime Band*, 1938.
b. May 05, 1915 in New York, New York

Leonard Geoffrey Feather
American composer–critic
• Leading jazz spokesman, 1940s-50s; hosted Jazz Club, US series; wrote jazz reference books.
b. September 13, 1914 in London, England

Daniel Paul Federici
(E Street Band; "Phantom")
American musician
• Plays keyboards, accordion with Bruce Springsteen's band since 1968.
b. January 23, 1950 in Flemington, New Jersey

Michael Jay Feinstein
American musician
• Recording, cabaret pianist; known for romantic works by George Gershwin, Cole Porter.
b. September 07, 1956 in Columbus, Ohio

Don(ald William) Felder
(The Eagles)
American musician–singer–songwriter
• Joined the Eagles as lead guitarist, songwriter, 1973; recorded title song from movie *Heavy Metal*, 1981.
b. September 21, 1947 in Gainesville, Florida

Morton Feldman
American composer
• Leading avant-garde composer noted for developing use of hypnotic repetition; operas include *Neither*.
b. January 12, 1926 in New York, New York
d. September 03, 1987 in Buffalo, New York

Jose Feliciano
American singer–musician
• Blind singer, guitarist; composed theme for TV show "Chico and the Man"; best-known single: "Light My Fire," 1968.
b. September 1, 1945 in Lares, Puerto Rico

Freddy Fender
(Baldermar Huerta)
American singer–songwriter
• Won Grammy, 1977, for "Before the Next Teardrop Falls."
b. June 04, 1937 in San Benito, Texas

Fania Fenelon
(Fanny Goldstein)
French author–singer–musician
• Memoirs, *Playing for Time* 1977, telling horrors of Nazi concentration camps, made into film starring Vanessa Redgrave, 1985.
b. September 02, 1918 in Paris, France
d. December 2, 1983 in Paris, France

Frederick Fennell
American conductor
• Founded Eastman Wind Ensemble, 1952, made numerous albums; guest conductor with Boston Pops.
b. July 02, 1914 in Cleveland, Ohio

Maynard Ferguson
Canadian jazz musician
• Headline trumpeter, 1950s; noted for powerful highnote work; led own bands, 1960s-70s; hit album, *Conquistador*, 1978.
b. May 04, 1928 in Verdun, Quebec

Arthur Ferrante
(Ferrante and Teicher)
American pianist–composer
• Member of two-piano team; popularity peaked in late 1960s, with many records, concerts.
b. September 07, 1921 in New York, New York

Kathleen Ferrier
English opera singer
• Considered remarkable contralto; Benjamin Britten created title roles for her.
b. April 22, 1912 in Higher Walter, England
d. October 08, 1953 in London, England

Bryan Ferry
(Roxy Music)
English singer–songwriter
• Lead vocalist, principal songwriter for Roxy Music; solo album *Let's Stick Together*, 1976 and several others.
b. September 26, 1945 in Durham, England

Francois Joseph Fetis
Belgian musicologist–composer
• Wrote biographies of musicians, theoretical works; founded *Revue Musicale*, 1827, first musical criticism periodical.
b. March 25, 1784 in Mons, Belgium
d. March 26, 1871 in Brussels, Belgium

Emanuel Feuermann
American musician
• Cellist, appeared with many leading US orchestras, 1935–; played chamber music with Rubenstein, Heifetz.
b. November 22, 1902 in Kolomea, Galicia
d. May 25, 1942 in New York, New York

Arthur Fiedler
American conductor
• Led Boston Pops Orchestra, 1930-79; credited with elevating it to status of nat. institution through TV series, holiday concerts.
b. December 17, 1894 in Boston, Massachusetts
d. July 1, 1979 in Brookline, Massachusetts

John Field
Irish pianist–composer
• Originated keyboard nocturnes, used as models by Chopin; lived mostly in Russia.
b. July 26, 1782 in Dublin, Ireland
d. January 11, 1837 in Moscow, Russia

Dorothy Fields
American songwriter
• Won Oscar for lyrics to "The Way You Look Tonight"; contributed lyrics to 400 film songs.
b. July 15, 1905 in Allenhurst, New Jersey
d. March 28, 1974 in New York, New York

Shep Fields
(Rippling Rhythm Orchestra)
American bandleader
• Led 1930s-40s orchestra, noted for distinctive bubbling sound.
b. September 12, 1910 in Brooklyn, New York
d. February 23, 1981 in Los Angeles, California

Fifth Dimension
(Daniel Beard; William Davis Jr; Florence LaRue Gordon; MarilynMcCoo; Lamonte McLemore; Ronald Townson)
American music group
• Hits include "Up, Up and Away," 1967; "Aquarius," 1969.

Sylvia Fine
(Mrs Danny Kaye)
American lyricist–producer
• Wrote comedy scripts for husband; songs include "The Moon Is Blue," "Anatole of Paris."
b. August 29, 1893 in New York, New York

Ted Fiorito
American bandleader–songwriter
• Had 50-yr. career as pianist, bandleader; wrote song "Toot, Toot, Tootie, Goodbye."
b. December 2, 1900 in Newark, New Jersey
d. July 22, 1971 in Scottsdale, Arizona

Louis Firbank
(Velvet Underground)
American jazz musician–songwriter
• Lead guitarist, Velvet Underground, 1967-70; albums include *Walk on the Wild Side*.
b. March 02, 1942 in Brooklyn, New York

Firefall
(Mark Andes; Jock Bartley; Larry Burnett; Michael Clarke; Rick Roberts)
American music group
• Pop-country group formed 1974; hit single "You Are the Woman," 1976.

Rudolf Firkusny
American musician
• Celebrated 60 yrs. as int'l. concert pianist, 1983; favored Czech composers.
b. February 11, 1912 in Napajedla, Czechoslovakia

Eddie (Edwin Jack) Fisher
American singer
• "O, My Papa," 1953 million-selling hit; married to Debbie Reynolds, Elizabeth Taylor, Connie Stevens.
b. August 1, 1928 in Philadelphia, Pennsylvania

Fred Fisher
American composer
• Co-wrote "Peg 'O My Heart," 1913.
b. September 3, 1875 in Cologne, Germany
d. January 14, 1942 in New York, New York

Ella Fitzgerald
American singer
• Jazz singer adept at improvising, scat; has won eight Grammys.
b. April 25, 1918 in Newport News, Virginia

The Fixx
(Charlie Barrett; Cy Curnin; Rupert Greenall; Jamie West-Oram; Adam Woods)
English music group
• New wave group who released albums *Shattered Room*, 1982; *Reach the Beach*, 1983.

Robert Fizdale
American musician
• Pianist teamed with Arthur Gold since 1944; toured extensively, with works written for them; wrote *Misia*, 1979.
b. April 12, 1920 in Chicago, Illinois

Roberta Flack
American singer
• Won Grammys for "The First Time Ever I Saw Your Face," 1972; "Killing Me Softly," 1973.
b. February 1, 1940 in Black Mountain, North Carolina

Kirsten Flagstad
Norwegian opera singer
• Considered greatest Wagnerian soprano of day; "Isolde" most celebrated role.
b. July 12, 1895 in Oslo, Norway
d. December 07, 1962 in Oslo, Norway

Lester Raymond Flatt
(Flatt and Scruggs)
American musician–singer
• Teamed with Earl Scruggs 25 yrs.; hits include "Roll in My Sweet Baby's Arms"; "The Ballad of Jed Clampett," theme from TV's "Beverly Hillbillies."
b. June 28, 1914 in Overton County, Tennessee
d. May 11, 1979 in Nashville, Tennessee

Mick Fleetwood
(Fleetwood Mac)
English musician
• Drummer since 1967; recorded 1980 solo album *The Visitor* in Ghana.
b. June 24, 1942 in Cornwall, England

Fleetwood Mac
(Lindsey Buckingham; Mick Fleetwood; Christine McVie; John McVie;Stevie Nicks; Bob Welch; Robert Weston)
English music group
• Album *Rumours*, 1977, second biggest selling album of all time.

Leon Fleisher
American pianist–conductor
• Brilliant concert pianist, 1952-64; right hand paralyzed, 1965; successful conductor, 1970s; comeback as bimanual pianist, 1982.
b. July 23, 1928 in San Francisco, California

Karl Flesch
Hungarian violinist–teacher
• Founded Curtis String Quartet; wrote classic text on violin playing, 1924-30, translated into 22 languages.
b. October 09, 1873 in Moson, Hungary
d. November 15, 1944 in Lausanne, Switzerland

Flock of Seagulls
(Frank Maudsley; Paul Reynolds; Ali Score; Mike Score)
British music group
• Hit single, "I Ran," 1982; only British band to win Grammy, 1983.

Myron Floren
American musician
• Accordion player on "The Lawrence Welk Show."
b. November 05, 1919 in Webster, South Dakota

Carlisle Sessions Floyd
American composer
• His opera *Wuthering Heights* had NY premiere, 1959; also wrote *Of Mice and Men*, 1970.
b. June 11, 1926 in Latta, South Carolina

The Flying Burrito Brothers
(Chris Ethridge; Chris Hillman; Sneaky Pete Kleinow; Gram Parsons)
American music group
• Band formed 1969 to introduce country music to rock enthusiasts; hit album *Gilded Place of Sin*, 1969.

Eugene Nicholas Fodor
American violinist
• Popular concert soloist; shared top honors at Moscow's Tchaikovsky competition, 1974.
b. March 05, 1950 in Denver, Colorado

Josef Bohuslav Foerster
Czech composer
• Wrote five symphonies, six operas including *Nepremozeni*, 1918.
b. December 3, 1859 in Prague, Czechoslovakia
d. May 29, 1951 in Novy Vestec, Czechoslovakia

Dan(iel Grayling) Fogelberg
American composer–singer
• First hit song "Part of the Plan," 1975; recent hit "Leader of the Band," 1982.
b. August 13, 1951 in Peoria, Illinois

Foghat
(Roger Earl; David Peverett; Rod Price; Anthony Stevens)
British music group
• Formed, 1971; hit single "Slow Ride," 1976.

Red (Clyde Julian) Foley
American singer
• Founding father of country music; starred in "Ozark Mountain Jubilee," 1955-61; Hall of Fame, 1967.
b. June 17, 1910 in Bluelick, Kentucky
d. September 19, 1968 in Fort Wayne, Indiana

Frank Fontaine
American comedian–singer
• Best known for appearances on "The Jackie Gleason Show," 1960s.
b. April 19, 1920 in Haverhill, Massachusetts
d. August 04, 1978 in Spokane, Washington

Arthur William Foote
American composer–organist
• Wrote overture *In the Mountains*, 1887.
b. March 05, 1853 in Salem, Massachusetts
d. April 08, 1937 in Boston, Massachusetts

Mary Ford
(Irene Colleen Summers; Les Paul and Mary Ford)
American singer–musician
• Popular in early 1950s with husband, Les Paul; known for multiple harmony effects: "How High the Moon," 1951.
b. July 07, 1924 in Waukesha, Wisconsin
d. September 3, 1977 in Los Angeles, California

Tennessee Ernie (Ernest J) Ford
American singer
• TV star, 1950s-60s; sang gospel, country music; hit song, "Sixteen Tons," 1955.
b. February 13, 1919 in Bristol, Tennessee

Foreigner
(Dennis Elliott; Ed Gagliardi; Lou Gramm; Al Greenwood; Mick Jones; Ian McDonald; Rick Wills)
English music group
• Pop-rock hits include "Waiting for a Girl Like You," 1981.

Helen Forrest
American singer
• Big band vocalist, 1930s-40s; made films with Harry James; hosted radio show with Dick Haymes, 1940s.
b. April 12, 1918 in Atlantic City, New Jersey

David Foster
Canadian musician–songwriter
• Keyboardist; recorded many hits with various artists including "Thriller," 1983; won five Grammys.
b. 1950 in Canada

Pops (George Murphy) Foster
American jazz musician
• Dixieland bassist; 60 yr. career covered pioneer jazz days to 1960s.
b. May 19, 1892 in McCall, Louisiana
d. October 3, 1969 in San Francisco, California

Stephen Collins Foster
American composer
• Best known songs "Oh Susannah," 1848; "My Old Kentucky Home," 1853.
b. July 04, 1826 in Pittsburgh, Pennsylvania
d. July 13, 1864 in New York, New York

Susanna Foster
(Suzanne De Lee Flanders Larson)
American singer–actress
• Best known for remake of *Phantom of the Opera*, 1943.
b. December 06, 1924 in Chicago, Illinois

Pete(r Dewey) Fountain
American jazz musician
• Dixieland clarinetist; starred on Lawrence Welk's show, 1957-60; owned New Orleans club, 1960s-70s.
b. July 03, 1930 in New Orleans, Louisiana

The Four Freshmen
(Ken Albers; Don Barbour; Ross Barbour; Ray Brown; Bill Comstock;Ken Errair; Bob Flanagan; Hal Kratzch)
American music group
• Innovators of tight harmony sound, late 1940s; hit singles "It's a Blue World," 1952; "Graduation Day," 1956.

The Four Lads
(James Arnold; Frank Busseri; Connie Codarini; Bernard Toorish)
Canadian music group
• Former choirboys; hit singles "Moments to Remember"; "No Not Much."

The Four Seasons
(Tommy DeVito; Bob Gaudio; Nick Massi; Frankie Valli)
American music group
• Doo-wop group, begun 1956; number one hits "Sherry"; "Big Girls Don't Cry"; "Rag Doll."

Four Tops
(Renaldo Benson; Abdul Fakir; Lawrence Payton; Levi Stubbs)
American music group
• Hits include "Baby I Need Your Loving," 1964; "Reach Out I'll Be There," 1966.

Pierre Fournier
French musician
• International concert cellist, 1940s-60s.
b. June 24, 1906 in Paris, France
d. January 08, 1986 in Geneva, Switzerland

Peter Frampton
(Humble Pie)
American singer–songwriter
• Album *Frampton Comes Alive!* 1976, sold over 12 million copies.
b. April 22, 1950 in Beckenham, England

Jean Francaix
French composer–musician
• Works include opera: *La Princesse de Cleves*, 1965.
b. May 23, 1912 in Le Mans, France

Zino Rene Francescatti
French musician
• Brilliant concertist, 1920s-60s; played Beethoven's violin concerto with orchestra at age 10.
b. August 09, 1902 in Marseilles, France

Connie Francis
(Concetta Maria Franconero)
American singer
• Popular, award-winning vocalist, 1950s-60s; made eight gold records; starred in, sang title song for *Where the Boys Are*, 1963.
b. December 12, 1938 in Newark, New Jersey

Cesar Auguste Franck
French organist–composer
• Notable works include piano pieces, oratorios, "Symphony in D-minor," 1888.
b. December 1, 1822 in Liege, Belgium
d. November 08, 1890 in Paris, France

Franco
(L'Okanga La Ndju Pene Luambo Makladi)
African bandleader–musician
• One of Africa's most popular, influential musicians; created soukous style, a fusion of Afro-Cuban music with jazz, gospel, and African rhythms.
b. 1938
d. October 12, 1989 in Brussels, Belgium

Aretha Franklin
American singer
• Popular Motown star; hits include "Respect," 1967; "Freeway of Love," 1985.
b. March 25, 1942 in Memphis, Tennessee

Mel(vin) Franklin
(The Temptations)
American singer
• Top Motown group, formed 1962; hits include "My Girl," 1965.
b. October 12, 1942 in Montgomery, Alabama

Dallas June Frazier
American singer–songwriter
• Songs include country hits "Elvira"; "Fourteen Carat Mind," 1982; songwriter international Hall of Fame, 1976.
b. October 27, 1939 in Spiro, Oklahoma

Stan Freberg
American composer–author
• Satire on soap operas, "John and Martha," became nat. hit, 1951; developed TV puppet show "Time for Beanie," 1949-54.
b. August 07, 1926 in Pasadena, California

Free
(Rabbit Bundrick; Tetsu Kamauchi; Kirke; Wendell Richardson; Paul Rodgers)
British music group
• High-energy band known for understated music; formed, 1968; songs include "All Right Now," 1970; "Free," 1978.

Alan Freed
American radio performer–songwriter
• Unorthodox 1950s dj who introduced term "rock and roll"; career ruined by payola scandal, early 1960s.
b. December 15, 1922 in Johnstown, Pennsylvania
d. January 2, 1965 in Palm Springs, California

Bud (Lawrence) Freeman
American jazz musician
• Great tenor saxist, 1930s-60s; prolific recorder; charter member, "World's Greatest Jazz Band."
b. April 13, 1906 in Chicago, Illinois

Ace Frehley
(Kiss)
American singer–musician
• Guitarist; released solo album, 1978.
b. April 27, 1951 in Bronx, New York

Jay Jay French
(Twisted Sister)
American musician
• Guitarist with heavy metal group formed 1976.
b. July 2, 1954 in New York, New York

Mirella Freni
Italian opera singer
• Soprano; sang Mimi in La Scala's film version of *La Boheme*, 1963.
b. February 27, 1935 in Modena, Italy

Girolamo Frescobaldi
Italian organist–composer
• Organist at St. Peters; noted for keyboard compositions, monothematic writings; greatly influenced Baroque music.
b. 1583 in Ferrara, Italy
d. March 02, 1644 in Rome, Italy

Glenn Frey
(The Eagles)
American musician–songwriter–singer
• Released solo album *No Fun Aloud*, 1982; hits include "You Belong To The City," 1985.
b. November 06, 1948 in Detroit, Michigan

Janie Frickie
American singer–musician
• Had hit single "Down to My Last Broken Heart," 1980; CMA's female vocalist of year, 1982, 1983.
b. December 18, 1950 in Whitney, Indiana

Gerald Fried
American composer
• Won Emmy for score of TV mini-series "Roots," 1977.
b. February 13, 1928 in New York, New York

Frijid Pink
(Thomas Beaudry; Thomas Harris; Richard Stevers; Gary Thompson; Jon Wearing; Craig Webb; Lawrence Zelanka)
American music group
• Heavy-metal band, 1970s; biggest hit a remake of "House of the Rising Sun," 1970.

Rudolf Friml
American musician–composer
• Noted for Broadway operettas *Rose Marie*, 1924; *Vagabond King*, 1925; wrote songs "Indian Love Call," 1924; "The Donkey Serenade," 1937.
b. December 07, 1879 in Prague, Bohemia
d. November 12, 1972 in Hollywood, California

Lefty (William Orville) Frizzell
American singer
• Had number-one country hit, "Saginaw, Michigan," 1964; four singles on top-ten list at once, 1952.
b. March 31, 1928 in Corsicana, Texas
d. July 19, 1975 in Nashville, Tennessee

Jane Froman
American actress–singer
• Suffered crippling injuries in 1943 plane crash en route to entertain troops; inspiration for film *With a Song in My Heart*, 1952.
b. November 1, 1907 in Saint Louis, Missouri
d. April 22, 1980 in Columbia, Missouri

Joseph Fuchs
American violinist
• International concertist, 1950s-60s; performed new works of modern composers.
b. April 26, 1900 in New York, New York

The Fugs
(John Anderson; Lee Crabtree; Pete Kearney; Tuli Kupferberg; Charles Larkey; Vinny Leary; Bob Mason; Ken Pine; Ed Sanders; Peter Stampfield)
American music group
• Formed theater, music group, 1965; satirized politics, rock, sexual repression.

Funkadelic
(Mickey Atkins; Tiki Fulwood; Edward Hazel; William Nelson Jr; Lucas Tunia "Tawl")
American music group
• Dance band founded 1969; worked with George Clinton, Parliament; hits include "Knee Deep," 1979.

Richie Furay
(Buffalo Springfield; Poco; The Souther-Hillman-Furay Band)
American musician
• Country-rock singer in various bands; solo single "I Still Have Dreams," 1979.
b. May 09, 1944 in Yellow Springs, Ohio

Wilhelm Furtwangler
German conductor
• Led Vienna Symphony, Berlin State Opera, 1930s; absolved of pro-Nazi activities, 1946; noted for interpretations of Wagner, Beethoven.
b. January 25, 1886 in Berlin, Germany
d. November 3, 1954 in Eberstein, Germany (West)

Billy Fury
(Ronald Wycherly)
English singer
• Began as rock singer, found success in ballads; hits include "That's Love," 1960; "In Thoughts of You," 1965.
b. April 17, 1941 in Liverpool, England
d. January 29, 1983 in London, England

Peter Gabriel
(Genesis)
English singer–songwriter
• Genesis main vocalist, songwriter, 1968-75; noted for bizarre theatricals; hit album *Sledgehammer*, 1986.
b. May 13, 1950 in England

Giovanni Gabrieli
Italian composer–musician
• Developed multiple-choir technique; works mark start of modern orchestration; an organist at St. Mark's, Venice.
b. 1557 in Venice, Italy
d. August 12, 1612 in Venice, Italy

Ossip Gabrilowitsch
American conductor-pianist
• Led Detroit Symphony, 1918-36; wed to Mark Twain's daughter, often appeared in concert with her.
b. January 26, 1878 in Saint Petersburg, Russia
d. September 14, 1936 in Detroit, Michigan

Niels Wilhelm Grade
Danish composer
• Wrote romantic style symphonies, cantatas; founded modern Scandinavian school of composition.
b. February 22, 1817 in Copenhagen, Denmark
d. December 21, 1890 in Copenhagen, Denmark

(Otho) Lee Gaines
(Delta Rhythm Boys)
American composer–singer
• Founded gospel-blues quartet, Delta Rhythm Boys, 1933; popular, 1940s-50s.
b. April 21, 1914 in Houston, Mississippi
d. July 15, 1987 in Helsinki, Finland

Steve Gaines
(Lynyrd Skynard)
American musician
• Joined band as guitarist, 1976; killed in a private plane crash.
b. 1949
d. October 2, 1977 in Mississippi

Gallagher and Lyle
(Benny Gallagher; Graham Lyle)
British music group
• Duo formed, 1972-79; Lyle wrote Tina Turner's hit "What's Love Got to do With It?"

Rory Gallagher
Irish musician
• Blues-rock guitarist who formed trio Taste, 1965-71; Gallagher band, 1971.
b. March 02, 1949 in Ballyshannon, Ireland

Baldassare Galuppi
Italian composer
• Thirty comic operas include *Filosofo di Campagna*, 1754.
b. October 18, 1706 in Burano, Italy
d. January 03, 1785 in Venice, Italy

James Galway
Irish musician
• Celebrated flutist; with Royal Philharmonic, 1960s; concert artist, 1970s-80s; made numerous TV appearances.
b. December 08, 1939 in Belfast, Northern Ireland

Gang of Four
(Hugo Burnham; Andy Gill; Jon King; Sara Lee)
British music group
• Rhythm and blues/disco group, formed 1978; albums include *At the Palace*, 1984.

Jan Garber
American bandleader
• Led sweet-style dance band, especially popular, 1930s.
b. 1895
d. October 05, 1977 in Shreveport, Louisiana

Jerry (Jerome John) Garcia
(The Grateful Dead)
American musician–singer
• Founder, lead guitarist of acid-rock band, 1960s.
b. August 01, 1942 in San Francisco, California

Manuel del Popolo Vincente Garcia
Spanish opera singer–composer
• Famed tenor; starred in first US performance of *Don Giovanni*, 1820s.
b. January 22, 1775 in Seville, Spain
d. June 02, 1832 in Paris, France

Mary Garden
Scottish opera singer
• Soprano chosen by Debussy for premiere performance of *Pellas et Melisande*, 1902; awarded French Legion of Honor.
b. February 2, 1874 in Aberdeen, Scotland
d. January 04, 1967 in Aberdeen, Scotland

Art(hur) Garfunkel
(Simon and Garfunkel)
American singer–actor–poet
• Best-known songs with Paul Simon include "Bridge Over Troubled Water," 1969; "Mrs. Robinson," 1968.
b. October 13, 1942 in Forest Hills, New York

Erroll Garner
American jazz musician–songwriter
• Self-taught pianist; popular on TV, 1950s-60s; wrote music to "Misty," 1955.
b. June 15, 1921 in Pittsburgh, Pennsylvania
d. January 02, 1977 in Los Angeles, California

Gale Garnett
New Zealander actress–singer
• Wrote, performed, "We'll Sing in the Sunshine," 1964, which won Grammy.
b. July 17, 1942 in New Zealand

Leif Garrett
American actor–singer
• Teen idol whose hit single was a re-make of "Surfin' USA."
b. November 08, 1961 in Hollywood, California

John Gary
(John Gary Strader)
American singer
• 1960s balladeer on TV, radio, records; still active in nightclubs, known for mellow delivery; invented Aqualung diving aid.
b. November 29, 1932 in Watertown, New York

Gary Puckett and the Union Gap
(Dwight Cement; Kerry Chater; Gary Puckett; Paul Wheatbread; Mutha Withem)
American music group
• Late 1960s rock group known for wearing Civil War uniforms; hits include "Young Girl," 1968, "This Girl Is a Woman Now," 1969.

David Gates
(Bread)
American singer–songwriter
• Solo guitarist, lead singer of soft-rock group Bread, 1969-73.
b. December 11, 1940 in Tulsa, Oklahoma

Larry Wayne Gatlin
American singer–songwriter
• Lead singer in country-pop group Gatlin Brothers; won Grammy for single "Broken Lady," 1976.
b. May 02, 1948 in Seminole, Texas

Bob Gaudio
(The Four Seasons)
American musician–songwriter
• Keyboardist with original Four Seasons, 1962-69; wrote group hit songs "Who Loves You," 1975, "December, 1963 (Oh, What a Night)," 1975.
b. November 17, 1942 in Bronx, New York

Marvin Pentz Gaye
American singer
• Had several gold, platinum hits, 1962-83; won two Grammys, 1983; hits include "Ain't That Peculiar," 1965; "Sexual Healing," 1982.
b. April 02, 1939 in Washington, District of Columbia
d. April 01, 1984 in Los Angeles, California

Crystal Gayle
(Mrs Vassilios Gatzimos; Brenda Gail Webb)
American singer
• Country-pop singer; sister of Loretta Lynn, known for trademark long hair; won Grammy, 1978, for "Don't It Make My Brown Eyes Blue."
b. January 09, 1951 in Paintsville, Kentucky

Gloria Gaynor
American singer
• Hits include "Never Can Say Goodbye," 1974; "I Will Survive," 1979.
b. September 07, 1949 in Newark, New Jersey

Mitzi Gaynor
(Francesca Mitzi Marlene de Charney von Gerber)
American singer–dancer
• Starred in film version of *South Pacific*, 1958.
b. September 04, 1931 in Chicago, Illinois

Ricky Gazda
(Southside Johnny and the Asbury Jukes)
American musician
• Trumpeter with group since 1974.
b. June 18, 1952

Giuseppe Gazzaniga
Italian composer
• Wrote numerous opera buffa; noted for one-act *Don Giovanni Tenorio*, 1786.
b. 1743 in Verona, Italy
d. February 01, 1818 in Crema, Italy

Severino Gazzelloni
Italian musician
• Internationally noted flutist, largely responsible for renaissance of instrument.
b. January 05, 1919 in Roccasecca, Italy

Bob Geldof
(Boomtown Rats; "Saint Bob")
Irish actor–musician–singer
• Organizer of Live-Aid, which raised $84 million for African famine, July 1985.
b. October 05, 1954 in Dublin, Ireland

Peter Gellhorn
German conductor
• Led BBC Chorus, 1961-72; conductor for several opera companies.
b. October 24, 1912 in Breslau, Germany

Francesco Geminiani
Italian violinist–composer
• Virtuoso; wrote first published violin method, 1730.
b. February 05, 1687 in Lucca, Italy
d. December 17, 1762 in Dublin, Ireland

Maurice Gendron
French musician
• Internationally known concert cellist who recorded with Pablo Casals.
b. December 26, 1920 in Nice, France

Genesis
(Tony Banks; Bill Bruford; Phil Collins; Peter Gabriel; Steve Hackett; John Mayhew; Anthony Phillips; Michael Rutherford; John Silver)
English music group
• Formed 1966 as theatrical cult band; currently pop group with Phil Collins as lead singer.

Bobbie Gentry
(Roberta Streeter)
American singer–songwriter
• Wrote, recorded "Ode to Billy Joe," 1967; won three Grammys, adapted to film, 1976.
b. July 27, 1942 in Chicasaw County, Mississippi

Don George
American songwriter
• Best known for "The Yellow Rose of Texas," 1955, adapted from 1860s minstrel song.
b. August 27, 1909 in New York, New York

Graham Elias George
English composer
• Wrote opera *Evangeline*, ballet, *Peter Pan*, 1948; several anthems.
b. April 11, 1912 in Norwich, England

Gerry and the Pacemakers
(John Chadwick; Les Maguire; Freddie Marsden; Gerry Marsden)
English music group
• Pop group from Liverpool; had hits "Don't Let the Sun Catch You Crying," 1964; "Ferry Cross the Mersey," 1965.

George Gershwin
(Jacob Gershvin)
American composer
• Wrote innovative folk opera *Porgy and Bess*, 1935; semiclassical orchestral works include *Rhapsody in Blue*, 1924; won first Pulitzer for a musical: *Of Thee I Sing*, 1931; often worked with lyricist brother, Ira.
b. September 26, 1898 in Brooklyn, New York
d. July 11, 1937 in Hollywood, California

Ira Gershwin
(Authur Francis pseud)
American lyricist
• Brother of George; wrote lyrics for *Porgy and Bess; An American in Paris*.
b. December 06, 1896 in New York, New York
d. August 17, 1983 in Beverly Hills, California

Stan Getz
American jazz musician
• Tenor saxist, "cool" jazz exponent popular 1950s-70s; won several awards for bossa-nova recordings.
b. February 02, 1927 in Philadelphia, Pennsylvania

Vittorio Giannini
American composer
• Operas include *The Scarlet Letter*, 1938.
b. October 19, 1903 in Philadelphia, Pennsylvania
d. November 28, 1966 in New York, New York

Felice de Giardini
Italian musician–composer–impresario
• Violin virtuoso; directed Italian Opera at London's King Theater, 1755-95.
b. 1716
d. 1796

Andy Gibb
(The Bee Gees)
English singer–songwriter–musician
• Albums include *Shadow Dancing*, 1970s.
b. March 05, 1958 in Manchester, England
d. March 1, 1988 in Oxford, England

Barry Gibb
(The Bee Gees; Douglas Gibb)
English singer–songwriter
• Guitarist, songwriter; album *Saturday Night Fever* soundtrack sold 50 million copies, 1976-79.
b. September 01, 1946 in Manchester, England

Maurice Gibb
(The Bee Gees)
English singer–songwriter
• With group of brothers won six Grammys, 1977, 1978, for such hits as *Saturday Night Fever* Soundtrack.
b. December 22, 1949 in Manchester, England

Robin Gibb
(The Bee Gees)
English singer–songwriter
• Best known for hit album *Saturday Night Fever*, 1977.
b. December 22, 1949 in Manchester, England

Georgia Gibbs
American singer
• 1940s-50s pop singer; first hit: "If I Knew You Were Coming I'd've Baked You a Cake."
b. August 26, 1926 in Worcester, Massachusetts

Terri Gibbs
American singer–musician
• Blind country singer; hit single "Somebody's Knockin'," 1981.
b. June 15, 1954 in Augusta, Georgia

Bob Gibson
American singer–musician
• Folk singer, guitarist; with Bob Camp, 1960s.
b. November 16, 1931 in New York, New York

Debbie (Deborah Ann) Gibson
American singer
• Teen singer; had hit album, *Out of the Blue*, 1988.
b. August 31, 1970 in Brooklyn, New York

Don(ald) Gibson
American singer–songwriter
• Prolific country writer, performer; wrote songs "Sweet Dreams," 1956; "I Can't Stop Loving You," 1958.
b. April 03, 1928 in Shelby, North Carolina

Walter Wilhelm Gieseking
German musician
• Developed Leimer-Gieseking method of piano study.
b. November 05, 1895 in Lyons, France
d. October 26, 1956 in London, England

Roland Gift
(Fine Young Cannibals)
English actor–singer
• Lead vocalist for music group Fine Young Cannibals, 1983–.
b. 1962 in Birmingham, England

Beniamino Gigli
Italian opera singer
• Much-loved tenor; considered Caruso's successor; with NY Met., 1920-32, 1938-39; acclaimed as Lohengrin.
b. March 2, 1890 in Recanati, Italy
d. November 3, 1957 in Rome, Italy

Nick Gilder
English singer
• Had number-one single "Hot Child in the City," 1978, from album *City Nights*.
b. November 07, 1951 in London, England

Emil Grigorevich Gilels
Russian musician
• Pianist known for rich tone, virtuosic power; performed Romantic, classical works, sometimes playing all five Beethoven concertos in succession.
b. October 19, 1916 in Odessa, Russia
d. October 14, 1985 in Moscow, U.S.S.R.

Dizzy (John Birks) Gillespie
American jazz musician
• Trumpeter responsible for "Be-Bop" sound; wrote *To Be or Not...to Bop*, 1979.
b. October 21, 1917 in Cheraw, South Carolina

Mickey Leroy Gilley
American musician
• Club named Gilley's was setting for film *Urban Cowboy*; had 1980 pop hit "Stand By Me."
b. March 09, 1936 in Natchez, Mississippi

Don Gillis
American composer
• Produced NBC Toscanini-conducted concerts, 1950s; wrote *Symphony No. 5 1/2*.
b. June 17, 1912 in Cameron, Missouri
d. January 1, 1978 in Columbia, South Carolina

Patrick Sarsfield Gilmore
American bandleader
• Noted for flamboyant showmanship, wrote "When Johnny Comes Marching Home," 1863.
b. December 25, 1829 in County Galway, Ireland
d. September 24, 1892 in Saint Louis, Missouri

Dave (David) Gilmour
(Pink Floyd)
English singer–musician
• Joined group, 1968; his guitar playing is one of band's trademarks.
b. March 06, 1944 in Cambridge, England

Jakob Gimpel
American musician
• Brilliant concert pianist, noted for Schumann, Chopin repertoire; won Ben-Gurion award.
b. April 16, 1906 in Lemberg, Austria
d. March 12, 1989 in Los Angeles, California

Alberto Ginastera
American composer
• Modern eclectic-style operas include *Beatrix Cenci*, 1971; *Bomarzo*, 1967, was banned from Argentina for its sexual violence content.
b. April 11, 1916 in Buenos Aires, Argentina
d. June 25, 1983 in Geneva, Switzerland

James Peter Giuffre
American jazz musician
• Clarinetist, saxist; led own trio, 1950s; a major proponent of free-jazz style.
b. April 26, 1921 in Dallas, Texas

Carlo Maria Giulini
Italian conductor
• Led LA Philharmonic from 1978; Grammy winner, 1971.
b. May 09, 1914 in Basletta, Italy

Gladys Knight and the Pips
(Langston George; Eleanor Guest; William Guest; Brenda Knight; Gladys Knight; Merald Knight)
American music group
• Family group formed in Atlanta, 1952; biggest hit "Midnight Train to Georgia," 1973.

Peggy Glanville-Hicks
American composer–critic
• Wrote opera *The Transposed Heads*, 1954; ballet *A Season in Hell*, 1967.
b. December 29, 1912 in Melbourne, Australia
d. June 25, 1990 in Sydney, Australia

Philip Glass
American composer
• Noted for avant-garde style, use of electric wind instruments; commissioned by NY Met. to create work for 1992 celebration of Columbus' discovery.
b. January 31, 1937 in Baltimore, Maryland

David Glazer
American musician
• Int'l. clarinet soloist; member, NY Woodwind Quintet, 1951–.
b. May 07, 1913 in Milwaukee, Wisconsin

Alexander Constantinovich Glazunov
Russian composer
• Last of Russian National school; master of counterpoint; noted for ballet, *Raymonda*.
b. August 1, 1865 in Saint Petersburg, Russia
d. March 21, 1936 in Paris, France

Carroll Glenn
American violinist
• With husband, pianist Eugene List, founded Southern Vermont Music Festival.
b. 1922
d. April 25, 1983 in New York, New York

Mikhail Ivanovich Glinka
Russian composer
• Wrote first Russian nat. opera, *A Life for the Czar*, 1836; *Russlan and Ludmilla*, 1842, after Pushkin's fairy tale.
b. June 01, 1804 in Novospaskoi, Russia
d. February 15, 1857 in Berlin, Germany

Gloria Estefan and Miami Sound Machine
(Juan Marcos Avila; Betty Cortez; Emilio Estefan Jr; Gloria M Estefan; Enrique E Garcia; Roger Fisher; Gustavo Lezcano; Victor Lopez; Wesl)
Cuban music group
• Local club band whose Latin rhythms became popular, 1984; first number one hit "Anything for You" from album *Let it Loose*, 1988.

Alma Gluck
(Reba Fiersohn)
American opera singer
• NY Met. soprano, 1909-12; her recording, "Carry Me Back to Old Virginny," sold two million copies; wife of Efrem Zimbalist.
b. May 11, 1884 in Bucharest, Romania
d. October 27, 1938 in New York, New York

Christoph Wilibald Gluck
German composer
• Best-known operas: *Orfeo ed Eurydice*, 1762; *Iphigenie en Aulide*, 1772.
b. July 02, 1714 in Erasbach, Germany
d. November 15, 1787 in Vienna, Austria

The Go-Go's
(Charlotte Caffey; Belinda Carlisle; Gina Schock; Kathy Valentine; Jane Wiedlin)
American music group
• Most successful all-female rock group ever, 1978-85; had hit single "We Got the Beat" from album *Beauty and the Beat*, 1982.

Tito Gobbi
Italian opera singer
• Baritone, best known for portrayal of Scarpia in Puccini's *Tosca*, 1956.
b. October 24, 1915 in Bassano del Grappo, Italy
d. May 05, 1984 in Rome, Italy

Benjamin L P Godard
French composer
• Wrote operas *La Vivandiere*, 1895; *Jocelyn*, 1888, featuring the famous "Berceuse."
b. 1849
d. 1895

Leopold Godowsky
Polish musician
• Concert pianist who wrote many pieces, arrangements for instrument; developed weight and relaxation theory in piano teaching.
b. February 13, 1870 in Wilma, Russia
d. November 21, 1938

Andrew Gold
American singer
• Guitarist, arranger for Linda Ronstadt; wrote hit singles "Lonely Boy," "Thank You for Being a Friend," 1978.
b. August 02, 1951 in Burbank, California

Arthur Gold
Canadian pianist
• Part of piano duo with Robert Fizdale for 40 years; known for contemporary music.
b. 1919
d. January 03, 1990 in Manhattan, New York

William Lee Golden
(The Oak Ridge Boys)
American singer
• Baritone with country-pop group.
b. January 12, 1939 in Brewton, Alabama

Golden Earring
(Rinus Gerritsen; Barry Hay; George Kooymans; Robert Jan Stips; Cesar Zuiderwijk)
Dutch music group
• Holland's top rock band since, 1964; hit single "Twilight Zone," 1982.

Edwin Franko Goldman
American bandleader–composer
• Composed over 100 marches: "On the Mall," 1924; band held summer outdoor concerts in NYC, 1918-55.
b. January 01, 1878 in Louisville, Kentucky
d. February 21, 1956 in New York, New York

Richard Franko Goldman
American composer–bandleader
• Wrote "A Sentimental Journey," 1941, numerous works for ensembles.
b. December 07, 1910 in New York, New York
d. January 19, 1980 in Baltimore, Maryland

Karl Goldmark
Hungarian composer
• Noted for opera, *Queen of Sheba*, 1875; overture, *Sakuntala*, 1865.
b. May 18, 1830 in Keszthely, Hungary
d. January 02, 1915 in Vienna, Austria

Bobby Goldsboro
American singer–songwriter
• CMA star of year, 1968; hits include "Honey"; "The Straight Life."
b. January 18, 1941 in Marianna, Florida

Jerry Goldsmith
American composer
• Won Oscar, 1976, for *The Omen*; won 1981 Emmy for "Masada."
b. February 1, 1929 in Los Angeles, California

Benny Golson
American jazz musician–bandleader
• Tenor saxist; formed jazztet; first to take band on US State dept. tours.
b. January 25, 1929 in Philadelphia, Pennsylvania

Benny (Benjamin David) Goodman
American bandleader–musician
• World-renowned clarinetist, band leader during Big Band era; most popular songs "Stompin' at the Savoy"; "Sing, Sing, Sing."
b. May 3, 1909 in Chicago, Illinois
d. June 13, 1986 in New York, New York

Steve(n Benjamin) Goodman
American songwriter
• Best known as author of Arlo Guthrie's 1972 hit "City of New Orleans."
b. July 25, 1948 in Chicago, Illinois
d. September 2, 1984 in Seattle, Washington

Leon Jean Goossens
English musician
• Oboist; wrote oboe compositions, popularizing it as a solo performer; brother of Eugene.
b. June 12, 1897 in Liverpool, England
d. February 12, 1988 in Tunbridge, England

Dexter Keith Gordon
American jazz musician
• Tenor saxophonist; starred in film *Round Midnight*, 1986 and recorded soundtrack; received Oscar nomination, 1987.
b. February 27, 1923 in Los Angeles, California
d. April 25, 1990 in Philadelphia, Pennsylvania

Berry Gordy, Jr
American music executive–film executive
• Founded Motown Records, 1959; signed The Temptations; The Supremes; Hall of Fame, 1988; sold company for $61 million, 1988.
b. November 28, 1929 in Detroit, Michigan

Lesley Gore
American singer
• Early 1960s rock hits include "She's a Fool," 1963; "Young Love," 1966.
b. May 02, 1946 in Tenafly, New Jersey

Igor Gorin
American composer–singer–actor
• Baritone; had radio, operatic roles; made NY Met debut in *La Traviata*, 1964.
b. October 26, 1908 in Grodak, Russia
d. March 24, 1982 in Tucson, Arizona

Eydie Gorme
(Edith Gormenzano; Steve and Eydie; Mrs Steve Lawrence)
American singer
• Won Grammys 1960, 1966; won Emmy for "Steve and Eydie Celebrate Irving Berlin," 1979.
b. August 16, 1932 in New York, New York

Francois Joseph Gossec
French composer
• First French symphonist; wrote string quartets, operas, marches, hymns of Revolution.
b. January 17, 1734 in Vergnies, Belgium
d. February 16, 1829 in Passy, France

Glenn Herbert Gould
Canadian pianist–composer
• First N American to play in USSR; noted for idiosyncracies, Brahms interpretations; concentrated on recording after 1964.
b. September 25, 1932 in Toronto, Ontario
d. October 04, 1982 in Toronto, Ontario

Morton Gould
American composer–conductor
• Acclaimed versatile composer; works include ballet *Fall River Legend*, 1947; led radio's "Chrysler Hour," 1940s.
b. December 1, 1913 in Richmond Hill, New York

Robert Gerard Goulet
American actor–singer
• Broadway debut in *Camelot*, 1960; won Tony, 1968, for *The Happy Time*.
b. November 26, 1933 in Lawrence, Massachusetts

Charles Francois Gounod
French composer
• Wrote operas *Faust*, 1859; *Romeo and Juliet*, 1967; known for lyric rather than dramatic qualities.
b. June 17, 1818 in Paris, France
d. October 17, 1893 in Paris, France

Gary Graffman
American musician
• Internationally known concert pianist, 1950s-60s.
b. October 14, 1928 in New York, New York

Bill Graham
(Wolfgang Grajonca)
American producer
• Promotes music groups including the Rolling Stones, Santana; produced Live Aid concert, 1986.
b. January 08, 1931 in Berlin, Germany

Larry (Lawrence, Jr) Graham
(Sly and the Family Stone)
American singer–musician
• Bass guitarist with Sly and the Family Stone until 1972; solo performer since 1980.

Ronny Graham
American composer–actor–director
• Film scores include *To Be Or Not To Be*, 1983; *Finders Keepers*, 1984.
b. August 26, 1919 in Philadelphia, Pennsylvania

Graham Parker and the Rumour
(Bob Andrews; Martin Belmont; Andrew Bodnar; Stephen Goulding; Graham Parker; Brinsley Schwarz)
English music group
• Back-up band for Graham Parker, 1975-81; first album *Howlin' Wind*, 1976.

Percy Aldridge Grainger
American pianist–composer
• Experimented with electronic music, novel harmonies; made frequent use of folk tunes: *Children's March*.
b. July 08, 1882 in Melbourne, Australia
d. February 2, 1961 in White Plains, New York

Enrique Granados
Spanish composer–musician
• Noted for series of piano pieces, *Goyescas*, 1916, inspired by Goya's etchings.
b. July 27, 1867 in Lerida, Spain
d. March 24, 1916

Grand Funk Railroad
(Donald Brewer; Mark Farner; Craig Frost; Mel Schacher)
American music group
• Formed, 1969; most commercially successful heavy metal group, 1970-76; first group to have 10 consecutive platinum albums; sold over 20 million.

Amy Grant
American singer
• Christian rock singer whose album *Age to Age*, 1983, sold one million copies; *Unguarded* contained hit "Find a Way," 1985.
b. November 25, 1960 in Augusta, Georgia

Earl Grant
American musician
• A leading popular organist of 1960s.
b. January 2, 1931 in Idabelle, Oklahoma
d. June 1, 1970 in Lordsburg, New Mexico

Eddy (Edmond Montague) Grant
Guyanese singer–composer
• Music has reggae flavor; hits include "Living on the Front Line," 1979; "Electric Avenue," 1983.
b. March 05, 1948 in Plaisance, Guyana

Gogi Grant
(Myrtle Audrey Arinsberg; Audrey Grant)
American singer
• Best known for "The Wayward Wind," one of the most popular records of 1950s.
b. September 2, 1924 in Philadelphia, Pennsylvania

Norman Granz
American impresario–producer
• Promoted international jazz concerts; produced jazz records.
b. August 06, 1918 in Los Angeles, California

Stephane Grappelli
French jazz musician
• Jazz violinist; prominent in Europe for "Le Jazz hot," 1930s.
b. January 26, 1908 in Paris, France

The Grass Roots
(Creed Bratton; Rick Coonce; Warren Entner; Robert Grill; Reed Kailing; Joel Larson; Dennis Provisor)
American music group
• Hits include "Temptation Eyes," 1971; "Heaven Knows," 1969.

The Grateful Dead
(Jerry Garcia; Donna Godchaux; Keith Godchaux; Bill Kreutzmann; Phil Lesh; Ron McKernan; Robert Hall Weir)
American music group
• Psychedelic band formed, 1965, whose fans are known as "Dead Heads."

Dobie Gray
(Leonard Victor Ainsworth Jr)
American singer
• Husky-voiced country musician; hits include "Drift Away," 1973.
b. July 26, 1942 in Brookshire, Texas

Glen Gray
(Glen Gray Knoblaugh; "Spike")
American bandleader
• Led popular dance band, Casa Loma Orchestra, 1929-50.
b. June 07, 1906 in Roanoke, Illinois
d. August 23, 1963 in Plymouth, Massachusetts

Buddy (Armando) Greco
American singer–songwriter–pianist
• Jazz-styled vocalist, 1950s-70s; on TV, 1950-60.
b. August 14, 1926 in Philadelphia, Pennsylvania

Adolph Green
American dramatist–songwriter
• Won Tonys for *Hallelujah, Baby*, 1968; *Applause*, 1970; *On the Twentieth Century*, 1978; Songwriter's Hall of Fame, 1980.
b. December 02, 1915 in New York, New York

Al Green
American singer–songwriter
• Hits include "Let's Stay Together," 1972; "I'm Still In Love With You," 1972.
b. April 13, 1946 in Forest City, Arkansas

Johnny (John W) Green
American songwriter
• Wrote "Body and Soul," 1930; won Oscars for scores to *Easter Parade*, 1951; *American in Paris*, 1953; *West Side Story*, 1961.
b. October 1, 1908 in New York, New York
d. May 15, 1989 in Beverly Hills, California

Peter Green
(Peter Greenbaum)
English singer–musician
• Guitarist with Fleetwood Mac in original group, 1967; troubled history resulted in institutionalization; later recordings never matched prior success.
b. October 29, 1946 in London, England

Norman Greenbaum
American singer–songwriter
• Hit single, "Spirit in the Sky," sold two million copies, 1970.
b. November 2, 1942 in Malden, Massachusetts

Howard Greenfield
American songwriter
• Co-wrote Grammy-winning "Love Will Keep Us Together," with Neil Sedaka, 1975.
b. 1937
d. March 04, 1986 in Los Angeles, California

Lee Greenwood
American singer–songwriter
• Country performer who recorded single "I O U," 1983.
b. October 27, 1942 in Los Angeles, California

Sonny (William Alexander) Greer
American musician
• Drummer, Duke Ellington Orchestra for over 30 years.
b. December 13, 1903 in Long Branch, New Jersey
d. March 23, 1982 in New York, New York

The Greg Kihn Band
(Greg Douglass; Greg Kihn; Larry Lynch; Gary Phillips; Steve Wright)
American music group
• Rock band formed 1975; eighth album *Kihnspiracy* contained hit single "Jeopardy," 1983.

Aleksandr Tikhonovich Gretchaninov
(Aleksandr Tikhonovich Grechaninov)
American composer
• Music rooted in Russian national tradition; wrote popular song "Over the Steppes."
b. October 25, 1864 in Moscow, Russia
d. January 03, 1956 in New York, New York

Andre Ernest Modeste Gretry
French composer
• Founded French opera-comique; 50 operas included *Lucile*, 1769.
b. February 09, 1741 in Liege, Belgium
d. September 24, 1813 in Montmorency, France

Edvard Hagerup Grieg
Norwegian composer–musician
• Considered founder, Norwegian National School of Composition; 100 works include *Peter Gynt* suites.
b. June 15, 1843 in Bergen, Norway
d. September 04, 1907 in Bergen, Norway

Charles Tomlinson Griffes
American composer
• Impressionist works, often adapted from Oriental, Russian schools include *The White Peacock*, 1917.
b. September 07, 1884 in Elmira, New York
d. April 08, 1920 in Elmira, New York

Dale Griffin
(Mott the Hoople; "Buffin")
English musician
• Drummer with hard-rock group, 1969-74.
b. October 24, 1948 in Ross-on-Wye, England

Guilia Grisi
Italian opera singer
• Celebrated prima donna soprano; made annual London appearances, 1830s-50s.
b. July 28, 1811 in Milan, Italy
d. November 29, 1869 in Berlin, Germany

Ferde Grofe
American composer
• Wrote *Grand Canyon Suite*, 1931.
b. March 27, 1892 in New York, New York
d. April 03, 1972 in Santa Monica, California

Sir Charles Barnard Groves
English composer
• Leads major British operas, orchestras; with Royal Philharmonic since 1967.
b. March 1, 1915 in London, England

Louis Gruenberg
American composer
• Wrote opera *The Emperor Jones*, 1933.
b. August 03, 1884 in Russia
d. June 09, 1964 in Beverly Hills, California

Hugh Grundy
(The Zombies)
English singer–musician
• Drummer with "beat group" band, 1963-67; hits include "She's Not There," 1964.
b. March 06, 1945 in Winchester, England

Dave Grusin
American composer–filmmaker
• Oscar nominee for film scores: *Heaven Can Wait*, 1978; *On Golden Pond*, 1981; *Tootsie*, 1982.
b. 1934 in Littleton, Colorado

Johnny (John Albert) Guarnieri
American jazz musician
• Jazz pianist who performed with Benny Goodman and Artie Shaw bands during the Swing Era.
b. March 23, 1917 in New York, New York
d. January 07, 1985 in Livingston, New Jersey

Hilde Gueden
Austrian opera singer
• Soprano; former Vienna State Opera star; with NY Met., 1951-60; noted for Mozart, Strauss roles.
b. September 15, 1917 in Vienna, Austria
d. September 17, 1988 in Vienna, Austria

Guess Who
(Chad Allan; Bob Ashley; Randy Bachman; Burton Cummings; Bruce Decker; David Inglish; Jim Kale; Greg Leskiw; Vance Masters; Don McDougall;)
Canadian music group
• Top Canadian band, 1960s-70s; hit singles "These Eyes," 1969; "No Time," 1970.

Guido d'Arezzo
(Guido Aretinus; Fra Guittone; Guy of Arezzo)
Italian musician–religious figure
• Benedictine music theorist; devised four-line staff, system of solmization.
b. 990?
d. 1050

Yvette Guilbert
French singer
• Favorite Paris, London cabaret performer whose long black gloves were trademark.
b. 1867 in Paris, France
d. February 02, 1944 in Aix-en-Provence, France

David Wendel Fentress Guion
American songwriter
• Wrote Western melodies including "Home On the Range," 1908.
b. December 15, 1892 in Ballinger, Texas
d. October 17, 1981 in Dallas, Texas

Friedrich Gulda
Austrian pianist
• Brilliant classic concertist, 1940s-50s; wrote, performed jazz pieces, 1960s-70s.
b. 1930

Joseph Gungl
Hungarian composer–bandleader
• Bandmaster; composed over 300 popular dances, marches.
b. December 01, 1810 in Zsambek, Hungary
d. January 31, 1889 in Weimar, Germany

Arlo Guthrie
American singer
• Son of Woody Guthrie; best known for hit "Alice's Restaurant," 1969.
b. July 1, 1947 in Brooklyn, New York

Woody (Woodrow Wilson) Guthrie
American songwriter
• Folksinger, balladeer; wrote over 1000 songs, 1930s-40s, including "This Land is Your Land," 1956; Hall of Fame, 1988; father of Arlo.
b. July 14, 1912 in Okemah, Oklahoma
d. October 04, 1967 in New York, New York

Bobby (Robert Leo) Hackett
American jazz musician
• Guitarist, cornetist; led own band, 1940s-50s.
b. January 31, 1915 in Providence, Rhode Island
d. June 07, 1976 in Chatham, Massachusetts

Steve Hackett
(Genesis)
English musician
• Guitarist with Genesis, 1970-77.
b. February 12, 1950 in England

Henry Kimball Hadley
American composer
• Romantic operas include *Cleopatra's Night*, 1920; foundation organized for music advancement, 1938.
b. December 2, 1871 in Somerville, Massachusetts
d. September 06, 1937 in New York, New York

Sammy Hagar
(Van Halen)
American singer–musician
• Lead singer, second guitarist with Van Halen, 1986–; released 10 albums during nine yr. solo career.
b. October 13, 1949 in Monterey, California

Hakan Hagegard
Swedish opera singer
• Lyric baritone; starred in Igmar Bergman's film version of *The Magic Flute*, 1975.
b. November 25, 1945 in Karlstad, Sweden

Merle Ronald Haggard
American singer–songwriter
• Gravelly voiced country singer; hits include "Okie from Muskogee," 1969; won Grammy, 1984.
b. April 06, 1937 in Bakersfield, California

Bob Haggart
(Robert Sherwood)
American composer–musician
• Bassist with Bob Crosby, 1935-42; co-led World's Greatest Jazz Band, 1970s.
b. March 13, 1914 in New York, New York

Bernard Haitink
Dutch conductor
• Director, Amsterdam's Concertgebouw, since 1964; led London's Philharmonic, 1976-79; knighted, 1978.
b. March 04, 1929 in Amsterdam, Netherlands

Jacques Francois Fromental Halevy
(Jacques Francois F Elie Levy)
French composer
• Wrote "grand" opera *La Juive*, 1835; comic opera *L'Eclair*, 1835.
b. May 27, 1799 in Paris, France
d. March 17, 1862 in Nice, France

Bill (William John Clifford, Jr) Haley
(Bill Haley and the Comets; "Father of Rock 'n' Roll")
American singer–musician
• Hits "Rock Around the Clock," 1955; "Shake, Rattle, and Roll," 1954; paved way for Elvis Presley, The Beatles.
b. July 06, 1925 in Highland Park, Michigan
d. February 09, 1981 in Harlingen, Texas

Daryl Hall
(Hall and Oates)
American singer–musician
• With John Oates, recorded "Rich Girl" on first platinum album *Bigger Than Both of Us*, 1976.
b. October 11, 1948 in Pottstown, Pennsylvania

Juanita Hall
American singer–actress
• Best known for Broadway role of Bloody Mary in *South Pacific*, 1949
b. November 06, 1901 in Newport, New Jersey
d. February 28, 1968 in Keyport, New Jersey

Tom T Hall
American singer–songwriter
• Wrote song "Harper Valley PTA"; sold over 4.5 million copies.
b. May 25, 1936 in Olive Hill, Kentucky

Hall and Oates
(Daryl Hall; John Oates)
American music group
• Pop-rock hits include "Rich Girl," 1977; "Maneater," 1982.

Sir Charles Halle
English pianist–conductor
• Founded, led Halle Concerts, 1858-95, in Manchester, England; became famed Halle Orchestra.
b. April 11, 1819 in Hagen, Germany
d. October 25, 1895 in Manchester, England

Johnny Halliday
(Jean-Phillippe Smet)
French singer
• European rock star, 1960s; hit "Let's Twist Again," 1961.
b. June 15, 1943 in Paris, France

Ivar Hallstrom
Swedish composer
• Many operas, operettas include *The Vikings*, 1877.
b. June 05, 1826 in Stockholm, Sweden
d. April 11, 1901 in Stockholm, Sweden

Leonid Hambro
American pianist
• Official pianist, NY Philharmonic Orchestra, 1948–; concerts with Victor Borge, 1960–.
b. June 26, 1920 in Chicago, Illinois

Roy Hamilton
American singer
• Baritone of 1950s; hits include "Ebb Tide," 1954; "Unchained Melody," 1955.
b. April 16, 1929 in Leesburg, Georgia
d. July 2, 1969 in New Rochelle, New York

Marvin Hamlisch
American composer–musician
• Won Oscars for scoring *The Way We Were*, *The Sting*, 1973; won Tony, Pulitzer for *A Chorus Line*, 1975.
b. June 02, 1944 in New York, New York

Jan Hammer
(Mahavishnu Orchestra)
Czech musician–composer
• Pianist with Mahavishu Orchestra, 1971-73; best known for soundtrack performances, production for TV series "Miami Vice," 1984–.
b. April 17, 1948 in Czechoslovakia

M C Hammer
American singer
• Rap singer; album *Please Hammer Don't Hurt 'Em* has sold more than 6 million copies to become rap's all-time best seller.
b. 1962 in Oakland, California

Oscar Hammerstein, II
(Rodgers and Hammerstein)
American lyricist
• Wrote lyrics for *Oklahoma!*, 1943; *Carousel*, 1945; *South Pacific*, 1949; with Richard Rogers, one of Broadway's most respected, successful teams.
b. July 12, 1895 in New York, New York
d. August 23, 1960 in Doylestown, Pennsylvania

John Henry Hammond, Jr
American music executive
• VP, Columbia Records; discovered Billie Holiday, Aretha Franklin, Bob Dylan; contributed to development of jazz.
b. December 15, 1910 in New York, New York
d. July 1, 1987 in New York, New York

Lionel Leo Hampton
American bandleader–jazz musician
• Top vibraphonist pioneer who formed big band, 1937; theme song: "Flying Home."
b. April 12, 1913 in Birmingham, Alabama

Herbie (Herbert Jeffrey) Hancock
American jazz musician–composer
• Pianist who won Grammy, 1984, for electronic jazz composition "Rockit."
b. April 12, 1940 in Chicago, Illinois

George Frederick Handel
(Georg Friedrich Handel)
English composer
• Master of baroque music who composed 46 operas; best-known work: *The Messiah*, 1742.
b. February 23, 1685 in Halle, Germany
d. April 14, 1759 in London, England

W(illiam) C(hristopher) Handy
American songwriter–bandleader
• First to compile, publish "blues" music; led own band, 1903-21; wrote "St. Louis Blues," 1914; "Memphis Blues," 1912.
b. November 16, 1873 in Florence, Alabama
d. March 29, 1958 in New York, New York

Howard Harold Hanson
American composer–conductor–educator
• Directed Rochester, NY's School of Music, 1924-64; varied works include opera, *Merry Mount*, 1934; Pulitzer-winner *Fourth Symphony*, 1944.
b. October 28, 1896 in Wahoo, Nebraska
d. February 26, 1981 in Rochester, New York

Otto Abels Harbach
American lyricist
• Often collaborated with Oscar Hammerstein; hits include "Smoke Gets in Your Eyes," 1933.
b. August 18, 1873 in Salt Lake City, Utah
d. January 24, 1963 in New York, New York

John Harris Harbison
American composer–educator
• MIT music professor, 1962–; wrote opera *Full Moon in March*, 1979.
b. December 2, 1938 in Orange, New Jersey

E(dgar) Y(ipsel) Harburg
American lyricist
• Wrote lyrics for "Somewhere Over the Rainbow," from *Wizard of Oz*, 1939; also wrote lyrics for song "Only a Paper Moon," play *Finian's Rainbow*.
b. April 08, 1896 in New York, New York
d. March 05, 1981 in Los Angeles, California

Louis Thomas Hardin
American musician
• Blinded at 13, he invented new string instrument, new drum.
b. May 26, 1916 in Marysville, Kansas

Tim Hardin
American songwriter–singer
• Wrote song "If I Were a Carpenter," recorded by Bobby Darin, Bob Seger, others.
b. December 23, 1941 in Eugene, Oregon
d. December 29, 1980 in Hollywood, California

Rebekah West Harkness
American philanthropist–composer
• Founded Harkness Ballet, 1964-74; Rebekah Harkness Foundation, to support dance companies, 1959.
b. April 17, 1915 in Saint Louis, Missouri
d. June 17, 1982 in New York, New York

Benjamin Robertson Harney
American composer
• Known for early ragtime compositions.
b. March 06, 1871
d. March 01, 1938 in Philadelphia, Pennsylvania

Sheldon Mayer Harnick
American lyricist
• Won Tony awards for *Fiorello*, 1960; *Fiddler on the Roof*, 1964.
b. April 3, 1924 in Chicago, Illinois

Lynn Morris Harrell
American musician
• Cello soloist with major US symphonies since 1970.
b. January 3, 1944 in New York, New York

Emmylou Harris
American singer
• Won Grammys, 1976, 1977; CMA female vocalist of year, 1980.
b. April 02, 1947 in Birmingham, Alabama

Phil Harris
American comedian–bandleader
• Showman who led band from 1930s; with Jack Benny's radio show, 1936-46; husband of Alice Faye; popularized song "That's What I Like About the South."
b. June 24, 1904 in Linton, Indiana

Roy Ellsworth Harris
American composer
• Numerous works include *Symphony No. 3*, 1937; overture, *When Johnny Comes Marching Home*, 1935.
b. February 12, 1898 in Lincoln County, Oklahoma
d. October 1979 in Santa Monica, California

George Harrison
(The Beatles)
English singer–songwriter
• Most mysterious of group who launched solo career with gold album *All Things Must Pass*, 1970; known for benefits for Bangladesh, interest in Eastern mysticism; had revival with album *Cloud Nine*, 1987.
b. February 25, 1943 in Liverpool, England

Debbie (Deborah Ann) Harry
(Blondie)
American singer
• First punk star to appear in commercial; hit songs with Blondie include "Call Me," 1980; solo singles: "Backfired," 1981.
b. July 01, 1945 in Miami, Florida

Charles Hart
English lyricist–composer
• Wrote lyrics for Tony-winner *The Phantom of the Opera*, 1986.
b. June 03, 1961 in London, England

Lorenz Milton Hart
(Rogers and Hart)
American lyricist
• Collaborated with Richard Rogers for 18 yrs.; wrote lyrics for musicals; songs include "Blue Moon"; "Where or When."
b. May 02, 1895 in New York, New York
d. November 22, 1943 in New York, New York

Mickey Hart
(The Grateful Dead)
American singer–musician
• Drummer with group since 1967; released solo album, *Rolling Thunder*, 1972.
b. 1950 in New York, New York

John Cowan Hartford
American singer–songwriter
• Wrote "Gentle on My Mind," 1967; recorded by Glen Campbell, 200 others.
b. December 3, 1937 in New York, New York

Dan Hartman
American singer–musician–songwriter
• Pop singer who had hit single "I Can Dream About You," 1984.

Rudolph Hartmann
German producer–manager
• Led noted German orchestras, 1920s-60s; revised many Strauss works.
b. October 11, 1900 in Ingolstadt, Germany

Johann Adolph Hasse
German composer
• Wrote over 100 operas including *Sesostrate*, 1726; wed to prima donna Faustina Bordoni.
b. March 25, 1699 in Bergedorf, Germany
d. December 16, 1783 in Venice, Italy

Bobby Hatfield
(Righteous Brothers)
American singer
• With Bill Medley had hit single "Unchained Melody," 1965.
b. August 1, 1940 in Beaver Dam, Wisconsin

Donny Hathaway
American singer–songwriter
• Best known for duets with Roberta Flack: "Where Is the Love," 1972; "The Closer I Get to You," 1978.
b. October 01, 1945 in Chicago, Illinois
d. January 13, 1979 in New York, New York

Richie Havens
American singer–musician
• Black folksinger who had hit single "Here Comes the Sun," 1971. Performed at Woodstock.
b. January 21, 1941 in Brooklyn, New York

Bean (Coleman) Hawkins
American jazz musician
• Tenor saxist, noted for 1939 recording of "Body and Soul"; led own band, 1940s.
b. November 21, 1904 in Saint Joseph, Missouri
d. May 19, 1969 in New York, New York

Erskine Ramsey Hawkins
American songwriter–bandleader
• Big band leader noted for high-note trumpet playing; theme was "Tuxedo Junction."
b. July 26, 1914 in Birmingham, Alabama

Ronnie Hawkins
American singer
• Rock 'n' roll hits include "Forty Days," "Mary Lou," 1959.
b. January 1, 1935 in Huntsville, Arkansas

Screamin' Jay (Jalacy) Hawkins
American singer–pianist
• Known for wild stage antics; albums include *Frenzy*, 1982.
b. July 18, 1929 in Cleveland, Ohio

Hawkwind
(Dave Brock; Alan Davey; Clive Deamer; Huw Lloyd Langton)
British music group
• Noted for live performances, rock band formed 1969; success tainted by bad publicity, drug use; hit single, "Silver Machine," 1972.

Franz Joseph Haydn
Austrian composer
• Composed *Surprise Symphony*, 1791; influenced work of Beethoven, Mozart.
b. March 31, 1732 in Rohrau, Austria
d. May 31, 1809 in Vienna, Austria

Isaac Hayes
American musician–songwriter
• Won Grammy, Oscar for score of *Shaft*, 1971; rhythm, blues vocalist.
b. August 2, 1942 in Covington, Tennessee

Roland Hayes
American opera singer
• Tenor who sang arias, folk songs, 1920s-40s; pioneered black singers on concert stage.
b. June 03, 1887 in Curryville, Georgia
d. December 31, 1976 in Boston, Massachusetts

Richard Hayman
American musician
• Led pop concerts with Detroit Symphony, 1970–; St. Louis Symphony, 1976–.
b. March 27, 1920 in Cambridge, Massachusetts

Dick (Richard) Haymes
American singer
• Star film vocalist noted for mellow voice, 1940s; rivaled by Crosby, Sinatra; hosted radio show with Helen Forrest, sang "Little White Lies,"
b. September 13, 1917 in Buenos Aires, Argentina
d. March 28, 1980 in Los Angeles, California

Lee Hays
(The Weavers)
American singer–songwriter
• Folk singer with The Weavers, 1948-63; co-wrote "If I Had a Hammer," with Pete Seeger.
b. 1914 in Little Rock, Arkansas
d. August 26, 1981 in North Tarrytown, New York

Lennie (Leonard George) Hayton
American composer–conductor
• Noted pianist-arranger, 1920s-60s; MGM music director, 1940-53; once wed to singer Lena Horne.
b. February 13, 1908 in New York, New York
d. April 24, 1971 in Palm Springs, California

Lee Hazelwood
American singer–songwriter
• Best known for duets with Nancy Sinatra: "Jackson," 1967; "Some Velvet Morning," 1968.
b. July 09, 1929 in Mannford, Oklahoma

Heart
(Mark Andes; Denny Carmassi; Mike Derosier; Roger Fisher; Steve Fossen; Howard Lesse; Ann Wilson; Nancy Wilson)
American music group
• Heavy metal band led by sisters, Ann, Nancy Wilson since 1972; album *Dreamboat Annie*, sold 2.5 million copies, 1976.

Ted Heath
English bandleader–musician
• Trombonist who led own band from 1945; in films, 1960s.
b. 1902 in London, England
d. November 18, 1969 in Virginia Water, England

Joey Heatherton
American actress–singer–dancer
• Films include *Happy Hooker Goes to Washington*, 1977; *Bluebeard*, 1972.
b. September 14, 1944 in Rockville Centre, New York

Ray(mond Joseph) Heatherton
American actor–singer
• Broadway, radio vocalist, 1930s; led dance combo, 1940s; hosted children's TV show, "Merry Mailman"; father of Joey.
b. June 01, 1910 in Jersey City, New Jersey

Neal Paul Hefti
American composer–publisher
• Trumpeter, Big Band arranger, 1940s-50s; film scores include *Barefoot in the Park*, 1967.
b. October 29, 1922 in Hastings, Nebraska

Jascha Heifetz
American violinist
• Child prodigy who had debut at age five; considered best classical violinist of c.; playing noted for silken tone, careful regard for composer's markings.
b. February 02, 1901 in Vilna, Russia
d. December 1, 1987 in Los Angeles, California

Fred Hellerman
(The Weavers)
American singer–musician–songwriter
• Folksinger; original member, The Weavers, 1948-64; co-wrote song "Kisses Sweeter Than Wine," 1951.
b. May 13, 1927 in New York, New York

Levon Helm
(The Band)
American musician–singer–actor
• Played Loretta Lynn's father in *Coal Miner's Daughter*, 1980.
b. May 26, 1943 in Marvell, Arkansas

Frieda Hempel
German opera singer
• Brilliant soprano; with NY Met., 1912-19; noted for Jenny Lind recitals, 1920s.
b. June 26, 1885 in Leipzig, Germany
d. October 07, 1955 in Berlin, Germany (West)

Fletcher Hamilton Henderson
American bandleader–composer
• Pianist; first jazzman to use written arrangements; organized his first band, 1921.
b. December 18, 1897 in Cuthbert, Georgia
d. December 29, 1952 in New York, New York

Ray Henderson
American songwriter
• Noted pianst-composer; often teamed with B DeSylva, Lew Brown; scored Jolson films; portrayed in film *Best Things in Life Are Free*, 1956.
b. December 01, 1896 in Buffalo, New York
d. December 31, 1971 in Greenwich, Connecticut

Skitch (Cedric) Henderson
(Lyle Henderson)
American bandleader–pianist
• Played piano on Sinatra, Crosby radio shows; led band on TV's "Tonight Show," 1960s.
b. January 27, 1918 in Halstad, Minnesota

Jimi (James Marshall) Hendrix
American musician–singer
• Psychedelic guitarist with hits "Purple Haze," "Hey Joe," 1967;died of drug overdose. Revered as one of all-time great guitarists.
b. November 27, 1942 in Seattle, Washington
d. September 18, 1970 in London, England

Don Henley
(The Eagles)
American singer–musician
• As solo performer, won 1990 Grammy for "The End of the Innocence."
b. July 22, 1947 in Gilmer, Texas

Robert Henrit
(Argent)
English musician
• Drummer with Argent, 1969-76.
b. May 02, 1946 in Boxbourne, England

Clarence Henry
American singer
• Rhythm and blues singer best known for froglike voice, hit single "Ain't Got No Home," 1956.
b. March 19, 1937 in Algiers, Louisiana

Hans Werner Henze
German composer
• Works include operas *Boulevard Solitude*, 1951; *The Bassarids*, 1966; *La Cubana*, 1973.
b. July 01, 1926 in Gutersloh, Germany

Victor Herbert
American conductor–composer
• Wrote over 40 operettas including *Babes in Toyland*, 1903.
b. February 01, 1859 in Dublin, Ireland
d. May 27, 1924 in New York, New York

Jerry Herman
American songwriter
• Won Tony, two Grammys for *Hello Dolly!* 1964.
b. July 1, 1933 in New York, New York

Woody (Woodrow Charles) Herman
American bandleader–musician
• Directed high-quality swing orchestras for over 50 yrs.; recording of "Woodchopper's Ball" sold over one million copies; won three Grammys.
b. May 16, 1913 in Milwaukee, Wisconsin
d. October 29, 1987 in Los Angeles, California

Herman's Hermits
(Karl Greene; Keith Hopwood; Derek Leckenby; Peter Noone; Barry Whitwam)
English music group
• Part of "British Invasion," 1960s; had ten hits, 1964-66: "Mrs. Brown You've Got a Lovely Daughter," 1965.

Louis Joseph Ferdinand Herold
French composer
• Wrote operas *La Clochette*, 1817; *Marie*, 1826; *Zampa*, 1831.
b. January 28, 1791 in Paris, France
d. January 19, 1833 in Les Ternes, France

Bernard Herrmann
American composer
• Wrote over 60 radio, movie scores; known for themes of Hitchcock films: *Psycho*, 1960.
b. June 29, 1911 in New York, New York
d. December 24, 1975 in Los Angeles, California

Arthur Herzog, Jr
American songwriter
• Wrote blues song "God Bless the Child," made famous by Billie Holiday.
b. 1901 in New York, New York
d. September 01, 1983 in Detroit, Michigan

Phillip Arnold Heseltine
(Peter Warlock pseud)
English composer–author
• Musical writings include *The English Ayre*, 1926; composed song cycle *The Curlew*.
b. October 3, 1894 in London, England
d. December 17, 1930 in London, England

Dame Myra Hess
English pianist
• Among great performers of her day; made London debut, 1907; created Dame, 1941.
b. February 25, 1890 in London, England
d. December 26, 1965

Eddie Heywood, Jr
American musician–composer
• Jazz pianist; recorded "Begin the Beguine," 1944; wrote "Canadian Sunset," 1956.
b. December 04, 1915 in Atlanta, Georgia
d. January 01, 1989 in Miami Beach, Florida

Al Hibbler
American singer
• Popular baritone with Duke Ellington's orchestra, 1943-51.
b. August 16, 1915 in Little Rock, Arkansas

Elvira de Hidalgo
Spanish opera singer–teacher
• Last of Spanish soprani d' agilita; only teacher of Maria Callas.
b. 1882 in Barcelona, Spain

Jack (Jay C) Higginbotham
American musician
• Trombonist, vocalist; recorded with Fletcher Henderson, Louis Armstrong, from 1930s; led own band, 1960s.
b. May 11, 1906 in Atlanta, Georgia
d. May 26, 1973 in New York, New York

Bertie (Elbert) Higgins
American singer–songwriter
• Recorded hit single, "Key Largo," 1982.
b. 1946 in Tarpon Springs, Florida

Loretta Sell Hildegarde
American singer
• Nightclub, radio pianist, vocalist; popular, 1940s; wore evening gowns, long gloves.
b. February 01, 1906 in Adell, Wisconsin

Billy Hill
American songwriter
• Numerous hits include "The Last Round-Up," 1933; "Empty Saddles," 1936.
b. July 14, 1899 in Boston, Massachusetts
d. December 24, 1940 in Boston, Massachusetts

Chippie (Bertha) Hill
American jazz musician
• Vocalist with Ma Rainey's troupe; made numerous recordings with Louis Armstrong.
b. 1905 in Charleston, South Carolina
d. May 07, 1950 in New York, New York

Dan Hill
Canadian singer
• Soft rock singer; had hit single "Sometimes When We Touch," 1977.
b. June 03, 1954 in Toronto, Ontario

Joe Hill, pseud
(Joel Emmanuel Haaglund; Joseph Hillstrom)
American labor union official–songwriter
• Member, IWW; best known for song "The Preacher and the Slave," which contained phrase "pie in the sky."
b. October 07, 1879 in Sweden
d. November 19, 1915 in Salt Lake City, Utah

Johann Adam Hiller
Prussian composer
• Credited with originating the singspiel; his singspiels include "Die Jagd," 1770.
b. December 25, 1728 in Wendisch-Ossig, Prussia
d. June 16, 1804 in Leipzig, Germany

Chris Hillman
(The Byrds; The Flying Burrito Brothers; The Souther-Hillman-Furay Band)
American musician
• Blue-grass mandolinist; solo works include "Slippin' Away."
b. December 04, 1942 in Los Angeles, California

Paul Hindemith
German musician–composer
• Music banned by Nazis; best known for opera *Mathis the Painter*, 1938.
b. November 16, 1895 in Hanau, Germany
d. December 28, 1963 in Frankfurt, Germany (West)

Natalie Leota Henderson Hinderas
American pianist
• One of first black musicians to establish a solid career in classical music.
b. 1927 in Oberlin, Ohio
d. July 22, 1987 in Philadelphia, Pennsylvania

Fatha (Earl Kenneth) Hines
American jazz musician
• Member, Down Beat Magazine Hall of Fame; leading influence in swing, jazz piano styles.
b. December 28, 1905 in Duquesne, Pennsylvania
d. July 22, 1983 in Oakland, California

Jerome Hines
American opera singer
• A leading basso, MY Met., from 1947; noted for *Boris Godunov*.
b. November 09, 1921 in Hollywood, California

Al Hirt
American jazz musician
• Trumpeter whose hits include "Bourbon Street," 1961; "Cotton Candy," 1964.
b. November 07, 1922 in New Orleans, Louisiana

Robert Ernest Hite, Jr
(Canned Heat; "The Bear")
American singer
• Blue-grass vocalist; hit song "On the Road Again."
b. January 26, 1943 in Torrance, California
d. April 1981 in Los Angeles, California

Don Ho
American singer
• Best known entertainer in Hawaii; popularized song "Tiny Bubbles," 1967.
b. August 13, 1930 in Kakaako, Hawaii

Johnny Hodges
American jazz musician
• Alto saxist with Duke Ellington, 1928-51.
b. July 25, 1906 in Cambridge, Massachusetts
d. May 11, 1970 in New York, New York

Al Hoffman
American composer–author
• Wrote popular stage scores, 1930s-50; hit songs include "Mairz Doats," 1944.
b. September 25, 1902 in Minsk, Russia
d. July 21, 1960 in New York, New York

Susanna Hoffs
(The Bangles)
American singer
• Lead vocalist with all-female rock group, 1981–; hits include "Walk Like an Egyptian," 1986.
b. January 17, 1962 in California

Josef Hofmann
American musician
• Child prodigy, int'l. concert pianist; famous for Chopin, Liszt interpretations.
b. January 2, 1876 in Krakow, Poland
d. February 16, 1957 in Los Angeles, California

Christopher Hogwood
English conductor–musician
• Founded Academy of Ancient Music, 1974.
b. September 1, 1941 in Nottingham, England

Lee Hoiby
American composer–pianist
• Virtuoso concert pianist/romantic composer best known for opera *Summer and Smoke*, 1971, based on play by Tennessee Williams.
b. February 17, 1926 in Madison, Wisconsin

Josef Holbrooke
English composer
• Wrote Celtic-type trilogy, *The Cauldron of Anwyn*, 1912-29.
b. July 05, 1878 in Croydon, England
d. August 05, 1958 in London, England

Billie Holiday
(Eleanora Fagan; "Lady Day")
American singer
• Renowned jazz vocalist; autobiography, *Lady Sings the Blues*, 1956, inspired film, 1972.
b. April 07, 1915 in Baltimore, Maryland
d. July 17, 1959 in New York, New York

Charles Holland
American opera singer
• Expatriate; first black man to perform in Paris Opera House; Carnegie Hall debut, 1982.
b. 1910
d. 1987 in Amsterdam, Netherlands

Jennifer Yvette Holliday
American singer–actress
• Star of Broadway's *Dream Girls*, who had hit single from show: "And I'm Telling You I'm Not Going," 1982.
b. October 19, 1960 in Riverside, Texas

The Hollies
(Bernie Calvert; Allan Clarke; Bobby Elliott; Eric Haydock; TonyHicks; Graham Nash; Mikael Rikfors; Terry Sylvester)
English music group
• Most consistently successful band after The Beatles; hit single "He Ain't Heavy, He's My Brother," 1970.

Heinz Holliger
Swiss musician
• International prize-winning oboist.
b. May 21, 1939 in Langenthal, Switzerland

Buddy (Charles Hardin Holley) Holly
(Buddy Holly and the Crickets)
American singer–songwriter
• Pioneered early, upbeat rock-and-roll: "Peggy Sue," 1957. Died in plane crash.
b. September 07, 1936 in Lubbock, Texas
d. February 03, 1959 in Clear Lake, Iowa

Libby Holman
American singer–actress
• In Broadway musicals, 1920s-30s; torch singer known for sultry rendition of "Body and Soul."
b. May 23, 1906 in Cincinnati, Ohio
d. June 18, 1971 in Stamford, Connecticut

Louise Homer
(Louise Dilworth Beatty)
American opera singer
• Leading contralto with NY Met., 1900-19; starred with Enrico Caruso in *Samson and Dalila*.
b. April 28, 1871 in Sewickley, Pennsylvania
d. May 06, 1947 in Winter Park, Florida

Sidney Homer
American composer
• Published over 100 songs: "Song of the Shirt," "Sweet and Low"; husband of Louise.
b. December 09, 1864 in Boston, Massachusetts
d. July 1, 1953 in Winter Park, Florida

Arthur Honegger
(Les Six)
French composer
• Member of avant-garde "Group of Six"; wrote *Le Roi David*, 1921; *Pacific 231*, 1923, describing a locomotive; composed several film scores.
b. March 1, 1892 in Le Havre, France
d. November 27, 1955 in Paris, France

The Honeycombs
(Denis Dalziel; John Lantree; Ann Honey Lantree; Martin Murray; Alan Ward)
English music group
• "British Invasion" group, formed 1963; first to have female drummer.

The Honeydrippers
(Jeff Beck; Jimmy Page; Robert Plant; Nile Rodgers)
English music group
• Formed to record album of old rock songs: hit single "Sea of Love," 1984.

James (Jimmy) Honeyman-Scott
(The Pretenders)
English musician
• Guitarist, keyboardist with British pop group, 1980-82.
b. November 04, 1956 in Hereford, England
d. June 16, 1982 in London, England

Brian Hooker
American dramatist–librettist
• Wrote librettos for Broadway shows, 1920s-30s, including *Vagabond King*, 1925.
b. November 02, 1880 in New York, New York
d. December 28, 1946 in New London, Connecticut

John Lee Hooker
American singer
• Had rhythm and blues million-seller, 1948, "Boogie Chillin'."
b. August 22, 1917 in Clarkdale, Mississippi

Mary Hopkin
Welsh singer
• Discovered by the Beatles; best-known song: "Those Were the Days," 1968.
b. May 03, 1950 in Ystradgynlais, Wales

Claude Hopkins
American musician
• Pianist who led popular swing band, 1930s-50s.
b. August 03, 1903 in Washington, District of Columbia

Lightnin' (Sam) Hopkins
American singer–musician
• Blues singer, guitarist, whose nickname was derived from partner "Thunder" Smith; recorded 100 singles.
b. March 15, 1912 in Centerville, Texas
d. January 3, 1982 in Houston, Texas

Telma Louise Hopkins
(Tony Orlando and Dawn)
American actress–singer
• Part of singing group Dawn; co-stars in TV series "Gimme a Break."
b. October 28, 1948 in Louisville, Kentucky

Francis Hopkinson
American continental congressman–lawyer–poet–composer
• Signed Declaration of Independence for NJ, 1776; wrote satires against British; helped design American flag, 1777; considered among first American composers.
b. September 21, 1737 in Philadelphia, Pennsylvania
d. May 09, 1791 in Philadelphia, Pennsylvania

Paul Joseph Horn
American musician
• Flutist, Grammy Award winner, 1966; made recordings in Taj Mahal, Giza pyramids, 1976.
b. March 17, 1930 in New York, New York

Lena Calhoun Horne
American singer–actress
• Nightclub entertainer known for song "Stormy Weather"; starred on Broadway in "Lena Horne: The Lady and Her Music," 1980-82; won Spingarn, 1982. Known for her ageless beauty.
b. June 3, 1917 in Brooklyn, New York

Marilyn Horne
American opera singer
• Mezzo-soprano who dubbed Dorothy Dandridge's voice in *Carmen Jones*, film, 1954.
b. January 16, 1934 in Bradford, Pennsylvania

Bruce Hornsby
(Bruce Hornsby and the Range)
American singer–songwriter–musician
• Had number one single "Way It Is" from debut album of same name, 1986.
b. 1954 in Williamsburg, Virginia

Vladimir Horowitz
American pianist
• Dominated 20th-c. concert pianism with delicate pedaling, daring finger work; left Soviet Union, 1925, returning to Moscow to perform, 1986; won numerous Grammys.
b. October 01, 1904 in Kiev, Russia
d. November 05, 1989 in New York, New York

Johnny Horton
American singer
• Country singer who crossed over to pop charts; hit single "Battle of New Orleans," 1959.
b. April 3, 1927 in Tyler, Texas
d. November 05, 1960 in Austin, Texas

Hot Tuna
(Jack Casady; Papa John Creach; Jorma Kaukonen; Sammy Piazza; Will Scarlett; Bob Steeler)
American music group
• Satellite group of Jefferson Airplane, 1972-78.

Cissy (Emily Drinkard) Houston
(Sweet Inspirations)
American singer
• Gospel-soul singer; first to record "Midnight Train to Georgia"; mother of Whitney Houston.
b. 1932 in Newark, New Jersey

Whitney Houston
American singer
• Won Grammy, 1986, for top female pop vocalist; hits include "How Will I Know," 1987; won Emmy for performance on "The Grammy Awards," 1986.
b. August 09, 1963 in Newark, New Jersey

Alan Hovhaness
American composer
• Numerous works include "And God Created Great Whales," 1970, with recorded humpback whale voices.
b. March 08, 1911 in Somerville, Massachusetts

Eddy Howard
American bandleader–songwriter–actor
• Vocalist, 1930s; led band, 1940s-50s; wrote "Careless."
b. September 12, 1909 in Woodland, California
d. May 23, 1963 in Palm Desert, California

Joseph Edgar Howard
American entertainer–songwriter
• Wrote songs "Hello, My Baby"; "I Wonder Who's Kissing Her Now."
b. February 12, 1878 in New York, New York
d. May 19, 1961 in Chicago, Illinois

Howlin' Wolf
(Chester Burnett)
American singer–songwriter
• Had rhythm and blues hits, 1954-64: "Little Red Rooster"; "Back Door Man."
b. June 1, 1910 in West Point, Mississippi
d. January 1, 1976 in Chicago, Illinois

Bronislaw Huberman
Austrian violinist
• Int'l. concertist; founded Palestine Symphony Orchestra, 1936, composed largely of Jewish musicians; exiled by Nazi oppression.
b. December 19, 1882 in Czestochowa, Poland
d. June 16, 1947 in Nant Corsier, Switzerland

Mick Hucknall
(Simply Red; "Red")
British singer
• Known for flaming red hair; had number one hit "Holding Back the Years," 1986.
b. June 08, 1960 in Manchester, England

The Hudson Brothers
(Brett Hudson; Bill Hudson; Mark Hudson)
American music group
• Hit singles include "Rendevous," 1975; starred in own weekly TV show, "The Razzle Dazzle Comedy Hour," 1975.

Huey Lewis and the News
(Mario Cipollina; Johnny Colla; Bill Gibson; Chris Hayes; Sean Hopper; Huey Lewis)
American music group
• Pop/rock group formed 1982; hits include "Heart and Soul," 1983; "If This Is It," 1984.

The Human League
(Ian Burden; Joe Callis; Joanne Catherall; Phil Oakey; Susanne Sulley; Philip Wright)
English music group
• Electro-pop band formed 1977; best successes in US: "Don't You Want Me," 1982; "Human," 1987.

Humble Pie
(David Clem Clemson; Peter Frampton; Steve Marriott; Gregory Ridley; Jerry Shirley)
English music group
• Hard-rock band, 1968-75; had hit album Smokin', 1972.

Helen Humes
American singer
• Jazz singer who sang with Count Basie, 1938-42; had hit song "Be Baba Leba," 1945.
b. June 23, 1913 in Louisville, Kentucky
d. September 13, 1981 in Santa Monica, California

Johann Nepomuk Hummel
German composer–pianist
• Helped develop art of piano playing; wrote opera Mathilde von guise, 1810.
b. November 14, 1778 in Pressburg, Germany
d. October 17, 1837 in Weimar, Germany

Engelbert Humperdinck
German composer
• Wrote opera Hansel and Gretel, 1893.
b. September 01, 1854 in Siegburg, Germany
d. September 27, 1921 in Neustrelitz, Germany

Engelbert Humperdinck
(Arnold Gerry Dorsey)
English singer
• Nightclub, TV singer, most popular 1960s-70s; picked stage name from music dictionary; albums include Release Me, 1968.
b. May 03, 1936 in Madras, India

Lois Hunt
American actress–singer
• Soprano, NY Met., 1949-53; on Broadway in Sound of Music, 1961-62.
b. November 26, 1925 in York, Pennsylvania

Pee Wee (Walter) Hunt
American jazz musician
• Trombonist; vocalist with Glen Gray, 1929-43; led Dixieland combos, 1950s-60s.
b. May 1, 1907 in Mount Healthy, Ohio

Alberta Hunter
American singer–songwriter
• Blues singer; performed with jazz greats, wrote own songs; remarkable comeback at age 82.
b. April 01, 1897 in Memphis, Tennessee
d. October 17, 1984 in New York, New York

Ian Hunter
(Mott the Hoople)
English singer–musician
• Leader of Mott the Hopple; had solo hit "Just Another Night," 1979.
b. June 03, 1946 in Shrewsbury, England

Ivory Joe Hunter
American singer–songwriter
• Rhythm and blues singer-pianist, 1950s; had gold record "Since I Met You Baby," 1956.
b. 1911 in Kirbyville, Texas
d. November 08, 1974 in Memphis, Tennessee

Mississippi John Hurt
American singer–musician
• Hits include "Candy Man Blues," 1928; dropped out of business for 35 yrs., made comeback in 1963.
b. March 08, 1892 in Teoc, Mississippi
d. November 02, 1966 in Grenada, Mississippi

Ferlin Husky
American singer
• Country, pop recording star on radio, TV.
b. December 03, 1927 in Flat River, Missouri

Michael Hutchence
(INXS)
Australian singer
• Lead singer; had top 10 singles "New Sensation," "Devil Inside" from album Kick, 1988.
b. January 22, 1960 in Sydney, Australia

Ina Ray Hutton
American bandleader–singer
• Founded one of first all-female orchestras, 1935-40.
b. March 03, 1916 in Chicago, Illinois
d. February 19, 1984 in Ventura, California

Brian Hyland
American singer
• Pop singer who had novelty hit, "Itsy Bitsy Teenie Weenie Yellow Polkadot Bikini," 1960.
b. November 12, 1943 in Woodhaven, New York

Chrissie (Christine Elaine) Hynde
(The Pretenders)
American singer–songwriter
• Founded British rock group The Pretenders, 1978.
b. September 07, 1951 in Akron, Ohio

Janis Ian
(Janis Fink)
American singer–songwriter
• Won Grammy, 1975, for "At Seventeen."
b. May 07, 1950 in New York, New York

Ian and Sylvia
(Sylvia Fricker; Ian Tyson)
Canadian music group
• Husband-wife folksinging duo, formed 1959; sang country music, 1960s.

Jacques Ibert
French composer
• Director, Paris Opera, French Academy in Rome; wrote music for films, 1937-55.
b. August 15, 1890 in Paris, France
d. February 05, 1962 in Paris, France

Billy Idol
(William Board)
English singer
• Punk rock teen idol; hit singles "Eyes Without a Face," 1984; "Rebel Yell," 1985.
b. November 3, 1955 in Surrey, England

Julio Iglesias
(Julio Iglesias de la Cueva)
Spanish singer–songwriter
• Master of love song; has sold over 100 million albums.
b. September 23, 1943 in Madrid, Spain

Ike and Tina Turner
American music group
• Husband-wife rock and roll singing duo; first hit: "A Fool in Love," 1960. Known for domestic disaccord.

The Impressions
(Fred Cash; Sam Gooden; Ralph Johnson; Reggie Torrian)
American music group
• Soul vocal group formed 1958; pre-Temptations hits include "Gypsy Woman," 1961; "It's Alright," 1963.

The Incredible String Band
(Gerard Dott; Mike Heron; Malcolm Le-Maistre; Licorice (Christina) McKechnie; Rose Simpson; Robin Williamson)
Scottish music group
• Albums include *Changing Horses; I Looked Up.*

Paul (Marie Theodore Vincent d') Indy
French composer–author
• Wrote opera *Le Chant de la Cloche,* 1883; revived interest in Gregorian chant; made Wagner known in France.
b. March 27, 1851 in Paris, France
d. December 02, 1931 in Paris, France

James Ingram
American singer–songwriter
• With Patti Austin, had hit single "Baby Come to Me," 1982.
b. February 16, 1956 in Akron, Ohio

The Ink Spots
(Billy Bowen; Charlie Fuqua; Orville Jones; Bill Kenny; Herb Kenny; Ivory Watson)
American music group
• Biggest hit "If I Didn't Care," 1939.

INXS
(Garry Gary Beers; Andrew Farriss; Jon Farriss; Tim Farriss; Michael Hutchence; Kirk Pengilly)
Australian music group
• Hit single "Original Sin," 1984, featured Daryl Hall on back-up vocals.

John Ireland
English composer
• Wrote piano pieces, orchestral works, 100 songs to words of noted authors.
b. August 13, 1879 in Inglewood, England
d. June 12, 1962 in Washington, England

Iron Butterfly
(Erik Braun; Ronald Bushy; Lee Dorman; Doug Ingle; Michael Pinera; Lawrence Reinhardt)
American music group
• Heavy metal group; albums include *Sun and Steel,* 1975; *Iron Butterfly,* 1970. Known for 18-minute "In A Gadda Da Vida," off album of same name, which became one of Atlantic largest-selling rock albums.

Iron Maiden
(Clive Burr; Paul Di'Anno; Steve Harris; Dave Murray; Adrian Smith; Dennis Stratton)
British music group
• Heavy metal band named after medieval torture device; formed in 1977; albums include *Piece of Mind,* 1983.

Robert Augustine Irving
American conductor
• Led NYC Ballet, 1958–; England's Royal Ballet, 1949-58.
b. August 28, 1913 in Winchester, England

The Isley Brothers
(O'Kelly Isley; Ronald Isley; Rudolph Isley; Ernie Isley; MarvinIsley; Chris Jasper)
American music group
• Soul-rock group formed, 1957; hits include "It's Your Thing," 1969; "Harvest For the World," 1976.

Eugene George Istomin
American musician
• Int'l concert soloist; with Pablo Casals, annual Casals Festivals, from 1950.
b. November 26, 1925 in New York, New York

Amparo Iturbi
Spanish pianist
• Often performed with brother, Jose.
b. 1899
d. April 21, 1969 in Beverly Hills, California

Konstantin Konstantinovich Ivanov
Russian conductor
• Led USSR State Symphony, 1946-75; has had numerous world tours.
b. May 21, 1907 in Efremov, Russia

Burl Ives
(Icle Ivanhoe)
American actor–singer
• Foremost folksinger since 1940s; won 1959 Oscar for *The Big Country;* noted for role of Big Daddy in *Cat on a Hot Tin Roof,* 1958.
b. June 14, 1909 in Hunt, Illinois

Charles Edward Ives
American composer
• Unconventional style of composition included polytonal harmonies, unusual rhythms; won 1947 Pulitzer for *Symphony Number Three.*
b. October 2, 1874 in Danbury, Connecticut
d. May 11, 1954 in New York, New York

The J Geils Band
(Stephen Jo Bladd; Magic Dick; Jerome Geils; Seth Justman; DannyKlein; Peter Wolf)
American music group
• Combined blues, doo-woop, rhythm and blues, pop; had hit album *Freeze-Frame,* single "Centerfold," 1981.

Aunt Molly Jackson
(Mary Magdalene Garland)
American singer
• Songs include "The Death of Harry Simms," 1931; prominent figure in coal mine union organization, 1930s.
b. 1880 in Clay City, Kentucky
d. September 01, 1960

Jackie (Sigmund Esco) Jackson
(The Jackson Five; The Jacksons)
American singer
• Oldest in group of singing brothers; first hit, "I Want You Back," 1970, sold over two million copies; solo album *Jackie Jackson,* 1973.
b. May 04, 1951 in Gary, Indiana

Janet Damita Jackson
American singer–actress
• Youngest sister of Michael; albums *Control,* 1986, *Rhythm Nation: 1814,* 1989, have sold 5 million copies each; 7 singles from *Rhythm Nation* have made Billboard top 10, making her first female artist to accomplish this.
b. May 16, 1966 in Gary, Indiana

Jermaine La Jaune Jackson
(The Jackson Five; The Jacksons)
American singer–musician
• Has had consistent solo career: "Let's Get Serious," 1980.
b. December 11, 1954 in Gary, Indiana

Joe Jackson
English singer
• Had hit single "Steppin' Out," 1982.
b. August 11, 1955 in Burton-on-Trent, England

Mahalia Jackson
American singer
• Best known for gospel songs "I Believe," "He's Got the Whole World in His Hands."
b. October 26, 1911 in New Orleans, Louisiana
d. January 27, 1972 in Evergreen Park, Illinois

Marlon David Jackson
(The Jackson Five; The Jacksons)
American singer
• Biggest selling hit was "I'll Be There," 1970.
b. March 12, 1957 in Gary, Indiana

Michael Joseph Jackson
(The Jackson Five; The Jacksons; "Peter Pan of Pop" "Smelly")
American singer–actor
• Lead singer with group of brothers; solo career made him cult figure: best-selling album of all time *Thriller*, 1982; followed by *Bad*, 1987.
b. August 29, 1958 in Gary, Indiana

Milt(on) Jackson
American jazz musician
• Pioneer bop vibist; helped develop progressive jazz.
b. January 01, 1923 in Detroit, Michigan

Randy (Steven Randall) Jackson
(The Jacksons)
American singer
• Joined singing brothers as drummer, 1974.
b. October 29, 1961 in Gary, Indiana

Tito (Toriano Adaryll) Jackson
(The Jackson Five; The Jacksons)
American singer–musician
• Had 13 top 20 singles: "ABC" was number one, 1970.
b. October 15, 1953 in Gary, Indiana

The Jackson Five
(Jermaine Jackson; LaToya Jackson; Marlon Jackson; Michael Jackson; Jackie Jackson; Tito Jackson)
American music group
• Motown group from Gary, IN; hits include "ABC," "I'll Be There," 1970.

The Jacksons
(Jackie Jackson; Marlon Jackson; Michael Jackson; Randy Jackson;Tito Jackson)
American music group
• Family singing group formed 1976 after leaving Motown label as The Jackson Five; hit albums include *Triumph*, 1981; *Victory*, 1984.

Al(bert T) Jacobs
American lyricist–composer
• Wrote over 300 songs including "This Is My Country," "There'll Never Be Another You."
b. January 22, 1903 in San Francisco, California
d. February 13, 1985 in Laurel, Maryland

Illinois Jacquet
American jazz musician
• Tenor saxist; led own combos, 1940s-70s; recorded "Flying Home."
b. October 31, 1922 in Broussard, Louisiana

Mick (Michael Philip) Jagger
(The Rolling Stones)
English singer–musician
• Formed Rolling Stones, 1962; hits include "Satisfaction," "Honky Tonk Woman."
b. July 26, 1943 in Dartford, England

Ahmad Jamal
American jazz musician
• Pianist known for concerts, recordings; only artist to have album on nat. top-10 list for 108 straight weeks: *But Not for Me*.
b. July 07, 1930 in Pittsburgh, Pennsylvania

Bob James
American jazz musician
• Uses funk influence in music; hit albums include *Foxie*, 1983.
b. December 25, 1939 in Marshall, Montana

Harry James
American bandleader
• Brilliant trumpeter; led popular dance band for 40 yrs; wed to Betty Grable, 1943-65.
b. March 15, 1916 in Albany, Georgia
d. July 05, 1983 in Las Vegas, Nevada

Rick James
(James Johnson)
American singer
• Double platinum album *Street Songs*, 1981, included single "Super Freak."
b. February 01, 1952 in Buffalo, New York

Skip (Nehemiah) James
American musician–singer
• Blues pioneer, rediscovered, 1960s; hit song "I'm So Glad."
b. June 09, 1902 in Bentonia, Mississippi
d. October 03, 1969 in Philadelphia, Pennsylvania

Sonny James
(Jimmy Loden; "The Southern Gentleman")
American singer
• Country vocalist; recorded best-selling "Young Love," 1957.
b. March 01, 1929 in Hackleburg, Alaska

James Gang
(Tom Bolin; James Fox; Phil Giallombardo; Bubba Keith; Roy Kenner; Dale Peters; Richard Shack; Dom Troiano; Joseph Fidler Walsh; Bob Webb)
American music group
• Vocal, instrumental rock group; albums include *Yer Album*, 1969.

Jan and Dean
(Jan Berry; Dean Torrance)
American music group
• Surf music duo, 1958-66; hit debut single "Jennie Lee," sold 10 million albums.

Leos Janacek
Czech composer
• A leading exponent of musical nationalism; wrote *From House of the Dead*, 1930.
b. July 03, 1854 in Hukvaldy, Moravia
d. August 12, 1928 in Prague, Czechoslovakia

Antonio Janigro
Italian musician–conductor
• International cello soloist; founded ensemble, Solisti di Zagreb, 1950.
b. January 21, 1918 in Milan, Italy

Byron Janis
American pianist
• First American sent in cultural exchange to USSR, 1960, 1962; discovered unknown Chopin waltzes.
b. March 24, 1928 in McKeesport, Pennsylvania

Al(lan) Jardine
(The Beach Boys)
American singer–musician
• Vocalist, guitarist; hits with group include *Ten Years of Harmony*, 1981.
b. September 03, 1942 in Lima, Ohio

Maurice Jarre
French composer
• Won Oscars for scores *Lawrence of Arabia*, 1962; *Doctor Zhivago*, 1966.
b. September 13, 1924 in Lyons, France

Al Jarreau
American singer
• Won Grammys for best jazz vocalist, 1978, 1979.
b. March 12, 1940 in Milwaukee, Wisconsin

Keith Jarrett
American musician
• Noted jazz pianist, 1960s-70s; specialized in Bartok performances, 1980s.
b. May 08, 1945 in Allentown, Pennsylvania

Jay and the Americans
(David Jay Black; Sandy Deane; Howie Kane; Marty Sander; JohnJay "Traynor; Kenny Vance)
American music group
• Clean-cut, Brooklyn-based group; hits included "Cara Mia," 1965; "This Magic Moment," 1969.

Renee Marcelle Jeanmaire
French actress–dancer–singer
• Wife of Roland Petit and leading dancer of Ballets Roland Petit, Casino de Paris.
b. April 29, 1924 in Paris, France

Blind Lemon Jefferson
American singer
• Country-blues singer, 1920s; album issued 1968: *Blind Lemon Jefferson: 1926-29.*
b. 1897 in Wortham, Texas
d. 1930 in Chicago, Illinois

Jefferson Starship
(Marty Balin; Jack Casady; Joey Covington; Spencer Dryden; Paul Katner; Jorma Kauoknen; Grace Slick)
American music group
• Founded, 1966, as Jefferson Airplane; several members formed Starship, 1985.

Garland Jeffreys
American singer–songwriter
• Soul singer who blends rock, jazz, reggae; album *Escape Artist*, 1981.
b. 1944 in Brooklyn, New York

Gordon Jenkins
American composer–conductor
• Best known for 1945 composition *Manhattan Tower Suite*, in praise of NY.
b. May 12, 1910 in Webster Groves, Missouri
d. May 01, 1984 in Malibu, California

Waylon Jennings
American singer
• Albums of country music include *Take It to the Limit;* narrator for TV series "The Dukes of Hazzard," 1979-86.
b. June 15, 1937 in Littlefield, Texas

Adolph Jensen
German composer
• Published about 160 songs; similar to Schumann's works.
b. January 12, 1837 in Konigsberg, Germany
d. January 23, 1879 in Baden-Baden, Germany

Jerry Murad's Harmonicats
(Al Fiore; Don Les; Jerry Murad)
American musicians
• Harmonica group best known for 1947 hit "Peg o' My Heart."

Jethro Tull
(Mick Abrahams; Ian Anderson; Barriemore Barlowe; Martin Barre; Clive Bunker; Glenn Cornick; John Evan; Jeffrey Hammond-Hammond)
English music group
• Successful rock band; popular 1970s singles include "Living in the Past," 1972. Led by Anderson's flute playing.

Joan Jett
(Joan Jett and the Blackhearts; Joan Larkin; The Runaways)
American singer–musician
• Had pop-heavy metal single "I Love Rock 'n Roll," 1982.
b. September 22, 1960 in Philadelphia, Pennsylvania

Joseph Joachim
Hungarian violinist–composer
• Violin virtuoso; founded famed Joachim Quartet, 1869; wrote "Hungerian Concerto," 1857.
b. June 28, 1831 in Kisstee, Hungary
d. August 15, 1907 in Berlin, Germany

Joan Jett and the Blackhearts
(Ricky Byrd; Lee Crystal; Joan Jett; Gary Ryan)
American music group
• Had hit single "I Love Rock 'n Roll," 1982.

Billy (William Martin) Joel
American singer–songwriter
• Had five #1 songs from album *An Innocent Man*, 1983; singles include "You're Only Human," 1985.
b. May 09, 1949 in Bronx, New York

Grant Johannesen
American pianist
• International concertist, 1950s-60s; esteemed for French, American works.
b. 1921 in Salt Lake City, Utah

Elton John
(Reginald Kenneth Dwight)
English singer–songwriter
• All albums are gold; hits include "Rocket Man," 1972; "Philadelphia Freedom," 1975; "Wrap Her Up," 1985.
b. March 25, 1947 in Pinner, England

Bunk (William Geary) Johnson
American jazz musician
• Early Dixieland trumpeter; rediscovered, 1937, by jazz aficionados.
b. December 27, 1879 in New Orleans, Louisiana
d. July 07, 1949 in New Iberia, Louisiana

Dink (Oliver) Johnson
American jazz musician
• Drummer, pianist, clarinetist with Kid Ory, 1920s.
b. October 28, 1892 in New Orleans, Louisiana
d. November 29, 1954 in Portland, Oregon

Hall Johnson
American composer
• Organized Hall Johnson Choir heard in movie *Lost Horizon;* founded Negro Choir, 1925.
b. March 12, 1888 in Athens, Georgia
d. April 3, 1970 in New York, New York

J J (James Louis) Johnson
American jazz musician
• Noted bop era trombonist; with Count Basie, 1940s.
b. January 22, 1924 in Indianapolis, Indiana

James Price Johnson
American songwriter–pianist
• Wrote lyrics, music for hit "Charleston," 1923; song gave its name to popular 1920s dance.
b. February 01, 1891 in New Brunswick, New Jersey
d. November 17, 1955 in New York, New York

Al Jolson
(Asa Yoelson)
American singer
• Starred in *The Jazz Singer*, 1927, the first talking film.
b. May 26, 1886 in Saint Petersburg, Russia
d. October 23, 1950 in San Francisco, California

Niccolo Jommelli
Italian composer
• Developed more progressive, realistic Italian opera; wrote church music, opera *Armida*, 1770.
b. September 1, 1714 in Aversa, Italy
d. August 25, 1774 in Naples, Italy

Allan Jones
American singer
• Father of Jack Jones, famous for song "Donkey Serenade," 1937.
b. October 14, 1907 in Old Forge, Pennsylvania

Billy (William Reese) Jones
(The Happiness Boys; The Interwoven Pair)
American singer
• Early radio star, part of team with Ernie Hare; famous for performing some of first commercial jingles for many products.
b. March 15, 1889
d. November 23, 1940

Brian Jones
(The Rolling Stones)
English singer–musician
• One of original Rolling Stones; found dead in swimming pool from drug overdose.
b. February 26, 1943 in Cheltenham, England
d. July 03, 1969 in London, England

Davy (David) Jones
(The Monkees)
English actor–singer
• Vocalist with The Monkees on popular TV series, 1966-68.
b. December 3, 1945 in Manchester, England

George Jones
American singer
• Named best male vocalist by CMA, 1980, 1981; married to Tammy Wynette, 1968-75.
b. September 12, 1931 in Saratoga, Texas

Grace Jones
Jamaican singer–actress–model
• In James Bond film *A View to a kill,* 1985; star of *Vamp,* 1986; hit album *Living My Life,* 1982.
b. May 19, 1952 in Spanishtown, Jamaica

Grandpa (Louis Marshall) Jones
American musician–TV personality
• Known for banjo solos on TV series "Hee Haw," since 1969.
b. October 2, 1913 in Henderson County, Kentucky

Gwyneth Jones
Welsh opera singer
• Dramatic soprano with Covent Garden Royal Opera since 1966; noted for Verdi, Wagner roles.
b. November 07, 1936 in Pontnewynydd, Wales

Howard Jones
English singer
• Dance music hits include "What Is Love," 1983; "Things Can Only Get Better," 1985.
b. February 23, 1955 in Southampton, England

Isham Jones
American bandleader–songwriter
• Led outstanding dance band that was most popular, 1930-35; wrote "It Had to be You," 1924.
b. January 31, 1894 in Coalton, Ohio
d. October 19, 1956 in Hollywood, California

Jack Jones
American singer
• Nightclub entertainer; best known for hit title song for film *Love with the Proper Stranger,* 1964.
b. January 14, 1938 in Beverly Hills, California

Jo(nathan) Jones
American jazz musician
• Drummer with Count Basie band, 1935-48; innovative swing-era techniques were major influence on jazz drummers.
b. October 07, 1911 in Chicago, Illinois
d. September 03, 1985 in New York, New York

John Paul Jones
(John Baldwin; Led Zeppelin)
English musician
• Keyboardist, bassist, Led Zeppelin rock group, 1968-80.
b. January 03, 1946 in Sidcup, England

Jonah (Robert E) Jones
American musician
• Trumpeter, fine showman; with Cab Calloway, 1941-51; recorded show tunes, jazz hits.
b. December 31, 1909 in Louisville, Kentucky

Matilda Sissieretta Joyner Jones
American singer
• First Negro prima donna; star of Black Patti Troubadours, 1896-1916.
b. January 05, 1869 in Portsmouth, Virginia
d. June 24, 1933 in Providence, Rhode Island

Quincy Delight Jones
American composer
• Wrote scores for over 50 films including *In Cold Blood,* 1967; *The Wiz,* 1978; worked on "We Are the World," 1985; won five Grammys.
b. March 14, 1933 in Chicago, Illinois

Rickie Lee Jones
American singer–songwriter
• Combines rhythm and blues, jazz, folk music; hit single "Chuck E's in Love," 1979.
b. November 08, 1954 in Chicago, Illinois

Spike (Lindsay Armstrong) Jones
American bandleader–musician
• With City Slickers Band was noted, 1940s-60s for lampooning popular songs, using zany sound effects.
b. December 14, 1911 in Long Beach, California
d. May 01, 1964 in Los Angeles, California

Thad(deus Joseph) Jones
American musician
• Soloist, jazz drummer with Count Basie Orchestra, 1954-63.
b. March 28, 1923 in Pontiac, Michigan
d. August 2, 1986 in Copenhagen, Denmark

Tom Jones
American dramatist–songwriter
• Known for musical comedies; books, lyrics include *The Rainmaker,* 1963; plays include *The Bone Room.*
b. February 17, 1928 in Littlefield, Texas

Tom Jones
(Thomas Jones Woodward)
Welsh musician–singer
• Hits include "It's Not Unusual," 1964; "What's New Pussycat," 1965. Known for tight pants.
b. June 07, 1940 in Pontypridd, Wales

Janis Joplin
(Big Brother and the Holding Company)
American singer
• Hits include "Me and Bobby McGee," 1971; died of drug overdose; life story was filmed: *The Rose,* 1979.
b. January 19, 1943 in Port Arthur, Texas
d. October 03, 1970 in Hollywood, California

Scott Joplin
American musician–composer
• Developed ragtime music; wrote "The Entertainer," 1902; music revived in score of *The Sting,* 1973.
b. November 24, 1868 in Texarkana, Texas
d. April 04, 1917 in New York, New York

Louis Jordan
American jazz musician–singer
• Alto saxist who led Tympany Five, 1940s; noted for novelty, blues recordings; starred in all-black movie musical, *Beware,* 1946.
b. July 08, 1908 in Brinkley, Arkansas
d. February 04, 1975 in Los Angeles, California

Journey
(Jonathan Cain; Aynsley Dunbar; Steve Perry; Gregg Rolie; Neil Schon; Steve Smith; Ross Valory)
American music group
• Rock band called "America's most popular rock band," 1983; hit single "Send Her My Love," 1983.

Eileen Joyce
Australian pianist
• Played with London Philharmonic in blitzed British towns, WW II.
b. November 21, 1912 in Zeehan, Tasmania

Judas Priest
(K K Downing; Rob Halford; Ian Hill; Dave Holland; Glenn Tipton)
British music group
• Heavy metal band formed mid-1970s; album *Screaming for Vengeance,* 1982.

Naomi Judd
(The Judds)
American singer
• The mother in the mother-daughter country group formed 1982; won three Grammys.
b. January 11, 1946 in Ashland, Kentucky

Wynonna Judd
(Christina Ciminella; The Judds)
American singer–musician
• The daughter in the mother-daughter country duo formed 1982; first hit singles were "Had a Dream (for the Heart)" and "Mama, He's Crazy," both 1984.
b. May 03, 1964 in Ashland, Kentucky

The Judds
(Naomi Judd; Wynonna Judd)
American music group
• Mother-daughter country duo formed 1982; have two platinum albums *Why Not Me* and *Rockin' with the Rhythm*.

K C and the Sunshine Band
(Oliver Brown; H(arry) W(ayne) Casey; Rick Finch; Robert Johnson;Denvil Liptrot; Jerome Smith; Ronnie Smith; James Weaver; Charles Williams)
American music group
• Formed 1973; hits nominated for Grammys: "That's the Way," 1975; "Shake Your Booty," 1976.

Dmitri Borisovich Kabalevsky
Russian composer
• Wrote piano concertos, symphonies, operas including *Colas Breugnon*, 1938.
b. December 3, 1904 in Saint Petersburg, Russia
d. February 17, 1987 in U.S.S.R.

Bert Kaempfert
German musician
• With band, known for "easy listening" albums, 1960s-70s; had hit single "Three O'Clock in the Morning," 1965; arranged recording debut of Beatles, 1961, as back-up group.
b. October 16, 1923 in Hamburg, Germany

Gus Kahn
American songwriter
• Wrote Broadway scores, songs including "My Blue Heaven," "Mammy"; produced average of six hit songs annually for 20 yrs.
b. November 06, 1886 in Koblenz, Germany
d. October 08, 1941 in Beverly Hills, California

Kitty Kallen
American singer-actress
• Vocalist with Big Bands; had hit "Little Things Mean a Lot," 1954.
b. May 25, 1926 in Philadelphia, Pennsylvania

Martin Kalmanoff
American composer–conductor–musician
• Wrote works for TV, musical theater, 17 operas.
b. May 24, 1920 in Brooklyn, New York

Bert Kalmar
American lyricist
• With Harry Ruby wrote hit songs "Who's Sorry Now?" 1923; "Three Little Words," 1930.
b. February 16, 1884 in New York, New York
d. September 18, 1947 in Los Angeles, California

Um Kalthoum
Egyptian singer
• Arab world's most beloved songstress.
b. 1898 in Tamay-al-Zahirah, Egypt
d. February 03, 1975 in Cairo, Egypt

Max Kaminsky
American jazz musician
• Star trumpeter; peaked in 1940s with Dixieland group; led own bands, 1960s-70s.
b. September 07, 1908 in Brockton, Massachusetts

John Kander
American composer
• With Fred Ebb, wrote song "New York, New York"; won Tonys for *Cabaret*, 1967, *Woman of the Year*, 1980.
b. March 18, 1927 in Kansas City, Missouri

Helen Kane
(Helen Schroder; "The Boop-Boop-a-Doop Girl")
American singer–actress
• Baby-voiced performer, 1920s-30s; portrayed by Debbie Reynolds in *Three Little Words*, 1950.
b. August 04, 1908 in New York, New York
d. September 26, 1966 in Jackson Heights, New York

Paul Kantner
(Jefferson Airplane; Jefferson Starship)
American singer–musician
• Rock 'n roll performer; with Jefferson Starship, 1972-84.
b. March 12, 1942 in San Francisco, California

Bronislau Kaper
American composer
• Won Oscar, 1953, for score of *Lili*.
b. February 05, 1902 in Warsaw, Poland
d. May 1983 in Beverly Hills, California

Gertrude Kappel
German opera singer
• A leading Wagnerian soprano; with NY Met., 1928-36.
b. September 01, 1893 in Halle, Germany
d. April 1971 in Munich, Germany (West)

Herbert von Karajan
Austrian conductor
• Director of the Berlin Philharmonic, 1954-89; made more than 800 recordings; criticized for Nazi past.
b. April 05, 1908 in Salzburg, Austria
d. July 16, 1989 in Anif, Austria

Terry Kath
(Chicago)
American singer–musician
• Guitarist, formed group with Walter Parazaider, 1967; died of accidental self-inflicted gun wound.
b. January 31, 1946 in Chicago, Illinois
d. January 23, 1978 in Los Angeles, California

Milton Katims
American musician–conductor
• Led Seattle Orchestra, 1954-76; first violinist under Toscanini, NBC Symphony, 1940-54.
b. 1909 in Brooklyn, New York

Jorma Kauokenen
(Jefferson Airplane)
American singer–musician
• Vocalist, guitarist with Jefferson Airplane, 1965-71; with Jack Casady, formed band Hot Tuna, 1970.
b. December 23, 1940 in Washington, District of Columbia

Kevin Kavanaugh
(Southside Johnny and the Asbury Jukes)
American singer–musician
• Keyboardist with group since 1974.
b. August 27, 1951

Hershy Kay
American composer
• Wrote hit scores for ballet, Broadway, screen: *Coco*, 1969; *Evita*, 1978.
b. November 17, 1919 in Philadelphia, Pennsylvania
d. December 02, 1981 in Danbury, Connecticut

Sammy Kaye
American bandleader
• Noted for "swing and sway" rhythms, 1930s-60s; star of TV show "Sammy Kaye Show," 1950-59.
b. March 13, 1913 in Lakewood, Ohio
d. June 02, 1987 in Ridgewood, New Jersey

Lainie Kazan
(Lainie Levine)
American singer–actress
• Broadway appearances include *Seesaw; The Women*.
b. May 15, 1942 in New York, New York

Buell H(ilton) Kazee
American musician–singer
• Folk music performer, 1930s; recorded "Rock Island Line."
b. August 29, 1900 in Burton Fork, Kentucky
d. August 31, 1976

Reinhard Keiser
German composer
• Wrote over 120 Baroque operas, many sacred works.
b. January 09, 1674 in Teuchern, Germany
d. September 12, 1739 in Hamburg, Germany

Edgar Stillman Kelley
American composer
• Wrote "Alice in Wonderland" suite, 1919; "Gulliver" symphony, 1936.
b. April 14, 1857 in Sparta, Wisconsin
d. November 12, 1944 in New York, New York

Rudolf Kempe
German conductor
• Led London's Royal Philharmonic, 1961-75; conducted BBC Symphony from 1975.
b. June 14, 1910 in Niederpoyritz, Germany
d. May 11, 1976 in Zurich, Switzerland

(Wilhelm) Walter Friedrich Kempff
German pianist–composer
• Made US debut, 1964; epitomized old tradition of German pianism.
b. November 25, 1895 in Juterbog, Germany

Eddie Kendrick
(The Temptations)
American singer
• Lead tenor, Temptations, 1963-71; successful solo career on rhythm and blues charts.
b. December 17, 1940 in Union Springs, Alabama

Nick Kenny
American songwriter–journalist
• Hit songs include "While a Cigarette Was Burning"; pioneered early amateur radio show.
b. February 03, 1895 in Astoria, New York
d. December 01, 1975 in Sarasota, Florida

Kenny G
(Kenny Gorelick)
American jazz musician
• Saxophonist; hit "Songbird," 1987, is one of only two instrumentals to reach top 10 without being connected with movie or TV.
b. 1956

Louis Philip Kentner
English musician
• Int'l. concert pianist; played with Menuhin, 1950s; Liszt authority.
b. July 19, 1905 in Karwin, Silesia

Stan(ley Newcomb) Kenton
American bandleader
• Led outstanding jazz bands since 1941; wrote "And Her Tears Flowed Like Wine."
b. February 19, 1912 in Wichita, Kansas
d. August 25, 1979 in Hollywood, California

Freddie Keppard
American jazz musician
• New Orleans cornetist; co-led Original Creole Orchestra, 1910s.
b. February 15, 1899 in New Orleans, Louisiana
d. July 15, 1933 in Chicago, Illinois

Jerome David Kern
American composer
• Important in transition from operettas to modern musical comedies; known for Show Boat, 1927; song "Ol' Man River," 1927.
b. January 17, 1885 in New York, New York
d. November 11, 1945 in New York, New York

Doug(las James) Kershaw
American musician
• Cajun fiddler, known for classic "Louisiana Man."
b. January 24, 1936 in Tel Ridge, Louisiana

Francis Scott Key
American composer
• Wrote "The Star-Spangled Banner," Sep 13-14, 1814; adopted by Congress as national anthem, 1931.
b. August 01, 1779 in Carroll County, Maryland
d. January 11, 1843 in Baltimore, Maryland

Aram Khachaturian
(Aram Ilych Khachaturyan)
Russian composer
• Outstanding Soviet composer, noted for internationally popular "Saber dance," 1942.
b. June 06, 1903 in Tiflis, Russia
d. May 01, 1978 in Moscow, U.S.S.R.

Ali Akbar Khan
Indian musician–director
• Int'l. tours include collaborations with Yehudi Meduhin, Duke Ellington, others.
b. April 14, 1922 in Shivpur, India

Chaka Khan
(Rufus; Yvette Marie Stevens)
American singer
• Lead singer with Rufus, 1972-78; solo hit "Through the Fire," 1985.
b. March 23, 1953 in Chicago, Illinois

Tikhon Nikolaevich Khrennikov
Russian composer
• Major spokesman for Soviet musical policy; works often based on folk music; operas include Mother, 1957.
b. June 1, 1913 in Elets, Russia

Kid Creole and the Coconuts
(August Darnell; Taryn Haegy; Andy Hernandez; Adriana Kaegi; Cheryl Poirier)
American music group
• Music is Latin based with pop-rock influences: album Tropical Gangsters, 1982.

Edward Kilenyi, Sr
American musician–composer
• Hollywood music director for 30 yrs.; Gershwin's teacher.
b. January 25, 1884 in Hungary

Albert King
(Albert Nelson)
American musician
• Started guitarist career in 1948; had 1960s hit "Born Under A Bad Sign."
b. April 25, 1923 in Indianola, Mississippi

B B (Riley B) King
("Bassman of the Blues"; "The Boy from Beale Street"; "King of the Blues"; "The Beale Street Blues Boy")
American singer–musician
• Frequent Grammy Award winner; more than 50 hit albums include Six Silver Strings, 1985.
b. September 16, 1925 in Itta Bena, Mississippi

Ben E King
(The Drifters; Benjamin Earl Nelson)
American musician–singer
• Lead singer with The Drifters before becoming soloist; had hit single "Stand By Me," 1961.
b. September 28, 1938 in Henderson, North Carolina

Carole King
(Carole Klein)
American singer–songwriter
• Won four Grammys, 1972, for album Tapestry, , one of the best-sellingalbums of all time. Hit singles include "One Fine Day," 1980.
b. February 09, 1941 in Brooklyn, New York

Claude King
American musician–singer
• Country guitarist, songwriter, popular 1960s; had hit single "The Burning of Atlanta," 1962.
b. February 05, 1933 in Shreveport, Louisiana

Evelyn King
("Champagne")
American singer
• Recorded disco hit "Shame," 1977.
b. July 01, 1960 in Bronx, New York

Wayne King
American bandleader
• Led dance band, 1930s-40s; famous for waltzes, slow, dreamy style; recorded "Josephine," 1937.
b. February 16, 1901 in Savanna, Illinois
d. May 16, 1985 in Phoenix, Arizona

William King
(The Commodores)
American singer
• Plays brass instruments, writes songs for black pop group formed 1968.
b. 1947 in Birmingham, Alabama

King Crimson
(Robert Fripp; Mike Giles; Greg Lake; Ian McDonald; Pete Sinfield)
English music group
• Heavy metal space band, 1969-74; debut album *In The Court of Crimson King*, 1969.

King Sisters
American music group
• Vocal quartet sang with Big Bands, 1930s-40s; made comeback, 1960s, with "The King Family" TV series.

The Kingston Trio
(Roger Gambill; George Grove; Bob Shane)
American music group
• Rose to fame, late 1950s, with ballad "Tom Dooley."

The Kinks
(Mick Avory; John Beechman; Laurie Brown; David Davies; Raymond Davies; John Gosling; Alan Holmes; Peter Quaife)
English music group
• British rock group, 1963-; "You Really Got Me," 1964, first big US hit.

Igor Kipnis
American musician
• Award-winning harpsichordist; revived interest in fortepiano; son of Alexander.
b. September 27, 1930 in Berlin, Germany

John Kirby
American musician
• Led sextet, "The Biggest Little Band in the Land," 1930s-40s; on "Duffy's Tavern" radio show, early 1940s.
b. December 31, 1908 in Baltimore, Maryland
d. 1952 in Hollywood, California

Lisa Kirk
American singer
• Featured in Broadway's *Kiss Me Kate*, 1949; in TV, nightclubs, 1950s.
b. February 25, 1925 in Brownsville, Pennsylvania
d. November 11, 1990 in New York, New York

Ralph Kirkpatrick
American musician
• Selected to record all of Bach's keyboard music, 1956.
b. January 1, 1911 in Leominster, Massachusetts
d. April 13, 1984 in Guilford, Connecticut

Don Kirshner
American music executive
• Founded Aldon Music, 1958-63, launching songwriting careers of Neil Sedaka, Neil Diamond, others.
b. April 17, 1934 in Bronx, New York

Kiss
(Eric Carr; Peter Criss; Ace Frehley; Gene Simmons; Paul Stanley)
American music group
• Formed 1972, known for makeup, mystery image; hit song "Beth," 1976.

Eartha Mae Kitt
American singer
• Sang earthy songs in low-key monotone; films include *St. Louis Blues*, 1958.
b. January 16, 1928 in North, South Carolina

Edward Lawrence Kleban
American lyricist
• Won Tony, Pulitzer for writing lyrics for *A Chorus Line*, which opened on Broadway, 1975.
b. April 3, 1939 in New York, New York
d. December 28, 1987 in New York, New York

Giselher Klebe
German composer
• Widely diverse works include fairy-tale opera *Das Marchen von der Schonen Lilie*, 1968.
b. June 28, 1925 in Mannheim, Germany

Otto Klemperer
German conductor–composer
• Led German, US symphonies; noted interpreter of German Romantics.
b. May 14, 1885 in Breslau, Germany
d. July 06, 1973 in Zurich, Switzerland

Earl Klugh
American musician
• Jazz guitarist recording since 1977; albums include *Two of a Kind*, 1982.
b. 1953 in Detroit, Michigan

Gladys Maria Knight
(Gladys Knight and the Pips)
American singer
• Won two Grammys, 1973, for "Midnight Train to Georgia."
b. May 28, 1944 in Atlanta, Georgia

Mark Knopfler
(Dire Straits)
Scottish musician–composer
• Formed rock group, 1977; hits include Grammy winner "Money for Nothing," 1986.
b. August 12, 1949 in Glasgow, Scotland

Heinrich Knote
German opera singer
• Famed, handsome Heldentenor; compared to Enrico Caruso; with NY Met., 1904-08.
b. November 26, 1870 in Munich, Germany
d. January 15, 1953 in Germany (West)

Leonid Borisovich Kogan
Russian musician
• Violin virtuoso; played US tours on cultural exchange program; won Lenin Prize, 1965.
b. October 14, 1924 in Dnepropetrovsk, U.S.S.R.
d. December 17, 1982 in U.S.S.R.

Barbara Anne Kolb
American composer
• First US woman to win Prix de Rome, 1969; wrote *Soundings*.
b. February 1, 1939 in Hartford, Connecticut

Kool and the Gang
(Cliff Adams; George Brown; Kool Bell; Ronald Bell; Spike Mickens; Michael Ray; Claydes Smith; J T Taylor; Dennis Thomas; Rickey West)
American music group
• Began, 1964, as jazz group; currently rhythm and blues-pop group; had platinum single "Celebration," 1980.

Al Kooper
(Blood Sweat and Tears)
American musician–producer
• Rock singer, organist, guitarist, 1960s; formed Blood, Sweat, and Tears, 1968.
b. February 05, 1944 in Brooklyn, New York

Alexis Korner
(Alexis Koerner; "Grandfather of British Rhythm and Blues")
English musician
• Known for discovering musicians Mick Jagger, Ginger Baker, Robert Plant, etc.
b. April 19, 1928 in Paris, France
d. January 01, 1984 in London, England

Erich Wolfgang Korngold
Austrian composer
• Won Oscars for scores of *Anthony Adverse*, 1936; *Adventures of Robin Hood*, 1938.
b. May 29, 1897 in Brunn, Austria
d. November 29, 1957 in Hollywood, California

Andre Kostelanetz
American conductor
• Led Columbia Broadcasting Orchestra, 1930s; NY Philharmonic, 1952-79; helped general audiences appreciate classics.
b. December 22, 1901 in Saint Petersburg, Russia
d. January 13, 1980 in Port-au-Prince, Haiti

Leo Kottke
American musician
• One of top acoustic guitarists, popular in Europe; recorded album *Time Step*, 1983.
b. in Athens, Georgia

Serge Alexandrovich Koussevitzky
American conductor-composer
• Led Boston Symphony, 1924-49; founded Berkshire Music Festival, 1934; championed modern composers.
b. July 26, 1874 in Vyshni Volochek, Russia
d. June 04, 1951 in Boston, Massachusetts

Kraftwerk
(Karl Bartos; Wolfgang Flur; Ralf Hutter; Florian Schneider)
German music group
• Electronic band, formed 1968; hit album *Autobahn*, 1974.

Alfredo Kraus
Spanish opera singer
• One of the most renowned lyric tenors of his generation; regular with NY Met. since mid-1960s.
b. November 24, 1927 in Las Palmas, Canary Islands

Lili Kraus
New Zealander musician
• Int'l. concert pianist since 1925; recorded entire Mozart, Schubert piano repertory; Japanese prisoner, WW II.
b. March 04, 1908 in Budapest, Hungary
d. November 06, 1986 in Asheville, North Carolina

Bernie (Bernard Leo) Krause
(The Weavers)
American singer-songwriter
• Member, folk group The Weavers, 1963-64; pres., Parasound, Inc., 1968-; sonic artist on several albums.
b. December 08, 1938 in Detroit, Michigan

Fritz Kreisler
American violinist-composer
• One of most renowned virtuosos of 20th c.; American debut, 1888; wrote operettas, popular violin music.
b. February 02, 1875 in Vienna, Austria
d. January 29, 1962 in New York, New York

Gidon Kremer
Russian musician
• Gold medal violinist in Moscow Tchaikovsky competition, 1970; repertoire stresses contemporary composers.
b. February 27, 1947 in Riga, Latvia

Ernst Krenek
American composer
• Created sensation with first jazz opera, *Jonny Spielt Auf*, 1927; greatly influenced modern composers.
b. August 23, 1900 in Vienna, Austria

Rodolphe Kreutzer
German musician-composer
• A founder of French school of violin playing; wrote 40 operas, 20 violin concertos; Beethoven wrote "Kreutzer Sonata" for him.
b. November 16, 1766 in Versailles, France
d. January 06, 1831 in Geneva, Switzerland

Bill Kreutzmann
(The Grateful Dead; Bill Sommers)
American musician
• Drummer with psychedelic band, formed 1965.
b. June 07, 1946 in Palo Alto, California

Robby Krieger
(The Doors)
American musician
• Guitarist with group, 1965-73, known for jazz innovations; had number one hit "Light My Fire," 1966.
b. January 08, 1946 in Los Angeles, California

Kris Kristofferson
(Kris Carson)
American actor-singer-songwriter
• Wrote song "Help Me Make It Through the Night"; films include *A Star Is Born*, 1976; *Heaven's Gate*, 1980.
b. June 22, 1937 in Brownsville, Texas

Gene Krupa
American bandleader-musician
• Legendary jazz drummer; noted for virtuoso solos with Benny Goodman, 1934-38; led own band, 1940s.
b. January 15, 1909 in Chicago, Illinois
d. October 16, 1973 in Yonkers, New York

Jan Kubelik
Hungarian violinist
• Int'l. noted virtuoso; regarded as Paderewski's counterpart; active until WW I.
b. July 05, 1880 in Michle, Czechoslovakia
d. December 05, 1940 in Prague, Czechoslovakia

Rafael Kubelik
Swiss conductor-composer
• Controversial conductor of Chicago Symphony, London's Covent Garden Opera, 1950s; music director, NY Met., 1973-74; son of Jan.
b. June 29, 1914 in Bychory, Czechoslovakia

Anton Kuerti
Austrian pianist
• Concert performer; founded Parry Sound; Festival of Sound.
b. 1938 in Vienna, Austria

Kay (James King Kern) Kyser
American musician-bandleader
• Best known as host of radio's "Kollege of Musical Knowledge," 1933-49.
b. June 18, 1906 in Rocky Mount, North Carolina
d. July 23, 1985 in Chapel Hill, North Carolina

Patti LaBelle
(Patricia Louise Holte)
American singer
• Solo artist since 1977; hits include "New Attitude," 1985; "On My Own," 1986.
b. October 04, 1944 in Philadelphia, Pennsylvania

Luigi Lablache
Italian opera singer
• Foremost bass singer of his time; Schubert, others wrote songs for him.
b. December 06, 1794 in Naples, Italy
d. January 23, 1858 in Naples, Italy

Tommy Ladnier
American jazz musician
• Cornetist, adept at blues; recorded jazz classics with Bechet, Mezz Mezzrow.
b. May 28, 1900 in Mandeville, Louisiana
d. June 04, 1939 in New York, New York

Francis Lai
French composer
• Won Oscars for scores to *Love Story*, 1970; *Oliver's Story*, 1970.
b. 1933 in France

Cleo Laine
(Clementina Dinah Campbell; Mrs John Dankworth)
English singer-actress
• Popular jazz singer who made American debut, 1973, Carnegie Hall.
b. October 28, 1927 in Southall, England

Frankie Laine
(Frank Paul LoVecchio)
American singer
• Hit songs from 1950s include "Mule Train," 1948; "Sixteen Tons," 1956.
b. March 3, 1913 in Chicago, Illinois

Rick (Richard Quentin) Laird
(The Mahavishnu Orchestra)
Irish singer–musician
• Bassist who cofounded Mahavishnu Orchestra, 1971-73.
b. in Dublin, Ireland

Greg(ory) Lake
(Emerson Lake and Palmer; King Crimson)
English singer–musician
• Guitarist, bassist, vocalist with group formed 1970-79; known for acoustic ballads.
b. November 1, 1948 in Bournemouth, England

Constant Lambert
English composer
• Created ballet as art form in England; director, Sadler's Wells, 1931-47; composed *Romeo and Juliet*, 1926.
b. 1905 in London, England
d. August 21, 1951 in London, England

Robert Lamm
(Chicago)
American singer–musician
• Keyboardist, unofficial leader of group; had solo album *Skinny Boy*, 1974.
b. October 13, 1944 in Brooklyn, New York

Abbe Lane
American actress–singer
• Ex-wife of Xavier Cugat who starred with him in TV's "Xavier Cugat Show," 1957.
b. December 14, 1932 in Brooklyn, New York

Burton Lane
(Burton Levy)
American composer
• Wrote scores for *Finian's Rainbow*, 1947; *On a Clear Day You Can See Forever*, 1965.
b. February 02, 1912 in New York, New York

Frances Langford
(Frances Newbern)
American singer–actress
• Popular 1930s-40s vocalist; co-starred with Bob Hope on WW II broadcasts.
b. April 04, 1913 in Lakeland, Florida

Snooky Lanson
(Roy Landman)
American singer
• Star of TV's "Hit Parade," 1950s.
b. March 27, 1919 in Memphis, Tennessee
d. July 02, 1990 in Nashville, Tennessee

Mario Lanza
(Alfredo Arnold Cocozza)
American opera singer–actor
• Tenor who starred in MGM musical *The Great Caruso*, 1951.
b. January 31, 1921 in Philadelphia, Pennsylvania
d. October 07, 1959 in Rome, Italy

Raoul Laparra
French composer
• Opera *Las Torreras*, 1929, used Spanish folk elements; killed in air raid.
b. May 13, 1876 in Bordeaux, France
d. April 04, 1943 in Paris, France

Ronald LaPread
(The Commodores)
American musician
• Trumpeter, bassist with black pop group; had hit singles "Sail On," "Still," 1979.
b. 1948 in Tuskegee, Alabama

Jaime Laredo
Bolivian violinist
• Prize-winning virtuoso, 1950s-60s; first performed at age eight; pictured on Bolivian airmail stamp.
b. June 07, 1941 in Cochabamba, Bolivia

Ruth Laredo
(Ruth Meckler)
American pianist
• Commissioned to edit works of composers; first volume, *The Preludes*, was released, 1985.
b. November 2, 1937 in Detroit, Michigan

Julius LaRosa
American singer
• Pop singer; became folk hero after Arthur Godfrey fired him on the air, 1953.
b. January 02, 1930 in New York, New York

Alicia de Larrocha
Spanish pianist
• Noted for renditions of Spanish composers Albeniz, Granados.
b. May 23, 1923 in Barcelona, Spain

Nicolette Larson
American singer
• Has recorded songs with many other singers; hit single "I Only Want to Be With You," 1982.
b. July 17, 1952 in Helena, Montana

Lily Laskin
French musician
• Credited with popularizing and making harp a featured solo instrument; revived many musical scores for harp.
b. August 31, 1893 in Paris, France
d. January 05, 1988 in Paris, France

Orlandus de Lassus
(Roland Delattre; Orlando di Lasso)
Belgian composer
• Ranks after Palestrina, as leading Renaissance composer; wrote over 1,500 works.
b. 1532 in Mons, Netherlands
d. June 14, 1594 in Munich, Germany

Jacob Lateiner
American musician
• Soloist in annual US, European tours since 1950; gave first concert at age eight.
b. May 31, 1928 in Havana, Cuba

Stacy Lattisaw
American singer
• Recorded first album at age 12: *Young and In Love*, 1978.
b. November 25, 1966 in Washington, District of Columbia

Harry MacLennan Lauder, Sir
(Harry MacLennan; "The Laird of the Halls")
Scottish singer
• Famed music-hall comedian, noted for "Roamin' in the Gloamin'."
b. August 04, 1870 in Portobello, Scotland
d. February 25, 1950 in Lenarkshire, Scotland

Cyndi (Cynthia) Lauper
American singer
• Five hits from first album *She's So Unusual*, broke record for most Top 10 singles from debut album; won Grammy, 1984.
b. June 2, 1953 in Queens, New York

Carol Lawrence
(Carol Maria Laraia)
American singer–actress
• Played Maria in Broadway's *West Side Story*, 1957-60.
b. September 05, 1935 in Melrose Park, Illinois

Jack Lawrence
American composer–lyricist–producer
• Wrote lyrics, music for "If I Didn't Care," 1939; "All or Nothing at All," 1940.
b. April 07, 1912 in New York, New York

Steve Lawrence
(Sidney Liebowitz)
American actor–singer
• Won seven Emmys for specials with
wife Eydie Gorme.
b. July 08, 1935 in New York, New York

Yank (John R) Lawson
(John R Lausen)
American jazz musician
• Trumpeter who was a founder of Bob
Crosby band, 1935; co-led World's
Greatest Jazz Band.
b. May 03, 1911 in Trenton, Missouri

Bernie Leadon
(The Eagles)
American singer–musician
• Played guitar, mandolin, banjo for Eagles, 1971-76; formed own band, recorded album Natural Progressions, 1977.
b. July 19, 1947 in Minneapolis, Minnesota

Simon LeBon
(Duran Duran)
English singer
• Lead singer, Duran Duran since 1978,
who is popular teenage pin-up boy.
b. October 27, 1958 in Bushey, England

Stanley Richard Lebowsky
American musician–composer
• Wrote popular song "The Wayward
Wind," 1956; Tony nominee for Irma
La Douche, 1961.
b. November 26, 1926 in Minneapolis, Minne-
sota
d. October 19, 1986 in New York, New York

Led Zeppelin
(John Bonham; John Paul Jones; Jimmy
Page; Robert Plant)
English music group
• Heavy-medal band formed, 1968; dis-
banded, 1980, after death of John Bon-
ham.

Huddie Ledbetter
("Leadbelly")
American singer–musician
• Famed blues singer; wrote "Good
Night, Irene," 1943.
b. 1885 in Mooringsport, Louisiana
d. December 06, 1949 in New York, New
York

Brenda Lee
(Brenda Mae Tarpley; "Little Miss Dyna-
mite")
American singer
• Began singing professionally at age six;
1969 Grammy nominee for "Johnny One
Time."
b. December 11, 1944 in Atlanta, Georgia

Geddy Lee
(Rush)
Canadian singer
• Guitarist, bass player with progressive
trio, 1974–; had many gold records; won
two Junos, 1978, 1979.
b. July 29, 1953 in Toronto, Ontario

Johnny Lee
American singer
• Had hit song "Lookin' for Love,"
1980, from film Urban Cowboy.
b. 1947 in Texas City, Texas

Peggy Lee
(Norma Delores Egstrom)
American singer–actress
• Hits include "Fever," 1958; "Is That
All There Is?," 1969.
b. May 2, 1920 in Jamestown, North Dakota

Christopher Kaye LeFleming
English composer–educator
• Wrote "Five Psalms"; orchestral suite
London River.
b. February 26, 1908 in Wimborne Minister,
England
d. June 19, 1985 in Woodbury, England

Leginska
American conductor–musician
• One of first women symphony conductors; founded Boston Philharmonic, 1926.
b. April 13, 1880 in Hull, England
d. February 26, 1970 in Los Angeles, California

Michel Jean Legrand
French composer–conductor
• Composed scores of over 50 films including Summer of '42, 1971.
b. February 24, 1932 in Paris, France

Franz Lehar
Hungarian composer
• Numerous popular operettas include
The Merry Widow, 1905.
b. April 3, 1870 in Romorn, Hungary
d. October 24, 1948 in Bad Ischl, Austria

Tom (Thomas Andrew) Lehrer
American songwriter
• Satirical ditties collected in album An
Evening Wasted With Tom Lehrer, 1959;
songs popular again in "Tom Foolery"
revue, 1980s.
b. April 09, 1928 in New York, New York

Carolyn Leigh
American songwriter
• Wrote lyrics to songs "Hey, Look Me
Over"; "The Best is Yet to Come";
"Young at Heart."
b. April 21, 1926 in Bronx, New York
d. November 19, 1983 in New York, New
York

Mitch Leigh
(Irwins Michnick)
American composer
• Notable works include "Man of La
Mancha" featuring "The Impossible
Dream," 1965.
b. January 3, 1928 in Brooklyn, New York

Erich Leinsdorf
American conductor
• Led Boston Symphony, 1962-69; NY
Met., 1957-62; made many recordings.
b. February 04, 1912 in Vienna, Austria

Dianne Lennon
(Lennon Sisters)
American singer
• With sisters, regulars on "The Lawrence Welk Show," 1955-71.
b. December 01, 1939 in Los Angeles, California

Janet Lennon
(Lennon Sisters)
American singer
• With sisters, had hit song "Sad Movies
Make Me Cry," 1961.
b. November 15, 1946 in Culver City, Califor-
nia

John Winston Lennon
(The Beatles)
English singer–songwriter–musician
• "Love Me Do," 1962 first song writ-
ten with Paul McCartney; solo career,
1970, included hit "Imagine," 1971.
Murdered.
b. October 09, 1940 in Liverpool, England
d. December 08, 1980 in New York, New
York

Julian (John Charles Julian) Lennon
English musician–singer
• Son of John Lennon; Paul McCartney
wrote song "Hey Jude" for him; hit album Valotte, 1983.
b. April 08, 1963 in Liverpool, England

Kathy Lennon
(Lennon Sisters)
American singer
• With sisters, had hit song "Tonight
You Belong to Me," 1956.
b. August 22, 1942 in Santa Monica, Califor-
nia

Peggy Lennon
(Lennon Sisters)
American singer
• With sisters, regulars on "The Law-
rence Welk Show," 1955-71.
b. April 08, 1940 in Los Angeles, California

Annie Lennox
(Eurythmics)
Scottish singer
• Androgynous-look singer with Eurythmics; singles include "Here Comes the Rain Again," 1984.
b. December 25, 1954 in Aberdeen, Scotland

Lotte Lenya
(Karoline Blamauer; Mrs Kurt Weill)
Austrian actress–singer
• Raspy-voiced star; won Tony for revival of *Threepenny Opera*, 1955.
b. October 18, 1900 in Vienna, Austria
d. November 27, 1981 in New York, New York

Leonardo Leo
Italian composer
• Wrote over 60 operas; played important role in development of pre-classical symphony.
b. August 05, 1694 in San Vito, Italy
d. October 31, 1744 in Naples, Italy

Ruggiero Leoncavallo
Italian composer
• Best known for opera *I Pagliacci*, 1892.
b. March 08, 1858 in Naples, Italy
d. August 09, 1919 in Montecatini, Italy

Raymond John Leppard
English conductor
• Harpichordist; director, English Champer Orchestra, 1959-77; conductor, BBC N. Symphony, 1972-80.
b. August 11, 1927 in London, England

Alan Jay Lerner
(Lerner and Loewe)
American dramatist–lyricist–composer
• Known for collaborations with Loewe; won two Tonys, two Oscars, one Grammy including film/play *Gigi*, 1958, 1974.
b. August 31, 1918 in New York, New York
d. June 14, 1986 in New York, New York

Les Six
(George Auric; Louis Durey; Arthur Honegger; Darius Milhaud; Francois Poulenc; Germaine Tailleferre)
French composers
• Avant-garde group, led by Honegger, popular after WW I.

Phil Lesh
(Grateful Dead)
American singer–musician
• Rock bassist, composer of electronic music; with Grateful Dead since 1965.
b. March 15, 1940 in Berkeley, California

Edgar Leslie
American songwriter
• Wrote songs for films; collaborated with Irving Berlin, Harry Warren, others.
b. December 31, 1885 in Stamford, Connecticut
d. January 22, 1976 in New York, New York

The Lettermen
(Tony Butala; Gary Pike; Jim Pike)
American music group
• Ballad style vocalists, formed 1960; favorite of college students; nine gold albums include *Song for Young Lovers*, 1962.

Ray Lev
American pianist
• Concertist known for her extensive repertoire; made US debut, 1933.
b. May 08, 1912 in Rostov-on-Don, Russia
d. May 2, 1968 in New York, New York

Oscar Levant
American composer–musician
• Concert pianist, caustic wit; films include *Rhapsody in Blue*, 1945; wrote autobiography *Smattering of Ignorance*, 1944.
b. December 27, 1906 in Pittsburgh, Pennsylvania
d. August 14, 1972 in Beverly Hills, California

James Levine
American conductor
• Music director, Met. Opera, 1975–; frequent guest conductor, piano soloist.
b. June 23, 1943 in Cincinnati, Ohio

Henry Jay Lewis
American conductor
• First black director of a US symphony orchestra; led NJ Symphony, 1968-76.
b. October 16, 1932 in Los Angeles, California

Huey Lewis
(Hugh Anthony Cregg III; Huey Lewis and the News)
American group
• Founded group, 1979; hits include "I Want a New Drug," 1983; "The Power of Love," 1984; "Hip to Be Square," 1986.
b. July 05, 1951 in New York, New York

Jerry Lee Lewis
American singer–musician
• Country-rock hit singles include "Whole Lotta Shakin' Goin' On," 1957; "Breathless," 1958.
b. September 29, 1935 in Ferriday, Louisiana

John Aaron Lewis
American musician
• Jazz pianist, played with Dizzy Gillespie, Miles Davis, etc; formed Modern Jazz Quartet, 1952-74.
b. May 03, 1920 in La Grange, Illinois

Meade Anderson Lux Lewis
American jazz musician–composer
• Pianist who popularized boogie-woogie; wrote "Honky Tonk Train Blues," 1930s.
b. September 05, 1905 in Chicago, Illinois
d. June 07, 1964 in Minneapolis, Minnesota

Ramsey Emanuel Lewis, Jr
American musician–composer
• Hits include "The In Crowd," 1965.
b. May 27, 1935 in Chicago, Illinois

Ted Lewis
(Theodore Leopold Friedman)
American bandleader
• Cane, top-hat dance man; noted for "Me and My Shadow."
b. June 09, 1892 in Circleville, Ohio
d. August 25, 1971 in New York, New York

Josef Lhevinne
American pianist–teacher
• Virtuoso, won Rubinstein prize, 1895; widely acclaimed in US for two-piano recitals with wife, Rosina, 1906-20s.
b. December 03, 1874 in Moscow, Russia
d. December 02, 1944 in New York, New York

Rosina L Lhevinne
(Mrs Joseph Lhevinne)
American musician–teacher
• Taught at Juilliard School of Music, NYC, 1924-76; performed two-piano recitals with husband, 1906-20s.
b. March 29, 1880 in Moscow, Russia
d. November 09, 1976 in Glendale, California

Liberace
(Wladziu Valentino Liberace; "Walter Busterkeys")
American musician–entertainer
• Pianist, known for elaborate costumes, flashy pianos topped by candelabras; highest paid entertainer in 1960s-70s.
b. May 16, 1919 in West Allis, Wisconsin
d. February 04, 1987 in Palm Springs, California

George J Liberace
American musician–celebrity relative
• Conductor, violinist; was silent, straight man for flamboyant younger brother; ran Liberace's enterprises.
b. July 31, 1911 in Menasha, Wisconsin
d. October 16, 1983 in Las Vegas, Nevada

Rolf Liebermann
Swiss composer–manager
• Paris Opera Co.'s first foreign administrator, 1973-80; wrote operas *Penelope,* 1954; *Leonore,* 1952.
b. September 14, 1910 in Zurich, Switzerland

Enoch Henry Light
American musician–record executive–composer
• Headed award-winning recording companies, 1950s-60s; wrote popular songs.
b. August 18, 1907 in Canton, Ohio
d. July 31, 1978 in New York, New York

Gordon Meredith Lightfoot
Canadian singer–songwriter
• Wrote songs "If You Could Read My Mind," 1970; "Sundown," 1974.
b. November 17, 1939 in Orillia, Ontario

Abbey Lincoln
(Gaby Lee; Anna Marie Wooldrigde)
American singer–actress
• Dance band vocalist; made recordings, night club appearances, 1950s.
b. August 06, 1930 in Chicago, Illinois

Jenny (Johanna Maria) Lind
(Mrs Otto Goldschmidt; "Swedish Nightingale")
English opera singer
• Coloratura soprano, brought to US for concert tour, 1850-52, by P T Barnum.
b. October 06, 1820 in Stockholm, Sweden
d. November 02, 1887 in Wynd's Point, England

Lisa Lisa and Cult Jam
(Mike Hughes; Alex Mosley; Lisa Velez)
American music group
• Latin band; had three top 40 hits including "Head to Toe," 1987.

Eugene List
American pianist
• Int'l concertist; debut at age 12.
b. July 06, 1918 in Philadelphia, Pennsylvania
d. March 01, 1985 in New York, New York

Franz (Ferencz) Liszt
Hungarian pianist–composer
• Piano virtuoso; created the symphonic poem; works include song: "Liebestraume," 1850; 20 Hungarian Rhapsodies, 1851-86.
b. October 22, 1811 in Raiding, Hungary
d. July 31, 1886 in Bayreuth, Germany

Little Jack Little
(John Leonard)
American bandleader
• His band featured on radio, in nightclubs, 1920s-30s; wrote song "Shanty in Old Shanty Town."
b. May 28, 1900 in London, England
d. April 09, 1956 in Hollywood, California

Little Anthony and the Imperials
(Clarence Collins; Anthony Gourdine; Sammy Strain; Ernest WrightClarence Collins; Tracy Lord; Glouster Rogers)
American music group
• Popular, 1950s-60s; hit singles include "Tears On My Pillow," 1958; "Goin' Out of My Head," 1964.

Little Esther
(Esther Phillips)
American singer
• Hits include "What a Difference a Day Makes"; "Double Crossing Blues"; "Release Me."
b. December 23, 1935 in Houston, Texas
d. August 07, 1984 in Los Angeles, California

Little Eva
(Eva Narcissus Boyd)
American singer
• Hits include "The Loco-Motion," 1962; words, music written by Gerry Goffin, Carole King for their babysitter.
b. June 29, 1945 in Bellhaven, North Carolina

Little Richard
(Richard Wayne Penniman; "Georgia Peach")
American singer
• Hits include "Tutti Frutti," 1955; "Good Golly Miss Molly," 1957; "Long Tall Sally,"1956.
b. December 25, 1935 in Macon, Georgia

The Little River Band
(Beeb Birtles; David Briggs; John Farnham; Rick Formosa; Graham Goble; Steve Housden; Mal Logan; George McArdle; Roger McLachan)
Australian music group
• Vocal harmony, country-pop group begun 1975; had single "Take It Easy On Me," 1981.

Jerry Livingston
(Jerry Levinson)
American songwriter
• Wrote novelty tune "Mairzy Doats," 1943; love song "The Twelfth of Never," 1956.
b. 1909 in Denver, Colorado
d. July 1, 1987 in Los Angeles, California

Frank Loesser
American composer
• Wrote Broadway musicals *Guys and Dolls,* 1951; *Most Happy Fella,* 1956.
b. June 29, 1910 in New York, New York
d. July 28, 1969 in New York, New York

Frederick Loewe
(Lerner and Loewe; "Fritz")
Austrian composer
• Noted for collaboration with lyricist Alan Lerner; hits include 1956 Tonywinner, *My Fair Lady; Camelot,* 1968.
b. June 1, 1904 in Vienna, Austria
d. February 14, 1988 in Palm Springs, California

Nils Lofgren
(E Street Band; "Lefty")
American musician–singer–songwriter
• Pop-rock singer, guitarist; formed band Grin, 1969-74; acclaimed album *Nils Lofgren,* 1975.
b. June 21, 1951 in Chicago, Illinois

Kenny (Kenneth Clarke) Loggins
(Loggins and Messina)
American singer–musician–songwriter
• Pop-rock singer; solo albums include *Celebrate Me Home,* 1977; *Nightwatch,* 1978.
b. January 07, 1948 in Everett, Washington

Loggins and Messina
(Kenny Loggins; Jim Messina)
American music group
• Country-rock duo, 1971-76; hit albums included single "Your Mama Don't Dance," 1972.

Nicola Logroscino
Italian composer
• Buffo-style operas included *Ricciardo,* 1743.
b. October 1698 in Bitonto, Italy
d. 1765 in Palermo, Sicily

Carmen Lombardo
American songwriter–musician–celebrity relative
• Saxophonist in brother, Guy's band, 1929-71; co-wrote classic "Boo Hoo."
b. July 16, 1903 in London, Ontario
d. April 17, 1971 in North Miami, Florida

Guy Albert Lombardo
Canadian bandleader
• Known for New Year's Eve performances with band, The Royal Canadians.
b. June 19, 1902 in London, Ontario
d. November 05, 1977 in Houston, Texas

Julie London
(Julie Peck)
American singer–actress
• Nightclub, film, TV performer, noted for blues song "Cry Me A River."
b. September 26, 1926 in Santa Rosa, California

Avon Long
American actor–singer
• Danced at Cotton Club in Harlem; appeared in *Porgy and Bess,* 1942.
b. June 18, 1910 in Baltimore, Maryland
d. February 15, 1984 in New York, New York

Claudine Georgette Longet
French actress–singer
• Was married to Andy Williams; accused of shooting lover, Spider Sabich.
b. January 29, 1942 in Paris, France

Trini(dad, III) Lopez
American singer
• Best known for "If I Had a Hammer," 1963.
b. May 15, 1937 in Dallas, Texas

Vincent Lopez
American bandleader–composer
• Started regular broadcasts of dance band music, 1921; popularized song "Nola"; wrote "Knock, Knock Who's There?"
b. December 3, 1895 in New York, New York
d. September 2, 1975 in Miami Beach, Florida

Lee Loughname
(Chicago)
American musician
• Trumpeter with group; had hit single "Does Anyone Really Know What Time It Is?" 1970.
b. October 21, 1946 in Chicago, Illinois

Mike Love
(The Beach Boys)
American singer–musician
• Lead vocalist for The Beach Boys, 1961–.
b. March 15, 1941 in Los Angeles, California

Lovin' Spoonful
(John Boone; Joe Butler; John Sebastian; Zal Yanovsky)
American music group
• Hit songs include "Do You Believe in Magic?," 1965.

Jack Warren Lowe
(Whittemore and Lowe)
American pianist–composer
• With Arthur Whittemore, member of two-piano team popular, 1940s-60s; wrote orchestra, chamber works.
b. December 25, 1917 in Aurora, Colorado

Nick Lowe
(Rockpile)
English singer–musician
• Hit single "Cruel to Be Kind," came from debut solo album *Pure Pop for Now People,* 1978.
b. March 25, 1949 in Suffolk, England

Pierre Luboshutz
Musician–Composer–Pianist
• With wife, formed popular piano duo, Luboshutz and Nemenoff, from 1937.
b. June 22, 1894 in Odessa, Russia
d. April 18, 1971 in Rockport, Maine

Lorna Luft
(Mrs Jake Hooker)
American singer–celebrity relative
• Daughter of Judy Garland and Sid Luft; half-sister of Liza Minnelli; films include *Where the Boys are '84,* 1984.
b. November 21, 1952

Jean-Baptiste Lully
(Giovanni Battista Lulli)
French composer
• Considered father of National French Opera; head of Paris Opera, 1672-87; wrote ballets, opera *Alceste,* 1674.
b. November 28, 1632 in Florence, Italy
d. March 22, 1687 in Paris, France

Lulu
(Marie McDonald McLaughlin)
Scottish singer–actress
• Best known for 1967 hit single "To Sir with Love," introduced in movie of same name.
b. November 03, 1948 in Glasgow, Scotland

Jimmy (James Melvin) Lunceford
American jazz musician–actor
• Black band leader of 1930s; members included Cy Oliver; made film *Blues in the Night,* 1941.
b. June 06, 1902 in Fulton, Mississippi
d. July 13, 1947 in Seaside, Oregon

Radu Lupu
Romanian pianist
• Won first prize, Van Cliburn Piano Competition, 1966; appeared with orchestras worldwide.
b. November 3, 1945 in Galati, Romania

Witold Lutoslawski
Polish composer
• First Government Prizewinner, 1955; works include "Concerto," 1954, children's songs.
b. 1913

Abe Lyman
American bandleader
• Society band leader, 1930s; featured in film *Mr. Broadway.*
b. August 04, 1897 in Chicago, Illinois
d. October 23, 1957 in Beverly Hills, California

Frankie Lyman
(Frankie Lyman and the Teenagers)
American singer
• Had top-ten hit "Why Do Fools Fall in Love?" 1956.
b. September 3, 1942 in Washington Heights, New York
d. February 28, 1968

Moura Lympany
English pianist
• Int'l concertist; won Ysaya competition, 1938; championed works of British composers.
b. August 18, 1916 in Saltash, England

David Lynch
(The Platters)
American singer
• Second tenor in vocal group founded in 1953; best known hit "Only You," 1955.
b. 1930 in Saint Louis, Missouri
d. January 02, 1981 in Long Beach, California

Annifrid Lyngstad-Fredriksson
(ABBA)
Swedish singer
• First solo album *Something's Going On,* produced by Phil Collins, 1982.
b. November 15, 1945 in Stockholm, Sweden

Loretta Lynn
(Loretta Webb; Mrs Oliver Lynn Jr)
American singer
• Movie *Coal Miner's Daughter,* 1977 based on her life.
b. April 14, 1935 in Butcher Hollow, Kentucky

Jeff Lynne
(Electric Light Orchestra)
English musician
• Leader of Electric Light Orchestra; solo single "Video," 1984.
b. December 3, 1947 in Birmingham, England

Phil(ip) Lynott
(Thin Lizzy)
Irish singer–musician
• Founded band, 1970; wrote most of group's songs which celebrate comic-book heroism.
b. August 2, 1951 in Dublin, Ireland
d. January 04, 1986 in Salisbury, England

Lynyrd Skynyrd
(Robert Burns; Allen Collins; Steve Gaines; Ed King; William Powell; Gary Rossington; Ronnie VanZant; Leon Wilkeson)
American music group
• Hit songs include "Free Bird," 1974. Most of band was lost in air crash.

Southside Johnny Lyon
(Southside Johnny and the Asbury Jukes)
American singer–musician
• Harmonica player, vocalist, friend of Bruce Springsteen; group has recorded some of Springsteen's songs.
b. December 04, 1948 in Neptune, New Jersey

Yo-Yo Ma
American musician
• Internationally acclaimed cello virtuoso; on TV at age seven; Avery Fisher winner, 1978.
b. October 07, 1955 in Paris, France

Lorin Maazel
American conductor–violinist
• Led major American orchestras at age nine to 11; director, Cleveland orchestra, 1972-82; guest conductor, London Philharmonia, from 1976.
b. March 05, 1930 in Paris, France

Moms (Jackie) Mabley
(Loretta Mary Aiken)
American singer–comedienne
• Noted for "dirty old lady" comedy routine; starred in Amazing Grace, 1974.
b. March 19, 1894 in Brevard, North Carolina
d. May 23, 1975 in White Plains, New York

Galt MacDermot
Canadian composer
• Won Grammy for score of Hair, 1968.
b. December 19, 1928 in Montreal, Quebec

Sir Alexander Campbell Mackenzie
Scottish composer
• Compositions which introduce Scottish elements include "Tam o' Shanter," 1911; "Scottish Rhapsodies," 1880.
b. August 22, 1847 in Edinburgh, Scotland
d. April 28, 1935 in London, England

Gisele MacKenzie
(Marie Marguerite La Fleche)
Canadian singer–actress
• Star of "Your Hit Parade," 1953-57; "Gisele Mackenzie Show," 1957-58.
b. January 1, 1927 in Winnipeg, Manitoba

Gordon MacRae
American actor–singer
• Gained musical movie fame as baritone star of Oklahoma, 1955; Carousel, 1956.
b. March 12, 1921 in East Orange, New Jersey
d. January 24, 1986 in Lincoln, Nebraska

Sheila MacRae
(Sheila Stephens)
American actress–singer
• In TV series "Jackie Gleason Show," 1966-70; first husband was Gordon MacRae.
b. September 24, 1923 in London, England

Madonna
(Madonna Louise Ciccone)
American singer–actress
• Top new performer, 1980s; hits include "Who's That Girl," 1987; "Papa Don't Preach," 1986; in films Desperately Seeking Susan, 1985; Dick Tracy, 1990.
b. August 16, 1959 in Bay City, Michigan

Charles Magnante
American composer–musician
• Accordionist; first to give full accordion concert, Carnegie Hall, 1939.
b. December 05, 1905 in New York, New York

The Mahavishnu Orchestra
(Billy Cobham Jr; Jerry Goodman; Jan Hammer; Rick Laird; John McLaughlin)
American music group
• Name of two rock groups founded by guitar virtuoso John McLaughlin, 1970s; album Apocalypse, 1974.

Gustav Mahler
Austrian composer–conductor
• Composer of nine operas; conducted NY Met., 1908-10.
b. July 07, 1860 in Kalischt, Bohemia
d. May 18, 1911 in Vienna, Austria

Gaetano Majorano
Italian opera singer
• Famed male soprano, 1740s-50s; highest paid soloist of his time.
b. April 12, 1710 in Bitonto, Italy
d. January 31, 1783 in Naples, Italy

Miriam Makeba
South African singer
• Sang African melodies; often starred with Harry Belafonte, 1960s.
b. March 04, 1932 in Prospect Township, South Africa

Tommy Makem
(The Clancy Brothers)
Irish singer
• Recording, touring star, 1960s; his Irish folk singing with Clancy Brothers seen in several TV shows.
b. 1932 in Keady, Ireland

Witold Malcuzynski
Polish musician
• Best known for interpretations of Chopin; debuted in US at Carnegie Hall, 1942.
b. August 1, 1914 in Warsaw, Poland
d. July 17, 1977 in Majorca, Spain

The Mamas and the Papas
(Dennis Doherty; Cass Elliot; Elaine Spanky McFarlane; John Phillips; Mackenzie Phillips; Michelle Gilliam Phillips)
American music group
• Original group formed 1965; had light CA folk-pop beat; hits include "Monday, Monday," 1966.

Melissa Toni Manchester
American singer–songwriter
• Began career as back-up singer for Bette Midler; hit songs "Midnight Blue"; "Don't Cry Out Loud."
b. February 15, 1951 in New York, New York

Henry Mancini
American composer
• Won Oscars, 1961, 1962, for songs "Moon River" and "Days of Wine and Roses"; won Oscar for Victor/Victoria, 1982.
b. April 16, 1924 in Cleveland, Ohio

Barbara Ann Mandrell
(Mrs Ken Dudney)
American singer–musician
• Country-pop singer; first number one hit "Sleeping Single in a Double Bed," 1978.
b. December 25, 1948 in Houston, Texas

Chuck (Charles Frank) Mangione
American jazz musician–composer
• Plays flugelhorn; hit song "Feels So Good," 1978.
b. November 29, 1940 in Rochester, New York

Jim Dandy Mangrum
(Black Oak Arkansas)
American singer
• Lead singer known for long-hair, shirtless performances.
b. March 3, 1948 in Black Oak, Arkansas

Manhattan Transfer
(Cheryl Bentyne; Tim Hauser; Laurel Masse; Alan Paul; Janis Siege)
American music group
• Won three Grammys for *Vocalese*, 1985.

Barry Manilow
American singer–songwriter
• Wrote commercial jingles, accompanied Bette Midler before first hit, "Mandy," 1975.
b. June 17, 1946 in Brooklyn, New York

Eddie Manion
(Southside Johnny and the Asbury Jukes)
American musician
• Baritone saxophonist with group since 1974.
b. February 28, 1952

Herbie Mann
(Herbert Jay Solomon)
American jazz musician
• Flutist, formed afro-jazz sextet, 1959; had numerous hit albums.
b. April 16, 1930 in New York, New York

Shelly (Sheldon) Manne
American jazz musician
• Hit drummer, 1940s-50s; with Woody Herman, Stan Kenton; opened own Hollywood club, 1960s.
b. June 11, 1920 in New York, New York
d. September 26, 1984 in Los Angeles, California

Sir August Manns
English conductor
• For 45 seasons, led London's Saturday Concerts, which were started at Crystal Palace, 1856.
b. March 12, 1825 in Stettin, Germany
d. March 02, 1907 in London, England

Wingy (Joseph) Manone
American jazz musician
• Left-handed, Louis Armstrong-style trumpeter; lost right arm, age eight; popular, 1920s-50s.
b. February 13, 1904 in New Orleans, Louisiana
d. July 09, 1982 in Las Vegas, Nevada

Annunzio Mantovani
(Annunzio Paolo)
Italian conductor
• Noted for "Mantovani sound"; orchestral arrangements of light classics include "Donkey Serenade."
b. November 05, 1905 in Venice, Italy
d. March 3, 1980 in Tunbridge Wells, England

Ray Manzarek
(The Doors)
American singer–musician
• Formed group in 1966; keyboard player, 1966-73.
b. February 12, 1935 in Chicago, Illinois

Benedetto Marcello
Italian composer
• Wrote 400 cantatas, 10 masses; known for settings of paraphrases of first 50 psalms, 1724-26.
b. 1686 in Venice, Italy
d. 1739 in Brescia, Italy

Igor Markevitch
Russian conductor
• Specialist in Russian, French, Spanish music; wrote first symphony at age 11; conducted leading orchestras for over 50 yrs.
b. July 27, 1912 in Kiev, Russia
d. March 07, 1983 in Antibes, France

Johnny (John David) Marks
American composer–lyricist–songwriter
• Wrote Christmas classic "Rudolph the Red-Nosed Reindeer"; has sold over 150 million records.
b. November 1, 1909 in Mount Vernon, New York
d. September 03, 1985 in New York, New York

Bob (Robert Nesta) Marley
(Bob Marley and the Wailers)
Jamaican musician–composer
• Combined reggae music, Rastafarian faith; sold over 20 million albums at time of death.
b. February 05, 1945 in Kingston, Jamaica
d. May 11, 1981 in Miami, Florida

Sylvia Marlowe
(Mrs Leonid Berman)
American musician
• Harpsichordist; founded Harpsichord Music Society, 1957.
b. September 26, 1908 in New York, New York
d. December 1, 1981 in New York, New York

Joe Marsala
American musician–composer
• Clarinet, sax player with numerous bands, 1930s-60s; wrote "Little Sir Echo."
b. January 05, 1907 in Chicago, Illinois

Bradford Marsalis
American musician
• Jazz saxophonist whose first break was an appearence with Sting in the documentary *Bring on the Night*. Has since collaborated with Sting on several albums; nominated for 2 Grammies; brother of Wynton.
b. August 26, 1960 in New Orleans, LA

Wynton Marsalis
American musician
• Classical, jazz trumpeter; first artist ever to win Grammys for albums in both categories, 1984.
b. October 18, 1961 in New Orleans, Louisiana

Gerry Marsden
(Gerry and the Pacemakers)
English singer–musician
• Founded group, 1959; managed by Brian Epstein.
b. September 24, 1942 in Liverpool, England

The Marshall Tucker Band
(Tommy Caldwell; Toy Caldwell; Jerry Eubanks; Doug Gray; George MCorkle; Paul Riddle)
American music group
• Dixie-rock band, formed 1972.

Martha and the Vandellas
(Rosalind Ashford; Betty Kelly; Lois Reeves; Martha Reeves; Annette Sterling; Sandra Tilley)
American music group
• Motown group popular for dance records; hit singles "Dancing in the Streets," 1964; "I'm Ready for Love," 1966.

Dean Martin
(Dino Crocetti)
American singer–actor
• Crooner best known for comedy films with Jerry Lewis, 1948-57; starred in 1960s-70s TV series.
b. June 17, 1917 in Steubenville, Ohio

Freddy Martin
American bandleader
• Band leader, 1932-83; theme song was hit "Tonight We Love," 1941.
b. December 09, 1906 in Cleveland, Ohio
d. September 3, 1983 in Newport Beach, California

Tony Martin
(Alfred Norris Jr)
American singer–actor
• Popular big-band era baritone; husband of Cyd Charisse.
b. December 25, 1913 in San Francisco, California

Giovanni Martinelli
American opera singer
• Sang over 50 tenor roles with NY Met., 1913-46; starred with Flagstad, 1939.
b. October 22, 1885 in Montagnana, Italy
d. February 02, 1969 in New York, New York

Al Martino
(Alfred Cini)
American actor–singer
• Starred in, sang theme song, *The Godfather*, 1972.
b. November 07, 1927 in Philadelphia, Pennsylvania

Bohuslav Martinu
Czech composer
• Wrote six symphonies, chamber music, radio operas, ballet *Istar*, 1921.
b. December 08, 1890 in Policka, Czechoslovakia
d. August 28, 1959 in Liestal, Switzerland

John Martyn
Scottish singer–musician
• Guitarist; albums include *Sapphire*, 1984.
b. June 28, 1946 in Glasgow, Scotland

The Marvelettes
(Katherine Anderson; Juanita Cowart; Gladys Horton; Georgeanna Tillman; Wanda Young)
American music group
• Motown rock group's hit singles include "Please Mr. Postman," 1961; "Beechwood 4-5789," 1962.

Richard Marx
American singer
• Pop singer; had hit single "Endless Summer Nights," 1988.
b. September 16, 1963 in Chicago, Illinois

Hugh Ramapolo Masekela
American musician
• Trumpeter whose jazz-rock album *Grazin' in the Grass*, 1968, sold four million copies.
b. April 04, 1939 in Witbank, South Africa

Daniel Gregory Mason
American composer–author–educator
• Wrote three symphonies, chamber music, piano pieces; grandson of Lowell.
b. November 2, 1873 in Brookline, Massachusetts
d. December 04, 1953

Dave Mason
(Traffic)
English musician
• Guitarist; helped form Traffic, 1967; solo albums include *Alone Together*, 1970.
b. May 1, 1946 in Worcester, England

Lowell Mason
American composer–teacher
• Established first public school music program, 1838; hymns include "Nearer, My God to Thee."
b. January 08, 1792 in Medfield, Massachusetts
d. August 11, 1872 in Orange, New Jersey

Nick Mason
(Pink Floyd)
English singer–musician
• Drummer; oversees special audio effects in studio, concerts.
b. January 27, 1945 in Birmingham, England

D Curtis Massey
American singer–songwriter
• Had own radio, TV show; music director, "Petticoat Junction"; "Beverly Hillbillies."
b. May 03, 1910 in Midland, Texas

Nick Massi
(Nicholas Macioci; The Four Seasons)
American singer–musician
• Bass player, arranger for popular 1960s group, the Four Seasons.
b. September 19, 1935 in Newark, New Jersey

Amalia Materna
Austrian opera singer
• Soprano chosen by Wagner for his *Brunhilde*, first Bayreuth Festival, 1876.
b. July 1, 1844 in Saint Georgen, Austria
d. January 18, 1918 in Vienna, Austria

Johnny (John Royce) Mathis
American singer
• Smooth ballader; recorded 76 albums; hits include "Too Much Too Little Too Late," 1978.
b. September 3, 1935 in San Francisco, California

Matty (Julian Clifton) Matlock
American jazz musician
• Clarinet, sax player with Bob Crosby, 1942; 1950s-60s.
b. April 27, 1909 in Paducah, Kentucky
d. June 14, 1978 in Los Angeles, California

Billy (E William) May
American jazz musician
• Trumpeter, arranger with Charlie Barnet, Glenn Miller, 1940s.
b. November 1, 1916 in Pittsburgh, Pennsylvania

John Brumwell Mayall
American jazz musician
• Singer, organist, harmonica player; led band, The Bluesbreakers, 1960s; wrote over 200 songs.
b. November 29, 1933 in Manchester, England

Curtis Mayfield
American singer–songwriter
• Hit soundtrack album *Superfly*, 1972.
b. June 03, 1942 in Chicago, Illinois

Dorothy Maynor
American singer
• Soprano who had NY debut, 1939; founded Harlem School of Arts for Underprivileged Children, 1963.
b. September 03, 1910 in Norfolk, Virginia

MC 5 (Motor City Five)
(Michael Davis; Wayne Kramer; Fred Sonic Smith; Rob Tyner; Denis Thompson)
American music group
• Revolutionary, high-energy rock group formed 1967.

Andrea McArdle
American singer–actress
• Original Annie, Broadway musical *Annie*, 1976.
b. November 04, 1963 in Philadelphia, Pennsylvania

Linda Louise Eastman McCartney
(Mrs Paul McCartney; Wings)
American musician–photographer
• Married Paul McCartney, 1969; keyboardist, vocalist for Wings, formed 1971 by husband.
b. September 24, 1942 in New York, New York

Paul (James Paul) McCartney
(The Beatles; Wings)
English singer–songwriter
• Most successful of the Beatles, best-selling composer, recording artist of all time; greatest hit: "Yesterday."
b. June 18, 1942 in Liverpool, England

Delbert McClinton
American singer
• Rhythm and blues performer highlighted in NBC's "Saturday Night Live," 1980s.
b. 1940 in Lubbock, Texas

Marilyn McCoo
(Mrs Billy Davis Jr; The Fifth Dimension)
American singer–actress
• With Fifth Dimension, 1966-73; co-host of "Solid Gold."
b. September 03, 1943 in Jersey City, New Jersey

John McCormack
American opera singer
• Tenor noted for Irish folksongs, ballads; concert performer honored by US, Irish stamps, 1984.
b. June 14, 1884 in Athlone, Ireland
d. September 16, 1945 in Dublin, Ireland

Clyde McCoy
American jazz musician
• Trumpeter who led band, 1930s-60s; theme song: "Sugar Blues."
b. December 29, 1903 in Ashland, Kentucky

Van McCoy
American composer–musician
• Recorded disco hit "The Hustle," 1975.
b. January 06, 1944 in Washington, District of Columbia
d. July 06, 1979 in Englewood, New Jersey

Country Joe McDonald
American singer–songwriter–musician
• Member of best known political rock group of mid-1960s; convicted in MA for chanting obscenities.
b. 1942 in El Monte, California

Michael McDonald
(Doobie Brothers)
American singer–songwriter
• Has successful solo career including hit single with Patti LaBelle "On My Own," 1986.
b. in Saint Louis, Missouri

Reba McEntire
American singer
• Country singer named CMAs Entertainer of Year, 1986; hit album: *Whoever's in New England*, 1986; won Grammy, 1986. Most of band went down in air crash, 1991.
b. March 28, 1954 in Chockie, Oklahoma

Bobby McFerrin
American singer
• Acapella singer; won three Grammys, 1989, for calypso-style song "Don't Worry, Be Happy."
b. March 11, 1950 in New York, New York

Maureen Therese McGovern
American singer
• Known for singing film themes: "The Morning After," 1973, from *The Poseidon Adventure*; "Can You Read My Mind?," 1979, from *Superman*.
b. July 27, 1949 in Youngstown, Ohio

Roger McGuinn
(The Byrds)
American musician–singer–songwriter
• Lead vocalist, founder of The Byrds, 1965-72. Known for distinct 12-string guitar playing. Now has solo career.
b. July 13, 1942 in Chicago, Illinois

McGuire Sisters
(Christine McGuire; Dorothy McGuire; Phyllis McGuire)
American music group
• Popular vocal group, 1950s; had hit single "Sincerely," 1954.

Jimmy (James) McHugh
American songwriter
• Hits include "I Can't Give You Anything But Love," 1928; "On the Sunny Side of the Street," 1930.
b. July 1, 1894 in Boston, Massachusetts
d. May 23, 1969 in Beverly Hills, California

Hal (Harold W) McIntyre
American jazz musician
• Altoist with Glenn Miller, 1937-41; led own band, 1940s-50s.
b. November 29, 1914 in Cromwell, Connecticut
d. May 05, 1959 in Hollywood, California

Red (William) McKenzie
American singer
• Vocalist, kazoo player; led novelty act *Mound City Blue Blowers*, 1920s.
b. October 14, 1907 in Saint Louis, Missouri
d. February 07, 1948 in New York, New York

Ron McKernan
(The Grateful Dead; "Pigpen")
American singer–musician
• Vocalist; harmonica, percussion player; original member, Grateful Dead, 1967-73.
b. September 08, 1946 in San Bruno, California
d. March 08, 1973 in Corte Madera, California

Ray McKinley
American singer–musician–bandleader
• Drummer, vocalist who led new Glenn Miller Band, 1956-66.
b. June 18, 1910 in Fort Worth, Texas

Bill (William) McKinney
American musician
• Drummer for jazz band called McKinney's Cotton Pickers, 1920s.
b. 1894 in Paducah, Kentucky
d. October 14, 1969

John McLaughlin
(Mahavishnu Orchestra)
English musician
• First jazz-rock group to attain fame in both types of music, 1972-74.
b. January 04, 1942 in Yorkshire, England

Don McLean
American singer–songwriter
• Hit songs "American Pie," 1971; "Vincent," 1972.
b. October 02, 1945 in New Rochelle, New York

James Lawrence McMurtry
American singer–songwriter–musician
• Folksinger; debut album *Too Long in the Wasteland*, 1989; son of novelist Larry.
b. March 18, 1962 in Fort Worth, Texas

Jimmy (James Duigald) McPartland
American jazz musician–bandleader
• Dixieland cornetist who led own band, 1940s-50s.
b. March 15, 1907 in Chicago, Illinois

Margaret Marian McPartland
English pianist–songwriter
• Had own jazz trio, 1950s-60s; founded Halcyon record label; once married to James; hosts own weekly radio show on National Public Radio.
b. March 2, 1918 in Slough, England

Clyde McPhatter
(The Drifters)
American singer
• Former lead tenor in group, 1953-56; began solo career, 1956.
b. November 15, 1933 in Durham, North Carolina
d. June 13, 1972 in New York, New York

Carmen McRae
American singer
• Jazz singer, who cut first album, 1954.
b. April 08, 1922 in New York, New York

Christine Perfect McVie
(Fleetwood Mac)
English singer–songwriter
• First solo album, *Christine McVie*, contained hit single "Got a Hold on Me." 1984.
b. July 12, 1943 in Birmingham, England

John McVie
(Fleetwood Mac)
English musician
• Bass guitarist with Fleetwood Mac, 1967–; albums include *Mr. Wonderful*, 1969.
b. November 26, 1946 in England

Meat Loaf
(Marvin Lee Aday)
American musician–actor
• Sang with Amboy Dukes; weighs 260 pounds.
b. September 27, 1947 in Dallas, Texas

Bill Medley
(Righteous Brothers)
American singer
• With Bobby Hatfield had hit "Soul and Inspiration," 1966; solo hit "Brown-Eyed Woman," 1968.
b. September 19, 1940 in Santa Ana, California

Zubin Mehta
Indian conductor
• Conductor, LA Philharmonic, 1962-78; NY Philharmonic, 1978–.
b. April 29, 1936 in Bombay, India

Etienne Nicolas Mehul
French composer
• Wrote over 40 operas including *Ariodant*, 1799; *Joseph*, 1807.
b. June 22, 1763 in Givet, France
d. October 18, 1817 in Paris, France

Randy Meisner
(The Eagles; Poco)
American singer–musician
• Bass player with Eagles, 1971-77; left to pursue solo career.
b. March 08, 1946 in Scotts Bluff, Nebraska

George Miltiades Melachrino
English bandleader
• Formed group, Melachrino Strings, known for unique smooth sound; played every instrument except harp, piano.
b. May 01, 1909 in London, England
d. June 18, 1965 in London, England

Melanie
(Melanie Safka)
American singer–songwriter
• Singer, guitarist, often in folk vein; hit song "Brand New Key," 1971.
b. February 03, 1948 in New York, New York

Dame Nellie Melba
(Helen Porter Mitchell Armstrong)
Australian opera singer
• Outstanding coloratura of her day; star of London's Covent Garden, NY Met. from 1890s; made Dame, 1918; desert, "peaches melba" was created in her honor.
b. May 19, 1859 in Melbourne, Australia
d. February 23, 1931 in Sydney, Australia

Lauritz Melchior
American opera singer
• Famed Wagnerian tenor with NY Met., 1926-50; considered finest heldentenor of the day.
b. March 2, 1890 in Copenhagen, Denmark
d. March 18, 1973 in Santa Monica, California

Jose Melis
Cuban bandleader–pianist
• Music director for Jack Paar's "Tonight Show" who made several recordings.
b. February 27, 1920 in Havana, Cuba

John Cougar Mellencamp
American singer–songwriter–musician–artist
• Rock singer whose career skyrocketed with heavy cable-TV exposure: "Hurt So Good," 1982. Often sings tales of small-town life.
b. October 07, 1951 in Seymour, Indiana

Memphis Slim
(Peter Chatman)
American pianist–singer
• Int'l. blues performer; hits include "Beer Drinking Woman."
b. 1916
d. February 24, 1988 in Paris, France

Men at Work
(Greg Ham; Colin Hay; John Rees; Jerry Speiser; Ron Strykert)
Australian music group
• Album *Business As Usual*, 1982, included hits "Who Can It be Now?"; "Down Under."

Felix Mendelssohn
(Felix Mendelssohn-Bartholdy)
German composer–conductor–musician
• Works include five symphonies; wrote famed overture to *Midsummer Night's Dream*, 1826.
b. February 03, 1809 in Hamburg, Germany
d. November 04, 1847 in Leipzig, Germany

Sergio Mendes
(Sergio Mendes and Brasil '66)
Brazilian musician–bandleader
• Hits include "The Look of Love."
b. February 11, 1941 in Niteroi, Brazil

Willem (Josef Willem) Mengelberg
Dutch conductor
• Noted for leading Amsterdam's Concertgebouw for 50 yrs.; often led NY Philharmonic, 1920s.
b. March 28, 1871 in Utrecht, Netherlands
d. March 22, 1951 in Zuort, Switzerland

Peter Mennin
American composer–educator
• Pres., Julliard School, 1962-83; wrote nine symphonies.
b. May 17, 1923 in Erie, Pennsylvania
d. June 17, 1983 in New York, New York

Gian Carlo Menotti
Italian composer
• Foremost composer-librettist of modern opera; wrote Pulitzer Prize-winning operas *The Consul*, 1950, *The Saint of Bleecker Street*, 1955; also wrote Christmas opera *Amahl and the Night Visitors*, 1954.
b. July 07, 1911 in Cadigliano, Italy

Yehudi Menuhin
American violinist
• Child prodigy, debut with San Francisco Symphony at age seven.
b. April 22, 1916 in New York, New York

Saverio Mercadante
Italian composer
• Wrote nearly 60 operas including *Elisa e Claudio*, 1821; *Il Giuramento*, 1837.
b. September 1795 in Altamura, Italy
d. December 17, 1870 in Naples, Italy

Johnny (John H) Mercer
American singer–songwriter
• Won Oscars for the lyrics to "On the Atchison," 1946; "Moon River," 1961; wrote "That Old Black Magic," 1942.
b. November 18, 1909 in Savannah, Georgia
d. June 25, 1976 in Bel Air, California

Mabel Mercer
American singer
• Gravel-voiced cabaret performer at NYC nightclubs, 1940s-60s; annual Stereo Review award named for her.
b. January 1900 in Burton-on-Trent, England
d. April 21, 1984 in Pittsfield, Massachusetts

Freddie Mercury
(Frederick Bulsara; Queen)
English singer–musician
• Album *We Are the Champions* included single "Another One Bites the Dust."
b. September 08, 1946 in Zanzibar

Ethel Merman
(Ethel Zimmerman)
American singer–actress
• Starred on Broadway in *Annie Get Your Gun*, 1946; *Hello, Dolly*, 1970.
b. January 16, 1909 in Astoria, New York
d. February 15, 1984 in New York, New York

Robert Merrill
American opera singer
• Baritone who became first American to sing 500 performances at NY Met., 1973.
b. June 04, 1919 in New York, New York

Nan Merriman
American opera singer
• Mezzo-soprano; soloed with Toscanini on broadcasts, recordings, 1940s.
b. 1920

Olivier Messiaen
French composer–musician
• His music glorifying beauty of UT resulting in mountain named for him, 1978; studies bird songs.
b. December 1, 1908 in Avignon, France

Jim Messina
(Buffalo Springfield; Loggins and Messina; Poco)
American singer–songwriter
• Bass player, vocalist; directed Buffalo Springfield at age 19; part of Loggins and Messina, 1972-77.
b. December 05, 1947 in Maywood, California

Pietro Metastasio
(Pietro Trapassi)
Italian dramatist–poet–librettist
• Viennese court poet, from 1729; wrote librettos for many operas, melodramas including *Attilio Regolo*, 1750.
b. January 03, 1698 in Rome, Italy
d. April 12, 1782 in Vienna, Austria

The Meters
(Joseph Modeliste; Art Neville; Leo Nocentelli; George Porter)
American music group
• Off-beat funk hits include "Sophisticated Sissy," 1968.

Joseph Meyer
American composer
• Wrote songs "If You Knew Susie," 1925; "Crazy Rhythm," 1928.
b. March 12, 1894 in Modesto, California

Giacomo Meyerbeer
(Jakob Liebmann Beer)
German composer
• Very popular in his day; wrote spectacular French operas *Les Huguenots*, 1836; *Le Prophete*, 1849.
b. September 05, 1791 in Berlin, Germany
d. May 02, 1864 in Paris, France

Mezz (Milton) Mezzrow
American jazz musician
• Saxophonist-clarinetist; led Harlem's first mixed band, 1937; wrote "Really the Blues," 1946.
b. November 09, 1899 in Chicago, Illinois
d. August 05, 1972 in Paris, France

George Michael
(George Michael Panayiotou; George Michael Panos; Wham)
English singer
• Hits with Wham! include "Careless Whisper," 1984; solo hits include "Faith," 1987.
b. June 25, 1963 in Radlett, England

Arturo Benedetti Michelangeli
Italian musician
• Piano virtuoso who toured US, 1950, 1966; noted for love of dangerous sports, idiosyncracies.
b. January 05, 1920

Midnight Oil
(Peter Garrett; Peter Gifford; Rob Hurst; Jim Moginie; Martin Rotsey)
Australian music group
• Debut US album *10, 9, 8, 7, 6, 5, 4, 3, 2, 1*, 1983.

Julia Migenes-Johnson
American actress–opera singer
• Starred in original Broadway version of *Fiddler on the Roof*, 1964-67; had NY Met. debut, 1980.
b. 1945

Buddy Miles
American singer–musician
• Drummer, known for husky voice; albums include *Sneak Attack*, 1981.
b. September 05, 1946 in Omaha, Nebraska

Darius Milhaud
(Les Six)
French composer–actor
• Member of jazz group Les Six, 1920s; 400 works include ballet *La Creacion du Monde*, 1923, first use of blues, jazz in symphonic score.
b. September 04, 1892 in Aix-en-Provence, France
d. June 22, 1974 in Geneva, Switzerland

Frankie Miller
Scottish singer
• Rhythm and blues, rock songs include "Darlin'," 1978.
b. 1950 in Glasgow, Scotland

Glenn Miller
American bandleader
• Leading figure of Big Band era, 1930s-40; hits include "In the Mood"; "Chattanooga Choo-Choo."
b. March 01, 1904 in Clarinda, Iowa
d. December 15, 1944

Mitch(ell William) Miller
American conductor
• Host of TV series "Sing Along with Mitch," 1961-66; hit single "Yellow Rose of Texas," 1955.
b. July 04, 1911 in Rochester, New York

Roger Dean Miller
American singer–songwriter
• Country-pop singer who won 11 Grammys; hit single "King of the Road," 1965.
b. January 02, 1936 in Fort Worth, Texas

Steve Miller
(The Steve Miller Band)
American musician–singer
• Hit songs include "Heart Like a Wheel," 1981; "Abracadabra," 1982.
b. October 05, 1943 in Dallas, Texas

Milli Vanilli
(Fabrice Morvan; Rob Pilatus)
German music group
• Eurodisco duo, known for dancing and long cornrow hair; debut album *Girl You Know It's True*, 1989, sold 7 million copies; revealed that group never sang, only lip-synced songs; stripped of Grammy, 1990.

Donald Mills
(The Mills Brothers)
American singer
• Member of the family vocal group, 1930s-70s; often on Bing Crosby radio shows; hits include "Lazy River," 1931.
b. April 29, 1915 in Piqua, Ohio

Harry Mills
(The Mills Brothers)
American singer
• Member of vocal group, popular 1930s-70s; noted for stage presence, pleasing personalities.
b. August 19, 1913 in Piqua, Ohio
d. June 28, 1982 in Los Angeles, California

Herbert Mills
(The Mills Brothers)
American singer
• Member of family vocal group; hits include "Glow Worm," 1952.
b. April 02, 1912 in Piqua, Ohio
d. April 12, 1989 in Las Vegas, Nevada

Irving Mills
American musician–composer
• Discovered, managed Duke Ellington, 1926; wrote "Minnie the Moocher."
b. January 16, 1894 in New York, New York
d. April 21, 1985 in Palm Springs, California

John Mills
(The Mills Brothers)
American singer
• Replaced son in family vocal group, 1936-56.
b. February 11, 1889 in Bellefonte, Pennsylvania
d. December 08, 1967 in Ohio

Stephanie Mills
American actress–singer
• Made Broadway debut in *The Wiz*, 1975, revival, 1984; hit songs include "You're Putting a Rush on Me," 1987; won Grammy, 1980.
b. March 22, 1957 in Brooklyn, New York

The Mills Brothers
(Donald Mills; Harry Mills; Herbert Mills; John Mills)
American music group
• First black vocal group to break the color barrier, 1930s; hits include million-seller "Paper Doll," 1943; noted for radio, TV, club appearances.

Sherrill Eustace Milnes
American opera singer
• Outstanding Verdi baritone; joined NY Met., 1965 in debut *Faust*, 1965.
b. January 1, 1935 in Downers Grove, Illinois

Ronnie Milsap
American singer
• Blind country singer whose hits include "Any Day Now," 1982.
b. January 16, 1944 in Robinsville, North Carolina

Nathan Milstein
American violinist
• Noted concertist; toured with Horowitz in Russia; made US debut, 1929; won Grammy, 1975.
b. December 31, 1904 in Odessa, Russia

Charles Mingus
American jazz musician–band leader
• Bass virtuoso who elevated bass to melody carrier; led sextet, 1960s.
b. April 22, 1922 in Nogales, Arizona
d. January 05, 1979 in Cuernavaca, Mexico

Liza Minnelli
(Mrs Mark Gero)
American actress–singer
• Daughter of Judy Garland, Vincente Minnelli; won Oscar for *Cabaret*, 1972; other films include *Arthur*, 1981.
b. March 12, 1946 in Los Angeles, California

Mischa Mischakoff
(Mischa Fischberg)
American violinist
• Concertmaster, NBC Symphony Orchestra under Toscanni, 1937-51; Detroit Symphony, 1951-68.
b. April 03, 1895 in Proskurov, Russia
d. February 01, 1981 in Petoskey, Michigan

Missing Persons
(Dale Bozzio; Terry Bozzio; Warren Cuccurullo; Patrick O'Hearn)
American music group
• New wave group who had gold debut album *Spring Session M*, 1983.

Mitch Ryder and the Detroit Wheels
(John Badenjek; Joe Cubert; Earl Eliot; Jimmy McCartney; Mitch Ryder)
American music group
• Leading teenage blue-eyed soul band of mid-1960s; first hit "Jenny Take a Ride," 1965.

Chad (William Chad) Mitchell
(Chad Mitchell Trio)
American singer
• Founded trio, 1959; biggest hit "Lizzie Borden," 1962; replaced in group by John Denver, 1965-69.
b. December 05, 1936 in Portland, Oregon

Guy Mitchell
(Al Cernik)
American singer
• Hits include "My Heart Cries for You," 1950; "Heartaches by the Number," 1959.
b. February 27, 1927 in Yugoslavia

Joni Mitchell
(Roberta Joan Anderson)
Canadian singer–songwriter
• Wrote, recorded first hit, "Chelsea Morning," 1962.
b. November 07, 1943 in McLeod, Alberta

Willie Mitchell
American musician
• Trumpeter, keyboard player; rhythm and blues/soul albums include *Best Of...*, 1980.
b. 1928 in Ashland, Mississippi

The Modern Jazz Quartet
(Kenny Clarke; Percy Heath; Milt Jackson; John Lewis)
American music group
• Black group founded by Jackson, Lewis, 1952.

The Modernaires
(Ralph Brewster; Bill Conway; Hal Dickinson; Chuck Goldstein)
American music group
• Vocal quartet; introduced by Charlie Barnet, 1936; recorded "Chattanoog Choo Choo" with Glenn Miller.

Anna Moffo
American opera singer
• Soprano who made debut at Met., 1959; made numerous recordings, films, TV appearances.
b. June 27, 1934 in Wayne, Pennsylvania

Molly Hatchet
(Barry Borden; Danny Joe Brown; Bruce Crump; Jimmy Farrar; Dave Hlubek; Steve Holland; Duane Rolland; Banner Thomas; Riff West)
American music group
• Southern blues-boogie, heavy-metal band formed 1975; album *Beating the Odds* sold over two million copies.

Federico Mompou
Spanish composer
• Wrote over 200 piano works, mostly in unique folklike idiom.
b. April 1, 1893 in Barcelona, Spain
d. June 3, 1987 in Barcelona, Spain

Thelonius Sphere Monk
American songwriter–musician
• Leading jazz pianist who helped develop "bop," 1940s; known for chord structures, active into 1970s. *Straight No Chaser*, 1990 based on Monk's life.
b. October 1, 1920 in Rocky Mount, North Carolina
d. February 17, 1982 in Englewood, New Jersey

The Monkees
(Mickey Dolenz; Davy Jones; Mike Nesmith; Peter Tork)
American music group
• Prefabricated 1960s pop group formed by TV executives; had hit TV series, 1966-68, hit singles "Last Train to Clarksville," 1966, "I'm a Believer," 1967.

Bill (William Smith) Monroe
American singer–songwriter
• Wrote Elvis Presley hit "Blue Moon of Kentucky," 1947.
b. September 13, 1911 in Rosine, New York

Lucy Monroe
American singer
• Called "star-spangled soprano," for her rendition of national anthem in over 5,000 performances.
b. October 23, 1906 in New York, New York
d. October 13, 1987 in New York, New York

Vaughn Monroe
American singer–bandleader
• Noted for songs "Racing with the Moon," "Ballerina."
b. October 07, 1911 in Akron, Ohio
d. May 21, 1973 in Stuart, Florida

Pierre-Alexandre Monsigny
French composer
• Noted French comic opera writer: *Les Aveux Indiscrets*, 1759.
b. October 17, 1729 in Fauquembergue, France
d. January 14, 1817 in Paris, France

Patsy Montana
American singer–composer
• Called Queen of Country Western Music, 1973; wrote over 200 songs.
b. October 3, 1914 in Hot Springs, Arkansas

Pierre Monteux
American conductor
• Conducted 60 orchestras including the one in San Francisco, 1935-52.
b. April 04, 1875 in Paris, France
d. July 01, 1964 in Hancock, Maine

Claudio Monteverdi
Italian composer
• Wrote opera *Orfeo*, 1607; considered greatest composer of his day.
b. May 15, 1567 in Cremona, Italy
d. November 29, 1643 in Venice, Italy

Melba Montgomery
American singer–songwriter
• Country singer; paired with George Jones, 1963-67.
b. October 14, 1938 in Iron City, Tennessee

Wes Montgomery
American jazz musician
• Guitarist who used thumb as plectrum; recorded album *Movin' Wes*, 1965.
b. March 06, 1925 in Indianapolis, Indiana
d. June 15, 1968 in Indianapolis, Indiana

Carlos Montoya
American musician
• Internationally renowned flamenco guitarist, soloist.
b. December 13, 1903 in Madrid, Spain

Moody Blues
(Graeme Edge; Justin Hayward; Denny Laine; John Lodge; Michael Pinder; Ray Thomas; Clint Warwick)
English music group
• Hits include "Nights in White Satin," 1967; "The Voice," 1981.

Keith Moon
(The Who)
English musician
• Drummer who helped create rock opera *Tommy*.
b. August 23, 1946 in Wembley, England
d. September 07, 1978 in London, England

Douglas Moore
American composer
• Wrote 1951 Pulitzer-winning opera *Giants in the Earth*; folk opera *Ballad of Baby Doe*, 1956.
b. August 1, 1893 in Cutchoque, New York
d. July 25, 1969 in Greenport, New York

Grace Moore
American singer
• Popular opera, film soprano, 1930s; hosted own radio show; killed in plane crash; 1953 film based on her life.
b. December 01, 1901 in Tennessee
d. January 26, 1947 in Copenhagen, Denmark

Melba Moore
American singer–actress
• Won Tony for *Purlie*, 1970.
b. October 29, 1945 in New York, New York

Sam(uel David) Moore
(Sam and Dave)
American singer
• With Dave Prater, one of leading soul acts, 1960s; hit song "Soul Man," 1967, popularized again, late 1970s, by Dan Aykroyd, John Belushi as Blues Brothers.
b. October 12, 1935 in Miami, Florida

Max Edward Morath
American entertainer–musician
• Ragtime pianist who revived vintage music on TV, Broadway, national tours, 1960s-70s.
b. October 01, 1926 in Colorado Springs, Colorado

Helen Riggins Morgan
American singer–actress
• Broadway, nightclub star, 1920s-30s; the original "torch singer"; noted for "My Bill."
b. August 02, 1900 in Danville, Illinois
d. October 09, 1941 in Chicago, Illinois

Jane Morgan
American singer
• Popular vocalist, 1940s-50s; hit ballad "Fascination," 1957.
b. 1920 in Boston, Massachusetts
d. 1974

Jaye P Morgan
American singer
• Husky-voiced popular vocalist, 1950s-70s; frequent TV guest.
b. December 03, 1932 in Denver, Colorado

Russ Morgan
American songwriter–bandleader
• Trombonist, arranger, who led band, 1930s-40s; known for sweet, sentimental sound; wrote "You're Nobody Till Somebody Loves You," 1944.
b. 1904 in Scranton, Pennsylvania
d. August 07, 1969 in Las Vegas, Nevada

Jim (James Douglas) Morrison
(The Doors; "Lizard King")
American singer–songwriter
• Best-selling albums include *Waiting for the Sun*, 1969; *An American Prayer*, 1978. In 1991, subject of Oliver Stone film "The Doors."
b. December 08, 1943 in Melbourne, Florida
d. July 03, 1971 in Paris, France

Van Morrison
(George Ivan; Them)
Irish singer–songwriter
• First solo US hit, 1967, "Brown-Eyed Girl"; best-selling album *Moondance*, 1970.
b. August 31, 1945 in Belfast, Northern Ireland

Buddy Morrow
American musician
• Trombonist noted for tone, range; led big band, 1950s.
b. February 08, 1919 in New Haven, Connecticut

Ella Mae Morse
American singer
• Jazz-style vocalist, 1940s; had comeback, early 1950s, with "The Blacksmith Blues."
b. September 12, 1924 in Mansfield, Texas

Arthur Morton
American composer
• Composer with film companies since 1948; scores include *Superman*, 1978; *Poltergeist II*, 1986.
b. August 08, 1908 in Duluth, Minnesota

Jelly Roll (Joseph Ferdinand) Morton
American jazz musician–songwriter
• Pianist considered inventor of orchestral jazz, early 1900s; wrote "Jelly Roll Blues," 1917.
b. September 2, 1885 in Gulfport, Louisiana
d. July 1, 1941 in Los Angeles, California

Jerry (Jerome Sheldon) Moss
American music executive
• Co-founder, A & M Records, Inc.; hits include *Taste of Honey*, 1965.
b. 1935 in Brooklyn, New York

The Motels
(Martha Davis; Brian Glascock; Michael Goodroe; Marty Jourard; Guy Perry)
American music group
• Songs they popularized include "Only the Lonely," 1982; "Remember the Night," 1983.

Bennie Moten
American bandleader
• Led swinging Kansas City band, 1920s; Count Basie's band patterned after his.
b. November 13, 1894 in Kansas City, Missouri
d. April 02, 1935 in Kansas City, Missouri

The Mothers of Invention
(Jimmy Carl Black; Ray Collins; Roy Estrada; Bunk Gardner; Don Preston; James Sherwood; Ian Underwood; Frank Zappa)
American music group
• Backup group for Frank Zappa, often changed by him.

Motley Crue
(Tommy Lee; Mick Mars; Vince Neil; Nikki Sixx)
American music group
• Heavy metal band; albums include *Shout at the Devil*, 1983.

Mott (the Hoople)
(Verden Allen; Ariel Bender; Nigel Benjamin; Morgan Fisher; Dale "Buffin" Griffin; Ian Hunter; Ray Major; Mick Ralphs; Rick Ronson)
English music group
• Hard rock group formed 1969 in Hereford, England; had success with David Bowie-produced albums.

Mountain
(Corky Laing; Felix Pappalardi; David Perry; Leslie West)
American music group
• Heavy-metal group formed, 1969; albums include *Twin Peaks*, 1977.

(Johann Georg) Leopold Mozart
Austrian musician–composer
• Court composer, 1757; devised violin technique; father of Wolfgang.
b. 1719 in Augsburg, Germany
d. 1787 in Salzburg, Austria

Wolfgang Amadeus Mozart
(Johannes Chrysostomus Wolfgangus Theophilus Mozart)
Austrian composer
• Composed over 600 works, including *The Marriage of Figaro*, 1896.
b. January 27, 1756 in Salzburg, Austria
d. December 05, 1791 in Vienna, Austria

Eugene Mravinsky
(Evgeni Mravinsky)
Russian conductor
• Led Leningrad Philharmonic; noted for performances of Tchaikovsky.
b. 1903 in Saint Petersburg, Russia

Robert Muczynski
American composer–musician
• Works, influenced by Russian modern school, include *Dovetail Overture*, 1960.
b. March 19, 1929 in Chicago, Illinois

Maria Muldaur
American singer
• Noted for hit "Midnight at the Oasis," 1974; nominated for Grammys.
b. September 12, 1943 in New York, New York

Gerry (Gerald Joseph) Mulligan
American jazz musician–composer
• Noted baritone saxophonist, arranger; formed own pianoless quartet, 1950s; developed "cool" jazz.
b. April 06, 1927 in New York, New York

Charles Munch
French conductor
• Led Boston Symphony, 1949-62; founded Paris Philharmonic, 1930s.
b. September 26, 1891 in Strasbourg, France
d. November 06, 1968 in Richmond, Virginia

Karl Munchinger
German conductor
• Founded Stuttgart Chamber Orchestra, 1945; the "Klassische Philharmonie," 1966.
b. May 29, 1915 in Stuttgart, Germany

Patrice Beverly Munsel
American singer
• Soprano who at 18, was youngest singer ever accepted at NY Met.; in films, Broadway musicals.
b. May 14, 1925 in Spokane, Washington

Turk (Melvin) Murphy
American jazz musician–bandleader
• Traditional jazz trombonist, noted for reviving earlier jazz, ragtime hits.
b. December 16, 1915 in Palermo, California
d. May 3, 1987 in San Francisco, California

Anne Murray
(Mrs David Langstruth; Morna Anne Murray)
Canadian singer
• Former physical education teacher; first gold record "Snowbird," 1970.
b. June 2, 1945 in Springhill, Nova Scotia

Thea Musgrave
Scottish composer
• Operas include *The Decision*, 1967; *Mary, Queen of Scots*, 1977.
b. May 27, 1928 in Edinburgh, Scotland

Riccardo Muti
Italian conductor
• Music director, Philadelphia Orchestra, 1980-.
b. July 28, 1941 in Naples, Italy

Anne-Sophie Mutter
German musician
• Child prodigy violinist; soloist performing with orchestras worldwide, known for technical command, accurate intonation, and rich sound.
b. June 29, 1963 in Rheinfelden, Germany (West)

Milton Nascimento
Brazilian singer–songwriter–musician
• Sings original pop in sophisticated folk style; has recorded 18 albums, three available in US.
b. 1942 in Rio de Janeiro, Brazil

Graham Nash
(The Hollies; Crosby Stills Nash and Young)
English musician–singer
• Member of two well-known groups, 1960s-70s; solo career spent helping antinuclear power movement; helped define soft CA sound, 1960s.
b. February 02, 1942 in Blackpool, England

Johnny Nash
American singer
• Brought reggae to attention of American public with number one hit "I Can See Clearly Now," 1972.
b. August 19, 1940 in Houston, Texas

Fats (Theodore) Navarro
American jazz musician
• Bop trumpeter, active in 1940s; recorded with Goodman, Eckstine.
b. 1923
d. 1950

Nazareth
(Peter Agnew; Manny Charlton; Dan McCafferty; Darrell Sweet)
Scottish music group
• Hard rock group formed, 1969; known for making quiet versions of other artists music close to heavy-metal.

Rick (Eric Hilliard) Nelson
(Stone Canyon Band)
American singer–actor
• Sold 35 million records before age 21; son of Ozzie, Harriet; killed in plane crash.
b. May 08, 1940 in Teaneck, New Jersey
d. December 31, 1985 in Dekalb, Texas

Willie Nelson
American musician–singer–actor
• Won Grammys for "Blue Eyes Crying in the Rain," 1975; "Georgia on My Mind," 1978.
b. April 3, 1933 in Abbott, Texas

Peter Nero
American pianist–conductor
• Known for nightclub, pop concert performances; leader of over 150 orchestras since 1971; with Philadelphia Pops since 1979.
b. May 22, 1934 in New York, New York

Mike (Michael) Nesmith
(The Monkees)
American singer–songwriter
• Vocalist with The Monkees on popular TV series, 1966-68; known for trademark wool cap.
b. December 3, 1942 in Houston, Texas

Victor E Nessler
German composer
• Wrote popular opera *Der Trompeter von Sachingen*, 1884.
b. January 28, 1841 in Baldenheim, Germany
d. May 28, 1890 in Strassburg, Germany

Ethelbert Woodbridge Nevin
American composer
• Piano pieces included "Narcissus"; wrote music for "The Rosary"; "Mighty Lak a Rose."
b. November 25, 1862 in Edgeworth, Pennsylvania
d. February 17, 1901 in New Haven, Connecticut

New Kids on the Block
(Jon Knight; Jordan Knight; Joe McIntyre; Donnie Wahlberg; DannyWood)
American music group
• Teen pop group formed in Boston, 1985; dominated music charts, 1989, with two songs simultaneously in top 10; all albums have platinum sales including *Hangin' Tough*, 1989.

New Order
(Joy Division; Bernard Albrecht; Peter Hook; Stephen Morris)
American music group
• New wave, dance music hits include "Blue Monday," 1983.

Anthony George Newley
English actor–singer–songwriter
• Stage productions include *Stop the World, I Want to Get Off*, 1961-63; won Grammy for "What Kind of Fool Am I?" 1962.
b. September 24, 1931 in London, England

Phyllis Newman
American actress–singer
• Won Tony, 1962, for *Subways are for Sleeping.*
b. March 19, 1935 in Jersey City, New Jersey

Randy Newman
American singer–songwriter
• Known for sarcastic hit single, "Short People," from 1978 album *Little Criminals.*
b. November 28, 1943 in Los Angeles, California

Juice Newton
(Judy Cohen)
American singer
• Country-pop singer; hit singles include "Angel of the Morning," 1981; "Break It to Me Gently," 1982.
b. February 18, 1952 in Virginia Beach, Virginia

Wayne Newton
American singer
• Hit singles include "Danke Schoen," 1963; "Daddy Don't You Walk So Fast," 1972; highly successful nightclub performer, 1970s–.
b. April 03, 1942 in Roanoke, Virginia

Olivia Newton-John
English singer–actress
• Hit songs include "Physical," 1981; "Heart Attack," 1982; starred in *Grease; Xanadu.*
b. September 26, 1948 in Cambridge, England

Red (Ernest Loring) Nichols
(The Five Pennies)
American musician–radio performer
• Popular 1920s-30s jazz trumpeter; biographical film, *The Five Pennies*, 1959.
b. May 08, 1905 in Ogden, Utah
d. June 28, 1965 in Las Vegas, Nevada

Stevie (Stephanie) Nicks
(Fleetwood Mac)
American singer–songwriter
• First solo album was *Bella Donna*, 1981.
b. May 26, 1948 in Phoenix, Arizona

Carl Otto Ehrenfried Nicolai
German composer
• Wrote popular opera *Merry Wives of Windsor*, 1849.
b. June 09, 1810 in Konigsberg, Germany
d. May 11, 1849 in Berlin, Germany

Night Ranger
(Jack Blades; Alan Fitz Fitzgerald; Brad Gillis; Kelly Keagy; Jeff Watson)
American music group
• Album *Midnight Madness*, 1983, produced hit single "Sister Christian."

Alwin Nikolais
American choreographer–composer
• Wrote electronic ballet scores, won acclaim for portrayal of extraterrestrial creatures in Monetti's opera, *Help! Help! the Globolinks.*
b. November 25, 1912 in Southington, Connecticut

Birgit Nilsson
Swedish opera singer
• Considered one of finest Wagnerian sopranos of all time, 1950s-60s.
b. May 17, 1918 in West Karup, Sweden

The Nitty Gritty Dirt Band
(Ralph Barr; Chris Darrow; Jimmie Fadden; Jeff Hanna; Jim Ibbotson; Bruce Kunkel; John McEven; Leslie Thompson)
American music group
• Group formed in 1960s; plays blue grass to hard rock; had triple album, *Dirt, Silver and Gold*, 1976.

Marni Nixon
American opera singer
• "Ghost-sang" for film stars including Audrey Hepburn, Natalie Wood, others.
b. February 22, 1929 in Altadena, California

Ray Noble
English bandleader
• Led dance bands, 1930s-40s; wrote "Cherokee," 1938; popular radio actor, 1940s-50s.
b. December 17, 1903 in Brighton, England
d. April 02, 1978 in London, England

Bob Nolan
(Sons of the Pioneers)
American songwriter–singer
• Credited with performing, writing over 1,000 gospel, country, western songs including "Cool Water," 1936.
b. 1908 in Canada
d. June 16, 1980 in Costa Mesa, California

Jimmie Noone
American jazz musician
• Early jazz clarinetist who led his own band, 1920s-30s.
b. April 23, 1895 in Cut Off, Louisiana
d. April 19, 1944 in Los Angeles, California

Peter Noone
(Herman's Hermits)
English singer–musician
• Herman of Herman's Hermits, 1963-71; number one hit "I'm Henry the Eighth, I Am," 1965.
b. November 05, 1947 in Manchester, England

Lillian Nordica
(Lillian Norton; "The Lily of the North")
American opera singer
• Celebrated Wagnerian soprano with NY Met., 1896-1907; first American singer widely acclaimed in Europe.
b. May 12, 1859 in Farmington, Maine
d. May 1, 1914 in Batavia, Indonesia

Jessye Norman
American opera singer
• "A soprano of magnificent presence," with Metropolitan Opera Co., 1983–.
b. September 15, 1945 in Augusta, Georgia

Red (Kenneth) Norvo
American jazz musician
• Vibraphonist who led own band, 1930s-40s; once wed to his vocalist, Mildred Bailey.
b. March 31, 1908 in Beardstown, Illinois

Jean Nougues
French composer
• Wrote popular opera *Quo Vadis*, 1909.
b. April 25, 1875 in Bordeaux, France
d. August 28, 1932 in Paris, France

Guiomar Novaes
Brazilian musician
• Outstanding pianist; noted for deep concentration, colorful performances; had US debut, 1915.
b. February 28, 1895 in Sao Paulo, Brazil
d. March 07, 1979 in Sao Paulo, Brazil

Ivor Novello
(David Ivor Davies)
Welsh songwriter–actor
• Wrote song "Keep the Home Fires Burning"; appeared in film *Once a Lady*, 1932.
b. January 15, 1893 in Cardiff, Wales
d. March 06, 1951 in London, England

Carlo Novi
(Southside Johnny and the Asbury Jukes)
Mexican musician
• Tenor saxophonist with group since 1974.
b. August 07, 1949 in Mexico City, Mexico

Ted (Theodore Anthony) Nugent
(The Amboy Dukes; Damn Yankees; "Motor City Mad Man")
American singer
• Known for wild antics, wearing earplugs while performing; songs include "Journey to the Centre of the Mind," 1968.
b. December 13, 1948 in Detroit, Michigan

Gary Numan
(Gary Anthony James Webb)
English singer–musician
• Considered first superstar of the synthesiser; albums include *She's Got Claws*, 1981.
b. March 08, 1958 in London, England

Bobby Nunn
American musician
• Bass player; original member of pop group the Coasters, 1955-58; hits include "Yakety Yak," 1958.
b. 1925
d. November 05, 1986 in Los Angeles, California

Ervin Nyiregyhazi
American pianist
• Held first piano concert at age six; wrote over 100 works for piano.
b. January 19, 1903 in Budapest, Hungary
d. April 13, 1987 in Los Angeles, California

Laura Nyro
American singer–songwriter
• Best known for writing pop music, 1960s-70s, with poetic lyrics; albums include *NY Tendaberry*, 1969.
b. October 18, 1947 in Bronx, New York

The Oak Ridge Boys
(Duane Allen; Joe Bonsall; Bill Golden; Richard Sterban)
American music group
• Country-pop group known for four-part harmonies; hit single "Elvira," 1981.

John (William) Oates
(Hall and Oates)
American singer–songwriter
• Known for award-winning rock, R&B hits recorded with Daryl Hall: "I Can't Go for That," 1981.
b. April 07, 1948 in New York, New York

Billy Ocean
(Leslie Sebastian Charles)
English singer
• Co-wrote number one single, "Caribbean Queen," 1984.
b. January 21, 1950 in Trinidad

Phil(ip David) Ochs
American singer–political activist
• Song "I Ain't Marching Anymore," 1963, protested Vietnam War.
b. December 19, 1940 in El Paso, Texas
d. April 09, 1976 in Far Rockaway, New York

Helen O'Connell
American singer
• Popular vocalist with Jimmy Dorsey, 1939-43; made comeback, 1950s.
b. May 23, 1921 in Lima, Ohio

Donald O'Connor
American dancer–singer
• Best known for 1940s-50s Hollywood musicals: *Singin' in the Rain*, 1952.
b. August 28, 1925 in Chicago, Illinois

Sinead O'Connor
Irish singer–songwriter
• Pop singer; combines pop, jazz, Celtic sounds; hit single "Nothing Compares to You," 1990; known for clean-shaven head and uninhibited tongue.
b. 1967 in Dublin, Ireland

Anita O'Day
(Anita Colton)
American singer
• Popular, 1940s, with hit "And Her Tears Flowed Like Wine."
b. December 18, 1919 in Chicago, Illinois

Odetta
(Odetta Homes Felious Gordon)
American singer–musician
• Films include *The Last Time I Saw Paris*, 1954.
b. December 31, 1930 in Birmingham, Alabama

Jacques Offenbach
(Jacques Eberst)
French musician–composer
• Best known for four-act opera *The Tales of Hoffmann*; credited with creating the French operetta.
b. June 2, 1819 in Cologne, Germany
d. October 04, 1880 in Paris, France

The O'Jays
(Walter Williams; Sam Strain; Edward Levert)
American music group
• Hits include "Use Ta Be My Girl," 1977; "Girl, Don't Let It Get You Down," 1980.

Chauncey (Chancellor) Olcott
American singer–songwriter
• Popular tenor; wrote Irish songs including "When Irish Eyes Are Smiling," 1913; film *My Wild Irish Rose*, 1947, portrays life.
b. July 21, 1860 in Buffalo, New York
d. March 18, 1932 in Monte Carlo, Monaco

Mike Oldfield
English composer
• Wrote song that was used for theme to film *The Exorcist*, 1973: "Tubular Bells."
b. May 15, 1953 in Reading, England

Joe (Joseph) Oliver
American musician–bandleader
• Jazz pioneer whose band featured Louis Armstrong, Johnny Dodds; hits include "Dixieland Blues"; first black jazz band to record, 1923.
b. May 11, 1885 in Abend, Louisiana
d. April 08, 1938 in Savannah, Georgia

Sy (Melvin James) Oliver
American musician
• Trumpeter, vocalist, bandleader; composer, arranger for Jimmy Lunceford, 1930s; Tommy Dorsey, 1940s.
b. December 17, 1910 in Battle Creek, Michigan
d. May 27, 1988 in New York, New York

Roy Orbison
American singer–musician
• Ballad rock singer often compared with Elvis Presley; best-selling sone "Oh, Pretty Woman," 1964; known for trademark dark glasses.
b. April 23, 1936 in Wink, Texas
d. December 06, 1988 in Hendersonville, Tennessee

Carl Orff
German composer
• Known for innovative three-part oratorio *Carmina Burana*, 1937.
b. July 1, 1895 in Munich, Germany
d. March 29, 1982 in Munich, Germany (West)

Tony Orlando
(Michael Anthony Orlando Cassavitis; Tony Orlando and Dawn)
American singer
• With Dawn, had biggest selling single, 1973, "Tie a Yellow Ribbon Round the Old Oak Tree."
b. April 03, 1944 in New York, New York

Eugene Ormandy
(Jeno Blau)
American conductor
• One of world's greatest conductors, who led Philadelphia Orchestra 44 yrs., longest of any conductor in US history; won Grammy, 1967.
b. November 18, 1899 in Budapest, Hungary
d. March 12, 1985 in Philadelphia, Pennsylvania

Kid (Edward) Ory
American jazz musician
• Noted "tailgate" trombonist; wrote "Muskrat Ramble."
b. December 25, 1886 in La Place, Louisiana
d. January 23, 1973 in Honolulu, Hawaii

Jeffrey Osbourne
American singer
• Had hit single "On the Wings of Love," 1982.
b. October 09, 1948 in Providence, Rhode Island

Ozzie (John) Osbourne
(Black Sabbath)
English singer
• Lead singer Black Sabbath; solo albums have all gone gold.
b. December 03, 1949 in Birmingham, England

K(ay) T(oinette) Oslin
American singer
• Country singer; had hit single, gold debut album *80's Ladies*, 1987; won Grammy, 1988.
b. 1942 in Crossit, Arkansas

Donny (Donald Clark) Osmond
(The Osmonds)
American singer
• Co-starred with sister on "Donny & Marie Show," 1976-79; performed with family since age four.
b. December 09, 1958 in Ogden, Utah

Marie (Olive Marive) Osmond
(The Osmonds)
American singer
• Co-starred with brother on "Donny & Marie Show," 1976-79; performed with family since age seven; solo albums include *Paper Roses*.
b. October 13, 1959 in Ogden, Utah

The Osmonds
(Alan Osmond; Donny Osmond; Jay Osmond; Jimmy Osmond; Marie Osmond; Merrill Osmond; Wayne Osmond)
American music group
• Vocal, instrumental family group formed, 1959; hits include "Down by the Lazy River," 1972.

Gilbert O'Sullivan
(Raymond Edward O'Sullivan)
Irish singer
• Had two hits, 1972: "Alone Again (Naturally)"; "Clair."
b. December 01, 1946 in Waterford, Ireland

The Outlaws
(Harvey Dalton Arnold; Rick Cua; David Dix; Billy Jones; Henry Paul; Hughie Thomasson; Monte Yoho)
American music group
• Merged country rock with Southern rock; hit single "(Ghost) Riders in the Sky," 1980.

Buck (Alvis Edgar, Jr) Owens
American singer–musician
• Co-hosted long-running country music variety TV show "Hee Haw," 1969-85.
b. August 12, 1929 in Sherman, Texas

Harry Owens
American bandleader
• Known for radio show, 1930s; song "Sweet Leilani," 1934, won two Oscars.
b. April 18, 1902 in O'Neill, Nebraska
d. December 12, 1986 in Eugene, Oregon

Seiji Ozawa
Japanese conductor
• Music director, Boston Symphony Orchestra, 1973–; won Emmy for musical direction of "Central Park in the Dark/A Hero's Life," 1976.
b. September 01, 1935 in Hoten, Japan

Pablo Cruise
(Bud Cockrell; David Jenkins; Cory Lerios; Steve Price)
American music group
• Band formed in 1973 with a mellow rock sound; songs include "Cool Love," 1981.

Gasparo Pacchierotti
Italian opera singer
• Male soprano popular in London, 1770s; among greatest castrati of day.
b. May 1740 in Fabriano, Italy
d. October 28, 1821 in Padua, Italy

Giovanni Pacini
Italian composer
• Wrote oratorios, chamber music, operas including *Medea*, 1843.
b. February 17, 1796 in Catania, Sicily
d. December 06, 1867 in Pescia, Italy

Ignace Jan Paderewski
Polish pianist–statesman
• Popular pianist who was foremost interpreter of Chopin; pres. of Poland, 1919.
b. November 18, 1860 in Kurilovka, Poland
d. June 29, 1941 in New York, New York

Ferdinando Paer
Italian composer
• Best known of 43 operas include *La Griselda*, 1796; *Agnes*, 1819.
b. June 01, 1771 in Parma, Italy
d. May 03, 1839 in Paris, France

Niccolo Paganini
Italian violinist–composer
• Revolutionized violin technique, fingering methods.
b. October 27, 1782 in Genoa, Italy
d. May 27, 1840 in Nice, France

Hot Lips (Oran Thaddeus) Page
American jazz musician
• Jazz, blues trumpeter; blues singer with Artie Shaw, early 1940s.
b. January 27, 1908 in Dallas, Texas
d. November 05, 1954 in New York, New York

Jimmy (James Patrick) Page
(Honeydrippers; Led Zeppelin; Yardbirds)
English musician
• Guitarist with heavy-metal groups; best known for Led Zeppelin tours, albums: *Led Zeppelin III*, 1970.
b. January 09, 1944 in Helston, England

Patti Page
(Clara Ann Fowler; "The Singing Rage")
American singer
• Popular vocalist, 1950s; hits include "Confess," 1948.
b. November 08, 1927 in Clarence, Oklahoma

Giovanni Paisiello
Italian composer
• Wrote over 100 operas including *Il Barbiere di Siviglia*, 1782, a rival to Rossini's later masterpiece.
b. May 08, 1740 in Taranto, Italy
d. June 05, 1816 in Naples, Italy

Giovanni Palestrina
Italian composer
• Among greatest Renaissance composers noted for Motets, Masses including *Missa Papae Marcelli*.
b. December 27, 1525 in Palestrina, Italy
d. February 02, 1594 in Rome, Italy

Tony Palligrosi
(Southside Johnny and the Asbury Jukes)
American musician
• Trumpeter with group since 1974.
b. May 09, 1954

Carl Palmer
(Asia; Emerson Lake and Palmer)
English musician
• Drummer with Emerson, Lake, and Palmer, 1970-79; formed group Asia, 1981.
b. March 2, 1951 in Birmingham, England

Robert Palmer
English singer
• Hit singles "Bad Case of Loving You," 1979; "Some Like It Hot," 1985.
b. January 19, 1949 in Batley, England

James Pankow
(Chicago)
American musician
• Trombonist with group; hit single "Wishing You Were Here," 1974.
b. August 2, 1947 in Chicago, Illinois

Walter Parazaider
(Chicago)
American musician
• With Terry Kath, formed group, 1967; hits include "Saturday in the Park," 1972.
b. March 14, 1945 in Chicago, Illinois

Paul Paray
French conductor
• Director, Detroit Symphony, 1952-63.
b. May 24, 1886 in Treport, France
d. October 1, 1979 in Monte Carlo, Monaco

Christopher William Parkening
American musician
• Classical guitarist, began playing as a child; noted for int'l. concert tours.
b. December 14, 1947 in Los Angeles, California

Charlie (Charles Christopher) Parker
American jazz musician
• Alto-saxophonist; co-creator of bebop.
b. August 29, 1920 in Kansas City, Kansas
d. March 12, 1955 in New York, New York

Graham Parker
(Graham Parker and the Rumour)
English singer-songwriter
• Punk-rock musician often compared to Bob Dylan, Elvis Costello, Bruce Springsteen for angry, eloquent songs.
b. 1950 in London, England

Ray Parker, Jr
American singer
• Versatile performer, record producer; had number one hit "Ghostbusters," 1984.
b. May 01, 1954 in Detroit, Michigan

Parliament
(George Clinton; Raymond Tiki Fulwood; Eddie Hazel; Junie Morrison; Gary Shider: Bernie Worrell)
American music group
• Rock/funk hits include "One Nation under a Groove," 1978.

Gram Parsons
(Cecil Connor; The Byrds; The Flying Burrito Brothers)
American singer-songwriter
• Tried to blend country, rock styles; compositions later recorded by Emmylou Harris; died of drug overdose.
b. November 05, 1946 in Winter Haven, Florida
d. September 19, 1973 in Joshua Tree, California

Harry Partch
American composer
• Formulated 43 microtonal scale; invented unusual instruments; avante-garde works included *Oedipus*, 1952.
b. June 24, 1901 in Oakland, California
d. September 03, 1974 in San Diego, California

Dolly Rebecca Parton
(Mrs Carl Dean)
American singer-songwriter-actress
• First gold record, 1978, for "Here You Come Again"; movie debut in *Nine to Five*, 1980.
b. January 19, 1946 in Sevierville, Tennessee

Joe Pass
(Joseph Anthony Passalaqua)
American jazz musician
• Jazz guitarist, 1960s-; teamed with Oscar Peterson, Ella Fitzgerald.
b. January 13, 1929 in New Brunswick, New Jersey

Giuditta Negri Pasta
Italian opera singer
• Legendary soprano with amazing range; noted for Rossini roles, 1820s-30s.
b. April 09, 1798 in Saronno, Italy
d. April 01, 1865 in Como, Italy

Tony Pastor
(Antonio Pestritto)
American bandleader
• Saxist, singer with Artie Shaw, 1930s; led band, 1940s; noted for rhythm vocals.
b. October 26, 1907 in Middletown, Connecticut
d. October 31, 1969 in New London, Connecticut

Jaco (John Francis Anthony, III) Pastorius
American musician
• Jazz-rock bass guitarist known for rapid-fire fingering techniques.
b. December 01, 1951 in Norristown, Pennsylvania
d. September 21, 1987 in Fort Lauderdale, Florida

Adelina Juana Maria Patti
Italian opera singer
• Famed coloratura; most popular, best paid singer of her day.
b. February 19, 1843 in Madrid, Spain
d. September 27, 1919 in Brecknock, Wales

Carlotta Patti
Italian singer
• Popular concert soprano; US debut, 1861; sister of Adelina.
b. October 3, 1835 in Florence, Italy
d. June 27, 1889 in Paris, France

Julius Patzak
Austrian opera singer
• Outstanding tenor; appeared over 1,000 times, Munich State Opera, 1928-45.
b. April 09, 1898 in Vienna, Austria
d. January 26, 1974 in Rottach-Egern, Germany

Les Paul
(Les Paul and Mary Ford; Lester William Polfus)
American musician–inventor
• Jazz guitarist; duo with wife, 1950s; developed eight-track tape recorder; credited with inventing electric guitar, 1941; Hall of Fame, 1988.
b. June 09, 1916 in Waukesha, Wisconsin

Paul Revere and the Raiders
(Charlie Coe; Joe Correrro; Mark Lindsay; Paul Revere; Freddy Weller)
American music group
• Late 1960s-early 1970s pop hits include "Indian Reservation," 1971.

Luciano Pavarotti
Italian opera singer–actor
• Best selling classical vocalist today; starred in *Yes, Giorgio*, 1982; won three Grammys, one Emmy.
b. October 12, 1935 in Modena, Italy

Tom (Thomas R) Paxton
American singer–musician–songwriter
• Albums include *Outward Bound*, 1966; *In the Orchard*, 1985.
b. October 31, 1937 in Chicago, Illinois

Johnny Paycheck
(Don Lytle)
American singer
• Best known for hit country single "Take This Job and Shove It," 1978.
b. May 31, 1941 in Greenfield, Ohio

Freda Payne
American singer
• Hits include "Band of Gold," 1970.
b. September 19, 1945 in Detroit, Michigan

Leon Payne
American songwriter
• Singer, one-man band, 1920s-30s; blind from childhood.
b. June 15, 1917 in Alba, Texas
d. September 11, 1969 in San Antonio, Texas

Lawrence Payton
(The Four Tops)
American singer
• With group, 1954–; first hit "Baby I Need Your Loving," 1964.
b. 1930 in Detroit, Michigan

Eddie Peabody
American musician
• Most famous banjoist during, 1930s-40s.
b. 1902
d. November 07, 1970 in Covington, Kentucky

Krzysztof Penderecki
Polish composer
• Wrote controversial avant-garde opera *Devils of Loudun*, 1969; won many awards, including Grammys.
b. November 23, 1933 in Debica, Poland

Teddy (Theodore D) Pendergrass
American singer
• Album *Life Is a Song Worth Singing*, 1978, was double platinum; paralyzed in car accident.
b. March 26, 1950 in Philadelphia, Pennsylvania

Kenny Pentifallo
(Southside Johnny and the Asbury Jukes)
American musician
• Drummer with group since 1974.
b. December 3, 1940

Art(hur Edward) Pepper
American jazz musician
• Top altoist; with Stan Kenton, 1948-52; received long jail sentences for narcotics violations.
b. September 01, 1925 in Gardena, California
d. June 15, 1982 in Los Angeles, California

Murray Perahia
American pianist–conductor
• Won many awards for performing complete Mozart concertos; won first Avery Fisher Award, 1975.
b. April 19, 1947 in New York, New York

Giovanni Battista Pergolesi
Italian composer
• Noted for intermezzos, comic operas: *La Serva Pardona*, 1733.
b. January 04, 1710 in Jesi, Italy
d. March 16, 1736 in Pozzuoli, Italy

Jacopo Peri
Italian composer
• Wrote *Dafne*, 1597, considered the first opera.
b. August 2, 1561 in Rome, Italy
d. August 12, 1633 in Florence, Italy

Carl Lee Perkins
American songwriter–singer
• Wrote hit song "Blue Suede Shoes," 1955; sung by Elvis Presley, 1956.
b. April 09, 1932 in Jackson, Tennessee

Itzhak Perlman
Israeli violinist
• Concert performer; won 10 Grammys, 1970s-80s.
b. August 31, 1945 in Tel Aviv, Palestine

Steve Perry
(Journey)
American singer
• Had hit single "Foolish Heart," on first solo album *Street Talk*, 1984.
b. January 22, 1949 in Hanford, California

Walt Perry
(Chicago)
American musician
• Plays brass instruments for group Chicago.
b. 1945 in Chicago, Illinois

Vincent Persichetti
American composer
• Wrote over 150 pieces including nine symphonies: *The Creation*, 1970; taught at Juilliard, NYC, for 40 yrs.
b. June 06, 1915 in Philadelphia, Pennsylvania
d. August 14, 1987 in Philadelphia, Pennsylvania

Louis Persinger
American musician–conductor
• Concert master, San Francisco Symphony, 1916-28; violinist, taught Menuhin.
b. February 11, 1888 in Rochester, Illinois
d. December 31, 1966 in New York, New York

Peter and Gordon
(Peter Asher; Gordon Waller)
English music group
• Folk-pop duo, 1961-68; hits include "World without Love," 1964, written by Paul McCartney; "Lady Godiva," 1966.

Peter, Paul, and Mary
(Noel Paul Stookey; Mary Travers; Peter Yarrow)
American music group
• Won Grammy, 1963, for "Blowin' in the Wind"; group disbanded, 1971.

Roberta Peters
(Roberta Peterman)
American opera singer
• Outstanding soprano; had NY Met. debut, age 20, 1950; has made many TV appearances.
b. May 04, 1930 in New York, New York

Oscar Emanuel Peterson
Canadian jazz musician
• Classically trained jazz pianist known for ability to play at fast speed; most recorded pianist of all time; best known composition is "Canadian Suite."
b. August 15, 1925 in Montreal, Quebec

Oscar Pettiford
American jazz musician–songwriter
• Bass player; developed pizzicato jazz cello.
b. September 3, 1922 in Okmulgee, Oklahoma
d. September 08, 1960 in Copenhagen, Denmark

Tom Petty
(Tom Petty and the Heartbreakers)
American musician
• Hit songs include "Refugee," 1980; "Don't Do Me Like That," 1979; founded The Heartbreakers rock group, 1975.
b. October 2, 1952 in Gainesville, Florida

Esther Phillips
(Esther Mae Jones; "Little Esther")
American singer
• Best known for album *From a Whisper to a Scream*, 1972.
b. December 23, 1935 in Galveston, Texas
d. August 07, 1984 in Los Angeles, California

John Phillips
(The Mamas and the Papas)
American singer
• Formed "goodtime rock 'n' roll" group, 1965; hits include "Monday, Monday," 1966; re-organized band, 1980s.
b. August 3, 1935 in Parris Island, South Carolina

Michelle Gillam Phillips
(The Mamas and the Papas)
American actress–singer
• Hits with group include "California Dreamin'," 1966; married to John Phillips, 1962-70.
b. April 06, 1944 in Long Beach, California

Sam Phillips
American music executive
• Began Sun Records, 1952; first recorded Elvis Presley, Carl Perkins.
b. January 05, 1923 in Florence, Alabama

Edith Piaf
(Edith Gassion)
French singer
• Known for tragic love songs: "La Vie en Rose."
b. December 1915 in Paris, France
d. October 11, 1963 in Paris, France

Gregor Piatigorsky
American musician
• Cellist who debuted in US, 1929; with Berlin Philharmonic, 1924-28; often duoed with Heifetz.
b. April 17, 1903 in Ekaterinoslav, Russia
d. August 06, 1976 in Los Angeles, California

Francesco Maria Piave
Italian librettist
• Wrote over 70 librettos, including Verdi's *Rigoletto*, 1832; *La Traviata*, 1852.
b. May 18, 1810 in Mureno, Italy
d. March 05, 1876 in Milan, Italy

Nicola Piccinni
(Nicola Piccini)
Italian composer
• Wrote 139 operas including comic opera, *La Buona Figliuola*, 1760.
b. January 16, 1725 in Bari, Italy
d. May 07, 1800 in Passy, France

Wilson Pickett
American singer–songwriter
• Hits include "In the Midnight Hour," 1965; "Funky Broadway," 1967.
b. March 18, 1941 in Prattville, Alabama

Webb Pierce
American singer
• Country recording star, 1950s-60s; hits include "Slowly," 1954.
b. August 08, 1926 in West Monroe, Louisiana
d. February 24, 1991 in Nashville, Tennessee

Gabriel Pierne
French composer
• His eight operas included *Sophie Arnould*, 1927.
b. August 16, 1863 in Metz, France
d. July 17, 1937 in Ploujean, France

Gary Pike
(The Lettermen)
American singer
• Joined group as replacement, late 1960s; younger brother of Jim.
b. in Twin Falls, Idaho

Jim Pike
(The Lettermen)
American singer
• A founder of group, got its name from his high school football experience; first big hit single: "The Way You Look Tonight," 1961.
b. November 06, 1938 in Saint Louis, Missouri

Pink Floyd
(Syd Barrett; Jon Carin; Rachel Furay; Dave Gilmour; Nick Mason;Scott Page; Guy Pratt; Tim Renwick; Gary Wallis; Roger Waters)
English music group
• Album *Dark Side of the Moon*, 1973, was on *Billboard* list of top LPs for over 500 weeks.

Ezio Pinza
(Fortunato Pinza)
American opera singer
• Celebrated bass; NY Met., 1926-48; starred in Broadway's *South Pacific*, 1949.
b. May 18, 1892 in Rome, Italy
d. May 09, 1957 in Stamford, Connecticut

Walter Piston
American musician–composer
• Won Pulitzers, 1948, 1961 for symphonies.
b. January 2, 1894 in Rockland, Maine
d. November 12, 1976 in Belmont, Massachusetts

Gene Pitney
American singer–songwriter
• Pop, rock balladeer; wrote "Hello Mary Lou," for Rick Nelson, 1961; had number two hit single "Only Love Can Break a Heart," 1962.
b. February 17, 1941 in Rockville, Connecticut

Robert Anthony Plant
(Honeydrippers; Led Zeppelin)
English singer–songwriter
• With hard-rock group Led Zeppelin since 1968; solo albums include *Shaken 'n' Stirred*, 1985.
b. August 2, 1948 in Bromwich, England

The Plasmatics
(Jean Beauvoir; Wes Beech; Stu Deutsch; Richie Stotts; Wendy O(rlean) Williams)
American music group
• Punk band with theatrical antics; albums include *Coup d'Etat*, 1982.

The Platters
(David Lynch; Herb Reed; Paul Robi; Zola Taylor; Tony Williams)
American music group
• Formed 1953, hits include "Only You," 1955; "Smoke Gets in Your Eyes," 1958.

Paul Peter Plishka
American opera singer
• Bass; NY Met. debut, 1967.
b. August 28, 1941 in Old Forge, Pennsylvania

Poco
(Paul Cotton; Richie Furay; George Grantham; Jim Messina; Randy Meisner; Tim Schmit; Rusty Young)
American music group
• Albums include *Deliverin'*, 1970; *Crazy Eyes*, 1973; *Ghost Town*, 1982.

Anita Pointer
(The Pointer Sisters)
American singer
• With sisters, first black woman to perform at Grand Ole Opry, Nashville.
b. 1948 in East Oakland, California

Bonnie Pointer
(The Pointer Sisters)
American singer
• Left sister group, 1978, to pursue solo career; hit single "I Can't Help Myself," 1979.
b. July 11, 1951 in East Oakland, California

June Pointer
(The Pointer Sisters)
American singer
• With sisters, hits include "He's So Shy," 1980; "I'm So Excited," 1982.
b. 1954 in East Oakland, California

Ruth Pointer
(The Pointer Sisters)
American singer
• With sisters, first pop act to perform at San Francisco Opera House.
b. 1946 in East Oakland, California

The Pointer Sisters
(Anita Pointer; Bonnie Pointer; June Pointer; Ruth Pointer)
American music group
• Pop, rhythm and blues group; hit singles include "Fire," 1979; "Break Out," 1984.

The Police
(Stewart Copeland; Andy Summers; Gordon Sting Sumner)
British music group
• Group blended New Wave rock, Jamaican, int'l rhythms, melodic pop, 1977-83; hit song "Every Breath You Take," from *Synchronicity*, 1983.

Lily Pons
French opera singer
• Colatura soprano, reigning diva, NY Met.,, 1928-53; wife of Andre Kostelanetz.
b. April 12, 1904 in Cannes, France
d. February 13, 1976 in Dallas, Texas

Rosa Ponselle
(Rose Ponzillo)
American opera singer
• Outstanding NY Met. soprano, 1918-37; debuted with Caruso, made several recordings.
b. January 22, 1894 in Meriden, Connecticut
d. May 25, 1981 in Stevenson, Maryland

Jean-Luc Ponty
French violinist
• Former classical, now jazz, rock, and fusion violinist credited with increased popularity of jazz violin.
b. September 29, 1942 in Avranches, France

Iggy Pop
(James Newell Osterberg; "Iggy Stooge"; "Godfather of Punk")
American singer–songwriter–actor
• Early proponent of punk rock known for primitive sound, outlandish stage antics; albums include *Choice Cuts*, 1984, *Brick by Brick*, 1990.Known in late sixties for work with band "The Stooges."
b. April 21, 1947 in Ann Arbor, Michigan

Cole Porter
American composer–lyricist
• Wrote musicals *Kiss Me, Kate; Can-Can; Silk Stockings;* song "Night and Day."
b. June 09, 1892 in Peru, Indiana
d. October 15, 1964 in Santa Monica, California

Quincy Porter
American composer
• Won Pulitzer for "Concerto for Two Pianos & Orchestra," 1954.
b. February 07, 1897 in New Haven, Connecticut
d. November 12, 1966 in New Haven, Connecticut

Francis Poulenc
(Les Six)
French composer
• Best known for *Dialogues des Carmelites.*
b. January 07, 1899 in Paris, France
d. January 3, 1963 in Paris, France

Maud Powell
American violinist
• One of the few female violinist of her time; brought classical music to small towns, outposts in US by touring.
b. August 22, 1867 in Peru, Illinois
d. January 02, 1920 in Uniontown, Pennsylvania

Teddy Powell
American bandleader–musician
• Violinist, vocalist, arranger, who led dance bands, 1940s; wrote "Bewildered."
b. March 01, 1906 in Oakland, California

Dave (David) Prater
(Sam and Dave)
American singer
• With Sam Moore, one of leading soul acts, 1960s; hit song "Soul Man," 1967, popularized again, late 1970s, by Dan Aykroyd, John Belushi as Blues Brothers.
b. May 09, 1937 in Ocilla, Georgia
d. April 09, 1988 in Sycamore, Georgia

Josephine Premice
American actress–singer–dancer
• Tony nominee for *A Hand Is on the Gate,* 1967.
b. July 21, 1926 in New York, New York

Elvis Aaron Presley
("The King"; "Elvis the Pelvis")
American singer–actor
• Rock 'n roll idol; hit songs include "Hound Dog," 1956; "All Shook Up," 1957.
b. January 08, 1935 in Tupelo, Mississippi
d. August 16, 1977 in Memphis, Tennessee

Billy (William Everett) Preston
American singer
• Hits include "You Are So Beautiful," 1975; "With You I'm Born Again," 1979.
b. September 09, 1946 in Houston, Texas

The Pretenders
(Martin Chambers; Pete Farndon; Malcolm Foster; James Honeyman-Scott; Chrissie Hynde; Robbie McIntosh)
English music group
• Early 1980s English rock band best known for hit album *The Pretenders,* 1980.

Andre Previn
American composer–pianist–conductor
• Won two Oscars, seven Grammys; conductor, Pittsburgh Symphony, 1976-84; music director, LA Philharmonic, 1984–.
b. April 06, 1929 in Berlin, Germany

Alan Price
(The Animals)
English singer–songwriter
• Left The Animals, 1965; solo albums include *Travellin' Man,* 1986.
b. April 19, 1942 in Fairfield, England

Florence Beatrice Smith Price
American composer
• First black woman symphonic composer in US; work performed 1933.
b. April 08, 1888 in Little Rock, Arkansas
d. June 03, 1953 in Chicago, Illinois

Leontyne Price
American opera singer
• Soprano star in *Porgy and Bess*, 1952-54; with NY Met. since 1960; won Spingarn, 1964.
b. February 1, 1927 in Laurel, Mississippi

Ray Price
(Noble Ray Price; "The Cherokee Cowboy")
American musician–singer
• Pop-country hits include "For the Good Times," 1970, nominated for Grammy.
b. January 12, 1926 in Perryville, Texas

Charley Pride
American singer
• Won Grammy for "Kiss an Angel Good Morning," 1972; first black country music star.
b. March 18, 1938 in Sledge, Mississippi

Louis Prima
American musician
• Popular bandleader, jazz trumpeter, 1940s-50s; known for zany singing in films.
b. December 07, 1912 in New Orleans, Louisiana
d. August 24, 1978 in New Orleans, Louisiana

William Primrose
American violinist
• Organized Primrose Quartet, 1938; wrote autobiography, 1978.
b. August 23, 1904 in Glasgow, Scotland
d. May 01, 1982 in Provo, Utah

Prince
(Prince Roger Nelson; "His Royal Badness")
American musician–singer–songwriter
• New-wave funk singer whose movie, *Purple Rain*, won Oscar for Best Original Score, 1985.
b. June 07, 1958 in Minneapolis, Minnesota

Yvonne Printemps
(Yvonne Wigniolle)
French actress–singer
• Former Folies Bergere performer, graduated to theater; played first title role appearance in *Mozart*, 1926.
b. July 25, 1898 in Ermont, France
d. January 18, 1977 in Paris, France

John Michael Pritchard, Sir
English conductor
• Leading international conductor; led BBC Symphony, 1982-89.
b. February 05, 1921 in London, England
d. December 04, 1989 in San Francisco, California

Procol Harum
(Gary Brooker; Matthew Fisher; Robert Harrison; David Knights; Keith Reid; Ray Royer; Robin Trower; Barry Wilson)
English music group
• British classical rock band, late 1960s; had biggest hit song with "A Whiter Shade of Pale," 1967.

Sergei Sergeevich Prokofiev
Russian composer
• Concert pianist best known for composing fairy tale for narrator, orchestra, *Peter and the Wolf*, 1936.
b. April 23, 1891 in Sontsovka, Russia
d. March 05, 1953 in Moscow, U.S.S.R.

Giacomo Puccini
Italian composer
• Wrote many operas with exotic settings including *La Boheme*, 1896; *Madame Butterfly*, 1904.
b. December 22, 1858 in Lucca, Italy
d. November 29, 1924 in Brussels, Belgium

Tito Puente
American bandleader
• Led dance band, 1950s; often named musician of month; won Grammys, 1978, 1983.
b. April 2, 1923 in New York, New York

Henry Purcell
English composer
• Noted Baroque composer; "English Operas" include *Fairy Queen*, 1692.
b. 1658 in London, England
d. November 21, 1695 in Westminster, England

Bernard Purdie
American musician
• Session drummer for Aretha Franklin, Steely Dan, others; albums include *Shaft*, 1976.
b. June 11, 1939 in Elkton, Maryland

Pure Prairie League
(Michael Connor; Billy Hands; Michael Reilly; Jeff Wilson)
American music group
• Country-rock band formed 1971; albums include *Something in the Night*, 1981.

Flora Purim
Brazilian singer
• Leading jazz interpreter, 1970s; albums include *Butterfly Dreams*, 1973.
b. March 06, 1942 in Rio de Janeiro, Brazil

QuarterFlash
(Jack Charles; Rick DiGiallonardo; Rich Gooch; Marv Ross; Rindy Ross; Brian David Willis)
American music group
• Had 1981 hit single "Harden My Heart."

Suzi Quatro
(Suzi Soul; The Pleasure Seekers; Cradle)
American singer
• Promoted as the "first raunchy female rock star"; songs include "The Wild One," 1974.
b. June 03, 1950 in Detroit, Michigan

Queen
(John Deacon; Brian May; Freddie Mercury; Roger Taylor)
English music group
• Hard-rock band formed in 1972; albums include *Bohemian Rhapsody*, 1975.

Quicksilver Messenger Service
(John Cipollina; Gary Duncan; Gregory Elmore; David Freiberg; Nicky Hopkins; Dino Valenti)
American music group
• Formed in 1965; albums include *Happy Trails*, 1969.

Quiet Riot
(Frankie Banal; Carlos Cavazo; Kevin DuBrow; Rudy Sarzo)
American music group
• Heavy metal band whose debut album *Mental Health*, 1983, sold over four million copies.

Eddie (Edward Thomas) Rabbitt
American singer–songwriter
• Wrote over 300 songs including "Kentucky Rain"; hit single "I Love a Rainy Night."
b. November 27, 1941 in Brooklyn, New York

Michael Rabin
American violinist
• Internationally known virtuoso; debuted at age fourteen.
b. May 02, 1936 in New York, New York
d. January 19, 1972 in New York, New York

Sergei Vasilyevich Rachmaninoff
Russian composer
• Last of romantic composers; best known for *Second Piano Concerto*, 1901.
b. April 01, 1873 in Oneg, Russia
d. March 28, 1943 in Beverly Hills, California

Gerry Rafferty
Scottish singer–songwriter
• Had hit single "Baker Street," 1978; albums include *Sleepwalking*, 1982.
b. 1945 in Scotland

Raffi
(Raffi Cavoukian)
Canadian singer–songwriter
• Popular children's performer since 1974; albums include *Singable Songs for the Very Young,* 1976.
b. July 08, 1948 in Cairo, Egypt

Ma (Gertrude) Rainey
(Gertrude Malissa Nix Pridgett)
American singer
• Blues pioneer who recorded in 1920s–30s; Bessie Smith was her protege.
b. April 26, 1886 in Columbus, Georgia
d. December 22, 1939 in Columbus, Georgia

Bonnie Raitt
American singer–songwriter
• Blues singer; won four Grammys, 1990, for *Nick of Time.* Daughter of John.
b. November 08, 1949 in Los Angeles, California

John Emmet Raitt
American singer
• Stage, TV vocalist, 1940s-60s; starred in Broadway's *Carousel,* 1945.
b. January 19, 1917 in Santa Ana, California

Torsten Ralf
Swedish opera singer
• Tenor, noted for Wagner, Verdi repertories; NY Met. star, 1940s.
b. January 02, 1901 in Malmo, Sweden
d. April 27, 1954 in Stockholm, Sweden

Jean-Philippe Rameau
French composer
• Wrote *Treatise on Harmony,* 1722, which became cornerstone of modern music theory.
b. September 25, 1683 in Dijon, France
d. September 12, 1764 in Paris, France

The Ramones
(Dee Dee Ramone; Joey Ramone; Johnny Ramone; Marky Ramone)
American music group
• New wave band, formed 1974; provided most of music for, starred in 1979 film *Rock 'n' Roll High School;* members unrelated.

Jean-Pierre Rampal
French musician
• Noted flutist; many French composers wrote works for him.
b. January 07, 1922 in Marseilles, France

Boots (Homer Louis, III) Randolph
American musician
• Hit song "Yakety Sax," 1963.
b. in Paducah, Kentucky

Danny Rapp
(Danny and the Juniors)
American singer
• Had hit single "At the Hop," 1957.
b. 1941 in Philadelphia, Pennsylvania
d. April 04, 1983 in Quartzside, Pennsylvania

Rare Earth
(Gil Bridges; Edward Cuzman; Peter Hoorelbeke; Kenny James; Ray Monette; Mark Olson; John Persh; Rob Richards; Michael Urso)
American music group
• Detroit group, reportedly first white act signed by Motown; known for recording earlier Motown hits: "Get Ready," 1970.

The Rascals
(Eddie Brigati; Felix Cavaliere; Gene Cornish; Dino Danelli; Buzzy Feiten; Robert Popwell; Ann Sutton)
American music group
• Blue-eyed soul group formed 1965; number one hits "Good Lovin'," 1966; "Groovin'," 1967.

Judith Raskin
American opera singer
• Soprano; popular first on TV; NY Met., 1962-72; noted Mozart singer.
b. June 21, 1928 in New York, New York
d. December 21, 1984 in New York, New York

The Raspberries
(Jim Bonfanti; Wally Bryson; Eric Carmen; Michael McBride; ScottMcCord; David Smalley)
American music group
• Formed 1970 in Cleveland; most hits written, sung by Eric Carmen.

Maurice Joseph Ravel
French composer
• Best known for ballet *Bolero,* 1928, used as theme for movie *10,* 1981.
b. March 07, 1875 in Ciboure, France
d. December 28, 1937 in Paris, France

Lou(is Allen) Rawls
American singer
• Began career as gospel singer; known for smooth, love ballads including "You'll Never Find," 1976, "Lady Love," 1978; has won numerous Grammys.
b. December 01, 1936 in Chicago, Illinois

Johnnie (John Alvin) Ray
American singer
• Emotionally charged 1950s singing idol; had number 1 hit single, "Cry," 1952.
b. January 1, 1927 in Dallas, Oregon
d. February 24, 1990 in Los Angeles, California

Vladimir Ivanovich Rebikov
Russian composer
• Wrote short opera *The Christmas Tree;* fairy-tale opera *Yolka,* 1903.
b. May 31, 1866 in Krasnoyarsk, Russia
d. December 01, 1920 in Yalta, U.S.S.R.

Otis Redding
American singer–songwriter
• Hits include "Dock of the Bay," 1968. Killed in plane crash.
b. September 09, 1941 in Dawson, Georgia
d. December 1, 1967 in Madison, Wisconsin

Helen Reddy
Australian singer–songwriter
• Hit single, "I Am Woman," 1972, became feminist movement theme song.
b. October 25, 1942 in Melbourne, Australia

Don Redman
American jazz musician–composer
• Saxophonist; arranger; led own band, 1930s; director for Pearl Bailey.
b. July 29, 1900 in Piedmont, West Virginia
d. November 3, 1964 in New York, New York

Dean Reed
American singer
• Sang "Tutti Frutti," "Blue Suede Shoes," in Russia.
b. 1939 in Denver, Colorado
d. June 17, 1986 in Germany (East)

Jerry Reed
(Jerry Hubbard; "The Alabama Wild Man")
American songwriter–singer
• Country music guitarist; wrote popular, offbeat song "When You're Hot, You're Hot," 1971.
b. March 2, 1937 in Atlanta, Georgia

Lou Reed
(Velvet Underground)
American singer–songwriter–musician
• Had hit single "Walk on the Wild Side," 1973, although not primarily known for hit singles. Hit album *New York* , 1989. Seminal punk rock influence.
b. March 02, 1944 in New York, New York

Della Reese
(Delareese Patricia Early)
American singer–actress
• Gold records include "Don't You Know?," 1959; first woman to host TV variety show, "Della," 1969-70.
b. July 06, 1932 in Detroit, Michigan

Jim Reeves

American singer
• Influential country-western performer, 1950s-60s; biggest hit: "He'll Have to Go," 1960; killed in plane crash.
b. August 2, 1924 in Galloway, Texas
d. July 31, 1964 in Tennessee

Martha Reeves

(Martha and the Vandellas)
American singer
• Lead singer, Martha and the Vandellas, 1962-72; hit single "Heat Wave," 1964.
b. July 18, 1941 in Detroit, Michigan

Phil Regan

American singer
• Theme song was "Happy Days Are Here Again," which he sang at Harry Truman's inauguration.
b. May 28, 1906 in Brooklyn, New York

Steve Reich

American composer
• One of best known exponents of "minimal" music; often created overlapping rhythms; wrote "Desert Music," 1984.
b. October 03, 1936 in New York, New York

Fritz Reiner

Hungarian conductor
• Noted Wagner, Strauss interpreter; director of Metropolitan Opera, 1948-53; Chicago Symphony, 1953-62.
b. December 1, 1888 in Budapest, Hungary
d. November 15, 1963 in New York, New York

Django (Jean Baptiste) Reinhardt

Belgian jazz musician–composer
• Swing guitarist with gypsy heritage; first European to influence American jazz.
b. January 23, 1910 in Liverchies, Belgium
d. May 16, 1953 in Fontainebleau, France

Eduard Remenyi

Hungarian musician–composer
• Violin soloist to Queen Victoria, 1854; had brilliant American tour, 1880s; said to be unexcelled for vigor, pathos.
b. July 17, 1830 in Heves, Hungary
d. May 15, 1898 in San Francisco, California

REO Speedwagon

(Kevin Cronin; Neal Doughty; Alan Gratzer; Bruce Hall; Gregg Philbin; Gary Richrath)
American music group
• Album *High Infidelity*, 1981, sold over six million copies; hit single "Can't Fight This Feeling," 1985.

Elizabeth Rethberg

(Elizabeth Sattler)
American opera singer
• Described as "world's most perfect singer"; with NY Met., 1922-42.
b. September 22, 1894 in Schwarzenburg, Germany
d. June 06, 1976 in Yorktown Heights, New York

Alvino Rey

(Alvin McGurney)
American bandleader–musician
• Pioneer in development of electric guitar; featured guitarist on King Family TV series, 1960s.
b. July 01, 1911 in Oakland, California

Emil von Reznicek

Austrian composer
• Wrote comic operas *Donna Diana*, 1894; *Til Eulenspiegel*, 1902.
b. May 04, 1860 in Vienna, Austria
d. August 02, 1945 in Berlin, Germany

Ruggiero Ricci

American violinist
• Child prodigy; repertoire included all of Paganini's works; celebrated "Golden Jubilee" of performing, 1978.
b. July 24, 1918 in San Francisco, California

Tim(othy Miles Bindon) Rice

English librettist
• Wrote lyrics for popular rock musical *Jesus Christ, Superstar*, 1971; won Tony, Grammy for *Evita*, 1980.
b. November 1, 1944 in Amersham, England

Buddy (Bernard) Rich

American jazz musician
• All-time great drummer, with Tommy Dorsey, 1939-42; formed Buddy Rich band, 1960s.
b. June 3, 1917 in New York, New York
d. April 02, 1987 in Los Angeles, California

Charlie (Charles Allan) Rich

American musician–singer
• Pop-country star whose hits include "Behind Closed Doors," 1973; won Grammy.
b. December 14, 1932 in Forrest City, Arkansas

Cliff Richard

(Harry Roger Webb)
British singer
• Hit singles include "Devil Woman," 1976; "She's So Beautiful," 1985.
b. October 14, 1940 in Lucknow, India

Keith Richard

(The Rolling Stones; Keith Richards; Nanker Phelge joint pseud)
English musician–singer
• Wrote "Satisfaction" with Mick Jagger, 1965; song's success brought superstardom to Rolling Stones.
b. December 18, 1943 in Dartford, England

Lionel (Brockman) Richie

American singer
• Former lead singer, Commodores; had nine number one songs in nine consecutive years; won five Grammys; won Oscar for best song, 1985.
b. June 2, 1949 in Tuskegee, Alabama

Harry Richman

American singer
• Top nightclub entertainer, 1920s-30s; noted for cane, top hat.
b. August 1, 1895 in Cincinnati, Ohio
d. November 03, 1972 in Burbank, California

Hans Richter

Hungarian conductor
• Bayreuth conductor, 1876-1912; then regarded as finest interpreter of Wagner, German classics.
b. April 04, 1843 in Raab, Hungary
d. December 05, 1916 in Bayreuth, Germany

Karl Richter

German musician–conductor
• Leader, developer, Munich Bach Choir, Orchestra, 1950s.
b. October 15, 1926 in Plauen, Germany
d. February 16, 1981 in Munich, Germany (West)

Sviatoslav Theofilovich Richter

Russian pianist
• Int'l. concertist; hero of Socialist Labour, 1975; noted for impeccable style.
b. March 2, 1915 in Zhitomir, Russia

Nelson Riddle

American musician–composer
• Known for collaborations with Frank Sinatra, 1950s; won Oscar, 1974, for score of *The Great Gatsby*.
b. June 01, 1921 in Oradell, New Jersey
d. October 06, 1985 in Los Angeles, California

Wallingford Riegger

American composer
• Wrote orchestral works, ballet, film scores; composed "Symphony No. 3," 1948; developed electronic instruments.
b. April 29, 1885 in Albany, Georgia
d. April 02, 1961 in New York, New York

The Righteous Brothers
(Bobby Hatfield; Bill Medley)
American music group
• Duo formed 1962; personified "white soul" with harmony ballads; hit song "You've Lost That Lovin' Feelin'," 1964.

Jeannie C Riley
(Jeannie C Stephenson)
American singer
• 1960s pop-country hits include "Harper Valley PTA."
b. October 19, 1945 in Anson, Texas

Nikolai Andreevich Rimsky-Korsakov
Russian composer
• Known for brilliant instrumentation in symphonies; wrote 16 operas including *The Snow Maiden*, 1881.
b. March 18, 1844 in Tikhvin, Russia
d. June 21, 1908 in Saint Petersburg, Russia

Ottavio Rinuccini
Italian poet–librettist
• Wrote text for Peri's *Dafne*, 1594; considered first true opera.
b. January 2, 1562 in Florence, Italy
d. March 28, 1621 in Florence, Italy

Minnie Riperton
American singer
• Had five-octave voice range; hits include "Lovin' You," 1974.
b. November 08, 1948 in Chicago, Illinois
d. July 12, 1979 in Los Angeles, California

Johnny Rivers
American singer
• Songs include "Poor Side of Town," 1966.
b. November 07, 1942 in New York, New York

Max(well Lemuel) Roach
American jazz musician
• Modern jazz pioneer who played drums for Dizzie Gillespie, Coleman Hawkins at first behop recording session, 1944.
b. January 1, 1924 in Elizabeth City, North Carolina

Marty Robbins
(Martin David Robinson)
American singer
• Country-western star won Grammy, 1959, for "El Paso."
b. September 26, 1925 in Glendale, Arizona
d. December 08, 1982 in Nashville, Tennessee

Don Robertson
American songwriter
• Country music hits include "I Really Don't Want to Know"; "Please Help Me I'm Falling."
b. December 05, 1922 in Peking, China

Robbie (Jaime) Robertson
(The Band)
Canadian musician–actor
• Guitarist, vocalist with The Band, 1966-76.
b. July 05, 1944 in Toronto, Ontario

Leo Robin
American lyricist
• Wrote lyrics for Bob Hope's theme song "Thanks for the Memory," which won 1938 Oscar.
b. April 06, 1895 in Pittsburgh, Pennsylvania
d. December 29, 1984 in Woodland Hills, California

Earl Hawley Robinson
American composer–singer
• Wrote famous "Ballad for Americans," 1939, recorded by Paul Robson.
b. July 02, 1910 in Seattle, Washington

Smokey (William, Jr) Robinson
(Smokey Robinson and the Miracles)
American singer–songwriter
• Hits include "Shop Around," 1961; "Tracks of my Tears," 1965; "Tears of a Clown," 1970.
b. February 19, 1940 in Detroit, Michigan

Tom Robinson
(Tom Robinson Band)
British singer–musician
• Formed group to voice political views; songs include "War Babies," 1983.
b. 1948

George Rochberg
American composer
• Acclaimed for award-winning "Night Music," 1948; "Violin Concerto," 1975.
b. July 05, 1918 in Paterson, New Jersey

Rockpile
(Billy Bremer; Dave Edmunds; Nick Lowe; Terry Williams)
British music group
• Pub-rock group, 1976-81; recorded one album *Seconds of Pleasure*, 1980.

Jim (James) Rodford
(Argent; Kinks)
English musician
• Bassist with Argent, 1969-76; Kinks, since 1978.
b. July 07, 1945 in Saint Albans, England

Jimmie C Rodgers
American singer–songwriter
• Father of modern country music; had million-selling single "Blue Yodel"; country music Hall of Fame, 1961.
b. September 08, 1897 in Meridian, Mississippi
d. May 26, 1933 in New York, New York

Jimmy F Rodgers
American singer
• Hits include "Kisses Sweeter Than Wine," 1957; "Honeycomb," 1957.
b. September 18, 1933 in Camas, Washington

Nile Rodgers
(Honeydrippers)
American musician
• Guitarist who produces albums for other musicians, including Madonna.
b. September 19, 1952 in New York, New York

Richard Rodgers
(Rodgers and Hart; Rodgers and Hammerstein)
American composer
• Won Pulitzers for *Oklahoma*, 1943; *South Pacific*, 1949; wrote music for 40 Broadway hits.
b. July 28, 1902 in New York, New York
d. December 3, 1979 in New York, New York

Johnny Rodriguez
(John Raul Davis Rodriguez)
American singer
• Country music star, who mixed Spanish, English lyrics in his hits, including "You'll Always Come Back to Hurting Me."
b. December 1, 1951 in Sabinal, Texas

Tommy Roe
American singer
• Styled singing after Buddy Holly; had hit singles "Sheila," 1962; "Sweet Pea," 1966; "Dizzy," 1969.
b. May 09, 1942 in Atlanta, Georgia

Kenny (Kenneth Ray) Rogers
(Kenny Rogers and The First Edition)
American singer
• Pop-country hits include "Lady," 1980; "She Believed in Me," 1970.
b. August 21, 1938 in Houston, Texas

Shorty (Milton M) Rogers
American jazz musician
• Trumpeter, bandleader; noted as outstanding arranger for Woody Herman, 1940s.
b. April 14, 1924 in Lee, Massachusetts

The Rolling Stones
(Mick Jagger; Brian Jones; Keith Richard; Mick Taylor; Charlie Watts; Ron Wood; Bill Wyman)
English music group
• Group formed, 1962; first US single "Not Fade Away," 1964.

Sonny (Theodore Walter) Rollins
American jazz musician
• Outstanding tenor saxist. Wrote music, played soundtrack for film *Alfie*, 1965.
b. September 07, 1930 in New York, New York

Felice Romani
Italian librettist
• Foremost of his time; wrote approximately 100 librettos.
b. January 31, 1788 in Genoa, Italy
d. January 28, 1865 in Moneglia, Italy

The Romantics
(Coz (George) Canler; Rich Cole; Jimmy Marinos; Wally Palmer; Mike Skill)
American music group
• Gold album *In Heat*, 1983; top ten single "Talking in Your Sleep."

Sigmund Romberg
American composer
• Wrote operettas *Maytime*, 1917; *Student Prince*, 1924; 2000 songs including "Stout Hearted Men."
b. July 29, 1887 in Nagykanizsa, Hungary
d. November 09, 1951 in New York, New York

Harold Jacob Rome
American songwriter
• Wrote score for *Call Me Mister*, 1946; song "Fanny," 1954.
b. May 27, 1908 in Hartford, Connecticut

Linda Ronstadt
American singer
• Has six platinum albums; starred on Broadway in *The Pirates of Penzance*, 1981.
b. July 15, 1946 in Tucson, Arizona

Ned Rorem
American composer
• Won 1976 Pulitzer for Bicentennial commission: *Air Music*; published many diaries.
b. October 23, 1923 in Richmond, Indiana

Billy Rose
(William S Rosenburg)
American producer–lyricist
• Musicals included *Jumbo*, 1935; *Carmen Jones*, 1943; opened NYC's famed nightclub Diamond Horseshoe, 1938; wed to Fanny Brice.
b. September 06, 1899 in New York, New York
d. February 1, 1966 in Montego Bay, Jamaica

David Rose
English songwriter–conductor
• Music director for many TV shows; won 22 Grammys, four Emmys; wrote "Holiday for Strings," 1943; once wed to Judy Garland.
b. June 15, 1910 in London, England
d. August 23, 1990 in Burbank, California

Fred Rose
American singer
• Popularized country music, 1940s-50s; often collaborated with Gene Autry.
b. August 24, 1897 in Evansville, Indiana
d. December 01, 1954 in Nashville, Tennessee

Vincent Rose
American bandleader–songwriter
• Led dance bands, 1920s-30s; wrote "Avalon," 1920; "Pretty Baby," 1931.
b. June 13, 1880 in Palermo, Italy
d. May 2, 1944 in Rockville Centre, New York

Nathaniel Rosen
American musician
• First American cellist to win coveted Tchaikovsky award, Moscow, 1978.
b. 1948

Moriz Rosenthal
Polish pianist
• Pupil of Chopin, Liszt; made US debut, 1888; called "perfect pianist."
b. December 18, 1862 in Bemberg, Poland
d. September 03, 1946 in New York, New York

Diana Ross
(Diane Ross; The Supremes; Mrs Arne Naess)
American singer
• Lead vocalist with The Supremes; group had 15 consecutive hits over 10-yr. period; went solo, 1969; appeared in films, stage; won special Tony for *Th Wiz*, 1977.
b. March 26, 1944 in Detroit, Michigan

Lanny (Lancelot Patrick) Ross
American singer
• Popular radio tenor, 1930s-50s; had own TV show, early 1950s.
b. January 19, 1906 in Seattle, Washington
d. April 26, 1988 in New York, New York

Renzo Rossellini
Italian composer
• Wrote 130 movie scores including *Open City*, 1945; brother of Roberto.
b. February 02, 1908 in Rome, Italy
d. May 14, 1982 in Monte Carlo, Monaco

Gaetano Rossi
Italian librettist
• Wrote over 120 librettos for noted composers.
b. 1780 in Verona, Italy
d. January 27, 1855 in Verona, Italy

Gioacchino Antonio Rossini
Italian composer
• Best-known operas include *Barber of Seville*, 1816; *William Tell*, 1829.
b. February 29, 1792 in Pesaro, Italy
d. November 13, 1868 in Passy, France

Mstislav Leopoldovich Rostropovich
Russian musician–educator–conductor
• Renowned cellist; director, Washington's National Symphony, 1977–; won Lenin Prize, 1963.
b. August 12, 1927 in Baku, U.S.S.R.

Helge Roswaenge
Danish opera singer
• Celebrated dramatic tenor; with Berlin State Opera, 1920s-40s; often compared to Caruso.
b. August 29, 1897 in Copenhagen, Denmark
d. August 1972 in Denmark

David Lee Roth
(Van Halen)
American singer–musician
• Lead singer, Van Halen, 1974-76; had best-selling solo album *Crazy from the Heat*.
b. October 1, 1955 in Bloomington, Indiana

Lillian Roth
American singer
• Broadway performer at age eight; wrote autobiography *I'll Cry Tomorrow*, 1954, filmed 1955.
b. December 13, 1910 in Boston, Massachusetts
d. May 12, 1980 in New York, New York

Claude Joseph Rouget de Lisle
French songwriter
• Known for writing words, music to French national anthem "La Marseillaise," 1792.
b. May 1, 1760 in Lons-le-Saunier, France
d. June 2, 1836 in Choisy le Roi, France

Albert Roussel
French composer
• Wrote opera ballet *Padmavati*, 1918; often used Oriental scales, rhythms.
b. April 05, 1869 in Tourcoing, France
d. August 23, 1937 in Royan, France

The (The Irish Rovers) Rovers
(Jimmy Ferguson; Wilcil McDowell; George Millar; Joe Millar; WillMillar)
Canadian music group
• Hits include "The Unicorn," 1968; "Wasn't That a Party," 1981; N Ireland-born musicians have had TV series, concert successes.

Roxy Music
(Brian Eno; Bryan Ferry; John Gustafson; Eddie Jobson; Andrew MacKay; Phil Manzanera; Paul Thompson)
English music group
• Hit singles include "The Same Old Scene," 1980; "Avalon," 1982.

Miklos Rozsa
American composer
• Arranged film background music, 1930s-70s; scored *Ben Hur*, 1959.
b. April 18, 1907 in Budapest, Hungary

Anton Gregorovitch Rubinstein
Russian pianist
• Virtuoso who rivaled Liszt; established prize for piano playing, composition, 1890.
b. November 28, 1829 in Kherson, Russia
d. November 2, 1894 in Peterhof, Russia

Arthur Rubinstein
American pianist
• Ranked with Rachmaninoff, Horowitz among greatest pianists of 20th c.; considered world's finest interpreter of Chopin.
b. January 28, 1887 in Lodz, Poland
d. December 2, 1982 in Geneva, Switzerland

Harry Ruby
American songwriter
• Prolific Broadway composer; collaborated with Bert Kalmar on "Three Little Words," 1930; film based on their partnership, 1950.
b. January 27, 1895 in New York, New York
d. February 23, 1974 in Woodland Hills, California

Jimmy Ruffin
American singer
• Hits include "What Becomes of the Brokenhearted," 1966; "Hold on to My Love," 1980. Brother of David, formerly of Temptations.
b. May 07, 1939 in Meridian, Mississippi

Titta Ruffo
(Ruffo Cafiero Titta)
Italian opera singer
• Famed baritone, noted for Verdi roles.
b. June 09, 1877 in Pisa, Italy
d. July 06, 1953 in Florence, Italy

Carl Ruggles
American composer-artist
• Controversial atonal musical works include *Sun-Treader*, 1931; had recent popularity.
b. March 11, 1876 in Marion, Massachusetts
d. October 24, 1971 in Bennington, Vermont

Todd Rundgren
American musician-singer
• Music influenced by "British Invasion"; songs include "Hello It's Me," 1973.
b. June 22, 1948 in Upper Darby, Pennsylvania

Rush
(Geddy Lee; Alex Liefson; Neil Peart; John Rutsey)
Canadian music group
• Formed 1971; use laser, visual projections; hit album *Power Windows*, 1985.

Billy Rush
(Southside Johnny and the Asbury Jukes)
American musician
• Guitarist with Southside Johnny and the Asbury Jukes since 1974.
b. August 26, 1952

Tom Rush
American singer-songwriter
• Blues albums include *Late Night Radio*, 1985.
b. February 08, 1941 in Portsmouth, New Hampshire

Patrice Louise Rushen
American pianist-singer
• Child prodigy; studied music at age three; jazzy dance hits include "Feels So Real," 1984.
b. September 3, 1954 in Los Angeles, California

Jimmy Rushing
American jazz musician
• Major blues singer, toured with swing bands; with Count Basie, 1935-48, 1960s.
b. August 26, 1903 in Oklahoma City, Oklahoma
d. June 08, 1972 in New York, New York

Anna Russell
English comedienne-singer
• Wrote *The Power of Being a Positive Stinker*; popular satirist of opera stars; had many hit recordings.
b. December 27, 1911 in London, England

Leon Russell
(Hank Wilson)
American singer
• Country-rock star, 1960s-70s; honky-tonk pianist; did duo with Willie Nelson "One for the Road."
b. April 02, 1941 in Lawton, Oklahoma

Lillian Russell
(Helen Louise Leonard; "The American Beauty")
American singer-actress
• In vaudeville, light opera, including Tony Pastor shows from 1880.
b. December 04, 1861 in Clinton, Iowa
d. June 06, 1922 in Pittsburgh, Pennsylvania

Pee Wee (Charles Ellsworth) Russell
American jazz musician
• Clarinetist; popular soloist in Dixieland bands, small combos for over 40 yrs.
b. March 27, 1906 in Saint Louis, Missouri
d. February 15, 1969 in Alexandria, Virginia

Michael Rutherford
(Genesis; Mike and the Mechanics)
English singer-musician
• Guitarist, bassist, vocalist, original member of Genesis.
b. October 02, 1950 in England

Bobby Rydell
(Robert Ridarelli)
American musician
• Singer, drummer; popular, 1959-65; hits include "Forget Him," 1963.
b. April 26, 1942 in Philadelphia, Pennsylvania

Mitch Ryder
(William S Levise Jr; Mitch Ryder and the Detroit Wheels)
American singer
• Lead vocalist in mid-60s blue-eyed soul band; had less-successful solo career.
b. February 26, 1945 in Detroit, Michigan

Jean Georges Sablon
French singer-composer
• Has appeared in musicals, variety shows, and nightclubs worldwide.
b. March 25, 1909 in Nogent-sur-Marne, France

Hans Sachs
German composer-poet
• Famed poet of the Meistersinger; wrote over 6000 works; main figure in Wagner's opera.
b. November 05, 1494 in Nuremberg, Germany
d. January 19, 1576 in Nuremberg, Germany

Sade
(Helen Folasade Adu)
Nigerian singer
• Debut album *Diamond Life*, 1984 sold over six million copies; second album *Promise*, 1985, was platinum.
b. January 16, 1960 in Nigeria

Barry Sadler
American singer
• Wrote and sang popular Vietnam-era song, "The Ballad of the Green Berets," 1966.
b. 1941 in Leadville, Colorado
d. November 05, 1989 in Murfreesboro, Kentucky

Carole Bayer Sager
(Mrs Burt Bacharach)
American singer–songwriter
• Won 1986 Grammy for "That's What Friends Are For."
b. March 08, 1947 in New York, New York

(Charles) Camille Saint-Saens
French musician–composer
• Best known for opera *Samson et Delila*, 1877, several symphonies.
b. October 09, 1835 in Paris, France
d. December 16, 1921 in Algiers, Algeria

Buffy (Beverly) Sainte-Marie
American Indian singer–composer
• Won Oscar for best song from *An Officer and a Gentleman*, 1982; has composed over 300 songs.
b. February 2, 1941 in Craven, Saskatchewan

Nadja Salerno-Sonnenberg
Italian violinist
• Concert star, 1981–; youngest to win the Naumburg competition.
b. January 1, 1961 in Rome, Italy

Antonio Salieri
Italian conductor–composer
• Thirty five operas include *Tarare*, 1787; his envy of Mozart depicted in 1985 Oscar-winning film, *Amadeus*.
b. August 18, 1750 in Legnano, Italy
d. May 07, 1825 in Vienna, Austria

Sam and Dave
(Sam Moore; Dave Prater)
American music group
• Black singing duo known for pop, soul hits including "Soul Man," 1967.

Sam the Sham and the Pharaohs
(Butch Gibson; David Martin; Jerry Patterson; Domingo Samudio; Ray Stinnet)
American music group
• 1960s rock-and-roll band best known for first hit, "Wooly Bully," 1965.

Olga Samaroff
American pianist
• Ranked among best pianists, early 1900s; wed to Leopold Stokowski, 1911-23.
b. August 08, 1882 in San Antonio, Texas
d. May 17, 1948 in New York, New York

Julia Sanderson
(Julia Sackett; The Singing Sweethearts)
American singer–actress
• Often starred with husband, Frank Crumit, on stage, radio, 1900-40s; started Battle of Sexes Game Show, 1939-43.
b. August 22, 1887 in Springfield, Massachusetts
d. January 27, 1975 in Springfield, Massachusetts

Sandler and Young
(Tony Sandler; Ralph Young)
American music group
• Popular singing duo, 1960s-70s, combining suave European Tony Sandler and comedic American Ralph Young.

Tommy (Thomas Adrian) Sands
American singer–actor
• Had hit song "Teenage Crush," 1957; film, TV star, 1950s-60s; first husband of Nancy Sinatra.
b. August 27, 1937 in Chicago, Illinois

Santana
(Jose Areas; David Brown; Michael Carabello; Ndugu Chancler; TomCoster; Armando Pereza; Gregg Rolie; Carlos Santana; Michael Shrieve;)
American music group
• Music is a mix of latin, jazz, rock; hits include "Evil Ways," 1970; "Hold On," 1982.

Carlos (Devadip Carlos) Santana
(Santana)
Mexican musician
• Guitarist, founder of rock band Santana, 1966.
b. July 2, 1947 in Autlan, Mexico

Pablo de Sarasate
(Martin Meliton S y Navascuez)
Spanish violinist–composer
• Celebrated virtuoso; had enormously successful worldwide tours, many noted works written for him.
b. March 1, 1844 in Pamplona, Spain
d. September 2, 1908 in Biarritz, France

Sir Malcolm Sargent
English conductor
• Led British orchestras, 1920s-60s; made frequent int'l. tours; commemorative stamp issued in his honor, 1980.
b. April 29, 1895 in Stamford, England
d. October 03, 1967 in London, England

Arthur Edward Satherly
American music executive
• Record industry pioneer; helped launch careers of Gene Autry, Tex Ritter, Roy Rogers.
b. October 19, 1889 in Bristol, England
d. February 1, 1986 in Fountain Valley, California

Eddie (Edward Ernest) Sauter
American jazz musician–songwriter
• Trumpeter; arranged for Benny Goodman, Red Norvo, 1930s-40s; co-led Sauter-Finegan band, 1950s.
b. December 02, 1914 in Brooklyn, New York
d. April 21, 1981 in Nyack, New York

Savoy Brown
(Miller Anderson; Eric Dillon; James Leverton; Kim Simmonds; StanWebb)
British music group
• Heavy rock group formed 1966; albums include *Rock & Roll Warriors*, 1981.

Bidu Sayao
Brazilian opera singer
• Soprano prima donna with NY Met., 1937-52; noted for Manon role, jewel collection.
b. May 11, 1902 in Rio de Janeiro, Brazil

Leo (Gerald) Sayer
English singer
• Pop-rock hits include "Have You Ever Been In Love," 1982.
b. May 21, 1948 in Shoreham, England

Boz (William Royce) Scaggs
American musician–singer
• Won Grammy for "Lowdown," 1976; other hits include "Miss Sun," 1980.
b. June 08, 1944 in Dallas, Texas

Joey Scarbury
American singer
• Hit single "Believe It or Not," 1981, theme from TV show "Greatest American Hero.
b. June 07, 1955 in Ontario, California

Alessandro Scarlatti
Italian composer
• Established Italian opera overture; wrote 200 masses, 115 operas, including *Il Tigrane*, 1715; father of Domenico.
b. May 02, 1660 in Palermo, Sicily
d. November 24, 1725 in Naples, Italy

Domenico Girolamo Scarlatti
Italian composer
• Founded modern keyboard technique; first to use arpeggios in performances; wrote over 500 harpsichord sonatas.
b. October 26, 1685 in Naples, Italy
d. July 23, 1757 in Naples, Italy

Peter Schickele
American composer–musician
• Created mythical, zany composer, PDQ Bach, who lampoons music classics; wrote score, lyrics for *Oh, Calcutta*.
b. July 17, 1935 in Ames, Iowa

Lalo Claudio Schifrin
Argentine composer
• Wrote for films, TV; four Grammys include score for TV's "Mission Impossible."
b. June 21, 1932 in Buenos Aires, Argentina

Peter Schilling
German singer
• First single, "Major Tom (Coming Home)," was int'l. hit, 1983.
b. January 28, 1956 in Stuttgart, Germany (West)

Joseph Schillinger
American composer–musician
• Composers Gershwin, Levant and others used his musical system.
b. September 01, 1895 in Kharkov, Russia
d. March 23, 1943 in New York, New York

Martha Schlamme
Austrian singer–actress
• Known for singing folk songs in 12 languages; made Broadway debut, 1968, in *Fiddler on the Roof*.
b. 1930 in Vienna, Austria
d. October 06, 1985 in Jamestown, New York

Timothy B Schmidt
(The Eagles; Poco)
American singer–musician
• Joined The Eagles, 1977, replacing Randy Meisner. Member of Poco.
b. October 3, 1947 in Oakland, California

Alexander Schneider
American musician
• First to present all of Bach's unaccompanied violin works in concert; often accompanied Casals.
b. October 21, 1908 in Vilna, Russia

Arnold Schoenberg
American composer
• Invented 12-tone musical system, 1921; wrote opera *Moses und Aron*, 1951, song cycle *Pierrot Lunaire*, 1912.
b. September 13, 1874 in Vienna, Austria
d. July 13, 1951 in Brentwood, California

Tom Scholz
(Boston)
American singer–musician
• Founded hard-rock group Boston, 1975; hits include "Amanda," 1986; has also invented, made electronic equipment for musicians.
b. March 1, 1947 in Toledo, Ohio

Franz Schreker
German composer
• Operas include *Der Ferne Klang*, 1912; *Christophorous*, cancelled by Nazis, 1933, first performed, 1978.
b. March 23, 1878 in Monaco
d. March 21, 1934 in Berlin, Germany

Franz Peter Schubert
Austrian composer
• Created the German lieder; symphonies include B Minor (*The Unfinished*, 1822) and C Major; wrote "Ave Maria."
b. January 31, 1797 in Vienna, Austria
d. November 19, 1828 in Vienna, Austria

Gunther Schuller
American composer–conductor
• Noted horn player, 1940s-50s; popularized "cool jazz" style; instrumental in ragtime revival; wrote operas, third-stream music.
b. November 22, 1925 in New York, New York

William Howard Schuman
American composer
• Pres. emeritus, Juilliard School, 1962–; Lincoln Center, 1969–; first to receive Pulitzer in music, 1943.
b. August 04, 1910 in New York, New York

Clara Josephine Wieck Schumann
German pianist
• Brilliant performer; wife of Robert Shumann, friend of Brahms.
b. September 13, 1819 in Leipzig, Germany
d. May 2, 1896 in Frankfurt, Germany

Robert Alexander Schumann
German composer
• Led Romantic movement; career as pianist ended due to hand injury.
b. June 08, 1810 in Zwickau, Germany
d. July 29, 1856 in Endenick, Germany

Ernestine Rossler Schumann-Heink
American opera singer
• Brilliant contralto; famed for Wagnerian roles, German Lieder; noted radio performer.
b. June 15, 1861 in Lieben, Czechoslovakia
d. November 16, 1936 in Hollywood, California

Heinrich Schutz
German composer
• Regarded as finest German composer before Bach; wrote first German opera, *Daphne*, 1627; composed over 500 sacred works.
b. October 08, 1585 in Kostritz, Germany
d. November 06, 1672 in Dresden, Germany

Gustav Schutzendorf
German opera singer
• Best known of four brothers, all operatic baritones; with NY Met., 1922-35; wed to soprano Grete Stuckgold.
b. 1883 in Cologne, Germany
d. April 27, 1937 in Berlin, Germany

Arthur Schwartz
American songwriter
• With Howard Dietz, wrote over 500 songs, including "Dancing in the Dark," "That's Entertainment."
b. November 25, 1900 in Brooklyn, New York
d. September 03, 1984 in Kintnersville, Pennsylvania

Jean Schwartz
American songwriter
• Prolific Broadway composer, 1900-1930s; wrote "Rock-a-Bye Your Baby to a Dixie Melody," 1918; "Chinatown My Chinatown," 1910.
b. November 04, 1878 in Budapest, Hungary
d. November 3, 1956 in Sherman Oaks, California

Stephen L(awrence) Schwartz
American dramatist–composer
• Wrote music, lyrics for *Godspell*, 1971; *Butterflies Are Free*, 1969.
b. March 06, 1948 in Roslyn, New York

Gerard Schwarz
American composer–musician
• Trumpet virtuoso who is one of most sought-after conductors in US.
b. August 19, 1947 in Weehawken, New Jersey

Elisabeth Schwarzkopf
German opera singer
• Soprano who performed in US, 1950s-70s; renowned Mozart singer.
b. December 09, 1915 in Jarotschin, Poland

Patty Scialfa
(E Street Band; "Red")
American singer
• Has sung background vocals with Bruce Springsteen's band since 1984.
b. July 29, 1956 in Deal, New Jersey

Scorpions
(Francis Buchholz; Matthias Jabs; Klaus Meine; Herman Rarebell; Rudolph Schenker)
German music group
• Formed in 1971; first American tour, 1979-80.

Hazel Dorothy Scott
(Mrs Adam Clayton Powell Jr)
American jazz musician
• Pianist, singer, popular in 1940s; sang "FDR Jones"; had own TV show.
b. June 11, 1920 in Port of Spain, Trinidad
d. October 02, 1981 in New York, New York

Raymond Scott
(Harry Warnow)
American songwriter–bandleader
• Led quintet, 1940s; with TV's "Your Hit Parade," 1950s; wrote "In an 18th Century Drawing Room."
b. September 1, 1909 in New York, New York

Tony Scott
American musician
• Top jazz clarinetist, 1950s-60s; adapted folk songs to jazz.
b. June 17, 1921 in Morristown, New Jersey

Earl Eugene Scruggs
(Flatt and Scruggs)
American musician–songwriter
• Won Grammy, 1969, for "Foggy Mountain Breakdown."
b. January 06, 1924 in Flint Hill, North Carolina

Jim (James) Seals
(Seals and Crofts)
American singer–songwriter
• Guitarist, vocalist with Seals and Crofts; had hit album *Diamond Girl*, 1973.
b. 1942 in Sindey, Texas

Seals and Crofts
(Dash Crofts; Jim Seals)
American music group
• Hit rock duo, popular during 1970s; songs show social concern.

The Searchers
(Billy Adamson; Frank Allen; Bob Jackson; John McNally; Mike Pender)
British music group
• Second to The Beatles in popularity, 1960s; hits include "Love Potion No. 9," 1964.

John Sebastian
(Lovin' Spoonful)
American singer
• Co-founder, rock-folk group, Lovin' Spoonful, 1965.
b. March 17, 1944 in New York, New York

Harry Secombe
Welsh actor–comedian–singer
• With Spike Mulligan, Peter Sellers, originated, performed in BBC radio series, "The Goon Show," 1951-56.
b. September 08, 1921 in Swansea, Wales

Sholom Secunda
Russian conductor
• Wrote over 40 operettas for NYC Yiddish Theater; noted for "Bei Mir Bist Du Schon," 1933.
b. August 23, 1894 in Alexandria, Russia
d. June 13, 1974 in New York, New York

Neil Sedaka
American singer–songwriter
• Wrote songs "Breaking Up is Hard to Do," 1960; "Love Will Keep Us Together," 1975.
b. March 13, 1939 in Brooklyn, New York

Pete(r) Seeger
(The Weavers)
American singer–songwriter
• Folksinger, guitarist, social activist; founded The Weavers, 1948; wrote modern folksong "If I Had a Hammer," 1958, popularized by Peter, Paul, and Mary, 1962.
b. May 03, 1919 in New York, New York

Bob (Robert Clark) Seger
(The Silver Bullet Band)
American singer–musician–songwriter
• Triple platinum albums *Stranger in Town*, 1978; *Against the Wind*, 1980. First band was "The Lost Herd."
b. May 06, 1945 in Ann Arbor, Michigan

Andres Segovia
Spanish musician
• Brought classical guitar into mainstream of musical world during 71-yr. career.
b. February 18, 1894 in Linares, Spain
d. June 02, 1987 in Madrid, Spain

Michael Sembello
American singer–musician
• Guitarist for Stevie Wonder, 1973-79; had hit single "Maniac" from film *Flashdance*, 1983.
b. 1956 in Philadelphia, Pennsylvania

Tullio Serafin
Italian conductor
• Led Milan's La Scala, Rome Opera Co., 1909-50s; helped launch Maria Callas.
b. December 08, 1878 in Rottanova, Italy
d. February 02, 1968 in Rome, Italy

Danny (Daniel Peter) Seraphine
(Chicago)
American musician
• Drummer with group since 1967; had number one hit "Hard to Say I'm Sorry," 1982.
b. August 28, 1948 in Chicago, Illinois

Peter A(dolf) Serkin
American pianist
• Noted for chamber music, contemporary compositions, fresh interpretations of classic, romantic music; son of Rudolph.
b. July 24, 1947 in New York, New York

Rudolph Serkin
(Rudolf Serkin)
American pianist
• Made US debut, 1933; specialized in Viennese classics.
b. March 28, 1903 in Eger, Czechoslovakia

Roger Huntington Sessions
American composer
• Most popular work was first major composition *The Black Masters*, 1923.
b. December 28, 1896 in Brooklyn, New York
d. March 16, 1985 in Princeton, New Jersey

Doc (Carl H) Severinsen
American musician–bandleader
• Joined "Tonight Show" orchestra, 1962; music director since 1967.
b. July 07, 1927 in Arlington, Oregon

David Seville
(Ross S Bagdasarian)
American singer
• Wrote "The Chipmunk Song," 1958; led to animated TV series "The Alvin Show," 1960.
b. January 27, 1919 in Fresno, California
d. January 16, 1972 in Beverly Hills, California

The Sex Pistols
(Paul Cook; Steve Jones; Johnny Rotten; Sid Vicious)
English music group
• Hit songs include "God Save the Queen," 1977; was banned from radio in England.

Sha Na Na
(Lenny Baker; John Bowser Bauman; Johnny Contrado; Dennis Frederick Greene; "Jocko" John; Dan McBride; "Chico" Dave Ryan; T)
American music group
• Formed in 1969; albums include *Remember Then*, 1978.

Paul Shaffer
Canadian musician–composer
• Best known as keyboardist, bandleader on TV show "Late Night with David Letterman," 1982–.
b. November 28, 1949 in Thunder Bay, Ontario

Daniel Shafran
Russian musician
• Remarkable cellist, concertist; won first prize in Moscow competition, 1937.
b. February 13, 1923 in Leningrad, U.S.S.R.

Ravi Shankar
Indian musician–composer
• Sitarist; first Indian instrumentalist to be internationally known; gave lessons to George Harrison who introduced the sitar to popular music.
b. April 07, 1920 in Benares, India

Del Shannon
(Charles Weeden Westover)
American composer–songwriter
• Early rock singer; wrote, recorded no. 1 hit "Runaway," 1961; popularity waned with Beatles-led British Invasion; suicide victim.
b. December 3, 1939 in Coopersville, Michigan
d. February 08, 1990 in Santa Clarita, California

Artie Shaw
(Arthur Arshowsky)
American musician
• Clarinetist, prominent "swing" bandleader, 1930s-40s; had biggest hit with Cole Porter's "Begin the Beguine," 1938.
b. May 23, 1910 in New York, New York

Robert Lawson Shaw
American conductor
• Founder, director, Robert Shaw Chorale, 1948-65; leader of Atlanta Symphony, 1967-; won many Grammys.
b. April 3, 1916 in Red Bluff, California

Rodion Konstantinovich Shchedrin
Russian composer
• Extremely popular works include Bizet's *Carmen* written as a ballet for ballerina wife, Maya Plisetskaya.
b. December 16, 1932 in Moscow, U.S.S.R.

George Albert Shearing
American musician
• Popular blind pianist known for block chords; wrote jazz classic "Lullaby of Birdland."
b. August 13, 1919 in London, England

Sheila E
(Sheila Escovedo)
American singer–musician
• Has worked with Prince; had solo single "The Glamorous Life," 1984.
b. December 12, 1959 in San Francisco, California

T G Sheppard
(Bill Browser)
American singer–musician
• Country singer, guitarist who sang "Make My Day," with Clint Eastwood, 1984.
b. July 2, 1944 in Jackson, Tennessee

Bobby Sherman
American singer–actor
• 1960s teen hero; first single, "Little Woman," 1969, went gold; starred in TV's "Here Come the Brides," 1968-70.
b. July 22, 1945 in Santa Monica, California

Richard Morton Sherman
American composer–lyricist
• Won Oscars for score of *Mary Poppins* and song "Chim, Chim, Cheree," 1964.
b. June 12, 1928 in New York, New York

Larry Shields
American jazz musician
• Pioneered hot-style clarinet; star of Chicago's Original Dixieland Band, 1916.
b. May 17, 1893 in New Orleans, Louisiana
d. November 22, 1953 in Hollywood, California

David (Lee) Shire
American composer
• Won best song Oscar for *Norma Rae*, 1979; Grammy for *Saturday Night Fevver*, 1978.
b. July 03, 1937 in Buffalo, New York

The Shirelles
(Doris Kenner Jackson; Beverly Lee; Addie Micki Harris McFadden; Shirley Alston Owens)
American music group
• Their 1961 hit, "Dedicated to the One I Love," was the first million-selling single by an all-girl group.

John Stanton Shirley-Quirk
American opera singer
• Bass-baritone who sang multiple roles in *Death in Venice*, 1973; made NY Met. debut, 1974.
b. August 28, 1931

Dinah Shore
(Frances Rose Shore; "Fannie")
American singer–actress
• Began singing, 1938; won ten Emmys for various TV shows.
b. March 01, 1917 in Winchester, Tennessee

Bobby (Robert Waltrip) Short
American pianist
• Known for supper-club singing; specializes in songs of 1920s-30s; wrote autobiography *Black and White Baby*, 1971.
b. September 15, 1926 in Danville, Illinois

Dmitri Dmitryevich Shostakovich
Russian composer
• Best-known symphony, *Fifth*, celebrated 20th anniversary of Russian Revolution, 1937.
b. September 25, 1906 in Saint Petersburg, Russia
d. August 09, 1975 in Moscow, U.S.S.R.

Maxim Shostakovich
Russian conductor
• Son of Dmitri; led USSR State Orchestra, 1960s; noted for interpretating his father's works; defected to US, 1981.
b. May 1, 1938 in Leningrad, Russia

Jean Sibelius
Finnish composer
• Romantic composer who drew themes from nature, folklore; known for seven symphonies, 1899-1924.
b. December 08, 1865 in Tavastehus, Finland
d. September 2, 1957 in Jarvenpaa, Finland

Elie Siegmeister
American composer–conductor
• Stage, orchestral works include *Ozark Set*, 1943; founded, led American Ballad singers, 1939-44; wrote on music.
b. January 15, 1909 in New York, New York
d. March 1, 1991 in Manhasset, New York

Beverly Sills
(Mrs Peter B Greenough; Belle Silverman; "Bubbles")
American opera singer
• Coloratura soprano, made operatic debut, 1947; director, NYC Opera, 1979-88; won two Emmys, Medal of Freedom, 1980.
b. May 25, 1929 in Brooklyn, New York

Horace Ward Martin Tavares Silver
American jazz musician
• Oustanding pianist, accompanist; noted for "funky" style popular in late 1950s.
b. September 28, 1928 in Norwalk, Connecticut

Harry Simeone
American composer
• Arranger for Fred Waring; co-wrote "The Little Drummer Boy," 1958.
b. May 09, 1911 in Newark, New Jersey

Guilietta Simionato
Italian opera singer
• La Scala's leading contralto, 1939-59; with NY Met., 1959-65.
b. May 12, 1916 in Forli, Italy

Gene Simmons
(Gene Klein; Kiss)
American singer–musician
• Co-founded Kiss, 1972; dressed as fire-breathing, blood-spewing ghoul; invented Axe bass guitar, 1980.
b. August 25, 1949 in Haifa, Israel

Ginny (Virginia E) Simms
American singer–radio performer
• Popular vocalist, Kay Kyser's band, 1930s-40s; own radio, TV show, early 1950s.
b. May 25, 1916 in San Antonio, Texas

Carly Simon
American singer–songwriter
• Hits include "You're So Vain," 1972; "Jesse," 1980; "Coming Around Again," 1987.
b. June 25, 1945 in New York, New York

Joe Simon
American singer
• Rhythm and blues, soul singer; hit single "The Chokin' Kind," 1966.
b. September 02, 1943 in Simmesport, Louisiana

Paul Simon
(Simon and Garfunkel)
American songwriter–singer–actor
• Has successful solo career; won 1987 Grammy for South African album *Graceland*.
b. November 05, 1942 in Newark, New Jersey

Simon and Garfunkel
(Arthur Garfunkel; Paul Simon)
American music group
• Sixth grade classmates who formed folk-rock duo; number one hits "Mrs. Robinson," 1967; "Bridge Over Troubled Waters," 1970.

Nina Simone
(Eunice Wayman)
American singer
• Jazz/soul singer, noted for club, festival performances; albums include *Fodder On My Wings*, 1984.
b. February 21, 1933 in Tryon, North Carolina

Simple Minds
(Charlie Burchill; Mel Gaynor; John Giblin; Jim Kerr; Mick Mac Neil)
Scottish music group
• Punk-dance style hits include "Alive and Kicking," 1985. Recent release *Real Life*, 1991.

Valerie Simpson
(Mrs Nickolas Ashford; Ashford and Simpson)
American singer
• With husband, contributed original material to soundtrack of *The Wiz*; recorded two solo albums.
b. August 26, 1948 in Bronx, New York

Zoot (John Haley) Sims
American jazz musician
• Saxophonist with Big Bands, 1940s; won Grammy, 1977.
b. October 29, 1925 in Inglewood, California
d. March 23, 1985 in New York, New York

Frank (Francis Albert) Sinatra
American singer–actor
• Regarded as biggest entertainment attraction in 20th c.; won Oscar, 1953, for *From Here to Eternity*.
b. December 12, 1915 in Hoboken, New Jersey

Frank Sinatra, Jr (Francis Albert)
American singer–celebrity relative
• Son of Frank; nightclub performer, cameo roles in TV, films.
b. January 1, 1944 in Jersey City, New Jersey

Nancy Sinatra
American singer–celebrity relative
• Recorded "Something Stupid," with father, 1969.
b. June 08, 1940 in Jersey City, New Jersey

Zutty (Arthur James) Singleton
American musician
• Drummer with leading jazz groups for over 50 yrs.
b. May 14, 1898 in Bunkie, Louisiana
d. July 14, 1975 in New York, New York

Noble Sissle
American bandleader–lyricist
• Led Sizzling Syncopators, 1930s-60s; often collaborated with Eubie Blake; wrote "I'm Just Wild About Harry."
b. July 1, 1889 in Indianapolis, Indiana
d. December 17, 1975 in Tampa, Florida

Sister Sledge
(Debbie Sledge; Joni Sledge; Kathy Sledge; Kim Sledge)
American music group
• Sister quartet known for hit "We Are Family," 1979, which became theme for world champ Pittsburgh Pirates, 1979.

Ricky Skaggs
American musician–singer
• Won 1982 CMA awards for best male vocalist and newcomer of year.
b. July 18, 1954 in Cordell, Kentucky

Leonard Slatkin
American conductor
• Most promising American-born conductor since Leonard Bernstein; music director, St. Louis Symphony since 1979.
b. September 01, 1944 in Los Angeles, California

Ruth Slenczynska
American pianist
• Acclaimed protege; stopped performing at early age; wrote memoirs *Forbidden Childhood*, 1957, recounts problems.
b. January 15, 1925 in Sacramento, California

Grace Wing Slick
(Jefferson Airplane; Mrs Skip Johnson; Grace Barnett Wing)
American singer
• Lead vocalist, Jefferson Starship, 1966-78; rock hits include "White Rabbit," 1967; persued solo career.
b. October 3, 1943 in Chicago, Illinois

Sly and the Family Stone
(Gregg Errico; Lawrence Graham Jr; Jerry Martini; Cynthia Robinson; Fred Stone; Rose Stone; Sly Stone)
American music group
• Dance-rock hits include "Family Affair," 1971.

The Small Faces
(Kenny Jones; Ian MacLagan; Steve Marriott; Rick Wills)
British music group
• Styled after rock group The Who; hits include "Tin Soldier," 1967.

Charlie Smalls
American composer–lyricist
• Won Tonys for music, lyrics of *The Wiz*, 1975.
b. October 25, 1943 in New York, New York
d. August 27, 1987 in Bruges, Belgium

Olga Smaroff
American pianist–critic
• Founded Schubert Memorial, 1928; wrote music texts; once wed to Leopold Stokowski.
b. August 08, 1882 in San Antonio, Texas
d. May 17, 1948 in New York, New York

Bessie Smith
American singer–songwriter
• Blues singer, 1920s, discovered by Ma Rainery; first recording "Gulf Coast Blues," 1923.
b. April 15, 1894 in Chattanooga, Tennessee
d. September 26, 1937 in Clarksdale, Mississippi

Clarence Smith
American jazz musician
• Pianist, vocalist; wrote "Pine Top's Boogie Woogie," 1928; accidentally murdered.
b. June 11, 1904 in Troy, Alabama
d. March 14, 1929 in Chicago, Illinois

Joe Smith
American jazz musician
• Trumpeter with Fletcher Henderson, McKinney's Cotton Pickers, 1920s.
b. June 1902 in Ohio
d. December 02, 1937 in New York, New York

Kate (Kathryn Elizabeth) Smith
American singer
• Recorded over 2,000 songs, had 19 number one hits, best known for rendition of "God Bless America."
b. May 01, 1909 in Greenville, Virginia
d. June 17, 1986 in Raleigh, North Carolina

Keely Smith
American singer
• Pop vocalist with husband, Louis Prima, 1950s-60s.
b. March 09, 1932 in Norfolk, Virginia

Paul Joseph Smith
American composer
• Won Oscar, 1940, for work on Walt Disney classic *Pinocchio*.
b. October 3, 1906 in Calumet, Michigan
d. January 25, 1985 in Glendale, California

Patti Smith
American singer–poet
• Hit single "Because the Night," written with Bruce Springsteen, 1978.
b. December 31, 1946 in Chicago, Illinois

Rex Smith
American actor–singer
• Had hit single "You Take My Breath Away," 1981; starred in Broadway, film versions of *Pirates of Penzance*, 1980.
b. 1956 in Jacksonville, Florida

Sammi Smith
American singer
• Won best female country vocalist Grammy, 1972, for "Help Me Make It Through the Night."
b. August 05, 1943 in Orange, California

William Smith
(William Henry Joseph Berthol Bonaparte Smith; "Willie the Lion")
American jazz musician–songwriter
• One of great "stride" pianists, active from 1920s; subject of two short films, 1900s.
b. November 23, 1897 in Goshen, New York
d. April 18, 1973 in New York, New York

Smokey Robinson and the Miracles
(Pete Moore; Claudette Rogers Robinson; William Smokey Robinson; Bobby Rogers; Ronnie White)
American music group
• All-Detroit group, formed 1957; hit singles "I Second That Emotion," 1965; "The Tears of a Clown," 1970.

Dee (Daniel Dee) Snider
(Twisted Sister)
American singer–songwriter
• Lead singer, Twisted Sister, 1976–; composes most of group's original songs.
b. March 15, 1955 in Massapequa, New York

Hank (Clarence Eugene) Snow
American singer
• Country music star, popular, 1950s; wrote hit "I'm Movin' On."
b. May 09, 1914 in Liverpool, Nova Scotia

Phoebe Laub Snow
American singer
• Albums include *Never Letting Go*, 1977; *Rock Away*, 1980.
b. July 17, 1952 in New York, New York

Elisabeth Anna Soderstrom
Swedish opera singer
• Soprano, who is also versatile actress known for more than 50 operatic roles in ten languages.
b. May 07, 1927 in Stockholm, Sweden

Soft Cell
(Marc Almond; Dave Ball)
English music group
• Formed 1979; hit single "Tainted Love," 1982, was on charts for 43 straight weeks.

Soft Machine
(Roy Babbington; Elton Dean; Hugh Hopper; Phil Howard; John Marshall; Mike Ratledge)
British music group
• Jazz sounding group; albums include *The Land of Cockayne*, 1981.

Solomon
(Solomon Cutner)
English pianist
• Child prodigy; concert repertoire focused on Mozart, Brahms, Shubert; retired, 1956.
b. August 09, 1902 in London, England
d. February 22, 1988 in London, England

Sir Georg Solti
English musician–conductor
• Winner of 22 Grammys, 1962-83.
b. October 21, 1912 in Budapest, Hungary

Judith Somogi
American conductor
• Music director, conductor, Utica (NY) Symphony, 1977-88; first female to conduct an opera in US.
b. May 13, 1937 in New York, New York
d. March 23, 1988 in Long Island, New York

Stephen Joshua Sondheim
American composer–lyricist
• One of America's most acclaimed lyricists; wrote lyrics for *West Side Story*, 1957; *Gypsy*, 1959.
b. March 22, 1930 in New York, New York

Sonny and Cher
(Sonny Bono; Cher)
American music group
• 1960s pop hits include "I Got You Babe."

Sons of the Pioneers
(Pat Brady; Roy Lanham; Rob Nolan; Lloyd Perryman; Rusty Richards; Roy Rogers; Tim Spencer; Dale Warren)
American music group
• One of first highly successful, durable Western singing groups, 1930s; hits include "Cool Water," 1948.

Robert B(andler) Sour
American lyricist
• Hit songs include "Body and Soul," 1930.
b. October 31, 1905 in New York, New York
d. March 06, 1985 in New York, New York

John Philip Sousa
American composer–conductor
• Wrote 140 marches, including "Stars and Stripes Forever," 1897.
b. November 06, 1854 in Washington, District of Columbia
d. March 06, 1932 in Reading, Pennsylvania

Joe South
American musician–singer–songwriter
• Won two Grammys, 1969, for "Games People Play."
b. February 28, 1942 in Atlanta, Georgia

J(ohn) D(avid) Souther
(The Souther-Hillman-Furay Band)
American singer–songwriter
• Guitarist, vocalist with country-rock band, 1973-75.
b. in Detroit, Michigan

The Souther-Hillman-Furay Band
(Richie Furay; James Gordon; Paul Harris; Chris Hillman; Al Perkiins; J(ohn) D(avid) Souther)
American music group
• Country-rock band formed 1973; first album was gold; disbanded, 1975, with members going on to solo careers.

Southside Johnny and the Asbury Jukes
(Gene Bacia; Steve Becker; Al Berger; Ricky Gazda; Kevin Kavanaugh; "Southside" Johnny Lyon; Eddie Manion; Carlo Novi; Tony Palligr)
American music group
• Rhythm and blues influenced rock band formed 1974; albums featured Bruce Springsteen songs.

David Soyer
American musician
• Cellist; won five Grammys for Guarneri Quarter recordings, 1965-74.
b. February 24, 1923 in Philadelphia, Pennsylvania

Albert Spalding
American violinist
• Int'l. concertist, 1910-40s; wrote violin pieces; son of Albert Goodwill.
b. August 15, 1888 in Chicago, Illinois
d. May 26, 1953 in New York, New York

Spandau Ballet
(Tony Hadley; John Keeble; Gary Kemp; Martin Kemp; Steve Norman)
English music group
• Formed 1979; known for flamboyant, then classic dress; hit single "True," 1983.

Muggsy (Francis Joseph) Spanier
American jazz musician
• Noted Dixieland cornetist; with Ted Lewis, 1929-36; led own band, early 1940s; used plunger mute.
b. November 09, 1906 in Chicago, Illinois
d. February 12, 1967 in Sausalito, California

The Spencer Davis Group
(Spencer Davis; Muff Winwood; Stevie Winwood; Pete York)
English music group
• Hits include "Gimme Some Lovin'," 1967.

Phil Spitalny
American bandleader
• Conducted female orchestra, 1935-55.
b. November 07, 1890 in Odessa, Russia
d. October 11, 1970 in Miami, Florida

Charlie Spivak
American bandleader–musician
• Played lead trumpet with his popular band, 1940s-50s; disbanded with demise of big bands.
b. February 17, 1906 in New Haven, Connecticut
d. March 01, 1982 in Greenville, South Carolina

Tossy Spivakovsky
Russian musician
• Concert master of Berlin Philharmonic pre Nazism; violin soloist, 1941-.
b. February 04, 1907 in Odessa, Russia

Dusty Springfield
(Mary Isobel Catherine O'Brien)
English singer
• Popular vocalist, 1963-69; hits include "Wishin' and Hopin,'" 1964.
b. April 16, 1939 in Hampstead, England

Rick (Richard) Springfield
Australian actor–musician–singer
• Former star of soap opera "General Hospital" who had Grammy-winning hit "Jessie's Girl," 1981.
b. August 23, 1949 in Sydney, Australia

Bruce Springsteen
("The Boss")
American singer–songwriter–musician
• Album *Born in the USA*, most popular rock album of all time, 1985. Solo album *Tunnel of Love*, 1988.
b. September 23, 1949 in Freehold, New Jersey

Squeeze
(John Bentley; Paul Carrack; Chris Difford; Julian Holland; HarryKakoulli; Gilson Lavis; Don Snow; Glenn Tilbrook)
English music group
• Formed 1974 in London; had hit album *East Side Story*, 1981.

Billy Squier
American singer–musician
• Guitarist whose singles include "Everybody Wants You," 1982; "Eye On You," 1984.
b. May 12, 1950 in Wellesley, Massachusetts

Chris Squire
(Yes)
English singer–musician
• Self-taught bassist who formed Yes, 1968; had solo album *Fish Out of the Water*, 1975.
b. March 04, 1948 in London, England

Mariano Stabile
Italian opera singer
• Baritone; sang Falstaff more than 1,000 times; retired, 1960.
b. May 12, 1888 in Palermo, Sicily
d. January 11, 1968 in Milan, Italy

Jim (James Wayne) Stafford
American singer–songwriter
• Novelty songwriter; had hit singles "Spiders and Snakes," 1974; "My Girl Bill," 1974.
b. January 16, 1944 in Eloise, Florida

Jo Stafford
American singer
• Popular performer, 1940s-50s; sang with Tommy Dorsey through mid-1944.
b. November 12, 1918 in Coalinga, California

Paul Stanley
(Paul Eisen; Kiss)
American singer–musician
• Guitarist who co-founded Kiss, 1972.
b. January 2, 1949 in Queens, New York

Singers Staple, The
(Cleotha Mavis Pervis Roebuck Pop and Yvonne Staple)
American music group
• Family group formed, 1954; soul hits include "Let's Do It Again," 1975.

Janos Starker
Hungarian musician
• Cello virtuoso; int'l. reputation as first cellist with many symphonies.
b. July 05, 1924 in Budapest, Hungary

Kay Starr
(Kathryn Stark)
American singer
• Popular vocalist, 1940s-50s; combined blues, country, swing; hit single: "Wheel of Fortune," 1952.
b. July 21, 1924 in Doughtery, Oklahoma

Ringo Starr
(The Beatles; Richard Starkey)
English singer–musician
• Drummer with legendary rock group; started solo career, 1970; starred in film *Caveman*, 1981.
b. July 07, 1940 in Liverpool, England

Starship
(Don Baldwin; Craig Chaquico; Pete Sears; Grace Slick; Mickey Thomas)
American music group
• Made up of members of Jefferson Starship; hit album *Knee Deep in the Hoopla*, 1985.

Statler Brothers
(Phillip Balsley; Lew C DeWitt; Don S Reid; Harold W Reid)
American music group
• Durable country harmony group; hit singles since early 1960s.

Eleanor Steber
American opera singer
• Soprano; NY Met., 1940-66; noted for Mozart, Verdi, Puccini roles.
b. July 17, 1916 in Wheeling, West Virginia
d. October 03, 1990 in Langhorne, Pennsylvania

Steeleye Span
(Martin Carthy; Bob Johnson; Kemp; John Kirkpatrick; Peter Knight; Maddy Prior)
British music group
• Pioneered electronic folk music; albums include *Sails of Silver*, 1980.

Steely Dan
(Jeff Baxter; Walter Becker; Denny Dias; Donald Fagen; James Hodder; David Palmer)
American music group
• Formed, 1972; lively, bluesy jazz hits include "FM," 1978; "Deacon Blues," 1978.

Joseph Stein
American dramatist–librettist
• Won Tony for play *Fiddler on the Roof*, 1965; wrote film version, 1972.
b. May 3, 1912 in New York, New York

William (Hans Wilhelm) Steinberg
American conductor
• Director, Pittsburgh Symphony, 1952-76; Boston Symphony, 1968-72.
b. August 01, 1899 in Cologne, Germany
d. May 16, 1978 in New York, New York

Max Steiner
Austrian composer–conductor
• Wrote music for *Gone With the Wind*, 1939; Oscar-winning scores for *The Informer*, 1935; *Now, Voyager*, 1942.
b. May 1, 1888 in Vienna, Austria
d. December 28, 1971 in Hollywood, California

Steppenwolf
(George Biondo; Robert Cochran; Wayne Cook; Jerry Edmonton; JohnKay)
American music group
• Songs include "Born to Be Wild," 1968.

Isaac Stern
American violinist
• Made debut age 11; int'l. concertist; made soundtrack for *Fiddler on the Roof*, 1971; French Legion of Honor, 1979.
b. July 21, 1920 in Kreminiecz, U.S.S.R.

Cat Stevens
(Stephen Demetri Georgiou; Yosef Islam)
English singer–songwriter
• Rock-folk singer; had hits "Moon Shadow," 1971, "Morning Has Broken," 1972; quit music business, became Muslim, 1981.
b. July 21, 1948 in London, England

Ray Stevens
(Harold Ray Ragsdale)
American musician–singer
• Pianist, country-western singer, 1970s.
b. January 24, 1939 in Clarksdale, Georgia

Al Stewart
British singer–songwriter
• Hit singles include "Year of the Cat," 1977; "Time Passages," 1978.
b. 1945 in Glasgow, Scotland

David Stewart
(The Eurythmics)
English musician
• Guitarist with Eurythmics; singles include "Would I Lie to You?" 1985.
b. September 19, 1952 in Sunderland, England

John Stewart
American singer–songwriter
• Best known for writing song "Daydream Believer," 1967, which was number one hit for The Monkees, 1967; member of Kingston Trio, 1961-67.
b. September 05, 1939 in San Diego, California

Rod(erick David) Stewart
English singer–songwriter
• Singer with Jeff Beck Group, 1968-69; Faces, 1969-75; solo performer, 1975-.
b. January 1, 1945 in North London, England

Slam (Leroy) Stewart
American jazz musician–composer
• Innovative bassist with Art Tatum, Benny Goodman; recorded "Flat Foot Floogie" with Slim Gaillard, 1938.
b. September 21, 1914 in Englewood, New Jersey
d. December 1, 1987 in Binghamton, New York

Wynn Stewart
American singer–songwriter
• Formed country-western band, The Tourists, 1960s; hit single "Something Pretty," 1968.
b. June 07, 1934 in Morrisville, Missouri
d. July 17, 1985 in Hendersonville, Tennessee

Teresa Stich-Randall
American opera singer
• Soprano; NY Met debut, 1961; sang Aida at age 15.
b. December 24, 1927 in West Hartford, Connecticut

William Grant Still
American composer–conductor
• First black to lead major US orchestra, LA Philharmonic, 1936; wrote "Afro-American Symphony," 1931.
b. May 11, 1895 in Woodville, Mississippi
d. December 03, 1978 in Los Angeles, California

Stephen Stills
(Buffalo Springfield; Crosby, Stills, Nash and Young)
American musician–singer–songwriter
• Guitarist, keyboardist; solo hits include "Love the One You're With," 1971.
b. January 03, 1945 in Dallas, Texas

Sting
(Gordon Matthew Sumner; The Police)
English singer–songwriter–actor
• Self-taught musician, force behind success of Police; played villain in films *Brimstone and Treacle*, 1982; *Dune*, 1984. Released *Soul Cages*, 1991.
b. October 02, 1951 in Wallsend, England

Sonny (Edward) Stitt
American jazz musician
• Saxophonist with Dizzy Gillespie, 1940s; led own combo, 1950s-60s.
b. February 02, 1924 in Boston, Massachusetts
d. July 22, 1982 in Washington, District of Columbia

Frederick A Stock
American conductor
• Led Chicago Symphony for 48 yrs.
b. November 11, 1872 in Dulich, Germany
d. October 2, 1942 in Chicago, Illinois

Karlheinz Stockhausen
German composer
• Avant-garde works emphasize time-space music, electronic devices, audience participation; *Sirius* dedicated to space pioneers, 1976.
b. August 28, 1928 in Modrath, Germany

Leopold (Anton Stanislaw) Stokowski
American conductor–musician
• Led Philadelphia Orchestra, 1914-36; formed American Symphony Orchestra, 1962; film *Fantasia*, 1940, helped popularize the classics.
b. April 18, 1882 in London, England
d. September 13, 1977 in Hampshire, England

George E Stoll
American composer
• Film scores include *For Me and My Gal*, 1942; won Oscar for *Anchors Aweigh*, 1945.
b. May 07, 1905 in Minneapolis, Minnesota
d. January 18, 1985 in Monterey, California

Richard Leslie Stoltzman
American musician
• Clarinet virtuoso, known for combining traditional, contemporary material from classical, jazz sources.
b. July 12, 1942 in Omaha, Nebraska

Robert Stolz
German composer
• Wrote 2,000 songs, 50 operettas, music for films; won Oscars, 1941, 1944.
b. August 25, 1886 in Graz, Austria
d. June 27, 1975 in Berlin, Germany (West)

Sly Stone
(Sylvester Stewart; Sly and the Family Stone)
American singer–musician
• Led rock/blues group, 1970s; hits include "Family Affair," 1971; nominated for Grammy, 1973.
b. March 15, 1944 in Dallas, Texas

Paul (Noel Paul) Stookey
(Peter Paul and Mary)
American singer–songwriter
• Member, folk-singing group, 1961–; wrote, recorded "The Wedding Song" ("There Is Love,") 1971.
b. November 3, 1937 in Baltimore, Maryland

Alessandro Stradella
Italian composer
• Adventuresome life subject of 19th-c. operas, books; wrote opera *Il Corispeo*.
b. 1642 in Naples, Italy
d. February 28, 1682 in Genoa, Italy

George Strait
American singer
• Country singer; CMA entertainer of year, 1989, 1990; album *Does Fort Worth Ever Cross Your Mind* was CMA album of year, 1985.
b. May 1, 1952 in Pearsall, Texas

Teresa Stratas
(Anastasia Strataki)
Canadian opera singer
• Soprano; NY Met., since late 1950s; won three Grammys, one Tony.
b. May 26, 1939 in Toronto, Ontario

Oskar Straus
Austrian composer
• Wrote 50 operettas including *Chocolate Soldier*, 1909; filmed, 1941.
b. April 06, 1870 in Vienna, Austria
d. January 11, 1954 in Bad Ischl, Austria

Johann Strauss, Sr
Austrian composer–conductor
• Published 152 waltzes; led orchestra at Viennese dance halls.
b. March 14, 1804 in Vienna, Austria
d. September 25, 1849 in Vienna, Austria

Johann Strauss, Jr
Austrian composer–conductor–violinist
• Wrote 16 operettas, 400 waltzes, including *The Blue Danube*, 1864.
b. October 25, 1825 in Vienna, Austria
d. June 03, 1899 in Vienna, Austria

Richard Strauss
German conductor–composer
• Wrote operas *Salome*, 1905; *Rosenkavalier*, 1911; one of last German romantics.
b. June 11, 1864 in Munich, Germany
d. September 08, 1949 in Garmisch, Germany (West)

Igor Fedorovich Stravinsky
American composer
• Noted for ballets *The Firebird*, 1910, *Rite of Spring*, 1913; greatly influenced modern music.
b. June 17, 1882 in Oranienbaum, Russia
d. April 06, 1971 in New York, New York

Strawbs
(Rod Coombes; Dave Cousins; Chas Cronk; Dave Lambert)
British music group
• Music mixes folk/bluegrass; songs include "Part of the Union," 1973.

Stray Cats
(Lee Rocker; Brian Setzer; Slim Jim Phantom (Jim McDonnell))
American music group
• Rock group formed, 1979; albums include *Built for Speed*, 1982.

Billy (William) Strayhorn
American jazz musician
• Pianist, arranger, Duke Ellington's band, 1938-67; wrote "Take the ₉A' Train," 1941.
b. November 29, 1915 in Dayton, Ohio
d. May 31, 1967 in New York, New York

Barbra Joan Streisand
American singer–actress
• Won Oscar, 1968, for *Funny Girl*; albums include *The Lodgers*, 1985.
b. April 24, 1942 in New York, New York

Giuseppina Strepponi
Italian opera singer
• Famed soprano, late 1830s; wife of Verdi.
b. September 18, 1815 in Lodi, Italy
d. November 15, 1897 in Busseto, Italy

Charles Strouse
American composer
• Won Tonys for *Bye Bye Birdie*, 1959; *Applause*, 1970; *Annie*, 1977.
b. June 07, 1928 in New York, New York

Levi Stubbs
(The Four Tops)
American singer
• Original member of group.
b. in Detroit, Michigan

Jule (Julius Kerwin Stein) Styne
American songwriter
• Won best song Oscar for "Three Coins in the Fountain," 1954; other songs included in films *I'll Walk Alone*, 1945; *Funny Girl*, 1968.
b. December 31, 1905 in London, England

Styx
(John Curulewski; Dennis DeYoung; Chuck Panozzo; John Panozzo; Tommy Shaw; James Young)
American music group
• Hard pop group formed 1963, popular among young teens; hit single "Babe," 1979.

Dana Nadine Suesse
American composer–musician
• Child prodigy pianist; composed orchestral pieces as well as pop tunes: "You Oughta Be in Pictures," 1934.
b. December 03, 1911 in Shreveport, Louisiana
d. October 16, 1987 in New York, New York

Sir Arthur Seymour Sullivan
(Gilbert and Sullivan)
English composer–author
• With W S Gilbert produced 14 comic operas; wrote "Onward Christian Soldiers," 1871.
b. May 14, 1842 in London, England
d. November 22, 1900 in London, England

Tom Sullivan
American singer–actor–composer
• Blind performer who wrote *If You Could See What I Hear*, 1976; made into movie, 1982.
b. March 27, 1947 in Boston, Massachusetts

Yma Sumac
Peruvian singer
• Flamboyant concertist, billed as Inca princess; voice ranged five octaves.
b. September 1, 1928 in Ichocan, Peru

Donna Summer
(LaDonna Andrea Gaines; Mrs Bruce Sudano)
American singer
• Disco hits include "Hot Stuff," 1979; "Last Dance," 1978; "Dinner With Gershwin," 1987.
b. December 31, 1948 in Boston, Massachusetts

Supertramp
(Bob C Benberg; Richard Davies; John Anthony Helliwell; Rodger Hodgson; Dougie Thompson)
English music group
• Albums include *...Famous Last Words*, 1982.

The Supremes
(Florence Ballard; Cindy Birdsong; Diana Ross; Jean Terrell; MaryWilson)
American music group
• Detroit trio, formed 1962; hits include "Baby Love," 1964; Hall of Fame, 1988.

Survivor
(Dave Bickler; Marc Droubay; Stephan Ellis; Dennis Keith Johnson;; Jim Peternik; R Gary Smith; Frankie Sullivan)
American music group
• Had number one hit "Eye of the Tiger," theme song from *Rocky III*, 1982.

Dame Joan Sutherland
Australian opera singer
• Leading coloratura soprano, 1960s-70s; won Grammy for best classical vocalist, 1981.
b. November 07, 1929 in Sydney, Australia

Elizabeth A (Liz) Swados
American author–composer–director
• Composer, director for *Nightclub Cantata*, 1977.
b. February 05, 1951 in Buffalo, New York

Donald Ibrahim Swann
Welsh composer–lyricist–entertainer
• Starred with Michael Flanders in two-man show *At the Drop of a Hat*, 1950s.
b. September 3, 1923 in Llanelly, Wales

Kay Swift
American musician–songwriter
• Pianist-arranger; songs include "Forever and a Day."
b. April 19, 1905 in New York, New York

The Sylvers
(Charmaine Sylver; Edmund Sylver; Foster Sylver; James Sylver; Joseph Sylver; Leon Sylver; Olympia-Ann Sylver)
American music group
• Family group of singers, began recording, 1972; soul hits include "Boogie Fever," 1976; "Hot Line," 1977.

Henryk Szeryng
Mexican violinist
• Int'l. concertist since 1933; recorded nearly 250 works, mostly in Romantic style.
b. September 22, 1921 in Zelazowa Wola, Poland
d. March 03, 1988 in Kassel, Germany (West)

T Rex
(Marc Bolan; Steven Currie; Mickey Finn; Jack Green; Bill Legend;Steven Peregrine Took)
English music group
• Rock group formed 1967; up and down career eventually landed hit song "Bang A Gong (Get it On)," 1972.

Germaine Tailleferre
(Les Six)
French composer
• Only woman composer in group of post-WW I composers.
b. April 19, 1892 in Pau-St. Maur, France
d. November 07, 1983 in Paris, France

Otar Vasilevich Taktakishvili
Russian composer
• Music shows Caucasus influence; has written piano concertos, symphonicpoems.
b. 1924

The Talking Heads
(David Byrne; Chris Frantz; Jerry Harrison; Martina Weymouth)
American music group
• New wave group begun, 1977; combine traditional rock styles with Afro-American music; had hit single "Burning Down the House," 1983.

Garry Wayne Tallent
(E Street Band)
American musician
• Bassist who joined Bruce Springsteen's band, 1971.
b. October 27, 1949 in Detroit, Michigan

Thomas Tallis
(Thomas Tallys; "Father of English Cathedral Music")
English organist–composer
• Among first to set English words to music for Anglican liturgy; organist of the chapel royal.
b. 1515 in Greenwich, England
d. November 23, 1585 in Greenwich, England

Francesco Tamagno
Italian opera singer
• Probably greatest tenor di forza of all time; created role of Othello, 1887.
b. December 28, 1850 in Turin, Italy
d. August 31, 1905 in Varese, Italy

Antonio Tamburini
Italian opera singer
• Celebrated baritone, idol of London, Paris, 1830s-40s; created many roles.
b. March 28, 1800 in Faenza, Italy
d. November 09, 1876 in Nice, France

Giuseppe Tartini
Italian composer–violinist
• Wrote 50 violin sonatas; developed "Tartini harmonic" for finer intonation.
b. April 08, 1692 in Istria, Italy
d. February 26, 1770 in Padua, Italy

Art(hur) Tatum
American jazz musician
• All-time great jazz pianist, noted for original technique, improvisation; led trio, 1943-55; recorded "Sweet Lorraine."
b. October 13, 1910 in Toledo, Ohio
d. November 04, 1956 in Los Angeles, California

Richard Tauber
British opera singer–actor
• Tenor, noted for Mozart, Lehar operetta roles; films include *Blossom Time*, 1932.
b. May 16, 1892 in Linz, Austria
d. January 08, 1948 in London, England

Bernie Taupin
English lyricist
• Wrote lyrics for Elton John's gold records.
b. May 22, 1950 in Sleaford, England

Billy (William Edward) Taylor
American jazz musician
• Noted jazz pianist, since 1937; had weekly TV show, 1960s; member, Jazz Hall of Fame, 1979.
b. July 24, 1921 in Greenville, North Carolina

Cecil Percival Taylor
American musician
• Jazz pianist, who combines classical, contemporary music; innovator in harmony rhythm.
b. March 15, 1933 in Long Island, New York

James Vernon Taylor
American singer–songwriter
• Has nine gold albums, four platinum albums, three gold singles for his folk-rock songs.
b. March 12, 1948 in Boston, Massachusetts

Livingston Taylor
American singer–celebrity relative
• Brother of James Taylor; hit single "I Will Be in Love with You," 1978.
b. November 21, 1950 in Boston, Massachusetts

Mick Taylor
(The Rolling Stones)
English musician
• Guitarist; replaced Brian Jones, 1969-74.
b. January 17, 1948 in Hertfordshire, England

Peter Ilyich Tchaikovsky
(Petr Ilich Chaikovshy)
Russian composer
• Known for classical ballet scores *Swan Lake*, 1877; *Nutcracker Suite*, 1892; *Sleeping Beauty*, 1889.
b. May 07, 1840 in Votiwsk, Russia
d. November 06, 1893 in Saint Petersburg, Russia

Alexander Tcherepnin
American pianist–composer
• Experimented with nine-note scale, rhythmic polyphony; wrote opera, *Farmer and the Nymph*, 1952.
b. January 2, 1899 in Saint Petersburg, Russia
d. September 29, 1977

Dame Kiri Te Kanawa
New Zealander opera singer
• Soprano; performed at wedding of Prince Charles, Lady Diana Spencer, 1981.
b. March 06, 1947 in Gisborne, New Zealand

Charles Teagarden
(Little T)
American jazz musician
• Trumpeter with Big Bands, late 1920s-63; brother of Jack.
b. July 19, 1913 in Vernon, Texas
d. December 1, 1984 in Las Vegas, Nevada

Jack (Weldon John) Teagarden
(Big T)
American jazz musician–bandleader
• Great jazz trombonist, vocalist; led own band, 1939-46; in film *Birth of the Blues*, 1941.
b. August 2, 1905 in Vernon, Texas
d. January 15, 1964 in New Orleans, Louisiana

Tears for Fears
(Roland Orzabal; Curt Smith)
English music group
• Bath, England duo; had number one hit "Everybody Wants to Rule the World," 1985.

Renata Tebaldi
Italian opera singer
• Outstanding postwar soprano; noted for Verdi, Puccini roles.
b. February 01, 1922 in Pesaro, Italy

Teena Marie
(Mary Christine Brockert; "Lady T")
American singer
• Often works with Rick James; hits include "I Need Your Lovin'"; "It Must be Magic."
b. 1957 in Santa Monica, California

Louis Teicher
(Ferrante and Teicher)
American pianist–composer
• Part of Ferrante and Teicher piano team, 1947–.
b. August 24, 1924 in Wilkes-Barre, Pennsylvania

Georg Philipp Telemann
German composer
• Wrote over 600 overtures, 50 operas, including *Sokrates*, 1721.
b. March 14, 1681 in Magdeburg, Germany
d. June 25, 1767 in Hamburg, Germany

Alec Templeton
American pianist
• Famed blind entertainer, noted for piano parodies, novelty vocals, 1930s-40s; own radio show, 1940.
b. July 04, 1910 in Cardiff, Wales
d. March 28, 1963 in Greenwich, Connecticut

The Temptations
(Dennis Edwards; Melvin Franklin; Eddie Kendricks; Otis Williams;Paul Williams)
American music group
• Group formed in 1964; hits include "My Girl"; "Just My Imagination."

Ten CC
(Paul Burgess; Lol Creme; Kevin Godley; Graham Gouldman; Eric Stewart; 10 CC)
English music group
• Formed in 1972; albums include *Windows in the Jungle*, 1983.

Ten Years After
(Chick Churchill; Alvin Lee; Rick Lee; Leo Lyons)
British music group
• Major blues band, 1967-75; albums include *Goin' Home*, 1975.

Toni Tennille
(Mrs Daryl Dragon; Captain and Tennille)
American singer
• Had 1975 hit "Love Will Keep Us Together," written by Neil Sedaka.
b. May 08, 1943 in Montgomery, Alabama

Klaus Tennstedt
German conductor
• Musical director, conductor of London Philharmonic Orchestra, 1983–.
b. June 06, 1926 in Merseburg, Germany

Tammi Terrell
American singer
• Best known for duets with Marvin Gaye: "Your Precious Love," 1967; "Ain't Nothing Like the Real Thing," 1968.
b. 1946 in Philadelphia, Pennsylvania
d. March 16, 1970

Joe Tex
(Joseph Arrington Jr)
American singer
• Had 1964 hit "Hold On to What You've Got."
b. August 08, 1933 in Rogers, Texas
d. August 13, 1982 in Navasota, Texas

Mikis Theodorakis
Greek composer
• Revitalized modern Greek music; wrote score for *Zorba the Greek*, 1964.
b. July 29, 1925

Thin Lizzy
(Eric Bell; Brian Downey; Scott Gorham; Phil Lynott; Garry Moore;Brian Robertson; Midge Ure; Darren Wharton; Snowy White)
Irish music group
• Hard-nosed rock band, known for successful album *Jailbreak*, 1976.

Third World
(Bunny Rugs Clarke; Michael Ibo Cooper; Stephen Cat Coore;Richard Daley; Orvin "Carrot" Jarrett; Willie Stewart)
Jamaican music group
• Reggae band formed 1973; hits include "Sense of Purpose," 1985.

Thirty-Eight Special
(Don Barnes; Steve Brookins; Jeff Carlisi; Jack Grondin; Larry Junstron; Donnie Van Zandt)
American music group
• Formed 1979; albums include *Tour de Force*, 1984.

B(illy) J(oe) Thomas
American singer
• Hits include "Raindrops Keep Fallin' On My Head," 1970; "Somebody Done Somebody Wrong Song," 1974.
b. August 07, 1942 in Houston, Texas

Michael Tilson Thomas
American conductor
• Principal guest conductor, LA Philharmonic, 1981-85; principal conductor, London Symphony, 1989–.
b. December 21, 1944 in Hollywood, California

Hank Thompson
American singer–musician–bandleader
• Led country music-swing band, Brazos Valley Boys, 1950s-70s; had 100 hit-chart records by 1966.
b. September 03, 1925 in Waco, Texas

Kay Thompson
American singer
● Noted for singing career with Williams Brothers, 1947-53; invented popular character in book, *Eloise*, 1955.
b. November 09, 1913 in Saint Louis, Missouri

Thompson Twins
(Tom Bailey; Alannan Currie; Joe Leway)
English music group
● Chesterfield, England group; hit singles include "Hold Me Now," 1984; "King for Just One Day," 1986.

Virgil Garnett Thomson
American composer–musician–critic
● Wrote 100 musical portraits; opera *Four Saints in Three Acts*, 1934; won Oscar for score of *Louisiana Story*, 1948.
b. November 25, 1896 in Kansas City, Missouri
d. September 3, 1989 in New York, New York

Kerstin Thorborg
Swedish opera singer
● Sometimes considered greatest Wagnerian Mezzo-soprano of all time; NY Met., 1936-50.
b. May 19, 1896 in Hedemora, Sweden
d. April 12, 1970 in Falun, Sweden

Claude Thornhill
American songwriter–bandleader
● Led major dance band, 1940s; noted for novelty arrangements.
b. August 1, 1908 in Terre Haute, Indiana
d. July 01, 1965 in Caldwell, New Jersey

Willie Mae Thornton
American singer
● Known for renditions of "Have Mercy Baby"; "Hound Dog"; "Ball and Chain."
b. December 11, 1926 in Montgomery, Alabama
d. July 25, 1984 in Los Angeles, California

Three Dog Night
(Michael Allsup; James Greenspoon; Daniel Hutton; Skip Konte; Charles Negron; Joseph Schermine; Floyd Sneed; Cory Wells)
Australian music group
● Rock band formed, 1968; hits include "Joy to the World," 1971.

Tiffany
(Tiffany Renee Darwish)
American singer
● Teen singer; had million-selling debut album, 1987, that included single hits "Could've Been," "I Think We're Alone Now."
b. October 02, 1971

Glenn Tilbrook
(Squeeze)
English singer–musician
● Guitarist, vocalist; collaborated with Chris Difford on over 600 songs.
b. August 31, 1957 in London, England

Mel(vin) Tillis
American singer–songwriter
● Has written over 450 songs; CMA entertainer of year, 1976.
b. August 08, 1932 in Pahokee, Florida

Dimitri Tiomkin
American composer–pianist
● Wrote music for over 100 films; four Oscar-winning scores include *High Noon*, 1952.
b. May 1, 1899 in Saint Petersburg, Russia
d. November 11, 1979 in London, England

Sir Michael Kemp Tippett
English composer
● Works include oratorio *A Child of Our Time*, 1941; opera *The Knot Garden*, 1970.
b. January 02, 1905 in London, England

Cal(len Radcliffe, Jr) Tjader
American jazz musician
● Vibist; with Brubeck octet, 1949-51, George Shearing, 1950s; won 1981 Grammy.
b. July 16, 1925 in Saint Louis, Missouri
d. May 05, 1982 in Philippines

Ernst Toch
American composer–musician
● Seven symphonies include 1956 Pulitzer-winning *Third Symphony*; wrote piano pieces, film scores.
b. December 07, 1887 in Vienna, Austria
d. October 01, 1964 in Los Angeles, California

Tom Petty and the Heartbreakers
(Ron Blair; Mike Campbell; Stan Lynch; Tom Petty; Benmont Tench)
American music group
● Rock group formed by Tom Petty, 1975; album *Damn the Torpedoes*, 1979, sold over 2.5 million copies.

Pinky Tomlin
American songwriter
● Co-wrote popular hit, "The Object of My Affection," 1934; used in film *Times Square Lady*, 1935.
b. September 09, 1908 in Eros, Arkansas
d. December 15, 1987 in Los Angeles, California

Tone-Loc
(Anthony Terrell Smith)
American singer
● Rap singer; had multi-platinum hit single "Wild Thing," 1988; won several Grammys, 1990.
b. 1966 in Los Angeles, California

Toots and the Maytals
(Raleigh Gordon; Frederick Toots Hibbert; Nathaniel Jerry Mathias)
Jamaican music group
● Reggae band, 1962-83; hit albums include *Reggae Greats*, 1985.

Peter Tork
(The Monkees)
American singer–musician
● Bass guitarist, vocalist with The Monkees on popular TV series, 1966-68.
b. February 13, 1944 in Washington, District of Columbia

Mel(vin Howard) Torme
American singer–songwriter
● Versatile film, TV entertainer from 1940s; wrote "The Christmas Song"; won 1983 Grammy.
b. September 13, 1925 in Chicago, Illinois

Dean Torrence
(Jan and Dean)
American singer
● Formed singing duo with junior high school friend, Jan Berry, 1958; has designed album covers.
b. March 1, 1941 in Los Angeles, California

Arturo Toscanini
Italian conductor
● Considered finest maestro of his time; director, La Scala, from 1898; NBC Symphony, 1937-54; directed from memory.
b. March 25, 1867 in Parma, Italy
d. January 16, 1957 in New York, New York

Peter Tosh
(Winston Hubert MacIntosh; Bob Marley and the Wailers)
Jamaican singer
● Original Wailer; one of the founding fathers of Jamaica's vibrant music of revolution–reggae.
b. October 09, 1944 in Westmoreland, Jamaica
d. September 11, 1987 in Kingston, Jamaica

Francesco Paolo Tosti
Italian composer
● Singing teacher to Britain's royal family; wrote "Goodbye Forever and Forever."
b. April 07, 1846 in Ortona, Italy
d. December 06, 1916 in Rome, Italy

Toto
(Bobby Kimball; Steve Lukather; David Paich; Jeff Porcaro; Mike Porcaro; Steve Porcaro)
American music group
• Formed late 1970s; hits include "Rosanna," 1982, "Africa," 1983.

Dave Tough
American jazz musician
• A top drummer, 1940s; with Spivak, Goodman, Woody Herman, others.
b. April 26, 1908 in Oak Park, Illinois
d. December 06, 1948 in Newark, New Jersey

Joan Peabody Tower
American composer
• Works include *Percussion Quartet*, 1963; *Hexachords for Flute*, 1972.
b. September 06, 1938 in New Rochelle, New York

Peter Dennis Blandford Townshend
(The Who)
English musician–singer–songwriter
• Called one of rock music's most intelligent, inventive songwriters; wrote opera *Tommy*.
b. May 19, 1945 in London, England

Arthur Tracy
American singer
• Appeared with accordion on radio shows, films, 1930s-50s: film *The Big Broadcast*, 1932.
b. June 25, 1903 in Philadelphia, Pennsylvania

Traffic
(Jim Capaldi; Dave Mason; Stevie Winwood; Chris Wood)
English music group
• Rock band formed 1967; known for hit albums: *Traffic*, 1968.

Walter Trampler
American musician
• Viola virtuoso; known for performances with Budapest String Quartet.
b. August 25, 1915 in Munich, Germany

Maria Augusta von Trapp
American singer–author
• Fled Nazi-occupied Austria, formed Trapp Family Singers, 1930s; life story was inspiration for play *The Sound of Music*, 1959.
b. January 26, 1905 in Vienna, Austria
d. March 28, 1987 in Morrisville, Vermont

Helen Traubel
American opera singer
• Leading NY Met. Wagnerian soprano, 1939-53; forced to resign due to nightclub appearances.
b. June 2, 1899 in Saint Louis, Missouri
d. July 28, 1972 in Santa Monica, California

Mary Travers
(Peter Paul and Mary)
American singer
• Member of folk music trio, popular in 1960s; hits include number-one single "Leavin' on a Jet Plane," 1969.
b. November 07, 1937 in Louisville, Kentucky

Merle Robert Travis
American musician–singer
• Country Music Hall of Fame, 1977; compositions include "16 Tons," "Old Mountain Dew"; created "Travis-style" guitar playing.
b. November 29, 1917 in Rosewood, Kentucky
d. October 2, 1983 in Park Hill, Oklahoma

Randy Travis
(Randy Traywick)
American singer
• Country singer; had number one single "Forever and Ever, Amen," 1987.
b. May 04, 1959 in Marshville, North Carolina

John Jay Traynor
(Jay and the Americans)
American singer
• Lead singer, original "Jay" of Jay and the Americans, 1961-62.

Leonard Joseph Tristano
American jazz musician
• Blind avant-garde pianist, active, late 1940s; noted for jazz improvisations.
b. March 19, 1919 in Chicago, Illinois
d. 1978 in Jamaica, New York

Triumph
(Rick Emmet; Mike Levine; Gil Moore)
Canadian music group
• Albums include *Best Of*, 1985.

The Troggs
(Ronnie Bond; Chris Britton; Tony Murray; Reg Presley)
British music group
• Cabaret, club performers since 1966; albums include *Love is All Around*, 1967. Single "Wild Thing."

John Scott Trotter
American musician–songwriter
• Pianist, arranger for Bing Crosby radio shows, 1930s-40s; won Oscar for scoring *Pennies From Heaven*, 1961.
b. June 14, 1908 in Charlotte, North Carolina
d. October 29, 1975 in Los Angeles, California

Bobby (Robert William) Troup
American actor–songwriter–singer
• Former bandleader who played Dr. Joe Early in TV series "Emergency," 1972-77; wrote "Daddy," 1941; "Route 66," 1946.
b. October 18, 1918 in Harrisburg, Pennsylvania

Robin Trower
(Procol Harum)
English musician
• Albums include *Beyond the Mist*, 1985.
b. March 09, 1945 in London, England

Tatiana Troyanos
American opera singer
• Mezzo-soprano; starred in *Ariodante*, opening of Kennedy Center, 1971.
b. September 12, 1938 in New York, New York

Frank(ie) Trumbauer
American songwriter–bandleader
• C-melody saxist; with Paul Whiteman, 1927-36; recorded classics with Beiderbecke.
b. May 3, 1901 in Carbondale, Illinois
d. June 11, 1956 in Kansas City, Missouri

Ernie (Ernest) Tubb
American singer–musician–songwriter
• Country music legend who wrote over 150 songs including hit "Walking the Floor over You," 1941.
b. February 09, 1914 in Crisp, Texas
d. September 06, 1984 in Nashville, Tennessee

The Tubes
(Rich Anderson; Michael Cotten; Prairie Prince; Bill Spooner; Roger Steen; Re Styles; Fee Waybill; Vince Welnick)
American music group
• Begun late 1960s, combining rock, theater, satire; appeared in film *Xanadu*, 1980.

Orrin Tucker
American bandleader
• Led dance bands, 1930s-40s; recorded "Oh, Johnny, Oh" with Bonnie Baker, 1939.
b. February 17, 1911 in Saint Louis, Missouri

Richard Tucker
(Reuben Tickel)
American opera singer–actor
• Considered best operatic tenor, 1940s-
50s.
b. August 28, 1913 in Brooklyn, New York
d. January 08, 1975 in Kalamazoo, Michigan

Sophie Tucker
(Sophia Kalish)
American singer
• Vaudeville performer billed as "last of
the red-hot Mamas."
b. January 13, 1884 in Russia
d. February 09, 1966 in New York, New
York

Tanya (Denise) Tucker
American singer
• First hit at age 14; millionaire by 16;
hit song "Delta Dawn," 1973.
b. October 1, 1958 in Seminole, Texas

Tommy Tucker
American bandleader
• Led hotel-style dance bands, 1930s-
50s; best known song was "I Don't
Want to Set the World on Fire."
b. May 18, 1908 in Souris, North Dakota
d. July 11, 1989 in Sarasota, Florida

Alice Tully
American singer–philanthropist
• Former operatic soprano; donated Alice
Tully Hall, chamber music recital hall in
Lincoln Center for Performing Arts,
NYC.
b. October 11, 1902 in Corning, New York

Rosalyn Tureck
American pianist
• Specialized in Bach; founded Int'l.
Bach Society, 1966.
b. December 14, 1914 in Chicago, Illinois

Dame Eva Turner
English opera singer
• Dramatic soprano; 35-year career
earned her the unofficial title of England's greatest soprano; won renown in
title role in Puccini's "Turandot."
b. March 1, 1892 in Oldham, England
d. June 16, 1990 in London, England

Ike Turner
(Ike and Tina Turner)
American singer–songwriter
• Wrote, sang hit songs "A Fool in Love
(Tell Me What's Wrong)," 1960; "Good-
bye, So Long," 1971.
b. November 05, 1931 in Clarksdale, Missis-
sippi

Joe Turner
American jazz musician
• Blues vocalist; rock pioneer; recorded
classic "Shake, Rattle, and Roll," 1954.
b. May 18, 1911 in Kansas City, Missouri
d. November 24, 1985 in Hollywood, California

Tina Turner
(Anna Mae Bullock; Ike and Tina Turn-
er)
American singer
• Won Grammys for "Proud Mary,"
1972; "What's Love Got to Do With
It?," 1984.
b. November 26, 1938 in Nutbush, Tennessee

The Turtles
(Howard Kaylan; Don Murray; Al Nichol;
Jim Pons; Chuck Portz; John Seiter; Jim
Tucker)
American music group
• Underrated cult band during Beatles
era; hits include "Happy Together,"
1967.

Twisted Sister
(Jay Jay French; Mark the Animal Men-
doza; Eddie Fingers Ojeda; A J Pero;
Dee Snider)
American music group
• Heavy metal group formed 1976,
known for wild attire, hard rock sound;
first single "We're Not Gonna Take It,"
1984.

Conway Twitty
(Harold Lloyd Jenkins; "The High Priest
of Country Music")
American singer–songwriter
• Began as rock-n-roll singer, later
turned to country music: "Lonely Boy
Blue," 1960.
b. September 01, 1933 in Friars Point, Mississippi

Bonnie Tyler
(Gaynor Hopkins)
Welsh singer
• Raspy-voiced singer who had number
one hit "Total Eclipse of the Heart,"
1983.
b. June 08, 1953 in Swansea, Wales

Steve Tyler
(Aerosmith)
American musician–singer
• Vocalist with heavy-metal band since
1970; hit album *Toys in the Attic*,
1975, went platinum.
b. March 26, 1948 in Boston, Massachusetts

Ian Tyson
(Ian and Sylvia)
Canadian singer–songwriter
• Former rodeo performer; played blues,
folk material; formed duo, 1959.
b. September 25, 1933 in Victoria, British
Columbia

Sylvia Fricker Tyson
(Ian and Sylvia; Mrs Ian Tyson)
Canadian singer–songwriter
• With husband formed folksinging coun-
try duo; hits include "You Were on My
Mind," 1964.
b. September 19, 1940 in Chatham, Ontario

U2
(Adam Clayton; The Edge (David Howell
Evans); Larry Mullen Jr; "Bono Vox"
(Paul Hewson))
Irish music group
• Third album *War*, 1983, described vio-
lence in N Ireland.

UB 40
(Astro (Terence Wilson); James Brown;
Ali Campbell; Robin Campbell; Earl Fal-
coner; Norman Hassan; Brian Travers;
Michael Virture)
English music group
• Reggae group formed 1978; named for
number of British unemployment benefits
card.

UFO
(Neil Carter; Paul Chapman; Phil Mogg;
Andy Parker; Michael Schenker; Pete
Way)
British music group
• Formed 1971; hard-rock band whose
hits include *The Wild, the Willing, and
the Innocent*, 1982.

Leslie (Marian Crayne) Uggams
American singer–actress
• Won Tony for *Hallelujah Baby*, 1968;
played Kizzy in TV epic, "Roots," 1977.
b. May 25, 1943 in New York, New York

Hermann Uhde
German opera singer
• Noted bass-baritone, noted for Wagnerian roles; died on stage.
b. July 2, 1914 in Bremen, Germany
d. October 1, 1965 in Copenhagen, Denmark

James Ulmer
("Blood")
American musician
• Sound based on blues, hard rock,
avant-garde jazz; albums include *Free
Lancing*, 1982.
b. 1942 in Saint Matthews, South Carolina

Bjorn Ulvaeus
(ABBA)
Swedish singer–musician
• With group since 1973; hits include "Dancing Queen," 1977; "Take a Chance on Me," 1978.
b. April 25, 1945 in Stockholm, Sweden

Caroline Unger
Austrian opera singer
• Contralto known for turning Beethoven around to see audience applause after first performance of ninth symphony, 1824.
b. October 28, 1803 in Vienna, Austria
d. March 23, 1877 in Florence, Italy

Uriah Heep
(Mick Box; David Byron; Ken Hensley; Al Napier; Paul Newton)
English music group
• Rock group whose albums include *Demons And Wizards*, 1972; not liked by critics.

Viorica Ursuleac
Romanian opera singer
• Considered the ideal soprano by R Strauss; noted also for Mozart, Wagner roles.
b. March 26, 1899 in Czernowitz, Romania

Vladimir Ussachevsky
Composer
• Works using electronic sound include *The Creation*, 1961; a founder, Princeton Electronic Music Center, 1959.
b. October 21, 1911 in Hailar, China
d. January 04, 1990 in New York, New York

Jerry Vale
(Gerano Louis Vitaliamo)
American singer
• Hit singles include "Innamorata," 1956; "Dommage, Dommage," 1966.
b. July 08, 1932 in Bronx, New York

Ritchie Valens
(Richard Valenzuela)
American singer
• Had number one single "La Bamba," 1958; life story filmed, 1987. Killed in plane crash.
b. May 13, 1941 in Pacoima, California
d. February 03, 1959 in Clear Lake, Iowa

Rudy (Hubert Prior) Vallee
American actor–singer
• Saxophonist, vaudeville performer; known for using megaphone, theme song "My Time Is Your Time."
b. July 28, 1901 in Island Pond, Vermont
d. July 03, 1986 in Hollywood, California

Frankie Valli
(Francis Castelluccio; The Four Seasons)
American singer
• Hits include "Sherry"; "Big Girls Don't Cry"; "My Eyes Adored You."
b. May 03, 1937 in Newark, New Jersey

Egbert Anson VanAlstyne
American songwriter–musician
• Wrote over 700 songs, including "In the Shade of the Old Apple Tree."
b. March 05, 1882 in Chicago, Illinois
d. July 09, 1951 in Chicago, Illinois

Luther Vandross
American singer–musician
• First album *Never Too Much*, 1971 was platinum; vocal arranger of Donna Summer/Barbra Streisand duet "Enough Is Enough."
b. April 2, 1951 in New York, New York

Vangelis
(Evangelos Papathanassiou)
Greek composer
• Won Oscar for score of *Chariots of Fire*, 1982.
b. March 29, 1943 in Volos, Greece

Van Halen
(Michael Anthony; Sammy Hagar; David Lee Roth; Alex Van Halen; Eddie Van Halen)
American music group
• California-based, heavy metal rock band; first number-one hit was "Jump," 1984.

Alex Van Halen
(Van Halen)
American musician
• Drummer, brother of Eddie Van Halen.
b. May 08, 1955 in Nijmegen, Netherlands

Eddie (Edward) Van Halen
(Van Halen)
American musician–singer
• One of world's top guitarists with band Van Halen since 1974.
b. January 26, 1957 in Nijmegen, Netherlands

Jimmy (James) Van Heusen
(Edward Chester Babcock)
American songwriter
• "Architect of melody," known for collaborations with Sammy Kahn; with Kahn, won Oscars for "All the Way," 1957, "High Hopes," 1959, "Call Me Irresponsible," 1963.
b. January 26, 1913 in Syracuse, New York
d. February 06, 1990 in Rancho Mirage, California

Vanilla Fudge
(Carmine Appice; Tim Bogert; Vincent Martell; Mark Stein)
American music group
• One of first heavy-rock bands, formed 1966; known for psychedelic light shows.

Vanity
(Denise Mathews)
American singer–actress
• Recorded album *Nasty Girl* with Vanity 6; solo *Wild Animal*, 1985; in film *The Last Dragon*, 1985.
b. in Niagara Falls, New York

Gino Vannelli
Canadian singer–songwriter
• One of first pop artists to perform without guitars or bass; "Wheels of Life," 1979; "Living Inside Myself."
b. June 16, 1952 in Montreal, Quebec

Ronnie (Ronald) Van Zant
(Lynyrd Skynard)
American musician–singer
• Founding member of classic southern rock band, 1973-77; group ended when he and others were killed in plane crash.
b. 1949
d. October 2, 1977 in Mississippi

Edgar Varese
American composer–author
• Founded, directed International Composers Guild, 1921-27; developed electronic music, 1917.
b. December 22, 1883 in Paris, France
d. November 06, 1965 in New York, New York

Sergei Vassilenko
Russian composer
• Wrote operas *Christopher Columbus*, 1933; *Buran*, 1939; works inspired by Russian folk songs, the East.
b. March 3, 1872 in Moscow, Russia
d. March 11, 1956 in Moscow, U.S.S.R.

Jimmy Vaughan
American musician
• Former guitarist for *Fabulous Thunderbirds*, known for blues-driven sound; with brother Stevie Ray recorded *Family Style* in 1990.
b. March 20, 1951 in Dallas, Texas

Sarah Lois Vaughan
American singer
• Jazz vocalist, pianist; career took off after winning contest at Apollo Theater, NYC, 1942.
b. March 27, 1924 in Newark, New Jersey
d. April 03, 1990 in Los Angeles, California

Stevie Ray Vaughan
American musician–singer–songwriter
• Premier blues guitarist. Died in helicopter crash leaving a concert. Won Grammy in 1984 for *Texas Flood;* in 1989 for *In Step.*
b. 1956 in Dallas, Texas
d. August 27, 1990 in East Troy, Wisconsin.

Bobby Vee
(Robert Velline)
American singer
• Teen idol singer similar to Frankie Avalon, Fabian; songs include "Take Good Care of My Baby," 1961.
b. April 3, 1943 in Fargo, North Dakota

Suzanne Vega
American singer–songwriter
• Blends jazz, rock and roll, and minimalism; had hit single "Luka," 1987.
b. July 11, 1959 in Santa Monica, California

Giovanni Battista Velluti
Italian opera singer
• Male soprano, considered last great castrato; shocked, fascinated Londoners, 1820s.
b. January 28, 1780 in Monterone, Italy
d. January 22, 1861 in Sambruson, Italy

The Velvet Underground
(John Cale; Sterling Morrison; Lou Reed; Marueen Tucker)
American music group
• Formed, 1965; never sold many records but influenced David Bowie, the Cars, the Sex Pistols, and countless others.

Charlie Ventura
American jazz musician
• Noted tenor saxist; with Gene Krupa, 1940s.
b. December 02, 1916 in Philadelphia, Pennsylvania

The Ventures
(Bob Bogle; Johnny Durrill; Nokie Edwards; Howie Johnston; JerryMcGee; Mel Taylor; Don Wilson)
American music group
• Instrumental rock group, formed 1960; hits include "Walk, Don't Run," 1960; "Hawaii Five-O," 1969.

Giuseppe Fortunino Francesco Verdi
Italian composer
• Composed 27 operas, including *Rigoletto; La Traviata; Aida.*
b. October 1, 1813 in Le Roncole, Italy
d. January 27, 1901 in Milan, Italy

Shirley Carter Verrett
American opera singer
• Mezzo-soprano; made NY Met. debut, 1968; 1955 Marion Anderson winner.
b. May 31, 1933 in New Orleans, Louisiana

Sid Vicious
(John Simon Ritchie; The Sex Pistols)
English singer
• Bass player, vocalist with punk rock group, 1977-78; arrested for murder, 1978; died of drug overdose.
b. 1957
d. February 02, 1979 in New York, New York

Jon Vickers
Canadian opera singer
• Among finest postwar heroic tenors; made recordings, operatic films; had NY Met. debut, 1960.
b. October 29, 1926 in Prince Albert, Saskatchewan

Heitor Villa-Lobos
Brazilian composer
• Wrote over 1,400 works including *Bachianas Brasileiras,* 1930-44, featuring national folk music.
b. March 05, 1887 in Rio de Janeiro, Brazil
d. November 17, 1959 in Rio de Janeiro, Brazil

Gene Vincent
(Vincent Eugene Craddock)
American singer
• Known for wild habits on/off stage; recorded "Pistol Packin' Mama," 1960.
b. February 11, 1935 in Norfolk, Virginia
d. October 12, 1971 in Hollywood, California

Cleanhead (Eddie) Vinson
American jazz musician–singer
• Saxophonist, vocalist; sang with Cootie Williams, 1940s; own band, 1960s.
b. December 18, 1917 in Houston, Texas
d. July 02, 1988 in Los Angeles, California

Bobby (Stanley Robert) Vinton
American singer
• Hits include "Blue Velvet"; had sold over 25 million records by 1974.
b. April 16, 1935 in Canonsburg, Pennsylvania

Giovanni Battista Viotti
Italian musician–composer
• Foremost violinist of his time; played for royalty, directed the Paris Opera.
b. May 23, 1753 in Vercelli, Italy
d. March 03, 1824 in London, England

Galina (Pavlovna) Vishnevskaya
Russian opera singer
• First Russian diva to sing with Metropolitan Opera, 1961, in title role of *Aida.*
b. October 25, 1926 in Leningrad, U.S.S.R.

Antonio Lucio Vivaldi
Italian musician–composer
• Violinist, famous for over 100 concertos including *The Four Seasons.*
b. March 04, 1675 in Venice, Italy
d. July 27, 1741 in Vienna, Austria

Heinrich Vogl
German opera singer
• Leading Wagnerian tenor at Bayreuth, 1876-97.
b. January 15, 1845 in Aue, Germany
d. April 21, 1900 in Munich, Germany

The Vogues
(Charles Blasko; William Burkette; Hugh Geyer; Don Miller)
American music group
• Formed, 1960; hits include "Turn Around Look At Me," 1968.

Andreas Vollenweider
Swiss musician
• Cult harpist who combines jazz, classical styles; has million-selling albums *Behind the Gardens,* 1981; *Caverna Magica,* 1982.
b. 1953 in Zurich, Switzerland

Frederica VonStade
(Mrs Peter Elkus; "Flicka")
American opera singer
• Mezzo-soprano; had NY Met. debut in 1970; noted for Wagner, Rossini roles.
b. June 01, 1945 in Somerville, New Jersey

Albert Von Tilzer
(Albert Gumm)
American composer
• Best known for song "Take Me Out to the Ball Game."
b. March 29, 1878 in Indianapolis, Indiana
d. October 01, 1956 in Los Angeles, California

Harry Von Tilzer
(Harry Gumm)
American publisher–songwriter
• Published two thousand songs including "Wait Till the Sun Shines, Nellie"; "In the Sweet Bye-and-Bye."
b. July 08, 1872 in Detroit, Michigan
d. January 1, 1946 in New York, New York

Vitya Vronsky
(Victoria Vronsky; Vronsky and Babin)
American pianist
• Performed two-piano concerts with husband, Victor, since 1937.
b. August 22, 1909 in Evpatoria, Russia

Vladimir Semyonovich Vysotsky
Russian actor–singer–songwriter
• Best known as ballad singer whose songs were mildly critical of Soviet officials.
b. 1938 in U.S.S.R.
d. July 25, 1980 in Moscow, U.S.S.R.

Richard Wagner
(Wilhelm Richard Wagner)
German composer–librettist–poet
• Opera themes derived from medieval legends; wrote *Lohengrin, Tristan, Die Meistersinger;* founded Bayreuth Festival, 1876.
b. March 22, 1813 in Leipzig, Germany
d. February 13, 1883 in Venice, Italy

Rudolf Wagner-Regeny
Romanian composer
• Operas include *Johanna Balk,* 1941; director of the State Conservatory in East Berlin, 1950.
b. August 28, 1903 in Regen, Romania
d. September 18, 1969 in Berlin, Germany

Porter Wagoner
American singer
• With Grand Ole Opry, 1957–; won three CMA awards with Dolly Parton.
b. August 12, 1927 in West Plains, Missouri

Bea Wain
American singer
• Famous for renditions of "My Reverie," "Deep Purple," 1938; popular in 1930s-40s.
b. April 3, 1917 in New York, New York

Loudon Wainwright III
American musician–singer–songwriter
• Acoustic guitarist; albums include *Fame and Wealth,* 1983.
b. September 05, 1947 in Chapel Hill, North Carolina

John Waite
(The Babys)
English singer–songwriter
• Had hit single, "Missing You," 1984.
b. July 04, 1955 in England

Tom Waits
American musician
• Beatnik revivalist; was opening act for Frank Zappa, 1970s; appeared as pianist in film *Paradise Alley,* 1979.
b. December 07, 1949 in Pomona, California

Jimmy Wakely
American actor–singer–songwriter
• Starred in movie westerns, 1940s; had CBS radio show, 1952-57.
b. February 16, 1914 in Mineola, Arkansas
d. September 23, 1982 in Los Angeles, California

Rick Wakeman
(Yes)
English musician
• Wrote film scores for *The Burning,* 1981; *Journey to the Center of the Earth,* 1974.
b. May 18, 1949 in London, England

Edyth Walker
American opera singer
• Mezzo-soprano, noted for Wagner roles; among first Americans accepted in European opera houses.
b. March 27, 1867 in Hopewell, New York
d. February 19, 1950 in New York, New York

Junior (Autrey de Walt) Walker
(Jr Walker and the All-Stars)
American musician–singer
• Saxophonist; hits include "Shotgun," 1965; "How Sweet It Is," 1966.
b. 1942 in Blythesville, Arkansas

T-Bone (Aaron) Walker
American singer–musician–songwriter
• Blues guitarist who popularized the use of the electric guitar.
b. May 28, 1910 in Linden, Texas
d. March 16, 1975 in Los Angeles, California

Sippie Wallace
(Beulah Thomas; "Texas Nightingale")
American singer
• Major 1920s blues singer; received Grammy nomination for *Sippie,* 1983.
b. November 01, 1898 in Houston, Texas
d. November 01, 1986 in Detroit, Michigan

Alfred Franz Wallenstein
American musician–conductor
• Cellist; one of first native American symphonic conductors to gain national status; directed LA Philharmonic, 1943-56.
b. October 07, 1898 in Chicago, Illinois
d. February 08, 1983 in New York, New York

Fats (Thomas Wright) Waller
American jazz musician–songwriter
• Stride pianist, famed entertainer, singer; wrote "Ain't Misbehavin'," "Honeysuckle Rose."
b. May 21, 1904 in New York, New York
d. December 15, 1943 in Kansas City, Missouri

Gordon Waller
(Peter and Gordon)
Scottish singer–musician
• Part of Peter and Gordon duo, 1961-68; biggest hit "World without Love," 1964, written by Paul McCartney.
b. June 04, 1945 in Braemar, Scotland

Joe (Joseph Fidler) Walsh
(The Eagles; The James Gang)
American musician–singer
• Joined James Gang, 1971; Eagles, 1976-82; solo albums include *The Confessor,* 1985.
b. November 2, 1947 in Cleveland, Ohio

Bruno Walter
(Bruno Schlesinger)
American conductor–pianist
• An authority on the interpretation of the works of Mahler, Mozart.
b. September 15, 1876 in Berlin, Germany
d. February 17, 1962 in Beverly Hills, California

Sir William Turner Walton
English composer
• Composed "Orb and Sceptre" (Coronation March), 1953, for coronation of Elizabeth II.
b. March 29, 1902 in Oldham, England
d. March 08, 1983 in Ischia, Italy

Wang Chang
(Darren Costin; Nick Feldman; Jack Hues)
English music group
• Jazz/rock group formed 1981; name is Chinese for "perfect pitch."

William Caesar Warfield
American singer
• Best known for roles in *Showboat,* 1951; *Porgy & Bess,* 1952; husband of Leontyne Price.
b. January 22, 1920 in West Helena, Arkansas

Jennifer Warnes
American singer
• Sang Oscar-winning song "Up Where We Belong," 1983, with Joe Cocker.
b. 1947 in Orange County, California

Harry Warren
(Salvatore Guaragna)
American songwriter
• Wrote hundreds of popular songs for plays, films; won Oscars for hits "Lullaby of Broadway," 1935; "You'll Never Know," 1940; "On the Atchinson, Topeka and the Santa Fe," 1946.
b. December 24, 1893 in New York, New York
d. September 22, 1981 in Los Angeles, California

Leonard Warren
American opera singer
• Leading baritone from 1940s; noted for Rigoletto role; died on stage at NY Met.
b. April 21, 1911 in New York, New York
d. March 04, 1960 in New York, New York

Dionne Warwick
American singer
- Three-time Grammy winner; hits include "Alfie," 1967; "That's What Friends are For," 1985.
b. December 12, 1941 in East Orange, New Jersey

Buck (Ford Lee) Washington
(Buck and Bubbles)
American jazz musician–comedian
- Part of comedy team with John Sublett, 1919-53.
b. October 16, 1903 in Louisville, Kentucky
d. January 31, 1955 in New York, New York

Dinah Washington
(Ruth Jones; "Queen of the Blues")
American singer
- Adapted blues style to pop songs; with Lionel Hampton's band, 1943-49.
b. August 29, 1924 in Tuscaloosa, Alabama
d. December 14, 1963 in Detroit, Michigan

Grover Washington, Jr
American musician
- Jazz saxophonist; crossed over to pop with 1981 hit "Just the Two of Us," with Bill Withers.
b. December 12, 1943 in Buffalo, New York

Muddy Waters
(McKinley Morganfield)
American singer–musician
- Won five Grammys; hits include "I'm a Man"; "I've Got My Mojo Working."
b. April 04, 1915 in Rolling Fork, Mississippi
d. April 3, 1983 in Downers Grove, Illinois

Jody Watley
American singer
- Won Grammy for best new artist, 1988; hits include "Looking for a New Love," 1987; granddaughter of Jackie Wilson.
b. January 3, 1961 in Chicago, Illinois

Doc (Arthel Lane) Watson
American musician
- Country music entertainer, considered finest interpreter of guitar flat-picking in world; with son, Merle, won two Grammys, 1970s.
b. March 02, 1923 in Deep Gap, North Carolina

Douglas Benjamin Watt
American composer–author
- Drama critic for NY Daily News, 1937-70; contributor, New Yorker mag.; wrote After All These Years.
b. January 2, 1914 in New York, New York

Andre Watts
American musician
- Internationally famous pianist; played at Nixon's inaugural concert, 1969.
b. June 2, 1946 in Nuremberg, Germany

Charlie (Charles Robert) Watts
(The Rolling Stones)
English singer–musician
- Drummer, original member of Rolling Stones, 1964-.
b. June 02, 1941 in Islington, England

Fee Waybill
(The Tubes; John Waldo)
American singer
- Lead singer for The Tubes since late 1960s.
b. September 17, 1950 in Omaha, Nebraska

Weather Report
(Alejandro Acuna; Alphonso Johnson; Jaco Pastorius; Wayne Shorter; Chester Thompson; Norada Walden; Josef Zawainul)
American music group
- Modern jazz instrumental hit "Birdland," 1978.

Teddy Weatherford
American jazz musician
- Pianist, leading exponent of "Chicago-style" jazz, 1920s.
b. October 11, 1903 in Bluefield, West Virginia
d. April 25, 1945 in Calcutta, India

The Weavers
(Erik Darling; Lee Hays; Fred Hellerman; Bernie Krause; Pete Seeger)
American music group
- Popular folk group, 1948-63; hits include "On Top of Old Smoky," 1951; "Good Night Irene," 1950; pioneered in making folk music commercially successful.

Chick (William) Webb
American jazz musician
- Drummer, bandleader, 1920s-30s; noted for "Stompin' at the Savoy"; introduced Ella Fitzgerald.
b. February 1, 1902 in Baltimore, Maryland
d. 1939 in Baltimore, Maryland

Jim Webb
American composer
- Wrote songs "Up, Up, and Away," 1967; "MacArthur Park," 1968; "Galveston," 1969.
b. August 15, 1946 in Elk City, Oklahoma

Andrew Lloyd Webber
American composer
- Musicals include Jesus Christ Superstar, 1970; Cats, 1981; Phantom of the Opera, 1988, won seven Tonys; leader of "British invasion" on Broadway.
b. March 22, 1948 in London, England

Carl Maria von Weber
German composer
- Founder, German Romantic school; wrote operas Der Freishutz, 1821; Oberon, 1826.
b. November 18, 1786 in Eutin, Germany
d. June 05, 1826 in London, England

Paul Francois Webster
American lyricist
- Wrote over 500 songs including Oscar-winning "Shadow of Your Smile," 1965.
b. December 2, 1907 in New York, New York
d. March 22, 1984 in Beverly Hills, California

Robert Weede
American singer
- Baritone with NY Met., San Francisco Opera; starred in Broadway's Most Happy Fella, 1956; Tony nominee for Cry for Us All, 1970.
b. February 22, 1903 in Baltimore, Maryland
d. July 1, 1972 in Walnut Creek, California

Kurt Weill
American composer
- Best known work Threepenny Opera, 1928; also wrote One Touch of Venus, and "September Song."
b. March 02, 1900 in Dessau, Germany
d. April 03, 1950 in New York, New York

George Theodore Wein
American musician–producer
- Founded Newport Jazz Festival, 1954; produces jazz festivals throughout country.
b. October 03, 1925 in Boston, Massachusetts

Max M Weinberg
(E Street Band; "Mighty Max")
American musician
- Drummer with Bruce Springsteen's band since 1974. Known for big whopping beat.
b. April 13, 1951 in South Orange, New Jersey

Jaromir Weinberger
American composer
- Wrote immensely popular Bohemian-style opera, Schwanda the Bagpiper, 1927.
b. January 08, 1896 in Prague, Czechoslovakia
d. August 06, 1967 in Saint Petersburg, Florida

Bob (Robert Hall) Weir
(The Grateful Dead)
American singer–musician
• Recorded solo album *Bombs Away*, 1978.
b. October 16, 1949 in San Francisco, California

Alexis Sigismund Weissenberg
American pianist
• Gives over 85 int'l. concerts yearly; has made several records.
b. July 26, 1929 in Sofia, Bulgaria

Bob Welch
(Fleetwood Mac)
American musician
• Guitarist with Fleetwood Mac, 1971-75; had solo single "Sentimental Lady," 1977.
b. July 31, 1946 in Los Angeles, California

Ken Welch
American writer–composer–songwriter
• With wife, Mitzie, won Emmys for music for TV specials including "Linda in Wonderland," 1981.
b. February 04, 1926 in Kansas City, Missouri

Mitzie Welch
(Marilyn Cottle)
American writer–composer–songwriter
• With husband, Ken, won several Emmys including "Carol Burnett Show," 1976.
b. July 25, in McDonald, Pennsylvania

Lawrence Welk
American bandleader
• Started band, 1927; host of TV's "The Lawrence Welk Show," 1955-59.
b. March 11, 1903 in Strasburg, North Dakota

Egon Wellesz
Austrian composer–musicologist
• Expert on Byzantine music; wrote many operas.
b. October 21, 1885 in Vienna, Austria
d. November 09, 1974 in Oxford, England

Kitty Wells
(Muriel Deason Wright)
American singer
• Award-winning Grand Ole Opry star since 1950s; Country Music Hall of Fame, 1976.
b. August 3, 1919 in Nashville, Tennessee

Mary Wells
American singer
• Sang "Bye, Bye, Baby," 1961; "Two Lovers," 1962; "My Guy," 1964.
b. May 13, 1943 in Detroit, Michigan

Percy Wenrich
American songwriter
• Wrote songs "Moonlight Bay," "Put on Your Old Gray Bonnet."
b. January 23, 1887 in Joplin, Missouri
d. March 17, 1952 in New York, New York

Dottie West
(Dorothy Marie Marsh; Mrs Alan Winters)
American singer
• Country music star known for duets with Jim Reeves, Jimmy Dean, Kenny Rogers; won Clio for cowriting "Country Sunshine" for commercials, 1973, the first awarded to a country artist.
b. October 11, 1932 in McMinnville, Tennessee

Wham
(George Michael; Andrew Ridgeley)
English music group
• Childhood friends who formed group, 1982-86; had three number one hits, including "Everything She Wants," 1985.

Barry White
American singer
• Hits include "Never, Never Gonna Give You Up," 1973; "My First, My Last, My Everything," 1974.
b. September 12, 1944 in Galveston, Texas

Josh(ua Daniel) White
American singer
• Folk singer who recorded, performed internationally, 1930s-60s; known for ballads: "Ballad of John Henry."
b. February 11, 1908 in Greenville, South Carolina
d. September 05, 1969 in Manhasset, New York

Paul Whiteman
American bandleader
• Popularized jazz music, 1920s-30s; commissioned, introduced George Gershwin's *Rhapsody in Blue*, 1924; had radio show, 1930s-40s.
b. March 28, 1891 in Denver, Colorado
d. December 29, 1967 in Doylestown, Pennsylvania

Margaret Whiting
American singer
• Popular pop vocalist, 1940s-50s; daughter of Richard.
b. July 22, 1924 in Detroit, Michigan

Richard Armstrong Whiting
American composer
• Leading composer for 1930s movies; hits include "Sleepy Time Gal," 1925.
b. November 12, 1891 in Peoria, Illinois
d. February 1, 1938 in Beverly Hills, California

Arthur Austin Whittemore
(Whittemore and Lowe; "Buck")
American pianist
• With Jack Lowe, member of two-piano team popular, 1940s-60s.
b. October 23, 1916 in Vermillion, South Dakota
d. October 23, 1984 in Long Island, New York

The Who
(Roger Daltry; John Entwistle; Kenny Jones; Keith Moon; Peter Towshend)
English music group
• Leading rock band, 1960s-70s; hits ranged from hard rock and country to rock opera *Tommy*, 1969.

Henri (Henryk) Wieniawski
Polish violinist–composer
• Virtuoso; toured US with Anton Rubinstein, 1870s; wrote violin classics.
b. July 1, 1835 in Lublin, Poland
d. April 02, 1880 in Moscow, Russia

Earl Wild
American pianist–composer
• Pianist with NBC Orchestra; performed first piano recital on TV.
b. November 26, 1915 in Pittsburgh, Pennsylvania

Kim Wilde
English singer
• Hit singles include "Kids in America," 1981; "Rage To Love," 1985.
b. November 18, 1960 in London, England

Alec (Alexander Lafayette Chew) Wilder
American composer
• Writer of lyrical pop, jazz, classical works; arranged for Frank Sinatra, Judy Garland, Jimmy Dorsey, others.
b. February 17, 1907 in Rochester, New York
d. December 24, 1980 in Gainesville, Florida

Andy Williams
(Howard Andrew Williams)
American singer
• Award-winning crooner known for easy-going style; hits include "Where Do I Begin?," 1971; "Lonely Street," 1959.
b. December 03, 1930 in Wall Lake, Iowa

Cootie (Charles Melvin) Williams
American jazz musician
• Last surviving member of Duke Ellington Orchestra of 1920s; known for growling, muted trumpet.
b. July 24, 1908 in Mobile, Alabama
d. September 15, 1985 in Long Island, New York

Deniece Williams
American singer
• Number one hits "Too Much, Too Little, Too Late," with Johnny Mathis, 1978; "Let's Hear It for the Boy," 1984.
b. June 03, 1951 in Gary, Indiana

Don Williams
American musician–singer
• Guitarist; laid-back style in hits *Cafe Carolina*, 1984.
b. May 27, 1939 in Floydada, Texas

Hank (Hiram King) Williams
(hakespeare ")
American singer–songwriter
• Instrumental in popularizing country-western music; hits include "Your Cheatin' Heart"; "Jambalaya."
b. September 15, 1923 in Georgiana, Alabama
d. January 01, 1953 in West Virginia

Hank Williams, Jr
American singer
• Country-western star since 1960s; hits include "Texas Women," 1981; Country Music Entertainer of the Year, 1987, 1988.
b. May 26, 1949 in Shreveport, Louisiana

Joe Williams
(Joseph Goreed)
American singer
• Blues, jazz, ballads singer, known for hits with Count Basie, including "Everyday I Have the Blues," 1955.
b. December 12, 1918 in Cordele, Georgia

John Williams
(Sky)
Australian musician
• Classical guitarist; solo album *Echoes of London*, 1986.
b. April 24, 1941 in Melbourne, Australia

John Towner Williams
American composer–conductor
• Conductor, Boston Pops, 1980–; won Oscars for scores of *Jaws*, 1975; *Star Wars*, 1977.
b. February 08, 1932 in Flushing, New York

Mary Lou Williams
American composer–musician
• Contributed to growth of bebop style, 1940s; wrote for Benny Goodman, Duke Ellington.
b. May 08, 1910 in Pittsburgh, Pennsylvania
d. May 28, 1981 in Durham, North Carolina

Mason Williams
American composer–musician–author
• Won Grammy, 1969, for "Classical Gas."
b. August 24, 1938 in Abilene, Texas

Milan Williams
(The Commodores)
American musician–singer
• Drummer since group's founding, 1971; wrote hit instrumental "Machine Gun," 1974.
b. 1947 in Mississippi

Patrick Williams
American composer
• Won Emmys for theme songs for TV shows "Lou Grant," 1980; "The Princess and the Cabbie," 1982.
b. April 23, 1939 in Bonne Terre, Missouri

Paul Hamilton Williams
American singer–songwriter
• Won 1976 Oscar for best song: "Evergreen."
b. September 19, 1940 in Omaha, Nebraska

Roger Williams
American pianist
• Popular hits include "Autumn Leaves," 1955; "Born Free," 1966.
b. October 01, 1926 in Omaha, Nebraska

Tex Williams
American musician–actor
• Country-western singer popular in films, 1930s-50s; best-selling hit singles include "Smoke! Smoke! Smoke!"
b. August 23, 1917 in Ramsey, Illinois
d. October 11, 1985 in Newhall, California

Robin Williamson
(Incredible String Band)
Scottish musician
• Sang, played many instruments for rock band, 1967, then began solo career; albums include *Journey's Edge*, 1977.
b. in Glasgow, Scotland

Bob Wills
American musician–songwriter
• Pioneered Western swing music; best known for song "San Antonio Rose," 1940.
b. March 06, 1906 in Limestone County, Texas
d. May 13, 1975 in Fort Worth, Texas

Meredith Willson
American composer
• Best known for Broadway hits *The Music Man*, 1957; *The Unsinkable Molly Brown*, 1960.
b. May 18, 1902 in Mason City, Iowa
d. June 15, 1984 in Santa Monica, California

Ann Wilson
(Heart)
American singer–musician
• Lead singer of Heart since 1972.
b. June 19, 1951 in San Diego, California

Brian Douglas Wilson
(The Beach Boys)
American singer–songwriter
• Vocalist, bassist, pianist with "CA rock" group; hits include "Help Me, Rhonda," 1965.
b. June 2, 1942 in Hawthorne, California

Carl Dean Wilson
(The Beach Boys)
American singer
• Vocalist, guitarist with the Beach Boys since 1961; famous "CA rock" hits include "Surfin USA," 1963.
b. December 21, 1946 in Hawthorne, California

Dennis Wilson
(The Beach Boys)
American musician–singer
• Drummer, keyboardist, singer; only member to release solo album, *Pacific Ocean Blue*.
b. December 01, 1941 in Hawthorne, California
d. December 28, 1983 in Marina del Rey, California

Jackie Wilson
American singer
• Hits include "Lonely Teardrops," 1959; "Higher and Higher," 1967.
b. June 09, 1932 in Detroit, Michigan
d. January 21, 1984 in Mount Holly, New Jersey

Mary Wilson
(The Supremes)
American singer
• Original member of 1960s-70s pop group; hits include "Where Did Our Love Go?," 1964.
b. March 06, 1944 in Greenville, Mississippi

Nancy Wilson
American singer
• Hit singles since 1963 include "Tell Me the Truth," 1963; "Face It Girl, It's Over," 1968.
b. February 2, 1937 in Chillicothe, Ohio

Nancy Wilson
(Heart)
American singer–musician
• Featured guitarist with Heart since 1972.
b. March 16, 1954 in San Francisco, California

Teddy (Theodore) Wilson
American jazz musician
• Pianist who played with Benny Goodman, 1935-39; one of first blacks to be accepted playing with white musicians.
b. November 24, 1912 in Austin, Texas
d. July 31, 1986 in New Britain, Connecticut

Jesse (James Ridout) Winchester
Canadian singer–songwriter
• Wrote pop songs, 1970s, that became hits for others: "Brand New Tennessee Waltz," "Isn't That So"; moved to Canada to avoid draft, 1967.
b. May 17, 1944 in Bossier City, Louisiana

Kai Chresten Winding
American jazz musician
• Instrumental in creating Be-Bop style of jazz; leading trombonist, 1940s-50s'; with World's Greatest Jazz Band, 1960s.
b. May 18, 1922 in Aarhus, Denmark
d. May 06, 1983 in Yonkers, New York

Hermann Winkelmann
German opera singer
• Brilliant tenor of Vienna Opera, 1880-1900; excelled in Wagnerian roles.
b. March 08, 1849 in Brunswick, Germany
d. January 18, 1912 in Vienna, Austria

Arthur Winograd
American conductor
• Founder, member, Julliard String Quartet, 1946-55; staff conductor, MGM Records, 1954-58.
b. April 22, 1920 in New York, New York

Edgar Holand Winter
(Edgar Winter Group; White Trash)
American singer–musician
• Album *They Only Come Out at Night*, 1973, had hit "Frankenstein."
b. December 28, 1946 in Beaumont, Texas

Johnny (John Dawson, III) Winter
American singer–musician
• Noted blues guitarist; produced albums for Muddy Waters.
b. February 23, 1944 in Beaumont, Texas

Paul Theodore Winter
American musician
• Leader of Paul Winter Sextet, 1961-65; first jazz group to perform at White House, 1962.
b. August 31, 1939 in Altoona, Pennsylvania

Hugo Winterhalter
American bandleader
• Arranger of 11 gold records, 1950s; songs performed by Perry Como, Doris Day.
b. August 15, 1909 in Wilkes-Barre, Pennsylvania
d. September 17, 1973 in Greenwich, Connecticut

Steve (Stevie) Winwood
(Blind Faith; The Spencer Davis Group; Traffic)
English musician–singer
• R&B vocalist; performed with several groups before solo career; hit songs include "While You See a Chance," 1982.
b. May 12, 1948 in Birmingham, England

Bill Withers
American singer–songwriter
• Hits include "Ain't No Sunshine," 1971; "Lean On Me," 1972; "Lovely Day," 1978.
b. July 04, 1938 in Slab Fork, West Virginia

Isidore Witmark
American music executive–publisher
• Internationally known music publisher, 1880s-1920s; big promoter of ragtime music.
b. June 15, 1869 in New York, New York
d. April 09, 1941 in New York, New York

Paul Wittgenstein
American pianist
• One-armed virtuoso who played left-hand concertos; brother of Ludwig.
b. November 05, 1887 in Vienna, Austria
d. March 03, 1961 in Long Island, New York

Hugo Wolf
Austrian composer
• Wrote *Italienische Serenade*, 1893; died in an asylum for the insane.
b. March 13, 1860 in Windischgraez, Austria
d. February 22, 1903 in Vienna, Austria

Peter Wolf
(J Geils Band)
American singer
• Lead vocalist, J Geils Band until 1984; solo single "I Need You Tonight," 1984.
b. March 07, 1946 in Boston, Massachusetts

Stevie Wonder
(Steveland Morris Hardaway)
American singer–musician–songwriter
• Consistently successful performer; hits include "Part-time Lover," 1985; "Skeletons in Your Closet," 1987.
b. May 13, 1951 in Saginaw, Michigan

Ron(ald) Wood
(The Rolling Stones)
English musician
• Guitarist with rock band since 1975; hits include "Going to a Go-Go," 1982.
b. June 01, 1947 in London, England

Cobina Wright
American journalist–singer
• Had leading roles in several operas; columnist for Hearst Newspapers.
b. August 14, 1921 in Lakeview, Oregon
d. April 09, 1970 in Hollywood, California

Gary Wright
(Spooky Tooth)
American musician
• Left rock band Spooky Tooth, 1970, for solo career; hit albums include *Dream Weaver*, 1976; *Really Wanna Know You*, 1981.
b. April 26, 1943 in Englewood, New Jersey

Rick (Richard) Wright
(Pink Floyd)
English singer–musician
• Keyboard player with band on and off since its formation.
b. July 28, 1945 in London, England

Syretta Wright
American singer–songwriter
• Ex-wife of Stevie Wonder; had hit "With You I'm Born Again," 1980 with Billy Preston.
b. 1946 in Pittsburgh, Pennsylvania

John Wummer
American musician
• First flutist, NY Philharmonic Orchestra, 1942-65; original member of NBC Orchestra under Arturo Toscanini, 1937.
b. 1899 in Philadelphia, Pennsylvania
d. September 06, 1977 in San Francisco, California

Bill (William George) Wyman
(The Rolling Stones)
English musician
• Bass player with The Rolling Stones; hits include *Paint It Black*, 1966; *Hang Fire*, 1982.
b. October 24, 1941 in London, England

Tammy Wynette
(Wynette Pugh)
American singer
• CMA female vocalist of year, 1968, 69, 70; autobiography *Stand by Your Man*, 1979.
b. May 04, 1942 in Tupelo, Mississippi

X
(D(on) J Bonebrake; John Doe; Exene (Christine Cervenka); Billy Zoom)
American music group
• Group formed 1977; influenced by punk, heavy metal, rockabilly, country music.

Iannis Xenakis
French composer
• Avant-garde musical theorist who developed computerized music; wrote compositions for all media including "Kottos," 1977.
b. May 29, 1922 in Braila, Romania

Jimmy (James Edward) Yancey
American jazz musician
• Pianist who helped develop boogie woogie, 1930s-40s.
b. 1894 in Chicago, Illinois
d. September 17, 1951 in Chicago, Illinois

Weird Al (Alfred Matthew) Yankovic
American singer–comedian
• Best known for satirizing rock hits: "Like a Surgeon," 1985; "I'm Fat," 1988.
b. October 23, 1959 in Los Angeles, California

Glenn Yarbrough
American singer–musician
• Best known for top-ten hit "Baby, the Rain Must Fall," from 1965 film.
b. January 12, 1930 in Milwaukee, Wisconsin

Yardbirds
(Jeff Beck; Eric Clapton; Chris Dreja; James McCarty; Jimmy Page;Keith Relf; Paul Samwell-Smith; Anthony Sopham)
English music group
• Blues-based rock band, formed 1963; albums include *Little Games*, 1967.

Peter Yarrow
(Peter Paul and Mary)
American composer–author–singer
• With group Peter, Paul and Mary, 1962-70, 1978–; won Grammy 1963; solo albums include *That's Enough for Me.*
b. May 31, 1938 in New York, New York

Jack Yellen
American author–songwriter
• Wrote "Happy Days Are Here Again," 1929.
b. July 06, 1892 in Razcki, Poland

Yes
(Jon Anderson; Peter Banks; Bill Bruford; Geoff Downes; Trevor Horn; Steve Howe; Tony Kaye; Patrick Moraz; Chris Squire; Rick Wakeman)
English music group
• Biggest hit single "Owner of a Lonely Heart," 1983.

Vincent Youmans
American composer
• Wrote song "Tea for Two," 1926; Broadway scores include *No, No, Nanette*, 1925.
b. September 27, 1898 in New York, New York
d. April 05, 1946 in Denver, Colorado

Angus Young
(AC-DC)
Scottish musician
• Knickers-clad guitarist with AC-DC since 1973.
b. March 31, 1959 in Glasgow, Scotland

Faron Young
American singer–musician
• Recorded over 60 albums, 105 singles, including 32 number-one hits; wrote "I Miss You Already," 1957.
b. February 25, 1932 in Shreveport, Louisiana

Lester Willis Young
American jazz musician
• Leading tenor saxist, prominent 1930s-40s; pioneered modern "cool" style.
b. August 27, 1909 in Woodville, Mississippi
d. March 15, 1959 in New York, New York

Malcolm Young
(AC-DC)
Scottish musician
• Guitarist, who helped form AC-DC, 1973.
b. January 06, 1953 in Glasgow, Scotland

Neil Young
(Buffalo Springfield; Crosby, Stills, Nash and Young; Crazy Horse)
Canadian musician–songwriter–singer
• Albums include *Live Rust*, 1980; *Hawks and Doves*, 1980; *Ragged Glory*, 1990. Known for lack of singing voice, excellent guitar work, and body of songwriting.
b. November 12, 1945 in Toronto, Ontario

Paul Young
(Q-Tips; Streetband)
English singer
• Lead singer turned soloist who had hit single "Everytime You Go Away," 1985.
b. 1956 in Bedfordshire, England

Ralph Young
(Sandler and Young)
American singer
• Partner with Tony Sandler, 1960s-70s; albums include *More and More.*

Trummy (James Osborne) Young
American jazz musician
• Brash trumpeter; prominent, 1930s-50s.
b. January 12, 1912 in Savannah, Georgia

Florian Zabach
American violinist
• Noted for sometimes whistling while performing in concert; mastered classic music then turned to pop.
b. August 15, 1921 in Chicago, Illinois

Nicanor Zabaleta
Spanish musician
• Known as king of the harpists; harp works written for him include *Aria and Passepied*, 1965.
b. January 07, 1907 in San Sebastian, Spain

Pia Zadora
(Mrs Meshulam Riklis)
American actress–singer
• Had successful first album *Pia and Phil*, 1985.
b. 1955 in New York, New York

Riccardo Zandonai
Italian composer
• Wrote operas *Francesca da Rimini*, 1914; *Giuliette e Romeo*, 1922; *I Cavalieri di Ekebu*, 1925.
b. May 28, 1883 in Sacco, Italy
d. June 05, 1944 in Pesaro, Italy

Frank (Francis Vincent, Jr) Zappa
(The Mothers of Invention)
American musician–singer–songwriter
• Early leader of hard-rock style; founded Mothers of Invention, 1964.
b. December 21, 1940 in Baltimore, Maryland

Moon Unit Zappa
American singer
• Daughter of Frank Zappa; had hit song "Valley Girl," 1982.
b. 1968

Nicola Antonio Zingarelli
Italian composer–musician
• Wrote 34 operas including comic opera, *Berenice*, 1811.
b. April 04, 1752 in Naples, Italy
d. May 05, 1837 in Torre del Greco, Italy

The Zombies
(Rod Argent; Paul Atkinson; Colin Blunstone; Hugh Grundy; Chris Taylor White)
English music group
• Formed, 1963; hits include "Tell Her No," 1964; "Time of the Season," 1968.

Ellen Taaffe Zwilich
American composer
• First woman to win Pulitzer for music, 1983, for *Three Movements for Orchestra.*
b. April 3, 1939 in Miami, Florida

ZZ Top
(Frank Beard; Billy Gibbons; Dusty Hill)
American music group
• Texan group, formed 1970; frequent tours have made all albums gold or platinum.

POTENTATES, POLITICIANS & MILITANTS

Communists,

Kings, Queens,

Presidents,

Revolutionaries...

Ferhat Abbas
Algerian political leader
• President of Algeria's first provisional government, 1958-61; wrote *Manifesto of the Algerian People,* 1943.
b. October 24, 1899 in Taher, Algeria
d. December 24, 1985

Sheik Mohammad Abdullah
Indian political leader
• Struggled to free country from political domination of India.
b. December 05, 1905 in Soura, Kashmir
d. September 08, 1982 in Srinagar, Kashmir

Abdullah Ibn Hussein
Jordanian ruler
• King of Jordan, 1946-51; supported pro-British policies; assassinated.
b. 1882 in Mecca, Saudi Arabia
d. July 2, 1951 in Jerusalem, Israel

Isao Abe
Japanese political leader
• Founder, Japanese Socialist Party, who introduced baseball to Japan.
b. 1865 in Tokyo, Japan
d. February 1, 1949 in Tokyo, Japan

Creighton Williams Abrams
American military leader
• Commanding general, US forces in Vietnam, 1968-72.
b. September 15, 1914 in Springfield, Massachusetts
d. September 04, 1974 in Washington, District of Columbia

Luigi Amedeo Abruzzi
(Duke of Abruzzi; Prince of Savoy-Aosta)
Italian explorer–military leader
• Explored N Pole, 1899; commanded Italian fleet, WW I; helped colonize Italian Somaliland.
b. January 29, 1873 in Madrid, Spain
d. March 18, 1933 in Duca degli Abruzzi, Italian Somaliland

Dean Gooderham Acheson
American cabinet member
• Turman's secretary of state, 1949-53; primary creator of NATO; won Pulitzer for *Present at the Creation,* 1969.
b. April 11, 1893 in Middletown, Connecticut
d. October 12, 1971 in Sandy Spring, Maryland

Abigail Smith Adams
(Mrs John Adams; Diana; Portia)
American first lady
• Only woman to be wife of one pres., mother of another, John Quincy Adams.
b. November 11, 1744 in Weymouth, Massachusetts
d. October 28, 1818 in Quincy, Massachusetts

John Adams
American US president
• Signed Declaration of Independence, 1776; second US pres., 1797-1801; helped draw up Treaty of Paris, 1793, ending American Revolution.
b. October 3, 1735 in Braintree, Massachusetts
d. July 04, 1826 in Quincy, Massachusetts

John Quincy Adams
("Publicola"; "The Second John")
American US president
• Son of John Adams, sixth US president, 1825-29; catalyst behind Monroe Doctrine, 1823.
b. July 11, 1767 in Braintree, Massachusetts
d. February 23, 1848 in Washington, District of Columbia

Louisa Catherine Adams
(Mrs John Quincy Adams)
American first lady
• Married John Quincy Adams, 1797; when Congress adjourned to attend her funeral it was first time a woman was so honored.
b. February 12, 1775 in London, England
d. May 14, 1852 in Washington, District of Columbia

Sherman Llewellyn Adams
American presidential aide
• Rep. governor of NH, 1949-53; chief of White House staff, 1953-58; resigned over "gift" scandal, 1958.
b. January 08, 1899 in East Dover, Vermont
d. October 27, 1986 in Hanover, New Hampshire

Joseph Patrick Addabbo
American political leader
• Dem. congressman from NY, 1961-86; adamant watchdog for military spending.
b. March 17, 1925 in Queens, New York
d. April 1, 1986 in Washington, District of Columbia

Hugh Joseph Addonizio
American political leader
• Dem. con. from NJ, 1949-61; mayor of Newark, NJ, 1962-70; convicted of extortion, 1970.
b. January 31, 1914 in Newark, New Jersey
d. February 02, 1981 in Red Bank, New Jersey

Konrad Adenauer
German political leader
• First Chancellor of Federal German Republic (West Germany), 1949-63.
b. January 05, 1876 in Cologne, Germany
d. April 19, 1967 in Rhondorf, Germany (West)

Spiro Theodore Agnew
American US vice president
• Nixon's vp; resigned, 1973, pleading no contest to income tax evasion charges.
b. November 09, 1918 in Baltimore, Maryland

Agrippina
Roman ruler
• Mother of Nero who was murdered by her son.
b. 16
d. 59 in Baige, Italy

Ahmadou Ahidjo
Cameroonian political leader
• Five-term president of Cameroon, 1961-82; died in exile.
b. August 1924 in Garoua, Cameroon
d. November 3, 1989 in Dakar, Senegal

Akbar
(Jalalud din Muhammad; "The Great")
Arabian ruler
• Greatest of Indian Moghul emperors who extended empire to N India; instituted new religion, Din-i-Ilahi.
b. October 14, 1542 in Umarkot, Pakistan
d. October 15, 1605 in Agra, India

(Tsugonomiya) Akihito
Japanese ruler
• Succeeded father, Hirohito, as Japan's 125th emperor, 1989.
b. December 23, 1933 in Tokyo, Japan

Alaric I
Ruler
• Visigothic king, 395-410, who sacked Rome, 410.
b. 370
d. 410 in Consentia, Italy

Albert
(Prince of Liege)
Belgian prince
• Brother of Baudouin, king of Belgium; heir to throne.
b. June 06, 1934 in Brussels, Belgium

Albert
(Albert Alexandre Louis Pierre Grimaldi)
Monacan prince
• Son of Prince Rainier and Princess Grace who is heir to Monacan throne.
b. March 14, 1958 in Monte Carlo, Monaco

Albert I
(Albert Leopold Clement Marie Meinrad)
Belgian ruler
• King who reigned 1909-34; personally commanded Belgian army during WW I.
b. April 08, 1875 in Brussels, Belgium
d. February 17, 1934 in Namur, Belgium

Carl Bert Albert
American political leader
• Dem. majority leader, 1962-71; Speaker of House, 1971-76.
b. May 1, 1908 in McAlester, Oklahoma

Affonso de Albuquerque
("The Portuguese Mars")
Portuguese political leader
• Viceroy of India; founded Portuguese empire in the East.
b. 1453 in Alhandra, Portugal
d. December 16, 1515 in Goa, India

Miguel Aleman
Mexican political leader
• First civilian pres. following 1917 revolution, 1946-52.
b. September 29, 1903 in Sayula, Mexico
d. May 14, 1983 in Mexico City, Mexico

Alexander I
(Aleksandr Pavlovich; "The Northern Telemaque")
Russian ruler
• Grandson of Catherine the Great; czar of Russia, 1801-25; succeeded by brother Nicholas I.
b. December 23, 1777 in Saint Petersburg, Russia
d. December 01, 1825 in Taganrog, Russia

Alexander II
(Aleksandr Nikolaevich)
Russian ruler
• Son of Nicholas I; czar of Russia, 1855-81; freed serfs, 1861; sold Russia, 1867.
b. April 29, 1818 in Moscow, Russia
d. March 13, 1881 in Saint Petersburg, Russia

Alexander III
(Aleksandr Aleksandrovich)
Russian ruler
• Younger son of Alexander II; czar of Russia, 1881-94; reign known for repression of liberal ideas, persecution of Jews.
b. March 1, 1845 in Russia
d. November 01, 1894 in Livadia, Russia

Alexander of Tunis
(Harold Rupert Leofric George Alexander)
English military leader–political leader
• Charismatic commander of Allied forces in WW II Italian invasion, 1943; governor-general of Canada, 1946-52.
b. December 1, 1891 in County Tyrone, Ireland
d. June 16, 1969 in Slough, England

Alexander the Great
(Alexander III; "The Conqueror of the World" "The Emathian Conqueror"; "Macedonia's Madman")
Macedonian ruler
• King who forged largest western empire of ancient world, from Greece to N India.
b. September 2, 356 in Pella, Macedonia
d. June 13, 323 in Babylon

Clifford L Alexander, Jr
American political leader
• Secretary of Army, 1977-80; first black in US history to serve as civilian head of military branch.
b. September 21, 1933 in New York, New York

Alexius Comnenus
(Alexius I)
Byzantine ruler
• Emperor of Eastern Roman Empire, 1081-1118.
b. 1048
d. August 15, 1118

Raul Ricardo Alfonsin Foulkes
Argentine political leader
• Elected pres., 1983, defeating Peronist Party for first time in 38 yrs.; pursued human rights reforms, democratization.
b. March 31, 1926 in Chascomus, Argentina

Alfonso XIII
Spanish ruler
• King of Spain, 1886-1931; reign marked by social unrest, several assassination attempts.
b. May 17, 1886 in Madrid, Spain
d. February 28, 1941 in Rome, Italy

Alfred the Great
English ruler
• King of Wessex, 871-99; revived learning, Old English literary prose.
b. 849 in Wantage, England
d. October 28, 901

Saul David Alinsky
American political activist
• Established Industrial Area Foundation, 1940; wrote *Rules for Radicalis*, 1971.
b. January 3, 1909 in Chicago, Illinois
d. June 12, 1972 in Carmel, California

Ethan Allen
American military leader
• Organized Green Mountain Boys, 1770, to harass New Yorkers in land dispute between NY and NH.
b. January 21, 1738 in Litchfield, Connecticut
d. February 11, 1789 in Burlington, Vermont

Richard Vincent Allen
American presidential aide
• Nat. security adviser under Ronald Reagan, 1981-82; resigned amid controversy, replaced by William Clark.
b. January 01, 1936 in Collingswood, New Jersey

Edmund Henry Hynman Allenby
(1st Viscount Allenby; "The Bull")
English military leader
• WW I field marshal in Middle East; armies captured Jerusalem, defeated Turks, 1917-18.
b. April 23, 1861 in Southwell, England
d. May 14, 1936 in London, England

Salvador (Gossens) Allende
Chilean political leader
• Socialist pres. of Chile, 1970-73; overthrown in violent coup.
b. July 26, 1908 in Valparaiso, Chile
d. September 11, 1973 in Santiago, Chile

Yigal Allon
(Yigal Paicovich)
Israeli army officer–statesman
• Proposed restoration of heavily populated Arab areas of West Bank to Jordan.
b. October 1, 1918 in Kfar Tabor, Israel
d. February 29, 1980 in Afula, Israel

Juan Alvarez
Mexican military leader
• Indian general; led revolt which ousted Santa Anna, 1854; temporary president of Mexico, 1855.
b. January 27, 1780 in Guerrero Territory, Mexico
d. August 21, 1867

Hamilton Shirley Amerasinghe
Sri Lankan diplomat–government official
• Pres., UN General Assembly, 1967.
b. March 18, 1913 in Colombo, Ceylon
d. December 04, 1980 in New York, New York

Jeffrey Amherst
English army officer
• Commander-in-chief, British forces, 1780; Amherst College named for him.
b. January 29, 1717 in Riverhead, England
d. August 03, 1797 in Kent, England

Idi Amin
(Idi Amin Dada Oumee; "Big Daddy" "The Wild Man of Africa")
Ugandan political leader
• Overthrew Milton Obote; president of Uganda, 1971-80; known for torture, murder of dissidents.
b. 1925 in Koboko, Uganda

Toney Anaya
American political leader
• Dem, governor of NM, 1983–; only hispanic governor in US.
b. April 29, 1941 in Moriarty, New Mexico

John Bayard Anderson
American political leader
• Liberal Rep. con. from IL, 1960-80; Independent Party presidential candidate, 1980.
b. February 15, 1922 in Rockford, Illinois

Robert Anderson
American military leader
• General who surrendered Ft. Sumter to Confederates, Apr 13, 1861.
b. June 14, 1805 in Louisville, Kentucky
d. October 27, 1871 in Nice, France

Andrew
(Andrew Albert Christian Edward; Earl of Inverness; Baron Killyleagh; Duke of York; "Randy Andy")
English prince
• Third child of Queen Elizabeth II and Prince Philip; fought in Faukland Islands War, 1982; currently fourth in line to British throne.
b. February 19, 1960 in London, England

John Albion Andrew
American political leader
• Organized 54th MA Regiment, 1863, first black unit during Civil War.
b. May 31, 1818 in Windham, Maine
d. October 3, 1867 in Boston, Massachusetts

Andrew Prince of Russia,
(Andrew Romanov)
Russian prince
• Was oldest surviving relative of Czar Nicholas II.
b. 1897 in Saint Petersburg, Russia
d. May 08, 1981 in Teynham, England

Frank M(axwell) Andrews
American military leader
• General who commanded US forces in Europe succeeding Eisenhower, 1943.
b. February 03, 1884 in Nashville, Tennessee
d. May 03, 1943 in Iceland

Mark N Andrews
American political leader
• Popular Rep. con. since 1963; ND senator, 1980–.
b. May 19, 1926 in Fargo, North Dakota

Yuri Vladimirovich Andropov
Russian political leader
• General Secretary, Communist Party, after death of Brezhnev, 1982-84.
b. June 15, 1914 in Nagutskaia, Russia
d. February 09, 1984 in Kuntsevo, U.S.S.R.

Anne
English ruler
• Reigned 1702-14; with no heirs, succession passed to Hanoverian line-George I.
b. February 06, 1665 in London, England
d. August 01, 1714 in Kensington, England

George Anson
(Lord Anson Baron Soberton; "Father of the Navy")
English naval officer
• Circumnavigated globe, 1740-44; adventures described in *Anson's Voyage*.
b. April 23, 1697 in Shugborough, England
d. June 06, 1762 in Moor Park, England

Ion Antonescu
Romanian political leader
• Dictator, 1940-44; forced abdication of King Carol II, aligned Romania with Nazis; executed by firing squad.
b. June 15, 1882 in Pitesti, Romania
d. June 01, 1946 in Bucharest, Romania

Antoninus Pius
(Titus Aurelius Fulvus Boionius Arrius Antoninus)
Roman ruler
• Emperor of Rome, 138-161; Wall of Antonius built in his honor to protect against British invasion, 142.
b. September 19, 86 in Lanuvium, Italy
d. March 07, 161

Marc Antony
(Marcus Antonius; Marc Anthony)
Roman soldier–political leader
• Prominent soldier, politician under Julius Caesar; defeated by Octavius, 31 BC; committed suicide with Cleopatra.
b. 83?BC
d. 30BC in Egypt

Benigno Simeon Aquino, Jr
Philippine political leader
• Bitter rival of Ferdinand Marcos, assassinated upon return to Manila after three years exile in US.
b. November 27, 1932 in Concepcion, Philippines
d. August 21, 1983 in Manila, Philippines

Corazon Cojuangco Aquino
Philippine political leader
• Widow of Benigno Aquino; opposed Ferdinand Marcos in 1986 elections; became president, Feb 1986.
b. January 25, 1933 in Tarlac, Philippines

Yasir Arafat
Palestinian political leader
• Head of PLO, 1969–; has sought recognition of a Palestinian homeland through both legal and violent means.
b. 1929 in Jerusalem, Palestine

Pedro Eugenio Aramburu
Argentine political leader
• Pres., Argentina, 1955-58; replaced Peron's constitution with original democratic constitution.
b. May 21, 1903 in Buenos Aires, Argentina
d. July 16, 1970 in Timote, Argentina

Leslie Cornelius Arends
American political leader
• Rep. congressman, 1934-74; was House Whip for record 30 yrs.
b. September 27, 1895 in Melvin, Illinois
d. July 16, 1985 in Naples, Florida

Moshe Arens
Israeli government official–political leader
• Ambassador to US, 1982-83; succeeded Ariel Sharon as defense minister, 1983-84; minister without portfolio, 1984–.
b. December 27, 1925 in Kaunas, Lithuania

Arnulfo Arias Madrid
Panamanian political leader
• Civilian president of Panama, 1940-41, 1949-51, 1968, each time ousted by military; died in exile.
b. 1901 in Panama
d. August 1, 1988 in Miami, Florida

Oscar Arias Sanchez
Costa Rican political leader
• Pres. of Costa Rica, 1986–; won Nobel Peace Prize for leadership in peace plan involving five Central American countries, 1987.
b. September 13, 1941 in Heredia, Costa Rica

Henry Harley Arnold
American military leader
• First general of Air Force, 1949; used air power as weapon during WW II.
b. June 25, 1886 in Gladwyne, Pennsylvania
d. January 15, 1950 in Sonoma, California

Klas Pontus Arnoldson
Swedish political activist
• Shared 1908 Nobel Peace Prize for working for peace for 35 yrs.
b. October 27, 1844 in Goteborg, Sweden
d. February 2, 1916 in Stockholm, Sweden

Earl of Arthur Kattendyke Strange David Archibald Gore Arran
English journalist–political leader
• Sponsored 1966 Sexual Offences Bill, legalizing homosexual acts between consenting adults; author *Lord Arran Writes*, 1964.
b. July 05, 1910
d. February 23, 1983 in Hemel Hempstead, England

Artemisia
Persian ruler
• Erected one of seven wonders of ancient world, Mausoleum at Halicarnassus, honoring husband Mausolus.

Chester Alan Arthur
American US president
• Twenty-first pres., who succeeded James Garfield, 1881-84; supported civil service reform, 1883.
b. October 05, 1829 in Fairfield, Vermont
d. November 18, 1886 in New York, New York

Jacob Meyer Arvey
American political leader
• Dem. party chief from IL, 1946-53; launched political career of Adlai Stevenson Jr.
b. November 03, 1895 in Chicago, Illinois
d. August 25, 1977 in Chicago, Illinois

Reubin O'Donovan Askew
American government official–political leader
• Dem. governor of FL, 1971-79; sought Dem. presidential nomination, 1984.
b. September 11, 1928 in Muskogee, Oklahoma

Asoka the Great
Indian ruler
• King of Magadha, 273-232 BC; reign marked by prosperous times; made Buddhism a world religion.
b. 300BC
d. 232BC

Les(lie, Jr) Aspin
American political leader
• Dem. congressman from WI, 1970–; chm. of powerful Armed Services Com.
b. July 21, 1938 in Milwaukee, Wisconsin

Herbert Henry Asquith
(1st Earl of Oxford and Asquith)
English political leader
• Liberal prime minister, 1908-16; introduced social welfare programs.
b. September 12, 1852 in Morley, England
d. February 15, 1928 in Sutton Courtney, England

Hafez al Assad
Syrian political leader
• Minister of Defense, 1966-70; led coup that made him pres., 1971.
b. October 06, 1930 in Qardaha, Syria

Nancy Witcher Langhorne Astor
(Mrs William Waldorf Astor; Viscountess Astor)
English political leader
• First woman to sit in House of Commons, 1919-45; advocated temperance, opposed socialism; wrote *My Two Countries*, 1923.
b. May 19, 1879 in Greenwood, Virginia
d. May 02, 1964 in Lincoln, England

Nora Gadea Astorga
Nicaraguan revolutionary–diplomat
• Best known for role in assassination of Reynaldo Perez Vegas, 1978; ambassador to US, 1986-87.
b. 1949 in Managua, Nicaragua
d. February 14, 1988 in Managua, Nicaragua

Atahualpa
Peruvian ruler
• Incan emperor, 1532-33, captured by Pizarro; killed in spite of paid ransom.
b. 1500 in Quito, Ecuador
d. August 29, 1533 in Cajamarca, Peru

Kemal Ataturk
(Mustafa Kemal)
Turkish soldier–political leader
• Founder, first president, Turkish Republic, 1923-38.
b. 1880 in Thessalonica, Greece
d. November 1, 1938 in Ankara, Turkey

David R Atchison
American political leader
• As pres. pro tem of Senate, served as US pres. for one day, Mar 4, 1849.
b. August 11, 1807 in Frogtown, Kentucky
d. June 26, 1886 in Gower, Missouri

Attila
Ruler
• King of the Huns known for attacks on Europe during last stages of Roman Empire.
b. 406
d. 453

Earl Clement Richard Attlee
English political leader
• Labour prime minister, 1945-51; directed formulation of welfare state, nationalization of industry; led Labour opposition, 1951-55.
b. January 03, 1883 in London, England
d. October 08, 1967 in London, England

Augustus
(Octavius Caesar)
Roman ruler
• Emperor who returned Rome to constitutional rule after death of Caesar, 44 BC.
b. September 23, 63 in Rome, Italy
d. August 19, 14 in Nola, Italy

Augustus II
(Frederick Augustine I; Augustus the Strong)
Polish ruler
• King of Poland, 1697-1733; known for architectural beautification of Dresden.
b. May 12, 1670 in Dresden, Germany
d. February 01, 1733 in Warsaw, Poland

Aurangzeb
Indian ruler
• Last Mogul emperor of India, 1658-1707; contributed to collapse of empire.
b. October 24, 1618 in Dohad, India
d. February 2, 1707 in Ahmednuggur, India

Vincent Auriol
French political leader
• Socialist Party leader; first pres. of Fourth Republic, 1947-54.
b. August 25, 1884 in Revel, France
d. January 01, 1966 in Paris, France

Obafemi Awo Awolowo
Nigerian political leader
• A leader in Nigerian independence; prime minister, under British rule, Western Nigeria, 1954-59; ran for president of Nigeria, 1979, 1983.
b. March 06, 1909 in Ikenne, Nigeria
d. May 09, 1987 in Ikenne, Nigeria

Patricio Aylwin (Azocar)
Chilean political leader
• Succeeded Augusto Pinochet as president of Chile, 1990–, returning country to democracy.
b. November 26, 1918 in Vina del Mar, Chile

Mohammad Ayub Khan
Pakistani political leader
• Pres. of Pakistan, 1958-69; wrote *Friends Not Masters: A Political Autobiography*, 1967.
b. May 14, 1907 in Rehana, Pakistan
d. April 19, 1974 in Islamabad, Pakistan

Jose Simon Azcona Hoyo
Honduran political leader
• President of Honduras, 1986–.
b. January 26, 1927 in La Ceiba, Honduras

Nnamdi Azikiwe
(Zik Azikiwe; "Father of Modern Nigerian Nationalism")
Nigerian political leader
• First head of independent Nigeria, 1963; overthrown by military coup, 1966.
b. November 16, 1904 in Zungeri, Nigeria

Ibrahim Badamasi Babangida
Nigerian political leader
• Military president of Nigeria, brought to power in bloodless coup, 1985–.
b. August 17, 1941 in Minna, Nigeria

Sir Douglas Robert Steuart Bader
English air force officer
• Legless pilot who shot down at least 22 German planes, WW II.
b. February 21, 1910 in London, England
d. September 05, 1982 in London, England

Pietro Badoglio
Italian military leader
• Led forces that defeated Austria, WW I; prime minister, 1943-44.
b. September 28, 1871 in Monferrato, Italy
d. October 31, 1956 in Monferrato, Italy

Ivan Christofovorich Bagramian
Russian military leader
• Commanded 1st Baltic Army which drove Nazis from Lithuania, 1943-45; given title Hero of Soviet Union twice, Order of Lenin five times.
b. December 02, 1897 in Gyandzha, Armenia
d. September 21, 1982 in Moscow, U.S.S.R.

Jean Sylvain Bailly
French astronomer–politician
• Calculated Halley's Comet orbit, 1759; briefly pres. of national assembly, mayor of Paris; guillotined.
b. September 15, 1736 in Paris, France
d. November 12, 1793 in Paris, France

Bobby (Robert Gene) Baker
American political leader
• Senate Dem. majority secretary who was convicted, 1967, of tax evasion, theft, conspiracy to defraud govt.
b. November 12, 1928 in Easley, South Carolina

Howard Henry Baker, Jr
American political leader–government official
• Rep. senator from TN, 1966-85; White House Chief of Staff under Reagan, 1987-88.
b. November 15, 1925 in Huntsville, Tennessee

James Addison Baker, III
American presidential aide–government official
• Secretary of State under Bush, 1989–; Reagan's Treasury secretary, 1985-88, chief of staff, 1981-85.
b. April 28, 1930 in Houston, Texas

Shahpur Bakhtiar
Iranian political leader
• Leader of Bakhtiaris, Iran's oldest, largest tribe.
b. 1916

Ahmad Hasan al Bakr
Iraqi political leader
• Pres., of Iraq, 1968-79.
b. 1914 in Tikrit, Iraq
d. October 04, 1982 in Baghdad, Iraq

Joaquin Balaguer
Dominican political leader
• Pres., Dominican Republic, 1960, 1966-78, 1986–.
b. September 01, 1907 in Villa Bisono, Dominican Republic

Malcolm (Howard Malcolm, Jr) Baldrige
American cabinet member
• US secretary of Commerce under Reagan, 1981-87; killed in rodeo accident.
b. October 04, 1922 in Omaha, Nebraska
d. July 25, 1987 in Walnut Creek, California

Michael Balopoulos
Greek political leader
• Colonel who led 1967 military coup to overthrow democratic govt.
b. 1920
d. March 03, 1978 in Athens, Greece

Sirimavo Ratwatte Dias Bandaranaike
Sri Lankan political leader
• World's first female prime minister, 1959-65, 1970-77.
b. April 17, 1916 in Kandy, Ceylon

Abolhassan Bani-Sadr
Iranian political leader
• First pres. elected in Iran's 2,500 year history, 1980; lost power to Khomeini, 1981.
b. March 22, 1933 in Hamadan Province, Persia

William Brockman Bankhead
American political leader
• Dem. congressman from AL, 1917-40; Speaker of House, 1936-40; father of Tallulah.
b. April 12, 1874 in Moscow, Alabama
d. September 15, 1940 in Bethesda, Maryland

Hugo Banzer-Suarez
Bolivian political leader
• Pres. of Bolivia, 1971-78; overthrown in coup, Jul, 1978.
b. July 1, 1926 in Santa Cruz, Bolivia

Alben William Barkley
American US vice president
• Dem. con., 1912-26; Truman's vp, 1949-53.
b. November 24, 1877 in Graves County, Kentucky
d. April 3, 1956 in Lexington, Virginia

Ross Robert Barnett
American political leader
• Governor of MS, 1960-64; known for racism; attempted to defy US courts; caused riots, 1960-62.
b. January 22, 1898 in Standing Pine, Mississippi
d. November 06, 1987 in Jackson, Mississippi

Comte de Paul Francois Jean Nicolas Barras
French politician
• Helped to overthrow Robespierre, 1794; arranged for marriage between Josephine, Napoleon.
b. June 3, 1755 in Fox-Amphoux, France
d. January 29, 1829 in Chaillot, France

Raymond Barre
French government official
• Prime minister of France, 1976-81.
b. April 12, 1924 in Saint-Denis, France

Errol Walton Barrow
Barbadian political leader
• Prime minister, Barbados, 1961-76, 1986-87; led island to independence, Nov, 1966.
b. January 21, 1920 in Saint Lucy, Barbados
d. June 01, 1987 in Bridgetown, Barbados

Marion Shepilov Barry, Jr
American political leader
• Democratic mayor of Washington, DC, 1979–; sentenced to six months in prison for cocaine possession, 1990.
b. March 06, 1936 in Itta Bena, Mississippi

Tom Barry
Irish military leader
• Leader in Irish War for Independence, 1919-22, who helped develop guerilla warfare.
b. July 01, 1897 in Rosscarbery, Ireland
d. July 02, 1980 in Cork, Ireland

Fulgencio Batista y Zaldivar
Cuban political leader
• Dictator who came to power, 1952; overthrown by Fidel Castro, 1959.
b. January 16, 1901 in Banes, Cuba
d. August 06, 1973 in Guadalmina, Spain

Batu Khan
Mongolian military leader
• Grandson of Genghis Khan who conquerded Russia, 1240; organized Mogul state Golden Horde.

Albert Charles Baudouin
Belgian ruler
• King of Belgium, 1951–; proclaimed independence of Zaire, 1960.
b. September 07, 1930 in Brussels, Belgium

Beatrix
(Beatrix Wilhelmina Armgard)
Dutch ruler
• Daughter of Juliana who was invested as queen, Apr 30, 1980.
b. January 31, 1938 in Soestdijk, Netherlands

Earl David Beatty
English naval officer
• Commander of successful naval action during WW I; first sea lord of navy, 1919-27.
b. 1871 in Nantwich, England
d. 1936

Pierre Gustav Toutant de Beauregard
American military leader
• Confederate general who directed bombing of Ft. Sumter to start Civil War, 1861.
b. May 28, 1818 in Saint Bernard, Louisiana
d. February 2, 1893 in New Orleans, Louisiana

Cesare Beccaria
Italian explorer–political leader
• Argued against capital punishment of criminals in *Essay on Crimes and Punishment*, 1767.
b. March 15, 1738 in Milan, Italy
d. November 28, 1794 in Milan, Italy

Joseph Bech
Luxembourg diplomat
• Foreign minister, 1926-59; instrumental in founding of Benelux, Common Market follwing WW II.
b. February 17, 1887 in Diekirch, Luxembourg
d. March 08, 1975 in Luxembourg

Menachem Wolfovitch Begin
Israeli political leader
• Prime minister, 1977-83; shared 1978 Nobel Peace Prize with Anwar Sadat for signing historic Camp David agreement, 1978.
b. August 16, 1913 in Brest-Litovsk, Poland

Ayatollah Mohammad Beheshti
Iranian political leader
• Founder of Islamic Republican Party, 1979; killed in bomb blast.
b. 1929 in Isfahan, Persia
d. June 28, 1981 in Teheran, Iran

Fernando Belaunde-Terry
Peruvian political leader
• Pres. of Peru, 1963-68, 1980-85.
b. October 17, 1912 in Lima, Peru

Belisarius
Byzantine army officer
• One of great military leaders, responsible for much of Justinian I's success.
b. 505
d. March 565

John Bell
American political leader
• Southern Whig leader; senator, 1847-59; unsuccessful presidential candidate, 1860, defeated by Lincoln.
b. February 15, 1797 in Nashville, Tennessee
d. September 1, 1869 in Stewart County, Tennessee

Fabian Gottlieb von Bellinghausen
(Faddei F Bellinsgauzen)
Russian naval officer–explorer
• First to see Antarctica, 1820; founded Russian Geographic Society, 1845.
b. August 3, 1779 in Oesel, Russia
d. January 25, 1852 in Kronstadt, Russia

Mehdi Ben Barka
Moroccan political leader
• Exiled left-wing revolutionary, murdered in France by Moroccan agents.
b. 1920
d. 1965 in France

Ahmed Ben Bella
Algerian revolutionary–political leader
• First premier, pres. of Algeria, 1962-65, and of independent Algeria after ouster of French.
b. December 1916 in Marnia, Algeria

Eliahu Ben-Elissar
Israeli diplomat
• First Israeli ambassador to Arab country, Egypt, 1980.
b. 1932 in Poland

Avigdor Ben-Gal
Israeli army officer
• Led Israeli troops into Lebanon, 1978.
b. 1936

David Ben-Gurion
(David Grun)
Israeli political leader
• Emigrated to Palestine, 1906; Israel's first prime minister, 1948-53.
b. October 16, 1886 in Plonsk, Poland
d. December 01, 1973 in Tel Aviv, Israel

William Bennett
Canadian politician
• Social Credit Party premier of British Columbia, 1975-86.
b. April 14, 1932 in Kelowna, British Columbia

W(illiam) A(ndrew) C(ecil) Bennett
Canadian political leader
• Social Credit premier of British Columbia, 1952-72.
b. September 06, 1900 in Hastings, New Brunswick
d. February 23, 1979 in Kelowna, British Columbia

William John Bennett
American cabinet member
• Chm., National Endowment for the Humanities, 1981-85; secretary of Education, 1985-88; director, Office of National Drug Control Policy, 1989-90.
b. July 31, 1943 in Brooklyn, New York

Thomas Hart Benton
American political leader
• Dem. Senate leader, 1821-51; lost office for opposing extension of slavery.
b. March 14, 1782 in Hillsboro, North Carolina
d. April 1, 1858 in Washington, District of Columbia

Lloyd Millard Bentsen, Jr
American political leader
• Dem. VP candidate, 1988; senator from TX, 1971–.
b. February 11, 1921 in Mission, Texas

Bob (Robert Selmer) Bergland
American cabinet member–farmer
• Secretary of Agriculture, under Carter, 1977-81; first farmer to fill post since 1945.
b. July 22, 1928 in Roseau, Minnesota

Lavrenti Pavlovich Beria
Russian communist leader
• Head of Soviet Intelligence, 1934-53; executed in power struggle after Stalin's death.
b. March 29, 1899 in Georgia, Russia
d. December 23, 1953

Nabih Berri
Lebanese government official
• Leader of Shiite Muslims-Amal-in Lebanon since 1980, known for role in Beirut TWA hostage crisis, 1985.
b. 1938 in Freetown, Sierra Leone

Daniel J Berrigan
American poet–political activist–clergyman
• Convicted of destroying draft records with brother Philip, 1968.
b. May 09, 1921 in Virginia, Minnesota

Elizabeth McAlister Berrigan
(Mrs Philip Berrigan)
American political activist
• Former nun, member of Catholic anti-war movement, who was indicted for plotting to kidnap Henry Kissinger, 1971.
b. 1939

Philip Francis Berrigan
American political activist
• With brother Daniel, was first Catholic priest imprisoned for peace agitation in US, 1968.
b. October 05, 1923 in Minneapolis, Minnesota

Belisario Betancur
(Belisario Betancur Cuartas)
Colombian political leader
• Conservative party leader elected pres. of Colombia, 1982.
b. 1923 in Amaga, Colombia

Aneurin Bevan
British political leader–orator
• Labor party leader; introduced British socialized medicine system, 1948.
b. November 15, 1897 in Tredagar, Wales
d. July 06, 1960 in Chesham, England

Ernest Bevin
English political leader–government official
• Labor party leader who helped found NATO, 1940s.
b. March 09, 1881 in Winsford, England
d. April 14, 1951 in London, England

Adulyadej Bhumibol
(Rama IX King)
Thai ruler
• King of Thailand, 1946–.
b. December 05, 1927 in Cambridge, Massachusetts

Benazir Bhutto
Pakistani political leader
• Prime minister of Pakistan, 1988-90; first woman head of Moslem nation; daughter of Zulfikar Ali Bhutto.
b. June 21, 1953 in Karachi, Pakistan

Zulfikar Ali Bhutto
Pakistani political leader
• Served as pres., prime minister, 1970s, building nation's economy, prestige; overthrown, 1977, executed.
b. January 05, 1928 in Larkana, Pakistan
d. April 04, 1979 in Rawalpindi, Pakistan

Mario Biaggi
American political leader
• Dem. representative from NY, 1969-88; resigned following racketeering conviction.
b. October 26, 1917 in New York, New York

Joe (Joseph Robinette, Jr) Biden
American political leader
• Dem. senator from DE, 1973–; early presidential candidate, 1988.
b. November 2, 1942 in Scranton, Pennsylvania

Reynaldo Benito Antonio Bignone
Argentine political leader
• Mild-mannered general thrust into presidency, 1981, to lead Argentine civilian government.
b. January 21, 1928 in Moron, Argentina

Dzemal Bijedic
Yugoslav political leader
• Prime minister, 1971-77; killed in plane crash.
b. April 12, 1917 in Mostar, Yugoslavia
d. January 18, 1977 in Yugoslavia

Steven Biko
South African political activist
• A leader of Black Consciousness Movement; died while in custody of S African security police; subject of 1987 film *Cry Freedom.*
b. 1947 in Pretoria, South Africa
d. September 12, 1977 in South Africa

Shah Dev Birendra Bir Bikram
Nepalese ruler
• One of few remaining monarchs with absolute power; inherited throne from father, Mahendra Bir Bikram Shah Dev, 1972, crowned, 1975.
b. December 28, 1945 in Kathmandu, Nepal

Billy (William Avery) Bishop
Canadian military leader
• WW I ace who shot down 72 enemy aircraft; wrote *Winged Warfare,* 1918.
b. February 08, 1894 in Owen Sound, Ontario
d. September 11, 1956 in Palm Beach, Florida

Maurice Bishop
Grenadian political leader
• Marxist who became prime minister in 1979 coup; led invasion, 1983.
b. May 29, 1944 in Aruba
d. October 19, 1983 in Saint George's, Grenada, West Indies

Robert Blake
English military leader
• Captured the Scilly Islands, 1651; sank the Spanish Fleet at Santa Cruz, 1657.
b. 1599
d. August 07, 1657

(Jean Joseph Charles) Louis Blanc
French political leader–author
• Considered father of state socialism; wrote *History of French Revolution,* 1847-62.
b. 1811 in Madrid, Spain
d. 1882

Jim (James Johnston) Blanchard
American political leader
• Democratic governor of MI, 1983-91, defeated in upset by John Engler.
b. August 08, 1942 in Detroit, Michigan

Captain William Bligh
English naval officer
• Captain, HMS *Bounty* when mutiny occurred; cast adrift for 4,000 miles.
b. September 09, 1754 in Plymouth, England
d. December 07, 1817 in London, England

Ray C(harles) Bliss
American political leader
• Chm., GOP, 1966-68; credited with rebuilding party after defeat of Goldwater, 1964.
b. December 16, 1907 in Akron, Ohio
d. August 06, 1981 in Akron, Ohio

Tasker H Bliss
American military leader
• As chief of staff, WW I, transformed army from small peacetime organization to huge war machine.
b. December 31, 1853 in Lewisburg, Pennsylvania
d. November 09, 1930 in Washington, District of Columbia

Claude Charles Bloch
American military leader
• Admiral at Pearl Harbor during Japanese attack, 1941.
b. July 12, 1878 in Woodbury, Kentucky
d. October 06, 1967 in Washington, District of Columbia

John Rusling Block
American cabinet member
• Millionaire farmer who was secretary of Agriculture under Ronald Reagan, 1981-86.
b. February 15, 1935 in Galesburg, Illinois

Gebhard Leberecht von Blucher
Russian military leader
• Led Prussian army in Napoleon's defeat at Laon; entered Paris, 1814; aided British at Waterloo.
b. December 16, 1742 in Rostock, Germany
d. September 12, 1819 in Schlesian, Germany

W Michael Blumenthal
American business executive–cabinet member
• Secretary of Treasury under Jimmy Carter, 1977-79; chm. of Burroughs Corp., 1981–.
b. January 03, 1926 in Berlin, Germany

Boadicea
(Boudicca)
Ruler
• Queen of Iceni, AD60, who raised rebellion against Romans in Britain.

Hale (Thomas Hale) Boggs
American political leader
• Dem. con. from LA, 1941-43, 1947-72; lost in Alaska plane crash.
b. February 15, 1914 in Long Beach, Mississippi
d. October 1972 in Alaska

Lindy Boggs
(Mrs Hale Boggs)
American political leader
• Entered Congress as widow, replacing husband; chairwoman of Democratic National Convention, 1976.
b. March 13, 1916 in Brunswick, Louisiana

Bokassa I (Jean Bedel)
African political leader
• Took control of Central African Empire, 1966; named pres., for life, 1972; crowned emperor, 1977.
b. February 21, 1921 in Boubangui, Africa

Edward Patrick Boland
American political leader
• Dem. congressman from MA, 1953–; sponsored Boland amendments, 1983-86, which restricted US covert aid to Nicaraguan Contras.
b. October 01, 1911 in Springfield, Massachusetts

Frances Payne Bolton
American political leader
• Held 28-yr. term in Congress as Rep. representative; her grandfather, husband and son have also served.
b. March 29, 1885 in Cleveland, Ohio
d. March 09, 1977 in Lyndhurst, Ohio

Francois Charles Joseph Bonaparte
(L'Aiglon; Napoleon II)
French political leader
• Son of Napoleon Bonaparte; titular king of Rome, 1811-14; prince of Parma, 1814-18.
b. 1811 in Paris, France
d. 1832 in Austria

Jerome Bonaparte
French ruler
• Youngest brother of Napoleon; king of Westphalia, 1807-13.
b. November 15, 1784 in Corsica
d. June 24, 1860 in Paris, France

Joseph Bonaparte
French ruler–celebrity relative
• Older brother of Napoleon; king of Naples, 1806-08; king of Spain, 180808-13.
b. January 07, 1768 in Corte, Comoros
d. July 28, 1844 in Florence, Italy

Margaret Grace Bondfield
English government official
• First British woman cabinet minister: minister of labor, 1929-31.
b. 1873 in Furnham, England
d. June 16, 1953 in Sanderstead, England

Francois Bonivard
Swiss patriot
• Led Genevese revolt against Charles III, 1528; imprisoned, 1530-36; subject of Lord Byron's "Prisoner of Chillon."
b. 1494
d. 1570

Lord Robert John Graham Boothby
Scottish politician
• British conservative who served on Parliament 62 yrs; private secretary to Winston Churchill, 1926-29.
b. 1900 in Edinburgh, Scotland
d. July 16, 1986 in London, England

Sir Robert Laird Borden
Canadian political leader
• Twice prime minister; headed Conservative govt., 1911-17; Union govt., 1917-20.
b. June 26, 1854 in Grand Pre, Nova Scotia
d. June 1, 1937 in Ottawa, Ontario

Cesare Borgia
Italian military leader
• Said to be prototype for Machiavelli's *The Prince.*
b. 1475 in Rome, Italy
d. March 12, 1507 in Navarre, France

Rodrigo Cevallos Borja
Ecuadorean political leader
• Founded Democratic Left Party, 1970; succeeded Leon Febres-Cordero as president of Ecuador, 1988–.
b. June 19, 1935 in Quito, Ecuador

Subhas Chandra Bose
Indian politician
• Headed puppet regime planned for India by Japan, 1943.
b. 1897
d. August 19, 1945

Louis Botha
South African military leader–political leader
• Boer military leader, who helped form Union of S Africa; became first premier, 1910-19.
b. September 27, 1862 in Honigfontein, South Africa
d. August 27, 1919 in Pretoria, South Africa

Pieter Willem Botha
South African political leader
• Eighth prime minister of S Africa, elected 1978.
b. January 12, 1916 in Paul Roux, South Africa

Georges Ernest Jean Marie Boulanger
French soldier–politician
• Popular minister of war, 1886; plotted to overthrow Third Republic, condemned for treason.
b. 1837 in Rennes, France
d. 1891 in Brussels, Belgium

Houari Boumedienne
Algerian political leader
• President of Algeria, 1976-78; helped country gain independence from France, 1962; major Third World spokesman.
b. August 23, 1932 in Clauzel, Algeria
d. December 27, 1978 in Algiers, Algeria

Robert Bourassa
Canadian politician
• Liberal Party premier of Quebec, 1970-76, 1985–.
b. July 14, 1933 in Montreal, Quebec

Leon-Victor Auguste Bourgeois
French politician
• Won 1920 Nobel Peace Prize for pioneering the League of Nations.
b. May 29, 1851 in Paris, France
d. September 29, 1925 in Epernay, France

Habib Ben Ali Bourguiba
(Father of Tunisian Independence)
Tunisian political leader
• Tunisia's first president, 1957–; pro-West, liberal leader gave up day-to-day control of govt. due to illness, 1969.
b. August 03, 1903 in Monastir, Tunisia

Bill (William Warren) Bradley
American basketball player–political leader
• Forward, NY Knicks, 1967-77; Hall of Fame, 1982; US senator from NJ, 1979.
b. July 28, 1943 in Crystal City, Missouri

Omar Nelson Bradley
American military leader
• Last five-star general; first permanent chm., Joint Chiefs of Staff, 1949-53.
b. February 12, 1893 in Clark, Missouri
d. April 08, 1981 in New York, New York

Tom (Thomas J) Bradley
American political leader
• First black mayor of predominantly white city, Los Angeles, 1973–; won Spingarn, 1983.
b. December 29, 1917 in Calvert, Texas

James Scott Brady
American presidential aide
• Press secretary shot during Reagan assassination attempt, 1981.
b. August 29, 1940 in Centralia, Illinois

Nicholas Frederick Brady
American government official–cabinet member
• Succeeded James Brady as Treasury secretary, 1988–.
b. April 11, 1930 in New York, New York

Braxton Bragg
American military leader
• Commander-in-chief, Confederate Army, 1864-65.
b. March 22, 1817 in Warrenton, North Carolina
d. September 27, 1876 in Galveston, Texas

Willy Brandt
(Herbert Ernst Karl Frahm)
German political leader
• Chancellor of W Germany, 1969-74; won Nobel Peace Prize, 1971; mayor of W Berlin, 1957-66.
b. December 18, 1913 in Lubeck, Germany

Karl Hjalmar Branting
Swedish astronomer–political leader
• Shared Nobel Peace Prize, 1921; prime minister of Sweden, 1889-1925.
b. November 23, 1860 in Stockholm, Sweden
d. February 24, 1925 in Stockholm, Sweden

Heinrich Alfred Brauchitsch
German military leader
• Commander-in-chief of German Army, 1938-41; made scapegoat for failure to capture Moscow, removed from command, 1941.
b. October 04, 1881 in Berlin, Germany
d. October 18, 1948

Leonid Ilyich Brezhnev
Russian communist leader
• General secretary of Soviet Communist Party, 1966-82; presided over first attempts at detente, signed SALT I treaty with Nixon, 1972.
b. December 19, 1906 in Kamenskoye, Russia
d. November 1, 1982 in Moscow, U.S.S.R.

Brian Boru
Irish ruler
• High king of Ireland through conquest, 1002-1014; defeated Norse in battle, broke Norse power in Ireland.
b. 926
d. April 23, 1014 in Clontarf, Ireland

Styles (Henry Styles) Bridges
American political leader
• Governor, NH, 1935-37; leading Rep. senator, 1937-54.
b. September 09, 1898 in West Pembroke, Maine
d. November 26, 1961 in Concord, New Hampshire

John Bright
English government official–author
• Founded Anti-Corn Law League, 1839; supported Northern cause in American Civil War.
b. November 16, 1811 in Greenbank, England
d. March 27, 1889 in Greenbank, England

Robert Briscoe
Irish political leader
• First Jewish Lord Mayor of Dublin, 1956; a founder of the Fianna Fail Party, 1926.
b. September 25, 1894 in Dublin, Ireland
d. May 3, 1969

Ed (John Edward) Broadbent
Canadian political leader
• Leader, New Democratic Party, 1975–; MP, 1968–; wrote *The Liberal Rip-off*, 1970.
b. March 21, 1936 in Oshawa, Ontario

Edward William Brooke
American political leader
• Rep. senator, MA, 1967-79; first black man elected to Senate since reconstruction.
b. October 26, 1919 in Washington, District of Columbia

Sir James Brooke
British political leader
• First rajah, (Borneo), 1841.
b. April 29, 1803 in Benares, India
d. June 11, 1868 in England

Angie Elizabeth Brooks
Liberian diplomat
• Member, UN General Assembly, 1954–; first African woman pres., 1969.
b. August 24, 1928 in Virginia, Liberia

Manilo Giovanni Brosio
Italian diplomat
• Leader of Liberal party, ambassador to US, 1955-61; NATO secretary-general, 1964-71.
b. July 1, 1897 in Turin, Italy
d. March 14, 1980 in Turin, Italy

George Alfred Brown
English political leader
• Controversial MP, 1945-70; deputy leader of Labour Party, 1960-70.
b. September 02, 1914 in London, England
d. June 02, 1985

George Scratchley Brown
American military leader
• Commanded Seventh Air Force, Vietnam, 1968-70; controversial chm., Joint Chiefs of Staff, 1974-78.
b. August 17, 1918 in Montclair, New Jersey
d. December 05, 1978 in Washington, District of Columbia

Harold Brown
American businessman–cabinet member
• Secretary of Defense under Jimmy Carter, 1977-81.
b. September 19, 1927 in New York, New York

Jacob Jennings Brown
American military leader
• Commanded Battle of Niagara, War of 1812; commanding general of US Army, 1821-28.
b. May 09, 1775 in Bucks County, Pennsylvania
d. February 24, 1828 in Washington, District of Columbia

Jerry (Edmund Gerald, Jr) Brown
American political leader
• Dem. governor of CA, 1975-82; succeeded by George Deukmejian; son of Pat Brown.
b. April 07, 1938 in San Francisco, California

John Young Brown, Jr
American businessman–political leader
• Bought Kentucky Fried Chicken from Colonel Sanders, 1964, for $2 million; governor of KY, 1980-83.
b. 1933 in Lexington, Kentucky

Sir Frederick A(rthur) M(ontague) Browning
British army officer–military leader
• Organized Red Devils Airborne Division, WW II; husband of author Daphne DuMaurier.
b. December 2, 1896
d. March 14, 1965 in Cornwall, England

Gro Harlem Brundtland
Norwegian political leader
• Prime minister, Feb-Oct, 1981, 1986; youngest woman to run modern govt.
b. April 2, 1939 in Oslo, Norway

Marcus Junius Brutus
Roman politician–assassin
• Principal assassin, with Cassius, of Julius Caesar, 44BC.
b. 85BC
d. 42BC

James Buchanan
American US president
• Fifteenth pres., 1857-61; opposed slavery in principle, but defended it under Constitution.
b. April 23, 1791 in Mercersburg, Pennsylvania
d. June 01, 1868 in Lancaster, Pennsylvania

John Buchanan
Canadian politician
• Progressive-Conservative Party premier of Nova Scotia, 1978–.
b. April 22, 1931 in Sydney, Nova Scotia

Patrick Joseph Buchanan
American presidential aide
• Conservative director of communications, under Reagan, 1985-87.
b. November 02, 1938 in Washington, District of Columbia

Lloyd Mark Bucher
American naval officer–military leader
• Commander, USS *Pueblo*, seized by N Korea, 1968.
b. September 01, 1927 in Pocatello, Idaho

Simon Buckner, Jr
American military leader–politician
• Commanded American 10th Army, Pacific Theater; killed few days before Okinawa conquest.
b. July 18, 1886 in Munfordville, Kentucky
d. June 18, 1945 in Okinawa, Japan

Don Carlos Buell
American army officer–military leader
• Civil War major general, 1862; failed to pursue Confederates in KY; resigned, 1864.
b. March 23, 1818 in Marietta, Ohio
d. November 19, 1898 in Rockport, Kentucky

John Buford
American military leader
• Major-general; took part in Sioux Expedition, 1855; chief of cavalry, Army of Potomac, 1862.
b. March 04, 1826 in Woodford County, Kentucky
d. December 16, 1863 in Washington, District of Columbia

Nikolai Ivanovich Bukharin
Russian communist leader
• Co-edited Communist Party organ *Pravda* with Lenin; executed in purges of 1938.
b. 1888 in Moscow, Russia
d. March 13, 1938

Vladimir Bukovsky
Russian political activist
• Released from Soviet labor camp in exchange for Chilean Communist Party leader, Luis Corvalan.
b. December 3, 1942 in Moscow, U.S.S.R.

Robert Lee Bullard
American military leader
• WW I Commander of Second Army; wrote famous message at Battle of the Marne, turning point of the war, 1918.
b. January 15, 1861 in Youngsboro, Alabama
d. September 11, 1947 in New York, New York

Bernhard H M Bulow
German political leader
• Chancellor, 1900-09; isolated Germany in foreign policy which led to French-British-Russian alliance.
b. May 03, 1849 in Altona, Germany
d. October 28, 1929 in Rome, Italy

Dale Leon Bumpers
American political leader
• Governor of AR, 1970-74; Dem. senator from AR, 1975–.
b. August 12, 1925 in Charleston, Arkansas

Ellsworth Bunker
American diplomat–political leader
• Ambassador to Vietnam, 1967-73; chief negotiator, Panama Canal Treaties, 1973-78.
b. May 11, 1894 in Yonkers, New York
d. September 27, 1984 in Brattleboro, Vermont

Jim (James Paul David) Bunning
American baseball player–political leader
• Pitcher, 1955-71; threw perfect game, 1964; Rep. con. from KY, 1987–.
b. October 23, 1931 in Southgate, Kentucky

Sir John Burgoyne
English army officer–dramatist
• Defeated by Americans, surrendered at Saratoga, 1777.
b. 1722
d. June 04, 1792 in London, England

Forbes (Linden Forbes Sampson) Burnham
Guinean political leader
• First prime minister of newly independent Guyana, 1966-70, of Co-operative Republic of Guyana, 1970-80.
b. February 2, 1923 in Kitty, Guyana
d. August 06, 1985 in Georgetown, Guyana

Ambrose Everett Burnside
American military leader–political leader
• As general, commanded Army of the Potomac, 1862; governor of RI, senator; term "sideburns" named for him.
b. May 23, 1824 in Liberty, Indiana
d. September 13, 1881 in Bristol, Rhode Island

Aaron Burr
American US vice president
• VP under Thomas Jefferson who shot, killed Alexander Hamilton in duel,1804.
b. February 06, 1756 in Newark, New Jersey
d. September 14, 1836 in New York, New York

Phillip Burton
American political leader
• Dem. con. from CA, 1964-83; lost bid for House leadership by one vote, 1976.
b. June 01, 1926 in Cincinnati, Ohio
d. April 1, 1983 in San Francisco, California

Barbara Pierce Bush
(Mrs George Bush)
American first lady
• Married George Bush, 1945; as first lady, has focused on reading and illiteracy.
b. June 08, 1925 in Rye, New York

George Herbert Walker Bush
American US president
• 41st US president, 1989–; VP under Reagan, 1981-89; CIA director under Ford, 1976-77.
b. June 12, 1924 in Milton, Massachusetts

Kofi A(brefa) Busia
Ghanaian political leader
• Prime minister of Ghana, 1969-72; prominent intellectual promoted African self-respect.
b. July 11, 1913 in Wenchi, Ghana
d. August 28, 1978 in Oxford, England

Sir William Alexander Clarke Bustamante
Jamaican political leader
• Prime minister, 1962-77; led Labour Party, 1943-77.
b. February 24, 1884
d. August 06, 1977 in Irish Town, Jamaica

Gatsha Mangosuthu Buthelezi
South African political leader
• Descendant of Zulu royalty; has served as head of Kwazulu, semi-autonomous Zulu homeland within S Africa since 1970.
b. August 27, 1928 in Mahlabatini, South Africa

Earl Lauer Butz
American cabinet member
• Secretary of Agriculture, 1971-76; sentenced to five years in prison for tax evasion, 1981.
b. July 03, 1909 in Noble County, Indiana

Harry Flood Byrd
American political leader–editor
• Dem. governor of VA, 1926-30; US senator, 1933-65.
b. June 1, 1887 in Martinsburg, West Virginia
d. October 2, 1966

Harry Flood Byrd, Jr
American political leader
• Dem. senator from VA, 1965-83; son of Harry Flood.
b. December 2, 1914 in Winchester, Virginia

Robert C(arlyle) Byrd
American political leader
• Dem. senator from WV, 1959–; majority leader, 1977-79, 1987–.
b. January 15, 1918 in North Wilkesboro, North Carolina

Jane Margaret Burke Byrne
(Mrs Jay McMullen)
American political leader
• Dem. mayor of Chicago, 1979-83.
b. May 24, 1934 in Chicago, Illinois

James Francis Byrnes
American cabinet member
• Appointed to Supreme Court by FDR, 1941-42; secretary of State under Truman, 1945-47; governor of SC, 1951-55.
b. May 02, 1879 in Charleston, South Carolina
d. April 09, 1972 in Columbia, South Carolina

Adolfo Calero (Portocarrero)
Nicaraguan political activist
• Supported by US, led rebels in attempt to overthrow Sandinista regime in Nicaragua, 1988.
b. 1932 in Nicaragua

John Caldwell Calhoun
American US vice president
• Secretary of War 1817-25; VP under Adams, 1824-32; promoted southern unity, state's rights.
b. March 18, 1782 in Calhoun Mills, South Carolina
d. March 31, 1850

Caligula
(Gaius Caesar Germanicus)
Roman ruler
• Succeeded Tiberius as Roman emperor, 37-41; main character in Camus' play *Caligula*, 1944.
b. August 31, 12 in Antium, Italy
d. January 24, 41 in Rome, Italy

James (Leonard James) Callaghan
English government official
• Labor Party leader; prime minister, 1976-79.
b. March 27, 1912 in Portsmouth, England

Plutarco Calles
Mexican statesman–army officer
• Pres., of Mexico, 1924-28; sponsored agrarian reforms; exiled in US, 1936-41.
b. September 25, 1877
d. October 19, 1945 in Mexico City, Mexico

William Laws Calley
American army officer–military leader
• Convicted of mass murder of Vietnamese civilians at My Lai, 1974.
b. 1943

Cambyses II
Persian ruler
• Son, successor of Cyrus the Great, 529-522 BC; added Eygpt to Persian empire, 525 BC.

Simon Cameron
American political leader–cabinet member
• Controlled PA Republican politics, 1857-77; US Secretary of War, 1861; censured by Congress, 1862, for questionable awarding of army contracts.
b. March 08, 1799 in Lancaster County, Pennsylvania
d. June 26, 1889 in Donegal Springs, Pennsylvania

Sir Henry Campbell-Bannerman
English political leader
• Prime minister, 1905-08, after Balfour's resignation; furthered liberal measures, criticized British methods in S Africa.
b. September 07, 1836 in Glasgow, Scotland
d. April 22, 1908 in London, England

Hector Jose Campora
Argentine political leader
• Peronist, who resigned presidency after seven wks. allowing Peron's return to power, 1973.
b. March 26, 1909 in Mercedes, Argentina
d. December 19, 1980 in Mexico City, Mexico

Wilhelm Canaris
German military leader–spy
• Director of German military intelligence; killed in plot against Hitler.
b. January 01, 1887 in Aplerbeck, Germany
d. April 09, 1945 in Flossenburg, Germany

Earl Charles John Canning
English political leader
• Governor-general of India during Sepoy Mutiny, 1857; first viceroy, 1858-62; son of George.
b. December 14, 1812 in London, England
d. June 17, 1862 in London, England

Joseph Gurney Cannon
American political leader
• Conservative Rep. congressman from IL, 1870s-1920s; House speaker, 1903-11; autocratic rule led to loss of much of speaker's power.
b. May 07, 1836 in New Garden, North Carolina
d. November 12, 1926 in Danville, North Carolina

Canute
(Canute of Denmark; Canute the Great)
English ruler
• Conquered England, ruled, 1016-35; Denmark, 1018-35; Norway, 1028-35.
b. 995
d. November 12, 1035 in Shaftesbury, England

Marcus Aurelius Antonius Caracalla
Roman ruler
• Ruled, 211-217; murdered brother to gain control of throne.
b. April 04, 186
d. April 08, 217

Hattie Wyatt Caraway
American political leader
• First woman elected to Senate, 1932; Dem. represented AR, 1932-45.
b. February 01, 1878 in Bakerville, Tennessee
d. December 21, 1950 in Falls Church, Virginia

Lazaro Cardenas
Mexican political leader
• Inaugurated 6-yr. program of agrarian reform and industrialization, 1934-40.
b. May 21, 1895 in Jiquilpan, Mexico
d. October 19, 1970 in Mexico City, Mexico

James T Brudenell Earl of Cardigan,
British army officer–military leader
• Led disastrous charge immortalized in "The Charge of the Light Brigade," 1854; cardigan sweater named for him.
b. 1797
d. 1868

Hugh Leo Carey
American political leader
• Dem. governor of NY, 1974-81; prevented default by selling bonds.
b. April 11, 1919 in Brooklyn, New York

Carl Gustaf XVI
(Carl Gustaf Folke Hubertus)
Swedish ruler
• Became king, Sep 19, 1973, as world's youngest reigning monarch.
b. April 3, 1946 in Stockholm, Sweden

Carlota
(Charlotte; Marie Charlotte A V C)
Belgian ruler
• Wife of Maximilian, empress of Mexico, 1864-67; went insane after realizing failure of husband's cause, 1866.
b. 1840 in Brussels, Belgium
d. 1927 in Belgium

Ingvar Gosta Carlsson
Swedish political leader
• Prime minister of Sweden, 1986-.
b. November 09, 1934 in Boras, Sweden

Frank Charles Carlucci, III,
American cabinet member
• Govt. service veteran; succeeded Caspar Weinberger as defense secretary under Reagan, 1987.
b. October 18, 1930 in Scranton, Pennsylvania

Robert Bostwick Carney
American naval officer–military leader
• Appointed NATO commander-in-chief of Allied Forces in Mediterranean by Eisenhower, 1951; planned key Pacific naval battles, WW II.
b. March 26, 1895 in Vallejo, California
d. June 25, 1990 in Washington, District of Columbia

Carol II
Romanian ruler
• Reigned, 1930-40; noted for abolishing political parties, founding Front of National Rebirth; ousted by Germans.
b. October 16, 1893 in Sinaia, Romania
d. April 04, 1953 in Estoril, Portugal

Baron Peter Alexander Rupert Carrington
English politician
• NATO secretary-general, 1984-88; foreign secretary, 1979-82; awarded Presidential Medal of Freedom, 1988.
b. June 06, 1919 in London, England

Karl Walter Carstens
German political leader
• President, Federal Republic of Germany, 1979-84.
b. December 14, 1914 in Bremen, Germany

Jimmy (James Earl, Jr) Carter
American US president
• Dem. 39th president, 1977-81; first elected from deep South; Iran hostage crisis contributed to defeat, 1980.
b. October 01, 1924 in Plains, Georgia

Rosalynn (Eleanor Rosalynn Smith) Carter
(Mrs Jimmy Carter)
American first lady
• Married Jimmy Carter, 1946; wrote memoirs: *First Lady from Plains*, 1984.
b. August 18, 1927 in Plains, Georgia

Roger David Casement
Irish diplomat
• Irish Nationalist, opposed Irish participation in WW I; hanged for treason by British.
b. September 01, 1864 in Dun Laoghaire, Ireland
d. August 03, 1916 in London, England

Cassius
(Caius Cassius Longinus; "The Last of the Romans")
Roman army officer–political leader
• Led conspiracy to murder Caesar, 44 BC.

Humberto Castello Branco
Brazilian political leader
• Pres. of Brazil, 1964-67; developed new constitution increasing presidential power.
b. September 2, 1900 in Fortaleza, Brazil
d. July 18, 1967

Barbara Anne Betts Castle
English politician
• Labour member, House of Commons, 1945-79; wrote *The Castle Diaries*, 1980.
b. October 06, 1911 in Chesterfield, England

Frederick W Castle
American army officer–military leader
• Medal of Honor recipient, 1944; Air Commander, leader of 2,000 heavy bombers against German airfields; killed in action.
b. October 14, 1908 in Manila, Philippines
d. December 24, 1944 in Liege, Belgium

Viscount Robert Stewart Castlereagh
British statesman–politician
• Foreign secretary, 1812-22; led coalition against Napoleon, having him confined to St. Helena; suicide victim.
b. 1769 in Dublin, Ireland
d. 1822

Fidel Castro (Ruz)
Cuban communist leader
• Led campaign to overthrow Batista regime, 1959; premier of Cuba 1959–.
b. August 13, 1926 in Mayari, Cuba

Clifton Bledsoe Cates
American military leader
• US Marine, 1917-54; distinguished veteran of WW I and II.
b. August 31, 1884 in Tiptonville, Tennessee
d. June 06, 1970 in Annapolis, Maryland

Catherine the Great
(Catherine II; Sophia Augusta Frederike of Anhaltzerbst)
Russian ruler
• Empress, 1762-96; worked toward westernization, expansion; made St. Petersburg cultural rival with Paris.
b. April 21, 1729 in Stettin, Germany
d. November 06, 1796

Nicolae Ceausescu
Romanian political leader
• Last hard-line communist leader in Warsaw Pact, 1974-89; chased from power, found guilty of grave crimes against Romania; executed by firing squad.
b. January 26, 1918 in Scornicesti-Olt, Romania
d. December 25, 1989 in Bucharest, Romania

Edgar Algernon Robert Cecil
English statesman–author
• Won Nobel Peace Prize, 1937; among architects of League of Nations.
b. September 14, 1864 in London, England
d. November 24, 1958 in Turnbridge Well, England

Richard F Celeste
American political leader
• Democratic governor of OH, 1983-91, succeeded by George Voinovich.
b. November 11, 1937 in Cleveland, Ohio

Emanuel Celler
American political leader
• Liberal Dem. congressman from NY, 1923-72; wrote, fought for Civil Rights Acts of 1957, 1960, 1964.
b. May 06, 1888 in Brooklyn, New York
d. January 15, 1981 in Brooklyn, New York

(Marco) Vinicio Cerezo (Arevalo)
Guatemalan political leader
• President of Guatemala, 1986–; first elected civilian since 1970.
b. December 26, 1942 in Guatemala City, Guatemala

Anton Joseph Cermak
American political leader–victim
• Mayor of Chicago, 1931-33; killed by bullet intended for FDR.
b. May 09, 1873 in Prague, Bohemia
d. March 06, 1933 in Miami, Florida

John Hubbard Chafee
American political leader
• Rep. senator from RI, 1977–; first Rep. elected from RI in 46 yrs.
b. October 22, 1922 in Providence, Rhode Island

Adna Romanza Chaffee
American army officer–military leader
• Led US troops in capture of Peking, Boxer Rebellion, 1900; military governor of Philippines, 1901-02.
b. April 14, 1842 in Orwell, Ohio
d. November 14, 1914 in Los Angeles, California

Adna Romanza Chaffee
American army officer–military leader
• Organized first US mechanized brigade, 1934; headed Armored Force, 1940; son of Adna R.
b. September 23, 1884 in Junction City, Kansas
d. August 22, 1941 in Boston, Massachusetts

Chaka
African political leader
• Founded Zulu Empire, mid-1820s; ruled 50,000 people.
b. 1773
d. September 1828

Neville (Arthur Neville) Chamberlain
English political leader
• Conservative prime minister, 1937-40; sought "peace in our time" thru appeasement of Hitler.
b. March 18, 1869 in Edgbaston, England
d. November 09, 1940 in Odiham, England

Violeta Barrios de Chamorro
Nicaraguan political leader
• Defeated Sandinista leader Daniel Ortega to become first elected female president of a Central American nation, 1990–.
b. October 18, 1929 in Rivas, Nicaragua

Camille N(imer) Chamoun
Lebanese political leader
• Maronite Christian leader; pres. of Lebanon, 1952-58; founded National Liberal party, 1958; followers called "Chamounists."
b. 1900 in Deir el-Kamar, Lebanon
d. August 07, 1987 in Beirut, Lebanon

Happy (Albert Benjamin) Chandler
American political leader–baseball executive
• Dem. governor of KY, 1935-39, 1955-59; baseball commissioner, 1945-51.
b. July 14, 1898 in Corydon, Kentucky

Chang Tso-Lin
Chinese military leader
• Manchurian leader from 1918; his army driven from Peking by Nationalists, 1928.
b. 1873 in Fengtien, China
d. June 04, 1928 in China

Charlemagne
(Charles the Great)
Ruler
• Conquered, ruled almost all Christian lands of Europe, 768-814.
b. April 02, 742
d. January 28, 814

Charles
(Charles Philip Arthur George; Prince of Wales)
English prince
• First child of Queen Elizabeth II and Prince Philip; currently heir to British throne.
b. November 14, 1948 in London, England

Charles I
English ruler
• King of Great Britain, Ireland, 1625-49; need for money, power led to English Civil Wars.
b. November 19, 1600
d. January 3, 1649

Charles II
(Charles the Bald)
French ruler
• Holy Roman emperor, 875-77; successfully invaded Italy, 875; failed to take over German kingdom.
b. 823
d. 877

Charles II
English ruler
• King of Great Britain, Ireland, 1660-85; wanted to strengthen monarchy, reduce financial power of Parliament.
b. May 29, 1630
d. February 06, 1685

Charles V
Ruler
• Hapsburg King of Spain, 1516-50; Holy Roman emperor, 1519; signed the Treaty of Crecy, 1544; Peace of Augsburg, 1555.
b. February 24, 1500 in Ghent, Flanders
d. September 21, 1558 in Spain

Charles VII
(Charles Albert; Charles of Bavaria)
Ruler
• Holy Roman emperor, 1742-45; in War of Austrian Succession, 1740-48.
b. August 06, 1697
d. January 2, 1745

Charles XII
Swedish ruler
• King of Sweden, 1697-1718; lost battle of Poltaua, 1709, which ended Swedish Supremacy.
b. June 27, 1682
d. December 11, 1718 in Fredriksten, Norway

Charles Martel
(Charles the Hammer)
Ruler
• Head of Frankish empire later ruled by grandson Charlemagne.
b. 689
d. 741

Mary Eugenia Charles
Dominican political leader
• Prime minister of Dominica, 1980-; requested US invasion of Grenada, 1983.
b. May 15, 1919 in Pointe Michel, Dominica

Charlotte Aldegonde E M Wilhelmine
Luxembourg ruler
• Grand Duchess of Luxembourg, 1919-64; helped to found European Common Market.
b. January 23, 1896 in Chateau de Berg, Luxembourg
d. July 09, 1985 in Luxembourg

William Curtis Chase
American military leader
• Major general; led first American troops to enter Tokyo, 1945; advocate of Nationalist China.
b. March 09, 1895 in Providence, Rhode Island
d. August 21, 1986 in Houston, Texas

Isaac Chauncey
American military leader
• Served with US Navy, 1798-1840; commander of naval forces on lakes Ontario, Erie during War of 1812.
b. February 2, 1772 in Black Rock, Connecticut
d. January 27, 1840 in Washington, District of Columbia

Camille Chautemps
French political leader
• Prime minister of France, 1930-38.
b. February 01, 1885 in Paris, France
d. July 01, 1963 in Washington, District of Columbia

Dick (Richard Bruce) Cheney
American cabinet member
• US Secretary of Defense, Bush administration, 1989-.
b. January 3, 1941 in Lincoln, Nebraska

Cheops
(Khufu)
Egyptian ruler
• Builder of the Great Pyramid at Giza.

John A(ndrew) Cherberg
American political leader
• Lt. governor of WA, 1957-; has served longer in position than anyone in US.
b. October 17, 1910 in Pensacola, Florida

Konstantin Ustinovich Chernenko
Russian political leader
• Called first Siberian, first peasant to lead USSR; oldest man elected general secretary of USSR's Communist Party; succeeded Andropov, Feb 13, 1984.
b. September 24, 1911 in Bolshaya Tes, Russia
d. March 1, 1985 in Moscow, U.S.S.R.

Viktor Mikhailovich Chernov
(Boris Olenin pseud)
Russian journalist
• Founded Social Revolutionary party, 1902; pres., All-Russian Constituent Assembly, 1918.
b. 1876
d. April 15, 1952 in New York, New York

Lionel Chevrier
Canadian politician
• Known as father of St. Lawrence Seaway; Seaway president, 1945-57.
b. April 02, 1903 in Cornwall, Ontario
d. July 08, 1987 in Montreal, Quebec

Ching Chiang
(Chiang Ching Mao; Ping Lan)
Chinese actress–political leader
• Wife of Mao Tse-tung, sentenced to death as member of "gang of four," 1976.
b. 1913 in Chucheng, China

Chiang Ching-Kuo
Chinese political leader
• President, Republic of China (Taiwan), 1978-88; liberalized policies, dropped martial law; son of Chiang Kai-Shek.
b. March 18, 1906 in Fenghua, China
d. January 13, 1988 in Taipei, Taiwan

The Chicago Seven
(Rennie Davis; David Dellinger; John Radford Froines; Tom Hayden;Abbie Hoffman; Jerry Rubin; Lee Weiner)
American political activists
• Disrupted 1968 Democratic National Convention, Chicago, with antiwar demonstrations; courtroom proceedings described in Hayden's book *Trial*, 1970.

Lawton Mainor Chiles, Jr
American political leader
• Democratic governor of FL, 1991-, defeated incumbent Bob Martinez; US senator, 1971-88.
b. April 03, 1930 in Lakeland, Florida

Truong Chinh
Vietnamese political leader
• Pres., Council of State, Vietnam, 1981-86.
b. 1906
d. September 3, 1988 in Hanoi, Vietnam

Jacques Rene Chirac
French politician
• Mayor of Paris, 1977-83; prime minister of France, 1974-76, 1986-88.
b. November 29, 1932 in Paris, France

Shirley Anita St Hill Chisholm
American political leader–author
• First black woman elected to Congress, 1968; Dem. from NY, 1969-83; wrote *Good Fight*, 1973.
b. November 3, 1924 in Brooklyn, New York

Joaquim Alberto Chissano
Mozambican political leader
• Succeeded Samora Machel as president of Mozambique, Nov 1986.
b. October 22, 1939 in Malehice, Mozambique

Chou En-Lai
Chinese pollitical leader
• With Mao Tse-Tung, founded Chinese Communist Party; premier, 1949-76.
b. 1898 in Shaohsing, China
d. January 08, 1976 in Peking, China

Christian IV
Danish ruler
• Reigned 1588-1648; city of Christiania, now Oslo, named after him.
b. April 12, 1577 in Denmark
d. February 28, 1648 in Copenhagen, Denmark

Christian X
Danish ruler
• King from 1912; enfranchised women, 1915; granted independence to Iceland, 1918; symbolized resistance to Nazis during 1943-45 imprisonment.
b. September 26, 1870 in Copenhagen, Denmark
d. April 2, 1947 in Copenhagen, Denmark

Christina
Swedish ruler
• Daughter of Gustav II Adolphus; ruled, 1632-54; abdicated throne to cousin Charles X Gustav.
b. 1626 in Stockholm, Sweden
d. 1689 in Rome, Italy

Christina
Dutch princess
• Daughter of Queen Juliana, Prince Bernhard; sister of Irene.
b. February 18, 1947 in Soestdijk, Netherlands

Henri Christophe
Haitian ruler
• Revolutionary who ruled, 1811-20; shot himself after having a stroke.
b. 1767 in Grenada, West Indies
d. 1820 in Haiti

Chu Te
Chinese army officer–military leader
• Became commander, military forces, under Mao Tse-tung 1927.
b. December 18, 1886 in Szechwan, China
d. August 06, 1976 in Peking, China

Vasili Ivanovitch Chuikov
Russian military leader
• Fought in Red Army during Russian Revolution, 1918-21; defended Stalingrad against Hitler, 1942.
b. February 12, 1900 in Serebryanye Prudy, Russia
d. March 18, 1982 in Moscow, U.S.S.R.

Chun Doo Hwan
Korean government official
• Pres. of Republic of Korea, 1980-88.
b. January 23, 1931 in Naechonri, Korea

Arthur (Raymond Arthur) Chung
Guyanese government official
• First pres. of Republic of Guyana, 1970-80.
b. January 1, 1918 in Demerara, Guyana

Il-Kwon Chung
Korean diplomat–politician
• Prime minister, 1964-70; adviser to pres. of Democratic Republic, 1979-80.
b. November 21, 1917

Sir Winston Leonard Spencer Churchill
English political leader–author
• Conservative WW II prime minister, 1940-55; rallied English, Americans to confront Hitler; won 1953 Nobel in literature, wrote *The Second War*, 1948-53, in six vols.
b. November 3, 1874 in Woodstock, England
d. January 24, 1965 in London, England

Cicciolina
(Ilona Staller)
Italian actress–politician
• Hard-core porn star elected to Italian parliament, 1987; wrote autobiography, *Confessions*, 1988.
b. in Budapest, Hungary

Henry Gabriel Cisneros
American political leader
• Mayor, San Antonio, TX, 1981-89; first Mexican-American to head major US city.
b. June 11, 1947 in San Antonio, Texas

Champ (James Beauchamp) Clark
American political leader
• Democratic leader, 1909-11; House Speaker, 1911-19.
b. March 07, 1850 in Lawrenceburg, Kentucky
d. March 02, 1921 in Washington, District of Columbia

Joe (Charles Joseph) Clark
Canadian political leader
• Prime minister, 1979-80.
b. June 05, 1939 in High River, Alberta

Joseph Sill Clark
American political leader
• First dem. mayor of Philadelphia in 67 yrs., 1952-56; senator from PA, 1956-68.
b. October 21, 1901 in Philadelphia, Pennsylvania
d. January 12, 1990 in Philadelphia, Pennsylvania

Mark Wayne Clark
American military leader
• Led Allied invasion of Italy during WW II; commanded UN forces in Korea, 1952-53; signed Korean armistice July 27, 1953.
b. May 01, 1896 in Madison Barracks, New York
d. April 17, 1984 in Charleston, South Carolina

Ramsey (William Ramsey) Clark
American cabinet member
• Attorney general under Lyndon Johnson, 1967-69.
b. December 18, 1927 in Dallas, Texas

Sir Ellis Emmanuel Innocent Clarke
Trinidadian political leader
• Pres. of Trinidad and Tobago, 1976–.
b. December 28, 1917 in Trinidad

Claudius I
(Tiberius Claudius Nero Germanicus)
Roman ruler
• Ruled, AD 41-54, began Roman occupation of Britain, AD 43; adopted son Nero who became emperor upon his death, by poison.
b. August 01, 10
d. October 13, 54 in Rome, Italy

Karl von Clausewitz
Prussian author–military leader
• Book *On War* expounded philosophy of war; had enormous effect on military strategy, tactics, in World Wars.
b. June 01, 1780 in Burg, Prussia
d. November 16, 1831

Lucius du Bignon Clay
American army officer–military leader
• Leader of Berlin Airlift, 1948-49; commander-in-chief, US forces in Europe, 1947-49.
b. April 23, 1897 in Marietta, Georgia
d. April 16, 1978 in Chatham, Massachusetts

William Perry Clements, Jr
American political leader
• Rep. governor of Texas, 1979-83, 1987-.
b. April 03, 1917 in Dallas, Texas

Cleopatra VII
Macedonian ruler
• Mistress of Julius Caesar, Marc Antony; killed herself with asp.
b. 69BC in Alexandria, Egypt
d. August 3, 30 in Alexandria, Egypt

Frances Folsom Cleveland
(Mrs Grover Cleveland)
American first lady
• Youngest first lady, first White House bride, 1886.
b. July 21, 1864 in Buffalo, New York
d. October 29, 1947 in Baltimore, Maryland

Grover (Stephen Grover) Cleveland
American US president
• Dem. 22nd, 24th president, 1885-89, 1893-97; worked to stablilize currency.
b. March 18, 1837 in Caldwell, New Jersey
d. June 24, 1908 in Princeton, New Jersey

Clark McAdams Clifford
American cabinet member
• Special adviser to presidents Truman, Kennedy, Johnson; defense secretary under Johnson, 1968-69.
b. December 25, 1906 in Fort Scott, Kansas

Bill (William Jefferson) Clinton
American political leader
• Dem. governor of AR, 1979-81, 1983-.
b. August 19, 1946 in Hope, Arkansas

George Clinton
American US vice president
• VP under Jefferson, 1805-12; NY governor, 1777-95, 1801-04; opposed adoption of US Constitution.
b. July 26, 1739 in Little Britain, New York
d. April 2, 1812 in Washington, District of Columbia

Sir Henry Clinton
British military leader
• Commander-in-chief of British troops in American Revolution, 1778-81, succeeding Howe.
b. 1738 in Newfoundland
d. December 23, 1795 in Gibraltar

Jacqueline Cochran
(Mrs Floyd B Odlum)
American aviatrix–journalist–military leader
• Organized Women's Air Force Service (WASP), 1943; first woman to break sonic barrier, 1953.
b. 1910 in Pensacola, Florida
d. August 09, 1980 in Indio, California

Jacques Coeur
French merchant–diplomat
• Wealthy, influential financial adviser to Charles VII; falsely condemned, imprisoned.
b. 1395
d. 1456

Jean-Baptiste Colbert
French statesman–government official
• Powerful minister under Louis XIV, 1665-85; created French navy, 1668.
b. August 29, 1619 in Reims, France
d. September 06, 1683

William Egan Colby
American government official–political leader
• Director, CIA, 1973-76.
b. January 04, 1920 in Saint Paul, Minnesota

Schuyler Colfax
American US vice president
• VP under U S Grant, 1869-73; involvement in scandal ended career.
b. March 23, 1823 in New York, New York
d. January 13, 1885 in Mankato, Minnesota

General Joseph Lawton Collins
American army officer–military leader
• Army chief of staff, 1949-53; head of army during Korean War; Ambassador to Viet Nam, 1954-55.
b. May 01, 1896 in New Orleans, Louisiana
d. September 12, 1987 in Washington, District of Columbia

Martha Layne Hall Collins
American political leader
• First woman governor of KY, 1983–; chaired Dem. National Convention, 1984.
b. December 07, 1936 in Bagdad, Kentucky

Fernando Affonso Collor de Mello
Brazilian political leader
• Moderate conservative president of Brazil, 1989–; first popularly elected president in three decades.
b. August 12, 1949 in Rio de Janiero, Brazil

Constantine I
(Constantine the Great; Flavius Valerius Aurelius Constantinus)
Roman ruler
• Ruled, 306-377; adopted Christianity, tried to extend rights to Christians; banished Arius, Arianism.
b. 280 in Naissus
d. March 22, 337

Constantine V
(Copronymus)
Byzantine ruler
• Son of Leo III; during reign, 741-755, summoned council on image worship, 754.
b. 718
d. 775

Constantine VI
Byzantine ruler
• Last of Isaurian emperors; throne seized by mother, Irene, who had him killed.
b. 770
d. 820

Palaeologus Constantine XI
(Dragases)
Byzantine ruler
• Last emperor of the Eastern Roman Empire, 1449-53.
b. 1404
d. 1453

Constantine XII
Greek ruler
• Succeeded to throne, 1964; left Greece, 1967; deposed, 1973.
b. June 02, 1940 in Athens, Greece

John Conyers, Jr
American political leader
• Dem. congressman from MI, 1964–; wrote *Anatomy of an Undeclared War*, 1972.
b. May 16, 1929 in Detroit, Michigan

Grace Anne Goodhue Coolidge
(Mrs Calvin Coolidge)
American first lady
• Popular, sociable White House hostess, the opposite of her retiring husband.
b. January 03, 1879 in Burlington, Vermont
d. July 08, 1957 in Northampton, Massachusetts

(John) Calvin Coolidge
American US president
• 30th pres.; Rep. assumed office on death of Harding, 1923; re-elected, 1924.
b. July 04, 1872 in Plymouth, Vermont
d. January 05, 1933 in Northampton, Massachusetts

John Sherman Cooper
American diplomat–political leader
• UN delegate 1949-51, 1968, 1981; former ambassador to India, Nepal, E Germany. Drafted Cooper-Church amendment aimed at barring further U.S. military action in Cambodia during Vietnam War.
b. August 23, 1901 in Somerset, Kentucky
d. February 21, 1991 in Washington, District of Columbia

Lewis Corey
(Louis C Fraina)
Italian author–critic
• Founded American Communist Party, 1918; changed to democratic principles demonstrated in book, *The Unfinished Task*, 1942.
b. October 13, 1894 in Italy
d. September 16, 1953 in New York, New York

Erastus Corning, III
American political leader
• Mayor of Albany, NY, 1942-83; longest tenured mayor in US.
b. October 07, 1909 in Albany, New York
d. May 28, 1983 in Boston, Massachusetts

Marquis Charles Cornwallis
English army officer–military leader
• Surrendered to George Washington at Yorktown, 1781.
b. December 31, 1738 in London, England
d. October 05, 1805 in Ghazipur, India

Liam Cosgrave
Irish political leader
• Irish prime minister, 1973-77.
b. April 3, 1920 in Dublin, Ireland

Nicanor Costa Mendez
Argentine government official
• Foreign minister who led Argentine attack on Falkland Islands, 1982.
b. October 3, 1922 in Buenos Aires, Argentina

Arthur da Costa e Silva
Brazilian army officer–political leader
• Led 1964 revolution; pres., 1967-69.
b. October 03, 1902 in Taquari, Brazil
d. December 17, 1969 in Rio de Janeiro, Brazil

John Aloysius Costello
Irish political leader
• Prime minister of first coalition government of Eire, 1948-51; head of the Government of Ireland, 1954-76.
b. June 2, 1891 in Dublin, Ireland
d. January 05, 1976 in Dublin, Ireland

Sir Zelman Cowen
Australian political leader
• Governor general of Australia, 1977-82; author of books on legal, political subjects.
b. October 07, 1919 in Melbourne, Australia

Malin Craig
American military leader–government official
• Commanded every type of military unit; US Army chief of staff, 1935-39.
b. August 05, 1875 in Saint Joseph, Missouri
d. July 25, 1945

Daniel B Crane
American political leader
• Rep. congressman from IL, 1978–; censured by US House, Jul 1983, for sexual relations with page.
b. January 1, 1936 in Chicago, Illinois

Alan MacGregor Cranston
American political leader
• Dem. senator from CA, 1969–.
b. June 19, 1914 in Palo Alto, California

Marcus Licinius Dives Crassus
Roman army officer
• With Pompey and Caesar organized First Triumvirate, 60; governor of Syria, 54.
b. 115BC
d. June 06, 53 in Carrhae, Mesopotamia

Bettino (Benedetto) Craxi
Italian political leader
• First Socialist to become prime minister of Italy, 1983-86.
b. February 24, 1934 in Milan, Italy

Croesus
Ruler
• Last king of Lydia, defeated by Cyrus the Great, 546 BC; known for great wealth.
b. 560BC
d. 546BC

Oliver Cromwell
English ruler–military leader
• Ruled England as Lord Protector, 1653-58, after execution of Charles I; favored religious freedom. Remembered for atrocities committed against Irish.
b. April 25, 1599 in Huntingdon, England
d. September 03, 1658

William James Crowe, Jr
American military leader
• Navy admiral; rose from submarine service to succeed John Vessey as chairman of Joint Chiefs of Staff, 1985-89; succeeded by Colin Powell.
b. January 02, 1925 in La Grange, Kentucky

Arturo Cruz
(Arturo Jose Cruz Porras)
Nicaraguan politician–diplomat
• Disgust with Sandinistas led to alignment with Contras, early 1980s; aborted candidacy in controversial 1984 pres. election.
b. December 18, 1923 in Jinotepe, Nicaragua

Cuauhtemoc
Aztec ruler
• Last Aztec ruler who defended empire against Spanish; hanged by Cortes.
b. 1495 in Tenochtitlan, Mexico
d. February 26, 1525 in Itzancanal, Mexico

Viscount Andrew Browne Cunningham
Irish military leader
• One of great sea commanders of Britain; led Allied naval forces in N Africa, Sicily campaigns, WW II; head of naval staff, 1943-46.
b. January 07, 1883 in Dublin, Ireland
d. June 12, 1963 in London, England

Mario Matthew Cuomo
American political leader
• Dem. governor of NY, 1982–.
b. June 15, 1932 in Queens County, New York

Mike (Michael Charles) Curb
American political leader
• Chm., Rep. National Committee, 1982–; lt. gov. of CA, 1979-83; pres., MGM Records, 1968-74.
b. December 24, 1944 in Savannah, Georgia

James Michael Curley
American political leader
• Boston Dem. boss, 1900-47; four-time mayor; governor of MA, 1935-37.
b. November 2, 1874 in Boston, Massachusetts
d. November 12, 1958 in Boston, Massachusetts

William Barker Cushing
American military leader
• Union naval hero of the Civil War; known for sinking confederate warship, *Albermarle*, 1864.
b. November 04, 1842 in Delafield, Wisconsin
d. December 17, 1874 in Washington, District of Columbia

Josef Cyrankiewicz
Polish political leader
• Premier, 1947-52, 1954-70.
b. April 23, 1911 in Tarnow, Poland
d. January 2, 1989

Cyrus the Great
(Cyrus the Elder)
Persian political leader
• Founded Persian empire, ca. 550 BC;
captured Babylon, 538 BC.
b. 600BC
d. 529BC

Richard Joseph Daley
American political leader
• Dem. mayor of Chicago, 1955-76;
considered last of big-city bosses.
b. May 15, 1902 in Chicago, Illinois
d. December 2, 1976 in Chicago, Illinois

George Mifflin Dallas
American US vice president
• Second in command under JK Polk,
1844-48.
b. July 1, 1792 in Philadelphia, Pennsylvania
d. December 31, 1864 in Philadelphia, Pennsylvania

John Nichols Dalton
American political leader
• Rep. governor of VA, 1978-82; helped
build state's Rep. party into one of
South's strongest.
b. July 11, 1931 in Emporia, Virginia
d. July 3, 1986 in Richmond, Virginia

Alfonse Marcello D'Amato
American political leader
• Rep. senator from NY, who upset Javits, 1981–.
b. August 01, 1937 in Brooklyn, New York

John Claggett Danforth
American political leader
• Moderate Rep. senator from MO,
1976–; heir to Ralston Purina fortune.
b. September 05, 1936 in Saint Louis, Missouri

Darius I
(Darius the Great)
Persian ruler
• King, 521-486 BC; army defeated by
Greeks at Battle of Marathon, 490 BC.
b. 558BC
d. 486BC

Jean Francois Darlan
French government official
• Ex-Vichy commissioner for French and
W Africa; assassinated.
b. August 07, 1881 in Nerac, France
d. December 24, 1942 in Algiers, Algeria

Roberto D'Aubuisson
Salvadoran politician
• Head of ultra-right Nationalist Republican Alliance Party, pres., Constituent Assembly, 1982–.
b. 1944 in Santa Tecla, El Salvador

Angela Yvonne Davis
American revolutionary–author
• On FBI's ten most-wanted list, 1970;
wrote autobiography, 1974.
b. January 26, 1944 in Birmingham, Alabama

Benjamin Oliver Davis, Jr
American air force officer–military leader
• Member, first group of blacks admitted
to air corps, 1941; first black general in
air force, 1954.
b. December 18, 1912 in Washington, District
of Columbia

Benjamin Oliver Davis
American military leader
• First black general in US Army, 1940.
b. July 01, 1877 in Washington, District of
Columbia
d. November 26, 1970 in North Chicago, Illinois

Dwight Filley Davis
American cabinet member
• Secretary of War under Coolidge; governor general, Philippine Islands, 1929-32; donor, 1900, of Davis Cup for
world champion tennis.
b. July 05, 1879 in Saint Louis, Missouri
d. November 28, 1945 in Washington, District
of Columbia

Jefferson Davis
American political leader
• Pres. of Confederacy, 1861-65.
b. June 03, 1808 in Christian County, Kentucky
d. December 06, 1889 in New Orleans, Louisiana

Charles Gates Dawes
American US vice president–statesman
• Developed Dawes Plan for German war
reparations, 1920s, VP under Calvin
Coolidge, 1925-29; shared 1925 Nobel
Peace Prize.
b. August 27, 1865 in Marietta, Ohio
d. April 23, 1951 in Evanston, Illinois

William L(evi) Dawson
American political leader
• Dem. rep. from IL, 1943-70; first
black man to chair major House com.
b. April 26, 1886 in Albany, Georgia
d. November 09, 1970 in Chicago, Illinois

William Frishe Dean
American army officer–military leader
• Highest ranking officer held captive in
Korean War, 1950-53.
b. August 01, 1899 in Carlyle, Illinois
d. August 24, 1981 in Berkeley, California

Michael Keith Deaver
American presidential aide
• Close adviser to Reagan, deputy chief
of staff, 1981-85; involved in controversial lobbying activities.
b. April 11, 1938 in Bakersfield, California

Regis (Jules Regis) Debray
French government official
• Radical leader in France; appointed as
foreign policy adviser by the French
pres.
b. September 02, 1940 in Paris, France

Michel Jean Pierre Debre
French political leader
• Prime minister of France, 1959-62;
Minister of Defence, 1969-73.
b. January 15, 1912 in Paris, France

**Charles Andre Joseph Marie
DeGaulle**
French political leader
• Army general, 1940, who assumed
leadership after WW II; first pres., Fifth
Republic, 1959-69.
b. November 22, 1890 in Lille, France
d. November 09, 1970 in Colombey les deux
Egloses, France

F(rederik) W(illem) De Klerk
South African political leader
• President of South Africa, 1989–, succeeding P W Botha.
b. March 18, 1936 in Johannesburg, South
Africa

Martin Robinson Delany
American author–social reformer–soldier
• Advocated colonization as solution to
slavery; first black commissioned in US
Army, 1865.
b. 1812
d. 1885

David T (Dave) Dellinger
(The Chicago 7)
American author–editor–political activist
• Chairman, National Mobilization Committee to End War in Vietnam, 1967-71.
b. August 22, 1915 in Wakefield, Massachusetts

Demetrius I
(Demetrius Poliorcetes)
Macedonian ruler
• King of Macedonia, 294-285 BC; destroyed Egyptian fleet, 306 BC.
b. 337BC
d. 283BC

Suleyman Demirel
Turkish political leader
• Four-time prime minister detained after
Sep 1980 coup; known as moderate man
of the people.
b. October 06, 1924 in Islamkoy, Turkey

Sir Miles Christopher Dempsey
English army officer–military leader
• Led Second Army in D-Day invasion, 1944; commanded forces in South East Asia, Middle East, 1945-47.
b. December 15, 1896 in Hoylake, England
d. June 06, 1969 in Yattendon, England

Joop (Johannes Marten) Den Uyl
Dutch politician
• Prime minister of The Netherlands, 1973-77, 1977-81, 1982-87.
b. 1919 in Amsterdam, Netherlands
d. December 24, 1987 in Amsterdam, Netherlands

Deng Tiaoping
Chinese political leader
• VP of Chinese Communist Party, 1977-87; most powerful member.
b. August 22, 1904 in Kuangan, China

Jeremiah Andrew Denton, Jr
American political leader
• Rep. senator from AL, 1981-87; first POW to return from Vietnam.
b. July 15, 1924 in Mobile, Alabama

Jaime DePinies
Spanish diplomat
• President of UN General Assembly, 1985–.
b. November 18, 1917 in Madrid, Spain

Jan E DeQuay
Dutch political leader
• One of founders of Dutch Union, 1940; prime minister of Netherlands, 1959-63.
b. 1901 in S'Hertogenbosch, Netherlands
d. July 04, 1985 in Beers, Netherlands

Jean Jacques Dessalines
(Jacques I)
Haitian ruler
• Brought to Haiti as slave; with British help, overthrew French, declared himself emperor of the new republic, 1804-06.
b. 1758 in Guinea
d. October 17, 1806 in Haiti

George (Courken George, Jr) Deukmejian
American political leader
• Conservative Republican governor of CA, 1983-90; succeeded Jerry Brown; succeeded by Pete Wilson.
b. June 06, 1928 in Menands, New York

Jacob Loucks Devers
American army officer–military leader
• Influential in revitalizing armed forces, WW II; retired as four-star general, 1949.
b. September 08, 1887 in York, Pennsylvania
d. October 15, 1979 in Bethesda, Maryland

Donald Devine
Canadian politician
• Progressive-Conservative Party premier of Saskatchewan, 1982–.
b. July 05, 1944 in Regina, Saskatchewan

Bernadette Josephine Devlin
(Bernadette Devlin McAliskey)
Irish political activist
• At age 21, youngest woman elected to British Parliament, 1969-74.
b. April 23, 1947 in Cookstown, Northern Ireland

George Dewey
American naval officer–military leader
• Admiral who destroyed eight Spanish warships in Spanish-American War, 1898, to become nat. hero.
b. December 26, 1837 in Montpelier, Vermont
d. January 16, 1917 in Washington, District of Columbia

Thomas Edmund Dewey
American political leader
• Lost close presidential race against Harry Truman, 1948; Rep. governor of NY, 1943-55.
b. March 24, 1902 in Owosso, Michigan
d. March 16, 1971 in Bal Harbour, Florida

Porfirio Diaz
(Jose de la Cruz Porfirio)
Mexican political leader
• Overthrew govt., ruled as dictator, 1876-80, 1884-1911.
b. September 15, 1830 in Oaxaca, Mexico
d. July 02, 1915 in Paris, France

Gustavo Diaz Ordaz
Mexican political leader
• Pres. of Mexico, 1964-72; ambassador to Spain, 1977; known for bloody handling of student demonstrations, 1968.
b. March 12, 1911 in Puebla, Mexico
d. July 15, 1979 in Mexico City, Mexico

Charles Coles Diggs, Jr
American political leader
• Dem. con. from MI, 1954-80; convicted of defrauding govt. in payroll kickback, 1980.
b. December 02, 1922 in Detroit, Michigan

Sir John Greer Dill
Irish military leader
• Senior British representative on combined Chiefs of Staff committee, WW II.
b. December 25, 1881 in Lurgan, Northern Ireland
d. November 04, 1944 in Washington, District of Columbia

John David Dingell, Jr
American political leader
• Dem. congressman from MI, 1956–; chm., Energy and Commerce Com. investigating toxic waste.
b. July 08, 1926 in Colorado Springs, Colorado

David Norman Dinkins
American political leader
• Succeeded Ed Koch as New York City's 106th and first black mayor, 1990–.
b. July 1, 1927 in Trenton, New Jersey

Diocletian
(Gaius Aurelius Valerius Diocletianus)
Roman ruler
• Ruled, 284-305; persecuted Christians; retired, became interested in gardening.
b. 245
d. 313

Dionysius the Elder
Greek ruler
• Tyrant of Syracuse whose reign was maintained by obedience through fear.
b. 430BC
d. 367BC in Syracuse, Sicily

Abdou Diouf
Senegalese political leader
• Prime minister of Senegal, 1970-80; pres., 1981–.
b. September 07, 1935 in Louga, Senegal

Everett McKinley Dirksen
American political leader
• Rep. senator, party leader from IL, 1950s-60s; played major role in passage of civil rights legislation, 1960s; known for oratory.
b. January 04, 1896 in Pekin, Illinois
d. September 07, 1969 in Washington, District of Columbia

Benjamin Disraeli
(Benjamin Disraeli Beaconsfield Earl of; "Dizzy")
English statesman–author
• Prime minister, 1868, 1874-80; founded modern Conservative Party; popular novels include Lothair, 1870.
b. December 21, 1804 in London, England
d. April 19, 1881 in London, England

Robert Ellington Dixon
American military leader
• WW II pilot who signalled sinking of first Japanese carrier: "Scratch one flattop."
b. 1906
d. October 21, 1981 in Virginia Beach, Virginia

Anatoly Fedorovich Dobrynin
(Anatoliy Federovich Dobrynin)
Russian diplomat
• Soviet ambassador to US, 1962-86.
b. November 16, 1919 in Krasnaya Gorka, U.S.S.R.

Christopher John Dodd
American political leader
• Dem. senator from CT, 1981–; son of former senator Thomas Dodd.
b. May 27, 1944 in Willimantic, Connecticut

Thomas Joseph Dodd
American political leader
• Dem. senator from CT, 1959-71; censured by Senate for financial irregularities, 1967.
b. May 15, 1907 in Norwich, Connecticut
d. May 24, 1971 in Old Lyme, Connecticut

Samuel Kanyon Doe
Liberian political leader
• Army officer; overthrew white leader, Tolbert and assumed leadership, 1980; captured by rebels and died of wounds during civil war.
b. May 06, 1951 in Tuzon, Liberia
d. September 09, 1990 in Monrovia, Liberia

Karl C Doenitz
(Karl C Dönitz)
German naval officer–political leader
• Hitler's successor who declared Germany's surrender, 1945; tried, sentenced for war crimes.
b. September 16, 1891 in Berlin, Germany
d. December 24, 1980 in Hamburg, Germany (West)

Bernadine Rae Dohrn
(The Weathermen)
American political activist
• Led militant Weathermen group, 1960s-70s; fled prosecution for breaking antiriot laws; indictments eventually dropped, 1970s.
b. January 12, 1942 in Chicago, Illinois

Bob (Robert Joseph) Dole
American political leader
• Rep. senator from KS, 1969–; senate majority leader, 1981-87.
b. July 22, 1923 in Russell, Kansas

Elizabeth Hanford Dole
(Mrs Robert Dole; "Liddy")
American cabinet member
• First woman secretary of transportation, 1983-87; secretary of labor, 1989-90; president, American Red Cross, 1990–.
b. July 2, 1936 in Salisbury, North Carolina

Engelbert Dollfuss
Austrian political leader
• Chancellor, 1932-34; killed by Austrian Nazis.
b. October 04, 1892 in Texing, Austria
d. July 25, 1934

Pete V(ichi) Domenici
American political leader
• Conservative Rep. senator from NM, 1973–; head of Senate Budget Committee, 1981.
b. May 07, 1932 in Albuquerque, New Mexico

Raymond James Donovan
American cabinet member
• Secretary of labor under Ronald Reagan, 1981-85.
b. August 31, 1930 in Bayonne, New Jersey

James Harold Doolittle
American military leader–army officer
• Led first aerial raid on Japan, WW II.
b. December 14, 1896 in Alameda, California

Andrea Doria
Italian military leader–statesman
• One of greatest Italian military leaders, conquerors of his day; drove French from Genoa, 1528; name given to luxury liner that sank, 1956.
b. November 3, 1466
d. November 25, 1560

Sir James Douglas
Canadian businessman–political leader
• First governor of newly created colony of BC, 1858-64; in office during gold rush.
b. August 15, 1803 in Demerara, New Guiana
d. August 02, 1877 in Victoria, British Columbia

Sholto (William Sholto) Douglas
(Baron Douglas of Kirtleside)
English military leader
• Master of Royal Air Force; chm., British European Airways; wrote *Years of Combat*, 1963.
b. December 23, 1893 in Oxford, England
d. October 29, 1969 in Northampton, England

Sir Alexander Frederick Douglas-Home
English politician
• Member, House of Lords, 1951; disclaimed peerages for life, 1965; held various political posts, 1960s-70s.
b. July 02, 1903 in London, England

Baron Hugh Caswell Tremenheere Dowding
British air force officer–military leader
• Victorious director, Battle of Britian, 1940; designed improvements to fighter planes.
b. April 22, 1882 in Moffat, Scotland
d. February 15, 1970 in Kent, England

James Lee Dozier
American military leader
• Five-star general, kidnapped by Red Brigade terrorists, 1981; freed by Italian police after 42 days.
b. April 1, 1931 in Arcadia, Florida

Draco
Greek politician
• Called founder of Athenian civilization; gave Athens first written code of law, 621 BC.

Dracula
(Vlad the Impaler)
Hungarian prince
• Alleged vampire whose life has been subject of many horror films.
b. 1431
d. 1476

Sir Francis Drake
English naval officer–navigator
• First Englishman to circumnavigate globe, 1577-80; helped defeat Spanish Armada, 1588.
b. 1540 in Tavistock, England
d. January 28, 1596 in Portobelo, Panama

Jean Drapeau
Canadian politician
• Mayor of Montreal, 1954-57, 1960-86.
b. February 18, 1916 in Montreal, Quebec

Willem Drees
Dutch political leader
• Country's longest-serving prime minister, 1948-58; introduced comprehensive welfare system; ended colonial role in Indonesia, 1949.
b. July 05, 1886 in Amsterdam, Netherlands
d. May 14, 1988 in The Hague, Netherlands

Alfred Dreyfus
French army officer
• Wrongly convicted of high treason, 1895, vindicated in 1906; defended by Emile Zola in *J'Accuse*, 1898.
b. October 09, 1859 in Mulhouse, Alsace
d. July 12, 1935

Jose Napoleon Duarte (Fuentes)
Salvadoran political leader
• Christian Democrat president of El Salvador, 1981-82, 1984-89; struggled to bring democracy to country.
b. November 23, 1926 in San Salvador, El Salvador
d. February 23, 1990 in San Salvador, El Salvador

Yuri Vladimirovich Dubinin
Russian diplomat
• Soviet ambassador to US, 1986–.
b. October 07, 1930 in Moscow, U.S.S.R.

W(illiam) E(dward) B(urghardt) DuBois
American author–reformer
• Prominent in early movements for racial equality; helped create NAACP, 1909; advocated Pan-Africanism.
b. February 23, 1868 in Barrington, Massachusetts
d. August 27, 1963 in Accra, Ghana

Jacques Duclos
French communist leader
• Among founding members of French Communist Party; party secretary, 1931-64.
b. October 02, 1896 in Louey, France
d. April 25, 1975 in Paris, France

Alene B(ertha) Duerk
American naval officer–military leader
• First woman to receive flag rank in US Navy: rear admiral, 1972.
b. March 29, 1920 in Defiance, Ohio

Bertrand Du Guesclin
French military leader
• Considered greatest French warrior of his day; Constable of France, 1370.
b. 1320 in Dinan, France
d. July 13, 1380 in Languedoc, France

Michael Stanley Dukakis
American political leader
• Democratic governor of MA, 1975-79, 1983-91; Democratic presidential candidate, 1988, defeated by George Bush.
b. November 03, 1933 in Brookline, Massachusetts

Duncan I
Scottish ruler
• Succeeded Malcolm II, 1034; overthrown, killed by Macbeth.

Lord Edwin Duncan-Sandys
British diplomat–politician
• Negotiated independence for many British territorial colonies, 1960-64; Conservative member of Parliament, 1930s-70s.
b. January 24, 1908
d. November 26, 1987 in London, England

Duong Van Minh
Vietnamese army officer–political leader
• Pres. of Vietnam, 1975.
b. February 19, 1916 in My Tho, Vietnam

Maurice le Noblet Duplessis
Canadian political leader
• Premier of Quebec, Canada, 1936-39, 1944-59; founded National Union Party.
b. April 2, 1890 in Three Rivers, Quebec
d. September 07, 1959 in Schefferville, Quebec

Pierre Samuel DuPont, IV
American political leader
• Rep. governor of DE, 1977-85; first to declare candidacy for 1988 pres. election, 1986.
b. January 22, 1935 in Wilmington, Delaware

Francois Duvalier
("Papa Doc")
Haitian political leader
• Dictator of Haiti, 1957-71; during reign economy declined, terror increased.
b. April 14, 1907 in Port-au-Prince, Haiti
d. April 21, 1971 in Port-au-Prince, Haiti

Jean-Claude Duvalier
("Baby Doc")
Haitian political leader
• Became "pres. for life" of Haiti, 1970; overthrown in coup, 1986, fled into exile.
b. July 03, 1951 in Port-au-Prince, Haiti

Thomas Francis Eagleton
American political leader
• George McGovern's running mate, 1972; withdrew due to past history of nervous exhaustion.
b. September 04, 1929 in Saint Louis, Missouri

Antonio dos Santos Ramaiho Eanes
Portuguese political leader
• Pres. of Portugal, 1976-86; first freely elected in 50 yrs.
b. January 25, 1935 in Alcains, Portugal

Jubal Anderson Early
American military leader
• Confederate general who led Washington, DC raid, 1864.
b. November 03, 1816 in Franklin County, Virginia
d. March 02, 1894 in Lynchburg, Tennessee

James Oliver Eastland
American political leader
• Dem. senator from MS, 1941-78; opposed civil rights legislation.
b. November 28, 1904 in Doddsville, Mississippi
d. February 19, 1986 in Greenwood, Mississippi

John Henry Eaton
American political leader
• Youngest ever sworn into Senate; Dem. from TN, 1818-29; secretary of War, 1829-31.
b. June 18, 1790 in Halifax County, North Carolina
d. November 17, 1856 in Washington, District of Columbia

Theophilus Eaton
English colonial figure–politician
• Founded New Haven, CT, 1638; governor of New Haven colony from 1639.
b. 1590 in Stony Stratford, England
d. January 07, 1658 in New Haven, Connecticut

Abba Eban
(Aubrey Solomon)
Israeli diplomat
• UN representative, 1949-59; ambassador to US, 1950-59; wrote *Israel in the World*, 1966.
b. February 02, 1915 in Cape Town, South Africa

Friedrich Ebert
German political leader
• First pres. of German republic, 1919; leading proponent of Weimar constitution.
b. February 04, 1871 in Heidelberg, Germany
d. February 28, 1925

Louis Echeverria Alvarez
Mexican political leader
• Pres. of Mexico, 1970-76.
b. January 17, 1922 in Mexico City, Mexico

Saint Edmund
(Eadmund; Edmund the Martyr)
Ruler
• Ruled East Anglia, 855-870; refused to renounce faith while being tortured to death.
b. 840 in Nurnberg, Germany
d. 870

Edward
(Edward Antony Richard Louis)
English prince
• Youngest child of Queen Elizabeth II and Prince Philip; currently seventh in line to British throne.
b. March 1, 1964 in London, England

Edward I
English ruler
• Ruled England, 1272-1307; eldest son of Henry III; buried in Westminster Abbey.
b. 1239 in Westminster, England
d. 1307

Edward II
(Edward of Carnarvon)
English ruler
• Ruled England, 1307-27; fourth son of Edward I; captured, imprisoned, forced to resign, murdered, 1327.
b. 1284 in Carnarvon, England
d. 1327

Edward III
(Edward of Windsor)
English ruler
• Ruled England, 1327-77; eldest son of Edward II; claimed French crown in name of mother, Isabella, 1337, assumed title, 1340.
b. 1312 in Windsor, England
d. 1377

Edward IV
English ruler
• Ruled England, 1461-70, 1471-83; during reign increased trade, improved public administration.
b. April 28, 1442 in Rouen, France
d. 1483 in London, England

Edward V
English ruler
• Crown was seized by uncle, Richard III, 1483; deposed, imprisoned on grounds of illegitimacy.
b. 1470 in Westminster, England
d. 1483 in London, England

Edward VI
English ruler
• Ruled England, Ireland, 1547-53; only child of Henry VIII, Jane Seymour; Henry VIII's only legitimate son.
b. 1537 in Hampton Court, England
d. 1553 in London, England

Edward VII
(Edward Albert)
English ruler
• Son of Queen Victoria who ruled 1901-10; popular monarch known as peacemaker.
b. 1841 in London, England
d. 1910 in London, England

Edward VIII
(Edward Albert Christian George Andrew Patrick David; Duke of Windsor)
English ruler
• Reigned, Jan-Dec, 1936; abdicated to marry twice-divorced American Wallis Simpson.
b. June 23, 1894 in Richmond, England
d. May 18, 1972 in Paris, France

Edward the Black Prince
(Prince of Wales; Edward IV; Edward of Woodstock)
English prince
• Eldest son of Edward III; started hearth tax which led to revolt in 1368.
b. 1330 in Woodstock, England
d. 1376 in London, England

Edward the Confessor
(Eadward)
English ruler
• Ruled the English, 1042-66; supervised rebuilding of Westminster Abbey; canonized, 1161; feast day, Oct 13.
b. 1002 in Oxford, England
d. January 05, 1066

Edwy
(Eadwig)
English ruler
• Son of Edmund I; succeeded uncle, Eadred, as king, 955.

Dwight David Eisenhower
American US president–military leader
• Allied European military leader, WW II; popular, conservative 34th pres., 1953-61.
b. October 14, 1890 in Denison, Texas
d. March 28, 1969 in Washington, District of Columbia

John Sheldon Doud Eisenhower
American diplomat–celebrity relative
• Son of Dwight and Mamie Eisenhower, father of David; in US Army, 1944-63, in reserves as brigadier general; ambassador to Belgium, 1969-71; author of books about WW II.
b. August 03, 1922 in Denver, Colorado

Mamie Geneva Doud Eisenhower
(Mrs Dwight David Eisenhower)
American first lady
• Her short bangs were fashion fad; served as honorary pres. of Girl Scouts.
b. November 14, 1896 in Boone, Iowa
d. November 01, 1979 in Washington, District of Columbia

David Elazar
Israeli army officer
• Commanded Israeli troops, October War, 1973; resigned.
b. 1925 in Sarajevo, Yugoslavia
d. April 15, 1976 in Tel Aviv, Israel

Kristjan Eldjarn
Icelandic politician
• Pres. of Iceland, 1968-80.
b. December 06, 1916 in Tjorn, Iceland
d. September 13, 1982 in Cleveland, Ohio

James Bruce Elgin
(Eighth Earl of Elgin)
English political leader
• As governor-general of Canada, 1847-54; applied concept of "responsible govt."; viceroy of India, 1862-63.
b. July 2, 1811 in London, England
d. November 2, 1863 in Dharmsala, India

Elizabeth I
English ruler
• Daughter of Henry VIII, Anne Boleyn; ruled Great Britain, N Ireland, 1558-1603; during reign England became world power.
b. September 07, 1533 in Greenwich, England
d. March 24, 1603

Elizabeth II
(Elizabeth Alexandra Mary)
English ruler
• Succeeded father George VI to throne upon his death, 1952; noted horsewoman; allowed TV coverage of royal family.
b. April 21, 1926 in London, England

Daniel Ellsberg
American author–economist–political activist
• Leaked Pentagon Papers to press, 1971; wrote *Papers on the War*, 1972.
b. April 07, 1931 in Chicago, Illinois

Guillermo Endara
Panamanian political leader
• Elected president of Panama, May 1989; sworn into office following overthrow of Manuel Noriega, December 1989.

Epaminondas
Greek military leader
• Theban commander; brilliant tactician; defeated Spartans, 371, 362 BC.
b. 410BC
d. 362BC

Ludwig Erhard
German economist–political leader
• West German chancellor, 1960s, who guided country's post-WWII economic recovery.
b. February 04, 1897 in Fuerth, Germany
d. May 07, 1977 in Bonn, Germany (West)

Eric IX
(Eric the Saint; Erik IX Jedvardsson)
Swedish ruler
• King of Sweden, c. 1150-60, who led Christian crusade to Finland, c. 1157; killed by a Danish prince while attending mass; feast day, May 18.

Tage Fritiof Erlander
Swedish politician
• Prime minister, 1946-69; instituted comprehensive school system, social security in Sweden.
b. June 13, 1901 in Ransater, Sweden
d. June 21, 1985 in Huddinge, Sweden

Sam(uel James, Jr) Ervin
American political leader
• Folksy Dem. senator from NC, 1954-74; known for role in 1973 Watergate hearings.
b. September 27, 1896 in Morganton, North Carolina
d. April 23, 1985 in Winston-Salem, North Carolina

Levi Eshkol
(Levi Shkolnik)
Israeli political leader
• A founder of the state of Israel, 1948; premier, 1963-67.
b. October 25, 1895 in Oratova, Ukraine
d. February 26, 1969 in Jerusalem, Israel

Comte d' Charles Henri Hector Estaing
French naval officer
• Commanded National Guard at Versailles, 1789; testified in favor of Marie Antoinette during her trial; guillotined as a royalist.
b. November 28, 1729 in Auvergne, France
d. April 28, 1794 in Paris, France

Eugenie
(Eugenia Marie de Montijo de Guzman; Comtessa de Teba)
French ruler
• Wife of Napoleon III and empress, 1853-71; fashion trendsetter of her time.
b. 1826 in Granada, Spain
d. 1920

Laurent Fabius
French political leader
• Conservative prime minister, 1984–, who aims to modernize France.
b. August 2, 1946 in Paris, France

Fahd ibn Abdul Aziz
Saudi ruler
• Formerly Crown Prince, 1973-82; succeeded throne after sudden death of brother, 1982–.
b. 1922 in Riyadh, Saudi Arabia

Charles Warren Fairbanks
American US vice president
• Served as vp under Theodore Roosevelt, 1905-09.
b. May 11, 1852 in Unionville Center, Ohio
d. June 04, 1918 in Indianapolis, Indiana

Thomas Fairfax
(Baron of Cameron)
English army officer–military leader
• Commanded New Model Army, 1645, fought against defeated Charles I.
b. January 17, 1612 in Leeds Castle, England
d. November 12, 1671 in Winchester, Virginia

Faisal II
Iraqi ruler
• King, 1939-58; killed during overthrow of monarchy.
b. May 02, 1935 in Baghdad, Iraq
d. July 14, 1958

Faisal (Ibn Abdul-Aziz al Saud)
Saudi ruler
• King 1964-75; resisted radical political forces in Arab world; assassinated by nephew.
b. 1906 in Riyadh, Saudi Arabia
d. March 25, 1975 in Riyadh, Saudi Arabia

Faisal ibn Musaed
Saudi prince–assassin
• Nephew of Faisal; murdered his uncle.
b. 1947
d. 1975

Albert Bacon Fall
American cabinet member
• Secretary of Interior, 1921-23; imprisoned for involvement in Teapot Dome scandal, 1930-32.
b. November 26, 1861 in Frankfort, Kentucky
d. November 3, 1944 in El Paso, Texas

Thorbjorn Nils Olof Falldin
Swedish political leader
• First non-Socialist prime minister, 1976-78.
b. April 24, 1926 in Vastby, Sweden

Amintore Fanfani
("Little Professor"; "Tom Thumb of Italian Politics")
Italian political leader
• Five-time prime minister; resigned April 1983; wrote over 40 books.
b. February 06, 1908 in Tuscany, Italy

Frances T(arlton) Farenthold
American political activist
• First woman ever to have name placed in nomination as Dem. VP candidate, 1972.
b. October 02, 1926 in Corpus Christi, Texas

Farouk I
Egyptian ruler
• Ruled, 1936-52; incompetent, corrupt; overthrown, forced to abdicate.
b. February 11, 1920 in Cairo, Egypt
d. March 18, 1965 in Rome, Italy

David Glasgow Farragut
American military leader
• Civil War hero remembered for saying "Damn the torpedoes, full speed ahead," 1864.
b. July 05, 1801 in Knoxville, Tennessee
d. August 14, 1870 in Portsmouth, New Hampshire

Walter E Fauntroy
American social reformer–politician
• Dem. con. from DC, 1971–; chm., Congressional Black Caucus, 1981-83.
b. February 06, 1933 in Washington, District of Columbia

Francois Felix Faure
French political leader
• Sixth pres. of French Republic, in office during Dreyfus Affair, 1895-99.
b. January 3, 1841 in Paris, France
d. February 16, 1899 in Paris, France

Leon Febres-Cordero
Ecuadorean political leader
• Social Christian president of Ecuador, 1984-88; succeeded by Rodrigo Cevallos Borja.
b. March 09, 1931 in Guayaquil, Ecuador

Dianne Feinstein
American political leader
• Mayor of San Francisco, 1978-88; succeeded assassinated George Moscone.
b. June 22, 1933 in San Francisco, California

Rebecca Ann Latimer Felton
American political leader
• Appointed senator from GA, 1922; first woman to sit in Senate.
b. June 1, 1835 in Decatur, Illinois
d. January 24, 1930 in Atlanta, Georgia

Ferdinand I
Roman ruler
• Brother of Charles V; raised in Spain; ruled Holy Roman Empire, 1558-64.
b. 1503
d. 1564

Ferdinand V
(Ferdinand II; Ferdinand the Catholic; Ferdinand III)
Spanish ruler
• Best known for marrying Isabella of Castile, uniting Spain; established the Inquisition, 1478; aided Columbus.
b. March 1, 1452 in Sos, Spain
d. January 23, 1516 in Madrigalejo, Spain

Geraldine Anne Ferraro
(Mrs John Zaccaro)
American political leader
• Walter Mondale's running mate, 1984 presidential election; first woman vp candidate.
b. August 26, 1935 in Newburgh, New York

Joao Baptista de Oliveira Figueiredo
Brazilian political leader
• Pres. of Brazil, 1979-85.
b. January 15, 1918 in Rio de Janeiro, Brazil

Jose Figueres Ferrer
Costa Rican political leader
• President of Costa Rica, 1953-58, 1970-74, advocating equal treatment for all.
b. September 25, 1906 in San Ramon, Costa Rica
d. June 08, 1990

Abigail Powers Fillmore
(Mrs Millard Fillmore)
American first lady–teacher
• While in office set up first White House library.
b. March 13, 1798 in Stillwater, New York
d. March 3, 1853 in Washington, District of Columbia

Millard Fillmore
American US president
• Became 13th pres. upon death of Zachary Taylor; Whig, 1850-53; sent Commodore Perry to open up Japan, 1852; supported divisive Compromise of 1850.
b. January 07, 1800 in Summerhill, New York
d. March 08, 1874 in Buffalo, New York

Vigdis Finnbogadottir
Icelandic political leader
• Iceland's first female head of state, 1980–.
b. April 15, 1930 in Reykjavik, Iceland

Hamilton Fish, III
American political leader
• Rep. con. from NY, 1919-45; known for outspokenness, isolationist views.
b. December 07, 1888 in Garrison, New York
d. January 18, 1991 in Cold Spring, New York

Garret FitzGerald
Irish political leader
• Prime minister of Ireland, 1981-1987; signed historic Anglo-Irish Agreement, 1985.
b. February 09, 1926 in Dublin, Ireland

John Francis Fitzgerald
American businessman–political leader
• Father of Rose Kennedy; mayor of Boston, 1905-14.
b. February 11, 1863 in Boston, Massachusetts
d. October 02, 1950 in Boston, Massachusetts

Marlin (Max Marlin) Fitzwater
American presidential aide
• Replaced Larry Speakes as presidential press secretary, 1987–.
b. November 24, 1942 in Salinas, Kansas

Titus Quinctius Flamininus
Roman military leader
• Proclaimed independence of Greek city-states, 196, after defeating Macedonian King Philip V at Cynoscephalae.
b. 230?BC
d. 175?BC

Ralph Edward Flanders
American political leader
• Rep. senator from VT who introduced censure resolution against Joseph McCarthy, 1954.
b. September 28, 1880 in Barnet, Vermont
d. February 19, 1970 in Springfield, Vermont

Daniel John Flood
American political leader
• Dem. congressman from PA, 1944-46, 1948-52, 1954-80.
b. November 26, 1904 in Hazelton, Pennsylvania

Edward Joseph Flynn
American political leader
• NY City Democratic "boss," 1922-53.
b. September 22, 1891 in Bronx, New York
d. August 18, 1953 in Dublin, Ireland

Elizabeth Gurley Flynn
American political leader
• Professional revolutionary, 1906-64; first woman nat. chm., US Communist Party, 1961.
b. August 07, 1890 in Concord, New Hampshire
d. September 05, 1964 in Moscow, U.S.S.R.

Ferdinand Foch
French military leader
• Supreme commander of Allied forces, 1918; directed final victorious offensive, WW I.
b. October 02, 1851 in Tarbes, France
d. March 2, 1929 in Paris, France

Thomas Stephen Foley
American political leader
• Dem. congressman from WA, 1965–; House majority leader, 1987–.
b. March 06, 1929 in Spokane, Washington

James E(lisha) Folsom
American political leader
• Dem. governor of AL, 1947-51, 1955-59; helped pass law to stifle Ku Klux Klan, 1949.
b. October 09, 1908 in Elba, Alabama
d. November 21, 1987 in Cullman, Alabama

Marion Bayard Folsom
American government official–cabinet member
• Chief drafter of Social Security Act, 1935; HEW secretary, 1953-61.
b. November 23, 1894 in McRue, Georgia
d. September 28, 1976 in Rochester, New York

Manuel Deodoro da Fonseca
Brazilian political leader
• First president of Brazil, 1891.
b. August 05, 1827 in Alagoas, Brazil
d. August 23, 1892 in Rio de Janeiro, Brazil

John Forbes
British army officer
• Took over Fort Duquesne, 1758, renaming it Fort Pitt; later became Pittsburgh.
b. 1710 in Dunfermline, Scotland
d. March 11, 1759 in Philadelphia, Pennsylvania

Betty (Elizabeth Anne Bloomer) Ford
(Mrs Gerald Ford)
American first lady
• Co-founder, pres., Betty Ford Center for drug rehabilitation, 1982–; wrote *The Times of My Life*, 1978.
b. April 08, 1918 in Chicago, Illinois

Gerald Rudolph Ford
(Gerald King)
American US president
• Rep., 38th pres., 1974-77; succeeded Nixon after his resignation, pardoned him, 1974; withdrew US in fall of S Vietnam, Cambodia, 1975.
b. July 14, 1913 in Omaha, Nebraska

Nathan Bedford Forrest
American military leader
• Conferedate war general; first head of original Klu Klux Klan.
b. July 13, 1821 in Chapel Hill, Tennessee
d. October 29, 1877 in Memphis, Tennessee

James Vincent Forrestal
American cabinet member
• First secretary of Defense, 1947-49.
b. February 15, 1892 in Beacon, New York
d. May 22, 1949 in Bethesda, Maryland

Joe (Joseph Jacob) Foss
American political leader–football executive
• WW II ace; governor of SD, 1955-63; commissioner of AFL, 1959-66, until league merged with NFL.
b. April 17, 1915 in Sioux Falls, South Dakota

Francis I
French ruler
• King, 1515-47; known for patronizing arts, letters; Renaissance in France occured during reign.
b. 1494
d. 1547

Francisco Franco
Spanish political leader
• Dictator who overthrew republican opposition, headed oppressive regime, 1936-75.
b. December 04, 1892 in El Ferrol, Spain
d. November 2, 1975 in Madrid, Spain

Benjamin Franklin
(Richard Saunders pseud)
American political leader–scientist–author
• Published *Poor Richard's Almanack*, 1732-57; invented lightning rod, bifocal glasses; helped draft Declaration of Independence, Constitution.
b. January 17, 1706 in Boston, Massachusetts
d. April 17, 1790 in Philadelphia, Pennsylvania

Franz Ferdinand
Austrian political leader
• Archduke, whose assassination, 1914, led to outbreak of WW I.
b. December 18, 1863 in Graz, Austria
d. June 28, 1914 in Sarajevo, Yugoslavia

Franz Joseph I
Austrian ruler
• Emperor of Austria, 1848-1916, king of Hungary, 1867-1916, whose reign was last great age of Austrian political, cultural preeminence.
b. 1830
d. 1916

Franz Joseph II
(Prince of Liechtenstein)
Liechtenstein ruler
• Head of State, 1938-84; oversaw country develop from poor, rural to wealthy tax, banking haven; passed power to son, Crown Prince Hans Adam.
b. August 16, 1906 in Liechtenstein
d. November 13, 1989 in Vaduz, Liechtenstein

Sir Bruce Austin Fraser
(Lord Fraser of North Cape; "Tubby")
English naval officer–military leader
• Commander, British Home Fleet, WW II; credited with sinking German battleship *Scharnhorst*, 1943.
b. February 05, 1888 in Acton, England
d. February 12, 1981 in London, England

John Malcolm Fraser
Australian political leader
• Liberal Party prime minister of Australia, 1975-83.
b. March 21, 1930 in Melbourne, Australia

Frederick I
(Frederick Barbarossa)
German ruler
• Thought to be one of greatest German kings, 1152-90; ruled Italy, 1155-90, Holy Roman Empire, 1152-90.
b. 1123
d. 1190

Frederick II
German ruler
• Son of Henry VI; ruled Holy Roman Empire, 1212-50; noted for interests in science, literature.
b. 1194
d. 1250

Frederick III
German ruler
• Ruled Holy Roman Empire, 1440-93; reign marked by conflict between German princes, Austrian nobles.
b. 1831 in Potsdam, Germany
d. June 15, 1888 in Berlin, Germany

Frederick IX
Danish ruler
• King, 1947-72; known for resisting Germans, allowing female succession to throne, making parliament one house.
b. March 11, 1899 in Copenhagen, Denmark
d. 1972

Frederick the Great
(Frederick II)
German ruler
• King of Prussia, 1740-86; son of Frederick William I; noted for social reforms.
b. January 24, 1712 in Berlin, Germany
d. August 17, 1786 in Berlin, Germany

Frederick Louis
(Prince of Wales)
English prince
• Father of King George III of England; had strained relationship with his father, George II.
b. January 2, 1707 in Hannover, Germany
d. March 2, 1751 in London, England

Frederick William I
Prussian ruler
• King, 1713-40; reign marked by internal improvements of kingdom; ordered mandatory schooling, 1717.
b. August 15, 1688 in Berlin, Germany
d. May 31, 1740 in Potsdam, Germany

Paul Lamar Freeman
American military leader
• Four-star general, US Army; headed NATO, 1962-65; highly decorated for WW II service.
b. 1907
d. April 17, 1988 in Monterey, California

Elias Freij
Jordanian politician
• Mayor of Bethlehem, 1972–.
b. 1920 in Bethlehem, Jordan

John Charles Fremont
American explorer–political leader
• Led three Western expeditions, 1840s; one of first two CA senators; first Rep. candidate for pres., 1856.
b. January 21, 1813 in Savannah, Georgia
d. July 13, 1890 in New York, New York

John Radford Froines
(The Chicago 7)
American political activist
• Took part in antiwar demonstrations during 1968 Democratic National Convention in Chicago.
b. June 13, 1939 in Oakland, California

Mitsuo Fuchida
Japanese naval officer–military leader
• Imperial Navy commander who led attack on Pearl Harbor, Dec 1941.
b. 1903
d. May 3, 1976 in Kashiwara, Japan

Alberto Fujimori
Peruvian political leader
• President of Peru, 1990–, succeeding Alan Garcia Perez; first person of Japanese descent to lead Latin American nation.
b. July 28, 1938 in Lima, Peru

Takeo Fukuda
Japanese political leader
• Acquited of 1947 political crimes, 1958; prime minister, 1976-78.
b. January 14, 1905 in Japan

James William Fulbright
American political leader
• Dem. senator from AR, 1945-74; books include *The Arrogance of Power*, 1966.
b. April 09, 1905 in Sumner, Missouri

Thomas Gage
English army officer
• Governor of MA, 1774-75; used troops to restrain colonial resistance, which led to bloodshed.
b. 1721 in Firle, England
d. April 02, 1787 in England

Sir Eric Matthew Gairy
West Indian political leader
• Prime minister of Grenada, 1974-79; deposed in coup.
b. February 18, 1922 in St. Andrew's, Grenada, West Indies

Sir Richard Nelson Gale
English army officer–military leader
• Led 6th airborne division during Allied invasion of Normandy, 1944.
b. July 25, 1896 in London, England
d. July 29, 1982 in Kingston-on-Thames, England

Joseph Simon Gallieni
French army officer–military leader
• Led counterattack against Germans at the Marne, 1914; minister of war, 1915-16; made marshal posthumously.
b. 1849 in Saint-Beat, France
d. 1916

Leopoldo Fortunato Galtieri
Argentine political leader
• Pres. of Argentina, 1976-82; resigned after unsuccessful war with Great Britain over Falkland Islands.
b. July 15, 1926 in Caseros, Argentina

Maurice Gustave Gamelin
French army officer–military leader
• Head of Allied forces at outbreak of WW II.
b. September 2, 1872 in Paris, France
d. April 18, 1958 in Paris, France

Indira Priyadarshini Nehru Gandhi
Indian political leader
• Prime minister, 1966-77, 1978-84; worked for economic planning, social reform; assassinated; daughter of Nehru.
b. November 19, 1917 in Allahabad, India
d. October 31, 1984 in New Delhi, India

Rajiv Ratna Gandhi
Indian political leader
• Son of Indira Gandhi and grandson of Jawaharlal Nehru. Became India's sixth and youngest prime minister in 1984 after assassination of his mother. Ousted in 1989. Assassinated by bomb blast while making political comeback, campaigning for prime minister.
b. August 2, 1944 in Bombay, India
d. May 21, 1991 in Sriperumpudur, India

Alan Garcia Perez
Peruvian political leader
• President of Peru, 1985-90; succeeded by Alberto Fujimori.
b. May 23, 1949 in Lima, Peru

Alfonso Garcia Robles
Mexican diplomat
• Shared Nobel Peace Prize, 1982, for work on disarmament; his Treaty of Tlateloco banned nuclear arms from Latin America, 1960s.
b. March 2, 1911 in Zamora, Mexico

James Abram Garfield
American US president
• Rep., 20th pres., Mar 4 - Sep 9, 1881; shot in Washington railway station by Charles J Guiteau.
b. November 19, 1831 in Cuyahoga County, Ohio
d. September 19, 1881 in Elberon, New Jersey

Lucretia Rudolph Garfield
(Mrs James A Garfield)
American first lady
• In White House less than seven months; survived husband by 30 yrs.
b. April 19, 1832 in Hiram, Ohio
d. March 14, 1918 in Pasadena, California

Giuseppe Garibaldi
Italian political leader–soldier
• Major figure in Risorgimento movement for Italian unity, mid-1800s.
b. July 04, 1807 in Nice, France
d. June 02, 1882

Jake (Edwin Jacob) Garn
American political leader
• Rep. senator from UT, 1974–; first politician in space, Apr 12, 1985 on space shuttle *Discovery*.
b. October 12, 1932 in Richfield, Utah

John Nance Garner
American US vice president
• VP under Franklin Roosevelt, 1933-41.
b. November 22, 1868 in Blossom Prairie, Texas
d. November 07, 1967 in Uvalde, Texas

Marcus Moziah Garvey
Jamaican political leader
• Led Back to Africa movement; founded Universal Negro Improvement Assn., 1911.
b. August 17, 1887 in Saint Ann's Bay, Jamaica
d. June 1, 1940 in London, England

Alcide de Gasperi
Italian statesman–political leader
• Progressive prime minister, 1945-53, who brought Italy into NATO, tried major reforms.
b. April 03, 1881 in Terentino, Italy
d. August 19, 1954

Horatio Gates
American army officer–military leader
• Commanded Americans, defeated British at Saratoga, 1777.
b. July 26, 1728 in Maldon, England
d. April 1, 1806 in New York, New York

James Maurice Gavin
American army officer–military leader
• Paratroop general; commanded 82nd Airborne, took part in D-Day invasion, WW II; served twice as ambassador to France under John F Kennedy.
b. March 22, 1907 in New York, New York
d. February 23, 1990 in Baltimore, Maryland

Amin Gemayel
Lebanese political leader
• Succeeded assassinated brother as president, 1982-88.
b. 1942 in Bikfaya, Lebanon

Bashir Gemayel
Lebanese political leader
• Pres.-elect who was assassinated in bomb attack before taking office.
b. November 1, 1947 in Bikfaya, Lebanon
d. September 14, 1982 in Beirut, Lebanon

Sheikh Pierre Gemayel
Lebanese politician
• Founder of Phalange party, 1936; held parliamentary posts, 1958-70; party started civil war, 1975.
b. November 01, 1905 in Lebanon
d. August 3, 1984 in Bikfaya, Lebanon

George I
(George Louis)
English ruler
• First king of house of Hanover; succeeded Queen Anne, 1714.
b. March 28, 1660 in Hanover, Prussia
d. June 12, 1727 in Germany

George II
(George Augustus)
English ruler
• King, 1727-60; son of George I.
b. November 1, 1683 in Prussia
d. October 25, 1760 in London, England

George II
Greek ruler
• Unpopular king, 1922-23, 1935-47; son of Constantine I; deposed by military junta, 1923.
b. July 2, 1890
d. April 01, 1947

George III
(George William Frederick)
English ruler
• King, 1760-1820; grandson of George II; known for mental attacks, support of policy that led to loss of American colonies.
b. June 04, 1738 in London, England
d. January 29, 1820 in Windsor, England

George IV
(George Augustus Frederick)
English ruler
• Prince regent when George III became mentally deranged, 1811-20; King, 1820-30.
b. August 12, 1762 in London, England
d. June 25, 1830 in Windsor, England

George V
(George Frederick Ernest Albert)
English ruler
• Grandson of Queen Victoria who ruled 1910-36; succeeded by son Edward VIII.
b. 1865 in London, England
d. January 2, 1936 in London, England

George VI
(Albert Frederick Arthur George; Duke of York)
English ruler
• Ascended to throne, Dec 11, 1936, upon abdication of brother Edward VIII; father of Queen Elizabeth II.
b. December 14, 1895 in Sandringham, England
d. February 06, 1952 in Sandringham, England

George Edward Alexander Edmund
(Duke of Kent)
English prince
• Youngest brother of King George VI.
b. December 2, 1902 in London, England
d. August 25, 1942 in Scotland

Richard Andrew Gephardt
American political leader
• Moderate Dem. congressman from MO, 1977–; first Dem. to declare 1988 presidential candidacy, 1987.
b. January 31, 1941 in Saint Louis, Missouri

Einar Gerhardsen
Norwegian political leader
• Prime minister, 1940s-60s; helped determine nation's pro-West stance after WW II.
b. May 1, 1897 in Oslo, Norway
d. September 19, 1987 in Oslo, Norway

Erno Gero
Hungarian government official
• Member, Hungarian Communist Party, 1918-62; as first secretary, called in Soviet troops to quell uprising, 1956.
b. August 17, 1898 in Budapest, Hungary
d. March 12, 1980 in Budapest, Hungary

Elbridge Gerry
American US vice president
• Signed Declaration of Independence; Madison's vp, 1812-14; actions gave rise to term "gerrymander."
b. July 17, 1749 in Marblehead, Massachusetts
d. November 23, 1814 in Washington, District of Columbia

Donald Getty
Canadian politician
• Progressive-conservative party premier of Alberta, 1985–.
b. August 3, 1933 in Westmount, Quebec

Gheorghe Gheorghiu-Dej
Romanian communist leader
• Head of state, 1961-65; established Rumania's independence from Soviet Union.
b. November 08, 1901 in Barlad, Romania
d. March 19, 1965

Joseph A Ghiz
Canadian political leader
• Liberal Party premier of Prince Edward Island, 1986–.
b. January 27, 1945 in Charlottetown, Prince Edward Island

Robert Lee Ghormley
American naval officer–military leader
• Commanded American, Allied naval forces in Southwest Pacific, WW II; led attack on Solomon Islands, 1942.
b. October 15, 1883 in Portland, Oregon
d. June 21, 1958 in Washington, District of Columbia

Sadegh Ghotbzadeh
Iranian government official
• Foreign minister who was executed in plot to kill Khomeini and topple government.
b. 1936
d. September 15, 1982 in Teheran, Iran

Kenneth Allen Gibson
American political leader
• First black mayor of Newark, NJ, 1970-86.
b. May 15, 1932 in Enterprise, Alabama

Newt(on Leroy) Gingrich
American political leader
• Republican congressman from GA, and House Minority Whip, 1979–; known for guerrilla-style tactics.
b. June 17, 1943 in Harrisburg, Pennsylvania

Henri Honore Giraud
French army officer–military leader
• Escaped German prison camp, re-establishing French army; military chief, North African campaign, 1943.
b. January 18, 1879
d. March 11, 1949 in Dijon, France

Valery Giscard d'Estaing
French politician
• Pres. of France, 1974-81.
b. February 02, 1926 in Koblenz, Germany

Rudolph William Giuliani
American political leader
• US attorney, NYC, 1983-89; prosecuted major organized crime, corruption, fraud cases: Ivan Boesky stock-fraud conviction, 1986.
b. May 28, 1944 in New York, New York

William Ewart Gladstone
English political leader–author
• Four-time British prime minister, 1868-1894; most prominent man in politics of his time.
b. December 29, 1809 in Liverpool, England
d. May 19, 1898 in Hawarden, England

Carter Glass
American statesman–political leader
• Dem. senator, con. for 44 yrs.; helped draft Federal Reserve Bank Act, 1913.
b. January 04, 1858 in Lynchburg, Virginia
d. May 28, 1946 in Washington, District of Columbia

Florizel Augustus Glasspole
Jamaican political leader
• Governor general of Jamaica, 1973–.
b. September 25, 1909 in Kingston, Jamaica

John Herschel Glenn, Jr
American astronaut–political leader
• First man to orbit Earth, Feb 20, 1962; Dem. senator from OH, 1975–.
b. July 18, 1921 in Cambridge, Ohio

Sir John Bagot Glubb
English military leader–author
• Commanded Arab Legion/Jordanian Army, 1939-56; wrote books on Mideast.
b. April 16, 1897 in Preston, England
d. March 17, 1986 in Mayfield, England

Godfrey of Bouillon
French ruler–soldier
• Led First Crusade, 1096; captured Jerusalem and became first king, 1099; subject of *Chansons de Geste*.
b. 1058 in Baisyin Brabant, France
d. July 18, 1100 in Jerusalem, Palestine

Boris Fedorovich Godunov
Russian ruler
• Czar of Russia, 1598-1605; life was subject of play by Pushkin, opera by Mussorgski.
b. 1551 in Moscow, Russia
d. April 23, 1605

George Washington Goethals
American army officer–engineer–political leader
• Chief engineer, Panama Canal, 1913; first governor of Canal Zone, 1914-17.
b. June 29, 1858 in Brooklyn, New York
d. January 21, 1928 in New York, New York

Louis Malesherbes Goldsborough
American naval officer–military leader
• Commanded fleet that destroyed Confederate fleet, 1862.
b. February 18, 1805 in Washington, District of Columbia
d. February 2, 1877 in Washington, District of Columbia

Barry Morris Goldwater
American political leader–author
• Rep. senator from AZ, 1953-87; defeated by Lyndon Johnson in landslide 1964 presidential election; father of modern conservatism.
b. January 01, 1909 in Phoenix, Arizona

Barry Morris Goldwater, Jr
American political leader
• Son of Barry Goldwater, Rep. congressman from CA, 1969-.
b. July 05, 1938 in Los Angeles, California

Wladyslaw Gomulka
Polish political leader
• Led Poland's Communist Party, 1956-70.
b. February 06, 1905 in Krosno, Poland
d. September 01, 1982 in Warsaw, Poland

Felipe Gonzalez Marquez
Spanish political leader
• First Socialist premier since 1936-39 Civil War; elected 1982-.
b. March 05, 1942 in Seville, Spain

Wilson (Willie Wilson) Goode
American political leader
• First black mayor of Philadelphia, 1984-.
b. August 19, 1938 in Seaboard, North Carolina

Andrew Jackson Goodpaster
American army officer–military leader
• Commander-in-chief, Supreme Allied Command, Europe, 1969-74, 1977-81.
b. February 12, 1915 in Granite City, Illinois

Mikhail Sergeyevich Gorbachev
Russian political leader
• Named secretary general of USSR Communist Party following death of Chernenko, Mar 1985; initiated policy of glasnost, attempting to revive Soviet society; won Nobel Peace Prize, 1990.
b. March 02, 1931 in Privolnoye, U.S.S.R.

Albert Arnold Gore
American political leader
• Dem. senator from TN, 1953-70.
b. December 26, 1907 in Granville, Tennessee

Albert Gore, Jr
American political leader
• Moderate Dem. senator from TN, 1985-; presidential candidate, 1988. Known also for music sticker crusade of wife, Tipper.
b. March 31, 1948 in Washington, District of Columbia

Joao Goulart
Brazilian political leader
• Last civilian president of Brazil, 1961-64.
b. March 01, 1918 in Sao Borja, Brazil
d. December 06, 1976

Yakubu Gowon
Nigerian army officer–political leader
• Crushed Biafran secessionist revolt, 1967-70; head of state, 1966-75.
b. October 19, 1934 in Pankshin, Nigeria

William Alexander Graham
American political leader
• A founder of Whig party; senator, governor, secretary of navy.
b. September 05, 1804 in Lincoln County, North Carolina
d. August 11, 1875 in Saratoga Springs, New York

(William) Phil(ip) Gramm
American economist–political leader
• Rep. senator from TX, 1984-; co-author of Gramm-Rudman budget balancing law, 1985.
b. July 08, 1942 in Fort Benning, Georgia

Julia Dent Grant
(Mrs Ulysses S Grant)
American first lady
• Unpretentious army wife; buried with husband in NY's monumental tomb.
b. January 26, 1826 in Saint Louis, Missouri
d. December 14, 1902 in Washington, District of Columbia

Ulysses S(impson) Grant
(Hiram Ulysses Grant)
American US president–military leader
• Union commander-in-chief, Civil War; forced surrender of R E Lee; 18th pres., Rep., 1869-77; term marred by scandals.
b. April 27, 1822 in Point Pleasant, Ohio
d. July 23, 1885 in Mount McGregor, New York

Ella Grasso
(Ella Tambussi)
American political leader
• First woman elected governor in US; Dem., CT, 1975-80.
b. May 1, 1919 in Windsor Locks, Connecticut
d. February 05, 1981 in Hartford, Connecticut

Gratian
(Flavius Gratianus)
Roman ruler
• Ruled empire of Gaul, Spain, Britain; later in reign neglected public affairs for hunting; killed by Maximus followers.
b. 359
d. 383

Mike Gravel
American political leader
• Dem. senator from Alaska, 1969-75; "Pentagon Papers" affair brought him to wide public attention, 1971.
b. May 13, 1930 in Springfield, Massachusetts

Samuel Lee Gravely, Jr
American naval officer–military leader
• First black admiral in US, 1971; retired 1980.
b. June 04, 1922 in Richmond, Virginia

Louis Patrick Gray
American FBI director
• Acting director, FBI, 1972-73, who resigned over Watergate; indicted for illegal practices, 1978.
b. July 18, 1916 in Saint Louis, Missouri

Rodolfo Graziani
(Marchese DiNeghelli)
Italian military leader
• Minister of Defense for Mussolini, WW II; imprisoned by Italian court, 1950.
b. August 11, 1882 in Frosinone, Italy
d. January 11, 1955 in Rome, Italy

Edith S(tarrett) Green
American political leader
• Powerful Dem. congressman from OR, 1955-75; worked on education, women's rights, anti-poverty legislation.
b. January 17, 1910 in Trent, South Dakota
d. April 21, 1987 in Tualatin, Oregon

Richard Grenville
English naval officer
• Led colonizing expedition to Roanoke Island, NC, 1585; subject of Tennyson's poem "The Revenge"; cousin of Sir Walter Raleigh.
b. 1541 in Cornwall, England
d. 1591

Lady Jane Grey
English ruler
• Ruled for nine days; imprisoned, beheaded by Mary I's troops.
b. October 1537 in Bradgate, England
d. February 12, 1554 in London, England

Marvin (Samuel Marvin) Griffin
American political leader
• Governor of GA, 1955-59; George Wallace's VP running mate, 1968.
b. September 04, 1907 in Bainbridge, Georgia
d. June 13, 1982 in Tallahassee, Florida

Arthur Griffith
Irish political leader
• Founded Sinn Fein movement, 1902; president, Irish Free State, 1922.
b. March 21, 1872 in Dublin, Ireland
d. August 12, 1922 in Dublin, Ireland

George Theodorus Grivas
Cypriot military leader
• Led right-wing guerilla group, EOKA, to unite Cyprus with Greece, 1955-59.
b. March 23, 1898 in Trikomo, Cyprus
d. January 27, 1974 in Limassol, Cyprus

Andrei Andreevich Gromyko
Russian diplomat
• Pres., USSR, 1985-88; Soviet foreign affairs minister, 1957-85.
b. July 05, 1909 in Starye Gromyky, Russia
d. July 02, 1989 in Moscow, U.S.S.R.

James E Groppi
American political activist–clergyman
• Former priest who gained national attention by leading 200 consecutive marches in support of open housing in Milwaukee, 1960s.
b. 1930 in Milwaukee, Wisconsin
d. November 04, 1985 in Milwaukee, Wisconsin

Karoly Grosz
Hungarian communist leader
• Succeeded Janos Kadar as Communist Party chief, 1988–.
b. August 01, 1930 in Miskolc, Hungary

Leslie Richard Groves
American army officer–military leader
• Director of Manhattan Project, which developed atomic bomb, 1942-47.
b. August 17, 1896 in Albany, New York
d. July 13, 1970 in Washington, District of Columbia

Alfred Maximillian Gruenther
American military leader
• Youngest four-star general in US history; Supreme Military Commander, NATO, 1953-56.
b. March 03, 1899 in Platte Center, Nebraska
d. May 3, 1983 in Washington, District of Columbia

Heinz Wilhelm Guderian
German military leader
• Army general who developed concept of blitzkrieg warfare during WW II.
b. July 17, 1888 in Kulm, Prussia
d. May 15, 1954 in Fussen, Germany (West)

Gustaf Adolf VI
(Gustavus)
Swedish ruler
• Reigned 1950-73; founded Swedish Institute in Rome; succeeded by grandson, Carl Gustaf XVI.
b. November 11, 1882 in Stockholm, Sweden
d. September 15, 1973 in Helsingborg, Sweden

Gustavus Adolphus
(Gustavus II Adolph)
Swedish ruler
• Son of Charles IX; ruled, 1611-32; victorious in battle with Russia, 1613-17.
b. December 09, 1594 in Stockholm, Sweden
d. November 16, 1632 in Lutzen, Germany

Antonio Guzman
(Silvestre Antonio Guzman Fernandez)
Dominican political leader
• Pres., 1978-82; freed political prisoners, abolished state censorship.
b. February 12, 1911 in La Vega, Dominican Republic
d. July 04, 1982 in Santo Domingo, Dominican Republic

Haakon VII
Norwegian ruler
• First king of independent Norway after separation from Sweden, 1905-57.
b. August 03, 1872 in Charlottenlund, Denmark
d. September 21, 1957 in Oslo, Norway

George Habash
Palestinian political leader
• Founded Popular Front for Liberation of Palestine (PFLP), radical Marxist faction of PLO, 1967.
b. 1925 in Lydda, Palestine

Hissene Habre
Chadian political leader
• Pres. of Chad, 1982–; took office after military coup.

Saad Haddad
Lebanese army officer–military leader
• Renegade army major; formed own militia, made seperate peace with Israel to keep Syria from annexing Lebanon.
b. 1937 in Marjayoun, Lebanon
d. January 14, 1984 in Marjayoun, Lebanon

Hadrian
(Publius Aelius Hadrianus)
Roman ruler
• Emperor, 117-38; during reign erected many buildings, including temple of Venus and Roma.
b. January 24, 76 in Spain
d. 138

Frank Hague
American political leader
• Dem. mayor, political boss of Jersey City, 1917-47.
b. January 17, 1876 in Jersey City, New Jersey
d. January 01, 1956 in Jersey City, New Jersey

Alexander Meigs Haig, Jr
American military leader–cabinet member
• Commander in chief, US European Command, 1974-78; Reagan's secretary of State, 1981-82; Rep. presidential candidate, 1987-88.
b. December 02, 1924 in Philadelphia, Pennsylvania

Haile Selassie I
(Lij Tafari Makonnen; "Lion of Judah")
Ethiopian ruler
• Autocratic ruler of Ethiopia, 1930-74.
b. July 17, 1891 in Harar, Ethiopia
d. August 27, 1975 in Addis Ababa, Ethiopia

Gus Hall
(Arvo Kusta Halberg)
American political activist
• Leading American communist; two-time presidential candidate.
b. October 08, 1910 in Iron, Minnesota

Walter Hallstein
German diplomat–statesman
• Founder of European Economic Community (Common Market), pres., 1958-67.
b. November 17, 1901 in Mainz, Germany
d. March 29, 1982 in Stuttgart, Germany (West)

Alexander Hamilton
American political leader–author
• First US treasury secretary, 1789-95; strong federalist, planned US fiscal system.
b. January 11, 1757 in Nevis, West Indies
d. July 11, 1804 in Weehawken, New Jersey

Sir Ian Standish Monteith Hamilton
British army officer–author
• British commander at Gallipoli, WW I.
b. 1853
d. October 12, 1947 in London, England

Lee Herbert Hamilton
American political leader
• Dem. congressman from IN, 1964–; foreign affairs expert; co-chaired Iran Contra hearings, 1987.
b. April 2, 1931 in Daytona Beach, Florida

Hannibal Hamlin
American US vice president
• VP under Lincoln, 1861-65.
b. August 27, 1809 in Paris Hill, Maine
d. July 04, 1891 in Bangor, Maine

Knut Hjalmar Leonard Hammarskjold
Swedish political leader
• Prime minister, 1914-17; chm., Nobel Prize Foundation, 1929-47; father of Dag.
b. 1862
d. October 12, 1953 in Stockholm, Sweden

Hammurabi
Babylonian ruler
• Started to build tower of Babel; established written code of law.
b. 1955BC
d. 1913BC

Wade Hampton
American army officer–military leader
• Confederate leader whose troops of artillery, infantry, cavalry were known as "Hampton's Legion."
b. March 28, 1818 in Charleston, South Carolina
d. April 11, 1902 in Columbia, South Carolina

Winfield Scott Hancock
American military leader
• Battle of Gettysburg, Indian Wars hero; Dem. presidential candidate, 1880, lost to Garfield.
b. February 14, 1824 in Montgomery County, Pennsylvania
d. February 09, 1886 in Governor's Island, New York

Thomas Troy Handy
American army officer–military leader
• Deputy chief-of-staff to generals Marshall, Eisenhower; commander of all US troops in Europe, 1944-54.
b. March 11, 1892 in Spring City, Tennessee
d. April 14, 1982 in San Antonio, Texas

Hannibal
Military Leader
• Carthaginian general, who with 35,000 soldiers, elephants, crossed Alps into Italy, 221 BC; known for tactical genius.
b. 247BC
d. 183BC

Takashi Hara
Japanese political leader
• First commoner, professional politician to be prime minister, 1918-21; assassinated.
b. 1856 in Mariola, Japan
d. November 04, 1921 in Tokyo, Japan

Harald
Norwegian ruler
• Son of King Olav V; succeeded father to throne upon his death, 1991.
b. February 21, 1937 in Oslo, Norway

William Joseph Hardee
American army officer–military leader
• Confederate general, surrendered to Sherman in NC, Apr, 1865; wrote *Rifle and Light Infantry Tactics*, 1855, used as army textbook.
b. November 1, 1815 in Savannah, Georgia
d. November 06, 1873 in Wytheville, Virginia

Florence Kling De Wolfe Harding
(Mrs Warren G Harding)
American first lady
• Ambitious divorcee who pushed Warren into presidency; burned his executive papers.
b. August 15, 1860 in Marion, Ohio
d. November 21, 1924 in Marion, Ohio

Warren G(amaliel) Harding
American US president
• Rep., 29th pres., 1921-23; administration was plagued with corruption, scandal.
b. November 02, 1865 in Blooming Grove, Ohio
d. August 02, 1923 in San Francisco, California

Baron William David Ormsby-Gore Harlech
British diplomat
• Confidant of John F Kennedy who was British ambassador to Washington, 1961-65.
b. May 2, 1918
d. January 26, 1985 in Shrewsbury, England

Bryce Nathaniel Harlow
American presidential aide–business executive
• Powerful adviser to Ford, Nixon, Eisenhower; lobbiest, governmental relations expert.
b. August 11, 1916 in Oklahoma City, Oklahoma
d. February 17, 1987 in Washington, District of Columbia

Ernest N(ason) Harmon
American army officer–military leader
• Commanded First Armored Division, North African, Italian campaigns, WW II; one of army's most decorated officers.
b. February 26, 1894 in Lowell, Massachusetts
d. November 13, 1979 in White River Junction, Vermont

Harold II
British ruler
• King who reigned after brother-in-law, Edward the Confessor's death, 1066; conquered Wales, killed in battle.
b. 1022
d. October 15, 1066 in Hastings, England

Sir Arthur Travers Harris
English military leader
• Head of Britain's Bomber Command, WW II; believed key to victory was massive night bombing raids on German cities.
b. April 13, 1892 in Cheltenham, England
d. April 05, 1984 in London, England

Joseph Pratt Harris
American political activist–educator
• Invented automatic voting machine, Harris Votamatic, 1962.
b. February 18, 1896 in Candor, North Carolina
d. February 13, 1985 in Berkeley, California

Anna Tuthill Symmes Harrison
(Mrs William Henry Harrison)
American first lady
• Wife of William Henry, grandmother of Benjamin Harrison.
b. July 25, 1775 in Morristown, New Jersey
d. February 25, 1864 in North Bend, Ohio

Benjamin Harrison
American US president
• Rep., 23rd pres., 1889-93; grandson of William Henry; election decided by electoral college; popular vote favored Grover Cleveland.
b. August 2, 1833 in North Bend, Ohio
d. March 13, 1901 in Indianapolis, Indiana

Caroline Lavinia Scott Harrison
(Mrs Benjamin Harrison)
American first lady
• First wife of Benjamin Harrison; died in White House two weeks before husband was defeated for second term.
b. October 01, 1832 in Oxford, Ohio
d. October 25, 1892 in Washington, District of Columbia

William Henry Harrison
American US president
• Ninth pres., Mar 4-Apr 4, 1841; first pres. to die in office.
b. February 09, 1773 in Charles City, Virginia
d. April 04, 1841 in Washington, District of Columbia

William Kelly Harrison, Jr
American military leader
• General; influential negotiator in truce talks that ended Korean War, 1951-52.
b. September 07, 1895 in Washington, District of Columbia
d. May 25, 1987 in Bryn Mawr Terrace, Pennsylvania

Gary Warren Hart
(Gary Warren Hartpence)
American political leader
• Dem. senator from CO, 1975-87; vied for presidential nomination, 1984, 1988; scandal-ridden 1988 campaign rocked party.
b. November 28, 1936 in Ottawa, Kansas

Philip Aloysius Hart
American political leader
• Popular liberal Dem. senator from MI, 1958-76.
b. December 1, 1912 in Bryn Mawr, Pennsylvania
d. December 26, 1976 in Washington, District of Columbia

Harun-Al-Rashid
(Caliph of Bagdad)
Arabian political leader
• Fifth caliph of Abbasia dynasty, 785-803; reign marked by grandeur and noble style.
b. 764 in Rey, Persia
d. March 24, 809 in Tus, Persia

Ali Nasir Muhammad Hasani
Political Leader
• Pres., People's Democratic Republic of Yemen, 1980-86.
b. 1938

Hassan II
(King of Morocco)
Moroccan ruler
• King since 1961; son of King Mohammed V.
b. July 09, 1929

Orrin Grant Hatch
American political leader
• Conservative Rep. senator from UT, 1977–.
b. March 22, 1934 in Pittsburgh, Pennsylvania

Richard Gordon Hatcher
American political leader
• First black mayor of Gary, IN, 1967–.
b. July 1, 1933 in Michigan City, Indiana

Mark Odom Hatfield
American political leader
• Moderate Rep. senator from OR, 1967–; wrote *Between a Rock and a Hard Place*, 1977.
b. July 12, 1922 in Dallas, Oregon

Richard Hatfield
Canadian politician
• Progressive-Conservative Party premier of New Brunswick, 1970-87.
b. April 09, 1931 in Woodstock, New Brunswick

Sibyl Collings Hathaway
(Dame of Sark)
British ruler–author
• Feudal master of Channel Island; Seigneur of Sark, 1927-74; wrote *Maid of Sark*, 1939.
b. January 13, 1884
d. July 14, 1974 in London, England

Charles James Haughey
Irish political leader
• Prime minister during prison hunger strikes, 1979-81; ousted by Fitzgerald.
b. September 16, 1925 in Castlebar, Ireland

Vaclav Havel
Czech dramatist–political leader
• Dissident playwright; won Obie for *The Increased Difficulty of Concentration*, 1970; named interim president of Czechoslovakia, 1989; first freely elected president in 55 years, 1990.
b. October 05, 1936 in Prague, Czechoslovakia

Bob (Robert James Lee) Hawke
Australian political leader
• Labor Party leader, succeeded Malcolm Fraser as prime minister, 1983–.
b. December 09, 1929 in Bordertown, Australia

Gus (Augustus Freeman) Hawkins
American political leader
• Dem. congressman from CA, 1962–; co-author, Humphrey-Hawkins Full Employment and Balanced Growth Act.
b. August 31, 1907 in Shreveport, Louisiana

Sir John Hawkins
(Sir John Hawkyns)
English naval officer
• Naval expeditions with relative, Sir Francis Drake, brought about break between England and Spain, defeated Spanish Armada, 1587.
b. 1532 in Plymouth, England
d. November 12, 1595 in West Indies

Paula Fickes Hawkins
(Mrs Walter E Hawkins)
American political leader
• Rep. senator from FL, 1980-87; first woman elected to Senate based on own career.
b. January 24, 1927 in Salt Lake City, Utah

Carl Trumball Hayden
American political leader
• Dem. senator from AZ, 1927-69; credited with longest senatorial tenure.
b. October 02, 1877 in Tempe, Arizona
d. January 25, 1972 in Mesa, Arizona

Tom (Thomas Emmett) Hayden
(The Chicago 7)
American political activist
• Co-founded SDS (Students for Democratic Society), 1961; liberal Dem. CA assemblyman, 1982–; wrote *Reunion: A Memoir*, 1988; ex-husband of Jane Fonda.
b. December 11, 1939 in Royal Oak, Michigan

Lucy Webb Hayes
(Mrs Rutherford B Hayes; "Lemonade Lucy")
American first lady
• First president's wife to graduate from college; refused to serve alcohol at White House.
b. August 28, 1831 in Chillicothe, Ohio
d. June 25, 1889 in Fremont, Ohio

Rutherford B(irchard) Hayes
American US president
• Rep., 19th pres., 1877-81; won by one vote in newly created electoral college; ended Reconstruction period in South.
b. October 04, 1822 in Delaware, Ohio
d. January 17, 1893 in Fremont, Ohio

Wayne Levere Hays
American political leader
• Congressman who retired from office after involvement with Elizabeth Ray, 1976.
b. June 13, 1911 in Bannock, Ohio

William Babcock Hazen
American military leader
• Army's chief signal officer, 1880; organized Adolphus Greely's polar expedition, 1881; court-martialed for criticizing superiors, 1885.
b. September 27, 1830 in West Hartford, Vermont
d. January 16, 1887 in Washington, District of Columbia

Timothy Michael Healy
Irish political leader
• Led anti-Parnell nationalists; first governor general, Irish Free State, 1922-28.
b. May 17, 1855 in Bantry, Ireland
d. March 26, 1931 in Chapelizod, Ireland

Edward Richard George Heath
English political leader
• Prime minister, 1970-74.
b. July 09, 1916 in Broadstairs, England

William Heath
American military leader
• Last surviving Revolutionary War major general; commanded Eastern Department, Hudson Valley, 1777-79.
b. March 02, 1737 in Roxbury, Massachusetts
d. January 24, 1814 in Roxbury, Massachusetts

Margaret Mary Heckler
American cabinet member–diplomat
• Secretary of Health and Human Services under Reagan, 1983-85; ambassador to Ireland, 1985–.
b. June 21, 1931 in Flushing, New York

Gustav Walter Heinemann
German political leader
• First Social Democrat to be elected pres. of Germany, 1969-74; opposed Hitler.
b. July 23, 1899 in Schwelm, Germany (West)
d. July 07, 1976 in Essen, Germany (West)

Heliogabalus
(Elagabalus; Varius Avitus Bassianus)
Roman ruler
• King, 218-221; imposed Baal worship on Rome; adopted Alexander as heir; killed when he tried to depose Alexander.
b. 204 in Emesa, Syria
d. 222

Richard McGarrah Helms
American government official–political leader
• CIA Deputy Director, 1965-73; ambassador to Iran, 1973-76.
b. March 3, 1913 in Saint Davids, Pennsylvania

Thomas Andrews Hendricks
American US vice president
• VP under Grover Cleveland, 1885.
b. September 07, 1819 in Zanesville, Ohio
d. November 25, 1885 in Indianapolis, Indiana

Henry I
(Henry Beauclerc)
English ruler
• King of England, 1100-35, ascending to throne following death of brother, William II; long suspected of arranging brother's death; youngest son of William the Conqueror.
b. 1068 in Yorkshire, England
d. December 01, 1135 in France

Henry II
English ruler
• First Plantagenet king of England, 1154-89; began development of common law.
b. March 05, 1133
d. 1189

Henry III
English ruler
• Plantagenet king, 1216-72; captured during Baron's War, 1264; rescued by son Edward I, 1265, who later succeeded him.
b. 1207
d. 1272

Henry IV
(Henry Bolingbroke; Henry of Lancaster)
English ruler
• King of England, 1399-1413.
b. 1367
d. March 2, 1413

Henry V
English ruler
• Lancastrian king of England, 1413-22; acquired Norway, France, 1417-20.
b. 1387
d. 1422

Henry VI
English ruler
• King of England, son of Henry V; ruled during War of Roses.
b. 1421
d. 1471

Henry VII
(Henry Tudor)
English ruler
• King of England, 1485-1509; first Tudor monarch; marriage of daughter to James IV of Scotland brought two countries together.
b. January 28, 1457
d. April 21, 1509 in Richmond, England

Henry VIII
English ruler
• Most renowned of English kings, 1509-47; break with Roman church led to English Reformation; father of Elizabeth I.
b. June 28, 1491 in Greenwich, England
d. January 28, 1547 in Westminster, England

Henry of Wales
(Henry Charles Albert David; "Harry")
English prince
• Second son of Prince Charles and Princess Diana; third in line to British throne behind father and brother, William of Wales.
b. September 15, 1984 in London, England

Henry the Navigator
Portuguese prince
• Never went on voyage but established school of navigation, improved compass, helped voyagers in costal African trips.
b. March 04, 1394 in Porto, Portugal
d. November 13, 1460 in Sagres, Portugal

Henry William Frederick Albert
(Duke of Gloucester)
English prince
• Uncle of Queen Elizabeth II, last surviving son of King George V; best known as soldier, horseman.
b. March 31, 1900 in Sandringham, England
d. June 09, 1974 in Northamptonshire, England

Patrick Henry
American revolutionary–patriot
• Led radical faction in VA, 1775; famous for saying, "Give me liberty or give me death."
b. May 29, 1736 in Hanover County, Virginia
d. June 06, 1799 in Charlotte County, Virginia

Anthony B Herbert
American military leader
• Much-decorated lieutenant colonel; in book *Soldier*, 1973, described US Army atrocities in Vietnam; sued "60 Minutes" for libel.
b. 1930

Nicholas Herkimer
American military leader
• Revolutionary war hero; killed in Battle of Oriskany; NY town named for him.
b. November 1, 1728 in Herkimer, New York
d. August 19, 1777 in Little Falls, New York

Steingrimur Hermannsson
Icelandic political leader
• Prime minister of Iceland, 1983–.
b. June 22, 1928 in Iceland

Rafael Hernandez-Colon
Puerto Rican politician
• Governor of Puerto Rico, 1973–.
b. October 24, 1936 in Ponce, Puerto Rico

Herod Antipas
Palestinian ruler
• Son of Herod the Great who executed John the Baptist, sent Jesus to Pontius Pilate.
b. 4BC
d. 39AD

Herod the Great
Ruler–Biblical Character
• King of Judea who ordered the killing of all males under age two for fear of losing throne to Jesus.
b. 73BC
d. 4BC

Luis Herrera Campins
Venezuelan political leader
• Member of Partido Social Christiano, 1946–; pres. of Venezuela, 1979-83.
b. May 04, 1925 in Acarigua, Venezuela

Chaim Herzog
Israeli political leader
• Pres., 1983–; ambassador to UN, 1975-78.
b. September 17, 1918 in Belfast, Northern Ireland

Michael Ray Dibdin Heseltine
British government official–political leader
• Defense minister in Margaret Thatcher's Conservative gov't., 1983-86.
b. March 21, 1933 in Swansea, Wales

Henry Kent Hewitt
American naval officer–military leader
• Led naval operations, invasion of N Africa, WW II; invasion of S France, 1944; appointed Admiral, 1949.
b. February 11, 1887 in Hackensack, New Jersey
d. September 15, 1972 in Middlebury, Vermont

Walter Joseph Hickel
American cabinet member
• Nixon's secretary of interior, 1969-70; governor of AK, 1966-69.
b. August 18, 1919 in Claflin, Kansas

Ambrose Powell Hill
American military leader
• Confederate lt. general; led first attack, Battle of Gettysburg; killed in action.
b. November 09, 1825 in Culpeper, Virginia
d. April 02, 1865 in Petersburg, Virginia

Lester Hill
American political leader
• Dem. senator from AL, 1938-68.
b. December 29, 1894 in Montgomery, Alabama
d. December 2, 1984 in Montgomery, Alabama

Patrick John Hillery
Irish political leader
• Pres. of the Republic of Ireland, 1976–.
b. May 02, 1923 in Miltown-Malbay, Ireland

Carla Anderson Hills
American cabinet member
• US Trade Representative in George Bush's cabinet, 1989–; secretary of HUD, 1975-77.
b. January 03, 1934 in Los Angeles, California

Paul von Hindenburg
German army officer–political leader
• Pres., 1925-34, who appointed Adolph Hitler chancellor, 1933.
b. October 02, 1847 in Posen, Germany
d. August 02, 1934 in Neudeck, Germany

Hirohito
Japanese ruler
• Japan's longest-reigning emperor, 1926-89; surrendered to US to end WW II, 1945; wrote monographs on marine biology.
b. April 29, 1901 in Tokyo, Japan
d. January 07, 1989 in Tokyo, Japan

Hitotsubashi
(Tokugawa Keiki Yoshinobu)
Japanese ruler
• Last shogun of Japan, 1866-67; aided in peaceful transition of power to emperor; became prince, 1902.
b. 1837
d. 1902

Ho Chi Minh
(Nguyen That Thank; "Uncle Ho")
Vietnamese communist leader–revolutionary
• Founder, first pres., N Vietnam, 1954-69; legendary figure instrumental in spread of Communism throughout Southeast Asia.
b. May 19, 1890 in Kim Lien, Vietnam
d. September 03, 1969 in Hanoi, Vietnam (North)

Richmond Pearson Hobson
American military leader
• Commander of Merrimac during famous naval maneuver, 1898.
b. August 17, 1870 in Greensboro, Alabama
d. March 16, 1937 in New York, New York

John Reed Hodge
American army officer–military leader
• Led American Division in Pacific during WW II.
b. June 12, 1893 in Golconda, Illinois
d. November 12, 1963 in Washington, District of Columbia

Courtney Hodges
American military leader
• Commander, US First Army, WW II.
b. January 05, 1887 in Perry, Georgia
d. January 16, 1966 in San Antonio, Texas

Andreas Hofer
Austrian miltiary leader
• Prominent in organization of Tyrol militia, late 1700s; led insurrection against Bavaria, 1809; betrayed to French, court-martialed, shot.
b. November 22, 1767 in Saint Leonhard, Austria
d. February 2, 1810 in Mantua, Italy

Ernest Frederick Hollings
American political leader
• Progressive Dem. senator from SC, 1966–.
b. January 01, 1922 in Charleston, South Carolina

Harold Edward Holt
Australian political leader
• Prime minister, 1966-67; supported Lyndon Johnson's escalation of Vietnam War.
b. August 05, 1908 in Sydney, Australia
d. December 17, 1967 in Port Philip Bay, Australia

Sir Keith Jacka Holyoake
New Zealander political leader
• Prime minister, 1960-72; governor general, 1977-80.
b. February 11, 1904 in Pahiatua, New Zealand
d. December 08, 1983 in Wellington, New Zealand

Erich Honecker
German politician
• First, general secretary, central committee, Socialist Unity Party; most powerful man in E Germany, 1971–.
b. August 25, 1912 in Wiebelskirchen, Germany

John Bell Hood
American military leader
• Confederate general; led Confederate Army in unsuccessful defense of Atlanta, 1864.
b. June 01, 1831 in Owingsville, Kentucky
d. August 3, 1879 in New Orleans, Louisiana

Joseph Hooker
American military leader
• Union general in Civil War; commanded Army of the Potomac, 1862-63.
b. November 13, 1814 in Hadley, Massachusetts
d. October 31, 1879 in Garden City, New York

Herbert Clark Hoover
American US president
• 31st pres., Rep., 1929-33; administration dominated by early yrs. of Great Depression.
b. August 1, 1874 in West Branch, Iowa
d. October 2, 1964 in New York, New York

J(ohn) Edgar Hoover
American FBI director
• Director of FBI, 1924-72; established fingerprint file, crime lab.
b. January 01, 1895 in Washington, District of Columbia
d. May 02, 1972 in Washington, District of Columbia

Lou Henry Hoover
(Mrs Herbert Hoover)
American first lady
• Dignified, brilliant White House hostess; she and husband translated *De Re Metallica*.
b. March 29, 1875 in Waterloo, Iowa
d. January 07, 1944 in New York, New York

Grace Brewster Murray Hopper
American military leader–mathematician–educator
• Rear admiral who was oldest active military officer, 1943-86; co-invented computer language COBOL.
b. December 09, 1906 in New York, New York

Sir Brian Gwynne Horrocks
British army officer–military leader
• Helped to defeat Rommel's forces in Africa, 1942; his forces annihilated at Arnhem, 1944.
b. September 07, 1895 in Rainkhet, India
d. January 06, 1985 in Fishbourne, England

Nicholas Horthy de Nagybanya
(Miklos von Nagybanya)
Hungarian naval officer–political leader
• Dictator of Hungary, 1920-44; aided Hitler in WW II.
b. June 18, 1868 in Kenderes, Hungary
d. March 09, 1957 in Estoril, Portugal

Felix Houphouet-Boigny
African politician
• President of Republic of the Ivory Coast, 1960–.
b. October 18, 1905 in Ivory Coast

Sam(uel) Houston
American miltiary leader–political leader
• First pres., Republic of Texas, 1836-38, 1841-44; hero of Battle of San Jacinto, 1836.
b. March 02, 1793 in Lexington, Virginia
d. July 26, 1863 in Huntsville, Texas

Amir Abbas Hoveyda
Iranian political leader
• Prime minister of Iran, 1965-77, who was Shah's adviser; executed by Islamic court.
b. February 18, 1919 in Teheran, Persia
d. April 07, 1979 in Tehran, Iran

Oliver Otis Howard
American military leader
• Union Civil War general; founded Howard Univ., 1867, in Washington, DC.
b. November 08, 1830 in Leeds, Maine
d. October 26, 1909 in Burlington, Vermont

Richard Howe
(Military Leader)
British naval officer
• Led British navy in America, 1776-78.
b. March 19, 1725
d. August 05, 1799

Enver Hoxha
Albanian political leader
• Founded Albanian Communist Party, 1941; prime minister, 1944-54; kept country internationally isolated.
b. October 16, 1908 in Gjinokaster, Albania
d. April 11, 1985 in Tirana, Albania

Kuo-Feng Hua
Chinese political leader
• Premier, chm., Chinese Communist Party, 1976-80.
b. 1919 in Shansi Province, China

Orville Liscum Hubbard
American political leader
• Mayor of Dearborn, MI, 1941-77; holder national record for full-time mayor, until passed by Erastus Corning, III.
b. April 02, 1903 in Union City, Michigan
d. December 16, 1982 in Detroit, Michigan

Clarence R Huebner
American army officer–military leader
• Commander, First Division, campaigns in Sicily, France, Germany, WW II.
b. November 24, 1888 in Bushton, Kansas
d. September 23, 1972 in Washington, District of Columbia

Hugh Capet
French ruler
• Succeeded Louis V, 987, over Charles of Lower Lorraine.
b. 938
d. 996

Jessie Wallace Hughan
American political activist
• Active pacifist, socialist party member; founder, War Resister's League, 1923-55.
b. December 25, 1876 in Brooklyn, New York
d. April 1, 1955 in New York, New York

Hulagu Khan
Mongolian ruler
• Grandson of Genghis Khan, brother of Kublai Khan; fought for control of Baghdad and Syria.
b. 1217
d. 1265

Hubert Horatio Humphrey, Jr
American US vice president
• Thirty-two yr. public service career included 23 yrs. as Dem. senator from MN, 5 yrs. as VP under Johnson.
b. May 27, 1911 in Wallace, South Dakota
d. January 13, 1978 in Waverly, Minnesota

Gustav Husak
Czech political leader
• Pres., Czechoslovak Socialist Republic, 1975–.
b. January 1, 1913 in Bratislava, Czechoslovakia

Hussein (Ibn Talal)
(King of Jordan; Hussein I)
Jordanian ruler
• Descendant of Mohammed, who succeeded father to throne, 1953–.
b. November 14, 1935 in Amman, Jordan

Saddam Hussein
Iraqi political leader
• Pres. of Iraq, 1979–. His 1990 invasion of Kuwait prompted "Desert Storm" war with U.S. and allies.
b. April 28, 1937 in Tikrit, Iraq

Haj Amin Husseini
Palestinian political leader
• Anti-Zionist leader of Arab world, 1940s-50s; Nazi collaborator, WW II.
b. 1893 in Jerusalem, Palestine
d. July 04, 1974 in Beirut, Lebanon

Ibn Saud
(Abdul Aziz ibn Saud)
Saudi ruler
• Founder of Saudi Arabia, 1932, who was king, 1932-53.
b. 1880 in Riyadh, Saudi Arabia
d. November 09, 1953 in Saudi Arabia

Idris I
(Sayyid Muhammad Idris as-Sanusi)
Liberian ruler
• First, only king of Libya, 1951-69; deposed by Khadafy.
b. March 13, 1890 in Jaghbub, Libya
d. May 25, 1983 in Cairo, Egypt

Pharaoh Ikhnaton
(Akhenaton)
Egyptian ruler
• Ruled ancient Egypt ca. 1379-1362 BC; changed religious beliefs from polytheism to monotheism.
b. 1372BC
d. 1354BC

Arturo Umberto Illia
Argentine political leader
• Won first Argentinian presidential election based on proportional representation, 1963; ousted in coup, 1966.
b. August 04, 1900 in Cordoba, Argentina
d. January 18, 1983 in Cordoba, Argentina

Daniel Ken Inouye
American political leader
• Dem. senator from HI, 1963–; co-chaired Iran-Contra hearings, 1987.
b. September 07, 1924 in Honolulu, Hawaii

Isabella I
(Isabelala Catolica)
Spanish ruler
• Queen of Castile, 1474; financed Columbus' voyage, 1492.
b. April 22, 1451 in Madrigal, Spain
d. November 26, 1504 in Medina del Campo, Spain

Isabella II
(Maria Isabella Louisa)
Spanish ruler
• Queen of Spain, 1833-1868; had strifeful reign; abdicated in favor of son, Alfonso XII; 1870.
b. October 1, 1830 in Madrid, Spain
d. April 19, 1904 in Paris, France

Yusof bin Ishak
Singaporean political leader
• First elected pres. of Singapore, 1963-70.
b. August 12, 1910
d. November 23, 1970 in Singapore

Baron Hastings Lionel Ismay
English military leader
• A leading military advisor to Churchill, WW II; secretary-general, NATO, 1952-57.
b. June 21, 1887 in Naini Tal, India
d. December 17, 1965 in Wormington Orange, England

Augustin de Iturbide
(Augustin I)
Mexican army officer–ruler
• Won Mexican independence from Spain, 1821; Emperor, 1822-23.
b. September 27, 1783 in Valladolid, Mexico
d. July 19, 1824

Ivan III
("Ivan the Great")
Russian ruler
• Czar of Russia, 1462-1505; compiled first Russian code of law.
b. January 22, 1440
d. October 27, 1505

Ivan IV
("Ivan the Terrible")
Russian ruler
• Grandson of Ivan III; czar of Russia at age three; assumed title 1547.
b. August 25, 1530
d. March 17, 1584

Sheikh Mohammed Ali Jaabari
Palestinian politician
• Mayor of Hebron, Israel for 36 yrs.
b. 1900 in Jordan
d. May 29, 1980 in Hebron, Israel

Andrew Jackson
American US president
• First Dem. pres., 1829-37; military hero of War of 1812; introduced spoils system, boosted expansionism.
b. March 15, 1767 in Waxhaw, South Carolina
d. June 08, 1845 in Nashville, Tennessee

Henry Martin Jackson
("Scoop")
American political leader
• Dem. senator from WA, 1953-83; prominent member, Armed Services Committee.
b. May 31, 1912 in Everett, Washington
d. September 01, 1983 in Everett, Washington

Maynard Holbrook Jackson, Jr
American political leader
• First black mayor of Atlanta, GA, 1974-82.
b. March 23, 1938 in Dallas, Texas

Rachel Donelson Robards Jackson
(Mrs Andrew Jackson)
American first lady
• Caused scandal when she married Jackson before divorcing first husband.
b. June 15, 1767 in Pittsylvania County, Virginia
d. December 22, 1828 in Nashville, Tennessee

Stonewall (Thomas Jonathan) Jackson
American military leader
• Outstanding Confederate general; defeated Union at second Battle of Bull Run, 1862; killed by fire from his own troops.
b. January 21, 1824 in Clarksburg, West Virginia
d. May 1, 1863 in Guinea Station, Virginia

James I
Scottish ruler
• King of Scotland, 1406-37.
b. July 1394 in Dunfermline, Scotland
d. February 2, 1437 in Perth, Scotland

James I
(James VI)
English ruler
• As James I, King of England, 1603-25; as James VI, King of Scotland, 1567-1625; son of Mary Queen of Scots.
b. June 19, 1566 in Edinburgh, Scotland
d. March 27, 1625 in Theobalds, England

James II
Scottish ruler
• King of Scotland, 1437-60.
b. 1430 in Edinburgh, Scotland
d. 1460 in Roxburgh Castle, Scotland

James II
English ruler
• King of England, Scotland, Ireland, 1685-88.
b. October 14, 1633 in London, England
d. September 16, 1701 in Saint-Germain-en-Laye, France

James III
Scottish ruler
• King of Scotland, 1460-88.
b. 1452 in Stirling, Scotland
d. 1488 in Sauchieburn, Scotland

James IV
Scottish ruler
• King of Scotland, 1488-1513; marriage to Margaret Tudor led to union of crowns of England, Scotland.
b. 1473
d. September 09, 1513

James V
Scottish ruler
• King of Scotland, 1513-42.
b. 1512 in Linlithgow, Scotland
d. 1542 in Solway Moss, England

Daniel James, Jr
American military leader
• First black four-star general in US, 1975.
b. February 11, 1920 in Pensacola, Florida
d. February 25, 1978 in Colorado Springs, Colorado

Sir Leander Starr Jameson
British political leader
• S African statesman; led unsuccessful Jameson raid, 1895, to overthrow Boer govt.; prime minister, Cape Colony, 1904-08; helped found Unionist Party, 1910.
b. February 03, 1853 in Edinburgh, Scotland
d. November 26, 1917 in London, England

Piotr Jaroszewicz
Polish politician
• Chm., Council of Ministers, 1970-80; pres., Chief Council of Union of Fighters for Freedom and Democracy, 1972-80.
b. October 08, 1909 in Nieswicz, Poland

Wojciech Witold Jaruzelski
Polish political leader
• Career soldier; head of Poland, 1981-1990.
b. July 06, 1923 in Kurow, Poland

Jacob Koppel Javits
American political leader
• Liberal Rep. senator from NY, 1956-80, who championed civil rights, ERA.
b. May 18, 1904 in New York, New York
d. March 07, 1986 in West Palm Beach, Florida

Sir Alhaji Dawda Kairaba Jawara
Gambian political leader
• First prime minister, 1963-70, pres., 1970–, Gambia.
b. May 16, 1924 in Barajally, Gambia

Junius Richard Jayewardene
Ceylonese political leader
• Exec. pres., Sri Lanka, 1977–; committed to Western-style democracy, free enterprise system.
b. September 17, 1906 in Colombo, Ceylon

Prince Jean
(Jean Benoit Guillaume Marie Robert Louis Antoin Adolphe Marc d'Aviano)
Luxembourg ruler
• Grand Duke of Luxembourg, 1964–; son of Charlotte, Felix; married Princess Josephine Charlotte.
b. January 05, 1921 in Colmar, France

Thomas Jefferson
American US president
• Third pres., 1801-09; wrote Declaration of Independence, 1776; negotiated LA Purchase, 1803; organized Lewis, Clark expedition, 1803.
b. April 13, 1743 in Albemarle, Virginia
d. July 04, 1826 in Albemarle County, Virginia

Jahangir
(Jehangir; Conqueror of the World)
Indian ruler
• Son of Akbar; ruled India, 1605-27; pleasant ruler who enjoyed the arts.
b. 1569
d. 1627

John Rushworth Jellicoe
English naval officer–military leader
• Commanded Atlantic Fleet, 1910-16; governor general of New Zealand, 1920-24.
b. December 05, 1859 in Southampton, England
d. November 2, 1935

Roy Harris Jenkins
Welsh political leader
• Co-founded Social Democratic Party in Britain, Mar 1981.
b. November 11, 1920 in Abersychan, Wales

John Wilson Jenrette, Jr
American political leader
• Former congressman convicted in AB-SCAM scandal, 1980; served two-year sentence, 1984-86.
b. May 19, 1936 in Conway, South Carolina

Jezebel
Phoenician princess
• Wife of King Ahab; name is used symbolically for a wicked woman.
b. 9thBC
d. ?

Mohammed Ali Jinnah
Indian political leader
• Principal founder, first governor-general of Pakistan, partitioned from India, 1947.
b. December 25, 1876 in Karachi, Pakistan
d. September 11, 1948 in Karachi, Pakistan

Joseph Jacques Cesaire Joffre
French military leader
• Commander of French army credited with directing orderly French retreat before German advance, 1914.
b. January 12, 1852 in Rivesaltes, France
d. January 13, 1931 in Paris, France

John, King of England
English ruler
• Son of Henry II; forced by English barons to sign Magna Carta, 1215.
b. December 24, 1167 in Oxford, England
d. October 29, 1216 in Newark, England

Sobieski John III
Polish ruler
• King of Poland, 1674-96; later years unsuccessful because of poor political conditions.
b. August 17, 1624 in Olesko, Poland
d. June 17, 1696

Andrew Johnson
American US president
• Dem., 17th pres., 1865-69; succeeded Lincoln on his assassination; survived impeachment by Congress, 1868.
b. December 29, 1808 in Raleigh, North Carolina
d. July 31, 1875 in Carter Station, Tennessee

Eliza McCardle Johnson
(Mrs Andrew Johnson)
American first lady
• Taught Andrew to read, write; semi-invalid unable to assume White House duties.
b. October 04, 1810 in Leesburg, Tennessee
d. January 15, 1876 in Greeneville, Tennessee

Hiram Warren Johnson
American political leader
• A founder of Progressive Party, ran as Theodore Roosevelt's VP candidate, 1912; firmly isolationist senator from CA, 1917-47.
b. September 02, 1866 in Sacramento, California
d. August 06, 1945 in Bethesda, Maryland

Lady Bird (Claudia Alta Taylor) Johnson
(Mrs Lyndon Johnson)
American first lady
• Promoted national conservation programs; wrote *White House Diary*, 1971.
b. December 22, 1912 in Karnack, Texas

Lyndon Baines Johnson
American US president
• Dem., 36th pres., 1963-69; domestic improvements overshadowed by US involvement in S. Vietnam. Originated "Great Society."
b. August 27, 1908 in Stonewall, Texas
d. January 22, 1973 in Johnson City, Texas

Pierre Marc Johnson
Canadian politician
• Conservative who succeeded Rene Levesque as leader of Parti Quebecois; opposition leader, Dec 1985–.
b. July 05, 1946 in Montreal, Quebec

Albert S Johnston
American military leader
• Served in Mexican War for the Union 1845; served in Civil War for Confederate Army, 1861.
b. February 02, 1803 in Washington, Kentucky
d. April 06, 1862 in Shiloh, Tennessee

Joseph Eggleston Johnston
American military leader
• Left Union Army during Civil War to join Confederate Army as brigadier general; credited for victory at first battle of Bull Run, 1861.
b. February 03, 1807 in Prince Edward, Virginia
d. February 21, 1891 in Washington, District of Columbia

Franz Jonas
Austrian political leader
• Pres. of Republic of Austria, 1965-74.
b. October 04, 1899 in Vienna, Austria
d. April 24, 1974 in Vienna, Austria

David Charles Jones
American army officer–military leader
• Chm., Joint Chiefs of Staff, 1978-82; commander, US Air Force, Washington, 1974-78.
b. July 09, 1921 in Aberdeen, South Dakota

Jesse Holman Jones
American cabinet member–real estate executive
• Secretary of Commerce, 1940-45; built over 30 Houston, TX skyscrapers; wrote *Fifty Billion Dollars*, 1951.
b. April 05, 1874 in Robertson County, Tennessee
d. June 01, 1956 in Houston, Texas

John Paul Jones
American military leader
• Founded American naval tradition; said "I have not yet begun to fight," during Revolutionary War.
b. July 06, 1747 in Kirkcudbright, Scotland
d. July 18, 1792 in Paris, France

Hamilton Jordan
(William Hamilton McWhorter Jordan; "Ham" "Hannibal Jerkin")
American presidential aide
• Chief of staff under Carter, 1979-81; int'l. communications consultant, 1984–.
b. September 21, 1944 in Charlotte, North Carolina

Salvador Jorge Blanco
Dominican political leader
• Pres. of Dominican Republic, 1982-86.
b. July 05, 1926 in Santiago, Dominican Republic

Anker Henrik Jorgensen
Danish political leader
• Prime minister of Denmark, 1972-82.
b. July 13, 1922 in Copenhagen, Denmark

Joseph I
Hungarian ruler
• King of Hungary, 1687-1711; king of Germany, 1690-1711; Holy Roman emperor, 1705-11.
b. 1678
d. 1711

Helen Joseph
South African author–political activist
• Active in South African politics; charged with treason, 1956, acquitted, 1961; first S African to be put under house arrest, 1962-67, 1967-71.
b. 1905 in England

Josephine
(Marie Josephe Rose Tascher de la Pagerie)
French ruler
• Marriage to Napoleon, 1796, annulled 1809; played prominent part in social life of time.
b. June 24, 1763 in Les Trois-Ilets, Martinique
d. May 29, 1814 in Malmaison, France

Flavius Josephus
(Joseph Ben Matthias; "The Greek Livy")
Hebrew historian–political leader
• Governor of Galilee; wrote *History of the Jewish War*.
b. 37 in Jeruselum, Israel
d. 101 in Rome, Italy

Juan Carlos I
(Prince Juan Carlos Borbon y Borbon; "Juan Carlos the Brief")
Spanish ruler
• King of Spain, 1975–.
b. January 05, 1938 in Rome, Italy

Benito Pablo Juarez
("The Mexican Washington")
Mexican political leader
• Pres. of Mexico, 1861-63, 1867-72; passed reform laws that reduced power of army, church.
b. March 21, 1806 in Oaxaca, Mexico
d. July 18, 1872 in Mexico City, Mexico

Julian (Flavius Claudius Julianus)
Roman ruler
• General, proclaimed emperor by troops, 361; enemy of Christianity.
b. 331
d. 363

Juliana
(Juliana Emma Maria Wilhelmina)
Dutch ruler
• Ruled 1948-80; supported int'l. efforts such as Marshall Plan, NATO; abolished the curtsy.
b. April 3, 1909 in The Hague, Netherlands

Julius Caesar
Roman army officer–statesman
• Conquered all Gaul, Britain, 58-49 BC; Roman dictator, 49-44 BC, known for reforms; wrote on Gallic wars; assassinated by Brutus; month of July named for him.
b. July 12, 100 in Rome, Italy
d. March 15, 44 in Rome, Italy

Kamal Fouad Jumblatt
Lebanese political leader
• Powerful head of Druze sect, leader of Progressive Socialist Party, 1949-77; won Lenin Peace Prize, 1972. Assassinated.
b. January 06, 1917 in Mukhtara, Lebanon
d. March 16, 1977 in Beirut, Lebanon

Walid Jumblatt
Lebanese political leader
• Leader of Lebanese Druze community, pres., National Socialist Party, since father's assassination, 1977.
b. 1949

Justinian I (Flavius Anicius Justinianus)
Byzantine ruler
• Byzantine emperor, 527-65; completed codification of Roman law.
b. 483
d. 565

Janos Kadar
Hungarian communist leader
• Head of Communist Party, 1956-88.
b. May 26, 1912 in Fiume, Hungary
d. July 06, 1989 in Budapest, Hungary

David Kalakaua
Hawaiian ruler
• Ruled HI, 1874-91; his ideas sparked revolution, 1887; new constitution restricted his powers, 1887.
b. November 16, 1836
d. January 3, 1891 in San Francisco, California

Mikhail (Ivanovich) Kalinin
Russian political leader
• Considered "grandfather" of Russian revolution; pres., USSR, 1923-46.
b. November 2, 1875 in Upper Troitsa, Russia
d. June 03, 1946 in Moscow, U.S.S.R.

Kamehameha I
(Kamehameha the Great)
Hawaiian ruler
• Ruled Hawaiian Islands, 1810-19; preserved ancient customs, religious beliefs; united islands, 1795.
b. 1758 in Kohala, Hawaii
d. May 05, 1819 in Kailua, Hawaii

Kamehameha II
(Liholiho)
Hawaiian ruler
• Son of Kamehameha I; ruled 1819-24; rid islands of ancient religion, taboo system.
b. 1797 in Hawaii
d. July 14, 1824 in London, England

Kamehameha III
(Kauikeaouli)
Hawaiian ruler
• Reigned, 1825-54; established island independence from US, Britain, France, 1842-43; promulgated constitution, 1840.
b. March 07, 1813
d. December 15, 1854 in Honolulu, Hawaii

Kamehameha IV
(Alexander Liholiho)
Hawaiian ruler
• Popular, efficient king, 1854-63; aimed at establishing independence.
b. February 09, 1834
d. November 3, 1863 in Honolulu, Hawaii

Kamehameha V
(Lot Kamehameha)
Hawaiian ruler
• Last of direct line of monarchs, 1863-72.
b. December 11, 1830
d. December 11, 1872

Constantine Karamanlis
(Constantinos Caramanlis; "Costas")
Greek political leader
• Premier, 1955-63; pres., 1980-85.
b. February 23, 1907 in Prote, Greece

Rashid Abdul Hamid Karami
Lebanese political leader
• Leader of Sunni Muslims, member Lebanese parliament, 1951-87; killed in bomb attack.
b. December 3, 1921 in Tripoli, Lebanon
d. June 01, 1987 in Jubayl, Lebanon

Babrak Karmal
Afghan political leader
• Pro-Soviet pres. of Afghanistan, 1979-87; forced out by Soviets.
b. 1929

Nancy Landon Kassebaum
American political leader
• Rep. senator from KS, 1979–; daughter of Alf Landon.
b. July 29, 1932 in Topeka, Kansas

Abdul Karim (el) Kassem
Iraqi politician
• Premier of Iraq, 1958-63; overthrown, killed by military junta.
b. November 21, 1914 in Baghdad, Iraq
d. February 09, 1963 in Baghdad, Iraq

Kenneth David Kaunda
Zambian political leader
• First pres. of Zambia, 1964–.
b. April 28, 1924 in Chinsali, Rhodesia

Estes Kefauver
American political leader
• Headed televised Senate crime investigation, 1950-51; Dem. candidate for VP, 1956.
b. July 26, 1903 in Madisonville, Tennessee
d. August 1, 1963 in Bethesda, Maryland

Urho Kaleva Kekkonen
Finnish political leader
• Pres. of Finland, 1956-82, known for skilled neutrality, friendship with USSR.
b. August 03, 1900
d. August 31, 1986 in Helsinki, Finland

Sir Vernon Kell
English government official
• First director of MI 5, 1909-40, British equivalent of FBI.
b. 1873 in Yarmouth, England
d. 1942

Clarence Marion Kelley
American FBIdirector
• First permanent FBI director since death of J Edgar Hoover, 1973-78.
b. October 24, 1911 in Kansas City, Missouri

Petra Karin Kelly
German politician
• Spokesman, strategist for W German political party, the "Greens."
b. November 29, 1947 in Gunzberg, Germany (West)

Jack (John French) Kemp
American political leader
• Quarterback, 1957-70, mostly with Buffalo; Rep. con. from NY, 1970–.
b. July 13, 1935 in Los Angeles, California

Edward Moore Kennedy
American political leader
• Liberal Democratic senator from MA, 1962–; brother of John and Robert Kennedy; involved in Chappaquiddick incident, car accident which killed Mary Jo Kopechne, 1969.
b. February 22, 1932 in Brookline, Massachusetts

John Fitzgerald Kennedy
American US president
• First Roman Catholic pres., 1961-63; won 1957 Pulitzer for *Profiles in Courage;* assassinated while in office.
b. May 29, 1917 in Brookline, Massachusetts
d. November 22, 1963 in Dallas, Texas

Joseph Patrick Kennedy, Sr
American financier–diplomat–political leader
• Self-made millionaire; US ambassador to England, 1938-40; romantically linked to actress Gloria Swanson; father of Kennedy family.
b. September 06, 1888 in Boston, Massachusetts
d. November 18, 1969 in Hyannis Port, Massachusetts

Robert Francis Kennedy
American political leader
• US Attorney General, 1961-64, appointed by brother, JFK; Dem. senator from NY, 1964-68; assassinated following victory in CA primary.
b. November 2, 1925 in Brookline, Massachusetts
d. June 06, 1968 in Los Angeles, California

Rose Fitzgerald Kennedy
(Mrs Joseph Patrick Kennedy)
American celebrity relative–author
• Matriarch of politically prominent Kennedy family; wrote autobiography *Times to Remember,* 1974.
b. July 22, 1890 in Boston, Massachusetts

George Churchill Kenney
American military leader
• Commander, Allied Air Forces under MacArthur, 1942-45; participated in Japanese defeat at New Guinea.
b. August 06, 1889 in Yarmouth, Nova Scotia
d. 1974

Jomo (Johnstone) Kenyatta
(Johstone Kamau; Kamau wa Ngengi; "Mzee")
Kenyan political leader
• Terrorist organizer who was first pres. of Kenya, 1964.
b. October 2, 1891 in Kenya
d. August 22, 1978 in Mombasa, Kenya

Francis Keppel
American educator–government official–political leader
• Dean, Harvard U Graduate School of Education, 1948-62; US commissioner of education, 1962-66; tried to enforce Civil Rights Act, opposed racial segregation of public schools.
b. April 16, 1916 in New York, New York
d. February 19, 1990 in Cambridge, Massachusetts

Alexander Fedorovitch Kerensky
(Aleksandr Feodorovich Kerenski)
Russian political leader
• Premier, Jul-Nov 1917, whose indecisiveness enabled Bolsheviks to seize power.
b. April 22, 1881 in Simbirsk, Russia
d. June 11, 1970 in New York, New York

Bob (Joseph Robert) Kerrey
American political leader
• Democratic senator from NE, 1989–; governor, 1983-86.
b. August 27, 1943 in Lincoln, Nebraska

Moammar Khadafy
(Moamar al-Gaddafi; Mu'ammar al-Qadhafi)
Liberian political leader
• Led military coup against monarchy, 1969; pres., Mar 1977–.
b. 1942 in Misurata, Libya

Khalid Ibn Abdul Aziz Al-Saud
Saudi ruler
• Ruled Saudi Arabia, 1975-82, following King Faisal's assassination.
b. 1913 in Riyadh, Saudi Arabia
d. June 13, 1982 in Taif, Saudi Arabia

Mustafa Khalil
Egyptian political leader
• Held many govt. positions including prime minister, 1978-80.
b. 1920

Seretse M Khama
Botswana political leader
• First pres. of Botswana, 1966-80.
b. July 01, 1921 in Serowe, Botswana
d. July 13, 1980 in Gaborone, Botswana

Hojatolislam (Sayed) Ali Khamenei
Iranian political leader
• President, Islamic Republic of Iran, 1981-89; replaced Khomeini as Iran's supreme religious leader, 1989.
b. 1939 in Khorasan, Iran

Abdul Ghaffar Khan
Pakistani political activist
• Helped Gandhi gain independence for India through passive resistance; opposed Pakistani separation, 1947.
b. 1891
d. January 2, 1988 in Peshawar, Pakistan

Genghis Khan
(Genchiz Khan; Jenghiz Khan)
Mongolian conqueror
• Defeated much of present-day Asia with bold, brilliant moves.
b. 1162
d. 1227

Liaquat Ali Khan
(Liaquat Ali Khan)
Pakistani political leader
• Head of Moslem League, prime minister of Pakistan, 1947-51; assassinated.
b. October 01, 1895 in Karnal, Pakistan
d. October 16, 1951 in Rawalpindi, Pakistan

Kim Dae Jung
Korean politician
• Opposition leader who has struggled to restore human rights, economic justice to S Korea.
b. January 06, 1924 in Hayi-do, Korea

Il Sung Kim
Korean political leader
• Founder, first head of state, North Korea, 1948-72, pres., 1972-.
b. April 15, 1912 in Mangyongdae, Korea

Husband Edward Kimmel
American military leader
• Commanded naval fleet at Pearl Harbor, Feb-Dec, 1941; after Japanese attack, found quilty of "dereliction of duty"; retired from navy, 1942.
b. February 26, 1882 in Henderson, Kentucky
d. May 15, 1968 in Groton, Connecticut

Ernest Joseph King
(Colleen, code name)
American military leader
• Principal strategist of naval policy, WW II.
b. November 23, 1878 in Lorain, Ohio
d. June 25, 1956 in Portsmouth, New Hampshire

William Lyon Mackenzie King
Canadian political leader
• Leader of Canadian Liberal party, 1919-48; prime minister, 1921-30; 1935-48.
b. December 17, 1874 in Berlin, Ontario
d. July 22, 1950 in Kingsmere, Ontario

William Rufus de Vane King
American US vice president
• Elected with Franklin Pierce; took oath of office in Cuba where he went to find cure for TB.
b. April 07, 1786 in Sampson County, North Carolina
d. April 18, 1853 in Cahaba, Alabama

Neil Gordon Kinnock
Welsh political leader
• Succeeded Michael Foot as head of Britain's Labor Party, 1983-.
b. March 28, 1942 in Tredagar, Wales

Rudolf Kirchschlager
Austrian political leader
• Pres. of Austria, 1974-86.
b. March 2, 1915 in Austria

Alan Goodrich Kirk
American military leader–diplomat
• Commanded naval task force landing troops on D-Day, 1944; foreign ambassador, 1946-62.
b. October 3, 1888 in Philadelphia, Pennsylvania
d. October 15, 1963 in New York, New York

Claude Roy Kirk, Jr
American political leader
• First Rep. governor of FL in 94 yrs., 1967-71.
b. January 07, 1926 in San Bernardino, California

Jeane Duane Jordan Kirkpatrick
American diplomat–political leader
• US permanent representative to UN, 1981; resigned, 1985.
b. November 19, 1926 in Duncan, Oklahoma

Nobusuke Kishi
Japanese political leader
• Prime minister of Japan, 1956-60; resigned amid protests after he signed security treaty with US.
b. November 13, 1896 in Japan
d. August 07, 1987 in Tokyo, Japan

Henry Alfred Kissinger
("Henry the K"; "The Iron Stomach"; "Super Kraut")
American government official–cabinet member
• Secretary of State under Nixon, Ford; won Nobel Peace Prize, 1973.
b. May 27, 1923 in Fuerth, Germany

Horatio Herbert Kitchener
English military leader
• Hero of victories in Africa who expanded British army as secretary of state for war, 1914.
b. June 14, 1850 in Ballylongford, Ireland
d. June 05, 1916

Thanom Kittikachorn
Thai political leader
• Prime minister, 1958, 1963-71, 1972-73; aggressively opposed communism.
b. August 11, 1911 in Tak, Thailand

Jean Baptiste Kleber
French army officer
• Commanded division in Napoleon's army; recaptured Cairo from Turks; assassinated.
b. March 09, 1753 in Strasbourg, France
d. June 14, 1800 in Cairo, Egypt

Richard Gordon Kleindienst
American government official–presidential aide
• Attorney general, 1972-73, who played key role in Richard Nixon's election, 1968.
b. August 05, 1923 in Winslow, Arizona

Henry Knox
American military leader–patriot–government official
• Succeeded Washington as commander of Continental Army, 1783; US secretary of War, 1785-94.
b. July 25, 1750 in Boston, Massachusetts
d. October 25, 1806 in Thomaston, Maine

Ed(ward Irwin) Koch
American political leader
• Flamboyant mayor of NYC, 1978-89.
b. December 12, 1924 in New York, New York

Helmut Michael Kohl
German political leader
• Chancellor, West Germany, 1982-.
b. April 03, 1930 in Ludwigshafen, Germany

Mauno Henrik Koivisto
Finnish political leader
• First socialist president; elected Jan 1982.
b. November 25, 1923 in Turku, Finland

Ivan S Konev
Russian military leader
• Supreme commander of Soviet land forces, 1946-60; founded Warsaw Pact.
b. December 27, 1897 in Ladeino, Russia
d. May 21, 1973 in Moscow, U.S.S.R.

Prince Fumimaro Konoye
Japanese political leader
• Three-time premier of Japan, 1933-41.
b. October 1891
d. December 15, 1945 in Tokyo, Japan

C(harles) Everett Koop
American political leader
• Surgeon-general of the US, 1982-89; leader of public education campaign to combat AIDS epidemic.
b. October 14, 1916 in Brooklyn, New York

Aleksei Nikolaevich Kosygin
Russian communist leader
• Led Soviet effort at economic modernization, 1960s.
b. February 2, 1904 in Saint Petersburg, Russia
d. December 19, 1980 in Moscow, U.S.S.R.

Seyni Kountche
Nigerian political leader
• President of Niger, 1974-87; ended Niger's reliance on imported, launched political reforms.
b. 1931 in Fandou, Niger
d. November 1, 1987 in Paris, France

Ron Kovic
American author–political activist
• Marine sergeant paralyzed in Vietnam War; wrote of experiences in autobiography *Born on the Fourth of July*, 1986, filmed starring Tom Cruise, 1989.
b. July 04, 1946 in Ladysmith, Wisconsin

Juscelino Kubitschek (de Oliveira)
Brazilian political leader
• Pres. of Brazil, 1956-61; administration known for economic achievements including construction of new capital, Brasilia, 1957.
b. September 12, 1902 in Diamantina, Brazil
d. August 22, 1976 in Rio de Janeiro, Brazil

Kublai Khan
Mongolian ruler
• Founded Mongol, Yuan dynasties in China; grandson of Genghis Khan; subject of poem by S T Coleridge.
b. 1216
d. 1294

Dennis John Kucinich
American political leader
• Youngest mayor in Cleveland history, 1977-80; presided over city's default.
b. October 08, 1946 in Cleveland, Ohio

Bela Kun
Hungarian communist leader
• Leader of Third International who tried to ignite worldwide revolution; liquidated by Stalin.
b. 1886
d. 1939

Madeleine May Kunin
American political leader
• Dem. governor of VT, 1985-91; state's first female governor; defeated by Richard Snelling.
b. September 28, 1933 in Zurich, Switzerland

Saburo Kurusu
Japanese diplomat
• Was negotiating to end tensions with US when Japanese attacked Pearl Harbor, precipitating war, Dec 7, 1941.
b. 1888 in Yokohama, Japan
d. April 07, 1954 in Tokyo, Japan

Vasili Vasilievich Kuznetzov
Russian politician–diplomat
• First vice president of USSR, 1977-86.
b. February 13, 1901 in Sofilovka, Russia
d. June 05, 1990 in Moscow, U.S.S.R.

Nguyen Cao Ky
Vietnamese political leader
• VP of S Vietnam, 1967-71; fled to US, 1975; wrote *Twenty Years and Twenty Days*, 1977.
b. September 08, 1930 in Son Tay, Vietnam

Spyros Achilles Kyprianou
Cypriot political leader
• President of Cyprus, 1977–.
b. October 28, 1932 in Limassol, Cyprus

Henry Richardson Labouisse
American political leader
• Main organizer of Marshall Plan; head of UNICEF, 1965-79; US ambassador to Greece, 1962-65.
b. February 11, 1904 in New Orleans, Louisiana
d. March 25, 1987 in New York, New York

Marquis Marie Joseph Paul Lafayette
French army officer–statesman
• Revolutionary war hero; negotiated French aid for American cause, 1779; close friend of George Washington.
b. September 06, 1757 in Chavaniac, France
d. May 2, 1834 in Paris, France

Robert Marion LaFollette
American political leader
• Progressive Rep. senator from WI, 1906-25; presidential candidate, 1924.
b. June 14, 1855 in Primrose, Wisconsin
d. June 18, 1925 in Washington, District of Columbia

Melvin Robert Laird
American cabinet member
• Secretary of defense under Richard Nixon, 1969-73.
b. September 01, 1922 in Omaha, Nebraska

Marc Lalonde
Canadian politician–economist
• Principal secretary to Pierre Trudeau, 1968-72; served in ministerial capacity, 1972-84.
b. July 26, 1929 in Ile Perrot, Quebec

Judy (Julia Verlyn) LaMarsh
Canadian politician–TV personality–author
• Canadian minister of Health and Welfare, 1963-65; only woman in Lester Pearson cabinet.
b. December 2, 1924 in Chatham, Ontario
d. October 27, 1980 in Toronto, Ontario

Richard Douglas Lamm
American political leader
• Dem. governor of CO, 1974-87; wrote *The Immigration Time Bomb*, 1985.
b. August 03, 1935 in Madison, Wisconsin

Bertha Ethel Landes
American political leader
• Mayor of Seattle, 1926-28; first woman to head sizable American city.
b. October 19, 1868 in Ware, Massachusetts
d. November 29, 1943 in Ann Arbor, Michigan

Alf(red Mossman) Landon
American businessman–political leader
• Rep. presidential candidate who lost overwhelmingly to Franklin Roosevelt, 1936.
b. September 09, 1887 in West Middlesex, Pennsylvania
d. October 12, 1987 in Topeka, Kansas

David Russell Lange
New Zealander political leader
• Moderate socialist head of Labour Party elected prime minister, 1984, succeeding Robert Muldoon.
b. August 04, 1942 in Otahuhu, New Zealand

Hans Langsdorff
German naval officer
• Graf Spee commander, trapped by Royal Navy, 1939; committed suicide.
b. 1890
d. 1939

Edward Geary Lansdale
American military leader
• Counterrevolution expert whose theories had great impact on US policies in Philippines, Vietnam, 1950s-60s.
b. February 06, 1908 in Detroit, Michigan
d. February 23, 1987 in McLean, Virginia

Lyndon Hermyle Larouche, Jr
American political leader
• Controversial right-wing Dem. activist; founded National Democratic Policy Committee, 1985.
b. September 08, 1922 in Rochester, New Hampshire

Jean de Lattre de Tassigny
French army officer–military leader
• Commanded first French Army, 1944; Western Europe Land forces, 1948-50.
b. February 02, 1889 in France
d. January 11, 1952

Sir Wilfrid Laurier
Canadian politician
• First French-Canadian to be prime minister, 1896-1911.
b. November 2, 1841 in Saint Lin, Quebec
d. February 17, 1919 in Ottawa, Ontario

Pierre Laval
French political leader
• Premier of Vichy govt., 1942; collaborated with Germany, executed for treason.
b. June 28, 1883 in Chatelden, France
d. October 15, 1945

Rita Marie Lavelle
American political leader
• Former head of EPA toxic waste clean-up program, indicted for conflict of interest, mismanagement, 1983; jailed 4.5 months.
b. September 08, 1947 in Portsmouth, Virginia

James Lawrence
American naval officer–military leader
• Wounded while attacking British frigate; known for crying, "Don't give up the ship," 1813.
b. October 01, 1781 in Burlington, New Jersey
d. June 01, 1813

Henry Ware Lawton
American military leader
• Indian fighter who captured Geronimo, 1886.
b. March 17, 1843 in Manhattan, Ohio
d. December 19, 1899 in Philippines

Le Duan
Vietnamese political leader
• Communist Party secretary-general who led Communists to victory in war for Vietnam, 1969-75.
b. April 07, 1908 in Annam, French Indochina
d. July 1, 1986 in Hanoi, Vietnam

Le Duc Tho
(Phan Dinh Khai)
Vietnamese government official
• First Asian and communist to win Nobel Peace Prize; shared with Henry Kissinger for work in negotiating Vietnam armistice, 1973; refused award, saying peace hadn't yet been achieved.
b. October 14, 1911 in Dich Le, Vietnam
d. October 13, 1990 in Hanoi, Vietnam

William Daniel Leahy
American naval officer–presidential aide
• Chief of staff for Roosevelt, Truman during WW II.
b. May 06, 1875 in Hampton, Iowa
d. July 2, 1959 in Bethesda, Maryland

Jacques-Philippe Leclerc
French army officer–military leader
• Commanded French Far Eastern Forces, 1945; signed Japanese surrender document for France.
b. November 28, 1902 in Belloy Saint Leonard, France
d. November 28, 1947 in Algeria

Charles Lee
American military leader–author
• Revolutionary War leader who gave British a plan for defeating Americans; constantly criticized Washington, dismissed from army, 1780.
b. 1731 in Dernhall, England
d. October 02, 1782 in Philadelphia, Pennsylvania

Henry Lee
American political leader
• Eulogized Washington as "First in war, first in peace, first in hearts of his countrymen," 1779; father of Robert E.
b. January 29, 1756 in Dunfries, Virginia
d. March 25, 1818 in Cumberland Island, Georgia

Kuan Yew Lee
Singaporean political leader
• Singapore's first and world's longest-serving prime minister, 1959-90; masterminded island's transformation from colonial outpost to thriving metropolis.
b. September 16, 1923 in Singapore

Robert E(dward) Lee
("Uncle Robert")
American army officer–military leader
• Led Army of Northern VA, 1862-65; commander, Confederate Army, 1865; pres., Washington College, 1865-70.
b. January 19, 1807 in Stratford, Virginia
d. October 12, 1870 in Lexington, Virginia

Teng-Hui Lee
Chinese political leader
• Succeeded Chiang Ching-Kuo as president of Republic of China, 1988; first native Taiwanese in post.
b. January 15, 1923 in Taipei, Taiwan

Thomas Sim Lee
American politician–military leader
• Revolutionary War leader; six-year governor of MD.
b. October 29, 1745 in Prince George's County, Maryland
d. November 09, 1819 in Frederick County, Maryland

John Francis Lehman, Jr
American military leader
• Youngest secretary of Navy when appointed by Reagan, 1981-87.
b. September 14, 1942 in Philadelphia, Pennsylvania

Mickey (George Thomas) Leland
American political leader
• Democratic congressman from TX, 1978-89; two-time chairman, Congressional Black Caucas; known for work with African famine; died in plane crash.
b. November 27, 1944 in Lubbock, Texas
d. August 07, 1989 in Gambela, Ethiopia

Curtis Emerson LeMay
American military leader–politician
• Air Force chief of staff; directed air assault over Japan in final days of WW II; commanded Berlin airlift after WW II; vice presidential running mate of George Wallace, 1968.
b. November 15, 1906 in Columbus, Ohio
d. October 01, 1990 in March Air Force Base, California

Nikolai Lenin
(Joseph Richter pseud; Vladimir Ilyich Ulyanov)
Russian communist leader–author
• Founder of Bolshevism; premier, 1918-24; established dictatorship of the proletariat; introduced socialist reforms.
b. April 09, 1870 in Simbirsk, Russia
d. January 21, 1924 in Gorki, U.S.S.R.

Leonidas I
Greek ruler
• Ruled Sparta, 491-480 BC; known for heroic stand against Xerxes I.

Leopold III
Belgian ruler
• Succeeded to throne, 1934, on death of father, Albert I; taken prisoner during German invasion, 1940; abdicated to son, Baudoin I, 1951.
b. November 03, 1901 in Brussels, Belgium
d. September 25, 1983 in Brussels, Belgium

Jean-Marie Le Pen
French politician
• Charismatic leader of French National Front Party, 1986–.
b. June 2, 1928 in La Trinite-sur-Mer, France

Sebastian Lerdo de Tejada
Mexican political leader
• President of Mexico, 1872-76, after death of Juarez; overthrown by Diaz; exiled.
b. April 25, 1825 in Jalapa, Mexico
d. 1889 in New York, New York

Ferdinand Marie de Lesseps
French engineer–diplomat
• Chief engineer for construction of Suez Canal, 1859-69.
b. November 19, 1805 in Versailles, France
d. December 07, 1894 in La Chanaie, France

Orlando Letelier
Chilean diplomat
• Ambassador to US, 1971-73; killed by bomb in car.
b. April 13, 1932 in Temuco, Chile
d. September 21, 1976 in Washington, District of Columbia

Rene Levesque
Canadian government official
• Parti Quebecois premier of Quebec, 1976-85; sought independence for province.
b. August 24, 1922 in New Carlisle, Quebec
d. November 01, 1987 in Montreal, Quebec

Carl Milton Levin
American political leader
• Dem. senator from MI, 1979–.
b. June 28, 1934 in Detroit, Michigan

David Levy
Israeli politician
• Vice-premier of Israel, 1984–; one of first Moroccan Jews to reach cabinet rank.
b. 1938 in Rabat, Morocco

Stephen Henry Lewis
Canadian government official
• Canadian ambassador to UN, 1984–; advocate of organization's preservation.
b. November 11, 1937 in Ottawa, Ontario

Karl Liebknecht
German communist leader–revolutionary
• Founded Spartacus League, 1918, forerunner of German Communist party; murdered with Rosa Luxemburg.
b. 1871 in Berlin, Germany
d. 1919

Wilhelm Liebknecht
German politician
• Co-founded Social Democratic Labor Party, 1869; father of Karl.
b. March 29, 1826 in Giessen, Germany
d. August 07, 1900 in Berlin, Germany

Lydia Kamekeha Liliuokalani
Hawaiian ruler
• Queen of Islands, 1891-93; against annexation; deposed, 1893; wrote song "Aloha Oe," 1898.
b. September 02, 1838 in Honolulu, Hawaii
d. November 11, 1917

Piao (Yu-Yung) Lin
Chinese government official
• Defense minister, 1959-72, killed in plane crash after failing in attempt to assassinate Mao Tse-Tung.
b. 1908 in Ungkung, China
d. September 12, 1971

Abraham Lincoln
American US president
• Rep., 16th pres., 1861-65; led Union during Civil War; author of Emancipation Proclamation, 1863; gave Gettysburg Address, 1863; assassinated by John W Booth.
b. February 12, 1809 in Hardin County, Kentucky
d. April 15, 1865 in Washington, District of Columbia

Mary Todd Lincoln
American first lady
• Suffered mental instability after husband's death; ruled insane, 1875.
b. December 13, 1818 in Lexington, Kentucky
d. July 16, 1882 in Springfield, Illinois

Charles Augustus Lindbergh
American political leader
• Progressive Rep. congressman, 1907-17; unpopular for denouncing war propaganda, 1917; father of the aviator.
b. 1859 in Stockholm, Sweden
d. 1924

Liu Shao-Ch'i
Chinese communist leader
• Chm., People's Republic of China, 1959, replacing Mao Tsetung; formally purged, 1968.
b. 1898 in Hunan, China
d. October 1974

Robert R Livingston
American cabinet member
• Administered first presidential oath of office to Washington; on committee of five that drew up Declaration of Independence, 1776; first secretary of State, 1781-83.
b. November 27, 1746 in New York, New York
d. February 26, 1813 in Clermont, New York

Alberto Lleras Camargo
Colombian political leader
• Liberal party president of Colombia, 1946-47, 1958-62; helped bring political peace to Colombia; head, Organization of American States, 1948-54.
b. July 03, 1906 in Bogota, Colombia
d. January 04, 1990 in Bogota, Colombia

John Alexander Logan
American soldier–political leader
• A founder, Grand Army of the Republic, 1865, who instituted Memorial Day, May 30, 1868.
b. February 09, 1826 in Murphysboro, Illinois
d. December 26, 1886 in Washington, District of Columbia

Earl Kemp Long
American political leader
• Governor of LA, 1939-40; 1948-52; 1956-60; brother of Huey.
b. August 26, 1895 in Winnfield, Louisiana
d. September 05, 1960 in Alexandria, Louisiana

Huey Pierce Long
American political leader
• Governor of LA, 1928-32; senator, 1932-35; assassinated; noted for "Every Man a King" campaign promise.
b. August 3, 1893 in Winnfield, Louisiana
d. September 1, 1935 in Baton Rouge, Louisiana

Russell Billiu Long
American political leader
• Dem. senator from LA, 1951-86; longtime finance committee chm.; son of Huey.
b. November 03, 1918 in Shreveport, Louisiana

James Longstreet
American military leader–public official–author
• Confederate general whose tardiness supposedly led to Lee's defeat at Gettysburg, 1863; wrote civil war histories.
b. January 08, 1821 in Edgefield District, South Carolina
d. January 02, 1904 in Gainesville, Georgia

Jose Lopez Portillo
Mexican political leader
• Pres. of Mexico, 1976-82.
b. July 16, 1920 in Mexico City, Mexico

Pal Losonczi
Hungarian political leader
• Head of State, 1967–.
b. September 18, 1919 in Bolho, Hungary

Peter Lougheed
Canadian politician
• Progressive-Conservative premier of Alberta, 1971-85.
b. July 26, 1928 in Calgary, Alberta

Louis I
Ruler
• Ruled Holy Roman Empire, 814-840; son of Charlemagne; twice deposed by his sons.
b. 778
d. June 2, 840

Louis IX
(Saint Louis)
French ruler
• King from 1226; led two crusades, 1248-54, 1270; canonized, 1297.
b. April 25, 1215 in Poissy, France
d. August 25, 1270 in Tunis, Tunisia

Louis XIV
French ruler
• Absolute monarch, ruled despotically; had longest reign in European history, 1643-1715; built Versailles.
b. September 16, 1638 in Saint-Germain-en-Laye, France
d. September 01, 1715

Louis XV
(The Well Beloved)
French ruler
• Ruled France, 1715-74; his failure to solve fiscal problems led to the Revolution; great-grandson of Louis XIV.
b. February 15, 1710 in Versailles, France
d. May 1, 1774

Louis XVI
French ruler
• Ruled from 1774; his reforms failed to stop Revolution; he and wife, Marie Antoinette, found guilty of treason, guillotined.
b. August 23, 1754 in Versailles, France
d. January 21, 1793

Louis Phillippe
French ruler
• Proclaimed king, 1830, in July revolution against Charles X; abdicated, 1848.
b. October 06, 1773 in Paris, France
d. August 26, 1850 in London, England

Robert A(bercrombie) Lovett
American cabinet member
• Secretary of Defense during Korean conflict, 1951-53; received Presidential Medal of Freedom, 1963.
b. September 14, 1895 in Huntsville, Texas
d. May 07, 1986 in Locust Valley, New York

Ruud (Rudolphus Franciscus Maria) Lubbers
Dutch political leader
• Prime minister of Netherlands, 1982-.
b. May 07, 1939 in Rotterdam, Netherlands

Count Felix von Luckner
German naval officer
• Exploits destroyed $25 million worth of allied shipping, WW I; Lowell Thomas wrote biography, 1927.
b. 1881
d. 1966

Lucius Licinius Lucullus
(Lucius Licinius Lucullus Ponticus)
Roman army officer
• Served in the East under Sulla; noted for banquets; term Lucullan derived from his extravagant living.
b. 110BC
d. 57BC

Ludwig II
(Louis II; "Mad King Ludwig")
Bavarian ruler–eccentric
• Patron of Wagner; built tourist-attraction castle; declared insane, committed suicide.
b. August 25, 1845 in Nymphenburg, Bavaria
d. June 13, 1886 in Lake Starnberg, Bavaria

Richard Green Lugar
American political leader
• Rep. senator from IN, 1977-.
b. April 04, 1932 in Indianapolis, Indiana

Patrice Emergy Lumumba
Congolese political leader
• First prime minister of Republic of Congo, June, 1960; deposed, Sept. 1960; believed killed by Katanga Province tribesmen.
b. July 02, 1925 in Oualua, Congo
d. January 18, 1961 in Elisabethville, Congo

Jaime Lusinchi
Venezuelan political leader
• Pres. of Venezuela, 1984-.
b. May 27, 1924 in Clarines, Venezuela

Douglas MacArthur
American army officer–military leader
• Accepted Japanese surrender, 1945; dismissed by Truman in Korea, 1951.
b. January 26, 1880 in Little Rock, Arkansas
d. April 05, 1964 in Washington, District of Columbia

Macbeth
Scottish ruler
• King of Scotland, 1040-57; slain by Malcolm III.
d. 1057

Maccabees
(Eleazar Maccabees; Jochanan Maccabees; Mattathias Maccabees; Simon Maccabes)
Patriots
• Jewish family who restored political, religious life from Syrian persecution; Hanukkah celebrates this event.

John Alexander MacDonald
Canadian political leader
• First prime minister of Canada, 1867-73, 1878-91; influential in passage of British N America Act, 1867.
b. January 11, 1815 in Glasgow, Scotland
d. June 06, 1891 in Ottawa, Ontario

Thomas MacDonough
American naval officer–military leader
• Captain who led one of most important battles in US navy; his victory caused British to lose claim of Great Lakes, 1814.
b. December 31, 1783 in New Castle County, Delaware
d. November 1, 1825

Gerardo Machado y Morales
Cuban political leader
• Involved in revolution against Spain, 1895-98; liberal pres. of Cuba, 1925-33; dictatorial powers caused popular revolt ending in his ousting.
b. September 29, 1871 in Santa Clara, Cuba
d. March 29, 1939 in Miami Beach, Florida

Samora Moises Machel
Mozambican political leader
• Installed as pres. of newly independent Mozambique, 1975; never faced coup attempt; died in plane crash.
b. September 29, 1933 in Chilembene, Mozambique
d. October 19, 1986 in Muzimi, South Africa

Niccolo Machiavelli
Italian philosopher–author
• Wrote *The Prince*, 1513, outlining pragmatic theory of govt.
b. May 03, 1469 in Florence, Italy
d. June 22, 1527 in Florence, Italy

Alexander Mackenzie
Canadian political leader
• First Liberal Party prime minister of Canada, 1873-78.
b. January 28, 1822 in Dunkeld, Scotland
d. April 17, 1892 in Toronto, Ontario

Harold (Maurice Harold) MacMillan
English political leader
• Conservative prime minister, 1957-63; helped Britain adapt to its reduced military, economic, diplomatic power.
b. February 1, 1894 in London, England
d. December 29, 1986 in Sussex, England

Lester Garfield Maddox
American political leader
• Segregationist Dem. governor of GA, 1967-71.
b. September 3, 1915 in Atlanta, Georgia

Francisco Indalecio Madero
Mexican revolutionary–political leader
• Liberal ruler of Mexico, 1911-13, succeeding Diaz; attempted social reforms.
b. 1873 in Mexico
d. 1913 in Mexico

Dolly Payne Todd Madison
(Mrs James Madison)
American first lady
• Popular, influential figure in Washington society; model for several historical romances, biographies.
b. May 2, 1768 in Guilford County, North Carolina
d. July 12, 1849 in Orange County, Virginia

James Madison
American US president
• Fourth pres., 1809-17; drafted Bill of Rights.
b. March 16, 1751 in Port Conway, Virginia
d. June 28, 1836 in Orange County, Virginia

Miguel de la Madrid Hurtado
Mexican political leader
• Pres. of Mexico, 1982-88.
b. December 12, 1934 in Colima, Mexico

Alvaro (Alfredo) Magana
Salvadoran political leader
• Pres. of El Salvador, 1982-84.
b. October 08, 1925 in Ahuchapan, El Salvador

Andre Maginot
French politician
• War minister, 1929-32 who planned system of fortifications called Maginot line.
b. February 17, 1877 in Paris, France
d. January 07, 1932 in Paris, France

Bir Bikram Shah Dev Mahendra
Nepalese ruler
• King of Nepal, 1956-72, who was world's only Hindu monarch.
b. June 11, 1920 in Kathmandu, Nepal
d. January 31, 1972 in Bharatpur, Nepal

Mahmud of Ghazni
Afghan ruler–conqueror
• Founded Ghaznavid dynasty, 999-1186; staunch Muslim, who destroyed Hindu temples, forced conversion.
b. 971
d. 1030

Archbishop Makarios III
(Michael Christedoulos Mouskos)
Cypriot religious leader–politician
• First pres., Republic of Cyprus, 1959-77; led political, religious life there for 25 yrs.
b. August 13, 1913 in Cyprus
d. August 02, 1977 in Nicosia, Cyprus

Daniel F Malan
South African politician
• Pres., Union of South Africa, 1948-54; advocated apartheid.
b. May 22, 1874 in Riebeck, South Africa
d. February 07, 1959 in Cape Town, South Africa

Yakov (Alexandrovich) Malik
Russian diplomat
• Outspoken, conservative Soviet ambassador to UN, 1948-75; expert on Far Eastern affairs.
b. February 11, 1906 in Kharkov, Russia
d. February 11, 1980 in Moscow, U.S.S.R.

Marvin Mandel
American political leader
• Dem. governor of MD, 1969-77; found guilty of political corruption, 1977; conviction overturned, 1979.
b. April 19, 1920 in Baltimore, Maryland

Nelson Rolihlahla Mandela
South African political activist
• Leader, African National Congress, sentenced to life in prison, 1964, for conspiracy to overthrow S African govt.; released from prison, 1990.
b. July 18, 1918 in Umtata, South Africa

Winnie Mandela
(Nkosikazi Nobandle Nomzano Madikizela; Mrs Nelson Mandela)
South African political activist
• With husband, has struggled for black liberation in S Africa since 1963.
b. 1936 in Transkei, South Africa

Michael Norman Manley
Jamaican political leader
• Prime minister of Jamaica, 1972-80, 1989–; wrote of political philosophy in *The Politics of Change: A Jamaican Testament*, 1974.
b. December 1, 1923 in Kingston, Jamaica

Baron Carl Gustav Emil Mannerheim
Finnish military leader–political leader
• President of Finland, 1944-46; nat. hero in three wars against USSR.
b. June 04, 1867 in Louhissaari, Finland
d. January 27, 1951 in Lausanne, Switzerland

Mike (Michael Joseph) Mansfield
American political leader
• Dem. senator from MT, 1953-76; ambassador to Japan, 1977-88.
b. March 16, 1903 in New York, New York

Al (Abu Jafar Ibn Muhammad) Mansur
Arabian political leader
• Second Abbasid calyph, 754-775, who built city of Baghdad, 762.
b. 712
d. October 775 in Mecca, Arabia

Manuel I
(Emanuel the Great; "The Fortunate")
Portuguese ruler
• Reigned during country's golden age, 1495-1521; centralized public administration.
b. 1469
d. 1521

Mao Tse-Tung
Chinese communist leader–author
• Peasant who founded People's Republic of China, 1949; controlled until death.
b. December 26, 1893 in Shaeshan, China
d. September 09, 1976 in Peking, China

Ferdinand Edralin Marcos
Philippine political leader
• Pres. of Philippines, 1966-86; abandoned presidency, Feb 25, 1986.
b. September 11, 1917 in Sarrat, Philippines
d. September 28, 1989 in Honolulu, Hawaii

Marcus Aurelius Antoninus
(Marcus Annius Verus)
Roman ruler–philosopher–author
• Roman emperor, A.D. 161-180; wrote *Meditations* advocating stoicism.
b. April 2, 121 in Rome, Italy
d. March 17, 180 in Vindobona, Austria

Margaret
(Margaret Rose)
English princess
• Sister of Queen Elizabeth II; currently 11th in line to British throne; children are Viscount Linley and Lady Sarah Armstrong-Jones.
b. August 21, 1930 in Glamis, Scotland

Margrethe II
Danish ruler
• First woman to rule Denmark; acceded to throne Jan 14, 1972.
b. April 16, 1940 in Copenhagen, Denmark

Maria Theresa
Austrian ruler
• Wed Francis I, Holy Roman Emperor; mother of Emperor Leopold II and Marie Antoinette.
b. May 13, 1717 in Vienna, Austria
d. November 29, 1780

Marie Alexandra Victoria
English ruler–author
• Queen of Ferdinand I, 1914-27; followed Rumanian armies as Red Cross nurse, WW I; wrote *My Country*, 1916, many Romanian fairy tales.
b. 1875 in London, England
d. 1938

Duke John Churchill Marlborough
English army officer–statesman
• Led forces against Louis XIV in War of the Spanish Succession.
b. 1650 in Devonshire, England
d. June 16, 1722 in Windsor, England

George Catlett Marshall
American military leader–government official
• Proposed Marshall Plan, to aid war-torn European countries, 1947; won Nobel Peace Prize, 1953; prominent WW II general.
b. December 31, 1880 in Uniontown, Pennsylvania
d. October 16, 1959 in Bethesda, Maryland

Thomas Riley Marshall
American US vice president
• VP under Wilson, 1913-21; said "What this country needs is a good five-cent cigar."
b. March 14, 1854 in North Manchester, Indiana
d. June 01, 1925 in Washington, District of Columbia

Wilfried Martens
Belgian political leader
• Prime minister of Belgium, 1979–.
b. April 19, 1936 in Sleidinge, Belgium

Bob (Robert) Martinez
American political leader
• Republican and first Hispanic governor of FL, 1987-91; succeeded by Lawton Chiles.
b. December 25, 1934 in Tampa, Florida

Mary I
(Mary Tudor; "Bloody Mary")
English ruler
• Daughter of Henry VIII and Katharine of Aragon; first English queen to rule in own right.
b. February 18, 1516 in Greenwich, England
d. November 17, 1558

Mary Queen of Scots
(Mary Stuart)
Scottish ruler
• Inherited Scottish throne at age of six days; beheaded by Elizabeth I.
b. December 1542 in Linlithgow, Scotland
d. February 08, 1587 in Fotherinhay, England

Spark Masayuki Matsunaga
American political leader
• Dem. senator from HI, 1977-90, representative, 1963-76; decorated Bronze Medal, Purple Heart.
b. October 08, 1916 in Kauai Island, Hawaii
d. April 15, 1990 in Toronto, Ontario

Matthias Corvinus
Hungarian ruler
• During reign improved internal conditions, army, 1458-90; throne constantly challenged by uncle, Frederick III.
b. 1443
d. 1490

Ion Gheorghe Maurer
Romanian diplomat
• Chm., Council of Ministers, 1961-74.
b. September 23, 1902 in Bucharest, Romania

Pierre Mauroy
French political leader
• Premier in Francois Mitterand's Socialist govt.
b. July 05, 1928 in Cartignie, France

Mausolus
Persian ruler
• Virtual ruler of Rhodes; enormous tomb, built for him by wife, Artemisia, Mausoleum at Halicarnassus, is one of world's wonders.

Samuel Augustus Maverick
American rancher–political leader
• Helped establish Republic of Texas, 1836; term "maverick" used for unbranded cattle wandering unattended.
b. July 25, 1803 in Pendleton, South Carolina
d. September 02, 1870 in San Antonio, Texas

Maximilian
(Ferdinand Maximilian Joseph)
Austrian ruler
• Archduke of Austria, emperor of Mexico, 1864-67; empire in Mexico denounced by US; Napoleon III withdrew support.
b. July 06, 1832 in Vienna, Austria
d. June 19, 1867 in Queretaro, Mexico

Maximilian I
German ruler
• King of Germany, 1486-1519; Holy Roman Emperor, 1493-1519; laid foundation of Hapsburg greatness.
b. March 22, 1459 in Vienna, Neustadt
d. January 12, 1519 in Upper Austria

Maximilian II
German ruler
• Holy Roman Emperor, 1564-76.
b. July 31, 1527
d. October 12, 1576

Norman D Mayer
American political activist
• Held Washington Monument hostage, Dec, 1982, to protest nuclear weapons.
b. March 31, 1916 in El Paso, Texas
d. December 08, 1982 in Washington, District of Columbia

Romano L Mazzoli
American political leader
• Dem. congressman from KY, 1971–; co-authored landmark Immigration Reform and Control Act of 1986.
b. November 02, 1932 in Louisville, Kentucky

Tom (Thomas Joseph) Mboya
Kenyan political leader
• Leader of Kenya Independence Movement, 1960s; assassination started widespread rioting.
b. August 15, 1930 in Rusinga Island, Kenya
d. July 05, 1969 in Nairobi, Kenya

William Gibbs McAdoo
American political leader
• Prominent Dem. candidate for pres., 1920, 1924; senator from CA, 1933-38.
b. October 31, 1863 in Marietta, Georgia
d. February 01, 1941 in Washington, District of Columbia

Anthony Clement McAuliffe
American military leader
• Noted for terse reply "Nuts" to German surrender ultimatum, 1944; commanded US forces in Europe, 1955-56.
b. July 02, 1898 in Washington, District of Columbia
d. August 11, 1975 in Washington, District of Columbia

Thomas Lawson McCall
American political leader
• Environmentalist Rep. governor of OR, 1967-74.
b. March 22, 1913 in Egypt, Massachusetts
d. January 08, 1983 in Portland, Oregon

Eugene Joseph McCarthy
American political leader
• Dem. senator from MN, 1958-70; Dem. presidential candidate, 1968, 1972.
b. March 29, 1916 in Watkins, Minnesota

Joe (Joseph Raymond) McCarthy
American political leader
• Rep. senator from WI, 1947-57; best known for early-1950s subcommittee investigations of alleged communist activities; censured by Senate, derided for "witch hunt" tactics, 1954.
b. November 14, 1908 in Grand Chute, Wisconsin
d. May 02, 1957 in Bethesda, Maryland

George Brinton McClellan
American military leader
• Indecisive Union general who was Dem. presidential candidate against Lincoln, 1864.
b. December 03, 1826 in Philadelphia, Pennsylvania
d. October 29, 1885 in Orange, New Jersey

John Little McClellan
American political leader
• Dem. senator from AR, 1943-77; second-longest serving senator; known for heading crime investigations, 1960s.
b. February 25, 1896 in Sheridan, Arkansas
d. November 27, 1977 in Little Rock, Arkansas

Paul Norton McCloskey, Jr
American political leader
• Moderate Rep. con. from CA, 1967-83.
b. September 29, 1927 in San Bernardino, California

Larry (Lawrence Patton) McDonald
American political leader–victim
• Archconservative Dem. congressman from GA, 1974-83; died aboard Korean jetliner shot down by Soviet Union.
b. April 01, 1935 in Atlanta, Georgia
d. September 01, 1983

Irvin McDowell
American military leader
• Union general, relieved of command after second battle of Bull Run, 1862; later exonerated.
b. October 15, 1818 in Columbus, Ohio
d. May 04, 1885 in San Francisco, California

Robert Carl McFarlane
American presidential aide
• Nat. security adviser to Ronald Reagan, 1983-85.
b. July 12, 1937 in Washington, District of Columbia

George Stanley McGovern
American political leader
• Liberal senator from SD, 1963-81; Dem. presidential candidate, 1972; lost to Richard Nixon in huge landslide.
b. July 19, 1922 in Avon, South Dakota

Martin McGuinness
Irish politician–political activist
• IRA leader currently an elected member of N Ireland Assembly.
b. 1950

Frank McKenna
Canadian politician
• Liberal premier of New Brunswick, 1985-.
b. January 19, 1948 in Apolaqui, New Brunswick

Ida Saxton McKinley
(Mrs William McKinley)
American first lady
• After tragic deaths of two children, she developed epilepsy; husband was devoted, caring.
b. June 08, 1847 in Canton, Ohio
d. May 26, 1907 in Canton, Ohio

William McKinley
American US president
• Rep., 25th to hold office, 1897-1901; led US through Spanish-American War; assassinated.
b. January 29, 1843 in Niles, Ohio
d. September 14, 1901 in Buffalo, New York

Stewart Brett McKinney
American political leader
• Rep. congressman from CT, 1971-87; championed liberal causes.
b. January 3, 1931 in Pittsburgh, Pennsylvania
d. May 07, 1987 in Washington, District of Columbia

John (Joseph) McLaughlin
American presidential aide
• Roman Catholic priest, who was a Nixon speechwriter, strong Watergate defender, 1971-74.
b. 1927

Robert S(trange) McNamara
American banker–cabinet member
• Defense secretary, 1961-68; president, World Bank, 1968-81.
b. June 09, 1916 in San Francisco, California

James Birdseye McPherson
American military leader
• Union general, 1862; led army of the Tennessee, 1864; killed in action.
b. November 14, 1828 in Green Creek, Ohio
d. June 22, 1864 in Atlanta, Georgia

George Gordon Meade
American military leader
• Union general who commanded army of the Potomac, 1863-65; repulsed Lee at Gettysburg.
b. December 31, 1815 in Cadiz, Spain
d. November 06, 1872 in Philadelphia, Pennsylvania

Evan Mecham
American political leader
• Rep. governor of AZ, 1987-88; his impeachment, 1988, was state's first, first in US since 1929.
b. May 12, 1924 in Duchesne, Utah

Cosimo de Medici
(Cosimo the Elder)
Italian ruler
• First of Medici family to rule Florence, 1433; known chiefly for generosity to scholars, artists.
b. September 27, 1389 in Florence, Italy
d. August 01, 1464 in Florence, Italy

Francesco de Medici
Italian ruler
• Successor as Grand Duke of Tuscany, 1574-87.
b. March 25, 1541
d. October 19, 1587

Lorenzo de Medici
(Lorenzo the Magnificent)
Italian poet–ruler–art patron
• Virtual Florentine ruler from 1470s; tyrannical, but made Florence prosperous, center of culture.
b. January 01, 1449 in Florence, Italy
d. April 08, 1492 in Florence, Italy

Ernest L Medina
American army officer–military leader
• Stood trial for ordering murder of Vietnamese civilians in My Lai, 1968.
b. 1936

Edwin Meese III
American government official–presidential aide
• US Attorney General, 1985-88.
b. December 02, 1931 in Oakland, California

Golda Meir
(Golda Myerson)
Israeli political leader
• First woman prime minister of Israel, 1969-74; wrote *My Life*, 1975.
b. May 03, 1898 in Kiev, Russia
d. December 08, 1978 in Jerusalem, Israel

Oscar Humberto Mejia Victores
Guatemalan political leader
• Seized presidency in Aug 1983 coup.
b. December 09, 1930 in Guatemala City, Guatemala

Viscount William Lamb Melbourne
English political leader
• Prime Minister, 1834; 1835-41; favored adviser of Queen Victoria; husband of Lady Caroline Lamb.
b. March 15, 1779 in Hertfordshire, England
d. November 24, 1848 in Hertfordshire, England

Andrew William Mellon
American financier–cabinet member
• Secretary of Treasury, 1921-32; ambassador to Great Britain, 1932-33; endowed Washington's National Gallery of Art.
b. March 24, 1855 in Pittsburgh, Pennsylvania
d. August 26, 1937 in Southampton, New York

Pedro Menendez de Aviles
Spanish naval officer–colonizer
• Founded St. Augustine, Florida, 1500s; attempted to establish Spanish rule in Florida.
b. February 15, 1519 in Aviles, Spain
d. September 17, 1574 in Santander, Spain

Menelik II
(Sahle Mariam)
Ethiopian ruler
• Emperor, 1889-1913; expanded realm; established country's independence; succeeded by regency due to illness, 1910.
b. 1844
d. 1913

Menes
(Mena)
Egyptian ruler
• Credited with uniting Egypt, its first king; founder of first dynasty; ruled 62 yrs.
b. fl. 3100BC

Haile Mariam Mengistu
Ethiopian political leader
• Marxist Ethiopian head of state, 1977–.
b. 1937 in Wollamo, Ethiopia

Sir Robert Gordon Menzies
Australian politician
• Served longest continuous term as Australia's prime minister, 1939-66.
b. December 2, 1894 in Jeparit, Australia
d. May 14, 1978 in Melbourne, Australia

Wesley Merritt
American military leader
• Led first US Philippine expedition; occupied Manila in Spanish-American War, 1898.
b. June 16, 1836 in New York, New York
d. December 03, 1910 in Natural Bridge, Virginia

John(Ioannis) Metaxas
Greek political leader
• Dictator of Greece, 1936-41, who led country into WW II against Germany, Italy.
b. April 12, 1871 in Cephalonia, Greece
d. January 29, 1941 in Athens, Greece

Ralph H Metcalfe
American track athlete–political leader
• Dem. congressman from IL, 1970-78; founding member, Congressional Black Caucus; finished second behind Jesse Owens in 100-meters, 1936 Olympics.
b. May 3, 1910 in Atlanta, Georgia
d. October 1, 1978 in Chicago, Illinois

Howard M(orton) Metzenbaum
American political leader
• Dem. senator from OH, 1977–.
b. June 04, 1917 in Cleveland, Ohio

Michael V
Romanian ruler
• Preceded (1927-30) and succeeded (1940-47) father, Carol II, to throne.
b. October 25, 1921

Robert H(enry) Michel
American political leader
• Rep. congressman from IL, 1957–; House minority leader, 1981–.
b. March 02, 1923 in Peoria, Illinois

Roland Michener
Canadian government official
• Governor general, commander-in-chief, 1967-74.
b. April 19, 1900 in Lacombe, Alberta

Nelson Appleton Miles
American military leader
• General; helped crush Indians in West, capturing Geronimo, 1886; commanded forces at Wounded Knee massacre, 1890.
b. August 08, 1839 in Westminster, Massachusetts
d. May 15, 1925 in Washington, District of Columbia

William E Miller
American political leader
• Rep. congressman from NY who was Barry Goldwater's running mate in 1964 presidential election.
b. March 22, 1914 in Lockport, New York
d. June 24, 1983 in Buffalo, New York

William G(rawn) Milliken
American political leader
• Moderate Rep. governor of MI, 1969-82; served longer than any governor in state history.
b. March 26, 1922 in Traverse City, Michigan

Wilbur Daigh Mills
American political leader
• Dem. con. from AR, 1939-77; chaired Ways and Means Committee, 1958-74; career ruined by 1974 sex scandal.
b. May 24, 1909 in Kensett, Arkansas

Baron George Francis Milne
British military leader
• WW I general who led campaign into Turkey, occupying Constantinople until 1920.
b. November 05, 1866 in Aberdeen, Scotland
d. March 23, 1948 in London, England

T'ai-Tsu Ming
(Yuan-Chang Chu; Hung Wu)
Chinese ruler
• Founder, first emperor of Ming dynasty, 1368-98; ended Yuan dynasty by capturing Peking; drove out Mongols, united China.
b. 1328 in Anhwei Province, China
d. 1398

Patsy Takemoto Mink
American political leader
• Liberal Dem. representative from HI, 1965-77.
b. December 06, 1927 in Paia, Hawaii

Billy (William) Mitchell
American military leader
• Commander, WW I air forces; vocal proponent of supremacy of air power; court-martialed for criticizing management of military air service, 1925.
b. December 29, 1879 in Nice, France
d. February 19, 1936 in New York, New York

Marc Andrew Mitscher
American military leader
• Naval aviator; commander-in-chief of Atlantic Fleet, 1946-47; commanded aircraft carrier *Hornet*, WW II; known as doer, preferring the offensive tactic.
b. January 26, 1887 in Hillsboro, Wisconsin
d. February 03, 1947 in Norfolk, Virginia

Constantine Mitsotakis
Greek political leader
• Prime minister of Greece, 1990–, succeeding Andreas Papandreou.
b. October 18, 1918 in Chania, Crete

Francois Maurice Marie Mitterrand
French political leader
• Socialist pres. who defeated Valery Giscard d'Estaing, 1981, ending 23 yrs. of Gaullist rule.
b. October 26, 1916 in Jarnac, France

Joseph Desire (Sese Seko) Mobutu
Congolese political leader
• Dictatorial pres. of Zaire, coming to power in coup, 1965–.
b. October 14, 1930 in Lisala, Belgian Congo

Rose Mofford
American political leader
• Dem. governor of Arizona, 1988–; became governor on impeachment of Evan Mecham.
b. June 1, 1922 in Globe, Arizona

Mohammed V
(Sidi Mohammed Ben Moulay Youssef)
Moroccan ruler
• Ruled, 1957-61, after France recognized country's independence.
b. August 1, 1910
d. February 26, 1961 in Rabat, Morocco

Mohammed Zahir Shah
Afghan ruler
• Crowned King, 1933; abdicated, 1973.
b. October 3, 1914 in Kabul, Afghanistan

Daniel Torotich Arap Moi
Kenyan political leader
• Succeeded Jomo Kenyatta as pres. of Kenya, 1978–.
b. September 1924 in Kuriengwo, Kenya

Viacheslav Mikhailovich Molotov, pseud
(V M Skryabin)
Russian communist leader
• Soviet Communist Party leader during Stalin's regime; negotiated WW II alliances with Great Britain, US, 1941-42. Crude incendiary device named after him.
b. March 09, 1890 in Kirov District, Russia
d. November 08, 1986 in Moscow, U.S.S.R.

Walter Frederick Mondale
American US vice president
• Dem. senator from MN, 1964-77; VP, 1977-80, under Carter; unsuccessful presidential candidate against Reagan, 1980.
b. January 05, 1928 in Ceylon, Minnesota

Ernesto Teodora Moneta
Italian political leader
• Shared 1907 Nobel Peace Prize for founding Lombard Peace Union, 1887.
b. September 2, 1833 in Milan, Italy
d. February 1, 1918 in Milan, Italy

Jean (Omer Gabriel) Monnet
French economist–diplomat
• Father of European Economic Community; helped reconstruction of France after WW II.
b. November 09, 1888 in Cognac, France
d. March 16, 1979 in Rambouillet, France

Elizabeth Kortright Monroe
(Mrs James Monroe)
American first lady
• Introduced more formal ways of White House entertaining.
b. June 3, 1768 in New York, New York
d. September 23, 1830 in Loudoun County, Virginia

James Monroe
American US president
• Fifth in office, 1817-25; declared Monroe Doctrine, 1823; term called "era of good feeling."
b. April 28, 1758 in Westmoreland, Virginia
d. July 04, 1831 in New York, New York

Mike (Aimer Stillwell) Monroney
American political leader
• Dem. senator from OK, 1951-69; opposed Joe McCarthy.
b. March 02, 1902 in Oklahoma City, Oklahoma
d. February 13, 1980 in Rockville, Maryland

Louis Joseph de Montcalm
French military leader
• Commander French forces in Canada; killed in defense of Quebec.
b. February 29, 1712 in Nimes, France
d. September 14, 1759 in Quebec

Montezuma I
Aztec ruler
• Emperor, 1440-64; rebuilt Tenochtitlan, 1446, following flood, plague; issued Draconian code of laws.
b. 1390 in Tenochtitlan, Mexico
d. 1464 in Tenochtitlan, Mexico

Montezuma II
Aztec ruler
• Emperor, 1502-19; conquered by Cortes.
b. 1480 in Tenochtitlan, Mexico
d. June 1520 in Tenochtitlan, Mexico

Simon de Montfort
English political leader
• Led revolt against Britain's Henry III; became virtual ruler; called Great Parliament, 1265.
b. 1208 in Normandy, France
d. August 04, 1265 in Evesham, England

Viscount Bernard Law Montgomery Montgomery of Alamein
English military leader
• Field marshal during WW II who defeated Germans at El Alamein, 1942; led Allied landings in Normandy, 1944.
b. November 17, 1887 in Kennington Oval, England
d. March 25, 1976 in Isington, England

Joseph Manuel Montoya
American political leader
• Dem. senator from NM, 1965-77; on Senate Watergate Committee, 1973.
b. September 24, 1915 in Pena Blanca, New Mexico
d. June 05, 1978 in Washington, District of Columbia

Thomas H(inman) Moorer
American naval officer–military leader
• Much-decorated chm., US Joint Chiefs of Staff, 1970-74; Chief of Naval Operations, 1967-70.
b. February 09, 1912 in Mount Willing, Alabama

William Singer Moorhead
American political leader
• Dem. congressman from PA, 1959-81.
b. April 08, 1923 in Pittsburgh, Pennsylvania
d. August 03, 1987 in Baltimore, Maryland

Jose M Morelos y Pavon
Mexican clergyman–military leader
• Led revolution against Spain after Hidalgo's execution, 1813; shot by royalists.
b. 1765
d. 1815

Daniel Morgan
American politician–army officer–military leader
• Best known for defeating Banastre Tarleton, 1781; helped supress Whiskey Rebellion, 1794.
b. 1736 in Bucks County, Pennsylvania
d. July 06, 1802 in Winchester, Virginia

Sir Frederick Morgan
English army officer–military leader
• Chief planner, Allied invasion of Europe, WW II; acted as Britain's controller of atomic energy.
b. February 05, 1894 in England
d. March 2, 1967

Ernest Nathan Morial
American political leader
• Dem., first black mayor of New Orleans, 1978-86.
b. October 09, 1929 in New Orleans, Louisiana
d. December 24, 1989 in New Orleans, Louisiana

Aldo Moro
Italian politician
• Leader, Christian Democratic Party; kidnapped, killed by Red Brigade terrorists.
b. September 23, 1916 in Maglie, Italy
d. May 09, 1978 in Rome, Italy

Justin Smith Morrill
American political leader
• Congressman, later senator, who sponsored Morrill Act, 1857; provided land for land-grant colleges, forerunners state universities.
b. April 14, 1810 in Strafford, Vermont
d. December 28, 1898 in Washington, District of Columbia

Levi Parsons Morton
American US vice president
• VP under Benjamin Harrison, 1889-93; governor of NY, 1895-97.
b. May 16, 1824 in Shoreham, Vermont
d. May 16, 1920 in Rhinebeck, New York

Oliver Perry Morton
American political leader
• Rep. senator from IN, 1867-77; played major role in passage of 15th Amendment, 1870, which enfranchised blacks.
b. August 04, 1823 in Salisbury, Indiana
d. November 01, 1877 in Indianapolis, Indiana

George Richard Moscone
American political leader
• Mayor of San Francisco, 1976-78; murdered by Daniel White.
b. November 24, 1929 in San Francisco, California
d. November 27, 1978 in San Francisco, California

Robert Moses
American political leader
• N.Y. city parks commissioner, 1934-60; developed bridges, playgrounds, state parks, highways, , Jones Beach, Shea Stadium etc.
b. December 18, 1888 in New Haven, Connecticut
d. July 29, 1981 in West Islip, New York

Moshoeshoe II
(Constantine Bereng Seeiso)
Ruler
• King, upon restoration of Lesotho's independence, 1966-; exiled from country, 1970; returned as head of state, 1970.
b. May 02, 1938 in Mokhotlong, Lesotho

Sir Oswald Ernald Mosley
English politician
• One-time potential candidate for prime minister; completely reversed loyalties to found British Union of Fascists, 1932-43.
b. November 16, 1896 in Staffordshire, England
d. December 02, 1980 in Orsay, France

Mohammed Mossadegh
Iranian political leader
• Premier of Iran, 1951-53; nationalized Britain's oil holdings.
b. 1879 in Teheran, Persia
d. March 05, 1967 in Teheran, Iran

William Moultrie
American political leader–politician
• Revolutionary war leader; defended Charleston, 1779; twice governor of SC.
b. December 04, 1730 in Charleston, South Carolina
d. September 27, 1805 in Charleston, South Carolina

Earl Louis Mountbatten Mountbatten of Burma,
English naval officer
• Great-grandson of Queen Victoria; killed in bomb explosion credited to IRA.
b. June 25, 1900 in Windsor, England
d. August 27, 1979 in Mullaghmore, Ireland

Daniel Patrick Moynihan
American political leader–diplomat
• Dem. senator from NY, 1976–; outspoken proponent of arms control.
b. March 16, 1927 in Tulsa, Oklahoma

(Muhamed) Hosni Mubarak
Egyptian political leader
• Succeeded Anwar Sadat as pres., 1981.
b. May 04, 1928 in Kafr-El Meselha, Egypt

Robert Gabriel Mugabe
South African political leader
• Prime minister of Zimbabwe, 1980–; co-founder, Zimbabwe African Nat. Union, 1963, pres., 1977–.
b. February 21, 1924 in Kutama, South Africa

Sir Robert David Muldoon
New Zealander political leader
• Prime minister, 1975-84.
b. September 25, 1921 in Auckland, New Zealand

Brian (Martin Brian) Mulroney
Canadian political leader
• Millionaire Conservative Party leader who defeated John Turner's Liberal Party to become prime minister, Sep 1984.
b. March 2, 1939 in Baie Comeau, Quebec

Mumtaz Mahal
(Arjumand Banu)
Hindu ruler
• Favorite wife of Mogul emperor Shah Jahan, who built Taj Mahal as her mausoleum, 1648.
b. 1593
d. 1630

Karl Earl Mundt
American educator–political leader
• Rep. senator from SD, 1949-72; chaired Senate's Army-McCarthy hearings, 1954.
b. June 03, 1900 in Humboldt, South Dakota
d. August 16, 1974 in Washington, District of Columbia

Luis Munoz Marin
Puerto Rican politician
• First elected governor of Puerto Rico, 1948-64.
b. February 18, 1898 in San Juan, Puerto Rico
d. April 3, 1980 in San Juan, Puerto Rico

Do Muoi
Vietnamese political leader
• Prime minister of Vietnam, 1988–.
b. 1917

Joachim Murat
French military leader–politician
• Brother-in-law of Napoleon I; king of Naples, 1808-15.
b. March 25, 1767 in La Baslide-Fortumiere, France
d. October 13, 1815 in Pizzo, Italy

John Michael Murphy
American political leader
• Dem. representative from NY, 1963-81; convicted in Abscam scandal, 1980.
b. August 03, 1926 in Staten Island, New York

John Patrick Murtha
American political leader
• Dem. rep. from PA, 1974–; first Vietnam veteran elected to Congress; named, not indicted, in Abscam scandal.
b. June 17, 1932 in New-Martinsville, West Virginia

Yoweri Kaguta Museveni
Ugandan political leader
• Succeeded Milton Obote as president of Uganda, 1986–.
b. 1944

Edmund Sixtus Muskie
American political leader
• Secretary of State under Carter, 1980-81; Dem. senator from ME, 1959-80; governor of ME, 1955-59.
b. March 28, 1914 in Rumford, Maine

Benito Mussolini
Italian political leader
• Founded Italian Fascist Party, 1919; prime minister, 1922-43; allied with Hitler, 1939.
b. July 29, 1883 in Dovia, Italy
d. April 28, 1945 in Milan, Italy

Mutesa I
Ugandan ruler
• Ruled Buganda, now Uganda, c. 1857-84; expanded trade, let Europeans into country.
b. 1838
d. 1884

Mutsuhito
(Meiji)
Japanese ruler
• Reign, 1867-1912, marked end of feudalism, birth of modern Japan.
b. 1852 in Kyoto, Japan
d. July 1912

Abel Tendekai Muzorewa
African political leader–clergyman
• Pres., African Nat. Council, 1971–; received UN Human Rights Award, 1973.
b. April 14, 1925 in Umtali, Rhodesia

Alva Reimer Myrdal
(Mrs Karl Gunnar Myrdal)
Swedish sociologist–diplomat
• Swedish ambassador to India, 1956-61; won Nobel Peace Prize, 1982, for advocating nuclear disarmament.
b. January 31, 1902 in Uppsala, Sweden
d. February 01, 1986 in Stockholm, Sweden

Ralph Nader
American political activist–author
• Founder of consumer rights movement in US, who wrote *Unsafe at Any Speed*, 1965.
b. February 27, 1934 in Winsted, Connecticut

Nadir Shah
(Nader Shah; Tahmasp Qoli Khan)
Persian ruler
• Ruled, 1736-47; deposed Tahmasp II in Afghanistan; made Sunni sect of Islam nat. religion.
b. 1688 in Khurasan, Persia
d. 1747

Mohammed Naguib
Egyptian political leader
• Became first pres. of Egypt, 1952, after military coup; removed from office, 1954.
b. February 2, 1901 in Khartoum, Sudan
d. August 28, 1984 in Cairo, Egypt

Sarojini Naidu
Indian poet–political leader–feminist
• First Indian woman pres. of Indian National Congress, 1925; wrote sentimental verse *The Bird of Time*, 1912.
b. February 13, 1879 in Hyderabad, India
d. March 02, 1949 in Lucknow, India

Ahmadzi Najib
Pakistani political leader
• President of Afghanistan, 1986–; installed by Soviets after forcing out Karmal.
b. 1947 in Paktia, Pakistan

Yasuhiro Nakasone
Japanese political leader
• Prime minister, 1982-87; introduced Western-style leadership through candor, aggressiveness.
b. May 27, 1918 in Takasaki, Japan

Palden Thondup Namgyal
Indian ruler
• King of Sikkim, 1963-75; deposed by India which annexed country.
b. May 22, 1923 in Gangtok, Sikkim
d. January 29, 1982 in New York, New York

Henri Namphy
Haitian political leader
• Succeeded Duvalier as president of Haiti, 1986–.
b. November 02, 1932 in Cap Haitien, Haiti

Charles Napier
British army officer–military leader
• Successful admiral who fell into disgrace after declining to attack in a major battle.
b. 1782
d. 1853

Napoleon I
(Napoleon Bonaparte)
French ruler
• Formed Napoleonic Code, 1804-10; overthrown at Waterloo, 1815.
b. August 15, 1769 in Ajaccio, Corsica
d. May 05, 1821 in Saint Helena

Napoleon III
(Charles Louis Napoleon Bonaparte; "Napoleon le Petit")
French ruler
• Proclaimed himself emperor, 1852; deposed in bloodless revolution, 1871; preceeded Bismarck.
b. April 2, 1808 in Paris, France
d. January 09, 1873 in Chislehurst, England

Gamal Abdel Nasser
Egyptian political leader
• Led coup that deposed King Farouk, 1952; pres. of Egypt, 1956-70.
b. January 15, 1918 in Beni Mor, Egypt
d. September 28, 1970 in Cairo, Egypt

Yitzhak Navon
Israeli political leader
• Labor party member, 1968–; pres. of Israel, 1978-83.
b. April 19, 1921 in Jerusalem, Palestine

Nebuchadnezzar II
Babylonian ruler
• King, 605-562 BC; destroyed city, temple of Jerusalem, 586 BC.

Nefertiti
Egyptian ruler
• Probably shared power of throne with pharoah husband Akhenaton; often shown wearing a pharoah's crown.
b. 1390BC
d. 1360BC

Juan Negrin
Spanish physician–politician
• Last premier, Second Republic, 1937-39; leader of Loyalists in Spanish Civil War until 1939.
b. 1892 in Spain
d. November 14, 1956 in Paris, France

Jawaharlal Nehru
Indian political leader
• Father of Indira Gandhi; India's first prime minister, 1947-64.
b. November 14, 1889 in Allahabad, India
d. May 27, 1964 in Allahabad, India

Nero
(Nero Claudius Caesar Germanicus)
Roman ruler
• Known for persecuting Christians; started fire that destroyed Rome.
b. 37
d. 68

Ngo dinh Diem
Vietnamese political leader
• Dictatorial anti-communist pres. of S Vietnam, 1954-63; assassinated in coup d'etat.
b. 1901 in Quang Bihn, Annam
d. November 02, 1963

Nicholas I
Russian ruler
• Ruled Russia, 1825-55; during reign Turkey declared war on Russia, 1853, which led to the Crimean War.
b. July 06, 1796 in Tsarkoe, Russia
d. March 02, 1855 in Saint Petersburg, Russia

Nicholas II
(Nikolai Aleksandrovich Romanov)
Russian ruler
• Last czar of Russia, 1894-1917, whose disorganization led to revolution of 1917; executed with family.
b. May 18, 1868 in Tsarskoe Selo, Russia
d. July 16, 1918 in Ekaterinburg, U.S.S.R.

Gaafar Mohammed al Nimeiry
Sudanese political leader
• Former revolutionary; arrested for suspicion of overthrowing govt.; pres. of Sudan, 1971-85, overthrown in coup.
b. January 01, 1930 in Wad Nubawi, Sudan

Chester William Nimitz
American naval officer–military leader
• Commander of Pacific Fleet, 1941-45, who planned strategy that defeated Japanese, WW II.
b. February 24, 1885 in Fredericksburg, Texas
d. February 2, 1966 in San Francisco, California

Francesco Saverio Nitti
Italian political leader
• Anti-fascist premier of Italy, 1919-20; exiled to France by Mussolini; retired to aid in postwar reconstruction, 1945.
b. July 19, 1868 in Melfi, Italy
d. February 2, 1953 in Rome, Italy

Robert N(elson) C(ornelius) Nix, Sr
American political leader
• First black Dem. congressman from PA, 1958-79.
b. August 09, 1905 in Orangeburg, South Carolina
d. June 22, 1987 in Philadelphia, Pennsylvania

Patricia (Thelma Catherine Patricia Ryan) Nixon
(Mrs Richard M Nixon)
American first lady
• High school teacher before marriage to Richard Nixon, Jun 21, 1940; biography written by daughter Julie, 1986.
b. March 16, 1912 in Ely, Nevada

Richard Milhous Nixon
American political leader–author
• 37th pres., Rep., 1969-74, first pres. to resign; ended US involvement in Vietnam, repaired relations with People's Republic of China, initiated detente with USSR; administration marred by Watergate scandal.
b. January 09, 1913 in Yorba Linda, California

Kwame Nkrumah
Ghanaian political leader
• Dictator; first pres. of Ghana, 1960-66.
b. September 21, 1909 in Nkroful, Ghana
d. April 27, 1972 in Bucharest, Romania

Philip John Noel-Baker
(Baron Noel-Baker of Derby)
English diplomat–author
• Won Nobel Peace Prize, 1959, for working toward world disarmament; Labor MP, 1929-70.
b. November 01, 1889 in London, England
d. October 08, 1982 in London, England

Lyn (Franklyn Curran) Nofziger
American presidential aide
• Conservative Rep. known for harsh words, unkept appearance; served as press secretary for Nixon, Reagan.
b. June 08, 1924 in Bakersfield, California

Lon Nol
Cambodian political leader
• Deposed Prince Sihanouk, ending 1,100-year old Cambodian monarchy, 1970-75.
b. November 13, 1913 in Preyveng, Cambodia
d. November 17, 1985 in Fullerton, California

Kichisaburo Nomura
Japanese diplomat
• Ambassador to US at time of Pearl Harbor attack, 1940-41; the attack ended his negotiations.
b. December 1877 in Wakayama-Ken, Japan
d. May 08, 1964 in Tokyo, Japan

Odvar Nordli
Norwegian political leader
• Held various political posts since 1952 including prime minister, 1976-81.
b. November 03, 1927 in Stange, Norway

Manuel Antonio Noriega (Morena)
Panamanian political leader
• Leader, Panamanian army, virtual dictator, 1983-89; overthrown in US invasion, 1989 and imprisoned in U.S.
b. 1934

Samdech Preah Norodom Sihanouk (Varman)
Cambodian ruler
• Ruled Cambodia three times between, 1941-76; gained independence from French rule, 1953.
b. October 31, 1922 in Pnompenh, Cambodia

Lauris Norstad
American air force officer–military leader
• Supreme commander of NATO, 1956-63.
b. March 24, 1907 in Minneapolis, Minnesota
d. September 12, 1988 in Tucson, Arizona

Frederick North North, Baron
English political leader
• Prime minister, 1770-82, known for reforms; his rigid colonial policies led Americans to revolt.
b. April 13, 1732 in London, England
d. August 05, 1792 in London, England

Oliver Laurence North, Jr
American presidential aide
• Marine colonel; his White House operations sparked Iran-Contra controversy, 1986.
b. October 07, 1943 in San Antonio, Texas

John William Frederic Nott
British government official
• Defense minister responsible for British Military operations in Falkland Islands, 1982.
b. February 01, 1932 in London, England

Antonia Coello Novello
American physician–political leader
• Succeeded C Everett Koop as surgeon general, 1989–; first woman, first Hispanic to hold post.
b. August 23, 1944 in Fajardo, Puerto Rico

Antonin Novotny
Czech political leader
• Communist party leader; pres. of Czechoslovakia, 1957-68.
b. December 1, 1904 in Prague, Czechoslovakia
d. January 28, 1975 in Prague, Czechoslovakia

Sam(uel Augustus, Jr) Nunn
American political leader
• Conservative Dem. senator from GA, 1972–; chm., senate armed forces committee, 1987–.
b. September 08, 1938 in Perry, Georgia

Julius Kambarage Nyerere
African political leader
• Son of tribal chief who became first pres. of Tanzania, 1964.
b. March 1922 in Butiama, Tanganyika

Milton (Apollo Milton) Obote
Ugandan political leader
• President of Uganda, 1966-71, deposed in military coup led by Idi Amin; succeeded Amin, 1980-86.
b. 1924 in Akokoro, Uganda

Larry (Lawrence Francis) O'Brien
American basketball executive–political leader
• Chairman, Democratic National Committee, 1968-69, 1970-72; directed John F Kennedy's presidential campaign; commissioner of NBA, 1975-84; Hall of Fame, 1984.
b. July 07, 1917 in Springfield, Massachusetts
d. September 27, 1990 in New York, New York

Leo W O'Brien
American political leader
• Democratic congressman from NY, 1952-66; led legislation granting statehood to Alaska, Hawaii.
b. September 21, 1900 in Buffalo, New York
d. May 04, 1982 in Albany, New York

Daniel O'Connell
Irish political leader
• Elected to Parliament, 1828; mayor of Dublin, 1841; convicted for establishing the Catholic Association, conspiracy.
b. August 06, 1775 in Cahirsiveen, Ireland
d. May 15, 1847 in Genoa, Italy

Masayoshi Ohira
Japanese political leader
• Prime minister of Japan, 1978-80.
b. March 12, 1910 in Toyohama, Japan
d. June 11, 1980 in Tokyo, Japan

Alvin E(dward) O'Konski
American political leader
• Rep. congressman from WI, 1943-73; co-wrote GI Bill of Rights.
b. May 26, 1904 in Kewaunee, Wisconsin
d. July 08, 1987 in Kewaunee, Wisconsin

Olav V
(Olaf V)
Norwegian ruler
• Succeeded father, King Haakon VII, Sep 21, 1957; role is mainly ceremonial, but is symbol of national unity; succeeded by son, Prince Harald.
b. July 02, 1903 in Sandringham, England
d. January 17, 1991 in Oslo, Norway

Sir Maurice Oldfield
English government official
• Chief of British Secret Intelligence Service, 1973-79; inspiration of John Le-Carre, Ian Fleming spy novels.
b. November 06, 1915 in Bakewell, England
d. March 1, 1981 in England

Jacqueline Lee Bouvier Kennedy Onassis
American editor–first lady
• Newspaper photographer before marriage to John Kennedy, 1953; married Aristotle Onassis, 1968; currently editor at Doubleday.
b. July 28, 1929 in Southampton, New York

Tip (Thomas Philip) O'Neill
American political leader–author
• Dem. congressman from MA, 1952-86; Speaker of House, 1976-86.
b. December 09, 1912 in Cambridge, Massachusetts

William Atchison O'Neill
American political leader
• Democratic governor of CT, 1979-91, succeeded by Lowell Weicker.
b. August 11, 1930 in Hartford, Connecticut

Kay Avonne Orr
American political leader
• Rep. governor of Nebraska, 1987-91, defeated by Ben Nelson; first elected Rep. woman governor in US history.
b. January 02, 1939 in Burlington, Iowa

Daniel Ortega Saavedra
Nicaraguan political leader
• Sandinista president of Nicaragua, 1979-90, defeated by Violeta Barrios de Chamorro.
b. November 11, 1945 in La Libertad, Nicaragua

Osman I
(Othman I)
Turkish political leader
• Founded dynasty that ruled Ottoman Empire.
b. 1259 in Bithynia
d. 1326

Sergio Osmena, Jr
Philippine political leader
• Governor, Cebu, Philippines, 1951-53; mayor, Cebu City; ran for pres. against Marcos, 1969.
b. September 09, 1878 in Cebu, Philippines
d. October 19, 1961 in Manila, Philippines

Mariano Ospina Perez
Colombian political leader
• President of Colombia, 1946-50; led Conservatives for 30 years.
b. November 24, 1891 in Medellin, Colombia
d. April 14, 1976 in Bogota, Colombia

Alfredo Ovando Candia
Bolivian political leader
• Organized 1967 military offensive against Che Guevara's forces; pres. of Bolivia, 1969-70.
b. April 06, 1918 in Coboja, Bolivia
d. January 24, 1982 in La Paz, Bolivia

Turgut Ozal
Turkish political leader
• Prime minister, 1983–; major objectives industrial growth, track expansion.
b. 1927 in Malatya, Turkey

Bob (Robert William) Packwood
American political leader
• Rep. senator from OR, 1969–.
b. September 11, 1932 in Portland, Oregon

Farah Diba Pahlevi
Iranian ruler
• Descendent of Mohammed, who married Shah of Iran, Dec 21, 1959.
b. October 14, 1938 in Teheran, Iran

Mohammed Riza Pahlevi
(Shah of Iran)
Iranian ruler
• Headed Iran, 1941-79; overthrown by Ayatollah Khomeini; died in exile.
b. October 26, 1919 in Teheran, Persia
d. July 27, 1980 in Cairo, Egypt

Riza Pahlevi
Persian ruler
• Founder, modern Iran who encouraged westernization, industrialization; Shah, 1925-41.
b. 1877 in South Africa
d. 1944

Emmett Paige, Jr.
American military leader
• First black soldier to become a general, 1976; head of Information Systems Command, 1984–.
b. February 2, 1931 in Jacksonville, Florida

Ian Richard Kyle Paisley
Irish clergyman–political leader
• Protestant minister who is most influential representative against Catholics in Ulster.
b. April 06, 1926 in Armagh, Northern Ireland

(Sven) Olof (Joachim) Palme
Swedish government official
• Leader of Sweden's socialist party; prime minister, 1969-76, 1982; assassinated.
b. January 3, 1927 in Stockholm, Sweden
d. February 28, 1986 in Stockholm, Sweden

Vijaya Lakshmi (Nehru) Pandit
Indian politician–diplomat
• First female pres., UN, 1953-54; wrote autobiography *The Scope of Happiness: A Personal Memoir*, 1979; sister of Jawahari.
b. August 18, 1900 in Allahabad, India
d. December 01, 1990 in New Delhi, India

George Papadopoulos
Greek political leader
• Headed a group of colonels that seized control of Greek government; premier, 1967-81.
b. May 05, 1919 in Eleochorian, Greece

Andreas George Papandreou
Greek political leader
• First Socialist prime minister of Greece, 1981-90; defeated by Constantine Mitsotakis; son of George.
b. February 05, 1919 in Chios, Greece

George Papandreou
Greek political leader
• Organized Democratic Socialist Party, 1935; premier, 1944-45; father of Andreas.
b. February 13, 1888 in Patras, Greece
d. November 01, 1968 in Athens, Greece

Louis-Joseph Papineau
Canadian political leader
• Led movement for political reform in Canada.
b. October 07, 1786 in Montreal, Quebec
d. September 25, 1871 in Montebello, Quebec

Chung Hee Park
Korean army officer–political leader
• Pres., 1963-79; assassinated.
b. September 3, 1917 in Sosan Gun, Korea
d. October 26, 1979 in Seoul, Korea (South)

Floyd Lavinius Parks
American military leader
• Commanded US sector of Berlin when American troops entered, Jul-Oct, 1945.
b. February 09, 1896 in Louisville, Kentucky
d. March 1, 1959 in Washington, District of Columbia

Charles Stewart Parnell
Irish political leader
• Promoted Irish independence by uniting Irish factions, introducing first Home Rule bill in Parliament, 1886. Opponents revealed he was having affair with married woman, leading to quick physical and political decline.
b. 1846 in Avondale, Ireland
d. October 06, 1891 in Brighton, England

Frederic Passy
French government official
• Held positions in French legislature, 1847-49, 1881-89; shared first Nobel Peace Prize, 1901.
b. May 2, 1822 in Paris, France
d. June 12, 1912 in Neuilly-sur-seine, France

Eden Pastora (Gomez)
Nicaraguan political leader
• Hero of 1979 revolution that toppled Anastasio Somoza.
b. January 22, 1937 in Dario, Nicaragua

John Orlando Pastore
American political leader
• Dem. senator from RI, 1950-76; best known for war on sex, violence on TV which resulted in "family viewing time," 1975.
b. March 17, 1907 in Providence, Rhode Island

George Smith Patton, Jr
American army officer–military leader
• Commanded 3rd Army, WW II; leader in "Battle of The Bulge," 1944; portrayed by George C Scott in Oscar-winning film Patton, 1970.
b. November 11, 1885 in San Gabriel, California
d. December 21, 1945 in Heidelberg, Germany

Ana Pauker
(Ana Rabinsohn)
Romanian political leader
• Foreign minister, 1947-52, ousted by Communists from Politburo during purge of Jewish officials.
b. 1894 in Bucharest, Romania
d. June 1960 in Bucharest, Romania

Paul I
Greek ruler
• Sixth monarch of Greece, 1947-64; succeeded by son, Constantine.
b. December 14, 1901 in Athens, Greece
d. March 06, 1964

Paul, Prince of Yugoslavia
Yugoslav ruler
• Ruled Yugoslavia as regent for nephew, Peter II, 1934-41; forced into exile after signing secret pact with Hitler.
b. 1893
d. September 14, 1976 in Paris, France

Friedrich von Paulus
German military leader
• Led German army which fell to Russians at Stalingrad, Feb 1943.
b. 1890
d. February 01, 1957 in Dresden, Germany (West)

Howard Russell Pawley
Canadian politician
• New Dem. Party premier of Manitoba, 1981–.
b. November 21, 1934 in Brampton, Ontario

Lester B(owles) Pearson
Canadian political leader–author
• Liberal prime minister of Canada, 1963-68; won Nobel Peace Prize, 1957, for helping to resolve Arab-Israeli War.
b. April 23, 1897 in Newtonbrook, Ontario
d. December 27, 1972 in Ottawa, Ontario

(Alfred) Brian Peckford
Canadian politician
• Progressive-conservative party premier of Newfoundland, 1979–.
b. August 27, 1942 in Whitbourne, Newfoundland

Pedro I
(Antonio Pedro de Alcantara Bourbon)
Brazilian ruler
• Fled to Brazil, 1807; later declared independence from Portugal, crowned emperor, 1822; abdicated, 1831.
b. October 12, 1798 in Lisbon, Portugal
d. September 24, 1834 in Lisbon, Portugal

Pedro II
(Pedro de Alcantara)
Brazilian ruler
• Crowned after abdication of father, Pedro I, 1841; forced to abdicate after Brazil became a republic, Nov 15, 1889.
b. December 02, 1825 in Rio de Janeiro, Brazil
d. December 05, 1891 in Paris, France

Pelopidas
Military Leader
• General who helped liberate Thebes from Sparta, 379.

John Clifford Pemberton
American military leader
• Although born in the North, served as officer in confederate army; surrendered to Grant at Vicksburg.
b. August 1, 1814 in Philadelphia, Pennsylvania
d. July 13, 1881 in Penllyn, Pennsylvania

Thomas Joseph Pendergast
American political leader
• Dem. political boss in Kansas City, 1920s-1930s; one of strongest political bosses in US.
b. July 22, 1870 in Saint Joseph, Missouri
d. January 26, 1945 in Kansas City, Missouri

Pepin III
(Pepin le Bref; Pepin the Short)
French ruler
• First Carolingian king of Franks, 751-68; son of Charles Martel; father of Charlemagne.
b. 715
d. 768

Claude Denson Pepper
American political leader
• Dem. senator from FL, 1936-51; congressman, 1963-89; oldest member of Congress; instrumental in passage of law against mandatory retirement based only on age, 1989.
b. September 08, 1900 in Dudleyville, Alabama
d. May 3, 1989 in Washington, District of Columbia

Sir William Pepperell
American army officer–military leader
• Led land forces that captured French fortress at Louisburg, 1745; first native American created baronet, 1746.
b. June 27, 1696 in Kittery, Maine
d. July 06, 1759 in Kittery, Maine

Charles Harting Percy
American political leader
• Moderate Rep. senator from IL, 1967-85.
b. September 27, 1919 in Pensacola, Florida

Shimon Peres
Israeli political leader
• Prime minister of Israel, 1984-86; alternating in office with Yitzhak Shamir, 1986–.
b. August 16, 1923 in Wolozyn, Poland

Carlos Andres Perez
Venezuelan political leader
• Social democratic president of Venezuela, 1974-79, 1989–.
b. October 27, 1922 in Rubio, Venezuela

Adolfo Perez Esquivel
Argentine political activist
• Surprise winner of 1980 Nobel Peace Prize; human rights activist jailed, abused by own govt.; Catholic lay leader.
b. November 26, 1931 in Buenos Aires, Argentina

Frances Perkins
American cabinet member
• First woman to serve in cabinet position: FDR's secretary of Labor, 1933-45.
b. April 1, 1882 in Boston, Massachusetts
d. May 14, 1965 in New York, New York

Eva Duarte Peron
(Mrs Juan Peron; "Evita")
Argentine political leader
• Co-governed with husband; play *Evita* based on her life.
b. May 07, 1919 in Los Toldos, Argentina
d. July 26, 1952 in Buenos Aires, Argentina

Isabel Martinez de Peron
(Mrs Juan Peron)
Argentine political leader
• First woman president in Argentina; succeeded husband, 1974-76; ousted in military coup.
b. February 04, 1931 in Las Rioja, Argentina

Juan Peron
Argentine political leader
• Pres. of Argentina, 1946-55, 1973-74.
b. October 08, 1895 in Lobos, Argentina
d. July 01, 1974 in Buenos Aires, Argentina

Rudy George Perpich
American political leader
• Democratic governor of MN, 1977-79, 1983-91, defeated by Arne Carlson.
b. June 27, 1928 in Carson Lake, Minnesota

Admiral Oliver Hazard Perry
American naval officer–military leader
• National hero who defeated British on Lake Erie, 1813; dispatched, "Have met the enemy and they are ours."
b. August 2, 1785 in South Kingstown, Rhode Island
d. August 23, 1819 in Angostura, Venezuela

John J(oseph) Pershing
American army officer–military leader
• Commander of American Expeditionary Force in Europe, 1917-19; won Pulitzer, 1932 for memoirs.
b. September 13, 1860 in Linn City, Missouri
d. July 15, 1948 in Washington, District of Columbia

Sandro (Alessandro) Pertini
Italian political leader
• President of Italy, 1978-86; considered one of the nation's most beloved leaders.
b. September 25, 1896 in Stella, Italy
d. February 24, 1990 in Rome, Italy

Henri Philippe Petain
French military leader–statesman
• Hero of Battle of Verdun, 1916; surrendered to Hitler, 1940, later headed Vichy govt.
b. April 24, 1856 in Cauchy a la Tour, France
d. July 23, 1951 in Island of Yeu

Peter II
(Petar Petrovic; Peter Karageorgeovitch)
Yugoslav ruler
• Succeeded throne on death of father, Alexander, 1934; reign ended, 1945, when country became a republic.
b. September 06, 1923
d. November 04, 1970 in Los Angeles, California

Peter the Great
(Peter I)
Russian ruler
• Introduced Western civilization into Russia; created regular Army, Navy; founded capital, St. Petersburg, 1703.
b. May 3, 1672 in Moscow, Russia
d. January 28, 1725 in Saint Petersburg, Russia

David Robert Peterson
Canadian politician
• Liberal Party premier of Ontario, 1985–.
b. December 28, 1943 in Toronto, Ontario

Pham Hung
(Pham Van Thien)
Vietnamese political leader
• Prime minister of Vietnam, 1987-88; instrumental in defeat of US in Vietnam War.
b. June 11, 1912 in Vinh Long Province, Vietnam
d. March 1, 1988 in Ho Chi Minh City, Vietnam

Pham van Dong
Vietnamese political leader
• Prime minister of Vietnam, 1976-87.
b. March 01, 1906 in Quang Nam, Vietnam

John Wolcott Phelps
American army officer–military leader
• Organized escaped slaves into first black Union troops, 1862.
b. November 13, 1813 in Guilford, Vermont
d. February 02, 1885 in Brattleboro, Vermont

Philip II
(Philip of Macedon)
Macedonian ruler
• Established federal system of Greek states; father of Alexander the Great.
b. 382BC in Macedonia
d. 336BC

Philip II
(Philip Augustus)
French ruler
• Ruled, 1179-1223; son of Louis VII; increased kingdom through various wars, 1181-85.
b. 1165
d. 1223

Philip V
Macedonian ruler
• Reign marked by wars with Rome, Balkans, 221-179 B.C.; attempted to rebuild kingdom.
b. 237BC
d. 179BC

Philip VI
(Philip of Valois)
French ruler
• First to rule from house of Valois, 1328-50; conflicts with Edward III led to Hundred Years' War, 1337.
b. 1293
d. 1350

Timothy Pickering
American political leader
• Federalist leader; secretary of state, 1795-1800, dismissed by Adams; in US Congress, 1803-17.
b. July 17, 1745 in Salem, Massachusetts
d. January 29, 1829 in Salem, Massachusetts

George Edward Pickett
American military leader
• Confederate general; led "Pickett's charge" at Gettysburg, 1863.
b. January 25, 1825 in Richmond, Virginia
d. July 3, 1875 in Norfolk, Virginia

Franklin Pierce
American US president
• Dem., 14th pres., 1853-57; tried unsuccessfully to end sectional controversy over slavery.
b. November 23, 1804 in Hillsboro, New Hampshire
d. October 08, 1869 in Concord, New Hampshire

Jane Means Pierce
(Mrs Franklin Pierce)
American first lady
• Always wore black in White House due to death of last surviving child, 1853.
b. March 12, 1806 in Hampton, New Hampshire
d. December 02, 1863 in Andover, Massachusetts

Samuel Riley Pierce, Jr
American cabinet member
• Reagan's secretary of HUD.
b. September 08, 1922 in Glen Cove, New York

Pontius Pilate
Roman political leader
• Procurator of Judaea, who tried to evade responsibility in trial of Jesus.
b. 26AD

Lynden Oscar Pindling
Bahamian government official
• First black prime minister of Bahamas, 1967-.
b. 1930 in Bahamas

William Pinkney
American political leader
• Influential in passage of Missouri Compromise, 1820; senator from MD, 1819-22, renowned for eloquence.
b. March 17, 1764 in Annapolis, Maryland
d. December 25, 1822 in Washington, District of Columbia

Augusto Pinochet Ugarte
Chilean political leader
• President of Chile, 1973-89; ousted Allende in bloody coup; succeeded by Patricio Aylwin.
b. November 25, 1915 in Valparaiso, Chile

William Pitt
English political leader–author
• Often considered Britain's greatest prime minister, 1783-1801, 1804-06; led England during French aggression.
b. May 28, 1759 in Hayes, England
d. January 23, 1806 in Putney, England

Francis Place
English political activist
• Influential, radical reformer; early advocate of birth control; instrumental in passage of Reform Bill, 1832, legalization of labor unions.
b. October 03, 1771 in London, England
d. January 01, 1854 in London, England

Milka Planinc
Yugoslav political leader
• First female prime minister of Yugoslavia, May 1982-83; received many decorations for yrs. of political service.
b. November 21, 1924 in Drnis, Yugoslavia

Galo Plaza Lasso
Ecuadorean political leader
• Pres., Ecuador, 1948-52; sec. gen., Organization of American States, 1968-75.
b. February 17, 1906 in New York, New York
d. January 28, 1987 in Quito, Ecuador

Pocahontas
(Matoaka; Mrs John Rolfe)
American Indian princess
• Daughter of Powhatan; supposedly saved life of Captain John Smith.
b. 1595 in Virginia
d. March 1617 in Gravesend, England

John Marlan Piondexter
American presidential aide
• Reagan's nat. security adviser, 1985-86; resigned amid controversy over his part in directing Iran-Contra operation.
b. August 12, 1936 in Washington, District of Columbia

Joel Roberts Poinsett
American cabinet member
• Secretary of War, 1837-40; amateur botanist whose name was given the poinsettia, traditional Christmas flower.
b. March 02, 1779 in Charleston, South Carolina
d. December 12, 1851 in Statesburg, South Carolina

Pol Pot
(Saloth Sar)
Cambodian political leader
• Prime minister of Cambodia, 1975-79, whose efforts to create agrarian society resulted in disease, starvation.
b. May 19, 1928

James K(nox) Polk
American US president
• Dem., 11th pres., 1845-49; led US in war against Mexico, resulting in annexation of Southwest.
b. November 02, 1795 in Mecklenburg County, North Carolina
d. June 15, 1849 in Nashville, Tennessee

Sarah Childress Polk
(Mrs James Polk)
American first lady
• Served as husband's official secretary; banned dancing, liquor from White House.
b. September 04, 1803 in Murfreesboro, Tennessee
d. August 14, 1891 in Nashville, Tennessee

Harry Pollitt
English political leader
• Chm., British Communist party, 1956-60; ran unsuccessfully for House of Commons, eight times.
b. November 22, 1890 in Droylesden, England
d. June 27, 1960

Pompey the Great
(Pompeius Magnus)
Roman army officer–statesman
• Rival of father-in-law, Julius Caesar; formed first Triumvirate, rulers of Rome, 60 BC.
b. 106BC
d. 48BC in Egypt

Georges Jean Raymond Pompidou
French political leader
• Prime minister, 1962-68; pres., 1969-74.
b. July 05, 1911 in Cantal, France
d. April 02, 1974 in Paris, France

David Dixon Porter
American military leader
• Commanded Civil War fleet; wrote book on experiences, 1887.
b. June 08, 1813 in Chester, Pennsylvania
d. February 13, 1891 in Washington, District of Columbia

William James Porter
American diplomat–political leader
• Chief US negotiator at Paris peace talks to end Vietnam War, 1971, 1972; ambassador to four countries in 40-yr. foreign service career.
b. September 01, 1914 in Staleybridge, England
d. March 15, 1988 in Fall River, Massachusetts

Grigori Alexsandrovich Potemkin
Russian military leader
• Conspirator in plot against Peter III, 1762; favored by Catherine III, 1774; created Prince of Tauris, 1787.
b. September 13, 1739 in Chizhovo, Russia
d. October 05, 1791 in Jassy, Romania

Adam Clayton Powell, Jr
American political leader–clergyman
• Dem. congressman since 1945; expelled, 1967, for misuse of funds but re-elected the same year.
b. November 29, 1908 in New Haven, Connecticut
d. April 04, 1972 in Miami, Florida

Colin Luther Powell
American military leader
• Army general; succeeded William Crowe as youngest and first black chairman of Joint Chiefs of Staff, 1989–; advised George Bush on Panama invasion, 1989, deployment of US troops to Saudi Arabia, 1990.
b. April 05, 1937 in New York, New York

Jody (Joseph Lester) Powell
American presidential aide–journalist
• Press secretary for Carter, 1976-81; nationally syndicated columnist.
b. September 3, 1943 in Vienna, Georgia

Rajendra Prasad
Indian politician
• First president of India, 1950-62.
b. December 03, 1884 in Bihar, India
d. February 28, 1963 in Patna, India

Samuel Prescott
American patriot–military leader
• Captured with Paul Revere on his famous ride; escaped, rode on to warn Concord; captured by British, 1777.
b. August 19, 1751 in Concord, Massachusetts
d. 1777 in Halifax, Nova Scotia

Larry Pressler
American political leader
• Target of "Abscam," 1980; rebuffed bribery overtures from FBI sting operation.
b. March 29, 1942 in Humboldt, South Dakota

Marthinus Wessel Pretorius
South African politician
• First pres. of S African Republic, 1857-60, 1864-71; Pretoria named after him.
b. 1819 in Graaff Reinet, South Africa
d. May 19, 1901 in Potchefstroom, South Africa

Melvin Price
American political leader
• Dem. congressman from IL, 1945-88; first chm. of House Ethics committee, known for support of military.
b. January 01, 1905 in East Saint Louis, Illinois
d. April 22, 1988 in Washington, District of Columbia

Sterling Price
American military leader
• Confederate major general, defeated at Westport, MO, 1864.
b. September 11, 1809 in Virginia
d. September 29, 1867 in Saint Louis, Missouri

Carlos Prio Socarras
Cuban political leader
• President of Cuba, 1948-52; overthrown by Batista.
b. July 14, 1903 in Bahia Honda, Cuba
d. April 05, 1977 in Miami Beach, Florida

John Dennis Profumo
English political leader
• Foreign affairs minister, 1959-60; secretary of War, 1960-63; resigned due to involvement in political-sex scandal known as Profumo affair.
b. January 3, 1915

William Proxmire
American political leader
• Dem. senator from WI, 1959-89; awarded "Golden Fleece" for bureaucratic waste.
b. November 11, 1915 in Lake Forest, Illinois

Henry Pu-Yi
(Hsuan T'ung; P'ui)
Chinese ruler
• Became last imperial emperor of China at age three; puppet emperor Kang Teh of Manchukuo, 1934-45; life story film, *The Last Emperor*, 1987, won many Oscars.
b. February 11, 1906 in China
d. October 17, 1967 in Peking, China

Kazimierz Pulaski
Polish nobleman–army officer
• Revolutionary War hero, organized Pulaski cavalry corps, 1778; mortally wounded at Savannah.
b. March 04, 1747 in Winiary, Poland
d. October 11, 1779 in Savannah, Georgia

Israel Putnam
American army officer–military leader
• Commander of American Revolutionary Army during battle of Long Island, 1776; was inspiration for Guiterman's poem, "Death and General Putnam," 1935.
b. January 07, 1718 in Salem, Massachusetts
d. May 29, 1790 in Brooklyn, Connecticut

Howard (John Howard) Pyle
American political leader
• Rep. governor of AZ, 1951-55; known for ordering raid on polygamous AZ community, Short Creek, 1953.
b. March 25, 1906 in Sheridan, Wyoming
d. November 29, 1987 in Tempe, Arizona

Quabus bin Saud
(Qaboos bin Said)
Ruler
• Sultan of Oman, 1970–; deposed father, Said bin Taimur.
b. November 18, 1940 in Salalah, Oman

Alex(ander) Quaison-Sackey
Ghanaian diplomat
• First black African to preside over UN General Assembly, 1964-65.
b. August 09, 1924 in Winneba, Ghana

(James) Dan(forth) Quayle
American US vice president
• Vice president under George Bush, 1989–; Republican senator from IN, 1981-89.
b. February 04, 1947 in Indianapolis, Indiana

Manuel Luis Quezon (y Molina)
Philippine political leader
• First pres. of Philippines, 1935-42.
b. August 19, 1878 in Baler, Philippines
d. August 01, 1944 in Saranac Lake, New York

Yitzhak Rabin
Israeli statesman–political leader
• Ambassador to US, 1968-73; Israeli prime minister, 1974-77.
b. March 01, 1922 in Jerusalem, Palestine

Karl Bernhardovich Radek
Russian communist leader
• One of co-authors of new Soviet Constitution, 1936; arrested, imprisoned for treason, 1937.
b. 1885 in Lvov, Poland
d. 1939

Baron Fitzroy James Henry Somerset Raglan
British military leader
• Led British forces in Crimean War, lost arm in battle; raglan sleeves named for him.
b. September 3, 1788 in Badminton, England
d. June 28, 1855 in Sevastopol, Russia

Prince Abdul Rahman
Indian political leader
• First king of Malaya, 1957-60.
b. February 08, 1903 in Alor Star, Malaya
d. April 01, 1960

Sheik Mujibur Rahman
Bangladeshi political leader
• Founding pres. of Bangladesh, 1975; prime minister, 1972-75; killed in military coup.
b. March 17, 1920 in Tungipara, India
d. August 15, 1975 in Dacca, Bangladesh

Joseph Hayne Rainey
American political leader
• First black man elected to House of Representatives from SC, 1870-79.
b. June 21, 1832 in Georgetown, South Carolina
d. August 02, 1887 in Georgetown, South Carolina

Prince Rainier III
(Louis Henri Maxence Bertrand; Prince of Monaco)
Monacan ruler
• Succeeded grandfather, 1949–; family is oldest reigning dynasty in Europe; founded Monaco Red Cross, 1948.
b. May 31, 1923 in Monaco

Sir Walter Raleigh
English courtier–navigator–historian
• Tried to colonize VA, introducing tobacco to England; favorite of Queen Elizabeth beheaded for treason.
b. 1552 in Devonshire, England
d. October 29, 1618 in London, England

Jagjivan Ram
Indian politician
• Served as minister of labor, agriculture, railways, defense, 1970-79; main force behind drive for independence.
b. April 05, 1908 in Chandwa, India
d. July 06, 1986 in New Delhi, India

Rameses II
Egyptian ruler
• Third king of 19th dynasty; made treaty of friendship with Hittites, left several monuments.

Sir Seewoosagur Ramgoolam
Mauritian political leader
• Founder, first prime minister of Mauritius.
b. September 18, 1900 in Belle River, Mauritius
d. December 15, 1985 in Port Louis, Mauritius

Samuel J Randall
American political leader
• Dem., Speaker of House, 1876-81; strengthened speaker's power by classifying rules of House of Representatives.
b. October 1, 1828 in Philadelphia, Pennsylvania
d. April 13, 1890 in Washington, District of Columbia

Charles Bernard Rangel
American political leader
• Dem. congressman from NY, 1970–; member, House on Ways and Means, 1975–.
b. June 11, 1930 in Harlem, New York

Jeannette Rankin
American suffragist–political leader
• First woman to serve in Congress, 1917-19; only memeber to oppose US entry into WW I, II.
b. July 11, 1880 in Missoula, Montana
d. May 18, 1973 in Carmel, California

Didier Ratsiraka
Political Leader
• Pres. of Madagascar since 1976.
b. November 04, 1936 in Madagascar

Jerry John Rawlings
Ghanaian political leader
• Led three military coups to overthrow govt., 1979-81; head of state, 1981–.
b. June 22, 1947 in Accra, Ghana

Dixy Lee Ray
American political leader–zoologist
• Dem. governor of WA, 1977-80; received UN Peace Medal, 1973.
b. September 03, 1914 in Tacoma, Washington

Sam(uel Taliaferro) Rayburn
American political leader
• Dem. Speaker of House for periods from 1940-61.
b. January 06, 1882 in Roane County, Tennessee
d. November 16, 1961 in Bonham, Texas

Albert Cushing Read
American naval officer–aviator–military leader
• Rear admiral, 1941-46; commanded first Atlantic crossing in air, from Newfoundland to Portugal, via Azores, May 1919.
b. March 29, 1887 in Lyme, New Hampshire
d. October 1, 1967 in Miami, Florida

Nancy Davis Reagan
(Anne Frances Robbins)
American first lady
• Appeared in high school play *First Lady*, 1939; last movie *Hellcats* with Ronald Reagan, 1957; active in anti-drug campaign.
b. July 06, 1921 in New York, New York

Ronald Wilson Reagan
American US president
• 40th pres., Rep., 1981-89; applied "Reaganomics" to spur economy; known for conservative policies and appointments; oldest, first divorced president in office.
b. February 06, 1911 in Tampico, Illinois

Donald Thomas Regan
American presidential aide
• White House Chief of Staff under Reagan, 1985-87; secretary of Treasury, 1981-86.
b. December 21, 1918 in Cambridge, Massachusetts

Simon (Sol Simon) Reisman
Canadian government official
• Canada's chief negotiator at historic free-trade talks with US, 1985-87.
b. June 19, 1919 in Montreal, Quebec

Louis Renault
French educator–diplomat
• Shared 1907 Nobel Peace Prize for work at The Hague Peace Conferences, 1899, 1907.
b. May 21, 1843 in Autun, France
d. February 08, 1918 in Barbizon, France

Ernst Reuter
German politician
• Mayor of West Berlin from 1948; foe of communism, supported German friendship with West.
b. July 29, 1889 in Apenrade, Germany
d. September 29, 1953 in Berlin, Germany (West)

Hiram R Revels
American political leader
• First black man sworn into Senate office; Rep. from MA, 1870-71.
b. September 1822 in Fayetteville, North Carolina
d. March 04, 1901 in Aberdeen, Mississippi

Paul Revere
American patriot–silversmith
• Rode from Boston to Lexington, MA to warn of British attack, Apr 18, 1775; famous cry: "The British are coming!"; famed silversmith.
b. January 01, 1735 in Boston, Massachusetts
d. May 1, 1818 in Boston, Massachusetts

Paul Reynaud
French politician
• Led committee that formed 1958 Constitution; premier, 1940.
b. October 15, 1878 in Barcelonayye, France
d. September 21, 1966 in Neuilly, France

Cecil John Rhodes
English political leader
• Prime minister, Cape Colony, South Africa, 1890-96; founded Rhodes scholarships.
b. July 05, 1853 in Bishop's Stortford, England
d. March 26, 1902 in Cape Town, South Africa

Abraham Alexander Ribicoff
American political leader
• Liberal Dem. senator from CT, 1963-81; HEW secretary under JFK, 1961-62.
b. April 09, 1910 in New Britain, Connecticut

Richard I
(Richard the Lionhearted)
English ruler
• Subject of many legends of chivalry; reigned, 1189-99.
b. September 08, 1157 in Oxford, England
d. April 06, 1199 in Chaluz, France

Richard II
English ruler
• Son of Edward the Black Prince, grandson of Edward III; succeeded grandfather, 1377-99.
b. 1367 in Bordeaux, France
d. 1400 in Leicester, England

Richard III
English ruler
• Ruled, 1483-85; killed during battle of Bosworth Field by Earl of Richmond, who became Henry VII.
b. October 02, 1452 in Fotheringay Castle, England
d. August 22, 1485 in Leicester, England

Richard Richards
American political leader
• Appointed GOP chm. by Ronald Reagan.
b. May 14, 1932 in Ogden, Utah
d. December 1988

Elliot Lee Richardson
American cabinet member
• Govt. posts include secretary of HEW, defense, commerce, under Nixon, Ford.
b. July 2, 1920 in Boston, Massachusetts

Hyman George Rickover
American naval officer–military leader
• Admiral who spent 63 yrs. in navy; oversaw navy's transition to nuclear equipment.
b. January 27, 1900 in Makow, Poland
d. July 08, 1986 in Arlington, Virginia

Donald Wayne Riegle, Jr
American political leader
• Dem. senator from MI, 1977–.
b. February 04, 1938 in Flint, Michigan

Jose Efrain Rios Montt
Guatemalan political leader
• Became pres. after bloodless coup, 1982; overthrown in another coup, 1983.
b. June 16, 1926 in Huehuetenango, Guatemala

L(ucius) Mendel Rivers
American political leader
• Conservative Dem. congressman from SC, 1940-70; champion of American military might, urged escalation of Vietnam war.
b. September 28, 1905 in Berkeley County, South Carolina
d. December 28, 1970 in Birmingham, Alabama

Jose Rizal
Philippine patriot
• Exiled by Spanish govt. for novel *The Lost Eden*, 1886, which criticized Spanish regime, clergy; executed.
b. 1861 in Calamba, Philippines
d. 1896 in Manila, Philippines

Frank Lazzaro Rizzo
American political leader
• Flamboyant law-and-order mayor of Philadelphia, 1972-80.
b. October 23, 1920 in Philadelphia, Pennsylvania

Robert I
(Robert the Bruce)
Scottish ruler
• Rules, 1306-1329; battles with England led to Treaty of Northampton, 1328, recognizing his throne.
b. March 21, 1274
d. June 1329 in Cardross, Scotland

Robert Guiscard
Norwegian ruler
• Fought to gain control of southern Italy, Rome, Sicily, Byzantine Empire.
b. 1015
d. 1085

Frederick Sleigh Roberts
British army officer–military leader
• Commander-in-chief of India, 1885-93, of Ireland, 1895-99; captured major S. African cities while in command there, 1899-1900.
b. 1832 in Cawnpore, India
d. 1914

Sir William Robert Robertson
English army officer–military leader
• Field Marshal, WW I, first man in British army to rise from private to highest rank.
b. January 29, 1860 in Welbourne, England
d. February 12, 1933 in London, England

Michel Louis Leon Rocard
French politician
• Moderate socialist prime minister of France, succeeding Jacques Chirac, 1988–.
b. August 23, 1930 in Courbevoie, France

Comte Jean Baptiste Donatien de Vimeur Rochambeau
French army officer–military leader
• Led French force aiding Americans in Revolution; helped defeat Cornwallis at Yorktown, 1781.
b. July 01, 1725 in Vendome, France
d. May 1, 1807

John D(avison) Rockefeller, IV
American political leader
• Dem. senator from WV, 1985–.
b. June 18, 1937 in New York, New York

Nelson A(ldrich) Rockefeller
American US vice president
• Moderate Rep. governor of NY, 1959-73; VP under Ford, 1974-76.
b. July 08, 1908 in Bar Harbor, Maine
d. January 26, 1979 in New York, New York

Winthrop Rockefeller
American political leader
• Governor of AR, 1967-71.
b. May 01, 1912 in New York, New York
d. February 22, 1973 in Palm Springs, California

George Lincoln Rockwell
American political activist
• Organized American Nazi Party, 1958; advocated extermination of all American Jews.
b. March 09, 1918 in Bloomington, Illinois
d. August 25, 1967 in Arlington, Virginia

Christopher Raymond Perry Rodgers
American naval officer–military leader
• Rear-admiral; superintendent, Naval Academy, 1874-81; pres. of Int'l. Conference which fixed prime (Greenwich) meridian time, universal day.
b. November 14, 1819 in Brooklyn, New York
d. January 08, 1892 in Washington, District of Columbia

Peter Wallace Rodino, Jr
American political leader
• Dem. con. from NJ, 1949–; chm., House Judiciary Committee during Nixon's impeachment hearings, 1974.
b. June 07, 1909 in Newark, New Jersey

Baron George Brydges Rodney
English naval officer–military leader
• His victories over French, Spanish, Dutch in Caribbean waters contributed to Britain's command of the seas, 1800s.
b. February 19, 1719 in Walton-on-Thames, England
d. May 24, 1792 in London, England

Bernard William Rogers
American military leader
• General who became supreme Allied commander in Europe, Jun 1979.
b. July 16, 1921 in Fairview, Kansas

William Pierce Rogers
American cabinet member
• Secretary of State under Nixon, 1969-73.
b. June 23, 1913 in Norfolk, New York

Ruth Bryan Owen Rohde
American political leader–diplomat
• Ambassador to Denmark, 1933; first American woman to hold major diplomatic post.
b. October 02, 1885 in Jacksonville, Illinois
d. July 26, 1958 in Copenhagen, Denmark

Roh Tae Woo
Korean political leader
• President of South Korea, 1988–; election tactic was called "political miracle."
b. December 04, 1932 in Taegu, Korea (South)

Konstantin Konstantinovich Rokossovsky
Russian army officer–military leader
• Soviet WW II general; commanded forces defending Moscow, crushing German resistance outside of Stalingrad.
b. December 21, 1896
d. August 03, 1968 in Moscow, U.S.S.R.

Jamie Roldos-Aguilera
Ecuadorean political leader
• Youngest pres. in Western Hemisphere, tried to lead country toward democracy.
b. November 05, 1940 in Guayaquil, Ecuador
d. May 24, 1981 in Guachanama, Ecuador

Carlos Humberto Romero
Salvadoran political leader
• President of El Salvador, 1977-79; ousted in coup.
b. 1924 in Chalatenango, El Salvador

Carlos Antonio Romero Barcelo
Puerto Rican politician
• Governor of Puerto Rico, 1977-85.
b. September 04, 1952 in San Juan, Puerto Rico

Erwin Johannes Eugin Rommel
German army officer–military leader
• Former Hitler bodyguard best known for commanding German forces in Africa, 1941-43.
b. November 15, 1891 in Swabia, Germany
d. July 18, 1944 in Herrlingen, France

George Wilcken Romney
American businessman–political leader
• Rep. governor of MI, 1962-69. Ran for presidential nomination in 1972; saw campaign fall apart after he claimed to be "brainwashed" about Vietnam.
b. July 08, 1907 in Chihuahua, Mexico

Carlos Pena Romulo
Philippine statesman–journalist
• One of the founders of UN, 1945; first Asian to serve as pres. of UN General Assembly.
b. April 14, 1899 in Manila, Philippines
d. December 15, 1985 in Manila, Philippines

Chester A Ronning
Canadian diplomat
• Instrumental in arranging peace talks between US and N Vietnam, 1966.
b. December 13, 1894 in China
d. December 31, 1984 in Camrose, Alberta

Edith Kermit Carow Roosevelt
(Mrs Theodore Roosevelt)
American first lady
• Second wife of Theodore Roosevelt; married 1886.
b. August 16, 1861 in Norwich, Connecticut
d. September 3, 1948 in Oyster Bay, New York

Franklin Delano Roosevelt
American US president
• Dem., 32nd pres.; served longest term, 1933-45; created New Deal to combat Depression; increased influence of federal govt. through expanded bureaucracy; died in office.
b. January 3, 1882 in Hyde Park, New York
d. April 12, 1945 in Warm Springs, Georgia

Franklin Delano Roosevelt, Jr
American politician–celebrity relative
• Fourth child of Franklin and Eleanor Roosevelt; Liberal Party congressman from NY, 1950-54.
b. August 17, 1914 in Campobello Island, New Brunswick
d. August 17, 1988 in Poughkeepsie, New York

Theodore Roosevelt
American US president
• Rep., 26th pres., 1901-09; promoted activist foreign policy, conservation; first American to win Nobel Peace Prize, 1906, for mediating end to Russo-Japanese War.
b. October 27, 1858 in New York, New York
d. January 06, 1919 in Oyster Bay, New York

Anna Marie Rosenberg
American government official–political leader
• Named assistant secretary of Defense by Truman, 1950, highest position ever held by woman in nat. military establishment.
b. July 19, 1900 in Budapest, Hungary
d. May 09, 1983 in New York, New York

Benjamin Stanley Rosenthal
American political leader
• Dem. congressman from NY, 1962-82; leader in saving NYC from bankruptcy, 1977.
b. June 08, 1923 in New York, New York
d. January 04, 1983 in Washington, District of Columbia

Nellie Taylor Ross
American political leader
• First woman governor in US, Dem. of WY, 1925-27; first woman director of US Mint, 1933-53.
b. November 29, 1876 in Saint Joseph, Missouri
d. December 19, 1977 in Washington, District of Columbia

Daniel David Rostenkowski
American political leader
• Dem. congressman from IL, 1959–; chm. of Ways and Means Committee, 1981–.
b. January 02, 1928 in Chicago, Illinois

Baron Lionel Nathan Rothschild Rothschild
English banker–political leader
• First Jewish member of Parliament, 1858-74; son of Nathan Mayer Rothschild.
b. November 22, 1808 in London, England
d. June 03, 1879

James Henry Rowe, Jr.
American presidential aide
• Assistant to FDR who helped form, carry out New Deal.
b. June 01, 1909 in Butte, Montana
d. June 17, 1984 in Washington, District of Columbia

Wallace Edward Rowling
New Zealander politician
• Pres., Labour Party, 1970-73; prime minister, 1974-75; leader of Opposition, 1975-.
b. November 27, 1927

Jerry Rubin
(The Chicago 7)
American author–political activist
• Original "yippie" member; one of first defendants tried, convicted under anti-riot provision in 1968 Civil Rights Act.
b. July 14, 1938 in Cincinnati, Ohio

Warren Bruce Rudman
American political leader
• Rep. senator from NH, 1981-; co-authored Gramm-Rudman deficit reduction law, 1985.
b. May 18, 1930 in Boston, Massachusetts

Rudolf II
Ruler
• Ruled Holy Roman Empire, 1576-1612; son of Maximilian II; granted Bohemians religious freedom, 1608.
b. 1552
d. 1612

Rudolf of Hapsburg
Austrian prince
• Archduke, prince of Austria; only son of Emperor Franz Joseph.
b. 1858 in Laxenberg, Austria
d. January 3, 1889 in Vienna, Austria

Mariano Rumor
Italian political leader
• Christian Democratic prime minister of Italy; led five coalition governments, 1968-75.
b. June 16, 1915 in Vicenza, Italy
d. January 22, 1990 in Vicenza, Italy

Donald (Harold) Rumsfeld
American government official–political leader
• Rep. congressman from IL, 1963-69; director, OEO, 1969-70; ambassador to NATO, 1973-74; received Presidential Medal of Freedom, 1977.
b. July 09, 1932 in Chicago, Illinois

Karl Rudolf Gerd von Rundstedt
German military leader
• WW II field marshal, 1940; commander-in-chief on Western front, 1942-45.
b. December 12, 1875 in Aschersleben, Germany
d. February 24, 1953 in Hanover, Germany (West)

Loret Miller Ruppe
American government official–political leader
• Director of Peace Corps, 1981-.
b. January 03, 1936 in Milwaukee, Wisconsin

Dean (David Dean) Rusk
American cabinet member
• Secretary of State, 1961-69; defended US involvement in Vietnam.
b. February 09, 1909 in Cherokee County, Georgia

Lord John Russell
British historian–politician
• Prime minister, 1846-52, 1865-66; wrote *Memoirs of Thomas Moore*, 1853-66.
b. August 18, 1792 in London, England
d. May 28, 1878

Richard Brevard Russell, Jr.
American political leader
• Dem. senator from GA, 1933-71; leader of Senate's Southern Bloc; ran for pres., 1952.
b. November 02, 1897 in Winder, Georgia
d. January 21, 1971 in Washington, District of Columbia

Leo Joseph Ryan
American political leader–victim
• Dem. congressman from CA murdered by member of Jim Jones' Peoples Temple.
b. May 05, 1925 in Lincoln, Nebraska
d. November 19, 1978 in Jonestown, Guyana

Nicola Sacco
(Sacco and Vanzetti)
Italian political activist
• Tried, executed for murder during robbery; case became most notorious of century due to widespread charges of mistrial.
b. April 22, 1891 in Apulia, Italy
d. August 23, 1927 in Boston, Massachusetts

Anwar el Sadat
Egyptian political leader
• Pres., 1970-81; awarded 1978 Nobel Peace Prize with Menachem Begin, for reaching Camp David peace agreement. Assassinated.
b. December 25, 1918 in Talah Maonufiya, Egypt
d. October 06, 1981 in Cairo, Egypt

Arthur Saint Clair
American military leader
• First governor of Northwest Territory, 1787-1802; removed from office by Jefferson, 1802, for criticizing act which made Ohio a state.
b. March 23, 1736 in Thurso, Scotland
d. August 31, 1818 in Ligonier, Pennsylvania

Louis Stephen Saint Laurent
Canadian political leader
• Prime Minister, Liberal Party, 1948-57.
b. February 01, 1882 in Compton, Quebec
d. July 24, 1973 in Quebec City, Quebec

Saladin Yusuf ibn Ayyub
(Salah al-Din)
Moslem ruler
• Sultan of Egypt, Syria, 1174; united Muslim territories; considered great Muslim hero.
b. 1138 in Mesopotamia
d. 1193

Saeb Salam
Lebanese political leader
• Prime minister, 1952-53, 1960-61, 1970-73.
b. 1905 in Beirut, Lebanon

Carlos Salinas de Gortari
Mexican political leader
• Succeeded Miguel de la Madrid as president of Mexico, 1988-.
b. 1948 in Mexico

Aleksandr Vasilievich Samsonov
Russian military leader
• General; defeated by Germans at Battle of Tannenberg; suicide victim.
b. 1859
d. August 29, 1914 in Tannenberg, Prussia (East)

John Montagu Sandwich
(4th Earl of Sandwich)
English politician–military leader
• First Lord of Admiralty, 1771-82; selfishness led to ruin of British navy; much-hated man in 18th c. England; supposed inventor of sandwich.
b. November 03, 1718
d. April 3, 1792 in London, England

Terry Sanford
American educator–political leader
• Governor of NC, 1961-65; pres. of Duke U., 1969-85; senator from NC, 1987-.
b. August 2, 1917 in Laurinburg, North Carolina

Antonio Lopez de Santa Anna
Mexican political leader
• Pres. of Mexico intermittently, 1833-55; captured the Alamo in TX revolution, 1836.
b. 1794 in Jalapa, Mexico
d. June 2, 1876 in Mexico City, Mexico

Giuseppe Saragat
Italian political leader
• One of founders of post-war Italian Republic; first socialist pres. of Italy, 1964-71.
b. September 19, 1898 in Turin, Italy
d. June 11, 1988 in Rome, Italy

Elias Sarkis
Lebanese political leader
• Pres. of Lebanon, 1976-82; also gained fame as head of Central Bank.
b. July 2, 1924 in Shibaniyah, Lebanon
d. June 27, 1985 in Paris, France

Jose Sarney
(Jose Ribamar Ferreira da Costa)
Brazilian political leader
• Brazil's first civilian pres. since 1964; assumed power, 1985.
b. April 3, 1930 in Sao Bento, Brazil

Benjamin H Sasway
American political activist
• First person indicted for violation of Selective Service Act since draft revival, 1980.
b. 1961 in Vista, California

Eisaku Sato
Japanese political leader
• Premier, 1964-72; developed Japan into major economic, industrial nation; shared 1974 Nobel Peace Prize for helping stabilize Pacific area.
b. March 27, 1901 in Tabuse, Japan
d. June 03, 1975 in Tokyo, Japan

Saud (Ibn Abdul Aziz al Saud)
Saudi ruler
• Ruled Saudi Arabia, 1953-64; deposed by brother, Faisal.
b. January 15, 1902 in Kuwait
d. February 23, 1969 in Athens, Greece

Jeanne Mathilde Benoit Sauve
(Mrs Maurice Sauve)
Canadian political leader
• First woman, 23rd governor-general (queen's representative) of Canada, 1984–.
b. April 26, 1922 in Prud'Homme, Saskatchewan

Jonas Malheiro Savimbi
Angolan political leader
• Founded National Union for the Total Independence of Angola, 1966–.
b. August 03, 1934 in Angola

Eugene Sawyer, Jr.
American political leader
• Alderman, elected acting mayor of Chicago replacing Harold Washington, 1987.
b. September 04, 1934 in Greensboro, Alabama

Maurice Saxe
French military leader
• One of greatest generals of his time for victories at Fontenoy, 1745, Racoux, 1746.
b. 1696 in Saxony, France
d. 1750

William Donald Schaefer
American political leader
• Dem. governor of MD, 1987–; mayor of Baltimore, 1971-87.
b. November 02, 1921 in Baltimore, Maryland

Walter Scheel
German political leader
• Pres., Federal Republic of Germany, 1974-79.
b. July 08, 1919 in Solingen, Germany

Philipp Scheidemann
German political leader
• Proclaimed start of Weimar Republic, 1918; first chancellor, 1919.
b. 1865
d. 1939 in Denmark

Kurt von Schleicher
German political leader
• Chancellor of Germany, 1932-33; succeeded by Hitler.
b. 1882 in Brandenburg, Germany
d. 1934

James Rodney Schlesinger
American government official–cabinet member
• Secretary of Defense, 1973-75; Energy, 1977-79.
b. February 15, 1929 in New York, New York

Winfield Scott Schley
American military leader
• Led battle of Santiago, Spanish-American War, 1898; controversy arose about credit of battle between him and W T Sampson.
b. October 09, 1839 in Frederick County, Maryland
d. October 02, 1909 in New York, New York

Graf von Alfred Schlieffen
German military leader
• WW I field marshal; developed "swinging door" plan to crush French resistance.
b. 1833
d. 1913

Helmut Heinrich Waldemar Schmidt
German political leader
• Chancellor, W Germany, 1974-82; author of several books on political affairs.
b. December 23, 1918 in Hamburg, Germany

John McAllister Schofield
American military leader
• Civil War general; commander of US Army, 1888-95, succeeding Sheridan.
b. September 29, 1831 in Gerry, New York
d. March 04, 1906 in Saint Augustine, Florida

Edward Richard Schreyer
Canadian political leader
• Premier of Manitoba, 1969-77; governor-general, 1979-84, succeeded by Jeanne Sauve.
b. December 21, 1935 in Beausejour, Manitoba

Gerhard Schroder
(Gerhard Schroeder)
German politician
• Christian Democratic Union leader; foreign affairs minister, 1961-66, defense minister, 1966-69.
b. September 11, 1910 in Saarbrucken, Germany
d. December 31, 1989 in Island of Sylt

Patricia Scott Schroeder
(Mrs James White Schroeder)
American political leader
• Liberal Dem. congresswoman from CO, 1973–.
b. July 3, 1940 in Portland, Oregon

General H Norman Schwarzkopf
("Stormin Norman")
American military leader
• Chief military commander for Operation Desert Storm; credited with developing strategy which led to the military defeat of Saddam Hussein.
b. August 22, 1934 in Trenton, New Jersey

Elisabeth Schwarzhaupt
German politician
• First woman cabinet member in West Germany, health minister, 1961-66.
b. January 07, 1901 in Frankfurt-am-Main, Germany
d. October 29, 1986 in Frankfurt, Germany (West)

Richard Schultz Schweiker
American cabinet member
• Rep. senator from PA, 1969-81; secretary of HHS, 1981-83.
b. June 01, 1926 in Norristown, Pennsylvania

Publius Cornelius Scipio Africanus
(Scipio the Elder)
Roman army officer–military leader
• Most famous Roman general before Julius Caesar, known for victory over Hannibal at Zama.
b. 234BC
d. 183BC

Winfield Scott
American army officer–military leader
• Led US in Mexican War, 1846-48; Whig candidate for pres., 1852.
b. June 13, 1786 in Petersburg, Virginia
d. May 29, 1866 in West Point, New York

Brent Scowcroft
American presidential aide
• Head of National Security Council, 1975-77; member of Tower commission investigating Iran-Contra scandal, 1986-87.
b. March 19, 1925 in Ogden, Utah

William Warren Scranton
American political leader
• Rep. governor of PA, 1963-66.
b. July 19, 1917 in Madison, Connecticut

Edward Phillip George Seaga
Jamaican political leader
• Prime minister of Jamaica, 1980-89.
b. May 28, 1930 in Boston, Massachusetts

Antonio Segni
Italian political leader
• Premier of Italy, 1955-57, 1959-60; pres., 1962-64; founder of Christian Dem. Party.
b. February 02, 1891 in Sardinia, Italy
d. December 01, 1972 in Rome, Italy

Don Stephen Senanayake
Ceylonese political leader
• First prime minister of Ceylon, 1947-52; regarded as father of country.
b. October 2, 1884 in Botale, Ceylon
d. March 22, 1952 in Colombo, Ceylon

Sennacherib
Assyrian ruler
• During reign destroyed Babylon, 689 BC, restored Nineveh; killed by son.
b. 705BC
d. 681BC

William Steele Sessions
American FBI director
• Director of FBI, 1987–.
b. May 27, 1930 in Fort Smith, Arkansas

William Henry Seward
American cabinet member
• Secretary of State, appointed by Lincoln, 1861-69; his purchase of Alaska from Russia, 1867, was called "Seward's Folly."
b. May 16, 1801 in Florida, New York
d. October 1, 1872 in Auburn, New York

William Rufus Shafter
American military leader
• Led volunteer expeditionary force which invaded Cuba, Spanish-American War, 1898.
b. October 16, 1835 in Kalamazoo County, Michigan
d. November 12, 1906 in Bakersfield, California

Alhaji Shehu Usman Aliyu Shagari
Nigerian political leader
• Overthrown in bloodless coup, Dec 31, 1983, by military leader Mohammed Buhari.
b. April 1925 in Shagari, Nigeria

Yitzhak Shamir
(Yitzak Yezernitsky)
Israeli political leader
• Prime minister of Israel, 1983-86; has alternated in office with Shimon Peres, 1986–.
b. November 03, 1914 in Kuzinoy, Poland

Moshe Sharett
(Moshe Shertok)
Israeli government official
• Zionist leader; foreign minister, 1948-56; premier, 1953-55.
b. October 03, 1894 in Kherson, Russia
d. July 07, 1965 in Jerusalem, Israel

Ariel Sharon
Israeli government official
• Defense minister forced to resign because of role in Beirut massacre, 1982.
b. 1928 in Kafr Malal, Palestine

Robert Gould Shaw
American military leader
• White commander of a black regiment, the 54th Massachusetts; his career and story of 54th featured in film *Glory*, 1989.
b. October 1, 1837 in Boston, Massachusetts
d. July 18, 1863 in Charleston, South Carolina

Zalman Shazar
Israeli political leader
• Third pres. of Israel, 1963-73; leader of Zionist movement.
b. November 24, 1889 in Mir, Russia
d. October 05, 1974 in Jerusalem, Israel

Benjamin Henry Sheares
Singaporean political leader
• Pres., 1971-81; former gynecologist.
b. August 12, 1907 in Singapore
d. May 12, 1981 in Singapore

Sheba
(Makeda)
Ruler
• Biblical queen who made visit to Solomon to improve relations with Israel.
b. fl. 950BC in North Africa

Philip Henry Sheridan
American military leader
• Civil War Union general credited with forcing Lee's surrender by blocking retreat from Appomattox, 1865.
b. March 06, 1831 in Albany, New York
d. August 05, 1888 in Nonquitt, Massachusetts

James Schoolcraft Sherman
American US vice president
• VP under William Howard Taft, 1909-12.
b. October 24, 1855 in Utica, New York
d. October 3, 1912 in Utica, New York

William Tecumseh Sherman
American military leader
• Civil War Union general famous for march through Atlanta to the sea, 1864; said "War is Hell," 1880.
b. February 08, 1820 in Lancaster, Ohio
d. February 14, 1891 in New York, New York

Eduard Amvrosiyevich Shevardnadze
Russian diplomat
• Replaced Gromyko as minister of foreign affairs, 1985-90; resigned amid controversy.
b. January 25, 1928 in Mamati, U.S.S.R.

Arkady Nikolayevich Shevchenko
Russian diplomat
• Adviser to Andrei Gromyko, UN official, who defected to US, 1978; wrote *Breaking with Moscow*, 1985.
b. October 11, 1930 in Gorlovka, U.S.S.R.

Walter Campbell Short
American military leader
• Commanded armed forces at Pearl Harbor, Feb-Dec 1941; retired 1942; found directly responsible for failure of defenses.
b. March 3, 1880 in Fillmore, Illinois
d. September 03, 1949 in Dallas, Texas

Henry Shrapnel
English army officer–military leader
• Invented shrapnel shells, c. 1804.
b. June 03, 1761 in Bradford-on-Avon, England
d. March 13, 1842 in Southampton, England

Ahmed Shukairy
Palestinian political leader
• Founder, first head of PLO, 1964-67.
b. 1908 in Acre, Palestine
d. February 26, 1980 in Amman, Jordan

George Pratt Shultz
American cabinet member
• Succeeded Alexander Haig as Reagan's secretary of state, 1982-89.
b. December 13, 1920 in New York, New York

Sigismund
Ruler
• Ruled Holy Roman Empire, 1433-37; German king, 1410-37; king of Hungary, 1387-1437; son of Charles IV.
b. 1368
d. 1437

Hernan Siles Zuazo
Bolivian political leader
• Leader of revolution, 1952; pres., 1956-60, 1982-85.
b. March 19, 1914 in La Paz, Bolivia

John Graves Simcoe
English government official
• First lt. governor of Upper Canada, 1792-74; established capital at York (now Toronto), 1793.
b. February 25, 1752 in Cotterstock, England
d. October 26, 1806 in Exeter, England

Paul M(artin) Simon
American political leader
• Dem. senator from IL, 1974–; 1988 presidential candidate.
b. November 29, 1928 in Eugene, Oregon

William E(dward) Simon
American cabinet member
• Secretary of Treasury, 1974-77.
b. November 27, 1927 in Paterson, New Jersey

Alan Kooi Simpson
American political leader
• Rep. senator from WY, 1979–; co-authored landmark Simpson-Mazzoli immigration law, 1986.
b. September 02, 1931 in Denver, Colorado

William Hood Simpson
American military leader
• Commanded 9th Army in German invasion, WW II; four-star general, 1954.
b. May 19, 1888 in Weatherford, Texas
d. August 15, 1980 in San Antonio, Texas

William Sowden Sims
American military leader
• Wrote navigation textbook, 1880; adopted convoy system, WW I; co-wrote *The Victory at Sea*, won Pulitzer, 1920.
b. October 15, 1858 in Port Hope, Ontario
d. September 25, 1936 in Boston, Massachusetts

Giani Zail Singh
Indian political leader
• Seventh president of India, 1982-87.
b. May 15, 1916 in Sandhwan, India

V(ishwanath) P(ratap) Singh
Indian political leader
• Succeeded Rajiv Gandhi as prime minister of India, 1989-90; succeeded by Chandra Shekhar.
b. June 25, 1931 in Daiya, India

Joey (Joseph Roberts) Smallwood
Canadian political leader
• Led Newfoundland into Confederation; province's first premier, 1949-72.
b. December 24, 1900 in Gambo, Newfoundland

Alfred Emanuel Smith
American political leader
• Four-term Dem. governor of NY; first Catholic to run for pres., 1928.
b. December 3, 1873 in New York, New York
d. October 04, 1944 in New York, New York

Edmund Kirby Smith
(Edmund Kirby-Smith)
American military leader
• Last Confederate general to surrender in Civil War, May 1865; pres., U of Nashville, 1870-75.
b. May 16, 1824 in Saint Augustine, Florida
d. March 08, 1893 in Sewanee, Tennessee

Holland McTeire Smith
American military leader
• Led Marine invasion of Iwo Jima, 1945; regarded as father of modern amphibious warfare; only third Marine in history to reach full general.
b. April 2, 1882 in Seale, Alabama
d. January 12, 1967 in San Diego, California

Howard Worth Smith
American political leader
• Congressman, 1931-36; wrote Smith Act, 1940, making illegal to be a Communist.
b. February 02, 1883 in Broad Run, Virginia
d. October 03, 1976 in Alexandria, Virginia

Ian Douglas Smith
Rhodesian political leader
• Last prime minister of Rhodesia, 1964-79; declared country's independence, 1965.
b. April 08, 1919 in Seluwke, Rhodesia

Margaret Chase Smith
American political leader
• Rep. senator from ME, 1948-72; served longer than any other woman.
b. December 14, 1897 in Skowhegan, Maine

William French Smith
American presidential aide
• US attorney general under Ronald Reagan, 1981-84.
b. August 26, 1917 in Wilton, New Hampshire
d. October 29, 1990 in Los Angeles, California

John Wesley Snyder
American banker–government official–cabinet member
• Influential Truman adviser who was Secretary of Treasury, 1946-53; hepled design reconstruction programs after WW II.
b. June 21, 1895 in Jonesboro, Arkansas
d. October 09, 1985 in Seabrook Is., South Carolina

Mitch Snyder
American political activist
• Active with Community for Creative Non-Violence since 1973, on behalf of homeless people; apparent suicide victim.
b. August 14, 1943 in Brooklyn, New York
d. July 05, 1990 in Washington, District of Columbia

(Arthur) Christopher (John) Soames
(Baron of Fletching)
English government official
• Governor of S Rhodesia, 1979-80; presided over its transition into independent Zimbabwe; son-in-law of Winston Churchill.
b. October 12, 1920 in Penn, England
d. September 16, 1987 in London, England

Mario Alberto Nobre Lopes Soares
Portuguese political leader
• First civilian president of Portugal in 60 yrs., 1986–.
b. December 07, 1924 in Lisbon, Portugal

Sobhuza II
Swazi ruler
• World's longest reigning monarch, 1921-82; estimated to have had nearly 100 wives, 500 children.
b. July 22, 1899 in Swaziland
d. August 21, 1982 in Mbabane, Swaziland

Stephen Joshua Solarz
American political leader
• Liberal Dem. congressman from NY, 1975–.
b. September 12, 1940 in New York, New York

Solomon
Hebrew ruler–author
• Ruled Israel; renowned for wisdom, wealth; during reign nation rose to its greatest; wrote *The Song of Solomon*.
b. 973?BC
d. 933?BC

Anastasio Somoza
Nicaraguan political leader
• President, 1937-47, 1951-56; assassinated.
b. February 01, 1896 in San Marcos, Nicaragua
d. September 29, 1956 in Managua, Nicaragua

Anastasio Somoza Debayle
Nicaraguan political leader
• Pres. of Nicaragua, 1967-72; 1974-79.
b. December 05, 1925 in Leon, Nicaragua
d. September 17, 1980 in Asuncion, Nicaragua

Prince Souphanouvong
Laotian political leader
• President of Laos, 1975–.
b. 1902

Carl Andrew Spaatz
American army officer–military leader
• In charge of strategic bombing against Germany, Japan, WW II.
b. June 28, 1891 in Boyertown, Pennsylvania
d. July 14, 1974 in Washington, District of Columbia

John Jackson Sparkman
American political leader
• Dem. senator from AL, 1947-79; Adlai Stevenson's vice presidential running mate, 1952.
b. December 2, 1899 in Morgan County, Alabama
d. November 16, 1985 in Huntsville, Alabama

Larry Melvin Speakes
American presidential aide
• Deputy press secretary under Reagan, 1981-87.
b. September 13, 1939 in Cleveland, Mississippi

Hans Speidel
German military leader
• Part of abortive plot to assassinate Hitler, 1944; commanded Allied land forces in central Europe for NATO, 1957-63.
b. October 28, 1897 in Metzingen, Germany
d. November 28, 1984 in Bad Honnef, Germany (West)

Marian Spychalski
Polish architect–political leader
• Organized Polish Worker's Party, 1942; mayor of Warsaw, 1944-45; marshal of Poland, 1963-80.
b. December 06, 1906 in Lodz, Poland
d. June 07, 1980 in Warsaw, Poland

Joseph Stalin
(Iosif Visarionovich Djugashvili)
Russian political leader
• Successor of Lenin who was dictator, 1929-53; attempted to establish socialism by force, terror.
b. December 21, 1879 in Gori, Russia
d. March 05, 1953 in Moscow, U.S.S.R.

Aleksandr Stambuliski
(Alexandr Stamboliski)
Bulgarian political leader
• Leader of Peasant's Party; premier, 1920-23, until assassinated.
b. March 01, 1879
d. 1923

Frederick Arthur Stanley, Earl of Derby
(Lord Stanley of Preston)
English political leader–sportsman
• Governor-general of Canada, 1888-93; donated Stanley Cup, presented to amateur hockey teams, 1893-1912, to pros ever since.
b. January 15, 1841 in England
d. June 14, 1908 in England

Harold Raynsford Stark
American naval officer–military leader
• Chief of US naval operations, 1939-41; relieved of command after Pearl Harbor attack.
b. November 12, 1880 in Wilkes-Barre, Pennsylvania
d. August 2, 1972 in Washington, District of Columbia

Claus (Schenk Graf) Von Stauffenberg
(Klaus Graf Schenk von Stauffenberg)
German army officer
• Part of conspiracy against Hitler; failed in assassination attempt, July 1944; shot, killed.
b. November 15, 1907 in Upper Franconia, Germany
d. July 2, 1944 in Rastenburg, Germany

John Cornelius Stennis
American political leader
• Democratic senator from MS, 1947-89.
b. August 03, 1901 in Kemper County, Mississippi

Stephanie
(Stephanie Marie Elisabeth Grimaldi)
Monacan princess
• Daughter of Princess Grace, Prince Rainier; designed swimsuits, 1985.
b. February 01, 1965 in Monaco-Ville, Monaco

Alexander Hamilton Stephens
American political leader
• Elected vice president of US Confederate States, 1862-65; imprisoned May-Oct 1865; served in US Congress following Civil War.
b. February 11, 1812 in Crawfordsville, Georgia
d. March 04, 1883 in Atlanta, Georgia

Siaka Probyn Stevens
Sierra Leonean political leader
• First president, prime minister, of Sierra Leone, 1971-85.
b. August 24, 1905 in Moyamba, Sierra Leone
d. May 29, 1988 in Freetown, Sierra Leone

Ted (Theodore Fulton) Stevens
American political leader
• Rep. senator from AK, 1968–.
b. November 18, 1923 in Indianapolis, Indiana

Adlai Ewing Stevenson
American US vice president
• Served under Grover Cleveland, 1893-97.
b. October 23, 1835 in Christian County, Kentucky
d. June 14, 1914 in Chicago, Illinois

Adlai Ewing Stevenson, II
American diplomat–political leader
• UN ambassador, 1961-65; lost to Eisenhower in presidential races, 1952, 1956.
b. February 05, 1900 in Los Angeles, California
d. July 14, 1965 in London, England

Coke Robert Stevenson
American political leader
• Prominent in TX politics, 1920s-40s; governor of TX, 1943-47.
b. March 2, 1888 in Mason County, Texas
d. June 28, 1975 in San Angelo, Texas

Joseph Warren Stilwell
American army officer–military leader
• Commander of the 6th Army; chief-of-staff to Chiang Kai-Shek; disagreement over role of Chinese forces led to his loss of command by FDR, 1944.
b. March 19, 1883 in Palatka, Florida
d. October 12, 1946 in San Francisco, California

Henry Lewis (Harry) Stimson
American cabinet member
• Secretary of War, 1940-45; led expansion, operation of US Army, WW II; advised use of atomic bomb on Japan.
b. September 21, 1867 in New York, New York
d. October 2, 1950 in Huntington, New York

Lord Stirling
(William Alexander)
American military leader
• Continental army general; defended the NYC area in various battles, Mar 1776-Jan 1780.
b. 1726 in New York, New York
d. September 15, 1783 in New York, New York

David Allen Stockman
American political leader
• Directed OMB, 1981-85; wrote *Triumph of Politics*, 1986.
b. November 1, 1946 in Fort Hood, Texas

Robert Field Stockton
American naval officer–military leader
• Captured Santa Barbara, Los Angeles in Mexican War; declared CA a territory of US; Stockton, CA named for him.
b. August 2, 1795 in Princeton, New Jersey
d. October 07, 1866 in Princeton, New Jersey

Carl Burton Stokes
American political leader
• Mayor of Cleveland, 1960s; one of the first big city black mayors in America.
b. June 21, 1927 in Cleveland, Ohio

George Stoneman
American military leader–politician
• Union general; commanded troops that brought on Battle of Williamsburg, 1862; part of Atlanta campaign, 1864; Dem. governor of CA, 1883-87.
b. August 08, 1822 in Busti, New York
d. September 05, 1894 in Buffalo, New York

General George E Stratemeyer
American military leader
• US Air Force general, commanding general China-Burma-India, WW II; Far East Air Forces, 1949-52.
b. November 24, 1890 in Cincinnati, Ohio
d. August 09, 1969

Franz Josef Strauss
German politician
• Controversial government official; minister president of Bavaria, 1978-88; one of founders of Christian Social Union, 1945.
b. September 06, 1915 in Munich, Germany
d. October 03, 1988 in Regensburg, Bavaria

Robert Strauss
American presidential aide
• Chm., Dem. Nat. Committee, 1972-77; worked to reelect Carter, 1979-81.
b. October 19, 1918 in Lockhart, Texas

Alfredo Stroessner
Paraguayan political leader
• President of Paraguay, longest ruling political leader in Latin America, 1954-89; ousted in military coup.
b. November 03, 1912 in Encarnacion, Paraguay

James Matthew Stronge
Irish politician
• Member, N Ireland Parliament, killed with father, by IRA terrorists.
b. June 21, 1932
d. January 21, 1981 in Armagh, Northern Ireland

Sir (Charles) Norman (Lockhart) Stronge
Irish politician
• Speaker of House of Commons, N Ireland, 1945-69; killed in terrorist attack on his home.
b. July 23, 1894 in Bryansford, Northern Ireland
d. January 21, 1981 in Armagh, Northern Ireland

Lubomir Strougal
Czech government official
• Prime minister of Czechoslovakia, 1970-88.
b. October 19, 1924 in Veseli nad Luznici, Czechoslovakia

Jeb (James Ewell Brown) Stuart
American army officer–military leader
• Commanded all Confederate cavalry, 1862-64.
b. February 06, 1833 in Patrick County, Virginia
d. May 12, 1864 in Richmond, Virginia

Gerry E(astman) Studds
American political leader
• Dem. congressman from MA, 1973–; censured by House, Jul 1983, for homosexual affair with page.
b. May 12, 1937 in Mineola, New York

Xavier Louis Suarez
Cuban political leader
• Mayor, Miami, FL, 1985–; first Cuban-American mayor in Miami.
b. May 21, 1949 in Las Villas, Cuba

General Suharto
Indonesian political leader
• President since 1968.
b. June 08, 1921 in Kemusa, Indonesia

Achmed Sukarno
Indonesian political leader
• First pres. of Indonesia, 1945-67, headed authoritarian government with strong ties to Communist China.
b. June 01, 1901 in Surabaya, Indonesia
d. June 21, 1970 in Djakarta, Indonesia

Suleiman I
(Suleiman the Magnificent)
Turkish ruler
• Ottoman sultan, 1520-66; empire reached height of power under him.
b. 1496
d. September 05, 1566

Lucius C Sulla
(Felix)
Roman army officer–political leader
• Used army to seize control of state, 82 BC; revived Roman office of dictator; his was notorious for cruelty.
b. 138BC
d. 78BC in Campania, Italy

Thomas Sumter
American army officer–political leader
• Brigadier general in Revolution; Dem. senator from SC, 1802-10; Fort Sumter, SC named for him.
b. August 14, 1734 in Hanover County, Virginia
d. June 01, 1832 in Stateburg, Virginia

Sun Yat-Sen
(Sun Wen; "Father of Modern China")
Chinese political leader
• Led revolution that overthrew Manchu dynasty, 1911; principal founder of Chinese Nationalist Party, 1912; pres., South China Republic, 1921.
b. November 12, 1866 in Macao, China
d. March 12, 1925

Madame Chingling Soong Sun Yat-Sen
(Ching-ling Sung Sun)
Chinese political leader
• Widow of Sun Yat-sen; deputy chairman of People's Republic of China; ardent communist.
b. 1890 in Shanghai, China
d. May 29, 1981 in Peking, China

John Henry Sununu
American presidential aide–politician
• Chief of staff under George Bush, 1989–; Republican governor of NH, 1983-89.
b. July 02, 1939 in Havana, Cuba

Aleksandr V Suvorov
Russian military leader
• Commanded Austro-Russian forces against French in French Revolutionary Wars, 1798-99; never beaten in battle.
b. November 25, 1729
d. 1800

Zenko Suzuki
Japanese political leader
• Prime minister, 1980-82.
b. January 11, 1911 in Yamada, Japan

Ludvik Svoboda
Czech communist leader
• Pres. of Czechoslovakia, 1968-75.
b. November 25, 1895 in Horznatin, Czechoslovakia
d. September 2, 1979 in Prague, Czechoslovakia

Charles Robberts Swart
South African political leader
• First South African state president, 1961-67; last governor general, 1960-61.
b. December 05, 1894 in Orange Free State
d. July 16, 1982 in Bloemfontein, South Africa

Jack (John Leonard, Jr) Swigert
American astronaut–political leader
• Commanded *Apollo 13;* elected to Congress from CO, 1982; died before sworn in.
b. August 3, 1931 in Denver, Colorado
d. December 27, 1982 in Washington, District of Columbia

Stuart (William Stuart) Symington
American political leader
• Democratic senator from MO, 1952-77; known champion of the military; first US Air Force secretary, 1947-50.
b. June 26, 1901 in Amherst, Massachusetts
d. December 14, 1988 in New Canaan, Connecticut

Helen Herron Taft
(Mrs William Howard Taft)
American first lady
• Persuaded mayor of Tokyo to donate 3,000 cherry trees to nation's capital.
b. June 02, 1861 in Cincinnati, Ohio
d. May 22, 1943 in Washington, District of Columbia

Robert A(lphonso) Taft
American political leader
• Rep. senator from OH, 1939-53; son of William Howard; sponsored Taft-Hartley Labor Relations Act, 1947.
b. September 08, 1889 in Cincinnati, Ohio
d. July 31, 1953 in New York, New York

William Howard Taft
American US president
• Rep., 27th pres., 1909-13; created labor dept., 1911; Supreme Court justice, 1921-30.
b. September 15, 1857 in Cincinnati, Ohio
d. March 08, 1930 in Washington, District of Columbia

Noboru Takeshita
Japanese political leader
• Succeeded Yasuhiro Nakasone as prime minister, 1987.
b. February 26, 1924 in Shimane, Japan

Herman Eugene Talmadge
American political leader
• Dem. governor of GA, 1948-55; US senator, 1957-81; son of Eugene.
b. August 09, 1913 in Telfair County, Georgia

Oliver Tambo
South African political activist
• Pres. of South Africa's outlawed African National Congress, 1949–.
b. October 27, 1917 in Johannesburg, South Africa

Sir Banastre Tarleton
English army officer–military leader
• Led British Troops in American Revolution; with Cornwallis at surrender; noted for cruelty.
b. August 21, 1754 in Liverpool, England
d. January 25, 1833 in Shropshire, England

Howard Tawley
Canadian politician
• New Democratic Party premier of Manitoba, 1981–.
b. November 21, 1934 in Brampton, Ontario

Kenneth Douglas Taylor
Canadian diplomat
• Ambassador to Iran, 1977-80; helped six Americans escape from Iran during hostage crisis, 1980.
b. October 05, 1934 in Calgary, Alberta

Margaret Smith Taylor
(Mrs Zachary Taylor)
American first lady
• Devoted wife without social ambition; daughter acted as White House hostess.
b. September 21, 1788 in Calvert County, Maryland
d. August 18, 1852 in Pascagoula, Kentucky

Maxwell Davenport Taylor
American army officer–military leader
• Played a major role in determining American military, diplomatic strategy from WW II to Vietnam War.
b. August 26, 1901 in Keytesville, Missouri
d. April 19, 1987 in Washington, District of Columbia

Zachary Taylor
American US president
• 12th pres., 1849-50; hero of US-Mexican War, 1846-48.
b. November 24, 1784 in Orange County, Virginia
d. July 09, 1850 in Washington, District of Columbia

Olin E Teague
American political leader
• Dem. senator from TX, 1946-79; identified with veterans affairs.
b. April 06, 1910 in Woodward, Oklahoma
d. January 23, 1981 in Bethesda, Maryland

Norman Beresford Tebbit
English political leader
• Conservative member of Parliament, 1970–; chm., Conservative Party, 1985-87.
b. March 29, 1931 in London, England

Edgar Zivanai Tekere
Zimbabwean government official
• Secretary general who was arrested for murder during guerrilla attacks in Zimbabwe, 1980.
b. April 01, 1937 in Rhodesia

Jerald Franklin TerHorst
American journalist–presidential aide
• White House press secretary under Ford, who resigned after 30 days because of Ford's pardon of Richard Nixon, 1974.
b. July 11, 1922 in Grand Rapids, Michigan

Ton Duc Thang
(Ton Duc Thang)
Vietnamese government official
• Pres., Vietnam, 1976-80.
b. August 2, 1888 in Long Xuyen Province, Vietnam
d. March 3, 1980 in Hanoi, Vietnam

Shiekh Khalifa Ben Hamad al Thani
Qatari ruler
• Amir of Qatar, 1972–; expanded economic, social reform; stopped most of royal family's extravagance, privileges.
b. in Qatar

Margaret Hilda Roberts Thatcher
English political leader
• Conservative prime minister of Britain, May 1979-November 1990; first woman in British history to serve as prime minister; resigned from office.
b. October 13, 1925 in Grantham, England

Themistocles
Greek military leader
• Athenian commander who developed naval strength; led victory against Persians at Salamis, 480 BC.
b. 524?BC
d. 460?BC

Theodosius I
(Theodosius the Great)
Roman ruler
• Ruled Holy Roman Empire before division of East, West, 379-395; proclaimed son, Honorius, emperor of the West, 395.
b. 346 in Spain
d. 395 in Milan, Spain

George Henry Thomas
American military leader
• Distinguished Civil War general; accepted surrender of Atlanta, 1864.
b. July 31, 1816 in Southampton County, Virginia
d. March 28, 1870 in San Francisco, California

Americo Thomaz
(Americo Deus Rodrigues Tomas)
Portuguese political leader
• Elected pres., 1958; twice again, under suspicious circumstances, until ousted in 1974.
b. November 19, 1894 in Lisbon, Portugal
d. September 18, 1987 in Cascais, Portugal

James Robert Thompson
American political leader
• Republican governor of IL, 1977-91, succeeded by Jim Edgar.
b. May 08, 1936 in Chicago, Illinois

Maurice Thorez
French politician
• Leader of French Communist party, secretary general, 1930-64, first pres., 1964.
b. April 28, 1900 in Noyelles Godault, France
d. July 11, 1964

Dick (Richard Lewis) Thornburgh
American political leader
• Rep. governor of PA, 1979-87; succeeded Edwin Meese as US attorney general, 1988–.
b. July 16, 1932 in Pittsburgh, Pennsylvania

Jeremy (John Jeremy) Thorpe
English political leader
• Liberal MP, 1959-79; held balance of power in govt., mid-1970s.
b. April 29, 1929 in London, England

(James) Strom Thurmond
American political leader
• Conservative Dem., then Rep. senator from SC, 1955–; led segregationists, 1940s-50s; conducted longest Senate filibuster, 24 hrs., 1957.
b. December 05, 1902 in Edgefield, South Carolina

Tiberius Julius Caesar Augustus
(Tiberius Claudius Nero)
Roman ruler
• Second Roman Emperor, AD 14-37.
b. 42BC in Rome, Italy
d. 37AD in Capri

Semen Konstantinovich Timoshenko
Russian army officer–military leader
• WW II hero helped defeat German troops on Soviet western front.
b. February 19, 1895 in Urmanka, Russia
d. March 31, 1970 in Moscow, U.S.S.R.

Tito
(Josip Broz Tito)
Yugoslav political leader
• Established Yugoslavia as communist state after WW II; pres., 1953-80.
b. May 25, 1892 in Kumrovec, Yugoslavia
d. May 04, 1980 in Ljubljana, Yugoslavia

Titus
Roman ruler
• Ruled, AD 79-81; empire was peaceful during reign; aided Pompeii after volcano, Rome after fires.
b. 40 in Rome, Italy
d. 81

Palmiro Togliatti
(Ercole Ercoli)
Italian communist leader
• A founder, head of Italian Communist Party, 1921-44; exiled under Mussolini for 18 yrs.
b. March 26, 1893 in Genoa, Italy
d. August 21, 1964 in Yalta, U.S.S.R.

Heihachiro Togo
Japanese naval officer–military leader
• Considered Japan's greatest naval hero; led Japanese fleet in Russo-Japanese War, 1904-05.
b. 1847
d. 1934

Hideki (Eiki) Tojo
Japanese army officer–political leader
• Prime minister, 1941; directed Japanese military operations, WW II.
b. 1884 in Tokyo, Japan
d. December 23, 1948 in Tokyo, Japan

William Richard Tolbert, Jr.
Liberian political leader
• Pres. of Liberia, 1971-80.
b. May 13, 1913 in Bensonville, Liberia
d. April 12, 1980 in Monrovia, Liberia

Fernando Alvarez de Toledo
(Duke of Alva)
Spanish army officer
• Through use of cautious tactics rose to chief of Spanish Army, 1541; governor-general of Netherlands, 1567-73.
b. 1508 in Piedrahita, Spain
d. 1582 in Thomar, Spain

Nagarta Francois Tombalbaye
Chadian political leader
• Pres. of Chad since 1960; killed in military coup.
b. 1918
d. April 13, 1975 in Fort Lamy, Chad

Ton-duc-thong
Vietnamese political leader
• World's oldest communist head of state; pres., Socialist Republic of Vietnam, 1969-80.
b. August 2, 1888 in Long Xuyen Province, Vietnam
d. 1980 in Hanoi, Vietnam

Omar Torrijos Herrera
Panamanian political leader
• Engineered 1968 coup, instituted reforms as Chief of Government, 1972-78; main architect of Panama Canal treaties with US, 1979; against opposition granted asylum to Shah of Iran, 1979; killed in plane crash.
b. February 13, 1929 in Santiago de Veraguas, Panama
d. July 31, 1981 in Panama

Ahmed Sekou Toure
Guinean political leader
• Leader of Guinea since its independence, 1958-72; black Africa's longest surviving head of state.
b. January 09, 1922
d. March 26, 1984 in Cleveland, Ohio

Pierre Dominique Toussaint l'Ouverture
Haitian slave–political leader
• Self-educated slave who played dominant role in Negro Rebellion, 1791, bringing law, order to Haiti by 1801.
b. 1743 in Cape Francois, Haiti
d. April 07, 1803 in Fort-de-Joux, France

Katherine Amelia Towle
American military leader–educator
• First director of Women's Marines; in regular Marine Corps, 1948-53.
b. April 3, 1898 in Towle, California
d. March 01, 1986 in Pacific Grove, California

Trajan
(Marcus Ulpius Trajanus)
Roman ruler
• Ruled, 98-117; known for building bridges, roads, Trajan's Forum, Trajan's Column.
b. 53 in Italica, Spain
d. 117 in Selinus, Cilicia

William Barret Travis
American military leader
• Hero of Texas Revolution; commanded The Alamo, where all were slain by Santa Anna.
b. August 09, 1809 in Red Banks, South Carolina
d. March 06, 1836 in San Antonio, Texas

Moussa Trore
Malian political leader
• President, Republic of Mali, 1968–.
b. September 25, 1936 in Kayes, Mali

First Viscount Hugh Montague Trenchard
English military leader
• Marshall of Royal Air Force from 1927.
b. February 03, 1873 in Taunton, England
d. February 1, 1956 in London, England

Leon Trotsky
(Lev Davidovitch Bronstein)
Russian communist leader–author
• Organized 1917 revolution; banished, 1929, after power struggle with Stalin.
b. November 08, 1879 in Elisavetgrad, Russia
d. August 21, 1940 in Mexico City, Mexico

Pierre Elliott Trudeau
Canadian political leader
• Colorful Liberal prime minister, 1969-79, 1980-84.
b. October 18, 1919 in Montreal, Quebec

Rafael Leonidas Trujillo (Molina)
Dominican politician
• Dictator of Dominican Republic, 1931-61; assassinated.
b. October 24, 1891 in San Cristobal, Dominican Republic
d. May 3, 1961 in Ciudad Trujillo, Dominican Republic

Bess Truman
(Mrs Harry S Truman; Elizabeth Virginia Wallace; "The Boss")
American first lady
• Publicity shy, gracious, unassuming White House hostess, married 1919.
b. February 13, 1885 in Independence, Missouri
d. October 18, 1982 in Kansas City, Missouri

Harry S Truman
American US president
• Dem., 33rd pres., 1945-53; made decision to drop atomic bomb on Japan, 1945.
b. May 08, 1884 in Lamar, Missouri
d. December 26, 1972 in Kansas City, Missouri

Constantinos Tsatsos
Greek political leader
• First elected pres. of the republic of Greece, 1975-80.
b. July 01, 1899 in Athens, Greece
d. October 08, 1987 in Athens, Greece

Philibert Tsiranana
African political leader
• Pres. of Madagascar, 1959-72; first of the republic; declared independence in 1960.
b. October 18, 1912
d. April 16, 1978 in Tananarive, Madagascar

Paul Efthemios Tsongas
American political leader
• Dem. senator from MA, 1979-1985; resigned during bout with cancer; first official presidential candidate for 1992.
b. February 14, 1941 in Lowell, Massachusetts

William Vacanarat Shadrach Tubman
Liberian political leader
• President of Liberia, 1944-71.
b. November 29, 1895 in Harper, Liberia
d. July 23, 1971 in Harper, Liberia

Mikhail Nikolayevich Tukhachevski
Russian military leader
• Commanded Russian offensive in Russo-Polish War, 1919-20; led modernization of Red Army, 1935; charged with treason by Stalin, executed.
b. 1893 in Saint Petersburg, Russia
d. June 1937

Julio Cesar Turbay Ayala
Colombian political leader
• Pres., 1978-82; permanent representative UN, 1967; ambassador to US, 1974-76.
b. June 18, 1916 in Bogota, Colombia

Vicomte Henri D'Auvergne Turenne
French military leader
• Fought in Thirty Years War; emphasized mobility, surprise in military operations.
b. September 11, 1611
d. July 27, 1675

John Napier Turner
Canadian political leader
• Liberal Party leader who succeeded Pierre Trudeau as prime minister, 1984; defeated by Conservative Brian Mulroney, Sep 1984.
b. June 07, 1929 in Richmond, England

Stansfield Turner
American military leader
• Retired Naval admiral; directed CIA, 1977-81.
b. December 01, 1923 in Chicago, Illinois

Tutankhamen
(Tut-Ankh-Amen; "King Tut")
Egyptian ruler
• Boy ruler of 18th Dynasty; tomb, with magnificent contents, found 1922, in Valley of Kings.
b. 1358BC
d. 1340BC

Boss (William Marcy) Tweed
American political leader
• Tammany Hall boss; stole millions from city treasury; exposed by Nast cartoons, 1870.
b. April 03, 1823 in New York, New York
d. April 12, 1878 in New York, New York

Millard Evelyn Tydings
American political leader
• Dem. senator from MD, 1927-51; headed McCarthy investigation which cleared State Dept., 1950.
b. April 06, 1890 in Havre de Grace, Maryland
d. February 09, 1961 in Havre de Grace, Maryland

John Tyler
American US president
• Took office after Harrison's death, 1841-45, making him first vice president to take such action.
b. March 29, 1790 in Charles City, Virginia
d. January 18, 1862 in Richmond, Virginia

Julia Gardiner Tyler
(Mrs John Tyler)
American first lady
• Became Tyler's second wife in secret ceremony, 1844.
b. May 04, 1820 in Gardiner's Island, New York
d. July 1, 1889 in Richmond, Virginia

Letitia Christian Tyler
(Mrs John Tyler)
American first lady
• First president's wife to die in White House.
b. November 12, 1790 in New Kent County, Virginia
d. September 1, 1842 in Washington, District of Columbia

Tz'u Hsi
(Yehomala)
Chinese ruler
• Empress Dowager 1861-1908, who resisted foreign encroachment, modernization; last great Manchu leader.
b. 1835 in Peking, China
d. November 14, 1908

Walter Ulbricht
German communist leader
• Member, People's Chamber, 1949-73; chm., Council of State of German Democratic Republic, 1960-73.
b. June 3, 1893 in Leipzig, Germany
d. August 01, 1973 in Berlin, Germany (East)

Umberto II
(Umberto Nicola Giovanni Maria of Savoy)
Italian ruler
• Italy's last king; reigned May 9-Jun 2, 1946; monarchy abolished by Mussolini.
b. September 15, 1904 in Racconigi, Italy
d. March 18, 1983 in Geneva, Switzerland

Jesse Marvin Unruh
American political leader
• Influential CA assemblyman who aided John, Robert Kennedy presidential campaigns.
b. September 3, 1922 in Newton, Kansas
d. August 04, 1987 in Marina del Rey, California

Martin Van Buren
American US president
• Eighth pres., Dem., 1837-41; opposed annexation of Texas, established independent treasury system.
b. December 05, 1782 in Kinderhook, New York
d. July 24, 1862 in Kinderhook, New York

William Vander Zalm
(Wilhelmus Nicholass Theodoros Maria Vander Zalm)
Canadian political leader
• Social Credit premier of British Columbia, 1986-.
b. May 29, 1934 in Noordwykerhout, Netherlands

Bartolomeo Vanzetti
(Sacco and Vanzetti)
Italian political activist
• Tried, executed for murder during robbery; case became most notorious of century due to widespread charges of mistrial.
b. June 11, 1888 in Villafalletto, Italy
d. August 23, 1927 in Boston, Massachusetts

Vashti
Persian ruler
• Dethroned, maybe beheaded, for refusing to flaunt her beauty for group of princes at her husband, the king's request.

Juan Velasco Alvarado
Peruvian political leader
• Pres. of Peru after 1958 coup; ousted in 1975 coup.
b. June 16, 1910 in Piura, Peru
d. December 24, 1977 in Lima, Peru

Jose Maria Velasco Ibarra
Ecuadorean political leader
• Served as pres. of Ecuador five times between 1934-72; ousted by military off and on.
b. March 19, 1893 in Quito, Ecuador
d. March 3, 1979 in Quito, Ecuador

Ramaswamy Venkataraman
Indian political leader
• President of India, 1987-.
b. December 04, 1910 in Rajamadam, India

Hendrik F Verwoerd
South African political leader
• Prime minister, 1958-66; assassinated.
b. September 08, 1901 in Amsterdam, Netherlands
d. September 06, 1966 in South Africa

Vespasian
(Titus Flavius Sabinus Vespasianus)
Roman ruler
• During reign, suppressed revolt of Batavians; began erection of Colosseum, AD 69-79.
b. 8BC in Reate, Italy
d. June 24, 79

John William Vessey, Jr
American military leader
• First man to rise through ranks from private to four-star general to chairman of Joint Chiefs of Staff, 1979-85; succeeded by William Crowe.
b. June 29, 1922 in Minneapolis, Minnesota

Victor Emmanuel II
Italian ruler
• First king of Italy, 1861-78, who freed Italy from Austrian domination.
b. March 14, 1820 in Turin, Italy
d. January 09, 1878

Victor Emmanuel III
Italian ruler
• King of Italy, 1900-46; relinquished power to son, 1944; abdicated, 1946.
b. 1869 in Naples, Italy
d. 1947

Victoria
(Alexandrina Victoria)
English ruler
• Had longest reign in British history, 1837-1901; featured growing industrialization, middle class prosperity.
b. May 24, 1819 in London, England
d. January 22, 1901 in Isle of Wight, England

Victoria Ingrid Alice Desiree
Swedish princess
• First child of King Carl Gustaf XVI of Sweden; will succeed father to throne.
b. July 04, 1977 in Stockholm, Sweden

Jorge Rafael Videla
Argentine political leader
• Pres. of Argentina, 1976-81; led coup that ousted Pres. Peron.
b. August 02, 1925 in Mercedes, Argentina

Aulus Vitellius
Roman ruler
• Roman emperor, 69, after death of Otho; defeated, killed by Primus.
b. 15
d. 69

Paul Adolph Volcker
American banker–government official
• Chm., Federal Reserve Board, 1979-87; known for reducing double-digit inflation.
b. September 05, 1927 in Cape May, New Jersey

Andrew J Volstead
American political leader
• Ten-term congressman who personified Prohibition with passage of Volstead Act, 1919.
b. October 31, 1860 in Kenyon, Minnesota
d. January 2, 1947 in Granite Falls, Minnesota

Kliment Efremovich Voroshilov
Russian soldier–politician
• In command on the Leningrad front at outbreak of war with Germany, 1941; succeeded Stalin as chm. of Presidium, 1953-57.
b. February 03, 1881 in Ukraine, Russia
d. December 02, 1968 in Moscow, U.S.S.R.

James Samuel Wadsworth
American military leader
• Brigadier general of volunteers from 1861; played key role in Union victory at Gettysburg, 1863.
b. October 3, 1807 in Genesco, New York
d. May 08, 1864 in Virginia

Robert F(erdinand) Wagner
American political leader
• Dem. senator from NY, 1926-49; helped draft several New Deal measures.
b. June 08, 1877 in Hesse-Nasseau, Germany
d. May 04, 1953 in New York, New York

Lech Walesa
Polish political leader–labor union official
• Organized Solidarity, only independent trade union in Communist world, 1980; won Nobel Peace Prize, 1983; elected president in Poland's first free election, 1990.
b. September 29, 1943 in Popow, Poland

Daniel Walker
American political leader
• Dem. governor of IL, 1973-77; convicted of fraud, perjury, 1987.
b. August 06, 1922 in San Diego, California

Jimmy (James John) Walker
American political leader–songwriter
• Colorful mayor of NYC, 1925-32; investigation of widespread corruption led to resignation.
b. June 19, 1881 in New York, New York
d. November 18, 1946 in New York, New York

George Corley Wallace
American political leader
• Four-term Dem. governor of AL, 1960s-80s; paralyzed in assassination attempt, 1972; gained renown as strong segregationist, but moderated views, becoming symbol of "New South."
b. August 25, 1919 in Clio, Alabama

Henry Agard Wallace
American US vice president
• VP under FDR, 1941-45; Progressive Party presidential candidate, 1948.
b. October 07, 1888 in Adair County, Iowa
d. November 18, 1965 in Danbury, Connecticut

Lurleen Burns Wallace
(Mrs George Wallace)
American political leader
• Succeeded husband to become first woman governor of AL, 1967.
b. September 19, 1926 in Tuscaloosa, Alabama
d. May 07, 1968 in Montgomery, Alabama

Raoul Gustav Wallenberg
Swedish diplomat
• Saved nearly 100,000 Budapest Jews in WW II.
b. August 04, 1912 in Sweden
d. July 17, 1947 in Moscow, U.S.S.R.

Sir William Walworth
English politician
• Lord mayor, London, 1374-1381; money lender to Richard II; defended London Bridge against the Kentish peasants, 1381.

Wang Hung-Wen
(Wang Hongwen)
Chinese communist leader
• Sentenced to life imprisonment for being member of "gang of four," 1981.
b. 1937 in China

John William Warner
American political leader
• Rep. senator from VA, 1979–; husband of Elizabeth Taylor, 1976-82.
b. February 18, 1927 in Washington, District of Columbia

Joseph Warren
American military leader
• Revolutionary general known for sending Paul Revere, William Dawes on their famous ride.
b. June 11, 1741 in Roxbury, Massachusetts
d. June 17, 1775 in Charlestown, Massachusetts

George Washington
American US president
• First president, 1789-97; commander-in-chief, Continental Forces, 1775-83; warned against foreign alliances.
b. February 22, 1732 in Westmoreland, Virginia
d. December 14, 1799 in Mount Vernon, Virginia

Harold Washington
American political leader
• First black Dem. mayor of Chicago, 1983-87; suffered massive heart attack in office.
b. April 15, 1922 in Chicago, Illinois
d. November 25, 1987 in Chicago, Illinois

Martha Dandridge Curtis Washington
(Mrs George Washington)
American first lady
• Widow who married George Washington, Jan 6, 1759.
b. June 02, 1732 in New Kent County, Virginia
d. 1802 in Mount Vernon, Virginia

James Gaius Watt
American cabinet member
• Outspoken secretary of Interior, 1981-83; known for controversial environmental policies.
b. January 31, 1938 in Lusk, Wyoming

Robert Clifton Weaver
American cabinet member
• First secretary of HUD, 1966-69; first black US cabinet member.
b. December 29, 1907 in Washington, District of Columbia

William Hedgcock Webster
American FBI director
• FBI director, 1978–; honorary director Big Brothers of America, 1978–.
b. March 06, 1924 in Saint Louis, Missouri

Albert Coady Wedemeyer
American military leader
• Army general, military planner; originated WW II "Victory Program," which eventually led to invasion of Normandy, June 1944.
b. July 09, 1897 in Omaha, Nebraska
d. December 17, 1989 in Fort Belvoir, Virginia

Lowell Palmer Weicker, Jr
American political leader
• Independent governor of CT, 1991–; Republican US senator, 1971-89.
b. May 16, 1931 in Paris, France

Caspar Willard Weinberger
American cabinet member
• Secretary of HEW, 1973-75; Secretary of Defense, 1981-87.
b. August 18, 1917 in San Francisco, California

Ted (Theodore S) Weiss
American political leader
• Dem. congressman from NY, 1976-87; advocates end to arms race.
b. September 17, 1927 in Budapest, Hungary

Chaim Weizmann
Israeli political leader–religious leader
• Provisional pres. of Israel, 1948-49; first elected pres., 1949-52; first pres., World Zionist Organization, 1923.
b. November 27, 1874 in Grodno, Russia
d. November 09, 1952 in Rehovot, Israel

Robert Henry Winborne Welch, Jr
American political activist
• Founder of ultraconservative, anti-communist John Birch Society, 1958.
b. December 01, 1899 in Chowan County, North Carolina
d. January 06, 1984 in Winchester, Massachusetts

Duke Arthur Wellesley Wellington
English army officer–statesman
• Commander, Peninsular War, 1808-14, fighting Napoleon; prime minister, 1828-30.
b. May 01, 1769 in Dublin, Ireland
d. September 14, 1852

William Childs Westmoreland
American military leader
• Commanded US forces in Vietnam, 1964-68; Army chief of staff, 1968-72.
b. March 16, 1914 in Spartanburg, South Carolina

Maxime Weygand
French military leader
• Supreme allied commander, 1939, known for unsuccessful attempt to create new front.
b. January 21, 1867 in Brussels, Belgium
d. January 28, 1965 in Paris, France

Earle G Wheeler
American military leader
• Served as Army chief of staff, 1962-64; confirmed in 1973 that Nixon ordered secret attacks over Cambodia, 1969.
b. January 13, 1908 in Washington, District of Columbia
d. December 18, 1975 in Frederick, Maryland

Joseph Wheeler
American military leader
• Resigned from US army to join Confederate army, 1861; tried to reconcile North, South.
b. September 1, 1836 in Augusta, Georgia
d. January 25, 1906 in Brooklyn, New York

Kevin Hagan White
American political leader
• Mayor of Boston. 1967-84.
b. September 25, 1929 in Boston, Massachusetts

Kathy Whitmire
(Kathryn Jean Niederhofer)
American political leader
• First woman mayor of Houston, TX, 1981-.
b. August 15, 1946 in Houston, Texas

Dick (Richard) Whittington
English politician
• Lord mayor of London, intermittently, 1397-1420; subject of nursery rhyme, legends.
b. 1358
d. 1423

Charles Z Wick
(Charles Zwick)
American presidential aide
• Member Ronald Reagan's "kitchen cabinet"; director, US Information Agency, 1981-89.
b. October 12, 1917 in Cleveland, Ohio

Douglas (Lawrence Douglas) Wilder
American political leader
• Democratic governor of VA, 1990-; first elected black governor in US.
b. January 17, 1931 in Richmond, Virginia

Wilhelm II
(Friedrich Wilhelm Viktor Albert; William II)
German ruler
• Emperor of Germany, king of Prussia, 1888-1918, whose aggressive colonial policy, expansion of navy contributed to WW I outbreak.
b. January 27, 1859 in Berlin, Germany
d. June 04, 1941 in Doorn, Netherlands

Wilhelmina
(Wilhelmina Helena Pauline Maria)
Dutch ruler
• Constitutional monarch, 1890-1948; symbol of Dutch resistance, WW II; established govt. in exile in England; abdicated to daughter Juliana.
b. August 31, 1880 in The Hague, Netherlands
d. November 28, 1962 in Het Loo, Netherlands

William
(William the Lion)
Scottish ruler
• Founded Arbroath Abbey, 1178, during reign, 1165-1214.
b. 1143
d. 1214

William II
(Rufus)
English ruler
• King of England, 1087-1100, succeeding father William the Conqueror; died in hunting accident possibly arranged by brother, Henry I, who succeeded him to throne.
b. 1056
d. August 02, 1100

William III
Dutch ruler
• Stadtholder, 1672-1702; ruled England, 1689-1702; signed many treaties, passed Act of Settlement, 1701.
b. 1650 in The Hague, Netherlands
d. 1702

William of Wales
(William Arthur Philip Louis; "Wills")
English prince
• First son of Prince Charles and Princess Diana; second in line to British throne.
b. June 21, 1982 in London, England

William the Conqueror
(William the Norman)
English ruler
• Conquered England, 1066, replacing English nobility with Norman followers; King of England, 1066-87, succeeded by son, William II.
b. 1027 in Falaise, France
d. 1087 in Rouen, France

John James Williams
American political leader
• Rep. senator from DE, 1947-71; led investigation to expose fraud in IRS, early 1950s.
b. May 17, 1904 in Frankford, Delaware
d. January 11, 1988 in Lewes, Delaware

Edith Bolling Galt Wilson
(Mrs Woodrow Wilson)
American first lady
• Married pres., 1915; nursed him after his 1919 stroke, virtually running country until his term expired.
b. October 15, 1872 in Wytheville, Virginia
d. December 28, 1961 in Washington, District of Columbia

Ellen Axson Wilson
(Mrs Woodrow Wilson)
American first lady
• Prodded Congress to improve Washington, DC slums; first wife of Woodrow Wilson.
b. May 15, 1860 in Savannah, Georgia
d. August 06, 1914 in Washington, District of Columbia

Henry Wilson
American US vice president
• VP under U S Grant, 1873-77.
b. February 16, 1812 in Farmington, New Hampshire
d. November 1, 1875 in Washington, District of Columbia

Pete Barton Wilson
American political leader
• Republican governor of CA, 1991-, succeeding George Deukmejian; US senator, 1983-91, mayor of San Diego, 1971-83.
b. August 23, 1933 in Lake Forest, Illinois

Woodrow (Thomas Woodrow) Wilson
American US president
• Dem., 28th pres., 1913-21; WW I leader awarded Nobel Peace Prize for Versailles Treaty, 1919; domestic reforms included 1914 creation of Federal Reserve.
b. December 28, 1856 in Staunton, Virginia
d. February 03, 1924 in Washington, District of Columbia

John Winthrop
English political leader
• Governor, Massachusetts Bay Colony, 12 times, 1629-48; helped banish Ann Hutchinson.
b. January 12, 1588 in Suffolk, England
d. March 26, 1649 in Boston, Massachusetts

James Wolfe
English military leader
• British commander who captured Quebec from French on Plains of Abraham, 1759; killed in battle.
b. January 02, 1727 in Westerham, England
d. September 13, 1759 in Quebec

Jim (James Claud, Jr) Wright
American political leader
• Dem. con. from TX, 1955-87; succeeded Tip O'Neill as Speaker of House, 1987.
b. December 22, 1922 in Fort Worth, Texas

Xerxes I
(Ahaseuerus)
Persian ruler
• Son, successor of Darius I, 486-465 BC.
b. 519BC
d. 465BC

Agha Muhammad Yahya Khan
Pakistani political leader
• Pres., Pakistan, 1969-71; sentenced to five yrs. house arrest after forced resignation.
b. February 04, 1917 in Peshawar, Pakistan
d. August 08, 1980 in Rawalpindi, India

Isoroku Yamamoto
Japanese military leader
• Admiral who planned attack on Pearl Harbor, 1941.
b. April 04, 1884 in Nagaoka, Japan
d. May 1943

Sheikh Ahmad Zaki Yamani
Saudi government official
• Minister of state, 1962–; pres., Supreme Advisory Council for Petroleum & Mineral Affairs, 1975–; influential OPEC spokesman, Western ally.
b. 1930 in Mecca, Saudi Arabia

Tomoyuki Yamashita
Japanese army officer–millitary leader
• Led Japanese troops in Philippines, 1944; executed for war atrocities.
b. 1888 in Kochi, Japan
d. February 23, 1946 in Luzon, Philippines

Ye Jianying
Chinese political leader
• A founder, People's Liberation Army; one of leaders of the "Long March," 1934-35.
b. May 14, 1897 in Meixien, China
d. October 22, 1986

Princess of York
(Beatrice Elizabeth Mary)
English princess
• First child of Duke and Duchess of York–Prince Andrew and Sarah Ferguson; currently fifth in line to British throne.
b. August 08, 1988 in London, England

Princess of York
(Eugenie Victoria Helena)
English princess
• Second child of Duke and Duchess of York–Prince Andrew and Sarah Ferguson; currently sixth in line to British throne.
b. March 23, 1990 in London, England

Sam(uel William) Yorty
American political leader
• Mayor of Los Angeles, 1961-73.
b. October 01, 1909 in Lincoln, Nebraska

Shigeru Yoshida
Japanese political leader
• Prime minister of Japan, 1946-47, 1948-49; signed peace treaty with Allied Nations, 1951.
b. September 22, 1878 in Tokyo, Japan
d. October 2, 1967 in Oisi, Japan

Yoshihito
(Taisho)
Japanese ruler
• Father of Hirohito; reigned as emperor, 1912-26.
b. August 31, 1879 in Tokyo, Japan
d. December 25, 1926 in Hayama, Japan

Charles Woodruff Yost
American diplomat
• One of founders of UN; chief American delegate, 1969-71.
b. November 06, 1907 in Watertown, New York
d. May 21, 1981 in Washington, District of Columbia

Andrew Jackson Young, Jr
American political leader
• Ambassador to UN, 1977-79; mayor of Atlanta, 1982–; awarded Spingarn Medal, 1980; French Legion of Honor, 1982.
b. March 12, 1932 in New Orleans, Louisiana

Coleman A(lexander) Young
American political leader
• First black mayor of Detroit, 1974–; served longer than any other mayor in city's history; won Spingarn, 1980.
b. May 24, 1918 in Tuscaloosa, Alabama

Shih-Kai Yuan
Chinese political leader
• Pres. of China, 1913-16; sought to be dictator, suppressing Sun Yat-sen, 1914.
b. 1859
d. 1916

Zhao Ziyang
Chinese political leader
• Premier, 1980-87; replaced Deng Ziaoping as chief of Chinese Communist Party, 1987.
b. 1919 in Henan Province, China

Todor Zhivkov
Bulgarian politician
• Prime minister, 1962-71; pres., 1971–.
b. September 07, 1911 in Bulgaria

Georgi Konstantinovich Zhukov
Russian military leader
• WW II hero; led defense of Moscow, Leningrad, capture of Berlin; minister of Defense, 1955-57.
b. December 02, 1896 in Stelkovka, Russia
d. June 18, 1974 in Moscow, U.S.S.R.

Mohammad Zia-ul-Haq
(Mohammad Zia Al-Haq)
Pakistani political leader
• Overthrew Bhutto government, 1977; president until death.
b. August 12, 1924 in Jullunder, India
d. August 17, 1988 in Bahawalpur, Pakistan

Ron(ald Louis) Ziegler
American presidential aide
• Press secretary to Richard Nixon, 1969-74.
b. May 12, 1939 in Covington, Kentucky

Zog I
(Ahmed Bey Zogu)
Albanian ruler
• King of Albania, 1928-39; formally deposed, 1946.
b. October 08, 1895 in Burgayeti, Albania
d. April 09, 1961 in Suresnes, France

Scribes: Shakespeare, Seuss & Salinger

Authors, Editors,

Journalists, Poets,

Publishers...

Verna Norberg Aardema
(Verna Norberg Aardema Vugteveen)
American children's author
• Known for rewriting African folk tales for children; won Caldecott Medal, 1976, for *Why Mosquitoes Buzz in People's Ears.*
b. June 06, 1911 in New Era, Michigan

Edward Abbey
American author
• Writings champion environmental concerns: *Desert Solitaire*, 1968, *The Monkey Wrench Gang*, 1975; called "the Thoreau of the American West," by Larry McMurtry.
b. January 29, 1927 in Home, Pennsylvania
d. March 14, 1989 in Tucson, Arizona

Jack (Rufus Jack Henry) Abbott
(Jack Eastman pseud)
American author–murderer
• Wrote *In the Belly of the Beast: Letters from Prison*, 1981.
b. January 21, 1944 in Oscoda, Michigan

Pierre Abelard
French author–theologian–educator
• Controversial writings, especially *Sic et Non*, explained theories of logic; best known for tragic love affair with Heloise.
b. 1079 in Pallet, France
d. April 21, 1142 in Chalon-sur-Saone, France

Lascelles Abercrombie
English author–poet–critic
• Writings include *Thomas Hardy: A Critical Study*, 1912.
b. January 09, 1881 in Cheshire, England
d. October 27, 1938 in London, England

Dannie Abse
Welsh author
• Wrote award-winning play *House of Cowards*, 1960.
b. September 22, 1923 in Cardiff, Wales

Abu Salms pseud
(Abd al-Karim al-Karmi; "Father of Peace" "Palestine Poet")
Palestinian poet
• Voice of exiled Palestinians, who wrote *The Homeless*, 1964.
b. 1906 in Tulkarm City, Palestine
d. September 13, 1980 in Washington, District of Columbia

Chinua Achebe
(Albert Chinualumogu)
Nigerian author
• Novels reveal Nigerian life, impact of civilization: *Things Fall Apart* , 1958; *Arrow of God*, 1964.
b. November 16, 1930 in Ogidi, Nigeria

Gerrit Achterberg
Dutch poet
• Most prominent Dutch poet of 20th century; won Nat. Prize for Literature, 1949.
b. May 2, 1905 in Neerlangbroek, Netherlands
d. January 17, 1962 in Leusden, Netherlands

Douglas Noel Adams
British author
• Wrote *The Hitchhiker's Guide to the Galaxy*, 1979; made into British TV series shown on PBS.
b. March 11, 1952 in Cambridge, England

Hannah Adams
American author
• Considered first professional American woman writer: *History of New England*, 1799.
b. October 02, 1755 in Medford, Massachusetts
d. December 15, 1831 in Brookline, Massachusetts

Harriet Stratemeyer Adams
(Victor Appleton II; Franklin W Dixon; Laura Lee Hope; Carolyn Keene, pseuds.)
American children's author
• Wrote 200 books for *Hardy Boys; Nancy Drew; Bobbsey Twins* series.
b. December 11, 1892 in Newark, New Jersey
d. March 27, 1982 in Pottersville, New Jersey

Henry Brooks Adams
American historian–author
• Won Pulitzer for *Education of Henry Adams*, 1919; grandson of John Quincy.
b. February 16, 1838 in Boston, Massachusetts
d. March 27, 1918 in Washington, District of Columbia

James Truslow Adams
American historian–author
• Wrote 1922 Pulitzer-winner *Founding of New England and Epic of America*, 1921.
b. October 18, 1878 in Brooklyn, New York
d. May 18, 1949 in Westport, Connecticut

Richard Adams
English author
• Wrote best-seller *Watership Down*, 1972.
b. May 09, 1920 in Newbury, England

William Taylor Adams
(Warren T Ashton; Irving Brown; Brooks McCormick; Oliver Optic pseuds.)
American children's author
• Highly successful boys' adventure tales, in many series, made him rival to Horatio Alger from 1850; one of his period's best-paid writers.
b. July 3, 1822 in Bellingham, Massachusetts
d. March 27, 1897 in Dorchester, Massachusetts

Joy Friederike Victoria Gessner Adamson
(Mrs George Adamson)
Kenyan author–animal expert
• Best known work, *Born Free*, 1960; filmed, 1966.
b. January 2, 1910 in Troppau, Silesia
d. January 03, 1980 in Shaba, Kenya

Aesop
Greek author
• Semi-legendary figure; hundreds of animal fables attributed to him.
b. 620?BC in Phrygia, Asia Minor
d. 560?BC

James Rufus Agee
American author–poet
• Won Pulitzer, 1958, for *A Death in the Family*.
b. November 27, 1909 in Knoxville, Tennessee
d. May 16, 1955 in New York, New York

Nan Hayden Agle
American children's author
• Co-writer of popular "Three Boys" series 1951–.
b. April 13, 1905 in Baltimore, Maryland

S(hmuel) Y(osef) Agnon
(Shmuel Yosef Czaczkes)
Israeli author
• Wrote *Days of Awe*, 1948; first Israeli to win Nobel Prize for literature, 1966.
b. 1888 in Buczacz, Galicia
d. February 17, 1970 in Rehovot, Israel

Marie Catherine Sophie d' Agoult
(Daniel Stern pseud)
French author
• Wrote romances and political, historical essays; mistress of Franz Liszt, friend of George Sand.
b. December 31, 1805 in Frankfurt am Main, Germany
d. March 05, 1876 in Paris, France

Joan Delano Aiken
(Nicholas Dee; Rosie Lee pseuds)
English author
• Popular juvenile, adult mystery writer, who wrote *Night Fall*, 1969.
b. September 04, 1924 in Rye, England

W(illiam) H(arrison) Ainsworth
(Cheviot Tichborne pseud)
English author–editor
• Prolific historic novelist; works include *Jack Sheppard*, 1839; *Tower of London*, 1840.
b. February 04, 1805 in Manchester, England
d. January 03, 1882 in Reigate, England

Anna Akhmatova, pseud
(Anna Andreyevna Gorenko)
Russian author–poet
• Works, which were banned by Soviets until 1959, include *The Willow Tree*, 1940; considered Russia's greatest woman poet.
b. June 11, 1888 in Odessa, Russia
d. March 05, 1966 in Moscow, U.S.S.R.

Alain-Fournier pseud
(Henri Alban Fournier)
French author
• Only completed novel, *Le Grand Meaulnes*, 1913; called outstanding novel of 20th c.
b. October 03, 1886 in La Chapelle-d'Angillon, France
d. September 22, 1914 in Bois de St. Remy, France

Pedro Antonio de Alarcon
Spanish author
• Wrote internationally famous novelette, *The Three-Cornered Hat*, 1874.
b. March 1, 1833 in Guadix, Spain
d. July 2, 1891 in Madrid, Spain

Martha Albrand, pseud
(Katrin Holland; Heidi Huberta other pseuds; Heide Huberta Freybe, given name; Mrs. Sydney J Lamon)
American author
• Mystery writer; wrote award-winning *Desperate Moment*, 1950.
b. September 08, 1914 in Rostock, Germany
d. June 24, 1981 in New York, New York

Louisa May Alcott
American author
• Her early life in New England described in *Little Women*, 1869.
b. November 29, 1832 in Germantown, Pennsylvania
d. March 06, 1888 in Boston, Massachusetts

Henry M Alden
American author–editor
• Dean of American magazine editors; edited *Harper's Monthly*, 1869-1919.
b. November 11, 1836 in Mount Tabor, Vermont
d. October 07, 1919 in New York, New York

Brian Wilson Aldiss
(Jael Cracken; Arch Mendicant; Peter Pica; John Runciman; C C Shackleton, pseuds.)
English author
• Hugo-winning writer who wrote *Moreau's Other Island*, 1980.
b. August 18, 1925 in Dereham, England

Sholom Aleichem, pseud
(Solomon J Rabinowitz; "Yiddish Mark Twain")
Russian author
• Wrote of Jewish Ukranian life; *Tevye* was basis for Broadway's *Fiddler on the Roof*, 1964.
b. February 18, 1859 in Pereyaslavl, Russia
d. May 13, 1916 in New York, New York

Vicente Aleixandre
Spanish poet
• Surrealist who often used metaphors from nature; won Nobel Prize, 1977.
b. April 26, 1898 in Seville, Spain
d. December 14, 1984 in Madrid, Spain

Lloyd Chudley Alexander
American author
• Award-winning children's books include *Westmark*, 1981; Newbery Prize for *The High King*, 1969.
b. January 3, 1924 in Philadelphia, Pennsylvania

Sue Alexander
American children's author
• Won McKenzie Award for children's literature, 1980; wrote *Witch, Goblin, and Ghost* series.
b. August 2, 1933 in Tucson, Arizona

Vittorio Alfieri
Italian poet
• Called Italy's greatest tragic poet; works are political in nature.
b. January 16, 1749 in Asti, Italy
d. October 08, 1803 in Florence, Italy

Nelson Algren
(Nelson Algren Abraham; "Poet of the Chicago Slums")
American author
• Realistic novels include *The Man with the Golden Arm*, about drug addiction, 1949; made into 1955 film with Frank Sinatra.
b. March 28, 1909 in Detroit, Michigan
d. May 09, 1981 in Sag Harbor, New York

Ahmed Ali
Indian author–diplomat
• Founder, Indian Progressive Writers, 1932, who wrote *Twilight in Delhi*, 1966.
b. July 01, 1908 in Delhi, India

Hervey (William Hervey) Allen
American author–poet
• Wrote best-seller, *Anthony Adverse*, 1933; Poe biography, *Israfel*, 1926.
b. December 08, 1889 in Pittsburgh, Pennsylvania
d. December 28, 1949 in Miami, Florida

James Lane Allen
American author
• Popularized Blue Grass KY life in novels *Kentucky Cardinal*, 1894; *The Choir Invisible*, 1897.
b. December 21, 1849 in Lexington, Kentucky
d. February 18, 1925 in New York, New York

Larry Allen
American journalist
• Called "most shot-at" foreign correspondent; won 1942 Pulitzer for war reporting.
b. October 19, 1908 in Mount Savage, Maryland
d. May 12, 1975 in Mexico City, Mexico

Norman William Alley
American photojournalist
• Documented Spanish Civil War, Ethiopian War, WW I, WW II on film.
b. January 22, 1895 in Chicago, Illinois
d. April 01, 1981 in Woodland Hills, California

Kenneth Allsop
English author–journalist–critic
• Popular books include *Bootleggers*, 1961; *Hard Travellin'*, 1967.
b. January 29, 1920 in Leeds, England
d. May 23, 1973 in West Milton, England

A L O E pseud
(Charlotte Maria Tucker; "A Lady of England")
English children's author
• Wrote didactic novels for children, 1850s-90s; noted for famous pen name.
b. May 08, 1821 in Barnet, England
d. December 02, 1893 in Amritsar, India

Joseph Wright Alsop, Jr
American journalist–author
• Noted political columnist, 1935-68; books include *We Accuse*, 1955; brother of Stewart.
b. October 11, 1910 in Avon, Connecticut
d. August 28, 1989 in Washington, District of Columbia

Stewart Johonnot Oliver Alsop
American journalist–author
• Editor, *Saturday Evening Post*, 1958-68; co-wrote *Stay of Execution*, 1973.
b. May 17, 1914 in Avon, Connecticut
d. May 26, 1974 in Washington, District of Columbia

Timothy Mofolorunso Aluko
Nigerian author
• *One Man, One Woman* was first novel published in English in Nigeria, 1959.
b. June 14, 1918 in Ilesha, Nigeria

Alfred Alvarez
English poet–critic
• Influential reviewer-critic who discussed literary suicides in *Savage God*, 1971.
b. August 05, 1929 in London, England

Jorge Amado
Brazilian author
• Brazil's greatest living novelist whose social conscious writings have been translated into more than 30 languages.
b. August 1, 1912 in Bahia, Brazil

Andrei Alekseyevich Amalrik
Russian author
• Human rights advocate who wrote many anti-Soviet works, spent six years in labor camp.
b. May 12, 1938 in Moscow, U.S.S.R.
d. November 11, 1980 in Guadalajara, Spain

Nathaniel Ames
American publisher
• Compiled *Astronomical Diary and Almanack*, 1725-64, model for Benjamin Franklin's *Poor Richard's Almanack*.
b. July 22, 1708 in Bridgewater, Massachusetts
d. July 11, 1764 in Dedham, Massachusetts

Edmond de Amicis
Italian author–essayist
• Most famous work *Cuore*, 1876, known for Tuscan style; used in US to teach Italian.
b. October 21, 1846 in Oneglia, Italy
d. March 12, 1908 in Bordighera, Italy

Kingsley William Amis
(Robert Markham pseud; "Angry Young Man")
English author
• Satirical novelist; several produced as movies, including *Lucky Jim*, 1954.
b. April 16, 1922 in London, England

Martin Amis
English author
• Works include novel, *The Rachel Papers*, 1973; short stories, *Einstein's Monsters*, 1987; son of Kingsley.
b. August 25, 1949 in Oxford, England

Jane Amsterdam
American editor
• First woman to edit major NY daily newspaper, *NY Post*, 1988.
b. 1952

Anacreon
Greek poet
- Lyric poet noted for verse celebrating wine, love.
b. 572?BC in Teos, Asia Minor
d. 488?BC

Hans Christian Andersen
Danish author–poet
- Produced 168 fairy tales, 1835-45; first English translation, 1846.
b. April 02, 1805 in Odense, Denmark
d. August 04, 1875 in Copenhagen, Denmark

C(larence) W(illiam) Anderson
American children's author
- Wrote, illustrated *Billy and Blaze* series, 1936-70.
b. April 12, 1891 in Wahoo, Nebraska
d. March 26, 1971

Jack Northman Anderson
American journalist
- Has written syndicated column, "Washington-Merry-Go-Round," since 1969.
b. October 19, 1922 in Long Beach, California

Sherwood Anderson
American author–poet
- Major work *Winesburg, Ohio*, 1919, short stories of small town life.
b. September 13, 1876 in Camden, Connecticut
d. March 08, 1941 in Colon, Panama

James Frederick Andrews
American editor–author
- Credited with discovering, launching comic strips "Doonesbury"; "Ziggy."
b. October 08, 1936 in Westfield, Massachusetts
d. October 19, 1980

Michael Alford Andrews
English author
- Wrote *The Flight of the Condor*, 1982.
b. June 14, 1939 in Bexhill, England

V(irginia) C(leo) Andrews
American author
- Wrote *Flowers in the Attic*, 1979, filmed 1987; *Petals in the Wind*, 1980.
b. June 06, 1924 in Portsmouth, Virginia
d. December 19, 1986 in Virginia Beach, Virginia

Leonid Nikolayevich Andreyev
(James Lynch pseud; "The Edgar Allan Poe of Russian Literature")
Russian author
- Created macabre, pessimistic short stories: *The Red Laugh*, 1904.
b. June 18, 1871 in Orel, Russia
d. September 12, 1919 in Helsinki, Finland

Ivo Andric
Yugoslav author
- Wrote epic trilogy of Slavic Balkavis *Bridge on the Driva*, 1959; won Nobel Prize for literature, 1961.
b. October 1, 1892 in Travnik, Yugoslavia
d. March 13, 1975 in Belgrade, Yugoslavia

Jerzy Andrzejewski
(George Andrzeyevski pseud)
Polish author
- Best known for novel *Ashes and Diamonds*, 1948.
b. August 19, 1909 in Warsaw, Poland
d. April 19, 1983 in Warsaw, Poland

Norman (Sir Ralph Norman) Angell
English author–lecturer
- Best known work *The Great Illusion*, 1910, describes futility of war; won Nobel Peace Prize, 1933.
b. December 26, 1874 in Holbeach, England
d. October 07, 1967 in Surrey, England

Joan Walsh Anglund
American children's author–illustrator
- Popular illustrator of mouthless children; wrote *A Friend is Someone Who Likes You*, 1958.
b. January 03, 1926 in Hinsdale, Illinois

Walter Hubert Annenberg
American publisher–diplomat
- Owns several newspapers, magazines; sold *TV Guide* to Rupert Murdoch, 1988; ambassador to UK, 1969-75.
b. March 13, 1908 in Milwaukee, Wisconsin

Jay Anson
American author
- Wrote *The Amityville Horror*, 1977; adapted to film, 1979.
b. 1924 in New York, New York
d. March 12, 1980 in Palo Alto, California

Robert Sam Anson
American journalist
- Known for feature articles on controversy surrounding assassination of John F Kennedy, published as book, 1975.
b. 1945

Evelyn Anthony, pseud
(Evelyn Bridget Patricia Stephens Ward-Thomas)
English author
- Writes historical novels, contemporary thrillers; *The Tamarind Seed*, 1971, adapted to film, 1974.
b. July 03, 1928 in London, England

Guillaume Apollinaire
(Guillaume Kostrowitsky)
French author–critic
- Avant-garde writer; coined word "surrealism," promoted early Cubist painters.
b. August 26, 1880 in Rome, Italy
d. November 1, 1918 in Paris, France

Daniel Appleton
American publisher
- Founded D Appleton & Co. Publishers, 1838.
b. December 1, 1785 in Haverhill, Massachusetts
d. March 27, 1849 in New York, New York

Louis Marie Antoine Alfred Aragon
French poet
- One of founders of French Surrealism, 1924.
b. October 03, 1897 in Paris, France
d. December 24, 1982 in Paris, France

Jeffrey Howard Archer
English author–politician
- MP, 1969-74; wrote *Kane and Abel*, 1979; *First Among Equals*, 1984.
b. April 15, 1940

Ludovico Ariosto
Italian poet
- Produced finest Italian romantic epic, *Orlando Furioso*, 1532.
b. September 08, 1474 in Reggio, Italy
d. July 06, 1533 in Ferrara, Italy

Aristotle
Greek author–philosopher
- Member Plato's Academy, 367-347 BC; created Logic, the science of reasoning.
b. 384BC in Chalcidice, Greece
d. 322BC in Chalcis, Greece

Richard Willard Armour
American poet
- Whimsical poet known for poking fun at everything; poems usually four lines long; had syndicated newspaper column "Armour's Armory."
b. July 15, 1906 in San Pedro, California
d. February 28, 1989 in Claremont, California

Charlotte Armstrong
American author
- Suspense murder-mystery writer; won Poe award for *A Dram of Poison*, 1956.
b. May 02, 1905 in Vulcan, Michigan
d. July 18, 1969 in Glendale, California

William Howard Armstrong
American children's author–educator
- Wrote 1972 Newbery winner, *Sounder*.
b. September 14, 1914 in Lexington, Virginia

Matthew Arnold
English author–critic
• Oxford professor, known for poem "Dover Beach," 1853; social criticism *Culture and Anarchy*, 1869; son of Thomas.
b. December 24, 1822 in Laleham, England
d. April 15, 1888 in Liverpool, England

Oren Arnold
American children's author–editor
• Wrote over 2,000 magazine articles, tales of western America: *Wit of the West*, 1980.
b. July 2, 1900 in Minden, Texas

Harriette Louisa Simpson Arnow
American author
• Wrote novels about Appalachian life: *The Dollmaker*, 1954, made into TV movie starring Jane Fonda, 1983.
b. July 07, 1908 in Wayne County, Kentucky
d. March 22, 1986 in Washtenaw County, Michigan

Herbert Asbury
American author
• Wrote *The Barbary Coast*, 1933; *The French Quarter*, 1936.
b. September 01, 1891 in Farmington, Missouri
d. February 24, 1963 in New York, New York

John Lawrence Ashbery
(Jonas Berry pseud)
American author
• Won 1976 Pulitzer for narrative verse, *Self-Portrait in a Convex Mirror*.
b. July 28, 1927 in Rochester, New York

Harry Scott Ashmore
American editor–author
• Pulitzer-winning editorial writer, 1958; books include *Hearts and Minds*, 1982.
b. July 27, 1916 in Greenville, South Carolina

Isaac Asimov
(Paul French pseud)
American author–biochemist
• Leading popular scientist; wrote over 200 books; coined term "robotics."
b. January 02, 1920 in Petrovichi, U.S.S.R.

Emma Alice Margot Asquith
(Countess of Oxford and Asquith)
English author
• Eccentric, outspoken, shrewd; great influence on social, fashionable English life.
b. February 02, 1864 in Peebleshire, England
d. July 28, 1945 in London, England

Gavin Astor
(Lord Astor of Hever)
British publisher
• Head of Astor dynasty; pres., Times Newspapers Ltd. from 1967.
b. June 01, 1918
d. June 28, 1984 in Tillypronie, Scotland

Miguel Angel Asturias
Guatemalan author–diplomat
• Won Nobel Prize, 1967; wrote *Strong Wind*, 1969; *Le Miroir de Lida Sal*, 1967.
b. October 19, 1899 in Guatemala City, Guatemala
d. June 09, 1974 in Madrid, Spain

Margaret Eleanor Atwood
Canadian author–poet
• The most widely read writer in Canada; wrote best-selling novel *The Handmaid's Tale*, 1966.
b. November 18, 1939 in Ottawa, Ontario

Louis Auchincloss
(Andrew Lee pseud)
American author
• Wrote over 30 books, including *The Indifferent Children*, 1947.
b. September 27, 1917 in Lawrence, New York

W(ystan) H(ugh) Auden
English poet
• Won Pulitzer for verse *Age of Anxiety*, 1948.
b. February 21, 1907 in York, England
d. September 28, 1973 in Vienna, Austria

Jacques Audiberti
French author–poet
• Wrote of man, nature: *La Na*, 1944; *Monorail*, 1964.
b. March 25, 1899 in Antibes, France
d. July 1, 1965 in Paris, France

Jean Marie Auel
American author
• Wrote *The Clan of the Cave Bear*, 1980; *The Valley of Horses*, 1982.
b. February 18, 1936 in Chicago, Illinois

Richard Aungervyle
(Richard de Bury)
English author–clergyman
• Bibliophile; wrote classic tribute to books: *Philobiblon*, 1473.
b. January 24, 1281 in Bury Saint Edmunds, England
d. 1345

Jane Austen
English author
• Her books on family life in rural England and comedies have withstood time in the changing outside world: *Pride and Prejudice*, 1813, *Sense and Sensibility*, 1811.
b. December 16, 1775 in Steventon, England
d. July 18, 1817 in Winchester, England

Alfred Austin
English poet–critic
• Succeeded Tennyson as poet laureate, 1896; wrote *The Human Tragedy*, 1862.
b. May 3, 1835 in Headingley, England
d. June 02, 1913 in Ashford, England

Mary Hunter Austin
American author
• Described American Indian life, literature: *Land of Little Rain*, 1903.
b. September 09, 1868 in Carlinville, Illinois
d. August 13, 1934 in Santa Fe, New Mexico

Michael Angelo Avallone, Jr
American author
• Wrote over 1,000 paperbacks under dozens of pseuds.; created sleuth Ed Noon.
b. October 27, 1924 in New York, New York

Marcel Ayme
French author
• Wrote *The Hollow Field*, 1933; *The Conscience of Love*, 1962.
b. March 28, 1902 in Joigny, France
d. October 14, 1967 in Paris, France

William Edmonstoune Aytoun
Scottish author–educator
• Popular *Blackwood* contributor; wrote *Firmilian*, 1854.
b. June 21, 1813 in Edinburgh, Scotland
d. August 04, 1865 in Elgin, Scotland

Irving Babbitt
American author–critic
• A leader of new humanism; wrote *Masters of Modern French Criticism*, 1912.
b. August 02, 1865 in Dayton, Ohio
d. July 15, 1933 in Cambridge, Massachusetts

Isaac Emmanuelovich Babel
Russian author
• Short stories collected in *Jewish Tales*, 1927; disappeared into concentration camp, 1939.
b. 1894 in Odessa, Russia
d. 1941 in Siberia, U.S.S.R.

Babrius
Greek author
• Wrote Greek fables similar to Aesop; many of these became known, 1800s.
b. 2ndAD

Bacchylides
Greek poet
• Only fragments of work still exist; some discovered in 1800s.
b. 516?BC
d. 450?BC

Bert Coates Bach
American author
• Wrote *Fiction for Composition*, 1968; *Drama for Composition*, 1973.
b. December 14, 1936 in Jenkins, Kentucky

Richard David Bach
American author
• Wrote allegorical novel *Jonathan Livingston Seagull;* filmed, 1973.
b. June 23, 1936 in Oak Park, Illinois

Bert(ram Mark) Bacharach
American journalist–author
• Father of Burt Bacharach; had syndicated column, "Now See Here!", 1959-83.
b. March 1, 1898 in Philadelphia, Pennsylvania
d. September 15, 1983 in New York, New York

Irving Bacheller
American author
• Wrote *Eben Holden*, 1900.
b. August 12, 1859 in Pierpont, New York
d. February 24, 1950 in White Plains, New York

Delia Salter Bacon
American author
• Developed theory that Shakespeare's plays were written by Francis Bacon.
b. February 02, 1811 in Tallmadge, Ohio
d. September 02, 1859 in Hartford, Connecticut

Leonard Bacon
American poet
• Verse volumes include 1940 Pulitzer-winner, *Sunderland Capture and Other Poems*.
b. May 26, 1887 in Solvay, New York
d. January 01, 1954 in South Kingston, Rhode Island

Karl Baedeker
German publisher
• Issued travel handbooks in German, 1820s; later published them in French, English.
b. November 03, 1801 in Essen, Germany
d. October 04, 1859 in Koblenz, Germany

Gamaliel Bailey
American social reformer–editor
• Edited antislavery periodicals, including *National Era*, which first serialized *Uncle Tom's Cabin*, 1851-52; died of illness at sea.
b. December 03, 1807 in Mount Holly, New Jersey
d. June 05, 1859

H(enry) C(hristopher) Bailey
English author
• Created fictional detectives Reggie Fortune, Joshua Clunk; wrote *Mr. Fortune's Practice*, 1922.
b. February 01, 1878 in London, England
d. March 24, 1961

Hugh Baillie
American journalist
• Influential war correspondent known for interviews with General MacArthur, Hitler, Mussolini, Emperor Hirohito.
b. October 23, 1890 in Brooklyn, New York
d. March 01, 1966 in La Jolla, California

Beryl Bainbridge
English author
• Works include fantasy about Hitler, *Young Adolphe*, 1978; prize-winning novel, *The Bottle Factory Outing*, 1974.
b. November 21, 1933 in Liverpool, England

Carlos Heard Baker
American author
• Wrote *Ernest Hemingway: A Life Story*, 1969.
b. May 05, 1909 in Biddeford, Maine
d. April 18, 1987 in Princeton, New Jersey

Charlotte Baker
American author
• Wrote *A Sombrero for Miss Brown*, 1941; *House on the River*, 1948.
b. August 31, 1910 in Nacogdoches, Texas

Dorothy Dodds Baker
American author
• Writings include *Young Man With a Horn*, 1938; *Cassandra at the Wedding*, 1962.
b. April 21, 1907 in Missoula, Montana
d. June 18, 1968 in Terra Bella, California

Laura Nelson Baker
American author
• Writings include *The Red Mountain*, 1946; *From Whales to Snails*, 1970.
b. January 07, 1911 in Humboldt, Iowa

Ray Stannard Baker
(David Grayson pseud)
American author
• Won Pulitzer for *Woodrow Wilson: Life and Letters*, 1940.
b. April 17, 1870 in Lansing, Michigan
d. July 12, 1946 in Amherst, Massachusetts

Russell Wayne Baker
American journalist–author
• Columnist, *NY Times;* won Pulitzer, 1982, for autobiography *Growing Up*.
b. August 14, 1925 in Loudoun County, Virginia

Samm Sinclair Baker
American author
• Called America's "leading self-help author"; wrote *The Complete Scarsdale Medical Diet*, 1979, with Herman Tarnower.
b. July 29, 1909 in Paterson, New Jersey

Nigel Marlin Balchin
(Mark Spade pseud)
English author–farmer
• Wrote novel *Small Back Room*, 1934; thriller *Mine Own Executioner*, 1945.
b. December 03, 1908 in Wiltshire, England
d. May 17, 1970 in London, England

Faith Baldwin
American author
• Romantic novelist; wrote *American Family*, 1935.
b. October 01, 1893 in New Rochelle, New York
d. March 19, 1978 in Norwalk, Connecticut

James Arthur Baldwin
American author
• Described black life in US; best known work *Go Tell It On the Mountain*, 1953.
b. August 02, 1924 in New York, New York
d. November 3, 1987 in Saint Paul-de-Vence, France

John Dudley Ball, Jr
American author
• Best known for mystery novel *In the Heat of the Night*, 1965, adapted into 1976 Oscar-winning film starring Sidney Poitier.
b. July 08, 1911 in Schenectady, New York
d. October 15, 1988 in Encino, California

Ian Ballantine
American publisher
• One of first to produce hardcover, paperback editions simultaneously.
b. February 15, 1916 in New York, New York

J(ames) G(raham) Ballard
English author
• Wrote best-selling novel *Empire of the Sun*, 1984; most books are surrealistic fiction, with apocalyptic themes.
b. November 15, 1930 in Shanghai, China

Margaret (Violet Margaret Livingstone) Ballinger

(Margaret Hodgson pseud)
South African author–politician
• MP, representing black Africans; wrote *From Union to Apartheid, Trek to Isolation*, 1970.
b. January 11, 1894 in Glasgow, Scotland
d. February 07, 1980 in Cape Province, South Africa

Honore de Balzac

French author
• Developed the realistic novel; describes French society in masterpiece *Comedie Humaine*, 1900.
b. May 2, 1799 in Tours, France
d. August 18, 1850 in Paris, France

Matteo (Matthew) Bandello

Italian author
• Short stories imitate Boccaccio, are probable source of Shakespeare's *Romeo and Juliet*.
b. 1485 in Castelnuovo Scrivia, Italy
d. September 13, 1562 in Bassens, France

Viscount Edward Henry Harold Ward Bangor

English journalist
• BBC foreign correspondent, 1946-60; wrote *Number One Boy*, 1969.
b. November 05, 1905 in England

Lester Bangs

American critic–author
• Rock critic *Rolling Stone, Village Voice*; editor *Creem* magazine; recorded album *Juke Savages on the Brazos*, 1981.
b. December 1948
d. April 3, 1982 in New York, New York

Helen Bannerman

Scottish children's author
• Wrote controversial classic *Story of Little Black Sambo*, 1900.
b. 1863 in Edinburgh, Scotland
d. October 13, 1946 in Edinburgh, Scotland

Margaret Culkin Banning

American author
• Wrote over 30 novels on marriage, parenthood: *Echo Answers*, 1960.
b. March 18, 1891 in Buffalo, New York
d. January 04, 1982 in Tryon, North Carolina

John Barbour

Scottish clergyman–poet
• Wrote epic poem *The Bruce*, 1375, celebrating Scottish emancipation from England.
b. 1316
d. March 13, 1395 in Aberdeen, Scotland

Alexander Barclay

English poet
• Known for *Ship of Fools*, 1509, based on Sebastian Brant's earlier satire.
b. 1475
d. June 1, 1552 in Croydon, England

Arturo Barea

Spanish author
• Wrote trilogy *Forging of a Rebel*, 1946.
b. September 2, 1897 in Spain
d. December 24, 1957 in Faringdon, England

Clive Barker

English author
• Writes horror fiction; works include *The Damnation Game*, 1985, *The Inhuman Condition*, 1986.
b. October 05, 1952 in Liverpool, England

George Granville Barker

English author–poet
• Works include *Eros in Dogma*, 1944; *Collected Poems*, 1957.
b. February 26, 1913 in Loughton, England

Joel Barlow

American diplomat–journalist
• Friend of Thomas Paine; best-known poem *The Hasty-Pudding*, 1793.
b. March 24, 1754 in Redding, Connecticut
d. December 24, 1812 in Zarnowiec, Poland

Clive Alexander Barnes

English journalist–critic–author
• Well-known dance, drama critic; with *NY Post* since 1978.
b. May 13, 1927 in London, England

Djuna Barnes

(Lydia Steptoe pseud)
American author–journalist
• Writings influenced by James Joyce and T S Eliot; wrote novel *Nightwood*, 1933.
b. June 12, 1892 in Cornwall-on-Hudson, New York
d. June 18, 1982 in New York, New York

Julian Patrick Barnes

English author
• Best known for novel *Flaubert's Parrot*, 1984; TV critic, 1977-86.
b. January 19, 1946 in Leicester, England

Margaret Ayer Barnes

American author–dramatist
• Wrote Pulitzer novel *Years of Grace*, 1930.
b. April 08, 1886 in Chicago, Illinois
d. October 26, 1967

Natalie Clifford Barney

American author
• Hostess of celebrated Parisian literary salon, 1920s-30s; wrote risque memoirs.
b. October 31, 1876 in Dayton, Ohio
d. February 02, 1972 in Paris, France

Rona Barrett

(Rona Burstein; Mrs William A Trowbridge)
American journalist
• Gossip columnist since 1957; fan magazines *Rona Barrett's Hollywood, Rona Barrett's Gossip* sold over one million copies, 1974.
b. October 08, 1936 in New York, New York

William Edmund Barrett

American author
• Two of his novels, *The Left Hand of God*, 1951, and *The Lilies of the Field*, 1962, were made into movies.
b. November 16, 1900 in New York, New York
d. September 17, 1986 in Denver, Colorado

Sir James Matthew Barrie

Scottish author
• Best known for *Little Minister*, 1897; *Peter Pan*, 1904.
b. May 9, 1860 in Kirriemuir, Scotland
d. June 19, 1937 in London, England

Clarence Walker Barron

American publisher–editor
• Published *Wall Street Journal*, starting 1901; *Barron's Financial Weekly*, starting 1921.
b. July 02, 1855 in Boston, Massachusetts
d. October 02, 1928 in Battle Creek, Michigan

Marjorie (Ruth) Barrows

(Jack Alden; Noel Ames pseuds)
American author–editor
• Magazine editor, 1922-66, whose writings include *Little Red Balloon*, 1979.
b. 1902 in Chicago, Illinois
d. March 29, 1983 in Evanston, Illinois

John Simmons Barth

American author
• Won National Book Award in Fiction, 1973; books include *The Open Decision*, 1970.
b. May 27, 1930 in Cambridge, Maryland

Donald Barthelme

American author
• Known for short stories, satires, novels describing absurdity of 20th c. life through use of understatement; gained national fame with novella *Snow White*, 1967, originally published in *New Yorker*.
b. April 07, 1931 in Philadelphia, Pennsylvania
d. July 23, 1989 in Houston, Texas

John Bartlett
American lexicographer–publisher
• Edited first edition of *Familiar Quotations;* published 1855.
b. June 14, 1820 in Plymouth, Massachusetts
d. December 03, 1905 in Cambridge, Massachusetts

Bruce Barton
American author–advertising executive
• Wrote best-seller *Man Nobody Knows,* 1925, depicting Jesus as prototype of successful businessman.
b. August 05, 1886 in Robbins, Tennessee
d. July 05, 1967 in New York, New York

Luigi Giorgio Barzini, Jr
Italian author
• Best known for works about Americans, Italians; *Americans Are Alone in the World; The Italians,* 1964.
b. December 21, 1908 in Milan, Italy
d. March 3, 1984 in Rome, Italy

Basho
Japanese poet
• Zen Buddhist haiku master.
b. 1644 in Ueno, Iga, Japan
d. November 28, 1694 in Osaka, Japan

Ben Bassett
American journalist
• Foreign news editor, Associated Press, 1948-73; supervised coverage of Korean, Vietnam wars.
b. October 3, 1909 in Topeka, Kansas
d. October 14, 1987 in New Rochelle, New York

Walter Jackson Bate
American educator–author
• Won Pulitzers for biographies of John Keats, 1963, Samuel Johnson, 1977.
b. May 23, 1918 in Mankato, Minnesota

H(erbert) E(rnest) Bates
English author
• Wrote over 50 books including *The Two Sisters,* 1926; books on WW II.
b. May 16, 1905 in Rushden, England
d. January 29, 1974 in Canterbury, England

Katherine Lee Bates
American poet–educator
• Best known for writing hymn-patriotic song "America the Beautiful," 1911.
b. August 12, 1859 in Falmouth, Massachusetts
d. March 28, 1929 in Wellesley, Massachusetts

Charles Pierre Baudelaire
French poet
• Best-known poems contained in *Les Fleurs du Mal,* 1857.
b. April 09, 1821 in Paris, France
d. August 31, 1867 in Paris, France

(Lyman) Frank Baum
American author–journalist
• Wrote *The Wizard of Oz,* 1900.
b. May 15, 1856 in Chittenango, New York
d. May 06, 1919 in Hollywood, California

Vicki Baum
American author
• Wrote best-seller *Grand Hotel,* 1929, film starred Greta Garbo, 1932.
b. January 24, 1888 in Vienna, Austria
d. August 29, 1960 in Hollywood, California

Nina Mary Mabey Bawden
(Nina Mary Mabey Kark)
English author
• Writings include *Eyes of Green,* 1953; *Familiar Passions,* 1979.
b. January 19, 1925 in London, England

Sylvia Beach
American publisher
• Printed James Joyce's *Ulysses,* 1919, when no other publisher would.
b. 1887 in Baltimore, Maryland
d. October 06, 1962 in Paris, France

Erastus Flavel Beadle
American publisher–printer
• Originated the dime novel with *Malaeska,* 1860.
b. September 11, 1821 in Pierstown, New York
d. December 18, 1894 in Cooperstown, New York

Alex W(inkler III) Bealer
American children's author
• Writings include *The Picture-Skin Story,* 1957; *The Log Cabin,* 1978.
b. March 06, 1921 in Valdosta, Georgia
d. March 17, 1980 in Atlanta, Georgia

James Andrews Beard
American chef–author
• Popularized American cooking; book *Beard on Bread,* 1973, was definitive text on home baking.
b. May 05, 1903 in Portland, Oregon
d. January 23, 1985 in New York, New York

Anne Beatts
American writer
• Won Emmys for "Saturday Night Live," 1976, 1977, 1980.
b. 1948

Sir John Beaumont
English poet
• Wrote *Metamorphosis of Tobacco,* 1602, *Bosworth Field,* 1629; introduced heroic couplet; brother of Francis.
b. 1583 in Grace-Dieu, England
d. April 19, 1627 in London, England

Simone de Beauvoir
French author
• Best known for attack on inferior role of women: *The Second Sex,* 1949.
b. January 09, 1908 in Paris, France
d. April 14, 1986 in Paris, France

Marilyn (Mohr) Beck
American journalist–editor
• Hollywood columnist who wrote *Marilyn Beck's Hollywood,* 1973.
b. December 17, 1928 in Chicago, Illinois

Stephen David Becker
(Steve Dodge pseud)
American author
• Writings include *The Season of the Stranger,* 1951; *The Last Mandarin,* 1979.
b. March 31, 1927 in Mount Vernon, New York

Burdetta Faye Beebe
(B F Johnson; B F Beebe pseuds)
American children's author
• Writings include *Run, Light Buck, Run!,* 1962; *African Elephants,* 1968.
b. February 04, 1920 in Marshall, Oklahoma

Max (Sir Henry Maximilian) Beerbohm
English drama critic–author
• Writings include essays; wrote novel *Zuleika Dobson,* 1911; vol. of pictorial caricatures: *Rossetti and His Circle,* 1922.
b. August 24, 1872 in London, England
d. May 2, 1956 in Rapallo, Italy

Brendan Behan
Irish dramatist–author
• His humorous, vibrant books capture spirit of Irish nationalism; best known for autobiographical *Borstal Boy,* 1958 and self-destructive behavior.
b. February 09, 1923 in Dublin, Ireland
d. March 2, 1964 in Dublin, Ireland

Rene Lucien Belbenoit
French author
• Account of conditions on Devil's Island, *My Escape from Devil's Island,* led to abolition of penal colony.
b. 1889 in Paris, France
d. February 26, 1959 in Lucerne Valley, California

Vissarion Belinsky
Russian author
• Best-known Russian critic; *Literary Reviews,* 1834, traced Russian literary development.
b. May 3, 1811 in Sveaborg, Finland
d. May 26, 1848 in Saint Petersburg, Russia

Saul Bellow
American author
• Won Pulitzer Prize, 1976, for *Humboldt's Gift;* won Nobel Prize in literature, 1976.
b. July 1, 1915 in Lachine, Quebec

Andrey Bely, pseud
(Boris Nikolayevich Bugayev)
Russian poet
• Symbolist; wrote poetic "symphony," *Popal,* 1909; novel, *Petersburg,* 1913.
b. October 14, 1880 in Moscow, Russia
d. January 08, 1934 in Moscow, U.S.S.R.

Ludwig Bemelmans
American author
• Wrote *Hotel Bemelmans,* 1946; *Madeline* children's stories, 1953-62; won Caldecott for *Madeline's Rescue,* 1954.
b. April 27, 1898 in Tirol, Austria
d. October 01, 1962 in New York, New York

Samuel Flagg Bemis
American historian–editor
• Won Pulitzers for *Pinckney's Treaty,* 1926; *John Quincy Adams and Foundation of American Foreign Policy,* 1949.
b. October 2, 1891 in Worcester, Massachusetts
d. September 26, 1973 in Bridgeport, Connecticut

Margot Benary-Isbert
American author
• Writings include award-winning children's books, *The Ark,* 1953; *Blue Mystery,* 1957.
b. December 02, 1899 in Saarbrucken, Germany

Nathaniel Goddard Benchley
American author
• Son of Robert Benchley; writer of humor, historical novels: *Lassiter's Folly,* 1971.
b. November 13, 1915 in Newton, Massachusetts
d. December 14, 1981 in Boston, Massachusetts

Peter Bradford Benchley
American author–journalist
• Wrote novels *Jaws,* 1974; *The Deep,* 1976; *The Island,* 1979, all of which were filmed.
b. May 08, 1940 in New York, New York

Robert Charles Benchley
(Guy Fawkes pseud)
American author
• Wrote *Chips Off the Old Benchley,* 1949; won Oscar, 1935, for *How to Sleep.*
b. September 15, 1889 in Worcester, Massachusetts
d. November 21, 1945 in New York, New York

David Benedictus
English author
• Satiric novels include *Rabbi's Wife,* 1976.
b. September 16, 1938 in London, England

Stephen Vincent Benet
American author–poet
• Won Pulitzers for poetry volumes *John Brown's Body,* 1928; *Western Star,* 1943.
b. July 22, 1898 in Bethlehem, Pennsylvania
d. March 13, 1943 in New York, New York

William Rose Benet
American author–journalist
• Won Pulitzer Prize, 1941, for autobiographical verse *The Dust Which Is God;* brother of Stephen V.
b. February 02, 1886 in Fort Hamilton, New York
d. May 04, 1950 in New York, New York

Curtis G Benjamin
American publisher
• Pres., chm., McGraw-Hill, 1928-66; excellence in publishing award named for him.
b. July 13, 1901 in Providence, Kentucky
d. November 05, 1983 in Norwalk, Connecticut

Arnold Bennett
English author
• Known for realistic novels: *Old Wives Tales,* 1908; *Five Towns* series.
b. May 27, 1867 in Staffordshire, England
d. March 27, 1931

James Gordon Bennett
American newspaper publisher
• Founded *NY Herald* with $500, 1835.
b. 1795 in Keith, Scotland
d. June 01, 1872 in New York, New York

James Gordon Bennett, Jr
American author–publisher
• Financed Stanley's expedition to find Livingstone, 1869-72.
b. May 1, 1841 in New York, New York
d. May 14, 1918 in Bealieu, France

Lerone Bennett, Jr
American editor
• Editor, *Ebony* magazine, 1958-; wrote *Challenge of Blackness,* 1972.
b. October 17, 1928 in Clarksdale, Mississippi

Sally Benson
American author
• Wrote best-sellers *Junior Miss,* 1941; *Meet Me In St. Louis,* 1942.
b. September 03, 1900 in Saint Louis, Missouri
d. July 19, 1972 in Woodland Hills, California

Edmund Clerihew Bentley
English author–journalist
• Wrote detective classic *Trent's Last Case,* 1912.
b. July 1, 1875 in London, England
d. March 3, 1956 in London, England

Richard Bentley
English author–clergyman–critic
• Proved *Epistles of Phalaris* were spurious, 1669; first to use philology as test of authenticity.
b. January 27, 1662 in Oulton, England
d. July 14, 1742

William Benton
American publisher–politician
• Dem. senator from CT 1949-53; started Voice of America broadcasts; owner, publisher, *Encyclopedia Britannica,* 1942-73.
b. April 01, 1900 in Minneapolis, Minnesota
d. March 18, 1973 in New York, New York

John Berger
English author
• Novels include *The Foot of Clive,* 1962; *Corher's Freedom,* 1964.
b. November 05, 1926 in London, England

Terry Berger
American author
• Juvenile writings include *Black Fairy Tales,* 1969; *I Have Feelings,* 1971.
b. August 11, 1933 in New York, New York

Thomas Louis Berger
American author
• Best known for style of dealing with absurdity of American life: *Little Big Man,* 1964, adopted to film, 1970.
b. July 2, 1924 in Cincinnati, Ohio

George Berkeley
Irish author–philosopher
• Wrote *Principals of Human Knowledge,* 1710.
b. March 12, 1685 in Ireland
d. January 14, 1753 in Oxford, England

Sir Isaiah Berlin
English author–educator–philosopher
• Breadth of his erudition is suggested in his books on philosophy, political theory, intellectual history, and biography *Historical Inevitability,* 1955, *The Age of Enlightenment,* 1956.
b. June 06, 1909 in Riga, Russia

Charles L Frambach Berlitz
(Charles Francois Bertin pseud)
American author
• Wrote controversial *The Bermuda Triangle,* 1974; grandson of Maximilian, founder of Berlitz School of Languages.
b. November 22, 1913 in New York, New York

Georges Bernanos
French author
• Father of modern theological novel who wrote *The Diary of a Country Priest*, 1937.
b. May 05, 1888 in Paris, France
d. July 05, 1948 in Paris, France

Andrew Milroy Bernard
(Andrew Milroy Fleming-Bernard; "Master Bernard the Blind Poet")
British poet
• Poet laureate to Henry VII, Henry VIII.
b. in Toulouse, France
d. 1523

Carl Bernstein
American journalist–author
• With Bob Woodward wrote account of Watergate break-in, cover-up, *All the President's Men*, 1974.
b. February 14, 1944 in Washington, District of Columbia

Robert L(ouis) Bernstein
American publisher
• President, Random House, 1966-75; chairman, 1975–.
b. January 05, 1923 in New York, New York

Sid(ney Ralph) Bernstein
American editor–business executive
• Chm., exec. committee, Crain Communications, 1973–; pres., 1964-73.
b. January 29, 1907 in Chicago, Illinois

Theodore Menline Bernstein
American journalist
• With *NY Times* since 1925; wrote *The Careful Writer*, 1965.
b. November 17, 1904 in New York, New York
d. June 27, 1979 in New York, New York

James Gomer Berry
(Viscount Kemsley)
Welsh publisher
• Largest newspaper proprietor in Britain; sold holdings to Roy H Thomson, 1959.
b. May 07, 1883 in Merthyr Tydfil, Wales
d. February 06, 1968 in Monte Carlo, Monaco

Wendell Berry
American poet
• Wrote *Gift of Good Land*, 1981.
b. August 05, 1934 in Henry County, Kentucky

John Berryman
American author–poet
• Won Pulitzer Prize, 1964, for *77 Dream Songs*.
b. October 25, 1914 in McAlester, Oklahoma
d. January 07, 1972 in Minneapolis, Minnesota

Sir Walter Besant
English author
• Wrote *All Sorts and Conditions of Men*, 1882; founded Society of Authors, 1884.
b. August 14, 1836 in Portsmouth, England
d. June 09, 1901 in London, England

Oswald Herbert Best
English children's author
• Educational books include *Carolina Gold*, 1961.
b. March 25, 1894 in Chester, England

Alfred Bester
American author
• Science fiction novelist; won first Hugo for *The Demolished Man*, 1953; best known work *Tiger! Tiger!*, later published as *The Stars My Destination*, 1974.
b. December 18, 1913 in New York, New York
d. 1987 in Doylestown, Pennsylvania

Sir John Betjeman
English poet
• Poet laureate, 1972-84; style of simple words in easy swinging rhythm sold more copies than any poet since Kipling.
b. August 28, 1906 in Highgate, England
d. May 19, 1984 in Trebetherick, England

Chaim Nachman Bialik
Israeli author–poet
• Greatest modern Hebrew poet; first work *In the City of Slaughter*, 1903.
b. January 09, 1873 in Rady, Russia
d. July 04, 1934 in Tel Aviv, Palestine

Margery Williams Bianco
American children's author
• Wrote popular "toy" stories for children: *Velveteen Rabbit*, 1922; *Poor Cecco*, 1925.
b. July 22, 1881 in London, England
d. September 04, 1944 in New York, New York

Earl Derr Biggers
American author
• Created Chinese fictional detective Charlie Chan; first appeared in *House Without a Key*, 1925.
b. August 26, 1884 in Warren, Ohio
d. April 05, 1933 in Pasadena, California

Stephen Birmingham
American author
• Writes histories of the rich: *Jacqueline Bouvier Kennedy Onassis*, 1978; *Duchess*, 1981.
b. May 28, 1931 in Hartford, Connecticut

Earle (Alfred Earle) Birney
Canadian poet–author–critic
• Wrote *David and Other Poems*, 1942; *Turvey*, 1949; *Trial of a City*, 1952.
b. May 13, 1904 in Calgary, Alberta

Elizabeth Bishop
American poet
• Won Pulitzer for *North and South: A Gold Spring*, 1955.
b. February 08, 1911 in Worcester, Massachusetts
d. October 06, 1979 in Boston, Massachusetts

Isabella Lucy Bird Bishop
English traveler–author
• First woman member, Royal Geographic Society, 1892; wrote *Unbeaten Tracks in Japan*, 1880.
b. 1832 in Yorkshire, England
d. 1904 in Edinburgh, Scotland

Jim (James Alonzo) Bishop
American author–journalist
• Syndicated newspaper columnist for 27 yrs.; wrote many historical books: *The Day Lincoln Was Shot*, 1955, sold over three million copies.
b. November 21, 1907 in Jersey City, New Jersey
d. July 26, 1987 in Delray Beach, Florida

Bjornstjerne Martinius Bjornson
Norwegian poet–political leader
• Nat. poet of Norway; shared Nobel Prize for literature, 1902.
b. December 08, 1832 in Kvikne, Norway
d. April 26, 1910 in Paris, France

Winifred Sweet Black
(Annie Laurie psued)
American journalist
• One of original women reporters; often wrote in first person; inaugurated many reforms.
b. October 14, 1863 in Wisconsin
d. May 26, 1936 in San Francisco, California

Richard Doddridge Blackmore
English author
• Romantic novels include classic *Lorna Doone*, 1869.
b. June 07, 1825 in Longworth, England
d. January 2, 1900 in Teddington, England

Sir William Blackstone
English judge–author
• Wrote *Commentaries on the Laws of England*, 1765-69, in four vols.
b. July 1, 1723 in London, England
d. February 14, 1780 in London, England

Sir Basil Henry Blackwell
English publisher
• BH Blackwell, Ltd., founder, chmn., 1922-69; pres., 1969–.
b. May 29, 1889 in Oxford, England
d. April 09, 1984 in Oxford, England

Betsy Talbot Blackwell

American editor
• Editor-in-chief, *Mademoiselle* magazine, 1937-71; raised literary standards of women's magazines.
b. 1905 in New York, New York
d. February 04, 1985 in Norwalk, Connecticut

Earl Blackwell

(Samuel Earl Blackwell Jr)
American author-publisher
• Organizer, first chmn., Theater Hall of Fame, 1972.
b. May 03, 1913 in Atlanta, Georgia

Quentin Blake

English children's author-illustrator
• Writings include *Jack and Nancy*, 1969; *The Bear's Water Picnic*, 1970.
b. December 16, 1932 in England

Vicente Blasco-Ibanez

Spanish author
• Wrote realistic novels *Blood and Sand*, 1913; *Four Horseman of the Apocalypse*, 1918.
b. 1867 in Valencia, Spain
d. 1928 in Menton, France

William Peter Blatty

American author
• Wrote *The Exorcist*, 1971; sold over 10 million copies; on best-seller list 55 weeks.
b. January 07, 1928 in New York, New York

Robert Marvin Bleiberg

American publisher-editor
• Publisher, editorial director, *Barron's National Business and Financial Weekly*.
b. June 21, 1924 in Brooklyn, New York

James Benjamin Blish

American author
• Science fiction writer; won Hugo for *A Case of Conscience*, 1958.
b. May 23, 1921 in East Orange, New Jersey
d. July 3, 1975 in Henley-on-Thames, England

Baroness Karen Christentze Blixen

(Pierre Andrezel; Isak Dinesen pseuds)
Danish author
• Known for memoirs of life in Kenya, *Out of Africa*, 1937; film version won best picture Oscar, 1985.
b. April 17, 1885 in Rungsted, Denmark
d. September 07, 1962 in Rungsted, Denmark

Allan David Bloom

American educator-author
• Wrote best-selling *Closing of the American Mind*, 1987, damning critique of American higher education.
b. September 14, 1930 in Indianapolis, Indiana

Harry Bloom

South African author-lawyer
• Imprisoned for writing award-winning, anti-apartheid novel *Episode*, 1956.
b. 1913 in South Africa
d. July 28, 1981 in Canterbury, England

Ursula Bloom

(Shiela Burns; Mary Essex; Rachel Harvey; Deborah Mann; Lozania Prole; Sara Sloane, pseuds.)
English author
• Prolific literary figure who wrote more than 500 novels, 1924-79, including *Secret Lover*, 1930.
b. 1893 in Chelmsford, England
d. October 29, 1984 in London, England

Charles Blount

English author
• Deist, known for *The Two First Books of Philostratus, Concerning Life of Apollonius Tyaneus*, 1680.
b. April 27, 1654 in Upper Holloway, England
d. August 1693

Judy Sussman Blume

American author
• Wrote *Are You There God? It's Me Margaret*, 1970; *Wifey*, 1978; books for children noted for sexual frankness.
b. February 12, 1938 in Elizabeth, New Jersey

Edmund Charles Blunden

English poet-critic
• Named to Oxford's poetry chair, 1966; wrote *War Poets, 1914-18*, 1962.
b. November 01, 1896 in London, England
d. January 2, 1974 in Sudbury, England

Wilfrid Scawen Blunt

English poet-politician-traveler
• Colorful Victorian, whose writings include lyric verse, *Love Sonnets of Proteus*, 1881.
b. August 14, 1840 in Crawley, England
d. September 1, 1922 in London, England

Nellie Bly, pseud

(Elizabeth Cochrane Seaman)
American journalist
• Wrote muckraking articles on prisons, asylums; author *Around the World in 72 Days*, 1890.
b. May 05, 1867 in Cochrane's Mill, Pennsylvania
d. January 27, 1922 in New York, New York

Robert Elwood Bly

American poet
• Won National Book Award for *The Light Around the Body*, 1968.
b. December 23, 1926 in Madison, Minnesota

Chay Blyth

British author-adventurer
• Circumnavigated globe alone in yacht, 1970-71; wrote *The Impossible Voyage*, 1972.
b. 1940 in Hawick, England

Enid Mary Blyton

(Mary Pollock psued)
English author
• Wrote over 400 children's stories, 1922-68, including *The Secret Seven* adventure series, 1949-54.
b. August 11, 1897 in East Dulwich, England
d. November 28, 1968 in London, England

Giovanni Boccaccio

Italian author
• Father of classical Italian prose; wrote *The Decameron*, 1353.
b. 1313 in Florence, Italy
d. December 21, 1375 in Certaldo, Italy

Lucien Albert Bodard

French journalist-author
• Wrote award-winning novel *Annie-Marie*, 1981.
b. January 03, 1914 in Chungking, China

Maxwell Bodenheim

American author-poet
• Sardonic writings include poem *Bringing Jazz*, 1930; novel *Crazy Man*, 1924; murdered with wife in Greenwich Village.
b. May 23, 1893 in Hermanville, Mississippi
d. February 06, 1954 in New York, New York

Matteo Maria Boiardo

Italian poet
• Famous for unfinished epic poem on Charlemagne, *Orlando Innamorato*, 1487.
b. 1441 in Scandiano, Italy
d. 1494 in Reggio Emilia, Italy

Nicolas Boileau(-Despreaux)

French author-poet-critic
• Wrote *Satires*, 1666; *Art Poetique*, 1674, which defined principles of classic French verse.
b. November 01, 1636 in Paris, France
d. March 13, 1711

Heinrich Boll

German author
• Won Nobel Prize, 1972, for works dealing with drift of German society during Nazi, post-war periods.
b. December 21, 1917 in Cologne, Germany
d. July 16, 1985 in Hurtgenwald, Germany (West)

Don F Bolles

American journalist
• Investigative reporter for *Arizona Republic*; killed in car bomb explosion.
b. 1928 in Milwaukee, Wisconsin
d. June 13, 1976 in Phoenix, Arizona

Robert Oxton Bolt

English author
• Plays include award-winning *Man for All Seasons*, 1960; won Oscar for *Dr. Zhivago* screenplay, 1965.
b. August 15, 1924 in Manchester, England

Sarah Tittle Barrett Bolton

American poet
• Wrote verse *Paddle Your Own Canoe*, 1851.
b. December 18, 1814 in Newport, Kentucky
d. August 04, 1893 in Indianapolis, Indiana

Erma Louise Bombeck

(Mrs William Bombeck)
American journalist–author–humorist
• Syndicated columnist, 1967–; wrote *If Life Is a Bowl of Cherries, What Am I Doing in the Pits?*, 1971.
b. February 21, 1927 in Dayton, Ohio

Arna Wendell Bontemps

American author
• Leader, "Harlem Renaissance" movement, 1920s; wrote *Black Thunder*, 1936.
b. October 13, 1902 in Alexandria, Louisiana
d. June 04, 1973 in Nashville, Tennessee

George Gough Booth

American editor
• Founded Booth newspaper syndicate, Cranbrook Foundation; published *Detroit News*, 1888-1949.
b. September 24, 1864 in Toronto, Ontario
d. April 11, 1949 in Detroit, Michigan

Henry Bordeaux

French author
• His 50 novels of provincial life were widely read: *The Gardens of Omar*, 1923; *Footprints Beneath the Snow*, 1912.
b. January 29, 1870 in Thonon, France
d. 1963

Petrus Borel d'Hauterive

French poet–author
• Led group of Romantics called *bousingos*; translated *Robinson Crusoe* into French.
b. June 28, 1809 in Lyons, France
d. July 14, 1859 in Mostaganem, Algeria

Jorge Luis Borges

Argentine author
• Leader, "Ultraismo" literary movement, combining surrealism, imagism.
b. August 24, 1899 in Buenos Aires, Argentina
d. June 14, 1986 in Geneva, Switzerland

Harold A Bosley

American clergyman–author
• Among his works were *The Deeds of Christ*, 1969; *Men Who Build Churches*, 1972.
b. February 19, 1907 in Burchard, Nebraska
d. January 21, 1975

Jean Bothwell

American children's author
• Wrote award-winning *The Thirteenth Stone*, 1946.
b. in Winside, Nebraska
d. March 02, 1977 in Missouri

Phyllis Bottome, pseud

(Mrs Ernan Forbes-Dennis)
English author
• A prolific writer, best known for anti-Nazi novel *The Mortal Storm*, 1937; *Private Worlds*, 1937.
b. 1884
d. August 23, 1963 in Hampstead, England

Pierre Francois Marie-Louis Boulle

French author
• Popular novels include *Bridge Over River Kwai*, 1952; *Planet of the Apes*, 1963.
b. February 2, 1912 in Avignon, France

Vance Bourjaily

American author
• Gained prominence in generation of young writers after WW II; novels include *Brill Among the Ruins*, 1970.
b. September 17, 1922 in Cleveland, Ohio

Margaret Bourke-White

American photojournalist
• *Life* photographer, 1936-69; first official woman photojournalist of WW II: *You Have Seen Their Faces*, 1937.
b. June 14, 1904 in New York, New York
d. August 27, 1971 in Stamford, Connecticut

Jim (James Alan) Bouton

American baseball player–author
• Pitcher, 1962-68; wrote best-selling baseball expose, *Ball Four*, 1970.
b. March 08, 1939 in Newark, New Jersey

Ben(jamin William) Bova

American author–editor
• Writer of science, science fiction books: *Kinsman*, 1979; *The Exiles Trilogy*, 1980.
b. November 08, 1932 in Philadelphia, Pennsylvania

Thomas Bowdler

English editor
• His expurgated editions of Shakespeare's works and Gibbon's *Decline & Fall* resulted in term "bowdlerize."
b. July 11, 1754 in Ashley, England
d. February 24, 1825 in Rhyddings, England

Catherine Drinker Bowen

American author
• Wrote best-selling *John Adams and the American Revolution*, 1950; biographies on Francis Bacon, Sir Edward Coke.
b. January 01, 1897 in Haverford, Pennsylvania
d. November 01, 1973 in Haverford, Pennsylvania

Elizabeth Dorothea Cole Bowen

Irish author
• Wrote *The Heat of the Day*, 1949; noted for sensitive use of language, character.
b. June 07, 1899 in Dublin, Ireland
d. February 22, 1973 in London, England

Jane Sydney Bowles

(Mrs Paul Bowles)
American author
• Noted "writer's writer," who did stories on women and their attempt at independence.
b. February 22, 1917 in New York, New York
d. May 04, 1973 in Malaga, Spain

Harold Vincent Boyle

American journalist
• Awarded Pulitzer for correspondence, WW II; called "the American infantryman's Boswell."
b. February 21, 1911 in Kansas City, Missouri
d. April 01, 1974 in New York, New York

Jack Boyle

American author
• Wrote mystery, *Boston Blackie*, 1919; title character became subject of films, TV series, radio shows, 1920s-50s; Boyle himself remains a mystery.

Kay Boyle

American author
• Writings include *Wedding Day*, 1931; *Generation without Farewell*, 1959.
b. February 19, 1903 in Saint Paul, Minnesota

Helen Dore Boylston

American author
• Used experience as nurse to write *Sue Barton* novels for girls, 1936-52.
b. April 04, 1895 in Portsmouth, New Hampshire
d. September 3, 1984 in Trumbull, Connecticut

Gerald Warner Brace
American author–educator
• Described New England life in his 11 novels including *Bell's Landing*, 1955.
b. September 23, 1901 in Islip, New York
d. July 2, 1978 in Blue Hill, Maine

Ray Douglas Bradbury
American author
• Has written over 1,000 science fiction stories, including *The Martian Chronicles*, 1950, *Fahrenheit 451*, 1954.
b. August 22, 1920 in Waukegan, Illinois

Ben(jamin Crowninshield) Bradlee
American journalist–editor
• VP, exec. editor, *Washington Post*, 1968–.
b. August 26, 1921 in Boston, Massachusetts

David Henry Bradley, Jr
American author
• Relates tragedy of black history in novel *Chaneysville Incident*, 1981.
b. September 07, 1950 in Bedford, Pennsylvania

Milton Bradley
American manufacturer–publisher
• First game, "The Checkered Game of Life" led to success of Milton Bradley Co.
b. November 08, 1836 in Vienna, Maine
d. May 3, 1911 in Springfield, Massachusetts

Anne Bradstreet
American poet
• Verse, published 1650, considered first significant literary work in Colonial Amercia.
b. 1612 in Northampton, England
d. September 16, 1672 in Andover, Massachusetts

James Winston Brady
American editor–publisher
• Publisher, *Women's Wear Daily*, 1964-71; editorial director, *Harper's Bazaar*, 1968-71; TV talk show host, 1973–.
b. November 15, 1928 in Brooklyn, New York

John Gerard Braine
English author
• One of the "angry young men"; wrote *Room at the Top*, 1957; filmed, 1958.
b. April 13, 1922 in Yorkshire, England
d. October 28, 1986 in London, England

Malcolm Braly
American author
• Wrote novel, screenplay *On the Yard*; filmed, 1979.
b. July 16, 1925 in Portland, Oregon
d. April 07, 1980 in Baltimore, Maryland

Max Brand, pseud
(Frederick Schiller Faust; "King of the Pulps")
American author–journalist
• Popular Westerns include *Destry Rides Again*, 1930; wrote Dr. Kildare films.
b. May 29, 1892 in Seattle, Washington
d. May 12, 1944 in Italy

Stewart Brand
American publisher
• Editor, publisher, *CoEvolution Quarterly*, 1973–; publishes *The Last Whole Earth Catalog*.
b. December 14, 1938 in Rockford, Illinois

Sebastian Brant
German poet
• His allegorical *Ship of Fools*, 1494, became big hit with several editions; basis for 1960s novel, film.
b. 1457 in Strasbourg, Germany
d. May 1, 1521 in Strasbourg, Germany

Rex Brasher
American ornithologist–artist–author
• Wrote 12-volumed *Birds and Trees of North America*, 1934.
b. July 31, 1869 in Brooklyn, New York
d. February 29, 1960 in Kent, Connecticut

Richard Brautigan
American author–poet
• Became campus hero, 1960s, with whimsical novel *Trout Fishing in America*, 1967. Master of the nonsequitur simile. Committed suicide.
b. January 3, 1933 in Tacoma, Washington
d. October 25, 1984 in Bolinas, California

Gerald (Edward Fitz-Gerald) Brenan
English author
• Definitive interpreter of Spanish literature, culture: *The Spanish Labyrinth*, 1943.
b. April 07, 1894 in Malta
d. January 16, 1987 in Malaga, Spain

Barbara Johnes Brenner
American children's author
• Free-lance writer of children's books: *Barto Takes the Subway*, 1960; *A Snake-Lover's Diary*, 1970.
b. June 26, 1925 in Brooklyn, New York

Jimmy Breslin
American author–journalist
• Pulitzer-winning NYC columnist who wrote *Table Money*, 1983.
b. October 17, 1930 in Jamaica, New York

Andre Breton
French poet
• Founded Surrealist movement, 1924; wrote *Surrealist of Manifesto*.
b. February 18, 1896 in Tinchebray, France
d. September 28, 1966 in Paris, France

George Platt Brett, Jr
American publisher
• Pres., Macmillan, 1931-58; published Mitchell's *Gone With the Wind*, 1936.
b. December 09, 1893 in Darien, Connecticut
d. February 11, 1984 in Southport, Connecticut

Jan Churchill Brett
American children's author–illustrator
• Self-illustrated children's books include *Good Luck Sneakers*, 1981.
b. December 01, 1949 in Hingham, Massachusetts

Simon Anthony Lee Brett
English author
• Wrote mystery novels, plays *So Much Blood*, 1977; created detective Charles Paris.
b. October 28, 1945 in Worcester, England

Breyten Breytenbach
South African poet–artist–political activist
• Wrote *True Confessions of an Albino Terrorist*, 1985, describing imprisonment, 1975-82, for anti-apartheid activities.
b. September 16, 1939 in Bonnievale, South Africa

Robert Seymour Bridges
English author–poet
• Poet laureate, 1913-30, who wrote philosophical poem "Testament of Beauty," 1929.
b. October 23, 1844 in Walmer, England
d. April 21, 1930 in Chilswell, England

Jean Anthelme Brillat-Savarin
French author–chef
• Wrote gastronomic classic *Physiology of Taste*, 1884.
b. April 01, 1755 in Bellay, France
d. February 02, 1826 in Paris, France

Carol Ryrie Brink
American author
• Prolific adult, children's writer; won Newbery for *Caddie Woodlawn*, 1936.
b. December 28, 1895 in Moscow, Idaho
d. August 15, 1981 in La Jolla, California

Hesba Fay Brinsmead
(Pixie Hungerford pseud)
Australian author
• Writings include *Pastures of the Blue Crane*, 1964; *Isle of the Sea Horse*, 1969.
b. March 15, 1922 in New South Wales, Australia

Arthur Brisbane
American journalist
• Articles swayed public opinion to contribute to outbreak of Spanish-American War, 1898.
b. December 12, 1864 in Buffalo, New York
d. December 25, 1936 in New York, New York

Fawn McKay Brodie
American author
• Wrote biographies of Sir Richard Burton, Joseph Smith, Thomas Jefferson; won Knopf biography award, 1943.
b. September 15, 1915 in Ogden, Utah
d. January 1, 1981 in Santa Monica, California

Joseph Alexandrovich Brodsky
(Iosif Alexandrovich Brodsky)
American author–poet
• Accused, sentenced to hard labor in USSR for dissent for his vocation, poetry, 1964; poet-in-residence, U. of MI, 1972-75, 1981-82; won Nobel Prize in literature, 1987.
b. May 24, 1940 in Leningrad, U.S.S.R.

Jane Ellen Brody
American author–journalist
• Syndicated columnist writing on nutrition, health: *Jane Brody's Nutrition Book*, 1981.
b. May 19, 1941 in Brooklyn, New York

Louis Brucker Bromfield
American author
• Developed experimental farming community; won Pulitzer for *Early Autumn*, 1926.
b. December 27, 1896 in Mansfield, Ohio
d. March 18, 1956 in Columbus, Ohio

Jacob Bronowski
English mathematician–author
• Wrote TV series for BBC: "The Ascent of Man," 1974.
b. January 18, 1908 in Poland
d. August 22, 1974 in East Hampton, New York

Anne Bronte
(Acton Bell pseud)
English author
• Sister of Charlotte and Emily; wrote *Agnes Grey*, 1847.
b. March 25, 1820 in Thornton, England
d. May 26, 1849 in Scarborough, England

Charlotte Bronte
(Currer Bell pseud; Mrs Arthur Bell Nicholls)
English author
• Most successful of sisters; wrote *Jane Eyre*, 1847.
b. April 21, 1816 in Thornton, England
d. March 31, 1855 in Haworth, England

Emily Jane Bronte
(Ellis Bell pseud)
English author
• Wrote *Wuthering Heights*, 1848.
b. August 2, 1818 in Thornton, England
d. December 19, 1848 in Haworth, England

Patrick Branwell Bronte
English poet
• Dissolute brother of the Bronte sisters.
b. 1817
d. September 26, 1848

Gwendolyn Brooks
American author–poet
• First black woman to win Pulitzer for poetry, 1950, for *Annie Allen*.
b. June 07, 1917 in Topeka, Kansas

Maria Gowen Brooks
(Maria del Occidente pseud)
American poet
• Wrote epic poem *Zophiel*, 1833.
b. 1794 in Medford, Massachusetts
d. November 11, 1845 in Cuba

Van Wyck Brooks
American author
• First to write of American cultural, literary development; won Pulitzer, 1936: *The Flowering of New England, 1815-1865* .
b. February 16, 1886 in Plainfield, New Jersey
d. May 02, 1963 in Bridgewater, Connecticut

Jim (James Patrick) Brosnan
American baseball player–author
• Pitcher, 1954-63; wrote one of first exposes on baseball, *The Long Season*, 1960.
b. October 24, 1929 in Cincinnati, Ohio

Joyce Diane Bauer Brothers
(Mrs Milton Brothers)
American psychologist–author
• Syndicated columnist, radio, TV show hostess; books include *What Every Woman Ought to Know About Love and Marriage*, 1984.
b. October 2, 1928 in New York, New York

(Matthew) Heywood (Campbell) Broun
American journalist–author
• Helped found "The Newspaper Guild," 1934, which presents annual reporting awards in his name; noted NYC newsman, 1908-40.
b. December 07, 1888 in Brooklyn, New York
d. December 18, 1939 in New York, New York

Carter Brown, pseud
(Alan Geoffrey Yates)
English author
• Wrote 270 detective novels.
b. August 01, 1923 in London, England
d. May 05, 1985 in Sydney, Australia

Charles Brockden Brown
American author–editor
• First American professional author; introduced Indians to US fiction; wrote six gothic romances.
b. January 17, 1771 in Philadelphia, Pennsylvania
d. February 22, 1810 in Philadelphia, Pennsylvania

Christy Brown
Irish author–poet
• Born with crippling cerebral palsy and only usable limb was left foot; wrote best-seller *Down All the Days*, 1970; film *My Left Foot*, 1989, was his life story.
b. June 05, 1932 in Dublin, Ireland
d. September 06, 1981 in Parbrook, England

Cecil B Brown
American broadcaster–journalist
• Newspaper reporter, WW II correspondent known for dramatic style; with CBS, 1940-43; NBC, 1960s.
b. September 14, 1907 in New Brighton, Pennsylvania
d. October 25, 1987 in Los Angeles, California

Dee (Alexander) Brown
American author–historian
• Has written on American West, conquest of Indians: *Bury My Heart at Wounded Knee*, 1971.
b. February 28, 1908 in Louisiana

George Mackay Brown
Scottish poet–author
• Wrote *Pictures in the Cave*, 1977; *Selected Poems*, 1977.
b. October 17, 1921 in Stromness, Scotland

James Brown
American publisher
• With Charles Little, formed Little, Brown and Co., 1837.
b. May 19, 1800 in Acton, Massachusetts
d. March 1, 1855

Marcia Brown
American children's author–illustrator
• Self-illustrated books include *Stone Soup*, 1947; *Skipper John's Cook*, 1951; three-time Caldecott winner.
b. July 13, 1918 in Rochester, New York

Margaret Wise Brown
American children's author
• Wrote popular *Noisy Book* series, 1939-51.
b. May 23, 1910 in New York, New York
d. November 13, 1952 in Nice, France

William Hill Brown
American author
• Wrote "first American novel," *The Power of Sympathy*, 1789.
b. December 01, 1765 in Boston, Massachusetts
d. September 02, 1793

William Wells Brown
American author–reformer
• First black American to publish novel.
b. 1815 in Lexington, Kentucky
d. November 06, 1884 in Chelsea, Massachusetts

Alice Crolley Browning
American educator–editor
• Wrote *Negro Story*, 1944; founded International Black Writers Conference, 1970.
b. November 05, 1907 in Chicago, Illinois
d. October 15, 1985 in Chicago, Illinois

Elizabeth Barrett Browning
(Mrs Robert Browning)
English poet
• Wrote *Sonnets from the Portuguese*, 1850, her own love story in verse.
b. March 06, 1806 in Durham, England
d. June 3, 1861 in Florence, Italy

Robert Browning
English poet
• Married Elizabeth Barrett, 1846; wrote *Pippa Passes*, 1841.
b. May 07, 1812 in London, England
d. December 12, 1889 in Venice, Italy

Susan Brownmiller
American author–feminist
• Wrote best-selling *Against Our Will*, 1975.
b. February 15, 1935 in Brooklyn, New York

Jean de Brunhoff
French children's author–illustrator
• Creator of the *Babar* series, 1931.
b. 1899 in France
d. October 16, 1937 in Switzerland

Giordano Bruno
Italian philosopher–author
• Wrote metaphysical *On the Infinite Universe and Its Worlds*, 1582; challenged dogma; burned at stake.
b. 1548 in Nola, Italy
d. February 17, 1600 in Rome, Italy

Sir Arthur W M Bryant
English author
• Historian and biographer of King Charles II and Samuel Pepys.
b. February 18, 1899 in Norfolk, England
d. January 22, 1985 in Salisbury, England

William Cullen Bryant
American poet–editor
• Best known poem *Thanatopsis*, 1811; edited, *NY Evening Post*, 1829-78.
b. November 03, 1794 in Cummington, Massachusetts
d. June 12, 1878 in New York, New York

Viscount James Bryce Bryce
British diplomat–author
• Ambassador to US, 1907-13; wrote classics *Holy Roman Empire*, 1864; *American Commonwealth*, 1888.
b. May 1, 1838 in Belfast, Northern Ireland
d. January 22, 1922 in Sidmouth, England

Martin Buber
Israeli philosopher–author
• Hasidic scholar whose philosophy of religious existentialism is described in book *I and Thou*, 1922.
b. February 08, 1878 in Vienna, Austria
d. June 13, 1965 in Jerusalem, Israel

Sir John Buchan
(Baron Tweedsmuir)
Scottish author–government official
• Canadian governor-general, 1935-40; adventure novels include classic *Thirty-Nine Steps*, 1915.
b. August 26, 1875 in Perth, Scotland
d. February 11, 1940 in Montreal, Quebec

George Buchanan
Scottish author
• Wrote *De Juri Regni*, 1579, stating that kings rule by popular will; had great impact on 16th-c. political thought.
b. February 01, 1506 in Killearn, Scotland
d. September 28, 1582 in Edinburgh, Scotland

Art(hur) Buchwald
American journalist
• Column syndicated in over 550 newspapers; wrote *The Buchwald Stops Here*, 1978.
b. October 2, 1925 in Mount Vernon, New York

Pearl S(ydenstricker) Buck
American author
• Won Pulitzer, 1932, Nobel Prize, 1938; wrote *The Good Earth*, 1930.
b. June 26, 1892 in Hillsboro, West Virginia
d. March 06, 1973 in Danby, Vermont

William F(rank) Buckley, Jr
American editor
• Editor, *National Review* mag., 1955-88; wrote *Atlantic High*, 1982.
b. November 24, 1925 in New York, New York

Frederick Buechner
American author–clergyman
• Prize-winning writer of psychological novels: *Long Days Dying*, 1950; *Return of Ansel Gibbs*, 1959.
b. July 11, 1926 in New York, New York

Emma Bugbee
American journalist–suffragette
• With *NY Herald Tribune*, 1911-66; broke barrier excluding women from newspaper city rooms.
b. 1888 in Shippensburg, Pennsylvania
d. October 06, 1981 in Warwick, Rhode Island

Vincent T Bugliosi
American lawyer–author
• Prosecutor in Manson family murder trials; wrote *Helter-Skelter*, 1974.
b. August 18, 1934 in Hibbing, Minnesota

Charles Bukowski
("Dirtiest Old Man in L.A.")
American author–poet
• Has published more than 40 books of poetry and prose, including *Ham on Rye*, 1982; *Hot Water Music*, 1983; and the screenplay for the movie *Barfly*, 1987.
b. 1920 in Andernach, Germany

Thomas Bulfinch
American author
• Published *The Age of Fable*, 1855, later called *Bulfinch's Mythology*; has become standard reference work.
b. July 15, 1796 in Newton, Massachusetts
d. May 27, 1867 in Boston, Massachusetts

Ivan Alekseevich Bunin
Russian author–translator
• First Russian to win Nobel Prize for literature, 1933; wrote novel *Derevnya*, 1910.
b. October 22, 1870 in Voronezh, Russia
d. November 08, 1953 in Paris, France

Basil Bunting
English poet
• Greatest popularity in 1960s as leader of British literary avant-garde.
b. March 01, 1900 in Scotswood, England
d. April 17, 1985 in Hexham, England

John Bunyan
English clergyman–author
• Wrote religious allegory *Pilgrim's Progress*, 1678, while in prison.
b. November 28, 1628 in Elstow, England
d. August 31, 1688 in London, England

Robert Joseph Burch
American author
• Juvenile fiction writer: *Ida Early Comes Over the Mountain*, 1980, Juvenile Literary Guild selection.
b. June 26, 1925 in Inman, Georgia

Eugene Leonard Burdick
American author
• Wrote controversial, political theory best sellers, *Ninth Wave*, 1956; *Ugly American*, 1958; *Fail Safe*, 1962.
b. December 12, 1918 in Sheldon, Louisiana
d. July 26, 1965

Anthony Burgess
English author–journalist
• His inventive, sophisticated novels include *Clockwork Orange*, 1962; *Napolean Symphony*, 1974.
b. February 25, 1917 in Manchester, England

Gelett (Frank Gelett) Burgess
American author
• Humorist whose best-known poem was "The Purple Cow."
b. January 3, 1866 in Boston, Massachusetts
d. September 18, 1951 in Carmel, California

Thornton Waldo Burgess
American children's author–journalist
• Wrote syndicated series of animal stories for children *Bedtime Stories*.
b. January 14, 1874 in Sandwich, Massachusetts
d. June 07, 1965 in Hampden, Massachusetts

John Burke
Irish author
• *Burke's Peerage* published annually since 1847, first systematic genealogical compilation.
b. 1787 in Tipperary, Ireland
d. March 27, 1848 in Aix-la-Chapelle, France

Ben Lucien Burman
American journalist–author
• Last of his 22 books was *Thunderbolt at Catfish Bend*, 1984.
b. December 12, 1895 in Covington, Kentucky
d. November 12, 1984 in New York, New York

Frances Eliza Hodgson Burnett
American author
• Wrote *Little Lord Fauntleroy*, 1886; *The Little Princess*, 1905; *The Secret Garden*, 1911.
b. November 24, 1849 in Manchester, England
d. October 29, 1924 in Plandome, New York

W(illiam) R(iley) Burnett
(James Updyke pseud)
American author
• Wrote gangster story *Little Caesar*, 1929; film script of *Asphalt Jungle*, 1949.
b. November 25, 1899 in Springfield, Ohio
d. April 25, 1982 in Santa Monica, California

Sheila (Philip Cochrane Every) Burnford
Scottish author
• Wrote *The Incredible Journey*, 1961.
b. May 11, 1918 in Scotland
d. April 2, 1984 in Bucklers Hard, England

James Burnham
American editor–author
• A founding editor of *National Review* mag., 1955-78; wrote books warning of communist threat: *The Struggle for the World*, 1947.
b. November 22, 1905 in Chicago, Illinois
d. July 28, 1987 in Kent, Connecticut

John Horne Burns
American author
• *The Gallery*, 1947, best example of his colorful, forceful expression.
b. October 07, 1916 in Andover, Massachusetts
d. August 1, 1953 in Leghorn, Italy

Robert Burns
(Bard of Ayrshire)
Scottish poet
• Beloved nat. poet; wrote songs "Auld Lang Syne" and "Comin' thro' the Rye"; most work in vernacular, praised lowland life.
b. January 25, 1759 in Alloway, Scotland
d. January 21, 1796 in Dumfroes, Scotland

Stanley Burnshaw
American author–poet–editor
• Pres., editor-in-chief, Holt, Rinehart & Winston, 1939-58; wrote first anthology of modern Hebrew poetry, *The Modern Hebrew Poem Itself*, 1965.
b. June 2, 1906 in New York, New York

Elihu Burritt
American reformer–author
• Self-taught lecturer on pacifist causes; traveled, wrote extensively for world peace: *Sparks from the Anvil*, 1846.
b. December 08, 1812 in New Britain, Connecticut
d. March 06, 1879 in New Britain, Connecticut

Edgar Rice Burroughs
American author–cartoonist
• Wrote *Tarzan* series; more than 35 million copies sold.
b. September 01, 1875 in Chicago, Illinois
d. March 1, 1950 in Los Angeles, California

William S(eward) Burroughs
American author
• A chief spokesman for the "beat movement," 1950s; wrote *Naked Lunch*, 1959.
b. February 05, 1914 in Saint Louis, Missouri

Abe (Abram Solman) Burrows
American dramatist–author
• Won Pulitzer, 1961, for *How to Succeed in Business Without Really Trying*.
b. December 18, 1910 in New York, New York
d. May 17, 1985 in New York, New York

Maxwell Struthers Burt
American author
• Wrote *Powder River*, 1939; *Along These Streets*, 1942.
b. October 18, 1882 in Baltimore, Maryland
d. August 28, 1954 in Jackson, Wyoming

Isabel Arundel Burton
English traveler–author
• Wrote books about her travels with husband Sir Richard Burton.
b. 1831 in London, England
d. 1896

Sir Richard Francis Burton
English author–explorer–orientalist
• Discovered Lake Tanganyika, 1858; noted for 16-vol. translation of *Arabian Nights*, 1885-88.
b. March 19, 1821 in Hertfordshire, England
d. October 2, 1890 in Trieste, Italy

Virginia Lee Burton
American children's author–illustrator
• Won 1943 Caldecott for *Little House*; wrote *Mike Mulligan and His Steam Shovel*, 1939.
b. August 3, 1909 in Newton Centre, Massachusetts
d. October 15, 1968

Leo (Felice Leonardo) Buscaglia
American educator–author
• Lecturer on interpersonal relationships who wrote *Living, Loving, Learning*, 1982.
b. March 31, 1925 in Los Angeles, California

Samuel Butler
English poet
• Famous for mock epic *Hudibras*, ridiculing the Puritans.
b. February 14, 1612 in Langar, England
d. September 25, 1680 in London, England

Samuel Butler
English author
• Wrote realistic novel *Way of All Flesh*, 1903; satire *Erewhon*, 1872.
b. December 04, 1835 in Nottinghamshire, England
d. June 18, 1902 in London, England

Michel Butor
French author
• Wrote *Passing Time*, 1957; *Second Thoughts*, 1957; *Degrees*, 1960.
b. September 14, 1926 in Mans-en-Baroeul, France

Betsy Byars
American children's author
• Won Newberry Medal for *Summer of the Swans*, 1971.
b. August 07, 1928 in Charlotte, North Carolina

William Newton Byers
American editor
• Issued first newspaper in Denver, CO, "Rocky Mountain News," 1859-1878.
b. February 22, 1831 in Madison County, Ohio
d. March 25, 1903

George Gordon Byron, 6th Baron Byron of Rochdale
(Lord Byron)
English poet
• Writer of Romantic narrative poems: "Childe Harold's Pilgrimage," 1812.
b. January 22, 1788 in London, England
d. April 19, 1824 in Missolonghi, Greece

Herb Caen
American journalist–author
• Has syndicated column in *San Francisco Chronicle*, 1958–; wrote *One Man's San Francisco*, 1976.
b. April 03, 1916 in Sacramento, California

James M(allahan) Cain
American author
• Wrote *The Postman Always Rings Twice*, 1934; filmed, 1946; *Mildred Pierce*, 1941; filmed, 1945.
b. July 01, 1892 in Annapolis, Maryland
d. October 27, 1977 in Hyattsville, Maryland

Sir Hall Caine
English author
• Wrote popular novels of biblical themes *The Eternal City*, 1901; *The Prodigal Son*, 1904.
b. May 14, 1853
d. August 31, 1931

Peter Ritchie Calder
(Lord Ritchie-Calder of Balmashannar)
Scottish journalist
• Newspaper, mag. articles bridged gap between scientist, layman, 1922-50s.
b. July 01, 1906 in Forfar, Scotland
d. January 31, 1982

Nigel David Ritchie Calder
English author
• Writer of popular science books: *The Restless Earth*, 1972; *The Comet Is Coming!* 1981.
b. December 02, 1931 in London, England

Erskine Preston Caldwell
American author
• Known for earthy depictions of rural poor: *God's Little Acre*, 1933; filmed, 1958; *Tobacco Road*, 1932; filmed, 1941.
b. December 17, 1903 in Moreland, Georgia
d. April 11, 1987 in Paradise Valley, Arizona

Taylor (Janet Miriam Taylor) Caldwell
(Mrs William Robert Prestie)
English author
• Wrote *Testimony of Two Men*, 1968; *The Captains and the Kings*, 1972.
b. September 07, 1900 in Manchester, England
d. August 3, 1985 in Greenwich, Connecticut

Hortense Calisher
(Mrs Curtis Harnack)
American author
• Novels include *The Bobby-Soxer*, 1986; *Eagle Eye*, 1972.
b. December 2, 1911 in New York, New York

Morley Edward Callaghan
Canadian author
• Best known for allegorical fiction written in 1930s: *Such Is My Beloved*, 1934; autobiographical memoir *That Summer in Paris*, 1963, describes friendship with Hemingway and Fitzgerald.
b. September 22, 1903 in Toronto, Ontario
d. August 25, 1990 in Toronto, Ontario

Italo Calvino
Italian author
• Writings include allegorical fantasy *If on a Winter's Night a Traveler*, 1979.
b. October 15, 1923 in Santiago de Las Vegas, Cuba
d. September 19, 1985 in Siena, Italy

Eleanor Francis Cameron
Canadian author
• Wrote prize-winning children's stories *Court of the Stone Children*, 1973; *Julia Redfern*, 1982.
b. March 23, 1912 in Winnipeg, Manitoba

Luis de Camoes
(Luis de Camoens)
Portuguese poet
• Best known work, epic poem *Os Lusiadas*, 1572.
b. 1524 in Lisbon, Portugal
d. 1580 in Lisbon, Portugal

Dino Campana
Italian poet
• Only verse published during lifetime *Orphic Songs*, 1914.
b. August 2, 1885 in Marradi, Italy
d. March 11, 1932 in Florence, Italy

Tommaso Campanella
(Domenico Giovanni)
Italian philosopher–poet–author
• Wrote *Civitas Solis*, 1623, his idea of Utopian society.
b. September 05, 1568 in Stilo, Italy
d. May 21, 1639 in Paris, France

Joseph Campbell
American author
• Best known book *The Hero of a Thousand Faces*, 1949; his mythological writings were inspiration for *Star Wars* film trilogy.
b. March 26, 1904 in New York, New York
d. October 31, 1987 in Honolulu, Hawaii

Thomas Campbell
Scottish poet
• Known for patriotic war song, "Ye Mariners of England," 1800; wrote *Pleasures of Hope*, 1799.
b. August 27, 1777 in Glasgow, Scotland
d. June 15, 1844 in Boulogne-sur-Mer, France

Walter Stanley Campbell
(Stanley Vestal pseud)
American author
• Books on southwestern frontier include *Sitting Bull*, 1928.
b. August 15, 1887 in Severy, Kansas
d. December 1957

William Edward March Campbell
(William March pseud)
American author
• Wrote *The Bad Seed*, 1954; dramatized by Maxwell Anderson, 1955.
b. September 18, 1893 in Mobile, Alabama
d. May 15, 1954 in New Orleans, Louisiana

Albert Camus
(Bauchart; Albert Mathe pseuds; Saetone joint pseud)
French author–philosopher
• Proponent of absurdism philosophy; major novel *L'Etranger*, 1942; won Nobel Prize in literature, 1957.
b. November 07, 1913 in Mondovi, Algeria
d. January 04, 1960 in Sens, France

John (Edwin John) Canaday
(Matthew Head pseud)
American critic–author
• Controversial *NY Times* art news editor, 1959-77; wrote classic text *Mainstreams of Modern Art*, 1959.
b. February 01, 1907 in Fort Scott, Kansas
d. July 19, 1985 in New York, New York

Vincent Canby
American journalist–critic
• *NY Times* film critic, 1969–.
b. July 27, 1924 in Chicago, Illinois

Elias Canetti
Bulgarian author
• Works include novel *Auto-da-Fe*, 1935; nonfiction *Crowds and Power*, 1960; won Nobel Prize, 1981.
b. July 25, 1905 in Ruschuk, Bulgaria

Cass Canfield
American publisher
• Spent entire career at Harper & Row, 1929-86; wrote biographies of Pierpont Morgan, Jefferson Davis.
b. April 26, 1897 in New York, New York
d. March 27, 1986 in New York, New York

Erwin Dain Canham
American newspaper editor–journalist
• Edited *Christian Science Monitor*, 1945-79.
b. February 03, 1904 in Auburn, Maine
d. January 03, 1982 in Agana, Guam

Karel Capek
Czech author–essayist
• His play *R.U.R.*, 1920, introduced word "robot."
b. January 09, 1890 in Male Svatonovice, Bohemia
d. December 24, 1938 in Prague, Czechoslovakia

Truman Capote
American author
• Wrote *Breakfast at Tiffany's* filmed, 1961; *In Cold Blood* filmed, 1968.
b. September 3, 1924 in New Orleans, Louisiana
d. August 26, 1984 in Los Angeles, California

Arthur Capper
American editor–publisher–politician
• World's largest publisher of farm journals; appointed DD Eisenhower to West Point.
b. July 14, 1865 in Garnett, Kansas
d. December 19, 1951 in Topeka, Kansas

Philip Joseph Caputo
American author–journalist
• Wrote *Rumor of War*, memoir of Vietnam; won Pulitzer, 1972.
b. January 1, 1941 in Chicago, Illinois

Roger Andrew Caras
American journalist
• Authority on nature, environment; ABC News animal, wildlife correspondent since 1975; wrote *The Forest*, 1979.
b. May 24, 1928 in Methuen, Massachusetts

Giosue Alessandro Guiseppe Carducci
Italian poet–critic
• Won Nobel Prize for literature, 1906; notable poems include "Barbaric Odes," "Hymn to Satan," "Rime."
b. July 27, 1835 in Val di Castello, Italy
d. February 16, 1907 in Bologna, Italy

Thomas Carew
English poet
• First of Cavalier poets; influenced by Donne and Jonson.
b. 1595 in West Wickham, England
d. 1639

Ernestine Moller Gilbreth Carey
(Mrs Charles E Carey)
American author–lecturer
• With brother, Frank, wrote reminiscences of their childhood, *Cheaper by the Dozen*, 1948.
b. April 05, 1908 in New York, New York

(William) Bliss Carman
Canadian author–poet
• Popular verse vols. include *Sappho*, 1902; *Songs from Vagabondia*, 1894.
b. April 15, 1861 in Frederickton, New Brunswick
d. June 08, 1929 in New Canaan, Connecticut

Dale Carnegie
American author
• Wrote *How to Win Friends and Influence People*, 1936; has sold over five million copies.
b. November 24, 1888 in Maryville, Missouri
d. November 01, 1955 in New York, New York

Robert A Caro
American author
• Wrote best-sellers about power: *The Power Broker: Robert Moses and the Fall of New York*, 1974; *The Path to Power* (about Lyndon Johnson), 1982.
b. October 3, 1936 in New York, New York

Leslie Carpenter
American journalist
• Syndicated Washington correspondent, 1944-74.
b. 1922
d. July 24, 1974 in Washington, District of Columbia

John Dickson Carr
American author
• Detective, mystery writer; created character of Dr. Gideon Fell, corpulent sleuth.
b. 1905 in Uniontown, Pennsylvania
d. February 27, 1977 in Greenville, South Carolina

Gladys Hasty Carroll
American author
• Regional novel *As the Earth Turns*, 1933, translated into 60 languages.
b. June 26, 1904 in Rochester, New Hampshire

Lewis Carroll, pseud
(Charles Lutwidge Dodgson)
English author
• Wrote *Alice's Adventures in Wonderland*, 1865; *Through the Looking Glass*, 1872.
b. January 27, 1832 in Cheshire, England
d. January 14, 1898 in Guildford, England

Rachel Louise Carson
American biologist–author
• Writings combine scientific accuracy with lyrical prose: *The Sea Around Us*, 1951, *Silent Spring*, 1962.
b. May 27, 1907 in Springdale, Pennsylvania
d. April 14, 1964 in Silver Spring, Maryland

Robert Carson
American author
• Won Oscar for screenplay for *A Star Is Born*, 1937.
b. October 06, 1909 in Clayton, Washington
d. January 19, 1983 in Los Angeles, California

Barbara Hamilton Cartland
English author
• World's top-selling romance novelist; step-grandmother of Princess Diana.
b. July 09, 1901 in England

Raymond Clevie Carver, Jr
American author
• One of best known short-story writers in US: *Will You Please Be Quiet, Please?* 1976; *Cathedral*, 1983.
b. May 25, 1938 in Clatskanie, Oregon
d. August 02, 1988 in Port Angeles, Washington

Joyce (Arthur Joyce Lunel) Cary
English author
• Wrote trilogies *The Horse's Mouth*, 1944; *Prisoner of Grace*, 1952.
b. December 07, 1888 in Londonderry, Northern Ireland
d. March 29, 1957 in Oxford, England

Giovanni Giacomo Casanova (de Seingalt)
Italian author–adventurer
• His bawdy accounts of career as charlatan, gambler, lover, *Memories*, 1826-38, were published, 1960.
b. April 02, 1725 in Venice, Italy
d. June 04, 1798 in Dux, Bohemia

Neal Cassady
American author
• One of people most responsible for Beat Generation; writings consisted chiefly of letters to friends. One of Ken Kesey's Merry Pranksters.
b. February 08, 1926 in Salt Lake City, Utah
d. February 04, 1968 in San Miguel de Allende, Mexico

R(onald) V(erlin) Cassill
American author
• Award-winning short stories include *The Prize*, 1968.
b. May 17, 1919 in Cedar Falls, Iowa

Igor Loiewski Cassini
American journalist
• Gossip columnist under the name "Cholly Knickerbocker"; brother of Oleg.
b. 1915

Jean Cassou
(Jean Noir pseud)
French author–critic
• Wrote *33 Sonnets Composes au Secret*, 1944, while imprisoned during German occupation.
b. July 09, 1897 in Deusto, France

Carlos Castaneda
American anthropologist–author
• Wrote *Teachings of Don Juan: The Yaqui Way of Knowledge*, 1968.
b. December 25, 1931 in Sao Paulo, Brazil

Conte Baldassare Castiglione
Italian diplomat–writer–courtier
• Writer of Renaissance Europe; chief work *The Courtier*, 1518.
b. December 03, 1478 in Casatico, Italy
d. February 02, 1529 in Toledo, Spain

Willa Sibert Cather
American author
• Won Pulitzer for novel *One of Ours*, 1923; wrote *Death Comes for the Archbishop*, 1927.
b. December 07, 1873 in Winchester, Virginia
d. April 24, 1947 in New York, New York

Arthur Catherall
(A R Channel; Dan Corby; Peter Hallard pseuds)
English author
• Wrote dozens of boys' adventure stories: *Rod o' the Rail*, 1936.
b. February 06, 1906 in Bolton, England
d. 1980

Bruce Catton
American author–journalist
• Historical works on the Civil War include 1953 Pulitzer winner, *A Stillness at Appomattox*.
b. October 09, 1899 in Petoskey, Michigan
d. August 28, 1978 in Frankfort, Michigan

Gaius Valerius Catullus
Roman poet
• Wrote over 100 lyric poems.
b. 84BC in Verona, Italy
d. 54BC

Charles Stanley Causley
English author
• Folk poetry is based on his Cornish childhood, later yrs. in the navy, as a teacher.
b. August 24, 1917 in Launceston, England

Betty (Elizabeth Allen) Cavanna
(Betsy Allen; Elizabeth Headley pseuds)
American children's author
• Has written books for girls for 30 yrs., including *Going on Sixteen*.
b. June 24, 1909 in Camden, New Jersey

Camilo Jose Cela
Spanish author
• Created *tremendismo*, style that emphasized violence, grotesque imagery; best known novel *The Family of Pascual Duarte*, 1942; won Nobel Prize in literature, 1989.
b. May 11, 1916 in Ira Flavia, Spain

Louis-Ferdinand Celine
(Louis-Ferdinand Destouches)
French author
• Misanthropic views expressed in *Journey to the End of Night*, 1932, *Death on the Installment Plan*, 1936.
b. May 27, 1894 in Courbevoie, France
d. July 04, 1961 in Meudon, France

Bennett Alfred Cerf
American publisher–journalist
• Co-founded Random House Publishers, 1927; panelist on TVs "What's My Line?", 1952-68.
b. May 25, 1898 in New York, New York
d. August 27, 1971 in Mount Kisco, New York

Miguel (de) Cervantes (Saavedra)
Spanish poet–dramatist
• Began writing *Don Quixote* in prison, 1605; forerunner of modern novel; considered Spain's equivalent of Shakespeare.
b. September 29, 1547 in Alcala, Spain
d. April 23, 1616 in Madrid, Spain

Norman Chandler
American newspaper publisher–business executive
• Third-generation publisher of *LA Times*, 1945-60; credited with paper's growth, phenomenal success; CEO of parent co., Times Mirror, 1961-68.
b. September 14, 1899 in Chicago, Illinois
d. October 2, 1973 in Los Angeles, California

Otis Chandler
American newspaper publisher–business executive
• Son of Norman and Dorothy; succeeded father as publisher, *LA Times*, 1960-80; editor in chief, Times Mirror Co., 1980-.
b. November 23, 1927 in Los Angeles, California

Raymond Thornton Chandler
American author
• Created private detective Philip Marlowe; wrote novel *The Big Sleep*, 1939.
b. July 23, 1888 in Chicago, Illinois
d. March 26, 1959 in La Jolla, California

Dickey Chapelle
American photojournalist
• Combat photojournalist; killed in Vietnam mine blast.
b. March 14, 1918 in Shorewood, Wisconsin
d. November 04, 1965 in Chulai, Vietnam (South)

Yuen Ren Chao
Chinese poet
• Best known for creating a phonetic alphabet to translate Chinese to English.
b. November 03, 1892 in Tientsin, China
d. February 24, 1982 in Cambridge, Massachusetts

Rene (Emile) Char
French poet
• Outspoken poet of the Resistance; wrote short, brilliant pieces including "Hammer without a Master," 1934.
b. June 14, 1907 in L'Isle Sorgue, France
d. February 19, 1988 in Paris, France

Pierre Francis Xavier de Charlevoix
French traveler–author
• Jesuit; wrote detailed accounts of travels across North America: *Journal Historique*, 1744.
b. October 29, 1682 in Saint-Quentin, France
d. February 01, 1761 in La Fleche, France

Henri Charriere
French author–murderer
• Escaped from Devil's Island, 1941; book *Papillion* sold over five million copies; Steve McQueen starred in movie, 1973.
b. 1906
d. July 29, 1973 in Madrid, Spain

Leslie Charteris
American author
• Best known for creating Simon Templar in *The Saint* series; films, TV shows have been based on the stories.
b. May 12, 1907 in Singapore

Edna Woolman Chase
American editor
• Editor-in-chief, *Vogue* mag., 1914-55; organized first US fashion show, 1944.
b. March 14, 1877 in Asbury Park, New Jersey
d. March 2, 1957 in Sarasota, Florida

Francois Rene de Chateaubriand
French author
• Pioneer of romantic movement; wrote *Memories from Beyond the Tomb*, 1850.
b. September 04, 1768 in Saint-Malo, France
d. July 04, 1848 in Paris, France

Thomas Chatterton
English poet
• Claimed his "Rowley Poems" were copies of 15th c. manuscripts.
b. November 2, 1752 in Bristol, England
d. August 25, 1770 in Bristol, England

Bruce (Charles Bruce) Chatwin
English author
• Known for distinctive travel books, novels; wrote *The Songlines*, 1987.
b. May 13, 1940 in Yorkshire, England
d. January 18, 1989 in Nice, France

Geoffrey Chaucer
English poet
• Wrote *The Canterbury Tales*, ca. 1387, never completed.
b. 1340 in London, England
d. October 25, 1400 in London, England

Haridas Chaudhuri
Indian author
• Books include *The Rhythm of Truth*, 1958; *Mastering the Problems of Living*, 1968.
b. May 24, 1913 in Calcutta, India
d. June 2, 1975 in San Francisco, California

John Cheever
American author
• Won Pulitzer, 1979; noted for subtle, comic style; short story collections include *World of Apples*, 1973. Becoming increasingly known posthumously as a confused and unhappy man, courtesy of offspring's memoirs and his own published notes and letters.
b. May 27, 1912 in Quincy, Massachusetts
d. June 18, 1982 in Ossining, New York

Marie-Andre de Chenier
French author–poet
• Early French Romanticist whose verse volumes include *La Jeune Captive*, 1795.
b. October 3, 1762 in Constantinople, Turkey
d. July 25, 1794

Anna Chan Chennault
(Mrs Claire Lee Chennault)
Chinese journalist–author
• US correspondent *Hsin Shen Daily News*, Taipei, 1958–; wrote best seller *Chennault and the Flying Tigers*, 1963.
b. June 23, 1925 in Peking, China

Maxine Cheshire
(Mrs Bert W Cheshire)
American journalist
• Reporter, Washington *Post*, 1954-65; columnist LA Times Syndicate since 1965.
b. April 05, 1930 in Harlan, Kentucky

Charles Waddell Chesnutt
American author–lawyer
• Works depicting struggle of American black include *The Conjure Woman*, 1899; awarded Spingarn Medal.
b. June 2, 1858 in Cleveland, Ohio
d. November 15, 1932 in Cleveland, Ohio

Earl Philip Dormer Chesterfield
(Philip Dormer Stanhope)
English author–statesman
• *Letters to His Son*, 1774, classic portrait of 18th-c. gentleman.
b. September 22, 1694 in London, England
d. March 24, 1773 in London, England

G(ilbert) K(eith) Chesterton
English poet–critic–essayist
• Wrote *Father Brown* detective stories, 1911-45; literary criticism.
b. May 29, 1874 in Kensington, England
d. June 14, 1936 in Chiltern Hills, England

Lydia Maria Child
American author–feminist
• Founded, edited *Juvenile Miscellany*, 1826-34, first children's monthly in US; wrote *Philothea*, 1836.
b. February 11, 1802 in Medford, Massachusetts
d. October 22, 1880 in Wayland, Massachusetts

(Robert) Erskine Childers
Irish author–rebel
• Wrote *The Riddle of the Sands*, 1903.
b. June 25, 1870 in London, England
d. November 24, 1922 in Dublin, Ireland

Marquis William Childs
American journalist–author
• Pulitzer-winning political columnist, 1969: *Ethics in a Business Society*.
b. March 17, 1903 in Clinton, Iowa
d. June 3, 1990 in San Francisco, California

Kate Chopin
(Katherine O'Flaherty)
American author
• Novels of Cajun, Creole life include *Bayou Folk*, 1894.
b. February 08, 1851 in Saint Louis, Missouri
d. August 22, 1904 in Saint Louis, Missouri

Chretien de Troyes
French poet–author
• Wrote earliest known Arthurian legends, first known version of Grail legend, *Perceval, ou Le Conte de Graal*.
b. 1130
d. 1183

Mary Blount Christian
American children's author
• Fiction writings include *Sebastian: Super Sleuth*, 1973; *The Doggone Mystery*, 1980.
b. February 2, 1933 in Houston, Texas

Dame Agatha Mary Clarissa Miller Christie
English author–dramatist
• Play *Mousetrap* longest running in British history; created detectives Miss Marple, Hercule Poirot; mysteries sold over 100 million copies.
b. September 15, 1890 in Torquay, England
d. January 12, 1976 in Wallingford, England

Matthew F Christopher
American children's author
• Writes children's sports novels: *Wild Pitch; Run Billy Run*, 1980.
b. August 16, 1917 in Bath, Pennsylvania

Marian Christy
American journalist
• Syndicated fashion, style columnist, 1952–; won several awards, honors.
b. November 09, 1932 in Ridgefield, Connecticut

Korney Ivanovich Chukovsky
(Nikolai Ivanovich Korneichuk)
Russian scholar–children's author
• One of first to translate English works into Russian; censors largely ignored children's books, due to his immense popularity.
b. March 31, 1882 in Saint Petersburg, Russia
d. October 28, 1969 in Moscow, U.S.S.R.

Charles Churchill
English poet–satirist
• Wrote biting verse: *The Rosciad*, 1761; *The Ghost*, 1762.
b. February 1731 in London, England
d. November 04, 1764 in Boulogne, France

Winston Churchill
American author
• Wrote novels on political, historical subjects: *The Crisis*, 1901; *The Crossing*, 1904.
b. 1871 in Saint Louis, Missouri
d. March 12, 1947 in Winter Park, Florida

John Anthony Ciardi
American poet–author
• Award-winning writer known for English translation of Dante's *Inferno*, 1954.
b. June 24, 1916 in Boston, Massachusetts
d. April 01, 1986 in Metuchen, New Jersey

Colley Cibber
English author–actor–dramatist
• Poet laureate, 1730; ridiculed in Alexander Pope's *The Dunciad*.
b. November 06, 1671 in London, England
d. December 12, 1757 in London, England

Craig Claiborne
American author–editor
• Food editor, *NY Times*; wrote *The New New York Times Cook Book*, 1979.
b. September 04, 1920 in Sunflower, Mississippi

Thomas L Clancy, Jr
American author
• Had surprise hit with first novel, *The Hunt for Red October*, 1984; other military thrillers include *Patriot Games*, 1987.
b. 1947 in Baltimore, Maryland

Patricia Clapp
American author
• Writes plays, novels mostly for juveniles: *Constance: A Story of Early Plymouth*, 1969, *Witches' Children*, 1982.
b. June 09, 1912 in Boston, Massachusetts

Raymond Lewis Clapper
American journalist
• Newspaper correspondent, commentator, Scripps-Howard chain, 1936-44; read by millions, he died in plane crash.
b. April 3, 1892 in La Cygne, Kansas
d. February 1944 in Marshall Islands

John Clare
English poet
• Romantic nature writer; wrote *Rural Muse*, 1835; declared insane, 1837.
b. July 13, 1793 in Helpstone, England
d. May 2, 1864 in Northampton, England

Barrett H Clark
American author
• Works include *Oedipus and Pollyanna*, 1927; *America's Lost Plays*, 1940-41, in 20 volumes.
b. August 26, 1890 in Toronto, Ontario
d. August 05, 1953 in Briarcliff, New York

Charles Badger Clark
American poet
• Specialized in western lore, cowboy life: "Sky Lines and Wood Smoke," 1935.
b. January 01, 1883 in Albia, Iowa
d. September 26, 1957

Sydney Clark
American author–traveler
• Popular travel writer known for *All the Best* series, 1939-72.
b. August 18, 1890 in Auburndale, Massachusetts
d. April 2, 1975

Walter van Tilburg Clark
American author
• Best known for book *The Ox-Bow Incident*, 1940; filmed, 1942.
b. August 03, 1909 in East Oreland, Maine
d. November 1, 1971 in Reno, Nevada

Arthur C(harles) Clarke
English author–scientist
• With Stanley Kubrick, wrote novel, screenplay *2001: A Space Odyssey*, 1968.
b. December 16, 1917 in Minehead, England

Austin Clarke
Irish poet
• Wrote verse plays, novels inspired by the Irish countryside, history, legends.
b. May 09, 1896 in Dublin, Ireland
d. March 2, 1974 in Dublin, Ireland

John Henrik Clarke
American author
• Co-founder, *Harlem Quarterly*, 1950.
b. January 01, 1915 in Union Springs, Alabama

Paul Louis Charles Claudel
French author–diplomat–poet
• Foremost Catholic writer of his era; wrote poetic dramas, *The Hostage*, 1909; *Satin Slipper*, 1931.
b. August 06, 1868 in Villenluve, France
d. February 23, 1955 in Paris, France

Claudian
Alexandrian poet
• Considered the last great classical Latin poet; wrote unfinished epic *Rape of Porserpine*.
b. 365 in Alexandria, Egypt
d. 408

James Dumaresq Clavell
American author
• Wrote *Taipan*, 1966; *Shogun*, 1975; *Noble House*, 1981.
b. October 1, 1924 in Sydney, Australia

Beverly (Atlee Bunn) Cleary
American children's author
• Won 1984 Newbery Award for *Dear Mr. Henshaw*; wrote *Henry Higgins, Ramona* series.
b. 1916 in McMinnville, Oregon

Eldridge Cleaver
American political activist–author
• Civil rights radical; wrote *Soul on Ice*, 1968; *Soul on Fire*, 1978.
b. August 31, 1935 in Little Rock, Arkansas

Vera Allen Cleaver
(Mrs William Joseph Cleaver)
American children's author
• With husband, co-wrote popular children's books: *Queen of Hearts*, 1978.
b. January 06, 1919 in Virgil, South Dakota

William Joseph (Bill) Cleaver
American author
• With wife Vera, co-wrote numerous children's books: *Trial Valley*, 1977.
b. March 2, 1920 in Hugo, Oklahoma
d. August 2, 1981 in Winter Haven, Florida

Sarah Norcliffe Cleghorn
American author
• Poems collected in *Poems and Protests*, 1917.
b. February 04, 1876 in Norfolk, Virginia
d. April 04, 1959 in Philadelphia, Pennsylvania

Stuart Cloete
South African author
• Novels of S Africa include *The Turning Wheels*, 1937; *Mamba*, 1956.
b. July 23, 1897 in Paris, France
d. March 19, 1976 in Cape Town, South Africa

Arthur Hugh Clough
English poet
• Wrote pastoral verse "Bothie of Toperna-Vuolich," 1848; subject of Matthew Arnold's elegy, "Thyrsis."
b. January 01, 1819 in Liverpool, England
d. November 13, 1861 in Florence, Italy

Robert Myron Coates
American author–critic
• Novels include *Eater of Darkness*, 1929; *Wisteria Cottage*, 1948.
b. April 06, 1897 in New Haven, Connecticut
d. February 08, 1973 in New York, New York

Elizabeth Jane Coatsworth
American poet–children's author
• Won Newbery Award for *The Cat Who Went to Heaven*, 1930.
b. May 31, 1893 in Buffalo, New York
d. August 31, 1986 in Nobleboro, Maine

J(ohn) M Coetzee
South African author
• Political novels include *From the Heart of the Country*, 1977.
b. February 09, 1940 in Capetown, South Africa

Robert Peter Tristram Coffin
American poet–author–biographer
• Won 1935 Pulitzer for verse *Strange Holiness;* many books concern ME life.
b. March 18, 1892 in Brunswick, Maine
d. October 29, 1956 in Raleigh, North Carolina

Nevill Henry Kendall Aylmer Coghill
English author–educator–scholar
• Chaucer authority who translated *Canterbury Tales* into modern English, 1951.
b. April 19, 1899 in Castletownshend, England
d. November 06, 1980 in Oxford, England

Margaret Louise Coit
American author
• Won Pulitzer for first book: *John C Calhoun: American Portrait*, 1951.
b. May 3, 1922 in Norwich, Connecticut

Carroll Burleigh Colby
American author–artist
• Known for juvenile nature, adventure stories: *Gobbit, the Magic Rabbit*, 1951.
b. September 07, 1904 in Claremont, New Hampshire
d. October 31, 1977

Lonnie William Coleman
American author
• Wrote *Beulah Land; Look Away, Beulah Land; The Legacy of Beulah Land.*
b. August 02, 1920 in Barstow, Georgia
d. August 13, 1982 in Savannah, Georgia

Hartley Coleridge
English poet–journalist
• Compiled biograhies: *Worthies of Yorkshire*, 1832; eldest son of Samuel Taylor.
b. September 19, 1796 in Bristol, England
d. January 06, 1849 in Grasmere, England

Mary Elizabeth Coleridge
(Anodos pseud)
English author–poet
• Wrote novel *Seven Sleepers of Ephesus*, 1893; verse *Gathered Leaves*, published, 1910.
b. September 23, 1861 in London, England
d. August 25, 1907 in Harrogate, England

Samuel Taylor Coleridge
English author–poet–critic
• Wrote "The Rime of the Ancient Mariner"; "Kubla Khan."
b. October 21, 1772 in Ottery St. Mary, England
d. July 25, 1834 in London, England

Manning Coles, pseud
(Cyril Coles and Adelaide Frances Oke Manning)
English authors
• Invented Tommy Hambleton, intelligence agent; mysteries include *Drink to Yesterday, Toast to Tomorrow*, 1959.

Colette pseud
(Sidonie Gabriellee Colette)
French author
• Best works include four volume *Claudine*, 1930; *GiGi*, 1943.
b. January 28, 1873 in Saint-Sauveur, France
d. August 03, 1954 in Paris, France

Peter Collier
American author
• Co-author with David Horowitz, *The Fords: An American Epic*, 1986.
b. June 02, 1939 in Hollywood, California

Jackie (Jacqueline Jill) Collins
American author
• Best-selling novels include *Hollywood Wives*, 1983; *Rock Star*, 1988; sister of actress Joan.
b. October 04, 1941 in London, England

Wilkie (William) Collins
English author
• Wrote mystery novels *The Woman in White*, 1860; *The Moonstone*, 1868.
b. January 08, 1824 in London, England
d. September 23, 1889 in London, England

Carlo Collodi, pseud
(Carlo Lorenzini)
Italian author
• Story *Pinocchio*, first appeared in newspaper, 1880; English translation, 1892.
b. November 24, 1826 in Tuscany, Italy
d. October 26, 1890 in Florence, Italy

Lillian Colonius
American children's author
• Books include *At the Library*, 1967; *Here Comes the Fireboat*, 1967.
b. March 19, 1911 in Irvine, California

Johann Amos Comenius
Czech author
• Developed new philosophy of education; wrote *Orbis sensualium pictus*, 1658, first illustrated textbook, used for 200 yrs.
b. March 28, 1592 in Unersky, Moravia
d. November 15, 1670 in Amsterdam, Netherlands

Alexander Comfort
English author
• Biologist, best known for books *The Joy of Sex*, 1972; *A Gormet's Guide to Making Love*, 1973.
b. February 1, 1920 in London, England

Dame Ivy Compton-Burnett
English author
• Wrote witty, chilling social comedies of Edwardian family life: *Mother and Son*, 1955.
b. June 05, 1892 in London, England
d. August 27, 1969 in London, England

Richard Thomas Condon
American author
• Best-selling novels include *Manchurian Candidate*, 1959; *Prizzi's Honor*, 1982.
b. March 18, 1915 in New York, New York

Evan Shelby Connell, Jr
American author
• Among his fiction writings *The Anatomy Lesson and Other Stories*, 1957; *The Patriot*, 1960.
b. August 17, 1924 in Kansas City, Missouri

James B Connolly
American author
• Realistic sea stories included *Out of Gloucester*, 1902.
b. 1868 in Boston, Massachusetts
d. January 2, 1957

Sir William Neil Connor
(Cassandra)
Irish journalist
• Columnist for London *Daily Mirror*, 1935-67.
b. 1910 in County Derry, Northern Ireland
d. April 06, 1967 in London, England

Robert Conquest
English author
• Writings include *The Pasternak Affair; Courage of Genius*, 1962; known for works of science fiction, history.
b. July 15, 1917 in Malvern, England

Joseph Conrad
(Teodor Josef Konrad Koreniowski)
Polish author
• Wrote *Lord Jim*, 1900; *Heart of Darkness*, 1902; *Victory*, 1915.
b. December 03, 1857 in Berdichev, Russia
d. August 03, 1924 in Bishopsbourne, England

Pat Conroy
American author
• Wrote autobiographical novels *The Great Santini*, 1976; *The Water is Wide*, 1972.
b. October 26, 1945 in Atlanta, Georgia

Bob (Robert Bernard) Considine
American journalist
• Syndicated newspaper columnist; wrote "On the Line" column for nearly 40 yrs.
b. November 04, 1906 in Washington, District of Columbia
d. September 25, 1975 in New York, New York

Edward Roger Cony
American journalist
• Pres., Dow Jones Publishing Co., 1976–; won Pulitzer, 1961 for national reporting.
b. March 15, 1923 in Augusta, Maine

Janet Cooke
American journalist
• Won Pulitzer for contrived story on heroin addiction, 1981; first fakery in Pulitzer history.
b. 1954 in Toledo, Ohio

John Esten Cooke
American author–historian
• Wrote prewar novels of early VA; served as Jeb Stuart's subordinate officer in Civil War, which was basis for more literature.
b. November 03, 1830 in Winchester, Virginia
d. September 27, 1886 in Boyce, Virginia

Dane Coolidge
American author
• Expert on Indians, cowboys; many novels on Western life were used as film themes.
b. March 24, 1873 in Natick, Massachusetts
d. August 08, 1940

Charles Ira Coombs
American children's author
• Children's information, adventure books include *Young Reader's* series, 1950s; *Be a Winner* series, 1973.
b. June 27, 1914 in Los Angeles, California

Barbara Cooney
American children's author–illustrator
• Caldicott winner for *Chanticleer*, 1958; *Ox-Cart Man*, 1980.
b. August 06, 1916 in Brooklyn, New York

James Fenimore Cooper
American author
• Wrote *The Spy*, 1821; *The Last of the Mohicans*, 1826; first important American novelist.
b. September 15, 1789 in Burlington, New Jersey
d. September 14, 1851 in Cooperstown, New York

Kenneth Hardy Cooper
Physician–Author
• Credited with coining word aerobics; wrote *Aerobics*, 1968.
b. 1931

Lester Irving Cooper
American writer
• Won Emmy, Peabody for "Animals, Animals, Animals," series, 1976.
b. January 2, 1919 in New York, New York
d. June 06, 1985 in New York, New York

Robert Coover
American author
• Wrote *The Origin of the Brunists*, 1966; *A Night at the Movies*, 1987.
b. February 04, 1932 in Charles City, Iowa

Scott (Winfield Scott) Corbett
American children's author
• Wrote over 60 books, including *Cutlass Island*, 1962.
b. July 27, 1913 in Kansas City, Missouri

Frances Crofts Darwin Cornford
American poet
• Books of poetry include *Spring Morning*, 1915; *Collected Poems*, 1954; granddaughter of Charles Darwin.
b. 1886
d. August 19, 1960 in Cambridge, Massachusetts

Gregory Corso
American poet
• One of the chief spokesmen of the beat movement, 1950s; anti-establishment works appear in "Gasoline," 1958.
b. March 26, 1930 in New York, New York

Julio Cortazar
French author
• Argentine writer known for intellectual fiction; lived in exile in Paris following election of Juan Peron.
b. August 26, 1914 in Brussels, Belgium
d. February 12, 1984 in Paris, France

John Russell Coryell
(Nick Carter pseud)
American author
• With writing team developed fictional detective, Nick Carter; first dime novel in the series, 1886.
b. 1848
d. July 15, 1924

Thomas B Costain
American author
• Wrote best-selling historical novels: *The Black Rose*, 1945; *The Silver Chalice*, 1952.
b. May 08, 1885 in Brantford, Ontario
d. October 08, 1965 in New York, New York

Charles Cotton
English author–translator
• Noted for treatise on fly-fishing, published in fifth edition of Walton's *Compleat Angler*, 1676; translation of Montaigne's *Essays*, 1685.
b. April 28, 1630 in Beresford Hall, England
d. February 16, 1687 in London, England

Louis (Marie Anne) Couperius
Dutch author–educator
• Wrote four-vol. epic *The Books of the Small Souls*, 1914-18.
b. June 1, 1863 in The Hague, Netherlands
d. July 16, 1923 in De Steeg, Netherlands

John Cournos
Author
• His immigrant life in England is background for books: *The Mask*, 1919; *The Wall*, 1921.
b. March 06, 1881 in Russia
d. August 29, 1966

Margaret Cousins
American children's author
• Books include *Uncle Edgar and the Reluctant Saint*, 1948; *Ben Franklin of Old Philadelphia*, 1952.
b. January 26, 1905 in Munday, Texas

Norman Cousins
American editor–author
• Editor *Saturday Review*, 1937-72; author of 25 books on the nature of illness: *Anatomy of an Illness as Perceived by the Patient*, 1979.
b. June 24, 1912 in Union Hill, New Jersey
d. November 3, 1990 in Westwood, California

Cyclone Covey
American author
• Wrote *The Gentle Radical*, 1966.
b. May 21, 1922 in Guthrie, Oklahoma

John Cowles, Sr
American publisher–business executive
• Owner of several daily newspapers, including *Minneapolis Star*.
b. December 14, 1898 in Algona, Iowa
d. February 25, 1983 in Minneapolis, Minnesota

William Hutchinson Cowles, Jr
American publisher
• Pres., Spokane Chronicle Co., 1935-68; Cowles Publishing Co., 1946-70.
b. July 23, 1902 in Sands Point, New York
d. August 12, 1971 in Spokane, Washington

Abraham Cowley
English poet
• Originator of English Pindaric ode; best known poem "Davideis," 1656.
b. 1618 in London, England
d. July 28, 1667 in Chertsey, England

George Harmon Coxe
American author
• Wrote over 60 mystery novels, had several series characters.
b. April 23, 1901 in Oleon, New York
d. January 3, 1984 in Hilton Head Island, South Carolina

Harold Coy
American children's author
• Non-fiction books include *The First Book of Presidents*, 1973.
b. September 24, 1902 in La Habre, California

James Gould Cozzens
American author
• Awarded Pulitzer for *Guard of Honor*, 1948.
b. August 19, 1903 in Chicago, Illinois
d. August 09, 1978 in Stuart, Florida

George Crabbe
English poet
• Wrote realistic narrative poems, "The Village," 1783; "The Borough," 1810.
b. December 24, 1754 in Aldeburgh, England
d. February 03, 1832 in Trowbridge, England

Helen Craig
English children's author–illustrator
• Wrote, illustrated prize-winning *Mouse House* series, 1978-83.
b. August 3, 1934 in London, England

Hart Crane
American poet
• Major poetry collections: *White Buildings*, 1926; *The Bridge*, 1930.
b. July 21, 1899 in Garrettsville, Ohio
d. April 27, 1932

Nathalia Clara Ruth Crane
American poet–author
• Wrote notable verse collection: *Janitor's Boy* at age 11.
b. August 11, 1913 in New York, New York

Stephen Crane
American author
• Wrote novels *Maggie: A Girl of the Streets*, 1893; *The Red Badge of Courage*, 1895.
b. November 01, 1871 in Newark, New Jersey
d. June 05, 1900 in Badenweiler, Germany

Adelaide Crapsey
American poet
• Her poetry was posthumously published in *Verse*, 1914; invented "cinquain" verse form.
b. September 09, 1878 in New York, New York
d. October 08, 1914 in Saranac Lake, New York

Christina Crawford
American actress–author
• Daughter of Joan Crawford; wrote *Mommy Dearest*, 1978; Faye Dunaway starred in movie, 1981.
b. June 11, 1939 in Hollywood, California

John Creasey
English author
• Crime novelist who wrote under 28 pen names; won Edgar, 1962, for *Gideon's Fire*.
b. September 17, 1908 in Southfields, England
d. June 09, 1973 in Salisbury, England

Robert White Creeley
American author–poet
• Edited *Black Mountain Review;* among his collections: *A Form of Women*, 1959.
b. May 21, 1926 in Arlington, Massachusetts

Harry Eugene Crews
American author
• Southern gothic novelist who wrote *Florida Frenzy*, 1982.
b. June 06, 1935 in Alma, Georgia

Robert Crichton
American author
• Wrote *The Great Imposter*, 1958; filmed, 1961; autobiography: *Memoirs of a Bad Soldier*, 1979.
b. January 29, 1925 in Albuquerque, New Mexico

Quentin Crisp, pseud
(Denis Pratt)
English author
• Noted for autobiography *The Naked Civil Servant*, 1968.
b. December 25, 1908 in Sutton, England

Rupert Croft-Cooke
English author
• Detective novels examples of classic British mystery.
b. June 2, 1903 in Edenbridge, England
d. 1979 in Bournemouth, England

Freeman Willis Crofts
Irish author
• Mystery tales include *French Strikes Oil*, 1952.
b. June 1879 in Dublin, Ireland
d. April 11, 1957

Herbert David Croly
American journalist
• Founder, first editor of liberal journal *The New Republic*, 1914-30.
b. January 23, 1869 in New York, New York
d. May 17, 1930 in Santa Barbara, California

A(rchibald) J(oseph) Cronin
American author
• Best known for *The Citadel*, 1937; *Keys of the Kingdom*, 1941.
b. July 19, 1896 in Helensburgh, England
d. January 06, 1981 in Glion, Switzerland

Alexander L Crosby
American children's author
• Books include *The Rio Grande*, 1966; *Steamboat Up the Colorado*, 1965.
b. June 1, 1906 in Catonsville, Maryland
d. January 31, 1980 in Quakertown, Pennsylvania

Harry Crosby
American publisher–poet
• Founder, Black Sun Press, 1927, which produced limited editions of T S Eliot, Joyce; obsession with death led to murder, suicide.
b. 1898 in Boston, Massachusetts
d. December 1, 1929 in New York, New York

Aleister (Edward Alexander) Crowley
English author–magician
• Writer of occult lore, Black Magic rites: *Diary of a Drug Fiend*, 1922.
b. October 12, 1875 in Leamington, England
d. December 01, 1947 in Brighton, England

Diane Crowley
American journalist
• Co-winner of nationwide search for Ann Landers' advice column replacement, 1986.
b. 1940

Francis Welch Crowninshield
(Arthur Loring Bruce)
American editor–publisher
• Edited *Vanity Fair*, 1914-35; one of founders of Museum of Modern Art.
b. June 24, 1872 in Paris, France
d. December 28, 1947 in New York, New York

Hugh Cudlipp
Welsh journalist
• Editor, England's *Daily Mirror*, 1952-63; wrote *Publish and Be Damned*, 1953.
b. August 28, 1913 in Cardiff, Wales

Countee Cullen
American poet
• Wrote *Color*, 1925; *The Black Christ*, 1930.
b. May 3, 1903 in New York, New York
d. January 1, 1946 in New York, New York

e(dward) e(stlin) cummings
American poet–author
• Noted for eccentricity of punctuation, typography; first published work was autobiographical *The Enormous Room*, 1922.
b. October 14, 1894 in Cambridge, Massachusetts
d. September 03, 1962 in North Conway, New Hampshire

Euclides da Cunha
Brazilian author
• Wrote *Os Sertoes*, 1902, which is considered the finest representation of the Brazilian cry for national unity, identity.
b. January 2, 1866 in Santa Rita, Brazil
d. August 15, 1909 in Rio de Janeiro, Brazil

Graham Robert Boutine Cunninghame
English author–traveler
• Wrote on S America: *Portrait of a Dictator*, 1933; city Don Roberto, Argentina named for him.
b. May 24, 1852 in London, England
d. March 2, 1936 in Buenos Aires, Argentina

Eve Curie
(Mrs Henry R Labouisse)
French author–journalist
• Wrote best-selling biography of her mother, *Madame Curie*, 1937.
b. December 06, 1904 in Paris, France

Cyrus Hermann Kotzschmar Curtis
American newspaper publisher
• Founded Curtis Publishing Co., 1891; published *Saturday Evening Post; Ladies Home Journal*.
b. June 18, 1850 in Portland, Maine
d. June 07, 1933 in Wyncote, Pennsylvania

Cynewulf
English poet
• Old English religious poet, most praised for "Elene," "Ascension."
b. 8th

Savinien de Cyrano de Bergerac
French poet–soldier
• Life romanticized by Edmond Rostand in *Cyrano de Bergerac*, 1897.
b. March 06, 1619
d. September 1655

Edward Dahlberg
American author
• Novels include *Bottom Dogs*, 1929; *Because I Was Flesh*, 1964.
b. July 22, 1900 in Boston, Massachusetts
d. February 27, 1977 in Santa Barbara, California

Janet Dailey
American author
• America's best-selling romance author; over 60 books include *Calder Born, Calder Bred*, 1987.
b. May 21, 1944 in Storm Lake, Iowa

Maureen Patricia Daly
Irish author
• Books, *Seventeenth Summer*, 1942; *The Ginger House*, 1964, have been filmed.
b. March 15, 1921 in Ulster, Northern Ireland

Clifton Daniel, Jr
American journalist
• With *NY Times*, 1944-80, associate editor, 1969-77; married to Margaret Truman.
b. September 19, 1912 in Zebulon, North Carolina

Nicholas Daniloff
American journalist
• Reporter with *US News & World Report*; jailed, accused of spying in Soviet Union, 1986.
b. December 3, 1934 in Paris, France

Frederic Dannay
(Ellery Queen Barnaby Ross joint pseuds; Daniel Nathan original name)
American author
• Wrote many *Ellery Queen* mysteries with cousin Manfred B Lee; won four Edgars.
b. October 2, 1905 in Brooklyn, New York
d. September 03, 1982 in White Plains, New York

Gabriele D'Annunzio
Italian poet–author–soldier
• Ardent fascist, courted by Mussolini; numerous writings include *Dead City*, 1902; famed WW I aviator.
b. March 12, 1863 in Pescara, Italy
d. March 01, 1938 in Vittoriale, Italy

Dante Alighieri
Italian poet
• Wrote celebrated masterpiece *The Divine Comedy*, 1307-21.
b. May 27, 1265 in Florence, Italy
d. September 14, 1321 in Ravenna, Italy

Olive Tilford Dargan
American poet–author
• Writings include poetic drama, lyric poetry, proletarian novels; best known for *A Stone Came Rolling*, 1935.
b. 1869 in Grayson County, Kentucky
d. January 22, 1968 in Asheville, North Carolina

Helen Fern Daringer
American children's author
• Writings include *Yesterday's Daughter*, 1964; *Just Plain Betsy*, 1967.
b. 1892 in Mattoon, Illinois

Robert Choate Darnton
American author
• Wrote award-winning *Literary Underground of the Old Regime*, 1982.
b. May 1, 1939 in New York, New York

Leon Daudet
French author–politician
• Wrote 40 books; co-editor, *L'Action Francaise*; supported French Royalist movement.
b. November 16, 1867
d. July 01, 1942

James Henry Daugherty
American children's author–illustrator
• Wrote, illustrated history books for children; won Newbery for *Daniel Boone*, 1939.
b. June 01, 1889 in Ashville, North Carolina
d. February 21, 1974

Marcia Davenport
American author–critic
• Wrote best-selling *Valley of Decision*, 1942; *East Side, West Side*, 1947.
b. June 09, 1903 in New York, New York

Donald Grady Davidson
American poet–critic–historian
• Founded Fugitive School of southern American literature, 1920's.
b. August 18, 1893 in Campbellsville, Tennessee
d. April 25, 1968 in Nashville, Tennessee

Hunter Davies
Scottish author–editor
• *Punch* columnist since 1979; wrote authorized biography of The Beatles, 1968; *London at Its Best*, 1984.
b. January 07, 1936 in Renfrew, Scotland

Leslie Purnell Davies
(Leslie Vardre pseud)
English author
• Writings include *The Paper Dolls*, 1964; *The Land of Leys*, 1979.
b. October 2, 1914 in Cheshire, England

Robertson (William Robertson) Davies
Canadian author
• One of Canada's most accomplished writers; known for Deptford trilogy.
b. August 28, 1913 in Thamesville, Ontario

Burke Davis
American children's author
• Writings include *Whisper My Name*, 1949; *Sherman's March*, 1973.
b. July 24, 1913 in Durham, North Carolina

Clyde Brion Davis
American journalist–author
• Best known for *The Great American Novel*, 1938.
b. May 22, 1894 in Unadilla, Nebraska
d. July 19, 1962 in Salisbury, Connecticut

Frederick C(lyde) Davis
(Murdo Coombs; Stephen Ransome; Curtis Steele pseuds)
American author
• Wrote several mysteries including *Warning Bell*, 1960.
b. June 02, 1902 in Saint Joseph, Missouri
d. 1977

Gerry Davis
English author
• Wrote science fiction series *Doctor Who*, 1974-78.
b. February 23, 1930 in London, England

Harold Lenoir Davis
American author
• Books include *Honey in the Horn*, 1935, Pulitzer winner.
b. October 18, 1896 in Yoncalla, Oregon
d. October 31, 1960 in San Antonio, Texas

Rebecca Blaine Harding Davis
American author–journalist
• Wrote *Waiting for the Verdict*, 1867; mother of Richard.
b. June 24, 1831 in Washington, Pennsylvania
d. September 29, 1910 in Mount Kisco, New York

Richard Harding Davis
American author–journalist
• War correspondent in six wars; wrote *The Bar Sinister*, 1903.
b. April 18, 1864 in Philadelphia, Pennsylvania
d. April 11, 1916 in Mount Kisco, New York

Geoffrey (George Geoffrey) Dawson
English editor
• Edited the London *Times*, 1911-41.
b. October 25, 1874 in Skipton-in-Craven, England
d. November 07, 1944 in London, England

Benjamin Henry Day
American publisher
• Founded *NY Sun*, 1833, the first one-cent daily paper.
b. April 1, 1810 in West Springfield, Massachusetts
d. December 21, 1889 in New York, New York

Cecil Day-Lewis
(Nicholas Blake pseud)
British poet–author
• Poet laureate, 1968, wrote numerous detective stories, verse collections. Father of actor Daniel.
b. April 27, 1904 in Ballintogher, Ireland
d. May 22, 1972 in London, England

Marguerite Lofft DeAngeli
American children's author–illustrator
• Won Newbery, 1950, for *A Door in the Wall*.
b. March 14, 1889 in Lapeer, Michigan
d. June 19, 1987 in Philadelphia, Pennsylvania

L(yon) Sprague DeCamp
American author
• Wrote many science-fiction *Conan* books based on character created by Robert E Howard; won Grand Master of Fantasy Award, 1976.
b. November 27, 1907 in New York, New York

Charles Theodore Henri Decoster
Belgian author
• Wrote one of the most important works in French-Belgian literature: *La Legende d'Ulenspiegel*, 1867.
b. August 2, 1827 in Munich, Germany
d. May 07, 1879 in Brussels, Belgium

Vladimir Dedijer
Yugoslav author
• Writings include *Letters from America*, 1945; *Sarajevo: 1914*, 1966.
b. February 02, 1914 in Belgrade, Yugoslavia

Daniel Defoe
English author
• Wrote *Robinson Crusoe*, 1719, based on adventures of Alexander Selkirk.
b. April 26, 1661 in London, England
d. April 26, 1731 in London, England

Robert F(air) DeGraff
American publisher
• Co-founded first American paperback co., Pocket Books, 1939.
b. June 09, 1895 in Plainfield, New Jersey
d. November 01, 1981 in Mill Neck, New York

Len (Leonard Cyril) Deighton
English author
• Best known for spy thrillers: *The Ipcress File*, 1962; movie starred Michael Caine, 1965.
b. February 18, 1929 in London, England

Meindert Dejong
American children's author
• Won Newbery for *Wheel on the School*, 1954; National Book Award for *Journey from Peppermint Street*, 1969.
b. March 04, 1906 in Wierum, Netherlands

George Thomas Delacorte, Jr
American publisher
• Established Dell Publishing Co., Inc., 1921; retired as chm., 1980.
b. June 2, 1894 in New York, New York

Samuel Ray Delany, Jr
American author
• Helped to make science fiction a respected literary genre.
b. April 01, 1942 in New York, New York

Stanton Hill Delaplane
American journalist
• Syndicated travel writer, *San Francisco Chronicle*, 1953-88; won Pulitzer for reporting, 1942.
b. October 12, 1907 in Chicago, Illinois
d. April 18, 1988 in San Francisco, California

Mazo DeLaRoche
Canadian author
• Best known for novel *Jalna*, 1927, first in a series of an Ontario family chronicle.
b. January 15, 1885 in Toronto, Ontario
d. July 12, 1961 in Toronto, Ontario

Grazia Deledda
(Grazia Madesani)
Italian author
• Writings depict Sardinian peasantry; won Nobel Prize, 1926.
b. September 27, 1875 in Nvoro, Sardinia
d. August 16, 1936 in Rome, Italy

Vina Croter Delmar
American author
• Novels include *The Laughing Stranger*, 1953; *Grandmere*, 1967.
b. January 29, 1905 in New York, New York

John Zachary DeLorean
American auto executive–author
• Founded DeLorean Motor Co., 1975; wrote *On a Clear Day you Can See General Motors*.
b. January 06, 1925 in Detroit, Michigan

Patrick Dennis, pseud
(Virginia Rowens pseud; Edward Everett Tanner III)
American author
• Known for *Auntie Mame*, which was adapted to film, Broadway musical *Mame*.
b. May 18, 1921 in Chicago, Illinois
d. November 06, 1976 in New York, New York

Thomas DeQuincey
English author
• Eloquent prose evident in masterpiece *Confessions of an English Opium Eater*, 1822.
b. August 15, 1785 in Greenheys, England
d. December 08, 1859 in Edinburgh, Scotland

Beatrice Schenk DeRegniers
American children's author
• Won Caldecott award for *May I Bring a Friend?* 1964; other books include *Waiting for Mama*, 1984.
b. August 16, 1914 in Lafayette, Indiana

Eustache Deschamps
French poet
• Wrote over 1,000 ballads; first critical treatise on French poetry, 1392.
b. 1346 in Vertus, France
d. 1406

Louis-Ferdinand Destouches
(Louis-Ferdinand Celine)
French author–physician
• Wrote *Journey to End of the Night*, 1934; *Death on Installment Plan*, 1938.
b. May 27, 1894 in Paris, France
d. July 04, 1961 in Paris, France

Aubrey Thomas DeVere
Irish poet–critic
• Promoted Celtic literary revival; wrote of Irish lore: *Legends of St. Patrick*, 1872.
b. January 1, 1814 in Curragh Chase, Ireland
d. January 21, 1902

Louis DeWohl
(Ludwig Von Wohl-Musciny)
German author
• Among his historical novels about saints, about 20 were filmed, dramatized.
b. January 24, 1903 in Berlin, Germany
d. June 02, 1961 in Lucerne, Switzerland

Michel Harry DeYoung
American newspaper editor
• With brother, founded what later became the *San Francisco Chronicle*, 1865, editor-in-chief, 1880-1925.
b. October 01, 1849 in Saint Louis, Missouri
d. February 15, 1925

Philip K(indred) Dick
(Richard Phillips pseud)
American author
• Science fiction writer who won 1962 Hugo award for *Man in the High Castle*.
b. December 16, 1928 in Chicago, Illinois
d. March 02, 1982 in Santa Ana, California

Charles John Huffam Dickens
(Boz pseud)
English author–dramatist
• Master storyteller who wrote classics *Pickwick Papers*, 1837; *Christmas Carol*, 1843; *Tale of Two Cities*, 1859.
b. February 07, 1812 in Portsmouth, England
d. June 09, 1870 in Godshill, England

Monica Enid Dickens
English author
• Wrote autobiographical series *One Pair of Hands*, 1939; *One Pair of Feet*, 1942.
b. May 1, 1915 in London, England

James Dickey
American poet–critic
• Wrote *Deliverance*, 1970; filmed, 1972, starring Burt Reynolds, Jon Voight.
b. February 02, 1923 in Atlanta, Georgia

Emily Elizabeth Dickinson
American poet
• Highly reclusive American literary giant; most works published posthumously.
b. December 1, 1830 in Amherst, Massachusetts
d. May 15, 1886 in Amherst, Massachusetts

Gordon Rupert Dickson
Canadian author
• Won Hugo for *Soldier, Ask Not*, 1965; other novels include *Wolfing*, 1969.
b. November 01, 1923 in Edmonton, Alberta

Denis Diderot
(Pantophile Diderot)
French editor–philosopher
• Editor, *Encyclopedie*, 1745, first modern encyclopedia; wrote novels, plays, art criticism.
b. October 05, 1713 in Langres, France
d. July 3, 1784 in Paris, France

Annie Doak Dillard
American author
• Won Pulitzer for *Pilgrim at Tinker Creek*, 1975.
b. April 3, 1945 in Pittsburgh, Pennsylvania

George Dillon
American author–editor
• Editor, *Poetry* Magazine, 1937-50; won 1931 Pulitzer for *Flowering Stone*.
b. November 12, 1906 in Jacksonville, Florida
d. May 09, 1968 in Charleston, South Carolina

Doris Miles Disney
American author
• Novel *Do Not Fold, Spindle, or Mutilate* adapted to film, 1971.
b. December 22, 1907 in Glastonbury, Connecticut
d. March 08, 1976 in Fredericksburg, Virginia

Isaac D'Israeli
English author–essayist
• First, considered best work: *Curiosities of Literature*, 1791-1823; father of Benjamin.
b. May 11, 1766 in London, England
d. January 19, 1848

Dorothy Dix, pseud
(Elizabeth Meriwether Gilmer)
American journalist–author
• Wrote syndicated column on advice to lovelorn, beginning 1896.
b. November 18, 1870 in Woodstock, Tennessee
d. December 16, 1951 in New Orleans, Louisiana

Jeane Pinckert Dixon
American astrologer–author
• Proponent of ESP known for horoscopes, annual predictions; began predicting at age eight.
b. January 05, 1918 in Medford, Wisconsin

Thomas Dixon
American author–clergyman
• His novel *The Clansman*, 1905, was basis for silent film epic *Birth of a Nation*, 1914.
b. January 11, 1865 in Shelby, North Carolina
d. April 03, 1946 in Raleigh, North Carolina

Milovan Djilas
Yugoslav author–politician
• VP of Yugoslavia, 1954; won US Freedom Award, 1968; books include *Tito*, 1980.
b. 1911 in Kolasin, Yugoslavia

E(dgar) L(aurence) Doctorow
American author–editor
• Combined historical figures, events with fiction in *Ragtime*, 1975.
b. January 06, 1931 in New York, New York

Mary Elizabeth Mapes Dodge
American children's author–editor
• Editor of children's magazine *St. Nicholas*, 1873-1905; wrote *Hans Brinker & the Silver Skates*, 1865.
b. January 26, 1831 in New York, New York
d. August 21, 1905 in Onteora Park, New York

Robert Dodsley
English bookseller–dramatist–publisher
• Founded *Annual Register*, 1758; helped finance Johnson's dictionary.
b. 1703 in Mansfield, England
d. 1764 in Durham, England

Stephen Reeder Donaldson
American author
• Won Fantasy Society Award for leper trilogy *Chronicles of Thomas Covenant*, 1978.
b. May 13, 1947 in Cleveland, Ohio

John Donne
English poet
• Metaphysical poet wrote sonnet "Death Be Not Proud"; poems neglected until 20th c.
b. 1573 in London, England
d. March 31, 1631 in London, England

Ignatius Donnelly
American politician–author
• *The Great Cryptogram*, 1888; *The Cipher in the Plays and on the Tombstone*, 1899, two studies on possibility of Bacon's authorship of Shakespeare's plays.
b. November 03, 1831 in Philadelphia, Pennsylvania
d. January 01, 1901 in Minneapolis, Minnesota

Hedley Williams Donovan
American journalist
• Editor in chief of all Time Inc. publications, 1964-79; wrote *Roosevelt to Reagan: A Reporter's Encounters With Nine Presidents*, 1985.
b. May 24, 1914 in Brainerd, Minnesota
d. August 14, 1990 in New York, New York

Rheta Childe Door
American journalist–feminist
• Covered Russian Revolution, WW I troops in France; wrote *Inside the Russian Revolution*, 1917.
b. November 02, 1866 in Omaha, Nebraska
d. August 08, 1948 in New Britain, Pennsylvania

Michael (Anthony) Dorris
American author
• Author of *The Broken Cord*, a largely autobiographical tale of fetal alcohol syndrome. Also *A Yellow Raft in Blue Water*, 1987. Currently working on *The Crown of Columbus* with wife Louise Erdrich.
b. January 30, 1945 in Dayton, Washington

Fyodor Mikhailovich Dostoyevsky
(Fyodor Dostoevski; Fedor Dostoevsky; Fyoder Dostoievsky)
Russian author
• Wrote novels *Crime and Punishment*, 1886; *The Idiot*, 1887; *Brothers Karamazov*, 1912.
b. November 11, 1821 in Moscow, Russia
d. February 09, 1881 in Saint Petersburg, Russia

Frank Nelson Doubleday
American publisher
• Founded Doubleday and Co., 1897.
b. January 08, 1862 in Brooklyn, New York
d. January 3, 1934 in Coconut Grove, Florida

Nelson Doubleday
American publisher
• Son of Frank Doubleday; founded Nelson Doubleday, Inc., 1910.
b. June 16, 1889 in Brooklyn, New York
d. January 11, 1949 in Oyster Bay, New York

Nelson Doubleday
American publisher–baseball executive
• CEO, Doubleday; majority owner, NY Mets, 1980-.
b. July 2, 1933 in Oyster Bay, New York

Lord Alfred Bruce Douglas
English author–poet
• Noted for intimate relationship with Oscar Wilde.
b. October 21, 1870
d. March 2, 1945 in Sussex, England

Gavin Douglas
Scottish poet–translator
• Noted for *Aeneid* translation, first classic work translated into English dialect.
b. 1474 in Tantallon Castle, Scotland
d. 1522 in London, England

Keith Castellain Douglas
English poet–soldier
• WW II casualty whose *Selected Poems*, were edited by Ted Hughes, 1964.
b. 1920 in Tunbridge Wells, England
d. June 1944 in St. Pierre, France

Lloyd Cassel Douglas
American author–clergyman
• Wrote best-sellers *Magnificent Obsession*, 1929; *Green Light*, 1935; *The Robe*, 1942, became first Cinema Scope film, 1953.
b. August 27, 1877 in Columbia City, Indiana
d. February 13, 1951 in Los Angeles, California

Charles Henry Dow
American financier–publisher
• With Edward D Jones started *Wall Street Journal*, 1889; laid basis for "Dow Theory," Dow-Jones average.
b. November 06, 1851 in Sterling, Connecticut
d. December 04, 1902 in Brooklyn, New York

Olin (Edwin Olin) Downes
American critic–author
• Music critic with *NY Times* for 32 yrs.; music books include *A Treasury of American Song*.
b. January 27, 1886 in Evanston, Illinois
d. August 22, 1955 in New York, New York

Fairfax Davis Downey
American author
• Wrote more than 50 books on historical, military, or animal themes including *Storming the Gateway*, 1960.
b. November 28, 1893 in Salt Lake City, Utah
d. May 31, 1990 in Springfield, New Hampshire

Sir Arthur Conan Doyle
Scottish author–physician
• Introduced Sherlock Holmes in *A Study in Scarlet*, 1887.
b. May 22, 1859 in Edinburgh, Scotland
d. July 07, 1930 in Crowborough, England

Margaret Drabble
English author
• Novels include *The Needle's Eye*, 1972; *The Middle Ground*, 1980.
b. June 05, 1939 in Sheffield, England

Theodore Dreiser
American editor–author
• Wrote *Sister Carrie*, 1900, *An American Tragedy*, 1925; books attacked as immoral.
b. August 27, 1871 in Terre Haute, Indiana
d. December 28, 1945 in Hollywood, California

Davis Dresser
(Brett Halliday pseud)
American author
• Mystery novels include *Framed in Blood*, 1951; *Violence Is Golden*, 1968.
b. July 31, 1904 in Chicago, Illinois
d. February 04, 1977 in Montecito, California

Rosalyn Drexler
American author
• Won 1979 Obie for *The Writer's Opera*, 1974 Emmy for *The Lily Show*.
b. November 25, 1926 in Bronx, New York

Hubert L(ederer) Dreyfus
American author
• Philosophy writings include *Sense and Nonsense*, 1964.
b. October 15, 1929 in Terre Haute, Indiana

Roscoe (James Roscoe) Drummond
American journalist
• Wrote newspaper column "State of the Nation" for 25 yrs.
b. January 13, 1902 in Theresa, New York
d. September 3, 1983 in Princeton, New Jersey

William Drummond of Hawthornden
Scottish poet
• Collections of Elizabethan verse include *Forth Feasting*, 1617; wrote *History of Scotland*, published in 1655.
b. December 13, 1585 in Hawthornden, Scotland
d. December 04, 1649 in Hawthornden, Scotland

Allen Stuart Drury
American author
• Background as Washington journalist was source for his Pulitzer-winning novel, *Advise and Consent*, 1960.
b. September 02, 1918 in Houston, Texas

John Dryden
English poet–dramatist
• Poet laureate, 1668-89; best-known play *Marriage a la Mode*, 1672.
b. August 09, 1631 in North Hamptonshire, England
d. May 01, 1700 in London, England

William Pene Du Bois
American children's author–illustrator
• Wrote, illustrated 1948 Newbery winner, *The Twenty-One Balloons;* son of Guy Pene.
b. May 09, 1916 in Nutley, New Jersey

Alan Dugan
American poet
• Verse vols. include *Collected Poems 1961-83*, 1983; won Pulitzer, 1963.
b. February 12, 1923 in Brooklyn, New York

Alexandre Dumas
(Dumas Pere)
French author–dramatist
• Best known works *The Three Musketeers*, 1844; *The Count of Monte Cristo*, 1845.
b. July 24, 1802 in Villers-Cotterets, France
d. December 05, 1870 in Puys, France

Daphne DuMaurier
(Lady Browning)
English author
• Classic gothic novels include *Rebecca*, 1938; *Jamaica Inn*, 1936.
b. May 13, 1907 in London, England
d. April 19, 1989 in Par, England

Paul Laurence Dunbar
American poet–author
• Published 24 volumes of fiction, poetry; poems used Negro folk material, dialect.
b. June 27, 1872 in Dayton, Ohio
d. February 09, 1906 in Dayton, Ohio

William Dunbar
Scottish poet
• Scottish Chaucerian who wrote *Dance of the Seven Deadly Sins*, 1503-08.
b. 1460
d. 1520

Robert Edward Duncan
American poet
• Considered one of greatest American lyric poets of his generation; wrote 14 books of poetry; received first National Poetry Award, 1985.
b. January 07, 1919 in Oakland, California

Finley Peter Dunne
American author–editor
• Best known as creator of Mr. Dooley, who commented on political issues for 30 years.
b. July 1, 1867 in Chicago, Illinois
d. April 24, 1936 in New York, New York

John Gregory Dunne
American author
• Wrote *True Confessions*, 1977; filmed, 1981.
b. May 25, 1932 in Hartford, Connecticut

Ariel (Ida Ariel Ethel Kaufman) Durant
(Mrs William James Durant)
American author
• Collaborated with husband, Will, on *Story of Civilization*.
b. May 1, 1898 in Proskurov, Russia
d. October 25, 1981 in Los Angeles, California

Will(iam James) Durant
American historian–author
• Produced, with wife Ida, 11-volume, 1926 Pulitzer winner *Story of Civilization*.
b. November 05, 1885 in North Adams, Massachusetts
d. November 07, 1981 in Los Angeles, California

Marguerite Duras, pseud
(Marguerite Donnadieu)
French author
• Acclaimed for novels, screenplays; film *Hiroshima Mon Amor*, 1954, won several awards; novel *L'Amant*, 1984, considered her best.
b. April 04, 1914 in Gia Dinh, French Indochina

Lawrence George Durrell
(Charles Norden pseud)
English author
• Chief work was four-part novel *Alexandria Quartet*, finished in 1960.
b. February 27, 1912 in Darjeeling, India
d. November 07, 1990 in Sommieres, France

E(dward) P(ayson) Dutton
American publisher
• Founded E P Dutton publishing house, 1858.
b. January 04, 1831 in Keene, New Hampshire
d. September 06, 1923

Roger Antoine Duvoisin
American children's author–illustrator
• Numerous works include 1948 Caldecott winner *White Snow, Bright Snow;* wrote *Happy Lion* series.
b. August 28, 1904 in Geneva, Switzerland
d. June 3, 1980 in Morristown, New Jersey

Cynthia Dwyer
American journalist
• Free-lance writer, imprisoned for attempting to free 52 American hostages in Iran; released, Feb 1981.
b. 1931 in Little Rock, Arkansas

Alexander Dyce
Scottish editor
• Noted for edition of Shakespeare, 1857, 1864-67; edited Collins's poems, 1827.
b. June 3, 1798 in Edinburgh, Scotland
d. May 15, 1869

Charles (Raymond) Dyer
English writer
• Novels include *Prelude to Fury*, 1959; screenplays include *Staircase*, 1969.
b. July 17, 1928 in Shrewsbury, England

Sir Edward Dyer
English diplomat–poet
• Most famous poem begins "My mind to me a kingdom is," a description of contentment.
b. 1545 in Somerset, England
d. May 1607 in London, England

Wayne Walter Dyer
American author
• Wrote *Your Erroneous Zones*, 1976; *The Sky's the Limit*, 1980.
b. May 1, 1940 in Detroit, Michigan

William (Derry) Eastlake
American author
• Writings include *The Bamboo Bed*, 1970; *Dancers in the Scalp House*, 1975.
b. July 14, 1917 in New York, New York

Mary Henderson Eastman
American author
• Wrote Indian tales, anti-Uncle Tom work *Uncle Phillis's Cabin*, 1852.
b. 1818 in Fauquier County, Virginia
d. February 24, 1887 in Washington, District of Columbia

Mignon Good Eberhart
American author
• Wrote over 50 detective fiction books, including *Murder in Waiting*, 1973; created sleuth nurse, Sarah Keate.
b. July 06, 1899 in Nebraska

Richard (Ghormley) Eberhart
American poet–dramatist
• Won Pulitzer for *Selected Poems 1930-1965*, 1965; also wrote *Ways of Light*, 1980.
b. April 05, 1904 in Austin, Minnesota

Irmengarde Eberle
(Allyn Allen; Phyllis Ann Carter pseuds)
American author
• Among 63 books are *Mustang on the Prairie*, 1968; *Moose Live Here*, 1971.
b. November 11, 1898 in San Antonio, Texas
d. February 27, 1979

Horst Eckert
(Janosch pseud)
Polish children's author–illustrator
• Writings, illustrations include *The Magic Auto*, 1971; *The Thieves and the Raven*, 1970.
b. March 11, 1931 in Zaborze, Poland

Leon (Joseph Leon) Edel
American author–journalist
• Writings include *The Middle Years*, 1963; *The Master*, 1972; won Pulitzer, 1963.
b. September 09, 1907 in Pittsburgh, Pennsylvania

Dorothy Eden
New Zealander author
• Wrote romantic fiction: *The Vines of Yarrabee*, 1969; *The Salamanca Drum*, 1979.
b. April 03, 1912 in Canterbury, New Zealand
d. March 04, 1982 in London, England

Maria Edgeworth
English children's author
• Novels depict Irish life, moral tales for children.
b. January 01, 1767 in Bourton Abbots, England
d. May 22, 1849 in Edgeworthstown, Ireland

Walter Dumaux Edmonds
American author
• Known for historical novels of NY; won 1942 Newbery for *Matchlock Gun*.
b. July 15, 1903 in Boonville, New York

India Moffett Edwards
American journalist–politician
• National Democratic Committee executive, 1940s; persuaded Harry Truman to appoint more women to federal posts; wrote memoirs *Pulling No Punches*, 1977.
b. 1895 in Chicago, Illinois
d. January 14, 1990 in Sebastopol, California

Fredrik Willem van Eeden
Dutch author
• Wrote novel trilogy *The Quest*, 1885-1907; founded Walden farm colony inspired by Thoreau, 1898.
b. May 03, 1860 in Haarlem, Netherlands
d. June 16, 1932 in Bussum, Netherlands

Ilya Grigoryevich Ehrenburg
(Ilya Ehrenbourg; Ilya Erenburg)
Russian author
• Prominent Soviet literary figure; 1954 novel *The Thaw* was precursor of expanded intellectual liberalism.
b. January 27, 1891 in Kiev, Russia
d. August 31, 1967 in Moscow, U.S.S.R.

Virginia Snider Eifert
American children's author
• Award-winning books include *Mississippi Calling*, 1957; *Journeys in Green Places*, 1963.
b. January 23, 1911 in Springfield, Illinois
d. June 16, 1966

T(homas) S(tearns) Eliot
English poet–critic
• Wrote *Murder in the Cathedral*, 1935, *The Cocktail Party*, 1950; won Nobel Prize, 1948.
b. September 26, 1888 in Saint Louis, Missouri
d. January 04, 1965 in London, England

Benjamin Elkin
American children's author
• Writings include *King's Wish and Other Stories*, 1960; *Magic Ring*, 1969.
b. August 1, 1911 in Baltimore, Maryland

Stanley (Lawrence) Elkin
American author
• Novels include *The Magic Kingdom*, 1985; *The Rabbi of Lud*, 1987.
b. May 11, 1930 in New York, New York

Stanley Ellin
American author
• Mystery writer whose books include *The Eighth Circle*, 1958; *The Key to Nicholas Street*, 1951.
b. October 06, 1916 in Brooklyn, New York
d. July 31, 1986 in New York, New York

Ebenezer Elliott
English poet
• Attributed all nat. problems to bread tax, which he condemned in influential *Corn Law Rhymes*, 1831.
b. March 17, 1781 in Masborough, England
d. December 01, 1849 in Great Haughton, England

Harlan Jay Ellison
American author
• Wrote 42 books including *Shatterday*, 1980; *An Edge in My Voice*, 1985.
b. May 27, 1934 in Cleveland, Ohio

Ralph Waldo Ellison
American author
• Novel *The Invisible Man*, 1952, proclaimed beginning of 1960s civil rights movement.
b. March 01, 1914 in Oklahoma City, Oklahoma

James Ellroy
American author
• Crime novels include *Blood on the Moon*, 1984; *The Black Dahlia*, 1987.
b. 1948

Robert Truscott Elson
American editor–journalist
• Editor, Time Inc., 1943-69.
b. June 21, 1906 in Cleveland, Ohio
d. March 11, 1987 in Southampton, New York

Sir Thomas Elyot
English author
• Wrote first Latin-English dictionary, 1538.
b. 1490 in Wiltshire, England
d. March 2, 1546 in Carleton, England

Odysseus Elytis
(Odysseus Elytis Alepoudhelis)
Greek poet–critic
• Awarded Nobel Prize in literature, 1979, for work in poetry.
b. November 02, 1911 in Iraklion, Crete

Ralph Waldo Emerson
American essayist–poet–philosopher
• A leading transcendentalist; wrote essay *Self-Reliance*, 1844.
b. May 25, 1803 in Boston, Massachusetts
d. April 27, 1882 in Concord, Massachusetts

Anne (McGuigan) Emery
American author
• Writings include *The Sky Is Falling*, 1970; *Step Family*, 1980.
b. September 01, 1907 in Fargo, North Dakota

Mihail Eminescu
(Mihail Emin)
Romanian poet
• Influential writer of over 60 poems, one novel; suffered from periods of insanity.
b. December 2, 1849 in Botosani, Romania
d. June 15, 1889 in Bucharest, Romania

Sir William Empson
English poet–critic
• Wrote *Collected Poems of William Empson*, 1949; *Milton's God*, 1961; *Using Biography*, 1985.
b. September 27, 1906 in Goole, England
d. April 15, 1984 in London, England

Shusaku Endo
Japanese author
• Oriental-Christian novelist, playwright who wrote *Shiroihito*, 1955; *Chinmoku*, 1966.
b. March 27, 1923 in Tokyo, Japan

Eloise Katherine Engle
American author
• Writings include *Dawn Mission*, 1962; *The Winter War*, 1973.
b. April 12, 1923 in Seattle, Washington

Paul (Hamilton) Engle
American author–poet
• Award-winning writings include *Embrace: Selected Love Poems*, 1969; *Who's Afraid?*, 1962.
b. October 12, 1908 in Cedar Rapids, Iowa

Kurt Enoch
American publisher
• Pioneer in paperback publishing with New American Library, Inc., 1947-60.
b. November 22, 1895 in Hamburg, Germany
d. February 15, 1982 in Puerto Rico

Dennis Joseph Enright
English author–poet
• Writings include *Daughters of Earth*, 1972; *The Joke Shop*, 1976.
b. March 11, 1920 in Leamington, England

Desiderius Erasmus
(Geert Geerts; Gerhard Gerhards)
Dutch author–philosopher–scholar
• Renaissance humanist who advanced reform in Catholic Church; best known for satire *The Praise of Folly*, 1509.
b. October 27, 1469 in Rotterdam, Netherlands
d. July 12, 1536 in Basel, Switzerland

Paul E(mil) Erdman
Canadian author–economist
• Mystery novels include *The Crash of '79*, 1976.
b. May 19, 1932 in Stratford, Ontario

Louise Erdrich
American author
• Lyrical prize-winning novelist; wrote *The Beet Queen*, 1987. Spouse of author Michael Dorris.
b. July 06, 1954 in Little Falls, Minnesota

John Erskine
American author–educator
• Wrote humorous versions of famous legends: *Galahad*, 1926.
b. October 05, 1879 in New York, New York
d. June 02, 1951 in New York, New York

Sergei Aleksandrovich Esenin
(Sergei Aleksandrovich Yesenin)
Russian poet
• Cult figure, imagist, who was attacked in literary world for "hooliganism" as a result of alcoholism: *Confessions of a Hooligan*, 1924.
b. February 21, 1895 in Konstantinovo, Russia
d. December 28, 1925 in Leningrad, U.S.S.R.

Eleanor Ruth Rosenfeld Estes
American children's author
• Won Newbery Medal for *Ginger Pye*, 1952.
b. May 09, 1906 in West Haven, Connecticut
d. July 15, 1988 in Hamden, Connecticut

Loren D Estleman
American author
• Best-selling mysteries feature tough-guy detective, Amos Walker.
b. September 15, 1952 in Ann Arbor, Michigan

Dennis (William Dennis) Etchison
(Jack Martin)
American educator–author
• Won World Fantasy Award for *Dark Country*, 1983.
b. March 3, 1943 in Stockton, California

Mark Foster Ethridge
American publisher
• Manager, publisher of Louisville papers, 1926-63; campaigned against racism, poverty.
b. April 22, 1896 in Meridian, Mississippi
d. April 05, 1981 in Moncure, North Carolina

Mark Foster Ethridge, Jr
American journalist
• Editor, *Detroit Free Press*, 1966-73, when paper won Pulitzer for riot coverage, 1968; outspoken critic of Vietnam war, advocated black political power.
b. July 29, 1924 in New York, New York
d. March 01, 1985 in Chapel Hill, North Carolina

Marie Hall Ets
American children's author
• Won Caldecott Medal, 1960, for *Nine Days to Christmas*.
b. December 16, 1895 in Milwaukee, Wisconsin

Rudolf Christoph Eucken
German philosopher–author
• Idealist whose philosophy centered on ethical activism; won Nobel Prize, 1908.
b. January 05, 1846 in Aurich, Germany
d. September 15, 1926 in Jena, Germany

Eupolis
Greek poet
• Comic poet; rival of Aristophanes; 19 titles survive.
b. 445?BC
d. 441?BC

Laurence Eusden
English poet
• Poet laureate, 1718-73.
b. 1688 in Spofforth, England
d. September 27, 1730 in Coningsby, England

Bergen Baldwin Evans
American lexicographer–author
• Master of ceremonies on radio, TV shows; wrote *Word A Day Vocabulary Builder*, 1963.
b. September 19, 1904 in Franklin, Ohio
d. February 04, 1978 in Highland Park, Illinois

Harold Matthew Evans
English author–editor
• Editor, London *Sunday Times*, 1967-81; editorial director, *US News & World Report*, 1984–.
b. June 28, 1927 in Manchester, England

Heloise Cruse Evans
American journalist
• Took over mother's nationally syndicated column "Hints from Heloise," 1977.
b. April 15, 1951 in Waco, Texas

Joni Evans
American publisher
• Chairman, Simon & Schuster, 1974-87; publisher, Random House, 1987–.
b. 1942

Orrin C Evans
American journalist
• Reporter, *Philadelphia Bulletin*; first black to cover major stories, 1930s; honored by NAACP, 1971.
b. in Steelton, Pennsylvania
d. August 07, 1971 in Philadelphia, Pennsylvania

Rowland Evans, Jr
(Evans and Novak)
American journalist
• Syndicated columnist, 1963–; wrote *The Reagan Revolution*, 1981, with Robert Novak.
b. April 28, 1921 in White Marsh, Pennsylvania

William Oliver Everson
(Brother Antoninus pseud)
American poet
• Writings include *The Masculine Dead: Poems 1938-40*, 1942; *Waldport Poems*, 1944.
b. September 1, 1912 in Sacramento, California

Frederic Ewen
American author
• Writings include *The Magic Mountain*, 1967; *The Unknown Chekhov*, 1968.
b. October 11, 1899 in Lemberg, Austria

Julianna Horatia (Gatty) Ewing
English children's author
• Wrote classic tale *Jackanapes*, 1884.
b. August 03, 1841 in Ecclesfield, England
d. May 13, 1885 in Bath, England

Sir Geoffrey Cust Faber
English publisher–author
• Founded Faber and Faber Publishers, 1927; wrote *Oxford Apostles*, 1933.
b. August 23, 1889 in Malvern, England
d. March 31, 1961 in Midhurst, England

John Burr Fairchild
American publisher
• Newspapers include *Women's Wear Daily; Daily News Record*, 1960–.
b. March 06, 1927 in Newark, New Jersey

Beatrice Fairfax, pseud
(Marie Manning)
American journalist
• Wrote syndicated column "Advice to the Lovelorn," 1898-1905, 1929-45.
b. 1878 in Washington, District of Columbia
d. November 28, 1945 in Allendale, New Jersey

Faiz Ahmad Faiz
Pakistani poet
• Considered Pakistan's poet laureate; wrote *Zindan Namah*, 1950s.
b. 1912 in Sialkot, British India
d. November 2, 1984 in Lahore, Pakistan

Oriana Fallaci
Italian journalist
• Interviews with nat. leaders collected in *Interviews with History*, 1976.
b. June 29, 1930 in Florence, Italy

Katherine Woodruff Fanning
American editor–journalist
• Editor, *Christian Science Monitor*, 1983-88.
b. October 18, 1927 in Chicago, Illinois

Eleanor Farjeon
English author
• Best known for children's fantasy tales *London Town*, 1916; *Martin Pippin* series, 1930s.
b. February 13, 1881 in London, England
d. June 05, 1965

Walter Lorimer Farley
American author
• Created *Black Stallion* series of children's novels; two have been filmed.
b. June 26, 1920 in Syracuse, New York
d. October 17, 1989 in Sarasota, New York

Philip Jose Farmer
American author
• Science-fiction books include *Maker of Universes*, 1965.
b. January 26, 1918 in Terre Haute, Indiana

John Chipman Farrar
American publisher–author
• Founded Farrar, Rinehardt, 1929; Farrar, Strause & Giroux, 1942.
b. February 25, 1896 in Burlington, Vermont
d. November 06, 1974 in New York, New York

James Thomas Farrell
American author
• Best known for *Studs Lonigan* trilogy, 1932-35.
b. February 27, 1904 in Chicago, Illinois
d. August 22, 1979 in New York, New York

Howard Fast
(E V Cunningham Walter Ericson pseuds)
American author
• Novels, *Spartacus; Mirage*, were adapted to film, 1960, 1965.
b. November 11, 1914 in New York, New York

William Faulkner
American author
• Wrote *The Sound and the Fury*, 1929; won Nobel Prize, 1949, Pulitzer Prize, 1962.
b. September 25, 1897 in New Albany, Mississippi
d. July 06, 1962 in Oxford, Mississippi

Jessie Redmon Fauset
American author
• First black woman elected to Phi Beta Kappa, 1905; among her works *Comedy: American Style*, 1934.
b. 1884 in Philadelphia, Pennsylvania
d. April 3, 1961

Frederick Schiller Faust
(Max Brand pseud)
American author–poet
• Wrote popular westerns; wrote *Dr. Kildare* films.
b. May 29, 1892 in Seattle, Washington
d. May 12, 1944 in Germany

Clay S Felker
American journalist
• Founder, editor, publisher, *New York* mag., 1967-77.
b. October 02, 1928 in Saint Louis, Missouri

Edna Ferber
American author
• Best-selling novels include 1925 Pulitzer-winning, *So Big; Show Boat*, 1926; *Giant*, 1952.
b. August 15, 1887 in Kalamazoo, Michigan
d. April 16, 1968 in New York, New York

Harvey Fergusson
American author
• Books include *Rio Grande*, 1933; *Home in the West*, 1945.
b. January 28, 1890 in Albuquerque, New Mexico
d. August 24, 1971

Eugene Field
American poet–journalist
• Popular children's verses include *Little Boy Blue; Wynken, Blynken, and Nod*.
b. September 02, 1850 in Saint Louis, Missouri
d. November 04, 1895 in Chicago, Illinois

Marshall Field, III
American publisher–philanthropist
• Established the *Chicago Sun*, 1941, Field Enterprises, Inc., 1944.
b. September 28, 1893 in Chicago, Illinois
d. November 08, 1956 in New York, New York

Marshall Field, IV
American publisher
• Pres., publisher, editor, *Chicago Daily News; Sunday Times*.
b. June 15, 1916 in New York, New York
d. September 18, 1965 in Chicago, Illinois

Marshall Field, V
American newspaper publisher
• Publisher, *Chicago Sun Times*, 1969-80; chm., Field Enterprises, 1972-84; chm., Field Corp., 1984–.
b. May 13, 1941 in Charlottesville, Virginia

Rachel Lyman Field
American children's author
• Writings include 1929 Newbery-winning *Hitty*; adult best-seller *All This and Heaven Too*, 1938.
b. September 19, 1894 in New York, New York
d. March 15, 1942 in Beverly Hills, California

Gabriel Fielding, pseud
(Alan Gabriel Barnsley)
English author
• Novels include *The Women of Guinea Lane*, 1986; *Brotherly Love*, 1954.
b. March 25, 1916 in Hexham, England
d. November 27, 1986 in Bellevue, Washington

Henry Fielding
English author
• Perfected English novel in his masterpiece *Tom Jones*, 1749.
b. April 22, 1707 in Sharpham Park, England
d. October 08, 1754 in Lisbon, Portugal

Temple Hornaday Fielding
American author
• Best known for producing *Fielding's Travel Guide to Europe*, annually since 1948.
b. October 08, 1913 in Bronx, New York
d. May 18, 1983 in Palma de Majorca, Spain

Jack Finney, pseud
(Walter Braden Finney)
American author
• Wrote science fiction classics *Invasion of the Body Snatchers*, 1954; *Time and Again*, 1970.
b. 1911 in Milwaukee, Wisconsin

Ronald Firbank
English author
• Wrote penetrating novels *Caprice*, 1917; *Prancing Nigger*, 1924.
b. January 17, 1886 in London, England
d. May 21, 1926 in Rome, Italy

Firdausi
(Firdousi; Firdusi)
Persian poet
• Wrote great epic *Shah Namah*, c. 1010, describing Persian kings.
b. 935?
d. 1020

Robert Lloyd Fish
(Robert L Pike pseud)
American author
• Winner of three Edgars Mystery writers awards: *Isle of Snakes*, 1963.
b. August 21, 1912 in Cleveland, Ohio
d. February 24, 1981 in Trumbull, Connecticut

Frances FitzGerald
American author–journalist
• Won Pulitzer for book about Vietnam, *Fire in the Lake*, 1972.
b. October 21, 1940 in New York, New York

F(rancis) Scott (Key) Fitzgerald
American author
• Wrote *This Side of Paradise*, 1920; *The Great Gatsby*, 1925; writings, lifestyle epitomized 1920s "Jazz Age."
b. September 24, 1896 in Saint Paul, Minnesota
d. December 21, 1940 in Hollywood, California

Robert Stuart Fitzgerald
American author–translator
• Poems known for rich imagery, vigorous language; translations of Homer's *Odyssey*, *Iliad* classics in own right.
b. October 12, 1910 in Geneva, New York
d. January 16, 1985 in Hamden, Connecticut

Zelda Fitzgerald
(Mrs F Scott Fitzgerald; Zelda Sayre)
American celebrity relative–author
• Wrote *Save Me the Waltz*, 1932.
b. July 24, 1900 in Montgomery, Alabama
d. March 1, 1948 in Asheville, North Carolina

James Fuller Fixx
American author–track athlete
• Dean of jogging craze, who collapsed, died while jogging; best selling book *Complete Book of Running*.
b. April 23, 1932 in New York, New York
d. July 2, 1984 in Hardwick, Vermont

Janet Flanner
(Genet pseud)
American journalist–author
• Correspondent, *New Yorker*, Paris, for 50 yrs.; wrote *Letter from Paris*.
b. March 13, 1892 in Indianapolis, Indiana
d. January 07, 1978 in New York, New York

Gustave Flaubert
French author
• Distinctive novelist of Realist school; prosecuted, acquited for *Madame Bovary*, 1857.
b. December 12, 1821 in Rouen, France
d. May 08, 1880 in Croisset, France

Martin Archer Flavin
American author
• Won Pulitzer for *Journey in the Dark*, 1943.
b. November 02, 1883 in San Francisco, California
d. December 27, 1967 in Carmel, California

Doris Fleeson
American journalist
• First syndicated woman political writer; columns appeared in 100 US papers, 1946-70.
b. May 2, 1901 in Sterling, Kansas
d. August 01, 1970 in Washington, District of Columbia

Raoul H(erbert) Fleishmann
American publisher–manufacturer
• Co-founder, publisher, *New Yorker* mag, 1924-69.
b. August 17, 1885 in Ischl, Austria-Hungary
d. May 11, 1969 in New York, New York

Ian Lancaster Fleming
English author
• Created James Bond adventure series; wrote *Dr. No*, 1958; *Goldfinger*, 1959.
b. May 28, 1908 in London, England
d. August 12, 1964 in Canterbury, England

Joan Margaret Fleming
English author
• Wrote over 30 mysteries, historical romances: *Young Man I Think You're Dying*, 1970.
b. March 27, 1908 in Horwich, England
d. November 15, 1980 in England

Rudolf (Franz) Flesch
American author
• Wrote *Why Johnny Can't Read*, 1955; expert on clear writing, literacy.
b. May 08, 1911 in Vienna, Austria
d. October 05, 1986 in Dobbs Ferry, New York

John Gould Fletcher
American poet–critic
• Won Pulitzer for *Selected Poems*, 1938.
b. January 03, 1886 in Little Rock, Arkansas
d. May 2, 1950 in Little Rock, Arkansas

Timothy Flint
American clergyman–author
• Missionary, described frontier life; his Daniel Boone biography, 1833, helped develop Boone legend.
b. July 11, 1780 in North Reading, Massachusetts
d. August 16, 1840 in North Reading, Massachusetts

Eugene Fodor
American editor–publisher
• Began publishing *Fodor's Travel Guides*, 1949.
b. October 05, 1905 in Leva, Hungary
d. February 18, 1991 in Torrington, Connecticut

Friedrich Wilhelm Foerster
German author–educator
• Books written by him were among first burned by the Nazis, 1930s; wrote *Europe and the German Question*, 1940.
b. June 02, 1869 in Berlin, Germany
d. January 09, 1966 in Kilchberg, Germany (West)

Antonio Fogazzaro
Italian author–poet
• Popular novels include *The Saint*, 1905; *Leila*, 1910.
b. March 25, 1842 in Vicenza, Italy
d. March 07, 1911 in Vicenza, Italy

Martha Foley
American journalist–editor
• Edited annual *Best American Short Stories*, 1958-76.
b. 1897 in Boston, Massachusetts
d. September 05, 1977 in Northampton, Massachusetts

Ken(neth Martin) Follett
(Myles Symon pseud)
Welsh author
• Mysteries feature industrial detective Piers Roper; best-seller *Eye of the Needle*, 1978.
b. June 05, 1949 in Cardiff, Wales

Theodor Fontane
German author
• Wrote historical novel, *Vor Dem Strum*, 1878; first master of realistic fiction in Germany.
b. December 3, 1819 in Neu-Ruppin, Germany
d. September 2, 1898 in Berlin, Germany

Bertie (Robert Charles) Forbes
Scottish journalist
• Founder, editor, *Forbes* mag., 1916; wrote on business, finance.
b. May 14, 1880 in Aberdeen, Scotland
d. May 06, 1954 in New York, New York

Kathryn Forbes, pseud
(Kathryn Anderson McLean)
American author
• Wrote *Mama's Bank Account*, 1943, which inspired TV series "I Remember Mama," 1949-57.
b. March 2, 1909 in San Francisco, California
d. May 15, 1966 in San Francisco, California

Malcolm Stevenson Forbes
American publisher–editor
• Millionaire publisher of *Forbes* magazine, 1957-90; known for extravagant parties.
b. August 19, 1919 in New York, New York
d. February 24, 1990 in Far Hills, New Jersey

Eileen Ford
American business executive–author
• With husband founded highly successful model agency, 1946–; author of syndicated column, *Eileen Ford's Model Beauty*.
b. March 25, 1922 in New York, New York

Ford Madox Ford
(Ford Madox Hueffer)
English author–poet
• Founded *English Review*, 1908; wrote *Good Soldier*, 1915, a study of emotional relationships.
b. December 17, 1873 in Merton, England
d. June 26, 1939 in Deauville, France

Cecil Scott Forester
English author
• Wrote *Horatio Hornblower* series; *The African Queen*, 1935.
b. August 27, 1899 in Cairo, Egypt
d. April 02, 1966 in Fullerton, California

James Douglas Forman
American author
• Wrote *A Ballad for Hogskin Hill*, 1979; *That Mad Game; War and the Chance for Peace*, 1980.
b. November 12, 1932 in Mineola, New York

E(dward) M(organ) Forster
English author
• Wrote *A Room with a View*, 1908; *A Passage to India*, 1924; both became Oscar-winning films, 1986, 1984.
b. January 01, 1879 in London, England
d. June 07, 1970 in Coventry, England

Frederick Forsyth
English author
• Won Poe for *The Day of the Jackal*, 1971; other thrillers: *The Odessa File*, 1972.
b. August 25, 1938 in Ashford, England

Timothy Thomas Fortune
American author–editor
• Ghost writer for Booker T Washington; writings include *The Negro in Politics*, 1885.
b. October 03, 1856 in Marianna, Florida
d. June 02, 1928

Michel Foucault
French author–philosopher
• Cultural historian who wrote award-winning *Madness and Civilization*, 1961.
b. October 15, 1926 in Poitiers, France
d. June 25, 1984 in Paris, France

Gene Fowler
American journalist–author
• Wrote outstanding biography of John Barrymore, *Goodnight Sweet Prince*, 1944.
b. March 08, 1890 in Denver, Colorado
d. July 02, 1960 in Los Angeles, California

Henry Watson Fowler
English lexicographer–author
• Compiled *Dictionary of Modern English Usage*, 1926; *Concise Oxford Dictionary*, 1911.
b. 1858
d. December 27, 1933 in London, England

John Fowles
English author
• Wrote best-sellers *The Collector*, 1963; *French Lieutenant's Woman*, 1969; both filmed, 1965, 1981.
b. March 31, 1926 in Leigh-on-Sea, England

Anatole France, pseud
(Jacques Anatole-Francois Thibault)
French author
• Wrote *Penguin Island*, 1908; won Nobel Prize, 1921.
b. April 16, 1844 in Paris, France
d. October 12, 1924 in Tours, France

Dick Francis
Welsh author
• Ex-champion steeplechase jockey; wrote horse racing mysteries: *Whip Hand*, 1979; *Break-In*, 1986; won Poe for *Forfeit*, 1969.
b. October 31, 1920 in Tenby, Wales

Bruno Frank
German author
• Best known for his short novels including *The Golden Man*, 1952.
b. June 13, 1887 in Stuttgart, Germany
d. June 2, 1945 in Beverly Hills, California

Gilbert Frankau
English author
• Best known for novel *World Without End*, 1943.
b. April 21, 1884 in London, England
d. November 04, 1952 in Hove, England

Pamela Frankau
(Mrs Eliot Naylor)
English author
• Popular novels include *Winged House*, 1953; *The Bridge*, 1957.
b. January 08, 1908 in London, England
d. June 08, 1967 in Hampstead, England

Max Frankel
American journalist
• Exec. editor *NY Times*, 1986–; won Pulitzer.
b. April 03, 1930 in Gera, Germany

Miles Franklin, pseud
(Stella Maria Sarah Franklin; "Brent of Bin Bin")
Australian author
• Best known work is autobiographical *My Brilliant Career*, written at 16.
b. October 14, 1879 in Talbingo, Australia
d. September 19, 1954 in Sydney, Australia

Antonia Pakenham Fraser, Lady
English author
• Wrote *Mary Queen of Scots*, 1969; mysteries featuring Jemima Shore.
b. August 27, 1932 in London, England

George MacDonald Fraser
English author
• Books include the continuing story of Harry Flashman: *Flashman*, 1969.
b. April 02, 1925 in Carlisle, England

Michael Frayn
English author
• Books include *The Tin Man*, 1965; *A Very Private Life*, 1968; *Sweet Dreams*, 1973.
b. September 08, 1933 in London, England

Louis-Honore Frechette
Canadian poet
• Best-known French-Canadian poet of 19th c.: *Les Oiseaux*, 1880.
b. November 16, 1839 in Levis, Quebec
d. May 31, 1908 in Montreal, Quebec

Russell Freedman
American author
• Won Newbery for *Lincoln: A Photobiography*, 1988.
b. October 11, 1929 in San Francisco, California

Nicolas Freeling
English author
• Mystery novels feature inspector Van der Valk: *The King of the Rainy Country*, 1966.
b. March 03, 1927 in London, England

Cynthia Freeman
(Beatrice Cynthia Freeman Feinberg)
American author
• Interior decorator-turned-romance novelist; first novel *A World Full of Strangers*, written at age 50.
b. 1915 in New York, New York
d. November 05, 1988 in San Francisco, California

Mary E Wilkins Freeman
American author
• Books on rural New England include *Pembroke*, 1894; *Jane Field*, 1893.
b. October 31, 1852 in Randolph, Massachusetts
d. March 13, 1930 in Metuchen, New Jersey

R(ichard) Austin Freeman
English author
• Detective writer; created scientific detective Dr. John Thorndyke: *The Cat's Eye*, 1927.
b. April 11, 1862 in London, England
d. September 3, 1943 in Gravesend, England

Brian Harry Freemantle
English author
• Mystery writer; created detective Charlie Muffin: *November Man*, 1976.
b. June 1, 1936 in Southampton, England

Marilyn French
(Mara Solwoska pseud)
American author
• Wrote *The Women's Room*, 1977; *The Bleeding Heart*, 1980.
b. November 21, 1929 in New York, New York

Philip Morin Freneau
American poet–journalist
• First professional US journalist; edited *National Gazetter* for Thomas Jefferson, 1791-93; revolutionary poems include "The British Prisonship," 1781.
b. January 02, 1752 in New York, New York
d. December 18, 1832 in Monmouth County, New Jersey

Jean Froissart
French author–poet
• Best-known work: *Chronicles*, originally in four vols., covering 1325-1400.
b. 1338 in Valenciennes, France
d. 1410 in Chimay, France

Robert Lee Frost
American poet
• Won four Pulitzers; wrote verses on rural New England.
b. March 26, 1874 in San Francisco, California
d. January 29, 1963 in Boston, Massachusetts

Carlos Fuentes
Mexican author–dramatist
• Writings include *Our Land*, 1974; *A Change of Skin*, 1968.
b. November 11, 1928 in Mexico City, Mexico

Robert Fulghum
American author
• With books *All I Really Need to Know I Learned in Kindergarten*, 1989, and *It Was on Fire When I Lay Down on It*, 1989, became first author ever to capture simultaneously the no. 1 and 2 spots on hardcover best-seller list
b. June 04, 1937 in Waco, Texas

Henry Blake Fuller
American author
• Realistic novels of Chicago life include *Cliff-Dwellers*, 1893.
b. January 09, 1857 in Chicago, Illinois
d. July 29, 1929 in Chicago, Illinois

Hoyt William Fuller
American critic–editor
• Editor, *Negro Digest*, 1970; later called *Black World;* started black aesthetic literary movement, 1960s-70s.
b. September 1, 1926 in Atlanta, Georgia
d. May 11, 1981 in Atlanta, Georgia

Isaac Kauffman Funk
American publisher
• Funk and Wagnalls Co. published *Standard Dictionary of the English Language*, 1893.
b. September 1, 1839 in Clifton, Ohio
d. April 04, 1912 in Montclair, New Jersey

Wilfred John Funk
American publisher
• Pres., Funk & Wagalls, 1925-40; wrote "Increase Your Word Power" for *Reader's Digest*, 1946-65; son of Isaac.
b. March 2, 1883 in Brooklyn, New York
d. June 01, 1965 in Montclair, New Jersey

Jacques Futrelle
American author
• Mystery writer whose books include *Blind Man's Bluff*, 1914; died on *Titanic*.
b. April 09, 1875 in Pike County, Georgia
d. April 15, 1912

Thomas (Eugene) Gaddis
American author–educator
• Wrote *The Birdman of Alcatraz*, biography on which 1962 hit film was based.
b. September 14, 1908 in Denver, Colorado
d. October 1, 1984 in Portland, Oregon

William Thomas Gaddis
American author
• Best known for first novel *The Recognitions*, 1955; others include *Carpenter's Gothic*, 1985.
b. December 29, 1922 in New York, New York

Wanda Gag
American children's author–illustrator
• Wrote, illustrated modern children's classic *Millions of Cats*, 1928.
b. May 11, 1893 in New Ulm, Minnesota
d. June 27, 1946 in New York, New York

Ernest J Gaines
American author
• Wrote novel, *The Autobiography of Miss Jane Pittman*, 1971; became Emmy-winning TV film, 1974.
b. January 15, 1933 in Oscar, Louisiana

William Maxwell Gaines
American businessman–publisher
• Founder, publisher *Mad* magazine, 1948–.
b. March 01, 1922 in New York, New York

Paul William Gallico
American author–journalist
• Wrote *The Snow Goose*, 1941; *The Poseidon Adventure*, 1969.
b. July 26, 1897 in New York, New York
d. July 15, 1976 in Monaco

John Galsworthy
(John Sinjohn pseud)
English author–dramatist
• Known for social satire: *The Forsyte Saga*, 1906-22; won Nobel Prize, 1932.
b. August 14, 1867 in Kingston, England
d. January 31, 1933 in Hampstead, England

Ernest Kellogg Gann
American author
• Wrote best-seller *High and the Mighty*, 1952.
b. October 13, 1910 in Lincoln, Nebraska

Frank Ernest Gannett
American newspaper publisher
• Founded Gannett Co., 1945; well known for media operations.
b. September 15, 1876 in Bristol, New York
d. September 03, 1957 in Rochester, New York

Gabriel Jose Garcia-Marquez
Colombian author
• Won 1982 Nobel Prize in literature for novels, short stories; wrote *One Hundred Years of Solitude*, 1967.
b. March 06, 1928 in Aracatacca, Colombia

Erle Stanley Gardner
(A A Fair pseud)
American author–lawyer
• Wrote Perry Mason detective stories series, basis for movies, radio, TV series.
b. July 17, 1889 in Malden, Massachusetts
d. March 11, 1970 in Temecula, California

Hy Gardner
American journalist
• Syndicated Broadway columnist, *NY Herald Tribune;* host of radio, TV shows, 1930s-40s.
b. December 02, 1908 in New York, New York
d. June 17, 1989 in Miami, Florida

Brian Wynne Garfield
American author
• Won Edgar for *Hopscotch*, 1975.
b. January 26, 1939 in New York, New York

Leon Garfield
English author
• Completed unfinished Dickens novel, *The Mystery of Edwin Drood*, 1980; won Carnegie Medal for *The God Beneath the Sea*, 1970.
b. July 14, 1921 in Brighton, England

Howard Roger Garis
American author
• Worked for Stratemeyer syndicate; wrote *Uncle Wiggly* series.
b. April 25, 1873 in Binghamton, New York
d. November 05, 1962 in Amherst, Massachusetts

David Garnett
(Leda Burke pseud)
English author
• Novelist, biographer, fantasy writer who co-founded Nonesuch Press, 1923; wrote award-winning *Lady into Fox*, 1922.
b. March 09, 1892 in Brighton, England
d. February 17, 1981 in Montucq, France

Richard Garnett
English author
• Works include *The Twilight of the Gods*, 1888, a collection of original fables; father of David.
b. February 27, 1835 in Staffordshire, England
d. April 13, 1906 in London, England

David Emery Gascoyne
English poet
• Writings include *Collected Poems*, 1982; *Free Spirits I*, 1982.
b. October 1, 1916 in Salisbury, England

William Campbell Gault
(Will Duke; Roney Scott pseuds)
American author
• Mystery novels include *Fair Prey*, 1958; works translated into 14 languages.
b. March 09, 1910 in Milwaukee, Wisconsin

Theophile (Pierre Jules Theophile) Gautier
French poet–author–critic
• Believed in "art for art's sake"; wrote psychological tale *Mademoiselle de Maupin*, 1835.
b. August 31, 1811 in Tarbes, France
d. October 23, 1872 in Neuilly, France

Martha Ellis Gellhorn
American author–journalist
• War correspondent, 1938-45; articles collected in *The Faces of War*, 1959; married to Ernest Hemingway, 1940-45.
b. 1908 in Saint Louis, Missouri

Jean Genet
French dramatist–author
• Wrote of sin, corruption: *Our Lady of the Flowers*, 1942, became cult classic.
b. December 19, 1910 in Paris, France
d. April 15, 1986 in Paris, France

Geoffrey of Monmouth
English author–religious figure
• His *Historia Regum Britanniae* (History of the Kings of Britain), c. 1135, was probably main source of Arthurian legend.
b. 1100 in Monmouth, Wales
d. 1154

Jean Craighead George
American artist–author
• Best-known self-illustrated book: *My Side of the Mountain*, 1960; made into movie, 1968.
b. July 02, 1919 in Washington, District of Columbia

Stefan Anton George
German poet
• Most famous work: *The Year of the Soul*, 1897.
b. December 12, 1868 in Budesheim, Germany
d. December 04, 1933 in Locarno, Switzerland

William Alexander Gerhardi
British author
• Writings include autobiographical novel, *Resurrective*, 1934.
b. November 21, 1895 in Saint Petersburg, Russia
d. July 05, 1977 in London, England

Noel Bertram Gerson
American author
• Wrote historical novels, westerns, biographies, juvenile works under many pseudonyms: *Fifty-Five Days at Peking* and *The Named Maja* both adapted to film.
b. November 06, 1914 in Chicago, Illinois
d. November 2, 1988 in Boca Raton, Florida

Frank Gervasi
American journalist
• Covered WW II in Europe, N Africa for *Collier's* magazine; information chief for Marshall Plan, 1950-54; author of 10 books; married to Georgia Gibbs.
b. February 05, 1908 in Baltimore, Maryland
d. January 21, 1990 in New York, New York

Georgie Anne Geyer
American journalist–author
• Syndicated columnist since 1975; wrote *Buying the Night Flight: The Autobiography of a Woman Foreign Correspondent*, 1983.
b. April 02, 1935 in Chicago, Illinois

Euell Gibbons

American author–naturalist
• Author of books on wild foods, including *Stalking the Good Life*, 1971; widely known as TV commercial spokesman for cereal.
b. September 08, 1911 in Clarksville, Texas
d. December 29, 1975 in Sunbury, Pennsylvania

Kahlil Gibran

American poet–artist
• Finest work *The Prophet* translated into 13 languages.
b. April 1, 1883 in Bechari, Lebanon
d. April 1, 1931 in New York, New York

Walter B(rown) Gibson

American author
• Used 12 pseudonyms; besides *Shadow* series, wrote on magic, games, astrology, etc.
b. September 12, 1897 in Philadelphia, Pennsylvania
d. December 06, 1985 in Kingston, New York

Sonia Gidal

(Mrs Tim Gidal)
German children's author
• Wrote "My Village" series with husband, 1950s-70.
b. September 23, 1922 in Berlin, Germany

Tim Gidal

German journalist
• Photojournalist whose collections are displayed internationally; wrote *Modern Photojournalism: Origin and Evolution*, 1972.
b. May 18, 1909 in Munich, Germany

Andre Paul Guillaume Gide

French author–critic
• Won Nobel Prize for literature, 1947.
b. November 22, 1869 in Paris, France
d. February 19, 1951 in Paris, France

Mildred Geiger Gilbertson

(Nan Gilbert; Jo Mendel pseuds)
American children's author
• Books include *The Strange New World Across the Street*, 1979.
b. June 09, 1908 in Galena, Illinois

Frank Bunker Gilbreth, Jr

American author–journalist
• With sister, Ernestine Carey, wrote of childhood in *Cheaper by the Dozen*, 1948; became film, 1950.
b. March 17, 1911 in Plainfield, New Jersey

Brendan Gill

American critic–author
• Contributor to *New Yorker* mag., 1936-.
b. October 04, 1914 in Hartford, Connecticut

Arnold Gingrich

American editor–author
• Published *Esquire*, 1952-76; emphasized magazine's literary qualities.
b. December 05, 1903 in Grand Rapids, Michigan
d. July 09, 1976 in Ridgewood, New Jersey

Haim Ginott

American author–psychologist
• Book *Between Parent and Child*, 1965, sold over 1.5 million copies, translated into more than 12 languages.
b. August 05, 1922 in Tel Aviv, Palestine
d. November 04, 1973 in New York, New York

Allen Ginsberg

American poet
• Associated with "Beat" movement; best-known poem *Howl*, 1956. Recently collaborated on work with composer/musician Phillip Glass.
b. June 03, 1926 in Newark, New Jersey

Aleksandr Ilich Ginzburg

Russian political activist–poet
• Published underground poetry that led to first arrest, jail sentence, 1960; set up fund for families of political prisoners, 1974.
b. 1936 in Leningrad, U.S.S.R.

Jean Giono

French author–dramatist
• Imprisoned for pacifist views, WW II; best-known novels adapted to screen: *Harvest*, 1937; *The Baker's Wife*, 1938.
b. March 3, 1895 in Manosque, France
d. October 09, 1970 in Manosque, France

John Giorno

American poet
• Writings include *Poems*, 1967; *Balling Buddha*, 1970.
b. December 04, 1936 in New York, New York

Nikki Giovanni

(Yolande Cornelia Jr)
American author–poet
• Writings include *My House*, 1972; *The Women and the Men*, 1975.
b. June 07, 1943 in Knoxville, Tennessee

Arturo Giovannitti

Italian poet
• Best-known work in *Arrows in the Gale*, 1914.
b. January 07, 1884 in Campobasso, Italy
d. December 31, 1959

Robert Giroux

American editor–publisher
• Chairman, Farrar, Straus, and Giroux, Inc, 1973-.
b. April 08, 1914 in New Jersey

George Robert Gissing

English author–critic
• Books dealt with poverty, despair: *The Private Papers of Henry Rycroft*, 1903.
b. November 22, 1857 in Wakefield, England
d. December 28, 1903 in Saint-Jean-de-Luz, France

Karl Adolf Gjellerup

(Epigonos pseud)
Danish author
• Wrote novel *The Pilgrim Kamanoto*, 1906, only work translated into English; shared Nobel Prize, 1917.
b. June 02, 1857 in Roholte, Denmark
d. October 11, 1919 in Klotzche, Germany

Ellen Anderson Gholson Glasgow

American author
• Novels were studies in Southern life; won Pulitzer for *In This Our House*, 1945.
b. April 22, 1874 in Richmond, Virginia
d. November 21, 1945 in Richmond, Virginia

Ralph Joseph Gleason

American journalist–critic
• Founded, edited *Rolling Stone* mag., 1967-75; first jazz critic to take rock music seriously.
b. March 01, 1917 in New York, New York
d. June 03, 1975 in Berkeley, California

Elinor Sutherland Glyn

English author
• Adapted her novels to film versions, 1920s; mentor of Clara Bow.
b. October 17, 1864 in Jersey, Channel Islands
d. September 23, 1943 in London, England

Rumer Godden

(Margaret Rumer Haynes Dixon)
English author–poet–dramatist
• Prolific writer of children's stories, adult fiction; six novels adapted for films and TV, including *In This House of Brede*, 1975.
b. December 1, 1907 in Sussex, England

Louis Antoine Godey

American publisher
• Established America's leading 19th-c. fashion mag., *Godey's Lady Book*, 1830.
b. June 06, 1804 in New York, New York
d. November 29, 1878 in Philadelphia, Pennsylvania

Edwin Lawrence Godkin

American journalist
• Founded *The Nation*, later *NY Evening Post*, 1881; fought campaign against Tammany Hall system, NYC.
b. October 02, 1831 in Wicklow, Ireland
d. May 21, 1902 in Brixham, England

Gail Godwin
American author
• Novelist, short story writer: *Glass People*, 1972.
b. June 18, 1937 in Birmingham, Alabama

Mary Wollstonecraft Godwin
English author–feminist
• Wrote feminist paper *The Vindication of the Rights of Women*, 1792; mother of Mary Shelley.
b. April 27, 1759 in London, England
d. September 1, 1797 in London, England

William Godwin
English author
• Father of Mary Shelley; radical nonconformist, wrote *An Enquiry Concerning Political Justice*, 1793.
b. March 03, 1756
d. April 07, 1836 in London, England

Johann Wolfgang von Goethe
German poet–dramatist–author
• Wrote *Faust*, 1770, 1831; *The Sorrows of Werther*, 1774.
b. August 28, 1749 in Frankfurt, Germany
d. March 22, 1832 in Weimar, Germany

Marilyn Goffstein
American children's author–illustrator
• *Goldie the Dollmaker*, 1969; *Me and My Captain*, 1974, are among her self-illustrated books.
b. December 2, 1940 in Saint Paul, Minnesota

Sir William Gerald Golding
English author
• Best known for allegorical cult novel *Lord of the Flies*, 1954; won Nobel Prize in literature, 1983.
b. September 19, 1911 in Cornwall, England

Eric Frederick Goldman
American author–historian
• US history authority; wrote *Rendevous with Destiny*, 1952; *The Tragedy of Lyndon Johnson*, 1969.
b. June 17, 1915 in Washington, District of Columbia
d. February 19, 1989 in Princeton, New Jersey

Witold Gombrowicz
American author
• Works include *Cosmos*, 1967; winner of International Prize for Literature.
b. September 04, 1904 in Moloszyee, Poland
d. July 25, 1969 in Nice, France

Edmond Louis Antoine Huot Goncourt
(Edmond Louis DeGoncourt)
French author
• Collaborated with brother Jules in Brothers Goncourt writing team; endowed annual Goncourt Prize for best prose.
b. May 26, 1822 in Nancy, France
d. July 16, 1896 in Chamrosay, France

Jules Alfred Huot de Goncourt
(Jules Alfred DeGoncourt)
French author
• Collaborated on social histories, novels with brother Edmond; wrote *Madame Gervaisais*, 1869; famed *Goncourt Diary*, 1851-96.
b. December 17, 1830 in Paris, France
d. June 2, 1870 in Paris, France

Ellen Holtz Goodman
American journalist
• Writes syndicated feature, "At Large," 1976–; won Pulitzer for commentary, 1980.
b. April 11, 1941 in Newton, Massachusetts

George Jerome Waldo Goodman
(Adam Smith)
American author
• His *The Money Game*, 1968, was published in five languages.
b. August 1, 1930 in Saint Louis, Missouri

Mitchell Goodman
American author
• Best known for war novel *The End of It*, 1961.
b. December 13, 1923 in New York, New York

Paul Goodman
American author–educator
• Books include *Growing Up Absurd*, 1960; plays include *The Young Disciple*, 1955.
b. September 09, 1911 in New York, New York
d. August 02, 1972 in North Stratford, New Hampshire

Samuel Griswold Goodrich
(Peter Parley pseud)
American publisher
• Published *The Tales of Peter Parley About America*, 1827, the first of over 100 books in series.
b. August 19, 1793 in Ridgefield, Connecticut
d. May 09, 1860 in New York, New York

Richard N(aradhof) Goodwin
(Bailey Lavid)
American lawyer–author
• Presidential speechwriter, 1960s; developed "Great Society" program.
b. December 07, 1931 in Boston, Massachusetts

Natalya Gorbanevskaya
Russian poet–translator
• Her involvement in 1968 protest, documented in *Red Square at Noon*, 1970.
b. 1936 in Moscow, U.S.S.R.

Nadine Gordimer
South African author
• Books include *Burger's Daughter*, 1979; *The Conservationist*, 1975.
b. November 2, 1923 in Springs, South Africa

Caroline Gordon
American author–critic
• Southern-theme writer whose novels include *The Malefactors*, 1956.
b. October 06, 1895 in Trenton, Kentucky
d. April 11, 1981 in Chiapas, Mexico

Mary Catherine Gordon
American author
• Novels of Roman Catholic manners include *Final Payments*, 1978; *Company of Women*, 1981.
b. December 08, 1949 in Far Rockaway, New York

Richard Gordon, pseud
(Gordon Ostlere)
English author
• Wrote comic series of novels on medical life: *Bedside Manners*, 1982; *Doctors in the Soup*, 1987.
b. September 15, 1921 in England

Helene Gordon-Lazareff
French journalist
• Editor-in-chief of fashion magazine, *Elle*, 1945-72.
b. September 21, 1909 in Rostov-on-Don, Russia
d. February 16, 1988 in Lavandou, France

Charles Henry Goren
American bridge player–journalist
• His method of bridge is most widely used; author *Bridge Is My Game*, 1965.
b. March 04, 1901 in Philadelphia, Pennsylvania

Gottfried von Strassburg
German poet
• Wrote unfinished love epic *Tristan and Isolde*, c. 1210.
b. 1170 in Strassburg, Germany
d. 1215

Robert A(dams) Gottlieb
American editor–business executive
• Pres., Alfred A Knopf Inc., 1973-87; editor, *New Yorker* magazine, 1987–.
b. April 29, 1931 in New York, New York

Elizabeth Goudge
English author
• Best-known novel *Green Dolphin Street*, 1944, was made into a film, 1947.
b. April 24, 1900 in Wells, England
d. April 01, 1984 in Henley-on-Thames, England

Ron(ald Joseph) Goulart
(Howard Lee; Kenneth Robeson; Frank S Shawn; Con Steffanson pseuds.)
American author
• Mystery, science fiction writer; received Edgar Award, 1971, for *After Things Fell Apart.*
b. January 13, 1933 in Berkeley, California

Beatrice Blackmar Gould
American editor–author
• With husband, Bruce, edited *Ladies Home Journal* magazine, 1935-62.
b. 1898 in Emmetsburg, Iowa
d. January 3, 1989 in Hopewell, New Jersey

Charles Bruce Gould
American editor–author
• Co-edited *Ladies Home Journal* magazine with wife, Beatrice, 1935-62.
b. July 28, 1898 in Luana, Iowa
d. August 27, 1989 in Hopewell, New Jersey

Stephen Jay Gould
American paleontologist–author
• Won American Book Award for *The Panda's Thumb,* 1981; National Book Critics Award for *The Mismeasure of Man,* 1982.
b. September 1, 1941 in New York, New York

Gwethalyn Graham, pseud
(Gwethalyn Graham Erichsen Brown)
Canadian author
• Novels include *Earth and High Heaven,* 1944; *Swiss Sonata,* 1948.
b. January 18, 1913 in Toronto, Ontario
d. November 24, 1965 in Montreal, Quebec

Kenneth Grahame
Scottish children's author
• Wrote children's classic *The Wind in the Willows,* 1908.
b. March 08, 1859 in Edinburgh, Scotland
d. July 06, 1932 in Pangbourne, England

Hardie Gramatky
American children's author–illustrator
• Award-winning watercolorist; his self-illustrated *Little Toot,* 1939, has become a perennial children's favorite.
b. April 12, 1907 in Dallas, Texas
d. April 29, 1979 in Westport, Connecticut

Harry Granick
(Harry Taylor)
American writer–critic
• Won Peabody for "Great Adventures" series, 1944; author of plays, books since 1937.
b. January 23, 1898 in Nova Kraruka, Russia

James Grant
Scottish author
• His fifty novels include *Romance of War,* 1845; *Harry Ogilvie,* 1856.
b. August 01, 1822 in Edinburgh, Scotland
d. May 05, 1887 in Edinburgh, Scotland

Jane Grant
American journalist
• First woman to cover "city room" desk; with *NY Times,* 1914-30; founded *New Yorker* mag., with husband Harold Ross, 1925.
b. May 29, 1895 in Joplin, Missouri
d. 1972 in Litchfield, Connecticut

Gunter Wilhelm Grass
German author
• Best known novel *The Tin Drum,* 1959; film version won best foreign film Oscar, 1980.
b. October 16, 1927 in Danzig, Germany

Shirley Ann Grau
American author
• Awarded Pulitzer for *The Keepers of the House,* 1965.
b. July 08, 1929 in New Orleans, Louisiana

Robert Ranke Graves
English poet–author
• Author of more than 135 novels, books of poetry, criticism, best known for historical novel, *I, Claudius,* 1934.
b. July 26, 1895 in London, England
d. December 07, 1985 in Majorca, Spain

Thomas Gray
English poet
• Poems concerned melancholy, love of nature; "Elegy Written in a Country Churchyard," 1751, best-known piece, epitome of Romantic period.
b. December 26, 1716 in London, England
d. July 3, 1771 in Cambridge, England

Andrew Moran Greeley
American author
• Controversial columnist, fiction, nonfiction writer; known for explicit novels with moral overtones: *The Cardinal Sins,* 1981.
b. February 05, 1928 in Oak Park, Illinois

Horace Greeley
American publisher
• Founded *NY Tribune,* 1834; popularized phrase "Go West, young man."
b. February 03, 1811 in Amherst, New Hampshire
d. November 29, 1872 in Pleasantville, New York

Anna Katharine Green
American author
• Wrote classic detective story *The Leavenworth Case,* 1878.
b. November 11, 1846 in Brooklyn, New York
d. April 11, 1935 in Buffalo, New York

Anne Green
American author
• Life in France subject of novels: *A Marriage of Convenience,* 1933; *The Old Lady,* 1947.
b. November 11, 1899 in Savannah, Georgia

Henry Green, pseud
(Henry Vincent Yorke)
English author
• Lyrical novelist; works include *Party Going,* 1939; *Loving,* 1945.
b. October 29, 1905 in Tewkesbury, England
d. December 13, 1973 in London, England

Joanne Greenberg
(Hannah Green pseud)
American author
• Wrote autobiographical novel *I Never Promised You a Rose Garden,* 1964; adapted to film, 1977.
b. September 24, 1932 in Brooklyn, New York

Bob (Robert Bernard, Jr) Greene
American journalist
• Syndicated columnist, 1976–; wrote *Billion Dollar Baby,* 1974, account of life on road with rock band.
b. March 1, 1947 in Columbus, Ohio

Graham Greene
English author
• Wrote *Brighton Rock,* 1938, *The End of the Affair,* 1951.
b. October 02, 1904 in Berkhampstead, England
d. April 3, 1991 in Vevey, Switzerland

Meg Greenfield
American journalist
• Columnist in *Newsweek;* won Pulitzer for editorial writing.
b. December 27, 1930 in Seattle, Washington

Germaine Greer
Australian author–educator
• Wrote one of the first successful feminist books *The Female Eunuch,* 1970.
b. January 29, 1939 in Melbourne, Australia

Arthur Gregor
American poet
• Writings include *Embodiment and Other Poems*, 1982.
b. November 18, 1923 in Vienna, Austria

Horace Victor Gregory
American poet
• Among prominent American poets; known for combining classic, contemporary lyrics; won 1965 Bollinger prize for *Collected Poems*.
b. April 1, 1898 in Milwaukee, Wisconsin
d. March 11, 1982 in Shelburne Falls, Massachusetts

Zane Grey
American author
• Sixty best-selling Westerns include *Riders of the Purple Sage*, 1912; books sold over 13 million copies during lifetime.
b. January 31, 1875 in Zanesville, Ohio
d. October 23, 1939 in Altadena, California

Grey Own pseud
((Archibald) George Stansfeld Belaney)
English naturalist–author
• Wrote best-seller on Indian lore: *Pilgrims on the Wild*, 1935.
b. September 1888 in Hastings, England
d. April 13, 1938 in Prince Albert, Saskatchewan

Arnold Griese
American author
• Juvenile books include *Do You Read Me*, 1976; *The Wind is Not a River*, 1979.
b. April 13, 1921 in Lakota, Iowa

John Howard Griffin
American author–photographer
• Chemically blackened skin to better understand racial problems in US; wrote *Black Like Me*, 1961.
b. June 16, 1920 in Dallas, Texas
d. September 09, 1980 in Fort Worth, Texas

Geoffrey (Edward Harvey) Grigson
English author–poet
• Poetry volumes include *Several Observations*, 1939; prose *Essays from the Air*, 1951.
b. March 02, 1902 in Pelynt, England
d. November 25, 1985

Martha Grimes
American author–educator
• Uses British pubs for the titles and settings of her mystery novels: *The Anodyne Necklace* 1983, *The Deer Leap*, 1985.
b. in Pittsburgh, Pennsylvania

Gilbert Hovey Grosvenor
American geographer–editor
• Driving force behind growth of *National Geographic* mag., 1899-1966.
b. October 28, 1875 in Constantinople, Turkey
d. February 04, 1966 in Baddeck, Nova Scotia

Melville Bell Grosvenor
American publisher
• Pres., National Geographic Society, 1957-67; edited mag., 1957-77.
b. November 26, 1901 in Washington, District of Columbia
d. April 22, 1982 in Miami, Florida

Henry Anatole Grunwald
American journalist–businessman
• Editor-in-chief, Time, Inc., 1979-87; US ambassador to Austria, 1987–.
b. December 03, 1922 in Vienna, Austria

Edgar A(lbert) Guest
American poet–journalist
• Popular homespun verse collections include *Heap o' Livin!*, 1916; hosted Detroit radio show, 1931-42.
b. August 2, 1881 in Birmingham, England
d. August 05, 1959 in Detroit, Michigan

Judith Ann Guest
American author
• Wrote *Ordinary People*, 1976; made into Oscar-winning movie, 1980.
b. March 29, 1936 in Detroit, Michigan

Jorge Guillen
Spanish poet
• Member, "Generation of 1927" group of Spanish poets; verses include *Cantico*; *Clamon*.
b. January 18, 1893 in Valladolid, Spain
d. February 06, 1984 in Malaga, Spain

Arthur Guiterman
American poet
• Known for humorous verse; American ballad *Brave Laughter*, 1943.
b. November 2, 1871 in Vienna, Austria
d. January 11, 1943

Nikolai Gumilev
Russian poet
• Writings include *Pearls*, 1910; *Pillar of Fire*, 1921; executed by Bolsheviks.
b. 1886
d. 1921

Thom Gunn
English poet
• Works include *The Passage of Joy*, 1982.
b. August 29, 1929 in Gravesend, England

A(lfred) B(ertram) Guthrie, Jr
American journalist–author
• Novels include Pulitzer-winner *The Way West*, 1949.
b. January 13, 1901 in Bedford, Indiana

Rosa Cuthbert Guy
American author
• Young adult books include *The Disappearance*, 1979; *I Heard a Bird Sing*, 1986.
b. September 01, 1928 in Trinidad

Albert Hackett
American author
• With wife won Pulitzer for play adaptation of *The Diary of Anne Frank*, 1955.
b. February 16, 1900 in New York, New York

Briton Hadden
American publisher
• Co-founded *Time* mag. with Henry Luce, 1923.
b. February 18, 1898 in Brooklyn, New York
d. February 27, 1929 in Brooklyn, New York

Shams-al-Din Muhammad Hafiz
Persian poet
• Considered greatest Persian lyric poet; principal work: "Divan."
b. 1320 in Shiraz, Persia
d. 1389

Sir Henry Rider Haggard
English author
• Wrote *King Solomon's Mines*, 1885; *She*, 1887.
b. June 22, 1856 in Bradenham, England
d. May 14, 1925 in London, England

Arthur Hailey
Canadian author
• Wrote *Hotel*, 1965; *Airport*, 1968; *Wheels*, 1971.
b. April 05, 1920 in Luton, England

David Halberstam
American journalist
• Won Pulitzer, 1964; critical writings of Vietnam War include *The Best and the Brightest*, 1972.
b. April 1, 1934 in New York, New York

Nancy Hale
American author–journalist
• Wrote fiction, biography, and memoirs, and short stories documenting changing American Upper-class manners: *The Prodigal Women*, 1942; was *New York Times'* first woman reporter, 1935.
b. May 06, 1908 in Boston, Massachusetts
d. September 24, 1988 in Charlottesville, Virginia

Sarah Josepha Hale
American journalist–author
• Edited *Godey's Lady Book*, 1837-77; wrote verse "Mary Had a Little Lamb," 1830.
b. October 24, 1788 in Newport, New Hampshire
d. April 3, 1879

Alex(ander) Palmer Haley
American author–journalist
• Pulitzer-winning novel *Roots*, 1977, had largest hard cover printing in US publishing history; became most-watched dramatic show in TV history; 1976 Spingarn winner.
b. August 11, 1921 in Ithaca, New York

Thomas Chandler Haliburton
(Sam Slick pseud)
Canadian judge–author
• Created humorous character Sam Slick who appears in *The Clockmaker*, 1836-40; Sam Slick series, 1840-53.
b. 1796 in Windsor, Nova Scotia
d. August 27, 1865 in Isleworth, England

James Norman Hall
American author
• Co-wrote novels of S Pacific with Charles Nordhoff: *Mutiny on the Bounty*, 1932.
b. April 22, 1887 in Colfax, Iowa
d. July 06, 1951 in Papeete, Tahiti

Radclyffe Hall
English author–poet
• Wrote *The Well of Loneliness*, 1928, censored for lesbian theme.
b. 1886 in Bournemouth, England
d. October 07, 1943 in London, England

Fritz-Greene Halleck
American poet
• Member, NYC's Knickerbocker group; wrote *Croaker Papers*, 1918.
b. July 08, 1790 in Guilford, Connecticut
d. November 19, 1867 in Guilford, Connecticut

Pete (William) Hamill
American journalist
• Wrote *The Gift*, 1973; *Flesh and Blood*, 1977.
b. June 24, 1935 in Brooklyn, New York

Charles Harold St John Hamilton
English author
• Wrote boys adventure series, weekly papers; used over 20 pseudonyms in 5,000 stories.
b. August 08, 1875 in Ealing, England
d. December 24, 1961

Virginia Hamilton
American author
• Won Edgar for *The House of Dies Drear*, 1969.
b. March 13, 1936 in Yellow Springs, Ohio

Richard Hammer
American author
• Won Edgars for fact crime books: *CBS Murders*, 1987; *The Vatican Connection*, 1983.
b. March 22, 1928 in Hartford, Connecticut

(Samuel) Dashiell Hammett
American author
• Created fictional detective Sam Spade in *The Maltese Falcon*, 1930.
b. May 27, 1894 in Saint Marys, Maryland
d. January 1, 1961 in New York, New York

Jupiter Hammon
American poet
• First black poet published in US, 1761.
b. 1720
d. 1800

Knut Pederson Hamsun
(Knut Pedersen)
Norwegian author
• Won 1920 Nobel Prize for *The Growth of the Soil*, 1917; wrote realistic novels of farmers, laborers.
b. August 04, 1859 in Lom, Norway
d. February 19, 1952 in Noerholmen, Norway

pseud Han Suyin
(Elizabeth Comber)
Chinese author
• Wrote "A Many Splendored Thing," 1952; "The Enchantress," 1985.
b. September 12, 1917 in Peking, China

Ernst Franz Sedgwick Hanfstaengl
German author
• Foreign press chief, 1932-37; friend of Hitler, who entertained Fuhrer on piano.
b. February 11, 1887 in Munich, Germany
d. November 06, 1975 in Munich, Germany (West)

Joseph Hansen
(Rose Brock; James Colton; James Coulton pseuds)
American author–poet
• Created detective character Dave Brandstetter; wrote novel *Skinflick*, 1980.
b. July 19, 1923 in Aberdeen, South Dakota

Elizabeth Hardwick
American author
• First woman recipient of Nathan Drama Criticism Award, 1967.
b. July 27, 1916 in Lexington, Kentucky

Thomas Hardy
English author–poet
• Wrote *Far From the Madding Crowd*, 1874; *Tess of the D'Ubervilles*, 1891.
b. June 02, 1840 in Higher Bockhampton, England
d. January 11, 1928 in Dorchester, England

Louis R Harlan
American author
• Won Pulitzer, 1984, for biography *Booker T Washington: The Wizard of Tuskegee*.
b. July 13, 1922 in West Point, Mississippi

Fletcher Harper
(Harper Brothers)
American publisher
• Member, famed published firm, from 1825; added *Harper's Weekly*, 1857; *Harper's Bazaar*, 1867; promoted schoolbook trade.
b. January 31, 1806 in Newton, New York
d. May 29, 1877 in New York, New York

Frances Ellen Watkins Harper
American poet
• Among earliest US black writers; wrote anti-slavery verse, 1850s-60s; co-organizer, National Assn. of Colored Women.
b. September 24, 1825 in Baltimore, Maryland
d. February 22, 1911 in Philadelphia, Pennsylvania

James Harper
(Harper Brothers)
American publisher
• Co-founded with brother John, J & J Harper, 1817; became reform mayor of NYC, 1844.
b. April 13, 1795 in Newton, New York
d. March 27, 1869 in New York, New York

John Harper
(Harper Brothers)
American publisher
• With brother James, co-founded J & J Harper, 1817; adopted firm name Harper Brothers, 1833.
b. January 22, 1797 in Newton, New York
d. April 22, 1875 in New York, New York

Joseph Wesley Harper
(Harper Brothers)
American publisher
• Admitted to brothers' firm, 1823; chief editor, critic.
b. December 25, 1801 in Newton, New York
d. February 14, 1870 in New York, New York

Michael (Edward Michael) Harrington
American politician–author
• Wrote *The Other America*, 1962, bringing poverty into arena of public discussion.
b. February 24, 1928 in Saint Louis, Missouri
d. July 31, 1989 in Larchmont, New York

Frank Harris
American author–journalist
• Works include *The Man Shakespeare*, 1909; controversial Wilde biography, 1916; erotic three-vol. *My Life and Loves*, 1925-27.
b. February 14, 1856 in Galway, Ireland
d. August 26, 1931

Joel Chandler Harris
American author
• Editor, *Atlanta Constitution*, 1890-1900; created Uncle Remus character.
b. December 09, 1848 in Eatonton, Georgia
d. July 03, 1908 in Atlanta, Georgia

Sydney J(ustin) Harris
American journalist–author
• Wrote syndicated column *Strictly Personal*, 1944-86; among several books since 1953: *Pieces of Eight*, 1982.
b. September 14, 1917 in London, England
d. December 07, 1986 in Chicago, Illinois

Leslie Poles Hartley
English author
• Best-known novel: *The Go-Between*, 1953.
b. December 3, 1895 in Whittlesea, England
d. December 13, 1972 in London, England

Franz Hartmann
German mystic–physician–author
• Wrote *Occult Science in Medicine*, 1893.
b. November 22, 1838 in Bavaria
d. August 07, 1912 in Kempten, Bavaria

Sadakichi Hartmann
American author
• "Bohemian" identified with NYC's Greenwich Village, Hollywood; wrote privately published plays: *Buddha*, 1897; *Moses*, 1934.
b. October 08, 1869 in Nagasaki, Japan
d. November 21, 1944 in Saint Petersburg, Florida

Jaroslav Hasek
Czech author
• Four-vol. series *The Good Soldier Schweik*, 1920-23, is considered a satirical masterpiece.
b. April 24, 1883 in Prague, Czechoslovakia
d. January 03, 1923 in Lipnice, Czechoslovakia

Gerhart Johann Hauptmann
German author–poet
• Leading Naturalist playwright: *The Weavers*, 1892; won Nobel Prize, 1912.
b. November 15, 1862 in Obersalzbrunn, Germany
d. June 06, 1946 in Schreiberlau, Germany

John Clendennin Burne Hawkes, Jr
American author
• Avant-garde novels include *The Cannibal*, 1949; *Passion Artist*, 1949.
b. August 17, 1925 in Stamford, Connecticut

Stephen Hawking
English educator–physicist–author
• Mathematics professor; has developed significant physics theories; wrote bestseller *A Brief History of Time*, 1988; suffers from Lou Gehrig's disease.
b. January 08, 1942 in Oxford, England

Cameron Hawley
American author
• Wrote best-selling novel *Executive Suite*, 1952; later film called *Cash McCall*, 1955.
b. September 19, 1905 in Howard, South Dakota
d. March 09, 1969 in Marathon, Florida

Julian Hawthorne
American author
• Wrote novel *Garth*, 1877, biographical *Hawthorne and His Circle*, 1903; son of Nathanial.
b. June 22, 1846 in Boston, Massachusetts
d. July 14, 1934 in San Francisco, California

Nathaniel Hawthorne
American author
• Wrote *The Scarlet Letter*, 1850; *The House of Seven Gables*, 1851.
b. July 04, 1804 in Salem, Massachusetts
d. May 19, 1864 in Plymouth, New Hampshire

Robert Earl Hayden
American poet
• Works include verse volume *Angle of Ascent: New and Selected Poems*, 1975.
b. August 04, 1913 in Detroit, Michigan
d. February 25, 1980 in Ann Arbor, Michigan

Alfred Hayes
American author
• Novels include *Shadow of Heaven*, 1947; *The Big Time*, 1944.
b. 1911 in London, England
d. August 14, 1985 in Sherman Oaks, California

Bessie Head
(Bessie Emery)
South African author
• Exiled from S Africa; wrote *Maru*, 1971; *A Question of Power*, 1974.
b. July 06, 1937 in South Africa
d. April 17, 1986 in Serowe, Botswana

Seamus Justin Heaney
Irish poet
• Volumes of poetry include *Eleven Poems*, 1965; *Bog Poems*, 1975.
b. April 13, 1939 in County Derry, Northern Ireland

Gerald (Henry FitzGerald) Heard
English author
• Writer on science, mystical religion; spiritual influence on Huxley, Isherwood: *Human Venture*, 1955.
b. October 06, 1889 in London, England
d. August 14, 1971 in Santa Monica, California

David W(hitmire) Hearst
American publisher
• Son of W R Hearst; published *LA Herald-Express*, 1950.
b. December 02, 1916 in New York, New York
d. May 13, 1986 in Los Angeles, California

William Randolph Hearst
American newspaper publisher
• Founder of newspaper chain with yellow journalism reputation; movie *Citizen Kane*, 1941, based on his life.
b. April 29, 1863 in San Francisco, California
d. August 14, 1951 in Beverly Hills, California

William Randolph Hearst, Jr
American editor–publisher
• Editor-in-chief, Hearst Newspapers, 1945–; won Pulitzer for international correspondence, 1956.
b. January 27, 1908 in New York, New York

F(elix) Edward Hebert
American politician–editor
• Dem. con. from LA, 1941-76; wrote award-winning expose of Huey Long, 1939.
b. October 12, 1901 in New Orleans, Louisiana
d. December 29, 1979 in New Orleans, Louisiana

Anthony Evan Hecht
American poet
• Won Pulitzer, 1968, for *The Hard Hours*, which featured empathetic perspective on human suffering.
b. January 16, 1923 in New York, New York

George Joseph Hecht
American publisher
• Founded *Parents' Magazine; Humpty Dumpty.*
b. November 01, 1895 in New York, New York
d. April 23, 1980 in New York, New York

Konrad Heiden
German historian–author
• Expert on Hitler, said to have coined term "Nazi" as derisive nickname.
b. August 07, 1901 in Munich, Germany
d. July 18, 1966 in New York, New York

Carl Gustaf Verner von Heidenstam
Swedish author–poet
• First volume of poetry *Pilgrimage and Wanderyears*, 1888, challenged contemporary Swedish literature; won Nobel Prize, 1916.
b. July 06, 1859 in Olshammar, Sweden
d. May 2, 1940 in Stockholm, Sweden

Heinrich Heine
German poet–critic
• Wrote satirical poetry including *The Harz Journey*, 1826.
b. December 13, 1797 in Dusseldorf, Germany
d. February 17, 1856 in Paris, France

Robert Anson Heinlein
American author
• Won four Hugos; classics include *The Moon is a Harsh Mistress*, 1966.
b. July 07, 1907 in Butler, Missouri
d. May 08, 1988 in Carmel, California

Andrew Heiskell
American publisher
• Chm., CEO, Time Inc., 1960-80.
b. September 13, 1915 in Naples, Italy

Joseph Heller
American author–dramatist
• Wrote contemporary American masterpiece, *Catch-22*, 1961.
b. May 01, 1923 in Brooklyn, New York

Mark Hellinger
American journalist
• News columnist, NYC, 1930s-40s; headed own film co. from 1937; Broadway theater named for him.
b. March 21, 1903 in New York, New York
d. December 21, 1947 in Hollywood, California

Felicia Dorothea Browne Hemans
English poet
• Wrote verses "The Boy Stood on the Burning Deck"; "England's Dead."
b. September 25, 1793 in Liverpool, England
d. May 16, 1835 in Dublin, Ireland

Ernest Miller Hemingway
American journalist–author
• Wrote *A Farewell to Arms*, 1929; *For Whom the Bell Tolls*, 1940; won Nobel Prize, 1954. Committed suicide.
b. July 21, 1899 in Oak Park, Illinois
d. July 02, 1961 in Ketchum, Idaho

Leicester Hemingway
American author
• Younger brother of Ernest Hemingway; wrote biography *My Brother, Ernest Hemingway.*
b. April 1915 in Oak Park, Illinois
d. September 13, 1982 in Miami, Florida

Mary Welsh Hemingway
(Mrs Ernest Hemingway)
American author–journalist
• Fourth wife of Ernest Hemingway; foreign correspondent during WW II; wrote autobiography *How It Was*, 1976.
b. April 05, 1908 in Walker, Minnesota
d. November 27, 1986 in New York, New York

Burton Jesse Hendrick
American biographer–journalist
• Won Pulitzers for *Victory at Sea*, 1920; *Life of Walter Page*, 1922; *Training of an American*, 1928.
b. December 28, 1870 in New Haven, Connecticut
d. March 23, 1949 in New York, New York

Henrietta Henkle
(Henrietta Buckmaster pseud)
American author–journalist
• Novels on black life include *Let My People Go*, 1941; *Deep River*, 1949.
b. 1909 in Cleveland, Ohio

Marguerite Henry
American children's author
• Won 1949 Newbery for *King of the Wind.*
b. April 13, 1902 in Milwaukee, Wisconsin

O Henry, pseud
(William Sydney Porter)
American author–journalist
• Wrote short stories with surprise endings; noted for tale *Gift of the Magi.*
b. September 11, 1862 in Greensboro, North Carolina
d. June 05, 1910 in New York, New York

William M Henry
American journalist
• Award-winning *Los Angeles Times* columnist, 1911-70.
b. August 21, 1890 in San Francisco, California
d. April 13, 1970 in Chatsworth, California

Lisa Henson
American publisher
• Daughter of Jim Henson; first woman pres. of *The Harvard Lampoon.*
b. 1960

George Alfred Henty
English children's author
• Wrote 80 boys adventure tales including *With Clive in India*, 1884.
b. December 08, 1832 in Trumpington, England
d. November 16, 1902 in Weymouth, England

Frank Patrick Herbert
American author
• Author of *Dune* series; won Nebula, 1965; Hugo, 1966; adapted to film, 1984.
b. October 08, 1920 in Tacoma, Washington
d. February 11, 1986 in Madison, Wisconsin

James Leo Herlihy
American author
• Works include *Midnight Cowboy*, 1965.
b. February 27, 1927 in Detroit, Michigan

Robert Herrick
English author–poet
• A major Cavalier poet; love lyrics, pastorals include "To Daffadils"; verse collection *Hesperides*, 1648.
b. August 24, 1591 in London, England
d. October 1674 in Dean Prior, England

James Herriot, pseud
(James Wight)
Scottish veterinarian–author
• Wrote *All Creatures Great and Small*, 1972; *All Things Bright and Beautiful*, 1974.
b. October 03, 1916 in Glasgow, Scotland

John Richard Hersey
American author–journalist
• Wrote *A Bell for Adano*, 1944; *Hiroshima*, 1946.
b. June 17, 1914 in Tientsin, China

Seymour Hersh
American journalist
• Won 1970 Pulitzer, int'l. reporting, for articles on My Lai massacre.
b. April 08, 1937 in Chicago, Illinois

Aleksandr Herzen
Russian author–revolutionary
• Published *The Bell*, 1857-67, leading journal of Russian reformers; wrote popular novel *Who is to Blame*, 1847.
b. 1812
d. 1870

Theodor Herzl
Hungarian journalist
• Founder of Zionism, 1897, who supported creation of Jewish settlement in Palestine.
b. May 02, 1860 in Budapest, Hungary
d. July 03, 1904 in Vienna, Austria

Hesiod
Greek poet
• Wrote *Works and Days, Theogony, The Shield of Heracles.*

Hermann Hesse
Swiss author
• Known for imagination, accuracy of psychological, cultural observations; won Nobel Prize, 1946.
b. July 02, 1877 in Calw, Germany
d. August 09, 1962 in Montagnola, Switzerland

Stefan Heym
German author
• Novels include *Five Days in June,* 1974.
b. April 1, 1913 in Chemnitz, Germany

Paul Johann Ludwig von Heyse
German author
• Master of novella; won Nobel Prize for literature, 1910.
b. March 15, 1830 in Berlin, Germany
d. April 02, 1914 in Munich, Germany

(Edwin) DuBose Heyward
American author
• Major writer of Harlem Renaissance; wrote *Porgy,* 1925; adapted as opera *Porgy and Bess,* 1935.
b. August 31, 1885 in Charleston, South Carolina
d. June 16, 1940 in Tryon, North Carolina

Eleanor Alice Burford Hibbert
(Philippa Carr; Elbur Ford; Victoria Holt; Kathleen Kellow; Jean Paidy; Ellalice Tate, pseuds.)
English author
• Prolific writer of Gothic romances since 1950s; best known as Victoria Holt.
b. 1906 in London, England

Ben Hibbs
American journalist
• Editor, *Saturday Evening Post,* 1942-62.
b. July 23, 1901 in Fontana, Kansas
d. March 29, 1975 in Penn Valley, Pennsylvania

Marguerite Higgins
American journalist
• Korean, Vietnam War correspondent who won 1951 Pulitzer for int'l. reporting.
b. September 03, 1920 in Hong Kong, China
d. January 03, 1966 in Washington, District of Columbia

Thomas Wentworth Higginson
American clergyman–author
• Unitarian minister, slavery opponent; led first colored regiment in Civil War, 1862-64; friend of Emily Dickinson.
b. December 22, 1823 in Cambridge, Massachusetts
d. May 09, 1911

Patricia Highsmith
American author
• Award-winning crime novels include *The Talented Mr. Ripley,* 1955.
b. January 12, 1921 in Fort Worth, Texas

Florence Josephine Cole Hightower
American children's author
• Wrote adventure mysteries for children: *Secret of the Crazy Quilt,* 1972.
b. June 09, 1916 in Boston, Massachusetts
d. March 06, 1981 in Boston, Massachusetts

Geoffrey Hill
English poet
• Award-winning verse vols. include *Mercian Hymns,* 1971.
b. June 18, 1932 in Bromsgrove, England

George Birkbeck Norman Hill
English author–educator
• Authority on life, works of Samuel Johnson; edited James Boswell's classic *Life of Johnson,* 1887.
b. June 07, 1835 in Tottenham, England
d. February 27, 1903 in London, England

Grace Livingstone Hill
American author
• Popular novels sold over three million copies: *April Gold,* 1936.
b. April 16, 1865 in Wellsville, New York
d. February 23, 1947 in Swarthmore, Pennsylvania

C K Hillegass
American publisher
• Publishes *Cliff Notes* study guides.
b. 1918 in Rising City, Nebraska

Tony Hillerman
American author
• Detective novelist concerned with American Indian culture: *Dance Hall of the Dead,* 1974.
b. May 27, 1925 in Sacred Heart, Oklahoma

Lee Hills
American editor
• Exec. editor, *Detroit Free Press,* 1951-69; editorial chm., Knight-Ridder Newspapers, 1979-81; won Pulitzer, 1956.
b. May 28, 1906 in Granville, North Dakota

Robert Hillyer
American poet–author–educator
• Poetry volumes include *The Seventh Hill,* 1928; won 1933 Pulitzer for *Collected Verses.*
b. June 03, 1895 in East Orange, New Jersey
d. December 24, 1961 in Wilmington, Delaware

James Hilton
English author
• Best-known novels are *Lost Horizon,* 1933; *Goodbye, Mr. Chips,* 1934.
b. September 09, 1900 in Leigh-on-Sea, England
d. December 2, 1954 in Long Beach, California

Chester Bomar Himes
American author
• Wrote detective novel *Cotton Comes to Harlem,* which became 1970 film.
b. July 29, 1909 in Jefferson City, Missouri
d. November 12, 1984 in Moraira, Spain

Thomas Hinde, pseud
(Sir Thomas Wiles Chitty)
English author
• Novels include *Daymare,* 1980.
b. March 26, 1926 in Felixstowe, England

S(usan) E(loise) Hinton
American author
• Writes books for teenagers: *The Outsiders,* 1967; *That Was Then, This Is Now,* 1971.
b. 1948 in Tulsa, Oklahoma

Shere Hite
(Shirley Diana Gregory)
American author
• Writings center on cultural research in human sexuality; controversial works known as "Hite Reports."
b. November 02, 1942 in Saint Joseph, Missouri

Edward Morley Hoagland
American author
• Novels include *Cat Man,* 1956; *The Moose on the Wall,* 1974.
b. December 21, 1932 in New York, New York

Thomas Hobbes
English author–philosopher
• Father of modern analytical philosophy; best-known work *Leviathan,* 1651.
b. April 05, 1588 in Malmesbury, England
d. December 04, 1679 in Hardwick, England

Samuel Goodman Hoffenstein
American poet
• Best-known work: *Poems in Praise of Practically Nothing*, 1928.
b. October 08, 1890 in Lithuania
d. October 06, 1947 in Hollywood, California

Eric Hoffer
American author–philosopher
• Wrote *The True Believer*, 1951; awarded Presidential Medal of Freedom, 1983.
b. July 25, 1902 in New York, New York
d. May 21, 1983 in San Francisco, California

Rob Hoffman
American publisher
• Co-founder of *National Lampoon* following graduation from Harvard, 1969.
b. 1948

Ernst Theodor Amadeus Hoffmann
German author
• Master of weird, macabre; Offenbach's opera *Tales of Hoffmann* based on his work.
b. January 24, 1776 in Konigsberg, Germany
d. June 25, 1822 in Berlin, Germany

Heinrich Hoffmann
German children's author
• Wrote children's classic *Struwwelpeter*, 1847, collection of graphic stories stressing morality.
b. June 01, 1809 in Frankfurt am Main, Germany
d. September 2, 1894 in Frankfurt am Main, Germany

James Fulton Hoge, Jr
American newspaper editor
• Publisher of *NY Daily News*, 1984–.
b. December 25, 1936 in New York, New York

Stewart Hall Holbrook
American author–journalist
• Made history entertaining, yet accurate in books such as *The Age of Moguls*, 1953; *Wyatt Earp: US Marshall*, 1956.
b. August 22, 1893 in Newport, Vermont
d. September 03, 1964 in Portland, Oregon

Raphael Holinshed
English editor
• Best-known work *The Chronicles of England, Scotlande, and Irelande*, 1578.

John Hollander
American author
• Poetry collections include *Tales Told of the Fathers*, 1975; edited *The Oxford Anthology of English Literature*, 1973.
b. October 28, 1929 in New York, New York

Emory Holloway
American author–educator
• Awarded Pulitzer Prize for biography of Walt Whitman, 1927.
b. March 16, 1885 in Marshall, Missouri
d. July 3, 1977 in Bethlehem, Pennsylvania

Albert Bernard Hollowood
English editor–economist
• Editor, *Punch* magazine, 1957-68; wrote *Funny Money*, 1975.
b. June 03, 1910 in Burslem, England
d. March 28, 1981 in Guildford, England

Constance Holme
English author
• Wrote of common folk of English country life: *The Lonely Plough*, 1914; *The Trumpet in the Dust*, 1921.
b. 1881 in Milnthorpe, England
d. June 17, 1955 in Arnside, England

John Clellon Holmes
American author
• Coined term "beat" describing literary, social rebels after WW II; *Nothing More to Declare*, 1967, regarded as definitive chronicle of Beat Generation.
b. March 12, 1926 in Holyoke, Massachusetts
d. March 3, 1988 in Middletown, Connecticut

Henry Holt
American publisher
• Founded Henry Holt & Co. publishers, 1873; books include *The Cosmic Relations and Immortality*, 1919.
b. January 03, 1840 in Baltimore, Maryland
d. February 13, 1926 in New York, New York

John Caldwell Holt
American educator–author
• Wrote *How Children Fail*, 1964; sparked debate about quality of education in US.
b. April 14, 1923 in New York, New York
d. September 14, 1985 in Boston, Massachusetts

Homer
Greek author
• Credited with writing *The Iliad*; *The Odyssey*.
b. 750BC

Theodore Edward Hook
English author–humorist
• Edited *John Bull*, 1820; popular racy novels include *Maxwell*, 1830.
b. September 22, 1788 in London, England
d. August 24, 1841 in London, England

Sir Anthony Hope-Hawkins
English author
• Books include *The Prisoner of Zenda*, 1894; *The Dolly Dialogues*, 1894.
b. February 07, 1863 in London, England
d. July 08, 1933 in Tadworth, England

Horace
(Quintus Horatius Flaccus)
Roman poet–satirist
• His *Ars Poetica* was used as style handbook by 16th-, 17th-c. neoclassicists.
b. December 08, 65 in Venosa, Lucania
d. November 27, 8

Paul Horgan
American author
• Won Pulitzers for *Great River*, 1954; *Lamy of Santa Fe*, 1975.
b. August 01, 1903 in Buffalo, New York

Ernest William Hornung
English author
• Best known for stories featuring A J Raffles and sidekick, Bunny, similar to Doyle's Holmes/Watson tales.
b. June 07, 1866 in Middlesbrough, England
d. March 22, 1921 in Saint-Jean-de-Luz, France

David Joel Horowitz
American author
• Co-author, with Peter Collier, *The Fords: An American Epic*, 1986.
b. January 1, 1939 in New York, New York

Aaron Edward Hotchner
American author–editor
• Long association with Ernest Hemingway resulted in memoir *Papa Hemingway*, 1966.
b. June 28, 1920 in Saint Louis, Missouri

Henry Oscar Houghton
American publisher
• Founded Houghton-Miflin publishing house, 1880.
b. April 3, 1823 in Sutton, Vermont
d. August 25, 1895 in North Andover, Massachusetts

Geoffrey Edward West Household
English author
• Wrote adventure stories: classic thriller *Rogue Male*, 1939.
b. November 3, 1900 in Bristol, England
d. October 04, 1988 in Oxfordshire, England

A(lfred) E(dward) Housman
English poet–scholar
• Best known for *A Shropshire Lad*, 1896.
b. March 26, 1859 in Fockbury, England
d. April 3, 1936 in Cambridge, England

Laurence Housman
English author–dramatist
• Brother of A E; wrote over 100 novels, fairy tales, self-illustrated books of verse; *Victoria Regina*, 1935, was one of his most successful plays.
b. July 18, 1865 in Bromsgrove, England
d. February 2, 1959 in Glastonbury, England

James Archibald Houston
Canadian author
• Best known for novel *White Dawn,* 1971; filmed, 1976.
b. June 12, 1921 in Toronto, Ontario

Barbara Howar
American journalist–author
• Her book, *Laughing All the Way,* 1973, tells inside story of Washington life during Kennedy, Johnson administrations.
b. September 27, 1934 in Nashville, Tennessee

Robert Ervin Howard
(Patrick Ervin pseud)
American author
• Fantasy writer known for popular *Conan the Barbarian* series.
b. January 22, 1906 in Peaster, Texas
d. June 12, 1936 in Cross Plains, Texas

Roy Wilson Howard
American journalist
• Pres., United Press, 1912-21; pres., chm., Scripps-Howard Newspapers, 1925-53.
b. January 01, 1883 in Gano, Ohio
d. November 2, 1964 in New York, New York

Susan Howatch
American author
• Books include *Penmarric,* 1971, adapted to BBC TV serial.
b. July 14, 1940 in Leatherhead, England

Edgar Watson Howe
American editor–author
• Wrote *Story of a Country Town,* 1883, early example of realism.
b. May 03, 1853 in Treaty, Indiana
d. October 03, 1937 in Atchison, Kansas

Julia Ward Howe
(Mrs Samuel Gridley Howe)
American author–social reformer
• Wrote poem, "Battle Hymn of the Republic," 1862; became theme for Union Army.
b. May 27, 1819 in New York, New York
d. October 17, 1910 in Newport, Rhode Island

Louis McHenry Howe
American journalist–secretary
• FDR's secretary, 1913-30; a political mentor who greatly influenced both Eleanor and Franklin's success.
b. January 14, 1871 in Indianapolis, Indiana
d. April 18, 1936 in Fall River, Massachusetts

Mark De Wolfe Howe
American editor–author
• Wrote nonfiction texts, biographies of New England life; won 1924 Pulitzer for *Barrett Wendell.*
b. May 22, 1906 in Boston, Massachusetts
d. February 28, 1967 in Cambridge, Massachusetts

Quincy Howe
American editor–broadcaster
• Pioneered in news commentary, analysis; wrote *A World History of Our Times,* 1947-53.
b. August 17, 1900 in Boston, Massachusetts
d. February 17, 1977 in New York, New York

Clark Howell
American journalist–editor
• Member of Democratic National Committee, 1892-1924; won Pulitzer, 1929, for campaign against municipal graft.
b. September 21, 1863 in Barnwell County, South Carolina
d. November 14, 1936 in Atlanta, Georgia

William Dean Howells
American author–editor
• Pre-eminent man of letters; edited *Atlantic Monthly,* 1871-81; *Harper's,* 1880s; wrote *Rise of Silas Lapham,* 1885.
b. March 01, 1837 in Martins Ferry, Ohio
d. May 1, 1920 in New York, New York

Lawrence W Hoyt
American publisher
• Founded Walden Book Co., 1962.
b. 1901 in Brighton, Massachusetts
d. December 17, 1982 in Bridgeport, Connecticut

Elbert Green Hubbard
(Fra Elbertus)
American author–publisher
• Established Roycroft Press and inspirational mags.; wrote *A Message to Garcia,* 1899; died on Lusitania.
b. June 19, 1856 in Bloomington, Illinois
d. May 07, 1915

Langston (James Langston) Hughes
American poet–author–journalist
• Expressed Negro view of America in *Shakespeare in Harlem,* 1942; 1959 Springarn winner.
b. February 01, 1902 in Joplin, Missouri
d. May 22, 1967 in New York, New York

Ted Hughes
English poet
• Poet laureate of England, 1984–; writer of award-winning children's verse.
b. August 17, 1930 in Mytholmroyd, England

Thomas Hughes
English reformer–author
• Wrote classic *Tom Brown's School Days,* 1857.
b. October 2, 1822 in Uffington, England
d. March 22, 1896 in Brighton, England

William Bradford Huie
American author–journalist
• Known for books dealing with violence in civil rights movement in South: *The Klansman,* 1967; also wrote *The Execution of Private Slovik,* 1954, later filmed.
b. November 13, 1910 in Hartselle, Alabama
d. November 23, 1986 in Guntersville, Alabama

Kathryn Cavarly Hulme
American author
• Wrote *The Wild Place,* 1953; best-selling biography *Nun's Story,* 1957.
b. January 06, 1900 in San Francisco, California
d. August 25, 1981 in Lihue, Hawaii

Rolfe (George Rolfe) Humphries
American poet
• Award-winning verse volumes include *Wind of Time,* 1951.
b. November 2, 1894 in Philadelphia, Pennsylvania
d. April 22, 1969 in Redwood City, California

Leigh Hunt
English author–poet
• Associated with Byron, Shelley, Keats; wrote verse "Abou Ben Adhem," 1834; edited literary periodicals.
b. October 19, 1784 in Southgate, England
d. August 28, 1859 in Putney, England

Fannie Hurst
American author
• Wrote popular novels including *Imitation of Life,* 1933; adapted to film, 1934.
b. October 19, 1889 in Hamilton, Ohio
d. February 23, 1968 in New York, New York

Zora Neale Hurston
American dramatist–author
• Her writings chronicle rural black life: *Mules and Men,* 1935; *Tell My Horse,* 1938.
b. January 07, 1903 in Eatonville, Florida
d. January 28, 1960 in Fort Pierce, Florida

Taha Hussein
Egyptian educator–author
• Outstanding Islamic scholar, author of over 40 books; blinded in childhood; wrote *An Egyptian Childhood,* 1932; *The Tree of Misfortune,* 1944.
b. November 14, 1889 in Maghagha, Egypt
d. October 28, 1973 in Cairo, Egypt

Aldous Leonard Huxley
English author–critic
• Best known for *Brave New World*, 1932; *Brave New World Revisited*, 1958.
b. July 26, 1894 in Godalming, England
d. November 22, 1963 in Los Angeles, California

Elspeth Josceline Grant Huxley
English author
• Books include *Man from Nowhere*, 1965; *Scott of the Antarctic*, 1978.
b. July 23, 1907 in London, England

Hammond Innes, pseud
(Ralph Hammond-Innes)
English author
• Writings include *Fire in the Snow*, 1947; *The Last Voyage*, 1978.
b. July 15, 1913 in Horsham, England

Robert W Irvin
American journalist
• Automotive writer for 30 yrs; editor, *Automotive News;* publisher, *Auto Week.*
b. March 03, 1933 in Highland Park, Michigan
d. December 01, 1980 in Chicago, Illinois

Clifford Michael Irving
American author–criminal
• Served 17 months in prison for writing false autobiography of Howard Hughes.
b. November 05, 1930 in New York, New York

John Irving
American author
• Best known work *The World According to Garp*, 1978; adapted to film, 1982.
b. March 02, 1942 in Exeter, New Hampshire

Washington Irving
(Diedrich Knickerbocker)
American author
• Wrote *Rip Van Winkle, Legend of Sleepy Hollow*, 1820.
b. April 03, 1783 in New York, New York
d. November 28, 1859 in Tarrytown, New York

Wallace (Admah) Irwin
American journalist–author
• Writings include *Pilgrims into Folly*, 1917; *Mated*, 1926; *Young Wife*, 1936; brother of Will.
b. March 15, 1875 in Oneida, New York
d. February 14, 1959 in Southern Pines, North Carolina

Will(iam Henry) Irwin
American journalist
• Books on his experiences as a WW I reporter include *Christ or Mars?*, 1923; brother of Wallace.
b. September 14, 1873 in Oneida, New York
d. February 24, 1948 in New York, New York

Kazuo Ishiguro
British author
• Writings deal with how people come to terms with past mistakes, failures; won Booker Prize, 1989, for *The Remains of the Day*.
b. November 08, 1954 in Nagasaki, Japan

Charles Reginald Jackson
American author
• Wrote novel, *The Lost Weekend*, 1944, which was filmed, 1945; won Oscar.
b. April 06, 1903 in Summit, New Jersey
d. September 21, 1968 in New York, New York

Helen Maria Hunt Fiske Jackson
American author
• Wrote *Ramona*, 1884; worked toward betterment of American Indians.
b. October 18, 1831 in Amherst, Massachusetts
d. August 12, 1885 in San Francisco, California

Shirley Jackson
American author
• Wrote stories dealing with supernatural in everyday setting: *The Lottery*, 1949.
b. December 14, 1919 in San Francisco, California
d. August 08, 1965 in North Bennington, Vermont

Max Jacob
French poet–artist
• Poems were written in surrealistic style before its actual beginning: *Le Cornet a Des*, 1917.
b. July 11, 1876 in Quimper, France
d. March 05, 1944 in Drancy, France

Joseph Jacobs
American author–folklorist
• Compiled *Celtic Fairy Tales*, 1891.
b. August 29, 1854 in Sydney, Australia
d. January 3, 1916 in Yonkers, New York

W(illiam) W(ymark) Jacobs
English author
• Wrote sea stories, humor; noted for tale *Monkey's Paw*, 1902.
b. September 08, 1863 in London, England
d. September 01, 1943 in London, England

Oswald Jacoby
American bridge player–journalist–author
• Called best card player in world, 1950; syndicated bridge columnist, 1949-84.
b. December 08, 1902 in New York, New York
d. June 27, 1984 in Dallas, Texas

Werner Wilhelm Jaeger
American philosopher–author
• Prominent 20th-c. classical humanist; *Paideia*, 1934, standard of classical studies.
b. July 3, 1888 in Lobberich, Prussia
d. October 19, 1961 in Boston, Massachusetts

Rona Jaffe
American author
• Wrote *The Last Chance*, 1976; *Class Reunion*, 1979.
b. June 12, 1932 in New York, New York

Gloria (Adelaide Love) Jahoda
American author
• Writings include *Annie*, 1960; *The Trail of Tears*, 1976.
b. October 06, 1926 in Chicago, Illinois
d. January 13, 1980 in Tallahassee, Florida

John Jakes
American author
• Wrote *The Bastard*, 1974; *The Rebels*, 1975.
b. March 31, 1932 in Chicago, Illinois

Henry James, Sr
American philosopher–writer–lecturer
• Writings on social, religious issues include *Christianity the Logic of Creation*, 1857.
b. June 03, 1811 in Albany, New York
d. December 18, 1882 in Cambridge, Massachusetts

Henry James, Jr
British author
• Master of psychological novel; wrote *The Aspern Papers*, 1888; *The Turn of the Screw*, 1898.
b. April 15, 1843 in New York, New York
d. February 28, 1916 in London, England

P(hyllis) D(orothy) James
English author
• Writings include *Cover Her Face*, 1962; *The Black Tower*, 1975.
b. August 03, 1920 in Oxford, England

Karl Jaspers
German author–philosopher–physician–educator
• Promoted existentialism; influenced modern theology, psychiatry.
b. February 23, 1883 in Oldenburg, Germany
d. February 26, 1969 in Basel, Switzerland

Robert Jastrow
American author–astronomer
• Writings include *Until the Sun Dies*, 1977; *The Enchanted Loom*, 1981.
b. September 07, 1925 in New York, New York

Richard Jeffries
English author
• Wrote classic autobiography *Story of My Heart*, 1883.
b. November 06, 1848 in North Wiltshire, England
d. August 14, 1887 in Worthing, England

Elizabeth Joan Jennings
English author
• Writings include *Let's Have Some Poetry*, 1960; *Selected Poems*, 1979.
b. July 18, 1926 in Boston, England

Gary (Gayne) Jennings
American author
• Books of juvenile non-fiction, self illustrated, include *March of the Gods*, 1976.
b. September 2, 1928 in Buena Vista, Virginia

Johannes Vilhelm Jensen
Danish author
• Won Nobel Prize in literature, 1944, for multi-volume *Himmerlandshistorier*.
b. January 3, 1873 in Farso, Denmark
d. November 25, 1950 in Copenhagen, Denmark

Oliver Ormerod Jensen
American author
• Co-founder, editor, *American Heritage* magazine, 1954–; wrote *Railroads in America*, 1975.
b. April 16, 1914 in Ithaca, New York

Virginia Allen Jensen
American author
• Books for children include *Lars Peter's Birthday*, 1959; *Sara and the Door*, 1975.
b. September 21, 1927 in Des Moines, Iowa

Richard Jessup
American author
• Wrote *The Cincinnati Kid*, 1964; movie starred Steve McQueen, 1965.
b. January 01, 1925 in Savannah, Georgia
d. October 22, 1982 in Nokomis, Florida

Sarah Orne Jewett
American author
• Stories depict New England countryside charm; works include *A Country Doctor*, 1884; *The Life of Nancy*, 1895.
b. September 03, 1849 in South Berwick, Maine
d. June 24, 1909 in South Berwick, Maine

Juan Ramon Jimenez
Spanish poet
• Best known for prose poem "Platero y Yo," 1917; won 1956 Nobel Prize.
b. December 24, 1881 in Monguer, Spain
d. May 29, 1958 in San Juan, Puerto Rico

John of Salisbury
English author
• Most learned scholarly writer of his time; wrote *Policraticus*, 1159.
b. 1120 in Salisbury, England
d. October 25, 1180

Charles Richard Johnson
American author
• Wrote novel *Oxherding Tale*, 1982.
b. April 23, 1948 in Evanston, Illinois

Eleanor M Johnson
American publisher
• Founded *The Weekly Reader*, 1928, which was read by two-thirds of today's US adults as children.
b. 1893
d. October 08, 1987 in Gaithersburg, Maryland

Eyvind Olof Verner Johnson
Swedish author
• Won 1974 Nobel Prize in literature for his novels, short stories.
b. July 29, 1900 in Overlvlea, Sweden
d. August 25, 1976 in Stockholm, Sweden

James Weldon Johnson
American author
• Wrote *The Book of American Negro Poetry*, 1921; *Negro Americans, What Now?* 1934.
b. June 17, 1871 in Jacksonville, Florida
d. June 26, 1938 in Wiscasset, Maine

John Harold Johnson
American publisher
• Publishing firm produces *Ebony*, *Jet*, *Ebony, Jr.* mags.; pres., Fashion Fair Cosmetics.
b. January 19, 1918 in Arkansas City, Arkansas

Josephine Winslow Johnson
(Mrs Grant G Cannon)
American author
• First novel, *Now in November*, won Pulitzer for fiction, 1935.
b. January 2, 1910 in Kirkwood, Missouri
d. February 27, 1990 in Batavia, Ohio

Pamela Hansford Johnson
(Baroness Pamela Hansford Johnson Snow; Mrs C P Snow)
English author–critic
• Versatile writer of psychological novels, literary studies: *Catherine Carter*, 1952.
b. May 29, 1912 in London, England
d. June 18, 1981 in London, England

James Jones
American author
• Wrote *From Here To Eternity*, 1951; adapted to film, 1953.
b. November 06, 1921 in Robinson, Illinois
d. May 09, 1977 in Southampton, New York

(Morgan) Glyn Jones
Welsh author
• Writings include *The Blue Bed, and Other Stories*, 1937; *The Learning Lark*, 1960.
b. February 28, 1905 in Wales

Erica Mann Jong
American author–poet
• Wrote *Fear of Flying*, 1973; *Parachutes & Kisses*, 1984.
b. March 26, 1942 in New York, New York

June Jordan
(June Meyer pseud)
American children's author
• Books for children include *Dry Victories*, 1972; *His Own Where*, 1971.
b. July 09, 1936 in Harlem, New York

Richard Joseph
American journalist
• Specialized in travel writing; travel editor, *Esquire* mag., 1947-76; books include *Your Trip Abroad*, 1950.
b. April 24, 1910 in New York, New York
d. September 3, 1976

William Iliya Jovanovich
American publisher
• Chm., CEO, Harcourt, Brace, Jovanovich, 1970–.
b. February 06, 1920 in Louisville, Colorado

James Augustus Aloysius Joyce
Irish author–poet
• Wrote *Ulysses*, 1922; banned in US as obscene until 1933.
b. February 02, 1882 in Dublin, Ireland
d. January 13, 1941 in Zurich, Switzerland

Emily Chubbock Judson
(Fanny Forester pseud)
American author–missionary
• Missionary to Burma, 1846-47; to Rangoon, 1847; wrote *My Two Sisters*, 1854.
b. August 22, 1817 in Eaton, New York
d. June 01, 1854 in Hamilton, New York

Elizabeth Rider Montgomery Julesberg
(Elizabeth Montgomery)
American children's author
• Wrote reading primers featuring Dick, Jane, Spot, 1940s.
b. July 12, 1902 in Huaras, Peru
d. February 19, 1985 in Seattle, Washington

Franz Kafka
Austrian author–poet
• His short stories, three novels characterized by themes of loneliness; most published posthumously: *Amerika*, 1927.
b. July 02, 1883 in Prague, Czechoslovakia
d. June 03, 1924 in Kierling, Austria

Roger Kahn
American journalist–author
• Sports editor *Newsweek*, 1956-60; editor *Saturday Evening Post*, 1963-68.
b. October 31, 1927 in Brooklyn, New York

Henry Kane
American author
• Mystery, crime novels include *The Little Red Phone*, 1982.
b. 1918 in New York, New York

Erik Axel Karlfeldt
Swedish poet
• Work is purposely archaic, bases in folklore, custom; refused Nobel Prize, 1918, awarded posthumously, 1931.
b. July 2, 1864 in Folkarna, Sweden
d. April 08, 1931 in Stockholm, Sweden

Erich Kastner
(Erich Kaestner)
German author–poet
• Wrote *Emil and the Detectives*, 1928; books burned in Germany, 1933.
b. February 23, 1899 in Dresden, Germany
d. July 29, 1974

Valentin Petrovich Katayev
Russian author
• Wrote satirical novel *The Embezzlers*, 1929; play *Squaring the Circle*, 1928.
b. January 28, 1897 in Odessa, Russia

Bel Kaufman
American author–educator
• Wrote *Up the Down Staircase*, 1965.
b. in Berlin, Germany

Sue Kaufman
(Sue Kaufman Barondess)
American author
• Writings on life's everyday pressures include *Diary of a Mad Housewife*, 1967.
b. August 07, 1926 in Long Island, New York
d. June 25, 1977 in New York, New York

Patrick Kavanagh
Irish poet
• Described Irish country life in poem "The Great Hunger," 1942; novel, *Tarry Flynn*, 1948.
b. 1905 in County Monaghan, Ireland
d. November 3, 1967 in Dublin, Ireland

Yasunari Kawabata
Japanese author
• First Japanese to win Nobel Prize in literature, 1968; known for impressionistic novels.
b. June 11, 1899 in Osaka, Japan
d. April 16, 1972 in Zushi, Japan

Mary Margaret Mollie Kaye
(Mollie Hamilton; M M Kaye)
English author
• Historical novels include best-seller *The Far Pavillions*, 1978.
b. 1909 in Simla, India

Sheila Kaye-Smith
English author
• Novels, describing life in Sussex, England, include *Sussex Gorse*, 1916.
b. February 04, 1887 in Hastings, England
d. January 14, 1956

Nikos Kazantzakis
Greek author
• Wrote *Zorba the Greek*, 1946; epic *Odysseia*, 1938.
b. December 02, 1883 in Crete
d. October 26, 1957 in Freiburg, Germany (West)

Mary Nesta Keane
(Molly Keane; M J Farrell pseuds)
Irish author
• Novel *Good Behaviour*, 1981, adapted for BBC TV production, 1982.
b. July 04, 1904 in County Kildare, Ireland

Ezra Jack Keats
American illustrator–children's author
• Known for use of collages in illustrating 32 books; won Caldecott Medal, 1963, for *The Snowy Day*.
b. March 11, 1916 in New York, New York
d. May 06, 1983 in New York, New York

John Keats
English poet
• Wrote *Ode on a Grecian Urn*, *Ode to a Nightingale*.
b. October 31, 1795 in London, England
d. February 23, 1821 in Rome, Italy

Helen Adams Keller
American author–lecturer
• How she learned to speak, write despite being blind, deaf told in *The Miracle Worker*, 1962.
b. June 27, 1880 in Tuscumbia, Alabama
d. June 01, 1968 in Westport, Connecticut

Kitty Kelley
American author
• Wrote unauthorized biographies: *Jackie Oh*, 1978, *His Way*, (about Frank Sinatra,) 1986; recently published scathing biography of Nancy Reagan.
b. April 04, 1942 in Spokane, Washington

Stephen Eugene Kelly
American publisher
• Publisher, *Saturday Evening Post; Holiday: McCalls* mags., 1960s-70s.
b. May 13, 1919 in Brooklyn, New York
d. April 06, 1978 in New York, New York

Alice Geer Kelsey
American children's author
• Children's books include *The Thirty Gilt Pennies; Land of the Morning*, 1968.
b. September 21, 1896 in Danvers, Massachusetts

Harry Kemelman
American author
• Won Edgar for *Friday the Rabbi Slept Late*, 1965, first of his popular detective series on Rabbi Small.
b. November 24, 1908 in Boston, Massachusetts

(Harry) Hibbard Kemp
American author–poet
• His worldly travels were basis for poems, novels: *More Miles*, 1926.
b. December 15, 1883 in Youngstown, Ohio
d. August 06, 1960 in Provincetown, Massachusetts

Margaret Kennedy
English author
• Works include *The Midas Touch*, 1967.
b. April 23, 1896 in London, England
d. July 31, 1967 in Adderbury, England

William (Joseph) Kennedy
American author
• Won 1983 Pulitzer for *Ironweed*, third novel of Albany trilogy; adapted to film, 1987.
b. January 16, 1928 in Albany, New York

X J Kennedy, pseud
(Joseph Charles Kennedy)
American children's author
• Best-known children's book: *One Winter Night in August*, 1975.
b. August 21, 1929 in Dover, New Jersey

Jack Kerouac
(Jean Louis Lebris de Kerouac; Jean-Louis Incogniteau)
American author–poet
• Leader of Beat Movement; wrote *On the Road*, 1957.
b. March 12, 1922 in Lowell, Massachusetts
d. October 21, 1969 in Saint Petersburg, Florida

Walter Francis Kerr
American critic–author
• Influential *NY Times* critic, 1966-83; won Pulitzer for criticism, 1978; entered Theater Hall of Fame, 1982.
b. July 08, 1913 in Evanston, Illinois

Ken Kesey
American author
• Wrote *One Flew Over the Cuckoo's Nest*, 1962; adapted to film, 1975.
b. September 17, 1935 in La Hunta, Colorado

Frances Parkinson Keyes
American author
• Best-known novel: *Dinner at Antoine's*, 1948.
b. July 21, 1885 in Charlottesville, Virginia
d. July 03, 1970 in New Orleans, Louisiana

Arthur W Keylor
American publisher
• VP in charge of mags., Time Inc., 1972-81; brought back *Life*, 1978; introduced *People*, 1974; *Discovery*, 1980.
b. 1920
d. August 17, 1981 in Manchester, Vermont

Faye Kicknosway
American poet
• Self-illustrated books of poetry include *Nothing Wakes Her*, 1978.
b. December 16, 1936 in Detroit, Michigan

Benedict Kiely
American author
• Writings focus on Ireland: *All the Way to Bantry Bay*, 1978.
b. August 15, 1919 in County Tyrone, Ireland

William X(avier) Kienzle
(Mark Boyle pseud)
American author
• Former priest who wrote *The Rosary Murders*, 1979; *Death Wears a Red Hat*, 1980.
b. September 11, 1928 in Detroit, Michigan

Soren Aabye Kierkegaard
(Soren Aabye Kjerkegaard)
Danish philosopher–author
• Regarded as founder of existentialism; attacked organized religion.
b. May 05, 1813 in Copenhagen, Denmark
d. November 11, 1855 in Copenhagen, Denmark

Baron John Raymond Godley Kilbracken
Irish author
• Books include *Bring Back My Stringbag*, 1979; *Living Like a Lord*, 1955.
b. October 17, 1920 in London, England

Bernard (Leslie Bernard) Kilgore
American journalist
• Pres., Dow, Jones & Co., 1945-67; built *Wall Street Journal* into major newspaper.
b. November 09, 1908 in Albany, Indiana
d. November 14, 1967 in Princeton, New Jersey

Joyce (Alfred Joyce) Kilmer
American poet–essayist
• Wrote poem *Trees*, 1913; killed in WW I.
b. December 06, 1886 in New Brunswick, New Jersey
d. July 3, 1918 in Seringes, France

James J(ackson) Kilpatrick, Jr
American journalist
• Nationally syndicated columnist; gained renown as conservative voice in commentary on "Sixty Minutes."
b. November 01, 1920 in Oklahoma City, Oklahoma

Francis Henry King
(Frank Cauldwell pseud)
Swiss author
• Short story writer known for chilling plots: *Hard Feelings*, 1976; *The Brighton Belle*, 1968.
b. March 04, 1923 in Adelboden, Switzerland

Stephen Edwin King
American author
• Master of popular horror tales: *Carrie*, 1974; *The Shining*, 1976; *Cujo*, 1981; *It*, 1986.
b. September 21, 1947 in Portland, Maine

Maxine Hong Kingston
American author
• Nonfiction books blend Chinese-American history, myth: *The Woman Warrior*, 1977; *China Men*, 1980.
b. October 27, 1940 in Stockton, California

Galway Kinnell
American poet
• Poems deal with life confronting death; won Pulitzer for *Selected Poems*, 1983.
b. February 01, 1927 in Providence, Rhode Island

(Joseph) Rudyard Kipling
English author–poet
• Won 1907 Nobel Prize; wrote *The Jungle Book*, 1894; *Just So Stories*, 1902.
b. December 3, 1865 in Bombay, India
d. January 18, 1936 in Burwash, England

Austin Huntington Kiplinger
American publisher
• Pres., Kiplinger Washington Editors, 1959–; editor-in-chief *Changing Times* mag., 1979–; son of WM.
b. September 19, 1918 in Washington, District of Columbia

W(illard) M(onroe) Kiplinger
American journalist–publisher
• Founded Kiplinger Washington Editors, Inc., 1923; publishes business newsletters, *Changing Times* mag.
b. January 08, 1891 in Bellefontaine, Ohio
d. August 06, 1967 in Bethesda, Maryland

Russell Kirk
American journalist
• Noted for works on political theory: *The Conservative Mind*, 1953; won awards for gothic, fantasy fiction.
b. October 19, 1918 in Plymouth, Michigan

Caroline Matilda Stansbury Kirkland
(Mrs Mary Clavers pseud)
American author
• First to write realistic fiction of American frontier: *A New Home*, 1839.
b. January 11, 1801 in New York, New York
d. April 06, 1864 in New York, New York

G(eorge) L(yman) Kittredge
American author
• Authority on English literature; wrote *Complete Works of Shakespeare*, 1936.
b. February 28, 1860 in Boston, Massachusetts
d. July 23, 1941 in Barnstable, Massachusetts

Otis Adelbert Kline
American author
• Prolific heroic-fantasy writer for *Weird Tales*, *Argosy* pulps.
b. 1891 in Chicago, Illinois
d. October 24, 1946 in New York, New York

Donald Simon Klopfer
American publisher
• Co-founded Random House publishers with Bennett Cerf, 1927-75.
b. January 23, 1902 in New York, New York
d. May 3, 1986 in New York, New York

Friedrich Gottlieb Klopstock
("The German Milton"; "The Milton of Germany")
German poet
• Baroque, emotional verses include religiously inspired masterpiece, *Messias*, 1748; translated: *The Messiah*, 1826.
b. July 02, 1724 in Quedlinburg, Germany
d. March 14, 1803 in Hamburg, Germany

Hilary Knight
American illustrator–children's author
• Illustrated *Eloise* and *Mrs. Piggle-Wiggle* books.
b. November 01, 1926 in Hempstead, New York

John Shively Knight, III
American author–newspaper editor
• Part of Knight Newspaper family; died before becoming firmly established in newspaper operations.
b. April 03, 1945 in Columbus, Georgia
d. December 07, 1975 in Philadelphia, Pennsylvania

John Shivley Knight
American newspaper publisher
• Founder, longtime editor, Knight-Ridder newspaper empire; won Pulitzer for column "Editor's Notebook," 1968.
b. October 26, 1894 in Bluefield, West Virginia
d. June 16, 1981 in Akron, Ohio

Alfred Abraham Knopf

American publisher
• With wife Blanche founded Alfred A Knopf, Inc., 1915.
b. September 12, 1892 in New York, New York
d. August 11, 1984 in Purchase, New York

John Knowles

American author
• Wrote *A Separate Peace*, 1960.
b. September 16, 1926 in Fairmont, West Virginia

E(dmund) G(eorge) V(alpy) Knox

(Evoe pseud)
British humorist
• Editor of *Punch* mag., 1932-71.
b. 1881
d. January 02, 1971 in London, England

Arthur Koestler

Hungarian author
• Most famous work: *Darkness at Noon*, 1940s anti-Stalinist novel.
b. September 05, 1905 in Budapest, Hungary
d. March 03, 1983 in London, England

Bernard Kops

English author–poet
• Works include *Awake for Mourning*, 1958; *The World Is a Wedding*, 1963.
b. November 28, 1926 in London, England

Michael Korda

American publisher
• Wrote *Charmed Lives*, 1979, focusing on the life of Uncle, Alexander.
b. 1919
d. December 24, 1973

Michael Vincent Korda

American editor
• Editor-in-chief, Simon & Schuster, 1958–; wrote *Worldly Goods*, 1982.
b. October 08, 1933 in London, England

Yuri Korinetz

Russian author
• Best-known work: *There, Far Beyond the River*, 1968; translated into 10 languages.
b. January 14, 1923 in Moscow, U.S.S.R.

Jerzy Nikodem Kosinski

(Joseph Novak pseud)
American author–essayist
• Wrote *Being There*, 1971; *The Painted Bird*, a story based on his nightmarish childhood in Nazi-occupied Eastern Europe. Committed suicide.
b. June 14, 1933 in Lodz, Poland
d. May 3, 1991 in New York, New York

Mikhail A(leksandrovich) Kovalev

(Riurik Ivnev pseud)
Russian author
• Writings *Love Without Love, The Open House* were banned from USSR, 1930s.
b. February 11, 1893 in Tbilisi, Russia
d. March 28, 1981 in Moscow, U.S.S.R.

Joseph Kraft

American journalist–author
• Internationally syndicated political columnist known for non-ideological approach to world affairs.
b. September 04, 1924 in South Orange, New Jersey
d. January 1, 1986 in Washington, District of Columbia

Judith Krantz

(Judith Tarcher)
American author
• Wrote *Scruples*, 1978; *Princess Daisy*, 1980; *Mistral's Daughter*, 1982.
b. January 09, 1928 in New York, New York

Paul Krassner

American journalist
• Former writer for *Mad* mag.; co-founded Youth International Party (Yippies), 1968; currently stand-up comic.
b. April 09, 1932 in Brooklyn, New York

Jiddu Krishnamurti

(Alcyone pseud)
Indian author–philosopher
• Advocate of self-knowledge; wrote books on subject: *The Future of Humanity*, 1986.
b. May 22, 1895 in Madanapelle, India
d. February 17, 1986 in Ojai, California

Arthur Krock

American journalist
• Editorial commentator, *NY Times*, 1953-67; won four Pulitzers; wrote several books: *The Consent of the Governed and Other Deceits*, 1971.
b. November 16, 1886 in Glasgow, Kentucky
d. April 12, 1974 in Washington, District of Columbia

Louis Kronenberger

American author–critic
• Drama critic, *Time*, 1938-61; theater arts professor, Brandeis U, 1953-70; author of many novels: *The Grand Manner*, 1929.
b. December 09, 1904 in Cincinnati, Ohio
d. April 3, 1980 in Wellesley, Massachusetts

Joseph (Quincy) Krumgold

American author
• Won Newberys for *And Now Miguel*, 1953; *Onion John*, 1960.
b. April 09, 1908 in Jersey City, New Jersey
d. July 1, 1980 in Hope, New Jersey

Ivan Andreyevich Krylov

Russian author
• His fables, published in collections beginning 1809, are classics in Russian literature.
b. February 14, 1768 in Moscow, Russia
d. November 21, 1844 in Saint Petersburg, Russia

Elisabeth Kubler-Ross

American psychiatrist–author
• Pioneered the advancement of thanotology, the study of death; wrote best-seller *On Death and Dying*, 1969.
b. July 08, 1926 in Zurich, Switzerland

Maxine Winokur Kumin

American author
• Best known for pastoral poetry; won Pulitzer, 1973, for *Up Country*.
b. June 06, 1925 in Philadelphia, Pennsylvania

Milan Kundera

Czech author
• Exile lived in France; could not be read, published in own country; wrote *The Book of Laughter and Forgetting*, 1980; novel *The Unbearable Lightness of Being* made into film, 1988.
b. April 01, 1929 in Brno, Czechoslovakia

Stanley Jasspon Kunitz

(Dilly Tante pseud)
American poet
• Won Pulitzer for *Selected Poems*, 1958; co-edited literary reference textbook.
b. July 29, 1905 in Worcester, Massachusetts

Aleksandr Ivanovich Kuprin

Russian author
• Traditionalist short story writer: *The River of Life*, 1916; *Sasha*, 1920.
b. September 07, 1870 in Narovchat, Russia
d. October 25, 1938 in Leningrad, U.S.S.R.

Harold Samuel Kushner

American religious leader–author
• Wrote *When Bad Things Happen to Good People*, 1981, after death of young son.
b. April 03, 1935 in Brooklyn, New York

Anatoli Vasilievich Kuznetsov

(A Anatoli)
English author
• Best known for *Babi Yar*, description of Nazi attacks on Russian Jews, 1966; defected to Britain, 1969, denouncing Soviet censorship.
b. August 18, 1929 in Kiev, U.S.S.R.
d. June 13, 1979 in London, England

Arthur Joseph LaBern
English author
• Wrote detective fiction, popular in England: *Goodbye Piccadilly, Farewell Leicester Square*, 1967; *It Always Rains on Sunday*, 1945.
b. February 28, 1909 in London, England

Jean de LaBruyere
French philosopher–author
• Wrote social satire on characters of Theophraste, 1688; later editions greatly enlarged.
b. August 16, 1645 in Paris, France
d. May 1, 1696 in Versailles, France

Robert Lacey
English author
• Wrote *Majesty: Elizabeth II and the House of Windsor*, 1977; *Ford: The Men and the Machine*, 1986.
b. January 03, 1944 in Guildford, England

(Pierre) Choderlos de Laclos
French author–army officer
• Wrote novel *Les Liaisons Dangereuses*, 1782, revealing immorality of his time.
b. October 19, 1741 in Paris, France
d. November 05, 1803 in Taranto, Italy

William Mackay Laffan
American newspaper publisher
• Started *NY Evening Sun*, 1887.
b. January 22, 1848 in Dublin, Ireland
d. November 19, 1909

Raphael Aloysius Lafferty
American author
• Science fiction works include 1973 short story Hugo winner *Eurema's Dam*.
b. November 07, 1914 in Neola, Iowa

Jean de LaFontaine
French author
• Noted for *Fables*, published in 12 books, 1668-94.
b. July 08, 1621 in Aisne, France
d. April 13, 1695 in Paris, France

Par Lagerkvist
Swedish dramatist–author–poet
• Wrote novels *Barabbas*, 1950; *The Dwarf*, 1945; won Nobel Prize, 1951.
b. May 23, 1891 in Vaxjo, Sweden
d. July 11, 1974 in Stockholm, Sweden

Selma Ottiliana Lovisa Lagerlof
Swedish author
• Wrote *Gosta Berling* saga, 1891; *Wonderful Adventures of Nils*, 1907; first woman to win Nobel Prize for literature, 1909.
b. November 2, 1858 in Marbacka, Sweden
d. March 16, 1940 in Marbacka, Sweden

John Lahr
American author–critic
• Award-winning drama critic; wrote *Automatic Vaudeville*, 1984; son of actor Bert.
b. July 12, 1941 in Los Angeles, California

Deirdre Susan Laiken
American author
• Won 1987 Edgar for her first mystery novel, *Death Among Strangers*; editor, *Scholastic Magazine*, 1974–.
b. January 21, 1948 in New York, New York

R(onald) D(avid) Laing
Scottish psychiatrist–author
• Guru of 1960s counter-culture; controversial views of schizophrenia discussed in book *The Divided Self*, 1960.
b. October 07, 1927 in Glasgow, Scotland
d. August 23, 1989 in Saint Tropez, France

Philip Lamantia
American author
• Volumes of surrealist verse include *Erotic Poems*, 1946; *Becoming Visible*, 1981.
b. October 23, 1927 in San Francisco, California

Alphonse Marie Louis de Prat de Lamartine
French poet–historian
• Noted for popular *Meditations poetiques*, 1820, which strongly influenced Romantic movement.
b. October 21, 1790 in Macon, France
d. March 01, 1869 in Paris, France

Mary Ann Lamb
English children's author
• Killed mother in fit of insanity, 1796; sister of Charles.
b. 1764 in London, England
d. May 2, 1847 in London, England

Eleanor Lambert
(Mrs Seymour Berkson)
American journalist
• Fashion publicist who started Best Dressed polls, 1940.
b. in Crawfordsville, Indiana

Richmal Crompton Lamburn
(Richmal Crompton pseud)
English author
• Writings include "Just William" children's series, 1920s-60s; novel *Dread Dwellings*, 1926.
b. November 15, 1890 in Bury, England
d. January 1, 1969

Louis Dearborn L'Amour
(Tex Burns pseud)
American author
• Popular writer of Western novels; wrote 101 books including *Hondo*, 1953, his first and best-selling novel.
b. March 22, 1908 in Jamestown, North Dakota
d. June 1, 1988 in Los Angeles, California

Evelyn Sibley Lampman
(Lynn Bronson pseud)
American children's author
• Wrote award-winning *Treasure Mountain*, 1949; *Cayuse Courage*, 1970.
b. April 18, 1907 in Dallas, Oregon
d. June 13, 1980 in Portland, Oregon

Ann Landers
(Esther Pauline Friedman Lederer; "Eppie")
American journalist
• Twin sister of Dear Abby; column syndicated in over 1,000 newspapers.
b. July 04, 1918 in Sioux City, Iowa

Sir Allen Lane
English publisher
• Founded Penguin Books, 1935; first British paperback publisher.
b. September 21, 1902 in Bristol, England
d. July 07, 1970

Rose Wilder Lane
American author
• Daughter of Laura Ingalls Wilder, who was agent, editor, collaborator with mother on *Little House* books.
b. December 05, 1887 in De Smet, South Dakota
d. October 3, 1968 in Danbury, Connecticut

Andrew Lang
(A Huge Longway; "A Well-Known Author")
Scottish author–poet
• Prolific writer of historical mysteries, folklore, mythology, fairy tales.
b. March 31, 1844 in Selkirk, Scotland
d. July 2, 1912 in Banchor, Scotland

William Langland
English author
• Credited with writing *Piers Plowman*, greatest pre-Chaucerian poem.
b. 1332 in Shropshire, England
d. 1400 in London, England

Ring(gold Wilmer) Lardner, Sr
American author–journalist
• Noted for satirical sketches, use of vernacular: *Treat 'Em Rough*, 1918.
b. March 03, 1885 in Niles, Michigan
d. September 25, 1933 in East Hampton, New York

Philip Larkin
English author–librarian–poet
• Writings include *Jill*, 1940; *High Windows*, 1974.
b. August 09, 1922 in Coventry, England
d. December 02, 1985 in Hull, England

Duc de Francois LaRochefoucauld
French author
• Wrote *Maxims*, 1665-85; biting observations on human conduct, desires.
b. September 15, 1613 in Paris, France
d. March 16, 1680 in Paris, France

Roy Edward Larsen
American publisher
• Pres., Time Inc., 1939-60, succeeding Henry Luce; published *Life* magazine, 1936-46.
b. April 2, 1899 in Boston, Massachusetts
d. September 09, 1979 in Fairfield, Connecticut

Joseph P Lash
American author
• Won 1971 Pulitzer for biography of the Roosevelts: *Eleanor and Franklin*.
b. December 02, 1909 in New York, New York
d. August 22, 1987 in Boston, Massachusetts

Jean Lee Latham
(Rose Champion joint pseud; Janice Gard; Julian Lee)
American children's author
• Numerous children's books include 1955 Newbery winner: *Carry On, Mr. Bowditch*.
b. April 19, 1902 in Buckhannon, West Virginia

Patrice de La Tour du Pin
French poet
• Wrote *Quest of Joy*, 1933; *Sum of Poetry*, 1946.
b. March 16, 1911 in Paris, France
d. October 28, 1975 in Paris, France

Margaret Jean Laurence
Canadian author
• Award-winning novelist, short story writer; *A Jest of God*, 1967, filmed as *Rachel, Rachel*.
b. July 18, 1926 in Neepawa, Manitoba
d. January 05, 1987 in Lakefield, Ontario

David Lawrence
American journalist
• Founder, editor, weekly *US News and World Report*, 1947.
b. December 25, 1888 in Philadelphia, Pennsylvania
d. February 11, 1973

D(avid) H(erbert) Lawrence
English author
• Wrote *Lady Chatterley's Lover*, 1928; banned in US, England many years.
b. September 11, 1885 in Eastwood, England
d. March 02, 1930 in Vence, France

Josephine Lawrence
American author
• Wrote popular fiction including *Under One Roof*, 1975.
b. 1897 in Newark, New Jersey
d. February 22, 1978 in New York, New York

Mildred Elwood Lawrence
American author
• Books for young girls include *Gateway to the Sun*, 1970; *Walk to a Rocky Road*, 1971.
b. November 1, 1907 in Charleston, Illinois

T(homas) E(dward) Lawrence
(Thomas Edward Shaw; "Lawrence of Arabia")
English author–soldier
• Spied against Turks in Arabia during WW I; wrote *The Seven Pillars of Wisdom*, 1926.
b. August 15, 1888 in Portmadoc, Wales
d. May 19, 1935 in England

Helen Brown Lawrenson
(Helen Brown Norder pseud)
American editor–author
• First woman to contribute to *Esquire* 1936, with article "Latins are Lousy Lovers."
b. October 01, 1907 in La Fargeville, New York
d. April 05, 1982 in New York, New York

Victor Fremont Lawson
American editor–publisher
• Owner, *Chicago Daily News; Chicago Record-Herald*; pres., Associated Press, 1894-1900; developed foreign news service.
b. September 09, 1850 in Chicago, Illinois
d. August 19, 1925

Halldor Kiljan Laxness
(Halldor Kiljan Gudjonsson)
Icelandic author–dramatist
• Leading modern Icelandic writer; won 1955 Noble Prize for Icelandic narratives.
b. April 23, 1902 in Reykjavik, Iceland

Camara Laye
African author
• Leading writer of French-speaking Africa: *Dark Child*, 1953.
b. January 01, 1928 in Kouroussa, French Guiana
d. February 04, 1980 in Dakar, Senegal

Emma Lazarus
American poet
• Wrote poem, "The New Colossus" that appears on Statue of Liberty.
b. July 22, 1849 in New York, New York
d. November 19, 1887 in New York, New York

Homer Lea
American author–soldier
• Sun Yat-sen's adviser; books predicted Japanese attack on Hawaii: *Valor of Ignorance*, 1909.
b. November 17, 1876 in Denver, Colorado
d. November 01, 1912 in Los Angeles, California

William Least Heat Moon, pseud
(William Lewis Trogdon)
American author
• Had critical, commercial success with first book *Blue Highways*, travel memoir, 1983.
b. August 27, 1939 in Kansas City, Missouri

F(rank) R(aymond) Leavis
English critic–author
• One of the Cambridge Critics, edited *Scrutiny*, 1932-53; wrote *Revolution*, 1936.
b. July 14, 1895 in Cambridge, England
d. April 14, 1978 in Cambridge, England

John LeCarre, pseud
(David John Moore Cornwell)
English author
• Introduced George Smiley, antithesis of James Bond, in *Call from the Dead*, 1962; also wrote *Little Drummer Girl*, 1983; *Perfect Spy*, 1986.
b. October 19, 1931 in Poole, England

William Julius Lederer
American author
• Wrote *Ensign O'Toole and Me*, 1957; *The Ugly American*, 1958.
b. March 31, 1912 in New York, New York

Harper (Nelle Harper) Lee
American author
• Won Pulitzer, 1961, for *To Kill a Mockingbird*; made into film, 1962.
b. April 28, 1926 in Monroeville, Alabama

Manfred B(ennington) Lee
(Manford Lepofsky; Ellery Queen pseud)
American author
• With cousin Frederic Dannay wrote *Ellery Queen* mysteries, beginning 1929.
b. January 11, 1905 in Brooklyn, New York
d. April 03, 1971 in Roxbury, Connecticut

Eugene Jacob Lee-Hamilton
English poet–translator
• Wrote over 200 sonnets: *Sonnets of the Wingless Hours*, 1894.
b. January 06, 1845 in London, England
d. September 07, 1907 in Bogni di Lucca, Italy

Margaret Kernochan Leech
(Mrs Ralph Pulitzer)
American author–historian
• Won Pulitzers for histories: *Reveille in Washington*, 1941; *In the Days of McKinley*, 1959.
b. November 07, 1893 in Newburgh, New York
d. February 24, 1974 in New York, New York

Sybil Leek
(Sybil Falk)
English astrologer–author
• Predicted assassinations of Kennedys, election of Nixon to presidency; wrote *Diary of a Witch*, 1968.
b. February 22, 1917 in Stoke-on-Trent, England
d. October 26, 1982 in Melbourne, Florida

Joseph Sheridan LeFanu
Irish author
• Eerie tales of supernatural include *House By the Churchyard*, 1863.
b. August 28, 1814 in Dublin, Ireland
d. February 07, 1873 in Dublin, Ireland

Richard LeGallienne
English poet–essayist
• Influenced by Oscar Wilde; best known work *From a Paris Garret*, 1936.
b. January 2, 1866 in Liverpool, England
d. September 14, 1947 in Menton, France

Alexis St Leger (Marie-Rene Alexis St Leger) Leger
(St John Perse)
French poet
• Verse collections include *Oiseaux*, 1962; won 1960 Nobel Prize.
b. May 31, 1887 in Guadeloupe, French West Indies
d. September 2, 1975 in Giens, France

Ursula Kroeber LeGuin
American author
• Writes science fiction, fantasy: *Left Hand of Darkness*, 1969; *Malafrena*, 1979.
b. October 21, 1929 in Berkeley, California

Rosamond Nina Lehmann
English author
• Novels include *The Ballad and the Source*, 1945; *The Sea-Grape Tree*, 1976; sister of John Frederick.
b. February 03, 1901 in London, England
d. March 12, 1990 in London, England

Fritz Leiber
(Francis Lathrop pseud)
American author
• Popular horror, science-fiction writer, noted for "Fafhrd and Gray Mouser" series; won numerous Hugo, Nebula awards.
b. December 25, 1910 in Chicago, Illinois

Mark Lemon
English journalist
• Co-founder, *Punch* mag.; editor, 1841-70.
b. November 3, 1809 in London, England
d. May 23, 1870 in Cranley, England

Madeleine L'Engle
(Madeleine L'Engle Camp; Madeleine Franklin)
American author
• Won 1963 Newbery for *A Wrinkle in Time*.
b. November 28, 1918 in New York, New York

Lois Lenski
American children's author–illustrator
• Numerous books include 1946 Newbery prize-winner: *Strawberry Girl*.
b. October 14, 1893 in Springfield, Ohio
d. September 11, 1974 in Tarpon Springs, Florida

Henry Cecil Leon
English author
• Prolific writer of crime novels, plays, including *Cross Purposes*, 1976.
b. September 19, 1902 in Middlesex, England
d. May 23, 1976

Elmore John Leonard, Jr
American author
• Prolific western, crime fiction writer: *City Primeval*, 1980; *La Brava*, 1983; *Glitz*, 1985.
b. October 11, 1925 in New Orleans, Louisiana

John Leonard
American author
• *NY Times* book review editor, 1971-76; wrote *Black Conceit*, 1973.
b. February 25, 1939 in Washington, District of Columbia

Max Lerner
American author–journalist
• Worldwide *NY Post* syndicated columnist, 1949–; books include *Ted and the Kennedy Legion*, 1980.
b. December 2, 1902 in Minsk, Russia

Gaston LeRoux
French author
• Popular mystery tales, featuring detective Rouletabille include *Le Mystere de la chambre jaunne*, 1908.
b. May 06, 1868 in Paris, France
d. April 15, 1927 in Nice, France

Doris May Lessing
English author
• Prize-winning works include five-volume *Children of Violence*, 1951-69; *African Stories*, 1964.
b. October 22, 1919 in Kermanshah, Persia

Sam(uel) Levenson
American author
• Hosted "Sam Levenson Show," 1959-64; wrote best-seller *Sex and the Single Child*, 1969.
b. December 28, 1911 in New York, New York
d. August 27, 1980 in Neponsit, New York

Albert Rice Leventhal
(Albert Rice pseud)
American publisher
• Forty yrs. in publishing; developed Little Golden Books.
b. October 3, 1907 in New York, New York
d. January 04, 1976 in New York, New York

Denise Levertov
American poet
• Works include verse volume *Jacob's Ladder*, 1961; essays *Poet in the World*, 1973.
b. October 24, 1923 in Ilford, England

Primo Levi
Italian writer–chemist
• Wrote Italian classic *Survival in Auschwitz*, 1961.
b. July 31, 1919 in Turin, Italy
d. April 11, 1987 in Turin, Italy

Bernard Levin
British critic–journalist
• Award-winning newspaper, mag., TV writer since 1953; books include *Enthusiasms*, 1983.
b. August 19, 1928

Ira Levin
American author
• Wrote thrillers *Rosemary's Baby*, 1967; *Stepford Wives*, 1972; won Poe for *A Kiss Before Dying*, 1954.
b. August 27, 1929 in Bronx, New York

Philip Levine
(Edgar Poe pseud)
American author–poet
• Verse vols. include *Ashes*, 1979; *One For the Rose*, 1981.
b. January 1, 1928 in Detroit, Michigan

Richard Leighton Levinson
American writer
• Noted for creating, writing TV mystery shows including "Colombo," 1971-76; won two Emmys, one Peabody, four Edgars.
b. August 07, 1934 in Philadelphia, Pennsylvania
d. March 12, 1987 in Los Angeles, California

Sonia Levitin
American children's author
• Wrote award-winning *Journey to America*, 1971.
b. August 18, 1934 in Berlin, Germany

Anthony Lewis
American journalist
• Won Pulitzer for nat. reporting, 1955, 1963; wrote award-winning crime book: *Gideon's Trumpet*, 1965.
b. March 27, 1927 in New York, New York

Boyd de Wolf Lewis
American editor–author
• Exec. editor, Newspaper Enterprise Assoc., 1945–; published *The World Almanac*, 1966-72.
b. August 18, 1905 in Boston, Massachusetts

C(live) S(taples) Lewis
(N W Clerk; Clive Hamilton pseuds)
English author–scholar
• Wrote literary studies, science fiction, children's fantasies, Christian apologetics including *Screwtape Letters*, 1942.
b. November 29, 1898 in Belfast, Northern Ireland
d. November 22, 1963 in Heddington, England

Elizabeth Foreman Lewis
American children's author
• Won 1983 Newbery for *Young Fu of the Upper Yangtze*.
b. May 24, 1892 in Baltimore, Maryland
d. August 07, 1958 in Arnold, Maryland

Janet Lewis
(Janet Lewis Winters)
American author–poet
• Novels include *The Invasion*, 1932; wife of Yvor Winters.
b. August 17, 1899 in Chicago, Illinois

Matthew Gregory Lewis
English author
• Wrote sensational spine-chilling Gothic novel *The Monk*.
b. July 09, 1775 in London, England
d. May 14, 1818

Oscar Lewis
American anthropologist–author
• Wrote prize-winning accounts of Mexican, Puerto Rican poor: *La Vida*, 1966.
b. December 25, 1914 in New York, New York
d. December 16, 1970 in New York, New York

Sinclair Lewis
American author–dramatist
• First American to win Nobel Prize for literature, 1930; wrote *Babbitt*, 1922, *Arrowsmith*, 1925.
b. February 07, 1885 in Sauk Centre, Minnesota
d. January 1, 1951 in Rome, Italy

Li Po
(Li T'ai-Pai; Li T'ai Peh; Li T'ai-Po)
Chinese poet
• Considered among China's greatest poets; noted for exquisite imagery, passionate lyrics.
b. 701 in Szechwan, China
d. 762

Doris Lilly
American journalist–author
• Syndicated gossip columnist, 1977–; wrote *Glamour Girl*, 1977.
b. December 26, 1926 in Pasadena, California

Victoria Endicott Lincoln
American author
• Popular novelist whose *A Private Disgrace*, 1967, concerns Lizzie Borden's trial.
b. October 23, 1904 in Fall River, Massachusetts
d. May 09, 1981 in Baltimore, Maryland

Anne Spencer Morrow Lindbergh
(Mrs Charles A Lindbergh)
American author–poet
• Wrote narrative *Listen! the Wind*, 1938; best-selling essays *Gift from the Sea*, 1955.
b. June 22, 1907 in Englewood, New Jersey

Astrid Lindgren
Swedish children's author
• Wrote *Pippi Longstocking* stories for children, 1950.
b. November 14, 1907 in Vimmerby, Sweden

David Lindsay
British author
• Wrote fantasy classic *A Voyage to Arcturus*, 1920.
b. March 03, 1878 in London, England
d. June 06, 1945 in Brighton, England

(Nicholas) Vachel Lindsay
American poet–author–lecturer
• Wrote verse *The Cargo*, 1914; *Johnny Appleseed*, 1928; committed suicide.
b. November 1, 1879 in Springfield, Illinois
d. December 05, 1931 in Springfield, Illinois

James A(lexander) Linen, III
American publisher
• Published *Time* magazine, 1945-60; pres. of Time Inc., 1960-69.
b. June 2, 1912 in Waverly, Pennsylvania
d. February 01, 1988 in Greenwich, Connecticut

Leo Lionni
Dutch designer–artist–children's author
• Popular self-illustrated juvenile books include Caldecott runner-up winner, *Inch by Inch*, 1961.
b. May 05, 1910 in Amsterdam, Netherlands

Joshua Ballinger Lippincott
American publisher
• Founded J B Lippincott & Co., 1836.
b. March 18, 1813 in Juliustown, New Jersey
d. January 05, 1886 in Philadelphia, Pennsylvania

Walter Lippmann
American editor–journalist–author
• Won Pulitzer, 1958, 1962, for syndicated column, "Today and Tomorrow."
b. September 23, 1889 in New York, New York
d. December 14, 1974 in New York, New York

Charles Coffin Little
American publisher
• Founded Little, Brown, and Co., 1847, with James Brown; published general and legal works.
b. July 25, 1799 in Kennebunk, Maine
d. August 09, 1869

(Flora) Jean Little
Children's Author
• Works include *Stand in the Wind*, 1975; *Listen For the Singing*, 1977.
b. January 02, 1932 in Taiwan

Freya Lota Littledale
American children's author
• Juvenile books include *The Elves and the Shoemaker*, 1975; *The Snow Child*, 1978.
b. in New York, New York

Emanuel Litvinoff
English author
• Works include *Blood on the Snow*, 1975; *The Face of Terror*, 1978.
b. June 3, 1915 in London, England

Livius Andronicus
Roman poet–dramatist–translator
• Founder of Roman epic poetry, drama; introduced Greek literature into Rome.
b. 284?BC in Tarentum, Italy
d. 204?BC

Arnold Stark Lobel
American children's author–illustrator
• Books include *Frog and Toad Together*; won Caldecott Medal, 1971.
b. May 22, 1923 in Los Angeles, California
d. December 06, 1987 in New York, New York

Alain Leroy Locke
American educator–author
• First black Rhodes scholar, 1907; numerous books include *Negro in America*, 1933.
b. September 13, 1886 in Philadelphia, Pennsylvania
d. June 09, 1954 in New York, New York

John Gibson Lockhart
Scottish biographer–editor
• Noted for classic seven-vol. biography of his father-in-law: *Life of Sir Walter Scott*, 1838.
b. July 14, 1794 in Lanarkshire, Scotland
d. November 25, 1854 in Abbotsford, Scotland

(Sir Robert Hamilton) Bruce Lockhart
Scottish author–diplomat–public official
• Works describing colorful career include *Memoirs of a British Agent*, 1932; knighted, 1943.
b. 1887 in Fifeshire, Scotland
d. February 27, 1970 in Brighton, England

Frances Louise Lockridge
American author
• Co-created, with husband Richard, popular sleuths, the Norths, who became subjects of film, radio, TV series.
b. 1896 in Kansas City, Missouri
d. February 17, 1963

Richard Lockridge
American author
• With wife, Francis Louise, wrote 27 humorous detective stories featuring the Norths.
b. September 26, 1898 in Saint Joseph, Missouri
d. June 19, 1982 in Tryon, North Carolina

William Loeb
American journalist–publisher
• Influential publisher, Manchester, NH *Union Leader* since 1946; noted for front page right-wing editorials.
b. December 26, 1905 in Manchester, New Hampshire
d. September 13, 1981 in Burlington, Massachusetts

Hugh Lofting
American children's author
• Wrote *Doctor Doolittle* series for children, 1920s-30s.
b. January 14, 1886 in Maidenhead, England
d. September 26, 1947

Norah Robinson Lofts
(Juliet Astley; Peter Curtis pseuds)
English author
• Wrote at least 50 historical romances, biographies including *Anne Boelyn*, 1979; *Day of the Butterfly*, 1979.
b. August 27, 1904 in Shipdham, England
d. September 1, 1983 in Bury St. Edmunds, England

John Logan
(John Burton Logan)
American poet–educator
• Verse volumes include *Zig-Zag Walk*, 1969; *Anonymous Lover*, 1972.
b. January 23, 1923 in Red Oak, Iowa
d. November 06, 1987 in San Francisco, California

Louis Lomax
American author–radio commentator–educator
• Wrote award-winning *The Reluctant Negro*, 1960.
b. August 06, 1922 in Valdosta, Georgia
d. July 1970 in Santa Rosa, New Mexico

Jack (John Griffith) London
American author
• Most books deal with brutal realism: *The Call of the Wild*, 1903.
b. January 12, 1876 in San Francisco, California
d. November 22, 1916 in Glen Ellen, California

Henry Wadsworth Longfellow
American poet–educator
• Among his many classic works: "Paul Revere's Ride," 1863; "The Song of Hiawatha," 1855; first American to have bust in Westminster Abbey.
b. February 27, 1807 in Portland, Maine
d. March 24, 1882 in Cambridge, Massachusetts

Longus
Greek author
• Supposedly wrote pastoral romance *Daphnis and Chloe.*
b. 3rd in Greece

Walter Lord
American author–historian
• Wrote authoritative books on *Titanic* sinking: *A Night to Remember*, 1955; *The Night Lives On*, 1986.
b. October 08, 1917 in Baltimore, Maryland

Pierre Loti, pseud
((Louis Marie) Julien Viaud)
French author–naval officer
• Noted for three novels of Breton peasant life including *An Iceland Fisherman*, 1886.
b. January 14, 1850 in Rochefort, France
d. June 1, 1923 in Hendaye, France

Pierre Louys, pseud
(Pierre Louis)
French poet–author
• Wrote verse volume *Astarte*, 1891; novel *Aphrodite*, 1896.
b. December 1, 1870 in Ghent, Belgium
d. June 04, 1925 in Paris, France

Elijah P Lovejoy
American journalist–abolitionist
• Newspaper editor whose presses were destroyed due to his anti-slavery editorials.
b. November 09, 1802 in Albion, Maine
d. November 07, 1837 in Alton, Illinois

Richard Lovelace
English poet–courtier
• Prototype of the dashing Cavalier; wrote verse volume *Lucasta*, 1649.
b. 1618 in Kent, England
d. 1658 in London, England

Peter Harmer Lovesey
(Peter Lear pseud)
English author
• Historical mystery writer, created Sergeant Cribb, Constable Thackeray; wrote *Wobble to Death*, 1970.
b. September 1, 1936 in Whitton, England

Amy Lowell
American poet–critic
• Dominating force in Imagist movement; most known poems "Patterns"; "Lilacs."
b. February 09, 1874 in Brookline, Massachusetts
d. February 09, 1925 in Brookline, Massachusetts

James Russell Lowell
American editor–diplomat
• First editor of *Atlantic Monthly*, 1857-61; ambassador to Spain, Great Britian, 1877-85.
b. February 22, 1819 in Cambridge, Massachusetts
d. August 12, 1891 in Cambridge, Massachusetts

Robert Trail Spence Lowell, Jr
American poet–dramatist
• Won Pulitzers for verse volumes *Lord Weary's Castle*, 1947; *The Dolphin*, 1974.
b. March 01, 1917 in Boston, Massachusetts
d. September 12, 1977 in New York, New York

Walter Lowenfels
American author–poet–editor
• Works include *To An Imaginary Daughter*, 1964; verse volume *American Voices*, 1959.
b. May 1, 1897 in New York, New York
d. July 07, 1976 in Tarrytown, New York

Marie Adelaide Belloc Lowndes
(Philip Curtin pseud)
English author
• Wrote *The Lodger*, 1913, novel about Jack the Ripper; later adapted into movie by Alfred Hitchcock.
b. 1868
d. November 11, 1947 in Eversley, England

Malcolm (Clarence Malcolm) Lowry
English author–poet
• Wrote *Under the Volcano*, 1947, autobiographical novel.
b. July 28, 1909 in Liverpool, England
d. June 1957 in Ripe, England

Yu Lu
Chinese poet
• Wrote nature, patriotic verse; extremely prolific; 9,000 of his 20,000 poems are extant.
b. 1125 in Shan-Yin, China
d. 1210

Lucan
(Marcus Annaeus Lucanus)
Roman poet–author
• Wrote epic *Pharsalia;* conspired against Nero.
b. June 03, 39 in Cordova, Spain
d. June 3, 65 in Rome, Italy

Clare Boothe Luce
(Mrs Henry Luce)
American author–politician–diplomat
• One of most influential women in 20th c.; congresswoman, 1943-47; ambassador to Italy, 1953-57; author of hit play *The Women*, 1936.
b. March 1, 1903 in New York, New York
d. October 09, 1987 in Washington, District of Columbia

Lucian
Greek author
• Wrote *Dialogues of the Gods; Dialogues of the Dead.*
b. 125 in Samosato, Syria
d. 200 in Egypt

Lucilius
Roman poet
• Considered founder of Latin satire; only fragments of work survive.
b. 180 in Campania, Italy
d. 102

Lucretius
Roman poet–philosopher
• Wrote six-books, unfinished didactic poem *De rerum natura* based on Epicurean doctrine.
b. 99BC
d. 55BC

Robert Ludlum
American author–actor–producer
• Wrote thrillers *The Gemini Contenders*, 1976; *The Aquitaine Progression*, 1983.
b. May 25, 1927 in New York, New York

Otto Ludwig
German author
• Early realist; wrote tragedy, *Der Erbforster*, 1850; coined term "poetic realism."
b. February 11, 1813 in Eisfield, Germany
d. February 25, 1865 in Dresden, Germany

Mabel Dodge Luhan
American author
• Wrote *Lorenzo in Taos*, 1932, which is an account of her relationship with D H Lawrence.
b. February 26, 1879 in Buffalo, New York
d. August 13, 1962

Alison Lurie
American author
• Won Pulitzer, 1984, for *Foreign Affairs*.
b. September 03, 1926 in Chicago, Illinois

Joseph Russell Lynes, Jr
American editor–author
• Managing editor *Harpers* mag., 1947-67; wrote *Snobs*, 1950; *The Tastemakers*, 1954.
b. December 02, 1910 in Barrington, Massachusetts

Eugene Lyons
American author–editor
• Moscow correspondent for UPI, one of first Americans to report from inside Soviet Union.
b. July 01, 1898 in Uslian, Russia
d. January 07, 1985 in New York, New York

Edward George Earle Lytton Bulwer-Lytton Lytton, 1st Baron Lytt
English author–poet
• Best remembered historical novels: *The Last Days of Pompeii*, 1834; *Rienzi*, 1835.
b. May 15, 1803 in London, England
d. January 18, 1873 in Torquay, England

Peter Maas
American author–editor
• Noted investigative reporter; wrote *Valachi Papers*, 1969; *Serpico*, 1973.
b. June 27, 1929 in New York, New York

George Mann MacBeth
Scottish poet
• Impressive verse collection *The Colour of Blood*, 1967, combines violence, elegance, wit.
b. January 19, 1932 in Shotts, Scotland

Hugh MacDiarmid, pseud
(Christopher Murray Grieve)
Scottish poet
• Verse volumes include *A Drunk Man Looks at the Thistle*, 1926.
b. August 11, 1892 in Langholm, Scotland
d. September 09, 1978 in Edinburgh, Scotland

Thomas MacDonagh
Irish poet–patriot
• Wrote *Of a Poet-Patriot;* executed after Easter Rebellion.
b. 1878 in Cloughjordan, Ireland
d. May 03, 1916 in Dublin, Ireland

John Dann MacDonald
American author
• Mystery writer known for Travis McGee detective stories; wrote suspense thriller *Condominium*, 1977.
b. July 24, 1916 in Sharon, Pennsylvania
d. December 28, 1986 in Milwaukee, Wisconsin

Antonio Machado
Spanish poet
• Sensitive to social problems of Spain, verse volumes, including *Campos de Castilla*, 1917, address morality, hope, despair.
b. July 26, 1875 in Seville, Spain
d. February 22, 1939 in Collioure, France

Helen MacInnes
American author
• Writer of spy fiction: *Above Suspicion*, 1941; *Ride a Pale Horse*, 1985.
b. October 07, 1907 in Glasgow, Scotland
d. September 3, 1985 in New York, New York

William MacKellar
American children's author
• Juvenile adventures include *Secret of the Sacred Stone*, 1970.
b. February 2, 1914 in Glasgow, Scotland

Compton (Sir Edward Montague) Mackenzie
English author
• Wrote *Whiskey Galore*, 1947; made into successful film *Tight Little Island*.
b. January 17, 1883 in West Hartlepool, England
d. November 3, 1972 in Edinburgh, Scotland

Henry Mackenzie
Scottish author
- Wrote popular *Man of Feeling*, 1771; *Man of the World*, 1773.
b. August 26, 1745 in Edinburgh, Scotland
d. January 14, 1831 in Edinburgh, Scotland

Alistair (Stuart) MacLean
Scottish author
- Wrote blood and thunder war stories that sold millions of copies: *The Guns of Navarone*, 1957.
b. 1922 in Glasgow, Scotland
d. February 02, 1987 in Munich, Germany (West)

Archibald MacLeish
American poet–journalist
- Won Pulitzers for *Conquistador*, 1932; *Collected Poems*, 1953; verse drama: *J.B.*, 1958.
b. May 07, 1892 in Glencoe, Illinois
d. April 2, 1982 in Boston, Massachusetts

Hugh (John Hugh) MacLennan
Canadian author
- Wrote nonfiction and novels, including *Two Solitudes*, 1945, whose title became a byword symbolizing tensions between French and English Canadians.
b. March 2, 1907 in Glace Bay, Nova Scotia
d. November 07, 1990 in Montreal, Quebec

Daniel MacMillan
Scottish publisher
- Established MacMillan and Co., publishers, 1843.
b. September 13, 1813 in Upper Corrie, Scotland
d. June 27, 1857 in Cambridge, England

James Macpherson
Scottish author–historian
- Noted literary forger; published *Fingal*, 1762; *Temora*, 1763, supposedly translations from Gaelic of ancient poet, Ossian.
b. October 27, 1736 in Ruthven, Scotland
d. February 17, 1796 in Ruthven, Scotland

Giulio Maestro
American children's author–illustrator
- Prize-winning illustrator of picture books, children's readers; wrote *Who's Said Meow?* 1975.
b. May 06, 1942 in New York, New York

Naguib Mahfouz
(Nagib Mahfuz)
Egyptian author
- Won Nobel Prize in literature, 1988; first Egyptian, Arab-language writer so honored.
b. December 11, 1911 in Cairo, Egypt

Norman (Kingsley) Mailer
American author
- Pearl Harbor attack inspired novel, *The Naked and the Dead*, 1948; won 1980 Pulitzer for *The Executioner's Song*.
b. January 31, 1923 in Long Branch, New Jersey

Clarence Major
American author
- Writings focus on scenes of violence, black issues; best-known novels include *No*, 1973; *Emergency Exit*, 1979.
b. December 31, 1936 in Atlanta, Georgia

Bernard Malamud
American author
- Wrote *The Natural*, 1952; adapted to film, 1984; won Pulitzer for *The Fixer*, 1967.
b. April 26, 1914 in New York, New York
d. March 18, 1986 in New York, New York

Curzio Malaparte
Italian author
- Wrote popular WW II novels *Kaputt*, 1945; *La Pelle*, 1949.
b. June 09, 1898 in Prado, Italy
d. July 19, 1957 in Rome, Italy

William Hurrell Mallock
English author
- Wrote satire on English life: *The New Republic*, 1877.
b. 1849 in Devonshire, England
d. April 05, 1923

Sir Max Edgar Lucien Mallowan
English archaeologist–author
- Wrote *Nimrud and Its Remains*, 1966, describing work, findings; married to Agatha Christie.
b. May 06, 1904 in London, England
d. August 19, 1978 in London, England

Dumas Malone
American author
- Won Pulitzer for multivolume biography of Thomas Jefferson, 1975.
b. January 1, 1892 in Coldwater, Mississippi
d. December 27, 1986 in Charlottesville, Virginia

Sir Thomas Malory
English author
- Wrote *Morte d'Arthur*, source for later versions of King Arthur legend.

Andre Malraux
French author–government official
- DeGaulle's minister of cultural affairs, 1958-69; wrote prize-winning novel *Man's Fate*, 1934; *Voices of Silence*, 1953.
b. November 03, 1901 in Paris, France
d. November 23, 1976 in Paris, France

William Raymond Manchester
American author
- Best known for historical books: *American Caesar: Douglas MacArthur*, 1978; *The Death of a President*, 1967.
b. April 04, 1922 in Attleboro, Massachusetts

Osip Emilyevich Mandelshtam
Russian poet
- Leader of Acheist school, known for impersonal, fatalistic poetry; died in concentration camp.
b. January 15, 1891 in Warsaw, Poland
d. December 28, 1943 in Vladivostok, U.S.S.R.

Frederick Feikema Manfred
(Feike Feikema pseud)
American author
- His novels of native area, "Siouxland," include *The Golden Bowl*, 1944; *The Wind Blows Free*, 1980.
b. January 06, 1912 in Doon, Iowa

Frank Fabian Mankiewicz
American journalist
- Press secretary to Robt. Kennedy, 1968; directed McGovern presidential campaign, 1972; wrote *Perfectly Clear: Nixon From Whittier to Watergate*, 1973.
b. May 16, 1924 in New York, New York

Thomas Mann
German author
- Known for narrative psychological studies, explorations in mythology; won Nobel Prize, 1929, for *The Magic Mountain*.
b. June 06, 1875 in Lubeck, Germany
d. August 12, 1955 in Zurich, Switzerland

Katherine Mansfield
(Kathleen Mansfield Beauchamp; Mrs John Middleton Murry)
New Zealander author
- Considered one of founders of modern short story; collections included in *Prelude*, 1918.
b. October 14, 1888 in Wellington, New Zealand
d. January 09, 1923 in Fontainebleau, France

Marco Polo
Italian traveler–author
- Medieval account of Asian travels was chief source of knowledge of East.
b. 1254 in Venice, Italy
d. January 09, 1324 in Venice, Italy

Filippo Tommaso Marinetti
Italian poet
- Founded Futurism; advocate of Fascism.
b. December 22, 1876 in Alexandria, Egypt
d. December 02, 1944 in Bellagio, Italy

Edwin Markham

American poet
• Wrote popular poem "The Man with the Hoe," 1899, inspired by Millet's painting.
b. April 23, 1852 in Oregon City, Oregon
d. March 07, 1940 in Staten Island, New York

Christopher Marlowe

English dramatist–poet
• Established blank verse in drama; wrote *Dr. Faustus*, 1604.
b. February 06, 1564 in Canterbury, England
d. May 3, 1593 in Deptford, England

Derek Marlowe

English author
• Books include *A Dandy in Aspic*, 1966; *Nightshade*, 1975.
b. May 21, 1938 in London, England

Clement Marot

Poet
• Introduced the elegy, epigram, sonnet into France; wrote *Temple de Cupido*, 1515.
b. 1496 in Cahors, France
d. September 1, 1544 in Turin, Italy

John Phillips Marquand

American author
• Wrote 1937 Pulitzer winner *The Late George Apley*.
b. November 1, 1893 in Wilmington, Delaware
d. July 16, 1960 in Newburyport, Massachusetts

Albert Nelson Marquis

American publisher
• Founded *Who's Who in America*, 1899.
b. January 12, 1854 in Brown County, Ohio
d. December 21, 1943 in Evanston, Illinois

Frederick Marryat

English author
• Among his sea adventures for boys: *Jacob Faithful*, 1834; published unflattering account of American Manners, *Diary in America*, 1839.
b. July 1, 1792 in London, England
d. August 09, 1848 in Langham, England

Catherine Marshall

(Mrs Peter Marshall)
American author
• Inspirational books have sold more than 18 million copies: *A Man Called Peter*, 1951.
b. September 27, 1914 in Johnson City, Tennessee
d. March 18, 1983 in Boynton Beach, Florida

S(amuel) L(yman) A(twood) Marshall

American army officer–journalist
• Major military historian; wrote *Pork Chop Hill* about Korean War, 1956.
b. July 18, 1900 in Catskill, New York
d. December 17, 1977 in El Paso, Texas

Martial

Roman poet
• Noted for 11 books of witty epigrams describing Roman life, published, 86-98.
b. 43 in Bilbilis, Spain
d. 104 in Bilbilis, Spain

John Bartlow Martin

American journalist
• Speechwriter for Democratic presidential candidates, 1950s-70s; wrote 15 books.
b. August 04, 1915 in Hamilton, Ohio
d. January 03, 1987 in Highland Park, Illinois

Harry Edmund Martinson

Swedish poet
• Won 1974 Nobel Prize for poetry; best-known poem is "Aniara."
b. May 06, 1905 in Jamshog, Sweden
d. February 11, 1978 in Stockholm, Sweden

Andrew Marvell

English author–poet–politician
• Great metaphysical poet; verse includes "To His Coy Mistress."
b. March 31, 1621 in Winestead, England
d. August 18, 1678 in London, England

Anne Loewenstein Marx

American poet
• Poems include "Face Lifts for All Seasons," 1980; "45 Love Poems for 45 Years," 1982.
b. in Bleicherode, Germany

Tsunenori Masaoka

(Masaoka Shiki pseud)
Japanese poet
• Revived haiku, tanka poetic forms; considered best haiku poet of modern times.
b. October 14, 1867 in Matsuyama, Japan
d. September 19, 1902 in Tokyo, Japan

John Masefield

English poet–dramatist–author
• Poet laureate of England, 1930-67.
b. June 01, 1878 in Ledbury, England
d. May 12, 1967 in Berkshire, England

F(rancis) van Wyck Mason

(Geoffrey Coffin; Frank W Mason; Van Wyck Mason; Ward Weaver pseuds.)
American author
• Wrote 58 novels during 40-yr. career; many mysteries contained character Hugh North, an Army intelligence officer: *Secret Mission to Bangkok*, 1960.
b. November 11, 1901 in Boston, Massachusetts
d. August 28, 1978 in Southampton, Bermuda

John Masters

American author
• Wrote about the British in India: *Bhowani Junction*, 1954; *Nightrunners of Bengal*, 1951.
b. October 26, 1914 in Calcutta, India
d. May 06, 1983 in Albuquerque, New Mexico

Robin (Robert Cecil Romer) Maugham

English author
• Wrote *Conversations with Willie*, 1978; nephew of Somerset.
b. May 17, 1916 in London, England
d. March 13, 1981 in Brighton, England

William Somerset Maugham

English author
• Wrote novels *Of Human Bondage*, 1915, filmed, 1934; *The Razor's Edge*, 1944, filmed, 1947.
b. January 25, 1874 in Paris, France
d. December 16, 1965 in Nice, France

Guy de (Henri Rene Albert Guy de) Maupassant

French author
• Recognized master of the short story who wrote *Pierre et Jean*, 1888.
b. August 05, 1850 in Dieppe, France
d. July 06, 1893 in Paris, France

(Ian) Robert Maxwell

(Jan Ludwig Hoch)
English publisher
• One of the richest men in Great Britain; founder and chairman, Robert Maxwell & Co. Ltd and Maxwell Communications Co.
b. June 10, 1923 in Selo Slatina, Czechoslovakia

William Maxwell

American author
• Novels include *They Came Like Swallows*, 1937; *The Chateau*, 1961.
b. August 16, 1908 in Lincoln, Illinois

Robert Lewis May
American advertising executive–author
• Wrote story "Rudolph the Red-Nosed Reindeer," 1939, to promote Montgomery Ward.
b. 1905
d. August 11, 1976 in Evanston, Illinois

Vladimir Mayakovsky
Russian poet–dramatist
• Futurist writer who wrote *The Cloud in Pants*, 1915; *The Bedbug*, 1929; committed suicide.
b. July 19, 1893 in Bagdadi, Russia
d. August 14, 1930 in Moscow, U.S.S.R.

Martin Prager Mayer
American author–music critic
• Works include *Fate of the Dollar*, 1980; *Money Bazaars*, 1984.
b. January 14, 1928 in New York, New York

Robert Clyve Maynard
American newspaper editor
• First black to own controlling interest in city daily newspaper when he bought Oakland, CA *Tribune*, 1983.
b. June 17, 1937 in Brooklyn, New York

Katherine Mayo
American author
• Wrote popular *Mother India*, 1927.
b. January 24, 1867 in Ridgeway, Pennsylvania
d. October 09, 1940 in Bedford, Pennsylvania

Judy Mazel
American author
• Wrote hugely successful *The Beverly Hills Diet*, 1981; opened weight-loss clinic catering to celebrities, 1979.
b. 1944 in Chicago, Illinois

Mary Therese McCarthy
American author–critic
• One of America's pre-eminent literary figures, 1930s-1970s; wrote autobiographical novels *Memories of a Catholic Girlhood*, 1957, *The Group*, 1963.
b. June 21, 1912 in Seattle, Washington
d. October 25, 1989 in New York, New York

Robert McCloskey
American children's author–illustrator
• Won 1942, 1948 Caldecott Medals for *Make Way for Ducklings; Time of Wonder*.
b. September 15, 1914 in Hamilton, Ohio

Anne (Elizabeth) O'Hare McCormick
American journalist
• With *NY Times*, 1922-54; best known as foreign correspondent; first woman to receive Pulitzer for journalism, 1937.
b. May 16, 1881 in Wakefield, England
d. May 29, 1954 in New York, New York

Johnston McCulley
(Raley Brien; George Drayne; Rowena Raley; Harrington Strong pseuds.)
American author
• Wrote *Zorro* adventure novels, 1924-58.
b. February 02, 1883 in Ottawa, Illinois
d. November 23, 1958 in Glendale, Ohio

Colleen McCullough
Australian author
• Wrote *The Thorn Birds*, 1977.
b. June 01, 1937 in Wellington, Australia

George Barr McCutcheon
American author–editor
• Popular novels include *Graustark*, 1901; *Brewster's Millions*, 1902; brother of John Tinney McCutcheon.
b. July 26, 1866 in South Raub, Indiana
d. October 23, 1928 in New York, New York

Thomas D'Arcy McGee
Canadian publisher–public official
• Founded newspapers *The Nation* (NYC), *The New Era* (Montreal); helped establish Dominion of Canada, served in Parliament, assassinated.
b. April 13, 1825 in Carlingford, Ireland
d. April 07, 1868 in Ottawa, Ontario

Ralph Emerson McGill
American journalist
• Editor, *Atlanta Constitution*, 1942-60, known for pro-civil rights editorials; won Pulitzer, 1959, Presidential Medal of Freedom, 1964.
b. February 05, 1898 in Soddy, Tennessee
d. February 03, 1969 in Atlanta, Georgia

Phyllis McGinley
American poet–author
• Light verse volumes include 1960 Pulitzer winner *Times Three*.
b. March 21, 1905 in Ontario, Oregon
d. February 22, 1978 in New York, New York

Joe McGinniss
American author
• Wrote *The Selling of the President 1968;* described mass market techniques of presidential campaign.
b. December 09, 1942 in New York, New York

William Peter McGivern
American author
• Wrote 23 mystery novels: *The Big Heat*, 1952; *Night of the Juggler*, 1974.
b. December 06, 1922 in Chicago, Illinois
d. November 18, 1982 in Palm Desert, California

Thomas Francis McGuane
American author–screenwriter
• Best known for novels *Ninety-Two in the Shade*, 1973; *Nobody's Angel*, 1982.
b. December 11, 1939 in Wyandotte, Michigan

William Holmes McGuffey
American educator–author
• Famous for six school books, *Eclectic Readers*, 1836-57, that had great influence on 19th-c. youth; over 122 million sold.
b. September 23, 1800 in Washington, Pennsylvania
d. May 04, 1873 in Charlottesville, Virginia

Claude McKay
American author
• Wrote *Home to Harlem*, 1928, first best-seller written by a black.
b. September 15, 1889 in Jamaica, British West Indies
d. May 22, 1948 in Chicago, Illinois

Rod Marvin McKuen
American poet–singer
• Wrote pop song, "Jean" for film *The Prime of Miss Jean Brodie*, 1969.
b. April 23, 1933 in San Francisco, California

Larry Jeff McMurtry
American author
• Writings portray Texas, the West; 1986 Pulitzer winner, *Lonesome Dove*, was filmed as TV miniseries, 1989.
b. June 03, 1936 in Wichita Falls, Texas

Andrew McNally, III
American publisher
• Rand-McNally, pres., 1948-74, chm., 1974–.
b. August 17, 1909 in Chicago, Illinois

Herman Cyril McNeile
(Sapper pseud)
English author
• Created detective hero *Bull-Dog Drummond*, 1920.
b. September 28, 1888 in Bodmin, England
d. August 14, 1937 in Pulborough, England

John Angus McPhee
American author
• Staff writer, *New Yorker*, 1965–; wrote best-seller: *Coming into the Country*, 1977.
b. March 08, 1931 in Princeton, New Jersey

A(lan) Ross McWhirter
English author–publisher
• Editor *The Guinness Book of World Records*, first edition, 1955.
b. August 12, 1925 in London, England
d. November 27, 1975 in London, England

Norris Dewar McWhirter
English author–publisher
• Twin brother of Alan; editor *The Guinness Book of World Records*,
b. August 12, 1925 in London, England

Walter R(obert) Mears
American editor–journalist–author
• Exec. editor, *Associated Press*, 1983–; won Pulitzer, 1977.
b. January 11, 1935 in Lynn, Massachusetts

Julius Meier-Graefe
German critic–author
• Wrote over 50 books on art, travel; founded four art mags.; favored Egyptian art.
b. June 1, 1867 in Resitza, Germany
d. July 1935

Frederic Gershon Melcher
American publisher
• R.R. Bowker exec.; established Newbery Medal for children's tales, 1921; Caldecott Medal for illustrations, 1937.
b. April 12, 1879 in Malden, Massachusetts
d. March 09, 1963 in Montclair, New Jersey

Herman Melville
American author
• Wrote *Moby Dick*, 1851.
b. August 01, 1819 in New York, New York
d. September 28, 1891 in New York, New York

H(enry) L(ouis) Mencken
American editor–satirist
• Known for biting satire, insult, debunking in *The American Mercury*, 1924-33; traced development of American English in *The American Language*, 1918.
b. September 12, 1880 in Baltimore, Maryland
d. January 29, 1956 in Baltimore, Maryland

Catulle (Abraham Catulle) Mendes
French author–critic
• Founded Parnassian school of poetry; wrote *Legende du Parnasse Contemporain*, 1884.
b. May 22, 1841 in Bordeaux, France
d. February 08, 1909 in Saint-Germain-en-Laye, France

George Meredith
English author–poet
• Wrote novel *Ordeal of Richard Feverel*, 1859; tragic poem *Modern Love*, 1862.
b. February 02, 1828 in Portsmouth, England
d. May 18, 1909 in Boxhill, England

Prosper Merimee
French author–historian–critic
• Wrote *Carmen*, 1846, later made into the famous opera by Bizet.
b. September 28, 1803 in Paris, France
d. September 23, 1870 in Cannes, France

Lee Meriwether
American author
• Wrote 1887 best-seller *A Tramp Trip: How to See Europe on Fifty Cents a Day*.
b. December 25, 1862 in Columbus, Mississippi
d. March 12, 1966 in Saint Louis, Missouri

Charles Merriam
American publisher
• With brother George founded G & C Merriam Co., 1832; published first Merriam-Webster dictionary, 1847.
b. 1806 in West Brookfield, Massachusetts
d. July 09, 1887 in Springfield, Massachusetts

James Merrill
American author
• Won Pulitzer for "Divine Comedies," 1977; son of Charles.
b. March 03, 1926 in New York, New York

Barbara Louise Gross Mertz
(Barbara Michaels; Elizabeth Peters pseuds)
American author
• Writes Gothic romances: *Patriot's Dream*, 1976.
b. September 29, 1927 in Canton, Illinois

W(illiam) S(tanley) Merwin
American poet
• Won Pulitzer for collection, *The Carrier of the Ladders*, 1971.
b. September 3, 1927 in New York, New York

Grace de Repentigny Metalious
American author
• Wrote *Peyton Place*, 1956; adapted into movie and TV series.
b. September 08, 1924 in Manchester, New Hampshire
d. February 25, 1964

Charlotte Mary Mew
English poet
• Wrote verse volumes *The Farmer's Bride*, 1916; *The Rambling Sailor*, 1929.
b. 1869
d. 1928

Alice Meynell
English poet–essayist
• Prose essays collected in *Colour of Life*, 1896; befriended poet Francis Thompson.
b. 1847 in London, England
d. November 27, 1922 in London, England

James A(lbert) Michener
American author
• Wrote *Tales of the South Pacific*, 1947; *Centennial*, 1974.
b. February 03, 1907 in New York, New York

Mihajlo Mihajlov
Yugoslav political activist–author
• Dissident, jailed for 13 years, unable to publish in native country; wrote *Underground Notes*, 1976.
b. September 26, 1934 in Pancevo, Yugoslavia

Sergei Vladimirovich Mikhalkov
Russian author
• Award-winning Soviet children's writer: *Krasny Galstuk*, 1947.
b. March 12, 1913 in Moscow, Russia

Margaret Ellis Millar
(Mrs Kenneth Millar)
Canadian author
• Mystery novels include 1956 Edgar-winner, *Beast in View*.
b. February 05, 1915 in Kitchener, Ontario

Edna St Vincent Millay
(Nancy Boyd pseud)
American author–poet
• Won Pulitzer for *The Ballad of the Harp Weaver*, 1922.
b. February 22, 1892 in Rockland, Maine
d. October 19, 1950 in Austerlitz, New York

Alice Duer Miller
American author
• Wrote *White Cliffs of Dover*, 1941.
b. July 28, 1874 in Staten Island, New York
d. August 22, 1942 in New York, New York

Caroline Miller
American author
• Wrote 1933 Pulitzer-winning novel *Lamb in His Bosom*.
b. August 26, 1903 in Waycross, Georgia

Henry Miller
American author
• Books *Tropic of Cancer*, 1934; *Tropic of Capricorn*, 1939, banned in US until 1960s.
b. December 26, 1891 in New York, New York
d. June 07, 1980 in Pacific Palisades, California

Joaquin Miller, pseud
(Cincinnatus Hiner Miller; "The Frontier Poet")
American poet–adventurer
• Wrote verse volumes *Specimens*, 1868; *Pacific Poems*, 1870.
b. September 08, 1837 in Liberty, Indiana
d. February 17, 1913 in Oakland, California

Jonathan (Wolfe) Miller
English author
• Wrote *Darwin for Beginners*, 1982; directed *Long Day's Journey Into Night*, 1985.
b. July 21, 1934 in London, England

Olive Beaupre Miller
American author
• Edited six-vol. children's classic, *My Bookhouse*, 1920-35.
b. 1883
d. 1968

A(lan) A(lexander) Milne
English author
• Wrote *Winnie-the-Pooh*, 1926; *The House at Pooh Corner*, 1928.
b. January 18, 1882 in London, England
d. January 31, 1956 in Hartfield, England

Christopher Robin Milne
English author
• The original Christopher Robin of his father's classic tale, *Winnie the Pooh*, 1926.
b. August 21, 1920 in London, England

Czeslaw Milosz
American author–educator
• Founded catastrophist school of Polish poetry; won Nobel Prize, 1980.
b. June 3, 1911 in Sateiniai, Lithuania

John Milton
English poet
• Wrote in four languages; known for masterpiece, written after losing eyesight, *Paradise Lost*, 1667.
b. December 09, 1608 in London, England
d. November 08, 1674 in London, England

Yukio Mishima, pseud
(Kimitake Hiraoka)
Japanese author
• Wrote modern Kabuki, no dramas; tetralogy *The Sea of Fertility*; committed public hara-kiri protesting Japan's westernization.
b. January 14, 1925 in Tokyo, Japan
d. November 25, 1970 in Tokyo, Japan

Frederic Mistral
French poet
• As member of Le Felibrige, influenced language, literature of Provence; wrote pastoral *Mireio*, 1859; won Nobel Prize, 1904.
b. September 08, 1830 in Maillane, France
d. March 25, 1914 in Maillane, France

Gabriela Mistral
(Lucila Godoy y Alcayaga)
Chilean poet–diplomat
• Verse volumes include *Lager*, 1954; *Sonnets of Death*; won 1945 Nobel Prize.
b. April 07, 1899 in Vicuna, Chile
d. January 1, 1957 in New York, New York

Margaret Mitchell
American author
• Won Pulitzer for her only book *Gone With the Wind*, 1936.
b. November 08, 1900 in Atlanta, Georgia
d. August 16, 1949 in Atlanta, Georgia

Arthur Moore Mizener
American author
• Noted for biographies of F Scott Fitzgerald: *The Far Side of Paradise*, 1951; Ford Maddox Ford: *The Saddest Story*, 1971.
b. September 03, 1907 in Erie, Pennsylvania
d. February 11, 1988 in Bristol, Rhode Island

Alice-Leone Moats
American author–journalist
• Wrote sassy etiquette book *No Nice Girl Swears*, 1933, reissued, 1983.
b. March 12, 1911 in Mexico City, Mexico
d. May 14, 1989 in Philadelphia, Pennsylvania

Clark Raymond Mollenhoff
American journalist
• Won Pulitzer for labor racketeering investigation, 1958, that ultimately led to Congressional probe; wrote of corruption in almost every presidential administration: *The President Who Failed: Carter Out of Control*, 1980.
b. April 16, 1921 in Burnside, Iowa

Maria Monk
American author
• Imposter; claimed scandalous nunnery practices in *Awful Disclosures by Maria Monk*, 1836.
b. June 01, 1816 in Saint John's, Quebec
d. September 04, 1849 in New York, New York

Harold Edward Monro
English author–businessman
• Opened London's Poetry Bookshop, 1913; founded *Poetry Review*, 1912.
b. March 14, 1879 in Brussels, Belgium
d. March 16, 1932 in Broadstairs, England

Nicholas John Turney Monsarrat
English author
• Wrote *The Cruel Sea*, 1951.
b. March 22, 1910 in Liverpool, England
d. August 07, 1979 in London, England

Lady Mary Wortley Montagu
English author
• Wrote witty, descriptive letters of Middle Eastern life; published posthumously, 1763.
b. May 26, 1689 in London, England
d. August 21, 1762 in London, England

Eugenio Montale
Italian poet–critic
• Won 1975 Nobel Prize; wrote *The Occasions*, 1939; *Satura*, 1963.
b. October 12, 1896 in Genoa, Italy
d. September 12, 1981 in Milan, Italy

Hubert Monteilhet
French author
• Wrote award-winning suspense novel *The Praying Mantises*, 1962.
b. 1928 in Paris, France

Lucy Maud Montgomery
Canadian author
• Wrote popular girls stories: *Anne of Green Gables*, 1908.
b. November 3, 1874 in Clifton, Prince Edward Island
d. April 24, 1942 in Toronto, Ontario

Brian Moore
Canadian author
• Novels attempt to come to terms with N Irish past: *The Lonely Passion of Judith Hearne*, 1956.
b. August 25, 1921 in Belfast, Northern Ireland

Julia A Davis Moore
American poet
• Popular during her day; now known as hilariously bad poet.
b. December 01, 1847 in Kent County, Michigan
d. June 05, 1920

Marianne Craig Moore
American poet–editor
• Verse volumes include *Observations*, 1924, won Pulitzer for *Collected Poems*, 1951.
b. November 15, 1887 in Saint Louis, Missouri
d. February 05, 1972 in New York, New York

Thomas Moore
Irish poet
• Noted for *Irish Melodies*, 1807-35; *Lalla Rookh*, 1817.
b. May 28, 1779 in Dublin, Ireland
d. February 25, 1852 in Bromham, England

Alberto Moravia, pseud
(Alberto Pincherle)
Italian author–journalist
• Italy's best-known contemporary novelist; wrote about women, sex, and the moral foibles of middle class Rome society; international reputation established with *Woman of Rome*, 1947.
b. November 28, 1907 in Rome, Italy
d. September 26, 1990 in Rome, Italy

Sir Thomas More
English author–statesman
• Leading figure of English humanism, defender of Roman Catholicism; best-known work: *Utopia*, 1516.
b. February 07, 1478 in London, England
d. July 06, 1535 in London, England

Edwin George Morgan
Scottish author–poet
• Poems include "The Vision of Cathkin Braes," 1952; "The Cape of Good Hope," 1955.
b. April 27, 1920 in Glasgow, Scotland

Christopher Darlington Morley
American author–journalist
• Works include best-selling novel *Kitty Foyle*, 1939; books on bookselling *Parnassus on Wheels*, 1917.
b. May 05, 1890 in Haverford, Pennsylvania
d. March 28, 1957 in Roslyn Heights, New York

Desmond Morris
English zoologist–author
• Pioneer in study of new science, comparative ethology; wrote best-selling *The Naked Ape*, 1967; other books include *The Human Zoo*, 1969; *Bodywatching*, 1985.
b. January 24, 1928 in Purton, England

Willie Morris
American author–editor
• Editor of *Harpers* mag, 1967-71; wrote award-winning autobiography *North Toward Home*, 1967.
b. November 29, 1934 in Jackson, Mississippi

Wright Marion Morris
American author
• Novels include *Love Among the Cannibals*, 1957; *A Life*, 1973.
b. January 06, 1910 in Central City, Nebraska

Theodore Morrison
American author
• Wrote four novels, four books of poetry; edited *The Portable Chaucer*, modern version of Chaucer's principal work, that has become a standard reference.
b. November 04, 1901 in Concord, New Hampshire
d. November 27, 1988 in Northampton, Massachusetts

Toni Morrison
(Chloe Anthony Wofford)
American author
• Wrote *Song of Solomon*, 1977; *Tar Baby*, 1981; awarded 1988 Pulitzer for *Beloved*.
b. February 18, 1931 in Lorain, Ohio

John Clifford Mortimer
English author–lawyer
• Wrote *Rumple of the Bailey*, 1978; adapted *Brideshaed Revisited* as PBS series.
b. April 21, 1923 in Hampstead, England

Frederic Morton
American author
• Novels include *An Unknown Woman*, 1976; non-fiction: *The Rothschilds*, 1962.
b. October 05, 1924 in Vienna, Austria

Barry Moser
American publisher–engraver
• Noted wood engraver; publisher of prestigious Pennyroyal Press, 1970–.
b. October 15, 1940 in Chattanooga, Tennessee

Arthur Harrison Motley
American publisher
• President, publisher of *Parade* mag., 1946-78.
b. August 22, 1900 in Minneapolis, Minnesota
d. May 29, 1984 in Palm Springs, California

Farley McGill Mowat
Canadian author
• Known for books about Northern Canada Eskimos; works in 60 languages have sold seven million copies.
b. May 12, 1921 in Belleville, Ontario

Edgar Ansel Mowrer
American journalist
• *Chicago Daily News* correspondent; won 1933 Pulitzer for describing Hitler's rise.
b. March 08, 1892 in Bloomington, Illinois
d. March 02, 1977 in Madeira, Portugal

Paul Scott Mowrer
American journalist–poet
• Won 1928 Pulitzer for foreign reporting; verse volumes include *Teeming Earth*, 1965; brother of Edgar.
b. July 14, 1887 in Bloomington, Illinois
d. April 05, 1971 in Beaufort, South Carolina

Patricia Moyes
(Mrs John S Haszard)
Irish author
• Won Edgar Allan Poe Award for *Many Deadly Returns*, 1970.
b. January 19, 1923 in Bray, Ireland

Malcolm Muggeridge
English author–broadcaster
• WW II counterintelligence spy; prolific writer of religious, political, personal themes; known for caustic commentaries on British royal family.
b. March 24, 1903 in Sanderstead, England
d. November 14, 1990 in London, England

Edwin Muir
Scottish author–critic
• Wrote *Estate of Poetry*, 1962; introduced Franz Kafta to English readers.
b. May 15, 1887 in Deerness, Scotland
d. January 03, 1959 in Cambridge, England

Malcolm Muir
American publisher
• Pres., editor-in-chief, *Newsweek*, 1937-61; pres., McGraw-Hill, 1928-37; founder, *Business Week*, 1929.
b. July 19, 1885 in Glen Ridge, New Jersey
d. January 3, 1979 in New York, New York

Lady Shikibu Murasaki
Japanese author
• Wrote one of earliest novels *Tale of the Genji*, c. 1020.
b. 978
d. 1031

Iris (Jean Iris) Murdoch
Irish author
• Wrote 22 thought-provoking novels: *Black Prince*, 1973; *The Good Apprentice*, 1985.
b. July 15, 1919 in Dublin, Ireland

Rupert (Keith Rupert) Murdoch
Australian publisher
• Controversial owner of British, American newspapers: *NY Post*; *Boston Herald*; *Times of London*.
b. March 11, 1931 in Melbourne, Australia

Warren B Murphy
American author
• Thrillers include co-authored "The Destroyer" series, 1971–.
b. September 13, 1933 in Jersey City, New Jersey

Gilbert (George Gilbert Aime) Murray
English author–translator
• Among most influential translators of Greek drama, wrote on public affairs.
b. January 02, 1866 in Sydney, Australia
d. May 2, 1957 in London, England

John Middleton Murry
English author
• Editor *The Adelphi*, 1923-48; wrote *Pencillings*, 1923; wed to Katherine Mansfield.
b. August 06, 1889 in London, England
d. May 13, 1957 in Bury St.Edmunds, England

Alfred de Musset
French writer
• Wrote lyric verse *Les Nuites*, 1835-37; play *Andrea del Sarto*, 1833; had love affair with George Sand, 1833-39.
b. December 11, 1810 in Paris, France
d. May 02, 1857 in Paris, France

Vladimir Nabokov
(Vladimir Sirin)
American author–translator
• Wrote *Lolita*, 1955, *Pale Fire*, 1962, and critical works; translated Russian authors.
b. April 23, 1899 in Saint Petersburg, Russia
d. July 02, 1977 in Montreux, Switzerland

John Naisbitt
American author
• Wrote *Megatrends;* one of most sought-after interpreters of contemporary scene.
b. 1929 in Salt Lake City, Utah

N Richard Nash
(Nathan Richard Nusbaum)
American writer
• Award-winning plays include *The Rainmaker*, 1957; wrote screenplay for *Porgy and Bess*, 1959.
b. June 07, 1913 in Philadelphia, Pennsylvania

Ogden Frederick Nash
American author
• Wrote poem, "Candy Is Dandy, But Liquor Is Quicker."
b. August 19, 1902 in Rye, New York
d. May 19, 1971 in Baltimore, Maryland

Robert Nathan
American author–composer
• Wrote romantic poetry, wry prose, including *Portrait of Jennie*, 1940.
b. January 02, 1894 in New York, New York
d. May 25, 1985 in Los Angeles, California

John Gneisenau Neihardt
American author
• Wrote verse, ficton on American Indians: *Song of the Messiah*, 1935.
b. January 08, 1881 in Sharpsburg, Illinois
d. November 03, 1973 in Columbia, Missouri

Nikolay Alexeyevich Nekrasov
Russian author
• Influential in radical wing of literature, using popular, social concerns rather than literary values; best-known poem: *The Pedlars*, 1861.
b. December 1, 1821 in Greshnevo, Russia
d. July 27, 1877 in Saint Petersburg, Russia

Howard Nemerov
American poet
• Verse volumes include *Mirrors and Windows*, 1958; among many awards is 1978 Pulitzer; US poet laureate, 1988–.
b. March 01, 1920 in New York, New York

Pablo Neruda
(Neftali Ricardo Reyes Basualto)
Chilean author–diplomat
• Won 1971 Nobel Prize in literature for surrealist poetry.
b. July 12, 1904 in Parral, Chile
d. September 23, 1973 in Santiago, Chile

Gerard de Nerval
(Gerard Labrunie)
French poet–translator–author
• Major influence on symbolists, surrealists through his use of fantasy in works: *Sylvie*, 1853.
b. May 22, 1808 in Paris, France
d. January 25, 1855 in Paris, France

Allen Harold Neuharth
American publisher–business executive–author
• CEO, Gannett Co., 1973–, largest, most profitable publicly held newspaper chain in US; wrote *S.O.B* .
b. March 22, 1924 in Eureka, South Dakota

John Newbery
English publisher
• Pioneer publisher of children's books: *Mother Goose's Nursery Rhymes*, c. 1760; Newbery Award for excellence in juvenile literature given in his honor since 1922.
b. 1713 in Berkshire, England
d. December 22, 1767 in London, England

Samuel Irving Newhouse
American newspaper publisher
• Owned 31 newspapers; bought Booth Newspapers, Inc. for $305 million.
b. May 24, 1895 in New York, New York
d. August 29, 1979 in New York, New York

Edwin Harold Newman
American author–broadcast journalist
• Won six Emmys; wrote *Strictly Speaking*, 1974; *Sunday Punch*, 1979.
b. January 25, 1919 in New York, New York

Beverley (John Beverley) Nichols
English writer
• Successful, witty works include novels, plays, nonfiction; best known for scandalous autobiography *Father Figure*, 1972.
b. September 09, 1898 in Bristol, England
d. September 15, 1983 in Kingston-upon-Thames, England

John George Nicolay
American author
• Private secretary to Lincoln, 1861-65; with John Hay, wrote first authoritative biography *Abraham Lincoln: A History*, published serially, 1886-90.
b. February 26, 1832 in Essingen, Bavaria
d. September 26, 1901 in Washington, District of Columbia

Friedrich Wilhelm Nietzsche
German philosopher–poet
• Glorified the "super man," denouncing Christianity; among most influential works: *Thus Spake Zarathustra*, 1891.
b. October 15, 1844 in Rocken, Saxony
d. August 25, 1900 in Weimar, Germany

Anais Nin
American author
• Best known for diaries; wrote *A Spy in the House of Love*, 1954; *Delta of Venus*, 1977.
b. February 21, 1903 in Paris, France
d. October 14, 1977 in Los Angeles, California

Nolan Christopher
Irish author
• Severely handicapped writer; awarded Britain's Whitbread Book of the Year Award, 1988, for autobiography *Under the Eye of the Clock.*
b. September 05, 1965 in Mullingar, Ireland

Charles Bernard Nordhoff
American author–traveler
• Co-wrote with James Hall popular S Seas adventures: *Mutiny on the Bounty*, 1932; *Pitcairn's Island*, 1934.
b. February 01, 1887 in London, England
d. April 11, 1947 in Santa Barbara, California

Kathleen Thompson Norris
American author
• Wrote *Mother*, 1911; her 82 novels sold 10 million copies.
b. July 16, 1880 in San Francisco, California
d. June 18, 1960 in San Francisco, California

Sterling North
American writer–critic
• Literary editor, *Chicago Daily News*, 1933-43; *NY Post*, 1943-49; noted for children's books: *Rascal*, 1963, filmed by Disney.
b. November 04, 1906 in Edgerton, Wisconsin
d. December 21, 1974 in Whippany, New Jersey

Andre Norton, pseud
(Alice Mary Norton)
American author
• Noted for original, complex fantasy, science fiction books; award-winning works include *Iron Butterflies*, 1980.
b. February 17, 1912 in Cleveland, Ohio

Novalis
(Friedrich von Hardenberg)
German poet
• Influenced *le romantisme* movement in France, which later developed into Romantic Movement; prose poems include *Hymns to the Night*, 1800.
b. May 02, 1772 in Halle, Germany
d. March 25, 1801 in Weissenfels, Germany

Alfred Noyes
English poet–author
• Noted for narrative verse based on English history; best-known poem, "The Highwayman."
b. September 16, 1880 in Wolverhampton, England
d. June 28, 1958 in Isle of Wight, England

Edgar Wilson (Bill) Nye
American author
• Comic works include *Bill Nye and Boomerang*, 1881; used puns, misquotes, scrambled sentences.
b. August 25, 1850 in Shirley, Maine
d. February 22, 1896 in Arden, North Carolina

Joyce Carol Oates
American author
• Prolific novelist, short story writer; wrote award-winning *Them*, 1969; *Bellefleur*, 1980.
b. June 16, 1938 in Lockport, New York

Edna O'Brien
Irish author
• Writings include *The Country Girls*, 1960; *Some Irish Loving*, 1979.
b. December 15, 1931 in Tuamgraney, Ireland

Adolph Simon Ochs
American newspaper publisher
• Published *NY Times*, 1896-1935; director, AP, 1900-35; introduced rotogravvre illustrations, book review supplements.
b. March 12, 1858 in Cincinnati, Ohio
d. April 08, 1935 in Chattanooga, Tennessee

Edwin Greene O'Connor
American author
• Won Pulitzer, 1962, for *The Edge of Sadness*.
b. July 29, 1918 in Providence, Rhode Island
d. March 23, 1968 in Boston, Massachusetts

Flannery O'Connor
American author
• Stories have Southern locales, originality, power; wrote collection of short stories *A Good Man Is Hard to Find*, 1955.
b. March 25, 1925 in Savannah, Georgia
d. August 03, 1964 in Milledgeville, Georgia

Thomas Power O'Connor
Irish journalist
• Held longest record of unbroken parliamentary service in his time, 1880-1929; wrote *The Parnell Movement*, 1886.
b. October 05, 1848 in Athlone, Ireland
d. November 18, 1929

Scott O'Dell
American author
• Wrote *Island of the Blue Dolphins*, 1960, *The Black Pearl*, 1967, and 24 other children's books; won three Newbery prizes.
b. May 23, 1903 in Los Angeles, California
d. October 15, 1989 in Mount Kisco, New York

Sean O'Faolain
("The Irish Chekov")
Irish author
• Writings include *Come Back to Erin*, 1940; *The Talking Trees*, 1970.
b. February 22, 1900 in Cork, Ireland
d. April 20, 1991 in Dublin, Ireland

Liam O'Flaherty
Irish author
• Best known for novel *The Informer*, 1926; became classic film, 1935.
b. August 28, 1896 in County Galway, Ireland
d. September 07, 1984 in Dublin, Ireland

John Henry O'Hara
American author
• Writings include *Butterfield 8*, *From the Terrace*; both filmed, 1960.
b. January 31, 1905 in Pottsville, Pennsylvania
d. April 11, 1970 in Princeton, New Jersey

Mary O'Hara
(Mary O'Hara Alsop; Mary Sture-Vasa)
American author
• Wrote *My Friend Flicka*, 1941.
b. July 1, 1885 in Cape May, New Jersey
d. October 15, 1980 in Chevy Chase, Maryland

Zoe Oldenbourg
French author
• Novels include *The Awakened*, 1956; *The Chains of Love*, 1958.
b. March 31, 1916 in Russia

Laurence Oliphant
English author
• Best known for *Piccadilly*, 1866.
b. 1829 in Cape Town, South Africa
d. December 23, 1888 in Twickenham, England

Margaret Oliphant
English author
• Books on English society include *Salem Chapel*, 1876.
b. April 04, 1828 in Musselburgh, Scotland
d. June 25, 1897 in Eton, England

Charles Olson
American poet
• Co-founded Black Mountain school of poetry; wrote *Call Me Ishmael*, 1947.
b. December 27, 1910 in Worcester, Massachusetts
d. January 1, 1970

Sydney Omarr
American astrologer–journalist
• Astrology columns appear in over 200 newspapers.
b. in Philadelphia, Pennsylvania

George Oppen
American poet
• Won 1969 Pulitzer for *On Being Numerous*.
b. April 24, 1908 in New Rochelle, New York
d. July 07, 1984 in Sunnyvale, California

James Oppenheim
American poet–author
• Poem volumes include *The Sea*, 1923; books include *Behind Your Front*, 1928.
b. May 24, 1882 in Saint Paul, Minnesota
d. August 04, 1932 in New York, New York

Baroness Emmuska Orczy
(Emma Madgalena Rosalia Maria Josefa Barbara Orczy)
British author
• Best known for *The Scarlet Pimpernel*, 1905.
b. September 23, 1865 in Tarna-Ors, Hungary
d. November 12, 1947 in London, England

Samuel Ornitz
(The Hollywood Ten)
American editor–author
• One of group of screenwriters jailed, 1950, for suspected Communist Party membership.
b. November 15, 1890 in New York, New York
d. March 11, 1957 in Los Angeles, California

George Orwell, pseud
(Eric Arthur Blair)
English author–critic
• Wrote *Animal Farm*, 1946; *1984*, 1949.
b. June 25, 1903 in Motihari, India
d. January 21, 1950 in London, England

Frances Sargent Locke Osgood
American poet
• Closely associated with Edgar Allan Poe; wrote *Casket of Fate*, 1840.
b. June 18, 1811 in Boston, Massachusetts
d. May 12, 1850 in New York, New York

Shaemas O'Sheel
(Shaemas Shields pseud)
American author
• Best known for poem "They Went Forth to Battle, But They Always Fell."
b. September 19, 1886 in New York, New York
d. 1954

Carl von Ossietzky
German journalist
• Won Nobel Peace Prize, 1935; prevented from accepting it by Hitler's decree.
b. October 03, 1889 in Hamburg, Germany
d. May 04, 1938 in Berlin, Germany

Will(iam Charles) Oursler
(Gale Gallager; Nick Marine pseuds)
American author
• Writings include *The Trail of Vincent Doon*, 1941; *One Way Street*, 1952.
b. July 12, 1913 in Baltimore, Maryland
d. January 07, 1985 in New York, New York

Bonaro Wilkinson Overstreet
American author
• Writings include *Search for a Self*, 1938; *The Iron Curtain*, 1963.
b. October 3, 1902 in Geyserville, California
d. September 1, 1985 in Arlington, Virginia

Ovid
(Publius Ovidius Naso)
Roman poet
• Noted works include *The Art of Love; Metamorphoses*.
b. 43BC in Sulmona, Italy
d. 17AD in Tomi, Romania

Guy Owen, Jr
American author
• Writings include *The Flim-Flam Man and Other Stories*, 1980.
b. February 24, 1925 in Clarkton, North Carolina
d. July 23, 1981 in Raleigh, North Carolina

Wilfred Owen
English poet
• Wrote about his hatred of war; best-known poem: *Strange Meeting*.
b. March 18, 1893 in Oswestry, England
d. November 04, 1918 in France

Amos Oz
(Amos Klausner)
Israeli author
• Work often documents Israeli society; best-known novel: *My Michael*, 1972.
b. May 04, 1939 in Jerusalem, Palestine

Koyo Ozaki, pseud
(Ozaki Tokutaro)
Japanese author
• Very popular during his time; known for unfinished masterpiece *Konjikiyasha*.
b. October 01, 1868 in Tokyo, Japan
d. October 3, 1903 in Tokyo, Japan

Clementine Haskin Paddleford
American editor–journalist
• Called "best known food editor" in America, 1953; 12 million estimated weekly readers; known for vivid descriptions of food.
b. September 27, 1900 in Stockdale, Kansas
d. November 13, 1967 in New York, New York

Albert Bigelow Paine
American author
• Wrote three-volume biography of *Mark Twain*, 1912.
b. July 1, 1861 in New Bedford, Massachusetts
d. April 09, 1937 in New Smyrna, Florida

Thomas Paine
American philosopher–author
• Advocated colonial independence in *Common Sense*, Jan 1776.
b. January 29, 1737 in Thetford, England
d. June 08, 1809 in New York, New York

LeRoy Lad Panek
American author
• Pioneer in sensational fiction; won Edgars for *Watteau's Shepherds: The Detective Novel in Britain, 1914-40*, 1979; *Introduction to the Detective Story*, 1987.
b. January 26, 1943 in Cleveland, Ohio

Giovanni Papini
Italian author
• Wrote popular *Life of Christ*, 1921; *Gog*, a satire on modern society, 1931.
b. January 09, 1881 in Florence, Italy
d. July 08, 1956 in Florence, Italy

Peggy (Margaret Cecile) Parish
American children's author
• Wrote more than 30 books, many of which featured her best-known character, Amelia Bedelia.
b. July 14, 1927 in Manning, South Carolina
d. November 18, 1988 in Manning, South Carolina

Sir Gilbert Parker
Canadian author
• Portrayed Canadian life in short stories *Pierre and His People*, 1892; novel, *The Weavers*, 1907.
b. November 23, 1862 in Addington, Ontario
d. September 06, 1932 in London, England

Francis Parkman
American historian–author
• Explored West; best known work, *The Oregon Trail*, 1849.
b. September 16, 1823 in Boston, Massachusetts
d. November 08, 1893 in Boston, Massachusetts

Lillian Rogers Parks
American author
• Wrote *My Thirty Years Backstairs at the White House*, 1961; TV mini-series, 1979.
b. 1897

Louella Oettinger Parsons
American journalist
• Influential Hollywood syndicated gossip columnist, 1922-65; rival of Hedda Hopper.
b. August 06, 1881 in Freeport, Illinois
d. December 09, 1972 in Santa Monica, California

Bellamy Partridge
American biographer–author
• Numerous light, popular books included *Country Lawyer*, 1939.
b. 1878 in Phelps, New York
d. July 05, 1960 in Bridgeport, Connecticut

Giovanni Pascoli
Italian poet
• Verse vols. include *Myricae*, 1891-1905; *Canti di Castelvecchio*, 1903.
b. December 31, 1855 in San Mauro, Italy
d. April 06, 1912 in Castelvecchio, Italy

Boris Leonidovich Pasternak
Russian author
• Forced to refuse Nobel Prize for literature, 1958; wrote *Doctor Zhivago*, 1957.
b. February 11, 1890 in Moscow, Russia
d. May 29, 1960 in Moscow, U.S.S.R.

Kenneth Patchen
American poet–author
• His surrealistic poems included in *Hurrah for Anything*, 1957; popular on college campuses.
b. December 13, 1911 in Niles, Ohio
d. January 08, 1972 in Palo Alto, California

Walter Horatio Pater
English author–critic
• Wrote *Studies in History of the Renaissance*, 1873; his masterpiece, *Marius the Epicurian*, 1885.
b. August 05, 1839 in Shadwell, England
d. July 3, 1894 in Oxford, England

Alan Stewart Paton
South African author–political activist
• Writings depict racial conflict in S Africa: *Cry, the Beloved Country*, 1948; founded doomed Liberal Party, 1950s.
b. January 11, 1903 in Pietermaritzburg, South Africa
d. April 12, 1988 in Durban, South Africa

Gilbert Patten
(Burt L Standish pseud)
American author
• His adventure books include the 200-vol. *Frank Merriwell* series, from 1896.
b. October 25, 1866 in Corinna, Maine
d. January 16, 1945 in Vista, California

Alicia Patterson
(Mrs Harry F Guggenheim)
American editor–publisher
• Founded *Newsday* magazine with husband, 1940.
b. October 15, 1909 in Chicago, Illinois
d. July 02, 1963 in New York, New York

Joseph Medill Patterson
American publisher
• With cousin Robert McCormick founded first US tabloid, *NY Daily News*, 1919; sole owner, from 1925; brother of Eleanor.
b. January 06, 1879 in Chicago, Illinois
d. May 26, 1946 in New York, New York

Robert (Pierre Stephen Robert) Payne
American author
• Published over 100 books; known for biographies.
b. December 04, 1911 in Saltash, England
d. February 18, 1983 in Hamilton, Bermuda

Octavio Paz
Mexican poet–critic
• Lyrical poetry uses rich imagery of Mexico's landscape to explore love, death, loneliness; poem "Sun Stone," 1957, inspired by a huge Aztec calendar stone; won Nobel Prize, 1990.
b. March 31, 1914 in Mexico City, Mexico

Thomas Love Peacock
English author–poet
• Works include satirical novel *Nightmare Alley*, 1818; Shelley's close friend.
b. October 18, 1785 in Weymouth, England
d. January 23, 1866 in Halliford, England

Norbert Pearlroth
American journalist
• Only researcher for "Ripley's Believe It or Not" newspaper feature, 1923-83.
b. May 1893 in Poland
d. April 14, 1983 in New York, New York

Padraic (Patrick Henry) Pearse
Irish poet–patriot
• Shot by British firing squad because of his part in the Easter Week rebellion, 1916; wrote *Collected Works*, 1916.
b. November 1, 1879 in Dublin, Ireland
d. May 03, 1916 in Dublin, Ireland

Sir Cyril Arthur Pearson
English publisher–philanthropist
• Founded mag *Pearson's Weekly*; newspapers *Daily Express*, 1900.
b. February 24, 1866 in Wells, England
d. December 09, 1921 in London, England

Drew Pearson
American journalist
• With Robert S. Allen wrote daily column "Washington Merry Go-Round," 1932-69.
b. December 13, 1897 in Evanston, Illinois
d. September 01, 1969 in Washington, District of Columbia

Westbrook Pegler
American journalist
• Outspoken, controversial reporter; won Pulitzer for reporting on racketeering in labor union, 1941.
b. August 02, 1894 in Minneapolis, Minnesota
d. June 24, 1969 in Tucson, Arizona

John Selman Pennington
American journalist
• Credited with helping launch Jimmy Carter's political career by exposing a vote fraud in state senate race, 1962.
b. 1924 in Andersonville, Georgia
d. November 23, 1980 in Saint Petersburg, Florida

Walker Percy
American author
• Southern author; wrote about search for faith and love in chaotic modern world: *Love in the Ruins*, 1971.
b. May 28, 1916 in Birmingham, Alabama
d. May 1, 1990 in Covington, Louisiana

S(idney) J(oseph) Perelman
American author
• Won 1956 Oscar for screenplay, *Around the World in Eighty Days*. Noted for scripts for Marx Brothers, humorous short stories.
b. February 01, 1904 in Brooklyn, New York
d. October 17, 1979 in New York, New York

Benjamin Peret
French author–poet
• One of first surrealist poets; collections include *Four Years After the Dog*, 1974.
b. 1899 in Nantes, France
d. 1959 in Paris, France

Isaac Loeb Peretz
Polish author
• Major force behind Yiddish literary movement, Jewish theater; plays include *The Golden Chain*, 1907; *The Hunchback*, 1414.
b. May 18, 1851 in Zamosc, Poland
d. April 03, 1915 in Warsaw, Poland

Benito Perez Galdos
Spanish author
• Father of modern Spanish novel; wrote 46-vol. *Episodios Nacionales*, 1873-1912, historical fiction of 19th c. Spain.
b. May 1, 1843 in Las Palmas, Canary Islands
d. January 04, 1920 in Madrid, Spain

Maxwell Evarts Perkins
American editor
• Scribner's editor who discovered Fitzgerald, Hemingway, Thomas Wolfe.
b. September 2, 1884 in New York, New York
d. June 17, 1947 in Stamford, Connecticut

Stuart Z Perkoff
American poet–artist
• Beat poet whose books of poetry include *Suicide Room*, 1956.
b. July 29, 1930 in Saint Louis, Missouri
d. June 14, 1974

Charles Perrault
French author–poet
• Known for his collection of fairy tales, including *Cinderella*, 1697.
b. January 12, 1628 in Paris, France
d. May 16, 1703 in Paris, France

Laurence Johnston Peter
American author
• Wrote best-seller on subject of human imcompetence: *The Peter Principle*, 1969.
b. September 16, 1919 in Vancouver, British Columbia
d. January 12, 1990 in Los Angeles, California

Julia Mood Peterkin
American author
• Books about South Carolina include 1928 Pulitzer winner *Scarlet Sister Mary*.
b. October 31, 1880 in Laurens County, South Carolina
d. August 1, 1961 in Orangeburg, South Carolina

Ellis Peters, pseud
(Edith Mary Pargeter)
English author
• Won 1963 Edgar for *Death and the Joyful Woman*.
b. September 28, 1913 in Horsehay, England

Maud Petersham
(Mrs Miska Petersham)
American children's author–illustrator
• With husband, won 1946 Caldecott Medal for *The Rooster Crows.*
b. August 05, 1890 in Kingston, New York
d. November 29, 1971

Francesco Petrarch
Italian poet
• Wrote *Canzoniere,* lyrics, love sonnets; crowned poet lauraete, Rome, 1341.
b. July 2, 1304 in Arezzo, Italy
d. July 19, 1374 in Arqua, Italy

Gaius Petronius
Roman author
• Reputed to be author of satire *Satyricon,* sometimes considerd first Western European novel.

Roger (Pierre Roger) Peyrefitte
French author
• Wrote best-seller, biography of Germaine Germain, *Manouche,* 1972.
b. August 17, 1907 in Castres, France

Phaedrus
Roman author
• Wrote fables in verse based on Aesop.
b. 15BC
d. 50AD

Harry Irving Phillips
American journalist
• Created WW II rookie Private Oscar Purkey; wrote *Private Purkey's Private Peace,* 1945.
b. November 26, 1889 in New Haven, Connecticut
d. March 15, 1965 in Milford, Connecticut

Francis Meredyth Pilkington
Irish children's author
• Noted for Irish fairy tales, legends: *The Three Sorrowful Tales of Erin,* 1965.
b. June 16, 1907 in Dublin, Ireland

Daniel Manus Pinkwater
American children's author–illustrator
• Books include *I Was a Second Grade Werewolf,* 1983; *Attila the Pun,* 1981.
b. November 15, 1941 in Memphis, Tennessee

H(enry) Beam Piper
American author
• Wrote science fiction tales: *Little Fuzzy,* 1962; *Space Viking,* 1963.
b. 1904 in Altoona, Pennsylvania
d. November 11, 1964

Walter Boughton Pitkin
American author–educator
• Wrote best seller *Life Begins at Forty,* 1932.
b. February 06, 1878 in Ypsilanti, Michigan
d. January 25, 1953 in Palo Alto, California

Belva Plain
American author
• Wrote *Evergreen,* 1978; *Random Winds,* 1980.
b. October 09, 1919 in New York, New York

Sylvia Plath
(Mrs Ted Hughes; Victoria Lucas pseud)
American author–poet
• Confessional verse collected in *Ariel,* 1965; wrote autobiographical novel, *The Bell Jar,* 1962; suicide victim.
b. October 27, 1932 in Boston, Massachusetts
d. February 11, 1963 in London, England

Plato
Greek philosopher–author
• Student of Socrates who founded the Academy, 387 BC; called world's most influential philosopher.
b. 427BC in Athens, Greece
d. 347BC in Athens, Greece

George Ames Plimpton
American author
• America's participatory journalist; wrote of experiences in several books including *Out of My League,* 1961, *Paper Lion,* 1966; founded *Paris Review,* 1953.
b. March 18, 1927 in New York, New York

William Charles Franklyn Plomer
South African author
• His opera *Gloriana* was performed during coronation of Queen Elizabeth,II, 1953.
b. December 1, 1903 in Pietersburg, South Africa
d. September 21, 1973 in England

Plutarch
Greek author
• Wrote hundreds of short pieces, especially biographies comparing Greek, Roman figures; has influenced philosophers, writers for hundreds of years.
b. 46 in Chaeronea, Greece
d. 120 in Chaeronea, Greece

Edgar Allan Poe
American poet–author–journalist
• Invented modern detective story; noted for macabre themes in poems, short stories: *The Raven,* 1845; *The Gold Bug,* 1843.
b. January 19, 1809 in Boston, Massachusetts
d. October 07, 1849 in Baltimore, Maryland

Frederik Pohl
American editor–author
• Science fiction books include *The Abominable Snowman,* 1963; *Man Plus,* 1977.
b. November 26, 1919 in New York, New York

Vasko Popa
Yugoslav poet
• Contemporary poet inspired by Serbian folk tradition: *Earth Erect,* 1973.
b. July 29, 1922 in Grebenac, Yugoslavia

Alexander Pope
English poet
• Verse satirist; wrote *The Rape of the Lock,* 1714; *Moral Essays,* 1731-35.
b. May 21, 1688 in London, England
d. May 3, 1744 in Twickenham, England

Eleanor H Porter
American author
• Best known for children's *Polyanna* books, 1913-18.
b. December 19, 1868 in Littleton, New Hampshire
d. May 21, 1920

Hal Porter
Australian author
• Best-known novel *The Tilted Cross,* 1961, considered an Australian classic.
b. February 16, 1911 in Victoria Park, Australia
d. September 29, 1984 in Australia

Katherine Anne Porter
American author
• Won Pulitzer, 1966, for her only full-length novel, *Ship of Fools.*
b. May 15, 1894 in Indian Creek, Texas
d. September 18, 1980 in Silver Spring, Maryland

Sylvia Field Porter
American journalist–author
• Syndicated financial columnist; wrote *Sylvia Porter's New Money Book for the 80's,* 1979.
b. June 18, 1913 in Patchogue, New York

Charles Portis
American author
• Best-known work, *True Grit,* 1968; John Wayne won Oscar in film, 1969.
b. December 28, 1933 in El Dorado, Arkansas

Elizabeth Lindley Post
American author
• Continues editing work of Emily Post, her husband's grandmother.
b. May 07, 1920 in Englewood, New Jersey

Emily Price Post

American author–journalist
• Wrote definitive work on proper social behavior, *Etiquette*, 1922.
b. October 3, 1873 in Baltimore, Maryland
d. September 25, 1960 in New York, New York

Chaim Potok

American author
• Best-sellers include, *The Chosen*, 1967, filmed, 1982; *The Promise*, 1969.
b. February 17, 1929 in New York, New York

Stephen Potter

English author
• Introduced new word to language with series of books: *One Upmanship*, 1952.
b. February 01, 1900 in London, England
d. December 02, 1969 in London, England

Anthony Dymoke Powell

English author
• Known for social satire in long series of novels, *A Dance to the Music of Time*.
b. December 21, 1905 in London, England

James Farl Powers

American author
• Short stories include *Prince of Darkness and Other Stories*, 1947; won Nat. Book Award for *Morte d'Urban*, 1962.
b. July 08, 1917 in Jacksonville, Illinois

John Cowper Powys

English writer
• Wrote *Meaning of Culture*; novel, *Wolf Solent*, 1929.
b. October 08, 1872 in Shirley, England
d. June 17, 1963 in Wales

Richard Scott Prather

American author
• Mystery books include *Dead Man's Walk*, 1965; *The Kubla Kan Caper*, 1966.
b. September 09, 1921 in Santa Ana, California

Edwin John Pratt

Canadian poet
• Best-known heroic narrative: *Behind the Log*, 1947.
b. February 04, 1883 in Western Bay, Newfoundland
d. April 26, 1964 in Toronto, Ontario

Fletcher Pratt

American author
• Prolific writer on military history, science fiction: *Alien Planet*, 1962; *Fleet Against Japan*, 1946.
b. April 25, 1897 in Buffalo, New York
d. June 1, 1956 in Long Branch, New Jersey

Reynolds (Edward Reynolds) Price

American author–educator
• Best known for *A Long and Happy Life*, 1962.
b. February 01, 1933 in Macon, North Carolina

Roger Taylor Price

American publisher
• Founded Price-Stern-Sloan Publishers, Inc., 1960; stand-up comedian, 1950-63.
b. March 06, 1920 in Charleston, West Virginia
d. October 31, 1990 in North Hollywood, California

Frederic Prokosch

American author–poet
• Had 60-year career that included his best-selling novel *The Asians*, 1935.
b. May 17, 1908 in Madison, Wisconsin
d. June 02, 1989 in Plan de Grasse, France

Marcel Proust

French author
• Wrote lengthy autobiography: *Remembrance of Things Past*, 1922-32.
b. July 1, 1871 in Paris, France
d. November 18, 1922 in Paris, France

Alice Rose Twitchell Provensen

American illustrator–children's author
• With husband Martin produced colorful self-illustrated children's books, including *Year at Maple Hill*, 1978.
b. August 14, 1918 in Chicago, Illinois

Martin Provensen

American illustrator–children's author
• Self-illustrated books include *Who's in the Egg*, 1968; *Our Animal Friends*, 1974.
b. July 1, 1916 in Chicago, Illinois
d. March 27, 1987 in Clinton Corners, New York

Rene-Francois-Armend Prudhomme

(Sully Prudhomme; Rene-Francois-Armend pseuds)
French poet
• Won Nobel Prize, 1901; best-known poem: "Vase Brise," 1865.
b. March 16, 1839 in Paris, France
d. September 06, 1907 in Chatenay, France

John Sleigh Pudney

English author–dramatist
• Wrote *Jacobson's Ladder*, 1938.
b. January 19, 1909 in Langley, England
d. November 1, 1977 in England

Manuel Puig

Argentine author
• Best known for all-dialogue novel, *Kiss of the Spider Woman*, 1979; filmed, 1985.
b. December 28, 1932 in General Villegas, Argentina
d. July 22, 1990 in Cuernavaca, Mexico

Luigi Pulci

Italian author
• Wrote comic masterpiece *The Morgante Maggiore*, 1483.
b. August 15, 1432 in Florence, Italy
d. November 1484 in Padua, Italy

Joseph Pulitzer

American editor–publisher
• Founded newspaper empire based on sensationalism, pro-labor policies; established Pulitzer Prizes, 1917.
b. April 1, 1847 in Mako, Hungary
d. October 29, 1911 in Charleston, South Carolina

Joseph Pulitzer, II

American journalist
• Editor, publisher, *St. Louis Post-Dispatch*, 1912-55.
b. March 21, 1885 in New York, New York
d. March 3, 1955 in Saint Louis, Missouri

Diana Pullein-Thompson

(Diana Fullein-Thompson Farr)
American children's author
• Books include *Ponies on the Trail*, 1978; *Ponies in Peril*, 1979.
b. in Wimbledon, England

James Purdy

American author
• Wrote *In a Shallow Grave*, 1975; *Sleepers in Moon-Crowned Valleys* trilogy, 1970-81.
b. July 17, 1923 in Ohio

Edward Bouverie Pusey

English author–clergyman
• Leader of Oxford Movement, co-writer *Tracts for the Times*, 1834.
b. March 22, 1800 in Pusey, England
d. September 14, 1882 in Ascot Priory, England

Merlo John Pusey

American author–editor
• Won Pulitzer 1952, for two-vol. biography of Charles Evans Hughes.
b. February 03, 1902 in Woodruff, Utah
d. November 25, 1985 in Washington, District of Columbia

Aleksandr Sergeyevich Pushkin
Russian author–poet
• Introduced Russian Romanticism; wrote *Boris Godunov*, 1831.
b. June 06, 1799 in Moscow, Russia
d. February 1, 1837 in Saint Petersburg, Russia

Mario Puzo
American author
• Won Oscars for screenplays of *The Godfather I, II*, 1972, 1974.
b. October 15, 1920 in New York, New York

Henry Pye
British poet
• Poet laureate, 1790; wrote epic *Alfred*, 1801.
b. 1745
d. 1813

Ernie (Ernest Taylor) Pyle
American journalist
• Won Pulitzer 1944 for WW II stories; killed by Japanese machine gun.
b. August 03, 1900 in Dana, Indiana
d. April 18, 1945 in Ie Shima, Okinawa

Barbara Mary Crampton Pym
English author
• Wrote seven novels including *Quartet in Autumn; Unsuitable Attachment*.
b. June 02, 1913 in Oswestry, England
d. January 11, 1980 in Oxford, England

Thomas Ruggles Pynchon, Jr
American author
• Challenging novels include prize-winning *V*, 1963; *Gravity's Rainbow*, 1973.
b. May 08, 1937 in Glen Cove, New York

Percy Qoboza
South African publisher
• Influential black publisher of several papers shut down by apartheid.
b. January 17, 1938
d. January 17, 1988 in Johannesburg, South Africa

Salvatore Quasimodo
Italian poet
• Won Nobel Prize for literature, 1959; poems noted for delicate phrases, tight structure.
b. August 2, 1901 in Syracuse, Sicily
d. June 14, 1968 in Naples, Italy

Ellery Queen, pseud
(Frederic Dannay; Manfred B Lee)
American author
• Fictitious detective used as pseudonym for popular mystery novels.

Jane Bryant Quinn
American journalist
• Financial business columnist, *Newsweek;* wrote *Everyone's Money Book*.
b. February 05, 1939 in Niagara Falls, New York

Sally Quinn
(Mrs Ben Bradlee)
American journalist
• Co-anchorperson, "CBS Morning News," 1973-74; reporter *Washington Post*, 1969-73, 1974–.
b. July 01, 1941 in Savannah, Georgia

Selwyn Raab
American journalist–author
• Reporter, *NY Times*, 1974–; news editor, NBC News, 1966-71; won many awards in field.
b. June 26, 1934 in New York, New York

Francois Rabelais
(Alcofribas Nasier pseud)
French author
• Noted for ribald humor; wrote *Gargantua and Pantagruel*.
b. 1494 in Chinon, France
d. 1553 in Paris, France

Ann Radcliffe
English author
• Gothic romances include *Mysteries of Udolpho*, 1794.
b. July 09, 1764 in London, England
d. February 07, 1823 in London, England

Dotson Rader
American author
• Novels include *Miracle*, 1978; *Beau Monde*, 1981.
b. 1942 in Minnesota

William MacLeod Raine
Author
• Wrote over 80 Western novels, including *Dry Bones in the Valley*, 1953.
b. June 22, 1871 in London, England
d. July 25, 1954 in Denver, Colorado

Allan Ramsay
Scottish poet
• Wrote popular pastoral, *The Gentle Shepherd*, 1725.
b. October 15, 1686 in Leadhills, Scotland
d. January 07, 1758 in Edinburgh, Scotland

Ayn Rand
American author
• Novels *The Fountainhead*, 1943; *Atlas Shrugged*, 1957, reflect "objectivist" philosophy.
b. February 02, 1905 in Saint Petersburg, Russia
d. March 06, 1982 in New York, New York

Dudley Randall
American poet
• Works include "The Black Poets," 1971; "After the Killing," 1973.
b. January 14, 1914 in Washington, District of Columbia

Robert Joseph Randisi
(Nick Carter; Tom Cutter; W B Longley; J R Roberts pseuds)
American author
• Won Shamus award for mystery novel *The Sterling Collection*, 1983.
b. August 24, 1951 in Brooklyn, New York

John Crowe Ransom
American poet
• Founder, editor *Kenyon Review*, 1939-59; wrote verse volume *Chills and Fevers*, 1924.
b. April 3, 1888 in Pulaski, Tennessee
d. July 05, 1974 in Gambier, Ohio

A(braham) H(enry) Raskin
Canadian journalist
• Reporter, columnist, editor for *NY Times*, 1934-77; regarded as dean of American labor reporters.
b. April 26, 1911 in Edmonton, Alberta

Ellen Raskin
American children's author–illustrator
• Won Newbery Medal for self-illustrated *Figgs and Phantoms*, 1975; *The Westing Game*, 1979.
b. March 13, 1928 in Milwaukee, Wisconsin
d. August 08, 1984 in New York, New York

William Raspberry
American journalist
• Syndicated columnist for *Washington Post*, 1966–; often writes about minority affairs.
b. October 12, 1935 in Okolona, Mississippi

Irina Ratushinskaya
American poet
• KGB political prisoner, 1983-86; wrote hundreds of poems in confinement; memoir of prison life, *Grey Is the Colour of Hope*, published in 1988.
b. March 04, 1954 in Odessa, U.S.S.R.

Marjorie Kinnan Rawlings
American author
• Won 1939 Pulitzer for *The Yearling*; filmed, 1946.
b. August 08, 1896 in Washington, District of Columbia
d. December 14, 1953 in Saint Augustine, Florida

Henry Jarvis Raymond
American politician–editor
• Co-founder, editor, NY *Times*, 1851-69; a founder of Republican Party, 1856.
b. January 24, 1820 in Lima, New York
d. June 18, 1869 in New York, New York

Claire Berenice Rayner
(Sheila Brandon pseud)
English author
• Former nurse who writes nonfiction books on medicine, sex.
b. January 22, 1931 in London, England

Charles Reade
English author–dramatist
• Wrote classic *The Cloister and the Hearth*, 1861.
b. June 08, 1814 in Ipsden, England
d. April 11, 1884 in London, England

Olivier Rebbot
French photojournalist
• Freelance photographer who covered Nicaraguan civil war, Iranian revolution; died of gunshot wounds in El Salvadorean civil war.
b. 1949 in France
d. February 1, 1981 in Hialeah, Florida

John Francisco Rechy
American author
• Novels concern underground homosexual life: *City of Night*, 1963.
b. March 1, 1934 in El Paso, Texas

Ishmael Scott Reed
American author
• Satirist; books include *Chattanooga*, 1973; *Flight to Canada*, 1976.
b. February 22, 1938 in Chattanooga, Tennessee

John Silas Reed
American author–journalist
• Wrote *Ten Days That Shook the World*, 1919, considered finest eyewitness account of Russian Revolution; film *Reds* based on his life, 1981; only American buried in Red Square, Moscow.
b. October 22, 1887 in Portland, Oregon
d. October 19, 1920 in Mosocw, U.S.S.R.

Myrtle Reed
(Katherine LaFarge Norton pseud)
American author
• Popular novelist; wrote best-selling *Lavender and Old Lace*, 1902.
b. September 27, 1874 in Chicago, Illinois
d. August 17, 1911 in Chicago, Illinois

Rex Reed
American critic–journalist
• Syndicated film critic noted for gossipy accounts of Hollywood greats.
b. October 02, 1939 in Fort Worth, Texas

Ennis (Samuel, Jr) Rees
American children's author
• Books include *Tiny Tall Tales*, 1967; *The Little Green Alphabet Book*, 1968.
b. March 17, 1925 in Newport News, Virginia

Lizette Woodworth Reese
American poet
• Wrote verse volume *Wild Cherry*, 1923; popular sonnet "Tears."
b. January 09, 1856 in Waverly, Maryland
d. December 17, 1935

Erich Maria Remarque
(Erich Paul Remark)
American author
• Wrote *All Quiet on the Western Front*, 1929; adapted to film, 1930.
b. June 22, 1898 in Osnabruck, Germany
d. September 25, 1970 in Locarno, Switzerland

James Barrett Reston
American journalist
• Wrote *NY Times* column, "Washington," 1974-87; won Pulitzers for nat. reporting, 1945, 1957.
b. November 03, 1909 in Clydebank, Scotland

David Robert Reuben
American psychiatrist–author
• Wrote *Everything You Always Wanted to Know About Sex*, 1969.
b. July 29, 1933 in Chicago, Illinois

Paul Julius Von Reuter
(Israel Beer Josaphat)
English journalist
• Founded news service using telegraph lines, carrier pidgeons, 1849; now called Reuter's News Agency.
b. 1816 in Kassel, Germany
d. February 25, 1899

Kenneth Rexroth
American poet
• Beat generation writer, 1950s; interested in mystical forms of experience.
b. December 22, 1905 in South Bend, Indiana
d. June 06, 1982 in Montecito, California

Margret (Elizabeth) Rey
American children's author
• Collaborated with husband, Hans, on *Curious George* books, 1941-66.
b. May 1906 in Hamburg, Germany

Wladyslaw Stanislaw Reymont
Polish author
• Known for *The Peasants*, 1902-09, prose epic of village life; won Nobel Prize, 1924.
b. May 1867 in Kobiele Wielkie, Poland
d. December 05, 1925 in Warsaw, Poland

Jean Rhys, pseud
(Ella Gwendolen Rees Williams)
English author
• Wrote *After Leaving Mr. MacKenzie*, 1931; *Good Morning, Midnight*, 1939.
b. August 24, 1894 in Rosea , Dominica, West Indies
d. May 14, 1979 in Exeter, England

Alice Caldwell Hegan Rice
American children's author
• Wrote classic *Mrs. Wiggs of the Cabbage Patch*, 1901.
b. January 11, 1870 in Shelbyville, Kentucky
d. February 1, 1942 in Louisville, Kentucky

Anne Rice
American author
• Wrote best-sellers, *Interview with a Vampire*, 1976; *The Feast of All Saints*, 1980.
b. October 04, 1941 in New Orleans, Louisiana

Craig Rice, pseud
(Georgiana Ann Randolph)
American author
• Wrote detective fiction with a comic touch: *Trial by Fury*, 1941.
b. June 05, 1908 in Chicago, Illinois
d. August 28, 1957 in Los Angeles, California

Grantland (Henry Grantland) Rice
American journalist–poet
• Coined term "the four horsemen" to describe U of Notre Dame football players; won 1943 Oscar for best one-reel film; wrote syndicated column "The Sportlight" from 1930.
b. November 01, 1880 in Murfreesboro, Tennessee
d. July 13, 1954 in New York, New York

Adrienne Cecile Rich
American poet
• Works explore themes of sexuality, relationships: *Diving into the Wreck: Poems 1971-72*.
b. May 16, 1929 in Baltimore, Maryland

Laura Elizabeth Howe Richards
(Mrs Henry Richards)
American author
• Daughter of Julia and Samuel Howe; wrote classic children's tale *Captain January*, 1910; movie starred Shirley Temple, 1936.
b. February 27, 1850 in Boston, Massachusetts
d. January 14, 1943 in Gardiner, Maine

Dorothy Miller Richardson
English author
• One of first to use "stream of consciousness" style; wrote 13-vol. novel, *Pilgrimage*.
b. May 17, 1873 in Abingdon, England
d. June 17, 1957 in Beckenham, England

Henry Handel Richardson, pseud
(Ethel Florence Lindsey Richardson; Henrietta Richardson Robertson)
Australian author
• Wrote trilogy of novels, *The Fortunes of Richard Mahony*, 1917-30.
b. January 03, 1870 in Melbourne, Australia
d. March 2, 1946 in Hastings, England

Samuel Richardson
English author
• Wrote *Pamela or Virtue Rewarded*, 1740, often considered first modern English novel.
b. July 31, 1689 in Derbyshire, England
d. July 04, 1761 in London, England

Mordecai Richler
Canadian author
• Wrote *The Apprenticeship of Duddy Kravitz*, 1959; filmed, 1974.
b. January 27, 1931 in Montreal, Quebec

Conrad Michael Richter
American author
• Won 1951 Pulitzer for *The Town*.
b. November 13, 1890 in Pine Grove, Pennsylvania
d. October 3, 1968 in Pottsville, Pennsylvania

Bernard Herman Ridder
American newspaper publisher
• Last of three surviving sons in Ridder Publications family; chm. emeritus, 1973; merged with Knight Newspapers, 1974.
b. March 2, 1883 in New York, New York
d. May 05, 1975 in West Palm Beach, Florida

Laura Riding
(Laura Riding Jackson)
American writer
• Wrote verse, fiction, criticism, including novel *Trojan Ending*, 1937; often collaborated with Robert Graves.
b. January 16, 1901 in New York, New York

Jeremy Rifkin
American author–political activist
• Wrote *Algeny*, 1983; *Declaration of a Heretic*, 1985.
b. 1945 in Chicago, Illinois

Jacob August Riis
American journalist
• NYC police reporter, 1877-88; exposed slum conditions; wrote autobiography, *Making of an American*, 1901.
b. May 03, 1849 in Ribe, Denmark
d. May 26, 1914 in Barre, Massachusetts

James Whitcomb Riley
American poet
• Wrote poems "Little Orphan Annie"; "The Raggedy Man."
b. October 07, 1849 in Greenfield, Indiana
d. July 22, 1916 in Indianapolis, Indiana

(Jean Nicolas) Arthur Rimbaud
French poet
• Wrote only from ages 16-19; great influence on Symbolist movement.
b. October 2, 1854 in Charlesville, France
d. November 1, 1891 in Marseilles, France

Frederick Roberts Rinehart
American publisher
• A founder, Farrar and Rinehart, 1929, with brother Stanley.
b. 1903 in Allegheny, Pennsylvania
d. June 15, 1981 in New York, New York

Mary Roberts Rinehart
American author–dramatist
• Wrote popular novels, mysteries including *The Circular Staircase*, 1908; *Tish*, 1916; mother of Frederick, Stanley.
b. August 12, 1876 in Pittsburgh, Pennsylvania
d. September 22, 1958 in New York, New York

Stanley Marshall Rinehart, Jr
American publisher
• A founder, Farrar and Rinehart, 1929, which became Holt, Rinehart & Winston, 1960.
b. August 18, 1897 in Pittsburgh, Pennsylvania
d. April 26, 1969 in South Miami, Florida

Robert J Ringer
American author
• Wrote *Looking Out for #1*, 1977.
b. 1938

Barbara Jean Rinkoff
American children's author
• First book, *A Map is a Picture*, 1965, used as elementary school text.
b. January 25, 1923 in New York, New York
d. February 18, 1975 in Mount Kisco, New York

Alexandra Ripley
American author
• Chosen by Margaret Mitchell's estate, 1988, to write sequel to *Gone with the Wind*.
b. January 08, 1934 in Charleston, South Carolina

Thomas Ritchie
American journalist
• Encouraged by Thomas Jefferson, he founded *Richmond Enquirer*, 1804; *Washington Union*, semi-official organ for President Polk, 1845; his journalism was powerful influence on nat. politics.
b. November 05, 1778 in Tappahannock, Virginia
d. December 03, 1854 in Washington, District of Columbia

Amelie Louise Rives
American author
• Wrote novel *Shadows of Flames*, 1915; one of earliest realistic accounts of drug addiction.
b. August 23, 1863 in Richmond, Virginia
d. June 15, 1945 in Charlottesville, Virginia

Garland Roark
(George Garland pseud)
American author
• Adventure stories include *Wake of the Red Witch*, 1946; *Should the Wind be Fair*, 1960.
b. July 26, 1904 in Grosebeck, Texas
d. February 09, 1985 in Nacogdoches, Texas

Harold Robbins
American author
• Known for commercially rather than critically successful novels, including one of the most read in history: *The Carpetbaggers*, 1961.
b. May 21, 1916 in New York, New York

Paul Robert
French lexicographer–author
• Compiled *Le Robert*, established as standard dictionary for contemporary French usage, 1964.
b. October 09, 1910 in Orleansville, Algeria
d. August 11, 1980 in Mougins, France

Sir Charles George Douglas Roberts
Canadian author
• Developed modern Canadian literature; wrote novels, verses of maritime provinces.
b. January 1, 1860 in Douglas, New Brunswick
d. November 26, 1943 in Toronto, Ontario

Kenneth Lewis Roberts
American author
• Noted for historical novels including *Northwest Passage*, 1937; adapted to film, 1940; won special Pulitzer, 1957.
b. December 08, 1885 in Kennebunk, Maine
d. July 21, 1957 in Kennebunkport, Maine

Denise Naomi Robins
(Ashley French; Harriet Gray; Julia Kane pseuds)
English author
• Her 200 romance novels include *Dark Corridor*.
b. February 01, 1897 in London, England
d. May 01, 1985 in London, England

Edwin Arlington Robinson
American poet
• Pulitzer winners include *Collected Poems*, 1921; *Man Who Died Twice*, 1924; narrative poem, *Tristram*, 1927.
b. December 22, 1869 in Head Tide, Maine
d. April 06, 1935 in New York, New York

Henry Morton Robinson
American author–poet
• Wrote best-selling novel *The Cardinal*, 1950.
b. September 07, 1898 in Boston, Massachusetts
d. January 13, 1961 in New York, New York

Joan Mary Gale Thomas Robinson
English children's author
• Self-illustrated books include *Teddy Robinson; Mary-Mary* series.
b. 1910 in Gerrards Cross, England

M(aurice) R(ichard) Robinson
American editor–publisher
• Founded Scholastic Magazines Inc., 1920.
b. December 24, 1895 in Wilkinsburg, Pennsylvania
d. February 07, 1982 in Pelham, New York

Selden Rodman
American writer
• Best known for narrative poem, "Lawrence: The Last Crusade," 1937; books include *Haiti: The Black Republic*, 1954.
b. February 19, 1909 in New York, New York

Edward Payson Roe
American clergyman–author
• Wrote best-selling novels *Barriers Burned Away*, 1872; *Opening a Chestnut Burr*, 1874.
b. March 07, 1838 in New Windsor, New York
d. July 19, 1888 in Cornwall-on-Hudson, New York

Theodore (Huebner) Roethke
American poet
• Among many award-winning works: *The Waking: Poems 1933-53*, 1954, won Pulitzer; *Words for the Wind*, 1958, won Bollingen.
b. May 25, 1908 in Saginaw, Michigan
d. August 01, 1963 in Bainbridge Isle, Washington

Carl Ransom Rogers
American psychologist–author
• Iconoclast who pioneered development of encounter groups, "self-actualization"; wrote *On Becoming a Person*, 1961.
b. January 08, 1902 in Oak Park, Illinois
d. February 04, 1987 in La Jolla, California

Rosemary Rogers
(Marina Mayson pseud)
American author
• Romantic, fantasy novels include *The Crowd Pleasers*, 1978; *Love Play*, 1981.
b. December 07, 1933 in Panadura, Ceylon

Sax Rohmer, pseud
(Arthur Sarsfield Ward)
English author
• Best known for "Fu-Manchu" series, which includes more than 30 novels.
b. February 15, 1883 in London, England
d. June 01, 1959 in London, England

Fernando de Rojas
Spanish author
• Wrote Spanish classic *La Celestina*, 1499, considered comparable to *Don Quixote*.
b. 1475 in Toledo, Spain
d. April 1541 in Talavera, Spain

Betty Rollin
American author–broadcast journalist
• Wrote *First, You Cry*, 1976; TV movie starred Mary Tyler Moore.
b. January 03, 1936 in New York, New York

Jules Romains
French author–philosopher
• Founded literary movement, Unanimisme, 1908; wrote 27-vol. *Men of Good Will*, 1932-46.
b. August 26, 1885 in Velay, France
d. August 14, 1972 in Paris, France

Irma von Starkloff Rombauer
American author
• Wrote *The Joy of Cooking*, first published 1931, the most popular American cookbook in mid-20th c.
b. October 3, 1877 in Saint Louis, Missouri
d. October 14, 1962 in Saint Louis, Missouri

Pierre de Ronsard
French poet
• Leader of the Pleiade; helped establish French sonnet; wrote *Amours*, 1552-59.
b. September 11, 1524 in Vendomois, France
d. December 26, 1585 in Touraine, France

Abraham Simon Wolf Rosenbach
American bookseller–author
• Legendary rare-book dealer; helped build America's finest book collections; wrote three memoirs.
b. July 22, 1876 in Philadelphia, Pennsylvania
d. July 01, 1952 in Philadelphia, Pennsylvania

Alvin Hirsch Rosenfeld
American editor–author
• Most of his writings deal with Holocaust: *A Double Dying: Reflections on Holocaust Literature*, 1980.
b. April 28, 1938 in Philadelphia, Pennsylvania

Abraham Michael Rosenthal
Canadian editor–author
• Executive editor of *NY Times* since 1977.
b. May 02, 1922 in Sault St. Marie, Ontario

Harry Roskolenko
(Colin Ross pseud)
American author
• Writings draw on his extensive travel; autobiography *When I Was Last on Cherry Street*, 1965 tells of his early life in NYC.
b. September 21, 1907 in New York, New York
d. July 17, 1980 in New York, New York

Harold Ross
American editor
• With financial backing from heir to Fleischman yeast fortune, founded *New Yorker* mag., 1925.
b. November 06, 1892 in Aspen, Colorado
d. December 06, 1951 in Boston, Massachusetts

Ishbel Ross
American author
• Wrote novels, biographies of famous women: *The President's Wife*, 1972.
b. 1897 in Scotland
d. September 21, 1975 in New York, New York

Christina Georgina Rossetti
English poet
• Often modeled for brother, Dante; best verse appears in *Goblin Market*, 1862.
b. December 05, 1830 in London, England
d. December 29, 1894 in London, England

Judith Rossner
American author
• Wrote *Looking for Mr. Goodbar*, 1975; filmed, 1977.
b. March 01, 1935 in New York, New York

Theodore Roszak
American historian–author
• Writings condemn technocratic culture: *The Making of a Counter Culture*, 1969.
b. 1933 in Chicago, Illinois

Henry Roth
American author
• Wrote novel recalling ghetto life: *Call It Sleep*, 1934; reprinted and rediscovered, 1960.
b. February 08, 1906 in Austria-Hungary

Philip Milton Roth
American author
• Won National Book Award for *Goodbye Columbus*, 1959, adapted to movie; wrote controversial best seller, *Portnoy's Complaint*, 1969.
b. March 19, 1933 in Newark, New Jersey

Esmond Cecil Harmsworth Rothermere, Viscount
English newspaper publisher–politician
• Owner of Britain's largest newspaper chain, inherited from his father, Harold S Harmsworth.
b. May 29, 1898 in London, England
d. July 12, 1978 in London, England

Harold Sidney Harmsworth Rothermere
English journalist
• Owner, publisher of several newspaper chains in Britain including *London Daily Mail*, 1890s-1940.
b. April 26, 1868
d. November 26, 1940 in Hamilton, Bermuda

Jean Jacques Rousseau
French philosopher–author
• Influential political, educational reformer; wrote *Social Contract*, 1762; *Confessions*, published, 1781.
b. June 28, 1712 in Geneva, Switzerland
d. July 02, 1778 in Ermenonville, France

Carl Thomas Rowan
American presidential aide–journalist
• First black man to sit on National Security Council, 1964-65; has written syndicated newspaper column since 1965.
b. August 11, 1925 in Ravenscraft, Tennessee

Nicholas Rowe
English poet–dramatist
• Poet laureate from 1715; tragic plays include *Tamerlane*, 1702; noted as first modern editor of Shakespeare.
b. June 2, 1674 in Little Barford, England
d. December 06, 1718 in London, England

Gabrielle Roy
Canadian author
• Wrote *The Tin Flute*, 1945; adapted to film, 1983.
b. March 22, 1909 in Saint Boniface, Manitoba
d. July 13, 1983 in Quebec City, Quebec

Anne Newport Royall
American journalist–traveler
• Sometimes called first American newspaperwoman; published Washington gossip sheet, 1830.
b. June 11, 1769 in Baltimore, Maryland
d. October 01, 1854 in Washington, District of Columbia

Mike Royko
American journalist
• Reporter, columnist with Chicago newspapers, 1959–; won Pulitzer for commentary, 1972.
b. September 19, 1932 in Chicago, Illinois

Vermont Connecticut Royster
American newspaper editor
• Columnist, *Wall Street Journal*, 1948–; won Pulitzer, 1953, for editorial writing.
b. April 3, 1914 in Raleigh, North Carolina

Vasili Rozanov
Russian author
• Published first detailed account of Dostoyevski: *Legend of the Grand Inquisitor*, 1890.
b. 1856 in Vetluga, Russia
d. 1919

Robert Chester Ruark
American author
• Best-selling works include *Horn of the Hunter*, 1953; wrote autobiography *Old Man and the Boy*, 1957.
b. December 29, 1915 in Wilmington, North Carolina
d. July 01, 1965 in London, England

Muriel Rukeyser
American poet
• Comprehensive collection of poetry released in 1979: *The Collected Poems of Muriel Rukeyser*; wrote on social themes, feminism.
b. December 15, 1913 in New York, New York
d. February 12, 1980 in New York, New York

William Simon Rukeyser
American editor
• Managing editor, *Fortune*, 1980-86; commentator, TV's "Good Morning America," 1978-85.
b. June 08, 1939 in New York, New York

Johan Ludwig Runeberg
Finnish poet
• Finland's greatest poet; composed national hymn; wrote in Swedish *Kung Fjalar*, 1844.
b. February 05, 1804 in Jakobstad, Finland
d. May 06, 1877 in Borga, Finland

Damon (Alfred Damon) Runyon
American journalist–author
• Used slang, metaphors in writings of romanticized underworld criminals; wrote *Guys and Dolls*, 1932.
b. October 04, 1884 in Manhattan, Kansas
d. December 1, 1946 in New York, New York

Salman Ahmed Rushdie
British author
• His novel *The Satanic Verses*, 1989, condemned by Muslims as blasphemous to Islam; sentenced to death by Ayatollah Khomeini, 1989; in hiding since sentence.
b. June 19, 1947 in Bombay, India

Bertrand Arthur William Russell
English mathematician–author
• Wrote popular books on philosophy, *Principia Mathematica*, 1910-13; won Nobel Prize, 1950.
b. May 18, 1872 in Monmouthshire, Wales
d. February 02, 1970 in Merionethshire, Wales

Solveig Paulson Russell
American children's author
• Informational books include *Johnny Appleseed*, 1967; *The Mushmen*, 1968.
b. March 1904 in Salt Lake City, Utah

Claude Ryan
Canadian journalist
• Publisher, *Le Devoir*, newspaper in Montreal, 1964-78; entered liberal politics, 1978–.
b. January 26, 1925 in Montreal, Quebec

Cornelius John Ryan
American journalist
• Noted for lively accounts of WW II history; writings include *The Longest Day: June 6, 1944*, 1959, co-wrote screenplay for film, 1972.
b. June 05, 1920 in Dublin, Ireland
d. November 23, 1974 in New York, New York

Ernesto Sabato
Argentine author
• Works examine human condition, survival of moral values; won Miguel de Cervantes Prize, 1985.
b. June 24, 1911 in Rojas, Argentina

Leopold von Sacher-Masoch
Austrian author
• Word "masochism" derived from abnormality often depicted in his novels.
b. January 27, 1836 in Lemberg, Austria
d. March 09, 1895

Nelly (Leonie) Sachs
German poet
• Won Nobel Prize in literature, 1966, for poetry, dramas.
b. December 1, 1891 in Berlin, Germany
d. May 12, 1970 in Stockholm, Sweden

Edward Charles Sackville-West
English author–critic
• Witty novels include *Piano Quintet*, 1925; *The Sun in Capricorn*, 1934; son of Victoria Mary.
b. November 13, 1901
d. 1965

Victoria Mary Sackville-West
(Mrs Harold Nicholson)
English poet–author
• Wrote *The Edwardians*, 1930, *Pepita*, 1937; mother of Nigel and Benjamin.
b. March 09, 1892 in Sevenoaks, England
d. June 02, 1962 in Cranbrook, England

Marquis (Donatien Alphonse Francoise) de Sade
French author
• Works first considered pornographic; believed sexual, criminal acts to be normal; term sadism derived from name.
b. June 02, 1740 in Paris, France
d. December 02, 1814 in Charenton, France

William L Safire
American author–journalist
• Washington columnist, *NY Times*, 1973–; won Pulitzer, 1978.
b. December 17, 1929 in New York, New York

Francoise Sagan, pseud
(Francoise Quoirez)
French author
• Wrote award-winning *Bonjour Tristesse*, 1945, filmed, 1958.
b. June 21, 1935 in Cajarc, France

Antoine (Jean Baptiste Marie Roger) de Saint-Exupery
French author–aviator
• Wrote fable *The Little Prince*, 1943; autobiography *Wind, Sand, and Stars*, 1939; opened transatlantic airmail routes to S America, Africa.
b. June 29, 1900 in Lyons, France
d. July 31, 1944 in France

J(erome) D(avid) Salinger
American author
• Best known for poignant human comedy, *Catcher in the Rye*, 1951, popular with teens at the time.
b. January 01, 1919 in New York, New York

Harrison Evans Salisbury
American journalist
• Staff writer with *NY Times*, 1949-73; won Pulitzer, 1955; best-sellers include *Black Nights, White Snow*, 1978.
b. November 14, 1908 in Minneapolis, Minnesota

Felix Salten, pseud
(Siegmund Salzmann)
Hungarian children's author
• Wrote *Bambi*, 1926, translated, 1928, as *Bambi: A Life in the Woods*.
b. September 06, 1869 in Budapest, Hungary
d. October 08, 1945 in Zurich, Switzerland

Ernest Samuels
American educator–author
• Won Pulitzer for three-vol. biography on Henry Adams, 1965.
b. May 19, 1903 in Chicago, Illinois

George Sand, pseud
(Amandine Aurore Lucie Dupin Dudevant)
French author
• Novels include *Lelia*, 1833; noted for her unconventionality, liaison with Chopin.
b. September 01, 1804 in Paris, France
d. June 08, 1876 in Nohant, France

Carl August Sandburg
American poet–author
• Won three Pulitzers in Poetry, 1918, 1940, 1951.
b. January 06, 1878 in Galesburg, Illinois
d. July 22, 1967 in Flat Rock, North Carolina

Helga Sandburg
American children's author
• Young adults novels include *Gingerbread*, 1964; daughter of Carl.
b. November 24, 1918 in Elmhurst, Illinois

Lawrence Sanders
American author
• Best-selling novels include *The Anderson Tapes*, 1970, filmed 1971; *The First Deadly Sin*, 1973.
b. 1920 in New York, New York

Mari Sandoz
American author
• Wrote *Old Jules*, 1935; books on Indians include *These Were the Sioux*, 1961.
b. 1900 in Sheridan County, Nebraska
d. March 1, 1966 in New York, New York

Paul Sann
American journalist
• Executive editor, *NY Post*, 1949-77; non-fiction books include *The Lawless Decade*, 1957.
b. March 07, 1914 in Brooklyn, New York

William Sansom
English author
• Best known for sketches of London life: *The Stories of William Sansom*, 1963.
b. January 18, 1912 in London, England
d. April 2, 1976 in London, England

George Santayana
American philosopher–author–educator
• Wrote philosophic *Realms of Being*, 1927-40; novel *Last Puritan*, 1935; memoirs *Persons and Places*, 1944-53.
b. December 16, 1863 in Madrid, Spain
d. September 26, 1952 in Rome, Italy

Inigo Lopez de Mendoza Santillana
Spanish poet
• First to write sonnets in Spanish.
b. August 19, 1398 in Carrion, Spain
d. March 25, 1458 in Guadalajara, Spain

Helen Hooven Santmyer
American author
• Wrote in obscurity for 60 yrs. before republication of fourth book "...And Ladies of the Club," 1984, became best-seller.
b. November 25, 1895 in Xenia, Ohio
d. February 21, 1986 in Xenia, Ohio

Sappho
Greek poet
• Lyric poet often compared to Homer; poems celebrate love of women.
b. 612BC in Greece
d. in Sicily

Jean Francois Sarasin
French author
• Wrote witty, satirical verse, popular with Parisian society, 1640s.
b. 1614
d. December 05, 1654

May Sarton
American author–poet
• Writings include verse vol. *A Durable Fire*, 1972; novel *As We Are Now*, 1973.
b. May 03, 1912 in Wondelgem, Belgium

Jean-Paul Sartre
French author–dramatist
• Major exponent of 20th-c. existentialism; wrote *Being and Nothingness*, 1943; refused Nobel Prize in literature, 1964.
b. June 21, 1905 in Paris, France
d. April 15, 1980 in Paris, France

Siegfried Sassoon
English poet–soldier–author
• Prize-winning *Memoirs of a Fox-Hunting Man*, 1928, best known of semi-autobiographical trilogy.
b. September 08, 1886 in Brenchley, England
d. September 01, 1967 in Purton, England

Marilyn vos Savant
(Mrs Robert Jarvik)
American journalist
• IQ of 228 is highest ever recorded; column, "Ask Marilyn," appears in *Parade* magazine.
b. August 11, 1946 in Saint Louis, Missouri

Ruth Sawyer
American children's author
• Won Newbery Medal for autobiography *Roller Skates*, 1936.
b. August 05, 1880 in Boston, Massachusetts
d. June 03, 1970

Richard Scarry
American children's author–illustrator
• Prolific writer of "best ever" picture books; won Edgar mystery award, 1976.
b. June 05, 1919 in Boston, Massachusetts

Jack Warner Schaefer
American author
• Wrote dozens of Western novels including *Shane*, 1949, adapted to film, 1953, translated into 35 languages.
b. November 19, 1907 in Cleveland, Ohio
d. January 24, 1991 in Santa Fe, Minnesota

Sydney H Schanberg
American journalist
• Columnist, associate editor, *NY Times*, 1959–; won Pulitzer, 1976.
b. January 17, 1934 in Clinton, Massachusetts

Robert Scheer
American journalist
• Anti-war activist, 1960s; wrote *How the United States Got Involved in Vietnam*, 1965; reporter, *LA Times*, 1976–.
b. April 14, 1936 in New York, New York

Harry Scherman
American publisher–author
• Co-founded Book of the Month Club, 1926.
b. February 01, 1887 in Montreal, Quebec
d. November 12, 1969 in New York, New York

Philip K(latz) Scheuer
American critic–editor
• Film, drama critic, LA *Times*, 1927-67.
b. March 24, 1902 in Newark, New Jersey
d. February 18, 1985 in Hollywood, California

Richard Schickel
American critic–author
• *Time* magazine movie critic, 1973–.
b. February 1, 1933 in Milwaukee, Wisconsin

Dorothy Schiff
American publisher–journalist
• First woman publisher in US; bought controlling interest in *New York Post*, 1939; responsible for turning it into a tabloid with scandal, glamour, columnists; sold to Rupert Murdoch, 1976.
b. March 11, 1903 in New York, New York
d. August 3, 1989 in New York, New York

Miriam Schlein
(Miriam Weiss)
American children's author
• Writer since 1952: *Giraffe: The Silent Giant*, 1976; *The Boy Who Became Pharaoh*, 1979.
b. June 06, 1926 in Brooklyn, New York

Arthur Meier Schlesinger, Jr
American historian–author
• Special asst. to presidents Kennedy, Johnson, 1961-64; wrote *A Thousand Days*, 1965; *Robert Kennedy and His Times*, 1978.
b. October 15, 1917 in Columbus, Ohio

Eduard Schmid
(Kasimir Edschmid pseud)
German author
• Wrote first German expressionist novellas.
b. October 05, 1890 in Darmstadt, Germany
d. August 31, 1966 in Vulpera, Switzerland

David Schoenbrun
American journalist
• War correspondent for CBS News, 1945-63; ABC News, 1963-79; author of seven best-selling books: *Soldiers of the Night*, 1980.
b. March 15, 1915 in New York, New York
d. May 23, 1988 in New York, New York

Jackson Volney Scholz
American track athlete–children's author
• Finished second in 1924 Olympic race which was adapted into 1981 film *Chariots of Fire*; wrote boys' sports books.
b. March 15, 1897 in Buchanan, Michigan
d. October 26, 1986 in Delray Beach, Florida

Hermann Otto Ludwig Schreiber
(Lujo Bassermann pseud)
Austrian historian–author
• Books include *Vanished Cities*, 1957; *The Oldest Profession*, 1967.
b. May 04, 1920 in Wiener Neustadt, Austria

Max Lincoln Schuster
American publisher
• Founded Simon and Schuster, with Richard Simon, 1924.
b. March 02, 1897 in Kalusz, Austria
d. December 2, 1970

Paul Mark Scott
English author
• Wrote novels *The Raj Quartet*, 1976, adapted for TV, 1982.
b. March 25, 1920 in London, England
d. March 01, 1978 in London, England

Sir Walter Scott
Scottish poet–author–historian
• Father of historical novel; writings include *Ivanhoe*, 1820.
b. August 15, 1771 in Edinburgh, Scotland
d. September 21, 1832 in Abbotsford, Scotland

Charles Scribner
American publisher
• Founded Baker and Scribner Publishers, 1846; changed to Charles Scribner's Sons, 1878.
b. February 21, 1821 in New York, New York
d. August 26, 1871 in Lucerne, Switzerland

Edward Wyllis Scripps
American newspaper publisher
• Formed Scripps-McRae League of Newspapers which evolved into Scripps-Howard Newspapers; developed United Press International.
b. June 18, 1854 in Rushville, Illinois
d. March 12, 1926 in Monrovia, Liberia

Robert Paine Scripps
American journalist
• Editorial director of Scripps-Howard newspaper chain from 1917.
b. October 27, 1895 in San Diego, California
d. March 02, 1938

Madeleine de Scudery
French author
• Wrote huge novels, which epitomized sentimental romances of her day: *Almahide, or the Slave as Queen*, 1660-63.
b. 1607 in Le Havre, France
d. June 02, 1701 in Paris, France

Jenny Seed
South African author
• Children's historical novels include *The Bushman's Dream*, 1974.
b. May 18, 1930 in Cape Town, South Africa

Alan Seeger
American poet
• Wrote "I Have a Rendevous with Death," 1916; killed in WW I.
b. June 22, 1888 in New York, New York
d. July 04, 1916 in Belloy en Senterre, France

Giorgos Styljanou Seferiades
Greek author–diplomat
• Won 1963 Nobel Prize in literature; best known for unique style of poetry.
b. February 22, 1900
d. September 2, 1971 in Athens, Greece

Henry Segal
American journalist
• Editor, publisher of *American Israelite*, 1930-85, oldest English-Jewish newspaper in US.
b. 1901
d. July 18, 1985 in Cincinnati, Ohio

Lore Groszmann Segal
American author
• Children's fiction include *Lucinella*, 1976; *Tell Me a Trudy*, 1977.
b. March 08, 1928 in Vienna, Austria

Jaroslav Seifert
Czech poet
• Won Nobel Prize for literature, 1984.
b. September 23, 1901 in Prague, Czechoslovakia
d. January 1, 1986 in Prague, Czechoslovakia

Hubert Selby, Jr
American author
• Wrote *Last Exit to Brooklyn*, 1964, subject of obscenity trial in England, banned in Italy.
b. July 23, 1928 in New York, New York

George Henry Seldes
American journalist
• Foreign correspondent, *Chicao Tribune*, 1919-28; advocate for freedom of the press; wrote *Even the Gods Cannot Change History*, 1976; *Witness to a Century*, 1987.
b. November 16, 1890 in Alliance, New Jersey

Gilbert Vivian Seldes
American critic–author–editor
• CBS program director, 1937-45; wrote *The Seven Lively Arts*, 1924; novel *The Wings of the Eagle*, 1929; brother of George.
b. January 03, 1893 in Alliance, New Jersey
d. September 29, 1970 in New York, New York

Samuel Dickson Selvon
(Sam Selvon pseud)
Trinidadian author
• Novels focus on Caribbean life: *Moses Ascending*, 1975; *I Hear Thunder*, 1963.
b. May 2, 1923 in Trinidad

Ramon Jose Sender
Spanish author
• Numerous strong novels include *Counterattack in Spain*, 1937; award-winning *Mr. Witt among the Rebels*, 1935.
b. February 03, 1902 in Alcolea de Cinca, Spain
d. January 15, 1982 in San Diego, California

John Herman Henry Sengstacke
American newspaper publisher
• President, editor of influential black newspaper *Chicago Defender* and affiliates since 1940; founded Negro Newspaper Publishers' Assn., 1940.
b. November 25, 1912 in Savannah, Georgia

Kate Seredy
Hungarian children's author–illustrator
• Won 1938 Newbery Medal for *The White Stag*.
b. November 1, 1899 in Budapest, Hungary
d. March 07, 1975 in Middletown, New York

Anya Chase Seton
American author
• Best-selling novels *Dragonwyck*, 1944, *Foxfire*, 1951, made into Hollywood movies; daughter of Ernest Thompson Seton.
b. 1916 in New York, New York
d. November 08, 1990 in Greenwich, Connecticut

Ernest Thompson Seton
American naturalist–author
• Noted animal fiction writer; instrumental in founding the Boy Scouts of America, 1910.
b. August 14, 1860 in South Shields, England
d. October 23, 1946 in Santa Fe, New Mexico

Doctor Seuss, pseud
(Theodore Seuss Geisel)
American children's author–illustrator
• Wrote *How The Grinch Stole Christmas*, 1957; *The Cat in the Hat*, 1957; *Green Egg and Ham*, 1960. Known for word play, rhymes.
b. March 02, 1904 in Springfield, Massachusetts

Anna Seward
English poet
• Wrote poetic novel *Louisa*, 1782; provided James Boswell gossip about Samuel Johnson.
b. December 12, 1747 in Eyam, England
d. March 25, 1809 in Lichfield, England

Anna Sewell
English author
• Wrote *Black Beauty*, 1877.
b. March 3, 1820 in Yarmouth, England
d. April 25, 1878 in Norwich, England

Anne Harvey Sexton
American poet
• Wrote "confessional" verse; won Pulitzer for *Live or Die*, 1967; committed suicide.
b. November 09, 1928 in Newton, Massachusetts
d. October 04, 1974 in Weston, Massachusetts

Anthony Shaffer
English author
• Won 1971 Tony for *Sleuth*.
b. May 15, 1926 in Liverpool, England

William Shakespeare
(Bard of Avon)
English dramatist-poet
• Considered greatest dramatist ever; wrote 154 sonnets, 37 plays.
b. April 23, 1564 in Stratford-on-Avon, England
d. April 23, 1616 in Stratford-on-Avon, England

Karl Jay Shapiro
American poet–critic
• Poems of WW II, *V-Letters & Other Poems*, won Pulitzer Prize, 1945.
b. November 1, 1913 in Baltimore, Maryland

Marjorie Weinman Sharmat
American children's author
• Prolific writer of books for juveniles: *Rex*, 1967, *Mooch the Messy*, 1976.
b. November 12, 1928 in Portland, Maine

William Sharp
(Fiona MacLeod pseud)
Scottish poet–author
• Wrote literary biographies, novels under own name; mystical verse prose under feminine pseudonym.
b. September 12, 1855 in Paisley, Scotland
d. December 12, 1905 in Sicily

Irwin Shaw
American author–dramatist
• Wrote *Rich Man, Poor Man*, 1970.
b. February 27, 1913 in Brooklyn, New York
d. May 16, 1984 in Davos, Switzerland

William Shawn
American editor
• Editor, *New Yorker* mag., 1952-88; second editor in mag.'s history.
b. August 31, 1907 in Chicago, Illinois

Gail Henion Sheehy
American journalist–author
• Wrote *Passages: Predictable Crises of Adult Life*, 1976.
b. November 27, 1937 in Mamaroneck, New York

Alice Hastings Bradley Sheldon
(Raccoona Sheldon; James Tiptree Jr pseuds)
American author
• Science fiction novelist; works include *Starry Rift*, 1986, *Brightness Falls from the Air*, 1985.
b. August 24, 1915 in Chicago, Illinois
d. May 19, 1987 in McLean, Virginia

Sidney Sheldon
American author
• Wrote *The Other Side of Midnight*, 1973; *Rage of Angels*, 1980; several screenplays, TV series, plays.
b. February 11, 1917 in Chicago, Illinois

Mary Wollstonecraft Shelley
(Mrs Percy Bysshe Shelley)
English author
• Wrote *Frankenstein*, 1818.
b. August 3, 1797 in London, England
d. February 01, 1851 in Bournemouth, England

Percy Bysshe Shelley
English poet
• Romantic lyricist known for *Prometheus Unbound*, 1820.
b. August 04, 1792 in Field Place, England
d. July 08, 1822 in Viareggio, Italy

Odell Shepard
American author
• Co-founder, Thoreau Society of America; won Pulitzer for *Pedlar's Progress, the Life of Bronson Alcott*, 1938.
b. July 22, 1884 in Rock Falls, Illinois
d. July 19, 1967 in New London, Connecticut

Mary Martha Sherwood

English children's author
• Wrote children's classic *History of the Fairchild Family*, 1818-47.
b. May 06, 1775 in Stamford, England
d. September 22, 1851 in Worcester, England

Leon Shimkin

American publisher
• Helped build Simon & Schuster into leading book publisher, eventually becoming owner; responsible for publishing Carnegie's *How to Win Friends and Influence People*, 1937.
b. April 07, 1907 in Brooklyn, New York
d. May 25, 1988 in New Rochelle, New York

William L(awrence) Shirer

American author–journalist
• Blacklisted during McCarthy era for supporting Hollywood Ten; wrote bestsellers *Berlin Diary*, 1941, *The Rise and Fall of the Third Reich*, 1960.
b. February 23, 1904 in Chicago, Illinois

Mikhail Aleksandrovich Sholokhov

Russian author
• Novel *And Quiet Flows the Don*, depicted civil war as experienced by Cossack villagers; won Nobel Prize in literature, 1965.
b. May 24, 1905 in Kruzhilin, Russia
d. February 21, 1984 in Veshenskaya, U.S.S.R.

Susan Richards Shreve

American author
• Won Edgar for juvenile mystery: *Lucy Forever and Miss Rosetree*, 1987.
b. May 02, 1939 in Toledo, Ohio

Irving Shulman

American author–educator
• Novels include *The Amboy Dukes*, 1947; biographies: *Harlow: An Intimate Biography*, 1964; adapted to film, 1965.
b. May 21, 1913 in Brooklyn, New York

Nevil Shute

(Nevil Shute Norway)
English author–aeronautical engineer
• Best known for novel of nuclear holocaust, *On the Beach*, 1963.
b. January 17, 1899 in Ealing, England
d. January 12, 1960 in Melbourne, Australia

Elizabeth Eleanor Siddal

(Mrs Dante Gabriel Rossetti; "Lizzie")
English model–artist
• Body exhumed after death to recover manuscript Rossetti had buried with her.
b. 1834 in Sheffield, England
d. February 1, 1862

Algernon Sidney

English politician–author
• First to write "God helps those who help themselves" in English in *Discourses Government*, 1698; charged with treason, executed for part in Ryehouse Plot.
b. 1622 in Penshurst, England
d. December 07, 1683 in London, England

Henryk Adam Aleksander Pius Sienkiewicz

(Litwos pseud)
Polish author
• Best known for historical novel *Quo Vadis*, 1895; won Nobel Prize for literature, 1905.
b. May 05, 1846 in Okrzejska, Poland
d. November 15, 1916 in Vevey, Switzerland

Jon Silkin

English poet
• Books of verse include *The Lapidary Poems*, 1979.
b. 1930 in London, England

Edward Rowland Sill

American poet–educator
• Best known for *The Hermitage and Other Poems*, 1868.
b. April 29, 1841 in Windsor, Connecticut
d. February 27, 1887 in Cleveland, Ohio

Frans E Sillanpaa

Finnish author
• Wrote novel *The Maid Silja*, 1931; won 1939 Nobel Prize in literature.
b. September 16, 1888 in Hameenkyro, Finland
d. June 03, 1964 in Helsinki, Finland

Alan Sillitoe

English author
• Novels, short stories adapted to film: *Saturday Night and Sunday Morning*, 1958.
b. March 04, 1928 in Nottingham, England

Ignazio Silone

(Secondo Tranquilli)
Italian author
• Founding member, Italian Communist Party, 1921; wrote *Bread and Wine*, 1936.
b. May 01, 1900 in Pescina, Italy
d. August 22, 1978 in Geneva, Switzerland

Robert Silverberg

American author
• Science fiction books include *Lord Valentine's Castle*, 1980.
b. January 15, 1935 in New York, New York

Sime Silverman

American publisher
• Founder, editor of show business newspaper, *Variety*, 1905-33.
b. May 18, 1873 in Cortland, New York
d. September 22, 1933 in Los Angeles, California

Alvin Silverstein

(Dr A)
American children's author
• Scientific, juvenile books include *Human Anatomy & Physiology*, 1980.
b. December 3, 1933 in New York, New York

Shel(by) Silverstein

American cartoonist–children's author–illustrator
• Self-illustrated best-sellers include *Where the Sidewalk Ends*, 1974; *A Light in the Attic*, 1981.
b. 1932 in Chicago, Illinois

Clifford Donald Simak

American author
• Wrote highly acclaimed science fiction, fantasy novels; won three Hugos; first in Fandom Hall of Fame, 1973; Grand Master, 1979.
b. August 03, 1904 in Millville, Wisconsin
d. April 25, 1988 in Minneapolis, Minnesota

Georges Simenon

(Georges Sim)
Belgian author
• Wrote over 500 books; created Chief Inspector Maigret, the Parisian detective featured in over 80 mysteries.
b. February 13, 1903 in Liege, Belgium
d. September 04, 1989 in Lausanne, Switzerland

Charles Simic

American poet
• Wrote award-winning verse, *Return to a Place Lit by a Glass of Milk*, 1975.
b. May 09, 1938 in Belgrade, Yugoslavia

William Gilmore Simms

American author
• Works include romantic novel *Master Faber*, 1833; popular SC histories.
b. April 17, 1806 in Charleston, South Carolina
d. June 11, 1870 in Charleston, South Carolina

Claude Eugene Henri Simon

French author
• Won Nobel Prize, 1985, for pioneering work in new novel style of 1950s.
b. October 1, 1913 in Tananarive, Madagascar

Norma Feldstein Simon
American children's author
• Children are sources for writings: *All Kinds of Families*, 1976.
b. December 24, 1927 in New York, New York

Richard Leo Simon
American publisher
• With Max Schuster, founded Simon & Schuster Publishers, 1924.
b. March 06, 1899 in New York, New York
d. July 29, 1960 in Stamford, Connecticut

Howard Simons
American newspaper editor
• Managing editor, *Washington Post*, 1971-84; wrote *Simm's List Book*, 1977.
b. June 03, 1928 in Albany, New York
d. June 13, 1989 in Jacksonville Beach, Florida

Louis Simpson
(Louis Aston Marantz Simpson)
American author–poet
• Won 1964 Pulitzer for verse volume *At the End of the Open Road*.
b. March 27, 1923 in Kingston, Jamaica

Jo Sinclair, pseud
(Ruth Seid)
American author
• Novelist, short story writer: *The Changelings*, 1955.
b. July 01, 1913 in Brooklyn, New York

Upton Beall Sinclair
(Clarke Fitch; Frederick Garrison; Arthur Stirling pseuds)
American author
• Wrote *The Jungle*, 1906; 1943 Pulitzer winner *Dragon's Teeth*.
b. September 2, 1878 in Baltimore, Maryland
d. November 25, 1968 in Bound Brook, New Jersey

Isaac Bashevis Singer
(Isaac Warshofsky pseud)
American author
• Foremost living writer of Yiddish literature; won Nobel Prize, 1978.
b. July 14, 1904 in Radzymin, Poland

Jane Sherrod Singer
American author
• Juvenile books include *Ernest Hemingway, Man of Courage*, 1963.
b. May 26, 1917 in Wichita Falls, Texas

Elsie Singmaster
American author
• Her novels describe Pennsylvania Dutch country she lived in.
b. August 29, 1897 in Schuylkill, Pennsylvania
d. September 3, 1958 in Gettysburg, Pennsylvania

Andrei Sinyavsky
(Abram Terts pseud)
Russian author–critic
• Tried, convicted for slander to the Soviet State for literary work, *The Makepeace Experiment*, 1966; exiled to Paris, 1973.
b. October 08, 1925 in Moscow, U.S.S.R.

L(ouis) E(dward) Sissman
American poet–essayist
• Writings include "Dying: An Introduction," 1968; "Pursuit of Honor," 1971.
b. January 01, 1928 in Detroit, Michigan
d. March 1, 1976 in Boston, Massachusetts

Charles Hubert Sisson
English poet
• Satirical, politically critical works include "Anchises," 1976; "Exactions," 1980.
b. April 22, 1914 in Bristol, England

Dame Edith Sitwell
English poet
• Wrote poetry volume *Street Songs*, 1943; biographical study *English Eccentrics*, 1933.
b. 1887 in Scarborough, England
d. December 09, 1964 in London, England

Sir Osbert Sitwell
English author
• Wrote novel *Before the Bombardment*, 1926; five-volume memoirs of his eccentric family, 1944-50.
b. December 06, 1892 in London, England
d. May 04, 1969 in Montagnana, Italy

Maj Sjowall
Swedish author–poet
• With husband, Per Wahloo, wrote detective novel series featuring Martin Beck as protagonist, 1965-75.
b. September 25, 1935 in Malmo, Sweden

John Skelton
British poet
• Poet laureate; tutor to Henry VIII; irregular rhyme-scheme called "skeltonic meter."
b. 1460
d. June 21, 1529 in Westminster, England

Robin Skelton
English poet
• Major books of poetry include *The Hunting Dark*, 1971; *Timelight*, 1978.
b. October 12, 1925 in Easington, England

Gloria Skurzynski
American author
• Juvenile books include *The Magic Pumpkin*, 1971; *What Happened in Hamelin*, 1979.
b. July 06, 1930 in Duquesne, Pennsylvania

David R Slavitt
(Henry Sutton pseud)
American author
• Wrote *Vital Signs*, 1975.
b. March 23, 1935 in White Plains, New York

Esphyr Slobodkina
American children's author–illustrator
• Self-illustrated books include *Long Island Ducklings*, 1961.
b. 1909 in Siberia, Russia

Christopher Smart
English poet–author
• Noted for poem, "A Song to David," 1763.
b. April 22, 1722 in Shipbourne, England
d. May 21, 1771 in Kings Bench, England

Alexander Smith
Scottish poet–essayist
• Labelled spasmodic poet; known for essays in *Dreamthorp*, 1863.
b. December 31, 1830 in Kilmarnock, Scotland
d. January 05, 1867 in Wardie, Scotland

A(rthur) J(ames) M(arshall) Smith
Canadian poet–critic
• Leading figure in modern Canadian poetry: *Poems New and Collected*, 1967.
b. November 08, 1902 in Montreal, Quebec
d. November 21, 1980 in East Lansing, Michigan

Betty Smith
(Betty Wehner)
American author
• Wrote best-seller *A Tree Grows in Brooklyn*, 1943; filmed, 1945; on Broadway, 1951.
b. December 15, 1904 in Brooklyn, New York
d. January 17, 1972 in Shelton, Connecticut

Dennis Smith
American author
• Wrote *Report from Engine Co. 82*, 1972, about his experiences as a firefighter.
b. September 09, 1940 in New York, New York

H(arry) Allen Smith
American author
• Thirty-six books of humor include *Low Man on a Totem Pole*, 1941.
b. December 19, 1907 in McLeansboro, Illinois
d. February 23, 1976 in San Francisco, California

Hedrick Laurence Smith
American journalist
• Chief Washington correspondent for *NY Times* since 1980; won Pulitzers for cowriting *The Pentagon Papers*, 1972, for int'l. reporting, 1974.
b. July 09, 1933 in Kilmacolm, Scotland

Iain Crichton Smith
Scottish poet
• Writes in English and Gaelic: *From Bourgeois Land*, 1969.
b. January 01, 1928 in Isle of Lewis, Scotland

Lillian Smith
American author
• Wrote popular novel *Strange Fruit*, 1944; banned in Boston.
b. December 12, 1897 in Jasper, Florida
d. September 28, 1966

Liz (Mary Elizabeth) Smith
American journalist
• Gossip column runs in *NY Daily News*, over 60 syndicated papers.
b. February 02, 1923 in Fort Worth, Texas

Martin Cruz Smith
(Simon Quinn; Martin Quinn; Jake Logan; Nick Carter pseuds)
American author
• Prolific writer of popular fiction, spy novels, westerns; wrote best-seller *Gorky Park*, 1981.
b. November 03, 1942 in Reading, Pennsylvania

Merriman Smith
American journalist
• Chief Washington correspondent for UPI, 1941-70; won Pulitzer, 1964, for coverage of John F Kennedy assassination.
b. February 1, 1913 in Savannah, Georgia
d. April 13, 1970 in Alexandria, Virginia

Samuel Francis Smith
American poet–clergyman
• Wrote patriotic hymn, "America," 1831.
b. October 21, 1808 in Boston, Massachusetts
d. November 16, 1895 in Boston, Massachusetts

Stevie (Florence Margaret) Smith
English poet
• Poems include "A Good Time Was Had by All," 1937; "Novel on Yellow paper," 1936.
b. 1903 in Hull, England
d. March 07, 1971 in Ashburton, England

William Jay Smith
American children's author–poet
• Wrote *The Tin Can and Other Poems*, 1966; honored for poetry, translations.
b. April 22, 1918 in Winnfield, Louisiana

Vernon John Sneider
American author
• Wrote *Teahouse of the August Moon*, 1951; became play, film.
b. October 06, 1916 in Monroe, Michigan
d. May 01, 1981 in Monroe, Michigan

W(illiam) D(eWitt) Snodgrass
(S S Gardens pseud)
American poet
• Won Pulitzer for *Heart's Needle*, 1959.
b. January 05, 1926 in Wilkinsburg, Pennsylvania

Sir C(harles) P(ercy) Snow
English scientist–author
• His series of 11 novels, *Strangers and Brothers*, depicts stresses of contemporary British life.
b. October 15, 1905 in Leicester, England
d. July 01, 1980 in London, England

Dorothea Johnston Snow
American children's author
• Wrote *Sequoyah: Young Cherokee Guide*, 1960; *Tomahawk Claim*, 1968.
b. April 07, 1909 in McMinnville, Tennessee

Edgar Parks Snow
American journalist
• Wrote of communism in China: *Red Star Over China*, 1937; *The Other Side of the River*, 1962.
b. July 19, 1905 in Kansas City, Missouri
d. February 15, 1972 in Eysins, Switzerland

Gary Sherman Snyder
American poet
• Won Pulitzer, 1975, for *Turtle Island*.
b. May 08, 1930 in San Francisco, California

Aleksandr Isayevich Solzhenitsyn
Russian author
• Exiled to Siberia, 1953; won Nobel Prize for literature, 1970; wrote *Gulag Archipelago*, 1973.
b. December 11, 1918 in Kislovodsk, U.S.S.R.

Susan Sontag
American author–critic
• One of most influential contemporary American critics, utilizing new sensibility to evaluate art; wrote novels *The Benefactor*, 1963; *Death Kit*, 1967.
b. January 16, 1933 in New York, New York

Virginia Sorensen
(Mrs Alec Waugh)
American children's author
• Won 1957 Newbery for *Miracles on Maple Hill*.
b. February 17, 1912 in Provo, Utah

Philippe Soupault
French author
• Wrote poem "The Magnetic Fields," 1919, with Andre Breton, considered the work that gave birth to the surrealist movement.
b. August 02, 1897 in Chaville, France
d. March 11, 1990 in Paris, France

Ivan Francis Southall
Australian author
• Novels for young adults deal with how children cope with various disasters: *Hills End*, 1962; *To the Wild Sky*, 1967.
b. June 08, 1921 in Canterbury, Australia

Terry Southern
American writer
• Writes satirical novels, screenplays; known for satire on pornography, *Candy*, 1958, later published as *Lollipop*, 1962; films include *Easy Rider*, 1969.
b. May 01, 1924 in Alvarado, Texas

Robert Southey
English poet–author
• One of "Lake Poets"; poet laureate, 1813-43.
b. August 12, 1774 in Bristol, England
d. March 21, 1843 in Keswick, England

Wole (Akinwande Oluwole) Soyinka
Nigerian author
• Works deal with life in Nigeria; first African, first black to win Nobel Prize for literature, 1986.
b. July 13, 1934 in Abeokuta, Nigeria

Muriel Sarah Spark
Scottish author
• Satirist; best-known novel, *The Prime of Miss Jean Brodie*, 1961, was adapted to film, stage.
b. February 01, 1918 in Edinburgh, Scotland

Elizabeth George Speare
American children's author
• Won Newbery Medals for *The Witch of Blackbird Pond*, 1959; *The Bronze Bow*, 1962.
b. November 21, 1908 in Melrose, Massachusetts

Stephen Spender
English author–poet
• Wrote autobiography *World Within World*, 1951; *Collected Poems*, 1954.
b. February 28, 1909 in London, England

Edmund Spenser
English poet
• Developed Spenserian stanza used in allegorical epic *The Faerie Queen*, 1596.
b. 1552 in London, England
d. January 13, 1599 in Westminster, England

Mickey (Frank Morrison) Spillane
American author
• Known for Mike Hammer detective stories.
b. March 09, 1918 in Brooklyn, New York

Joel Elias Spingarn
American author–educator
• Founded NAACP, 1913, pres., 1930-31; originated Spingarn Medal, 1914.
b. May 17, 1875 in New York, New York
d. July 26, 1939 in New York, New York

Karl Friedrich Georg Spitteler
(Felix Tandem pseud)
Swiss poet
• Best-known epic poem: *Olympischer Fruhling*, 1900-10; Nobelist, 1919.
b. April 24, 1845 in Liestal, Switzerland
d. December 28, 1924 in Lucerne, Switzerland

Benjamin McLane Spock
American physician–author
• Wrote *Common Sense Book of Baby Care*, 1946; sold over 11 million copies.
b. May 02, 1903 in New Haven, Connecticut

Axel Caesar Springer
German publisher
• Created Europe's largest newspaper empire, including *Die Welt, Bild Zeitung*.
b. May 02, 1912 in Hamburg, Germany
d. September 22, 1985 in Berlin, Germany (West)

Johanna Heuser Spyri
Swiss author
• Best known for ever-popular *Heidi*, 1880; adapted to films, TV shows.
b. June 12, 1827 in Hirzel, Switzerland
d. July 07, 1901 in Zurich, Switzerland

Baroness de Anne Louise Germaine Necker Stael-Holstein
French author
• Influenced French Romanticism; *Delphine*, 1802, *Corinne*, 1807, considered first modern, feminist, romantic novels; critic of Napoleon, consequently exiled from Paris many times.
b. April 22, 1766 in Paris, France
d. July 14, 1817 in Paris, France

Jean Stafford
American author
• Collection of short stories, *Collected Stories*, won Pulitzer, 1970.
b. July 01, 1915 in Covina, California
d. March 26, 1979 in White Plains, New York

William Edgar Stafford
American poet
• Poems deal with conflicts between natural, artificial worlds; won National Book Award, 1962, for *Traveling through the Dark*.
b. January 17, 1914 in Hutchinson, Kansas

Sir Henry Morton Stanley
(Stanley and Livingstone)
English explorer–journalist
• Best known for finding David Livingstone in Africa, 1871; fought on both sides in US Civil War.
b. January 31, 1841 in Denbigh, Wales
d. May 1, 1904 in London, England

Vincent (Charles Vincent Emerson) Starrett
American author–critic
• Books include *Bookman's Holiday*, 1942; *Private Life of Sherlock Holmes*, 1933.
b. October 26, 1886 in Toronto, Ontario
d. January 04, 1974 in Chicago, Illinois

Danielle Fernande Steel
American author
• Romantic best-sellers appeal to female readers: *Full Circle*, 1984.
b. August 14, 1947 in New York, New York

Sir Richard Steele
(Isaac Bickerstaff pseud)
British author–editor
• Founded periodical papers *Tatler*, 1709, *Spectator*, 1711, *Guardian*, 1713; wrote comedy *The Conscious Lover*, 1712.
b. March 1672 in Dublin, Ireland
d. September 01, 1729 in Carmarthen, Wales

Wallace Earle Stegner
American author
• Writings deal with American West; won Pulitzer, 1972, for *Angle of Repose*.
b. February 18, 1909 in Lake Mills, Iowa

William Steig
American cartoonist–illustrator–children's author
• Drawings featured in *The New Yorker*; won 1970, 1977 Caldecotts; wrote *The Amazing Bone*, 1977.
b. November 14, 1907 in New York, New York

Aaron Marc Stein
(George Bagby; Hampton Stone pseuds)
American author
• Mystery story writer; won Grand Master Edgar Award, 1979.
b. November 15, 1906 in New York, New York
d. August 29, 1985 in New York, New York

Gertrude Stein
American author
• Center of American expatriates in 1920s Paris; named members the "Lost Generation."
b. February 03, 1874 in Allegheny, Pennsylvania
d. July 27, 1946 in Neuilly, France

John Ernst Steinbeck
American author
• Won 1962 Nobel Prize; wrote *The Grapes of Wrath; Of Mice and Men; East of Eden*.
b. February 27, 1902 in Salinas, California
d. December 2, 1968 in New York, New York

Stendhal
(Marie Henri Beyle)
French author–critic
• Wrote *The Red and the Black*, 1831; *The Charterhouse of Parma*, 1839.
b. January 23, 1783 in Grenoble, France
d. March 23, 1842 in Paris, France

Ann Sophia Stephens
American author–editor
• Wrote first dime novel *Malaeska; or the Indian Wife of the White Hunter*, 1860.
b. May 3, 1810 in Seymour, Connecticut
d. August 2, 1886 in Newport, Rhode Island

George Sterling
American poet
• Leader of bohemian art colony, Carmel, CA, 1908-15.
b. December 01, 1869 in Sag Harbor, New York
d. November 18, 1926 in San Francisco, California

Philip Van Doren Stern
American author
• Novelist, historian, widely acclaimed for Civil War era books.
b. September 1, 1900 in Wyalusing, Pennsylvania
d. July 31, 1984 in Sarasota, Florida

Laurence Sterne
(Mister Yorick pseud)
English author–theologian
• Wrote *Tristram Shandy*, 1760-67; *Sentimental Journey*, 1768.
b. November 24, 1713 in Clonmel, Ireland
d. March 18, 1768 in London, England

Shane Stevens
American author
• Novels deal with life in Harlem: *Go Down Dead*, 1967.
b. October 08, 1941 in New York, New York

Wallace Stevens
American poet–author
• Won 1955 Pulitzer for *Collected Poems;* noted for verse theme: reality mixed with imagination.
b. October 02, 1879 in Reading, Pennsylvania
d. August 02, 1955 in Hartford, Connecticut

Janet Stevenson
American author
• Many of her writings deal with women in unexpected roles: *Woman Aboard,* 1969.
b. February 04, 1913 in Chicago, Illinois

Robert Louis Balfour Stevenson
Scottish author–poet–essayist
• Wrote *Treasure Island; A Child's Garden of Verses; Dr. Jekyll and Mr. Hyde.*
b. November 13, 1850 in Edinburgh, Scotland
d. November 13, 1894 in Vailima, Samoa

George Rippey Stewart
American author–educator
• Versatile writer, known for novels *Storm,* 1941; *Earth Abides,* 1951.
b. May 31, 1895 in Sewickley, Pennsylvania
d. August 22, 1980 in San Francisco, California

John Innes Mackintosh Stewart
(Michael Innes pseud)
Scottish author
• Wrote detective stories concerning sleuth Inspector Appleby: *The Spider Strikes,* 1939.
b. September 3, 1906 in Edinburgh, Scotland

Mary (Florence Elinor) Stewart
English author
• Wrote trilogy about Merlin, King Arthur: *The Last Enchantment,* 1979.
b. September 17, 1916 in Sunderland, England

Frank (Francis Richard) Stockton
American author
• Known for puzzling short story *The Lady or the Tiger,* 1884.
b. April 05, 1834 in Philadelphia, Pennsylvania
d. April 2, 1902 in Washington, District of Columbia

Bram Stoker
Irish author
• Published best-selling horror story *Dracula,* 1897.
b. 1847 in Dublin, Ireland
d. April 2, 1912

Irving Stone
American author
• Noted for biographical novels: *Lust for Life; The Agony and the Ecstasy; The Origin.*
b. July 14, 1903 in San Francisco, California
d. August 26, 1989 in Los Angeles, California

I(sidor) F(einstein) Stone
American journalist–author–pamphleteer
• Edited newsletter *I F Stone's Bi-Weekly,* 1953-71; wrote *Underground to Palestine,* 1946; *The Trial of Socrates,* 1988.
b. December 24, 1907 in Philadelphia, Pennsylvania
d. June 18, 1989 in Boston, Massachusetts

Robert Anthony Stone
American author
• Wrote *A Hall of Mirrors,* 1967; *Children of Light,* 1986.
b. August 21, 1937 in New York, New York

Rex Todhunter Stout
American author
• Founded Vanguard Press, 1926; created detective Nero Wolfe, 1934.
b. December 01, 1886 in Noblesville, Indiana
d. October 27, 1975 in Danbury, Connecticut

Adrien Pearl Stoutenburg
(Lace Kendall pseud)
American children's author
• Books include *Fee, Fi, Fo, Fum: Friendly & Funny Giants,* 1969; *A Cat Is,* 1971.
b. December 01, 1916 in Dafur, Minnesota

Harriet (Elizabeth) Beecher Stowe
American author
• Wrote *Uncle Tom's Cabin,* 1852.
b. June 14, 1811 in Litchfield, Connecticut
d. July 01, 1896 in Hartford, Connecticut

Mark Strand
American poet
• Publications include *Reasons for Moving,* 1968; won Edgar Award for *The Story of Our Lives,* 1974.
b. April 11, 1934 in Summerside, Prince Edward Island

Edward L Stratemeyer
American children's author
• Syndicate produced *The Rover Boys, Hardy Boys, Bobbsey Twins, Nancy Drew,* etc.
b. October 04, 1862 in Elizabeth, New Jersey
d. May 1, 1930 in Newark, New Jersey

Roger W(illiams) Straus, Jr
American publisher
• Founder, pres., Farrar, Straus & Co., 1945.
b. January 03, 1917 in New York, New York

Edward Streeter
American author
• Wrote *Father of the Bride,* 1949; *Chairman of the Bored,* 1961.
b. August 01, 1891 in New York, New York
d. March 31, 1976 in New York, New York

Thomas Sigismund Stribling
American author
• Trilogy depicting life in the South includes 1933 Pulitzer-winning novel, *The Store.*
b. March 04, 1881 in Clinton, Tennessee
d. July 08, 1965 in Florence, Alabama

Austin Strong
American author
• Wrote play *Seventh Heaven,* 1920, which was filmed, 1937.
b. January 18, 1881 in San Francisco, California
d. September 17, 1952 in Nantucket, Massachusetts

Philip Duffield Strong
American author
• Wrote *State Fair,* 1932; made into film several times.
b. January 27, 1899 in Keosauqua, Iowa
d. April 26, 1957

Richard Lee Strout
American journalist
• Known for political analyses in *Christian Science Monitor* and weekly column "TRB From Washington" in *New Republic.*
b. March 14, 1898 in Cohoes, New York
d. August 19, 1990 in Washington, District of Columbia

Jesse Hilton Stuart
American author–poet
• Prolific regional writer named poet laureate of KY, 1954; best-known work: *Man with a Bull-Tongue Plow,* 1934.
b. August 08, 1907 in W-Hollow, Kentucky
d. February 17, 1984 in Ironton, Ohio

Theodore Hamilton Sturgeon
(Edward Hamilton Waldo)
American author
• Books include *My People Is the Enemy,* 1964.
b. February 26, 1918 in Staten Island, New York
d. May 08, 1985 in Eugene, Oregon

William Clark Styron, Jr
American author
• Won Pulitzer for *The Confessions of Nat Turner,* 1968; wrote novel *Sophie's Choice,* 1979, filmed, 1982.
b. June 11, 1925 in Newport News, Virginia

Frank Sullivan
American journalist
• Best known for cliche phrases; wrote Christmas poems for *The New Yorker,* 1932-74.
b. September 22, 1892 in Saratoga, New York
d. February 19, 1976 in Saratoga, New York

Rene Francois Armand Sully-Prudhomme
French poet
• Won first Nobel Prize for literature, 1901.
b. March 16, 1839 in Paris, France
d. September 07, 1907 in Paris, France

C(yrus) L(eo) Sulzberger
American author
• Books include *Such a Peace: The Roots and Ashes of Yalta,* 1982.
b. October 27, 1912 in New York, New York

Linda Sunshine
American author
• Author *Plain Jane Works Out,* 1983, spoof of *Jane Fonda's Workout Book.*
b. 1948

Jacqueline Susann
American author–actress
• Wrote sex-filled novels *Valley of the Dolls,* 1966; *Once Is Not Enough,* 1973.
b. August 2, 1921 in Philadelphia, Pennsylvania
d. September 21, 1974 in New York, New York

Bertha Felicie Sophie Kinsky von Suttner
Austrian editor–writer
• First woman to win Nobel Peace Prize, 1905; wrote *Lay Down Your Arms,* 1889.
b. June 09, 1843 in Prague, Austria
d. June 21, 1914 in Vienna, Austria

Carol Sutton
American editor
• First woman to head news operation of major US daily newspaper, 1974.
b. June 29, 1933 in Saint Louis, Missouri
d. February 19, 1985 in Louisville, Kentucky

Horace (Ashley) Sutton
American author
• Travel books include *Travelers: The American Tourist from Stagecoach to Space Shuttle,* 1980.
b. May 17, 1919 in New York, New York

William Andrew Swanberg
American author
• Pulitzer-winning biographer whose books include *Citizen Hearst,* 1961; *Luce and His Empire,* 1972.
b. November 23, 1907 in Saint Paul, Minnesota

Glendon Fred Swarthout
American author
• Books include *Where the Boys Are,* 1960; *Skeletons,* 1979.
b. April 08, 1918 in Pinckney, Michigan

May Swenson
American poet
• Wrote *New and Selected Things Taking Place,* 1978.
b. May 28, 1919 in Logan, Utah

Jonathan Swift
(Isaac Bickerstaff pseud)
English satirist–author–clergyman
• Wrote *Gulliver's Travels,* 1726.
b. November 3, 1667 in Dublin, Ireland
d. October 19, 1745 in Dublin, Ireland

Laurence Swinburne
American children's author
• Books include *RFK: The Last Knight,* 1969; *Detli,* 1970.
b. July 02, 1924 in New York, New York

Julian Gustave Symons
English author
• Mystery writer; won 1961 Edgar for *Progress of a Crime.*
b. May 3, 1912 in London, England

Sir Rabindranath Tagore
(Ravindranath Thakur)
Indian poet
• Won Nobel Prize for literature, 1913; known for mysticism, religious feeling.
b. May 06, 1861 in Calcutta, India
d. August 07, 1941 in Calcutta, India

Gay Talese
American author–journalist
• Wrote *Honor Thy Father,* 1971; *Thy Neighbor's Wife,* 1980.
b. February 07, 1932 in Ocean City, New Jersey

Ida Minerva Tarbell
American author–editor
• Leader of "muckracking" movement in journalism; wrote *Life of Abraham Lincoln,* 1900.
b. November 05, 1857 in Erie County, Pennsylvania
d. January 06, 1944 in Bethel, Connecticut

Herman Tarnower
American physician–author
• Wrote *The Complete Scarsdale Medical Diet,* 1979; murdered by longtime companion, Jean Harris.
b. March 18, 1910 in New York, New York
d. March 1, 1980 in Purchase, New York

Torquato Tasso
Italian author
• Best-known epic *Jerusalem Delivered,* 1575; re-wrote because of criticism, 1587.
b. March 11, 1544 in Sorrento, Italy
d. April 25, 1595 in Rome, Italy

Allen (John Orley) Tate
American poet–critic
• Poems include *The Golden Mean and Other Poems,* 1923; novels include *The Fathers,* 1938.
b. November 19, 1899 in Winchester, Kentucky
d. February 09, 1979 in Nashville, Tennessee

Nahum Tate
British poet
• Poet laureate, 1692-1715, best known for "Panacea, a poem on Tea," 1700.
b. 1652 in Dublin, Ireland
d. August 12, 1715 in London, England

Jane Taylor
English poet
• Wrote *Twinkle, Twinkle Little Star;* sister of Ann.
b. September 26, 1783 in Holborn, England
d. April 12, 1824 in Ongar, England

Peter (Hillsman) Taylor
American author
• Master storyteller; won PEN/Faulkner best fiction award, 1985.
b. January 08, 1917 in Trenton, New Jersey

Phoebe Atwood Taylor
(Alice Tilton pseud)
American author
• Crime novels include *The Cape Cod Mystery,* 1931; *Punch with Care,* 1946.
b. May 18, 1910
d. January 09, 1976 in Boston, Massachusetts

Sydney Brenner Taylor
American children's author
• Wrote *All-of-a-Kind Family* series.
b. 1904 in New York, New York
d. February 12, 1978 in Queens, New York

Edwin Way Teale
American naturalist–author
• Wrote over 25 books; won Pulitzer for *Wandering Through Winter,* 1966.
b. June 02, 1899 in Joliet, Illinois
d. October 18, 1980 in Norwich, Connecticut

Sara Teasdale
American author–poet
• Writings include *Rivers to the Sea,* 1915; *Stars Tonight,* 1930.
b. August 08, 1884 in Saint Louis, Missouri
d. January 28, 1933 in New York, New York

Corrie Ten Boom
Dutch author
• Wrote of experiences in concentration camp: *The Hiding Place,* 1971; movie starred Julie Harris, 1975.
b. April 15, 1892 in Amsterdam, Netherlands
d. April 15, 1983 in Placentia, California

Lord Alfred Tennyson
English poet
• Poet laureate, 1850-92; wrote *Idylls of the King*, 1885; "Charge of the Light Brigade," 1854.
b. August 06, 1809 in Somersby, England
d. October 06, 1892 in Haslemere, England

Mary Virginia Terhune
American author
• Wrote romantic novels, household quotes; mother of Albert Payson.
b. December 31, 1831 in Dennisville, Virginia
d. June 03, 1922

Studs (Louis) Terkel
American author–journalist
• Books based on tape-recorded interviews include Pulitzer winner *The Good War*, 1985.
b. May 16, 1912 in New York, New York

Susan Terris
American children's author
• Writings include *The Upstairs Witch and the Downstairs Witch*, 1970; *Amanda, the Panda, and the Redhead*, 1975.
b. May 06, 1937 in Saint Louis, Missouri

Walter Terry
American critic–author
• Dance critic, 1936-82; wrote 22 books.
b. May 14, 1913 in Brooklyn, New York
d. October 04, 1982 in New York, New York

Walter Tevis
American author
• Wrote novel *The Hustler*, 1959, which became 1961 film, sequel *The Color of Money*, 1984.
b. February 28, 1928 in San Francisco, California
d. August 09, 1984 in New York, New York

Josephine Tey, pseud
(Elizabeth Mackintosh)
Scottish author
• Mystery novels include *Brat Farrar*, 1949; *To Love and Be Wise*, 1950.
b. 1897 in Inverness, Scotland
d. February 13, 1952

Ernest L Thayer
American author
• Wrote *Casey at the Bat*, 1888.
b. August 14, 1863 in Lawrence, Massachusetts
d. August 21, 1940 in Santa Barbara, California

Theocritus
Greek poet
• Originator of pastoral poetry; sensitivity to nature imitated by later poets.
b. 310BC in Syracuse, Sicily
d. 250BC

Ion N Theodorescu
(Tudor Arghezi pseud)
Romanian poet–translator
• Romania's poet laureate; wrote verse volume *Cuvinte Potrivite*, 1927.
b. May 2, 1880 in Bucharest, Romania
d. July 14, 1967 in Bucharest, Romania

Paul Edward Theroux
American author
• Wrote prize-winning novel *Picture Palace*, 1978; best-selling travel yarn *Kingdom By the Sea*, 1983.
b. April 1, 1941 in Medford, Mississippi

Caitlin Macnamara Thomas
(Mrs Dylan Thomas)
Welsh author
• Married Dylan Thomas, 1937; wrote of life together in *Leftover Life to Kill*, 1957.

Craig D Thomas
(David Grant)
Welsh author
• Best-selling novel *Firefox*, 1977, adapted to successful film, 1982.
b. November 24, 1942 in Cardiff, Wales

D(onald) M(ichael) Thomas
English author
• Wrote best-seller *The White House*, 1981.
b. January 27, 1935 in Carnkie, England

Dylan Marlais Thomas
Welsh author
• Wrote *A Child's Christmas in Wales; Under Milk Wood*, 1954.
b. October 27, 1914 in Swansea, Wales
d. November 09, 1953 in New York, New York

Edward Thomas
English poet–author
• Writings focus on nature, melancholy; wrote travel books, biographies before meeting, Robert Frost and switching to poetry.
b. March 03, 1878 in London, England
d. April 09, 1917 in Arras, France

Gwyn Thomas
Welsh author
• Wrote *Where Did I Put My Pity?; The Love Man; The Keep*.
b. July 06, 1913 in Porth, Wales
d. April 13, 1981 in Cardiff, Wales

Joyce Carol Thomas
American author
• Wrote 1982 award-winning young adult novel *Marked By Fire*.
b. May 25, 1938 in Ponca City, Oklahoma

Piri Thomas
American author
• Wrote autobiographies *Down These Mean Streets*, 1967; *Seven Long Times*, 1974.
b. September 3, 1928 in New York, New York

Robert B Thomas
American publisher
• Founded, edited *Old Farmer's Almanac*, 1792-1844.
b. April 24, 1766 in Grafton, Massachusetts
d. May 19, 1846 in West Bolyston, Massachusetts

Ronald Stuart Thomas
Welsh poet
• Poems express bleak view of man: *The Stones of the Field*, 1946.
b. March 29, 1913 in Cardiff, Wales

Ernest (Richard Ernest) Thompson
American author
• Wrote play *On Golden Pond*, 1978; won 1982 Oscar for screen adaptation.
b. 1950 in Bellows Falls, Vermont

Francis Joseph Thompson
English poet–essayist
• First volume *Poems*, 1893, contained best known poem "The Hound of Heaven."
b. December 18, 1859 in Preston, England
d. November 13, 1907 in London, England

George Selden Thompson
(George Selden)
American children's author
• Best known for *The Cricket in Times Square*, which won Newbery Medal, 1961, and was adapted to film, 1973.
b. May 14, 1929 in Hartford, Connecticut
d. December 05, 1989 in New York, New York

Hunter S(tockton) Thompson
(Sebastian Owl pseud)
American journalist–editor
• Wrote *Hell's Angels: A Strange and Terrible Saga*, 1966; nat. affairs editor, *Rolling Stone* mag, 1969-74. Pioneer of "gonzo" journalism.
b. July 18, 1939 in Louisville, Kentucky

Ruth Plumly Thompson
American historian–author
• Wrote 19 "Oz" books after Baum's death, including *The Enchanted Island of Oz*, 1976.
b. July 27, 1891 in Philadelphia, Pennsylvania
d. April 06, 1976

Thomas Thompson
American journalist
• At age 23 became youngest city editor with a major daily newspaper, *Houston Press*, 1957; wrote nonfiction best-sellers.
b. October 03, 1933 in Fort Worth, Texas
d. October 29, 1982 in Los Angeles, California

Vivian Laubach Thompson
American children's author
• Best known for book on the experience of moving: *Sad Day, Glad Day*, 1962.
b. 1911 in Jersey City, New Jersey

James Thomson
Scottish poet
• Best known collection *The Seasons*, 1730, emphasized blank verse, nature as a theme within itself.
b. September 11, 1700 in Ednam, Scotland
d. August 27, 1748 in Richmond, England

Roy Herbert Thomson
(Lord Thomson of Fleet)
English newspaper publisher–business executive
• Founded media empire, Thomson Organization Ltd; today has publishing, travel, oil.
b. June 05, 1894 in Toronto, Ontario
d. August 04, 1976 in London, England

Henry David Thoreau
American author
• Wrote essay *Civil Disobedience*, 1849; novel *Walden*, 1854.
b. July 12, 1817 in Concord, Massachusetts
d. May 06, 1862 in Concord, Massachusetts

Marcella Thum
American children's author
• Won Edgar for first book, *Mystery at Crane's Landing*, 1964; other books include *Margarite*, 1987.
b. in Saint Louis, Missouri

James Grover Thurber
American author
• Major contributor to *New Yorker* mag., 1927-52; known for whimsical writings, cartoons; best-known short story: "The Secret Life of Walter Mitty"; book: *The Thurber Carnival*, 1945.
b. December 08, 1894 in Columbus, Ohio
d. November 02, 1961 in New York, New York

Eunice Tietjens
American poet–author
• Wrote poems *Profiles on China*, 1917; novel *Jake*, 1921.
b. July 29, 1884 in Chicago, Illinois
d. September 06, 1944

Jacobo Timerman
Argentine author–journalist
• Wrote *Prisoner Without a Name, Cell Without a Number*, 1981, detailing events during capture in Argentina, 1977-79.
b. January 06, 1923 in Bar, U.S.S.R.

Comte de Alexis Tocqueville
French author
• Noted for classic, two-volume: *Democracy in America*, 1835.
b. July 29, 1805 in Vernevil, France
d. April 16, 1859 in Cannes, France

Mabel Loomis Todd
American author
• First editor of poems, letters of Emily Dickinson, 1890-95.
b. November 1, 1856 in Cambridge, Massachusetts
d. October 14, 1932 in Hog Island, Maine

Alvin Toffler
American author
• Wrote *Future Shock*, 1970; *The Third Wave*, 1980.
b. October 04, 1928 in New York, New York

John Willard Toland
American journalist–author–historian
• Historical works include 1970 Pulitzer winner *The Rising Sun*.
b. June 29, 1912 in La Crosse, Wisconsin

Ralph de Toledano
American journalist–author
• Syndicated columnist, King Features, 1960-71; publications include *RFK: The Man Who Would Be President*, 1967; *J Edgar Hoover: The Man & His Times*, 1973.
b. August 17, 1916 in Tangiers, Morocco

J(ohn) R(onald) R(euel) Tolkien
English author
• Wrote *The Hobbit*, 1938; *The Lord of the Rings*, 1954-56.
b. January 03, 1892 in Bloemfontein, South Africa
d. September 02, 1973 in Bournemouth, England

Alexey Nikolaevich Tolstoy
Russian author
• Historical novel, *Peter the Great*, 1929-34, called a masterpiece of Soviet literature.
b. December 2, 1882 in Nikolaevski-Samarskom, Russia
d. February 22, 1945 in Moscow, U.S.S.R.

Leo Nikolayevich Tolstoy
Russian author
• Wrote *War and Peace*, 1865-69; *Anna Karenina*, 1875-77.
b. August 28, 1828 in Yasnaya Polyana, Russia
d. November 2, 1910 in Astapovo, Russia

Guiseppe Tomasi di Lampedusa
Italian author
• Novelist; wrote of decline of Sicilian upper class in 1860s: *The Leopard*, published posthumously, 1960.
b. December 23, 1896 in Palermo, Sicily
d. July 26, 1957 in Rome, Italy

Henry Major Tomlinson
English author
• Noted for travel tale *The Sea and the Jungle*, 1912; novel *All Our Yesterdays*, 1930.
b. 1873 in London, England
d. February 05, 1958 in London, England

Jill Tomlinson
English children's author
• Animal tales include *Penguin's Progress*, 1975.
b. December 27, 1931 in Twickenham, England
d. 1976 in England

John Kennedy Toole
American author
• Wrote posthumously published best-seller *The Confederacy of Dunces*, 1980, which won Pulitzer. Suicide victim.
b. 1937 in New Orleans, Louisiana
d. March 26, 1969 in Biloxi, Mississippi

Jean Toomer
American author–poet
• A "Harlem Renaissance" writer; wrote *Cane*, 1923.
b. December 26, 1894 in Washington, District of Columbia
d. March 3, 1967

Charles Hanson Towne
American poet–editor
• Wrote *Pretty Girls Get There*, 1940; *Gentlemen Behave*, 1941.
b. February 02, 1877 in Louisville, Kentucky
d. February 28, 1949 in New York, New York

George Alfred Townsend
American author
• Wrote *Campaigns of a Non-Combatant*, 1865; *The Entailed Hat*, 1884.
b. January 3, 1841 in Georgetown, Delaware
d. April 15, 1914 in New York, New York

Philip (Theodore Philip) Toynbee
English author–critic–journalist
• Wrote *Tea with Mrs. Goodman*, 1947; *The Garden to the Sea*, 1953.
b. June 25, 1916 in Oxford, England
d. June 15, 1981

B Traven, pseud
(Berick Traven Torsvan)
Mexican author
• Wrote *Treasure of the Sierra Madre*, 1935; filmed, 1948.
b. 1890
d. March 27, 1969 in Mexico City, Mexico

P(amela) L(yndon) Travers
Australian author
• Wrote *Mary Poppins*, 1934; filmed by Walt Disney, 1964.
b. 1906 in Queensland, Australia

Lawrence Treat
(Lawrence Arthur Goldstone)
American author
• Mystery novels include *Venus Unarmed*, 1961; *Murder in the Mind*, 1967.
b. December 21, 1903 in New York, New York

Henry Treece
English author–poet–dramatist
• Versatile writer whose novels include *Red Queen, White Queen*, 1958; *Oedipus*, 1964.
b. 1911 in Staffordshire, England
d. June 1, 1966 in Barton-on-Humber, England

Richard William Tregaskis
American author
• Wrote best-selling *Guadalcanal Diary*, 1943.
b. November 28, 1916 in Elizabeth, New Jersey
d. August 15, 1973 in Honolulu, Hawaii

Richard Chenevix Trench
Irish poet–scholar
• Noted philologist who popularized study of language: *Study of Words*.
b. September 05, 1807 in Dublin, Ireland
d. March 28, 1886 in London, England

Elizabeth Borton de Trevino
American children's author
• Won Newbery Medal for *I, Juan de Pareja*, 1966.
b. September 02, 1904 in Bakersfield, California

William Trevor
(William Trevor Cox)
Irish author–dramatist
• Works deal with domestic, private relationships in English, Irish counties, towns; wrote book *The Children of Dynmouth*, 1976.
b. May 24, 1928 in Mitchelstown, Ireland

Yuri Valentinovich Trifonov
Russian author
• Major contributor to 20th-c. Russian literature; tales of Stalinist era include *The House on the Embankment*, 1983.
b. August 28, 1925 in Moscow, U.S.S.R.
d. March 21, 1981 in Moscow, U.S.S.R.

Calvin Marshall Trillin
American author
• *New Yorker* mag. staff writer, 1963–; books include *Uncivil Liberties*, 1982; *If You Can't Say Something Nice*, 1987.
b. December 05, 1935 in Kansas City, Missouri

Diana Rubin Trilling
American author–critic
• Wife of Lionel; wrote *Mrs. Harris: The Death of the Scarsdale Diet Doctor*, 1981.
b. July 21, 1905 in New York, New York

Anthony Trollope
English author
• Wrote 50 novels including *Barsetshire Chronicles*, 1850s-60s.
b. April 24, 1815 in London, England
d. December 06, 1882 in London, England

Frances Trollope
English author
• Wrote controversial, much resented *Domestic Manners of the Americans*, 1832; mother of Anthony.
b. March 1, 1780 in Bristol, England
d. October 06, 1863 in Florence, Italy

John Townsend Trowbridge
American journalist–author
• Best known for juvenile antislavery novels, *Cudjo's Cave*, 1864; *Jack Hazard Series*, 1871-74; narrative poem, "Darius Green and His Flying Machine," 1903.
b. September 18, 1827 in Ogdensburg, New York
d. February 12, 1916 in Arlington, Massachusetts

Margaret (Mary Margaret) Truman
(Mrs Clifton Daniel Jr)
American author–celebrity relative
• Daughter of Harry Truman; wrote *Letters from Father*, 1981.
b. February 17, 1924 in Independence, Missouri

John Trumbull
American poet–judge
• Most popular of Hartford Wits; wrote mock epic *M'Fingal*, 1782, satirizing stupidity of British.
b. April 24, 1750 in Watertown, Connecticut
d. May 11, 1831 in Detroit, Michigan

Marina Ivanovna Tsvetayeva
Russian poet
• Modernist poet influenced by Pasternak, folk music; suicide victim.
b. September 26, 1892 in Moscow, Russia
d. August 31, 1941 in Yelabuga, U.S.S.R.

Barbara Wertheim Tuchman
American author–historian
• Wrote about people at war or at brink of war; won Pulitzers for *The Guns of August*, 1962, *Stillwell and the American Experience in China, 1911-45*, 1971.
b. January 3, 1912 in New York, New York
d. February 06, 1989 in New York, New York

Ivan Sergeevich Turgenev
Russian author
• First major 19th-c. Russian novelist known abroad; wrote his masterpiece, *Fathers and Sons*, 1862; a popular comedy, *A Month in the Country*, 1850.
b. November 09, 1818 in Orel, Russia
d. September 03, 1883 in Bougival, France

Brinton Cassaday Turkle
American children's author
• Self-illustrated juvenile books include *The Adventures of Obadiah*, 1972; *Rachel & Obadiah*, 1978.
b. August 15, 1915 in Alliance, Ohio

Scott Turow
American author
• Lawyer-turned-best-selling author; wrote *The Burden of Proof*, 1990; *Presumed Innocent* filmed, 1990, starring Harrison Ford.
b. April 12, 1949 in Chicago, Illinois

Amos Tutuola
Nigerian author
• Novels with Yoruba folklore as background include *The Feather Woman of the Jungle*, 1962; *The Wild Herbalist of the Remote Town*, 1980.
b. June 1920 in Abeokuta, Nigeria

Mark Twain, pseud
(Samuel Langhorne Clemens; "The People's Author")
American author–journalist
• Wrote *Tom Sawyer*, 1876; *Huckleberry Finn*, 1885.
b. November 3, 1835 in Florida, Missouri
d. April 21, 1910 in Redding, Connecticut

Anne Tyler
American author
• Called chronicler of modern American family: *Morgan's Passing*, 1980; *Dinner at the Homesick Restaurant*, 1982.
b. October 25, 1941 in Minneapolis, Minnesota

Kenneth Peacock Tynan
English critic–author
• Reviewer for *London Observer*, 1954-58, 1960-63; wrote musical *Oh! Calcutta*, 1969.
b. April 02, 1927 in Birmingham, England
d. July 26, 1980 in Santa Monica, California

Tristan Tzara
Romanian author–poet
• Leader of Dada movement in French literature; edited *Dada* magazine, 1916-20.
b. April 04, 1896 in Moinesti, Romania
d. December 24, 1963 in Paris, France

Janice May Udry
American children's author
• Writings include *Danny's Pig*, 1960; *The Sunflower Garden*, 1969.
b. June 14, 1928 in Jacksonville, Illinois

Dorothy Uhnak
American author
• Crime novels include *The Ledger*, 1970.
b. 1933 in New York, New York

Sigrid Undset
Norwegian author
• Won Nobel Prize in literature, 1928; wrote three-vol. historical novel, *Kristin Lavranstadder*, 1922.
b. May 2, 1882 in Kalundborg, Denmark
d. June 1, 1949 in Lillehammer, Norway

Tomi (Jean Thomas) Ungerer
French children's author–illustrator
• Writings include *Moon Man*, 1967; *The Joy of Frogs*, 1985.
b. November 28, 1931 in Strasbourg, France

Kurt Unkelbach
American children's author
• Books on cats, dogs include *Uncle Charlie's Poodle*, 1975; wrote *Straw Hat*, 1937, which was produced on Broadway.
b. November 21, 1913 in New Britain, Connecticut

Jean Starr Untermeyer
American author
• Wrote *Growing Pains*, 1918; translated Hermann Broch's *The Death of Virgil*, 1945.
b. March 13, 1886 in Zanesville, Ohio
d. July 27, 1970

John Hoyer Updike
American author
• Won Pulitzer, 1981, for *Rabbit Is Rich*.
b. March 18, 1932 in Shillington, Pennsylvania

Leon Marcus Uris
American author
• Wrote *Exodus*, 1958; *Trinity*, 1976.
b. August 03, 1924 in Baltimore, Maryland

Chris VanAllsburg
American children's author–illustrator
• Won Caldecotts for *Jumanji*, 1981; *The Polar Express*, 1985.
b. June 18, 1949 in Grand Rapids, Michigan

Abigail Van Buren
(Pauline Esther Friedman; Mrs Morton Phillips; "Dear Abby" "Popo")
American journalist
• Wrote *Dear Abby on Marriage*, 1962; twin sister of Ann Landers.
b. July 04, 1918 in Sioux City, Iowa

Louis Joseph Vance
American author
• Wrote *The Lone Wolf*, 1914; *The Trembling Flame*, 1931.
b. September 19, 1879 in Washington, District of Columbia
d. December 16, 1933

Cornelius Vanderbilt, Jr
American journalist–filmmaker
• Founder, pres., Vanderbilt Newspapers, Inc., 1923; wrote *Park Avenue*, 1930; *Farewell to Fifth Avenue*, 1935.
b. April 3, 1898 in New York, New York
d. July 07, 1974 in Miami Beach, Florida

John Womack Vandercook
American author–broadcast journalist
• Writings include *Tom-Tom*, 1926; *Murder in New Guinea*, 1959.
b. April 22, 1902 in London, England
d. January 06, 1963 in Delhi, New York

Sir Laurens (Jan) Van Der Post
South African author
• Wrote *In a Province*, 1934; *The Heart of the Hunter*, 1961.
b. December 13, 1906 in Philioppis, South Africa

Dorothy Graffe Van Doren
American author
• Writings include *Strangers*, 1926; *The Country Wife*, 1950; *Men, Women and Cats*, 1962.
b. May 02, 1896 in San Francisco, California

Mark Van Doren
American poet–critic–author
• Won Pulitzer for poetry, 1939; writings include *That Shining Place*, 1969.
b. June 13, 1894 in Hope, Illinois
d. December 1, 1972 in Torrington, Connecticut

Hendrik Willem Van Loon
American historian–author
• Wrote six best-sellers including *The Story of Mankind*, 1921.
b. January 14, 1882 in Rotterdam, Netherlands
d. March 1, 1944 in New York, New York

Helen Lenore Vogt Van Slyke
American author
• Wrote best-sellers *A Necessary Woman*, 1979; *No Love Lost*, 1979.
b. July 09, 1919 in Washington, District of Columbia
d. July 03, 1979 in New York, New York

Carl Van Vechten
American author–critic
• Wrote *Parties*, 1930; *Pavlova*, 1947.
b. June 17, 1880 in Cedar Rapids, Iowa
d. December 21, 1964 in New York, New York

Giorgio Vasari
Italian architect–artist–author
• Published *Lives of Most Eminent Painters and Sculptors*, 1550, first work of art history.
b. July 3, 1511 in Arezzo, Italy
d. June 27, 1574 in Florence, Italy

Henry Vaughan
Welsh poet
• Best known for *The Retreat; The World*.
b. April 17, 1622 in Llansantfraed, Wales
d. April 23, 1695

Erico Lopes Verissimo
Brazilian author
• Novels set in Brazil, full of character, broad in scope include *Crossroads*, 1935.
b. December 17, 1905 in Rio Grande do Sul, Brazil
d. November 28, 1975 in Porto Alegre, Brazil

Jules Verne
French author
• Wrote *Twenty Thousand Leagues Under the Sea*, 1870; *Around the World in Eighty Days*, 1873; both adapted to film, 1954, 1956.
b. February 08, 1828 in Nantes, France
d. March 24, 1905 in Amiens, France

Peter Robert Edwin Viereck
American poet–educator
• Won 1949 Pulitzer for verse vol., *Terror and Decorum*.
b. August 05, 1916 in New York, New York

Peter Viertel
American author
• Writings include *The Canyon*, 1940; *White Hunter, Black Heart*, 1953.
b. November 16, 1920 in Dresden, Germany

Comte de Alfred Victor Vigny
French author–poet–dramatist
• Early exponent of French romanticism; wrote historical novel *Cliq-Mars*, 1826; verse *Les Destinees*, 1864.
b. March 27, 1797 in Loches, France
d. September 17, 1863 in Paris, France

Alan John Villiers
Australian adventurer–author
• Writings include *Whaling in the Frozen South*, 1925; *The Bounty Ships of France*, 1972.
b. September 23, 1903 in Melbourne, Australia
d. March 03, 1982

Francois Villon
(Francois de Montcorbier; Francois Des Loges)
French poet
• Wrote *Grand Testament*, 1461; became Rogue-hero of 19th c.
b. 1431 in Paris, France
d. 1463 in Paris, France

Judith (Stahl) Viorst
American author–poet
• Writings include *The Village Square*, 1965; *People and Other Aggravations*, 1971.
b. February 02, 1931 in Newark, New Jersey

Virgil
(Publius Vergilius Maro; Vergil)
Roman poet
• Unfinished epic poem *Aeneid* was about the founding of Rome.
b. October 15, 70 in Mantua, Gaul
d. September 21, 19 in Brundisium, Italy

William Lightfoot Visscher
American poet
• Wrote over 1,000 poems which were published in newspapers.
b. November 25, 1842 in Owingsville, Kentucky
d. February 1, 1924

John Donaldson Voelker
(Robert Traver pseud)
American judge–author
• Wrote *Anatomy of a Murder*, 1957; made into film, 1959.
b. June 29, 1903 in Ishpeming, Michigan
d. 1991, Michigan

Voltaire (Francois Marie Arouet de)
French author–philosopher
• Wrote *Candide*, 1759.
b. November 21, 1694 in Paris, France
d. May 3, 1778 in Paris, France

Erich Von Daeniken
Swiss author
• Wrote *Chariots of the Gods?* 1968; *Unsolved Mysteries of the Past*, 1969.
b. April 14, 1935 in Zofingen, Switzerland

Heimito Von Doderer
Austrian author
• Best known for novel *Die Strudelhofstiege*, 1951.
b. September 05, 1896
d. December 23, 1966 in Vienna, Austria

Nicholas Von Hoffman
American journalist
• Writings include *Mississippi Notebook*, 1964; *Two, Three, Many More*, 1969.
b. October 16, 1929 in New York, New York

Kurt Vonnegut, Jr
American author–journalist
• Wrote *Slaughterhouse Five*, 1969; *Breakfast of Champions*, 1973.
b. November 11, 1922 in Indianapolis, Indiana

Mark Vonnegut
American author
• Wrote *The Eden Express*, 1975; son of Kurt.
b. May 11, 1947 in Chicago, Illinois

Volodymyr Vynnychenko
Ukrainian author
• Known for realistic, unexpected conflicts; writings include *Nova Zapovid*, 1950.
b. 1880 in Kherson, Russia
d. 1951 in Paris, France

Adam Willis Wagnalls
American publisher
• With Isaac Funk founded publishing house, Funk & Wagnalls, 1890.
b. September 24, 1843 in Lithopolis, Ohio
d. September 03, 1924

John Barrington Wain
English author–critic
• Wrote novel, *Hurry on Down*, 1953; critical appraisal, *Living World of Shakespeare*, 1964.
b. March 14, 1925 in Stoke-on-Trent, England

Dan Wakefield
American author
• First novel, *Island in the City*, 1959, was an insight into the world of Spanish Harlem.
b. May 21, 1932 in Indianapolis, Indiana

Frederic Wakeman
American author
• Wrote best-seller *The Hucksters*, 1946.
b. December 26, 1909 in Scranton, Kansas

Alice Walker
American author
• Won Pulitzer for novel *The Color Purple*, 1982; filmed, 1985.
b. February 09, 1944 in Eatonton, Georgia

DeWitt Wallace
(William Roy DeWitt Wallace)
American publisher
• With wife, Lila, founded *Reader's Digest*, 1922.
b. November 12, 1889 in Saint Paul, Minnesota
d. March 3, 1981 in Mount Kisco, New York

Edgar Wallace
English author
• Wrote popular thrillers including *The Terror*, 1930.
b. December 1875 in Greenwich, England
d. February 1, 1932 in Hollywood, California

Irving Wallace
(Irving Wallechinsky)
American author
• One of best-read and best-selling 20th-century American authors; wrote *The Chapman Report*, 1960, filmed starring Jane Fonda, Shelley Winters, 1962.
b. March 19, 1916 in Chicago, Illinois
d. June 29, 1990 in Los Angeles, California

Lew(is) Wallace
American author–soldier
• Wrote best-sellers *Ben Hur*, 1880; *Prince of India*, 1893.
b. April 1, 1827 in Brookville, Indiana
d. February 15, 1905 in Crawfordsville, Indiana

Lila Bell Acheson Wallace
American publisher–editor
• Organizer, YWCA, 1921-22; co-founder, editor *Reader's Digest*, 1921-65.
b. December 25, 1889 in Virden, Manitoba
d. May 08, 1984 in Mount Kisco, New York

Edward Lewis Wallant
American author
• Wrote *The Pawnbroker*, 1961, filmed 1965.
b. October 19, 1926 in New Haven, Connecticut
d. December 05, 1962 in Norwalk, Connecticut

David Wallechinsky
American author
• Co-author: *The People's Almanac*, 1975; *The Book of Lists*, 1977; son of Irving Wallace.
b. February 05, 1948 in Los Angeles, California

Douglass (John Douglass, III) Wallop
American author
• Wrote *The Year the Yankees Lost the Pennant*, 1954, basis for hit musical *Damn Yankees*, 1955.
b. March 08, 1920 in Washington, District of Columbia
d. April 01, 1985 in Georgetown, Maryland

Horace Walpole
(Fourth Earl of Orford)
English author
• His work *The Castle of Otranto*, 1765, began fad for Gothic novels; brilliant prolific letter writer.
b. September 24, 1717 in London, England
d. March 02, 1797 in London, England

Sir Hugh Seymour Walpole
English author
• Novels include *The Dark Forest*, 1916.
b. March 13, 1884 in Auckland, New Zealand
d. June 01, 1941 in Brackenburg, England

John Walter
English newspaper publisher
• Founded *Daily Universal Register*, 1785, which was renamed London *Times*, 1788.
b. 1739
d. November 16, 1812

Joseph Aloysius Wambaugh, Jr
American author
• With LA police, 1960-74; wrote police novels *The New Centurions*, 1971; *The Blue Knight*, 1972; *The Choir Boys*, 1975.
b. January 22, 1937 in East Pittsburgh, Pennsylvania

Mary Jane Ward
American author
• Wrote novel *The Snake Pit*, 1946.
b. August 27, 1905 in Fairmount, Indiana

Charles Dudley Warner
American editor–author
• Best known for collaborating with Mark Twain on *The Gilded Age*, 1873; said, "Everybody talks about the weather but nobody does anything about it."
b. September 12, 1829 in Plainfield, Massachusetts
d. October 2, 1900 in Hartford, Connecticut

Sylvia Townsend Warner
English author–poet–biographer
• Best known for short stories in *New Yorker* mag.; wrote biography of Jane Austin.
b. December 06, 1893 in Harrow, England
d. May 01, 1978 in Maiden Newton, England

Robert Penn Warren
American author–poet–critic
• Three-time Pulitzer Prize winner, best known for *All the King's Men*, 1946; first US poet laureate, 1986-87.
b. April 24, 1905 in Guthrie, Kentucky
d. September 15, 1989 in Stratton, Vermont

Nathan Wartels
American publisher
• Founder of Crown Publishers Inc. and believed to be richest person in US publishing industry.
b. 1902
d. February 7, 1990 in New York, New York

Thomas Warton
English author
• Poet-laureate, 1785-90; wrote *Triumph of Iris*, 1749; brother of Joseph.
b. January 09, 1728 in Basingstake, England
d. May 21, 1790 in Oxford, England

Jakob Wassermann
German author
• Novelist best known for strange characters, startling plots: *Doctor Keerkhoven*, 1931.
b. March 1, 1873 in Nuremberg, Germany
d. January 01, 1934 in Aussee, Germany

Richard Martin Watt
American author
• Wrote *Dare Call It Treason*, 1963; *The Kings Depart*, 1969.
b. November 1, 1930 in Berwyn, Illinois

Alec (Alexander Raban) Waugh
English author
• Wrote best-seller *Island in the Sun*, 1955; brother of Evelyn Waugh.
b. July 08, 1898 in London, England
d. September 03, 1981 in Tampa, Florida

Evelyn Arthur St John Waugh
English author–satirist
• Wrote *Decline and Fall*, 1928; *Brideshead Revisited*, 1945.
b. October 28, 1903 in London, England
d. April 1, 1966 in Taunton, England

Jean Webster
American author
• Wrote *Daddy Long-Legs*, 1912.
b. July 24, 1876 in Fredonia, New York
d. June 11, 1916 in New York, New York

Noah Webster
American lexicographer–author
• Compiled *American Dictionary of the English Language*, 1828; his work helped standardize American pronunciation.
b. October 16, 1758 in West Hartford, Connecticut
d. May 28, 1843 in New Haven, Connecticut

Violet Brown Weingarten
American journalist–author
• Novels include *Half a Marriage*, 1976; films include *Debbie*, 1964.
b. February 23, 1915 in San Francisco, California
d. July 17, 1976 in New York, New York

Theodore (Russell) Weiss
American poet–editor
• Poem verses include *A Slow Fuse*, 1984; editor, publisher, *Quarterly Review Literature*, 1943–.
b. December 16, 1916 in Reading, Pennsylvania

Dorothy Violet Wellesley
(Duchess of Wellington)
English poet
• Wrote collection of poems, *Early Light*, 1956.
b. 1889
d. 1956

Paul Iselin Wellman
American journalist–author
• Novels include *Bowl of Brass*, 1944; *Magnificent Destiny*, 1962.
b. October 14, 1898 in Enid, Oklahoma
d. September 17, 1966 in Los Angeles, California

Walter Wellman
American journalist
• Founded *Cincinnati Post*, 1879; known for travels, record-breaking stunts.
b. November 03, 1858 in Mentor, Ohio
d. January 31, 1934 in New York, New York

Carolyn Wells
American author
• Wrote over 170 mysteries, nonsense tales, children's books.
b. June 18, 1869 in Rahway, New Jersey
d. March 26, 1942

H(erbert) G(eorge) Wells
English author
• Wrote *The Time Machine*, 1895; *The Invisible Man*, 1897; *The War of the Worlds*, 1898.
b. September 21, 1866 in Bromley, England
d. August 13, 1946 in London, England

Eudora Welty
American author
• Won Pulitzer for *The Optimist's Daughter*, 1972.
b. April 13, 1909 in Jackson, Mississippi

Jann Wenner
American journalist–publisher
• Founder, publisher *Rolling Stone* mag, 1967–; also owns *Us* mag.
b. January 07, 1946 in New York, New York

Franz Werfel
Austrian author
• Noted expressionist; wrote *The Song of Bernadette*, 1942; filmed, 1943.
b. September 1, 1890 in Prague, Bohemia
d. August 26, 1945 in Beverly Hills, California

Glenway Wescott
American author
• Novels include *The Grandmothers*, 1927; *The Pilgrim Hawk*, 1940.
b. April 11, 1901 in Kewaskum, Wisconsin
d. February 22, 1987 in Rosemont, New Jersey

Mathilde Luckemeyer Wesendonck
German poet–celebrity friend
• Friend of Richard Wagner; he set five of her poems to music as "The Wesendonck Songs."
b. 1828 in Traunblick, Austria
d. 1902

Morris Langlo West
Australian author
• Wrote *The Shoes of the Fisherman*, 1963; filmed, 1968.
b. April 26, 1916 in Melbourne, Australia

Nathanael West, pseud
(Nathan Wallenstein Weinstein)
American author
• Wrote *Miss Lonelyhearts*, 1933; *The Day of the Locust*, 1939.
b. October 17, 1903 in New York, New York
d. December 22, 1940 in El Centro, California

Rebecca Dame West, pseud
(Cecily Isobel Fairfield Andrews)
Irish author–journalist
• Wrote *The Fountain Overflows*, 1957; nonfiction *The Meaning of Treason*, 1949.
b. December 25, 1892 in County Kerry, Ireland
d. March 15, 1983 in London, England

Donald E(dwin) Edmund Westlake
American author
• Subjects include mystery, crime, humor, satire; wrote *Nobody's Perfect*, 1977.
b. July 12, 1933 in New York, New York

Edith Wharton
(Edith Newbold Jones)
American author
• Won Pulitzer, 1921, for *The Age of Innocence*; noted for *Ethan Frome*, 1911, and novels of NY society.
b. January 24, 1862 in New York, New York
d. August 11, 1937 in Paris, France

Phillis Wheatley
American poet
• Ex-slave; first black woman to have poetry published, 1770.
b. 1753 in Senegal
d. December 05, 1784 in Boston, Massachusetts

Hugh Callingham Wheeler
English writer
• Won Tonys for plays based on his books: *A Little Night Music*, 1973; *Candide*, 1974; *Sweeny Todd*, 1979.
b. March 19, 1912 in London, England
d. July 27, 1987 in Pittsfield, Massachusetts

John Hall Wheelock
American poet
• First book of poetry was *The Human Fantasy*, 1911.
b. September 09, 1886 in Far Rockaway, New York
d. March 22, 1978 in New York, New York

E(lwyn) B(rooks) White
American author
• Wrote children's classics *Charlotte's Web*, 1952; *Stuart Little*, 1945; awarded Laura Wilder Medal, 1970.
b. July 11, 1899 in Mount Vernon, New York
d. October 01, 1985 in North Brooklin, Maine

Patrick Victor Martindale White
Australian author
• Novels express religious philosophies, isolation themes; and contain complex symbols, myths, and allegories; won Nobel Prize, 1973, for *The Eye of the Storm*.
b. May 28, 1912 in London, England
d. September 3, 1990 in Sydney, Australia

T(erence) H(anbury) White
Irish author
• Fantasy writer, known for Arthurian epics; *The Sword in the Stone*, 1939 was filmed as *Camelot*, 1961.
b. May 29, 1906 in Bombay, India
d. January 17, 1964 in Piraeus, Greece

Theodore Harold White
American author
• Won Pulitzer for *The Making of the President, 1960*, 1961.
b. May 06, 1915 in Boston, Massachusetts
d. May 15, 1986 in New York, New York

William Allen White
American journalist
• World-famous, small-town newsman; won Pulitzers, 1922, 1946.
b. February 1, 1868 in Emporia, Kansas
d. January 29, 1944 in Emporia, Kansas

William Smith White
American journalist
• Nationally syndicated columnist, 1958-74; won Pulitzer for *The Taft Story*, 1955.
b. February 05, 1907 in De Leon, Texas

Don(ald Ford) Whitehead
American journalist
• Won two Pulitzers for international, 1950, domestic reporting, 1952; with Knoxville newspaper, 1957-81.
b. April 08, 1908 in Inman, Virginia
d. January 12, 1981 in Knoxville, Tennessee

William Whitehead
British poet
• Wrote play *A Charge to Poets*, 1762, in reply to hostile comments on his appointment as poet laureate, 1757.
b. 1715
d. 1785

Sarah Helen Power Whitman
American poet–essayist
• Once engaged to Edgar Allan Poe, ca. 1848; wrote *Poe and His Critics*, 1860.
b. January 19, 1803 in Providence, Rhode Island
d. June 27, 1878 in Providence, Rhode Island

Walt(er) Whitman
American poet
• Used free verse style in *Leaves of Grass*, 1855; became inspiration to other poets with his innovative style.
b. May 31, 1819 in West Hills, New York
d. March 26, 1892 in Camden, New Jersey

John Hay Whitney
American diplomat–publisher
• Published *NY Herald Tribune*, 1957-66; ambassador to Great Britain, 1957-66; joined with David O Selznick to form Selznick International Pictures, which made *Gone With the Wind*, 1939.
b. August 17, 1904 in Ellsworth, Maine
d. February 08, 1982 in Manhasset, New York

Phyllis Ayame Whitney
American author
• Won Edgar for *Mystery of the Hidden Hand*, 1964; other books include *Flaming Trees*, 1986; Grand Master, 1988.
b. September 09, 1903 in Yokohama, Japan

John Greenleaf Whittier
American poet–essayist
• Popular rural poet who devoted life to social causes and reform; wrote poem *Snow-Bound*, 1866.
b. December 17, 1807 in Haverhill, Massachusetts
d. September 07, 1892 in Hampton Falls, New Hampshire

Leonard Patrick O'Connor Wibberley

(Leonard Holton; Christopher Webb pseuds)
Irish author–journalist
• Author of *The Mouse That Roared*, 1955; filmed, 1959.
b. April 09, 1915 in Dublin, Ireland
d. November 22, 1983 in Santa Monica, California

Tom (Thomas Grey) Wicker

(Paul Connelly pseud)
American journalist–author
• Washington bureau chief, *NY Times*, 1964-68; author *Kennedy Without Tears: The Man Behind the Myth*, 1964.
b. June 18, 1926 in Hamlet, North Carolina

Margaret Widdemer

American author–poet
• Award-winning works include poem, "Lullaby," 1937; book series, "Winona," 1915-23.
b. September 3, 1897 in Doylestown, Pennsylvania
d. July 31, 1978 in Gloversville, New York

Kurt Wiese

American children's author–illustrator
• Illustrated 300 books by other authors; writings include *Buddy the Bear*, 1936.
b. April 22, 1887 in Minden, Germany
d. May 27, 1974

Elie(zer) Wiesel

American journalist–author
• Auschwitz concentration camp survivor whose books deal with Holocaust; won Nobel Peace Prize, 1986.
b. September 3, 1928 in Sighet, Transylvania

Simon Wiesenthal

Austrian author
• Survivor of Nazi death camps who founded Jewish Documentation Center; wrote *The Murderers Among Us*, 1967.
b. December 31, 1908 in Buczacz, Poland

Kate Douglas Wiggin

American children's author
• Wrote *Rebecca of Sunnybrook Farm*, 1903.
b. September 28, 1856 in Philadelphia, Pennsylvania
d. August 24, 1923 in Harrow, England

Richard Purdy Wilbur

American author–poet–educator
• Skilled writer who won 1957 Pulitzer for *Poems;* translated many of Moliere's works to English.
b. March 01, 1921 in New York, New York

John Wilcock

English author–newspaper editor
• One of the founders of *The Village Voice*, NYC; noted for one-dollar-a-day travel books.
b. 1927 in Shackhill, England

Ella Wheeler Wilcox

American poet
• Wrote almost 40 vols. of sentimental verse; most famous lines from "Solitude": "Laugh, and the World laughs with you; weep, and you weep alone."
b. November 05, 1850 in Johnstown, Wisconsin
d. October 31, 1919 in Short Beach, Connecticut

Laura Elizabeth Ingalls Wilder

(Mrs Almanzo James Wilder)
American author
• Published *Little House in the Big Woods*, 1932; books basis for TV series "Little House on the Prairie," 1974-82.
b. February 07, 1867 in Pepin, Wisconsin
d. January 1, 1957 in Mansfield, Missouri

Robert Ingersoll Wilder

American author–journalist
• Writings include *Flamingo Road*, 1942; *An Affair of Honor*, 1969.
b. January 25, 1901 in Richmond, Virginia
d. August 22, 1974

Brian Wildsmith

English illustrator–children's author
• Self-illustrated works include prize-winning, *Brian Wildsmith's ABC*, 1962.
b. January 22, 1930 in Penistone, England

J(ohn) Burke Wilkinson

American author
• Books include *By Sea and by Stealth*, 1956; *Night of the Short Knives*, 1964.
b. August 24, 1913 in New York, New York

Ben Ames Williams

American journalist–author
• Writings include *Crucible*, 1937; *The Unconquered*, 1953.
b. March 07, 1889 in Macon, Mississippi
d. February 04, 1953 in Brookline, Massachusetts

Jay Williams

(Michael Delving pseud)
American children's author
• Wrote *Danny Dunn* series of books for children.
b. May 31, 1914 in Buffalo, New York
d. July 12, 1978 in London, England

Kit Williams

British author–artist
• Wrote *Masquerade*, 1979, which sparked one of most exciting treasure hunts ever held on British soil.
b. 1947 in Romney Marshes, England

Ursula Moray Williams

English children's author
• Writings include *The Noble Hawks*, 1959; *The Three Toymakers*, 1946.
b. April 19, 1911 in Petersfield, England

William Carlos Williams

American author–poet
• Revolutionized American poetry; won 1963 Pulitzer for *Pictures From Brueghel*.
b. September 17, 1883 in Rutherford, New Jersey
d. March 04, 1963 in Rutherford, New Jersey

Calder Baynard Willingham, Jr

American writer
• His first novel, *End As a Man*, 1947, became film, play; wrote screenplay for *The Graduate*, 1967.
b. December 23, 1922 in Atlanta, Georgia

Garry Wills

American author–journalist
• Syndicated political columnist since 1970; books include *Bare Ruined Choirs*, 1972; *The Kennedy Imprisonment*, 1982.
b. May 22, 1934 in Atlanta, Georgia

Angus (Frank Johnstone, Sir) Wilson

English author
• Writings include *As If By Magic*, 1973; *Setting the World on Fire*, 1980.
b. August 11, 1913 in Bexhill, England

Colin Henry Wilson

English author
• Books include *Ritual in the Dark*, 1960; *The Space Vampires*, 1975.
b. June 26, 1931 in Leicester, England

Dorothy Clarke Wilson

American author
• Religious writings include over 70 plays; books include *Climb Every Mountain*, 1976.
b. May 09, 1904 in Gardiner, Maine

Earl Wilson

(Harvey Earl Wilson)
American journalist
• Best known for syndicated gossip column, "It Happened Last Night," 1943-83.
b. May 03, 1907 in Rockford, Ohio
d. January 16, 1987 in Yonkers, New York

Edmund Wilson

American author–critic
• Considered among this century's finest literary critics; wrote *Axel's Castle*, 1931.
b. May 08, 1895 in Red Bank, New Jersey
d. June 12, 1972 in Talcottville, New York

Hazel Hutchins Wilson
American children's author
• Series on Herbert character include *Herbert's Space Trip*, 1965; *Herbert's Stilts*, 1972.
b. April 08, 1898 in Portland, Maine

Margaret Wilson
American author–missionary
• Novels from women's perspective include 1924 Pulitzer winner, *The Able McLaughlins*.
b. January 16, 1882 in Traer, Iowa

Sloan Wilson
American author
• Best known for novels *The Man in the Gray Flannel Suit*, I and II, 1955, 1983.
b. May 08, 1920 in Norwalk, Connecticut

Walter Winchell
American journalist
• First of modern gossip columnists; had popular syndicated column, radio show, 1930s-50s; known for aggressive style, use of slang.
b. April 07, 1897 in New York, New York
d. February 2, 1972 in Los Angeles, California

William H Wise
American author
• Writings for juveniles include *The Cowboy Surprise*, 1961; *The Terrible Trumpet*, 1969.
b. July 21, 1923 in New York, New York

Owen Wister
American author
• Novel, *The Virginian*, 1902, has been the basis for long-running stage play, three movies.
b. July 14, 1860 in Germantown, Pennsylvania
d. July 21, 1938 in North Kingstown, Rhode Island

P(elham) G(renville) Wodehouse
English author
• Created characters Bertie Wooster and Jeeves; *The Inimitable Jeeves*, 1924.
b. October 15, 1881 in Guildford, England
d. February 14, 1975 in Long Island, New York

Thomas (Thomas Clayton) Wolfe
American author
• Wrote *Look Homeward, Angel*, 1929; *You Can't Go Home Again*, 1940.
b. October 03, 1900 in Asheville, North Carolina
d. September 15, 1938 in Baltimore, Maryland

Tom (Thomas Kennerly, Jr) Wolfe
American author
• Wrote *The Electric Kool-Aid Acid Test*, 1968; *The Right Stuff*, 1979; *Bonfire of the Vanities*, 1988.
b. March 02, 1931 in Richmond, Virginia

Helen Wolff
(Mrs Kurt Wolff)
American publisher
• Founded Pantheon Books, 1942-61; introduced European writer to US.
b. July 27, 1906 in Veskueb, Yugoslavia

Sarah Sayward Barrell Keating Wood
American author
• Published anonymous gothic romances: *Amelia, or Influence of Virtue*, 1802.
b. October 01, 1759 in York, Maine
d. January 06, 1855 in Kennebunk, Maine

Kathleen (Erin) Woodiwiss
American author
• Best-selling novels include *Shanna*, 1977; *Ashes in the Wind*, 1979.
b. June 03, 1939 in Alexandria, Louisiana

Donald Woods
South African journalist–author
• Active against apartheid; relationship with Steven Biko is subject of first major anti-apartheid film, *Cry Freedom*, 1987.
b. December 15, 1933 in Elliotdale, South Africa

Carter Godwin Woodson
American editor–author
• Wrote *The African Background Outlined*, 1936; *The Rural Negro*, 1930; won Spingarn, 1926.
b. December 19, 1875 in New Canton, Virginia
d. April 03, 1950

Bob (Robert Upshur) Woodward
American journalist
• With Carl Bernstein uncovered Watergate scandal; wrote *All the President's Men*, 1974.
b. March 26, 1943 in Geneva, Illinois

Leonard Sidney Woolf
English author–publisher
• Wrote novel *The Village in the Jungle*, 1913; play *Hotel*, 1939; founded Hogarth Press, 1917, with wife Virginia.
b. November 25, 1880 in London, England
d. August 14, 1969 in Rodmell, England

Virginia (Adeline Virginia Stephen) Woolf
English author–critic
• Greatest woman novelist of 20th c.; member, the "Bloomsburys."
b. January 25, 1882 in London, England
d. March 28, 1941 in Lewes, England

Alexander Humphreys Woollcott
American author–critic
• Model for egotist in Kaufman and Hart's *The Man Who Came to Dinner*.
b. January 19, 1887 in Phalanx, New Jersey
d. January 23, 1943 in New York, New York

William Wordsworth
English poet
• Wrote *Lyrical Ballads*, 1798, with Coleridge; poet laureate, 1843-50.
b. April 07, 1770 in Cockermouth, England
d. April 23, 1850 in Grasmere, England

Harold Bell Wright
American author
• Best known novels *The Shepherd of the Hills*, 1907; *The Winning of Barbara Worth*, 1911; works popular for moral lessons.
b. May 04, 1872 in Rome, New York
d. May 24, 1944 in La Jolla, California

James Arlington Wright
American poet
• Writings include *The Green Wall*, 1957; *Shall We Gather at the River*, 1968.
b. December 13, 1927 in Martins Ferry, Ohio
d. March 25, 1980 in New York, New York

Peter Maurice Wright
English author
• Memoirs of his yrs. as British counter-intelligence officer, *Spycatcher*, became int'l. best seller, 1987.
b. 1916 in Chesterfield, England

Richard Wright
American author
• Became country's leading black author with publication of *Native Son*, 1940.
b. September 04, 1908 in Natchez, Mississippi
d. November 28, 1960 in Paris, France

Patricia Wrightson
Australian author
• Wrote *The Crooked Snake*, 1955; *The Ice is Coming*, 1977.
b. June 19, 1921 in Lismore, Australia

Audrey May Wurdemann
American poet
• Won 1935 Pulitzer for verse *Bright Ambush*.
b. January 01, 1911 in Seattle, Washington
d. May 18, 1960 in Miami, Florida

Philip Gordon Wylie

American author
• Critic of US society known for attack on "momism" in *Generation of Vipers*, 1942.
b. May 12, 1902 in Beverly, Massachusetts
d. October 25, 1971 in Miami, Florida

Johann David Wyss

Swiss author
• Wrote classic shipwreck, adventure novel, *Swiss Family Robinson*, translated by son, Johann Rudolf.
b. 1743 in Bern, Switzerland
d. 1818 in Bern, Switzerland

Johann Rudolf Wyss

Swiss author
• Wrote Swiss national anthem, 1811; translated father's novel *Swiss Family Robinson* to English, making it adventure classic.
b. March 13, 1782
d. March 21, 1830

Elizabeth Yates

(Mrs William McGreal)
American children's author
• Won 1951 Newbery for *Amos Fortune, Free Man*.
b. December 06, 1905 in Buffalo, New York

William Butler Yeats

Irish poet–dramatist
• Leader, Irish literary renaissance; founded Abbey Theater, Dublin; won Nobel Prize for literature, 1923.
b. June 13, 1865 in Dublin, Ireland
d. January 28, 1939 in Menton, France

Frank Garvin Yerby

American author
• Popular historical romances include *Foxes of Harrow*, 1946.
b. September 05, 1916 in Augusta, Georgia

Charlotte Mary Yonge

English author
• Writings include *The Heir of Redclyffe*, 1853; *The Daisy Chain*, 1856.
b. August 11, 1823 in Otterbourne, England
d. March 24, 1901 in Elderfield, England

Ann Eliza Webb Young

American author–lecturer
• An ex-wife of Brigham Young, 1869; exposed Mormon polygamy: *Life in Mormon Bondage*, 1876.
b. September 13, 1844 in Nauvoo, Illinois
d. 1908

Andrew Young

Scottish author
• Writings include *Burning as Light*, 1967.
b. April 29, 1885 in Elgin, Scotland
d. November 26, 1971

Margaret Ann Buckner Young

American children's author
• Writings include *Black American Leaders*, 1969; *The Picture Life of Thurgood Marshall*, 1970.
b. March 2, 1922 in Campbellsville, Kentucky

Marguerite Yourcenar, pseud

(Marguerite de Crayencour)
French author
• Only woman ever admitted to Academie Francaise, 1980; masterpiece novel: *Memoires d'Hadrien*, 1951.
b. June 08, 1903 in Brussels, Belgium
d. December 17, 1987 in Bar Harbor, Maine

Nikolai Alekseevich Zabolotskii

Russian poet
• Now regarded as one of Soviet's finest poets; wrote verse *Stolbtsy*, 1929.
b. May 07, 1903 in Kazan, Russia
d. October 14, 1958 in Moscow, U.S.S.R.

Jeff Zaslow

American journalist
• Co-winner of nationwide search for Ann Landers' advice column replacement, 1986.
b. 1959

Marya Zaturenska

(Mrs Horace Gregory)
American poet
• Won Pulitzer, 1938, for *Cold Morning Sky*.
b. September 12, 1902 in Kiev, Russia
d. January 19, 1982 in Shelburne Falls, Massachusetts

John Peter Zenger

German printer–publisher–journalist
• His acquittal in famous libel trial, 1735, helped establish freedom of press in US.
b. 1697 in Germany
d. July 28, 1746 in New York, New York

Emile Edouard Charles Zola

French author–journalist
• Leader of French naturalism; defended Dreyfus, 1898; wrote novel, *Nana*, 1880.
b. April 02, 1840 in Paris, France
d. September 29, 1902 in Paris, France

Charlotte Shapiro Zolotow

American children's author
• Writings include *Big Brother*, 1960; *Say It!* 1980.
b. June 26, 1915 in Norfolk, Virginia

Maurice Zolotow

American author
• Writings include *Never Whistle in a Dressing Room*, 1944; *A Gift of Laughter*, 1965.
b. November 23, 1913 in New York, New York

Mortimer Benjamin Zuckerman

American publisher
• Owner, editor-in-chief, *US News & World Report*, 1984–.
b. June 04, 1937 in Montreal, Quebec

INDEX